LAWYERS' MEDICAL CYCLOPEDIA . . . .

of Personal Injuries and Allied Specialties

Editor
RICHARD M. PATTERSON, J.D.

VOLUME FOUR — FOURTH EDITION

PART B

Sections 30A.1–32A.99

LEXIS® LAW PUBLISHING
CHARLOTTESVILLE, VIRGINIA

6204511

PREFACE TO THE FOURTH EDITION

As in other volumes of *Lawyers' Medical Cyclopedia*, in this Fourth Edition of Volume 4B, emphasis has been placed upon the medical and medicolegal issues most frequently encountered in the practice of personal injury law and in the special fields of medical malpractice, life and health insurance claims, and claims for disability under workers' compensation and the Social Security Act.

The first chapter in this volume (Chapter 30A) covers diabetes mellitus. With its increasingly high incidence in the general population, diabetes continues to be a frequent legal as well as medical problem. Lawyers often encounter diabetic patients among personal injury victims and insurance and disability claimants. In the past ten years, there have been major changes in the way the diabetes is evaluated and managed. To incorporate these changes into the existing chapter — originally the work of endocrinologist Dorothy C. Rasinski, M.D., J.D. — we have been fortunate to obtain the services of Sandra C. Rice, M.D., of Bellevue, Washington, a specialist in diabetes care and treatment.

The chapter on organ and tissue transplants (Chapter 30B) should prove valuable to the malpractice attorney faced with controversial issues in this growing specialty that involves both surgery and medicine. This material has been revised and brought to date by the well-known surgical specialist and medicolegal consultant James A. Peterson, M.D., of Phoenix, Arizona.

The next chapter (Chapter 31) deals with plastic surgery, which includes cosmetic and reconstruction surgery, treatment of burn injuries, surgery of the hand, and replantation surgery. Our revisor of this chapter is a leading medicolegal expert in this area, plastic surgeon-attorney Michael S. Lehv, M.D., J.D., of Columbus, Ohio, a practitioner-consultant and a member of the faculties of Ohio State College of Medicine and Capital University School of Law.

The important topics of head injuries and injuries to the spinal cord and peripheral nerves (Chapter 32), which were revised and expanded in the previous edition by neurosurgeon Bruce L. Wilder, M.D., J.D. of the University of Pittsburgh, have been expertly updated by neurologist W. Steven Metzer, Jr., M.D., of the University of Arkansas College of Medicine.

The final chapter in the volume (Chapter 32A), which covers autopsies and related medicolegal issues, has been brought to date by John C. Hunsaker III, J.D., M.D., Associate Chief Medical Examiner, Division of Medical Examiner Services, Frankfort, Kentucky. Assisting Dr. Hunsaker, who is also director of the Division of Forensic Pathology at the University of Kentucky College of Medicine, Lexington, were forensic pathologists Donna M. Hunsaker, M.D., and Gregory J. Davis, M.D.

The editors extend their sincere thanks to the above authors, as well as to the other medical and surgical specialists who have contributed individual sections to this volume. Their unselfish efforts have produced for our readers another valuable edition of *Lawyers' Medical Cyclopedia.*

Richard M. Patterson
Editor

CONTRIBUTORS

(Current and Earlier Editions)

William L. Bourland, M.D., Memphis, TN.

Albert B. Butler, M.D., Northwestern University Medical School, Chicago, IL.

Gregory J. Davis, M.D., University of Kentucky College of Medicine, Lexington, KY.

Fritz Emanuel Dreifuss, M.B., M.R.C.P., F.R.A.C.P., University of Virginia Health Sciences Center, Charlottesville, VA.

Jack C. Fisher, M.D., University of California-San Diego School of Medicine, San Diego, CA.

James W. Fox IV, M.D., Jefferson Medical College, Philadelphia, PA.

J. William Futrell, M.D., University of Pittsburgh School of Medicine, Pittsburgh, PA.

Gerald T. Golden, M.D., Martinsburg, W.VA.

C. Thomas Gott, M.D., Ph.D., Las Vegas, NV.

Michael W. Hakala, M.D., Richmond, VA.

Donna M. Hunsaker, M.D., Frankfort, KY.

John C. Hunsaker III, J.D., M.D., University of Kentucky College of Medicine, Lexington, KY.

Michael S. Lehv, M.D., J.D., Ohio State University College of Medicine, Columbus, OH.

Jimmy A. Light, M.D., Washington Hospital Center, Washington, DC.

Frank C. McCue, M.D., University of Virginia Health Sciences Center, Charlottesville, VA.

W. Steven Metzer, Jr., M.D., University of Arkansas College of Medicine, Little Rock, AR.

Andrew H. Munster, M.D., Johns Hopkins University School of Mecicine, Baltimore, MD.

M. Louis Offen, M.D., Bethesda, MD.

John A. Owen, Jr., M.D., University of Virginia Health Sciences Center, Charlottesville, VA.

James A. Peterson, M.D., Phoenix, AZ.

Dorothy C. Rasinski, M.D., J.D., Irvine, CA.

Sandra C. Rice, M.D., Bellevue, WA.

Leslie E. Rudolf, M.D., University of Virginia Health Sciences Center, Charlottesville, VA.

Edward S. Sadar, M.D., Columbus, OH.

Alan E. Seyfer, M.D., Oregon Health Sciences University, Portland, OR.

Cyril H. Wecht, M.D., J.D., Central Medical Center and Hospital, Pittsburgh, PA.

Bruce L. Wilder, M.D., J.D., M.P.H., University of Pittsburgh School of Medicine, Pittsburgh, PA.

Gaylord S. Williams, M.D., University of Virginia Health Sciences Center, Charlottesville, VA.

CONTENTS

CHAPTER 30A

DIABETES MELLITUS

I. The Medical Problem

II. Related Topics

Annotations

CHAPTER 30B

ORGAN AND TISSUE TRANSPLANTATION

ANNOTATIONS

CHAPTER 31

BURN INJURIES, PLASTIC REPAIR, AND HAND SURGERY

I. BURN INJURIES AND THEIR TREATMENT

CONTENTS

ix

VII. Correction of Deformities

VIII. Surgical Sex Change

IX. The Hand

X. Related Topics

Annotations

CONTENTS

CHAPTER 32

INJURIES TO THE HEAD, SPINAL CORD,
AND PERIPHERAL NERVES

I. INTRODUCTION

VI. Trauma to the Cranial Nerves

VII. Evaluation and Treatment of Complications of Head Injury

VIII. Posttraumatic Epilepsy

IX. Anatomy and Physiology of the Spine and Spinal Cord

CONTENTS

XVIII. Electromyography

IXX. Related Topics

Annotations

CHAPTER 32A

AUTOPSIES

I. The Medicolegal Autopsy (Coroner or Medical Examiner)

II. The Hospital Autopsy

III. Autopsy Procedure — The Internal Examination

CONTENTS

IV. Legal Problems Associated With Autopsies

V. Autopsy Findings in the Medical Malpractice Case

VI. Related Topics

Annotations

COLOR PLATES

CHAPTER 30A

DIABETES MELLITUS*

I. THE MEDICAL PROBLEM

II. RELATED TOPICS

---

*Revised by Sandra C. Rice, M.D. Additional contributors to the current and earlier chapters include Dorothy C. Rasinski, M.D., J.D., John A. Owen, M.D., and Richard M. Patterson, J.D.

1

ANNOTATIONS

I. THE MEDICAL PROBLEM

§ 30A.1. General nature of diabetes.

Diabetes mellitus,[1] a chronic disorder of metabolism, is more easily described than defined; the diagnosis rests on relatively simple laboratory procedures, while the basic causes continue to be unraveled through intensive research. The diabetic patient characteristically has an abnormally high level of glucose (sugar) in the blood (hyperglycemia), and often this is associated with glucose in the urine (glycosuria). The spectrum of diabetes ranges from assymptomatic to severe illness. Severe diabetes may demonstrate greatly increased breakdown of fat and protein stores in the body. The products of fat breakdown, ketone bodies, may be present in high concentrations in blood and urine (ketonemia and ketonuria). This condition is called ketosis, or (if severe enough to cause derangement of acid-base balance) diabetic ketoacidosis, which will be discussed in more detail later.

The optimal functioning of all living creatures requires a smooth and efficient coordination of intake and dissipation of energy. In the human, energy is derived from the assimilation of the chemical components of foods with specific energy content (measured in calories), and is expended in muscular contraction, synthesis of structural and secretory materials, maintenance of body heat, and other work. Since food is taken in only at intervals and energy is expended continuously, efficient conservation of energy is essential for human health. Diabetes represents a complex departure from normal efficiency in this regard. Insulin, a hormone secreted by the beta cells in the islets of Langerhans of the pancreas (**Fig. 1**), restores normal efficiency, yet diabetes mellitus is more than simple insulin deficiency. In many cases, there seems to be a greater need for insulin in some metabolic processes than in others, so that many patients have "normal" insulin production, but some if not all of the biochemical stigmata of diabetes.

---

[1] Editor's Note: The complete term for the disease is "diabetes mellitus," although in this discussion the mellitus has been dropped for convenience. Alone, the word "diabetes" means merely excessive urination, while "mellitus," taken from the Greek, means sugary or sweet. Diabetes mellitus is evidenced not only by excessive urination, but also by excessive glucose, or sugar, in the blood or urine — hence, the lay term "sugar diabetes."

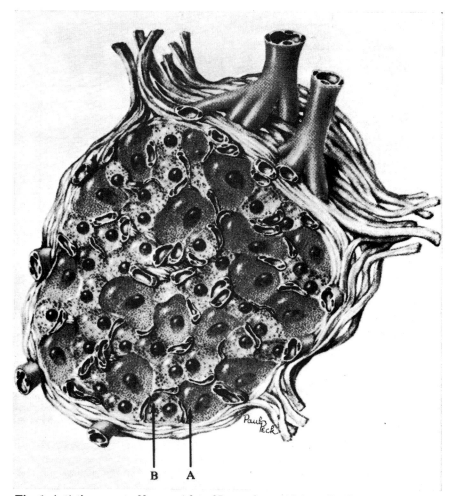

Fig. 1. Artist's concept of human islet of Langerhans. Alpha cells (A) and beta cells (B) are closely intermingled and lie in close proximity to a rich network of blood vessels.

Diabetes mellitus is not a single disease entity, but a clinical syndrome characterized primarily by an absolute or relatively deficiency of insulin, caused by various mechanisms resulting in hyperglycemia or elevated blood glucose. Most of the diabetic population can be divided into two general categories. Type I, or insulin-dependent diabetes mellitus (IDDM) which appears usually in younger age groups, requires lifelong treatment with insulin, since there is essentially no insulin production by or secretion from the pancreas in these individuals. Type II, noninsulin-dependent diabetes mellitus (NIDDM), which typically has an insidious onset after the age of forty, is often associated with obesity, and is commonly treated by dietary restriction and oral medication. In

3

this group, there may be decreased, normal, or excessive secretion of insulin. Strong familial aggregation is characteristic.

§ 30A.2. Normal intermediary metabolism.

The concept of efficient utilization of energy is analogous to the fuel system in a modern automobile. The "diabetic automobile" has multiple leaks in the fuel system so that gasoline drips out onto the road, or on the battery, leaks into the passenger area and possibly causes a continuous small fire, short-circuits certain electrical circuits, and most of all leads to poor carburetion and marked loss of horsepower.

The fuels for the body are protein, carbohydrate and fat. A typical diet contains these in a ratio that provides 15% of the calories from protein, 40% from carbohydrate, and 45% from fat. To store these calories, protein is built in the cellular structures of the body, carbohydrate is stored in the liver and as glycogen (starch) in the muscle, and fat is stored as globules of triglyceride in the fat cells.

Although insulin is generally regarded as a critical regulator of blood sugar, it is also necessary for protein and fat metabolism. Thus insulin deficiency causes derangement in all areas of the energy storage and retrieval process.

When carbohydrates are ingested, whether in the form of fruits, breads, candies, etc., they are broken down into glucose molecules in the stomach and then absorbed through the lining of the small intestine where they circulate in the blood stream. Circulating insulin affixes to the body's cells and facilitates the transfer of the glucose into the cells. The glucose then can be immediately utilized for energy or converted into glycogen or triglycerides and stored. This transfer of blood glucose from the blood stream into the cells lowers the concentration of circulating blood sugar.

Insulin, which is formed and stored in the pancreas, is released when sensors within the islets of Langerhans detect that the blood sugar reaches excessive levels. Conversely, no insulin is released when the blood sugar drops below a certain level. Thus the blood sugar concentration is precisely regulated minute to minute.

As noted, circulating insulin also facilitates the uptake and utilization of protein and fat that are similarly digested and absorbed in the small intestine after ingestion. The presence of insulin also impedes the breakdown of these nutrients once they are formed and stored within the cells.

Whereas insulin is the principle anabolic hormone (one that stores energy), the body has multiple catabolic hormones that work in opposition to insulin. These include steroid hormones and epinephrine produced by the adrenal glands and glucagon produced by the pancreas. When the body needs fuel, these hormones are secreted and cause (1) breakdown of glycogen to glucose, (2) release of glucose from the cells, (3) breakdown of stored fat to fatty acids, and (4) breakdown of protein in small units, amino acids. Normally, this process is balanced by insulin actions. But in cases of insulin deficiency, the process can accelerate and lead to an accumulation of fatty acids which then are converted to ketone bodies in the liver. The end result is life-threatening ketoacidosis.

Because hypoglycemia poses such an immediate threat to the body, the catabolic system is somewhat redundant, involving a number of hormones. The brain requires glucose as its energy source, and when levels fall below 50mg/dl, mental confusion occurs. Progressive deprivation of glucose leads to loss of consciousness and cell damage and death within hours. The outpouring of these hormones mediate the symptoms of low blood sugar, *i.e.* hunger, tremulousness, and sweating.

During periods of starvation, glycogen stores become exhausted as a source of glucose. Fat is broken down to fatty acids and converted to ketone bodies by the liver. Protein is broken down to amino acids that can be converted to glucose by the liver. Progressive inanition and muscle wasting ensue.

Figures 2, 3 and **4** schematically depict the interactions of the various bodily tissues and hormones during normal metabolism and during periods of caloric excess and deficit. Blood glucose concentration at any point in time represents a delicate balance between production and utilization. Minor alterations in any of these factors will alter the blood glucose and counter-regulatory mechanisms. The multiplicity of the factors involved is what makes diabetes such a complicated disease.

§ 30A.3. Incidence of diabetes.

There are eight million Americans diagnosed with diabetes, 90% to 95% of whom have Type II diabetes. Furthermore, it is estimated that another eight million persons meet the diagnostic criteria for diabetes, but remain undiagnosed. Diabetes occurs at any age, but the greatest number of cases come to light in the fifth and sixth decades of life. The prevalence of diabetes is 10% — 12% for those aged sixty-five or older.

The prevalence of diabetes is different among different countries and among racial and ethnic groups. Genetic factors predispose certain groups to a very high risk for diabetes. The "westernization" of less developed countries also plays a role. Obesity and decreased physical activity predispose to diabetes. Worldwide, the incidence of diabetes is increasing — by the year 2020 there will be an estimated 250 million people with diabetes.

§ 30A.4. Causes of diabetes.

Late in the nineteenth century, Von Mering and Minkowski produced diabetes in dogs by surgical removal of the pancreas. In 1921, Banting and Best were able to extract a substance from beef pancreas that would

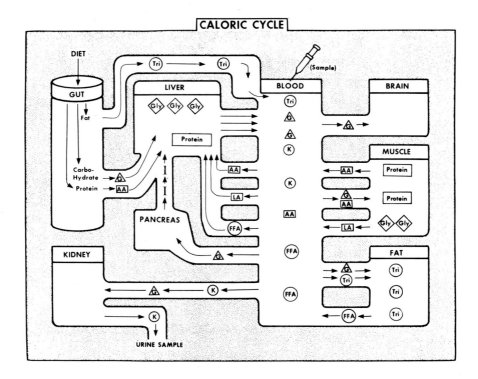

Fig. 2. The Caloric Cycle. Foodstuffs absorbed from the gut are processed in the liver and released into the blood stream. Representative organs utilizing energy are brain, muscle, and fat tissue. Energy stored in muscle and fat can be broken down and re-cycled to the liver. Blood glucose level serves as stimulus to insulin release. Excess glucose and ketones are excreted via the kidney.

Key to symbols: I—Insulin; Tri—Triglycerides (fat compound); FFA—Free fatty acids (fat compound); K—Ketones (fat compound); G—Glucose (carbohydrate compound); Gly—Glycogen (carbohydrate compound); LA—Lactic acid (carbohydrate compound); AA—Amino acids (protein compound).

lower the blood sugar in these animals. The active principle of these extracts proved to be insulin. Initially, it appeared that the disease was due to an insulin-deficiency state.

Surgical removal of the pancreas or damage from trauma leads to a diabetic state. In addition, repeated injury from inflammation to the pancreas (pancreatitis) or accumulation of deposits within the pancreas (such as iron deposition from hemochromatosis) lead to diabetes. However, the vast majority of patients are found to have grossly normal pancreas organs. It later was discovered that specialized cells, the beta cells, scattered throughout the interior of the pancreas produce insulin. Damage to these cells caused by the body's own immune system was found to be the basis for Type I, or insulin-dependent diabetes (IDDM).

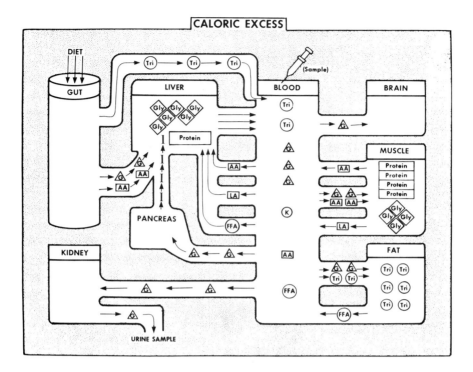

Fig. 3. Caloric Excess. The excess calories absorbed from the gut are stored in the liver, muscle, and fat, under the influence of increased insulin secretion. Breakdown of stored calories in muscle or fat is unnecessary, hence minimal. The spillage of excess glucose into the urine occurs only if blood glucose levels are high, which is unlikely if sufficient insulin is being secreted. For key to symbols, see Fig. 2.

It is believed that most patients with IDDM inherit one of a number of defective genes that predispose the person to diabetes. Several specific genetic markers on chromosome 6 (known as the DR3 or DR4 allele) have been traced to the disorder. Genes serve as the blueprint for proteins — one of which is an antibody. It is believed that these defective genes code for antibodies that attack the pancreatic beta cells causing an inflammatory response that eventually destroys them, rendering them unable to produce insulin. These antibodies, called islet cell antibodies can be detected in diabetic patients even before diabetes becomes clinically evident.

The fact that not all patients with these genes develop diabetes, as evidenced by twin studies, where one twin may develop the disease and one may not, speaks to the theory that environmental factors must also play a role in causing IDDM.

The more common type of diabetes is Type II Diabetes, or non-insulin dependent diabetes (NIDDM). This form is characterized by normal ap-

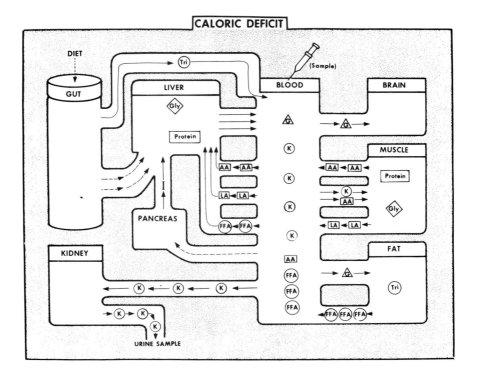

Fig. 4. Caloric Deficit. In starvation, energy needs are met by breakdown of protein and glycogen in liver and muscle. Fat breakdown produces increased blood levels of free fatty acids and ketones, with the latter appearing in the urine. Insulin secretion is minimal because blood sugar is low rather than high.

The metabolic picture of diabetes bears a close resemblance to that of caloric deficit, except that in diabetes dietary calories are absorbed as usual, and blood glucose is high because glucose does not enter muscle or fat in adequate quantities. With high blood glucose levels, urine may contain much glucose as well as ketones. For key to symbols, see Fig. 2.

pearing pancreatic tissue and beta cells. The cause for this type of diabetes lay in the inability of insulin to properly regulate glucose utilization in other tissues of the body. The term used to describe this dysfunction is "impaired glucose tolerance."

Patients with NIDDM generally have normal or even elevated levels of insulin circulating in the blood stream. Insulin needs to be able to chemically communicate with the body's cells and set off a chain of events that allows glucose to enter the cell and become utilized. In NIDDM, there appear to be any of several defects in this system, either with the way the insulin binds to the cell wall (attaches to the receptor) or interacts with other cellular elements. There is strong evidence that these defects are genetically acquired, and it appears that a number of different genetic patterns may predispose to this illness.

As in IDDM, other factors play a role in determining whether a genetically predisposed individual will acquire the disease. Obesity, aging, steroids, and other hormonal abnormalities appear to trigger this form of diabetes.

§ 30A.5. Noninsulin-dependent diabetes mellitus (NIDDM).

In the vast majority of cases, Type II diabetes, also sometimes called idiopathic, stable, adult-onset diabetes, develops rather insidiously and is discovered only fortuitously by routine measurement of blood or urine glucose. This is particularly true of the patient who is middle-aged, sedentary, and perhaps obese. In retrospect, such patients may have noted some unimpressive complaints of mild nocturia (excessive urination at night), blurred vision, malaise, skin infections with yeast or numbness and tingling of the feet. It is estimated that most Type II diabetics would manifest some laboratory evidence of diabetes as much as twelve years before the disease is eventually discovered. Thus the rationale for diabetes detection programs can be appreciated.

Environmental factors that play a contributing role are primarily nutritional, *i.e.* overeating and subsequent obesity. Whereas the body may be able to maintain normal blood sugar levels when one is of normal weight, the additional extra adipose tissue "overwhelms" the system leading to high blood sugar levels. Loosing weight frequently will restore blood sugars to normal ranges.

As noted, the primary defect in Type II diabetes involves insulin resistance. To overcome this phenomena, the beta cells initially increase insulin production. High circulating insulin levels can be seen (hyperinsulinemia). This, in itself, is felt to have potential deleterious effects on tissues. The diabetes gradually worsens because insulin resistance worsens and eventually the beta cells deteriorate.

The phenomena of insulin resistance has important implications with respect to treatment. It is apparent that exogenous insulin administration should not be the focus of treatment. Rather, medications that can improve insulin resistance by enhancing insulin's effects on the fat and muscle cells are being developed.

§ 30A.6. Insulin-dependent diabetes mellitus (IDDM).

Type I diabetes has historically been referred to as juvenile-onset diabetes. Usually the story unfolds from previous good health to serious symptoms and thus to medical diagnosis within a week or two. Often an intercurrent infection precipitates ketosis and even ketoacidosis, so that diabetes is already a life-threatening condition by the time it is discovered. (Occasionally this precipitous development of severe diabetes also occurs in adults.)

Often symptoms develop at or after a time when the child is growing rapidly. A marked increase in thirst and urination begins rather suddenly. A child previously well-trained may begin to wet the bed at night; older children usually must get up several times during the night to urinate. Appetite becomes voracious and yet the patient is easily fatigued and lacks endurance. His disposition may change. He begins to lose weight rapidly, and may become drowsy (because of early ketoacidosis) before medical attention is sought. Nausea, vomiting and abdominal pain are common findings. Usually the ketone bodies in the blood are high enough to allow the acetone to escape into exhaled air where it gives a characteristic odor to the breath.

If untreated, these patients will die from irreversible ketoacidosis. There is no way to reverse this fate except with insulin and replacement of fluid losses. This is what made the discovery of insulin such an earth-shaking event in 1921. The impact of adequate insulin and diet in these cases is dramatic. The symptoms disappear and the patient returns to his previous state of good health, growth, and development. Indeed, it often seems that diabetes becomes milder or may even seem to disappear in the first year or six months after treatment is started (the so-called honeymoon period). Invariably, however, it resumes its former severity and requires life-long management.

§ 30A.7. Diabetes due to specific causes.

Damage to the pancreas

There are some situations where known damage to the pancreas produces the expected picture of insulin deficiency, such as surgical removal of the pancreas for tumor or severe chronic recurrent pancreatitis. Since the pancreas is not functional, it cannot fulfill its other role of producing important digestive enzymes, so these patients can be chronically undernourished. Diabetes in these patients can be difficult to control.

Hemochromatosis

Hemochromatosis, a toxic deposition of iron in many tissues including the pancreas, gradually reduces the secretory capacity of the islets and produces a form of diabetes which is usually mild and fairly stable. This is caused by an inherited defect that affects about one in 1,000 people. The diagnosis is suspected when blood tests show an elevation in the liver function tests and can be confirmed by measuring the iron levels in the blood. Treatment involves frequent blood donations to eliminate iron stored within blood cells.

Drugs

Drugs rarely are implicated as true causes of diabetes. However, many drugs can potentiate hyperglycemia and worsen diabetic control. Diuretics containing thiazides or niacin, which is prescribed for decreasing cholesterol, can increase blood sugar. Hormones, especially steroids, which are used in arthritic conditions, asthma, allergy reactions, and many other conditions can have a major effect on blood sugar. Other hormones implicated are estrogens used in oral contraceptives and for treatment of menopausal symptoms. In women predisposed to diabetes, pregnancy can elevate blood sugar to diabetic levels (gestational diabetes) because of the high levels of estrogen produced during gestation, leading to the condition, gestational diabetes.

Hormone disorders

Diabetes is a well-known feature of *Cushing's syndrome*, a disorder characterized by high levels of cortisone inappropriately secreted by the adrenal glands. Patients with Cushing's syndrome tend to be obese, particularly around the abdomen, and have a characteristic "moon face" and high blood pressure.

Diabetes also occurs in *acromegaly*, where excessive growth hormone production seems to interfere with the peripheral effect of insulin. The exact mechanism is unknown.

Pheochromocytoma is a tumor of the adrenal medulla that produces excessive amounts of catecholamines, thus inhibiting secretion of insulin by the beta cells. The occasional diabetes occurring in thyrotoxicosis may be mediated by the increased sensitivity of all body tissues to catecholamines, which has been postulated by some.

In all of the above hormonal disorders, it is possible to correct the diabetes by prompt and effective control of the underlying endocrinopathy.

§ 30A.8. Diagnosing diabetes.

Discovery of diabetes may be fortuitous by finding glucose in the urine or an elevated blood sugar on routine lab testing. Screening programs as promoted by the American Diabetes Association not uncommonly lead to the diagnosis. These programs generally promoted at booths found at health fairs or hospitals whereby a simple finger stick blood test can alert an individual that his or her blood sugar is abnormal.

Not uncommonly the diagnosis follows confirmatory testing in patients who present with symptoms suspicious for diabetes. These include weight loss despite good food intake, frequent urination, increased thirst, blurred vision, numbness or tingling of the feet, or recurrent yeast infections. Patients who are obese and/or have a family history of diabetes are suspect.

Patients suspected of having diabetes are asked to obtain a fasting blood glucose level (no food or drink after midnight except water). If the level is over 126 mg/dl, then the diagnosis is confirmed. There is little need to proceed with the cumbersome glucose tolerance test (a test in which the patient is given a measured amount of glucose and then has his or her blood sugar levels tested at thirty- to sixty-minute intervals for the ensuing three hours).

Since the upper limits of normal for fasting glucose is 110 mg/dl., there is an occasional patient whose level is between 111 and 126. These individuals are classified as having "impaired glucose tolerance." Most of these patients progress to Type II diabetes at a rate of 7% per year.

The other diagnostic category of diabetes is gestational diabetes, in which diabetes occurs during pregnancy, generally in the third trimester. It is seen in about 4% of pregnancies and if not detected and treated, can cause increased risks to the fetus and newborn — including hypertensive problems for the mother — and an increased need for Cesarean section delivery.

Screening for gestational diabetes has been advised by the American Diabetes Association in all but the lowest-risk groups of mothers (*i.e.*, age less than twenty-five years, non-obese, low-risk ethnic groups, and no family history of diabetes). The screening test consists of administering 50 grams of glucose orally and testing the blood sugar in one hour. If the level is over 140, a diagnostic glucose tolerance test is performed. The criteria below define gestational diabetes. After 100 grams of glucose, two of four of the following values are exceeded:

Fasting	105mg/dl
One hour	190mg/dl
Two hours	165mg/dl
Three hours	145mg/dl

Women with gestational diabetes are at very high risk for developing Type II diabetes in later life and should be monitored and counseled on weight management.

§ 30A.9.   Treatment of diabetes.

Goals of Treatment

Regardless of the type or severity of diabetes, the goal of treatment is uniform. Simply stated, the goal is to maintain the blood sugar level within the range of a nondiabetic individual. This involves manipulating the various modalities that affect blood sugar, *i.e.* diet, exercise and medications to achieve the desired objective. Implicit in this goal is also to prevent excessive lowering of the blood sugar to values below a safe level (approximately 50mg/dl).

A landmark study published in 1993[2] by the Diabetes Control and Complications Trial (DCCT) group is the basis for this relatively new philosophy that meticulous glycemic control be the therapeutic goal. The results of the study demonstrated dramatic lessening of the risk for the chronic complications known to be associated with the disease. These will be discussed further, but include visual loss and blindness, kidney disease, nerve damage, and accelerated atherosclerosis.

Historically, it has been difficult to document if a patient's blood sugars have been in the normal range throughout time. Fortunately, another relatively new development has facilitated the ability of physicians to oversee this process. The glycosolated hemoglobin test (also known as glycated hemoglobin or hemoglobin A1c) is a readily available blood test that has been standardized to reflect how close to normal a diabetic's blood sugar has been over a two month period. Although there are slight variations among laboratories, a nondiabetic individual will show a level of 4%-7%. Values above this show increasing deviations from normal.

The DCCT confirmed that achieving and maintaining near normal glycosolated hemoglobin levels implies good control. Therefore, the diabetic should strive to achieve as close to normal levels on this test, recommended to be performed every four to six months.

Joint responsibility

For effective treatment of diabetes, both physician and patient must understand and accept their respective roles in the relationship. The patient must realize that he has a persistent, variable, life-long medical problem for which the therapeutic responsibility rests on him 99% of the time. He must utilize the physician as a medical resource for learning about his disease, for management overview, and for the crises, complexities, and complications that may be expected to occur throughout his life. The physician must treat the patient, explain the medical disease, demonstrate the methods of optimum therapy, transfer control of the disease to the patient, arrange for regular follow-ups, maintain a general overview of the management program, and treat the crises as they occur. The management of this changing relationship requires patience, flexibility, and sensitivity on both sides, plus a willingness to cooperate or compromise to reach mutually acceptable goals.

Patient education

Education of the patient starts at the time of diagnosis and should include an explanation of the nature of the disease and its complications,

---

[2] DCCT Research Group, *The Effect of Intensive Treatment of Diabetes on the Development and Progression of Long-term* *Complications in Insulin-Dependent Diabetes Mellitus*, 329 N. Engl. J. Med. 977, 1993.

the hereditary aspects, the theoretical and practical aspects of diet, the techniques of blood-urine testing, the details of drug treatment, the clinical picture of acidosis and hypoglycemia, the importance of weight-control, blood pressure and exercise, care of the feet, the medical-social implications of the disease in terms of employment, insurance, travel, sports, marriage, children, etc., the necessity of a continued doctor-patient relationship, and some idea of the long-term prognosis for well and poorly treated diabetics.

Specific education about techniques of testing for blood glucose levels should be provided quite early to (1) reinforce the point that diabetes is a permanent problem, (2) emphasize the value of dietary manipulation, and (3) provide proof of patient cooperation. The unstable diabetic should also be taught how to test the urine for ketone bodies.

One of the most important developments in the area of diabetes mellitus and patient control occurred with the introduction of blood glucose monitoring techniques available to patients for their own use away from the laboratory test setting. Both of these methods utilize testing one or two drops of blood the patient extracts from a fingertip, after pricking it with a sterile lancet. In both tests, the patient compares the results of a color reaction after the blood sample has been allowed to mix with reagents at the tip of a strip of testing paper. The less expensive, less reliable method involves comparing the color developed on the test strip with a chart that comes with the packet of reagent strips, showing a series of colors and the blood glucose levels they represent. The patient (or tester) can then get a reasonably close idea of the blood glucose at the moment of testing. Two things are critical for an accurate result: the timing at which the specimen is blotted and read, and the color vision of the reader. The better method, however, involves use of a small electronic blood glucose meter, which compares the colors automatically and gives the blood glucose level on a digital readout, thus eliminating the need to compare the colors visually on the strip to a color chart. This is particularly valuable for patients with vision problems and permits even tighter control because of its accuracy. The glucometer is a compact unit, small enough to fit in a patient's pocket and is easily utilized once the patient becomes familiar with the technique. Many monitors now feature a memory unit that stores readings — a feature that is useful for both the patient and the physician.

By the above means, patients have become more responsible for their own care. It is critical that the patients keep accurate records of blood glucose results and the time they are taken, so that their physicians can make appropriate decisions regarding adjustment of insulin dosage or other elements in the diabetic regimen. The more reliable patients can be instructed in protocols to adjust their own insulin dosage, depending on their individual patterns of blood glucose variation, as determined by their test results. The motivated patient thus can assume a greater degree of responsibility in the control of his diabetes and be much more aware of the effect that different foods or meal times, activities, medications, insulin dosage and timing, stress, and intercurrent illness can have upon his control and the progress of his disease. Based on the test results, adjustments can be made in the timing and content of meals, in activities, and in insulin timing and dosage levels, to keep the blood glucose as normal as possible.

Diet therapy

The explanation of diabetes as a disease of energy transfer helps prepare the patient for an appreciation of diet therapy as the foundation of all diabetic management. The Type II diabetic is usually at least mildly obese and may already have some early vascular disease. The diabetic diet, with its limitation of cholesterol, refined sugars, and total calories, is a prudent diet not only for him but for most nondiabetic middle-aged Americans. Although diet programs may be made as specific and detailed as patient acceptance permits, the essentials are (1) reduction of body weight to or slightly below ideal; (2) distribution of calories fairly evenly throughout the day; (3) distribution of calories in a way that minimizes highly refined carbohydrates, limits fats, and ensures adequate protein; (4) regular exercise to maintain body weight and general fitness; and (5) limited use of alcohol. Cigarette smoking should be discontinued. There is some evidence that increasing fiber intake contributes to the lowering of blood glucose levels.

Current recommendations of the American Diabetes Association include the following:

1. Calories should be prescribed to achieve and maintain desirable body weight.
2. Carbohydrate intake: a. Carbohydrate should be liberalized, up to 55% to 60% of the total calories, and individualized with the amount dependent upon the impact on blood glucose and lipid levels and upon individual eating patterns. b. Whenever acceptable to the patient, foods containing unrefined carbohydrate with fiber should be substituted for highly refined carbohydrates, which are usually low in fiber. c. In some individuals, modest amounts of sucrose and other refined sugars may be acceptable, contingent upon metabolic control and body weight.
3. Protein intake: 10% to 20% of the daily caloric intake should be from protein. The recommended daily allowance is 0.8 grams/kg of body weight for adults. Children, teenagers, pregnant females, and elderly persons may require more. There are situations where the protein intake may have to be reduced, especially in patients with incipient kidney disease.

4. Total fat and cholesterol intake should be restricted with total fat comprising less than 30% of caloric intake per day. Cholesterol intake should be less than 300 mg per day. Saturated fat should comprise less than 10% of calories, polyunsaturated fat should be less than 10% of calories, and the rest should be in the form of monounsatured fat. Patients with high cholesterol and/or triglyceride levels may be advised to reduce saturated fat intake to even lower levels.

5. The use of various nutritive and nonnutritive sweeteners is acceptable in diabetic management.

6. Recommended salt intake is 1,000 mg per 1,000 calories, not to exceed 3,000 mg per day. Most Americans eat more salt than is necessary. In hypertensive individuals, salt may be harmful, and its intake should be reduced. However, severe sodium restriction may be harmful in certain individuals with poorly controlled diabetes, postural hypotension, or fluid imbalance.

7. The same cautions regarding alcohol use that apply to the general public apply to individuals with diabetes. Specific problems may occur with hypoglycemia, neuropathy, control of blood sugar, obesity, and/or hyperlipemia.

8. Vitamins and minerals should meet the recommended requirements for health, with no evidence unique to the diabetic patient to warrant supplementation unless the patient is on a very low calorie diet or other special circumstances exist.

Exercise

Exercise should be emphasized as a major component of treatment of diabetes. Not only does it promote weight loss and improve cardiovascular health, it has been shown to decrease insulin resistance. As per the recent Surgeon General's Report on Physical Activity[3] it is recommended that individuals accumulate thirty minutes of moderate physical activity on most days of the week. Diabetics are not exempted, but a number of special considerations apply.

1. Patients at risk for cardiovascular disease should be evaluated for occult ischemic heart disease before embarking on an exercise program. This usually involves a graded exercise test supervised by a physician.

2. Strenuous exercises involving straining or jarring may be detrimental in patients with diabetic eye disease.

---

[3] U.S. Department of Health and Human Services, *Physical Activity and Health: A Report of the Surgeon General*, Centers for Disease Control and Prevention, National Health Promotion, Washington D.C., 1996.

3. Patients with neuropathy, which can cause numbness of the feet, should avoid forms of exercise such as jogging or prolonged walking that may predispose to blisters and foot injury.

4. Type I diabetics must take extra precautions to assess blood sugars levels before and after exercise and make proper adjustments in their insulin doses and food intake. General guidelines include: avoiding exercise if blood glucose levels are over 250 or ketosis is present; ingesting extra carbohydrate before exercise if levels are less than 100; learning how different levels of exercise affect their blood sugar; having available quickly absorbable carbohydrate foods during exercise and consuming them during or after exercise if needed.

Drug therapy

In newly diagnosed Type I diabetics, drug therapy with insulin is almost always initiated immediately. In Type II diabetics, most clinicians will attempt a period of diet and exercise therapy before initiating drugs. However, as new drugs are becoming available and their safety is being documented, there is a trend toward using medications earlier in the course of treatment. Since a long period of insulin resistance may have existed before diagnosing the diabetes, and this process likely has already accelerated atherosclerosis, there may be more of an urgency to improve control as soon as possible.

In mild Type II diabetes, weight loss and diet may achieve the goal of therapy, *i.e.* normalization of the blood sugar and normal glycosolated hemoglobin levels. (Note, although the DCCT study involved Type I diabetics, further studies involving Type II patients are confirming the generally held impression that good control benefits all diabetics). However, most diabetics with moderate to severe disease will require medications eventually.

Numerous factors affect the choice of the initial medication. Discussion of the characteristics of currently prescribed medications follows. Doses are generally initiated at low levels and gradually increased as necessary to control the blood sugar. There is an increasing trend to using combinations of medications. The rationale makes sense: since different medications address different deficiencies in the glucose regulatory pathway, combined use should have additive benefits. Studies are bearing this out.

§ 30A.10. Insulin.

Insulin is the drug of choice in Type I diabetes. Some clinicians prescribe insulin in Type II diabetics as initial treatment, but generally it is reserved for more severe cases that fail oral therapy. Not infrequently,

Type II diabetics will require temporary insulin therapy during periods of extreme stress, such as severe illness or injury.

Forms of Insulin

Insulin is available commercially in a number of forms: short-acting (regular of crystalline insulin, Semilente, Lispro), intermediate-acting (NPH, Lente) and long-acting (Ultralente, PZI). Insulin is mainly sold as U-100 insulin (100 units per cc.). Most patients inject a morning and evening shot of intermediate-acting insulin. Each dose is slowly absorbed and provides glucose lowering effects over approximately a twelve-hour period. Short acting-insulin, which lasts only several hours in the system, is given as a supplement before meals to lower the additional rise in sugar that follows food intake. The tightly controlled Type I diabetic generally takes three or more regular injections per day. The newest short acting-insulin is Lispro, which is absorbed very quickly and lowers the sugar more rapidly and predictably than regular insulin.

The original insulins were derived from beef and pork pancreatic extracts. Advancements in technology have allowed widespread availability of an exact replica of human insulins. These are (1) produced by chemically engineered alteration of pork insulin or (2) biochemically produced by altering bacterial and yeast organism DNA to make human insulin. Human insulins are considered the most desirable form for use because they do not elicit allergic reactions or stimulate antibodies that appear to have potential detrimental affects.

Injection and dosage

The patient (or someone in his family) must learn how to measure the proper dose of insulin into the syringe, make a satisfactory subcutaneous injection using aseptic technique, and keep the equipment clean and ready for use each day. These skills are difficult to achieve in patients who are blind, crippled with neuromuscular disease, intellectually challenged, living in extreme poverty, or traveling in undeveloped areas — but they are not impossible.

Response to insulin can usually be determined by gradual increase or decrease in dosage, with normal levels of glucose in the blood as the desired end-point. As control improves, subsequent changes in the intermediate- or long-acting insulin doses must be made more gradually and carefully — no more than a 10% change in dosage per day and no more often than once every three days. The dose of short-acting insulin is adjusted before each meal, depending on the pre-meal level of blood sugar and the size of the anticipated food intake. This form of treatment is referred to as a "sliding scale" of insulin use. Ideally, the blood sugar level should be continually monitored with appropriate administration of insulin minute-to-minute. The quest for this ideal level has stimulated the design of instrumentation for delivering insulin in a more physiological fashion, permitting the near normalization of the blood-glucose level in persons with diabetes for prolonged periods. Significant progress toward this goal has been made.

Two general classes of *insulin pumps* have been developed. The closed loop device consists of continuous blood-glucose monitoring, automatic, computer-regulated insulin delivery, and a catheter delivery system. Because of the unavailability of a reliable long-term glucose monitoring device, the closed loop pump is currently used only in short-term experimental studies. The open loop insulin delivery system is regulated by the patient in an attempt to deliver insulin at rates designed to accommodate meals, exercise, etc. Success of this new self-management tool is, however, totally dependent on intensive commitments not only by the patient to self-glucose measurement (up to seven times per day) for insulin adjustment, but also by a medical support team. Evidence in over 5,000 patients using open loop pumps shows that improved glucose control and other metabolic benefits are possible.

A major disadvantage of these devices is the potential for a sudden development of diabetic ketoacidosis in the event of a unnoticed mechanical failure of the pump. This occurs because there is no reservoir of long-acting insulin in the body as a "back-up" supply.

Since insulin is a small protein, if taken orally it is digested in the stomach and rendered unavailable for absorption as an intact functional molecule. Currently, it is administered primarily via injection by tiny hypodermic needles. Some patients, particularly children, use a jet injector with a device that delivers a fine stream of insulin through the skin under high pressure. Although there is generally no discomfort, these devices are more cumbersome, expensive, and do not deliver the insulin as predictably as with "shots." A form of nasally administered insulin may soon be available. However, this mode of treatment also appears to have inconsistent levels of insulin absorption and can cause irritation to the mucous membranes of the nose.

Adverse effects

Insulin therapy is sometimes associated with adverse effects. Some patients develop itching and redness at the site of injection a few weeks after treatment is started. This represents a local allergy to the insulin, which usually subsides spontaneously. Young people often show signs of localized atrophy or hypertrophy of subcutaneous fat at the sites of injection. All of these reactions are becoming rare now that the more highly purified insulins are being used.

Another uncommon phenomena is when the patient develops high levels of antibodies against insulin that block the insulin's effects. These patients may require hundreds of units of insulin compared to the normal daily requirements of less than sixty units that most diabetics receive.

The most common adverse reaction is the predictable one, hypoglycemia. (low blood glucose). Errors in dosage, inadequate diet, improper injection techniques, or excessive exercise may lead to a drop in blood glucose below the normal range, setting in motion a number of neurohormonal abnormalities, as described in Section 30A.2 on normal intermediary metabolism. These phenomena, called "insulin reaction" or "insulin shock," are best treated promptly by oral administration of sugar (if the patient is awake and alert), or by intravenous glucose or intramuscular glucagon. Aside from the inconvenience of regular injection, it is the ever-present fear of insulin reaction that constitutes the major disadvantage to this form of treatment. However, with the advent of blood glucose self-monitoring techniques, opportunities to check blood levels when symptoms begin to appear provide indications for intake of oral sugar or injection of glucagon to forestall the full "hypoglycemic reaction."

§ 30A.11. Oral hypoglycemic agents.

Sulfonylurea drugs

In 1944 a new anti-infective agent, a derivative of the sulfa drugs, was found by accident to cause hypoglycemia — low blood glucose — in normal subjects as well as in adult-onset diabetics. It was soon established that this drug stimulated the release of insulin from the beta cells. More recently there has been evidence also of the beneficial extra-pancreatic effect, mainly on hepatic metabolism. The sulfonylurea drugs are potent when given by mouth and soon became extremely popular, especially in the majority of middle-aged patients who were relatively asymptomatic despite hyperglycemia.

The original sulfonylurea drugs (Orinase, Diabenese, Dymelor and Tolinase) have now been largely replaced with "second generation" sulfonylureas that appeared on the market in the 1980s. These include glyburide (Micronase, Diabeta, Glynase), glipizide (Glucotrol), and glimepiride (Amaryl). All of these drugs bind to a receptor in the beta cells and stimulate the release of insulin. They differ slightly in their duration of action, method of elimination from the body and potency.

These drugs are generally well-tolerated. Some patients may complain of gastrointestinal upset and weight gain, and on rare occasions they cause a rash, liver damage, or adverse effects on blood cells. Like insulin, the most notable adverse effect is hypoglycemia. They should not be used in pregnancy or in patients known to be hypersensitive to sulfa-containing drugs.

Shortly after this class of drugs came into widespread use in the 1970s, a startling report came from the University Group Diabetes Program

(UGDP) that there was a significant increase in cardiovascular risk in patients on these drugs.[4] A significant controversy lingered for years over the safety of sulfonylureas, despite a general consensus that the study suffered from enough methodological and interpretive problems to render the conclusions invalid.

Metformin

In the late 1990s, a second orally prescribed drug for diabetes, metformin (Glucophage) became available in the United States. It belongs to a class of drugs known as biguanides. Its mechanism of action differs from the sulfonylureas in that it appears to act directly on muscle cells to facilitate the uptake and storage of glucose. It therefore seems to improve insulin sensitivity. It also suppresses glucose production by the liver. It has a low risk of hypoglycemia and has a favorable impact on lipids and weight gain.

Side effects include possible nausea and diarrhea. A major concern, however, is the risk of lactic acidosis, a serious and potentially life-threatening complication. The risk of this occurring is three episodes per 100,000 patient-years of treatment, which is very rare. Patients at risk for this problem are those with kidney or liver disease and in circumstances where a patient may become extremely dehydrated or deprived of oxygen. Judicial use of the medication renders it very safe in most circumstances.

Rezulin

Rezulin (troglitazone) became available for diabetic treatment in the United States in 1997. It belongs to a class of drugs known as thiazolidinediones. These drugs have been targeted to decrease insulin resistance by interacting with a receptor on muscle cells and affecting the way the cell metabolizes glucose. There appear to be other beneficial actions including beneficial effects on lipids and potential antioxidant effects.

It would appear that there are few side effects with treatment. Shortly after the drug was released, there were rare reports of serious liver damage, which caused some centers, notably in the United Kingdom, to advise caution in widespread use of the drug. Studies have shown that approximately 2% of individuals may develop reversible elevations of liver enzymes. The manufacturer recommends that patients be tested frequently during the initial phases of treatment to screen for liver function abnormalities. Also, these drugs may slightly reduce blood counts.

---

[4] University Group Diabetes Program, *A Study of the Effects of Hypoglycemic Agents on Vascular Complications in Patients with Adult-Onset Diabetes II — Mortality Results*, 19 Diabetes 789, 1970.

Precose

The 1990s saw yet another new class of drugs to treat diabetes become available. These drugs are known as alpha-glucosidase inhibitors, and Precose (acarbose) is the currently approved agent of this type. The major benefit of these drugs is their ability to decrease the rise in blood sugar seen following a meal. They act by blocking the enzymes in the first part of the small intestine that breaks down starch particles into glucose. Therefore, there is a delay in glucose absorption until the starch particles move further down the intestines where they eventually are absorbed. The main side effects are flatulence, diarrhea and abdominal discomfort.

Prandin

Prandin (repaglinide) was released in 1998. It acts similarly to the sulfonylureas and is being marketed as a more effective drug to stimulate the release of insulin quickly when given before meals. However, there are potential interactions between Prandin and certain drugs metabolized by the liver.

§ 30A.12. Choice of drug therapy.

Medical treatment of diabetes is going through major changes as the twentieth century comes to a close. Insulin continues to be the mainstay of Type I diabetes, but type II diabetic treatment is expanding rapidly. The doubts and hesitancy regarding the use of sulfonylureas that pervaded the 1970s has been replaced by a zeal to detect and treat hyperglycemia and hyperinsulinemia well before any diabetic symptoms appear. Studies have shown that at least half of Type II diabetics have atherosclerosis and that eye changes may be present in 15%-20% at the time of diagnosis.

Armed with a growing understanding of the pathophysiology of Type II diabetes and new drugs to choose from, treatment of these patients is becoming more successful. Whereas monotherapy has traditionally been the approach, combinations of drugs are being used more and more to try to treat difficult patients. The initial choice of drug is generally determined by the physician based on his or her familiarity with the drug and assessment regarding the risks and benefits as they apply to a specific patient. If the drug causes unacceptable side effects, an alternate is chosen.

The medication is then gradually increased until blood sugar control is achieved. Not uncommonly a second drug is added if the sugars remain higher than desirable. It has been shown that some combinations of drugs are synergistic at low doses (*i.e.* they work better together than either by itself). This approach seems logical when one considers that the drugs are acting at different sites of glucose metabolism. The most widely used oral combination is a sulfonylureas and metformin. Acarbose has also been added to both of these agents.

Type II diabetes patients not controlled on oral drugs are sometimes given insulin — usually at most one or two injections of a long-acting preparation. Conversely, some Type I patients on insulin will be given an oral agent if necessary. Acarbose can help prevent post meal hyperglycemia. Rezulin has been shown to decrease insulin doses in some Type I patients.

§ 30A.13. Replacement of pancreas.

Since insulin injections cannot possibly duplicate the sensitive, finely-modulated pancreatic control of blood glucose, modern science is attempting to construct an artificial pancreas. The essential components would include (1) a glucose-sensing device connected to an arterial blood supply, (2) a depot of crystalline insulin, (3) a mechanism for extruding insulin into the portal venous blood, (4) an energy source, and (5) a system that coordinates all of these components. Work is proceeding steadily along all these lines, and experimental "artificial pancreas" implants have been developed; however, they are still some distance from clinical application.

The alternative to an artificial pancreas is the option of pancreatic transplantation. The major drawback to this procedure is the requirement for life-long immunosuppresion that involves drugs that have potential toxic effects and can aggravate hyperglycemia. The main candidates for pancreatic transplants are diabetics with end-stage renal disease requiring a kidney transplant (who will require immunosuppresion anyway). Donor kidneys can come from cadavers or relatives; donor pancreases generally come from cadavers because the risk to a living relative donating part of a pancreas is felt to be unacceptable. Worldwide, nearly 8,000 pancreas transplants have been performed. The success rates improve steadily. Today, patients undergoing simultaneous kidney-pancreas transplantation show a 74% pancreatic graft survival and a 92% kidney survival at one year.[5]

Pancreatic transplantation for maintenance of insulin secretion holds the promise of providing the diabetic patient with optimal metabolic regulation through normal physiologic control mechanisms. As in transplantation of other tissue, immunologic rejection remains the major obstacle. However, exciting and fundamental advances have been made in

---

[5] Sutherland, D. E. R., et al., "Pancreas Transplant Results in the United Network for Organ Sharing (UNOS) USA Registry with a Comparison to Non-USA Data in the International Registry," in *Clinical Transplants* (P. Terasaki and G. Cecka, editors, UCLA Tissue Typing Laboratory, Los Angeles, 1993.

Editor's Note: On the transplantation of organs generally, see Chapter 30B of this Cyclopedia.

islet cell transplantation. This process involves recovering islet cells from pancreatic tissue, then infusing them into the vein going to the liver. The cells lodge within the liver tissue and presumably grow and become active secreting insulin. To date, this procedure is still considered highly experimental, with only a 20% chance of the patient becoming completely insulin-independent.

§ 30A.14. Extremes, complexities, and complications of diabetes.

The diabetic patient incurs the risk of many medical misadventures during his lifetime. These may be best understood if categorized as extremes, complexities, and complications of diabetes, as shown in **Table 1.**

Table 1
EXTREMES, COMPLEXITIES, AND COMPLICATIONS OF DIABETES

I. Extremes
    A. Hypoglycemia
    B. Diabetic coma
        1. Ketoacidosis
        2. Hyperosmolarity
        3. Lactic acidosis

II. Complexities
    A. Diabetes and growth
    B. Diabetes in pregnancy
    C. Diabetes and infection
    D. Trauma or surgery in the diabetic

III. Complications
    A. Microvascular complications
        1. Retinopathy
        2. Nephropathy
    B. Larger vascular complications
        1. Coronary artery disease
        2. Peripheral vascular disease
    C. Diabetic neuropathy
    D. Diabetic dermopathy
    E. Other complications

§ 30A.15. Diabetic extremes.

(A) HYPOGLYCEMIA

Hypoglycemia, or low-blood glucose, can occur in settings where the diabetic (1) takes too much insulin or oral medication, or (2) takes too little food, or (3) over-exercises. The increased utilization of glucose by muscle and adipose tissue lowers the blood glucose. Below 60 mg.% symptoms may develop; below 40 mg.% the symptoms are usually severe; and below 25 mg.% the patient is usually unconscious. Symptoms arise because the function of the central nervous system deteriorates from lack of energy supplied in the form of glucose; insulin has diverted this to muscle and adipose tissue at the expense of the brain. Symptoms affect first the higher centers of the brain, then lower and more primitive neurological functions. The patient may pass through typical stages: (1) hunger, "an inward trembling," weakness, anxiety, irritability, depression and emotional lability; (2) blurred vision, loss of coordination, and difficulty in walking or standing; (3) slurred speech or mutism; (4) loss of bladder or bowel control; and (5) stupor, convulsion, and deep coma. From this point the coma may proceed to death, or it may lighten but never fully lift, or the patient may recover, either completely or with varying neurological or personality defects.

Early in this course, a neurological reflex causes increased secretion of catecholamines (adrenalin) to effect muscle glycogen breakdown (thus restoring blood glucose), and this secretion causes secondary changes such as rapid heart beat, higher blood pressure, severe sweating, dilated pupils, pallor, tremors, etc. Hypoglycemia also causes increased glucagon secretion to effect breakdown of liver glycogen to glucose. Later on there is increased secretion of growth hormone and ACTH.

Hypoglycemia is an acute emergency, requiring immediate correction by giving the sufferer generous amounts of glucose by mouth in the form of sugar, honey, candy, or a sweetened beverage. If the patient is comatose, emergency personnel should be summoned who can administer intravenous glucose intravenously. Families of diabetics should also have injectable glucagon available. This can be injected into the subcutaneous tissue or muscle and will temporarily raise the blood sugar to allow the individual to consume glucose orally. Food should never be forced into the mouth of an unconscious person for fear of causing aspiration into the lungs and life-threatening breathing complications.

(B) DIABETIC COMA

Diabetic coma may occur in a number of forms. Treatment depends upon the underlying mechanism of the problem. As discussed above, severe and prolonged hypoglycemia can render a person unconscious, and is quickly reversible by glucose administration. Coma can also be caused by severe cases of diabetic ketoacidosis, hyperosmolarity, or lactic acidosis.

Ketoacidosis

Diabetic ketoacidosis is a condition brought on by insulin deficiency. It occurs exclusively in Type I diabetics. If there is inadequate insulin, and the blood sugar rises over about 200mg/dl, the kidney is unable to reabsorb glucose, and glucose spills into the urine (glycosuria). If the process goes unchecked, the urine, heavily laden with osmotically active sugar,

25

draws with it fluid from the body and leads to excessive urination and subsequent dehydration. The lack of insulin also leads to the breakdown of stored triglyceride, which leads to increased free fatty acids in the blood and increased production of ketone bodies by the liver (appearing in the blood as "ketonemia" and in the urine as "ketonuria"), and eventually systemic acidosis (acid-base imbalance). Although the blood glucose is high, the dehydration and acidosis combine to impair the utilization of glucose by the tissues of the central nervous system. Such patients become thirsty, weak and listless, nauseated (often with protracted vomiting), hot, dry and drowsy, then stuporous, and finally comatose. Through an auxiliary respiratory response to acidosis, they often breathe deeply and rapidly ("Kussmaul respiration"). The odor of acetone on the exhaled breath is classical. These patients will die unless prompt and continuous medical care can be obtained to provide the appropriate amounts of insulin, adequate intravenous fluid, electrolytes (especially potassium), and accessory therapeutic measures. Even then, improvement can rarely be detected earlier than six hours of intensive care, and most patients require several days to be stabilized, and placed back on a good maintenance program.

Ketoacidosis is sometimes the initial sign of unsuspected and untreated diabetes. It may also develop because of the omission of insulin injections, intercurrent infections, severe stress, gastrointestinal upsets, or accidental or surgical trauma without compensatory change in the therapeutic program.

Hyperosmolarity

Another form of diabetic coma is hyperosmolarity (also called hyperosmolar coma), which is now recognized as carrying a higher mortality rate (about 50%) than ketoacidosis. This problem occurs almost exclusively in elderly or middle-aged Type II diabetics. Generally, some event such as illness or incapacity leads to decreasing diabetic control and rising blood sugars with concomitant glycosuria and dehydration. Either because the patients have a diminished thirst response or are unable to access liquids, the process can accelerate, leading to blood sugar levels as much 1000 mg/dl. or more. Because these patients have some endogenous insulin production, fatty acid breakdown is spared, and ketoacidosis does not occur.

The sluggish circulation of thick, viscous blood, plus dehydration of the brain, may explain the neurological manifestations. These patients need correction of their massive dehydration and hyperosmolarity, which is best done by giving large amounts of intravenous fluids of less than physiological osmolarity. Since the heart, lungs, and circulatory tree can easily become overloaded by excessive hydration, the physician often finds it difficult if not impossible to strike the right balance between haste and restraint, which may contribute to the high mortality.

Lactic acidosis

A rare form of diabetic coma is lactic acidosis, which may occur in any patient with severe circulatory collapse and low oxygen levels. This situation is seen in patients with massive heart attacks, congestive heart failure, and severe infections and shock. Lactic acid is formed in large quantities by breakdown of muscle glycogen and by metabolism of pyruvate to lactate in the absence of oxygen. The result is intense acidosis with an extreme craving for air ("Kussmaul respiration"), dehydration, weakness, and coma, but these patients usually do not have excessive ketone body production and hyperglycemia may not be striking. Treatment should be prompt, intensive, and persistent, and aimed at correcting the circulatory impairment and the acidosis by giving intravenous bicarbonate.

Phenformin (a biguanide) was used in the United States for Type II diabetics until 1977, when it was withdrawn because of an association with an unacceptably high risk of lactic acidosis. Metformin, which has recently been approved, potentially can cause this disorder if used injudiciously in patients at high-risk patients for this condition.

§ 30A.16. Diabetic complexities.

Because diabetes is a life long condition, it will have a major impact on all phases of an individual's growth and development as well as be a factor in trauma and other illnesses.

(A) PERIOD OF GROWTH

Growth in childhood requires a generous intake of protein, a plentiful supply of calories, and a pattern of hormone secretion that favors building up body tissues. The juvenile diabetic must be given all the dietary necessities, and his insulin program must be tailored to allow for proper metabolism. Insulin requirements for children may rise two- or threefold during the adolescent growth spurt.

(B) PREGNANCY[6]

Pregnancy poses several special problems for the diabetic. There may be impaired fertility if diabetic control is poor. Once pregnant, the patient faces three threats: spontaneous abortion, stillbirth, and neonatal death. It is critical that insulin be used throughout. Oral hypoglycemic agents are not recommended. During the first six months of pregnancy,

---

[6] Editor's Note: See also Chapter 37, § 37.12c of this Cyclopedia with regard to pregnancy and diabetes.

27

insulin requirements, if any, should be minimal. During the third trimester, however, dosage may need to be increased every week or two to maintain good control, and the patient should be observed closely for hypertension or swelling of the ankles. It may be advisable to deliver the diabetic patient's baby early, at the 37th or 38th week of pregnancy, to avoid stillbirth or delivery of a large, edematous (swollen, with excessive fluid) infant with poor chance of survival. Pregnancy imposes a metabolic trauma on mother as well as child, and its severity increases with age, duration of the diabetes, and the number of pregnancies.

The infants of diabetic mothers are especially prone to respiratory distress, stillbirth, low serum glucose, low serum calcium, and birth injury. The incidence of congenital defects in the infants of diabetic mothers has been reported to be two to five times greater than in infants of nondiabetic mothers, depending on duration and severity of the mother's illness.

The pregnant patient with known diabetes also experiences personal medical problems such as an inreased risk of wide swings of blood sugar (between hyperglycemia with ketoacidosis and low blood sugar). Acceleration of kidney, eye, and neuropathic complications of diabetes during these pregnancies occurs when women are not meticulously cared for and when pregnancies are complicated by untreated hypertension.

Careful regulation of the pregnant patient with diabetes, frequent use of home glucose monitoring and either multiple injections of insulin daily or an insulin pump, along with significant advances in techniques for monitoring the fetus and placenta, has dramatically improved the outlook for the diabetic mother and her newborn infant. This intensive treatment has been facilitated by the establishment of specialized centers to manage high-risk pregnancies and the ability to identify fetal distress or compromise by specific hormone assays and stress tests.

The potential for improving pregnancy outcomes and increasing fetal survival in this group has changed dramatically in some large centers, in some cases approximating that of nondiabetic mothers.

(C) INFECTION

Infection with fever and prostration always upsets diabetic regulation and increases insulin requirements, because of increased secretion of adrenal gluco-corticoids and glucagon. The problem becomes even more complicated if loss of appetite, nausea, or vomiting interfere with proper nutrition; patients may then become dehydrated as well as hyperglycemic, and the transition into ketoacidosis can take place rapidly. The physician can handle some of these problems without hospitalization provided (1) the patient can take fluids by mouth, (2) blood glucose can be determined at frequent intervals and urine can be tested frequently for ketones, (3) regular insulin can be given frequently, and (4) the underlying infection can be handled adequately. Patients and their families must avoid the two most common mistakes: (1) delaying prompt contact with the physician and (2) omitting insulin because the patient is not eating.

(D) TRAUMA OR SURGERY

Trauma and surgery pose essentially the same metabolic threat in diabetes: a worsening mediated by increased secretion of catecholamines, adrenal glucocorticoids, and perhaps glucagon as well. Surgery is usually planned ahead, at least by a matter of hours, and during the planning phase every effort should be made to improve diabetic control. During surgery, generous amounts of calories should be given in intravenous fluids, and insulin should be administered at frequent, regular intervals, with close monitoring of blood glucose, until the patient is once again taking his usual diet by mouth. At this point, the patient will usually respond predictably to reinstitution of his former insulin or oral medication, so long as activity can be maintained to contribute to lowering of the blood glucose.

§ 30A.17. Diabetic complications.

Included in this discussion are those pathologic entities that are considered hallmarks of the disease. Whereas in previous years, these conditions were believed to be an inevitable consequence attributable to something intrinsic to the diabetic condition, these problems are now believed to be due to "glucotoxicity," which implies that it is the high circulating blood sugar that is the damaging factor. It is believed that many glucose molecules affix to various tissue proteins, which cause structural and functional alterations such as thickened tendons that limit flexibility or thickened blood vessel linings that impair oxygen flow to the cells.

The results of the ten-year Diabetes Control and Complications Trial (DCCT) and other studies support this concept and further conclude that these complications can be prevented, or at least minimized, by maintaining blood sugars in the near-normal range throughout the diabetic's life.

The complications of diabetes are classified as (1) microvascular (*i.e.*, small blood vessel or capillary damage) and (2) macrovascular (large blood vessel damage and nerve damage (neuropathy). Both Type I and Type II diabetics are at risk for developing these complications.

(A) MICROVASCULAR COMPLICATIONS

Although microvascular complications probably affect all tissues in the body, the most worrisome and disabling organ damage occurs in the retina (lining in the back of the eye) and the kidney. The pathologic process involves progressive thickening of the capillaries. Since these vessels are the final conduits of vital nutrients and oxygen from the circulatory system to the tissues, this process leads to cellular damage.

Retinopathy

As with other microvascular changes, diabetic retinopathy is generally not seen until the individual's diabetes has been present at least ten years. The initial changes are termed "nonproliferative" changes and include dilation of the capillaries and sluggish blood flow. Small aneurysms, hemorrhages and leakage of fluid can be seen within the retina. As the disease progresses, "proliferative retinopathy" can develop. This term implies growth of unchecked new blood vessels over the retina. All of these changes progressively impair vision by damaging the surface of the retina. Eventual blindness can be the end result. Diabetes is the second leading cause of blindness in the United States.[7]

Using laser treatments to prevent proliferation of the new blood vessels and to halt progression that has already begun has proven to be very effective. However, controlling blood sugar throughout the diabetic's lifetime is by far the most effective way to prevent blindness. The DCCT study showed that for every 10% reduction in the hemoglobin A1C, there is a 40% decline in the incidence of retinopathy. Controlling blood pressure also decreases this complication.

Since these changes can only be appreciated through direct visualization of the retina, an annual visit to an ophthalmologist is considered of paramount importance in managing diabetes.

Nephropathy

Nephropathy means kidney disease. Kidney lesions, unlike lesions in the retina, are not accessible by direct visualization. Routine urine and blood testing lead to the diagnosis. Normally, there should be no protein in the urine. Detection of even small amounts heralds the first sign of diabetic nephropathy. Once detected, the deterioration in kidney function follows a linear decline over the ensuring ten to twenty years resulting in increased proteinuria and rising levels of BUN and creatinine (the blood tests that measure kidney function).

The kidney performs many functions, the most important of which are elimination of toxins, control of bodily fluids, and regulation of blood pressure. Declining renal function leads to accumulation of organic acids and other chemicals that cause the patient to feel poorly, with fatigue, nausea and declining mental capacities. Prescription drugs, if not adjusted in dosage, can reach toxic levels. In addition, the patient's blood pressure will rise, fluid retention will occur, and he will become anemic.

---

[7] About 5,000 new cases of blindness related to diabetes are reported annually in the United States. After ten years of diabetes, half of all patients have retinopathy. After fifteen years, more than 80% of all patients have some diabetic retinopathy.

Eventually, when end-stage renal disease occurs, either dialysis or kidney transplantation will be necessary. The latter is the preferable alternative; however it is difficult to find suitable donors. Transplanted kidneys have traditionally come from cadavers or relatives, but improved anti-rejection therapies are now allowing nonrelated donors to successfully donate kidneys.[8]

Diabetes has become the most common cause of end-stage renal disease in the United States, with medical expenditures for the condition exceeding now $2 billion annually. Approximately 20%-30% of Type I diabetics who have had diabetes for more than twenty-five years develop nephropathy. The incidence is less in Type II diabetics, since these patients experience a later onset and thus shorter duration of the disease.

Recent studies are showing that controlling blood sugar and hypertension will have a significant impact on ameliorating and even preventing the onset and progression of diabetic nephropathy. Over the last ten years, a new class of hypertensive drugs, the ACE inhibitors, have been shown to significantly delay the progression of proteinuria and renal decline in not only diabetics, but other patients with renal disease. These medications are the drug of choice for diabetics with high blood pressure and are also now advocated for use in any diabetic with proteinuria.

(B) MACROVASCULAR COMPLICATIONS[9]

Larger vascular complications are those that present clinically as arterial atherosclerosis, a process by which there is a build up of cholesterol, calcium, and other material along the lining of blood vessels. This results in progressive narrowing of the vessel, limiting blood flow. Although the process occurs throughout the body, the most clinically significant vessels are the coronary arteries (supplying the heart), the carotid arteries (supplying the brain) and the major vessels to the lower extremities. Compromised blood flow to these areas leads to angina pectoris, prestroke syndromes, and claudication (leg pain), respectively. Complete blockage to these areas leads to heart attacks, completed strokes and gangrene of the lower extremities. It is unclear why diabetes, *per se*, accelerates this process but it is considered a major risk factor along with hypertension, smoking, and high cholesterol.

Coronary artery disease

Coronary artery disease causes angina pectoris, leads to myocardial infarction, and is a cause of cardiac enlargement and heart failure due to poor circulation. Hypertension, which is also common in diabetes, inten-

---

[8] Editor's Note: Kidney transplantation is discussed in Chapter 30B of this Cyclopedia.

[9] Editor's Note: For a detailed discussion of the heart and circulatory disorders mentioned in this section, see Chapter 34 of this Cyclopdia.

sifies all these problems. Their management requires a dedicated effort to eliminate smoking and overweight, to exercise regularly and to use cardiac drugs appropriately. In mild cases, "medical therapy" can be appropriate, i.e., the use of medications such as nitroglycerin and beta blockers. If the coronary arteries are significantly narrowed, more aggressive intervention has been shown to decrease symptoms and prevent heart attacks. Coronary artery bypass grafting (CABG) procedures have been performed routinely since the late 1970s. Veins taken from the legs, or rerouting an artery adjacent to the heart, can be used to bypass the blocked coronaries during an open heart surgical procedure. More recently, less invasive options such as a catheter inserted through the groin is threaded internally to the blocked area and either a balloon is inflated to dilate the artery (percutaneous balloon angioplasty) or a device mechanically chews away the plaque (atherectomy) is employed. Since blockages can reoccur following these latter procedures, cardiologists are now starting to place stents (small coils akin to one found in a ball point pen) within the dilated arteries to keep them open.

Peripheral vascular disease

Peripheral vascular disease is an insidious process that gradually reduces the blood flow to the feet and legs to and below the point of adequate nutrition. If a localized block in a large vessel is demonstrated, a vein or teflon graft may be used to reroute blood flow past the obstruction, but if small vessel disease is the basic problem, such surgery will be futile. In all cases, the physician must teach the diabetic patient scrupulous care of the feet: proper shoes and socks, care of the nails, prevention of trauma, and cleanliness at all times. If in spite of all precautions, tissue death, gangrene, or osteomyelitis still occur, amputation is the only recourse, usually just below or above the knee.[10] These patients can usually manage quite well on a prosthesis but, after a period of time (on the average about two years), they will often face similar surgery on the other leg.

Amputation for foot ulcers is much more common in diabetic patients as compared with the nondiabetic population. These lesions are caused by peripheral vascular disease, lead to an inadequate blood supply and neuropathy, and result in an insensitive and deformed foot. Their presence makes the diabetic foot highly susceptible to serious injuries, ulceration, gangrene, infection, and ultimately amputation.

Prevention methods include careful control of the diabetes itself, elimination or control of risk factors, elimination of vascular obstructions, careful and early treatment of foot lesions, and patient education. Where

---

[10] Editor's Note: For a discussion of amputation and the use of prostheses, see Chapter 35 of this Cyclopedia.

possible, smoking should be discontinued because of the role it plays in causing peripheral vascular spasm.

(C) DIABETIC NEUROPATHY

Diabetic neuropathy is a fairly common complication of diabetes, but its development is still poorly understood. There is evidence of vascular disease involving the nutrient vessels to the nerves, of biochemical abnormality, and of death of nerve tissue itself. There also is evidence of nerve swelling due to an accumulation of carbohydrate metabolites called polyols. Swelling can cause nerve damage because of the constraints of the fibrous sheath surrounding the nerve. Clinically, diabetic neuropathy is expressed in many ways, including involvement of cranial nerves, spinal cord, autonomic nervous system and the peripheral nervous system, which involves sensory and motor nerves.

Peripheral neuropathy

The nerves to the lower extremities are the most commonly affected sites of diabetic neuropathy. Early symptoms are burning pain and numbness in the feet and legs. This persists for a variable number of weeks or months and eventually disappears, usually leaving persistent numbness (*i.e.*, the nerve has become completely dead). These patients have most of their discomfort at night and are depressed and quite dependent on the physician for relief of even minor pain. These patients also experience difficulty in perceiving temperature changes, particularly in the feet. Because of this, they may burn their feet by improper use of heating pads or hot water bottles, or by plunging their feet into hot water without checking the temperature first.

Data suggest that careful diabetic control may improve neuropathic symptons, but there is no specific pharmacologic therapy for diabetic neuropathy. Treatment with some of the psychoactive drugs has been of some benefit in certain patients. It does not decrease the actual pain, but rather the perception of pain, primarily in the lower extremities. The drug used most frequently is amitriptyline, an antidepressant with sedative effects. Since it has been suggested that diabetic neuropathy may be due to polyol accumulation in nerve sheaths, an enzymatic agent that interferes with this accumulation — an aldose reductase inhibitor called sorbinil — has been tried. However, reports of its effectiveness have been mixed, and there has not been enthusiastic acceptance.

Autonomic neuropathy

The autonomic nervous system, comprised of the sympathetic and parasympathetic nervous system is responsible for controlling the unconscious functions of the circulatory, respiratory and digestive systems, as well as a myriad of other regulatory processes. Diabetic nerve damage can be manifested in any of these areas. The most common problems that develop are insufficiencies in controlling blood pressure with changes in position (orthostatic hypotension), which leads to dizziness and fainting; delay in gastric emptying, which can cause abdominal discomfort and nausea; acceleration of intestinal activity causing diarrhea; difficulties in bladder emptying; and erectile difficulties in men leading to impotence.

These problems are addressed individually, and various treatments may be helpful. Medications such as florinef may help control drops in blood pressure; support stockings are also useful. The distressing gastrointestinal symptoms, particularly the nocturnal diarrhea, may be partially controlled by changing meal patterns or also by using low-dose broad spectrum antibiotics. Impotence can by aided by implantation of a prosthesis into the penis, either rigid or inflatable, to permit intercourse. Rarely, the diabetic male may also have retrograde ejaculation, with sperm being lost into the bladder rather than ejected into the partner. This obviously impairs the ability to fertilize. At this time, there is no medical or surgical therapy for this particular problem.

Visceral neuropathic symptoms may also include "neurogenic bladder," as a result of which the patient experiences decreased sensation of the need to void, with occasional over-distention of the bladder and resultant "over-flow incontinence." In such situations, where urine accumulates in the bladder as a result of incomplete emptying, particularly if there is significant glycosuria, a fertile breeding ground for infection may develop. To control this problem, the patient can be taught to perform frequent self-catherization of the bladder to keep it as empty as possible, learn manual pressure techniques to help empty the bladder, or use low-dose oxybutynin (Ditropan) therapy to decrease bladder spasm. Unfortunately, this medication may cause severe side effects in the form of blurred vision, dryness of the mouth, and cardiac effects, which may contraindicate its use in some patients.

(D) DIABETIC DERMOPATHY

Diabetic dermopathy includes two rather innocuous but characteristic lesions of the lower extremities, *necrobiosis lipoidica diabeticorum* and diabetic "shin spots," neither of which cause symptoms or require therapy. Of more concern is the tendency for the diabetic to acquire superficial skin infections — namely boils, carbuncles, and cellulitis — because of the danger of these lesions in extremities with poor blood supply. The diabetic's response to infection is impaired anyway, and healing is slow, except in younger diabetics under good control. The combination of neuropathy (with decreased sensation of touch, pain, and temperature) and vascular insufficiency makes the feet particularly vulnerable to tight shoes, friction, blisters, badly trimmed nails, ill-advised attempts to "warm up" cold feet, and sharp objects on the floor, all of which can induce a break in the skin that allows infection that can go on to gangrene.

An annoying feature of uncontrolled diabetes is the increased susceptibility to infection by certain yeast organisms (Monilia) of warm moist mucous membranes, *i.e.*, mouth and genitalia. Balanitis in the male and vaginitis in the female cause severe itching, discharge, inflammation, and discomfort. Treatment should include control of the diabetes as well as the yeast infection.

II. RELATED TOPICS

§ 30A.18. Diabetes as a cause of accidents.

It has been suggested that a diabetic can live nearly as normally as the nondiabetic, and that with appropriate care he is not predisposed to more hazards than the nondiabetic.[11] The key, of course, is appropriate care. Common sense dictates that, because of the blurred vision and drowsiness that can be experienced by a diabetic who is insulin-deficient, and the possibility of dizziness or even blackout in the diabetic who suffers an insulin or oral hypoglycemic drug reaction, there may be a greater hazard involved under certain circumstances. Of greatest concern, of course, is the diabetic driver; next would be the diabetic who operates potentially dangerous industrial machinery.

Industrial accidents involving diabetics are relatively few, mainly because of strict safety regulations and the fact that diabetics generally have some warning of a severe attack. Automobile accidents are more common, especially in metropolitan areas with limited-access highways and congested traffic, and diabetic drivers are classified by some authorities as "accident-prone."[12] However, with the advent of self-monitoring techniques and the greater opportunity offered to tighter control, the well-motivated well-controlled diabetic is experiencing fewer reactions, and those that do occur can be anticipated and be controlled more easily. The end result could be fewer accidents and industrial problems related to diabetes and its control, particularly in those patients who had previously experienced severe hypoglycemic reactions but now self-monitor.

---

[11] In a three-year study of 7,599 diabetics insured under accident insurance policies, researchers in Denmark reported that the risk of accidents for diabetics was 0.7 per 1,000 person-years compared to an average of 5 per 1,000 person-years in two nondiabetic control groups. Mathiesen, B., and Borch-Johnsen, K., *Diabetes and Accident Insurance: A 3-Year Follow-Up of 7,599 Insured Diabetic Individuals*, 20 Diabetes Care 1781 (Nov.), 1997.

[12] See Annotation, "Denial, suspension, or cancellation of driver's license because of physical disease or defect," 38 A.L.R.3d 452; Annotation, "Physical defect, illness, drowsiness, or falling asleep of motor vehicle operator as affecting liability for injury, 28 A.L.R.2d 12. See also Chapter 13A, § 13A.9, this Cyclopedia. On accident-proneness generally, see Chapter 18, this Cyclopedia.

A driver who is unaware that he suffers from diabetes, and who because of his disease becomes drowsy and causes an accident, is not necessarily chargeable with negligence;[13] nor is a driver whose diabetes is well-regulated and whose reactions to insulin or oral hypoglycemic drugs are mild and preceded by a warning.[14] If, however, a diabetic knows that he is susceptible to the symptoms of his disease or an insulin or oral hypoglycemic drug reaction, his chances of being found liable for an accident arising out of such an occurrence are greatly increased.[15] A diabetic driver who blacked out from an insulin reaction and struck another automobile was deemed negligent "to an extreme degree" where it was discovered that, in the back seat of his car, he had both candy bars and a Coke which would have warded off his attack.[16]

In all states, if a driver suffers from a physical defect making him an obvious hazard on the highways, his driver's license may be suspended or revoked, subject to a proper administrative hearing. In several cases involving diabetic drivers who experienced insulin reactions while driving, courts have reinstated their driving privileges on the strength of an otherwise good driving record, medical testimony that there would be only a "slight possibility" of future attacks, and evidence that a person on insulin normally has adequate warning of a reaction.[17] In one case, the driver's own testimony to this effect was deemed sufficient.[18]

The U.S. Department of Transportation can prohibit insulin-dependent diabetic drivers to operate public and commercial vehicles in certain cases unless a waiver is obtained by the driver's employer.[19]

---

[13] Annotation, "Physical defect, illness, drowsiness, or falling asleep of motor vehicle operator as affecting liability for injury, 28 A.L.R.2d 12.

[14] See Porter v. Price (Utah, 1960) 355 P.2d 66.

[15] See Lutzkovitz v. Murray (Del. Super., 1975) 339 A.2d 64; Howle v. PYA/Monarch, Inc. (S.C. App., 1986) 344 S.E.2d 157.

[16] Gambino v. Lubel (La. App., 1966) 190 So. 2d 152.

[17] See Annotation, "Denial, suspension, or cancellation of driver's license because of physical disease or defect," 38 A.L.R.3d 452.

[18] Dehrone License (1959) 21 Pa. D. & C.2d 542.

[19] See, e.g., Daugherty v. City of El Paso (C.A.-5 Tex., 1995) 56 F.3d 695 (city bus driver); Baert v. Euclid Beverage, Ltd. (N.D. Ill., 1997) 954 F. Supp. 170 (truck driver-salesman).

The question of diabetic drivers and public safety came up in Canada in the early 1990s. The Nova Scotia Supreme Court struck down a legislative ban preventing diabetics from obtaining a license for driving tractor-trailer trucks. The court held that, while it is appropriate to inquire as to whether an individual's diabetes may affect the ability to drive, in view of new developments in the control of the disease, a blanket prohibition against licensing was unjustified. Hines v. Nova Scotia Registrar of Motor Vehicles (1990) 73 D.L.R.4th 91 (N.S.S.C., T.D.). Applying the same reasoning, Canada's Federal Court Trial Division struck down a federal regulation that categorically prevented diabetics from qualifying for a pilot's license if their diabetes could not be controlled by diet. The court held that the regulation was discriminatory in the absence of a showing that it was impossible to perform individualized assessments of would-be diabetic pilots. Bahlsen v. Minister of Transport (1995) F.C.J. No. 1026 (T.D.).

§ 30A.19. Trauma as a cause of diabetes.

There is general agreement that, in certain instances, trauma can cause diabetes mellitus, but probably only where the blood supply to the pancreas has been interrupted either by direct or blunt trauma, or where there has been destruction of the islet cells. Anecdotal instances have described blunt trauma with a child falling or being thrust over handle bars of a bicycle, with disruption of pancreatic blood supply, necessitating surgery, and ultimately resulting in diabetes mellitus. Obviously, in such a case, the patient would become insulin dependent automatically, and there would not be the genetic background or familial disposition normally attributed to Type I or Type II diabetes mellitus, as described in §§ 30A.5 and 30A.6 of this chapter.

In a 1969 Illinois case,[20] which involved a workman who fell from a scaffold and suffered severe internal injuries, medical evidence at the trial suggested that the claimant developed diabetes as a result of a direct injury to the pancreas. Also, in a 1973 Louisiana case,[21] $520,000 was awarded in an automobile accident claim in which it was alleged that a woman's total incapacity was the result of a minor blow to the pancreas. Commenting on the medical evidence, the Court of Appeals of Louisiana said:[22]

> Causation is also established by medical evidence as more probable than not. To the layman the chain of medical events seems incredible. Yet the experts were unanimous that a slight trauma to the pancreas could cause the excruciating journey through pseudo-cyst, diabetes, intestinal block, heart ailment, pneumonitis and stroke to the ultimate devastation of plaintiff wife's now surgery-ravaged, nigh-immobile, bladder-catheterized and colostomied body and severely brain-damaged, parrot-like mind. The opinion was nearly unanimous that in this case all problems were the foreseeable result of some trauma to the pancreas.

In another Illinois case, however, a plaintiff who developed diabetes following an accident recovered damages even though there was no apparent injury to her pancreas. The plaintiff, a fifty-seven-year-old woman in general good health, suffered a fractured tibia and a shoulder injury when struck by a motor vehicle. During a ten-day hospital stay, she was found to be suffering from diabetes and was placed on oral hypoglycemics. At the trial, three physicians testified that a diabetic condition could be triggered by trauma, although one of the physicians was of the opinion that this did not occur in the plaintiff's case. A fourth physician testified that traumatically induced diabetes could not be controlled by oral medication.[23]

---

[20] Kaspar v. Clinton-Jackson Corp. (1969) 118 Ill. App. 2d 364, 254 N.E.2d 826.

[21] Becnel v. Ward (La. App., 1973) 286 So. 2d 731.

[22] Id., at 732.

[23] Hehir v. Bowers, (Ill. App., 1980) 407 N.E.2d 149.

Lawsuits in which trauma-induced diabetes has been alleged successfully usually have involved a plaintiff with an existing or dormant diabetic condition that was activated by the trauma.[24] For example, see Missouri Pacific Railroad Company v. Diffee,[25] in which an eighteen-year-old boy developed diabetes after he was injured when a train struck his automobile. There was no injury to the pancreas. See also Mose v. Brewer,[26] in which the plaintiff developed diabetes mellitus shortly after being injured in an accident. At the trial, three physicians testified that such trauma could not be the direct cause of the plaintiff's diabetes, but trauma can precipitate the onset of diabetes in a genetically predisposed person.

Drug damage

In defining trauma, if one includes drug damage, there may be supporting evidence of "traumatic diabetes." In susceptible individuals, the following drugs may induce diabetic manifestations: cortisone-type steroids; ethacrynic acid; furosemide; indomethacin; lithium; oral contraceptives; phenothiazines; phenytoin; propranolol; thiazide diuretics; and tricyclic antidepressants.[27]

§ 30A.19a. Stress as a cause of diabetes.

Although some diabetics claim that they can trace the onset of their diabetes to a particularly stressful event, stress itself does not cause diabetes. However, severe stress can unmask the symptoms of diabetes in individuals who are predisposed to the disease. During times of stress, the body releases epinephrine, cortisone, and growth hormone as part of the "fight-or-flight" response.[28] These hormones raise blood-sugar levels in preparation for the brain and muscles to respond to the stressor, and they increase the body's need for insulin. In a person whose pancreas has lost the ability to produce sufficient amounts of insulin, elevated levels of these stress hormones may tax the pancreas enough to reveal diabetes as an underlying problem.[29]

---

[24] Enzer, N., *Trauma and the Diabetic II,* 11 For the Defense 33, 1970.

[25] (1947) 212 Ark. 55, 205 S.W.2d 458. See also Eichholz v. Niagara Falls Hydraulic Power & Mfg. Co. (1902) 68 App. Div. 441, 73 N.Y.S. 842, aff'd. (1903) 174 N.Y. 519, 66 N.E. 1107.

[26] (La. App., 1983) 428 So. 2d 1212.

[27] Long, J. W., and Rybacki, J. J., *The Es-* *sential Guide to Prescription Drugs,* Harper Perennial, New York, 1994, p. 70.

[28] Editor's Note: On the effects of stress on the body generally, see Chapter 19 of this Cyclopedia.

[29] Jeu, L. A., and Strauch, I., *Debunking the Top Diabetes Myths,* 15 Diabetes Self-Mgmt. 58 (Sept./Oct.), 1998.

§ 30A.20. Aggravation of preexisting diabetes.[30]

(A) PERSONAL INJURY CASES

A person with controlled diabetes can lose control of his disease through trauma, infection, or emotional disturbance.[31] One writer has reported seeing ketosis, which is over-production of ketone bodies and an indication that diabetes is out of control, brought on by a moderate sunburn.[32] Also, because of the diabetic's susceptibility to circulatory disturbances, infection, and the tendency not to heal, trauma presents a very severe hazard. For example, a 58-year-old woman with diabetes sustained a comminuted fracture of the thighbone. Her hospitalization covered seventeen months on four separate occasions and she underwent four operations. During hospitalization her diabetes was difficult to manage, and she developed a staphylococcus infection that did not respond to treatment. Her leg was still draining three years after the accident.[33]

In a 1989 Louisiana case, a fifty-seven-year-old male diabetic suffered electrical injuries when a T.V. antenna he was installing came in contact with a power line. The plaintiff suffered third-degree burns of his feet, hands, back, and abdomen. His diabetic condition delayed healing, he suffered posttraumatic stress, and decubitus ulcers developed on his lower legs that required extensive treatment. At the time of trial, it appeared that one leg might have to be amputated. The court awarded $229,669, and the defendant's insurer probably considered itself lucky.[34]

A case in Mississippi resulted in a $5,000 recovery for a minor bruise to a diabetic's foot.[35] In today's dollars, the same case would probably have brought $30,000. In a 1991 Ohio case, a minor trauma — injury to the little finger — became infected and the finger had to be amputated partly because of lack of circulation attributed to the plaintiff's preexisting diabetes. The plaintiff received $15,000 in damages.[36]

In personal injury cases involving diabetic plaintiffs, in addition to the complications that the plaintiff will likely suffer because of the disease, his medical expenses may also be higher because of a worsening of the disease itself, which is usually evidenced by an increased need for insulin.[37]

---

[30] See also § 30A.99 (B), (D).

[31] See § 30A.16, supra. For early medico-legal commentary, see also Tolstoi, E., "Diabetes Mellitus," in *Courtroom Medicine,* (M. Houts, editor), Charles C Thomas, Publisher, Springfield, Illinois, 1958; Enzer, N., *Trauma and the Diabetic I,* 11 For the Defense 21, 1970.

[32] Tolstoi, E., "Diabetes Mellitus," in *Courtroom Medicine,* (M. Houts, editor), Charles C Thomas, Publisher, Springfield, Illinois, 1958.

[33] Meagher v. Garvin (1964) 80 Nev. 211, 391 P.2d 507.

[34] Casanova v. Ballard (La. App., 1989) 533 So. 2d 1005.

[35] Walters v. Gilbert (1963) 248 Miss. 77 158 So. 2d 43.

[36] Pace v. Ohio Dep't of Transp. (Ohio Misc., 1991) 594 N.E.2d 187.

[37] See Bailey v. Barnett (Ky. App., 1971) 470 S.W.2d 331; Ziifle v. Allstate Ins. Co. (La. App., 1972) 262 So. 2d 122.

(B) WORKERS' COMPENSATION

Compensation for an on-the-job injury should not be affected by the fact that the employee suffered from preexisting diabetes where the resulting medical expenses or disability can be directly related to the injury.[38] Where a diabetic material handler for metal products company developed a blister on his foot from walking around on hot concrete all day, and the blister infected, eventually leading to gangrene and amputation, compensation was awarded for "injury by accident."[39] Also, where a diabetic accidentally bruised his toe while at work, and infection and gangrene developed with eventual death from a combination of the diabetes, pneumonia, and kidney failure, death benefits were upheld on the theory that the injury probably hastened the employee's death.[40]

But in a Delaware case, a diabetic who complained that a particle of paper material or dust got into his eye and caused an abrasion of the cornea was unsuccessful in his workers' compensation claim. The abrasion healed, but the claimant's sight remained impaired, and eventually a retinal detachment resulted. Compensation was denied on strong medical evidence that the retinal detachment was due to degeneration of the retina brought on by the preexisting diabetes independent of the injury and any other factor associated with employee's work, which included "strenuous" lifting of heavy bales. According to the medical testimony of one ophthalmologist, "the job is not a factor if a man is going to get into trouble with his retina from diabetes."[41]

A diabetic injured on the job as a result of fainting from an insulin reaction generally will be denied compensation unless it can be shown that his injuries were the result of some special hazard attributable to his work. For example, where a diabetic in insulin shock fell from a twelve-inch platform, striking his head on a concrete floor, compensation was denied because the platform on which the employee was required to

---

[38] See, e.g., Urban v. Morris Drywall Spray (Fla. App., 1991) 395 So. 2d 60; Tinker v. Veco, Inc. (Alaska, 1996) 913 P.2d 488.

[39] Paulley v. Industrial Comm'n (1962) 91 Ariz. 266, 371 P.2d 888. See also Williams v. Wilmore-Stanley Joint Venture (1972) 40 App. Div. 2d 744, 336 N.Y.S.2d 813 (claimant stood in wet sand mixing cement, which caused blisters and ulcers).

[40] Avignone Freres, Inc. v. Cardillo (1940) 73 App. D.C. 149, 117 F.2d 385. See also Snyder v. New York State Comm'n for Human Rights (1972) 31 N.Y.2d 284, 338 N.Y.S.2d 620, 290 N.E.2d 821 (compensa-

tion for breakage of blood vessels in eyes attributed to diabetes and tension aggravated by emotional episodes involving work); January v. Zielenski (1975) 27 Md. App. 390 (compensation for infection after foot injured from stepping on stone; Joseph Switken Co. v. Jackson (1975) 17 Pa. Commw. 554, 333 A.2d 500 (compensation for gangrene resulting from glass being embedded in toe; Burns v. Joyner (1975) 264 S.C. 207, 213 S.E.2d 734 (compensation for gangrene that developed from poor circulation during recovery of ankle sprain).

[41] Lawson v. Chrysler Corp. (Del. Super., 1964), 199 A.2d 749.

work presented no greater risk than he would have encountered outside his work.[42]

In a claim under the Mississippi compensation law, which provided for "apportionment" of compensation in certain cases complicated by pre-existing impairments, an award for an on-the-job heart attack was reduced by 50% because of contributing preexisting diabetes and its related vascular disorders.[43]

§ 30A.21. Insurance considerations.[44]

If an applicant for a life, accident, or health insurance policy knowingly fails to disclose at the time of application that he suffered from diabetes mellitus, it is grounds for denial of liability and for rescission of the policy by the insurance company.[45]

Disability policies generally provide greater benefits in the event of accidental injury as opposed to sickness. Also, many life insurance policies contain "double indemnity" or a rider that provides greater benefits should death result from an accident. Under such policies, claims involving diabetics frequently are contested because of the complications that often arise in the diabetic after a relatively minor injury.

In providing benefits for accidental injury, most policies are carefully worded to exclude coverage except where the disability or death following the accidental injury clearly is unassociated with a disease or pre-existing bodily infirmity of any kind. Where an applicant for a policy is known to be a diabetic, the insurer usually will require an endorsement excluding any coverage for any claim involving diabetes in any manner. Therefore, in most jurisdictions, but not all, for a claimant to recover proceeds on behalf of a diabetic under the accident benefit provision of a policy, he will have to prove that the accident, the medical expenses, and any disability or the insured's death would have resulted in the absence of his diabetes.[46]

Contested claims involving diabetic policyholders frequently arise under other than accident benefit provisions. Under almost any form of health insurance (hospitalization, surgical-medical expense, disability income, hospital indemnity plan, etc.), except where now prohibited by

---

[42] Howard v. Ford Motor Co. (Mo. App., 1962) 363 S.W.2d 61.

[43] Cuevas v. Sutter Well Works (1963) 245 Miss. 478, 150 So. 2d 524.

[44] See also § 30A.99 (C).

[45] Carmichael v. Nationwide Life Ins. Co. (Ark., 1991) 818 S.W.2d 39; Knysak v. Shelter Life Ins. Co. (Ill. App., 1995) 652 N.E.2d 852; Massachusetts Mut. Life Ins. Co. v. Manzo (N.J., 1991) 584 A.2d 190; Martin v. Mutual of Omaha Ins. Co. (1967) 198 Kan.

135, 422 P.2d 1009; Rhodes v. Metropolitan Life Ins. Co. (C.A.-5 La., 1949) 172 F.2d 183. See also Annotation, "What constitutes 'serious illness,' 'serious disease,' or equivalent language used in insurance applications," 28 A.L.R.3d 1255.

[46] Annotation, "Preexisting physical condition as affecting liability under accident policy or accident feature of life policy," 84 A.L.R.2d 176. See also § 30A.99(C) herein.

law, a diabetic applicant, if accepted as an insured, is usually accepted only with a rider excluding or limiting coverage for claims involving the disease.

When an insured diabetic files a claim for other than diabetes, he may expect exhaustive investigation by the insurance company to determine if his ailment is complicated by his diabetes. As in the case of the accidental injury, to be successful, a claim on behalf of a diabetic policyholder usually must show proof that the medical or hospital expenses, disability, or death was independent of the diabetes (if the disease was not covered under the policy. Many times this can be difficult, and usually these cases are won only with extensive and detailed medical evidence.

A common situation involves circulatory disturbances, which may or may not be the direct result of diabetes. Louisiana courts have been liberal in this regard. For a case in which recovery was allowed under a credit health policy for the amputation of a diabetic claimant's leg on grounds that a blocked artery could have resulted as easily in a nondiabetic as a diabetic, see Willis v. Continental Casualty Co.[47] Also, for a case in which a very liberal interpretation was given policy provisions to allow recovery for the loss of a diabetic's foot due to gangrene after a burn injury failed to heal, see McCray v. National Life and Accident Insurance Co.[48]

§ 30A.22. Evaluation of disability.

From the standpoint of permanent physical impairment of the whole person, according to the American Medical Association's Committee on Rating of Mental and Physical Impairment[49] a patient with diabetes mellitus should be rated as follows:

1. *Class 1 — Impairment of the whole person, 0% to 5%.* Type II diabetes (noninsulin-dependent), with or without evidence of diabetic microangiopathy, that can be controlled by diet.
2. *Class 2 — Impairment of the whole person, 5% to 10%.* Type II diabetes, with or without evidence of microangiopathy, if satisfactory control of the patient's plasma glucose level requires both a restricted diet and hypoglycemic medication (either an oral agent or insulin).
3. *Class 3 — Impairment of the whole person, 10% to 20%.* Type I diabetes (insulin-dependent) with or without evidence of microangiopathy.
4. *Class 4 — Impairment of the whole person, 20% to 40%.* Type I diabetes and hyperglycemia or hypoglycemia occurs frequently

---

[47] (La. App., 1967) 194 So. 2d 785.
[48] (La. App., 1971) 244 So. 2d 342.
[49] American Medical Association, *Guides* *to the Evaluation of Permanent Impairment*, 4th ed., American Medical Association, Chicago, 1993, pp. 270-71.

despite the conscientious efforts of both the patient and his or her physician.

Disability goes beyond physical impairment, however. A person suffering from diabetes may be much more disabled than the impairment ratings suggest. "Impairment" is purely a medical condition, a "deviation from normal in a body part or organ system and its functioning." "Disability," on the other hand, is defined by the AMA as "an alteration of an individual's capacity to meet personal, social, or occupational demands, or statutory or regulatory requirements, because of an impairment. Disability refers to an activity or task the individual cannot accomplish. Disability arises out of the interaction between impairment and external requirements, especially those of a person's occupation. Disability may be thought of as a gap between what a person *can* do and what the person *needs* or *wants* to do."[50]

Diabetics are well aware of the many problems that can be encountered because of their disease. Diabetes affects the person's insurability, may alter employability, and usually labels the person as a medical patient and not a well individual. The diabetic must accept the need for some level of life-long medical supervision, restrict his or her liberty and pleasures in eating and have more than ordinary concern for the outcome of any illness or injury. In younger persons, there even may be some hesitation about marriage and parenthood.[51] All of these possibilities must be considered in evaluating the diabetic's true disability.

Diabetics who claim disability under the Social Security Act have been denied benefits if their disease can be kept under control with proper insulin therapy and medical counsel.[52] Under the Act, a person is disabled only if he or she is unable to engage in substantial gainful work by reason of an impairment, and in most cases, a diabetic whose disease is under control is capable of performing substantial gainful work. Should a person's diabetes become uncontrollable, or progress to the point of gangrene and loss of a leg before control is maintained, he or she probably will be disabled for purposes of social security benefits in the absence of evidence to rebut such a finding.[53]

A person impaired by diabetes would be protected under the Americans with Disabilities Act of 1990[54] as a qualified individual with a disability.[55] Should a diabetic employee have difficulty in engaging in a particular occupation or in performing certain duties because of the dis-

---

[50] Id. at 2.

[51] Stearns, S., "Trauma, Stress, and Diabetes," *Medical Causation,* 6 Trial 61 (Dec./Jan.), 1969-70.

[52] See Perry v. Celebrezze (W.D. S.C., 1964) 236 F. Supp. 1.

[53] See the latest edition of *Disability Evaluation Under Social Security,* U.S. Department of Health and Human Services, Washington, D.C.

[54] See Chapter 27, § 27.79, this Cyclopedia.

[55] Wood v. Omaha Sch. Dist. (C.A.-8 Neb., 1993) 985 F.2d 437.

ease, under the act the employer would be required to make a reasonable attempt to accommodate him.[56]

§ 30A.23. Medical malpractice.[57]

Issues involving diagnosis

Diabetes is a detectible disease, and a physician will usually be found negligent for failing to determine its presence.[58] This would include obstetricians who failed to diagnose gestational diabetes in a pregnant patient.[59]

The case of Hill v. Stewart[60] involved a patient who was admitted to the hospital suffering from weight loss, frequent urination, excessive thirst, visual difficulties, nausea, and loss of appetite. His physician put down a preliminary diagnosis of multiple sclerosis and influenza. On the patient's admission, the physician ordered the usual laboratory tests, including an urinalysis, but did not specifically ask for a blood-glucose test. After he admitted his patient, the doctor did not return to the hospital to see him for twenty hours. When the patient's condition deteriorated, further tests were performed and it was discovered that he was suffering from uncontrolled diabetes. He died a short time later.

At the trial there was disputed medical testimony. An autopsy showed that the patient had died from (1) viral pneumonia with hyaline membrane disease, and (2) nonspecific optic neuropathy, possibly multiple sclerosis or diabetic neuropathy. Witnesses for the plaintiff, however, argued that an autopsy would not have shown that the patient was suffering from diabetic acidosis which, if unchecked, usually results in viral pneumonia. The trial court directed a verdict for the physician, but it was reversed on appeal and the reviewing court held there was a jury question on the negligence issue.

Proper care and treatment

Although diabetes is relatively simple to diagnose, proper treatment may be difficult in complicated cases, and general practitioners and family physicians run the risk of liability for failing to refer such patients to specialists.[61] Even an internist who does not specialize in treating diabe-

---

[56] See, e.g., Sarsycki v. United Parcel Serv. (W. D. Okla., 1994) 862 F. Supp. 336. See also § 30A.99(B) herein.

[57] See also § 30A.99(A) herein.

[58] See Gandianco v. Sobol (App. Div., 1991) 567 N.Y.S.2d 909 (medical specialist at psychiatric hospital failed to diagnose a patient's diabetic ketoacidosis). But see Conner v. Ofrenco (Ill. App., 1993) 628 N.E.2d 1150.

[59] Rodriguez v. Louisiana Med. Mut. Ins. Co. (La. App., 1993) 620 So. 2d 335. See also Booth v. Cathey (Tex. App., 1995) 893 S.W.2d 715. But see Stern v. Insurance Corp. of Am. (La. App., 1990) 56 So. 2d 1114.

[60] (Miss., 1968) 209 So. 2d 809.

[61] See Robinson v. Group Health Ass'n, Inc. (D.C. App., 1997) 691 A.2d 1147.

tes might find it wise in some instances to seek assistance from an endocrinologist.[62]

Apparently it is not just patients with the serious or complicated forms of the disease who may be undertreated. A survey of 3,000 general, family, and internal medicine practitioners revealed that up to 84% of older adult patients with diabetes are not receiving optimal care and thus run the risk of developing serious complications of the disease — especially diabetics being treated by rural physicians.[63] The researchers, who examined the medicare records of 100,000 diabetic patients, found that 84% had not received a simple glycohemoglobin test (used to determine how well the patient's glucose has been controlled during previous four to six weeks), 54% had not received a thorough eye examination within the past year, and 45% had not received adequate cholesterol monitoring. According to recommendations of the American Diabetes Association, for patients with Type II (noninsulin-dependant) diabetes, a glycohemoglobin test should be performed every six months, and for Type I (insulin-dependant) patients, every three to four months. As to eye examinations, which is important because of the tendency of diabetics to develop diabetic retinopathy and possible loss of sight, Type II diabetics should have yearly examinations by an ophthalmologist beginning not later than five years after their diabetes is diagnosed, and Type I diabetics should have yearly examinations beginning with the year they are diagnosed. Also, the ADA recommends that Type II diabetics be seen by their physician at least two times a year, and Type I patients at least three times a year.

Another problem arises when a physician, usually a general practitioner, loses contact with a diabetic patient who seeks treatment from another physician for a condition other than the diabetes. Medicolegal specialist Lawrence V. Jowers, M.D., LL.B., in a warning to physicians of diabetic patients, issued this cautionary advice on the problem of continued care:

> [A] physician cannot unilaterally terminate the continued care of the diabetic without timely notice. The patient *does not necessarily* terminate this relationship by employing another physician for an unrelated illness or condition. The obligation may persist, for example, when the diabetic patient develops appendicitis and goes to a surgeon with the knowledge of the physician treating the diabetes or when he is injured and referred to an orthopedist.
>
> Care must be continuing. If a physician has knowledge that his diabetic patient is under the emergency care of another physician — even if he is not called in on the case — he should, as a matter of

---

[62] Seitz v. Akron Clinic (Ohio App., 1990) 1990 Ohio App. LEXIS 606.

[63] Weiner, J. P., et al., *Variations in Office-Based Quality: A Claims-Based Profile of Care Provided to Medicare Patients with Diabetes*, 273 J.A.M.A. 1503 (May 17), 1995.

good medical practice communicate the fact of diabetes to the other physician. The failure to do so *could be* constructive abandonment.

The same would hold true in any referral of a diabetic for a non-diabetic illness or condition. In referring a pregnant diabetic for obstetrical care or in recommending a diabetic patient for minor surgery, such as removal of a wart or repair of a Colles' fracture, the physician must alert the consultant and continue the diabetic care or have an irrefutable agreement for someone else to do so. The responsibility follows the patient's diabetes. If trouble develops, it is no defense to say the disease was mild, someone else was taking over, or that the referring physician came to see the patient as soon as the diabetes caused serious problems. Foreknowledge obligates a physician to preventive management.[64]

Liability was found on the part of both a hospital and radiologists for allowing a diabetic to faint and injure herself during an X-ray examination, where the patient's physician had noted on her chart that she was subject to dizziness and possible fainting.[65]

A verdict for an obstetrician was reversed in an action for injuries to a diabetic mother and for the death of her child where it was alleged the defendant was negligent in failing to recognize that the mother's diabetic condition would have increased the size of the baby, which weighed eleven pounds at birth.[66] The infant died during the defendant's attempt to deliver it normally rather than by Cesarean section.

Lawsuits frequently arise over alleged negligent treatment of the feet of diabetics, which are prone to circulatory disturbances and infection. Most are quickly settled by the defendant's insurer. Among the reported cases, six involved chiropodists or podiatrists.[67]

In Richmond County Hospital Authority v. Haynes,[68] the patient was brought to the hospital in a diabetic coma, placed in bed, and leather restraining straps were applied to his wrists. When the straps were removed, the patient's wrists were found badly bruised and developing blisters. Because of the patient's diabetic condition, the blisters did not heal, and deep ulcerations formed and became infected. In the ensuing lawsuit, the plaintiff prevailed on the theory of res ipsa loquitur.

Without a blood-glucose or urine-glucose test, sometimes it can be difficult to distinguish hypoglycemia from an insulin reaction. In Domina v. Pratt,[69] the patient, a seven-year-old Type I diabetic was

---

[64]Jowers, L. V., *Medicolegal Aspects of Diabetes,* 3 J. Leg. Med. 25 (Feb.), 1975.

[65]Washington Hosp. Ctr v. Butler (1967) 127 App. D.C. 379, 384 F.2d 331.

[66]Dinner v. Thorp (1959) 54 Wash. 2d 90, 338 P.2d 137. See also James v. Wooley (Ala., 1988) 523 So. 2d 110; Dumas v. Genest (Mass., App., 1991) 568 N.E.2d 1179.

[67]Anderson v. Picciotti (N.J., 1996) 676 A.2d 127; Jambazian v. Borden (Cal. App.,

1994) 30 Cal. Rptr. 2d 768; Scales v. Tucker (N.C. App., 1985) 327 S.E.2d 306; Mathews v. Walker (Ohio App., 1973) 296 N.E.2d 569; Jones v. Stess (N.J. Super., 1970) 268 A.2d 292, 42 A.L.R.3d 475; Benz v. Levin (1948) 62 York Leg. Rec. 149, 64 Montg. Co. Law Repr. 216.

[68](1970) 121 Ga. App. 537, 174 S.E.2d 364.

[69](1940) 111 Vt. 166, 13 A.2d 198.

brought to the physician's office about two a.m. "in a cold sweat, extremely pale, and very restless." The boy's mother told the physician that the previous morning she gave him fifty-two units of insulin. That evening she gave him his usual daily urine test and it showed considerable sugar. Despite this, during the night, when he suddenly became unconscious, she gave him some maple syrup, which appeared to revive him. She then brought him to the physician's office. The physician felt the boy's eyeballs and pulse and said he thought the boy was in a diabetic coma. He did not run a urine test, which would have confirmed this fact. (The convenient blood-glucose monitor had yet to be developed.) The physician injected insulin at twenty-minute intervals until he had given 160 units. The boy grew worse and went into convulsions. He was taken to the hospital the next day where it was discovered he had suffered brain damage. The physician was found liable, mainly on medical testimony that he should have tested the boy's urine before he administered the insulin. The verdict was reversed, however, for the trial judge's failure to give a requested defense instruction on standard of care.

Informed consent

Informed consent problems can exist for physicians who place patients on insulin or oral hypoglycemic agents without warning them of the risk of an insulin reaction or hypoglycemia from too large a dose, taking too little food, or over-exercising.[70] Also, patients placed on oral hypoglycemic drugs should be cautioned to be aware of the possible side effects of these agents.[71]

---

[70] See § 30A.15(A).
[71] See § 30A.11.

ANNOTATIONS

§ 30A.96. Medical references.

The following references may aid in further research on the material covered in Chapter 30A. For a guide to the abbreviations used in references to periodicals, see Chapter 3, § 3.36.

(A) DIAGNOSIS AND TREATMENT GENERALLY

Allen, C., et al., *Risk of Diabetes in Siblings and Other Relatives of IDDM Subjects*, 40 Diabetes 831, 1991.

Barbash, G., et al., *Significance of Diabetes Mellitus in Patients with Acute Myocardial Infarction Receiving Thrombolytic Therapy*, 22 J. Am. Coll. Cardiol. 707 (Sept.), 1993.

Bell, D. S. H., *Exercise for Patients with Diabetes*, 92 Postgrad. Med. 183 (July), 1992.

Brechner, R. J., et al., *Ophthalmic Examination Among Adults with Diagnosed Diabetes Mellitus*, 270 J.A.M.A. 1714 (Oct. 13), 1993.

Cutfield, R. G., *Insulin-Dependent Diabetes Mellitus: Current Concepts and Future Trends*, 101 New Zealand Med. J. 761, 1988.

Dahlquist, G. G., et al., *Dietary Factors and the Risk of Developing Insulin-Dependent Diabetes in Childhood*, 300 Br. Med. J. 1302 (May 19), 1990.

Feher, M. D., et al., *Importance of Routine Measurement of HDL with Total Cholesterol in Diabetic Patients*, 85 J. Roy. Society Med. 8 (Jan.), 1992.

Gerken, K. L., et al., *Effectiveness of Screening for Diabetes*, 114 Arch. Pathol. Lab. Med. 201, 1990.

Gill, G. V., et al., *Problems of Diabetics in Prison*, 298 Br. Med. J. 221, 1989.

Gill, G. V., et al., *The Spectrum of Brittle Diabetes*, 85 J. Roy. Society Med. 259 (May), 1992.

Kassoff, A., et al., *Aspirin Effects on Mortality and Morbidity in Patients with Diabetes Mellitus*, 268 J.A.M.A. 1292 (Sept. 9), 1992.

Keen, H., *Gestational Diabetes: Can Epidemiology Help?*, 40 Diabetes 3 (Dec.), 1991.

Klein, B. E., et al., *Use of Cardiovascular Disease Medications and Mortality in People with Older Onset Diabetes*, 82 Am. J. Pub. Health 1142 (Aug.), 1992.

Linn, T., and Bretzel, R. G., *Diabetes in Pregnancy*, 75 Eur. J. Obstet. Gynecol. Reprod. Biol. 37 (Dec.), 1997.

Lundman, B. M., et al., *Smoking and Metabolic Control in Patients with Insulin-Dependent Diabetes Mellitus*, 227 J. Intern. Med. 101, 1990.

MacFarlane, I. A., et al., *Diabetics in Prison: Can Good Diabetic Care Be Achieved?*, 304 Br. Med. J. 152 (Jan. 18), 1992.

Margolis, S., and Saudek, C. D., *The Johns Hopkins White Papers 1994: Diabetes*, The Johns Hopkins Medical Institutions, Baltimore, 1994.

Martin, B. C., et al., *Familial Clustering of Insulin Sensitivity*, 41 Diabetes 850 (July), 1992.

Meng-Hee, T., et al., *Clinical Practice Guidelines for Treatment of Diabetes Mellitus*, 147 Can. Med. Assoc. J. 697 (Sept. 1), 1992.

Prosser, P. R. and Karam, J. H., *Diabetes Mellitus Following Rodenticide Ingestion in Man*, 239 J.A.M.A. 1148, 1978.

Quevedo, S. F., et al., *Standards of Medical Care for Diabetic Patients: A Panel Discussion*, 73 R.I. Med. J. 421 (Sept.), 1990.

Ratner, Re. E., and el-Gamassy, E. R., *Legal Aspects of the Team Approach to Diabetes Treatment*, 16 Diabetes Educ. 113 (Mar.-Apr.), 1990.

Rosenbloom, A. L. and Giordano, B. P., *Chronic Overtreatment With Insulin in Children and Adolescents*, 131 Am. J. Dis. Child 881 (Aug.). 1977.

Shaten, B. J., et al., *Risk Factors for the Development of Type II Diabetes Among Men Enrolled in the Usual Care Group of the Multiple-Risk Factor Intervention Trial,* 16 Diabetes Care 1331 (Oct.), 1993.

Singh, B. M., et al., *Delayed Diagnosis in Non-Insulin-Dependent Diabetes Mellitus,* 304 Br. Med. J. 1154 (May 2), 1992.

Summerson, J. H., et al., *Association Between Exercise and Other Preventive Health Behaviors Among Diabetics,* 106 Pub. Health Rep. 543 (Sept. 10), 1991.

Sutherland, D. E., and Pirenne, J., *Current Status of Pancreas Transplantation for Treatment of Type I Diabetes Mellitus,* 60 Acta Gastrenterol. Belg. 294 (Oct.-Dec.), 1997.

Will, J. C., et al., *The Preventability of "Premature Mortality": An Investigation of Early Diabetes Deaths,* 78 Am. J. Public Health 831, 1988.

Wood, W., et al., *Guidelines for Eye Care in Patients with Diabetes Mellitus: Results of A Symposium,* 149 Arch. Intern. Med. 769, 1989.

Yki-Jarvinen, H., et al., *Comparison of Insulin Regimens in Patients with Non-Insulin-Dependent Diabetes Mellitus,* 327 N. Engl. J. Med. 1426 (Nov. 12), 1992.

Yudkin, J. S., *The Deidesheimer Meeting: Significance of Classical and New Risk Factors in Noninsulin-Dependent Diabetes Mellitus,* 11 J. Diabetes Complications 100 (Mar./Apr.), 1997.

(B) COMPLICATIONS OF DIABETES

Abbott, R.D., et al., *Diabetes and the Risk of Stroke — The Honolulu Heart Program,* 257 J.A.M.A. 949, 1987.

Amiel, S. A., *Hypoglycaemia in Diabetes Mellitus: Protecting the Brain,* 40 Diabetologia (Suppl. 2) S62 (July), 1997.

Anastasio, A. S., *Role of the Podiatrist in the Management of Diabetic Foot Problems,* 39 Conn. Med. 357, 1975. 258, 1985.

Asbury, A. K., *Understanding Diabetic Neuropathy,* 319 N. Engl. J. Med. 577, 1988.

Aucott, J. N., et al., *Management of Gallstones in Diabetic Patients,* 10 Arch. Intern. Med. 1053 (May), 1993.

Balkau, B., et al., *Risk Factors for Early Death in Non-Insulin Dependent Diabetes and Men with Known Glucose Tolerance Status,* 307 Brit. Med. J. 295, 1993.

Beer, S. F., et al., *Neurosis Induced by Home Monitoring of Blood Glucose Concentrations,* 298 Br. Med. J. 362, 1989.

Bell, D. S., *Diabetic Nephropathy: Changing Concepts of Pathogenesis and Treatment,* 301 Am. J. Med. Sci. 195, 1991.

Bell, D. S., *Lower Limb Problems in Diabetic Patients: What Are the Causes? What Are the Remedies?,* 89 Postrad. Med. 237, 1991.

Brand, F. N., et al., *Diabetes, Intermittent Claudication, and Risk of Cardiovascular Events,* 38 Diabetes 504, 1989.

Brandt, K., et al., *Relationship Between Severity of Hyperglycemia and Metabolic Acidosis in Diabetic Ketoacidosis,* 63 Mayo Clin. Proc. 1071, 1988.

Classe, J. G., *Hypertension and Diabetes: A Clinicolegal Review,* 2 Optom. Clin. 15 (No. 2), 1992.

Clements, R. S., Jr., et al., *Complications of Diabetes: Prevalence, Detection, Current Treatment, and Prognosis,* 79 Am. J. Med. 2 (Suppl. 5A), 1985.

Connell, F. A., et al., *Lower Extremity Amputations Among Persons with Diabetes Mellitus,* 40 M.M.W.R. 737 (Nov. 1), 1991.

D.C.C.T. Research Group, *The Diabetes Control and Complications Trial,* 35 Diabetes 530 (May), 1986.

De Tejada, I. S., et al., *Impaired Neurogenic and Endothelium-Mediated Relaxation of Penile Smooth Muscle From Diabetic Men with Impotence,* 320 N. Engl. J. Med. 1025, 1989.

Dyck, P. J., et al., editors, *Diabetic Neuropathy*, W. B. Saunders Company, Philadelphia, 1987.

Dyck, P. J., *New Understanding and Treatment of Diabetic Neuropathy*, 326 N. Engl. J. Med. 1287 (May 7), 1992.

Edmonds, M. E., et al., *Improved Survival of the Diabetic Foot: Role of A Specialized Foot Clinic*, 60 Quarterly J. Med. 763, 1986.

Ewing, D. J., and Clarke, B. F., *Diabetic Autonomic Neuropathy: Present Insights and Future Prospects*, 9 Diabetes Care 648 (Nov.-Dec.), 1986.

Facchini, F. S., et al., *Insulin Resistance and Cigarette Smoking*, 339 Lancet 1128 (May 9), 1992.

Friedman, E. A., *Diabetic Renal-Retinal Syndrome*, 140 Arch. Intern. Med. 1149 (Sept.), 1980.

Frier, B. M., and Maher, G., *Diabetes and Hypoglycemia: Medicolegal Aspects of Criminal Responsibility*, 5 Diabet. Med. 521 (Sept.), 1988.

Garg, S. K., et al., *Oral Contraceptives and Renal and Retinal Complications in Young Women with Insulin-Dependent Diabetes Mellitus*, 271 J.A.M.A. 1099 (Apr. 13), 1994.

Ger, R., *Prevention of Major Amputations in the Diabetic Patient*, 120 Arch. Surg. 1317, 1985.

Goldman, M., et al., *Obstetric Complications with GDM [Gestational Diabetes Mellitus]: Effects of Maternal Weight*, 40 Diabetes 79 (Dec.), 1991.

Greene, D. A., *Acute and Chronic Complications of Diabetes Mellitus in Older Patients*, 80 Am. J. Med. 39 (Suppl. 5A), 1986.

Greene, D., et al., *Factors in Development of Diabetic Neuropathy: Baseline Analysis of Neuropathy in Feasibility Phase of Diabetes Control and Complications Trial (DCCT)*, 37 Diabetes 476, 1988.

Greenfield, S., et al., *Outcomes of Patients with Hypertension and Non-Insulin-Dependent Diabetes Mellitus Treated by Different Systems and Specialties*, 274 J.A.M.A. 1436, 1996.

Grunberger, G., et al., *Factitious Hypoglycemia Due to Surreptitious Administration of Insulin*, 108 Ann. Intern. Med. 254, 1988.

Haffner, S. M., *The Prediabetic Problem: Development of Noninsulin-Dependent Diabetes Mellitus and Related Abnormalities*, 11 J. Diabetes Complications 69 (Mar./Apr.), 1997.

Haider, R., et al., *Management of Acute Diarrhea in Diabetic Patients Using Oral Rehydration Solutions Containing Glucose, Rice, or Glycine*, 308 Brit. Med. J. 624, 1994.

Hansen, L. A., et al., *Pulmonary Complications in Diabetes Mellitus*, 64 Mayo Clin. Proc. 791, 1989.

Hart, N. D., et al., *Cardiovascular Disease in Women with Diabetes: Strategies for Reducing Its Toll*, 5 Adv. Nurse Pract. 32 (Aug.), 1997.

Hunter, D. J. S., et al., *Influence of Maternal Insulin-Dependent Diabetes Mellitus on Neonatal Morbidity*, 149 Can. Med. Assoc. J. 47 (July 1), 1993.

Julien, J., *Cardiac Complications in Noninsulin-Dependent Diabetes Mellitus*, 11 J. Diabetes Complications 123 (Mar./Apr.), 1997.

Kalter, H., *Perinatal Mortality and Congenital Malformations in Infants Born to Women with Insulin-Dependent Diabetes Mellitus: United States, Canada, and Europe 1940-1988*, 39 M.M.W.R. 363 (June 1), 1990.

Katcher, M. L., et al., *Lower Extremity Burns Related to Sensory Loss in Diabetes Mellitus*, 24 J. Fam. Pract. 149, 1987.

Kohner, E. M., *Diabetic Retinopathy and High Blood Pressure: Defining the Risk*, 10 Am. J. Hypertens. 181S (Sept.), 1997.

Kroc Collaborative Study Group, *Diabetic Retinopathy after Two Years of Intensified Insulin Treatment*, 260 J.A.M.A. 37, 1988.

Laakso, M., *Dyslipidemia, Morbidity, and Mortality in Noninsulin-Dependent Diabetes Mellitus: Lipoproteins and Coronary Heart Disease in Noninsulin-Dependent Diabetes Mellitus*, 11 J. Diabetes Complications 137 (Mar./Apr.), 1997.

Ladas, F., and Theodossiadis, G., *Long-Term Effectiveness of Modified Grid Laser Photocoagulation for Diffuse Diabetic Macular Edema*, 71 Acta Ophthalmol. 393, 1993.

Lau, D. C. W., *Atherosclerosis and Diabetes Mellitus*, 140 Can. Med. Assoc. J. 1466, 1989.

Lewis, E. J., et al., *The Effect of Angiotensin-Converting-Enzyme Inhibition on Diabetic Nephropathy*, 329 N. Engl. J. Med. 1456, 1993.

Lindstrom, T., et al., *Insulin Treatment Improves Microalbuminuria and Other Cardiovascular Risk Factors in Patients with Type 2 Diabetes Mellitus*, 235 J. Intern. Med. 253, 1994.

Lipman, T. H., et al., *Risk Factors for Cardiovascular Disease in Children with Type I Diabetes*, 12 J. Pediatr. Nurs. 265 (Oct.), 1997.

Lipsky, B. A., *Osteomyelitis of the Foot in Diabetic Patients*, 25 Clin. Infect. Dis. 1318 (Dec.), 1997.

Litzelman, D. K., et al., *Reduction of Lower Extremity Clinical Abnormalities in Patients with Non-Insulin-Dependent Diabetes Mellitus: A Randomized, Controlled Trial*, 119 Ann. Intern. Med. 36 (July), 1993.

MacCuish, A. C., *Early Detection and Screening for Diabetic Retinopathy*, 7 Eye 254, 1993.

Manson, J. E., et al., *A Prospective Study of Maturity-Onset Diabetes Mellitus and Risk of Coronary Heart Disease and Stroke in Women*, 151 Arch. Intern. Med. 1141, 1991.

Mathiesen, B., and Borch-Johnsen, K., *Diabetes and Accident Insurance: A 3-Year Follow-Up of 7,599 Insured Diabetic Individuals*, 20 Diabetes Care 1781 (Nov.), 1997.

Mathiesen, E. R., *Prevention of Diabetic Nephropathy: Microalbuminuria and Perspectives for Intervention in Insulin-Dependent Diabetes*, 40 Danish Med. Bull. 273 (June), 1993.

Mogensen, C. E., *How to Protect the Kidney in Diabetic Patients: With Special Reference to IDDM*, 46 Diabetes (Suppl. 2) S104 (Sept.), 1997.

Moren-Hybbinette, I., et al., *The Clinical Picture of the Painful Diabetic Shoulder — Natural History, Social Consequences and Analysis of Concomitant Hand Syndrome*, 221 Acta Med. Scand. 73, 1987.

Moren-Hybbinette, I., et al., *The Painful Diabetic Shoulder*, 219 Acta Med. Scand. 507, 1986.

Paetkau, M. E., et al., *Cigarette Smoking and Diabetic Retinopathy*, 26 Diabetes 46 (Jan.), 1977.

Parkhouse, N., et al., *Impaired Neurogenic Vascular Response in Patients with Diabetes and Neuropathic Foot Lesions*, 318 N. Engl. J. Med. 1306, 1988.

Pourmand, R., *Diabetic Neuropathy*, 15 Neurol. Clin. 569 (Aug.), 1997.

Primhak, R. A., et al., *Reduced Vital Capacity in Insulin-Dependent Diabetes*, 36 Diabetes 324, 1987.

Pullicino, P. M., et al., *Stroke Following Acute Myocardial Infarction in Diabetics*, 231 J. Intern. Med. 287, 1992.

Ram, Z., et al., *Vascular Insufficiency Quantitatively Aggravates Diabetic Neuropathy*, 48 Arch. Neurol. 1239 (Dec.), 1991.

Reiber, G. E., et al., *Risk Factors for Amputation in Patients with Diabetes Mellitus*, 117 Ann. Intern. Med. 97 (July 15), 1992.

Ruiz, J., *Diabetes Mellitus and the Late Complications: Influence of the Genetic Factors*, 23 Diabetes Metab. 57 (Mar., Suppl. 2), 1997.

Singer, D. E., et al., *Screening Guidelines for Diabetic Retinopathy*, 116 Ann. Intern. Med. 683 (Apr. 15), 1992.

Spangler, J. G., et al., *Prevalence and Predictors of Problem Drinking Among Primary Care Diabetic Patients*, 37 J. Fam. Prac. 370, 1993.

Stevens, A. B., et al., *Motor Vehicle Driving Among Diabetics Taking Insulin and Non-Diabetics*, 299 Br. Med. J. 591, 1989.

Teuscher, A. U., and Weidmann, P. U., *Requirements for Antihypertensive Therapy in Diabetic Patients: Metabolic Aspects*, 15 J. Hypertens. S67 (Mar., Suppl.), 1997.

Trail, K. C., et al., *Results of Liver Transplantation in Diabetic Recipients* 114 Surgery 650 (Oct.), 1993.

Wagner, F. W., Jr., *The Diabetic Foot,* 10 Orthopedics 163, 1987.

Warram, J. H., et al., *Excess Mortality Associated with Diuretic Therapy in Diabetes Mellitus,* 151 Arch. Intern. Med. 1350, 1991.

Wheat, J. L., et al., *Diabetic Foot Infections: Bacteriologic Analysis,* 146 Arch. Intern. Med. 1935, 1986.

Zoorob, R. J., and Hagen, M.D., *Guidelines on the Care of Diabetic Nephropathy, Retinopathy, and Foot Disease,* 56 Am. Fam. Physician 2021 (Nov. 15), 1997.

§ 30A.97.　Legal references.

The following additional references may aid in further research on the material covered in Chapter 30A.

Block, A. L., *Handling Internal Medicine Cases,* John Wiley & Sons, Inc., Somerset, N.J., 1992.

Bryce, R. I., *Diabetes and Crime,* 135 Solic. J. 934 (Aug. 16), 1991.

Classe, J. G., *Hypertension and Diabetes: A Clinicolegal Review,* 2 Optom. Clin. 15 (No. 2), 1992.

Contributory Negligence Peculiar to Diabetic Plaintiffs: A Case History, 1 Current Med. 30, 1954.

Enzer, N., *Trauma and the Diabetic,* 11 For the Defense 21, 33, 36, 1970.

Frier, B. M., and Maher, G., *Diabetes and Hypoglycemia: Medicolegal Aspects of Criminal Resonsibility,* 5 Diabet. Med. 521 (Sept.), 1988.

Gregory, D. R., *Diabetes Mellitus: Current Concepts,* 10 Law Med. J. 353 (Jan.), 1982.

Gregor, D. R., *The Oral Hypoglycemic Controversy,* Legal Aspects Med. Prac., Mar. 1979, p. 16.

Greyson, J., *Glucose Test Strips and Patient Self-Monitoring for Diabetes,* 18 Trial 14 (Oct.), 1982.

Jowers, L. V., *Medicolegal Aspects of Diabetes,* 3 J. Legal Med. 25 (Feb.), 1975.

Kabel, J., *Diabetes Self-Care: Potential Liability of the Treating Physician,* 5 J. Leg. Med. 253 (June), 1984.

Laidler, P., et al., *Diabetes Mellitus and Hypopituitarism,* 18 For. Sci. Intl. 169 (Sept.-Oct.), 1981.

Maher, G., *Automatism and Diabetes,* 99 Law Q. Rev. 511 (Oct.), 1983.

Medical Testimony in a Trauma-Diabetes Case, Showing the Direct and Cross-Examinations of the Plaintiff's Pediatrician and Expert Witness (an Internist), Med. Trial Tech. Q., 1973 Annual, 99, 191.

Quevedo, S. F., et al., *Standards of Medical Care for Diabetic Patients: A Panel Discussion,* 73 R.I. Med. J. 421 (Sept.), 1990.

Ratner, Re. E., and el-Gamassy, E. R., *Legal Aspects of the Team Approach to Diabetes Treatment,* 16 Diabetes Educ. 113 (Mar.-Apr.), 1990.

Reveno, W. S., *Trauma and Diabetes,* 36 Mich. St. B.J. 31, 1957.

Robins, B., et al., *Diabetes Mellitus: A Frequent Factor in Liability Claims,* 91 N.J. Med. 264 (Apr.), 1994.

Sippel, H. and Mottonen, M., *Combined Glucose and Lactate Values in Vitreous Humour for Postmortem Diagnosis of Diabetes Mellitus,* 19 For. Sci. Int'l 217 (May-June), 1982.

Tolstoi, E., "Diabetes Mellitus," in *Courtroom Medicine,* M. Houts, editor, Charles C Thomas, Publisher, Springfield, Ill., 1958.

Traumatic Diabetes, 2 Current Med. 14, 1955.

Vennum, M. K., *Home Blood Glucose Meter Accuracy and Precision: Liability and the Necessity of Refinement,* 40 Med. Trial Tech. Q. 547, 1994.

Wright, E., *Medical Testimony in a Diabetes and Trauma Case Showing the Direct and Cross-Examination of Plaintiff's Medical Witness — A Specialist in Internal Medicine,* 2 Med. Trial Tech. Q. 61, 1956.

§ 30A.98. American Law Reports.

84 A.L.R.2d 176. Preexisting physical condition as affecting liability under accident policy or accident feature of life policy. Diabetes, § 24.

12 A.L.R.3d 475. Excessiveness or adequacy of damages awarded to injured person for injuries to organic system and processes of body. Diabetes, § 63.

28 A.L.R.3d 1255. What constitutes "serious illness," "serious disease," or equivalent language used in insurance application. Diabetes, § 14.

38 A.L.R.3d 452. Denial, suspension, or cancellation of driver's license because of physical disease or defect. Diabetes, insulin reaction, § 10.

42 A.L.R.3d 482. Medical malpractice in connection with diagnosis, care, or treatment of diabetic.

20 A.L.R.5th 1. Necessity of expert testimony on issue of permanence of injury and future pain and suffering. Diabetes, § 21.

43 A.L.R.5th 87. Medical malpractice in connection with diagnosis, care, or treatment of diabetes.

80 A.L.R. Fed. 564. Social Security disability determinations: What is "severe" impairment under 20 CFR §§ 404.1520-404.1521. Diabetes, § 18[a].

97 A.L.R. Fed. 40. Who is "individual with handicaps" under Rehabilitation Act of 1973? Diabetes, § 11.

114 A.L.R. Fed. 141. Social Security: Right to disability benefits as affected by refusal to submit to, or coooperate in, medical or surgical treatment. Control of diabetes by diet and/or medication, § 9.

146 A.L.R. Fed. 1. Who is "qualified individual" under Americans with Disabilites Act provisions defi⸱ing and extending protection against employment discrimination to qualified indivi⸱ual with disability (42 U.S.C.A. §§ 12111(8), 12112(a). Diabetes, §§ 10, 12[a], 20, 26, 40[e, f], 47, 48[a], 49[b], 52, 53[a], 66, 68.

§ 30A.99. Cases.

In the following list of cases, no attempt has been made to include all the decisions on topics covered in Chapter 30A. The cases selected are those that the editors believe will best aid the reader in further research on the medicolegal issues involved.

Cases are arranged under the following headings:

(A) MEDICAL MALPRACTICE AND PRODUCT LIABILITY ACTIONS
(B) DISABILITY ISSUES
(C) LIFE AND HEALTH INSURANCE CLAIMS
(D) "TRAUMATIC DIABETES" AND AGGRAVATION OF PREEXISTING DIABETIC CONDITIONS
(E) DIABETICS AS DRIVERS OF MOTOR VEHICLES

(A) MEDICAL MALPRACTICE AND PRODUCT LIABILITY ACTIONS
[See also § 30A.23]

United States: Washington Hosp. Ctr. v. Butler (1967) 127 App. D.C. 379, 384 F.2d 331 (hospital and radiologists held liable for allowing diabetic patient to faint and injure herself during diagnostic X-ray examination; defendants failed to check patient's chart which contained attending physician's notation that she was subject to dizziness and possible fainting spells).

Maltempo v. Cuthbert (C.A.-5 Fla., 1974) 504 F.2d 325 (physician held negligent for failing to call jail physician about diabetic patient's condition after promising patient's family that he would let them know "if there were any problems"; patient died from aspiration of vomit).

Edwards v. United States (C.A.-5 Tex., 1975) 519 F.2d 1137 (suit by diabetic exprisoner for injuries allegedly suffered as result of negligent medical treatment at federal correctional institute, including reduction of insulin dosage, failure to provide proper diet, refusal to transfer him to medical facility, and failure to call in specialist).

Hemingway v. Ochsner Clinic (C.A.-5 La., 1979) 608 F.2d 1040 (issue whether drug Cafergot proper treatment for migraine for diabetic with peripheral vascular disease).

Knight v. United States (D. S.C., 1977) 442 F. Supp. 1069 (serviceman sued government for failure to discover his diabetic condition on induction into army).

In re Petition of Veteran's Affairs Med. Center (S.D. N.Y., 1990) 749 F. Supp. 495 (issue whether veteran's hospital was entitled to order authorizing amputation of leg of delirious and semiconscious diabetic's gangrenous foot in view of his earlier statement to wife that he would rather die than undergo amputation of a limb).

Alabama: Moon v. Harco Drugs (1983) 436 So. 2d 218 (cause of action against pharmacy for selling wrong type of insulin did not accrue when patient first discovered mistake, but accrued instead when she first became ill from using product, and limitations period could not be extended on theory of "continuous tort" because there were no repeated acts of negligence.

E.R. Squibb & Sons v. Cox (1985) 477 So. 2d 963 (manufacturer not liable for mispackaging or failure to warn in action by diabetic who took wrong insulin).

James v. Woolley (Ala., 1988) 523 So. 2d 110 (obstetricians chose to deliver obese, diabetic patient's baby by vaginal route, allegedly resulting in child suffering Erb's palsy).

Brackett v. Coleman (Ala., 1988) 525 So. 2d 1372 (unsuccessful action against physician engaged to treat patient for high blood pressure for failure to order blood and urine tests which would have revealed that patient was suffering from diabetic ketoacidosis and kidney failure; patient advised defendant on first visit that he was under care of another physician for diabetes).

Arizona: Hiser v. Randolph (1980) 126 Ariz. 608, 617 P.2d 774 (in action against physician "on call" in hospital emergency department, fact issue existed whether forty-minute delay in treating patient suffering from acute hyperglycemia proximately caused death).

Styles v. Ceranski (Ariz. App., 1996) 916 P.2d 1164 (malpractice action against a surgeon and a family practitioner for misdiagnosis of chronic pancreatitis and an unnecessary pancreatectomy, which resulted in the patient becoming an insulin-dependent diabetic).

California: Myers v. Quesenberry (1983) 144 Cal. App. 3d 388, 193 Cal. Rptr. 733 (pedestrian struck by defendant physician's patient while driving to hospital had cause of action against physician based on allegations that he negligently failed to warn patient against driving automobile while her diabetes remained uncontrolled and while she continued to suffer from psychological effects of learning that she was carrying dead fetus).

Pressler v. Irvine Drugs (1985) 169 Cal. App. 3d 1244, 215 Cal. Rptr. 807 (pharmacy liable for negligence of pharmacist who gave customer "Lente" insulin instead of "Semilente," a less potent product, but award of $325,000 reduced to $250,000 under California's statute limiting noneconomic loss recovery against health care providers).

Jambazian v. Borden (Cal. App., 1994) 30 Cal. Rptr. 2d 768 (in action for lack of informed consent, patient failed to establish that, had he been told that his foot surgery involved a greater risk than usual because of his diabetic condition, he would not have consented to the surgery; also, defendant offered evidence that patient had no symptoms of diabetes at time of surgery).

District of Columbia: Robinson v. Group Health Ass'n, Inc. (D.C. App., 1997) 691 A.2d 1147 (damages awarded against a group health provider (HMO) for failing to refer a diabetic patient for a vascular evaluation which, the opinion of the patient's medical expert, would have given patient a greater than 50% chance of avoiding a below-the-knee amputation).

Durphy v. Kaiser Foundation Health Plan of Mid-Atlantic States, Inc. (D.C. App., 1997) 698 A.2d 459 (diabetic patient's claim that the loss of his foot was due to his physicians' negligence in failing to diagnose osteomyelitis was not defeated by his failure to follow instructions regarding treatment where any such contributory negligence on the patient's part occurred after the defendants' alleged negligence).

Georgia: Albright v. Powell (1966) 113 Ga. App. 363, 147 S.E.2d 848 (laboratory analysis detected presence of sugar in patient's urine and report was inserted in patient's chart, but physician was not told by laboratory of positive findings and he did not consult chart; patient suffered several cerebrovascular accidents while on vacation and sued physician; verdict for defendant upheld).

Richmond County Hosp. Authority v. Haynes (1970) 121 Ga. App. 537, 174 S.E.2d 364 (patient brought to hospital in diabetic coma placed in leather restraining straps which badly bruised his wrists, causing ulcerations which became infected and failed to heal; res ipsa loquitur held applicable for award of $25,250).

Illinois: Benison v. Silverman (Ill. App., 1992) 599 N.E.2d 1101 (action by diabetic patient against family physician for negligent treatment that resulted in amputation of patient's foot).

Conner v. Ofreneo (Ill. App. 3d., 1993) 628 N.E.2d 1150 (unsuccessful action against physician for failure to diagnose and treat patient's diabetic ketoacidosis; evidence supported jury finding that defendant did not violate applicable standard of care in failing to consider possibility of diabetes and that patient's death could have been caused instead by fluid overload that developed while patient was being treated for dehydration).

Mundell v. La Pata (Ill. App., 1994) 635 N.E.2d 933 (obstetrician charged with negligence in failing to detect patient's gestational diabetes that resulted in large baby and brachial plexus injury on delivery).

Iowa: Correll v. Goodfellow (1964) 255 Iowa 1237, 125 N.W.2d 745 (chiropractor burned diabetic patient's foot with ultrasonic machine while attempting to treat ankle sprain; defendant assured patient machine would not injure her and that she did not have "that much diabetes"; directed verdict for defendant reversed).

Louisiana: Rajnowski v. St. Patrick's Hosp. (La., 1990) 564 So. 2d 671 (conflicting evidence as to whether diabetic patient developed ketoacidosis during last month of pregnancy that resulted in brain damage to baby or whether patient merely suffered from gestational diabetes that was under control).

Stein v. Insurance Corp. of Am. (La. App., 1990) 566 So. 2d 1114 (unsuccessful claim that eleven-pound ten-ounce baby's brachial plexus nerve injury during delivery was result of physician's negligence in failing to rule out mother's gestational diabetes and in failing to order ultrasound examination).

Rodriguez v. Louisiana Med. Mut. Ins. Co. (La. App., 1993) 620 So. 2d 335 (mother successfully sued her obstetricians for failing to properly test for and treat her gestational diabetes, which she claimed resulted in her 12-pound, 9-ounce baby suffering shoulder dystocia, respiratory distress, and fatal pneumonia).

Falkowski v. Maurus (La. App., 1993) 637 So. 2d 522 (claim that emergency medical technicians' negligence in establishing IV to treat nonresponsive diabetic patient caused damage to patient's ulnar nerve).

Head v. Pendleton Mem. Methodist Hosp. (La. App., 1996) 669 So. 2d 504 (diabetic's hand burned during wet-heat therapy, resulting in the amputation of two fingers).

Futch v. Attwood (La. App., 1997) 698 So. 2d 958 (where defendant's alleged negligence caused diabetic patient to suffer from painful complications of her disease, which worsened over a 62-hour period and finally resulted in her death, damages in the amount of $98,000 were not excessive).

Maryland: Miles v. Brainin (Md., 1961) 167 A.2d 117 (patient's loss of weight and excessive thirst misdiagnosed as virus infection).

Massachusetts: Dumes v. Genest (Mass. App., 1991) 568 N.E.2d 1179 (obstetrician accused of negligence in delivering obese and diabetic patient's infant, which resulted in child's Erb's palsy, contended that patient's prenatal records had not been available before he had to decide whether to perform C-section).

Michigan: Jennings v. Southwood (Mich. App., 1993) 499 N.W.2d 460 (question of emergency medical personnel's immunity under state's Emergency Medical Services Act in treating 13-year-old comatose diabetic; defendants accused of failing to administer glucose and failing to transport patient to hospital despite symptoms of hypoglycemia).

Minnesota: In re Muntner (Minn. App., 1991) 470 N.W.2d 717 (trial judge's authorization of involuntary administration of neuroleptic medication to schizophrenic patient despite absence of patient's guardian ad litem was appropriate where medication was needed and patient, a diabetic, refused to care for himself).

Mississippi: Erby v. North Miss. Med. Ctr. (Miss., 1995) 654 So. 2d 495 (hospital nursing staff charged with negligence in failing to properly monitor blood sugar of insulin-dependent diabetic patient following surgery to insert AV fistula and catheter for kidney dialysis).

Missouri: Gray v. Brock (Mo. App., 1988) 750 S.W.2d 696 (in action on behalf of diabetic patient whose condition was apparently misdiagnosed, the trial court erred in instructing the jury that the patient knew that his diabetes was out of control in view of evidence that prior to his hospitalization the patient believed that he had the flu and in view of no evidence that he realized that his increased fluid intake and frequent urination were attributable to his diabetes).

New Jersey: Jones v. Stess (1970) 111 N.J. Super. 283, 268 A.2d 292, 42 A.L.R.3d 475 (chiropodist clipped patient's toenails and toe despite knowledge that she was diabetic; infection developed leading to gangrene and amputation of leg at mid-thigh; motion to dismiss order reversed and new trial granted plaintiff with ruling that expert testimony on standard of care could be dispensed with because facts of case were within common knowledge and experience of laymen).

Ostrowski v. Azzara (1988) 111 N.J. 429, 545 A.2d 148 (unsuccessful malpractice action by diabetic for negligence of physician in removing toenail).

Anderson v. Picciotti (N.J., 1996) 676 A.2d 127 (malpractice action against podiatrist for improper treatment of diabetic's toe that had to be surgically amputated after accidentally being cut during nail trim).

New York: Greenstein v. Fornell (1932) 143 Misc. 880, 257 N.Y.S. 673 (physician failed to administer insulin before and after operation on diabetic patient; verdict for plaintiff).

Saron v. State (1965) 24 App. Div. 2d 771, 263 N.Y.S.2d 591 (issue whether psychiatric patient who also suffered from diabetes was properly treated while confined to state institution; judgment for defendant affirmed).

Himber v. Pfizer Laboratories (1981) 82 App. Div. 2d 776, 440 N.Y.S.2d 649 (insufficient evidence that ophthalmologist who prescribed daily dosage of buffered aspirin for approximately one week for patient complaint of "vitreous floaters" was liable for severe hemorrhaging in patient's eyes, loss of sight in one eye, and her death seventeen months later from problems related to longstanding diabetic condition).

Carlo v. Long Island College Hosp. (App. Div., 1990) 558 N.Y.S.2d 153 (22-year-old plaintiff who suffered from cerebral palsy claimed that condition was caused by physician's negligence in failing to monitor mother's blood sugar levels during pregnancy, and as a result, plaintiff was not properly treated for low blood sugar and respiratory distress at birth).

Gandianco v. Sobol (App. Div., 1991) 567 N.Y.S.2d 909 (evidence was sufficient to revoke physician's license on grounds of gross negligence and incompetence where record showed that physician, while employed as emergency medical care specialist at psychiatric hospital, failed to recognize that a patient was suffering from diabetic ketoacidosis).

Washington v. Community Health Plan (App. Div., 1995) 633 N.Y.S.2d 224 (hospital staff accused of misdiagnosing a patient's acute diabetes mellitus as a yeast infection).

North Carolina: Johnson v. Ruark Obstet. & Gynecol. Assocs. (N.C. App., 1988) 365 S.E.2d 909 (patient alleged obstetrician's failure to treat her diabetic condition during pregnancy caused her fetus to die in utero of malnutrition).

Ohio: Whitt v. Columbus Cooperative Enterprises (1980) 64 Ohio St. 2d 355, 415 N.E.2d 985 (action against optometrist for failing to discover diabetic retinal disease not governed by one-year statute of limitations to actions for "malpractice against a physician, podiatrist, or a hospital").

Seitz v. Akron Clinic (Ohio App., 1990) LEXIS 606 (question whether internist who chose to treat plaintiff for mild diabetes instead of referring her to an endocrinologist should be held to standard of care of internist or endocrinologist).

Newland v. Amin (Ohio App., 1991) 600 N.E.2d 357 (question whether family physician was negligent in failing to prevent an overweight 7-year-old child from developing diabetic ketoacidosis and in failing to provide adequate information concerning patient's medical history on referring him to endocrinologist).

Oregon: Dowell v. Mossberg (1960) 226 Or. 173, 355 P.2d 624 (56-year-old woman diabetic went to chiropractor for treatment after hearing radio commercial advertising defendant's clinic; patient's condition worsened for want of proper diagnosis and treatment and judgment for malpractice awarded; directed verdict for defendant later upheld on limitation of action issue [359 P.2d 541]).

Pennsylvania: Benz v. Levin (1948) 62 York Leg. Rec. 149, 64 Montg. Co. Law Rep. 216 (infection resulted and amputation necessary after chiropodist trimmed diabetic patient's toe and nail; directed verdict for defendant for want of evidence on violation of standard of care applicable to chiropodists).

South Carolina: Stokes v. Denmark Emer. Med. Servs. (S.C., 1993) 433 S.E.2d 850 (jury question whether failure of ambulance service to promptly transport diabetic patient to hospital with dialysis machine was proximate cause of her death).

Texas: Davis v. Manning (Tex. App., 1993) 847 S.W.2d 446 (unsuccessful malpractice action against physician for electing to treat patient's new-onset diabetes with oral hypoglycemic medication rather than with insulin).

Booth v. Cathey (Tex. App., 1995) 893 S.W.2d 715 (parents of stillborn child had cause of action against physician who failed to diagnose mother's gestational diabetes).

Vermont: Domina v. Pratt (1940) 111 Vt. 166, 13 A.2d 198 (physician failed to order test of patient's urine and misdiagnosed insulin shock as diabetic coma; evidence supporting verdict for plaintiff on this issue held sufficient but judgment reversed for failure to give defense instruction on standard of care).

Washington: Dinner v. Thorp (1959) 54 Wash. 2d 90, 338 P.2d 137 (diabetic mother sued obstetrician for her injuries and death of baby alleging negligence in failing to recognize that mother's condition would have increased size of baby which weighed eleven pounds at birth; verdict for defendant reversed).

West Virginia: Martin v. Charleston Area Med. Center (W. Va., 1989) 382 S.E.2d 502 (radiologist liable for death of patient from reaction to dye injection during urography; patient, who was not informed before test of risk of fatal reaction, was an untreated diabetic and had history of angina pectoris, asthma, bronchitis, and hypertension, and had previously suffered reactions to medications).

Wyoming: Siebert v. Fowler (1981) 637 P.2d 255 (unsuccessful action against ophthalmologist by diabetic who sought treatment for "vitreous floater" for defendant's failure to diagnose potential retinal separation).

(B) DISABILITY ISSUES

[See also §§ 30A.20 (B), 30A.22]

United States: Perry v. Celebrezze (W.D. S.C., 1964) 236 F. Supp. 1 (claimant denied Social Security disability benefits where diabetes could be kept under control with proper insulin therapy and medical counsel).

McCorpen v. Central Gulf Steamship Corp. (C.A.-5 Tex., 1968) 396 F.2d 547 (seaman who became ill when diabetes went out of control denied compensation under maintenance and cure provisions of general maritime law for failing to disclose existence of disease during pre-employment physical examination).

Director, Office of Workers' Comp. Programs v. Universal Terminal & Stevedoring Corp. (C.A.-3 N.J., 1978) 575 F.2d 452 (claimant's diabetes mellitus and heart disease were "manifest preexisting conditions," even though the claimant's employer did not have actual knowledge of these conditions, it being sufficient that their existence could have been established by a physical examination of the claimant or a review of his medical records).

Sprague v. Director, Office of Workers' Comp. Programs, U.S. Dep't of Labor (C.A.-1 Me., 1982) 688 F.2d 862 (question whether worker's diabetic condition or work-related bruising of leg caused infection which led to osteomyelitis.

Bentivegna v. United States Dept. of Labor (C.A.-9 Cal., 1982) 694 F.2d 619 (city of Los Angeles requirement of controlled blood sugar levels for diabetics discriminated against handicapped individuals under Rehabilitation Act of 1973).

Tome v. Schweiker (C.A.-8 Mo., 1984) 724 F.2d 711 (failure of diabetic claiming disability benefits under Social Security Act to strictly follow a dietary and insulin program did not disqualify her for noncompliance with the Act where the evidence established that she did not consciously chose not to follow her physician's orders but lacked the financial resources and discipline required to understand and follow a prescribed strict dietary and insulin regime).

Jones v. Heckler (C.A.-9 Cal., 1985) 760 F.2d 993 (in claim for social security disability benefits, administrative law judge was required to give specific reasons why diabetic was denied benefits in view of testimony of claimant's treating physician that she was unemployable).

Preston v. Heckler (C.A.-4 Md., 1985) 769 F.2d 988 (diabetic claimant for Social Security disability benefits was not guilty of noncompliance with the requirement that she submit to treatment where the evidence showed that she lacked the funds and mental acumen to appreciate and adhere to the established treatment program for her disease).

Davis v. Meese (E.D. Pa., 1988) 692 F. Supp. 505 (FBI's policy of excluding insulin-dependent diabetics from applying for the job classifications of special agent and investigative specialist did not violate the Rehabilitation Act of 1973 nor the due process clause of the Fifth Amendment).

Serrapica v. City of New York (S.D.N.Y., 1989) 708 F. Supp. 64 ("a poorly controlled diabetic poses an unpredictable risk of suffering a hypoglycemic reaction on the job, creating hazards to the individual, his or her co-workers and the public," and such an individual "simply could not safely operate the heavy and dangerous vehicles routinely employed by the Department of Sanitation").

Wood v. Omaha Sch. Dist. (C.A.-8 Neb., 1993) 985 F.2d 437 (persons impaired by diabetes are covered by the Americans with Disabilities Act of 1990).

Safranski v. Shalala (N.D. Ill., 1993) 1993 U.S. Dist. LEXIS 13033 (although it was well documented that claimant for social security disability benefits suffered from diabetes mellitus, and that related neuropathy had caused the amputation of all toes from his right foot, claimant presented no evidence of significant and persistent disorganization of motor functions, his foot had healed, he had good standing balance, he had normal strength and endurance, and he was capable of walking without assistance as well as climb and descend stairs).

Chandler v. City of Dallas (C.A.-5 Tex., 1993) 2 F.3d 1385 (in applying regulations under the federal Rehabilitation Act of 1973, the U.S. Court of Appeals, Fifth Circuit held as a matter of law that a driver with insulin-dependent diabetes presented a genuine substantial risk of injury to himself or others).

Bombrys v. City of Toledo (N.D. Ohio, 1993) 849 F. Supp. 1210 (under the Americans with Disabilities Act, a blanket exclusion of persons with insulin-dependent diabetes from becoming city police officers tended to discriminate against persons who could perform the essential functions of the job with reasonable accommodation on the part of the city).

Sarsycki v. United Parcel Serv. (W.D. Okla., 1994) 862 F. Supp. 336 (employer violated the Americans with Disabilities Act in demoting an insulin-dependent truck driver where: (1) U.S. Department of Transportation regulations barred insulin-dependent diabetics from driving commercial motor vehicles that weighed over 10,000 pounds and the plaintiff's route was served almost exclusively by vehicles weighing under that amount; (2) the employer had not conducted an individualized assessment of the plaintiff's abilities as required by the Act; (3) the plaintiff's diabetes was under control; (4) the plaintiff had never experienced a hypoglycemic episode; and (5) the physicians who examined the plaintiff found that he was qualified to drive motor vehicles weighing 10,000 pounds or less).

Lane v. Pena (D.D.C., 1994) 867 F. Supp. 1050 (the Merchant Marine Academy's rigid reserve requirements were not essential to its purpose, and therefore the Academy violated the federal Rehabilitation Act of 1973 when it expelled a student who could not fulfill reserve requirement because of insulin-dependent diabetes).

Myers v. Hose (C.A.-4 Md., 1995) 50 F.3d 278 (former bus driver whose diabetes could cause him to lose consciousness was not entitled to additional time to cure his disability; the Americans with Disabilities Act does not require an employer to wait an indefinite period of time for a "reasonable accommodation" to achieve its intended effect).

Dockery v. North Shore Med. Ctr. (S.D. Fla., 1995) 909 F. Supp. 1550 (where a former cook had to have four toes and part of her foot amputated because of diabetes, she was found not be be a "qualified individual with a disability" under the Americans with Disabilities Act when she testified that the only accommodation that would enable her to resume her employment was to be allowed a year-long leave of absence).

Daugherty v. City of El Paso (C.A.-5 Tex., 1995) 56 F.3d 695 (city did not violate the Americans with Disabilities Act in failing to obtain a waiver from the U.S. Department of Transportation that would allow an insulin-dependent diabetic driver to continue operating a city bus).

Riel v. Electronic Data Systems Corp. (C.A.-5 Tex., 1996) 99 F.3d 678 (in an action under the Americans with Disabilities Act by a systems engineer who claimed that he was fired for failing to meet interim deadlines on projects because of fatigue caused by his diabetes-related kidney disease, a question of fact was presented as to whether such interim deadlines were an essential function of the job in light of evidence that neither the written job description of the essential functions of the claimant's position nor an oral description of such functions given to the claimant's physician included meeting such interim deadlines).

Fritz v. Mascotech Automotive Systems Group, Inc. (E.D. Mich., 1996) 914 F. Supp. 1481 (an issue of fact existed as to whether an insulin-dependent diabetic automotive designer was discriminated against under the Americans with Disabilities Act where he had missed 30 full days of work during his 45-week period of employment, which he claimed was due to his insulin dosage not being adjusted to his work schedule and "onerous conditions" imposed upon him by his supervisor that included having to obtain a note from his physician each time he was absent or late and not allowing him flexible hours to accomplish his tasks).

Amariglioi v. National R.R. Pasenger Corp. (D.D.C., 1996) 941 F. Supp. 173 (passenger train attendant who suffered from uncontrolled diabetes and was subject to disorientation, blurred vision, and possible coma was not qualified under the Americans with Disabilities Act to perform the essential functions of the job, which included opening car doors to permit the loading and unloading of passengers, assisting passengers as they embark and disembark, and securing the car doors after the passengers have loaded, all of which duties entail long and stressful hours and travel for extended periods of time).

Baert v. Euclid Beverage, Ltd. (N.D. Ill., 1997) 954 F. Supp. 170 (truck driver who had insulin-dependent diabetes was not a "qualified individual with a disability" under the Americans with Disibilities Act because his disease prevented him from obtaining a renewal of his commercial driver's license and thus he could not "satisfy the prereqisites" of his position, which was required under the Act; furthermore, his employer could not retain him as a "helper" on the truck because the helper was also expected to drive).

Wells v. Apfel (C.A.-10, 1998) 1998 U.S. App. LEXIS 23247 (the denial of Social Security disability benefits was justified where a diabetic's high blood sugar, which she claimed caused chronic fatigue, was high only periodically in the evening, and her disease was otherwise well-controlled).

Alaska: Tinker v. Veco, Inc. (Alaska, 1996) 913 P.2d 488 (worker's diabetes would not have barred his compensation so long as the injury he received on the job aggravated, accelerated, or combined with his medical condition in a manner that resulted in the loss of his leg).

Arizona: Paulley v. Industrial Comm'n (1962) 91 Ariz. 266, 371 P.2d 888 ("injury by accident" found in compensation case where material handler suffering from diabetes developed blister from walking on hot concrete; blister became infected and led to gangrene and amputation).

Delaware: Lawson v. Chrysler Corp. (Del. Super., 1964) 199 A.2d 749 (worker suffering preexisting diabetes got particle of dust or paper material in eye causing abrasion of cornea; sight became impaired and retinal detachment resulted; compensation award denied on evidence that detachment unrelated to injury and probably due instead to degeneration caused by diabetes).

Florida: Urban v. Morris Drywall Spray (Fla. App., 1991) 595 So. 2d 60 (while there was some dispute as to whether a workers' compensation claimant's diabetes was causally related to his compensible accident, there was no dispute that the claimant's diabetic condition was aggravated, if only slightly, by the treatment he received for his compensable injuries or by the stress associated with the accident).

Fricker v. Department of Health & Rehab. Servs. (Fla. App., 1992) 606 So. 2d 446 (question whether patient's diabetes mellitus was severe impairment under state Medically Needy Program).

Iowa: Miller v. Sioux Gateway Fire Dep't, Div. of Dep't of Defense Military Div., State of Iowa (Iowa, 1993) 497 N.W.2d 838 (in action under Americans with Disabilities Act, the nature of a firefighter's duties justified finding that a diabetic who was not in control of his disease was not qualified for the position of firefighter).

Maryland: January v. Zielenski (1975) 27 Md. App. 390, 340 A.2d 381 (compensation awarded diabetic cab driver whose foot became infected and had to be amputated after stepping on stone).

Minnesota: Sigurdeon v. Carl Bolander & Sons Co. (Minn., 1995) 532 N.W.2d 225 (in an action under the Americans with Disabilities Act, the court held that, where an insulin-dependent diabetic had been able to obtain and retain employment for most of his adult years, his failure to obtain one job did not render him disabled).

Mississippi: Cuevas v. Sutter Well Works (1963) 245 Miss. 478, 150 So. 2d 524 (compensation award for heart attack occurring on job reduced by 50% because of contributing preexisting diabetes and related vascular degeneration).

Missouri: Howard v. Ford Motor Co. (App., 1962) 363 S.W.2d 61 (compensation denied diabetic worker who suffered insulin shock and fell from platform, striking head on concrete floor).

New York: Williams v. Wilmore-Stanley Joint Venture (1972) 40 App. Div. 2d 744, 336 N.Y.S.2d 813 (ulcers and blisters on feet of laborer who stood in wet sand while mixing cement and which, superimposed upon preexisting diabetic and circulatory condition, led to disabling partial amputation, were deemed accidental and covered by workmen's compensation).

Snyder v. New York State Comm'n for Human Rights (1972) 31 N.Y.2d 284, 338 N.Y.S.2d 620, 290 N.E.2d 821 (compensation award upheld where employee suffered breakage of blood vessels in eyes and resulting hemorrhages attributed to underlying diabetic condition and prolonged state of anxiety and tension aggravated by emotional episodes involving work).

Ohio: State ex rel. Greatorex v. Industrial Comm'n of Ohio (Ohio, 1997) 681 N.E.2d 916 (workers' compensation claimant was unsuccessful in arguing that, by reason of the allowance of his claim for aggravation of preexisting diabetes, he was entitled to have all aspects of his diabetic condition considered in determining whether he was permanently and totally disabled).

Pennsylvania: Joseph Switken Co. v. Jackson (1975) 17 Pa. Commw. 554, 333 A.2d 500 (glass embedded in diabetic workman's toe resulting in cellulitis, gangrene, and eventual amputation; work-related accident found despite argument that since claimant was suffering from diabetes it was possible that he might have eventually lost toe anyway).

Lombardo v. Workers' Comp. Appeal Bd. (Pa. Commw., 1997) 698 A.2d 1378 (workers' compensation judge could rely on the testimony of orthopedic surgeon that claimant's residual disability was due to her diabetes and not her injury, since under Pennsylvania law, an expert medical witness in a workers' compensation proceeding may testify outside his or her medical specialty, and any objection to such evidence goes to its weight and not to its competency).

South Carolina: Burns v. Joyner (1975) 264 S.C. 207, 213 S.E.2d 734 (diabetic pulpwood cutter sprained ankle and developed gangrene in toes necessitating amputation of leg; temporary disability benefits under workmen's compensation payable until he reached maximum recovery and was fitted with prosthesis).

Virginia: Woodward v. Amoco Oil Co. (Va. App., 1997) 1997 Va. App. LEXIS 617 (court did not err in rejecting an osteopath's testimony that a worker's cervical/thoracic strain precipitated his "diabetic gastroparesis," a form of stomach paralysis).

(C) LIFE AND HEALTH INSURANCE CLAIMS

[See also § 30A.21]

United States: Aetna Life Ins. Co. v. Hub Hosiery Mills (C.A.-1 Mass., 1948) 170 F.2d 547 (no misrepresentation by applicant for life insurance policy in failing to mention to company before delivery of policy a positive urine-sugar test where before test was taken applicant had eaten a pound of candy and where later test was negative).

Maryland Cas. Co. v. Morrow (C.A.-3 Pa., 1914) 213 Fed. 599 (under accident insurance policy limiting benefits to disability or death resulting solely from accidental injury "independently of all other causes," claimant could not recover for death of insured which resulted from concurring effect of an injury and preexisting diabetes).

Rhodes v. Metropolitan Life Ins. Co. (C.A.-5 La., 1949) 172 F.2d 183 (where in application for life insurance policy applicant falsely stated that he did not have diabetes, fact that he died from coronary thrombosis and not diabetes did not make misrepresentation immaterial so as to allow recovery by beneficiary under policy).

Moyer v. Mutual Benefit Health & Acc. Ass'n (C.A.-6 Ohio, 1938) 94 F.2d 457 (insured under accident policy died from blood poisoning; company argued death due primarily to preexisting diabetes that made him more susceptible to blood poisoning; judgment for company reversed).

Tingle v. Pacific Mut. Ins. Co. (W.D. La., 1993) 837 F. Supp. 186 (insurance company was not entitled to deny benefits for intentional deception on grounds that applicant had failed to state on application that his wife had noninsulin-dependant diabetes, in view of evidence that he had been instructed by agent to complete application while at work, and his wife had assured him that she was not diabetic).

Georgia: Gulf Life Ins. Co. v. Braswell (1960) 101 Ga. App. 133, 112 S.E.2d 804 (diabetic insured under accident policy suffered infected blister on toe that became gangrenous and necessitated amputation; medical evidence in dispute as to whether amputation due to blister alone, diabetes, a generally poor circulatory system, or a combination of these disorders).

Kansas: Martin v. Mutual of Omaha Ins. Co. (1967) 198 Kan. 135, 422 P.2d 1009 (false answer by health and accident insurance policy applicant to question asking whether he had ever had or received advice or treatment for diabetes barred recovery under policy for claim for expense of unrelated cataract operation; statute requiring that such a statement by an applicant must have "actually contributed to the contingency or event on which the policy is to become due and payable" held inapplicable because policy taken out prior to date statute became law).

Louisiana: Willis v. Continental Cas. Co. (La. App., 1967) 194 So. 2d 785 (under credit health insurance policy which excluded coverage for preexisting disease, benefits were held payable for amputation of diabetic claimant's leg on theory that cause of amputation, a blocked artery, could have resulted as easily in a nondiabetic individual as one who suffered from diabetes).

McCray v. National Life & Acc. Ins. Co. (La. App., 1971) 244 So. 2d 342 (insured who suffered loss of foot due to gangrene after burns failed to heal awarded benefits under health and accident policy despite preexisting diabetes; policy provision allowing benefits only if loss caused solely by disease or injuries contracted or sustained after the date of issue; "We find that the evidence shows that the chain of amputations subsequent to the initial burn and leading to the final amputation below the knee on plaintiff's leg were causally and directly related to the burn to plaintiff's toe. Were it not for the accident and toe injury to plaintiff, we do not believe that plaintiff's diabetic condition alone would have actively produced toe infections which never completely healed and subsequently spread elsewhere to plaintiff's leg. The accidental burn was certainly the predominant factor in bringing about the amputation. It is our opinion that the injury and not the disease was the *sine qua non* of plaintiff's loss of his right leg. The fact that plaintiff was suffering from diabetes does not presuppose that the loss of a limb necessarily would have resulted. Many diabetics live healthy, normal lives following prescribed diets and use of insulin.").

Brown v. State Mut. Life Ins. Co. of Am. (La. App., 1979) 377 So. 2d 355 (action to collect insurance benefits based on accidental death; diabetic allegedly stepped on staple, causing infection and eventually gangrene).

Chifici v. Riverside Life Ins. Co. (La. App., 1989) 546 So. 2d 811 (even though the insured was taking an oral hypoglycemic for high blood sugar because of "impaired glucose tolerance" when he applied for life insurance, the insurer was unsuccessful in refusing to pay death benefits for his denial on the application that he had never been treated for diabetes, since it could not be shown that he had ever been specifically told that he was diabetic).

Mississippi: Metropolitan Life Ins. Co. v. Williams (1938) 180 Miss. 894, 178 So. 477 (beneficiary could recover under accident policy where accident set in motion insured's dormant diabetic condition that contributed to death from septicemia).

American Funeral Assur. Co. v. Hubbs (Miss., 1997) 700 So. 2d 283 (where the insurer's agent filled in the answers to questions on the insured's application for the insured's policy, which included denying that she had ever been treated for diabetes, his conduct consisted of only ordinary or simple negligence and the "heightened circumstances" required for the imposition of punitive damages were not present).

Missouri: Christianson v. Metropolitan Life Ins. Co. (Mo. App., 1937) 102 S.W.2d 682 (judgment for plaintiff reversed where medical testimony was to effect that person could not contract "diabetic gangrene" without being afflicted with preexisting diabetes and that the number of diabetics who die from gangrene is much higher than the number of persons who die from gangrene without the complications of diabetes).

Harris v. New York Life Ins. Co. (Mo. App., 1974) 516 S.W.2d 303 (claimant under accident policy was successful where diabetic insured died following surgery from acidosis and cardiac arrest; death held to have result from "accidental bodily injury directly and independently of all other causes" on testimony that but for negligence of physician during postoperative period death would not have occurred).

New Jersey: Formosa v. The Equitable Life Assur. Soc'y of the U.S. (N.J. Super., 1979) 398 A.2d 1301 (insurer could deny death benefits to an insured who misrepresented on his application that he had never been treated for diabetes by showing that the misrepresentation was material to the risk the insurer assumed and did not have to prove that the diabetes — the fact misrepresented — resulted in the insured's death).

Massachusetts Mut. Life Ins. Co. v. Manzo (N.J., 1991) 584 A.2d 190 (rescission of the policy was in order where the applicant's failure to reveal his preexisting diabetes influenced the insurance company's judgment in estimating the extent of the risk in insuring his life and the amount of the premium).

Pennsylvania: Arnstein v. Metropolitan Life Ins. Co. (1938) 329 Pa. 158, 196 Atl. 491 (judgment affirmed for beneficiary under accident policy where diabetic died from streptococcic infection that developed after leg was burned from overexposure to heat lamp).

Tennessee: Parker v. Provident Life & Acc. Ins. Co. (1979) 582 S.W.2d 380 (nail puncture wound to insured's foot was held to be cause of amputation rather than preexisting diabetes).

Utah: Berger v. The Minnesota Mut. Life Ins. Co. of St. Paul, Minn. (Utah, 1986) 723 P.2d 388 (where an insurance company denied benefits for the death of the plaintiff's wife on grounds he did not disclose that she was a diabetic at the time he applied for her coverage, the jury was justified in finding that no misrepresentations were made if they found that the plaintiff, on completing the application, was only "representing and warranting as to his knowledge and belief" and not as to her actual health).

(D) "TRAUMATIC DIABETES" AND AGGRAVATION OF PREEXISTING DIABETIC CONDITIONS

[See also §§ 30A.19, 30A.20]

Arkansas: Missouri Pac. R. Co. v. Diffee (1947) 212 Ark. 55, 205 S.W.2d 458 (eighteen-year-old boy developed diabetes after being injured in train-car accident).

Illinois: Kaspar v. Clinton-Jackson Corp. (1969) 118 Ill. App. 2d 364, 254 N.E.2d 826 (among other severe injuries, worker who fell from scaffold claimed injury to pancreas caused diabetes).

Levin v. Welsh Bros. Motor Serv., Inc. (Ill. App., 1987) 518 N.E.2d 205 (neuropsychologist's testimony that plaintiff's diabetes could have resulted from accident was not within scope of witness' expertise, but admission was harmless error, because witness' limitations were amply disclosed on cross-examination).

Kentucky: Stallard v. Witherspoon (Ky. App., 1957) 306 S.W.2d 299 (65-year-old woman's diabetes aggravated by injury; leg previously amputated — use of crutch impaired; medical expenses $543; award of $3,000).

Bailey v. Barnett (Ky. App., 1971) 470 S.W.2d 331 (woman who suffered preexisting mild diabetes was required, after accident, to take daily insulin shots; $12,000 awarded).

Louisiana: Ziifle v. Allstate Ins. Co. (La. App., 1972) 262 So. 2d 122 (diabetic plaintiff in personal injury action suffered aggravation of condition because of "nervous agitation"; prior to accident patient was taking oral medication which had to be changed to insulin injections, and urine test had to be increased from one to three per day; $1,734 award increased to $3,500).

Becnel v. Ward (La. App., 1973) 286 So. 2d 731 (totally disabled woman awarded $520,000 in automobile accident case; claimed slight injury to pancreas caused chain of events leading to diabetes, stroke and brain damage).

Casanova v. Ballard (La. App., 1989) 533 So. 2d 1005 (57-year-old male diabetic suffered electrical injuries when T.V. antenna he was installing came in contact with power line; third-degree burns of feet, hands, back, and abdomen; posttraumatic stress syndrome; diabetic condition delayed healing; decubitus ulcers developed on lower extremities, requiring extensive treatment; medical expenses $29,669; right leg might have to be amputated; award of $229,669 affirmed).

Landry v. Melancon (La. App., 1989) 538 So. 2d 1143 (defense unsuccessful in attributing complications of plaintiff's whiplash injury to preexisting diabetes mellitus).

Clomon v. Monroe City Sch. Bd. (La. App., 1990) 557 So. 2d 110, aff'd (La., 1990) 572 So. 2d 571 (driver found 30% at fault in striking and killing child sued school board, claiming posttraumatic stress disorder and aggravation of diabetic condition).

Mississippi: Walters v. Gilbert (1963) 248 Miss. 77, 158 So. 2d 43 (73-year-old man sustained minor bruise to foot but because of preexisting diabetes injury did not heal and pain and swelling was continuous; $5,000 verdict upheld).

Missouri: Carnes v. Kansas City Southern Ry. Co. (1959) 328 S.W.2d 615 (55-year-old railroad engineer suffered hip injury and aggravated preexisting diabetes; leg amputated; complicating heart and circulatory disorder; $40,000 awarded).

Nevada: Meagher v. Garvin (1964) 80 Nev. 211, 391 P.2d 507 (58-year-old woman diabetic suffered comminuted fracture of femur; hospitalized seventeen months and operated upon four times; complications included staph infection; wound still drained three years after injury; hospital and medical bills exceeded $30,000; awards of $125,000 to woman and $17,500 to husband affirmed).

New York: De Paola v. Gitelman (Misc., 1954) 137 N.Y.S.2d 684 (woman involved in rear-end collision who alleged acceleration and aggravation of inactive diabetic condition was unsuccessful on this issue in view of evidence that diabetes was active just prior to accident and that any increase in the severity of the disease was of little consequence).

Ohio: Pace v. Ohio Dep't of Transp. (Ohio Misc., 1991) 594 N.E.2d 187 (passenger in automobile suffered injury to little finger when vehicle struck by snowplow; finger became infected and had to be amputated partly because of lack of circulation attributed to plaintiff's preexisting diabetic condition; $15,000 award affirmed).

(E) DIABETICS AS DRIVERS OF MOTOR VEHICLES

United States: Arnold v. Loose (C.A.-3 Pa., 1965) 352 F.2d 959 (where a physician who testified in a wrongful death action that an automobile driver's diabetes caused the accident admitted that he had never even read a text on diabetes or diabetic comas, his testimony was properly excluded).

Chandler v. City of Dallas (C.A.-5 Tex., 1993) 2 F.3d 1385 (in applying regulations under the federal Rehabilitation Act of 1973, the U.S. Court of Appeals, Fifth Circuit held as a matter of law that a driver with insulin-dependent diabetes presented a genuine substantial risk of injury to himself or others).

Sarsycki v. United Parcel Serv. (W.D. Okla., 1994) 862 F. Supp. 336 (employer violated the Americans with Disabilities Act in demoting an insulin-dependent truck driver where: (1) U.S. Department of Transportation regulations barred insulin-dependent diabetics from driving commercial motor vehicles that weighed over 10,000 pounds and the plaintiff's route was served almost exclusively by vehicles weighing under that amount; (2) the employer had not conducted an individualized assessment of the plaintiff's abilities as required by the Act; (3) the plaintiff's diabetes was under control; (4) the plaintiff had never experienced a hypoglycemic episode; and (5) the physicians who examined the plaintiff found that he was qualified to drive motor vehicles weighing 10,000 pounds or less).

Myers v. Hose (C.A.-4 Md., 1995) 50 F.3d 278 (former bus driver whose diabetes could cause him to lose consciousness was not entitled to additional time to cure his disability; the Americans with Disabilities Act does not require an employer to wait an indefinite period of time for a "reasonable accommodation" to achieve its intended effect).

Daugherty v. City of El Paso (C.A.-5 Tex., 1995) 56 F.3d 695 (city did not violate the Americans with Disabilities Act in failing to obtain a waiver from the U.S. Department of Transportation that would allow an insulin-dependent diabetic driver to continue operating a city bus).

Baert v. Euclid Beverage, Ltd. (N.D. Ill., 1997) 954 F. Supp. 170 (truck driver who had insulin-dependent diabetes was not a "qualified individual with a disability" under the Americans with Disibilities Act because his disease prevented him from obtaining a renewal of his commercial driver's license and thus he could not "satisfy the prerequisites" of his position, which was required under the Act; furthermore, his employer could not retain him as a "helper" on the truck because the helper was also expected to drive).

California: Smith v. Department of Motor Vehicles (1984) 163 Cal. App. 3d 321, 209 Cal. Rptr. 283 (determination as to whether decision to issue truck and bus driver's license to diabetics must be made on a case-by-case factual basis).

Louisiana: Gambino v. Lubel (La. App., 1966) 190 So. 2d 152 (diabetic driver who blacked out from insulin reaction and caused accident was held negligent "to an extreme degree" when evidence was introduced that he had in back seat of his automobile both candy bars and Coke which if taken would have prevented reaction).

Pennsylvania: Dehrone License (1959) 21 Pa. D. & C.2d 542 (diabetic suffered insulin reaction while driving and caused accident when he could not drive automobile out of heavy traffic; suspended license was restored by court on testimony that driver had blacked out only two or three times during fifteen years as diabetic and that loss of driving privileges would cause severe hardship, and because driver "appeared sincere" when he said he would heed warnings of impending attacks in the future").

Lunetta License (1964) 36 Pa. D. & C.2d 571 (where diabetic driver's single insulin reaction was preceded by dizziness, his license was reinstated on evidence that he was conscientious and carefully followed his physician's advice, and on his physician's testimony that his diabetes was "well controlled," suggesting that there was only slight possibility that he would experience such reactions in the future, and that if he did, he probably would have adequate warning).

Commonwealth, Dep't of Transp. v. Slater (Pa. Commw., 1983) 462 A.2d 870 (school bus driver's license revoked because he had diabetes mellitus).

Crosby v. Sultz (Pa. Super., 1991) 506 A.2d 1337 (where driver who struck plaintiff and her three children was under treatment for adult-onset diabetes and was subject to temporary lapses of consciousness, in third-party action against driver's physician, court held that physician had no duty to control his patient's driving habits or to protect third persons from injuries occasioned by an "unforeseeable" accident such as the one that occurred).

South Carolina: Howle v. PYA/Monarch, Inc. (S.C. App., 1986) 344 S.E.2d 157 (where "woozy" diabetic driver had not eaten lunch but did not stop driving nor eat candy he carried, his hypoglycemic blackout and resulting collision were not unforeseeable nor unavoidable).

Wisconsin: Bothum v. State Dep't of Transp. (1986) 134 Wis. 2d 378, 396 N.W.2d 785 (school bus driver's license could not be automatically revoked when he was diagnosed diabetic and prescribed hypoglycemic medication; case-by-case evaluation must be made regarding drivers' handicaps and particular job responsibilities).

CHAPTER 30B

ORGAN AND TISSUE TRANSPLANTATION*

§ 30B.1. Introduction.

The concept of replacing an old or diseased organ has intrigued men for years. Around 1770, the well-known surgeon John Hunter reported transplanting teeth from one person to another with some degree of success. He performed a number of other transplantation procedures, including grafting a rooster's testicle onto a hen "without altering the disposition of the hen."

The nineteenth century brought about an impressive number of reported transplant attempts. Fundamentally, however, there was little change in the outcome; in every case, the transplanted tissue was rejected promptly by the recipient or host animal. Notable transplant at-

---

*By James A. Peterson, Jr, M.D. Contributors to earlier editions of this chapter include Leslie E. Rudolf, M.D., Jimmy A. Light, M.D., and Richard M. Patterson, J.D.

tempts include the Swiss Reverdin's use of small, fine skin flaps for covering wounds (1869) and the contemporaneous attempts of Albert of Vienna and von Hippel to transplant nerve and corneal tissue. (The latter was successful.)

Organ transplantation grew to its present state during the twentieth century, as the biologic phenomena of tissue transplantation emerged and became better understood. Early investigators during this century were unable to distinguish between failures due to technical faults and those due to biologic factors, and many isolated claims of success were not repeatable (such as the transplantation of goat testicles to aging human males in attempts to restore virility).

§ 30B.2. · Definition of terms.

As the transplantation field is replete with terms not used in other areas of medicine, the following definitions should be helpful.

Transplantation (Grafting): Transfer of living matter (cells, organs) from one site to another in the same organism or to another organism.

Implantation: Transfer of nonviable animal or artificial material.

Autogeneic transplant (autograft; autotransplant; autologous transplant): Donor and recipient are the same individual.

Syngeneic transplant (isologous): Graft derived from an identical twin or clone.

Allogenic transplant (homologous graft; allograft; homograft): A graft derived from a genetically different individual of the same species.

Heterograft (xenograft): Transplant derived from an individual of an entirely different species.

MHC: the major histocompatibility complex; the cluster of genes on human chromosome 6 whose products are responsible for distinguishing "self" from "nonself." Designated the HLA system in humans.

Living related donor: Fully alive individual genetically related to the recipient.

Living unrelated donor: Fully alive individual genetically unrelated to the recipient.

Cadaveric donor with intact circulation: Dead brain but a live body because the beating heart continues to circulate blood and perfuse the tissues and organs.

Cadaveric non-heart-beating donor: dead brain, dead body. No circulating blood.

Orthotopic: Where the site of implantation of the tissue or organ corresponds to its normal site in the donor.

Heterotopic: Where the site of implantation differs from that in the donor.

To put these terms in some perspective: transplanting a kidney from a related living donor other than an identical twin would be a "renal allograft," whereas a graft from an indentical twin would be a "syngeneic renal graft," and transplanting a baboon kidney to a human would be a "xenograft" or "heterologous renal transplant."

§ 30B.3. The immune process.

In a universe covered with dangerous bacteria, viruses and fungal organisms, survival depends upon a body's ability to recognize these foreign invaders promptly and reject them by walling them off and eventually destroying them. The body's power to carry out this process is known as "immunity." This highly organized defense system is common to all higher forms of life (including all the vertebrates), and is particularly well-developed in primates. The defense system is a very complex, integrated cellular network, based on a component of white blood cells called lymphocytes. These lymphocytes recognize foreign invaders and respond with cellular and humoral (chemical) mechanisms (immune response).

In humans, this almost perfect system daily wards off many viruses, bacteria, and parasites that threaten the individual. While exposure to these invaders is common, only rarely is it necessary to supplement the body's immune system with other agents to help it fight off the attacks. In many instances, first exposure to an organism (e.g., the measles virus) will incite a mild disease process, arousing the body's immunity so that on the second exposure, no disease develops. In a way, this immune process develops a "memory" of the first exposure, and remains ready when the same organism is encountered again.

§ 30B.4. Antigens and antibodies.

The two main components of the immune process are the "antigen" and the "host." The antigen (literally, "a substance that generates antagonism") is usually a foreign protein. This is the key in the immune response system. When the antigen gains entry into the body, it is responsible for the development of specific antagonists: lymphocytes, antibodies and sensitized cells.

An antibody is also a protein, called an immunoglobulin. It is manufactured in a highly developed group of cells (lymphocytes) dispersed throughout the body that are responsible for developing the immune process. With the help of another protein called "complement," the antibody binds to precipitate, and may well inactivate, the invading protein and place it in a complex that can be removed by the body. The lymphocytes are also activated by antigen, and rapidly multiply and differentiate into cells that recognize and attack the foreign tissue. After the antigen is destroyed by the cellular and humoral action, the system is decelerated or "shutdown" by another lymphocyte network of "suppressor cells."

When threatened with infection, human survival depends upon winning the "war" between the invading antigen and the body's immune defense mechanism or antibodies. When the infection is mild and short-lived, the body's immune system responds by producing adequate numbers of antibodies to overcome the invading antigens. In situations where the invading antigens enter in large numbers or are particularly virulent, the disease is much more disastrous; the immune process may not be able to keep up, and in some cases death may occur.

§ 30B.5. Tissue rejection.

The "war" described in § 30B.4 switches from protective and beneficial to harmful and deadly when transplants are involved. Early investigators realized that tissues could elicit the same immune reaction as bacteria, only now the casualties were the cells of the transplant. The process whereby the recipient attacks the transplant is labeled "rejection." Rejection takes three forms — hyperacute, acute, and chronic.

Hyperacute rejection is the "most violent immune response known." Preexisting recipient antibodies directed against the graft bind to the cells lining the graft's blood vessels (endothelium) and trigger a cascade of chemical reactions that clot off the vessel (thrombosis). The graft can die within hours. Particularly sensitive to this type of response are the ABO blood group antigens and Class 1 MHC antigens such as are found in kidneys.

Acute rejection is a cellular attack against the graft that occurs during the first two months after operation. The recipient's lymphocyte defenders invade the graft, proliferate, and then destroy the graft's cells over a matter of days in a biological version of hand-to-hand combat. In the lung, patients present with nonspecific signs and symptoms that can mimic pneumonia, pulmonary edema, and reperfusion injury: fever, cough, shortness of breath, pulmonary infiltrates on chest Xray, and lowered arterial oxygen. In the liver, one sees fever, decreased bile output, a change in the character of the bile, increased white count, and increases in the battery of liver enzymes. The kidney will demonstrate dysfunction, but it is more prone to ABO-type problems than the liver for two postulated reasons: the liver derives its blood supply from two sources (arterial and portal vein) and the kidney is far more antigenic than the liver. The most definitive test for the diagnosis is organ biopsy which will reveal, for example, a "triad of portal lymphocytes, endotheliitis, and bile duct infiltration and damage" in the liver or perivascular mononuclear infiltrates with or without accompanying lymphocytic bronchiolitis in the lung. Vasculitis is difficult to demonstrate in the liver because few arterioles are present in the contrast to the highly vascular kidney. The importance of early diagnosis and effective treatment for acute rejection is reflected in data from the UCLA kidney transplant registry. In patients experiencing no rejection, the graft survival rate is 86% at one year postop and 72% at three years. Just one episode of rejection drops those figures to 68% and 53%, respectively. More than one episode lowers them even further to 57% and 46%, respectively.

Chronic rejection is an ill-defined, indolent, smouldering process that over months can render an organ nonfunctional. In the lung, obliterative bronchiolitis slowly but inexorably scars shut the tiniest air passages so that the patient suffocates. In the liver, the bile ducts are expecially vulnerable and eventually scar shut so that the patient once again becomes jaundiced. Its presence in the heart and the kidney suggests that injury to the graft exposes soluble human leukocyte antigens (HLA), which elicit a continual antibody response.[1]

Clearly, an ounce of prevention is worth a ton of cure.

§ 30B.6. Modification of immunity-rejection.

Thus far, only three ways exist to avoid or minimize rejection: a transplant between identical twins; immune tolerance; and proactive suppression (inhibition).

Because identical twins share identical genomes, each will recognize the other's tissues as "self." Clones in science fiction would do the same.

Many attempts have been made to induce immunologic tolerance in the recipient animal by small repeated injections of either living or dead cells from an allogenic donor prior to actual transplantation. This is comparable to allergy desensitization. While in certain situations this technique does produce tolerance and long-term graft survival, the outcome of these experiments depends largely on the genetic disparity between host and donor. The result may, unfortunately, be a heightened immunity on the part of the host and thus diminished survival time for the transplanted tissue. If such "tolerance" could be reliably produced, the next step would be developing "specific immunosuppression" so that the body's ability to deal with invading organisms would not be impaired.

The third approach centers on the fact that the antibodies to foreign antigens are produced chiefly in a group of white blood cells called lymphocytes. These cells circulate through the bloodstream continually and reside in very high concentrations in the spleen, liver, lymph nodes, and the thymus. Experiments have shown that depleting the total number of lymphocytes in the body can prolong graft survival. Lymphocytes come

---

[1] Wagner, R. B., and Johnston, M. R., *Why Should Thoracic Surgeons Understand Basic Biology*, 5 Chest Surg. Clin. N. Am. 1 (Feb.), 1995; Greenfield, L. J., Editor, *Surgery*, J. P. Lippincott Co., Philadelphia, 1989, pp. 538-9; Roitt, I. M., Editor, *Immunology*, C. V. Mosby Co., St. Louis, 1989; Rao, V. K., *Postransplant Medical Complications*, 78 Surg. Clin. N. Am. 113 (Feb.), 1998.

in two kinds — T and B cells. The T cells' ancestors developed in and migrated from the thymus to bone marrow and lymph nodes before the thymus atrophied and disappeared. B-cells (named originally for a chicken organ) colonize the bone marrow and are responsible for antibody production.

The mainstays of immunosuppression have been directed at depleting or interfering with the recipient's lymphocyte population. Irradiation, drugs, and antilymphocyte sera have been used. Additionally, tissue fluid — know as lymph — contains high concentrations of both T and B cells. Thus, some centers try to deplete the total body store of lymphocytes by cannulating the thoracic duct and siphoning off the lymph for a time.

The second generation of immunosuppression therapy takes two forms — induction and maintenance. Thus far, only two antilymphocyte antibody preparations (ATG and OKT3) have been approved for use in episodes of acute rejection. Otherwise, sequential quadruple induction therapy includes:

1. Starting the steroid methylprednisolone intravenously during the operation;
2. Starting azathioprine intravenously during the operation;
3. In some cases, substituting MMF (mycophenolate mofetil) for azathioprine;
4. Starting ATG or OKT3 immediately after the operation and continuing until the graft functions normally.

Maintenance therapy still employs steroids in combination with other agents such as azathioprine and the older version of cyclosporine. The problem with steroids is the development of hypertension and high serum lipid levels. However, once patients on those regimens are withdrawn from the steroids, anywhere from 26% to 74% will experience acute rejection.

Azathioprine has been the therapy workhorse for the past three decades. Reasons for discontinuing its use in a given patient include dropping white count, liver toxicity, severe infection (for which more white cells will be needed), and the appearance of a malignancy.

Cyclosporine has been the other workhorse since 1983. The original formulation has a narrow therapeutic window (margin for error) but in 1995 a new microemulsion format made bile absorption unimportant and increased the bioavailability of the drug by 15-to-30 percent.

Mycophenolate mofetil (MMF) joined the cause in 1995. Because MMF inhibits purine synthesis during cell division, T cells and B cells using that particular chemical pathway are particularly sensitive to this drug. Therefore, MMF impedes the proliferation of T and B cells, inhibits antibody production, and also interferes with the production of cytotoxic T cells. Though the optimal dose is yet undecided, the drug has demonstrated its effectiveness in large randomized trials in this country, Canada, Australia, and Europe.

Tacrolimus blocks activation of T cells about as effectively as does cyclosporine. In 1997, it was released for use first with liver transplants and then with renal cases. Its nephrotoxicity approximates that of cyclosporine but there are fewer rejection episodes. Major side effects, though, include a significant incidence (20%) of insulin-dependent diabetes plus tremors, hair growth, gum disease, and increased serum lipid levels. The incidence with cyclosporine is 4%. Speculation is that the drug's greatest value will be in combined kidney-pancreas transplants.

Concerning kidney transplants from living donors, recipients with identical HLA typing usually start the cyclosporine emulsion two or three days before the operation. Nonidentical HLA recipients in addition start MMF preoperatively as well.[2]

As always, while these immunosuppresion techniques have accounted for improved graft survival and patient quality of life, they must be balanced against the fact they alter the body's immune response so much as to leave the recipient facing an ever-present threat from bacteria, fungi, viruses, and parasites.

Finally, the intriguing concept of placing transplanted tissue in a "privileged site" has not met with significant success. The basic concept is that of placing the tissue in an environment where antibodies and cells carried by the blood cannot reach the transplant. While the method works with varying success using individual cells inside small plastic or metal chambers penetrable only by tissue fluid, it is clearly not an option for structures like the kidney, lung, or heart, which must have blood coursing through them to function, let alone survive.

§ 30B.7. Genetic similarity (histocompatibility) testing.

There are three major techniques to assess genetic similarity between donor and recipient. The closer this similarity (histocompatibility), the less immunosuppression is required to forestall rejection, and the fewer the risks associated with impeding the recipient's immune defenses. The end result — a transplant with longer survival and function.

The first technique is blood typing as for a transfusion. Each individual possesses either A, B, AB, or O type blood. When a transfusion is administered, the red cells must be compatible. For example, red cells with A antigens will elicit an antibody response from recipients with type B blood. Furthermore, it has been shown that skin grafts between individuals with incompatible blood types have a greatly shortened survival. The same phenomenon applies to transplants, but involves a greater number of antigens.

---

[2] Rao, V. K., *Postransplant Medical Complications*, 78 Surg. Clin. N. Am. 113 (Feb.), 1998.

The second technique investigates the similarities between this larger group of antigens designated the human leukocyte antigen (HLA) system. The genes coding for these antigens from the major histocompatibility complex (MHC) on chromosome 6. The genes — and therefore their products — are determined by one's pedigree and are essential to the body's immune recognition of "self" and "non-self." In particular, HLA-A and HLA-B are critical to confronting viral infections and transplants. The complexity involved is reflected in the HLA-B locus, which has four major interrelated cross-reactive antigen groups that involve 180 alleles.

The testing process is called tissue typing and is an indirect, back-door means of identifying the HLA antigens present in a person's cells. Basically, cells are mixed with a series of sera containing known HLA antibodies. If the cells possess the corresponding antigen, the antibodies bind to them, and the cells are destroyed. The results are documented under the microscope and recorded for future reference.

The third technique checks for preexisting recipient antibodies specifically directed against the cells of the proposed donor. This is the same procedure as the crossmatch for blood transfusions. In fact, it is prior exposure to donor antigens through transfusions or a previous transplant that elicits the production of these antibodies. If the crossmatch is positive, the transplant is canceled because the antibodies would trigger hyperacute rejection.[3]

There are more sophisticated methods of histocompatibility testing that require anywhere from twelve to sixty hours before the results are available. Understandably, when an individual is awaiting a cadaveric renal transplant, these tests are not appropriate, since the ability to keep the organ alive outside of the body is limited.

§ 30B.8. Recipient selection.

Physicians dealing with transplantation are frequently called upon to make value judgments relating to an individual's total suitability as an organ recipient. Physicians are usually not concerned with a general justification for transplant procedures, but they are concerned with individuals in the vital years of their lives who are threatened by irreversible failure of vital organs. In these cases, there is seldom any hesitation to consider the patient a potential recipient of an organ if he or she is otherwise healthy and can benefit from the procedure.

What treatment should be considered for older patients? Should they continue to have failing parts restored up to the point where (if and when it is feasible) all but the brain and central nervous system have been replaced? What about the individual who has been maintained on the

[3] Riott, I. M., editor, *Immunology*, C. V. Mosby Co., St. Louis, 1989; Lorentzen, D. F., et al., *A 25% Error Rate in Serologic Typing of HLA-B Homozygotes*, 50 Tissue Antigens 359 (Oct.), 1997.

artificial kidney for a long period, and who is brought to the hospital, only to refuse a cadaver kidney that has recently become available — at a time when this organ is not suitably matched with any other local recipient? When a cadaver donor kidney becomes available, should the person who has never received a previous transplant and is having trouble on the artificial kidney receive this organ, or should it be given to a more suitably matched recipient who has had a previous transplant, only to reject it? These questions frequently produce a dilemma; the physician must balance the probability of a successful transplant against the needs of a medically urgent patient who may require the transplant to survive, but who shows a lower probability that the transplant will succeed.

What are considered to be good long-term results of a kidney transplant procedure? Presently, approximately 60% of transplanted kidneys coming from cadaver donors are working at the end of five years. The results in renal transplantation have been improving steadily, as are the results in all solid organ transplants, thanks to modern immunosuppression and improved recipient preparation. In renal transplantation, failure of the transplanted organ does not mean death; the patient can be sustained on the artificial kidney while awaiting a second transplant. Failure of other transplanted organs, however, usually means death. Many such failures are directly related to attempts to suppress the immunologic reaction. As mentioned, all too often the patients die of infectious complications.

§ 30B.9. Indications for transplantation.

Indications for transplantation are as follows:

1. The procedure must serve a clearly defined therapeutic objective. Anything else would constitute unethical human experimentation.
2. The disease being dealt with must be localized. The presence of another or a secondary illness that is therapeutically unapproachable is, at present, a definite contraindication.
3. The patient must be well-advised of the hazards involved in the transplant surgery, and voluntary and informed consent must be obtained.
4. The organ to be replaced should be a vital organ in the final stage of irreversible failure. The disease in that organ should be such that it would be uninfluenced by all other attempts at cure.

Chronic glomerulonephritis, chronic pyelonephritis, polycystic renal (kidney) disease, and the traumatically damaged single kidney have been treated by renal transplant. There are other diseases, some familial and metabolic, that could cause end stage renal failure for which renal transplantation would be indicated. One metabolic disorder, however, oxalosis, cannot be treated with transplantation because the transplanted kidney soon succumbs to the original disease process.

Diseases that irreversibly damage the liver (congenital biliary atresia, postnecrotic cirrhosis, and primary hepatoma), the lung (pulmonary fibrosis, chronic obstructive emphysema, silicosis) and the heart (congenital cardiac malformation, advanced and extensive myocardial infarction, and cardiomyopathy) are a few of the disorders being cured with organ transplantation.

Pancreatic transplantation, either in the form of a whole organ transplant or possibly only the islet cells (those cells that produce insulin) may be indicated in the future for patients with diabetes mellitus who are developing severe complications of their disease.

§ 30B.10. Contraindications to transplantation.

Basically, any patient who has been declared brain dead or is to be withdrawn from life support should be considered a potential multiorgan donor.[4] However, in 1992 the United Network for Organ Sharing (UNOS) listed three absolute contraindications to organ donation.

1. Possible transmission of an infectious disease that will harm the recipient;
2. An active cancer that could be transferred to the recipient;
3. Donor characteristics that make it unlikely the organ will function.

The infectious disease could precede the donor's terminal illness or it could be a "co-morbid" to that illness. The proscribed antecedent diseases included HIV, active HBV, Jakob-Creutzfeldt's disease, malaria, disseminated tuberculosis, and encephalitis of unknown etiology. Certain viral (hepatitis C, Epstein-Barr, cytomegalovirus), bacterial, and fungal infections were considered "relatively" prohibited and on a case-by-case basis could be advanced to the "absolute" category. Co-morbid infections ranged from catheter-related urinary tract infections to outright sepsis.

Cancers of the viscera, blood, and bone marrow absolutely disqualified a donor. Limited (permissible) tumors included basal cell and early-stage squamous cell cancers, pre-invasive cancers of the uterus and cervix, and primary brain tumors that had not been subjected to extensive surgery and dissection. Because at times one cannot distinguish between a primary brain tumor and a brain metastasis from a visceral cancer, a complete autopsy at the time of organ removal eliminates the threat of unknowingly spreading the cancer to the recipient.[5]

---

[4] Rao, V. K., *Posttransplant Medical Complications*, 78 Surg. Clin. N. Am. 113 (Feb.), 1998.

[5] Kauffman, H. M., et al., *The Expanded Donor*, 11 Transplant. Rev. 165 (Oct.), 1997.

Accumulated experience, derived mostly from kidney transplants, now separates to some extent the above prohibitions between living donors and cadavers. The screening of cadaveric donors includes the following "absolute" prohibitions:

1. Cancer outside the brain and central nervous system;
2. Prolonged warm ischemia time;
3. Positive serology for Hepatitis B surface antigen;
4. Intravenous drug use;
5. A long history of hypertension.[6]

Originally included in the above list was donor sepsis, but a 1997 report from Ireland documented the successful transplantation of six livers, eleven kidneys, one heart-lung combination, and one kidney-plus-pancreas using organs from donors who died of bacterial meningitis and acute epiglottis.[7] The rationale was that intense antibiotic therapy and prolonged storage at four degrees Centigrade negated the infection's threat. Thus, it would seem that the push is on to switch some sepsis cases into the "relative" prohibition column, which includes the following:

1. Age over sixty;
2. Age under six;
3. Diabetes;
4. Mild hypertension;
5. Positive serology for hepatitis C;
6. Prolonged cold ischemia time;
7. Acute tubular necrosis (acute renal failure).

For living donors, a number of *potential* contraindications have been identified:

1. ABO blood group incompatibility;
2. Age under eighteen and over 65;
3. Cancer;
4. Severe hypertension;
5. Kidney stones;
6. Increased anesthetic/medical risk;
7. Positive blood crossmatch;
8. Diabetes;
9. Infection;
10. Significant protein in the urine;

---

[6] Rao, V. K., *Postransplant Medical Complications*, 78 Surg. Clin. N. Am. 113 (Feb.), 1998.

[7] Little, D. M., et al., *Donor Sepsis Is Not a Contraindication to Cadaveric Organ Donation*, 90 Q. J. Med. 641 (Oct.), 1997.

11. Primary kidney disease;

12. Mental incompetency;[8]

These criteria are not universal. The decision to accept or reject a given organ rests solely with the judgment of the transplant team. Organ-specific baseline laboratory tests similar to those for screening recipients also exist. The following significant alterations in some of the major criteria deserve attention.

Donor's age

The UNOS data indicate that the ideal kidney donor is between twelve and thirty years of age. Overall, increasing age of the donor kidney brings with it an increased risk of postoperative failure. Older kidneys do not function as well in young adult patients as in older patients. One explanation is that age-associated decline in renal function renders the old kidney more vulnerable to insults like ischemia and rejection. Another idea is that there is simply not enough functioning nephrons in an older kidney to handle the recipient's requirements. In some cases, two elderly kidneys are implanted to meet the demand. Generally, using old kidneys in an older recipient with a limited life expectancy amounts to palliation. In liver transplants, short-term survival has been comparable for grafts from donors on either side of age fifty.

For hearts, the situation is not clear. It has been said that there is no difference in survival whether a young heart or an old heart is used. Yet, recipients apparently do not fare as well with older hearts. Sometimes the discrepancy appears to rise from statistical gyrations on small amounts of data. On the other hand, a series of 10,783 transplanted hearts reported by the International Society for Heart and Lung Transplantation factored in donor and recipient elements such as ischemia time, hospital case-load, and the use of any ventricular assist devices. Using donors below age thirty-five as the control group, the Society calculated from the study that the recipient's mortality rate at one year postoperative was 26% greater where the donor was age thirty-five to forty-four. The increase was 73% for donors aged forty-five to fifty-nine, and 249% for donors age sixty and older.

Using older lung donors has not resulted in more operations being done or better outcomes.[9]

Hepatitis C

This topic is considered controversial and complicated. The incidence of hepatitis C (HCV) is low among the general population, accounting for

---

[8] Rao, V. K., *Postransplant Medical Complications*, 78 Surg. Clin. N. Am. 113 (Feb.), 1998.

[9] Kauffman, H. M., et al., *The Expanded Donor*, 11 Transplant. Rev. 165 (Oct.), 1997; Hanto, D. W., *Transplantation*, 186 J. Am. Coll. Surg. 232 (Feb.), 1998.

only 15% of acute viral hepatitis cases. However, HVC is considered the most important liver disease in the country because 85% of its victims remain infected with the virus. This amounts to some four million people in the United States. While HCV rarely causes acute liver failure, 20% of patients go on to develop cirrhosis and primary liver cancer. Remarkably, only 1.8% of kidney donors are HCV-positive. If a HCV-positive kidney is used in a HCV-negative recipient, there is a 55% chance the recipient will develop hepatitis. Therefore, some transplant teams will use such kidneys only for recipients who already have anti-HCV antibodies in their bodies.

Using HCV-positive organs is less controversial for recipients of life-sustaining transplants (heart, lung, or liver) than it is for kidney recipients. In liver transplants, organ and recipient survival go hand-in-hand. Placing HCV-positive livers into HCV-positive recipients have produced roughly the same frequency of recurrent hepatitis and the same four-year survival rate as placing them into HCV-negative recipients. In fact, some authors consider the subsequent hepatitis not to be a threat to the patient's long-term survival.[10]

Diabetes and hypertension

Despite some studies that show that kidneys from diabetic donors function perfectly well in nondiabetic recipients, one study demonstrated decreased graft survival when compared to nondiabetic kidneys. As yet, no appreciable numbers of cases have been done with diabetic hearts, livers, or lungs. As for hypertension, early results using donors with mild hypertension have demonstrated no appreciable difference from normotensive kidneys. At the University of Cincinnati, limited — and thus acceptable — kidney vascular disease is defined by renal biopsy showing less than 20% glomerulosclerosis plus minimal arteriolar sclerosis.

Preoperative organ function

Elevated agonal serum creatinine levels seem not to reflect any genuine problem with donor kidneys and should not be considered a contraindication. The same is not true for someone with chronically abnormal laboratory values. In livers, a variety of screening laboratory tests have proven unreliable and inconsistent, especially in obese donors, and so percutaneous liver biopsy is recommended. Specifically, pathologists check the degree of fatty change and infiltration present. Signs of severe

---

[10] Koff, R. S., *Hepatitis C*, 5 Sci. Med. 16, 1998; Kauffman, H. M., et al., *The Expanded Donor*, 11 Transplant. Rev. 165 (Oct.), 1997; Hanto, D. W., *Transplantation*, 186 J. Am. Coll. Surg. 232 (Feb.), 1998; Testa, G., et al., *Long-Term Outcomes of Patients Transplanted with Livers from Hepatitis C-Positive Donors*, 65 Transplantation 925 (Apr. 15), 1998.

fatty infiltration, ischemic necrosis, and chronic inflammation around the portal triads will disqualify a donor. Using such criteria has reduced the delayed function rate by 80%. To expand the pool of lung donors, the requirement for oxygenating capability was lowered by 25%, yet produced only a slight increase in the number of available donors. In the heart, two old criteria have bit the dust. First, drug support for effective contractility no longer automatically disqualifies a donor. Second, abnormal ventricular wall motion during heartbeats as visualized by echocardiograms and borderline ejection fractions also do not automatically eliminate a donor from consideration. As with many open heart procedures, the final assessment is made at the operating table under direct vision by the surgeon who may override the conclusions of other studies.[11]

Toxic exposure

Previously, it stood to reason that anything systemically damaging would certainly render any organ unusable for transplantation. However, case reports are accumulating which show that sometimes taking chances works. Successful transplants have been achieved with cadaver kidneys from donors who died from ethanol and methanol poisoning, lead poisoning, carbon monoxide, and cocaine and barbiturate overdoses. Perhaps the most dramatic case was a young man who committed suicide by ingesting a full vial of cyanide. The key to the outcome was that cyanide's bond to cytochrome oxidase is completely dissociable and thus reversible given the time and access to the antidote. Paramedics arrived fifteen minutes after ingestion, and the victim reached the hospital emergency room thirty minutes later. By that time, he had received Narcan intravenously, 100% oxygen by mask, and MAST trousers support, but he had unobtainable blood pressure, sinus bradycardia of forty beats, and no spontaneous respirations.

Upon transfer to the ICU, the patient's vital signs were restored through drug support, intense invasive monitoring, and mechanical ventilation. About three hours after ingestion, the Lilly Cyanide Antidote kit was administered and a follow-up half-dose was given an hour later. The patient's vital signs stabilized thereafter. At thirteen hours into the crisis, a head CT scan showed the typical signs of brain death from cyanide poisoning, and an EEG showed electrocerebral silence. Intensive donor management continued. Serum chemistries were satisfactory except for very abnormal liver function tests, which were judged to reflect anoxic damage to the liver. With the liver thus excluded, the heart, kidneys, and corneas were harvested and successfully transplanted.

---

[11] Kauffman, H. M., et al., *The Expanded Donor*, 11 Transplant. Rev. 165 (Oct.), 1997.

Cyanide poisoning is rapid in onset and just as quickly serum levels fall so that blood tests often give an artificially low result. In this case, the thiocyanate level at seven hours into the crisis was 2.0 mg/dl and at thirty hours was 1.0 mg/dl. The elapsed time without any cardiopulmonary support and later before vital signs stabilized was comparable or longer than most HBD (heart-beating donors) or NHBDs (nonheart-beating donors). Yet, while the brain is almost always a lost cause, other organs can recover from the insult. Despite the myocardium's exquisite susceptibility to cyanide anoxia, the almost complete dissociation of the cyanide-cytochrome complex can occur and leave no significant sequelae. Kidneys are particularly resilient as long as they remain well perfused and oxygenated. Corneas can survive the insult if their investing solution is high in glucose.[12]

§ 30B.11. Sources of organs and tissue.

The enabling legislation governing the procurement and distribution of transplant organs and tissues are the National Organ Transplant Act of 1984, the Omnibus Reconciliation Act of 1986, and the Transplants Amendment Act of 1990. The Department of Health and Human Services bears ultimate responsibility for the proper operation and conduct of this industry. In 1986, the United Network for Organ Sharing (UNOS) received a federal contract to administer the system as a nonprofit corporation and thus has front-line responsibility for the development, implementation, and monitoring of national transplantation policies. Moreover, the Health Care Financing Administration (HCFA) has the responsibility to certify (as well as recertify and decertify) all organ procurement organizations. As of 1994, there were eleven UNOS regions across the country involving 277 transplantation centers, 866 transplant programs, and 69 organ-procurement organizations. Each potential transplant recipient is registered with UNOS, sometimes through more than one transplant center. However, any given center can list a patient only once. UNOS approves the importation of organs only when all good-faith efforts to find a recipient within this country have failed.

With the overall success of transplantation, demand has steadily outpaced supply. For example, in the 1988, the number of waiting recipients was 25% higher than the number of operations performed. By 1994, the waiting list was 50% greater. As of October 31, 1996, there were 49,223 registered patients waiting for an organ.[13] Not surprisingly, the

---

[12] Barkoukis, T. J., et al., *Multiorgan Procurement from a Victim of Cyanide Poisoning*, 55 Transplantation 1434 (June), 1993; Rao, V. K., *Postransplant Medical Complications*, 78 Surg. Clin. N. Am. 113 (Feb.), 1998; Hauptman, P. J., and O'Connor, K. J.,

Procurement and Allocation of Solid Organs for Transplantation, 336 N. Engl. J. Med. 422 (Feb. 6), 1997.

[13] Hauptman, P. J., and O'Connor, K. J., *Procurement and Allocation of Solid Organs for Transplantation*, 336 N. Engl. J.

numbers of deaths occurring among waiting patients has also increased.[14]

(A) PROCUREMENT

The U.S. Department of Health and Human Services, through HCFA, originally specified that an organ-procurement organization had to provide a minimum fifty donors per year to be certified by the federal government. After much hue and cry, this requirement was reduced to providing a donor pool of "sufficient size" to maintain "effectiveness." (Apparently, it was then left to each administrator, supervisor, surgeon, and patient to define these terms for themselves.)

Efforts to increase the number of potential donors has focused on retrieving bodies heretofore lost to the process. Through the vigorous support of Pennsylvania's Delaware Valley Transplantation Program, legislation was enacted that required every acute care hospital within that region to routinely refer all near-death patients to the program for evaluation as possible donors. In a two-year period, significant results were obtained.

1. A 45% increase in the number of potential donors;
2. A 26% increase in the number of actual donations;
3. A 31% increase in the number of operations performed;
4. A 28% increase in the number of eye donations;
5. A 14% increase in the number of tissue donations.[15]

Because hospital-based providers have more contact with the donor patients and their families than anyone else, studies have looked at enhancing these providers' effectiveness in securing permission for donations. A study of emergency room physicians and personnel from the University of Southern California involved an intensive educational campaign on the procurement process with re-education every two to three months. As a result, the number of organs obtained yearly from that facility increased from none in 1994 to fourteen (five donors) in 1995 and thirty-two (nine donors) in 1996.[16]

Living, genetically related donors

The perfect donor is an identical twin who shares every bit of genetic code with the recipient. Next in line are fraternal twins and close blood relatives (siblings, parents, and children). As of 1997, 35% of donated

---

Med. 422 (Feb. 6), 1997; Steinbrook, R., *Allocating Livers: Devising a Fair System*, 336 N. Engl. J. Med. 436 (Feb. 6), 1997.

[14]Kauffman, H. M., et al., *The Expanded Donor*, 11 Transplant. Rev. 165 (Oct.), 1997; Hauptman, P. J., and O'Connor, K. J., *Procurement and Allocation of Solid Organs for*

Transplantation, 336 N. Engl. J. Med. 422 (Feb. 6), 1997.

[15]Hanto, D. W., *Transplantation*, 186 J. Am. Coll. Surg. 232 (Feb.), 1998.

[16]Henderson, S. O., et al., *Organ Procurement in an Urban Level I Emergency Department*, 31 Ann. Emer. Med. 466, 1998.

kidneys came from this category. Often, the optimum situation would find the donor and recipient in adjacent operating rooms, and the kidney would be hand-carried from one to the other. The time lapse from resection to the beginning of the vascular anastomoses would be but a matter of a few minutes. (Occasionally, a completely unrelated cadaveric donor with no major histocompatibility complex (MHC) mismatch will produce an equally good result. The next most frequent donations are transplants of portions of lung, liver, and pancreas.) The next most frequent donations are transplants of portions of lung, liver, and pancreas.[17]

Living, genetically unrelated donors

It should not be surprising that by far the most common donor in this category is the patient's spouse. Though not genetically related, the success rate for these organs exceeds that of the usual cadaveric donor because of the higher incidence of preexisting damage in the "unknown" donor. Ironically, the rarity of a nonspouse donating even a part of an organ to a total stranger is counterpoint to the widespread experience with blood donations. It is within this category that exists the greatest concern for unscrupulous and black market trading in organs.[18]

Cadaveric donors with intact circulation

Known as heart-beating donors (HBDs), these individuals, who have a dead brain but a living body, have been the number-one source for organs since the adoption of the "dead-brain" definition of death. There are two groups here — trauma victims with fatal head injuries, but a generally intact chest and trunk, and older patients who have succumbed to primary central nervous system problems such as strokes. Although the brain is lost, resuscitation efforts succeed in preserving effective blood oxygenation and circulation, thereby setting the stage for harvesting organs with the least possible time spent between removal and implantation. The percentage of such donors over age fifty doubled between 1988 and 1995.[19]

Asystolic cadaveric donors

In contrast to the HBDs, who are declared dead based on brain-based criteria, the nonheart-beating donors (NHBDs) are the traditional cadavers (dead brain, dead body) in whom blood circulation has ceased completely. In the beginning, the NHBD was the only alternative to a living donor. The primary obstacle to using the traditional cadaver was that tissue decay begins from the moment of asystole (cardiac standstill)

---

[17] Hauptman, P. J., and O'Connor, K. J., *Procurement and Allocation of Solid Organs for Transplantation*, 336 N. Engl. J. Med. 422 (Feb. 6), 1997.

[18] Id.
[19] Id.

and initiates a race against time (known as the "warm ischemia time"). The kidney was the only NHBD organ that could be reliably transplanted because it could remain viable and functional for up to forty-five minutes outside the body and away from arterial blood flow. The other major organs, however, could not.[20]

Clearly, there was no chance of enlarging the scope of organ transplantation unless the warm ischemia time could be shortened dramatically.[21] However, speed of operation had finite limits and so the solution was to cool the body to retard the process of disintegration. The principle is the same as in hypothermia victims whose cellular metabolism grinds to a halt such that oxygen demand and biochemical waste byproduct accumulation are minimal. With rewarming, life functions return to normal. Either whole body or regional cooling (or chilling) is used. Early methods included whole body cardiopulmonary bypass, direct renal artery cannulation and perfusion, and cold immersion of the whole body. The four contemporary methods of cooling are:

1. Femoral artery and vein cannulation and regional retrograde aortic flush;
2. Femoral artery and vein cannulation for formal cardiopulmonary bypass;
3. Open, direct cannulation of the aorta and flushing;
4. Peritoneal lavage with cold saline followed by direct aortic cannulation.[22]

In general, the donor is either in the intensive care unit or the operating room, depending on family preference. For the transplant team, the ideal is the operating room, with the femoral cannulas already placed and ready. Heparin and phentolamine (or phenoxybenzamine) are given intravenously to prevent blood clotting and renal artery spasm once life support is discontinued. The essential difference between the NHBD and the HBD is here — in the HBD, the organ is removed while the blood circulation is still operating, but in the asystolic donor, nothing can happen until the body has been without any blood circulation for a defined period of time.[23]

[20] Kootstra, G., *The Asystolic, or Non-Heartbeating Donor*, 63 Transplantation 917 (Apr. 15), 1997; Sainio, K., *Are Non-Heartbeating Donors Really Dead?*, 29 Ann. Med. 473, 1997; Hauptman, P. J., and O'Connor, K. J., *Procurement and Allocation of Solid Organs for Transplantation*, 336 N. Engl. J. Med. 422 (Feb. 6), 1997.

[21] Sainio, K., *Are Non-Heartbeating Donors Really Dead?*, 29 Ann. Med. 473, 1997; Kauffman, H. M., et al., *The Expanded Donor*, 11 Transplant. Rev. 165 (Oct.), 1997.

[22] Kauffman, H. M., et al., *The Expanded Donor*, 11 Transplant. Rev. 165 (Oct.), 1997.

[23] Rao, V. K., *Posttransplant Medical Complications*, 78 Surg. Clin. N. Am. 113 (Feb.), 1998; Kootstra, G., *The Asystolic, or Non-Heartbeating Donor*, 63 Transplantation 917 (Apr. 15), 1997; Hanto, D. W., *Transplantation*, 186 J. Am. Coll. Surg. 232 (Feb.), 1998; Kauffman, H. M., et al., *The Expanded Donor*, 11 Transplant. Rev. 165 (Oct.), 1997.

A physician not affiliated with the transplant team disconnects the ventilator and removes the endotracheal tube. At some point, that physician declares the patient dead. The time between the onset of asystole and the initiation of cooling (warm ischemia time) averages fifteen to twenty minutes. A formal but rapid laparotomy gains access to the aorta, if necessary, and to the target organs.

There are four etiologic categories of NHBD — dead on arrival (DOA), do not resuscitate (DNR), failed resuscitation (CPR$_f$), and unexpected cardiac arrest in a HBD. In the detached vernacular of the specialty, these four are reclassified into two: "controlled" and "uncontrolled" donations. "Controlled" donations are precisely that, patients who by prior arrangement through advance directives or family decision volunteer to be donors once their anticipated death occurs. These are the "do not resuscitate" patients. This situation allows for the greatest amount of preparation, all of which is geared toward minimizing the warm ischemia time. In stark contrast are the genuine, out-of-the blue, fatal emergencies that befall the DOA, CPR$_f$, and arrested HBD patients. There is absolutely no control over the length of time before CPR begins, how long it runs, and whether it is a genuine effort or merely a heroic gesture lasting far beyond the time when there could have been any reasonable hope.[24] Another way to think of the difference between these donor groups is that controlled donations are *proactive* while the uncontrolled are *reactive*.

At the University of Pittsburgh, the average warm ischemia time for "controlled" kidneys was twenty-three minutes; for "uncontrolled" kidneys, thirty-seven minutes. At the University of Wisconsin, the average warm ischemia time for all NHBD was fifteen minutes.[25]

The efforts to transplant other NHBD organs have had mixed results. Livers from "uncontrolled" donors have generally not fared well, while the "controlled" livers have worked satisfactorily. "Controlled" pancreatic transplants have had a high success rate attributable in large part to regional retrograde aortic cooling. Donated pediatric hearts have functioned satisfactorily if the donor was maintained on full cardiopulmonary bypass following the cessation of CPR. Thus far, the experience with lungs is too limited to draw any conclusions.[26]

As yet, there is no consensus on the proper time to begin the cooling process, let alone insert the femoral catheters. The Pittsburgh protocol

[24]Kootstra, G., *The Asystolic, or Non-Heartbeating Donor*, 63 Transplantation 917 (Apr. 15), 1997; Sainio, K., *Are Non-Heartbeating Donors Really Dead?*, 29 Ann. Med. 473, 1997; Hauptman, P. J., and O'Connor, K. J., *Procurement and Allocation of Solid Organs for Transplantation*, 336 N. Engl. J. Med. 422 (Feb. 6), 1997.

[25]Hauptman, P. J., and O'Connor, K. J., *Procurement and Allocation of Solid Organs for Transplantation*, 336 N. Engl. J. Med. 422 (Feb. 6), 1997; Hanto, D. W., *Transplantation*, 186 J. Am. Coll. Surg. 232 (Feb.), 1998.

[26]Kauffman, H. M., et al., *The Expanded Donor*, 11 Transplant. Rev. 165 (Oct.), 1997.

sets two minutes as the mandatory wait time between asystole and commencing the operation. However, others question how certain anyone can be that all neurologic activity has ceased by that point and suggest instead a ten-minute interval. However, that five-fold increase would return matters back to the very beginning because the nonrenal organs would not withstand the added minutes of warm anoxia.

Expanded donors

This group of donors have been described as imperfect, tainted, diseased, or marginal donors. Because these adjectives convey the implication that implanting organs from such donors suggests cutting corners to use damaged goods, the neutral word "expanded" was chosen to describe the campaign to increase the supply of cadaveric donors by altering, modifying, or lowering the standards for donor organs. An analogy would be installing Chevy parts in a Cadillac although the customer expected Cadillac parts would be used. The perspective fuelling this campaign is the concept that the comparison should not be between using these less-than-perfect donors and "ideal" donors, but between the recipient accepting these imperfect organs rather than dying while on the waiting list for the "ideal" match. In fact, in this decade, while the waiting list has grown 22% annually, the number of actual operations per year has increased only 8%, and the number of deaths on the waiting list has increased 18% per year. So the premise is that amelioration and palliation, though expensive, are better than death. The history of laparoscopic cholecystectomy draws an exact parallel to the change in standards. Originally, only patients meeting very restrictive criteria were deemed proper candidates for the new operation. As time passed and experience grew, the restrictions fell away, one by one, as more and more "prohibitive" patients were successfully treated. The key in transplantation is for all the participants to exercise uniformly sound judgment.

Traditionally, the "Big Four" donor criteria were (1) age between five and fifty-five, (2) normal blood pressure, (3) normal blood sugar, and (4) negative serology for Hepatitis C (HCV). The expanded criteria now include (1) ages younger than five and older than fifty-five, (2) high blood pressure, (3) clinical diabetes, and (4) positive HCV serology. A study from Louisiana demonstrated that, over a three year period, 200 additional transplants were made possible using the altered donor criteria.[27] This and other studies documented two unexpected results. First, hospital costs went up significantly when expanded donors were used. The loss leaders were the more extensive evaluations these donors command, extra expenses in placing the organs, and education programs to spur referrals. In a way, this is not surprising, because expanding the

---

[27] Jacobbi, L. M., et al., *The Risks, Benefits, and Costs of Expanding Donor Criteria,* 60 Transplantation 1491 (Dec. 27), 1995.

donor supply pool does place a higher degree of responsibility on the OPO (organ procurement organization) to provide a more detailed history and evaluation, as well as intensive and longer management, and it incurs an increase in liability. A major source of this liability is the industry-wide problem of high employee turnover within the procurement organizations. The Louisiana project saw a 200% turnover in the eighteen months of the study.

Clearly, handling extended donors entails more work, and apparently this is something many OPO employees find distasteful. Could it be that the OPOs are so obsessed with running "lean and mean" like modern for-profit corporations that they overwork their people into burnout? Whatever the cause, the immediate effect is that the system is often operating with rookies who are bound to make mistakes. That seems to be the weak link in the chain. Would it not seem advantageous to retain more veterans and utilize their experience? For specific modifications, see § 30B.10 herein.

Medical examiner cases

Major efforts to enlarge the donor pool have included:

1. Creation of the United Network for Organ Sharing (UNOS);
2. The Donor Opportunity Act;
3. The Uniform Anatomical Gift Act;
4. Organ Transplant Amendment Acts;
5. The National Organ Transplant Act;
6. Donor cards;
7. The National Task Force on Organ Transplantation;
8. Increased funding;
9. Public education;
10. Presumed consent programs.[28]

Despite the above efforts, demand for organs has exceeded supply, and frustrated, medical professionals have cast a jaundiced eye at whom they have perceived to be the villains: the medical examiner who seemed to deny access to so many possible donors. To ease the problem, New York, Tennessee, and New Jersey placed statutory limits on the extent of "interference" by a medical examiner (M.E.) or coroner. California's San Bernardino County and the city of Pittsburgh experimented with protocols to streamline the referral process involving coroner's cases. In the early 1990s, the Colorado Organs Recovery Systems (CORS) conducted a survey of coroners and medical examiners to confirm that unnecessary obstacles stood in the way of increased referrals. The survey found that the M.E.'s believed they were adhering to the philosophies of their local

---

[28] Wick, et al., *Pediatric Organ Donation: Impact of Medical Examiner Panel*, 27 Transplant. Proc. 2539 (Aug.), 1995.

district attorneys. More striking, though, was the discovery that the major concern expressed by district attorneys was that many delays were caused by physicians avoiding court dates. It is part and parcel of the process that the physician who pronounces the donor dead or whose responsibility is it to perform the resection or the transplant be prepared to testify in court as to the proper conduct of the proceedings. So in one aspect, the problem comes full circle — the physicians involved must stay fully involved.

The key to the successful protocol that CORS shepherded into being was to enlist the active participation of coroners and district attorneys. The two groups promoted the protocol because each had more than token input and thus felt at ease with its implementation. In addition, the improved communication eliminated the previous "them-versus-us" mentality. The result? In 1991, of fifty-five coroner's cases, twenty-two were denied. However, in 1993, after institution of the protocol, of fifty-six coroner's cases, only *nine* were denied. The forty-seven referred donors supplied thirty-seven hearts, thirty-eight livers, eighty-two kidneys, sixteen pancreases, and nine livers.[29]

The lack of pediatric donors for pediatric recipients sparked the greatest interest in M.E. cases. Indeed, one statistic revealed that, over a two-year period, M.E.s across the country had denied access to 562 donors and thus had deprived 1,893 recipients a transplant and presumably the gift of life. The cases most commonly withheld from donation involved suspected SIDS or child abuse victims.

Reports of studies in Virginia, Minnesota, and California may reflect the attitudes in these respective areas. The Virginia report concerns a two-part study: a national survey of recognized pediatric intensive care unit (PICU) directors and a chart audit of a 1,000-bed tertiary hospital with a 12-bed PICU. The 150 responses to the survey revealed some surprising information. For example, 56% of the PICU directors were under the jurisdiction of a medical examiner, 23% under a coroner (some of whom are not physicians), 18% worked with both types of officers, and 2% were under a justice of the peace. Alarmingly, 60% of the directors said the M.E. never or rarely came to the hospital; only 9% said the M.E. always or almost always came to the hospital. Also of concern was that only 6% of the PICU directors ever heard of any state laws applying to the medical examiner's responsibilities and prerogatives.

The Virginia study suggested that, while M.E. denial is a deterrent to donation, it is much less than expected. In fact, family refusal proved to be responsible for almost half the denials and outnumbered those by the M.E. Another significant factor was discontinuing life support before a determination of brain death had been made. The authors believe that,

---

[29]Jaynes, C. E., and Springer, J. W.,
Evaluating a Successful Coroner Protocol, 6
J. Transplant Coordination 28 (Mar.), 1996.

all tolled, recovering all the M.E. cases would not put a dent in the disparity in supply and demand. The following delineation of the M.E.'s position is edifying:

> The M.E. is placed in an unenviable position between two emotionally charged issues: a need to protect evidence for potential prosecution and a desire to provide organs for patients on the waiting list. The M.E.'s reluctance to allow blanket procurement centers around compromise of forensic standards, loss of evidence, and fear of legal ramifications. However ... no case has ever failed prosecution secondary to organ procurement ... As physicians, it is our responsibility to acknowledge the M.E.'s dilemma, provide a clear and complete presentation, ensure adequate documentation, and give the M.E. enough information with which to make an informed decision.[30]

The Minnesota study begins with a restatement of the "seriously conflicting interests" that an M.E. must confront, namely guarantee society that justice will be served while endeavoring to provide transplantable organs so that afflicted children may survive. Indeed, "[T]he pain of donor request denial ... is perhaps matched by the outrage that would ensue if a perpetrator of lethal childhood violence escaped justice due to limited forensic review." A survey of fifty-three M.E.s from thirty-one states involved evaluating three case scenarios. Remarkably, age, size of service area, forensic experience, types of assistance, case load, and presence or absence of formal credentialing played little part in the respondents' judgments on the three cases. The factors they did admit influenced their judgments were office policies that prohibited organ release and established working relationships with procurement teams. In fact, working relationships proved essential because most medical people view the M.E. as peripheral or "tangential" to the entire process. Nothing like expecting whole-hearted cooperation from someone looked upon as ancillary and inferior and is kept out of the loop. Notably throughout the study, the M.E.s stated they wanted more information than was provided. They expressed particular interest in ophthalmological exams of the retinas, skeletal X-rays, and a prospective statement from the procuring surgeon.

The authors of the Minnesota study developed six steps toward enhancing cooperation from the M.E.'s office. Among them is the caveat that the procurement team must make a commitment to be available for any subsequent legal proceedings. The greatest difficulty appears to come with cases of child abuse and homicide. However, a concerted effort at networking and maintaining active communication with the M.E.'s office cannot but help the situation. Especially important for the pro-

---

[30] Wick, et al., *Pediatric Organ Donation: Impact of Medical Examiner Panel*, 27 Transplant. Proc. 2539 (Aug.), 1995.

curement team is remaining vigilant for the subtle hints an M.E. might drop along the way indicating his desire for more information.

Another helpful facet of this article is that it contains twenty-two references for such topics as how to request organs, how to support the donating family, how to support non-procurement-team nurses unexpectedly thrust into the breach, and how to care for recipients.[31]

The California study emphasizes the high mortality rate among infants awaiting transplants and indicates that, despite a 1987 HCFA Medicaid mandate, 5% to 30% of eligible donor families are never approached on the subject. In addition, 39% of surveyed organ procurement organizations (OPOs) reported that medical examiners in their area did not release child abuse cases for donation. The study examined the effect of a protocol developed in San Diego County by the local M.E, the local OPO, and the children's hospital medical staff, and to some extent the district attorney. Mirroring experiences elsewhere, this cooperative venture had the following result — whereas in the five years prior to the protocol, only two cases in the entire county were released for donation, the first two and one-half years after the protocol's acceptance saw nineteen organs recovered for transplantation.[32]

Xenotransplants

Xenotransplants involve animal donors. At the opposite end of the spectrum from the identical twin donor is the donor from another species altogether, or what we generously call animals. Three theoretical advantages pertain to using animal donors:

1. The animal would be a "controlled" donor and there would be ample time to get the recipient in the best possible condition;
2. A possible reduced risk of recurrent human disease in the graft, since generally diseases are species-specific;
3. *Possible* genetic manipulation of the animals (as in the novel *Chromosome 6* in which a species of African primate is cultivated to carry the human MHC complex on its sixth chromosome). In that way, the animal's organs are a perfect match for the human patient for whom they were created.[33]

However, the rejection problems are more virulent than those when a human organ is used. In fact, "the strength of the cellular immune response to xenografts is so great that it is unlikely to be controlled by the

---

[31] Kurachek, S. C., et al., *Medical Examiners' Attitudes Toward Organ Procurement from Child Abuse/Homicide Victims*, 16 Am. J. Forensic Med. Pathol. 1, 1995.

[32] Duthie, S. E., et al., *Successful Organ Donation in Victims of Child Abuse*, 9 Clin. Transplant. 415, 1995.

[33] Platt, J. L., *New Directions for Organ Transplantation*, 392 Nature 11 (Supp., Apr. 30), 1998.

types of nonspecific immunosuppression used routinely to prevent allograft (human organ) rejection."[34]

Complicating the picture is the possibility that differences in biochemical pathways and cellular metabolism will render graft and recipient incompatible. Critical to the proper function of many cell types is the interaction between the cell and its surrounding matrix. Thus, conflicts between individual donor and recipient molecules may occur in such areas as growth factors and cellular adhesion. Another problem is that different kinds of grafts receive their blood supply in different ways. With isolated cells and free tissues (such as pig heart valves), the recipient's blood vessels supply the graft directly while the entire vasculature of a whole-organ graft is that of the donor, in direct contact with the recipient blood flowing through it. All too often what follows is an attack on the endothelium with the resulting devastating consequences. (See § 30B.5.)

The most obvious animal source — other primates — has not proven out. Aside from being relatively few in number and too small to supply organs large enough to meet the demands of the adult human, they are the reservoirs of some lethal viruses. So attention has focused on the pig because of organ size, availability, the ability to be genetically manipulated, and the lowered risk of accidentally transmitting a new disease to humans.[35]

(B) ALLOCATION

Although the procurement of organs is a national process, a patient's access to that process is not. Directly or indirectly, money rules. Some patients may be independently wealthy or have appropriate insurance coverage. Others benefit from charitable contributions from co-workers, relatives, neighbors, and fellow parishioners. Medicaid often restricts patients to centers within their state of residence. Managed care contracts can restrict access ever further. Generally, eight percent of waiting recipients die of their disease before an organ reaches them.

Generally, the process follows a master algorithm that incorporates such diverse factors as UNOS policies, acceptance criteria of individual centers (for example, distance between donor and recipient), and local "variances." Each recipient center has right of refusal based upon items such as whether the donor organ is too small or too large for the proposed recipient. Kidney distribution hinges in large part on the wait-time by the recipient and human leukocyte antigen (HLA) compatibility. Those recipients having no HLA mismatches get the highest priority simply because they have the greatest chance of long-term success. A notable

---

[34] Auchincloss, H., Jr., and Sachs, D. H., *Xenotransplantation*, 16 Annu. Rev. Immunol. 433, 1998.

[35] Platt, J. L., *New Directions for Organ Transplantation*, 392 Nature 11 (Supp., Apr. 30), 1998.

exception to this rule is when the kidney is part of a multiple-organ transplant — then allocation is determined by the status of the other organ(s).[36]

Altogether, "[T]he system's success hinges on its public and professional credibility and on the perception that it plays no favorites and rewards altruism."[37] Falsifying a recipient's severity of illness ("gaming the system") to gain earlier placement on the waiting list damages this credibility. Unfortunately, recent liver transplants to celebrity recipients whose illnesses came directly from flagrantly unhealthy lifestyles created the impression of favoritism and prompted calls for investigations and audits of the system. Questions were raised how these celebrities received their new livers within a few weeks or less when the wait-time across the country is commonly at least six months. Properly applied, the major factors deciding liver allocation are the wait time, the severity of illness (also known as urgency), the sizes of the donor and recipient, and their blood types. Perhaps in response to the cries of favoritism, in late 1996, UNOS amended its policy to give priority to three specific groups of recipients — patients in acute liver failure, those whose first transplanted liver failed within seven days of operation, and children facing permanent neurological damage. Included in the revision were standardized criteria for the waiting list, enlarging the regional distribution areas for each center, and establishing oversight regional review boards. Nevertheless, the bulk of transplanted livers will go to patients with chronic rather than acute, disease.[38]

§ 30B.12. The living donor — Some special problems.

Living, related kidney transplants have been performed since 1954, when the procedure was first successfully accomplished in Boston. Many of these transplants continue to function today, especially if they were well matched. In fact, at any point in time, more kidneys from living related donors (LRD) are functioning as compared to kidneys from cadaveric sources, because rejection is less frequent and less severe. Recipient survival is also better with LRD transplants, in part because less immunosuppression is needed, but also because donors and recipients can be optimally prepared for the surgery.

Despite the obvious advantages of LRD transplants, some transplant centers have sufficient concern that LRD's are rarely performed, whereas in others, LRD transplants predominate. Although experimental studies have raised concern that LRD's might be at risk for renal failure themselves, numerous long-term follow-up studies show that

---

[36] Hauptman, P. J., and O'Connor, K. J., *Procurement and Allocation of Solid Organs for Transplantation*, 336 N. Engl. J. Med. 422 (Feb. 6), 1997.

[37] Steinbrook, R., *Allocating Livers: Devising a Fair System*, 336 N. Engl. J. Med. 436 (Feb. 6), 1997.

[38] Id.

LRD's are not at excess risk, provided that the donor's initial health status and renal function was normal. Accordingly, LRD's must undergo an extensive evaluation prior to donation, especially if the recipient's renal failure was caused by a disease with hereditary or familial tendencies.

Potential LRD's may also feel substantial emotional turmoil or coercion from the recipient or other family members. Accordingly, care is taken to keep all medical information, including tissue-typing data, confidential. Donors, themselves, decide with whom to share the information. Medical reasons are cited if the donor is unable to donate.

In the United States, prior to 1974, there had been reports of five surgical deaths of persons attempting to donate organs, and there had been one death of a would-be donor after evaluation but before surgery. Between 1974 and 1988, there was one only one death of a living donor. Since 1988, however, seven more deaths have been reported during surgery or the postoperative period, possibly because of relaxation of eligibility criteria.

Bay and Herbert[39] studied sixteen series of kidney transplants and estimate the major complication rate for living donors to be 1-8% (pulmonary embolus, severe infection with sepsis, renal failure, hepatitis, and myocardial infarction). Although there have been some isolated cases of renal failure in persons who have donated a kidney, no large series has demonstrated progressive deterioration of renal function, and insurance companies do not increase premium rates for kidney donors. In most of the studies, however, the mean follow-up has usually been less than fifteen years, and many examples of renal functional deterioration require two to three decades to develop.

It is not yet clear whether donating a kidney causes an increase in a person's blood pressure. Proteinuria does seem to develop in some donors, but it is usually mild and not associated with renal dysfunction. Najarian et al.,[40] whose subjects were followed for an average of twenty-three years after donation, believe that renal transplant donors are not at increased risk for the development of renal failure.

§ 30B.13. The Uniform Anatomical Gift Act.

The Uniform Anatomical Gift Act (UAGA), which has been passed by all states, has been the guiding principle for organ and tissue donations. The UAGA, which provides the legal basis for the "donor card," allows any individual to assume responsibility for the disposition of his or her remains following death.[41]

[39] Bay, W. H., and Herbert, L. A., *The Living Donor in Kidney Transplantation*, 106 Am. Intern. Med. 719, 1987.

[40] Najarian, J. S., et al., *Twenty Years or More of Follow-Up of Living Kidney Donors*, 340 Lancet 807 (Oct. 3), 1992.

[41] Editor's Note: The essential provision of the Uniform Act is that any person of sound

In certain instances of sudden death, surgical teams in appropriate institutions can move quickly to retrieve the organs or tissues under authority of the card. Formerly, postmortem wishes were placed in "living wills," and by the time the donor's desires were uncovered, the organs or tissues were no longer viable.

§ 30B.14. Determination of death.

The transplantation industry constantly faces the dilemma of acquiring viable organs from dead, presumably deteriorating, bodies. One option for alleviating this problem is to modify the definition and criteria for diagnosing a body as dead.

Until the advent of effective medical resuscitation, life and death were uncomplicated concepts. Life was the capacity to obtain matter and energy from one's environment to maintain the body, grow, and propagate. Death was the loss of that capacity. A living person was warm to the touch, active, conscious, and healed wounds while a dead person was cold, inactive, unresponsive, and exhibited body-wide decay and disintegration. Long known was the fact that the absence of sustained blood flow through tissues brought on the hypoxic and then anoxic cellular damage that initiated the body's disintegration. Thus, the final common pathway to the state of being lifeless (and no longer needing one's own organs) was the halt to the circulation of the blood.

Cardiac death

Because the heart is the pump propelling the blood, cessation of effective heart action clearly produces a halt to that circulation which, under the traditional view, defined the state of nonlife. Death could, therefore, be easily determined by the absence of objective, measurable, heart-based criteria: blood pressure, pulse, and normal EKG waveforms.

Cardiac deaths are of two kinds — immediate and delayed. The immediate deaths are the trauma cases and unexpected collapses in which there were no appreciable impairments to health prior to the event. Clearly, the chances of acquiring a healthy organ are the greatest here. A delayed death occurs in that unfortunate patient who lingers over days and weeks, who dies inch by inch as systems and organs malfunction in a lethal decrescendo. Rarely can an undamaged, salvageable organ be found.[42]

---

mind and eighteen years of age (21 in some states) may donate all or part of his or her body for medical purposes, the gift to take effect after death. The Act provides that the wishes of the individual are paramount to those of the next of kin. If the individual has made no directions, next of kin may do-

nate according to a specified order of priority, beginning with the surviving spouse and including an adult son or daughter, either parent, an adult brother or sister, or a guardian of the decedent at the time of death.

[42]Taylor, R. M., *Reexamining the Defini-*

Brain (cerebral) death

The development of medical life support — ventilators, pacemakers, renal dialysis, tube feedings, intravenous nutrition, counterpulsation balloons, cardiopulmonary bypass, osmotic diuretics, arterial pressors, air mattresses, Stryker frames, and rotating beds — has created a new species of patient: warm, inactive, barely or nonresponsive, yet able to heal wounds. Previously these patients would have died outright, but now they survived indefinitely in a state of suspended animation. For the first time, the issue of quality of life was raised by many people who considered these patients "as good as dead," although their hearts functioned normally. The lightning rod in this debate was the case of Karen Ann Quinlan. However, the greatest impetus for redefining the criteria for declaring someone dead was the rise of the transplantation industry.

Medicine's official recommendation for the adoption of brain-death criteria came in a 1968 "Special Communication" from a Harvard study group to the *Journal of the American Medical Association.* Subsequently, every state of the Union endorsed this definition of death.[43]

The "whole-brain" criterion of death requires the irreversible cessation of hemispheric and brainstem neuronal functions. Physicians have devised both bedside and laboratory tests to show that this criterion has been satisfied. All require unresponsive coma, apnea, and the absence of brainstem (pupillary, corneal, vestibulo-ocular, gag, and cough) reflexes.[44]

With most cases of brain death, all measurable intracranial neuronal functions cease. In some cases, however, a critical number of neurons have been destroyed while a few continue to function in isolation. For example, some unequivocally whole-brain-dead patients continue to manifest rudimentary but recordable EEG activity or hypothalamic neuroendocrine activity sufficient to prevent diabetes insipidus.[45] Because these isolated nests of independently operating neurons no longer contribute critically to the functions of the organism as a whole, their continued activity remains consistent with the whole-brain criterion of death.

A number of philosophers and physicians have advocated replacing the whole-brain criterion of death with the "higher-brain" criterion of death. Under this theory, death represents "the irreversible loss of that which is significant to the nature of man." This group holds that irreversible loss of consciousness and cognition is necessary and sufficient for death. According to this formulation, the continued functioning of the brainstem

tion and Criteria of Death, 17 Semin. Neurol. 265, 1997.

[43] Id.

[44] Guidelines for the Determination of Death. Report of the Medical Consultants on the Diagnosis of Death to the President's Commission for the Study of Ethical Problems in Medicine and Biomedical and Behavioral Research, 32 Neurology 395, 1982.

[45] Bernat, J. L., How Much of The Brain Must Die in Brain Death? J. Clin. Ethics (in press).

is consistent with death; all that is required is cessation of functioning of the cerebral hemispheres.[46] Using this criterion, patients in persistent vegetative states, others with advanced forms of dementia, and anencephalic infants would be classified as dead.

Neurologist James L. Bernat, M.D., of Dartmouth Medical School, who has written extensively on determination of death,[47] finds the higher-brain formulation unsatisfactory as a concept of death because: (1) it classifies patients as dead who are considered alive in every society; (2) it is arbitrary to stipulate the degree of brain damage necessary for death because states of bilateral hemispheric neuronal damage form a continuum from mild to profound; (3) there is no reliable test for the higher-brain criterion (assessing prognosis with a high degree of certainty requires weeks or months of observation for patients in vegetative states,[48] and it is counterintuitive to argue that physicians must observe patients for that duration to determine whether or not they are dead); and (4) practical problems arise concerning burial practices (should the "dead" patient be buried while still exhibiting breathing, heartbeat, and gag and cough reflexes?).[49]

According to Bernat, the higher-brain formulation was devised to solve the problem of the patient in a persistent vegetative state. But he maintains that this is no longer a problem — that while many people do consider patients in states of permanent unawareness "as good as dead," and that most people would not want to continue living in a hopeless and meaningless state, acceptable medical practices exist today that permit termination of treatment that allows such patients to die,[50] and it is unnecessary to contrive that they are already dead. Bernat states that unjustifiably redefining live patients as dead destroys the serviceable concept of whole-brain death, which accurately portrays biological reality and has achieved a high level of acceptance by Western society.

A challenge to the whole-brain definition of death asserts that death is a biological event and not a utilitarian social construct. Neurologist Robert Taylor of Ohio State University agrees with Bernat that death is "the event that separates the process of dying from the process of disintegra-

---

[46] Zaner, R. M., editor, *Death Beyond Whole-Brain Criteria*, Kluwer Academic Publishers, Dordrecht, the Netherlands, 1988.

[47] Bernat, J. L., *The Definition, Criterion, and Statute of Death*, 4 Semin. Neurol. 45, 1984; Bernat, J. L., "Ethical Issues in Neurology," in Joynt, R.J., editor, *Clinical Neurology*, Philadelphia, J. B. Lippincott, 1991; Bernat, J. L., *How Much of The Brain Must Die in Brain Death?* J. Clin. Ethics (in press).

[48] Shewmon, D. A., and De Giorgio, C. M.,

Early Prognosis in Anoxic Coma: Reliability and Rationale, 7 Neurol. Clin. 823, 1989.

[49] Bernat, J. L., *Brain Death Occurs Only with Destruction of the Cerebral Hemispheres and the Brain Stem*, 49 Arch. Neurol. 569, 1992.

[50] Id. American Academy of Neurology, *Position of the American Academy of Neurology on certain aspects of the care and management of the persistent vegetative state patient*, 39 Neurology 125, 1989.

tion," but argues that the whole-brain concept "creates a legal convention that labels certain living (but permanently comatose) persons as dead and thereby legitimizes killing them by recovering their organs for transplantation into others." Taylor notes that, in fact, "most patients with severe, irreversible brain damage, notably those in the persistent vegetative state, do not meet the whole-brain criterion of death." Yet, he contends, "[T]he strongest argument for attempting to preserve the concept of brain death is the utilitarian argument that it is necessary for the continuation of our current program of organ transplantation." He blames logic and procedural flaws in the original Harvard paper for laying the foundation for the present situation and believes the only universally valid criterion for human death is the irreversible cessation of blood circulation.[51]

Taylor also argues that another social construct — legal blindness — is not as supportive an analogy as proponents like to think. Specifically:

1. Designating someone as "legally blind" accords that person the unique protection and social benefits of one who is biologically fully without sight.
2. Such designation usually results from the person's *voluntary* request.
3. Such designation creates obligations for society toward that person. Thus, altogether such designation is a positive act.
4. In contrast, no person *ever* requests being labeled "dead." Such a designation is completely involuntary.
5. The designation "dead" does not confer any privileges, benefits, or protection to that individual. "Rather, it eliminates most of them."
6. The designation "dead" creates little societal obligation and is anything but positive.

Taylor discusses three alternatives to the whole-brain definition in the absence of animal donors. (1) Follow the precedent in New Jersey and incorporate statutory religious objections on the grounds of wishing not to offend certain segments of society. Essentially this would be an "opting-out" provision. (2) Revert to the blood circulation criterion at the cost of an immediate worsening of the organ shortage. (3) Amend the dead-donor rule to permit harvesting from patients having no cerebral function whatsoever (with particular reference to anencephalic infants).

What does Taylor see as the ultimate solution? "The resolution of this debate cannot depend on which criteria are consistent with traditional concepts, since we have acknowledged that none of them is. Instead, the

---

[51] Taylor, R. M., *Reexamining the Definition and Criteria of Death*, 17 Semin. Neurol. 265, 1997.

resolution will depend on which criteria are most acceptable politically to a majority of people."[52]

Legally defined death

Approximately two-thirds of the states have either judicially or legislatively recognized brain death as death of the person, and it has been predicted that as additional courts are asked to decide the question, none will reject the precept.[53]

In August 1980, the National Conference of Commissioners on Uniform State Laws approved the Uniform Determination of Death Act. This Act states:

> An individual who has sustained either (1) irreversible cessation of circulatory and respiratory functions, or (2) irreversible cessation of all functions of the entire brain, including the brain stem, is dead. A determination of death must be made in accordance with accepted medical standards.[54]

The Uniform Determination of Death Act superseded the Uniform Brain Death Act, approved by the Commissioners in 1978, which did not include part (1) of the 1980 Act.

Over twenty-five states have adopted one or the other acts, or similar language patterned after statutory definitions suggested by the American Bar Association or the American Medical Association. The reader should consult the statutes of his or her state.

Basically, the criteria for brain death are as follows:

A. Clinical
  1. Unresponsive to painful stimuli;
  2. Absent cephalic reflexes, including fixed pupils nonreactive to light;
  3. No spontaneous respirations.
B. Confirmatory
  1. Electroencephalogram (EEG) should be "flat."[55]
  2. Absent blood flow by radionuclide study or arteriogram;
  3. Intracranial pressure in excess of mean arterial pressure.

It is important that these criteria be assessed at a time when the patient is not cold (hypothermic) or under the influence of sedatives such as barbiturates. These criteria must be present during two periods of observation at least six hours apart. When death has been declared,

[52] Id.

[53] In re Haymer (1983) 115 Ill. App. 3d 349, 71 Ill. Dec. 252, 450 N.E.2d 940.

[54] Uniform Determination of Death Act (U.L.A.) § 1.

[55] Editor's Note: For a discussion of electroencephalographic (EEG) evidence in the determination of death, see Chapter 22, § 22.13a, of this Cyclopedia.

assuming permission for donation has been obtained, organ recovery takes place before cardiorespiratory support is withdrawn.

§ 30B.15. Consent to donation.

Consent for organ donation can be obtained by anyone. In many institutions, the prospective donor's primary physician makes the family aware of impending death, and introduces the concept of donation. A member of the organ recovery team discusses the benefits and requirements of donation, and obtains consent. When the primary physician tries to obtain permission for donation, the family may question whether the physician is basically interested in maintaining the patient's life or in obtaining an organ for transplantation.

Required request (routine inquiry) legislation has been passed by nearly all states and by the federal government. This legislation requires that whenever deaths occur in a hospital the next of kin must be offered the opportunity to donate the deceased's organs or tissue. Furthermore, hospitals must have a relationship with the regional organ procurement organization (OPO) certified by the National Organ Procurement and Transplantation Network (OPTN). The laws do not specify who makes the request, but assigns the responsibility to the hospital administrator who is expected to establish a protocol and maintain suitable records. These laws arose in response to the public's overwhelming interest in donating organs and tissue. Over 80% would support donation, but organs are recovered from fewer than 20% of suitable donors. The presumption is that families are not being asked, despite the widely recognized organ shortage.

§ 30B.16. Informed consent.

Informed consent is probably the most important requisite of a valid donation of an organ or tissue by a living donor. A physician undertaking a transplantation procedure should obtain written consent of the donor, which should include a stipulation that the physician has explained, and the donor has understood, the nature and purpose of the operation, the risks involved, and the possible consequences and complications. The consent form should also include the donor's authorization to the physician to administer the necessary anesthesia for the procedure. The donor's signature should be witnessed.[56]

In the case of a proposed transplantation of organs or tissue from a deceased donor, it should be determined that a valid gift has been properly executed within the meaning of the applicable version of the Uni-

---

[56]Annotation, "Tort Liability of Physician or Hospital in Connection with Organ or Tissue Transplant Procedures," 76 A.L.R.3d 890.

form Anatomical Gift Act, preferably on forms designed for this purpose.[57]

§ 30B.17.   Organ and tissue preservation.

Organ preservation begins long before the organ leaves the donor's body. This stage in the process is called the "donor management" period.

Donor management

Once the brain is necrotic, no central sympathetic nervous system stimulation or control is possible. Consequently, within several hours, peripheral catecholamine levels drop by 90%. The result is marked vasodilation, peripheral pooling of blood, and severe cardiovascular instability. Through the loss of antidiuretic hormone, 75% of brain-dead patients can no longer conserve water in the kidneys. And 86% cannot regulate body temperature. In the face of such physiologic instability, it is not surprising that, in the absence of aggressive support, 20% sustain cardiac arrest within six hours of brain death. That figure rises to 50% at twenty-four hours. Lung dysfunction and consumptive coagulopathies frequently develop. All of these derangements contribute to what is known as "preservation injury."[58]

An aggressive coordinated effort is required to keep the target organ(s) viable and functional until the surgical team can remove them. Large volumes of warm intravenous fluids are needed to offset the poikilothermic hypothermia and the serious volume depletion that results from both the loss of brain control and the fluid restrictions so commonly employed in the management of brain-damaged patients. The threat of volume overload is very real because the body no longer makes its own instantaneous adjustments. Therefore, intensive monitoring with central venous pressure (CVP) lines, arterial lines, and sometimes central line pulmonary catheters are required. The absence of brain interaction often produces arrhythmias that do not reflect pathology in the heart itself but which require cardiac drug support to maintain adequate cardiac output without which there can be no effective tissue perfusion. Notably, bradycardia will not respond to atropine. Excessive use of positive end-expiratory pressure (PEEP) should be avoided. Steroid support and ADH (vasopressin) administration may be needed. Transfusions as needed should be given to produce a hematocrit of 25% to 30%. Ideal goals are a systolic blood pressure above 100 mm Hg, arterial oxygen greater than 100 mm Hg, and an hourly urine output greater than 100

---

[57] Id.

[58] Kauffman, H. M., et al., *The Expanded Donor*, 11 Transplant. Rev. 165 (Oct.), 1997; Hauptman, P. J., and O'Connor, K. J., *Procurement and Allocation of Solid Organs for Transplantation*, 336 N. Engl. J. Med. 422 (Feb. 6), 1997; Rao, V. K., *Posttransplant Medical Complications*, 78 Surg. Clin. N. Am. 113 (Feb.), 1998.

cc. Heart lung donors, however, should be controlled using no more than 40% inspired oxygen, tidal volumes of 10-to-15 ml/Kg, peak inspiratory pressures less than 30 cm of water, and PEEP less than 10 cm of water. In short, the CPR of donor management is more complicated and more difficult than one on a living body.[59]

Organ preservation

Cadaver organs are either deeply refrigerated — placed in static cold storage (SCS) — or maintained on active artificial life support, which is called continous pulsatile perfusion (CPP). Compared to the latter, SCS is technically much less complicated and less expensive.

The first concept for SCS was simply sealing the organ inside a sterile plastic specimen bag and then placing it in an ice chest. However, because one could not achieve a uniformly low temperature throughout the organ, zones of freezing and necrosis developed. The second concept added manual flushing of the organ's blood vessels with chilled intravenous fluids such as Ringers lactate. The flushing achieved uniform cooling, but too often cellular swelling and potassium leakage left the organ nonfunctional once implanted. The third concept involved the use of a flushing solution that imitated the chemical milieu inside the cell. The first successful formulation was the highly concentrated, high-potassium Collin's solution that routinely allowed kidney preservation to exceed twenty-four hours. Persistent problems with an unacceptably slow return of function in some recipients led to the adoption of a solution developed at the University of Wisconsin (U/W) that added ingredients to counter the swelling that accompanied hypothermia. Now, the standard for organs other than kidneys, the U/W solution[60] currently allows maximum preservation times of kidney, seventy-two hours; pancreas, seventy-two hours; liver, forty-eight hours; and heart, twelve hours.[61]

Continous pulsatile perfusion imitates the pulsatile blood flow in the body. The original perfusate used processed human plasma, which was later replaced by a synthetic hydroxymethyl starch product and then by a modified U/W solution. While the superiority of the U/W solution is well known for nonkidney organs, no one has yet demonstrated such clear superiority between cold storage and pulsatile perfusion. A major reason is each study uses different criteria, parameters, and variables, all of which makes meaningful comparisons impossible. However, one

[59] Kauffman, H. M., et al., *The Expanded Donor*, 11 Transplant. Rev. 165 (Oct.), 1997; Rao, V. K., *Postransplant Medical Complications*, 78 Surg. Clin. N. Am. 113 (Feb.), 1998.

[60] Potassium, potassium lactobionate, potassium hypophosphate, sodium, raffinose, hydroxyethyl starch, glutathione, adeno-sine, allopurinol, magnesium sulfate, penicillin, insulin, and dexamethasone.

[61] Kauffman, H. M., et al., *The Expanded Donor*, 11 Transplant. Rev. 165 (Oct.), 1997; Rao, V. K., *Postransplant Medical Complications*, 78 Surg. Clin. N. Am. 113 (Feb.), 1998.

study of note reviewed the United Network for Organ Sharing (UNOS) data on 19,804 kidneys and found that, while delayed function occurred more frequently with static cold storage kidneys, graft survival in the two groups was essentially identical. The question remains whether the lower rate of delayed function will offset CPP's higher cost. However, CPP's proven effectiveness in nonheart-beating donor (NHBD) kidneys strongly supports the idea of extending its application to all expanded donor organs. In fact, CPP may well obviate oxygen-free-radical-based reperfusion injury altogether.[62]

Generally, the maximal acceptable preservation times in many centers are kidney, thirty-six hours; pancreas eight to ten hours; liver, eight to ten hours; and heart/lung, four hours.[63] UNOS data on 23,104 kidneys indicates the two-year survival of kidneys placed within twenty-four hours surpassed that of those preserved longer than twenty-four hours. In addition, the odds of graft failure climb 6% to 8% for every additional ten hours of preservation. Livers supported for more than twenty hours have a higher failure rate than those implanted after shorter intervals. Reports for lungs should be interpreted with caution because of procedural limitations in those studies. The same problem plagues studies on hearts, which indicate that 300 minutes is the critical breakpoint. Registry data from the International Society for Heart and Lung Transplantation suggested that cold ischemia time greater than three hours increased the odds of mortality up to two years following surgery. The same was true for even longer cold ischemic periods.

Finally, UNOS has standardized the packaging, labeling, and shipping of all transplant organs, and transplant coordinators should be familiar with those requirements.[64]

Tissue preservation

The management of donated tissues is the same and yet different from the management of organs. Interestingly, unlike organ procurement in which sterility and aseptic techniques are always paramount, tissue procurement sometimes unavoidably involves contaminated material, which then must be sterilized.

Tissue banks may or may not be affiliated with organ procurement organizations. The oldest and best known are blood banks and service-organization-sponsored eye banks. Other tissues presently handled are bone, tendons, ligaments, fascia lata (quadriceps muscle fascia), cartilage, nerves, partial and whole joints, ear ossicles, skin, blood vessels,

---

[62] Id.

[63] Hauptman, P. J., and O'Connor, K. J., *Procurement and Allocation of Solid Organs for Transplantation*, 336 N. Engl. J. Med. 422 (Feb. 6), 1997.

[64] Kauffman, H. M., et al., *The Expanded Donor*, 11 Transplant. Rev. 165 (Oct.), 1997; Rao, V. K., *Posttransplant Medical Complications*, 78 Surg. Clin. N. Am. 113 (Feb.), 1998.

heart valves, pericardium, and dura mater. Animal tissue banks, such as those for pig skin and pig hearts, will not be discussed here.

Tissues must be excised no later than twenty-four hours after postmortem from refrigerated donors and twelve hours after death if not refrigerated. Preserving the cosmetic quality of the reconstructed portion of the body is of utmost importance pending funeral arrangements. Unlike organs that sometimes go straight into the recipient, most tissues must be processed, preserved, and then stored. Each tissue is immediately sampled for bacterial culture before being submitted for cutting, cleaning, sizing, and identification. Each specimen receives antibiotic treatment before being wrapped in saline gauze or similar material to begin the cooling process. Nonsterile specimens can be sterilized by gamma irradiation and ethylene oxide fumigation. However, such procedures are not infallible, and blind reliance on any sterilization method should be avoided. Thus, tests for sterility and chemical residues are highly recommended.

Storage options include simple hypothermia, deep freezing at temperatures below minus-sixty degrees Centigrade, controlled-rate freezing at one degree/minute, or preservation. Frozen tissue is stored at minus sixty to minus 196 degrees Centigrade. If viable cells are desired, the specimen undergoes controlled-rate freezing followed by storage in liquid nitrogen vapor. Freeze-dried tissue can be stored at room temperature.

Like organ donors, tissue donors are rigorously screened for a variety of illnesses, starting with aerobic and anaerobic blood cultures. If the specimen is coming from an organ donor, that protocol's workup will suffice. Otherwise, serologies for the major viruses — such as HCV, HBV, and HIV — and syphilis are determined. Blood typing is performed, and sometimes general chemical and toxicology screens are run. As with organ donors, autopsies should be performed on tissue donors except young trauma victims.

The following conditions are contraindications for tissue donation:

1. Clinical septicemia at death
2. Systemic fungal infections
3. Meningitis
4. Systemic viral disease
5. Active tuberculosis
6. Encephalitis
7. Syphilis
8. Bacterial infections (e.g. pyelonephritis, osteomyelitis)
9. Collagen diseases (e.g. rheumatoid arthritis, lupus, sarcoid, Grave's disease)
10. Intense toxic exposure
11. Prolonged steroid use
12. IV drug abuse

13. Long-standing insulin-dependent diabetes
14. Use of pituitary growth hormone
15. Degenerative neurologic disease
16. Metabolic bone disease
17. Anyone at high risk for AIDS
18. Acute rheumatic fever
19. Multiple open wounds or penetrating/blunt trauma to the abdomen
20. Any cancer except histologically proven *cured* basal cell of the skin and primary tumors confined to the central nervous system.[65]

§ 30B.18. · Complications in transplant surgery.

On the one hand, transplantation is an operation like any other, subject to traditional risks and hazards, while on the other hand, it can without warning present unusual complications. Perhaps the most important advance in reducing the incidence of such problems is simply having the recipient in optimal condition prior to receiving the new organ. Clearly, placing the transplant in a patient at death's door stands little chance of success and amounts to little more than a heroic gesture. For example, renal patients poisoned by full-blown uremia do far worse than patients who are routinely dialyzed to homeostatic levels and primed nutritionally. Granted, not all such objectives can be met in all patients, but the effort should be there. Organ rejection will not be considered in this section because it is an omnipresent phenomenon that is the crux of the entire process. (See §§ 30B.5, 30B.6.)

(A) DONORS

Because most donations come from deceased donors, these individuals are long past the time for concern on their behalf. However, too often living donors are essentially taken for granted because, after all, they are supposed to be perfectly healthy. Through assiduous care by the surgical team, the great majority of live donors recover uneventfully. However, significant numbers do encounter problems as indicated in a series of 871 live kidney donors over a ten-year period at the University of Minnesota.[66] Reflecting the expertise of that institution, there were no deaths or deep wound infections, and only two donors experienced "major" complications: one case of femoral nerve compression and one case of a retained surgical sponge. There were eighty six "minor" compli-

---

[65] Anderson, B. G., and Malinin, T. I., "Tissue Procurement for Transplantation," in *Organ Procurement, Preservation, and Distribution in Transplantation*, United Network for Organ Sharing, Richmond, Va., 1996.

[66] Johnson, E. M., et al., *Complications and Risks of Living Donor Nephrectomy*, 64 Transplantation 1124 (Oct. 27), 1997.

cations: two cases of suspected wound infection, thirteen pneumo-thoraces (collapsed lung), eleven unexplained fevers (requiring extra ob-servation and workup), eight cases with operative blood loss greater than 750 cc, eight cases of pneumonia, five wound hematomas/ seromas, four instances of phlebitis at the IV site, three episodes of atelectasis (lung congestion), two corneal abrasions, and one case each of epididymi-tis, accidental cut into the bowel, urethral injury during Foley catheter-ization, and colonic superinfection by *Clostridia difficile*.

(B) RECIPIENTS

Infections [67]

Infection has always been the potential bane of any operation. Whether direct contamination of the wound, colonization of the bladder, or proliferation in the congested mucus in airways, infection has some-times been inevitable, while at other times has signaled inadequate care. Transplant recipients face the same threat from the same organisms as do conventional surgical patients, but to a greater extent because of their suppressed immune system. Just as in diabetic or malnourished pa-tients, it is easier for an infection to start and more difficult to eradicate because the body's white cells are relatively ineffective. The answers to the dilemma lie with meticulous surgical technique and unremitting vigilance for the first hint of trouble. Such attention to detail will not always succeed in avoiding infections, but without such effort, the inci-dence would soar.

Any immunosuppressed patient — be it the result of a transplantation surgery, diabetes, malnutrition, cancer, or AIDS — also faces attack from opportunistic organisms, lazy bugs that find it too much work to assault a normal patient, but who seize the opportunity to wreak havoc in people whose guard is down. Much of transplantation research and management has centered on combating these exotic bacteria, viruses, fungi, and parasites. Many of these organisms can afflict any transplant recipient while others seem organ-specific due in large part to the evolu-tion for differing transplant management protocols for each organ. For example, toxoplasmosis seems to be a greater threat to heart transplant recipients than to other organ recipients. All tolled, a recipient's risk derives from actual exposure to the infectious agent and the net state of his or her preoperative immunosuppression.

Also important, if possible, is having the recipient free of infection at the time of operation. A report from the University of North Carolina concerning patients with advanced liver disease illustrates this point. To

---

[67] The primary source of this subsection is Rao, V. K., *Postransplant Medical Compli-cations*, 78 Surg. Clin. N. Am. 113 (Feb.), 1998. Additional sources are cited indepen-dently.

palliate a person's portal hypertension (high pressure in the veins bringing blood from the gut and spleen to the liver), a special jugular vein IV line is used to create a connection between branches of the portal vein and branches of the hepatic vein inside the liver itself. In technically difficult cases, clotting of the shunt may occur after the procedure and secondary infection with *Enterococcus* may develop. Antibiotic prophylaxis against this bacterium is recommend in these difficult cases because of the infection's high mortality and because liver transplantation should not be considered until the infection is cleared.[68]

Perhaps the most information in this area has come from kidney transplant patients. The first month after operation is characterized by the same infections seen in any other immunocompromised host because drug suppression of organ rejection is at its height. One of the most dangerous bacteria encountered is *Listeria monocytogenes*, an opportunistic bug whose portal of entry is the gut after eating contaminated food. Fortunately, the antibiotics penicillin, ampicillin, gentamicin, and bactrim can still eradicate the organism if administered in time. Conversely, after six months, immunosuppression is greatly reduced in most cases if not suspended so that the recipient's risk is essentially no different from the average person.

Reported incidences of specific infections are urinary tract (almost 70%), tuberculosis (about 5%), *Listeria* (up to 6%), Coccidiomycosis (8%), cytomegalovirus (18% to 67%), herpes simplex virus (50%), and varicella-zoster virus (up to 10%). Interestingly, these three viruses and the Epstein-Barr virus are all herpesviruses.[69]

Aside from tissue typing, the whole purpose of screening donors is to eliminate the chance of transmitting a disease to the recipient who is already in a relatively weakened state. Blood typing, coagulation studies, viral serologies, and serum chemistries are checked, and cultures of blood and urine are run during a workup that is no different from that applied to the recipient. Unique but vitally important regarding the donor, however, are the mechanism of death and the duration of CPR and any periods of hypotension.

In general, adult recipients should receive the following vaccinations before starting their preoperative immunosuppression — pneumovax, tetanus and diphtheria, influenza, hepatitis B, and varicella. The preoperative infectious disease assessment should cover the following:

1. Serology — Hepatitis B and C, anti-HIV, rapid plasma reagin, cytomegalovirus, herpes simplex, Epstein-Barr, varicella-zoster, *Toxoplasma*, anti-human T-cell lymphotropic virus, and endemic fungi;

[68]Brown, R. S., Jr., et al., *Enterococcal Bacteremia After Transjugular Intrahepatic Portosystemic Shunts (TIPS)*, 93 Am. J. Gastroenterol. 636 (Apr.), 1998.

[69]Greenfield, L. J., editor, *Surgery*, J. P. Lippincott Co., Philadelphia, 1993, p. 497.

2. Urine analysis and culture;
3. Chest X-ray;
4. Stool sample for ova and parasites;
5. Tuberculin and other skin tests.

Cytomegalovirus (CMV) afflicts at least one-third of all kidney recipients and is the most important of all the pathogens encountered by those patients. Portal of entry is either with the organ itself or transfused blood. Three forms of infection are recognized:

1. Primary infection: infected cells from a positive donor enter a seronegative patient.
2. Reactivation: recipient's own latent virus is reactivated by the operation.
3. Superinfection: latent virus in the donor organ reactivated in a seropositive patient.

Sometimes, the infection causes no symptoms and is detected through serial viral cultures. Acute illness involves fever, lowered white count, lowered platelet count, pneumonia, hepatitis, and ulcers. An alternative form involves a progressive chorioretinitis resulting in blurred or impaired vision and spots before the eyes. Another problem with CMV infection is a worsening of the patient's immunosuppression with the attendant threat of major simultaneous infections by opportunistic bugs like *Pneumocystis carinii* (parasite), *Aspergillosis* (fungus), and *Listeria* (bacterium). The risk of CMV infection increases with primary infection, the use of antilymphocyte antibodies, and overly aggressive immunosuppression. In addition, there is evidence that drug regimens headed by cyclosporine are more vulnerable to symptomatic disease than those based around tacrolimus. Two intravenous drugs — ganciclovir and foscarnet — remain effective in treating systemic infection.

Epstein-Barr virus at its best produces a mononucleosis-style illness of fever, lowered white count, mild hepatitis, atypical lymphocytes, and a negative heterophile test. At its worst, the virus triggers a variable postoperative lymphoproliferative disease (analogous to leukemias), which may range from a relatively mild polyclonal problem to a severe, rapidly progressive and fatal malignancy. Symptoms and signs include tonsillitis, fever, weight loss, lung infiltrates, abnormal liver function tests, gut bleeding or perforation, brain infiltrates, and infection of the the transplanted organ. Medical therapy is not predictable, but a reduction in the level of immunosuppression usually produces a "drastic effect" on the viral lesions.

Herpes simplex virus is seldom seen in the presence of generalized use of acyclovir prophylaxis. Its appearances represent activation of latent virus in the recipient within the first month after transplantation. Mouth ulcers can be complicated by secondary bacterial infections. Several laboratory tests are helpful in confirming the diagnosis — a Tzanck smear, direct immunofluorescence, and cultures of bodily fluids and secretions. Besides acyclovir, ganciclovir and foscarnet provide effective treatment.

Varicella-zoster virus usually produces a reactivation-style, shingles-like, skin eruption that follows the nerve dermatome patterns. Rarely seen is the deadly alternative, a primary infection in a seronegative recipient that represents either acute chickenpox or a disseminated viral attack producing hemorrhagic pneumonia, encephalitis, pancreatitis, hepatitis, coagulation disorders, and death. The appearance of vesicles on one side of the body, a Tzanck smear showing mulitnucleated giant cells, and positive direct immunofluorescence confirm the diagnosis. Preoperative vaccination of seronegative recipients is recommended. Acyclovir, valacyclovir, and famciclovir are the mainstays of therapy. Postexposure immune globulin, as for hepatitis, can be effective in preventing serious illness.

Hepatitis viruses B and C leave up to 15% of transplant recipients with chronic liver disease. The viruses are contracted through intimate mucosal contact, placing an infected organ, or contaminated blood products. Both viruses produce active hepatitis, cirrhosis, and primary liver cancer, and worsen the recipient's state of immunosuppression. The B virus carries a greater propensity for fulminant disease, liver failure, and death. Fortunately, the more benevolent C virus accounts for the majority of cases. Hepatitis C virus rarely produces an acute illness and the chronic version of the illness "proceeds at a slow pace."

HIV. While some recipients will follow the course of many HIV patients and show minimal effect for years, others will quickly develop full-blown AIDS shortly after the operation and die. Unanswered is the question whether HIV-positive patients should be recipients in the first place.

Papovavirus is particularly important in women recipients because of its association with increased occurrence of dysplastic, premalignant, and invasive malignant lesions of the cervix. The virus may also cause urethral papillomatosis.

Kidney recipients

Up to 15% of kidney transplant recipients develop a collection of lymphatic fluid called a lymphocele inside the abdomen, usually the pelvis. The phenomenon can occur in any operation involving extensive dissection around the major vessels coursing through the abdomen and pelvis. Because the extent and course of lymphatic vessels is highly variable, the problem is not a universal one, and only symptomatic lymphoceles require treatment.

Up to 7% of kidney patients will experience some mechanical problem such as a blockage to urine flow or a leak of urine from the ureter into the pelvis (a "urinoma"). Infection with its attendant swelling of surrounding tissues, hematoma, and lymphocele may all cause a direct compression of the new ureter. Leaving a twist or kink in the ureter at operation will seriously impede the flow of urine into the bladder. A stricture formed by scar tissue resulting from the healing of a segment of ureter deprived of sufficient blood supply and oxygen (ischemia) will feel as though someone had tied a thread around the ureter.

In fact, ischemia is the final common pathway leading to most of these complications. There can be many incipient causes, ranging from vascular problems within the organ itself to technical error by the surgeon. Urine leaks occur either at the anastomosis of the new ureter with the bladder or further upstream in the ureter itself. The latter are almost always due to vascular compromise (ischemia) in which the junctional problems are partially due to technical mistakes. Urine leaks usually appear early in the postoperative period. The constellation of reduced urine output, dysproportionate pain, abdominal swelling, and wound drainage "should prompt further investigation." As with obstructions, percutaneous pyelograms (direct into-the-kidney injections of contrast, producing a downstream IVP) will often demonstrate the site of the problem. The placement of stents into the ureter may or may not alleviate the problem.

Problems with the new kidney's artery and vein may also occur. A clotting off of the artery (thrombosis) almost always is the result of a technical error in the anastomosis or from leaving a twist or kink in the artery. The presence of multiple arteries (rather than the single one shown in the anatomy atlases) and preexisting athercosclerosis also contribute to the problem. Not infrequently, the new organ fails and dies. Thrombosis of the kidney's vein acts like a tourniquet on the arm and produces congestion of the kidney. Typical signs are palpable swelling and tenderness of the organ plus reduced urine output, but increased protein in the urine and creatinine in the serum. External compression of the vein by a mass such as a hematoma or lymphocele will have the same effect. Finally, despite good technique, sometimes late strictures of the arterial anastomosis develop. Because dense scar tissue encases the vessels, surgical repair is fraught with hazards and is generally undertaken as a last resort. Rather, the 60% to 85% success rate with angioplasty makes the indirect approach the first choice. The downside, though, is a 30% re-stenosis rate.

Remarkably, despite immunosuppression, less than five% of the renal transplant patients develop a wound infection. As mentioned earlier, optimizing the recipient's physical condition makes this low figure possible. Particularly important is to allow no or minimal anemia or uremia. Other important factors are intraoperative bladder irrigation with an antibiotic solution, the use of antibiotics before, during, and after the operation, meticulous surgical technique (which greatly reduces the chance of hematomas, seromas, etc.), and persistent awareness that prolonged wound healing is the norm.

Graft-versus-host disease

In this unique affliction, the transplanted organ attacks the recipient, creating lesions in the skin, intestine, and liver. Donor white cells come along for the ride with the transplanted organ and, if sensitized to recipient cell antigens, go on the attack. The problem is especially seen in some cases of bone marrow transplantation where the recipient's own white cells have been deliberately wiped out.

Various late complications

In a series from Hennepin County Hospital in Minneapolis, a fourth to half of the kidney recipients studied experienced late problems with infection, hypertension, cataracts, high serum lipids, musculoskeletal ailments, blood vessel problems, chronic liver disease, and cancer. Only 12% remained trouble-free.

Cancer

The incidence of cancer developing in patients who undergo organ or tissue transplantation ranges from 4% to 18%, with most tumors developing two to ten years after the advent of immunosuppression. Solid tumors with increased incidence in allograft recipients include squamous cell carcinomas of the skin, hepatoma, sarcoma, and carcinoma of the uterine cervix, vulva, and kidney. All of these malignancies are thought to arise from recipient tissue.[70]

Inadvertent transmission of malignant cells from donor to recipient has also been reported. Most of the tumors were carried in the kidneys.[71] In a tragic case, first reported in 1993, DNA tests revealed that at least twelve transplant recipients developed metastatic melanoma after receiving cadaveric allograft organs or tissues from a forty-two-year-old woman with unrecognized melanoma at the time the organs were harvested.[72] Four of the recipients died. Although the donor's husband could not recall any cancer in his wife's history, a careful review of her medical

---

[70] Loh, E., et al., *Development of Donor-Derived Prostate Cancer in a Recipient Following Orthotopic Heart Transplantation*, 277 J.A.M.A. 133 (Jan. 8), 1997. See also Penn, I., *The Problem of Cancer in Organ Transplant Recipients: An Overview*, 4 Transplant. Sci. 23, 1994.

[71] Id.; Gazdar, A. F., *Tumors Arising After Organ Transplantation: Sorting Out Their Origins*, 277 J.A.M.A. 154 (Jan. 8), 1997.

[72] Danovitch, G., "Transplantation in 1993: The Year in Review," in *Clinical Transplant 1993* (P. I. Teraski and J. M. Cecka, editors), University of California, Los Angeles, Los Angeles, 1994, p. 619.

records disclosed a surgical excision of a suspected skin cancer. Also, the cause of death listed on the donor's death certificate was cerebral hemorrhage, which is known to be consistent with metastatic melanoma. Further investigation revealed that the transplant coordinator was inexperienced and did not appreciate the significance of this information.[73]

Drug side effects

Immunosuppressive drugs have also been found to be associated with osteoporosis in transplant patients. The responsible drugs are the calcineurin phosphatase inhibitors, cyclosporine, tacrolimus, and the glucocorticoids. The incidence of the disease depends, in part, on which organ is transplanted. Kidney transplant patients seem to be less susceptible than do heart and liver recipients. The most critical period of bone loss appears to be within the first six months after transplantation. Cancellous bone of the spine seems to be the most at risk, with vertebral fractures being common.[74]

Team experience

The mortality rate at some transplantation centers is likely determined by the experience of key personnel. In a study reported in 1992, data was obtained from the registry of the International Society for Heart and Lung Transplantation and from other sources. The study included 1,123 patients who received a heart transplant at one of fifty-six hospitals in the United States during a two-year period ending in 1986. The authors found that patients who received one of a center's first five transplants had higher mortality rates than patients who received a subsequent transplant (20% versus 12%). Also, a correlation was found between the training of key personnel on the transplantation team and mortality at new transplantation centers. For example, new centers staffed by cardiologists with previous training in heart transplantation had lower mortality rates among heart-transplant recipients than centers without experienced cardiologists (7% versus 16%). By contrast, however, the previous training of the surgeons who performed the transplantations was not related to the mortality rate associated with the procedures.[75]

---

[73] Frickleton, J.C., *Transplanting Unsuspected Tumors: Reprieve Becomes a Death Sentence*, 2 Cancer Litig. 1 (May), 1996.

[74] Epstein, S., et al., *Organ Transplantation and Osteoporosis*, 7 Curr. Opin. Rheumatol. 255 (May), 1995.

[75] Laffel, G. L., et al., *The Relation Between Experience and Outcome in Heart Transplantation*, 327 N. Engl. J. Med. 1220, 1992.

§ 30B.19. Current status in transplant surgery.

Kidney

The United Network for Organ Sharing (UNOS) reported a ten-fold increase in the number of elderly kidney donors in the decade ending in 1995. Results have consistently shown that these older kidneys do not function all that well in young recipients. Therefore, matching the ages of donor and recipient seems to be the way to maximize the usefulness of these older organs. Not so well understood is the consistent finding that female kidneys do not function as well as male kidneys when placed into male recipients. The possibly chauvinistic explanation is that perhaps the female organs possess less renal mass than their male counterparts.

Because of the kidney's high antigenicity, accurate human leukocyte antigen (HLA) Class I tissue typing is critical for achieving optimal outcomes. Of concern, then, is the report that the standard microlymphocytotoxicity method can have as high as a 25% error rate, especially at the HLA-B locus. Researchers propose switching to rapid DNA-based methods such as polymerase chain reaction (PCR) with sequence-specific primers (SSP).

Acute rejection of cadaveric kidneys still occurs in 30% to 50% of transplants, depending on the immunosuppressive drug regimen being used. The drug micophenolate mofetil (MMF) appears to have particular value in preventing these episodes. Under investigation, beside monoclonal antibodies, are drugs with longer duration of action which, like antibiotics, would make possible a simpler, cheaper dosage schedule.

Laparoscopic nephrectomy has proven feasible in living donors but at this time falls into the Jurassic Park paradox — just because the laparoscopic procedure can be done, does that mean it should be done? Proponents cite the traditional advantages (for the donor) observed with many laparoscopic procedures: reduced blood loss, less postoperative pain, less time without food, a shorter length of hospital stay, and an earlier returned to work. However, there are two important concerns. First, the process of pneumoperitoneum (filling the abdominal cavity with carbon dioxide under pressure) has been shown to exert physiological effect on breathing and blood return to the heart. As yet unknown are the extent of similar effects on the kidney's hemodynamics, which should be maximal to provide the maximal chance for success. Second, the laparoscopic approach takes significantly longer than the open approach, which means a longer warm ischemic interval. The average time for the open operation is 183 minutes while the laparoscopic time is 227 minutes. Indeed, the question must be — after all the years and effort to shorten the warm ischemic time as much as possible, why now go out of our way to make it longer?[76]

---

[76]Kumar, M. S., et al., *Long-Term Function and Survival of Elderly Donor Kidneys* *Transplanted into Young Adults*, 65 Transplantation 282 (Jan. 27), 1998; Lorentzen,

Liver

As with kidneys, female livers have been found to fare worse in male recipients than do their male counterparts. Speculation attributes the difference to the older age of the female donors in the population studied.

Outcome studies have unexpectedly identified a subset of recipients who believe their quality of life worsened after the transplant. Researchers are trying to identify the reasons for such a paradoxical result, because such factors, if used prospectively, might influence future organ allocation.

For the time being, cluster allografts are confined strictly to the world of experimental surgery. In 1995, Dr. Starzl reported on his series of patients with extensive, otherwise traditionally unresectable gut cancers. The massive resection *en bloc* (in one piece) included the liver, pancreas, spleen, stomach, duodenum, and part of the colon. Originally, the patient received, in return, an *en bloc* transplant of liver, duodenum, and pancreas. Later patients received only a liver plus portal vein infusion of pancreatic islet cells. The greatest benefit was observed in patients with cancers of the endocrine glands and the least benefit in patients with cancers of the colon, pancreas, and gallbladder. The outcome was also very poor for primary liver cancer. However, importantly, the high morbidity and mortality rates must be viewed in the proper perspective, namely, that these were traditionally incurable patients in whom one-third were alive and functional five years after operation. In other words, their life expectancy had doubled or tripled compared to conventional therapy. Three obstacles currently preclude any general application of this approach. First, the precedent of massive, super-radical cancer operations was discarded for tumors of the breast, pelvis, head, and neck when the tumor's biology proved to be more determinant for the patient's outlook than how much tissue was removed. Second, primary liver tumors develop a four-fold increase in doubling time in immunosuppressed patients. And third, the competition for organs has generated "the logic that organs can be more efficiently invested to patients without carcinoma." Therefore, ready availability of animal organs (if achieved) may eventually provide the impetus to evaluate the cluster approach in greater detail.

One small step to alleviate the donor shortage has been to split the liver into its right and left lobes and give them separately to two recipients. Originally, the division was performed literally on a back table once the organ had been removed from the donor. The early experience of centers such as the University of Chicago was that, while the trans-

D. F., et al., *A 25% Error Rate in Serologic Typing of HLA-B Homozygotes*, 50 Tissue Antigens 359 (Oct.), 1997; Kauffman, H. M., et al., *The Expanded Donor*, 11 Transplant. Rev. 165 (Oct.), 1997; Rao, V. K., *Postransplant Medical Complications*, 78 Surg. Clin. N. Am. 113 (Feb.), 1998; Hanto, D. W., *Transplantation*, 186 J. Am. Coll. Surg. 232 (Feb.), 1998.

planted lobe functioned satisfactorily in the recipient, a variety of bile tract complications developed that were not seen in whole-liver transplants. Later on, there were also instances of shortened liver survival. A German study, however, has shown (sensibly) that the division can be accomplished while the liver is still in place in the donor and fully perfused. The survival and complication rates now seem comparable to those with whole liver transplants.

ABO blood grouping compatibility is still essential except in the most desperate of situations such as fulminant liver necrosis when the team has to grab whatever they can get their hands on. The absence of ABO compatibility between donor and recipient leads to an organ failure rate of 46% at thirty days after surgery. With ABO compatibility, the failure rate falls to 11%.

Data on the donor's length of hospital stay may have defined a new risk factor. Supposedly the incidence of postoperative graft nonfunction increases substantially if the donor has been in the hospital for more than three (some say four) days before the operation. The theory is that a non-feeding donor will quickly exhaust the liver's glycogen stores, leaving the liver depleted and much less able to withstand the stress of transplantation. A possible solution in such cases is infusing glucose solutions directly into the portal vein at operation on the assumption that the liver will just as quickly restore its glycogen supply.[77]

Heart

In most institutions, heart transplantation is considered an extension of routine cardiac surgery. This differs from other organ systems where surgeons specializing in transplantation provide the services. As with the liver, matching tissue types is impractical and does not appear to influence results. Rejection activity is monitored by frequent endomyocardial biopsies that guide the direction of immune therapy. With the advent of a variety of sometimes implantable assist/support devices, patients who formerly might have died can now be sustained while waiting for an appropriate donor.

Apoptosis, or "programmed cell death," was identified years ago, but only recently has it been recognized as a nearly omnipresent feature of many disease states as well as transplant rejection. Apoptotic cells have been found in transplanted hearts, kidneys, and livers. In hearts, factors known to induce apoptosis in mammalian cardiomyocytes are hyperten-

[77] Kauffman, H. M., et al., *The Expanded Donor*, 11 Transplant. Rev. 165 (Oct.), 1997; Goff, J. S., et al., *Measuring Outcome After Liver Transplantation: A Critical Review*, 4 Liver Transplant Surg. 189 (May), 1998; Alessiani, M., et al., *Assessment of Five-Year Experience with Abdominal Organ Cluster Transplantation*, 180 J. Am. Coll. Surg. 1 (Jan.), 1995; Barker, C. F., *"Cluster" Allografts*, 180 J. Am. Col. Surg. 88 (Jan.), 1995.

sive heart failure, infarction, rapid ventricular pacing, hypoxia, reperfusion injury, and mechanical stretch. Human conditions exhibiting apoptosis involve various cardiomyopathies. Furthermore, the degree of apoptosis has been strongly correlated with the presence and extent of cellular rejection. Also the speed of the process itself means that finding only a few apoptotic cells on biopsy may actually reflect a significant cumulative cell loss. There is also indication that apoptosis may play a role in transplantation tolerance.

An Australian study investigated how to maximize the viability of allograft valves. Logically, procuring the valve as soon as possible after asystole is important. In addition, valves from heart-beating donors (HBDs) were more viable than those from nonheart-beating donors (NHBDs). Valves destined not to be implanted for up to two days should be cryopreserved for that interval. Amphotericin B has a very adverse impact on the valves and should not be used. Paradoxically, storage at four degrees Centigrade after low-dose antibiotic sterilization lowered valve viability by almost 50%; amphotericin lowered it by more than 60%. Viability after a week of storage was down 98% from normal and after three weeks was zero.

Organ recipient compliance is perhaps more important than in any other patient group, and heart recipients are no exception. While overall results have been good, continued attention is needed to avoid complacency. Specifically, patients in a Chicago study assiduously took their medications on time, attended follow-up clinics as scheduled, and faithfully reported for and completed required tests. The authors found room for significant improvement in adhering to a prescribed diet, a prescribed exercise regimen, and maintaining a diary of their vital signs.[78]

A new entity known as the "domino transplant" is gaining favor and often involves the heart, liver, or kidney. Originating at Papworth Hospital in England in 1988, the double heart-lung procedure harvest's the recipient's heart as a donor graft for a second recipient. In other words, the heart-lung recipient becomes a living heart donor for another patient. The heart-lung graft is often a convenience that saves time compared to attaching two separate lungs to the recipient whose own heart is usually perfectly normal. The clear advantage goes to the second recipient who receives a heart that has been thoroughly studied prior to selection compared to the recipient/donor who is receiving cadaveric organs. The success with kidneys and livers has been comparable to one-stop recipients, but there have been two adverse results using hearts.

[78]Shaddy, R. E., *Apoptosis in Heart Transplantation*, 8 Coron. Artery Dis. 617, 1997; Kabelitz, D., *Apoptosis, Graft Rejection, and Transplantation Tolerance*, 65 Transplantation 869 (Apr. 15), 1998; Gall, K. L., et al., *Allograft Heart Valve Viability and Valve-Processing Variables*, 65 Ann. Thorac. Surg. 1032 (Apr.), 1998; Grady, K. L., et al., *Patient Compliance at One Year and Two Years After Heart Transplantation*, 17 J. Heart Lung Transplant. 383 (Apr.), 1998.

First, a review of UNOS data indicated that there was a significant decrease in graft survival for heart recipients of donors who had been previously transplanted. Second, the operative technique for excising the recipient/donor's heart makes a difference. Using the "right atrial cuff preservation" technique rather than the standard bicaval division method apparently damages the sinoatrial node, requiring the implantation of a permanent pacemaker. Excising a heart that is going to be discarded is one thing, but such an important detail is critical when that heart is going to be recycled into another patient.[79]

Lung

In 1990, Grossman et al.[80] reported an overall survival of 55% after single-lung transplantation, with one patient surviving for more than five years. A 1995 report of Center-Specific Graft and Patient Survival Rates, compiled by the United Network for Organ Sharing of Richmond, Virginia, showed an even more encouraging rate, 68.4%, for single-lung transplants after one year.[81] The one-year survival rate for heart-lung transplants remained about the same.[82]

As hoped and perhaps as expected, a successful lung transplant reverses the energy and physical mobility deficits endured by recipients prior to the operation. These improvements seem to persist for at least several years thereafter. Understandably, those unfortunate patients who develop obliterative bronchiolitis suffer a diminished quality of life. As in liver transplants, there is a push to explore quality of life parameters preoperatively as a means of forecasting and perhaps enhancing a recipient's *perception* about the quality of life after the operation. Could this endeavor evolve into assessing which patients should be selected for transplantation based upon the recipient's expectations, unreasonable or otherwise? Time may tell.[83]

Pancreas

Approximately 30% of juvenile onset insulin dependent (Type I) diabetics develop renal failure after 15-20 years of insulin therapy. In fact,

---

[79] Oaks, T. E., et al., *Domino Heart Transplantation: The Papworth Experience*, 13 J. Heart Lung Transplant. 433 (May/June), 1994; Lowell, J. A. et al., *Transplant Recipients as Organ Donors: the Domino Heart Transplant*, 29 Transplant. Proc. 3392, 1997; Rosado, L. J., et al., *Sinoatrial Node Dysfunction in Recipients of Domino Heart Transplants: Complication of a Surgical Technique*, 11 J. Heart Lung Transplant. 1078 (Nov./Dec.), 1992.

[80] Grossman, R. F., et al., *Results of Single-Lung Transplantation for Bilateral Pulmonary Fibrosis*, 322 N. Engl. J. Med. 727, 1990.

[81] *Organ Transplant Success Rate Continues High, HRSA Report Shows*, 110 Public Health Rep. 373 (May), 1995.

[82] Id.

[83] Gross, C. R., and Raghu, G., *The Cost of Lung Transplantation and the Quality of Life Post-Transplant*, 18 Clin. Chest Med. 391 (June), 1997.

about 30% of all patients developing renal failure are diabetic. These patients frequently have advanced retinopathy, disabling autonomic and peripheral neuropathies, and severe cardiovascular disease. Approximately 50% die within two years of developing renal failure.

Kidney transplantation is remarkably effective at reversing the uremic component of the diabetic's poor health, but it does nothing for the diabetic state. In recent years, the results of pancreas transplantation, which has been attempted for nearly twenty years with little success, have improved to the point where simultaneous kidney-pancreas transplantation is becoming standard therapy. Patients are already immunosuppressed for the kidney transplant, and recent technical advances have improved the operative success rate and provided a better method of monitoring for rejection activity. However, pancreas or islet cell (insulin-producing cells) transplantation to prevent secondary complications such as renal failure has not progressed as well. First, there is no method of reliably predicting which diabetic patients will develop complications. Secondly, islet cells seem very susceptible to the rejection process when transplanted separately from the whole pancreas. In contrast to heart, liver and kidney transplants, pancreas transplantation/islet cell replacement therapy is still evolving and is highly dependent on future research developments.

Combined pancreatic and renal transplantation (PRT) in diabetic patients remains controversial when compared to renal transplantation alone (RTA). Stratta et al.[84] analyzed the results and morbidity in four age-matched groups: thirty-one patients with Type I diabetes who underwent PRT before dialysis, thirty patients with diabetes dependent on dialysis who underwent PRT, thirty-one patients with Type I (insulin-dependent) diabetes who underwent RTA, and thirty-one patients without diabetes who underwent RTA. The four groups were comparable with respect to age, weight, gender, duration and severity of diabetes, dialysis type, number of retransplants, degree of sensitization, preservation time, and matching. The four groups differed, however, with regard to duration of dialysis and period of follow-up evaluation, pretransplant blood transfusions, racial distribution, and induction therapy.

The results of the study showed that PRT was associated with a greater morbidity rate as evidenced by a slightly higher incidence of rejections, infections, and reoperations. The number of readmissions and the hospitalization period during the first twelve months was also greater after PRT versus RTA. One the other hand, none of these differences were significant. No detrimental effect was noted on renal allograft function at one year, and patient and graft survival was actu-

---

[84]Stratta, R. J., et al., *The Analysis of Benefit and Risk of Combined Pancreatic and Renal Transplantation Versus Renal* *Transplantation Alone*, 177 Surg. Gynecol. Obstet. 163 (Aug.), 1993.

ally higher in the PRT group. Also, quality of life was improved in nearly ninety percent of the PRT recipients.

The authors concluded that the results showed that appropriate patient selection can overcome the morbidity associated with PRT, resulting in excellent patient and graft survival with the potential for complete rehabilitation.

Small intestine

Intestinal transplantation is for the patient 1) whose gut no longer works or is surgically absent, 2) who has exhausted vascular access sites for intravenous hyperalimentation, or 3) who has encountered serious complications with that hyperalimentation. Tacrolimus has improved graft survival but not enough to remove the incentive to find something better. For reasons unknown, incorporating the donor's own liver with the transplanted viscera appears to significantly ameliorate the rejection threat. However, due primarily to the severe shortage of donor livers, this double transplant has been infrequently performed except for domino transplants or cases with simultaneous end-stage liver disease. Finding donor leukocytes in the skin, blood, and lymph nodes of recipients of other organs suggested that the "2-way paradigm" of mutual acceptance, or tolerance, may be especially exploited in intestinal transplants. This co-existence, or detente, between two genetically different cell populations is called microchimerism. The absence of graft-versus-host disease in gut transplants has been all the more remarkable because the gut is saturated with lymphoid tissue. That this detente may be a legitimate entity is supported by a case report of the breakdown in that detente in a patient already compromised by a preexisting immune deficiency state in whom surgical complications mandated cessation of formal immunosuppression therapy. The donor white cells from the gut transplant then attacked in full force and the patient died from graft-versus-host disease.

ANNOTATIONS

§ 30B.96. Medical references.

The following additional references may aid in further research on the material covered in Chapter 30B. For a guide to the abbreviations used in references to periodicals, See Chapter 3, § 3.36.

(A) TRANSPLANTATION GENERALLY

Abouna, G. M., *Marginal Donors: A Viable Solution for Organ Shortage*, 29 Transplant. Proc. 2759 (Nov.), 1997.

Barbers, R. G., *Role of Transplantation (Lung, Liver, and Heart) in Sarcoidosis*, 18 Clin. Chest Med. 865 (Dec.), 1997.

Barone, G. W., et al., *Trauma Management in Solid Organ Transplant Recipients*, 15 J. Emerg. Med. 169 (Mar.-Apr.), 1997.

Boubenider, S., et al., *Incidence and Consequences of Post-Transplantation Lymphoproliferative Disorders*, 10 J. Nephrol. 136 (May-June), 1997.

Cantrill, S. V., *Brain Death*, 15 Emerg. Med. Clin. North Am. 713 (Aug.), 1997.

Corris, P. A., *Prophylaxis Post-Transplant. The Role of Monitoring Surveillance Bronchoscopy and Aintimicrobials*, 18 Clin. Chest Med. 311 (June), 1997.

DeChristopher, P. J., and Anderson, R. R., *Risks of Transfusion and Organ and Tissue Transplantation: Practical Concerns that Drive Practical Policies*, 107 Am. J. Clin. Pathol. (Supp. 1) S2 (Apr.), 1997.

Donnelly, J. P., *Bacterial Complications of Transplantation: Diagnosis and Treatment*, 36 J. Antimicrob. Chemother. 59 (Suppl. B, Oct.), 1995.

Dowie, M., *"We Have a Donor": The Bold New World of Organ Transplanting*, St. Martin's Press, New York, 1988.

Epstein, S., et al., *Organ Transplantation and Osteoporosis*, 7 Curr. Opin. Rheumatol. 255 (May), 1995.

Frickleton, J. C., *Transplanting Unsuspected Tumors: Reprieve Becomes a Death Sentence*, 2 Cancer Litig. 1 (May), 1996.

Frost, A. E., *Donor Criteria and Evaluation*, 18 Clin. Chest Med. 231 (June), 1997.

Gazdar, A. F., *Tumors Arising After Organ Transplantation: Sorting Out Their Origins*, 277 J.A.M.A. 154 (Jan. 8), 1997.

Griffiths, P. D., *Viral Complications After Transplantation*, 36 J. Antimicrob. Chemother. 91 (Suppl. B, Oct.), 1995.

Giuliano, K. K., *Organ Transplants. Tackling the Tough Ethical Questions*, 27 Nursing 34 (May), 1997.

Hadley, S., and Karchmer, A. W., *Fungal Infections in Solid Organ Transplant Recipients*, 9 Infect. Dis. Clin. North Am. 1045 (Dec.), 1995.

Hasse, J. M., *Diet Therapy for Organ Transplantation: A Problem-Based Approach*, 32 Nurs. Clin. North Am. 863 (Dec.), 1997.

Hiraga, S., *An Overview of Current Non-Heart-Beating Donor Transplantation*, 29 Transplant. Proc. 3559 (Dec.), 1997.

House, R. M., et al., *Psychiatric Aspects of Organ Transplantation*, 260 J.A.M.A. 535, 1988.

Houston, S. H., and Sinnott, J. T., *Management of the Transplant Recipient with Pulmonary Infection*, 9 Infect. Dis. Clin. North Am. 965 (Dec.), 1995.

Jason, D., *The Role of the Medical Examiner/Coroner in Organ and Tissue Procurement for Transplantation*, 15 Am. J. Forensic Med. Pathol. 192 (Sept.), 1994.

Jindal, R. M., et al., *Post-Transplant Diabetes Mellitus: The Role of Immunosuppression*, 16 Drug Saf. 242 (Apr.), 1997.

Jindal, R. M., *Post-Transplant Hyperlipidaemia*, 73 Postgrad. Med. J. 785 (Dec.), 1997.

Kelly, P. A., et al., *Sirolimus, a New, Potent Immunosuppressive Agent*, 17 Pharmacotherapy 1148 (Nov.-Dec.), 1997.

Klassen, A. C., and Klassen, D. K., *Who Are the Donors in Organ Donation? The Family's Perspective in Mandated Choice*, 125 Ann. Intern. Med. 70 (July), 1996.

Lechler, R., and Bluestone, J. A., *Transplantation Tolerance: Putting the Pieces Together*, 9 Curr. Opin. Immunol. 631 (Oct.), 1997.

Lucas, K. G., et al., *Post-Transplant EBV-Induced Lymphoproliferative Disorders*, 25 Leuk. Lymphoma 1 (Mar.), 1997.

Magee, C. C., and Sayegh, M. H., *Peptide-Mediated Immunosuppression*, 9 Curr. Opin. Immunol. 676 (Oct.), 1997.

Monaco, A. P., *Use of Donor-Specific Bone Marrow to Facilitate Tolerance in Clinical Solid Organ Transplantation: Old Facts and Future Prospects*, 29 Transplant. Proc. 2983 (Nov.), 1997.

Penn, I., *The Problem of Cancer in Organ Transplant Recipients: An Overview*, 4 Transplant. Sci. 23, 1994.

Perico, N., and Remuzzi, G., *Prevention of Transplant Rejection: Current Treatment Guidelines and Future Developments*, 11 J. Pediatr. Oncol. Nurs. 213 (Oct.), 1997.

Radecki, C. M., and Jaccard, J. *Psychological Aspects of Organ Donation: A Critical Review and Synthesis of Individual and Next-of-Kin Donation Decisions*, 16 Health Psychol. 183 (Mar.), 1997.

Singh, N., *Infections in Solid-Organ Transplant Recipients*, 25 Am. J. Infect Control. 409 (Oct.), 1997.

Singh, N., et al., *Infections Due to Dematiaceous Fungi in Organ Transplant Recipients: Case Report and Review*, 24 Clin. Infect. Dis. 369 (Mar.), 1997.

Spencer, C. M., et al., *Tacrolimus. An Update of Its Pharmacology and Clinical Efficacy in the Management of Organ Transplantation*, 54 Drugs 925 (Dec.), 1997.

Spital, A., *Ethical and Policy Issues in Altruistic Living and Cadaveric Organ Donation*, 11 Clin. Transplant. 77 (Apr.), 1997.

Starzl, T. E., et al., *Chimerism After Organ Transplantation*, 6 Curr. Opin. Nephrol. Hypertens. 292 (May), 1997.

Sturner, W. Q., *Can Baby Organs Be Donated in All Forensic Cases? Proposed Guidelines for Organ Donation from Infants Under Medical Examiner Jurisdiction*, 16 Am. J. Forensic Med. Pathol. 215 (Sept.), 1995.

Swinnen, L. J., *Treatment of Organ Transplant-Related Lymphoma*, 11 J. Hematol. Oncol. North Am. 963 (Oct.), 1997.

VanBuskirk, A. M., et al., *Transplantation Immunology*, 278 J.A.M.A. 1993 (Dec. 10), 1997.

Wainwright, S. P., and Gould, D., *Nonadherence with Medications in Organ Transplant Patients: A LIterature Review*, 26 J. Adv. Nurs. 968 (Nov.), 1997.

Wig, N., et al., *Brain Death and Organ Donation*, 10 Natl. Med. J. India 120 (May-June), 1997.

Youngner, S. J., et al., *Brain Death and Organ Retrieval*, 261 J.A.M.A. 2205, 1989.

(B) TRANSPLANTATION OF SPECIFIC ORGAN OR TISSUE

Abu-Elmagd, K., et al., *Three Years' Clinical Experience with Intestinal Transplantation*, 179 J. Am. Coll. Surg. 385 (Oct.), 1994.

Adachi, J. A., *Human Granulocytic Ehrlichiosis in a Renal Transplant Patient: Case Report and Review of the Literature*, 64 Transplantation 1139 (Oct.), 1997.

Anderson, B., et al., *Short-Term and Long-Term Changes in Renal Function after Donor Nephrectomy*, 145 J. Urol. 11, 1991.

Barnas, U., and Mayer, G., *Glomerular Proteinuria in Renal Transplant Patients: Mechanisms and Treatment*, 63 Kidney Int. Suppl. S78 (Dec.), 1997

Ben-Ari, Z. and Tur-Kaspa, R., *New Trends in Liver Transplantation for Viral Hepatitis*, 92 Am. J. Gastroenterol. 2155 (Dec.), 1997.

Carithers, R. L., Jr., *Recurrent Hepatitis C. After Liver Transplantation*, 3 Liver Transpl. Surg. (Supp. 1) S16 (Sept.), 1997.

Carson, K. L., and Hunt, C. M., *Medical Problems Occurring After Orthotopic Liver Transplantation*, 42 Dig. Dis. Sci. 1666 (Aug.), 1997.

Chertow, G. M., et al., *Antigen-Independent Determinants of Cadaveric Kidney Transplant Failure*, 276 J.A.M.A. 1732 (Dec. 4), 1996.

Chiavarelli, M., et al., *Cardiac Transplantation for Infants with Hypoplastic Left-Heart Syndrome*, 270 J.A.M.A. 2944 (Dec. 22), 1993.

Cho, Y. W., et al., "Fifteen-Year-Kidney Graft Survival" in *Clinical Transplants 1989*, P. Terasaki, editor, UCLA Tissue Typing Laboratory, Los Angeles, 1989.

Colonna, J. O., et al., *Infectious Complications in Liver Transplantation*, 123 Arch. Surg. 360, 1988.

Curtis, J. J., *Treatment of Hypertension in Renal Allograft Patients: Does Drug Selection Make a Difference?*, 63 Kidney Int. Suppl. S75 (Dec.), 1997.

Davison, J. M., and Milne, J. E., *Pregnancy and Renal Transplantation*, 80 Br. J. Urol.(Supp. 1) 29 (July), 1997.

Diethelm, A. G., et al., *Important Risk Factors of Allograft Survival in Cadaveric Renal Transplantation: A Study of 426 Patients*, 207 Ann. Surg. 538, 1988.

DiSesa, V. J., et al., *Management of General Surgical Complications Following Cardiac Transplantation*, 124 Arch. Surg. 539, 1989.

Donckier, V., et al., *Tolerance in Liver Transplantation: Facts and Perspectives*, 97 Acta Chir. Belg. 273 (Dec.), 1997.

Edelman, J. D., and Kotloff, R. M., *Lung Transplantation: A Disease-Specific Approach*, 18 Clin. Chest Med. 827 (Sept.), 1997.

Friend, P. J., *Liver Transplantation*, 29 Transplant. Proc. 2716 (Sept.), 1997.

Fung, J. J., *Tolerance and Chimerism in Liver Transplantation*, 29 Transplant. Proc. 2817 (Nov.), 1997.

Goulet, O., et al., *Intestinal Transplantation*, 25 J. Pediatr. Gastroenterol. Nutr. 1 (July), 1997.

Hertl., M., et al., *Surgical Approaches for Expanded Organ Usage in Liver Transplantation*, 29 Tansplant. Proc. 3683 (Dec.), 1997.

Improving Options in Kidney Treatment, 6 Johns Hopkins Med. Ltr. 5 (Apr.), 1994.

Kalayoglu, M., et al., *Long-Term Results of Liver Transplantation for Biliary Atresia*, 114 Surgery 711 (Oct.), 1993.

Katirsi, M. B., *Brachial Plexus Injury Following Liver Transplantation*, 39 Neurology 736, 1989.

Krom, R. A. F., et al., *The First 100 Liver Transplantations at the Mayo Clinic*, 64 Mayo Clinic Proc. 84, 1989.

Kusne, S., et al., *Infections after Liver Transplantation: An Analysis of 101 Consecutive Cases*, 67 Medicine 132, 1988.

Laffel, G. L., et al., *The Relation Between Experience and Outcome in Heart Translantation*, 327 N. Engl. J. Med. 120 (Oct. 22), 1992.

LaRocca, M. T., and Burgert, S. J., *Infection in the Bone Marrow Transplant Recipient and Role of the Microbiology Laboratory in Clinical Transplantation*, 10 Clin. Microbiol. Rev. 277 (Apr.), 1997.

Leigh, B. R., et al., *Solitary Extramedullary Plasmacytoma Five Years After Successful Cardiac Transplantation: Case Report and Review of the Lierature*, 9 Curr. Opin. Immunol. 631 (Oct.), 1997.

Levine, S. M., *Lung Transplantation: An Overview*, 23 Compr. Ther. 789 (Dec.), 1997.

Loh, E., et al., *Development of Donor-Derived Prostate Cancer in a Recipient Following Orthotopic Heart Transplantation*, 277 J.A.M.A. 133 (Jan. 8), 1997.

Luxon, B. A., *Liver Transplantation: Who Should be Referred — And When?*, 102 Postgrad. Med. 103 (Dec.), 1997.

Mallory, G. B., Jr., and Cohen, A. H., *Donor Considerations in Living-Related Donor Lung Transplantation*, 18 Clin. Chest Med. 239 (June), 1997.

Masetti, M., et al., *Current Indications and Limits of Pancreatic Islet Transplantation in Diabetic Nephropathy*, 10 J. Nephrol. 245 (Sept.-Oct.), 1997.

Michaels, M. G., et al., *Ethical Considerations in Listing Fetuses as Candidates for Neonatal Heart Transplantation*, 269 J.A.M.A. 401 (Jan. 20), 1993.

Najarian, J. S., et al., *Twenty Years or More of Follow-Up of Living Kidney Donors*, 340 Lancet 807 (Oct. 3), 1992.

Neumann, M., *Evaluation of the Pediatric Renal Transplant Recipient*, 24 A.N.N.A J. 515 (Oct.), 1997.

Nymann, T., et al., *Diagnosis, Management, and Outcome of Late Duodenal Complications in Portal-Enteric Pancreas Transplantation: Case Reports*, 185 J. Am. Coll. Surg. 560 (Dec.), 1997.

Overman, J. A., et al., *Role of the Nurse in the Multidisciplinary Team Approach to Care of Liver Transplant Patients*, 64 Mayo Clin. Proc. 690, 1989.

Palombo, J. D., *Assessment of the Cytokine Response in Liver Donors at the Time of Organ Procurement and Association with Allograft Function after Orthotopic Transplantation*, 179 J. Am. Coll. Surg. 209 (Aug.), 1994.

Patenaude, Y. G., et al., *Liver Transplantation. Review of the Literature: Medical Complications*, 48 Can. Assoc. Radiol. J. 333 (Dec.), 1997.

Peddi, V. R., and First, M. R., *Primary Care of Patients with Renal Transplants*, 81 Med. Clin. North Am. 767 (May), 1997.

Piskin, R., et al., *Renal Cell Carcinoma in Cadaver Donor Kidney*, 32 Urology 345 (Oct.), 1988.

Port, F. K., et al., *Comparison of Survival Probabilities for Dialysis Patients Versus Cadaveric Renal Transplant Recipients*, 270 J.A.M.A. 1339 (Sept. 15), 1993.

Salahudeen, A. K., et al., *High Mortality Among Recipients of Bought Living-Unrelated Donor Kidneys*, 336 Lancet 725 (Sept. 22), 1990.

Shapiro, L. M., et al., *Ten Years of Cardiac Transplantation at Papworth Hospital: Resource Management Pilot Schemes: Life-Sustaining Technology — Making the Decisions*, 298 Br. Med. J. 978, 1989.

Shaw, B. W., Jr., et al., *Stratifying the Causes of Death in Liver Transplant Recipients*, 124 Arch. Surg. 895, 1989.

Solez, K., et al., *Renal Transplant Biopsy: What Does It Tell?*, 6 Curr. Opin. Nephrol. Hypertens. 538 (Nov.), 1997.

Spital, A., *Life Insurance for Kidney Donors: An Update*, 45 Transplantation 819, 1988.

Sterioff, S., et al., *Retrieval of Donor Livers*, 64 Mayo Clin. Proc. 112, 1989.

Stewart, R. W., et al., *Cardiac Transplantation at the Cleveland Clinic Foundation: The First Twenty-Four Months*, 55 Cleve. Clin. J. Med. 49, 1988.

Sutherland, D. E., and Pirenne, J., *Current Status of Pancreas Transplanation for Treatment of Type I Diabetes Mellitus*, 60 Acta Gastroenterol. Belg. 294 (Oct.-Dec.), 1997.

Tabasco-Minguillan, J., et al., *Insulin Requirements after Liver Transplantation and FK-506 Immunosuppression*, 56 Transplantation 862 (Oct.), 1993.

Talsleth, T., et al., *Long-Term Blood Pressure and Renal Function in Kidney Donors*, 29 Kidney Int. 1072, 1986.

Terasaki, P. I., et al., *High Survival Rates of Kidney Transplants from Spousal and Living Unrelated Donors*, 333 N. Engl. J. Med. 333 (Aug. 10), 1995.

Trail, K. C., et al., *Results of Liver Transplantation in Diabetic Recipients*, 114 Surgery 650 (Oct.), 1993.

Thiel, G., *Emotionally Related Living Kidney Donation: Pro and Contra*, 12 Nephrol. Dial. Transplant. 1820 (Sept.), 1997.

Tilney, N. L., and Guttmann, R. D., *Effects of Initial Ischemia/Reperfusion Injury on the Transplanted Kidney*, 64 Transplantation 945 (Oct.), 1997.

Trail, K. C., et al., *Results of Liver Transplantation in Diabetic Recipients*, 114 Surgery 650 (Oct.), 1993.

Van Winter, J. T., et al., *Pregnancy After Pancreatic-Renal Transplantation Because of Diabetes*, 72 Mayo Clin. Proc. 1044 (Nov.), 1997.

Vasquez, M. A., *Southwestern International Medical Conference: New Advances in Immunosuppression Therapy for Renal Transplantation*, 314 Am. J. Med. Sci. 415 (Dec.), 1997.

Ventura, H. O., et al., *Cyclosporine-Induced Hypertension in Cardiac Transplantation*, 81 Med. Clin. North Am. 1347 (Nov.), 1997.

Wagoner, L. E., *Management of the Cardiac Transplant Recipient: Roles of the Transplant Cardiologist and Primary Care Physician*, 314 Am. J. Med. Sci. 173 (Sept.), 1997.

§ 30B.97. Legal references.

Abbing, H. D. C. R., *Transplantation of Organs: A European Perspective*, 21 J.L. Med. & Ethics 54 (Spring), 1993.

Allred, K. J., *Fetal Tissue Transplants: A Primer with a Look Forward*, 28 J. Health & Hosp. L. 193 (July-Aug.), 1995.

Anderson, M. F., *Encouraging Bone Marrow Transplants from Unrelated Donors: Some Proposed Solutions to a Pressing Social Problem*, 54 U. Pitt. L. Rev. 477 (Winter), 1993.

Anderson, W. L., and Copeland, J. D., *Legal Intricacies of Organ Transplantation: Regulations and Liability*, 50 J. Mo. B. 139 (May/June), 1994.

Anencephalic Newborns As Organ Donors: An Assessment of "Death" and Legislative Policy, 31 Wm. & Mary L. Rev. 197 (Fall), 1989.

Areen, J., *A Scarcity of Organs*, 38 J. Legal Educ. 555 (Dec.), 1988.

Ayres, I., et al., *Unequal Racial Access to Kidney Transplantation*, 46 Vand. L. Rev. 805 (May), 1993.

Barons, J., *Body Parts: FDA Regulation of Human Tissue Banks*, 13 Food Drug Cosm. & Med. Device L. Dig. 26 (Jan.), 1996.

Bauer, A. R., *Bioethical and Legal Issues in Fetal Organ and Tissue Transplantation*, 26 Hous. L. Rev. 955, 1989.

The Bell Tolls for Thee: But When? Legal Acceptance of "Brain Death" as a Criteria for Death, 9 Am. J. Trial Advoc. 331 (Fall), 1985.

Bernat, J., *Harvesting Organs from Anencephalic Infants for Transplantation: Are These Donors Dead or Alive?*, 28 J. Health & Hosp. L. 208 (July-Aug.), 1995.

Best, F. L., Jr., *Transfers of Bodies and Body Parts Under the Uniform Anatomical Gift Act*, 15 Real Prop. Prob. & Trusts J. 806 (Winter), 1980.

Beyer, G. W., *An Introduction to Anatomical Gifts*, 32 Prac. Law. 13 (June), 1986.

Biorck, G., *When Is Death?*, 1968 Wis. L. Rev. 484.

Blair, R. D., and Kaserman, D. L., *The Economics and Ethics of Alternative Cadaveric Organ Procurement Policies*, 8 Yale J. Reg. 403 (Summer), 1991.

Blood Transfusions and Human Transplants: A Problem of Proof and Causation, 4 Ind. Legal F. 518, 1971.

Brain Death — Illinois Judicially Adopts the Brain Death Standard, In re Haymer, 450 N.E.2d 940 (Ill.), 1984 S. Ill. U. L.J. 385, 1984.

Blumstein, J. F., *The Use of Financial Incentives in Medical Care: The Case of Commerce in Transplantable Organs*, 3 Health Matrix 1 (Spring), 1993.

Bouilier, W., *Sperm, Spleens, and Other Valuables: The Need to Recognize Property Rights in Human Body Parts*, 23 Hofstra L. Rev. 693 (Spring), 1995.

Brotherton v. Cleveland: Property Rights in the Human Body — Are the Goods Oft Interred with Their Bones?, 37 S.D. L. Rev. 429, 1992.

Burleson, I. L., *Uniform Anatomical Gift Act and Its Implications for Life and Health Insurance,* 5 Forum 171, 1970.

But, When Did He Die? Tucker v. Lower and the Brain-Death Concept, 12 San Diego L. Rev. 424, 1975.

Byrne, P. A., et al., *Anencephaly: Organ Transplantation?,* 9 Issues L. & Med. 23 (Summer), 1993.

Carrol, C., *Ethics of Transplantation,* 56 A.B.A. J. 137, 1970.

Charron, W. C., *Death: A Philosophical Perspective on the Legal Definitions,* 1975 Wash. U.L.Q. 979.

Childress, J.F., *Some Moral Connections Between Organ Procurement and Organ Distribution,* 3 J. Contemp. Health L. & Policy 85 (Spring), 1987.

Cohn, L. H., et al., *Five to Eight-Year Follow-Up of Patients Undergoing Porcine Heart-Valve Replacement,* 48 Ins. Couns. J. 484 (July), 1981.

Compulsory Removal of Cadaver Organs, 69 Colum. L. Rev. 693, 1969.

Consent and Organ Donation, 11 Rutgers Computer & Tech. L.J. 559, 1985.

Consent for the Legally Incompetent Organ Donor: Application of a Best-Interests Test, 12 J. Legal Med. 434 (Dec.), 1991.

The Constitutionality of "Presumed Consent" for Organ Donation, 9 Hamline J. Pub. L. & Pol'y 343, 1989.

Constitutional Law: Substantive Due Process and the Incompetent Organ Donor, 33 Okla L. Rev. 126 (Winter), 1980.

Corday, E., *Life-Death in Human Transplantation,* 55 A.B.A. J. 629, 1969.

Corrigan, A. T., *A Paper Tiger: Lawsuits Against Doctors for Nondisclosure of Economic Interests in Patients' Cells, Tissues and Organs,* 42 Case W. Res. L. Rev. 565, 1992.

Cotton, R. D., and Sandler, A. L., *The Regulation of Organ Procurement and Transplantation in the United States,* 7 J. Legal Med. 55 (Mar.), 1986.

Crespi, G. S., *Overcoming the Legal Obstacles to the Creation of a Future Market in Bodily Organs,* 55 Ohio St. L.J. 1, 1994.

Criteria for Determining Death in Vital Organ Transplants — A Medicolegal Dilemma, 38 Mo. L. Rev. 220, 1973.

Crothers, D J., and Uglem, C. G., *A Proposal for a Presumed Consent Organ Donation Policy in North Dakota,* 68 N.D. L. Rev. 637, 1992.

Davis, V. F., *Heavy Litigation Surrounds Autologous Bone Marrow Transplants, Other Experimental Procedures,* 7 Benefits L.J. 59 (Spring), 1994.

Death unto Life: Anencephalic Infants as Organ Donors, 74 Va. L. Rev. 1527, 1988.

Defining the Exact Moment of Death: A Changing Concept, Capital U. L. Rev. 405, 1978.

Definition of Irreversible Coma, 5 U. San Francisco L. Rev. 283, 1971.

Dickens, B. M., *Control of Living Body Materials,* 27 U. Toronto L.J. 142 (Summer), 1977.

Dickens, B. M., *Living Tissue and Organ Donors and Property Law: More on Moore,* 8 Contemp. Health L. & Pol'y 73 (Spring), 1992.

Douglass, L. E., *Organ Donation, Procurement and Transplantation: The Process, the Problems, the Law,* 65 UMKC L. Rev. 201 (Winter), 1996.

Dukeminier, J., Jr., *Supplying Organs for Transplantation,* 68 Mich. L. Rev. 811, 1970.

Featherstone, R. M., *Uniform Anatomical Gift Act: The Law's Approach to a Human Need,* 110 Trusts & Es. 468, 1971.

Frederickson, J. K., *He's All Heart ... and a Little Pig Too: A Look at the FDA Draft Xenotransplant Guideline,* 52 Food Drug L.J. 429, 1997.

Frickleton, J. C., *Transplanting Unsuspected Tumors: Reprieve Becomes a Death Sentence,* 2 Cancer Litig. 1 (May), 1996.

Friloux, C. A., Jr., *Death, When Does It Occur?,* 27 Baylor L. Rev. 10, 1975.

Gilmour, J. M., *"Our" Bodies: Property Rights in Human Tissue,* 8 Can. J. L. & Soc'y 113 (Fall), 1993.

Griner, R. W., *Live Organ Donations Between Siblings and the Best Interest Standard: Time for Stricter Judicial Intervention,* 10 Ga. St. U. L. Rev. 589 (Mar.), 1994.

Guiding Principles on Human Organ Transplantation, 42 Int'l Dig. Health Legis. 389, 1991.

Guttman, R. D., *The Meaning of "The Economics and Ethics of Alternative Cadaveric Organ Procurement Policies,"* 8 Yale J. Reg. 453 (Summer), 1991.

Hannemann, B. G., *Body Parts and Property Rights: A New Commodity for the 1990s,* 22 Sw. U. L. Rev. 399, 1993.

Havighurst, C. C., and King, N. M. P., *Liver Transplantation in Massachusetts: Public Policymaking as Morality Play,* 19 Ind. L. Rev. 955 (Fall), 1986.

Hirsh, H. L., *Brain Death,* 21 Med. Trial Tech. Q. 377, 1975.

Hoffman, A. C. and Van Cura, M. X., *Death — The Five Brain Criteria,* 24 Med. Trial Tech. Q. 377 (Spring), 1978.

Holder, A. R., "Organ Donation by Incompetent," in *The Best of Law & Medicine 70/73,* p. 77, American Medical Association, Chicago, 1974.

Holder, A. R., "Transplant Problems," in *The Best of Law & Medicine 70/73,* p. 79, American Medical Association, Chicago, 1974.

Hughes, M. A., *Life, Death, and the Law: Should the Anencephalic Newborn Be Considered a Source for Organ Donation?,* 6 Regent Univ. L. Rev. 299 (Fall), 1995.

Jacobs, D. J., *Organ Transplantation Issues: A Selective Bibliography,* 50 Rec. A.B. City N.Y. 707 (Oct.), 1995.

Kinney, J. H., *Restricting Nonative Choice: Fetal Tissue Transplantation and Respect for Human Life,* 10 J.L. & Health 259, 1995/96.

Korins, J. B., *Curran v. Bosze: Toward a Clear Standard for Authorizing Kidney and Bone Marrow Transplants Between Minor Siblings,* 5 Am. J. Fam. L. 269 (Winter), 1991.

Kress, J. M., *Xenotransplantation: Ethics and Economics,* 53 Food Drug L.J. 353, 1998.

Kurtz, S. F., and Saks, M. J., *The Transplant Paradox: Overwhelming Public Support for Organ Donation vs. Under-Supply of Organs. The Iowa Organ Procurement Study,* 21 J. Corp. L. 806 (Summer), 1996.

Kutner, L., *Due Process of Human Transplants: A Proposal,* 24 U. Miami L. Rev. 782, 1970.

Leavell, J. F., *Legal Problems in Organ Transplants,* 44 Miss. L.J. 865, 1973.

Liability Issues Arising Out of Hospitals' and Organ Procurement Organizations' Rejection of Valid Anatomical Gifts: The Truth and Consequences, 1990 Wis. L. Rev. 1655.

Little, J. W., *Research on Body Transplants,* 48 Mich. St. B.J. 11, 1969.

The Living Dead: Anencephaly and Organ Donation, 7 N.Y.L. Sch. J. Hum. Rts. 243 (Fall), 1989.

Louisell, D. W., *Procurement of Organs for Transplantation,* 64 Nw. U. L. Rev. 607, 1969.

MacDonald, A. C., *Organ Donation: The Time Has Come to Refocus the Ethical Spotlight,* 8 Stan. L. & Pol'y Rev. 177 (Winter), 1997.

Magnusson, R. S., *The Recognition of Proprietary Rights in Human Tissue in Common-Law Jurisdictions,* 18 Melb. U. L. Rev. 601 (June), 1992.

Marquis, D., *The Capron-Kass Definition of Death: Some Fatal Flaws,* Leg. Aspects of Med. Prac. 3 (Dec.), 1988.

Matter of Life and Death: A Definition of Death: Judicial Resolution or a Medical Responsibilities?, 19 How. L.J. 138 (Spring), 1976.

Medical Jurisprudence — Determining the Time of Death of the Heart Transplant Donor, 51 N.C. L. Rev. 172, 1972.

Meeker, H. L., *Issues of Property, Ethics, and Consent in the Transplantation of Fetal Reproductive Tissue,* 3 Am. U. J. Gender & L. 183 (Spring), 1995.

Merriken, J., and Overcast, T. D., *Governmental Regulation of Heart Transplantation and the Right to Privacy,* 11 J. Contemp. L. 481, 1985.

Miller, G. W., *Moral and Ethical Implications of Human Organ Transplants,* Charles C Thomas, Publisher, Springfield, Illinois, 1971.

Mills, D. H., *Statutory Brain Death?,* 229 J.A.M.A. 1225, 1974.

Moore v. Regents of the University of California: Insufficient Protection of Patients' Rights in the Biotechnological Market, 25 Ga. L. Rev. 489, 1991.

Morelli, M. N., *Organ Trafficking: Legislative Proposals to Protect Minors*, 10 Am. U.J. Int'l L. & Pol'y 917 (Winter), 1995.

Norrie, K. M., *Human Tissue Transplants: Legal Liability in Different Jurisdictions*, 34 Int'l & Comp. L.Q. 442 (July), 1985.

O'Carroll, T. L., *Over My Dead Body: Recognizing Property Rights in Corpses*, 29 J. Health & Hosp. L. 238 (July/Aug.), 1996.

Orentlicher, D., *Organ Retrieval from Anencephalic Infants: Understanding the AMA's Recommendation*, 23 J.L. Med. & Ethics 401 (Winter), 1995.

The Organ Supply Dilemma: Acute Responses to a Chronic Shortage, 20 Colum. J.L. & Soc. Probs. 363, 1986.

Overcast, T. D., et al., *Malpractice Issues in Heart Transplantation*, 10 Am. J. L. & Med. 3653 (Winter), 1985.

Pace, P. J., *Defining Human Death*, 126 New L.J. 1232 (Dec.), 1976.

Patient Selection for Artificial and Transplanted Organs, 82 Harv. L. Rev. 1322, 1969.

Pilarczyk, I. C., *Organ Donor Trusts and Durable Powers of Attorney for Organ Donation: New Twists on the Living Trust and Living Will*, 13 Prob. L.J. 29, 1995.

Price, D., and Mackay, R., *The Trade in Human Organs*, 141 New L.J. 1272 (Sept. 20), 1991; 1307 (Sept. 27), 1991.

Price, K., *Defining Death and Dying: A Bibliographic Overview*, 71 L. Lib. J. 49 (Feb.), 1978.

Prottas, J. M., *The Rules for Asking and Answering: The Role of Law in Organ Donation*, 63 U. Det. L. Rev. 183 (Fall), 1985.

Reagan, J. E., *Ethics Consultation: Anencephaly and Organ Donation*, 23 J.L. Med. & Ethics 398 (Winter), 1995.

The Regulation of Human Tissue and Organs (Symposium), 46 Food Drug Cosm. L.J. 1 (Special Issue), 1991.

Rettig, R. A., *Artificial Kidneys and Artificial Hearts*, 65 S. Cal. L. Rev. 503 (Nov.), 1991.

Robbennolt, J. K., et al., *Advancing the Rights of Children and Adolescents to be Altruistic: Bone Marrow Donation by Minors*, 9 J.L. & Health 213, 1994/95.

The Role of the Family in Cadaveric Organ Procurement, 65 Ind. L.J. 167 (Winter), 1989.

Regulating the Sale of Human Organs, 71 Va. L. Rev. 1015 (Sept.), 1985.

Rose, E. F., *Medicolegal Problems Associated with Organ and Tissue Transplantations*, 31 Med. Trial Tech. Q. 99 (Summer), 1984.

Ryan, K. J., *Tissue Transplantation from Aborted Fetuses, Organ Transplantation from Anencephalic Infants and Keeping Brain-Dead Pregnant Women Alive Until Fetal Viability*, 65 S. Cal. L. Rev. 683 (Nov.), 1991.

The Sale of Human Body Parts, 72 Mich. L. Rev. 1182, 1974.

Sanbar, S. S., *Medicolegal Aspects of Human Organ Transplantation*, 12 Leg. Aspects Med. Prac. 1 (Apr.), 1984.

Scott, R., *The Terrible Imbalance: Human Organs and Tissues for Therapy: A Review of Demand and Supply [Australia]*, 9 J. Contemp. Health L. & Pol'y 139 (Spring), 1993.

Segal, C. N., *Medical Malpractice in an Organ Transplant Case*, 15 Prac. Law. 65, 1969.

Sideman, R. J. and Rosenfeld, E. D., *Legal Aspects of Tissue Donations from Cadavers*, 21 Syracuse L. Rev. 825, 1970.

Sipes, D. D., *Does It Matter Whether There Is Public Policy for Presumed Consent in Organ Transplantation?*, 12 Whittier L. Rev. 505, 1991.

Smith, G. P., II, *Market and Nonmarket Mechanisms for Procuring Human and Cadaveric Organs: When the Price is Right*, 1 Med. L. Int'l 17, 1993.

Stason, E. B., *Uniform Anatomical Gift Act*, 23 Bus. Law. 919, 1968.

Stetter, R., *Kidney Donation from Minors and Incompetents*, 35 La. L. Rev. 551, 1975.

Survey of the Legal Aspects of Organ Transplantation, 50 Chi.-Kent L. Rev. 510, 1973.

Thorne, E. D., *When Private Parts Are Made Public Goods: The Economics of Market-Inalienability*, 15 Yale J. on Reg. 149 (Winter), 1998.

Time of Death — Legal, Ethical and Medical Dilemma, 18 Catholic Law. 243, 1973.

U.S. Congress, Office of Technology Assessment, *New Developments in Biotechnology: Ownership of Human Tissues and Cells.* Special Report, OTA-BA-337, U.S. Government Printing Office, Washington, D.C., Mar. 1987.

van Till-d'Aulnis de Bourouill, H. A. H., *Diagnosis of Death in Comatose Patients Under Resuscitation Treatment: A Critical Review of the Harvard Report,* 2 Am. J. L. & Med. 1 (Summer), 1976.

Walsh, L. A., *Judicial Recognition of Brain Death in New York: People v. Eulo [472 N.E.2d 286],* 36 Syracuse L. Rev. 1373, 1986.

Wasmuth, C. E., Jr., *Concept of Death,* 30 Ohio S. L.J. 32, 1969.

Wasmuth, C. E., Jr., *Medical-legal Problems of Organ Transplantation,* 11 Wm. & M. L. Rev. 636, 1970.

Weissman, S. I., *Why the Uniform Anatomical Gift Act Has Failed,* 116 Trusts & Es. 264 (Apr.), 1977.

Weisz, V., and Robbenolt, J. K., *Risks and Benefits of Pediatric Bone Marrow Donation: A Critical Need for Research,* 14 Behavioral Sci. & L. 375 (Autumn), 1996.

Williams, C. M., *Combatting the Problems of Human Rights Abuses and Inadequate Organ Supply Through Presumed Donative Consent,* 26 Case W. Res. J. Int'l L. 315 (Spring/Summer), 1994.

Williams, M. O., *The Regulation of Human Tissue in the United States: A Regulatory and Legislative Analysis,* 52 Food Drug L.J. 409, 1997.

§ 30B.98. American Law Reports.

35 A.L.R.3d 692. Transplantation: power of parent, guardian, or committee to consent to surgical invasion of ward's person for benefit of another.

76 A.L.R.3d 890. Tort liability of physician or hospital in connection with organ or tissue transplant procedures.

76 A.L.R.3d 913. Tests of death for organ transplant purposes.

54 A.L.R.4th 1214. Statutes authorizing removal of body parts for transplant: validity and construction.

4 A.L.R.5th 1000. Propriety of surgically invading incompetent or minor for benefit of third party.

114 A.L.R. Fed. 141. Social Security: Right to disability benefits as affected by refusal to submit to, or cooperate in, medical or surgical treatment. Organ transplants, § 14[a].

122 A.L.R. Fed. 1. Propriety of dental, or medical, or hospital benefits for investigative, educational, or experimental medical procedures pursuant to exclusion contained in ERISA-governed health plan. Transplants, §§ 10-14.5.

§ 30B.99. Cases.

In the following list of cases, no attempt has been made to include all the decisions on topics covered in Chapter 30B. The cases selected are those that the editors believe will best aid the reader in further research on the medicolegal issues involved.

[See also § 30B.16.]

United States: Campbell v. Wainwright (C.A.-5 Fla., 1969) 416 F.2d 949 (prison authorities had right to refuse inmate serving death sentence permission to travel to another state to donate kidney on ground that he might attempt to escape).

Karp v. Cooley (C.A.-5 Tex., 1974) 493 F.2d 408 (unsuccessful action against surgeon based on allegations that patient was not fully informed of risks of heart transplant).

Brotherton v. Cleveland (C.A.-6 Mich., 1991) 923 F.2d 477 (action by wife for wrongful removal of deceased husband's corneas for donation under Anatomical Gift Act).

Groft v. Health Care Corp. (D.C. Md., 1992) 792 F. Supp. 441 (even though the insured's treating surgeon claimed that a lung transplant was not experimental, a health insurer's denial of coverage for the procedure as treatment for the insured's end-stage emphysema was considered reasonable where the insurer's expert, a board-certified pulmonologist, testified that a consensus of pulmonologists considered lung transplantation for emphysema to be beyond the boundaries of ordinary therapy and that no such operations had been performed by the team of transplant surgeons who were to perform the operation on the insured).

Roseberry v. Blue Cross & Blue Shield of Neb. (D. Neb., 1992) 821 F. Supp. 1313 (Federal Employers' Health Benefit Act plans did not cover autologous bone marrow transplant for breast cancer).

Seymour v. Blue Cross/Blue Shield (C.A.-10 Utah, 1993) 988 F.2d 1020 (unsuccessful claim by policyholder that health insurer had unilaterally amended policy to exclude coverage for son's liver transplant).

Caudill v. Blue Cross & Blue Shield of N.C. (C.A.-4 N.C., 1993) 999 F.2d 74 (Federal Employers' Health Benefit Act plans did not cover autologous bone marrow transplant for breast cancer).

Heasley v. Belden & Blake Corp. (C.A.-3 Pa., 1993) 2 F.3d 1249 (district court erred in interpreting term "experimental procedure" in health insurance contract as referring generally to a liver transplant rather than to a surgical procedure specifically for treating Zollinger-Ellison's syndrome, a neuroendocrine liver cancer).

Miller v. Whitburn (C.A.-7 Wis., 1993) 10 F.3d 1315 (federal district court had jurisdiction to review state's decision that child's liver and bowel transplantation was experimental procedure and thus not covered by Medicaid).

Lyon v. United States (D. Minn., 1994) 843 F. Supp. 531 (where eye bank enucleator had been shown an apparently valid donation form and had no reason to believe there was a problem with the donation, eye bank was entitled to immunity under the Uniform Anatomical Gift Act in action by donor's family).

Perry v. St. Francis Hosp. & Med. Ctr. (D.C. Kan., 1994) 863 F. Supp. 724 (widow of the deceased was the only person who could pursue a claim against the Red Cross for converting bones and tissues that were removed from the deceased's body during a donation procedure that allegedly exceeded the family's authorization).

Barnett v. Kaiser Found. Health Plan, Inc. (C.A.-9 Cal., 1994) 32 F.3d 413 (administrator of health benefit plan governed by ERISA did not act arbitrarily in denying coverage of beneficiary's liver transplant where it based its judgment on (1) beneficiary's reduced survival rate because of his e-antigen status, (2) shortage of liver donors, and (3) medical profession's responsibility to distribute livers to patients with best chance of survival).

Shannon v. Jack Eckerd Corp. (C.A.-11 Fla., 1997) 113 F.3d 208 (a health insurance plan administrator's denial of benefits to an insured for a pancreas transplant on the grounds that the procedure was "investigation" was "arbitrary and capricious" in view of evidence that the administrator had simply accepted "bald assertions" of its medical consultant and advice from other insurers that they had denied such coverage rather than obtain additional relevant information).

Alabama: Green v. State (Ala. Crim. App., 1991) 591 So. 2d 576 (criminal defendant objected to trial court admitting photograph of murder victim taken after several organs had been removed for transplant purposes).

Hyde v. Humana Ins. Co. (Ala., 1992) 598 So. 2d 876 (question whether liver transplant criteria had been incorporated by reference into group medical coverage).

Wint v. Alabama Eye & Tissue Bank (Ala., 1996) 675 So. 2d 383 (deceased's family, which had refused to donate his eyes to eye bank, filed suit against eye bank when pathologist, in performing autopsy on deceased, discovered that both eyes were missing).

Arizona: Salgado v. Kirschner (Ariz., 1994) 878 P.2d 659 (federal law did not allow state to deny life-sustaining transplant coverage to otherwise eligible Medicaid recipient solely because she was over 21 years of age).

California: People v. Saldana (1975) 47 Cal. App. 3d 954, 121 Cal. Rptr. 243 (defense in second degree murder case argued that intervening cause of victim's death was removal from respirator at hospital, and that although "brain death" had been determined prior to such removal, death did not actually occur until removal from machine; court held medical evidence pointed to cessation of brain functions and therefore death).

Moore v. Regents of the Univ. of Cal. (Cal., 1990) 793 P.2d 497 (patient suffering from leukemia had causes of action for breach of fiduciary duty and lack of informed consent against physicians and university for unauthorized use of his samples of blood, blood serum, skin, bone marrow and sperm, which were of great commercial and scientific value).

Jacobsen v. Marin Gen. Hosp. (N.D. Cal., 1997) 963 F. Supp. 866 (parents of a Danish tourist whose organs were harvested following his death in California were unsuccessful in claiming the authorities were negligent in a 48-hour search for next-of-kin; the deceased carried no identification at the time of his death, and the search was deemed reasonable under California's version of the Uniform Anatomical Gift Act).

Colorado: Wota v. Blue Cross & Blue Shield (Colo., 1992) 831 P.2d 1307 (insured under health policy was not entitled to recover expenses for heart transplant where surgical provisions of policy that limited coverage of transplants to cornea, kidney, and bone marrow were unambiguous; also insurance company's initial payment of claims relating to insured's heart transplant did not establish an intention to cover such expenses where company, prior to the insured's operation, informed the insured that it had paid the claims without knowledge that they were related to a heart transplant and that further such expenses would not be covered).

Connecticut: Hart v. Brown (1972) 29 Conn. 368, 289 A.2d 386 (parents of identical twins could consent to transplant of kidney from one to the other).

District of Columbia: Bonner v. Moran (1941) 75 App. D.C. 156, 126 F.2d 121 (fifteen-year-old boy persuaded by aunt to donate skin to burned cousin; in action against surgeon, court held defendant should have obtained consent from donor's parent).

Georgia: Georgia Lions Eye Bank v. Lavant (1985) 335 S.E.2d 127 (hospital and eye bank not liable for arranging for removal of deceased infant's corneas without notifying mother where they otherwise acted under authority of state law).

Illinois: Smith v. Kurtzman (1982) 106 Ill. App. 3d 712, 436 N.E.2d 1 (a cause of action arising out of an unsuccessful kidney transplant was not time-barred where the plaintiff stated a cause of action for intentional misrepresentation within the limitation period in alleging that, following the unsuccessful transplant, the defendant surgeons informed the patient that it would be useless for him to undergo a second transplant because his body would again reject the kidney as it had the first time, when in fact the surgeons knew that the patient's body had rejected the first kidney because of allegedly negligent postoperative care).

In re Haymer (1983) 115 Ill. App. 3d 349, 450 N.E.2d 940 ("we recognize the nearly unanimous consensus of the medical community that when the whole brain no longer functions, the person is dead").

Curran v. Bosze (Ill., 1990) 566 N.E.2d 1319 (issue whether doctrine of substituted judgment should be applied to determine whether minors, if legally capable, would consent to bone marrow transplants in attempt to save life of sibling who suffered from leukemia).

Indiana: Smith v. Methodist Hosp. of Ind., Inc. (Ind. App., 1991) 569 N.E.2d 743 (action by parents for emotional distress against hospital for failing to inform them that their son was "brain dead" until after nuclear medicine brain-flow scan had been performed and son had been officially declared dead).

Kentucky: Strunk v. Strunk (Ky. App., 1968) 445 S.W.2d 145 (court had power to authorize mother, as "committee" of incompetent son, to subject son to operation calling for transplant of kidney to brother).

Michigan: Ravenis v. Detroit Gen. Hosp. (1975) 63 Mich. App. 79, 234 N.W.2d 411 (hospital liable for failure to maintain complete medical records of eye donor who apparently was source of infection which developed in recipient of corneal graft; first year ophthalmology resident who removed donor's eyes found not negligent).

Kelly-Nevils v. Detroit Receiving Hosp. (Mich. App., 1994) 526 N.W.2d 15 (hospital that harvested organs of patient on authorization of man who posed as his brother without verifying his identity did so in good faith and was not liable to patient's mother).

Minnesota: Rahman v. Mayo Clinic (Minn. App., 1998) 578 N.W.2d 802 (the Mayo Clinic was protected by the good faith provision of the Uniform Anatomical Gift Act when it removed a deceased patient's pelvic block for teaching purposes against the wishes of the deceased's family, when it was disclosed that the organ procurement agency had failed to note on the organ donation form that none of the patient's organs were to be used for medical research or education).

New Jersey: Strachan v. John F. Kennedy Mem. Hosp. (1988) 109 N.J. 523, 538 A.2d 346 (hospital held negligent for withholding release of "brain dead" son to his parents, allegedly in order to attempt to persuade parents to allow patient's organs to be removed for donation to transplant program).

Cavagnaro v. Hanover Ins. Co. (N.J. Super., 1989) 565 A.2d 728 (question whether hospital expenses incurred subsequent to confirmation of personal injury victim's irreversible brain death, and pending arrangements for transplantation of victim's organs, were compensable under New Jersey's no-fault act).

New York: Sirianni v. Anna (1967) 55 Misc. 2d 553, 285 N.Y.S.2d 709 (surgeon negligent in removing man's kidney prior to replacing it with kidney donated by patient's mother; although patient was adult and emancipated, and despite substantial settlement by defendant with patient, patient's mother sued defendant, claiming as damages harm done to son; court held donor of organ does not have cause of action against surgeon for negligence performed on recipient in removing organ).

New York City Health & Hosps. Corp. v. Sulsona (1975) 81 Misc. 2d 1002, 367 N.Y.S.2d 686, 76 A.L.R.3d 905 (court viewed brain death as "medically recognized concept" of death as opposed to "old" common-law definition consisting of "easily observable absence of heartbeat and respiration"; medical examiner's office issue guidelines relative to requests for organs and the Uniform Anatomical Gift Act).

People v. Eulo (N.Y., 1984) 472 N.E.2d 286 ("a defendant will not necessarily be relieved of criminal liability for homicide by the removal of victim's vital organs after victim has been declared dead according to brain-based criteria, notwithstanding that, at that time, victim's heartbeat and breathing were being continued by artificial means"; "recognition of brain-based criteria for determining death is not unfaithful to prior judicial definitions of 'death,' as presumptively adopted in the many statutes using that term. Close examination of the common-law conception of death and the traditional criteria used to determine when death has occurred leads inexorably to this conclusion.").

Oklahoma: Bill Hodges Truck Co. v. Gillum (Okla., 1989) 774 P.2d 1063 (workers' compensation claimant failed to establish that heart transplant was "reasonable and necessary" expense incident to recovery from compensable heart attacks).

South Dakota: Swanson v. Sioux Valley Empire Elec. Ass'n (S.D., 1995) 535 N.W.2d 755 (an insured who required a liver transplant was unsuccessful in suing the association through which he had obtained his health insurance coverage for negligently misrepresenting that the cost of such a procedure would be covered under the policy that replaced the coverage under which the plaintiff was originally insured).

Virginia: Tucker v. Lower (1972) No. 2831, Law and Equity Court, Richmond, Va. (accident victim's heart transplanted without locating relatives; verdict for surgeons with jury choosing "brain death" over "cardiac death" in determining time of death; consent question not decided due to running of statute of limitations).

Wisconsin: Williams v. Hofmann (1974) 66 Wis. 2d 145, 223 N.W.2d 844, 76 A.L.R.3d 880 (validity of liability limitation provision of Uniform Anatomical Gift Act challenged by husband whose deceased wife's kidneys were removed for transplantation).

CHAPTER 31

BURN INJURIES, PLASTIC REPAIR, AND HAND SURGERY*

I. BURN INJURIES AND THEIR TREATMENT

---

*Contibutors to the current and earlier editions of this chapter include Michael S. Lehv, M.D., J.D., Jack C. Fisher, M.D., Alan E. Seyfer, M.D., Gaylord S. Williams, M.D., Michael W. Hakala, M.D., Frank C. McCue III, M.D., and Richard M. Patterson, J.D.

V. COSMETIC SURGERY

VI. REPLANTATION SURGERY

VII. CORRECTION OF DEFORMITIES

VIII. SURGICAL SEX CHANGE

IX. THE HAND

I. BURN INJURIES AND THEIR TREATMENT

§ 31.1. Introduction.

The history of burn care might be characterized as an inexplicable compulsion to apply something to the wound surface. Over the years, an endless succession of ointments, creams, emolients, oils, and other materials have been applied without scientific basis and often with disastrous results. (**Table 1.**) Hippocrates, in 430 B.C., provided early advice for care of the burn wound, advocating application of "Swine's seam mixed with resin and bitumen." Throughout the nineteenth and early twentieth centuries, many topically applied materials achieved great popularity: alcohol and vitriolic ether were believed by many to eliminate inflammation because of the "cold" generated as these agents evaporated. Some physicians favored "coagulation" (*e.g.*, mercuric chloride, lime water, silver nitrate, and tannic acid). Later, the "harmful air" concept took hold, and various pliable films such as benzoin, castor oil, collodion, and even varnish were painted over the wound to seal the surface from the atmosphere.

Table 1

TOPICAL BURN THERAPY — HISTORICAL OUTLINE

EARLY NINETEENTH CENTURY

Alcohol	Gum Arabic	Olive Oil
Benzoin	Icthyol	Silver Nitrate
Carron Oil	Lard	Tallow
Castor Oil	Lime Water	Tannic Acid
Collodion	Mercuric Chloride	Vitriolic Ether
Flour	Molasses	Wax

LATE NINETEENTH CENTURY (after Lister introduced Antiseptics)

Bichloride of Mercury	Iodoform	Picric Acid
Boracic Acid	Lead Carbonate	Silver Nitrate
Carbolic Acid	Phenol	Zinc Oxide

TWENTIETH CENTURY (pre-World War II)

Acetic Acid	Gentian Violet	Silver Nitrate
Dakin's Solution	Paraffin	Tannic Acid

TWENTIETH CENTURY (Post-World War II)

Silver Nitrate (0.05%)	Coiloidal Silver Complex	Betadine Ointment
Sulfamylon (mafenide acetate)	Silver Lactate Cream	
Gentamycin Cream	Silver Sulfadiazine	

Sometime between 1835 and 1850, there developed a popular notion that toxins might be liberated from the burn wound surface and enter the blood stream, thus leading to death. Consequently, a variety of compresses were applied to "draw" these toxins out of the wound. Carron oil and various inorganic salts were dissolved in the compress fluid to achieve this noble but ill-conceived purpose.

After oils and salts, there came a period when foodstuffs such as molasses, flour, olive oil, lard, etc. were applied to improve the "nutritional status" of the burn wound. Dressings also entered into the empiricism of the day. Cotton and wool coverings were most widely used; gossamer (linen) was reserved for the wealthy who could afford it.

Since those early days, many lessons have been learned. Skin grafting has been introduced and accepted as the cardinal feature of wound care. In addition, the past several decades have seen the introduction of wound agents. Most of these incorporate antibiotics, and there appears to be a far more scientific basis for their application. Nevertheless, it is interesting to speculate how "modern day" wound care will be viewed one hundred years from now.

§ 31.2. Causes of burn injury.

In burn studies taken from the major medical centers, flame burns are the most frequent; in adults they usually result from smoking in bed and in children from parental carelessness. Next most frequent are scalds, usually occurring in children exposed to hot liquid near a stove. The so-called "attack burns" due to deliberate assaults with lye are infrequent and appear to be more characteristic of urban areas. Clothing ignition accounts for nearly 90% of the flame burns.

Patients with seizure disorders experience an uncommon number of burns — usually contact burns — which occur when they fall against a heat source — i.e., stove, etc. A frequent domestic source of electrical burn injury in children is the common wall socket or extension receptacle. Salivary contact with the contact points of a live plug will not produce large areas of burn, but they do result in significant localized disfigurement — usually around the corners of the mouth.[1]

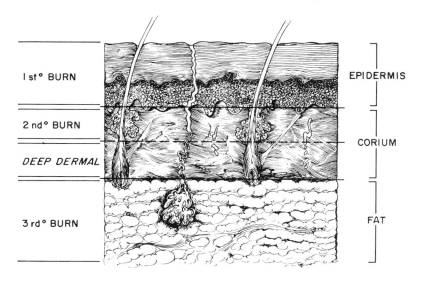

Fig. 1. Artist's drawing showing layers of skin with various depths of the four types of burns.

§ 31.3.   The burn wound.

Traditional classification

Traditionally, burns have been classified into three major categories according to the depth of injury: (1) first degree, characterized by erythema (redness) and painful skin sensitivity (e.g., sunburn); (2) second degree, a deeper burn that does not extend completely through the skin and ordinarily can be recognized by blister formation; and (3) third degree, meaning total destruction of the skin, often characterized by charring or coagulation of the surface. (**Figs. 1 and 2.**) Some surgeons also include a fourth degree burn, which involves destruction of muscle and other tissues beneath the skin.

Functional classification

More recently, surgeons have adopted a more functional classification — dividing all burns into two major categories: "partial thickness" and "full thickness." Here, the differentiation is more easily defined: partial

---

[1] Editor's Note: See also Chapter 26 of this Cyclopedia, § 26.17.

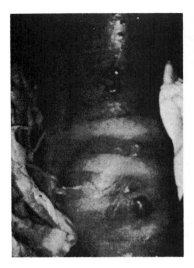 

Fig. 2. Left: First and second degree burns; the blistered areas are second degree. Right: Third degree burns.

thickness burns extend only part way through the skin elements and will heal spontaneously without skin grafts. Full thickness burns ordinarily do require application of skin grafts since all of the skin elements are destroyed. Nevertheless, although the classification sounds simple enough, determination of the depth of injury can be most difficult, particularly after the first 24 hours.

Determining depth of burn

Numerous techniques have been devised in recent years to determine accurately the depth of a burn. These include injections of fluorescein and other vital dyes intravenously or within the wound itself to see whether satisfactory circulation exists. Other methods include thermography (the measurement of heat conduction at the burn surface) and the uptake of radioactive isotopes by the burn wound. Unfortunately, none of these techniques have been found both practical and universally applicable to all types of burn injury. At present, there seems to be no substitute for early and careful observation of the wound together with precise determination of the sensitivity of the surface to a painful stimulus (e.g., pinprick).

Probability of survival

The factors that affect the mortality of burn patients have been the subject of numerous studies, from which the probability of an individual surviving an injury can be determined. One of the most accurate of these studies is the multifactorial probit analysis described by Zawacki and others.[2] The calculation of the chances of survival takes into account age, total burn area, percentage of third degree burn, prior pulmonary disease, and evidence of smoke inhalation on admission. Some appreciation of the severity of major burns can be garned from the *Rule of 50's*: "A fifty-year-old with a 50% burn has a 50% chance of dying."

§ 31.4. Early treatment.

Immediate care of the burn wound

Treatment of the superficial or partial thickness burn is relatively straightforward, since healing will occur without significant complications if the wound is given ordinary care. It is sometimes difficult for physicians to understand why patients continue to apply so many irritating substances to a minor burn. Not only is salt-containing butter still used, but also vinegar, caustic soda, and an endless variety of grease-containing ointments and salves. As one might predict, application of some of these materials occasionally can be damaging to the burned skin surface.

Numerous experiments have confirmed an early observation by many clinicians that immediate application of cold can diminish permanent tissue destruction. Accordingly, perhaps the only sensible treatment for a superficial burn is plain cold water or ice. However, care must be taken when applying cold water or ice to a burn, especially if the burn is large and if the patient is a child. Decrease in body temperature can occur and can increase the risk to the patient.

In the event of chemical burns, particularly those involving the eye, irrigation with large volumes of water is the hallmark of treatment. Alkali burns require longer periods of irrigation (sixty minutes or longer) than do acid burns. There should be no attempt to neutralize chemical burns (applying acid to an alkaline burn and vice versa), since the resulting damage usually will be worse.

After initial first aid, including cleansing and removal of loose blister fragments, burns should be wrapped loosely in a clean towel until examined by a physician. Patients with small burns (less than 5% of body surface) ordinarily are not admitted to the hospital. Those with full-thickness skin injury or burns involving more than 15 to 20% of the body surface (**Fig. 3.**) are usually admitted.[3]

---

[2] Zawacki, B. E., et al., *Multifactorial Probit Analysis of Mortality in Burned Patients,* 189 Ann. Surg. 1, 1979.

[3] Editor's Note: The extent of the burn usually is expressed in percentage of total body surface area, and the Lund and Browder chart (**Fig. 3**) often is incorporated into the patient's hospital record. A rapid method of estimating the extent of a burn is the "Rule of Nines," which states that the head, neck and upper extremities each constitute 9% of the total body surface area; the anterior trunk, posterior trunk, and lower extremities each constitute 18%; and

In making field or emergency room decisions with regard to triage and transportation of burn patients, burns of over 20% of the total body surface, burns with a 10 to 15% third-degree component, and burns in children exceeding 15% of the total body surface are considered life endangering. These are all best treated at specialized burn treatment facilities. In addition, high-voltage electrical injuries, chemical burns, and burns involving the face, hands, and perineum are best treated at burn centers.

Replacement of fluid loss

One of the most significant advances in burn care has been the realization that more must be treated than the burn wound itself. Observations made following World War II led to a more complete understanding of the importance of major shifts in body fluids that occur after a severe burn. Burn wounds may best be considered as three-dimensional spaces into which vast quantities of body fluids flow from other functional fluid compartments of the body. Thus the injured skin becomes swollen or "edematous." If this shift of fluid into the burn wound goes untreated, severe shock develops, leading to kidney failure. The reason is simple — there just is not enough fluid remaining in the body to perform necessary functions such as maintenance of blood volume. Fluids and proteins are sequestered into the burn wound where they usually remain for several days. Therefore, one essential therapeutic responsibility during the early hours following injury is replacement of the fluids that have been temporarily lost within the burn wound.

The components of this fluid loss have been analyzed which allows calculation of the needed fluids be they salt-containing solutions or colloidal fluids, such as plasma. The latter serve to replace lost tissue proteins. Current trends are toward greater use of salt-containing solutions and diminished use of plasma and its substitutes. There is little need for blood transfusion in the immediate post-burn period although red blood cell replacement does become important later when the severe nutritional deficiencies following burn injury progressively lead to anemia.

Fluid and acid-base balance must be monitored carefully during the first few days after injury. Methods now in use include body weight, urinary output, serum sodium concentration, central venous pressure, and percentage of cells within the circulating blood. These indicators are particularly important among the young and the elderly since the consequences of excessive fluid administration are more serious at these two age extremes. Other methods now in use regarding fluid and acid-base balance in the early care of the burn patient can also include cardiac output determinations and indirect measurement of left atrial pressure by means of the Swan-Ganz catheter. This is of particular value in patients who have cardiac disability or previous renal compromise.

---

the perineum (space between anus and scrotum) makes up the remaining 1%.

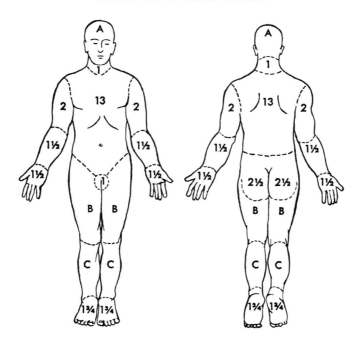

Relative Percentage of Areas Affected by Growth

	Age in Years					
	0	1	5	10	15	ADULT
A — ½ of head	9½	8½	6½	5½	4½	3½
B — ½ of one thigh	2¾	3¼	4	4¼	4½	4¾
C — ½ of one leg	2½	2½	2¾	3	3¼	3½

Total Per Cent Burned _____2°+ _____3°= _____

Fig. 3. Lund and Browder chart for determining extent of burns in terms of percentage of total body surface area. A burn covering the front half of the forearm would be 1½% of the total body surface area in either a child or an adult. A burn covering the front half of the thigh would be a 4¾% burn in an adult but would vary in a child depending on the age.

In addition to severe fluid accumulation within the burn wound, patients with full thickness injury experience a remarkable loss of water vapor and protein from the burn surface. This continues until the wound can be closed or sealed with skin grafts. Vaporization loss results in the wasted expenditure of calories leading to serious loss of energy from the body. Protein depletion also occurs from the burn surface leading to malnutrition unless there is adequate intake of high caloric foods. The importance of maintaining proper nutritional balance cannot be overemphasized. If patients are unwilling or incapable of eating sufficiently, food must be conveyed to the stomach by a nasal feeding tube. Methods are now available for maintaining good nutritional balance by intravenous feeding alone.

Treatment of lung damage

Lung damage following burn injury is not infrequent, particularly when the patient was located within an enclosed space at the time of injury and inhaled combustion products of the fire. In this instance, he must be watched closely and treated with oxygen and mechanical breathing aids whenever necessary. Whereas tracheostomy, a surgical opening in the neck to facilitate breathing, was once used commonly whenever burns involved the face, surgeons now realize that this is not always necessary. Only the occasional patient with a respiratory injury requires a tracheostomy.

One of the most useful ways to diagnose inhalation thermal injury is to assess the upper airway by means of the flexible bronchoscope. Since this injury is, in reality, a chemical tracheobronchitis, there will be direct visual evidence of irritation, swelling, and often carbonaceous deposits within the airways. The patient found unconscious within a closed space, or inebriated, is at greater risk for such injury.

Prevention of tetanus

Tetanus (lockjaw) continues to occur despite widespread immunization programs. Burns are one of the many types of wounds that precede the development of tetanus. A booster dose of tetanus toxoid should be given at the time of injury to anyone previously immunized. Certain segments of the population, however, have never been immunized for tetanus. For these individuals, the introduction of human tetanus immune globulin has usually resulted in more predictable and immediate protection from this often fatal and ordinarily preventable infectious disease.

Antibiotics

A notable advance in burn care has been the introduction of topical antibiotic-containing agents designed to control infection, the threat of which exists as long as the wound remains unhealed.

Antibiotics administered via the bloodstream have not been routinely effective in preventing infection, probably because they are not readily absorbed into the wound. It follows, therefore, that infection is better controlled by the application of an appropriate antibacterial drug directly to the wound surface.

Agents used on burn wounds include silver nitrate (in far weaker concentrations than were used in the nineteenth century), Sulfamylon cream (mafinide acetate cream), Garamycin ointment (gentamicin sulfate), silver sulfadiazine, silver lactate cream, Betadine Ointment (povidone iodine), and several others.

Bacteriologists now can measure the severity of infection within burned tissue, and many of these agents are known to limit this bacterial growth as long as they are applied continually throughout the healing period. Furthermore, the use of these agents can decrease evaporative water and energy losses from the burn surface.

No one knows which of these agents is best, nor whether they all have a beneficial effect in terms of ultimate survival among victims of the severest of burns. Evidence would suggest that patients with burns involving 20% to 40% of the body surface do better when topical antibiotics are used. But it is also well known that the use of these agents is not without complication, which has led many surgeons to limit their use only to the more serious cases. Sulfamylon cream is painful and can produce significant acid-base imbalances. Silver nitrate is difficult to use and may produce severe losses of sodium from the burn wound (which must be replaced). Garamycin ointment may lead to overgrowth of bacterial organisms that are resistant to the drug, thereby limiting the duration of its usefulness. Therefore, it is essential for all physicians treating burns to be aware of the inherent limitations of antibiotic drugs as well as their benefits, and to apply them only with good justification.

§ 31.5. Complications.

The victim of severe thermal injury remains a target for numerous complications as long as his wound remains open or ungrafted. Unfortunately, the prolonged nature of the recovery period after burn injury dictates that complications will be the rule rather than the exception in most burns of major consequence (*i.e.*, involving more than 20% of the body surface).

Although brief reference has already been made to burn shock, respiratory injury, and burn wound infection, these problems require more detailed consideration.

Shock and its consequences

If shock[4] is not avoided by prompt and adequate fluid replacement (See § 31.4), the kidneys will enter a phase of diminished function and eventually lead to kidney failure. Such an event necessitates the use of an artificial kidney dialysis unit to provide function until the kidneys re-

---

[4] Editor's Note: The several forms of shock are discussed in Chapter 30 of this Cyclopedia.

cover (ordinarily within one to two weeks). On the other hand, if excessive fluids are administered, particularly to elderly individuals whose circulatory tolerance is compromised, cardiac failure might result. Furthermore, disturbances in acid-base and nutritional balance can easily develop when burn patients begin to lose essential salts and proteins from the surface of the wound. The patient who lacks motivation to consume food in substantial quantities throughout the course of healing will soon present a critical problem in nutritional maintenance.

Respiratory complications

Respiratory complications may occur at any stage following burn injury.[5] Surveys of acute burn deaths show that asphyxia (suffocation) and smoke intoxication account for a significant percentage of fatalities. Even the patient who survives the initial consequences of a burn might later develop serious lung damage, particularly if exposure to combustion products occurred within an enclosed space. Then, at a time when natural resistance to infection decreases prior to closure of the burn wound, pneumonia is not an infrequent cause of death.

As more and more patients survive prolonged respirator care, the complications of endotracheal intubation are seen in the form of subglottic stenosis and tracheal esophageal fistula. It is the consensus of opinion that tracheostomy should probably be performed more often than in the past, and now it is not unusual to recommend a tracheostomy on patients who, after a week to ten days of respirator therapy, still show no signs of being capable of functioning independent of respirator support.

Stress ulcers

Even if burn shock and respiratory injury are avoided or treated, extensive thermal injury represents one of the severest forms of stress to the body as a whole, often resulting in gastrointestinal hemorrhage due to so-called "stress ulcers" located within the stomach and duodenum. This form of bleeding is exceedingly difficult to control and will often require surgical removal of a major portion of the ulcerated stomach. Mortality from emergency surgery of this type in an already severely ill patient understandably is high.

Infection

Burn wound infection still represents the most serious and most predictable consequence of burn injury. Infection within the burn wound can be controlled with topical antibiotic preparations only for a limited period of time (See § 31.4). Thus, the extensively burned patient stands

---

[5] Editor's Note: Respiratory problems are discussed in Chapter 33 of this Cyclopedia.

to experience greater risk of infection not only because of decreased host resistance, but simply because of the time required to cover a large wound with skin grafts.

Restrictive eschar

Circumferencial burns about an extremity or around the thoracic cage are capable of severely restricting circulation to the distal unburned extremity or of severely restricting ventilation mechanics. If there is any evidence of decreased circulation to an extremity, an escharotomy, or release of the unyielding burn eschar (remnants of burned skin) should be accomplished immediately. The escharotomy should be carried across the joints to relieve the circulation restriction. Likewise, if ventilatory mechanics are impaired due to the restrictive nature of the eschar, an escharotomy should be accomplished on the thorax as well. This can be done at the bedside with minimal discomfort to the patient.

Possible acceleration of tumor growth

Because a large burn suppresses the immune resistance of the patient, the possibility of tumor growth has to be considered in patients who have a dormant cancer. This possibility has been reported in several clinical settings and has been confirmed experimentally. The criteria for considering the possibility of burn-accelerated tumor growth are: (1) the burn must be larger than 20% of the total body surface; and (2) there must be reasonable evidence that the spread of malignant disease has occurred at a faster rate than would be normally expected of that type of tumor. There is no evidence that a burn injury is capable of inducing new cancer growth.

Delay in growth

An unexplained complication in pediatric burn patients is a period of growth delay. In a study by Rutan and Herndon,[6] the medical records of eighty pediatric burn patients two years or older were reviewed. All had sustained burns covering at least 40% of their total body surface. All patients were treated with early excision of their wounds within seventy-two hours of injury and they received standard postburn resuscitation and nutritional support. Yearly growth velocities were calculated for up to three years after injury. Despite adequate nutritional support and maximal exercise and/or long-bone stresses, a profound arrest in growth was observed during the first postburn year. This slowly resolved to near normal distribution by the third year. The exact cause of this phenomenon remains unknown.

---

[6] Rutan, R. L., and Herndon, D. N., *Growth Delay in Postburn Pediatric Patients,* 125 Arch. Surg. 392 (March), 1990.

§ 31.6a.   Preparation of the wound for skin grafts.

Once the severely burned patient has been brought into reasonable body fluid balance (usually within five to six days following injury), the major task that remains is closure of the wound. When the entire skin thickness has been irreparably injured, closure can be achieved only through application of thin pieces of skin taken from unburned areas of the patient's body. Before skin grafts can grow, however, all remnants of the burned skin (eschar) must be removed.

Since the eschar is quite thick and firmly attached to the underlying tissue layers, separation occurs spontaneously at a very slow rate and then only after bacterial growth yields enzymes that destroy the interface between burned and healthy tissue. This process may take as long as a month, and if topical antibiotics are used to limit bacterial growth, separation may be delayed even longer. Since the same bacterial proliferation that induces spontaneous separation of the eschar may also produce septic (infectious) complications, this period can be dangerous for the patient.

Temporary biologic dressings

A significant advance in burn care has been the use of banked skin from sources other than the patient. "Homografts" (also called "allografts") are skin grafts from genetically dissimilar individuals of the same species (stored skin from human donors). "Heterografts" (also called "xenografts") come from a different biological species (e.g., pig skin). Unlike skin from the patient himself ("autografts"), both types of foreign skin eventually are rejected by the body. Nevertheless, both allografts and xenografts are now in common use as temporary biologic dressings until the patient's own skin can be applied to the wound.

Some of the benefits of using temporary biologic dressings in the form of donor-stored skin grafts include: (1) control of infection within the burn wound; (2) limitation of vapor and protein losses from the burn surface; (3) reduction of the severe pain associated with second-degree burn wounds; and (4) preparation of the wound for final autografting. Since banked skin from nonpatient sources may become adherent temporarily to the burn surface after about six days, they must be removed and replaced at shorter intervals. If left in place, they will be rejected by the patient's body within four to six weeks.

§ 31.6b.   Skin grafts.

The techniques for grafting skin onto the surface of the burn wound have been in use for several decades. They involve the removal of razor thin sheets of skin from healthy areas of the patient's own body, and the transfer of these "grafts" to the raw wound (**Fig. 4**). Ideally, the graft donor site heals spontaneously in ten to fourteen days since the dermatome (**Fig. 5**) or skin knife (**Fig. 6**) used to cut the graft takes only a small thickness (20 to 50%) of the outer skin layer.[7] However, delayed donor-site healing due to infection or debilitation is not uncommon.

A burn victim's available donor sites may be limited, depending on the size of the burned area. A major problem in burn grafting, therefore, becomes skin availability. In order to distribute most economically what little skin may be available for grafting, it is sometimes necessary to use a device that converts solid skin grafts into an expandable mesh. With multiple blades, alternate perforations are cut in the skin, which is then spread out to cover wider areas of the burn wound. The small openings in the mesh heal quickly, and the final graft appearance is quite acceptable.

Special problems

Specific areas of the body present special problems to the surgeon applying grafts. The face has particular color tones and blush characteristics not shared by common donor sites such as the abdomen and leg. Therefore, facial grafts must be selected from areas as near to the face as possible to provide a satisfactory color match (*e.g.*, scalp, neck, upper chest wall). Burns overlying moving joints result in progressive contracture and limitations of movement. Therefore, it is essential to graft these sites as early as possible. Particularly troublesome also are burns involving the neck, armpit, and the space behind the knee. Hand burns are especially devastating since the continual functioning of any hand is dependent upon the movement of multiple joints. These must be treated with great care and as rapidly as possible.

Homografts

The only permanent solution to the lack of availability of patient skin donor sites (autografts) will eventually be the ability to obtain grafts from nonrelated individuals (homografts). But to date, despite remarkable advances in the field of organ transplantation, skin has not been permanently[8] exchanged between two individuals, except in a few cases involving identical twins. It is hoped that further research will yield methods for eliminating natural immunologic barriers to skin obtained from genetically dissimilar individuals.

---

[7] Editor's Note: These partial small-thickness grafts are called "split-thickness skin grafts" as opposed to "full-thickness grafts" in which the entire thickness of the skin is transplanted. Generally, full thickness grafts are done only in cases of small burn areas.

[8] Editor's Note: Skin transplants from donors are used as temporary biologic dressings. See § 31.6a, supra.

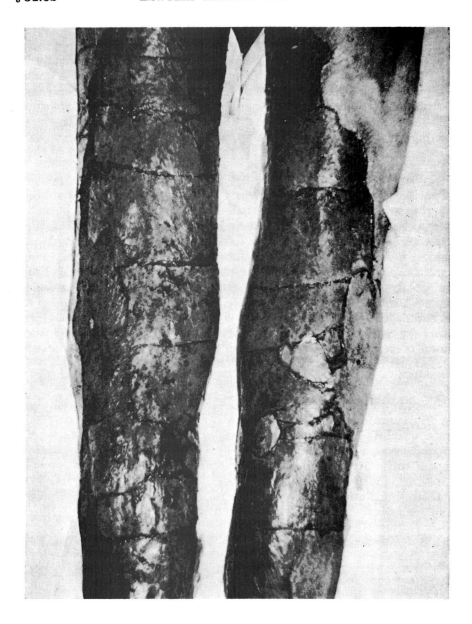

Fig. 4. Full-thickness burns of the leg shown soon after application of split-thickness skin grafts.

Fig. 5. Burns involving all skin elements require grafting of new skin. For this purpose, a dermatome is used to cut razor-thin sheets of skin from nearby uninjured sites.

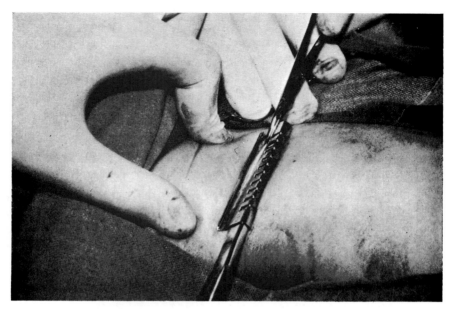

Fig. 6. Skin grafts also may be cut "free hand" with special knives.

§ 31.7a. Electrical burns.[9]

Electrical burns occur whenever some portion of the body (usually an extremity) completes an electrical circuit. If the power source supplying that circuit is direct current, there is no induction of muscular activity, but if the circuit is supplied by alternating current, tetanic (continuous, steady contraction) muscle spasms occur resulting in an unbreakable contact, especially if the body part involved is the hand. Electrical injuries are perhaps the most crippling of all burns, since they can destroy not only the skin of the surface but also the muscles, tendons, and blood vessels beneath.

Electrical injuries are more like a crush injury than a thermal injury. Myoglobinuria (excretion of muscle hemoglobin in the urine), due to the extensive destruction of muscle tissue as well as development of myonecrosis secondary to increased compartment pressures, are common findings after severe electrical injuries. The fluid requirements can be very great if there has been extensive damage to these muscle units.

The severity of electrical injuries is largely based on Ohm's Law, which states that the strength of an electric current varies directly as the electromotive force and inversely as the resistance. Therefore, cur-

9 Editor's Note: See also Chapter 26 of
this Cyclopedia regarding electrical injuries.

rent increases as resistance decreases, and it is the current that determines the extent of tissue damage, not the total number of volts emanating from the power source. Two factors that tend to decrease skin resistance are loss of integrity of the skin, and moisture. This is why an electrical injury within a bathtub might prove fatal: the resistance is lowered, and the final current available may be very high indeed.

Most electrical injuries occur in the home or industrial setting. Frequent domestic sources include television antenna installation mishaps and inadvertent contact with a live electrical receptacle. Industrial sources of injury usually involve contact with high tension wires. About 15% of electrical injuries prove fatal.

Treatment of electrically burned tissue must be conservative in nature. There is no place for immediate excision of damaged tissue, since it is exceedingly difficult to determine just how much vital deep anatomy has been destroyed. On the other hand, inordinate delay can lead to deep infection similar to gas gangrene. Whenever muscles, tendons, and bone are either destroyed or left uncovered, wound closure must be accompanied with thick flaps of skin moved from nearby regions. These procedures are infinitely more difficult and prolonged than skin grafting.

Electric plug burns of the mouth are rarely fatal but pose demanding problems for the plastic surgeon. Such incidents usually involve small children and the resulting scars can never be totally erased. Saliva is thought to act as the conductor of current, and the resulting spark gap usually produces a severe tissue-damaging burn at the corner of the mouth. Months later, accumulated scar tissue prevents complete opening of the mouth.

The attorney should remember that electrical injury, more than any kind of burn, probably is most directly related to individual carelessness, but usually on the part of the victim.

§ 31.7b.   Chemical burns.

In the first-aid management of chemical burns, it is imperative to have available facilities for early copious water lavage (irrigation) of the wound. It has been shown that chemical burns do much better when water irrigation is available within three to five minutes of injury. This reduces the extent of third degree injury and shortens hospital stay. Immediate water irrigation is the universal immediate treatment of all chemical burns and should take priority over any attempt to neutralize the chemical specifically or the administration of specific antidotes.[10]

Most chemical burns occur in laboratories and industrial plants. Also, the so-called "attack burn," involving thrown acid, is a commonly observed injury in any urban hospital emergency room. A majority of these

---

[10]Leonard, L. C., et al., *Chemical Burns.*
Effect of Prompt First Aid, 22 J. Trauma
420, 1982.

injuries are the result of assaults or personal quarrels and often involve the use of lye.

Lye

Lye burns differ from thermal burns in a number of ways. They are deeply erosive, and therefore can result not only in unusual manifestations, such as eardrum perforation and corneal ulceration, but also very severe secondary scarring. Treatment involves prolonged irrigation of all areas of contact with massive volumes of water. In the case of widespread injury, patients may be placed in a shower stall for twelve to twenty-four hours to achieve gradual dilution of the lye, which would otherwise continue to erode healthy tissue for many hours. Subsequent use of topical antibiotics may be helpful, but drugs should be selected with care since some may react adversely with any residual lye. Septic (infectious) complications are unusual, primarily because these burns rarely involve more than 20% of the body surface.

Phosphorus

White phosphorus burns have become an increasing problem in the military. This substance, an incendiary utilized in modern warfare, will ignite spontaneously in the air and then rapidly oxidize with resultant damage to all contiguous tissues. Small fragments of white phosphorus may be imbedded beneath the skin following the explosion of phosphorus-containing munitions. Emergency treatment includes irrigation with water and careful removal of all particles. Phosphorus cases can present a hazard to operating room personnel, since each particle removed can be expected to ignite promptly if not immersed promptly in water. Phosphorus is also used in the manufacture of insecticides and fertilizers, and burns of this type occasionally can be seen in industrial cases.

Magnesium

Magnesium burns produce ulcers that are small at first, but gradually enlarge to form extensive lesions. Magnesium may burn rapidly or slowly, depending on the size of the particles. If slow-burning embers penetrate deeper than the outer layers of the skin, they must be excised completely, and the wound must be closed by skin grafting.

Alkalis

Alkali burns are usually caused by sodium hydroxide, potassium hydroxide, or calcium oxide. Alkalis exert their damaging effect in three ways: by saponifying (liquefying) fat; by extracting considerable water from cells; and by dissolving and uniting with the proteins of the tissue.

The initial treatment for alkali burns is to wash the area with large quantities of water. Pouring the water over the area not only carries away the excess alkaline agents but also the heat they create. In lime (calcium oxide) burns, the dry lime should be brushed away before washing, so that the calcium oxide will not unite with water to form calcium hydroxide, which produces a tremendous amount of heat.

Acids

Concentrated acids withdraw water from cells and precipitate proteins. Sulfuric acid converts the corroded tissue into greenish black or dark brown slough (dead tissue). Nitric acid causes a yellow color, which becomes a yellowish brown. Hydrochloric acid is a much more severe caustic than nitric or sulfuric, and stains the skin yellowish brown. Trichloroacetic acid is the most corrosive of all organic acids; and forms a white, soft slough. Phenol, a poisonous acid, causes a white slough initially, that turns to a greenish black or copper color.

Acid burns should be treated by diluting or removing the acid as quickly as possible, usually by irrigating with large quantities of water. The remainder may be neutralized with a weak solution of baking soda.

Hydrofluoric acid is particularly troublesome, however, since it continues to inflict tissue destruction for several days after initial contact. Water irrigations are seemingly ineffective in reversing its effects, and a variety of methods have been introduced to neutralize its action. These include local application of magnesium oxide or subcutaneous injection of calcium gluconate. The use of a local anesthetic in conjunction with these reversing agents serves to control the unremitting pain that accompanies these burns. Some surgeons advocate early and total surgical removal of all injured tissue as the only means of curtailing further tissue destruction.

Petroleum derivatives

A form of chemical injury that is not only common but also frequently unrecognized is the cutaneous burn following contact with gasoline or other petroleum derivatives. Prolonged contact with nonburning gasoline, such as might occur following an automobile accident, can result in a burn that is indistinguishable from a typical flame burn. These burns, which are often mistakenly attributed to flame contact, can usually be prevented by those who first arrive at the accident scene to administer first aid.

§ 31.7c. Radiation burns.[11]

In radiotherapy, acute radiation burns involving the skin are no longer common. Two explanations can be found for this. First, current radiotherapeutic techniques involve the use of potent gamma irradiation sources such as cobalt 60, the Betatron, and the linear accelerator. Unlike the older conventional machines, these power sources can be focused successfully on deeper targets with less injury to the overlying skin. Second, the use of ionizing radiation has been restricted to those who are specifically trained to administer it, usually a radiologist or radiotherapist working together with a team of technicians in a large medical center. Gone are the days when X-ray machines could be found in the back of hairdressing shops for treatment of acne and excessive facial hair growth. Gone also are the portable fluoroscopy machines in shoe stores for the use of a sales clerk in checking the fit of a new shoe.

Nevertheless, patients who suffer the late-appearing chronic complications of misuse of ionizing radiation continue to inhabit the offices of plastic surgeons throughout the country. Chronic skin atrophy and ulceration, bone demineralization, unremitting pain, destruction of growth centers during childhood with resulting disfiguring deformity, and the development of skin and bone cancers are just a few of the consequences now seen twenty to thirty years after even small doses of X-ray therapy. It is, therefore, disquieting to see the use of extensive radiation for the early stages of some malignant diseases when the long-term consequences of high-dose radiation are not yet fully known.[12] The decision to take the "easier" therapeutic route, i.e., radiation therapy rather than surgery, might prove disastrous decades later to those who have been cured of their disease and look forward to normal longevity. Such thinking can be traced to the practice of measuring the success of cancer treatment by quantitating length of survival rather than the quality of the life so extended.

When radiation burns of the body surface develop, local treatment is similar to that applied to any other burn, together with the additional precaution of a careful survey of the patient's blood count for several weeks to detect any suppressive effects on the bone marrow. Radiation injury of the skin rarely requires grafting to achieve initial healing, but total skin resurfacing with grafts may be necessary years later should malignancies or chronic atrophic changes develop.

---

[11] Editor's Note: For an extensive discussion of the effects of radiation on the human body, see Chapter 29 of this Cyclopedia.

[12] One of the more common late manifestations of radiation therapy for breast cancer is the development of a chest wall ulceration that will not heal. Such ulcers enlarge with time and the optimum therapy is wide excision of the chest wall and replacement of the tissue with a healthy soft tissue flap.

§ 31.8. Repair of scars and contractures — Rehabilitation.

Reconstructive surgery

Even when freshly applied under ideal circumstances, skin grafts will never approach the quality and texture of the natural skin which existed before injury. Grafted skin inevitably contracts, later becoming both thin and taut. It lacks nervous sensation, will not develop normal color, and lacks the usual glands which provide for self-lubrication and other skin functions. As the skin over moving joints contracts, the range of motion of that joint decreases, leading to the development of a "contracture." Where skin grafting is delayed, or performed insufficiently, contractures are particularly severe.

Reconstructive surgery following burn injury is performed months and sometimes years after initial wound healing and closure by skin grafts. The surgeon in this repair process is largely concerned with the release of contractures, restoration of full joint movement, improvement of scars, resurfacing zones of poor skin quality with grafts of greater thickness and superior color match, and reconstruction of totally destroyed structures. **(Figs. 7 and 8.)**

Burn scars and contractures are troublesome because they represent an inherent shortage of tissue. This is a result of direct tissue loss from the burns (skin, fat, and muscle) plus shrinkage of split-thickness grafts used for initial burn wound coverage. The goal of reconstruction is to release or remove any constricting scar tissue and to add thicker and more pliable, normal tissue to fill in the defects. The following reconstruction techniques may also be used for reconstruction of new or old defects that result from other causes such as malignancy or trauma.

1. *Split-thickness skin grafts* are usually plentiful, easy to harvest, and easy to apply, but they tend to shrink, develop pigmentation, and lack pliability. Their "cosmetic" appearance is poor and patch-like. An example of their use in reconstruction would be the release of an old burn scar contracture that causes the elbow to "draw up." The elbow is stretched out and the defect is resurfaced with grafts.

2. *Full-thickness skin grafts* may be used to reconstruct small- to medium-sized defects on the face and hands. They do not shrink as much as split-thickness grafts and when harvested from areas above the collarbones, they maintain a good color-match with facial skin. Their major problem is that available donor skin is usually limited to the excess skin from behind the ears, the hollow above the collarbone, the upper eyelids, or penile foreskin. Example: replacement of traumatic eyelid loss with skin from behind the ear to allow the eyelid to close.

3. *Composite grafts* consist of more than one type of tissue — usually skin with attached cartilage, fat, or special tissues such as oral mucosa or eyelid conjunctiva. Example: reconstruction of tissue missing from a nostril using a wedge containing cartilage from the ear.

4. *Skin flaps* differ from skin grafts in that skin and underlying fat are shifted from one area to another while still remaining tethered at some point to the donor site. This preserves the necessary blood supply to these large, relatively bulky tissues that are too thick to survive as free grafts. Flaps provide a means of filling in skin and deeper defects and also of covering vital structures (vessels, nerves, and bones) with pliable, durable, normally textured skin, and soft tissue. The donor wound most often is closed directly, but may occasionally require its own skin graft. This type of surgery requires extensive planning and surgical expertise. Example: Tissue removed to treat cancer of the nasal tip is replaced with tissue rotated into the defect from the upper portions of the nose and lower forehead. The donor site is closed directly.

5. *Muscle flaps* add bulk and protection and are used where skin flaps are not feasible. They may be buried under existing skin or used on the surface by covering with skin grafts. *Myocutaneous flaps* include both skin and muscle in the mobilized tissues. The underlying muscle increases the blood supply to the skin and allows for larger tissue transfers and more durable coverage. *Composite flaps* may include bone or cartilage. *Island flaps* maintain their connection to the donor site solely through a set of arteries and veins. Example: a muscle flap from the lower leg is partially detached and rotated 180 degrees to cover an exposed orthopedic knee implant. A split-thickness skin graft is then used to cover the muscle flap.

6. *Free flaps* involve tissue transfers in which an island flap is temporarily created but the blood vessels are intentionally severed. The tissue is quickly moved to its recipient location and the vessels anastomosed (attached) to existing blood vessels in the area. Example: following a mastectomy, skin and fat from the abdomen are completely detached and then reattached to the chest wall area to reconstruct the missing breast. (See also § 31.27b.)

7. *Tissue expansion* is a multistage procedure that actually creates excess skin adjacent to an area of skin that requires resection. A balloon-like device called a tissue expander is inserted beneath the skin and gradually inflated by injecting saline into a self-sealing valve that has also been placed under the skin. This process is carried out over a period of several weeks with the skin gradually stretching as the balloon is periodically inflated. When the area appears ready, the tissue to be removed is excised, the

expander removed, and the newly created excess skin rearranged to cover the defect. An example would be a child with a large mole that covers part of the face and neck. One or more expanders are placed in the neck and normal skin there is gradually stretched. The mole and expanders are then removed and the defect is covered with the stretched skin.

Reconstruction procedures of this type are difficult, costly because of the need for repeated hospitalizations, and time-consuming to both patient and physician. Nevertheless, the need for such restorative work cannot be questioned. Careful acute burn care serves to assure preserved duration of life, but burn scar reconstruction serves to improve the quality of that life.

Emotional scars

Regardless of the cause, all but the most superficial burn wounds produce lasting emotional scars. The physician who ignores this sequelae of acute burn injury fails to provide one of the most essential aspects of total burn care: rehabilitation of the severely scarred burn survivor.

The emotional response and psychological adaptation to burn injury has been the subject of intensive study at a number of burn treatment centers. Implicit in the findings arising out of these studies is the severity of emotional trauma. This emotional trauma has been attributed to the following:

1. The fright of the injury;
2. Guilt over possible behavioral transgressions prior to the injury;
3. Severe pain associated with burns;
4. Prolonged hospitalization and inactivity;
5. Fear of death;
6. Disheartening comments by medical personnel inevitably overheard during hospitalization;
7. Irreversible effects on external appearance and bodily function.

There is little doubt that the services of psychiatrists, psychologists, psychiatric social workers, and a number of other related personnel are essential to the total care and rehabilitation of any seriously burned patient.

Physical rehabilitation

During the burn patient's period of prolonged immobilization while complete wound healing is being obtained, strenuous efforts should be made to initiate physical and possibly occupational therapy.

Physical therapy should include active and passive exercises of as many joints as possible to maintain full range of motion and to prevent contractures and calcification in and around the joints. The patient

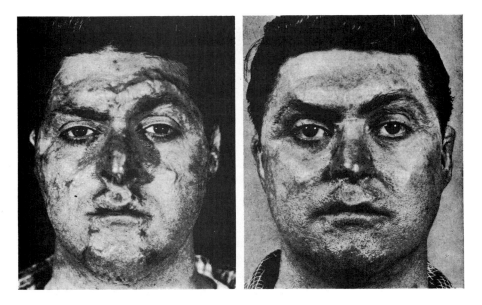

Fig. 7. Left: Photograph of patient with healed burn scars of nose, face and ears. Right: Same patient after reconstruction with skin grafts.

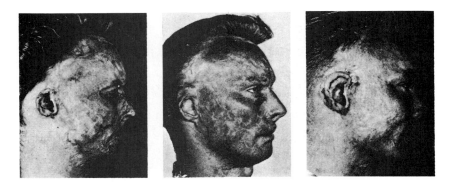

Fig. 8. Left: Photograph of patient with destruction of right ear by third degree burns. Center: Post-auricular skin flap raised and carved cartilage inserted beneath it. Right: Skin is folded and held by sutures to form helix (rim of ear). Skin graft has been placed behind for elevation.

should be kept ambulatory as much of the time as his condition permits, and every effort should be made to have him perform usual day-to-day personal functions. He should be encouraged to feed himself, shave himself, and to assist in his own bathing while in the hydrotherapy tank.

The above measures are necessary not only to preserve range of motion, but also to demonstrate to the patient that he is still capable of many of these maneuvers that should help minimize psychological dependence.

II. MEDICOLEGAL ASPECTS OF BURN INJURIES

§ 31.9. Burn injury claims.

The cause of the injury

When the attorney encounters a serious burn injury, he should be alert to the possibility of a products liability action. A defective or negligently designed product may have been the source of the burn or may have provided the medium for the rapid spread of fire (e.g., highly flammable carpeting or interior furnishings such as drapes). A products liability action must be considered a possibility whenever the burned victim's clothes caught fire after only brief exposure to a flame source. (See § 31.10.)

In fires involving wearing apparel, ease of ignition, rate of burning, and intensity of heat generated usually receive the most attention should litigation develop. A factor often overlooked is the inadequacy of the garment's design. Take, for example, children's sleepwear. A pull-over pajama top that fastens in the back with a complex arrangement of buttons and clasps would be a very poorly designed article in the event of fire. The child would have little chance to rid himself of this garment should it ignite. Even an adult coming to his assistance probably would not be able to remove the garment quickly enough to prevent serious injury.

Another example of a poorly designed garment would be "bell-type" sleeves on a woman's housecoat, which present a very serious hazard when working over a kitchen range.

In handling a flammable fabrics case, an attorney should consult federal and state statutes and regulations governing flammable products to determine the possibility of negligent design. In addition, he or she should check private regulatory standards, both within the defendant manufacturer's industry and those promulgated by safety organizations, such as the National Fire Protection Association. (Journals published by this association and similar organizations are invaluable research guides for the attorney involved in burn injury litigation.)

The injury itself

The treatment of major burns follows a fairly well-defined pattern, and each step of this treatment must be understood fully by counsel if he is to make an effective presentation of his case. The plaintiff's attorney will want to remember that the early stages of serious burn treatment, often lasting weeks or months, may be a true life-and-death struggle requiring around-the-clock attention of medical personnel. He will want to go beyond the common elements of the victim's hospital record and refer to nurses' notes and to fluid and medication charts, which often reveal the agony suffered by the burned patient. Also, the plaintiff's attorney will want to secure any plastic surgeon's records containing color photographs and slides of the patient at various stages of treatment and reconstruction. These materials are essential in presenting the case to the jury, especially where the plaintiff has made a good recovery with regard to appearance and function.

Jury verdicts involving burn injuries

The following is a comparison of median jury verdicts in personal injury actions involving burn injuries based upon type and severity of the injury for the period of 1990 to 1995.[13]

Facial burn injuries	$ 333,000
Mild burn injuries	30,110
Moderate burn injuries	200,000
Severe burn injuries	1,750,000
Catastrophic burn injuries	2,458,072

§ 31.9a. Rating burn impairment.[14]

For many years, the common medical measures of burn care and outcome have largely been physiologic values (*e.g.*, the measurement of fluid required to be given the patient during the first twenty-four hours of treatment), the patient's length of stay in the hospital, and extent of burned tissue. Such data is still important, but today physicians are more often being required to evaluate burn patients in terms of impairment and disability. Unfortunately, there is no universal agreement on the definitions of these terms, nor is there agreement on the methods of rating impairment and disability. The Rehabilitation Committee of the American Burn Association defines *burn impairment* as "a measure of the burn victim's physical and mental difference from accept standards" and *burn disability* as "the impact that the measured impairment has on the individual's activities in the interpersonal, family, school, work, social, and recreational environments," all of which may change as these environments change.

The most widely accepted general method of rating injury and disease is that established by the American Medical Association in its *Guides to the Evaluation of Permanent Impairment* (See Chapter 27 of this

---

[13] *Tracking Trends in Personal Injury Litigation*, 3 Pers. Inj. Verdict Rev. 1 (Aug. 7), 1995.

[14] Engrav, L. H., et al., *Rating Burn Impairment*, 19 Clin. Plast. Surg. 569 (July), 1992.

Cyclopedia). However, burn injuries receive scant coverage in these *Guides*. To assist in evaluating burn injuries, Loren H. Engrav, M.D., of the Division of Plastic Surgery, Department of Surgery, University of Washington Harborview Medical Center, Seattle, has used the AMA concept to construct an impairment-rating guide specifically for burn injuries, which includes detailed forms to be completed by the physician. This recommended guide can be found beginning at page 569 of Volume 19 of *Clinics in Plastic Surgery* (July 1992).

§ 31.10. Flammable fabrics.

Nearly one-half of all childhood burns are caused by flame contact, and nearly 90% of these are associated with clothing ignition. These statistics suggest that widespread use of flame retardant clothing would significantly decrease the frequency and severity of thermal injury.

During the late 1940s, a number of tragic accidents involving "high pile" rayon received widespread publicity. This fabric was found to be explosively flammable, giving rise to the term "torch sweater." Out of this experience arose the Flammable Fabrics Act of 1953, which succeeded in eliminating rayon "high pile" clothing from the market place. But this still left 99% of the children's clothing market untouched and did little to stimulate development of flame resistant clothing. (The concept of built-in flame retardancy in clothing was not new; the British had developed ignition-resistant clothing early in this century although it would not withstand simple laundering methods.)

Some members of the textile industry engaged in active resistance to further restrictive legislation during the 1950s and 60s, but others sought to develop marketable fabrics that would resist ignition. Among fabrics developed were Verel (Tennessee Eastmen), Dynel (Union Carbide), Nome (Dupont), Durrette (Monsanto), and Pyrovatex (Ciba). Another manufacturer, M. Lowenstein & Sons, developed a 100% cotton fabric with a flame retardant finish that withstood commercial laundering. This was marketed by Sears, Roebuck and Company, which was among the first companies to retail flame retardant children's sleepwear voluntarily. But the result was predictable: without mandatory legislation, the public was unwilling to pay the extra cost for such garments, regardless of the safety factor.

In 1967, amendments were added to the Flammable Fabrics Act[15] empowering the Federal Government to set additional standards of acceptable flammability. This amendment also put more bite into the law generally and resulted in highly successful carpet and mattress standards, as well as early steps toward a children's sleepwear standard.

---

[15] 15 U.S.C. 1191 et seq.

§ 31.11. Medical malpractice.

The method of treating the seriously burned patient, particularly with regard to the time for skin grafting and the choice of which burn areas are to receive the grafts, generally is a matter of individual judgment on the part of the surgeon, and his decision, even if eventually proven unwise, seldom has been challenged successfully. Thus, in order to prevail in malpractice actions against surgeons for improper treatment of burns, plaintiffs usually have to introduce convincing expert medical testimony that the defendants clearly violated acceptable standards of care.

A surgeon may be vulnerable, however, if the burn patient suffers additional injury or if his healing process is impaired because the surgeon does not choose the proper device for, or method of, grafting, or uses, to the patient's detriment, a new and unaccepted method of burn treatment.[16] Probably there are more new ideas and techniques introduced in burn therapy than in any other field of traumatic surgery, but most of these are abandoned within a short time. This would suggest a higher incidence of malpractice claims than in areas where there are fewer attempts to innovate, but the number of reported cases do not seem to bear this out.

Infections are always a serious complication in burn cases; even stethoscopes used in emergency rooms are a potential vector of infection for patients with burns. In one study, out of 150 stethoscopes examined, 133 were found to be contaminated with staphylococci. The primary reason was failure to clean the instruments properly. The seriousness of the finding lies in the fact that the instruments also can be a method of transmitting drug-resistant bacteria, a growing problem in hospitals.[17]

Treatment of a patient with major burn injuries should never be delegated to an inexperienced physician or surgeon unless absolutely necessary.[18]

III. THE FIELD OF PLASTIC SURGERY

§ 31.12. Misconceptions regarding plastic surgery.

Any survey of a medical specialty should be preceded by an attempt to define the boundaries of that specialty. This task is particularly difficult with the field of plastic and reconstructive surgery, since the protean interests of its members necessarily preclude any prospect of a universal

---

[16]See generally Annotation, "Malpractice in connection with care and treatment of burns," 97 A.L.R. 473.

[17]Jones, J. S., et al., *Stethoscopes: A Potential Vector of Infection?*, 26 Ann. Emerg. Med. 296 (Sept.), 1995.

[18]See Eastern v. Lexington Memorial Hosp., Inc. (1981) 303 N.C. 303, 278 S.E.2d 253 (obstetrician-gynecologist with no experience in treating serious burn cases assigned to treat severely burned emergency room patient who later died from tetanus).

definition. In addition, regional variations in the structure of plastic surgical practice, as well as the overlapping interests of several related surgical specialties, lead to confusion among those who wish to know exactly who does what.

The very name "plastic surgery" is a source of misunderstanding to many persons who have not required the services of a reconstructive surgeon. The general public commonly believes that implantable plastic materials are the primary ingredients of the trade. In truth, the term "plastic" is associated with the reconstructive surgeon only because it is a derivative of the Greek word "plastikos" meaning literally "to make or mold." Implantable materials are utilized by the reconstructive surgeon, but only in a small number of cases.

Lawyers often become involved with the plastic surgeon when their clients or their opponent's clients seek correction of facial deformities following accidents. And anyone who reads magazines knows that plastic surgeons perform "cosmetic" operations to improve appearance. The reconstructive surgeon, however, can and usually does far more than this.

As a specialty, plastic surgery derives its origin from groups of surgeons representing a number of specialties (dentistry, otolaryngology, general surgery, etc.) who were brought together in England and Continental Europe during World War I to treat the mounting number of jaw and facial injuries so characteristic of the trench warfare tactics of that conflict. Modern-day controversies among members of these disciplines regarding who should properly perform maxillofacial surgery tend to ignore the realities of how the specialty called plastic surgery came into existence.

§ 31.13. Scope of practice.

The practice of plastic surgery includes the treatment of burns, correction of birth defects, reconstructive surgery of the hand, treatment of traumatic facial injuries, control and reconstruction of head and neck malignant disease, as well as cosmetic or aesthetic surgery. If one were to select one word that pinpoints the substance of reconstructive surgical practice, that word would be "deformity." Plastic surgery is in essence the surgery of deformity, whether the deformity be congenital, traumatic, or malignant in origin.

In recent years, the development of new surgical techniques has broadened the scope of plastic surgery practice. Advances in the use of musculocutaneous flaps has opened up a wide new field of reconstructive possibilities. Progress with microvascular surgery has increased possibilities of free tissue transfer, replantation, and repair that were not considered possible several years ago. Plastic surgeons are now asked to participate in the repair of defects in all parts of the body. They are called upon to participate more frequently with orthopedic surgeons, gynecologists, urologists, general surgeons, and oncologists in the closure and repair of many large, soft tissue defects caused by trauma, infection, and malignant disease. Also, plastic surgeons are occasionally called upon to repair injured tendons, nerves, and blood vessels, and to set fractures of the small bones of the upper extremity.

IV. REPAIR OF FACIAL INJURIES

§ 31.14. Introduction.

Many of the basic techniques used today in all forms of plastic and reconstructive surgery were developed by surgeons attempting to rehabilitate patients with deformities of the head and neck that resulted from trauma sustained in war. The motor vehicle, however, has long since supplanted warfare as the major cause of head and neck trauma. Statistics show that nearly three-fourths of patients injured in automobile accidents are found to have some injury to the head and neck. Falls, accidents in the home, fights, and sporting injuries all contribute their share of head and neck trauma to the practice of a plastic surgeon.

§ 31.15. Initial care.

Trauma to the head and neck may produce injuries of any of the soft or meaty tissues or to the underlying bony framework. Facial lacerations, contusions, and even fractures are rarely, if ever, of themselves, fatal injuries. The surgeon must be mindful of the possibility of occult injury to other more significant parts of the anatomy. A physical examination should be performed on any patient in whom there is any question of multiple trauma before undertaking treatment of injuries to the face and neck.

Other injuries take precedence

Intrathoracic (within the chest) injuries and intra-abdominal injuries should take precedence in any therapeutic plan before the repair of facial lacerations or fractures. Similarly, fractures of long bones should be reduced and splinted as soon as they are detected. One of the most important therapeutic measures in the management of any trauma victim is the assurance and maintenance of an adequate airway. Occasionally, patients with central facial and mandibular (lower jaw) fractures have partial to almost total occlusion (blockage) of the upper airway in the throat and back of the mouth due to the tongue and other soft tissues falling backward into the throat from the loss of the support of the facial bones. Such patients may require an artificial airway to the lungs by means of a tube (endotracheal tube) inserted through the nose, mouth, or a surgical incision in the lower portion of the neck into the trachea or windpipe (tracheotomy). In emergency care this is the first order of business to which every physician should direct his or her immediate efforts.

Once an adequate airway has been established, the second most important general measure is the prevention or treatment of shock. This will include the application of pressure dressings, and perhaps, in the case of extremities: tourniquets, clamps, and occasionally ligatures (threads) to stop very brisk arterial bleeding. Once hemorrhage has been controlled, an immediate effort should be made to establish a cannula (tube for blood transfusion) in a vein so that lost blood and fluids can be replaced. As a general rule, it is rare for patients to die from hemorrhage from lacerations about the face and neck, unless one of the major carotid arteries has been lacerated.

A physician treating head and neck trauma also must be mindful of possible brain damage, and he or she must be aware of the generalized and localizing signs of this injury. He should suspect skull fractures in any patient who has absorbed enough force to his head to sustain facial fractures. Skull X-rays are usually indicated. Also, in such cases the physician must always suspect an injury to the cervical spine. The neck should be examined routinely in all cases of head and neck trauma, and X-rays of the cervical spine may be indicated in the presence of any facial fracture with the possible exception of nasal fractures.

The treatment of patients with obvious brain injury necessitates careful observation. At one time, this examination precluded the use of any narcotic, sedative, or general anesthetic. Lacerations about the face and neck had to be repaired under local anesthesia, and the treatment of facial fractures deferred until any neurological damage had been evaluated, treated, and stabilized. (In general, the reduction and stabilization of most facial fractures is feasible within the first ten days to two weeks following injury — most neurosurgical problems will have stabilized long before this time). Today, however, the development of the pressure screw for the constant monitoring of cerebrospinal fluid pressure has made it safer to administer narcotics, sedatives, and general anesthetics to patients with obvious or suspected brain injury. With such monitoring, it has been shown that barbiturates may have a protective effect on the traumatized brain tissue. With careful monitoring of cerebrospinal fluid pressure, patients with suspected brain injury may now be anesthetized for surgery to reduce and stabilize facial fractures at an earlier time than was previously considered safe.[19]

Prevention of tetanus

Any patient with wounds or lacerations that penetrate the skin should be given routine tetanus prophylaxis injections. The risk of tetanus is

---

[19]Editor's Note: Brain injuries are discussed in Chapter 32 of this Cyclopedia.

greater in deep wounds that have been contaminated by soil, animal feces, or garden mold. Local wound care should include the excision of all obviously devitalized tissue, dirt, and foreign material.

A good guide for systemic tetanus prophylaxis has been provided by the committee on trauma of the American College of Surgeons. This can be briefly summarized as follows: persons immunized against tetanus within the past ten years should be given 0.5 cc. of adsorbed tetanus toxoid booster. Patients whose last tetanus shot was more than ten years prior to the injury, and whose wounds are of the type in which the risk for tetanus is high, should also be given, in addition to the booster, 250 units of tetanus immune globulin (human). Also with these patients the systemic use of penicillin or oxytetracycline should be considered. For individuals not previously immunized against tetanus, the basic immunization schedule should be started at the time of initial wound treatment. This consists of 0.5 cc. of adsorbed or precipitated tetanus toxoid (first immunizing dose), followed in four to six weeks with a second injection of 0.5 cc. adsorbed toxoid and repeated again in six to twelve months. This is considered adequate prophylaxis for clean, minor wounds in patients not previously immunized. For patients not previously immunized with larger wounds containing devitalized tissue, considerable dirt, or other contamination, it is also recommended that 250 units of tetanus immune globulin (human) be given and that penicillin and oxytetracycline be considered as well.

Equine tetanus antitoxin (horse serum) has now been replaced by the safer human tetanus immune globulin in most areas. The equine tetanus antitoxin should be given only if the tetanus globulin is not available within twenty-four hours, and the possibility of tetanus outweighs the danger of reaction to the horse serum. If the equine tetanus antitoxin is given, it is recommended that at least 3,000 units be given. If the patient is sensitive to horse serum by history or skin test, the equine tetanus antitoxin should not be given. To attempt to desensitize the patient to horse serum is not recommended.

§ 31.16. Lacerations and soft tissue injury.

(A) EXAMINATION

The initial part of the examination of a patient with soft tissue trauma about the head and neck should consist of a brief history: how, when, and where the injury was sustained. With patients who are unable to give this history, the physician should attempt to collect this information from any source available. Further questioning as to the patient's age, place of residence or employment, etc., serve to give the physician a gross appraisal of the patient's mental status. A brief history may also point out the need for further diagnostic studies: for example, a patient with a small laceration of the forehead sustained in a high-speed automobile accident would deserve a more thorough work-up (with X-rays) than a patient with an identical laceration caused by an accidental cut with a knife.

The wounds should then be carefully examined by observation and palpation before any sedative, drugs, or local anesthetic agents are administered, and before the remainder of the face or neck is obscured by the placement of sterile drapes. The skin around the wound and along the distribution of cutaneous sensory nerves should be carefully tested for loss of sensation. The muscle groups around the wound and along the distribution of the motor nerves should be carefully checked for muscular paralysis — indicative of motor nerve injury. This can be done by asking the patient to raise his eyebrows, close his eyes, grimace, purse the lips, or perform other feats of facial expression.

Palpation with the gloved hand in large deep lacerations may reveal fractures of the underlying facial skeleton. Foreign bodies within the wound may also be revealed by this maneuver. Unless excessive swelling of the soft tissues has occurred, most significant fractures of the facial skeleton can be detected, or at least suspected, by palpation with the hand. If the injury is close to the eyes, the eyes should be carefully examined, and at least a gross check of visual acuity should be made. Any damage to the ocular globe should be referred to an ophthalmologist as soon as possible. A complete gross physical examination may or may not be indicated, depending on the history obtained.

(B) PREPPING AND DRAPING

Following the examination, uncomplicated soft tissue lacerations and wounds should be cleansed, the surrounding skin prepared (prepped) with a germicidal solution, and the wound isolated from surrounding, unprepped skin with sterile drapes. Some prefer to anesthetize the wound locally by injecting local anesthetic agents into the wound edges before prepping and draping. Wounds should be thoroughly washed out and irrigated with physiologic salt solutions to remove all dirt and foreign bodies. For cleansing, various topical germicidal agents, detergents, or soaps can be used, but strong prep solutions, which might damage the eyes, should be used with great caution on the face, if at all. The object of the sterile drapes is to prevent contamination of the wound by not allowing the instruments or sutures to come in contact with the unsterile surroundings during wound closure. Drapes should be of sufficient size to accomplish this end.

(C) EQUIPMENT AND SUPPLIES

Simple lacerations about the head and neck can be repaired in any well-equipped emergency department. Complex injuries involving the salivary ducts, tear ducts, nerves, or eyelids, or fractures of the facial skeleton, are usually repaired in the general operating room.

Uncomplicated lacerations are usually repaired under local anesthesia. Three recognized idiosyncratic reactions may occur when using injectable local anesthetic agents: (1) extreme central nervous system stimulation leading to seizures; (2) hemorrhagic or neurogenic shock leading to vascular collapse; and (3) marked depression leading to respiratory arrest. Therefore, a physician using these agents should have readily available an injectable barbiturate drug to control excitation, an injectable vasopressor drug to support shock and vascular collapse, and an oxygen source with a mask or intubation set to provide support for breathing.

There should be a syringe and needles for the injection of the anesthetic. Closure of the wound will require forceps or skin hooks, a needle holder, scissors or a knife. Most emergency room trays contain several hemostats for the control of bleeding vessels. Sterile gloves for the operating surgeon are considered essential, and a mask for the surgeon is usually advisable. Suture material varies with the preference of the surgeon. Sutures larger than size 3-0 should not be used. Most lacerations about the face and neck should be closed with sutures in the 5-0 to 6-0 range.

(D) ANESTHESIA

Most uncomplicated soft tissue lacerations about the head and neck may be repaired under local anesthesia. The technique for small, simple lacerations is to infiltrate the tissues around the wound edges with an injectable, local anesthetic agent such as procaine or lidocaine containing concentrations of epinephrine in the range of 1 to 50,000 through 1 to 100,000. The epinephrine in the anesthetic agent serves to slow down absorption, decrease bleeding from the wound and skin edges, and prolong the effect of the anesthetic agent. Epinephrine in these concentrations may be safely used in any of the soft tissues of the head and neck. For more extensive or multiple lacerations, specific regional nerve blocks of the sensory nerves of the face may be performed using these same injectable local anesthetic agents. Extremely large or complicated wounds requiring extremely delicate repair, such as nerves, lacrimal ducts, salivary ducts, and eyelids, and fractures of the facial skeleton other than the nose, usually require general anesthesia. Extremely uncooperative or inebriated patients may also require general anesthesia.

(E) WOUND CLEANSING AND DEBRIDEMENT

All soft tissue wounds should be thoroughly irrigated with physiologic salt solutions prior to closure to remove excessive blood clots, devitalized tissue, dirt, or foreign bodies. The wound edges should be carefully re-

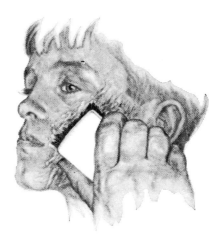

Fig. 9. Accidental tattoo. A scrub brush can be used to remove asphalt, dirt, grease, and gunpowder that has been ground into the skin. A No. 11 knife blade can also be used to remove deeply embedded particles. If all the pigment is not removed a permanent tattoo will result. (Courtesy of ETHICON, INC., Somerville, New Jersey).

tracted and every aspect of the wound explored. Attempts should be made to remove dirt ground into the skin in abrasion type injuries as this may produce a permanent blemish (traumatic tattoo). This dirt is best removed with a stiff brush or a "dermabrader" after the tissue has been anesthetized. **(Fig. 9.)**

In spite of the best efforts of competent physicians, it is not infrequent that small fragments of foreign material are left in deep and complicated lacerations. Bits of windshield glass following an automobile accident constitute one of the most frequently seen examples. Glass usually does not show on X-ray and may easily be missed in a deep, bleeding wound, particularly if the soft tissues have closed over it. Any foreign body left in a wound or laceration may carry with it bacterial organisms and serve as a source of infection. Therefore, all such debris should be removed if it can be found. All devitalized or detached tissue, with the possible exception of bone, should be removed from the wound as this tends to foster infection and retard healing. Ideally, a properly cleansed and debrided wound should contain only healthy, viable tissue at the time of closure.

(F) REPAIR

Properly cleansed and debrided soft tissue wounds about the head and neck may be safely closed without antibiotic coverage within the first eight hours. With systemic antibiotic coverage, such wounds may be safely closed within the first twenty-four hours. Wounds over twenty-four hours old should be dressed with wet dressings and the patient placed on systemic antibiotic therapy for three to four days. At this time, the wounds can be safely closed with a delayed primary closure. Antibiotics should then be continued for another five days. Small superficial

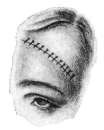

Fig. 10. Prevention of skin suture scars. Left: Wrong way. Suture scars are caused by tying sutures too tightly and leaving them in too long.

Right: Right way. Sutures should be tied just tight enough to approximate the wound edges, remembering that the tissues will swell with edema fluid. Sutures on the face can be removed by the fifth postoperative day, with alternate sutures even being removed on the third day. (Courtesy of ETHICON, INC., Somerville, New Jersey.)

wounds treated in this way may heal satisfactorily without a delayed closure. There is a generally recognized decreased tendency toward infection of wounds of the scalp, face, and neck presumably due to the abundant blood supply.

The suture repair of wounds about the head and neck should be accomplished as "atraumatically" as possible. Fine sutures should be used and they should be tied only tight enough to approximate (and not strangulate) the tissues. The sutures should be removed as soon as the wound has sufficient strength for the edges to remain approximated on their own. In general, most skin sutures can be removed from the head and neck by the fifth postoperative day. Alternate sutures may even be removed by the third day. Sutures in the hair-bearing portion of the scalp may be left for seven days. The typical "railroad tie" cross-hatching of a linear scar almost invariably is due to sutures that were too large, tied too tightly, left in place too long, or all of these. The byword for good cosmetic repair of facial lacerations is to use fine sutures with fine bites taken close to the wound edges, not tied too tightly, and to remove them as soon as they are no longer needed. **(Fig. 10.)**

Close skin edge approximation may be supported with adhesive tape strips following early removal of skin sutures. This is highly recommended. Superficial wounds require only a single layer closure of the skin. Deeper lacerations may require buried sutures. These are not removed. Some surgeons use absorbable sutures for the deep closure. Others prefer suture material that is not absorbed but remains in the deeper portions of the wound. It is important that the skin edges be approximated with a slight eversion of the wound edges. Later retraction of the scar, as it matures, will result in a flat, less noticeable scar. If the wound edges are approximated flat in an edge-to-edge fashion, or even worse, with a slightly rolled-in or inverted line of approximation, later scar contracture will produce a depression along the line of closure, making the scar more easily visible. Several well-known and easily performed suture techniques can readily accomplish this desirable eversion of the skin edges. Many surgeons prefer sutures of 3-0, 4-0, 5-0, or 6-0 Dexon, catgut, or nylon for approximation of the deeper tissues, and atraumatic sutures of 5-0, 6-0, or 7-0 nylon or silk for closure of the skin.

(G) SPECIAL WOUNDS

Multiple small glass cuts

Following federal legislation in 1965 that required the use of a thicker, more durable, middle layer in laminated automobile safety glass, the nature of facial lacerations caused by the victim's head striking the windshield was noted to change. Pre-1965 safety glass frequently allowed the victim's head to go completely through the windshield, causing large, flap-type lacerations about the head and neck as the weight of his body dragged his head back through the jagged opening. The newer, tougher, and more elastic safety glass rarely allows the victim's head to penetrate. The glass shatters into a myriad of crushed particles, which tend to remain attached to the plastic, middle layer. This extremely coarse and jagged abrasive surface tends to cause small and usually superficial lacerations over most of the skin surface. Small particles of glass may be driven into the skin and beneath it. These wounds require thorough cleansing and debridement and very careful exploration of each tiny wound to ensure that all particles are removed.

Many of these small lacerations are quite superficial and may not require suturing. Tiny, thin flaps of partial thickness skin may be elevated by these glass cuts. If properly dressed, these wounds occasionally will heal satisfactorily without suture. Larger wounds require careful exploration and suture closure.

If persistent irregular scarring results, patients with multiple, superficial, glass cuts about the face may be helped by abrading these areas with a dermabrasion cylinder (See § 31.23) after the wounds have completely healed.

Wounds with irregular edges

Slicing, tangential lacerations may produce wounds with beveled, irregular edges. The thin overlapping portion of the wound edge may be so thin as to be devitalized. Such wounds cannot be closed in the normal, everted manner, and where possible they should be sharply trimmed with scissors or a sharp knife to make the opposing skin edges square and of equal thickness at the point of approximation in wound closure. On the face, this trimming of precious skin must be moderated by a respect for preserving symmetry and balance in the facial features. The trimming of skin about the face should always be minimal, the general rule being that a secondary scar revision is always easier and the final results better when there is no deficit of tissue. Precious tissue about the nose, lips, and eyelids, if preserved and kept alive, may later prove invaluable at the time of scar revision. Small, thin flaps of tissue attached only by a frail, thin pedicle to the face may remain viable because of the abundant blood supply, where similar flaps in other regions of the body would not.

Trapdoor lacerations

These "U" shaped lacerations tend to heal with a central puckering or "pincushion" effect. All scars tend to shorten and contract somewhat during the process of wound healing and scar maturation. When the scar is in a semicircular or U-shaped configuration, shortening of the scar, as it contracts, tends to pucker the tissue in the central portion of the U as if it were caught within a constricting drawstring. Such wounds are probably best handled by primary closure of the wound as it appears and then a second operation at a later date to zigzag the edges to create angled closures along the line of the wound to break up the constricting effect of the contracting scar.

Wounds involving eyebrows, eyelids, nostril rims, and lips

Lacerations involving the eyebrows, eyelids, nostril rims, and lips require uncompromising exactness in realignment of the divided parts during wound closure. Eyebrows should never be shaved, since it is virtually impossible to properly realign the edges of a laceration through the eyebrow without the hairs. In addition, eyebrows grow at such an irregular and inconstant rate that the deformity from shaving the eyebrows may persist for a year or longer. In closing lacerations through eyebrows, it is wise to place the first several sutures at the upper and lower margin of the eyebrow to assure proper alignment. (**Fig. 11.**)

Eyelid lacerations may involve several important anatomical structures, a thorough knowledge of which is indispensable for the proper repair of eyelid lacerations. Suturing here must be extremely fine and exact. Any irregularity of the eyelid border produces a very noticeable deformity. Through-and-through lacerations of the lid should be closed in three layers: the conjunctical-tarsal layer (lining membrane on the inner aspect of the eyelid adjacent to the eyeball); the muscle layer; and the skin. The sutures should be very fine and placed so they cannot irritate the cornea of the eye as this may produce scarring and loss of vision.

Lacerations through the rim of the nostril require exact approximation of the nostril edge; here again, even the smallest irregularity in this

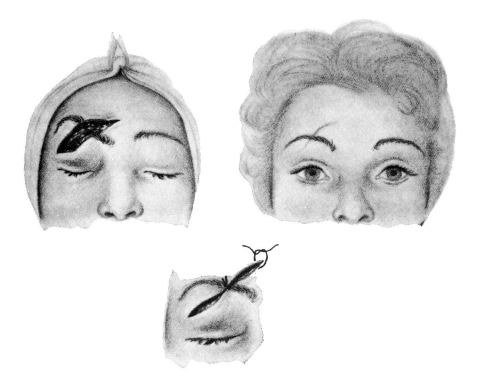

Fig. 11. Suturing eyebrow lacerations. Matching points on each side of the lacerated eyebrow should be aligned. It should be noted that the eyebrow hairs are slanted in a downward and outward direction. There is no reason ever to shave the eyebrow. (Courtesy of ETHICON, INC., Somerville, New Jersey.)

normally smooth line is very noticeable. It is recommended that the edges of the nostril rim be mortised with a V-shape cut on one edge to match a pointed shaped cut on the opposite edge, to provide a tongue-in-groove type closure. This tends to break up the straight line closure across the nostril rim, avoiding a notching effect due to scar contracture, thus serving to make the scar less noticeable.

Deep lacerations of the lips must also be carefully approximated as the line of juncture between the vermilion portion of the lip and the surrounding white skin provides another easily visible line that is extremely unforgiving of any irregularities in the closure. It is wise to determine carefully and accurately the vermilion cutaneous junction on either side of such a laceration and mark this point with a small, temporary tattoo of absorbable blue dye, such as methylene blue, prior to the injection of any local anesthetic agent. Any injections about the lip tend to fade out the color differential between the vermilion portion of the lip in the surrounding skin and make this line quite difficult to delineate. If this line is carefully determined before any injection, it is quite simple to

Fig. 12. Suture of lip laceration. The first suture should be placed at the vermilion-cutaneous border to obtain proper alignment. Deep scars in the vermilion of the upper lip tend to produce a redundancy of this tissue which usually requires a secondary wedge excision to revise it. (Courtesy of ETHICON, INC., Somerville, New Jersey.)

mark with a small hyperdermic needle dipped in methylene blue, and then thrust through the skin at the exact point of the vermilion cutaneous junction. Later, after the wound has been irrigated and debrided, these small dots of dye can be accurately approximated to each other with a single suture placed exactly through each dot, thus assuring accurate reapproximation of the vermilion cutaneous junction. (**Fig. 12.**) Because of the mobility of the mouth, lacerations through the lips frequently heal with contractures or areas of redundancy, which necessitate secondary scar revisions.

Avulsions

Larger areas of full thickness skin loss, which cannot be closed primarily without undue tension, should be closed with a split thickness skin graft. Split thickness skin grafts have a much better chance of taking and providing closure for the acutely traumatized wound than would a full thickness skin graft. After the wound has stabilized and healed, the split thickness skin graft can be excised and replaced with a full thickness skin graft or a flap for a better cosmetic result. Extensive avulsions and complex wounds may require multiple flap and grafting procedures to reconstruct lost parts.

Lacerations involving branches of the facial nerve

Deep wounds of the cheek or upper neck, from the level of the ear canal, posteriorly, to the region of an imaginary line dropped vertically from the outer angle of the eye, may divide major branches of the facial nerve. This nerve supplies motor innervation to the muscles of facial expression. When any branches of the facial nerve are divided, they should be repaired primarily within the first two to three days. During this period, the distal segment of the divided nerve is much easier to find because the muscles innervated by this segment of the nerve still respond to stimulation of the distal portion of the nerve. An electrical nerve stimulator is used as a probe in the wound and is a very significant aid in locating the distal end of the divided nerve.

After several days, response of the muscles to stimulation of the distal nerve segment with a nerve stimulator grows weak and variable and gradually disappears. The facial nerve, when repaired, shows remarkable regenerative powers, and results of facial nerve repair are generally considered among the best of motor nerve repairs. Successful results have been reported as late as two years following division of this nerve. Divisions of terminal branches of the facial nerve, anterior to the imaginary line dropped from the outer angle of the eye, are considered unnecessary and impractical. If the nerve is divided anterior to this line, spontaneous regeneration usually ensues. The tiny nerve filaments in this area are probably too small to repair without ultra-magnification and microsurgical techniques anyway. Nerve repair is usually accomplished by suturing the nerve sheath together with a number of very fine silk or nylon sutures. Following reapproximation of the nerve ends, regeneration of the nerve with eventual reanimation of the face occurs gradually and may take months for completion. Final results generally show some degree of residual weakness in the affected muscle group.

Lacerations involving the parotid salivary ducts

The parotid (Stensen's) duct runs from the major salivary gland, which is located in each cheek just anterior to the ear, forward through the cheek to emerge through a small papilla on the inner wall of the cheek, just opposite the upper second molar tooth. Divisions of this duct between the gland and its opening into the mouth may produce an external draining salivary fistula (opening). It is important to recognize this injury and to repair the duct primarily over a plastic tube with multiple sutures of silk or nylon. One of the major branches of the facial nerve runs in close juxtaposition with the parotid duct and, if divided, should be repaired. Divisions of the parotid duct should be suspected if salivary secretions are noted in deep, nonpenetrating wounds of the cheek, particularly if they increase with massage in the area of the parotid gland.

Divisions of the nasolacrimal duct system

Lacerations of the medial portions of the eyelids, about the inner canthus (angle at either end of slit between eyelids) of the eye, or along the lateral portion of the upper one-half of the nose, should point to the possibility of an injury to the nasolacrimal duct system. Such wounds should be carefully explored by dilating the lacrimal puncta near the medial angle of both the upper and lower eyelids and inserting probes into the duct system to see if they emerge into the wound. Colored solutions may also be injected through the puncta to see if these appear in the wound or drain normally into the nose. Similarly, radiopaque dyes may be injected and X-rays used to outline the entire nasolacrimal system. Divisions of any portion of the nasolacrimal duct system should be promptly repaired, primarily over a suitable nylon or polyethylene splint. These fine membrane-like ducts should be repaired with extremely fine sutures and splinted for an extended period to assure proper healing and maintain an open drainage system. Failure to repair results in blockage of the drainage of tears from that eye, and results in almost constant tearing. Totally successful results are difficult to obtain in the repair of these tiny, delicate structures.

Lacerations of the oral mucosa and tongue

These should be closed primarily. Deep lacerations involving muscle in the cheek or tongue should be closed in two layers using absorbable sutures in the muscles. Because of the wealth of pathogenic organisms in the human mouth, antibiotic coverage following closure of lacerations in this area is recommended. Extensive lacerations in this area may require the use of general anesthesia.

(H) SCAR REVISIONS AND LATE REPAIRS
(CORRECTIVE PLASTIC SURGERY)

Plastic surgeons are frequently called upon to "remove" scars resulting from traumatic lacerations. Actually, the terms "revise," "improve," or "minimize" would be more appropriate. Once the skin has been wounded to a depth sufficient to require healing by the formation of scar tissue, there will always be a scar of some sort in that area. Plastic surgeons can become quite adept at minimizing and camouflaging scars by techniques that tend to make the scars less visible. Surface irregularities can be smoothed out by careful wound approximation and by dermabrasion (See § 31.23). Scars that cross flexion creases and normal wrinkle lines can be redirected to lie within less noticeable normal skin lines. Sunken or depressed areas may be excised to give a smoother contour with a less visible deformity. Some results from surgical scar revision are truly impressive and, in favorable areas and with favorable tissue, scars can sometimes be made virtually invisible.

Patients are frequently referred to a plastic surgeon for revision of scars when the patient actually still has a healing wound. There is an inflammatory phase of wound healing that persists for many weeks and perhaps months following closure of the wound. It is generally agreed that scar revision during this period is undesirable. Most plastic surgeons prefer to wait until this phase of healing is complete, since they will be dealing with a softer, more pliable, mature scar in a bed of nonreactive, essentially normal surrounding skin. These scars are much more amenable to fine cosmetic revision, and the results obtained by late scar revision are generally superior to those from scars that have been revised too early. Unless scars are causing a gross deformity or limitation of function, a waiting period of several months is generally advisable prior to revision.

Scar revisions generally involve excision of the existing scar and closure of the resultant wound along the lines of relaxed skin tension or the natural crease lines in the skin. To accomplish this, the edges of the incision may be cut into tiny flaps that can be moved about and interdigitated to create closures that are zigzagged in configuration rather than formed in straight or curving lines. Such closure techniques are referred to as A-plasties or W-plasties. Subsequent dermabrasion or superficial shaving of the outer layers of the skin is often indicated as a secondary procedure following scar revision to produce a smoother surface at the site of the revision.

The development of a commercially available suspension of injectable bovine collagen (Zyderm) has provided plastic surgeons with yet another tool for flattening and thickening the skin in areas of depressed scars. The application of this material is limited to specific areas of the body, however. The effects of collagen injection may not be permanent, because some absorption of the material has been noted with the passage of time. Also, it cannot be used in patients allergic to bovine materials.

§31.17. Fractures of the facial bones.

Fractures of the facial bones usually result from blunt trauma (*e.g.*, automobile accidents and fights), and they tend to occur along fairly predictable lines of relative weakness in the facial bone structure. Most can be diagnosed, or at least suspected, by careful observation and palpation of the face and teeth. X-rays are usually taken to confirm the diagnosis and to establish a permanent record of the injury. Suspected fractures in different areas may require a number of X-ray projections to demonstrate adequately the bony detail in each area. No single X-ray projection is entirely adequate to demonstrate completely all possible abnormalities of the facial skeleton. (**Fig. 13.**) Nondisplaced fractures may be demonstrable only by X-ray and occasionally not even then. Physical examination should include also a check of the dental occlusion; the patient can tell quite readily whether his teeth come together in their usual occlusion.

Maxilla or mandible (jawbones)

Fractures of either the maxilla or mandible may produce dental malocclusion. Moderately displaced fractures in either the upper or lower dental arch can be readily observed. The inferior border of the mandible should be carefully palpated throughout its circumference. The examiner should check for irregularities of the bony surface, crepitance (crackling noise), or false motion. The area of the mandibular condyle, just anterior

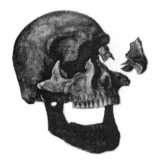

FACIAL BONE

Mandible
Condylar and coronoid processes, ascending ramus and body

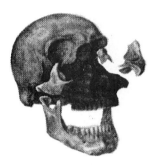

Maxilla and Zygoma
Symphysis, body and ascending rami

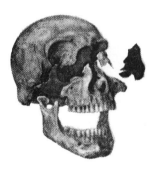

Zygomatic arch
Condylar and subcondylar

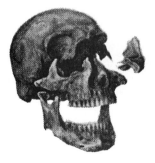

Nasal bone
Anterior mandible

Fig. 13. X-rays for suspected fracture of facial bones. (Courtesy of ETHICON, INC., Somerville, New Jersey.)

to the ear canal, should be carefully palpated for tenderness as the patient is asked to open and close his mouth. **(Fig. 14.)** Pain produced on this maneuver may be indicative of a condylar fracture. The examiner should grasp the anterior teeth or maxilla and attempt to move it up and down and in and out, while holding the head still. **(Fig. 15.)** Any motion of the maxilla independent of the head is indicative of a fracture.

Zygoma (cheek bone)

Fractures of the cheek bone (zygoma) may produce numbness of the cheek or upper lip on that side, visible depression of the cheek, lowering of the outer angle of the eyelids, and disturbances of vision. The area of the rim around the eyesocket should be carefully palpated with the finger for any bony irregularity or pain. **(Fig. 16.)**

Nasal bones

Fractures of the nasal bones are usually quite obvious on physical examination. There is usually swelling and displacement of the nose with marked tenderness and crepitation on palpation over the nasal bones. The nasal septum may be telescoped and driven under the nasal bones, producing shortening and uptilting of the nose. **(Fig. 17.)** Intranasal examination should be performed with a lighted speculum to determine deformity or hematoma (blood clot) formation within the nasal septum. If a septal hematoma is found, it should be promptly drained as this condition is prone to cause destruction of the nasal septum with a resultant "saddle nose" deformity. Severe nasal fractures may produce flattening and widening of the base of the nose and widening of the distance between the inner angles of the eyes.

Treatment

The treatment of facial fractures depends on their location, their displacement, and the general physical condition of the patient. Certain fractures require no treatment; these include fractures of the coronoid process of the mandible, stable undisplaced fractures of any facial bone (the patient with undisplaced fractures of the maxilla or mandible should be placed on a soft diet for one month), and simple fractures of the anterior wall of the maxillary sinus. Some fractures may be treated under local anesthesia in the emergency room. These include simple displaced fractures of the nasal bones and simple mandibular fractures that are treated by the application of arch bars and intermaxillary fixation (wiring the teeth together into occlusion, thus using the maxilla to stabilize the mandibular fracture). Some patients will require general anesthesia for this latter procedure, however. All other facial fractures should be treated in the operating room.

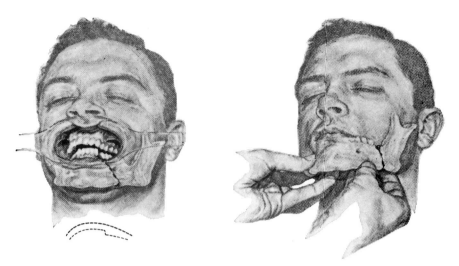

Fig. 14. Left: Occlusion of the teeth. The patient can readily tell whether his teeth come together in their usual occlusion. Abnormal occlusion may be due to a mandibular or maxillary fracture. Modernately displaced fractures can be readily identified by inspection of the teeth and alveolus.

Right: Palpation of the inferior border of mandible. The examiner's fingers can often palpate the step-like deformity of a moderately displaced mandibular fracture.

Below: Palpation of mandibular condyle. Subcondylar fractures are especially difficult to detect on examination. Pain upon palpation in this region when the jaw is being opened and closed must cause one to suspect a subcondylar fracture until proven otherwise by X-rays. (Courtesy of ETHICON, INC., Somerville, New Jersey.)

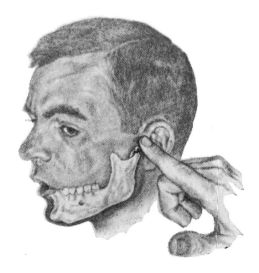

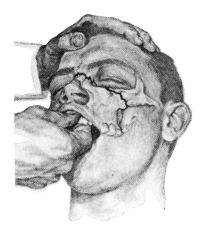

Fig. 15. Maxillary fractures. By grasping the anterior maxilla and attempting to move it in and out, a test of the solidity of the maxilla can be made. The fractured maxilla is usually quite freely movable. (Courtesy of ETHICON, INC., Somerville, New Jersey.)

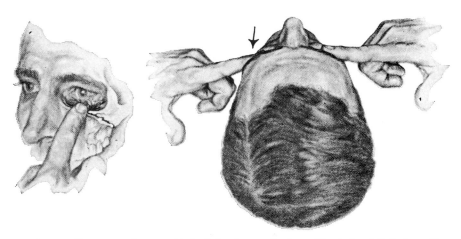

Fig. 16. Zygomatic fracture. Left: Palpation on the top of the infraorbital rim will easily reveal any separation of the zygomatico-maxillary suture lines. The fractured zygoma is commonly separated at its suture lines.

Right: By looking down over the patient's forehead the depression associated with a fractured zygoma can readily be seen by the level of the examiner's fingers resting on the malar eminence or lateral infraorbital rim. (Courtesy of ETHICON, INC., Somerville, New Jersey.)

Treatment of facial fractures must often be delayed while more serious injuries are stabilized. Also, if the patient has developed marked swelling of the facial soft tissues, open operations for the treatment of facial fractures are best delayed until this has been resolved. Any contraindication to general anesthesia such as a cerebral concussion or a full stomach, may also force delay of operative reduction and fixation of facial structures. Such delay is quite common. Most surgeons generally agree

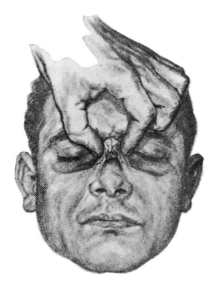
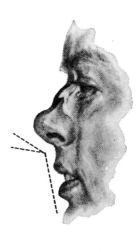

Fig. 17. Nasal fractures. Left: Palpation of the fractured nasal bones will usually reveal deformity and crepitus of these bones.

Right: Occasionally the fractured nasal septum is telescoped up and under the nasal bones. This deformity can be diagnosed by the increased naso-labial angle and the step deformity at the junction of the septum and nasal bones.

that facial fractures can be satisfactorily reduced and stabilized even after a delay of as much as two weeks after injury.

One of the most important requirements for the satisfactory treatment of facial fractures is the re-establishment and maintenance of normal dental occlusion. Even minimal irregularities of the teeth can cause great discomfort. Therefore, virtually all fractures of the upper or lower jaws are treated by wiring the teeth together (intermaxillary fixation) until the fractures have stabilized — usually four to six weeks. Certain fractures of the mandible also require open exposure of the fracture site and the placement of a steel wire directly across the fracture site through drill holes in the fracture fragments. Fractures of the upper jaw are usually further suspended by wires running down from the cheek bones or the bones at the margin of the orbit, downward to attach to the arch bars in the mouth. These wires prevent the upper face from sagging, opening the fracture site, and producing elongation of the face. Patients who have few or no teeth occasionally require the fabrication of temporary acrylic bridges, which are wired to the upper and lower jaws and fastened together with wires or rubber bands to maintain the proper occlusal relationship.

Fractures of the cheek bone (zygoma) usually require open surgical reduction and direct wiring. Extensively displaced fractures of this bone

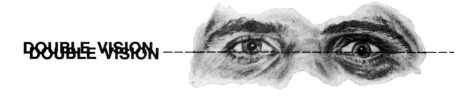

DOUBLE VISION

Fig. 18. Above: Diplopia (double vision) often accompanies a zygomatic fracture due to the eye on the fracture side being at a lower level. Diplopia is essentially severe on upward gaze.

Below: Anesthesia over the infraorbital nerve distribution due to contusion or laceration of the infraorbital nerve usually accompanies a zygomatic fracture. (Courtesy of ETHICON, INC., Somerville, New Jersey.)

occasionally cause shattering of the thin bones in the floor of the orbit. **(Fig. 18.)** Such fractures require exploration of the orbital floor with insertion of a thin implant on the orbital floor to prevent herniation of the fat around the eyeball into the maxillary sinus.

Beginning in the early 1980s, there has been a gradual trend toward the use of metal plates and screws in the fixation of facial fractures similar to developments in general orthopedic surgery. Small plates are usually fabricated from alloys of titanium, which larger plates are of stainless steel. Plating permits rigid fixation against the unrelenting pull of facial and jaw muscles. Long-term aesthetic and functional results are improved and prolonged immobilization of the jaw is often eliminated. Specially designed plates and eccentric screw positioning permits compression of bone fragments against each other, which greatly improves healing. The major disadvantage of plating is the necessity for larger access incisions and the expense and complexity of the proprietary plating systems.

One of the most challenging areas of reconstruction following facial trauma is the restoration of the proper level of the eyes and dealing with enophthalmos. This abnormal recession and lowering of the globe (eyeball) often necessitates correction by extensive exposure, release of the incarcerated globe, and restoration of orbital size and support through extensive bone grafting procedures.

Fractures of the nasal bones can usually be reduced by inserting an instrument in the nostrils and elevating the fracture fragments while molding them against external compression by the surgeon's other hand. These fractures are then further stabilized by the insertion of packing within the nose beneath the fragments and the application of an external splint, which is fixed to the nose with tape.

The development of miniature metal plates for the stable fixation of the displaced bony elements has in some ways revoluntionized the early treatment of facial bone fractures. In some cases, intermaxillary fixation will not be necessary due to the excellent stabilization attained by such miniature plates. Likewise, the exposure of these areas, sometimes employing a combined craniomaxillofacial approach, has afforded the surgeon much flexibility in the treatment of facial and craniomaxillofacial injuries.

Proper treatment of facial fractures should attempt to restore normal facial contour, re-establish and maintain proper dental occlusion, re-establish and maintain a normal nasal airway, and preserve functional mobility for the opening and closing of the jaws. Incisions placed in the face for the exposure of facial fractures should be placed in normal skin lines and closed with fine technique to minimize scarring.

V. COSMETIC SURGERY

§ 31.18. Introduction.

Surgery for the sole purpose of improving physical appearance is termed cosmetic surgery.[20] This type of surgery is growing rapidly in

---

[20] Editor's Note: After two years of debate, in 1974, the American Medical Association House of Delegates, approved an official AMA definition of "cosmetic surgery," intended to end confusion among physicians, insurance firms, and the public. The definition adopted is: "That surgery that is done to revise or change the texture, configuration, or relationship of contiguous structures of any feature of the human body which would be considered by the average prudent observer to be within the broad range of 'normal' and acceptable variation for age and ethnic origin; and in addition, is performed for a condition which is judged by competent medical opinion to be without potential for jeopardy to physical or mental health." *American Medical News,* December 9, 1974, p. 11.

Surgery for the sole purpose of improving the physical appearance of a "normal" individual is cosmetic surgery. Surgery which is performed to correct gross abnormalities of appearance caused by birth defects, trauma, cancer, or prior surgery is not cosmetic surgery because such patients are not "normal" to begin with. Cosmetic surgery, just like other cosmetics such as lipstick and eye shadow, is something applied to normal individuals in an attempt to make them feel as if they look better. Surgery performed to correct deformities or grossly abnormal appearing patients is "corrective" or "reconstructive" surgery. Most disputes between insurance companies and patients and physicians on this issue arise because of a lack of understanding of the true definition of cosmetic surgery. The AMA's defini-

popularity. Many older individuals feel the pressure to look younger to compete in the job market. Also, modern medicine and high standards of living are prolonging vigorous health well beyond arbitrarily assigned retirement ages. Many people seek cosmetic surgery merely to look better; to look as good to the rest of the world as they feel inside.

Younger individuals usually seek cosmetic surgery to alter some physical feature they think is unattractive. As we mature, we all develop a self-image, a personal concept of our bodies as we feel they appear to others. Any individual who feels his personal self-image is marred by his physical features is potentially a candidate for cosmetic surgery.

Cosmetic surgery patients are generally healthy. They come, not seeking a cure from disease nor restoration to health, but improvement in their appearance and in some cases relief from a personal, mental suffering. The psychological ramifications of cosmetic surgery are large and varied. This surgery, performed on the body to treat a distress of the mind, has been aptly termed psychosomatic medicine in reverse.

§ 31.19. Rhinoplasty.

Most patients seeking cosmetic rhinoplasty (plastic surgery on the nose) request a reduction in the size of the nose or of some of its topographical parts. Patients who request an augmentation or buildup in the size of the nose usually have some congenital or post-traumatic deformity that has either arrested growth or caused loss of bony or cartilaginous support. (Surgery for this latter group usually falls under the category of reconstructive or rehabilitative surgery, rather than cosmetic.)

Each patient who requests reduction rhinoplasty or cosmetic alteration of the shape of the nose has his or her own reasons for doing so. Most, however, believe that their noses are unattractive and are detracting from their general appearance. They invariably feel that altering the shape of the nose will improve their appearance and, hence, their acceptance by other individuals or society as a whole. Various external pressures, such as the ethnic implication, are often mentioned by patients seeking rhinoplasty.

It is most difficult for a patient who is unfamiliar with the techniques of rhinoplasty to describe to the surgeon exactly what changes he would like to have accomplished by surgery. The surgeon should attempt to extract this information prior to the operation, but ultimately the surgeon must determine the final shape at the time of surgery, tempered and modified by the patient's prestated desires. Most lawsuits following cosmetic rhinoplasty center about the surgeon having shaped a nose that the patient does not like. In these cases, the operation may be technically correct, and the final result may be pleasing to everyone except the

tion of cosmetic surgery states this quite
clearly.

patient. The surgeon, therefore, should strive to satisfy the patient's wishes rather than to produce what he or she considers a beautiful nose.

Technique and possible complications

Rhinoplasty may be performed under local or general anesthesia. The operative risk should not exceed the risk of the anesthetic method used. The incidence of postoperative complications is quite low. Postoperative hemorrhage may be seen, and if excessive, may require re-exploration or repacking of the nose. Infection is rarely seen, but when it occurs it may be disastrous. For this reason, antibiotics are recommended for five days following the operation. Another technical problem — resection of excessive cartilage or mucosal lining of the nose — may produce narrowing with obstruction of the nasal airway. This is a matter of judgment, but if too much tissue is resected, a secondary corrective operation may be required. Also, it is not unusual for patients to require a second "touchup" operation to correct minor asymmetries following a reduction rhinoplasty. Some surgeons routinely tell their patients that such a second minor procedure may be (or even will be) required.

In the classic rhinoplasty procedure currently used in the majority of operations, incisions are confined to the inside of the nose to avoid visible scars. The only external incisions are at the base of the nostril on either side, where a wedge of tissue may be excised if the surgeon believes the nostrils are too large or the lateral walls of the nostrils bulge outward too much following a reduction rhinoplasty. These small incisions are usually inconspicuous.

Through incisions within the nostrils, the skin over the dorsum of the nose is mobilized and elevated from the underlying bone and cartilage. This curving incision across the inner side of the dome of the nose is continued downward medially to expose the lower edge of the nasal septum, which divides the nasal cavity into two halves. The thin alar cartilages, which support the nasal tip and give it shape and form, may be exposed through these same incisions or through separate incisions placed closer to the rim of the nostril within the nasal vestibule. If the alar cartilages are too large, portions may be resected. If they are cleft and spread apart, they may be sutured together in the midline to add definition to the nasal tip. Removal of portions of the alar cartilage or modification of their shape allows the skin of the tip of the nose to drape inward to reduce the width of a bulbous tip. Excessive or total removal of these thin supporting cartilages may cause the nasal tip to appear pinched and may allow a collapse of the alar rims, producing inspiratory nostril obstruction. Varying amounts of nasal mucosa or lining may be removed along with portions of the alar cartilages, but excessive removal of lining mucous membrane may also cause narrowing of the nostril opening.

The tip of the nose may be elevated or tilted upward by resecting a wedge-shaped piece of cartilage from the lower border of the nasal septum. Excessive septal resection will produce too much uptilt and a "pug" nose. This effect is usually pronounced immediately following a rhinoplasty, but with time the tip tends to droop downward slightly. Therefore, patients are advised to wait several months following a rhinoplasty before assessing the final results.

If the nasal angle is satisfactory, but the nose is too long, a rectangular piece of cartilage may be excised from the lower portion of the nasal septum to allow for shortening. Some combinations of shortening and angle modification are usually indicated. The dorsal, nasal hump is removed with a saw or with a combination of scissors, a knife, and an osteotome. The upper portion of the hump is usually comprised of bone, while the lower portion is softer, nasal cartilage. Removal of the hump leaves the dorsum of the nose flat, much like the results of sawing off the top few feet of the roof of an A-frame house. Cuts must be made in the nasal bones on the sides of the nose so that the lateral walls can be compressed and fractured inward to again bring the edges of the bones on the dorsum of the nose together again to establish the A-frame effect and re-establish a thin, narrow ridge along the nasal dorsum. Following this maneuver, any irregularities of the bony surface can be smoothed with a rasp.

If the nasal reduction has been large, or if the tip is lowered significantly, the walls of the nostrils may flare outward, causing the nostril openings to appear too large. This can be corrected by full thickness wedge excisions of the skin and soft tissue from the lateral portions of the nostril floors. Incisions are closed with fine sutures and nasal packs are inserted in the nostrils on either side, and some form of rigid splint is applied over the outside of the nose and secured to the face, usually with tape.

There is usually some bleeding from the nose following a rhinoplasty, but this should not be excessive. There is almost always swelling of the cheeks and some bruising about the eyelids, but this usually resolves within two weeks. Some minor swelling may persist up to six weeks. After this, very little change will occur in the shape of the nose.

Unsuccessful rhinoplasties can result from both technical mistakes and errors of judgment. One of the most common mistakes is to resect too much tissue from the components of the nose — the dorsum, alar cartilages, or septum — an error that can result in both cosmetic and functional deformities. The defects that most often make the nose look unnatural are a shallow nasofrontal angle; an over-shortened nose; an over-reduced dorsum, which creates a "parrot's beak" deformity; and a round nasal tip with a short interdomal length that lacks definition. Furthermore, a deformity in one area of the nose is likely to affect other areas; for example, over-resection of the dorsum may also affect the tip of the nose. Usually, grafting is required to correct a nose that has been over-resected.[21]

Some patients have functional, anatomical abnormalities, such as obstruction to the nasal airway or to the drainage of the sinus cavities, which may require surgical correction at the time of a cosmetic rhinoplasty. In such case, the operation obviously is not entirely cosmetic in nature and may be properly billed, on a prorated basis, to health insurance companies as necessary (nonelective) surgery.

Open rhinoplasty

Although the traditional "closed rhinoplasty" described above has been the dominant technique in use since its development over one hundred years ago, the procedure has inherent limitations. Working through small incisions, surgeons are constrained in visualizing the underlying bones and cartilage of the nose. Symmetrical adjustments to these structures are often difficult, and placement and fixation of bone and cartilage grafts are hampered by the limited access.

Open rhinoplasty minimizes these limitations by exposing the entire nasal skeleton with minimal external incisions and scars. Incisions are made in the creases at the base of each nostril, and a third incision is made across the vertical skin structure (columella) that separates the nostrils. This permits the skin cover of the nose to be pulled upward toward the forehead, completely exposing the underlying structures. These structures may then be modified or augmented as necessary. The skin is replaced and the external incisions closed.

Advocates of open rhinoplasty claim improved results over the closed procedure, particularly when encountering difficult and unusual problems. The incisions in the nostril creases are no different than those used to reduce nasal width in traditional rhinoplasty, and the columellar scar heals reasonably well. On the downside, however, are the increased length and complexity of the surgery, increased healing time, and prolonged swelling. The open procedure is most commonly used on the noses of individuals with cleft lips, instances where previous operations or trauma have resulted in missing bone or cartilage, and in cases where the nasal tip is unusually flat or curved downward.

§ 31.20. Facial implants.

Mentoplasty

Many patients seeking reduction rhinoplasty also have a receding chin. Correction by augmentation "mentoplasty" enables the attainment of better balance and symmetry to the face. On profile, a large nose is

---

[21] Aiach, G., and Monghan, P., *Treatment of Over-Reduction of the Nose and Subse-* quent *Deformities*, 33 Br. J. Oral Maxillofac. Surg. 250 (Aug.), 1995.

accentuated by a receding chin. In some cases, reduction of the nose to match the receding chin is impossible, but progress in implantable prosthetics has given the surgeon a number of materials that may be implanted in the soft tissues anterior to the bone of the chin. This can greatly improve the patient's profile.

The most frequently used implants are silicone rubber or sponge. They may be inserted through external incisions beneath the chin, or through a hidden incision in the sulcus behind the lower lip. A pocket is developed in the soft tissues anterior to the periosteum covering the chin, and the implant is placed in the pocket, which is then closed with sutures.

The most feared complications of this procedure are infection and exposure of the implant through the wound, but with proper aseptic technique and antibiotic coverage, these complications are rarely seen. Silicone chin implants are available from a number of commercial distributors in varying sizes and shapes. Some surgeons prefer to cut and shape their own implants from silicone rubber or sponge, tailoring the implant to the needs of the individual patient.

Long-term follow-up studies on the fate of these implants have demonstrated that almost invariably they tend to erode the anterior surface of the bone of the chin and, over a number of years, gradually sink into the surface of the chin bone. This is believed to be due to the extra pressure exerted on the bone by the implant over a prolonged period. Such "sinking of the implant" eventually tends to negate the effects of the chin augmentation. This sinking effect is variable in degree in different patients, but seems to be less if the implant is placed outside the periosteum covering the bone of the chin.

Using nonporous silicone implants, plastic surgeons are now building up cheekbone areas and adding definition and width to "weak" jaws without having to make incisions on the patient's face. Instead, surgeons insert cheek and jaw implants through the inside of the patient's mouth. In addition to no scarring, in most cases recovery time is four weeks or less. About 95% of these implant patients are told by their surgeons that the results should last a lifetime. The remaining 5% may need more surgery to correct position or size.[22]

§ 31.21.   Face-lift.

This procedure may be called a "rhytidectomy." (A rhytid is a wrinkle; rhytidectomy, then, means to remove wrinkles.) However, face-lift is probably a better term, since the procedure does more to uplift sagging skin than to remove fine wrinkles. Both results are seen to a greater or lesser degree. Patients seeking the facelift are generally middle-aged or

---

[22] Seligson, S. V., *The Changing Face of Cosmetic Surgery*, 11 Health 87 (Mar.), 1997.

older individuals who desire to look younger. In most cases, a well performed procedure will accomplish this goal.

Contraindications

The contraindications in face-lift surgery include any physical disease or infirmity that might preclude major surgery. A second major contraindication that should always be considered is emotional instability. Some surgeons require psychiatric evaluation of all patients seeking cosmetic surgery, but this is impractical in some communities because of the shortage of competent psychiatrists. A plastic surgeon must, therefore, frequently rely on his or her own opinion regarding the psychic makeup of a patient. If the patient's expectations regarding the surgery are unrealistic, severe mental stress and depression may result from a perfectly performed operation. Careful exploration of the patient's life situation and reasons for wanting any form of cosmetic surgery, is very important in the preoperative evaluation.

Procedure

To elevate and tighten the skin about the face and neck and thereby reduce sagging and smooth out wrinkles, incisions must be made to permit the surgeon to "undermine" the skin — free it from its attachments to the underlying structures. The incisions are usually placed so that, as far as possible, they will not show, but these incisions, like all others, will leave scars. The final appearance depends not only on the skill of the surgeon, but also to a great deal on the patient's age, skin texture, and ability to heal.

In the usual face-lift, incisions on each side run from within the hair-bearing scalp in the region of the temples, above and just in front of the ears and downward just in front of the ears to the lobule at the inferior portion of the ear. The incision then curves upward in the groove of the ear. Approximately midway up behind the ear, the incision curves gently upward, backward, and then downward either to parallel or to enter the hairline behind the ears. All dissection is then anterior and downward from this incision. The skin is undermined and elevated from its bed as a very thin flap. Small bleeding vessels are controlled with ligatures or the electrocautery.

Care must be taken to avoid cutting, cauterizing, or ligating branches of the facial nerve that runs on the surface of the facial muscles within the fat. This nerve must be carefully dissected from the back side of the skin. The sensory nerve to the lower portion of the ear lies superficially just beneath the skin, behind and below the lobule of the ear. The skin flap must be dissected very thin in this area to avoid injury to this nerve.

The undermining of the skin may be carried as far anteriorly as the nasolabial fold (the crease running from the nose down just lateral to the mouth) on the face to a line dropped vertically from the outer angle of the mouth on the chin, and to the midline beneath the chin on the neck. This degree of undermining is the maximum; to undermine further anteriorly would distort the mouth and nostrils. Usually, a lesser degree of undermining than this is done.

After the skin flaps have been completely detached from the underlying structures, the skin of the face and neck is pulled backward and upward, overlapping the ear and the posterior edge of the incision. Here, a judgment decision must be made as to the proper tension to be placed on the skin. If it is pulled too tight, the blood supply to the skin edges may be compromised, causing necrosis and loss of skin. If it is left too loose, the effects of the face-lift will be lessened. After pulling the skin backward and upward to the desired degree, the excess skin around the ear is trimmed away. The resultant wounds are closed with sutures under slight tension. Some surgeons leave drains or suction catheters beneath the skin flaps at the time of closure. Usually, some form of compression dressing is placed over the area undermined and over the sites of incision closure. Care must be taken in the application of this dressing to avoid too much pressure over the edges of the skin flaps and over the ears. The drains are removed in a few days, and the sutures are usually removed in five to fourteen days.

In recent years, variations in the procedure for a face-lift have come into wide use by cosmetic surgeons. In an attempt to provide better and longer lasting support for the sagging facial skin, many surgeons now plicate or "reef up" the deeper layers of the fascia over the cheeks to suspend them in an elevated posterior position with sutures. This deeper layer, which is now frequently tightened, is termed the superficial musculo-aponeurotic system (SMAS). Many surgeons also dissect out the posterior portion of the platysma muscle, which lies immediately beneath the skin over the upper neck and lower face, and pull this muscle posteriorly and superiorly to tighten and better support the skin of the neck and lower face. Some surgeons routinely excise all possible subcutaneous fat in the lower face and neck. Also, procedures have evolved for removing this fat through hollow cannulas by a suction technique (See § 31.27), which some surgeons have combined with the usual face-lift surgery. When properly performed, these and other adjunctive techniques can improve the results of face-lift surgery; however, each also carries with it increased risk of complications.

Many plastic surgeons are now offering *endoscopic* face-lifts and brow-lifts to minimize the trauma of the procedure and recovery time. Use of an endoscope — a tube fitted with a miniature camera that is inserted into the tissue through tiny slits in the skin — does reduce the number and size of the incisions required for the procedure; however, some surgeons recommend limiting endoscopy to brow-lifts on the grounds that face-lifts require more control and visibility, which can usually be provided only with the larger incisions used in traditional facial surgery.[23]

Injections of soft tissue fillers such as collagen (a naturally occurring protein, usually obtained from cattle) and fat (taken from the patient's own body) to "plump up" facial skin can cause surface wrinkles, skin depressions, and scars to seem to disappear, and can make the patient's lips appear fuller. However, the effects are usually temporary, lasting from a few weeks to a year. The duration of the effects is nearly impossible to predict and seems to be determined in part by the patient's age, genetic background, skin quality, lifestyle, and the location of the area treated. Also, the patient faces the risk of an allergic reaction to the collagen, as well as the risk of infection, abscesses, open sores, skin-peeling, scarring, and lumpiness.[24]

Complications

Following a face-lift, a patient can expect some swelling and discoloration of the skin, particularly about the lower cheeks and upper neck, due to small amounts of blood deposited beneath and within the skin flaps. This is usually absorbed and clears within a few weeks. Patients usually note some decreased sensation in the posterior parts of the cheeks in front of the ears, and this may last for several months. Some decreased sensation of the ear lobules may be present for several weeks. Prolonged numbness of the lower half of the ears indicates severance of the sensory nerve to this area, in which event sensation in the area may be decreased for six months to a year.

The major complications of face-lift surgery include: (1) accidental damage of branches of the facial nerve in the course of dissection, cautery, or ligature of vessels; (2) skin loss attributable to excessive tension on the wound edges, or to elevating the flaps of skin too thinly, or to excessive pressure from the dressing; (3) excessive hemorrhage with hematoma (blood clot) formation within the wound; and (4) rarely, infection. Also, a face-lift, although usually performed under local anesthesia, is a major operation and may be followed by most of the complications of major surgery.

§ 31.22. Blepharoplasty.

Cosmetic surgery on the eyelids to remove wrinkles, excessive sagging skin, or "bags" is called a blepharoplasty. Eyelid changes typically precede, and may be more apparent, than aging of the face itself. Thus, blepharoplasty is often performed years before a face-lift would be appropriate. This is particularly true when "bags" under the eyes are the main problem, a condition that often develops as early as the twenties or

---

[23] *If You Are Considering Cosmetic Surgery*, 8 Johns Hopkins Med. Ltr. 4 (June), 1996.

[24] Id.

thirties. The executive or professional wishing to avoid an aging or tired appearance will usually opt for the relative simplicity and rapid recovery of a blepharoplasty. In older patients though, both blepharoplasty and face-lift are frequently indicated, and most surgeons will perform the blepharoplasty at the time of the face-lift, although some prefer to separate the procedures, usually performing the blepharoplasty first.

Occasionally, blepharoplasty may be indicated to correct hereditary conditions or the effects of disease. A hereditary condition called blepharochalasis produces marked excessive redundancy of the eyelid skin that may be so great as to interfere with vision. Severe hypothyroidism and a condition called myxedema may likewise produce large drooping folds of eyelid skin. Posttraumatic defects may also require correction by blepharoplasty. Blepharoplasty, therefore, is by no means always a cosmetic procedure.

There are three major correctable features that may be present in and about the eyelids of patients seeking blepharoplasty: (1) sagging or drooping of the eyebrows (usually due to normal process of aging); (2) loose, sagging, redundant skin of the upper or lower eyelids (usually due to hereditary factors governing the elasticity of the skin that tends to increase with age); and (3) herniations of orbital fat that produce rounded bulges and areas of swelling within the upper or lower lids (the eyeball rests on a cushion of globular fat that may bulge through weakened portions of the muscles and deep structures to present puffy areas of swelling just beneath the skin of the upper or lower eyelids). Patients may have any one or all three of these features.

Procedure

As an independent procedure, blepharoplasty is usually performed under local anesthesia, most often with oral or intravenous sedation. When performed in conjunction with another procedure, such as a face and/or brow lift, the type of anesthesia recommended for the dominant procedure will be used.

There has been an ongoing recognition that much of what might be thought of as excessive upper-eyelid skin is in reality the result of drooping (ptosis) of the eyebrows. In may cases, blepharoplasty may be combined with the brow lift. To avoid excessive eyelid skin resection with subsequent lid closure problems, the amount of eyelid skin to be resected is re-estimated after completion of the brow lift. The older procedure of correcting brow ptosis by removing a strip of skin above the eyebrows is seldom performed today. In any event, the final upper-lid incision ideally should lie hidden within the lid fold.

Whether general or local anesthesia is used, dilute concentrations of epinephrine are usually injected into the skin of the upper and lower lids to decrease bleeding. After the marked-out portion of excessive skin is removed from the upper lid, all small bleeding vessels are carefully coagulated with a fine electrocautery. If fat pads are to be dissected, the layers of muscle within the eyelid are carefully split along the direction of the fibers, and the protruding fat pads are dissected out and excised. The pedicle of the fat pads usually contains a small blood vessel that must be either ligated or cauterized. The muscle, if split along the direction of the fibers, will close spontaneously and need not be sutured. The skin edges of the wound in the lid are approximated with fine sutures, which are usually removed in two to five days. The lower lid incision usually runs just beneath the lower eyelashes. Both the upper and lower incisions may extend out lateral to the eye in the natural "crows feet" lines. Medially, the incisions in both the upper and lower lids should not extend beyond the lacrimal puncta (tiny openings on the edge of the eyelids through which tears drain), since incisions medial to these points may interfere with tear drainage.

From the incision beneath the eyelashes on the lower lid, the skin is usually dissected off of the muscle, downward toward the cheek for approximately three-fourths of an inch. Again, if fat pads are to be dissected, the muscle of the eyelid is split along the direction of the fibers and the fat is dissected out and removed. Here, some feel it unwise to close the deeper structures of the lid with sutures, as this may tend to pull the lower lid downward away from the eyeball. The skin of the lower lid is stretched upward and laterally with very, very slight tension, and the excess skin along the upper margin is trimmed away. This incision is likewise closed in a single layer with fine sutures, which are removed in two to five days. Some surgeons place an additional suture in the lower lid, near its free edge, which is then taped to the forehead with very slight tension to support the lower lid during the first few days of healing. Following blepharoplasty some surgeons apply compression dressings over the eyelids for the first few days to minimize bleeding and swelling.

For individuals in whom lower lid puffiness from protruding fat pads is the predominant problem, *trans-conjunctival* lower lid fat resection can be performed. Rather than incising the skin beneath the lashes, surgery is performed through an incision on the inside surface of the lid, and a shield is inserted temporarily to protect the eye. Minor lid skin wrinkles may simultaneously be treated with a chemical or laser "peel." (See §§ 31.24, 31.24a.)

Techniques have also been developed to minimize the tendency of the lower lid to droop slightly after an apparent well-performed operation to remove excess lower lid skin. These techniques include suspending lower lid muscle tissues lateral to the corner of the eye, relocating the tissues at the corner of the eye, and tightening the lower lid by a wedge resection.

Complications

Control of bleeding must be meticulous and complete. Hematomas (blood clots) developing within the lids following wound closure may produce swelling and discoloration for many weeks. If too much skin is resected from either the upper or the lower eyelids, the lid may be pulled away from the eyeball (a condition called ectropion), which causes irritation. If this is mild, it will usually correct itself within a few weeks, since all the swelling goes away and the skin stretches. If excessive, it may necessitate reoperation and the use of flaps or grafts to release the everted lid. If the lid is pulled away from the eyeball, it tends to cause excessive tearing and "watering" of the eyes. Sutures left in too long may cause small, white cysts within the skin of the eyelids at the site of the suture marks. There have been reports of loss sight following blepharoplasty; however, virtually all of these cases were associated with other systemic disease processes at the time of surgery. Infection is rarely seen.

§ 31.23. Dermabrasion.

In dermabrasion, the outer layers of the skin are literally "sanded down," usually with power-driven, rotating cylinders of sandpaper, diamond dust emery wheels, or wire brushes. The epidermis and part of the dermis is abraded away and surface irregularities and superficial marks within the skin, including fine wrinkles and freckles, are removed. This, of course, produces a raw surface to the skin, which requires one to two weeks to heal with new, thin, pink skin. Meanwhile, there is always scabbing and crusting about the abraded area. Usually, the skin is well enough within two weeks to allow the application of cosmetics. Dermabrasion can be performed satisfactorily under local anesthesia in small regional areas; however, if the entire face is to be abraded, general anesthesia is recommended.

Dermabrasion is frequently used in the treatment of post-acne scarring and usually some benefit is obtained; however, the results are rarely dramatic and patients may be disappointed. Dermabrasion is not a "magic eraser" for scars, but it can help to camouflage them by removing surface irregularities and blending them into the surrounding skin. The procedure also has been used for the removal of superficial tattoos, superficial nevi, and fine wrinkles about the mouth in elderly patients; in this last case, however, it is generally agreed that the process has a relatively transitory effect.

Immediate complications of dermabrasion consist of abrading too deeply into the skin and producing scars. Also, great care must be taken when abrading about the lips, nostrils, or eyelids, as these structures may be easily caught up in the rotating disc. Dermabrasion of eyelids is not recommended. Superficial infection in a thick, crusting scar following dermabrasion may cause deepening of the tissue lost and additional scarring. Many patients will develop multiple, tiny, white cysts within the abraded skin due to the rapid healing-over of skin pores. These cysts (milia), may require treatment with abrasive soaps, but usually disappear within six months. Dermabrasion removes much of the pigment-producing layer of the skin, and alters the ability to tan when exposed to the sunlight. Also, problems of increased pigmentation may be encountered also, with exposure to the sun. Patients should be counseled to avoid sunlight for three to six months. Sunscreen creams are advisable for this period. Some redness of the abraded skin usually persists for several months following a dermabrasion. This gradually fades and can usually be covered with cosmetics starting approximately two weeks following the dermabrasion.

§ 31.24. Chemical face-peel.

Chemical face-peeling may be used for treatment of fine wrinkling, abnormal pigmentation, damage due to radiation, freckles, superficial acne scarring, and hyperkeratoses (hypertrophy of the corneous layer of the skin). The technique consists of applying an acid solution to the skin, which produces an injury to the outer layers, much like a superficial burn. The outer tissues then peel away and, as the wound heals, there is a smoothing and tightening effect in the treated skin.

Techniques and solutions vary with physicians. Solutions of phenol or trichloracetic acid have been the most popular. An exact concentration of the solution is very critical since this determines the depth of tissue injury. Solutions of too strong a concentration may produce a deep burn with resultant scarring. Usually, waterproof adhesive tape is applied over the treated area immediately following application of the chemical solution, and left in place for forty-eight hours. The tape is then removed along with the superficial layer of the skin, leaving a raw, weeping surface much like a second-degree burn. This surface is usually treated with the application of topical bacterostatic powder, which is incorporated into a crust over the wound. The crust usually separates in several days with gentle washing of the skin. The face is usually quite swollen for several days following application, and the eyes are usually swollen shut. There is considerable discomfort during application of the solution, on removal of the tapes, and for several weeks or until all of the crusting has come off. It is usually three to four weeks following a face-peel before cosmetics can be applied. Following a face-peel, problems of abnormal pigmentation are encountered with exposure to the sun. The small, white, cystic milia seen following dermabrasion may also be present.

Chemical peeling can provide excellent results in the removal of fine wrinkles about the mouth or eyelids, and good results have also been obtained in treating fine wrinkles over the remainder of the face. But if chemical peeling is to be used as an accepted treatment modality, there can be no compromise in the exactness of the preparation of the solutions, the technique of application, and after-care of the wound. In addition, the patient must avoid sunlight for three to six months following treatment. Complications also include: decreased pigmentation in the treated area (bleaching effect); a general increased sensitivity to the sun; scarring; milia; prolonged redness of the skin; and adverse alteration of existing skin conditions.

§ 31.24a. Laser resurfacing.

Using a "pulsating laser," plastic surgeons can obtain results similar to a chemical peel, but during the procedure they can maintain more control over the depth of the peel than is possible with chemicals. Proponents of laser resurfacing point to other advantages over chemical peels: (1) the heat from the laser tightens collagen; (2) the recovery time for laser resurfacing is slightly shorter than for a peel; and (3) unlike chemical peels, which are not recommended for dark-skinned patients because of the tendency of the chemicals to sometimes lighten the skin, laser resurfacing is less likely to alter skin tone.[25] The major problem with laser resurfacing appears to be a prolonged redness of the skin that may persist for many months.

§ 31.25. Augmentation mammaplasty.

Augmentation mammaplasty may take the form of either a cosmetic procedure that provides an immediate improvement for women with small, drooping (ptotic), or asymmetric breasts, or as a reconstructive procedure — one of several available for the correction of defects that result from full or partial mastectomy. (See § 31.26a.) In the more common cosmetic version (80% of operations), an implant is placed either behind the breast or behind both the breast and the muscles of the chest wall. In reconstruction, the implant almost always lies beneath whatever chest wall cover remains following the ablative surgery.

From its inception in the mid-1960s through today, the breast implant has undergone a continuing evolution in shape, material, and construction, primarily in response to the overriding requirement that the implanted breast remain soft long after surgery. Early implants were composed of relatively firm silicone gel (a polysiloxane polymer) encased in a relatively thick silicone shell molded into a teardrop shape. Because pioneering surgeons believed that implants might shift or migrate, Decron™ patches were attached to the backs of implants to assure firm adherence to the chest wall. These implants were overly firm and tended

---

[25] Seligson, S. V., *The Changing Face of Cosmetic Surgery*, 11 Health 87 (Mar.), 1997.

to maintain their stereotypical breast-like shape regardless of body position. In response, manufacturers eliminated the patches and drastically decreased both shell and gel thickness. While in many cases the results were less firmness, there was a tendency to rupture. We now know that virtually all of these early soft implants eventually ruptured or at least leaked, either during or after (sometimes long after) the operation.

Despite the softness of these implants, "capsular contracture" remained a significant problem in from 5% to 50% of patients, depending upon the study methodology. In capsular contracture, the scar capsule that normally develops around any implanted device thickens and contracts and causes the breast to feel firm and often appear artificially round and tight. Innumerable theories and remedies have been proposed and tested in pursuit of a cure for capsular contracture. Because silicone gel may "bleed" through its implant shell, leaving an oily surface film, many surgeons have long believed gel-bleed to be an etiologic factor in capsular contracture. Attempts at implants with special impervious shells, or saline rather than gel-filled ("inflatable" implants), or multichambered gel-inflatables have not solved the problem. Another tack has been to alter the smooth surface of the implant, either by applying a polyurethane foam or by physically texturing the silicone shell. Hopes here were high, but any evidence of marked improvement in the rate of capsule formation has been questionable at best. In addition, subclinical infection became a problem, with various pre-, intra-, and postoperative antibiotic regimes having little success.

Unable to develop a contracture-free implant, surgeons have tried placing implants submuscularly behind the pectoralis major muscle rather than directly behind the breast. Unfortunately, any improvement in the contracture rate from this approach comes at the expense of breasts that appear unnaturally "full" superiorly or dynamically deformed by contraction of the pectoralis. Although surgeons are almost equally divided as to the ideal location for the implant, they no longer have a choice of implant composition because the FDA removed gel-filled implants from the market in 1993, leaving only saline inflatables available for cosmetic procedures. In the same year, polyurethane foam-covered implants were voluntarily withdrawn by the manufacturer. These events occurred in response to as yet unproven legal and medical claims that silicone gel somehow leads to connective tissue disorders and that polyurethane is carcinogenic.

Procedure

Cosmetic augmentation mammaplasty is an outpatient procedure and may be performed either under local anesthesia with sedation or general anesthesia. The most common incisions are *inframmary* (along the crease beneath the breast), *periareolar* (semicircularly above the areola), and *transaxillary* (through the axilla (armpit), often with endoscopic assistance). As mentioned earlier, some surgeons place the implant beneath the breast, while others place it submuscularly. In either event, an ample pocket is created using blunt and sharp dissection. Fiberoptic illumination and the electrocautery are essential, as is the infiltration of local anesthetic containing epinephrine for hemostasis. Many surgeons irrigate the pocket with antibiotics, antiseptics, or (to forestall contracture), steroids. Meticulous wound closure is the rule, as is the use of gentle postoperative breast compression with some type of brassiere.

Reconstruction of a missing breast. There are several ways to reconstruct a missing breast. The most popular methods are insertion of an implant; balloon expansion of the soft tissues over a period of weeks followed by insertion of the mammary prosthesis; conversion of the expander to a permanent prosthesis; or a variety of soft tissue operations utilizing the patient's own tissues or a combination of implant and their own tissues.

Reconstructive mammaplasty can be performed immediately after a mastectomy several months later. Currently, there is a strong trend toward immediate reconstruction. Usually the implant is placed partially or totally beneath the pectoralis and other chest wall muscles. "Expander implants" are available that include a buried, self-sealing valve that permits gradual inflation of the implant over a period of time. (The skin and muscle cover is usually quite tight following mastectomy.) Once the desired breast size has been reached and maintained, the expansion fill-port is removed during a second surgery. Depending upon current FDA regulations, the expander may be exchanged for a gel implant.

Soft tissue procedures include the rectus abdominis musculocutaneous flap in which a segment of loose abdominal fat and skin is moved to the breast region while still connected to its blood supply based on the rectus abdominis muscle. The breast is then sculptured into the size and shape that will give the best cosmetic result and sutured into place.

The latissimus dorsi musculocutaneous flap from the flank of the patient involves a similar concept in which a large muscle from the patient's back is moved anteriorly to the chest wall defect carrying a segment of skin and fat with it. A prosthesis is usually placed underneath this flap for an increase in volume and to attain a more symmetrical result.

Microsurgical free tissue transfers utilizing the buttock area, rectus abdominis, or a variety of other soft tissues are another alternative in the reconstruction of the missing breast. The nipple areola complex can be reconstructed, using a skin graft. This is usually done at a later date on an outpatient basis. Tattooing of the nipple areola complex can be done to attain a more natural color.

At first blush, the idea of transplanting to the breast fat that has been removed by liposuction from other areas of the body (§ 31.17) seems intriguing. Unfortunately, not only are the aesthetic results of this technique poor, subsequent detection of breast malignancies may be severely compromised. Injected fat is unevenly absorbed and eventually hardens (from scar tissue), leaving an asymmetrical breast filled with hard, rock-like lumps. Worse yet, the view on X-ray may mimic the appearance of breast cancer replete with calcifications. The procedure has been officially condemned by the American Society of Plastic and Reconstructive Surgery.

Complications

Bleeding, infection, and wound problems may occur with breast implants as in any other operation. Hematoma formation requires immediate reoperation and evacuation of the clotted blood. Infection may sometimes be controlled with antibiotics alone, but more often requires temporary removal of the implant. Serous fluid accumulation may be absorbed spontaneously or may require drainage. Wound dehiscence is uncommon in breast implants, but when it occurs, it is more serious with inframmary incisions because of the increased likelihood of implant exposure and requires temporary removal.

Complications specific to augmentation mammaplasty and related to leakage or implant rupture include gel migration and granuloma formation. Patients often note a change in the shape or feel of the breast when an implant ruptures. This event and occult leakage can be detected on mammography or magnetic resonance imaging (MRI). The ruptured or leaking implant should be removed, the gel evacuated, and the granulomata excised. A new implant can be placed immediately. Deflation of saline-filled implants also necessitates replacement.

Treatment of capsular contracture is problematic. Massage and Vitamin E administration have been tried, but are usually unsuccessful. The standard remedy in severe cases is removal and the insertion of a new implant, but even in these cases, some extent of recurrence is the rule.

Studies have shown an unexplained low incidence of breast cancer in women with implants. One possible reason — the impaired or delayed mammographic detection of the malignancy due to obscuration by the implant — has not been found in any of the studies. So far, no studies have demonstrated a statistically significant epidemiological correlation between breast implants and any connective tissue diseases (e.g. arthritis), although some woman have reported improvement in the symptoms of such diseases upon removal of the implant.

Despite a relative high incidence of major and minor complications, plus several years of adverse publicity,[26] augmentation mammaplasty

---

[26] Editor's Note: The silicone breast implant controversy is discussed in § 31.49.

remains popular as an elective procedure. This suggests that the psychological benefits of an enhanced body image should not be underestimated.

Injectable silicones

The augmentation of the female breast by an implantable prosthesis should be differentiated from injection into the female breast of various nonmedical silicone and other illicit preparations. At this time, there is no FDA-approved substance that may legally be injected into the female breast for cosmetic augmentation. Cases continue to surface where everything from impure commercial-grade silicone to melted paraffin has been injected by charlatans and quacks.

§ 31.26. Reduction mammaplasty.

Reduction mammaplasty is occasionally performed for purely cosmetic purposes. More often, women seek surgical relief from the discomfort caused by massive, heavy, pendulous breasts. The female breast can become large enough to restrict physical activity, interfere with breathing, prevent sleep, and cause constant pain. Operations to relieve such distress are certainly not purely cosmetic surgery. Sagging of the breast tissue (ptosis) tends to occur naturally with age. Ptosis occurs because a large breast is a heavy organ. The gland is somewhat loosely attached to the anterior chest wall, and with aging, these attachments stretch and loosen. The skin envelope that covers the breast is also distensible and will gradually stretch under the constant weight of the sagging, heavy gland. In older women the breast tissue tends to atrophy and decrease in size, leaving a thin, loose envelope of breast skin containing a decreased amount of glandular tissue that tends to droop. Reduction mammaplasty always involves removal of this excess breast skin and varying amounts of glandular tissue, depending on the size of the breast being operated on and the desired result.

Procedure

Numerous techniques have been described for the reduction mammaplasty. They differ in the configuration of the skin incisions; method of preserving the blood supply to the nipple and areola (area around the nipple), as these are moved upward; and methods of incising and reshaping glandular tissue. By this procedure, very large or ptotic breasts can be reduced and lifted into a more conical and elevated configuration that will satisfactorily renew youthfulness to the bosom. The results are usually quite good with the patient clothed. The nude breast, however, is invariably marked with visible scars.

With improved techniques, the majority of reduction mammaplasty procedures are now performed on an outpatient or short-stay basis. The

use of injected dilute solutions of epinephrine mixed with a local anesthetic has greatly reduced blood loss to the point that transfusion is
uncommon. Liposuction as an adjunct during breast reduction has enhanced the aesthetic results, particularly in the area where the breast
joins the sidewalls of the chest. Placement of buried but removable sutures has improved the appearance of scars, as has the postoperative use
of compression garments and external silicone sheeting.

Mastopexy

Breasts of normal size that sag, either naturally or as a consequence of
pregnancy, may be improved in appearance by a variety of techniques
designed to elevate and reshape. Collectively called "mastopexy," these
procedures frequently resemble a breast reduction in which only redundant skin and not breast tissue is removed. In many cases, the results
are improved by simultaneous augmentation with a small breast implant (§ 31.25). Mastopexy requries expert planning and meticulous surgical technique. It is a purely aesthetic operation that is usually judged
through extremely critical eyes.

Gynecomastia surgery

Enlargement of the male breast is called "gynecomastia." Virtually all
pubescent males experience a period of transient enlargement and/or
tenderness of a small button of breast tissue beneath the nipple. Hormonal problems (on rare occasions), certain medications, and liver disease may lead to gynecomastia, but in many individuals, one or both
breasts may enlarge to visible proportions without any systemic pathology. Breast cancer as a cause of male breast mass is extremely uncommon.

In thin and muscular individuals, the enlargement may consist of pure
breast tissue, but if the individual is obese with a fatty breast, it may
enlarge to the point of pendulosity. In these cases, the typical patient is
an adolescent who is greatly disturbed by his appearance in the gym
class and locker room.

Treatment consists of outpatient surgery, usually under general anesthesia. The procedure is aimed at near total removal of the breast tissue,
preferably through a semicircular incision around the areola. Extreme
cases with pendulosity and excess skin present a challenge in minimizing scars. While liposuction may be of some value in fine contouring, it
has generally been disappointing when applied to true breast tissue.
Although gynecomastia is psychological distressing and, by definition,
pathologic, corrective surgery is seldom covered by health plans.

Complications

Complications of breast reduction surgery include: marginal necrosis
(tissue destruction) of the edges of the skin flaps, due to excessive tension

in the wounds; hematoma (blood clot) formation within the breast; fat abscess formation within the breast; necrosis of the nipple and areola; plus any of the usual complications of major surgery under general anesthesia. There is usually some decreased sensation in the region of the nipple and areola, but this varies greatly with the techniques used and how much of the nerve supply to this area is interrupted. Some patients may develop totally anesthetic nipples while others may notice only slightly decreased sensation. This may improve within the first one to two years following surgery. Also, hypersensitivity of the nipples and areola may occur and is quite uncomfortable, but usually it is transitory.

§ 31.26a. Breast reconstruction.

It is now an accepted procedure for the patient facing a mastectomy for breast cancer to request consultation with a plastic surgeon to plan for restoration of the absent breast. Restoration can be performed at the same operation as the mastectomy, but more commonly it is done at a later date, after the mastectomy has healed. See the discussion of the procedure involved in augmentation mammaplasty in § 31.25.

§ 31.27. Reduction of trunk and extremities.

Liposuction is considered the standard technique for removal of fat from any subcutaneous location. This may be done as an independent procedure for contouring the trunk, thighs, or legs, or as an adjunct to other surgery, such as a face-lift, abdominoplasty, or breast reduction. The technique, also called involves the use of long metal cannulas inserted through small skin incisions through which fat is suctioned from subcutaneous tissues by means of a connecting tube to a strong vacuum suction machine. This technique appears to work well for localized fat collections in young patients with thick elastic skin. In general, the procedure is superior to and, except for the abdomen, has replaced open surgical excision previously employed for subcutaneous fat removal. In fact, as an independent procedure, liposuction is now the most commonly performed cosmetic surgical operation.

The independent (commonly called "standalone") liposuction procedure is typically performed on an outpatient basis for the purpose of altering body contours rather than for weight reduction. The thighs and abdomen are the most popular areas. Depending upon the desires and general health of the patient, the area of the body involved, the available facilities, and the preferences of the surgeon, either local anesthesia with sedation or general anesthesia is employed.

As experience with liposuction has increased, so too has the boldness of the surgeons with regard to the number of body areas treated and the total amount of fat removed. The appreciation of the need for the concomitant administration of large amounts of intravenous fluids has gone a long way toward insuring the safety of the procedure. Today, recovery from small to medium liposuction procedures is surprisingly trouble-free. Special compression garments minimize swelling and ecchymosis and facilitate the patient's rapid return to routine activities.

Evolutionary modifications of the basic liposuction technique and instrumentation are noteworthy. For example, *tumescent liposuction* involves the injection of large volumes of dilute local anesthetic solution with epinephrine. The subsequent turgidity of the tissues, coupled with epinephrine's vasoconstriction effect, minimizes blood loss and facilitates contouring. *Syringe liposuction* substitutes the use of supposedly more gentle and precise manually operated syringes for noisy and crudely powerful vacuum pumps. *Internal ultrasonic-assisted lipectomy* (UAL) utilizes a special cannula connected to an ultrasonic generator. The ultrasonic energy causes a disruption of fat cells (lipolysis) that may be of value in body areas where fibrous tissue makes standard liposuction mechanically difficult. (Although the liquified fat must still be conventionally suctioned.) Unfortunately, the burn potential of the ultrasonic energy; the large bore of the cannulae, which requires longer entry incisions; an increase in postoperative fluid accumulation; and high equipment costs limit the popularity of this technique. However, external ultrasonic devices are being tested that may provide similar benefits in liposuction pretreatment without the drawbacks of invasive cannulae.

Abdominoplasty

The simple accumulation of excess abdominal fat and "love handles" frequently seen on a person's sides above the hipbones is easily treated with liposuction alone. However, significant stretching and sagging (ptosis) of the abdominal skin, with or without accompanying laxity and protrusion of the muscular abdominal wall as a consequence of obesity or pregnancy, requires a different approach. Excess skin must be removed and the underlying muscle and fascia (fibrous muscle encasements) tightened or repaired. This is usually accomplished through a long horizontal incision above the groin and pubis, although occasionally a vertical incision is also required. Most often the umbilicus is transposed or reconstructed. Liposcution may also be used adjunctively, and less commonly, endoscopic techniques are utilized for abdominal wall reconstruction if excessive skin is not a problem. Cumulatively, these procedures are termed "abdominoplasty" or "abdominal dermatolipectomy."

By most techniques, the skin and underlying fat are separated from the muscles of the anterior abdominal wall over most of the abdomen. The excessive skin and fat is then pulled downward and cut away, and the low transverse incision is closed after transplanting the umbilicus to a higher point on the abdominal skin to leave it at its natural elevation.

By this technique, scars in the skin of the lower abdomen can be removed as can unsightly stretch marks that frequently result from multiple or frequent pregnancies. Laxity of the abdominal wall musculature or mid-line abdominal hernias can be repaired by direct suture while the fat-skin flap is elevated. Due to the extensive undermining of the skin and fat of the abdominal wall, drainage tubes are usually left beneath the flap when the wound is closed. A well fitting compression dressing is usually applied over the abdomen to avoid the accumulation of fluid or blood. Patients begin limited ambulation within a day or so, but may be unable to stand straight up for a week or more (to avoid tension on the incision). Although abdominoplasty was once strictly an inpatient hospital procedure, burgeoning costs have inspired a switch to alternative overnight facilities or an expeditious trip home. General anesthesia is usually required.

Abdominoplasty is usually a major surgical procedure with potentially serious complications, including pulmonary embolus, severe wound infections, hematoma from subcutaneous bleeding, and skin necrosis (death or gangrene of wound edges). Fortunately, pulmonary emboli are rare and may be minimized by appropriate patient selection, the use of compression hose, and perhaps by limiting the amount of intraoperative liposuctioning. The risk of infection is minimized by aseptic technique and prophylactic antibiotics. The risk of hematoma is minimized by careful control of intra-operative bleeding and draining the wound with suitable drainage tubes. Necrosis of the skin edges and separation of the wound is usually a result of too much tension at the site of closure — the surgeon resects too much skin and fat from the lower abdomen to allow the wound to close easily. A certain amount of tension in the closure is desirable for maximum benefit, but a judgment decision is necessary to define how tight is too tight. Allowing the patient to move about and ambulate too soon postoperatively also contributes to separation of the wound as does postoperative coughing, retching, and vomiting. The wounds are usually closed with numerous subcutaneous sutures left in place, and the skin stitches are usually left in from ten to fourteen days. Most patients can usually resume full normal activities in one month.

The reduction of thighs and buttocks by a similar surgical procedure is accomplished by taking out wedges of skin and fat through incisions in the gluteal crease just beneath the buttocks and carried downward through the full thickness of the subcutaneous fat to the underlying musculature. Depending on the extent of excess fat and skin, varying amounts can be excised and the wounds closed primarily. The wounds are closed with numerous subcutaneous sutures and skin sutures left in for a minimum of two weeks. Incisions should be placed high so as to be hidden under a bathing suit. The major complications of this procedure are the same as those for the abdominal dermolipectomy. Immediate postoperative results are usually quite gratifying. Long-term follow up studies have not yet been done.

Undesired results

There is concern over physicians rushing to perform liposuction without proper training. It has been claimed that practitioners of varying specialties and backgrounds are establishing liposuction practices after taking only brief training courses. In one case, it was reported that a family physician, after taking only a weekend course in the procedure, immediately began recruiting patients through advertisements on billboards and leaflets. Two of his patients died of postoperative infections and three others were hospitalized for complications.[27]

In March 1997, plastic surgeons removed twenty pounds of fat from a forty-seven-year-old Santa Anna, California, woman. The liposuction procedure lasted over ten hours, and the patient apparently lost a lot of blood. According to a petition asking for the suspension of the medical licenses of the physicians involved, when they finally called 911 and the patient was taken to the hospital, she was no longer breathing and had no pulse.[28]

The results in competent hands are better. Dillerud[29] reviewed 3,511 liposuction procedures performed on 2,009 patients over a five-year period and followed up for six to twelve months. He found that 88% of the procedures led to patient satisfaction and 3.4% led to dissatisfaction, with males being more dissatisfied than females. There were no deaths, deep thromboses, pulmonary emboli, hypotension, respiratory distress (fat emboli syndrome), hematoma, skin slough, or damage to adjacent organs. The most common general complaints involved excessive bleeding and complications of anesthesia. The most common local complications were hypertrophic scarring and skin problems. There was one clinical bacterial infection.

There were 379 complaints of "undesired results" at the six-month follow-up, and 213 revisions were required because of asymmetry, underresection, or skin problems. A total of 121 procedures unexpectedly required secondary suction, skin excision, or fat grafting. Forty-five sequelae were not corrected by revisions. The most difficult locations for undesirable results and complications were the medial thigh, buttock, ankle, and face.

[27] Pappas, *Body by Liposuction*, Hippocrates, May–June 1989, p. 26.

[28] *San Diego Union Tribune*, May 2, 1997.

[29] Dillerud, E., *Suction Lipoplasty: A Report on Complications, Undesired Results, and Patient Satisfaction Based on 3,511 Procedures*, 88 Plast. Reconstr. Surg. 329 (Aug.), 1991.

VI. REPLANTATION SURGERY

§ 31.27a. Replantation of limbs and digits.

Replantation of limbs and digits has flourished with the emergence of clinical microvascular surgery (see § 31.27b). The capability for microvascular surgery and, hence, replantation of severed limbs, is now available at most major medical centers and large hospitals throughout the country. While these techniques are not available in all community hospitals, most states have one or more centers where they can be performed.

The decision to replant a limb is predicated by:

1. Age of the patient (success rates drop drastically past the age of forty);
2. Method of amputation (cleanly cut amputations have greater than 85% survival rate, crush amputations 50%, and avulsion or ripping-type amputations about 10% survival);
3. Patient's occupation;
4. Dominance of the amputated limb;
5. Patient's wishes;
6. Length of warm ischemic time (length of time the amputated part has remained at room temperature; if this period exceeds six hours, the success rate for all types of amputations drops to less than 5%, but with cooling, this period can be stretched to twenty hours).

The replantation procedure is done by a team of surgeons. The usual procedure is to shorten the bones of the amputated part (so that the vessels and nerves can be approximated without tension), then repair (1) the muscles, (2) the tendons, and (3) the vessels in that order (with two veins repaired for every artery repaired). Next come the nerves, and the skin last, if it is present. Magnification (operating microscope) is used to repair the vessels and nerves.

Digital replantation indications follow those of major limb repair (method of amputation, length of warm ischemia, patient's age, etc.); however, because of the remarkable versatility of the hand, several exceptions are made. In multiple digital amputations and in single amputations of the thumb and index finger, replantation is indicated. But in single amputations or subtotal amputation of a single finger of any of the three ulnar digits (the third, fourth, and fifth fingers), special circumstances are required to warrant attempting replantation (patient's dominant hand, patient is piano player, left ring finger in a single girl, etc.), because the length of disability and amount of morbidity associated with these procedures often does not equate with the value served by these digits (of course, any amputated digit should be replanted if the patient so wishes).

The sequence of repairs in digital replantation is skeletal fixation, extensor tendon, dorsal veins, dorsal skin, digital artery, volar nerves, flexor tendons, palmar skin.

Postoperative care in replantation surgery includes antibiotic coverage, immobilization of the replanted part, and early active physical therapy and occupational therapy administered by trained personnel.

The long-term complications primarily involve decreased ranges of motion and changes in sensation (either increased or decreased) in the replanted part.

§ 31.27b. Free tissue transfer (microvascular surgery).

Successes gained in replantation surgery and the long history of transplanting skin from one part of the body to another, the next challenge to plastic surgeons has been transplanting large masses of tissue from one area to another. These masses of tissue can survive in their new location if their blood supply can be immediately instituted on transplantation. The operating microscope makes possible the suturing of the minute vessels, and the techniques and instruments used in limb and digit replantation (§ 31.27a) are applied.

Large flaps of tissue (skin, fat, muscle, bone, and even free segments of bowel) are transplanted to reconstruct breasts amputated for cancer, to reconstruct lower faces extirpated for cancer or lost to trauma, to replace missing segments of esophagus, etc. Success is predicated upon the transplanted tissue having a known single major blood vessel distribution, and the area receiving the transplant having adequate blood vessel with which to "hook-up."[30]

§ 31.27c. Indications for replantation of the hand or forearm.[31]

In general, the indications for replantation include (1) multiple digits, (2) a severed thumb, (3) amputation at the wrist or forearm, (4) sharp amputations with minimal to moderate avulsion proximal to the elbow, (5) single digits amputated between the proximal interphalangeal joint and the distal interphalangeal joint (distal to flexor digitorum superficialis insertion), and (6) amputations in children.

The level of amputation is important in replantation. In replantation of digits amputated distal to the insertion of the flexor digitorum superficialis between the proximal interphalangeal joint and distal interphalangeal joint, good motor and sensory function is often achieved. Replantation of the midpalm, wrist, or distal forearm also produce good function. Conversely, amputations proximal to the distal forearm and elbow are often complicated by severe avulsion or crush injury compo-

---

[30] Editor's Note: On transplantation of organs and tissue generally, see Chapter 30B.
[31] Schlenker, J. D., and Koulis, C. P., *Am-* *putations and Replantations*, 11 Emerg. Clin. N. Am. 739 (Aug.), 1993.

nents, making them prone to muscle necrosis, infection, and functional failure.

Although the thumb is the most important digit of the hand, motion of only the first carpometacarpal joint is required to preserve the function of opposition. Therefore, all thumb amputations should be considered for replantation regardless of the level of amputation or mechanism of injury.

All amputations in children should be considered for replantation. Sharp amputations in particular carry an improved prognosis in children for both survival of the replanted part and return of useful function.

VII. CORRECTION OF DEFORMITIES

§31.28. Introduction.

Impact of deformities

Plastic surgeons are frequently called upon to correct nature's blemishes, not only because of their obvious structural and functional impropriety but also because of the incalculable effects deformity may have on the mind. The first individual affected by the birth of a deformed child is, of course, the mother, who inevitably bears enormous guilt. She will be exposed to countless legends, most of them fallacious, that attempt to explain the appearance of the defect. No amount of reassurance or contradictory evidence seems to completely rid the mother (or father) of self-imposed blame.

After family members eventually adjust to a less than perfect child, the child begins to comprehend his or her own variance from accepted norm. Psychological inquiry is only now beginning to understand how behavioral patterns are affected by the presence of deformity. Children can be incredibly cruel to their peers — particularly when one among the group has physical abnormalities. Failure at social interaction may induce the child to withdraw entirely. Whatever else influences the surgeon's approach to childhood deformity, the need to preserve the patient's self-image is of paramount importance.

Causes of birth defects

Certain circumstances are known to result in congenital deformity. For example, abnormalities of the chromosomes can produce combinations of disfigurement that may or may not fall into familiar patterns. Specific genes that determine the presence of a single or multifaceted defect can either run in a family or appear spontaneously without warning. In addition to genetic reasons for birth defects, certain environmental influences are known to play a role. Drugs figure prominently in this category, thalidomide being the most notorious example, where judgments and settlements totaling nearly $75 million were obtained against the pharmaceutical firm that produced a drug introduced as a harmless sedative and later found to be responsible for tragic limb deformities in infants.[32] Even widely used agents, including antihistamines, anticonvulsants, antibiotics, and certain cancer agents have been found to adversely affect fetuses.[33] Because of the diversity of medications suspected of being cofactors in the genesis of deformity, women of childbearing age are often warned to use caution in their use of certain drugs, whether or not they believe they are pregnant.

Regardless of the precise cause of a birth defect, certain principles can be applied. Any child with one anomaly stands an excellent chance of having another. Associated deformities may be subtle, so that a careful diagnostic evaluation is in order whenever a deformity is first detected by the physician. At times, associated defects may not declare themselves for many years; an excellent example is the frequent coexistence of leukemia and related malignancies in Down's syndrome children. Knowledge of these principles sometimes permits the astute physician to recognize and successfully treat these sytemic disorders long before they would ordinarily become apparent.

Treatment

At one time, the traditional thinking among plastic surgeons was that aggressive correction of congenital defects must be deferred until maturity, lest the centers for normal growth be irreversibly injured surgically and the final result made more severe. Actually, little or no evidence in support of this contention has been found. To be sure, injury to certain anatomical zones (*e.g.*, the nasal septum or wall between the two nostrils) can result in significant growth arrest. But such an event is most unusual and easily avoidable during most reconstructive procedures.

Because of the emotional trauma that inevitably results from postponement of surgery until adolescence, many surgeons now advocate

---

[32] See "Thalidomide," in *Drugs in Litigation: Damage Awards Involving Prescription and Nonprescription Drugs*, LEXIS Law Publishing, Charlottesville, Va., 1998. Although thalidomide was banned for consumer use throughout the world, scientists continued to study its therapeutic effects. Clinical trials have shown that it is successful in treating erythema nodosum leprosum (ENL), an inflammatory complication of leprosy that results in painful skin lesions on the arms, legs, and face. About 30% of the world's twelve million leprosy victims suffer from ENL, and a committee of scientific advisors has recommended that the FDA approve the drug to treat this condition. Also, thalidomide is being tested as an experimental treatment for more than twenty other conditions, including several forms of cancer, macular degeneration, serious skin diseases, autoimmune disorders, tuberculosis, and mouth and esophageal ulcers in HIV patients. Id.

[33] Over two-dozen drugs have been involved in litigation because of birth defects in children born to mothers who took the product during pregnancy. For a summary of these cases, listed by generic and brand name of the drug involved, see *Drugs in Litigation: Damage Awards Involving Prescription and Nonprescription Drugs*, LEXIS Law Publishing, Charlottesville, Va., 1998.

correction of deformities prior to school. The work may not always be completed by that time, but experience has shown that a child's confidence and self-esteem can be improved significantly if he can be made to realize that someone shares his concern and has something to offer in the way of correction of his most visible defects.

§ 31.29. Cleft lip and palate.

Nearly one in every 800 live births yields a cleft of the upper lip, of the palate (roof of the mouth), or a combination of the two. Most occur without a family history of similar disorders, but some occur either in association with other heritable defects or within families known to be at higher than normal risk for such problems.

Facial features assume their final shape and profile during the sixth week of gestation when lateral growth processes meet or unite in midline with the earliest recognizable precursor of the nose. Failure of these zones to unite will result in a cleft or separation of such midline structures as the upper lip or palate. In more severe forms of malunion, the nose itself may even be absent or severely misshapen. Clefts of the lip are not only grotesque, but hinder the child's ability to nurse. Mothers, who must already struggle to overcome a natural rejection of their deformed offspring, are forced to work overtime to provide the infant with sufficient nourishment. Specially shaped nipples have been designed to facilitate the feeding process.

Clefts of the palate do not ordinarily interrupt normal feeding patterns appreciably, even though they can cause problems later. Without muscle integrity within the palate, speech patterns will not develop normally. Obstruction of the usual drainage routes from the ear to the throat can lead to hearing deficiencies of major significance. For these and other reasons, the cleft palate child is best treated by a team of specialists, including not only plastic surgeons, speech therapists, and otologists, but also dentists to handle the special problems resulting from interruption of the normal dental arches.

With regard to surgical correction of these deformities, there are a variety of acceptable approaches. Most surgeons try to correct the lip defect within the first three months of age. This not only serves the function of restoring normal eating habits, but also provides the mother with a more attractive child. Plastic surgeons rarely encounter a more grateful "patient" than the mother of a cleft lip child. Clefts of the palate are closed sometime between the first and second year of age. This assures the best structural condition before speech habits develop. Even though a major portion of reconstructive surgery should be completed before the second birthday, this does not mean that the surgeon's job is over. Often, secondary procedures are performed in future years, occasionally as late as the teenage years, to further improve appearance by means of scar revision or perhaps restoration of associated deformities of the nose, etc. It might even be stated that the job is not done until the surgeon has nothing more to offer or else the patient perceives no need for further improvement of residual defects.

§ 31.30.   Ear deformities.

Even the most subtle and seemingly inconsequential of nature's errors may serve to produce emotional stress. Such is the case with variations in the visible part of the ear. The most frequent example is the so-called "prominent ear." Children whose ears stick out usually become the targets of ridicule from their playmates. (Hearing function is rarely involved.) The folds of the cartilage forming the central skeleton or support for the external ear are simply incomplete, but they can ordinarily be corrected with relative ease through incisions hidden behind the ear. The operation is usually performed under local anesthesia if the patient is willing to co-operate and hold still.

Less commonly, ears may fail to develop at all, or else a small diminutive structure will be all that forms. This condition, called microtia or "small ear," is often associated with hearing loss. Surgical reconstruction of the external ear is exceedingly difficult. In fact, some surgeons maintain that it is virtually impossible and will resort to the use of a "glue-on" plastic or prosthetic ear. Techniques are available today for reconstruction of a reasonably acceptable ear. It is not a normal ear, but it does have natural outlines, normal color, a sense of touch, and in most instances, a high degree of patient acceptance. These surgical procedures involve the use of premolded pieces of silicone or an individually carved section of rib cartilage imbedded within a pocket beneath the skin surface.

Several surgical steps are necessary, but the final result appears to justify the work required.

§ 31.31.   Hand deformities.

Congenital malformations of the hand frequently accompany facial deformities, although they can also occur alone. The concurrent appearance of face and hand anomalies is probably due to both areas developing their detailed structure almost simultaneously between the fifth and sixth week of gestation. Presumably, whatever stimulus results in a structural variation in one place may exert an inhibitory influence elsewhere. Hand deformities assume several recognizable patterns. The fingers may either be reduplicated (polydactyly) or inappropriately united (syndactyly). They may be missing altogether (adactyly), foreshortened (brachydactyly) or elongated (macrodactyly). Most crippling of all are defects from thalidomide ingestion, termed phocomelia, which are characterized by total absence of the hand or peripheral arm.

There is no standardized treatment for hand deformities. Each child must be considered independently and his functional impairments corrected according to need. Since maintenance of hand function is the primary goal, aesthetic considerations must be designed in a manner that avoids loss of valuable function within the adjacent normal regions of the hand. In this regard, younger children have an advantage; their joints remain far more supple after surgery than do those of the adult.

Extra fingers are usually removed; care is taken to select the least functional digit for amputation. Fused fingers are separated.

Absence of digits can sometimes be disregarded, but never in the case of the thumb. Without the thumb to oppose the action of the fingers, the development of normal prehensile skills is impossible. However, procedures are available for repositioning the normal index finger so that it can assume the role of thumb. When performed successfully, the hand will have a pleasing appearance, and few will notice the absence of one finger. More extensive defects require elaborate, multistaged reconstructive efforts, often involving transfer of tissue from distant sites, bone grafting, tendon transferring, etc. In all cases however, the primary goal is to restore function at as early an age as possible. There is little need to wait until the patient "grows up," for by that time the tendency for joints to stiffen after surgery makes the final result less satisfactory.

§ 31.32. Hypertelorism, craniosynostosis, and other craniomaxillo facial defects.

Ocular hypertelorism is a condition characterized by a severe widening of eye position.[33] It is often associated with other major deformities including midline facial clefts, misshapen skulls, and palate defects. Craniosynostosis is the premature ossification of the skull and the obliteration of the sutures.

The standard approach to such defects that are considered amenable to surgical treatment is a bicoronal incision followed by removal of the segment of the frontal bone. The brain is then gently retracted posteriorly using an extradural approach, thereby exposing the orbital roofs and the base of the anterior fossa of the skull. After this approach, and with the vital structures out of the way, safe reconstruction of the entire upper and middle third of the face can be performed by the plastic surgeon. This approach usually requires extensive mobilization of the orbital contents through additional anterior incisions, reconstruction of the nasal complex, and removal or mobilization of large segments of the skull and facial bones.

---

[33] Contrary to popular belief, children suffering from this deformity are rarely retarded mentally. Not infrequently, they are inappropriately assigned to institutions, apparently under the presumption that "because a child looks stupid, he must be stupid."

§ 31.33. Birthmarks.

It has been estimated that as many as 10% of all live births involve some form of birthmark: usually a small blood vessel tumor (commonly referred to as a hemangioma) or occasionally an enlarged area of heavy pigmentation called a mole or nevus. When there are associated birth defects, the incidence may be as high as 25%. Fortunately, only a small proportion are readily visible. Birthmarks are almost never malignant, and there are no satisfactory explanations for their presence. Efforts to correlate their appearance with specific events at the time of conception or during pregnancy have been totally unsuccessful (regardless of what grandmother or the next-door neighbor thinks).

With regard to treatment, here is a situation where procrastination is fully justified. Hemangiomas ordinarily undergo a natural involution during the first three years of life and sometimes disappear altogether. Surgery is best applied after normal regression takes place, to assume the role of minimizing residual scarring. Surgery occasionally becomes necessary earlier if the birthmark demonstrates an aggressive growth pattern, lies in a vital site and interrupts normal function, or becomes a source of hemorrhage. In any event, it is ordinarily wise to complete most of the surgery by the time the individual starts school.

Radiation therapy of any form or source should *never* be administered to these lesions, not only because gamma irradiation is ineffective, but also because of the severe effects that X-rays impart to surrounding tissue and nearby growth centers.

VIII. SURGICAL SEX CHANGE

§ 31.33a. Gender dysphoria (transsexualism).

The assignment of sex at birth is a straightforward matter in most instances. Determination, however, is predicated on one basic assumption and presupposes another: The former is that external genitalia (sex organs) accurately reflect the chromosomal, gonadal, internal sexual, hormonal, and central nervous system parameters of sexuality; the latter is that social and pyschological events will lead to a gender identification compatible with sex of assignment. Formal assignment or reassignment surgical techniques are required when these underlying assumptions are invalid.

Beginning in the 1950s, as a consequence of an evolving freedom of sexual discussion and expression, "transsexualism," a condition in which there is psychological and social identification with the attributes of the opposite sex, has received increasingly greater attention. This condition has been known since antiquity, but was excluded from public and scientific discourse until brought into focus by the publicity surrounding the surgery in Sweden of Christine (George) Jorgenson in 1952.

Traditionally, issues of sex assignment and reassigment related exclusively to intersex or hermaphroditic conditions (individuals with incompletely defined sex organs or with reproductive organs of both sexes). Whereas intersex individuals are discordant in the *biological* variables of sex, the disharmony in the "transsexual" is between gender identity — the individual's subjective sense of maleness or femaleness — and physical sex. Superficially, it appears that intersex disorders raise physically based issues, while transsexuals raise issues that are psychologically based.

The transsexual patient (or gender dysphoric patient) must not be confused with the transvestite patient who assumes the opposite sex role only for fetishistic sexual arousal and otherwise lives in a heterosexual setting. The transsexual must also be differentiated from the effeminate homosexual or masculine lesbian. The homosexual and lesbian seek relationships with members of the same physical sex but enjoy and wish to keep their own sex organs. Transsexuals are often asexual and some are disgusted with their own sex organs (truly the body of one gender containing the mind of the opposite gender).

The treatment process of gender dysphoric (transsexual) patients usually includes a six-month to two-year course of cross-gender living in society while on the appropriate cross-gender hormone and under the care of a psychiatrist. If a patient passes the test, only then does he or she become a candidate for a surgical sex change. At the least, the standard of care would probably require that a psychiatrist conduct an extensive evaluation over an extended period of time with additional follow-up therapy after the surgery.[34]

§ 31.33b. The surgical procedure.

The male-to-female change includes filleting the penile shaft, turning the shaft inside-out, and burying the skin tube in the area immediately in front of the anal opening. The scrotum is filleted in the vertical midline, the testicles amputated, and the cut scrotal edges are attached back to themselves to form the new lips of the vagina. Breasts develop spontaneously secondary to the hormone treatment. Facial hair is permanently removed with electrolysis.

The female-to-male change is more difficult technically with a less satisfactory cosmetic result and more noticeable scars. The breasts, uterus, and ovaries are removed. A phallus is constructed of a tube of skin from the lower abdominal wall. A scrotum is made of flaps of tissue from the groins and silastic (plastic) prostheses are inserted for testicles. A long, thin pocket is made in the constructed phallic shaft into which a silastic rod is inserted before intercourse as a "stiffener" for erection.

---

[34]See Reisner v. Board of Regents of the State of New York (App. Div., 1988) 535 N.Y.S.2d 22.

None of the postoperative transsexual patients are capable of reproduction, but most report orgasm with sex play.

§ 31.33c.   Risk of civil or criminal liability.

An interesting legal question has been raised concerning surgical sex change. Does a surgeon's removal of a healthy, anatomically normal genital organ constitute a tort or crime? There once was speculation that such an operation may constitute the act of "mayhem"[35] which, at early common law, was the infliction of an injury that reduced the victim's "ability in physical combat," or as defined by Blackstone, an injury "violently depriving another of the use of such of his members as may render him less able in fighting."[36]

In a few states, the crime of mayhem is still on the statute books. In 1972, a federal court reviewing a defendant's conviction of "mayhem or maliciously disfiguring another" under a District of Columbia statute, described the act of mayhem as a "narrow common law offense" which, under today's statutes, has "considerably larger dimensions."[37] This transition, said the court, "has been accompanied, if not induced, by a shift in emphasis from the military and combative effects of the injury to the preservation of the human body in normal functioning."[38] This has led to speculation that *castration* could, under the right circumstances, be considered mayhem.[39]

No physician has been successfully prosecuted for mayhem in the United States for performing a sex change operation. It has been reported, however, that some years ago a surgeon in Argentina was convicted of assault following transsexual surgery.[40] In that case, the patient's consent was deemed invalid because of his low mental age and his "neurotic craving" for the operation. Had the charge been brought in this country it would likely have been dismissed for want of "malice" which, under most criminal statutes, is a required part of the offense.

On the civil side, a surgeon in this country might, under the circumstances of the Argentina case, have been found liable for operating on a patient who was incapable of giving his consent. Of interest is a ruling in a California case that voluntary vasectomies do not constitute mayhem. The court reasoned that there was no malice, and that the surgery did not render the patients impotent.[41]

---

[35] See Belli, M. M., *Transsexual Surgery: A New Tort?*, 239 J.A.M.A. 2143 (May 19), 1978.

[36] Blackstone, W., *Commentaries on the Law of England* (First English Edition, Oxford, 1765-1769, 4 Vols.) Oceana Publications, Inc., Dobbs Ferry, New York, 1966.

[37] United States v. Cook (1972) 149 App. D.C. 197, 462 F.2d 301, 303.

[38] Id.

[39] Belli, M. M., supra.

[40] Id.

[41] Jessin v. County of Shasta (1969) 274 Cal. App. 2d 737, 79 Cal. Rptr. 359, 35 A.L.R.3d 1433. This case did not involve a prosecution for the crime of mayhem, but a declaratory judgment proceeding to determine the legality of a welfare sterilization program.

Transsexual surgery changing a male to a female does render the patient impotent, but, as with voluntary vasectomies, it would be difficult to show malice. As to valid consent: surgeons who perform these operations do not do so indiscriminately. There is extensive psychiatric screening, usually at so-called "gender identity clinics," which includes stringent personality tests and an experiment in cross-gender living. As a result, only a relatively small number of applicants for the operation actually become candidates.

IX. THE HAND

§ 31.34. Introduction.

Although advances in surgical techniques, new antimicrobial drugs, and better anesthetic techniques and agents have made some of the more complex surgical procedures of the hand more reliable, nerve regeneration and tendon healing are among major areas where serious limitations still exist. The hand and arm may eventually be among the organs that will be most usefully transplanted once these problems are solved and the basic immunologic barriers are removed. There have been successes. The transfer of composite parts from one area of the hand to another has become routine, and hand surgery is now being done on diseases that previously were not treated at all or were treated only in their late stages. One example is rheumatoid arthritis.

§ 31.35. Anatomy of the hand.

The hand's sensitivity is such that it is capable of the finest discrimination of positional changes, temperature differentials, and surface variations. The specialized skin and facial covering on the palmar surface allows heavy wear. Mobility is obtained by a complex system of bones, joints, ligaments, and motor units.

The wrist (or carpus) articulates with the forearm bones (radius and ulna) and extending from it are five metacarpals or bony "rays." The thumb metacarpal is extremely mobile and is opposed by an almost similarly movable little finger metacarpal. **(Figs. 19 and 20.)** The keystone of the palmar arch formed by these five bones is the metacarpal of the index finger. **(Fig. 21.)** This bone is firmly anchored at the wrist. The next, the middle finger metacarpal, is almost as solidly fixed, but the ring and little finger metacarpals are much more mobile. This arch of the hand, with the bones connected by joints and ligaments and controlled by muscles, enables us to grasp objects of uneven shape or size with firmness and control and sensitivity. The terminal bones of the five

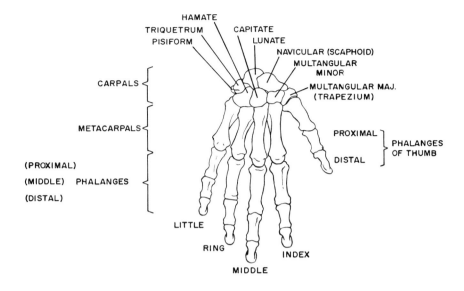

BONES OF THE HAND
DORSAL VIEW

Fig. 19. The bones of the wrist and hand as seen from the back of the hand. The digits are named instead of numbered to avoid confusion, and phalanges are identified as proximal, middle or distal referring to their position on the hand.

rays making up the digits are called phalanges. There are two in the thumb, and each other finger has three. In each finger they are called proximal, middle, and distal, referring to their respective position. There is no middle phalanx of the thumb.

Because of this intrinsic arch mechanism, the fingers tend to spread apart when they are extended; when they are closed or flexed, they converge towards the base of the palm. Therefore, when the mobility of this arch is lost or when any of the "rays" are not properly in line, there is a significant loss of skillful use of the hand. Following fractures or dislocations, the reduction and replacement of bones in the correct alignment is essential to maintain this function.

Motion of the hand at the wrist is described as flexion, extension, abduction (or radial deviation), and adduction (or ulnar deviation). These are measured in degrees by measuring the angle produced by the line of the middle finger metacarpal with the middle of the forearm. If the hand is straight in alignment with the forearm, it is said to be in the neutral (or zero) position. Motion of the hand bringing it palm-ward (toward the volar aspect) is designated flexion; bending in the opposite direction

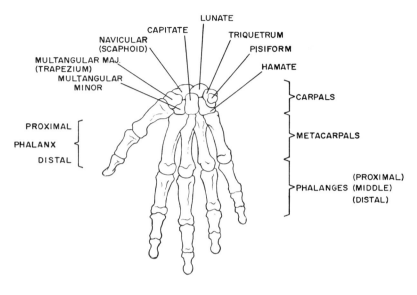

BONES OF THE HAND
PALMAR VIEW

Fig. 20. The bones of the hand as seen from the palm. The metacarpals are fixed to the carpals in varying degrees of stability; index metacarpal is the keystone of an arch and, therefore, firmly attached at its proximal end. The thumb and little finger metacarpals are very mobile, allowing the hand to be cupped around objects of irregular shape.

(backward) is extension (or dorsiflexion). Abduction (radial deviation) is angulation of the hand toward the thumb side. Adduction (ulnar deviation) is that motion occurring toward the little finger side. In the initial assessment and follow up of hand and wrist injuries, the angle of these motions is obtained and compared to the uninjured opposite side, thus giving a comparative measurement of the range of motion. (**Fig. 22.**)

Movements of fingers are usually described by stating what each particular finger is incapable of functioning normally in regard to motion. For example, if a finger and one of its joints cannot be straightened or extended, it is said to lack the measured number of degrees of extension to a straight line. (**Fig. 23.**) If a finger cannot be flexed so that its tip touches the palm, one measures this distance and describes the loss of function as a lack of flexion to the palm by that many inches or centimeters. (**Fig. 24.**) To be most specific, the complete flexion-extension arc of each joint of the finger can be measured, compared to the opposite hand, and the figures then converted to a percentage. This gives an easy to understand figure for the loss of motion in any part.

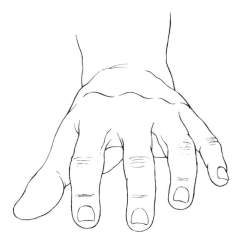

Fig. 21. The "dynamic tripod," the profile of the metacarpal arch. This view of the hand shows how the thumb and little finger metacarpals make up the corner of a tripod with its apex at the index metacarpal. Opening the fingers flattens out this arch, closing them accentuates it.

The grasping power of force of grip of the hand is measured on a "dynamometer" and represents the power of squeezing between the thumb and fingers. (**Fig. 25.**) These measurements are somewhat crude, and vary with the motivation of the subject. And of course they tell nothing of precision, skill, or the ability to sustain pressure during a long working period.

The motions of the hand at the wrist joint level are primarily controlled by the forearm muscles whose respective tendons attach to the bones of the hand proper. (**Fig. 26.**) The fingers themselves are controlled by two groups of muscles: the extrinsic muscles have their muscle origin in the forearm and their tendons reach down into the digits for their attachment, and the intrinsic muscles have their origin and insertion in the hand itself. One group of small intrinsic muscles lies between the metacarpals in the hand. These are called interossei. Another group on the thumb side is called the thenar muscles. A third group on the little finger side of the palm is the hypothenar muscle group. (**Fig. 27.**)

The extrinsic muscles primarily give the hand its strength of grasp, while the intrinsic muscles provide it with dexterity, skill, and coordination. Each separate muscle is a contractile motor unit, controlled through a nerve that originates in the spinal cord. The impulses from the nerve stimulate the muscle tissue to contract, thus activating motion in the distal part by means of the muscle's tendon, a gliding structure of tough inelastic tissue.

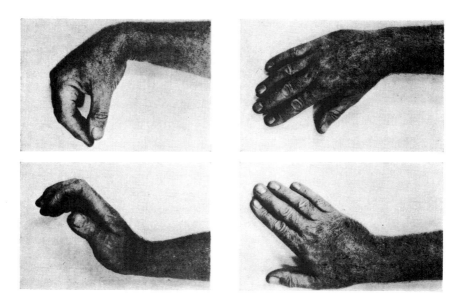

Fig. 22. Motions of the wrist. Palmar flexion (upper left) and extension or dorsi-flexion (lower left) are both described by measuring the angle made by the back of the hand with a line projected from the back of the forearm. Abduction or radial flexion (upper right): adduction or ulnar flexion (lower right) are measured by the angle made by the middle finger metacarpal with a line projected from the midline of the forearm.

Fig. 23. Lack of extension of the left index finger at its middle joint. Projecting a base line from the back of the proximal segment, the angle at which a line from the dorsal surface of the middle segment joins it will represent the degrees of loss of extension.

Where tendons pass around the concavity of a joint, such as on the palmar side of the wrist or finger, they are enclosed within a sheath. **(Fig. 28.)** Certain areas of this sheath, where the tendon would expand if not held in place, are thicker; these are called pulleys and are extremely important in the mechanical functioning of the hand. It is interference

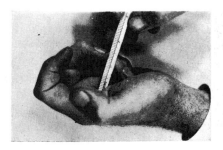

Fig. 24. The left middle finger lacks 11/8 inches of flexing to the midpalmar crease. This is a simple graphic way of describing limitation of flexion of a finger. By measuring how much the tip lacks of touching various parts such as the proximal or more distal palm, one can describe quite accurately the degree of this loss of function.

Fig. 25. Dynamometer for measuring force of grip. This model has adjustable spread of handles and is isometric, that is, there is no perceptible motion of the handle when squeeze pressure is applied. Thus any loss of range of motion in the fingers is not reflected in loss of power.

with this gliding structure caused by scar tissue during the healing process that results in the limited motion seen after tendon injuries in the hand. In other areas, such as on the back of the fingers where a true sheath mechanism is not present, the tendons glide because the surrounding soft tissue is elastic and moves with them.

The loose soft tissue beneath the skin of the hand is interspersed with fat, especially on the palmar surface. The covering skin on the palm is tough and horny, and like the skin on the sole of the foot, responds to wear by forming calluses. On a dorsal surface (back of the hand) the skin is less resistant to wear and is more pliable and elastic. This allows the fingers to be flexed into the palm without restraint. Following burns or significant full-thickness skin loss on the back of the hand, deep scarring limits flexion of the fingers.

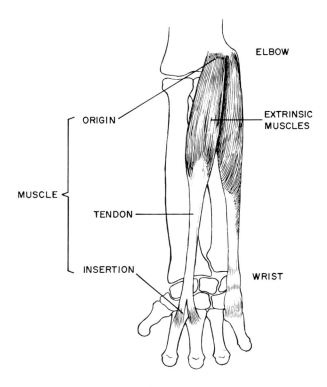

Fig. 26. Diagrammatic view of the dorsum of forearm and wrist, to show typical muscle tendon unit. Contraction of these muscles would result in extension or dorsiflexion of the wrist. They are extrinsic muscles as contrasted with intrinsic in Figure 27, and usually have relatively long tendons compared to the muscle mass.

The skin at the tip of each finger is highly specialized for touch and this pad once lost cannot be substituted for by any other skin. Loss of a finger tip, even when the small amputation stump is covered by otherwise good skin, results in loss of fine tactile sensibility.

§ 31.36. Finger joints.

The index, middle, ring, and little fingers each have three joints. From the hand outward, these are called the metacarpal phalangeal joint, the proximal interphalangeal joint, and the distal interphalangeal joint. More commonly, they are known as the proximal, middle, and distal joints of each finger. The thumb differs slightly in that it has a metacarpal phalangeal joint and only one interphalangeal joint.

The anatomy of the interphalangeal joints of the finger is complex. For such a small articulation it must be thoroughly understood to diagnose and treat injuries. The interphalangeal joints of the finger are of the

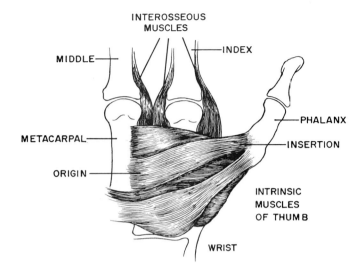

Fig. 27. Intrinsic muscles have all of their substance in the hand itself. Where they lie between the bones, they are called *interossei;* the group giving motion to the thumb is called *thenar,* and a similar group on the little finger side of the hand is called *hypothenar.* Intrinsics have relatively short tendons compared to their muscle mass, and are inserted in bone near the joint they act upon. This leverage enables rapid motion on the part. The extrinsic finger-moving muscles insert near the end of the digits, and allow a slower action but with greater power.

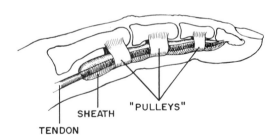

Fig. 28. Schematic drawing of a finger with flexor tendons enclosed in a sheath. A true sheath occurs where tendons pass around the concavity of a joint, and, therefore, sheaths are absent on the dorsum of the finger. The sheath, like a cylinder wall, allows the free gliding of the tendon, with areas of thickening at strategic points to prevent "bow-stringing" when the joint is flexed.

hinge type, allowing a varying range of motion in the plane perpendicular to that of the palm of the hand. For illustrative purposes, we will consider the anatomy of the proximal interphalangeal joint. The head of the proximal phalanx is bicondylar. **(Fig. 29.)** A pit is present on its dorsolateral aspect for the proximal attachment of the collateral liga-

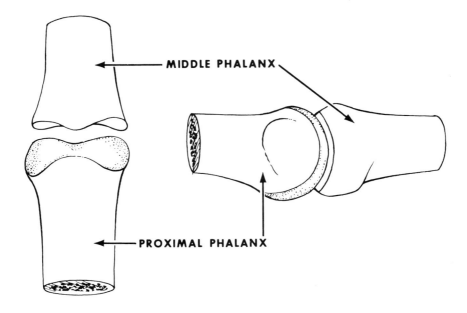

Fig. 29. Anteroposterior and lateral drawings of the bony constituents of the proximal interphalangeal joint of the finger. The head of the proximal phalanx contains its articulating surface which is in the shape of two condyles. The base of the middle phalanx is formed by two concavities separated by a vertical median bar; each concavity articulates with the corresponding condyle of the proximal phalanx. With this type of joint configuration it is easy to see that the primary motion is in the plane of flexion and extension. The shape of the articulating surfaces and the collateral ligaments on each side limit both rotation and motion in the radial and ulnar directions.

ment on both the radial and ulnar sides. As the finger flexes, this ligament glides volarly over a smooth flat area on the head of the phalanx. The base of the middle phalanx has a median ridge separating the two concavities that articulate with the condyles of the proximal phalanx. A lateral tubercle near the volar margin of the middle phalanx provides for the distal attachment of the collateral liagment.

The volar plate has a thick firm collagenous attachment to the volar lip of the middle phalanx and then thins out proximally into a membranous portion which attaches to the neck of the proximal phalanx. (**Fig. 30.**) At the palmar aspect of the base of the middle phalanx there is a roughened area with tubercles for the distal attachment of the volar plate. The joint cavity extends proximally into the dorsal and volar synovial pouches deep to the extensor tendon and flexor tendon sheath respectively. Dorsally, the common extensor expansion overlies the proximal interphalangeal joint. (**Fig. 31.**) On its lateral sides the capsule of

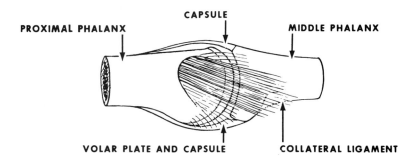

Fig. 30. A diagrammatic lateral view of the proximal interphalangeal joint show-ing the origin and insertion of the collateral ligament, the dorsal synovial pouch contained by the dorsal joint capsule and extensor tendon expansion, and the volar synovial pouch contained by the volar plate and joint capsule. Note that the volar plate is thick distally at its attachment to the middle phalanx and is much thinner proximally. Hyperextension injuries frequently damage the volar plate, while inju-ries resulting from lateral and torque stresses may damage the collateral ligaments.

the joint is covered by the lateral bands of the common extensor and by the medial and lateral band of the intrinsics.

The oblique retinacular ligament arises from the side of the proximal phalanx and passes laterally to the proximal interphalangeal joint cap-sule to join the lateral margin of the extensor bands on the dorsolateral aspect of the middle phalanx. This ligament has a free border at the level of the shaft of the middle phalanx which runs obliquely to insert into the extensor apparatus. The function of the oblique retinacular ligament is to extend the distal interphalangeal joint through a tenodesis effect as the middle or proximal interphalangeal joint is being flexed. The trans-verse retinacular ligament is superficial to the oblique. It runs from the volar aspect of the capsule and flexor tendon sheath dorsally to be at-tached to the lateral margin of the lateral tendon of the extensor mecha-nism.

The proximal interphalangeal joint of the finger is frequently injured during activities involving use of the hand. It is a particularly vulnera-ble joint because of its relatively long proximal and distal lever arms which transmit lateral and torque stresses without elevation by lateral flexibility. Because this joint and the distal joint are small, nonweight-bearing joints, there is often a tendency to minimize injuries to them. However, scarring or inflammation in the relatively dense soft tissue structures in their superficial location may cause persistent symptoms and limitation of motion after an injury. Stiffness and pain in the proxi-mal interphalangeal joint can be quite disabling.

§ 31.37. Nerves.

The nerves to the hand and upper extremity all originate in the spinal cord at various levels in the neck or cervical region. The upper curve

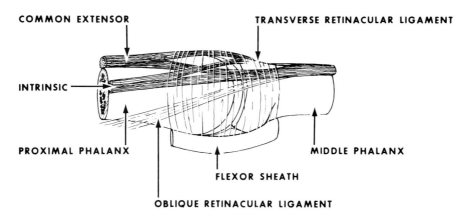

COMMON EXTENSOR   TRANSVERSE RETINACULAR LIGAMENT

INTRINSIC

PROXIMAL PHALANX   MIDDLE PHALANX

FLEXOR SHEATH

OBLIQUE RETINACULAR LIGAMENT

Fig. 31. A lateral schematic drawing of additional soft tissue structures which surround the proximal interphalangeal joint: 3 sets of tendons, the flexors, extensors and intrinsics; 2 additional ligaments, the transverse retinacular and oblique retinacular. The flexor tendons are not depicted, but lie within the flexor sheath. (See Fig. 28.) Note that the flexor sheath is intimately adherent to the volar (palmar) surface of the volar plate. The common extensor and the extensor apparatus with its extensor medial band cover the joint dorsally. Dorsolaterally, the capsule of the joint is covered by the medial and lateral bands of the intrinsic insertion and the lateral band of the common extensor. The oblique retinacular ligament takes origin from the proximal phalanx and the flexor tendon sheath and inserts distally into that portion of the extensor apparatus formed by the lateral bands of the common extensor and intrinsic tendons. When the proximal interphalangeal joint is flexed, this ligament produces tension in the extensor apparatus causing the distal interphalangeal joint to extend.

roots supply the shoulder with sensation and its muscle function; the next lower the elbow; and the lower roots supply the hand with sensation, and the small intrinsic muscles of the hand itself. The final branching of these nerve roots from the shoulder area results in three main nerve trunks in the forearm that supply the hand itself.

A nerve is composed of many fine fibrils called axones, each of which is actually a part of a nerve cell originating in the spinal cord. The axone transmits the electrical impulse. One set of fibers carrying impulses from the spinal cord to muscles is called "motor"; another set transmitting impulses from the specialized end organs in the hand to the spinal cord is called "sensory." Each type of fiber has a distinct function, but both may be incorporated into a large fasciculus (bundle) and several of these are fused into the nerve itself.

The transmission of electrical impulses is the function of the nerve. Such transmission can be impaired by scarring as well as direct cutting or division of the nerve. The loss of function resulting from injury to a nerve trunk will depend not only on the amount of damage, but also on which fibers are injured and which muscles or sensory areas they serve. Thus an injury at the wrist that results in loss of certain muscle func-

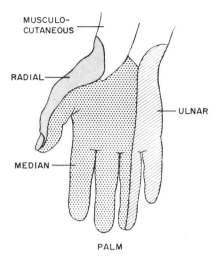

Fig. 32. The areas of skin on the palmar side which are supplied by the respective sensory nerves. This pattern, though quite constant, may show occasional variations, but these will not ordinarily cause confusion in diagnosis or treatment.

tions and loss of sensation in certain areas must have involved the nerve that supplies these specific functions. **(Figs. 32 and 33.)** Diagnosis of nerve injury is thus made from examination of the part supplied by the nerve.

The three nerves of the hand are the radial, median, and ulnar. Each nerve contains motor as well as sensory fibers but in varying proportions depending on the level of examination. Since these different fibers are not distinguishable to the surgeon, repair of a divided nerve by suture may result in some mismatching, due to incorrect rotation of the nerve trunk. If this occurs, the fiber's function is lost.

§ 31.38. Blood supply.

The hand is well nourished by blood through two main arteries, the radial and ulnar. **(Fig. 34.)** The radial artery is palpable as the "pulse" at the wrist. These two main arteries form arches for intercommunication, and, from these arches, the terminal branches supply each digit. Return flow of the blood is through veins and primarily toward the dorsum of the hand. Loss of arterial supply results in gangrene or death of the tissue, but obstruction of return flow causes stagnation of the blood in the dependent parts and is just as dangerous to the vitality of the part.

Although portions of the covering tissues can be replaced and survive as free grafts, it was not until the past decade that reimplantation of extremities was shown to be experimentally feasible. Reimplantation of extremities, especially digits, is extremely difficult and the cases must

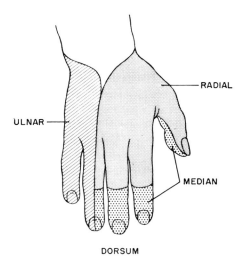

Fig. 33. Sensory patterns on the dorsum of the hand. Note that the median nerve, which supplies most of the important tactile areas on the palmar side, also supplies a portion of the dorsum of the index and middle fingers.

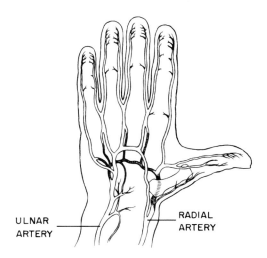

Fig. 34. The arterial blood supply of the hand, as seen from the palmar side. The two principal arteries, radial and ulnar, form two arches, a superficial and a deep (shaded in the diagram). Note that the radial artery, dividing at the wrist, has the larger branch passing behind the thumb metacarpal to supply the deep arch. The ulnar artery in contrast sends its larger division to the superficial arch. From the arches arise the digital branches.

229

be carefully selected. However, with better magnification and microsurgery techniques, even digits have been reimplanted successfully.

Because of the profuse supply of blood vessels in the hand, it is often possible to save a part when it remains attached by only a small pedicle. If this pedicle contains an artery of sufficient size to nourish the tissues, the part may live, and additional vessels will grow into it from the surrounding normal areas.

The principle of carrying the nourishment of a part on a narrow stem is utilized in the transplant of large blocks of tissues from one part of the body to another. The new growth of blood vessels that follows transplants in this way is often sufficient to carry the whole load, if time is given for it to develop. Thus a block of tissue, such as skin and fat from the abdomen, can be transplanted to the hand if, for three weeks, one end is left attached to the abdomen. When union of the graft with the hand is complete, the abdominal stem can be divided. These types of grafts are called pedicle transplants.

§ 31.39. Types of hand injuries.

Since the function of the hand is of such great importance in our daily lives; since this function depends on a very complicated mechanical arrangement of coordinated parts; and since motion depends on intact tendons and their gliding mechanism, the results of hand injury are magnified. A force that might disrupt a leg bone which, when healed, can satisfy the static structural requirements of the leg, can cause in the hand considerable interference with the delicate gliding tissues and thus be a major disability. Scars may bind and limit motion and skill, and coordination can be lost from an injury that might be trivial in other parts.

Injuries of the hand are common in manual workers and especially in industries using high speed machinery requiring the operator to manipulate the work. The time lost from injuries to the hand and the economic loss to the patient and industry far surpass those due to injuries to other parts of the body. Injuries to tendons from cuts and ruptures are diagnosed by determining the loss of function in the part supplied by that tendon. The presence of a wound over the course of a tendon and the patient's ability to make a motion performed solely by that tendon are presumptive evidence that the tendon is severed. Injuries higher up may damage a muscle nerve, and through paralysis of the muscle the function of the tendon is also lost.

Diagnosis is usually made by noting the position of the wound and what structures located there could be injured and by a test of the distal parts to determine the presence or absence of function in those parts. For example, after a cut in the forearm in a location where the ulnar nerve could be injured, tests are made of the sensation in the area supplied by this nerve, *i.e.*, the little finger and one-half of the ring finger, and of the function of the interosseus muscles, which are all supplied by the nerve. Without an exact knowledge of anatomy, it is impossible for the examining physician to determine the amount of damage to the hand and forearm from injury.

A tendon or nerve is sometimes compressed or injured by an external force without causing a break in the skin. A blow of sufficient force that compresses a tendon or nerve against a bony part can cause serious damage. Tissues react to trauma by swelling, and, in the case of a tendon, the scar following this swelling may interfere with its gliding. Nerves can be crushed to such an extent as to prevent transmission of the electrical impulses through the damaged part. Recovery may take place, but the amount of scar, especially if there is much hemorrhage, determines the amount of permanent loss of function.

Rupture of a normal tendon is a rare occurrence, and the term is often inaccurately used to designate a condition in which the tendon pulls from its bony attachment or its attachment to the contractile muscle. Tendons are extremely strong and resistant to stretch. If, however, a tendon is diseased as from arthritis or an infection, or if it is partially cut from a wound or weakened by attrition passing over a rough bony surface, it can rupture under ordinary stress. It is not uncommon to find that a patient can move a finger immediately after a cut over a tendon, yet a week or two later, after the tendon has parted, the motion is lost. This occurs because a few fibers remained intact at the time of injury only to soften and weaken later during the inflammatory healing period.

§ 31.40. Treatment of hand injuries.

Record of injury and treatment

Form 1 constitutes the type of record some medicolegal authorities recommend that physicians complete when treating wounds of the hand. To amplify and clarify the written record, it is also wise for a physician to rough-sketch the patient's wounded hand. Marginal notations adjacent to the sketch can then be made, explicit in terms of the exact size of the wound, area involved, etc. The illustration in **Figure 35** is a printed version of part of such a record.

Included in the record should be the presence of any disease and the existence of any deformity or condition, such as arthritis or a systemic disease, that might have an effect on the degree of rehabilitation or successful repair of the hand. Take the case of the physician who advises a fracture patient that she suffers from arthritis, and that it might complicate the repair. Later the patient's hands and fingers are partially disabled as a result of wearing a cast for three weeks. The physician may be unable to document that he had advised the patient about her arthritis at the time he treated the fracture.

The record should also contain the results of the examination, particularly information relating to fractures and nerve and tendon injuries. Suppose that one month after the repair of a fractured finger, the patient returns and points out that he has a loss of sensation in the finger. Unless the records note that the patient was examined at the time of his injury and was found to have nerve involvement, it may be difficult for the physician to prove that his surgery or treatment was not responsible for the impairment.

RECORD OF HAND WOUND AND TREATMENT

History of present injury:
Patient's age? _____ Sex? _____
Occupation? _____
Type of injury? _____
_____
Where the injury occurred? _____
_____
When the injury occurred? _____
How it happened? _____
At work or not? _____
Minor or major hand? _____
Previous injury and accidents, especially of the involved extremity? _____
Systemic disease present, if any, especially involving the hands? _____
Previous surgery? _____
General condition of the hand prior to the injury? _____
Patient's hobbies? _____

Chief complaint:
Patient's description of the injury, loss of function, etc. _____
_____

Physical examination:
Joints of the extremity proximal to the injured part: _____
Sites of injuries: _____
Type of wound (sharp-to-crush ratio): _____
Loss of function (list as range of motion in degrees of the involved joints): _____
_____
Individual tendon loss: _____
Sensation (pin prick or soft touch): _____
Vascular condition: _____
Clinical fracture or dislocation (stability): _____
Skin condition: _____
Amount of swelling: _____

Primary treatment:
By whom? _____
Where (hospital or office)? _____
Location (town)? _____
Findings of M.D. on exam? _____
What was done? _____
Dressings used? _____
Tetanus, X-ray or lab work? _____

Other action taken:

Again, be specific as to treatment of each digit: _____

Referral or consultation (who, when): _____

Follow-up care: _____

Plan of future reconstruction, including stages and alternatives, if possible: _____

General comments and impression:

Nature of the injuries (be specific in each involved digit as well as general picture overall):_

Describe the injured digits in generally understood fashion, i.e., thumb, index, middle or long, ring, little: _____

Form 1. Specimen form for complete record of care of hand wound. Reprinted through the courtesy of the publishers of Patient Care.

Methods of treatment

Treatment of an injury to the hand aims to restore lost function and to protect the hand against further disability. In most injuries, it is necessary to immobilize a part or all of the hand. Even without injury, such immobilization in an adult will often result in stiffness and loss of function, sometimes permanent. It is important, therefore, that the treatment should be such that it gives the best chance for restoration of the lost function while at the same time is the least likely to cause changes that would bring other disability. Many factors, therefore, have to be taken into consideration in deciding upon a course of treatment.

If there has been a break in the protective covering of the hand, there is danger of infection. Infection may result in much loss of function, far more than the injuring force itself caused. In open wounds, the first aim of treatment is to forestall this contamination, and prevent the invasion by bacteria.

The loss of function such as might come from damage to a tendon, bone, or nerve, is a separate problem. Many times this loss may be treated at the same time as the wound itself, but often treatment of the wound is all that should be done immediately. The treatment of loss of function becomes secondary to protecting the wound from infection.

Treatment of the wound consists of converting it from a surgically contaminated to a surgically clean wound, then closing the surface defect, either by suture or by skin from another part of the body. The essential steps are mechanical cleansing of the wound and surrounding parts by soap and water or surgical detergents, removal of foreign bodies, and the excision of devitalized tissue.

Many wounds cannot be made absolutely sterile, yet they will heal because the body defenses and the normal inflammatory reaction of the healing process will protect the organism against invasion by bacteria. The conditions of the wound, however, must be suitable for this defensive mechanism to function. Dead tissue or tissue so traumatized that its

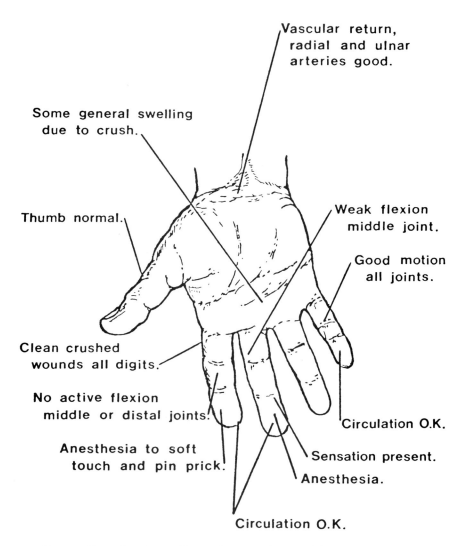

Fig. 35. Chart showing condition of a patient's injured hand. It is recommended that the physician make a sketch of the patient's injuries to amplify written record. (Chart adapted from sketch supplied through the courtesy of the publishers of Patient Care.)

recovery is impossible provides a culture medium which allows bacteria to gain a foothold. These same bacteria under optimum conditions of the wound would probably be destroyed by the body's own protective mechanisms.

Wounds are classified by type as incised, lacerating, avulsed, and crushing. Incised wounds, such as result from a cut with a sharp knife or glass, cause very little tissue destruction. They can be cleansed readily and closed by suture. Lacerating or tearing wounds may often present deceptive appearances. The stretching and tearing of the tissues even some distance from the actual skin wound result in impaired blood supply and changes in the healing process. Such wounds often consist of a flap of tissue with considerable undercutting of the surface, and may show on closer inspection extreme damage to the deeper tissues.

Crushing wounds are most serious and difficult to treat. The tissues are pulped and, with the reactive healing and scar, all parts tend to congeal into a mass of fibrous tissue destroying the mobility and especially interfering with tendon and joint motion. Avulsed wounds consist of the loss of some of the covering tissue such as seen in some wringer injuries or in the so-called "degloving" of a hand caught in rollers or when a finger catches by a ring. Here, if there is sufficient vitality of the remaining deeper structures, one may attempt to replace the lost cover by an immediate skin graft or transfer. Wounds of the crushing and avulsing type may be accompanied by thermal or chemical burning, compounding the damage and complicating the treatment.

The primary function of the surgeon is to treat the wound so as to prevent infection and further disability. His secondary aim is to restore the continuity of the parts damaged by the injuring force and to treat the loss of function. If the wounds are of such a nature that, by their type and location and with the facilities present, healing will be uncomplicated, the additional treatment of the loss of function can be provided at the first sitting. In many instances, however, due to the type of wound, the amount of contamination, its location, or accompanying injuries such as chest, abdomen, and head, it is sound judgment to confine the treatment to that of the wound alone.

This decision of the surgeon is based on many factors. In addition to the type and location of the wound, the surgeon should consider the amount of contamination in the wound and the facilities available. Without proper facilities such as operating room, anesthesia, and experienced assistants, it is impossible to carry out a proper repair of the many damaged structures. In these instances, it is only the surgeon who can decide that the treatment of the wound is all that should be accomplished at the time.

Treatment of the loss of function, from tendon or nerve damage, can be carried out secondarily after the wound has healed. The results of such treatment, when the danger of wound infection has passed, are as good and in many instances better than when carried out at the time of injury. This is especially true of tendon injuries on the palmar side of the fingers.

It is, therefore, wrong to say that every structure in the hand damaged by some force should be repaired at the time of injury. Not only is this attempted primary repair unnecessary to obtain a good return of function, but under certain conditions, such an attempt may add to the total disability. There are some specific conditions in which good surgical judgment would dictate some other procedure, such as a reconstruction, rather than direct repair. An example is in flexor tendon injuries near the distal segment of the finger. In general, it is best to think of the treatment of the injured hand as primarily the treatment of the wound and then later treatment of the loss of function. The goals of the latter is not to repair a divided structure, but to restore a loss of function, and not to repair a divided flexor tendon, but to restore flexion to the part (perhaps with a tendon graft).

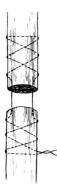

Fig. 36. Tendons are joined by nonabsorbable sutures. The material is woven back and forth to grasp the fibers of the tendon, and placed in such a way as to approximate the ends, and to cause a minimum of damage to the gliding surface.

§ 31.41.   Tendon injuries.

Tendons are strong inelastic fibrous structures extending from a muscle and attached to bone. The short fibers of the tendon that hold the muscle at its proximal end to the bone are attached at a point called the origin. From the distal end of the muscle, the tendon extends as a cord or as a flat ribbon to attach to the bone at a point called the insertion. When a muscle contracts, it shortens, pulls on the tendon, and the point of insertion is drawn toward the point of origin. Motion occurs at the joints between these two points. When tendons are severed, the motion or function is lost but the muscle contracts and stays in the shortened position separating the tendon ends. In repair, it is necessary to close this gap in the tendon and maintain an approximation of the tendon end until healing is complete.

Tendons heal by scar tissue through which tendon fibers then develop to restore continuity. This process requires at least three weeks, so that tension upon the healing ends must be prevented for this period. This is accomplished by using nonabsorbable material for suture, placing it in such a way as to hold the tendon ends together, and then restraining the pull of the muscle by protective external splinting. **(Fig. 36.)**

When healed, the tendon is expected to glide in the surrounding tissues; otherwise the motion of the part will be impaired. Thus the aim is

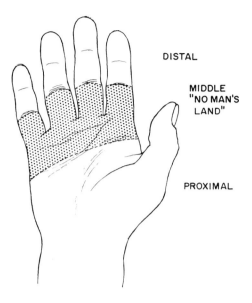

Fig. 37. The palmar surface of the hand, divided into three zones. When flexor tendons are severed, the time and method of repair varies depending on which of these areas is involved.

to obtain healing of the divided ends of the tendon, yet not to have such scarring as to act as a restraint on the gliding.

If a tendon surrounded by a sheath is cut, repair is most difficult because the healing process here involves not only the tendon but the sheath as well. It is as if one would attempt to weld a crack in a piston and the adjoining cylinder wall at the same time. Fusion of the two scars prevents motion. The problem of tendon repair in the sheathed tendon as seen in the flexor side of the finger and palm is not yet solved.

Under presently available methods, a plan of treatment can be stated as follows: The hand is divided into three zones. **(Fig. 37.)** Repair by suture is carried out in the proximal zone primarily if other factors of wound and facilities are favorable.

In the middle zone, commonly called "no man's land," the results of primary repair, even under the most ideal conditions, are not so good as secondary reconstruction; therefore, in this area only the skin is sutured at the time of injury, and the loss of function resulting from the tendon or nerve damage is restored by a reconstruction operation performed under elective conditions at a later date. Many repairs are attempted in this area with the result that so much scar is deposited from the additional surgical trauma that secondary surgery is made more difficult. This is particularly true in those cases where, under the delusion that it is necessary to join every divided structure, the inexperienced surgeon attempts to repair both flexor tendons (sublimis and profundus or superficial and deep) in this most vulnerable area. However, with the more precise microsurgical techniques now available, some experienced hand surgeons will repair both flexor tendons in certain select cases under very ideal conditions. Again, in some isolated instances, the experienced surgeon may properly attempt the repair of one of the divided tendons in this area. If so, he or she will confine the repair to the profundus tendon and will remove the sublimis in an attempt to prevent the scarring in the sheath that will compromise the gliding function. The surgeon will do only the required surgery and will not jeopardize a secondary reconstruction which can be done later if the primary repair fails. Such a method of treatment can be justified only if done by a surgeon of experience under ideal circumstances. Whatever the procedure selected, preservation of gliding simultaneous with end-to-end healing of tendons remains the goal.

In the distal zone, only one flexor tendon (profundus) is present in the finger, and motion of this tendon results in movement only at the terminal joint. Here stability of this joint will improve the function of the finger so that primary repairs under suitable conditions can be done. There are certain conditions, however, which alter the specific type of repair. If the profundus tendon is severed near the insertion and a repair is done, the scarring at the point of suture will usually adhere to the volar aspect of the distal joint capsule, making the effective pull here instead of at the true insertion. Under these circumstances, it is advisable to remove the short stub left of the insertion and reattach the tendon directly to the bone. This is called "advancement of the tendon," and the resultant shortening of the muscle tendon unit, due to the removal of this short portion, can be overcome by slight lengthening of the muscle. This adaptation takes place with ordinary use, but occasionally some corrective splinting in the postoperative period will aid. Usually about one centimeter of shortening can be overcome easily.

If the severance of the tendon is more proximal but still in the distal part of the finger, one of two conditions will be found: (1) both tendon ends will be found lying in the finger at the site of injury, or (2) if there was strong muscular contraction in the forearm at the time of injury, the proximal cut end will have been drawn up into the palm. Treatment depends on which condition is found. When both ends are found in the finger, direct suture of the two divided ends with the removal of the overlying pulley and sheath will result in limited but useful control of the distal segment.

If the proximal cut end of the tendon is retracted into the palm, an attempt to thread it into the finger through the bifurcation of the normal sublimis will usually damage the latter. It is much better to leave the proximal end alone and give stability to the distal joint. This can be done by using the distal end of the tendon, already attached at its normal insertion, and fastening it to the middle segment of the finger. Here it will act as a checkrein across the volar surface of the distal joint. This plan of treatment of flexor tendon injuries takes into consideration the type and location of the wound and the essential functions of the hand.

Extensor tendons heal by the same method as flexor tendons, but because one can overcome the muscular pull by splinting, the simple approximation of the tendon ends by suture is all that is required.

Where these extensor tendons lie beneath the thin skin on the dorsum of the knuckles or over the back of the hand, the suture is passed through the overlying skin and then through the tendons, thus approximating and holding tendon ends until healing is complete. All the suture is then removed, avoiding the foreign body reaction which is apt to occur when nonabsorbable material lies too close to the surface of the skin.

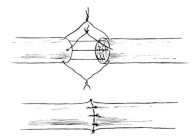

Fig. 38. Diagrammatic representation of nerve suture. Nerves are joined as accurately as possible, with the finest caliber suture material passed through the sheath or outer covering of the nerve. Tension is relieved by positioning of the nearby joints.

§31.42. Nerve injuries.

When a nerve is severed and the divided ends are approximated by sutures, healing is again by scar tissue. Because of the structure of the nerve and the necessity for a regrowth past the scar of the regenerating axonal processes, it is important that the scar be minimal. Suturing is done using the smallest caliber of material, and only the sheath or outer covering of the nerve is approximated. (Fig. 38.) Tension on this suture line is relieved by bending the accompanying joints. Union of nerve ends is completed in a few weeks, but regrowth of axones in the sutured nerve is slower and is about one millimeter a day or one inch a month. Some variation in this rate occurs, depending on age of the patient and the condition of the tissues.

If the regenerating axone is a motor fiber, not only must it grow down to the muscle, but also the muscle, once reinnervated, must develop and hypertrophy to gain enough strength to move the part before there is clinical evidence of recovery. When the motor nerve of a muscle is severed, the muscle loses all activity and shrinks and atrophies. This process is not entirely reversible and is progressive.

As a general rule, if a muscle has been without nerve supply for two years, it is useless to suture the nerve and hope for any recovery of useful motion. If the axones involved carry sensory fibers from a part, such an area will not show evidence of returning sensation until the axones reach the end organs involved. When sensation does begin to return, it is not of normal quality. A disturbed quality of sensation is called "paresthesia" and may persist for a long period after recovery of gross sensation. Paresthesias may be manifested by tingling, burning, and even pain.

There is some evidence that, when a sensory nerve does regenerate, it is never to the normal degree, and thus there is left some residual, though often slight, disability. This is most noticeable in the areas that are most highly specialized for touch, such as the tips of the thumb, index, and middle fingers. Clinically these complaints are difficult to evaluate, since the ordinary tests for sensation involve only gross determinations of touch, pain, and temperature.

The residual major stumbling block in restorative surgery of the extremity is the inability of surgeons to perfect means of gaining regular and reliable return of function after nerve section. When nerve regeneration can be reliably assured, the major problems in reimplantation and multiple nerve sections in severe injuries will be overcome. Furthermore, the optimum time for repair after a recognized injury is not fully known. Analysis of statistical data reveals no clinically predictable difference in recovery between primary and delayed repairs done within one year of injury. A great deal of energy has been invested in studies of nerve grafting and the conclusion remains that the autograft nerve is the most reliable. Nerve homografts in human subjects have not done well.

§ 31.42a. Carpal tunnel syndrome.

The carpal tunnel syndrome is caused by pressure on the median nerve as it travels through the fibro-osseous tunnel of the wrist. (**Fig. 39.**) At this point, the median nerve is in a canal with nine tendons surrounded on three sides by bone and on the fourth by the nonyielding transverse carpal ligament. Any increase in volume in this compartment causes pressure on the nerve and results in the typical pain and tingling sensations.

The most common individual cause of the carpal tunnel syndrome is swelling of the synovial lining of the flexor tendors that occupy the canal with the median nerve. The swelling is usually of unknown etiology but can follow trauma to the wrist either minor or major. Systemic diseases that have been found to cause the syndrome include rheumatoid arthritis, hypothyroidism, pregnancy, osteoarthritis, gout, diabetes mellitus,

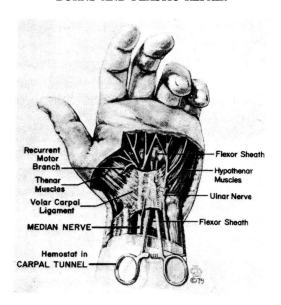

Fig. 39. The carpal tunnel. The carpal tunnel syndrome is caused by pressure on the median nerve as it travels through this fibro-osseous tunnel of the wrist.

amyloidosis, and myeloma. Also, symptoms can be caused by local encroachment in the carpal tunnel, such as by anomalous muscles or tumors.

The usual symptoms associated with carpal tunnel syndrome are tingling, numbness and pain in the hand in the distribution of the median nerve. While this can affect the thumb, index, long and radial half of the ring finger, the long and index fingers are the ones most commonly affected. The symptoms are found more frequently in women (about five-to-one), especially in the thirty- to sixty-year age group, and are usually worse at night. Symptoms can be aggravated by a repetitive activity or by sudden unusual stressful activity.

Some surgeons believe that the carpal tunnel syndrome can be work-induced if a job requires continuous repetitive motion of the hand. Also, position of the hand and wrist and vibrational stimuli are felt to be contributing factors when the syndrome occurs as an occupational disease.

Clinical examination will usually reveal decreased sensation to pin prick over the distribution of the median nerve. Frequently gentle tapping over the median nerve at the wrist will reproduce pain and tingling in the hand (Tinel's sign) as will acute flexion of the wrist for thirty seconds (Phalen's sign). In the advanced stages of the carpal tunnel syndrome, an obvious decrease in the size of the small muscles at the base of

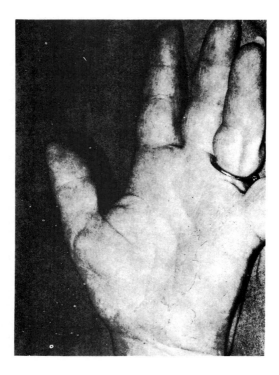

Fig. 40. In the advanced stages of carpal tunnel syndrome, an obvious decrease in the size of the small muscles at the base of the thumb can be seen.

the thumb is noted (**Fig. 40**), accompanied by a definite weakness of those muscles.

The patient can also experience pain in the shoulder and forearm that may or may not seem to radiate from the wrist. While no objective neurological findings are present in the arm when this is associated with carpal tunnel syndrome, the pain is relieved following surgical release.

Electromyelographic and nerve conduction studies can aid in the diagnosis of carpal tunnel syndrome; however, they are not always necessary. These tools are most helpful when there is some question concerning the exact point of pathology. Primarily, the diagnosis will be determined by history and physical examination.

Conservative treatment usually consists of splinting the wrist in extension and local injection of a cortisone preparation into the carpal tunnel canal. *Care must be taken not to inject directly into the median nerve.*

Surgical therapy consists of dividing the transverse carpal ligament that serves the roof of the carpal tunnel. This ligament is sometimes released through a transverse incision at the wrist; however, this approach gives a very limited view of the surgical area. The generally preferred incision is the longitudinal approach along the case of the thumb muscles, which allows complete inspection of the carpal tunnel canal. Some surgeons believe that this incision should extend into the wrist for complete exposure of the median nerve.[42]

Other medical problems can cause symptoms identical to a carpal tunnel syndrome and must be excluded when making the diagnosis. These conditions include a cervical disc syndrome, thoracic outlet syndrome, peripheral neuritis, cervical rib, and syringomyelia. The treatment of these conditions is significantly different from that of a carpal tunnel syndrome.

Workers who perform repetitive tasks are at risk for carpal tunnel syndrome and include garment workers, butchers, grocery checkers, electronics assembly workers, typists, musicians, packers, housekeepers, cooks, and carpenters. However, no reliable data exists on the frequency of work-related carpal tunnel syndrome in the general working population. Surveillance of work-related carpal tunnel syndrome is limited because of inadequate training of health professionals and underreporting of recognized cases.[43]

In 1988, the California Occupational Health Program (COHP) surveyed health-care practitioners to measure the occurrence of carpal tunnel syndrome in Santa Clara County (1987 population, 1.4 million), which has a variety of service and manufacturing industries. The survey was conducted as part of the Sentinel Event Notification System for Occupational Risks (SENSOR) program — a collaborative effort involving the National Institute for Occupational Safety and Health (NIOSH) and ten state health departments — which is intended to improve occupational disease surveillance at the state and local levels.

---

[42] Editor's note: Most articles dealing with carpal tunnel syndrome advocate surgery for relief of symptoms if conservative therapy fails. All authors stress immediate and lasting relief of symptoms following operation, but seldom mention any complications. In the January, 1978 issue of The Journal of Hand Surgery, Rodney I. MacDonald, M.D., and his associates reported on a series in which 186 operative cases of carpal tunnel release revealed 34 complications in 22 patients, for an incidence of 12%. Complications were grouped into seven categories: (1) inadequate section of the transverse carpal ligament (associated with both transverse and curved incisions); (2) symptoms related to damage to the palmar cutaneous branch of the median nerve; (3) reflex sympathetic dystrophy; (4) unsightly hypertrophic scar due to inappropriate incision; (5) damage to the superficial palmar arch following blind sectioning of the transverse carpal ligament; (6) bowstringing of the flexor tendons after excision of the transverse carpal ligament; and (7) adherence of the flexor tendons following excision of the mesotendon. Most complications encountered can be prevented by proper operative technique.

[43] The Centers for Disease Control, Occupational Disease Surveillance: Carpal Tunnel Syndrome, 262 J.A.M.A. 886 (Aug. 18), 1989.

The COHP staff members identified 1,698 Santa Clara County health-care providers who practiced in specialties and settings considered to be relevant to the care of carpal tunnel patients. Practitioners were administered questionnaires. Of 515 (30%) providers who responded, 489 (95%) reported caring for a total of 7,214 patients in 1987. Of these, responding providers believed 3,413 (47%) cases may have been work-related. Work-related cases were seen by 377 providers in various settings, including internal medicine, industrial and occupational medicine, chiropractic, and physical therapy.[44]

Work-related carpal tunnel syndrome is considered a cumulative trauma disorder caused by job tasks that subject the hand and wrist to biomechanical stresses, including (1) repetitive movements of the hand, (2) forceful grasping or pinching of tools or other objects, (3) awkward positions of the hand and wrist, (4) direct pressure over the carpal tunnel, and (5) use of vibrating hand-held tools. Because repetitive hand movements are required in many occupations, new high-risk groups for the syndrome and other cumulative trauma disorders continue to be identified. Patients with nonoccupational risk factors are also at risk for work-related carpal tunnel syndrome.[45] (See *infra*.)

Even though the disorder can often be managed with conservative measures (*e.g.*, wrist immobilization and nonsteroidal anti-inflammatory medications), recognition of work-related carpal tunnel syndrome is important, since without job redesign or reassignment, symptoms are likely to recur when the patient resumes the precipitating tasks. For all patients with symptoms suggestive of the disorder, an occupational history should be obtained that includes a description of tasks involving use of the hands. Failure to eliminate contributory job factors can result in recurrence or progression of symptoms, impaired use of the hand, and the need for surgical treatment. Redesign of tools, workstations, and job tasks can prevent occurrence of the syndrome among co-workers.[46]

Nonoccupational risk factors

Attribution of carpal tunnel syndrome to cumulative trauma is not always clear-cut. A random sample of workers at a poultry-processing plant whose tasks entailed significant repetitive hand usage were compared with a control group of applicants for employment. No significant differences in median-nerve motor and sensory latencies were detected between the two groups. Other researchers have evaluated obesity, age, sex, and hand dominance as risk factors for slowing of sensory conduction of the median nerve and have found that individual characteristics rather than job-related factors were the principal determinant. For example, patients who displayed the "clencher syndrome" (*i.e.*, those who

---

[44] Id.
[45] Id.

[46] Id.

habitually clench their jaw, hands, or rectum) and who drive long distances to work were more prone to work-related injury, particularly where the workplace was stressful. Furthermore, poor head, neck, or upper-body posture and forward-thrusting of the head and shoulders may accentuate symptoms of the disorder.[47]

In addition to the systemic disorders mentioned at the beginning of this section, other nonoccupational conditions associated with carpal tunnel syndrome include menopause and fibromyalgia.[48] Also, in 1993 physicians at a Barcelona, Spain hospital published a report linking carpal tunnel syndrome with hyperthyroidism. The authors found that the clinical and neurophysiologic evolution suggests such a relationship and that in patients with both CTS and hyperthyroidism, the symptoms of CTS went into remission when the endocrine problem was controlled. In such patients, the authors found that surgery was usually not necessary.[49]

§ 31.42b. Ulnar tunnel syndrome.

The ulnar tunnel syndrome is much less frequently seen than the carpal tunnel syndrome. (§ 31.42a.) Like the carpal tunnel syndrome, the symptoms are pain, tingling, and numbness in the distribution of the ulnar nerve to the hand. Advanced cases can show involvement of the small muscles of the hand innervated by the ulnar nerve.

The ulnar nerve at the wrist runs through a fibro-osseous canal, known as the canal of Guyon, along with the ulnar artery. Any increase in volume in the canal results in pressure on the ulnar nerve and produces symptoms. Ulnar tunnel syndrome can be the result of trauma, either caused by swelling or bleeding into the canal or by direct trauma to the nerve. Also damage to the ulnar artery can cause increased pressure on the ulnar nerve.

As in the carpal tunnel syndrome, surgical relief of pressure on the nerve usually alleviates the problem. This is accomplished by dividing the ligamentous roof of the canal of Guyon and removing the offending problems.

§ 31.42c. Cubital tunnel syndrome.

This syndrome is characterized by loss of sensation, paresthesias, or weakness over the distribution of the ulnar nerve. Often, there is a history of previous trauma to the elbow, sometimes many years prior to the present symptoms.

The ulnar nerve, as it passes through the tight tunnel between the medial epicondyle and the olecranon, is often incarcerated in scar tissue

---

[47]Sheon, R. P., *Repetitive Strain Injury*, 102 Postgrad. Med. 72 (Oct.), 1997.
[48]Id.

[49]Roquer, J., and Cono, J.F., *Carpal Tunnel Syndrome and Hyperthyroidism*, 88 Acts Neurol. Scand 149, 1993.

and must be transferred to an area away from the trauma and scar. The nerve is usually transposed anteriorly under a subcutaneous flap of tissue or within the flexor muscle mass in the forearm.

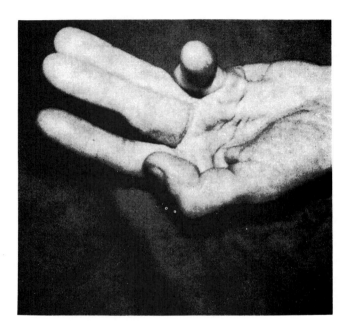

Fig. 41. Dupuytren's contracture involving primarily the little finger with bands and nodules in the palm.

§ 31.42d. Dupuytren's contracture.

The role of trauma in causing Dupuytren's disease or contracture has been the subject of much controversy since Baron Dupuytren described the condition in 1831. This disorder in its classic form is characterized by fibrous bands and nodules in the palm that often cause contractures of the fingers, especially the ring and little fingers. (**Fig. 41.**) This can progress to where the fingers cannot be moved away from the palm. (**Fig. 42.**) The disorder has been the target of research for many years, yet its basic etiology has continued to elude us.

Certain facts about this condition are known, however, and have been well documented. There is a definite hereditary factor, which was clearly demonstrated in 1963 by Ling,[50] who obtained a positive family history

[50] Ling, R. S. M., *Genetic Factor in Dupuytren's Disease*, 45B J. Bone & Joint Surg. 709, 1963. See also Boyes, J. H., *Dupuytren's Contracture, Notes on the Age of Onset and the Relationship to Handedness*, 88 Am. J. Surg. 147, 1954; Clarkston, P.,

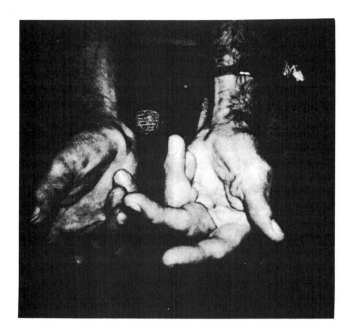

Fig. 42. Dupuytren's contracture. Bilateral disease involving little and ring fingers.

of only 16% when he questioned those affected, but found an actual incidence of 68% when he examined those patients' relatives himself.

Depuytren's contracture is a disorder of the older age group; it rarely appears before the age of forty and afflicts a larger percentage of people in each succeeding decade, so that approximately 20% of those over the age of sixty-five are afflicted. Males predominate by a ratio of seven to one. Another characteristic of Dupuytren's disease is its affinity for the Caucasian race, its occurrence in blacks and orientals being very rare. Northern Europeans, or populations colonized by them, have the highest incidence.

Many investigators have found the disease among epileptics and alcoholics much higher than in the general population, and the deformity is likely to be more severe in these groups. No satisfying explanation of these associations is known. The deformity in the palm and fingers is

Aetiology of Dupuytren's Disease, 110 Guy's Hosp. Rep. 52, 1961; Hueston, J. T. and Tubiana, R. T., *Dupuytren's Disease,* Constable Limited, Edinburgh, 1974; Larsen, R. D., et al., *Pathogenesis of Dupuytren's Contracture: Experimental and Further Clinical Observations,* 42A J. Bone & Joint Surg. 993, 1960; Moorehead, J. J., *Dupuytren's Contracture: Review of the Disputed Etiology 1831-1956,* 56 N.Y. St. J. Med. 3686, 1956; Skoog, T., *Pathogenesis and Etiology of Dupuytren's Contracture,* 31 Plastic & Recon. Surg. 258, 1963.

often associated with fibrous deformities elsewhere on the body including (1) nodules on the soles of the feet; (2) "knuckle pads," or fibrous deposits over the knuckles; and (3) fibrous plaques causing deviation of the penis, known as Peyronie's disease. The presence of any of these lesions often signifies a more aggressive form of the disease.

The question of the cause of the disease has been disputed since Dupuytren, in his original description, ascribed the cause in his patient, a coachman, to the repeated trauma by the butt of his whip against his palm. Most early authorities supported the idea that trauma, including that incurred in the manual labor of some occupations, was the cause, or at the least an aggravator, of this condition. The reasons for this lay in the fact that it was much more prevalent in males, its incidence in older populations is much higher, and often patients give a history of the deformity beginning soon after a specific traumatic incident or the beginning of a certain type of employment. In addition, some early investigators found a higher percentage of manual laborers were involved, and that the dominant hand was the one most affected. Microscopic examination of the tissue involved in the disease has demonstrated some evidence suggestive of trauma to a few authorities, but this has not been confirmed by later investigators.

During the past few decades, evidence has piled up against occupation or trauma as an instigator, or even an aggravator, of the disease. More thorough studies have shown that the condition is not more prevalent among manual workers, but, in fact, is more common among clerical workers. The disease is bilateral in the majority of cases, not restricted to the dominant, or trauma bearing hand, and in many cases the non-dominant hand is affected while the dominant hand remains disease-free. Also against the theory of traumatic etiology is the strong heredity pattern that appears to play the dominant role. The fact that there are accompanying lesions on other parts of the body not subjected to trauma suggests that there is a systemic rather than local cause. (If one wanted to implicate trauma as the cause, the fact that Dupuytren's disease does not follow many cases of obvious trauma would also have to be explained.) Also appearing to contradict the role of trauma in etiology is the fact that many cases seem to begin or become worse during forced inactivity, for example, in nursing homes.

Although there are cases of isolated, significant trauma to the hand followed by the appearance of Dupuytren's disease, most authorities now concur that the role of occupation with repeated stress and trauma to the hand plays no part in either the precipitation or aggravation of the disease.

While a number of treatment conservative measures have been tried, surgery to excise the diseased tissue once contracture has developed is recognized as the treatment of choice by nearly all authorities. There is some debate as to the extent of surgery that should be performed, but even in the most radical of operations, there is a significant chance of recurrence.

§ 31.43. Complications of treatment and residual disability.

In addition to the danger of infection common to all injuries involving wounds and the other results of the original injuring force, the most common and most disabling result of a hand injury is stiffness of the joints. As mentioned earlier, some stiffness is almost inevitable and, fortunately, especially in the younger individuals, it is temporary. If, however, the immobilization of the parts is prolonged for whatever reason or the joints are maintained in a prolonged nonfunctional position, then some stiffness may remain as a permanent residue. This complication can usually be prevented by proper treatment but, once developed, it cannot usually be completely relieved.

Malalignment of the body skeleton from either single or multiple fractures and dislocations of the hand results in varying disability due to upsetting the balance of muscular forces.

It is almost impossible to injure a hand and expect to have complete recovery of all function. Any severe injury will leave some disability. The disability may be manifested by limited motion, deformity, impaired sensation, instability, or weakness of grasp. If there is significant injury to the articulating surfaces and structures of a joint, the possibility of return to normal function is minimal. Scarred tissue may be more susceptible to sunlight, detergents, and cleansing agents. The effect is always either to reduce the function of the hand or to diminish its value as a sensory organ of perception.

The effect on the patient depends to a considerable degree on the specific uses of the hand necessary to him in his occupation or profession. A mild limitation of motion, not disabling to a clerk or office worker, might be a tragic loss to a pianist or highly skilled technician.

Residual disability in the hand is evaluated by determining the loss of motion as compared to the opposite normal hand, measuring the range of motion of various joints, and comparing the strength of grasp and pinch (**Fig. 43**), the two elements of power and precision grip, and determining the extent of lost sensation. The objective findings must be weighed against the specific occupational needs in the hand, the age, motivation, and adaptability of the patient, and whether it is the patient's dominant hand. The sole use of arbitrary tables of percentage loss for a certain digit is not realistic because the tables fail to take into account these various personal factors.

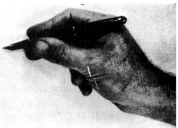

Fig. 43. The power grasp (left) and the precision grasp (right). In strong grasp, the fingers are flexed by the powerful extrinsic forearm muscles, and the thumb is more or less in the plane of the fingers. For precision work, the intrinsic muscles are utilized. Here the thumb is in opposition to the finger pulps; its tactile surface and that of the index and middle fingers hold an object like the three jaws of the machinist's chuck. These two types of grasp give the hand its prehensile function.

§ 31.44. Preexisting conditions.

There are many conditions that can be present in the hand which will alter the results of injury. These include developmental variations that occur in the hands as well as changes due to local or systemic disease processes.

Age is an important factor. In the young, the recuperative and regenerative powers are greater and there is less tendency to develop the disabling stiffness after injury. In the elderly, stiffness comes quickly and there is the added factor of impaired nutrition from diminished blood supply. In senile patients, the skin is thinner, is more easily damaged, and recovers more slowly after injury. Age is normally accompanied by attritional changes in the joints or tendons that cause them to become more prone to injury. In some instances, this is to such a degree that the injuring force is no more than the ordinary use or wear-and-tear. Since it is human nature to attempt to blame any change from the normal on some abnormal incident, many patients with changes in the hand due entirely to advancing age and this wear-and-tear phenomenon claim the disability as a result of some "accident."

It is difficult in many instances to determine the causal relationship between an injury and a disabling condition. Beyond this is the question of aggravation. Assuming a preexisting condition and then an injury, did the injury cause an alteration of the normal development of this preexisting condition? The answer to such questions involves a great deal of experience and knowledge regarding what is normal for that age and condition.

Many generalized body disease processes can affect the hand as well. Among these are arthritis, diabetes, tuberculosis, Dupuytren's contracture, and gout. Arthritis especially — the rheumatoid form — can result in a severe crippling deformity. In other types of body disease or injury, the basic process affects the nerves that control the hand, as in spinal cord injury or tumors, syringomyelia, poliomyelitis, and brain lesions from strokes or cerebral palsy.

Any disease process that affects the coordination of the hand, or more importantly, one that impairs its sensation, makes the hand more liable to injury. A numb area is susceptible to burning and, once damaged, the resultant wound heals slowly because of the loss of sensation and trophic changes that are dependent upon an intact nerve supply.

§ 31.45. Rehabilitation.

Today, the return of a worker with an injured hand to his or her former occupation or to a new trade or skill can be accomplished in several ways. In the past, the natural motivation to take care of one's own economic needs caused an injured to exercise, develop, and retrain if necessary, the remaining parts of the extremity. At present, there is a great tendency to try to relieve these persons of this duty and pass them through rehabilitation centers. Though these facilities have considerable value in many forms of disability, including the actual loss of a hand, most patients with ordinary hand injuries usually need only the desire and will to be able to return to work. The average patient can carry out so-called physiotherapy himself. If instructions are given and accompanied by the proper motivation, the results can be satisfactory. In many hand injury cases, there is little need for certain forms of physiotherapy such as diathermy, ultrasound, and passive stretching and massage following injuries to the hand; in fact, in certain hand injuries, the patient's disability may be prolonged by over-zealous physiotherapy measures.

X. RELATED TOPICS

§ 31.46. Anxiety disorders in cosmetic surgery patients.

Cosmetic surgery is an especially intense psychological experience. In addition to having the usual concerns about surgical complications and side effects, these patients come to the plastic surgeon filled with hope and expectations for an improved self-image, which puts them at risk for added anxiety and disappointment. This anxiety plus the perception of vulnerability can cause significant psychological reactions that can complicate the outcome for the patient.[51]

---

[51] Rankin, M., and Borah, G. L., *Anxiety Disorders in Plastic Surgery*, 100 Plast. Reconstr. Surg. 535 (Aug.), 1997. In an attempt to evaluate suggestions of personality disturbances in cosmetic surgery patients, Dunofsky compared a group of women over the age of 30 who had undergone single or multiple facial cosmetic surgery with a control group. The cosmetic surgery patients were found to be more narcis-

Through careful questioning and psychosocial assessment, the plastic surgeon, using appropriate indicators of abnormal anxiety, should be able to identify the majority of patients who are at an increased risk for postoperative psychological problems. However, some patients may mask concerns that may later manifest in anger and hostility. Close follow-up care by the plastic surgeon team is essential to the proper postoperative treatment of an overly anxious patient, and it is imperative that problematic patients be referred promptly to a qualified mental health professional to limit their adverse experience and to promote their well-being.[52]

§ 31.47. The psychological effect of facial disfigurement.

Wherever social interaction occurs, it is the face of the other person upon which we center attention. Not only does the face represent the person — his or her identity — it is also the source of vocal communication and the revealer of emotions. From the face's contour and expressive features we receive and interpret signals, and tend to form impressions and make judgments about personality and character traits — judgments that "turn us on or off" and operate adversely toward those whose faces happen to be ugly or "different."[53]

Because a disfigured person looks different, he or she is thought to be different, i.e., inferior, and receives differential treatment. If a person's appearance is a stimulus to feelings of shock and aversion — common reactions toward those whose faces have been burned or mutilated — he or she is avoided.[54]

The emotional prejudice surrounding the facially crippled, coupled with our obsession with physical attractiveness, exerts social and psychological pressures of such magnitude that to adapt and adjust to disfigurement is extremely difficult. Socially the disfigured are deprived of experiencing the pleasures and opportunities normally available to the nondisfigured for interpersonal relations, sex, and jobs.[55]

Studies indicate that employers are less likely to hire persons who are not superficially attractive. Regardless of their education, experience, or personality, one whose face is cruelly scarred or twisted invariably suffers employment discrimination. Employers are reluctant to place such

---

sistic and to have more problems with separation-individuation than the control group, but no differences were found on measuring self-esteem and social anxiety. Also, there were no differences between the single- and multiple-surgery patients. Dunofsky, M., *Psychological Characteristics of Women Who Undergo Single and Multiple Cosmetic Surgeries*, 39 Ann. Plast. Surg. 223 (Sept.), 1997.

[52] Rankin, M., and Borah, G. L., *Anxiety Disorders in Plastic Surgery*, 100 Plast. Reconstr. Surg. 535 (Aug.), 1997.

[53] Macgregor, F. C., *Psychic Trauma of Facial Disfigurement*, 33 Trial 90, 1984.

[54] Id.

[55] Id.

persons in positions that require direct contact with others. This is an unfortunate fact of human behavior that simply cannot be ignored.[56]

Excluded from the mainstream of a society hostile to those whose faces do not conform, the psychological consequences of facial disfigurement can be severe. This fact has been well established. Studies of several hundred plastic surgery patients whose facial defects were classified as slight, moderate, marked, or gross, revealed that the majority of patients suffered from psychological disturbances ranging from feelings of inferiority, anxiety, shame, self-consciousness, paranoid complaints, hostility, and behavioral problems to partial or total withdrawal and psychotic states.[57]

§ 31.48. Wound healing and scars.[58]

There has existed in the lay population and, even more unfortunately, in the medical community, the belief that a plastic surgeon can leave a healed wound with no visible scar. This is impossible. It is important for the attorney, both in counseling clients and in reviewing personal injury or malpractice cases, to bear this in mind. Even today, plastic surgeons are often called to the emergency room where the emergency room physician says something to the effect that "We could repair this patient's laceration, but she said she did not want a scar, so we thought you had better come treat it." This does a disservice to the patient, her family, and the plastic surgeon.

An acceptable scar is dependent on a number of variables. A "good" scar is one that is level with and essentially the same color as the surrounding uninvolved skin. It is ideally a fine line, but this can vary with location. In terms of a combination of physical and cosmetic concepts, a scar should not cause a tethering, distortion, or contracture of any surrounding landmarks or joints. An example of a location that generally leaves the least scars is the eyelid. Probably the worst areas for scarring are the anterior chest, shoulders, and upper back. These scars generally are quite wide and often remain hypertrophic for an extended period of time, sometimes permanently.

Another myth is that children "make better scars" than adults. It is true that children seem to heal more quickly and often with less tissue loss in even a compromised wound. However, the scars on children and adolescents remain much redder for much longer than similar scars in older patients. For this reason, early scar revision is more reasonable in an elderly patient than in an infant or child. The best advice that can be

---

[56] Defense Research Institute, Inc., *Plaintiff's Strategy,* June, 1987, p. 1.

[57] Macgregor, F. C., *Psychic Trauma of Facial Disfigurement,* 33 Trial 90, 1984.

[58] Mangold, W. J., "Plastic Surgery," in

Wecht, C. H., et al., editors, *Handling Soft Tissue Injury Cases: Medical Aspects,* Vol. 3, 2d ed., The Michie Co., Charlottesville, Va., 1993.

given parents of two- through fourteen-year-old children with an unsightly scar is simply to *wait.* Not only will a better result be achieved by scar revision when the child is older, it will allow the child to mature to the stage where he or she will be able to agree to, and participate actively in, the decision making involving both the revision and the often inconvenient postoperative care. In most cases, however, wound healing and scar formation and maturation follow a fairly predictable pattern.

With respect to the scars themselves, they can be expected to remain reddened from a few weeks after repair in areas such as the eyelids and face, and to as much as a year or two in areas such as the chest, shoulders, and knees. Most of the surface irregularities, early minimal "hypertrophy," and color disparity will resolve in the first six to twelve months. Thus, a scar that appears to need revision when viewed a few days or weeks after repair may ultimately require no further surgical attention.

Though the healing process has not been completed until the scar is soft and the redness has disappeared, there are some things that can be done to help enhance this process or, in some instances, speed it.

Massage seems to provide some benefit by simply allowing patients to feel that they are accomplishing something while awaiting the natural healing process. However, firm, continuous pressure, such as with a pressure garment, as is used in many instances on burn scars, may have significant value. Pressure also can be used with scars of flexion surfaces, such as the anterior neck, the anterior elbows, and around the knees. Though the pressure garments are uncomfortable and require some getting used to, they can be of immeasurable benefit in the severely scarred patient.

Long-term immobilization of a scarred area has also been shown to be of benefit, but in most instances the price paid in inconvenience is greater than the benefit reaped. The young girl who desires to have a better scar on her arm or leg may be told that long-term immobilization can help, but rarely will she be willing to have an arm or leg splinted for weeks or months. There is some suggestion currently that the use of an adherent, clear, plastic dressing, especially on scars of the arm or leg, may be of benefit in achieving an improved scar result. However, this has not yet been proven and will require further study.

In most instances, relatively heroic measures are simply not warranted. In areas such as the face, where the best result is hoped for, all reasonable measures should be taken in terms of initial wound care. However, if this still proves to leave a less than satisfactory scar, patients can benefit most by simply allowing the scar to mature completely and then consider surgical revision.

Probably the single most important thing a patient can do, and should always be encouraged to do, is to protect the fresh scar from overexposure to sun.

There are bleaching agents that many patients have been made aware of through the advertising media, if not from their doctor. They should be told that these products cannot, with any degree of certainty, be used to lighten *hyperpigmented* scars, since the amount of "bleaching" of the increased pigmentation cannot be controlled. More often than not, the resulting treated area is lighter than the surrounding area. Thus, the patient has simply replaced an unsightly darker area with an unsightly lighter one.

Development of malignancies from unstable scars is also a possibility. For this reason, in addition to the problems of cosmetic result and wound management, unstable scars should receive medical attention and such things as Z-plasty release or dermabrasion "sanding," combined with overgrafting, or simply excising and skin grafting may be relevant considerations.

One often unavoidable wound-healing problem is "trapdoor" deformity. This occurs with a U-shaped wound and resulting scar. With a U-shaped scar, shortening tends to contract and lessen the surface area within the concave portion of the scar. This tends to bulge the skin and soft tissue within this arch. The resulting defect is a bulge or "biscuit" of skin that often remains elevated and becomes a permanent defect. Though attempts have been made to avoid this result, no amount of layering of the closure or of support of the subcutaneous tissue seems to alter the result. The only effective management is a revision procedure, either by creating multiple Z-plasty releases of the line of the scar or, in some cases, by resecting a portion of the fullness and converting the scar to a more straight line or less acute arch.

Another bothersome problem of wound healing and scarring is that of permanent suture marks. The single most important determining factor in this regard seems to be the length of time sutures are left in place. Tension of the sutures on the wound is also of importance, but in most situations in which a wound has been closed by a competent surgeon, if excessive tension becomes exerted, it is more likely due to swelling and edema of the wound than to the fact that the sutures were simply placed too tightly. However, sutures left in as much as two weeks will cause permanent suture marking, while those that are removed perhaps as early as seven days, and most certainly as early as five days after placement, will generally not cause permanent marking.

Keloids and hypertrophic scars[59]

A study of sixty-five patients with 100 treated keloids and hypertrophic scars was undertaken to assess the value of (1) beta radiation alone,

---

[59] Karzi, M. A., et al., *Evaluation of Various Methods of Treating Keloids and Hy-* *pertrophic Scars: A 10-Year Follow-Up Study*, 45 Br. J. Plast. Surg., 374, 1992.

(2) beta radiation in combination with surgical treatment, and (3) triamcinolone acetonide administered to the lesion.

The authors found that primary irradiation seemed to relieve the symptoms of keloids and hypertrophic scars (55% response) without much influence on the size of the lesions. Postoperative irradiation, however, provided better control of keloids, with some recurrences, and combined preoperative and postoperative radiation yielded similar results, which suggests that the preoperative irradiation contributed little to the success rate. Triamcinolone acetonide was found to be effective in most lesions, reducing symptoms in 73% of the patients and flattening the lesion in 64%.

§ 31.49. The silicone breast implant controversy.

In December 1991, a San Francisco jury found that a ruptured silicone implant made by Dow Corning Corporation caused "mixed connective tissue disease" in a patient and awarded her $840,000 in compensatory damages and $6.5 million in punitive. In reaching its decision, the jury found that Dow Corning's implants were defectively designed and manufactured, that Dow Corning "failed to warn of a known or knowable risk of harm of the type plaintiff alleged occurred to her," and that the company was guilty of malice and fraud.[60] Dow Corning had vigorously defended the action, claiming that the medical evidence showed that the plaintiff's connective tissue disease had predated her implant surgery.

In January 1992, a special FDA advisory panel recommended a temporary ban on the use of gel-filled silicone implants pending further study. In early February, Dow Corning, the leading manufacturer of the more than one million implants in use, announced a change in top corporate management personnel and a change in policy; the company would begin new efforts to answer questions about implant safety and would consider providing financial assistance to women who wanted to have their implants removed.[61]

Two weeks later, the FDA advisory panel issued further recommendations. It officially classified the implants as "experimental," and recommend that the temporary ban for women seeking breast augmentation be continued. Women seeking implants for reconstruction after breast cancer surgery would be required to participate in supervised clinical trials in order to obtain the devices.[62]

---

[60] "Dow Corning Breast Implant Recipient Awarded $7.3 Mil. in Damages; Firm Appealing," F-D-C Reports, The Gray Sheet, Dec. 16, 1991, p. 10.

[61] Hilts, P. J., *Implant Company Ousts Top Executive as Controversy Grows*, New York Times, Feb. 11, 1992.

[62] Foreman, J., *Implants Seen as Experimental; As Result of FDA Review, Access to Silicone Gel Breast Implants to Be Curbed*, The Boston Globe, Feb. 23, 1992, p. 4.

The panel also recommended that if an implant ruptures, a woman should have it removed.[63] (Dow Corning warned that it is common for plastic surgeons to advise their patients to massage implants to reduce the formation of scar tissue, a practice that can be hazardous because of the risk of rupture.)[64] The panel did not recommend that women undergo mammograms to search for ruptures, but did advise that they follow established recommendations for routine mammography for breast cancer screening, which can pick up signs of ruptured implants. It also urged these women to be sure to get mammograms that use a special technique that helps the X-rays to "see" past the implant to underlying tissue, and that the mammograms be performed at facilities accredited by the American College of Radiology.[65]

Dow Corning officials said that the reported rupture rate for their implants was only 0.5%; however, independent researchers placed the rate at 5% to 6%. Rupture usually occurs between seven and ten years after implantation, especially after a trauma.[66] In March 1992, Dow Corning quit the implant business, saying that it had $250 million in insurance to apply to claims.

In addition to the clinical trials for breast cancer surgery patients, the FDA panel recommended "look back" studies of patients who already have implants.[67]

Some observers believed that the charges against silicone implants are exaggerated, that the evidence supporting such claims was poorly documented, and that the FDA has acted with insensitivity to the needs of women who can benefit from implants following cancer surgery and for cosmetic reasons.[68]

In September 1993, Winer and his associates[69] reported on a survey of women with a history of breast cancer who have undergone breast reconstruction with silicone implants. The purpose of their study was to determine the concerns of these women regarding their breast reconstructions and to assess the impact on them of the silicone implant controversy. They randomly selected 174 women and interviewed them by telephone from February through May 1992. The women, a subset of 359 mastectomy/reconstruction patients of one university-based plastic surgeon, had their first permanent prostheses placed between 1985 and 1990.

All study participants were aware of the controversy surrounding silicone implants. Seventy-six percent stated that breast reconstruction helped them cope with cancer, and only 16% had regrets about reconstruction. Many of the respondents had misconceptions about the nature

[63] Id.
[64] Hilts, supra.
[65] Foreman, supra.
[66] Id.
[67] Id.
[68] Fisher, J., *The Silicone Controversy:*
When Will Silicone Prevail?, 326 N. Engl. J. Med. 1696 (June 18), 1992.
[69] Winer, E. P., et al., *Silicone Controversy: A Survey of Women with Breast Cancer and Silicone Implants,* 85 J. Nat'l Cancer Inst. 1407 (Sept. 1), 1993.

of possible complications from silicone implants. Fifty-five percent were worried about the implants, yet only 13% considered having them removed as a result of the controversy. Only 27% indicated they would definitely choose silicone implants again. The majority of the women were unwilling to accept substantial risks of complications from implants, but there was variability in the level of risk that the respondents would tolerate.

In March 1994, Dow Corning and other breast implant makers put up $4.25 billion for women claiming injury. In May 1995, the company filed for Chapter 11 bankruptcy. Five months later, on October 28, a Nevada jury awarded an ill silicone breast implant claimant $4 million in compensatory damages and $10 million in punitive damages against Dow Chemical Company, the parent company of Dow Corning. Dow Chemical Company was drawn into the litigation with the argument that it helped its subsidiary company conceal known dangers of silicone.[70]

The plaintiff in the Nevada case did not suffer from cancer, but from what appeared to be an autoimmune disease in which the immune system attacks the body's own tissues. Dow Chemical argued that no one has shown that silicone causes autoimmune disease. In fact, in a 1994 study, researchers at the Mayo Clinic reviewed the medical records of 749 Minnesota women who had received implants over a 27-year period and found that they were not more likely than other women to develop autoimmune diseases. The following year, Harvard researchers reviewed the medical histories of over 87,000 nurses, including 876 who had received silicone implants, and likewise concluded that no evidence of silicone-related illness existed. In October 1995, the American College of Rheumatology issued a statement that these two studies "provide compelling evidence that silicone implants expose patients to no demonstrable additional risk for connective tissue or rheumatic disease."[71]

On February 14, 1996, a Michigan jury found thirty insurance companies liable to Dow Corning for costs associated with the breast cancer litigation.[72] The insurers had denied liability, which involved a total of approximately $700 million, on the ground that Dow Corning had concealed from them the health risks of the silicone gel implants.

On February 28, 1996, Hennekens et al.[73] reported on a retrospective cohort study of 395,543 female health professionals who completed mailed questionnaires for potential participation in a women's health program. A total of 10,830 women reported breast implants and 11,805 reported connective-tissue diseases between the years 1962 and 1991. In

---

[70] Cowley, G., *Silicone: Juries vs. Science,* Newsweek, Nov. 13, 1995, p. 75.

[71] Id.

[72] Hartford Acc. & Indem. v. Dow Corning Corp., No. 93-325788CK (Circuit Ct., Wayne Cty, Mich., Feb. 14, 1996).

[73] Hennekens, C. H., et al., *Self-Reported Breast Implants and Connective-Tissue Disease in Female Health Professionals: A Retrospective Cohort Study,* 275 J.A.M.A. 616 (Feb. 28), 1996.

comparing the reports of the women with connective-tissue diseases who had breast implants with those who did not, the authors found a statistically significant association between such diseases and breast implants; however, the authors concluded that, while this very large study made chance an unlikely explanation for the results, bias due to differential overreporting of connective-tissue diseases or selective participation by affected women with breast implants remained a plausible alternative explanation.

Researchers at Tulane University Medical School and representatives of Autoimmune Technologies jointly announced in February 1997 that they had developed a test that detects an association between silicone breast implants and autoimmune disease. The test, called the Anti-Polymer Antibody Assay or APA Assay, was made available to physicians for investigational use. According to Tulane and Autoimmune Technologies researchers, a double-blind study found 68% of silicone breast implants patients who claimed to be severely ill were found to be "reactive" on the APA Assay test, while only 3% of the implant patients who claimed only mild illness were reactive. A spokesman for Autoimmune Technologies, which has been granted an exclusive license for the APA Assay, stated that the test "proves that the illnesses are real, not something made up."[74]

In May 1997, it was reported that a team of investigators from the Mayo Clinic examined the medical records of 749 Minnesota women who received breast implants between 1964 and 1991 and found that 24% required additional implant-related surgery within five years of receiving the implant. The rate of complications was nearly three times higher among women whose implants followed breast removal for cancer than among women who received implants for cosmetic reasons only. The most frequent reasons for additional surgery were shrinkage of the outer capsule that surrounds the implant, rupture of the implant, and the formation of a blood clot around the implant. The complications did not appear related to the type of implant.[75]

According to a February 1998 report from Scotland, researchers at St. John's Hospital, Livingston, conducted a cross-sectional study of the prevalence of connective tissue diseases or their symptoms in women who had received a silicone gel-filled breast implant for either breast augmentation or reconstruction compared to women without implants. They found no increased incidence of antinuclear antibodies or rheumatoid factor in the implant group. They did find one case of rheumatoid arthritis in the reconstructed breast group and one in the non-implant group, but no differences were found in symptoms or physical signs of

---

[74]PR Newswire, Feb. 14, 1997, LEXIS, News Library, ASAPII File.

[75]*Breast Implants Commonly Cause Lo-* *cal Complications*, 15 Mayo Clinic Health Ltr. 4 (May), 1997.

connective tissue diseases between the implant patients and the controls.[76]

In a Canadian study reported the same month, 1,576 women who underwent cosmetic breast implants between 1978 and 1986, including 1,112 who had received silicone gel-filled implants, were compared to 726 controls with regard to the prevalence of rheumatoid arthritis, systemic lupus erythematosus, scleroderma, or Sjogren's syndrome. While the breast implant recipients self-reported significantly a greater rate of symptoms than the controls, the rate of postsurgical diagnoses of the principal targeted conditions did not indicate an increased incidence of typical or atypical connective tissue disease, leading the authors of the report to conclude that their study did not support the hypothesis that silicone gel-filled implants induce or promote connective tissue disease.[77]

Dow Corning Corporation announced in November 1998 that it had increased its settlement offer to the approximately 600,000 women who claimed that the company's silicone gel breast implants caused them one illness or another. Dow submitted to the court overseeing the company's Chapter 11 bankruptcy a proposal to pay the sum of $3.2 billion. Under the terms of the offer, each claimant would receive from $12,000 to $300,000.[78] The following month, a court-appointed panel of scientists reported that it had found no difinitive link between silicone breast implants and disease. The panel members, consisting of an epidemiologist, a toxicologist, an immunologist, and a rheumatologist, after reviewing approximately 2,000 studies at the request of the United States District Court in Birmingham, Alabama, stated that they believe that most of their peers in the scientific community will agree with their conclusion, but they cannot anticipate what research findings may appear in the future. A representative of Dow Corning announced that the panel's report is good news, but it will not affect the pending negotiations to settle the claims already filed against the company.[79]

---

[76] Park, A. J., et al., *Silicone Gel-Filled Breast Implants and Connective Tissue Diseases,* 101 Plast. Reconstr. Surg. 261 (Feb.), 1998.

[77] Edworthy, S. M., *A Clinical Study of the Relationship Between Silicone Breast Implants and Connective Tissue Disease,* 25 J. Rheumatol. 254 (Feb.), 1998.

[78] *Breast Implant Deal Is Final,* The National Law Journal, Nov. 23, p. A8.

[79] Sissell, K., *Panel Finds No Link to Disease; Breast Implants,* Chem. Week 9 (Dec. 9), 1998.

ANNOTATIONS

§ 31.96. Medical references.

The following additional references may aid in further research on the material covered in Chapter 31. For a guide to the abbreviations used in references to periodicals, see Chapter 3, § 3.36.

(A) BURN INJURIES

Berthod, F., and Damour, O., *In Vitro Reconstructed Skin Models for Wound Coverage in Deep Burns*, 136 Br. J. Dermatol. 809 (June), 1997.

Beushausen, T., and Mucke, K., *Anesthesia and Pain Management in Pediatric Burn Patients*, 12 Pediatr. Surg. Int. 321 (July), 1997.

Bowden, M. L., and Feller, I., editors, *The Psycho-Social Aspects of a Severe Burn: A Review of the Literature*, National Institute for Burn Medicine, Ann Arbor, Mich., 1979.

Brodzka, W., et al., *Burns: Causes and Risk Factors*, 66 Arch. Phys. Med. Rehabil. 746, 1985.

Carlson, D. E., et al., *Resting Energy Expenditure in Patients with Thermal Injuries*, 174 Surg. Gynecol. Obstet. 270 (Apr.), 1992.

Carrougher, G. J., *Management of Fluid and Electrolyte Balance in Thermal Injuries: Implications for Perioperative Nursing Practice*, 6 Semin. Perioper. Nurs. 201 (Oct.), 1997.

Cortiella, J., and Marvin, J. A., *Management of the Pediatric Burn Patient*, 32 Nurs. Clin. North Am. 311 (June), 1997.

Crawford, M. E., and Rask H., *Prehospital Care of the Burned Patient*, 3 Eur. J. Emerg. Med. 247 (Dec.), 1996.

Davies, J. W., *Physiological Responses to Burning Injury*, Academy Press, Inc., New York, 1982.

Davis, S. T., and Sheely-Adolphson, P., *Burn Management. Psychosocial Interventions: Pharmacologic and Psychologic Modalities*, 32 Nurs. Clin. North Am. 331 (June), 1997.

Dimick, P., et al., *Anesthesia-Assisted Procedures in a Burn Intensive Care Unit Procedure Room: Benefits and Complications*, 14 J. Burn Care Rehab. 446 (July-Aug.), 1993.

Dougherty, W., and Waxman, K., *The Complexities of Managing Severe Burns with Associated Trauma*, 76 Surg. Clin. North Am. 923 (Aug.), 1996.

Edwards-Jones, V., and Shawcross, S. G., *Toxic Shock Syndrome in the Burned Patient*, 54 Br. J. Biomed. Sci. 110 (June), 1997.

Edwards, M. J., et al., *Squamous Cell Carcinoma Arising in Previously Burned or Irradiated Skin*, 124 Arch. Surg. 115, 1989.

Engrav, L. H., et al., *Rating Burn Impairment*, 19 Clin. Plast. Surg. 569 (July), 1992.

Finlayson, E., and McArthur, E., *Treatment of Unhealed Burns with Severe Complications*, 6 J. Wound Care 260 (June), 1997.

Flint, L., *What's New in Trauma and Burns*, 182 J. Am. Coll. Surg. 177 (Feb.), 1996.

Garner, W. L., et al., *Effect of Triglycyl-Lysine-Vasopressin on Skin Blood Flow and Blood Loss During Wound Excision in Patients with Burns*, 14 J. Burn Care Rehab. 458 (July-Aug.), 1993.

German, G., et al., *Post-Burn Reconstruction During Growth and Development*, 12 Pediatr. Surg. Int. 321 (July), 1997.

Gordon, M., and Goodwin, C. W., *Burn Management: Initial Assessment, Management, and Stabilization*, 32 Nurs. Clin. North Am. 247 (June), 1997.

Greenfield, E., and Jordan, B., *Advances in Burn Wound Care*, 8 Crit. Care Nurs. Clin. North Am. 203 (June), 1996

Grover, R., and Morgan, B. D., *Management of Hypopigmentation Following Burn Injury*, 22 Burns 627 (Dec.), 1996.

Halebian, P. H., et al., *Improved Burn Center Survival of Patients with Toxic Epidermal Necrolysis Managed Without Corticosteroids*, 204 Ann. Surg. 503, 1986.

Heimbach, D., et al., *Artificial Dermis for Major Burns*, 208 Arch. Surg. 313, 1988.

Helm, P. A., et al., *Return to Work Following Hand Burns*, 67 Arch. Phys. Med. Rehabil. 297, 1986.

Herndon, D. N., et al., *A Comparison of Conservative Versus Early Excision: Therapies in Severely Burned Patients*, 209 Ann. Surg. 547, 1989.

Hinshaw, J. R., *Why Burn Severity Is Often Misjudged*, 83 Arch. Surg. 549, 1961.

Jones, W. G., et al., *Enterococcal Burn Sepsis: A Highly Lethal Complication in Severely Burned Patients*, 121 Arch. Surg. 649, 1986.

Jordan, B. S., and Harrington, D. T., *Management of the Burn Wound*, 32 Nurs. Clin. North Am. 251 (June), 1997.

Katcher, M. L., et al., *Lower Extremity Burns Related to Sensory Loss in Diabetes Mellitus*, 24 J. Fam. Pract. 149, 1987.

Klein, G. L., et al., *The Management of Acute Bone Loss in Servere Catabolism Due to Burn Injury*, 48 Horm. Res. (Suppl.) 83, 1997.

Kravitz, M., et al., *Improperly Sterilized Fine-Mesh Gauze Associated with Donor Site Infections in Skin-Grafted Burn Patients*, 13 Am. J. Infect. Control 178, 1985.

Laing, H. J., *Perioperative Burn Nursing*, 6 Semin. Perioper. Nurs. 210 (Oct.), 1997.

Le Boucher, J., and Cynober, L., *Protein Metabolism and Therapy in Burn Injury*, 41 Ann. Nutr. Metab. 69 (No. 2), 1997.

Martens, D. M., et al., *Outpatient Burn Management*, 32 Nurs. Clin. North Am. 343 (June), 1997.

Mason, S., *Young, Scarred Children and Their Mothers — A Short-Term Investigation into the Practical, Psychological, and Social Implications of Thermal Injury to the Preschool Child. Part I: Implications for the Mother*, 19 Burns 495, 1993.

Mason, S., and Hillier, V. F., *Young, Scarred Children and Their Mothers — A Short-Term Investigation into the Practical, Psychological, and Social Implications of Thermal Injury to the Preschool Child. Part II: Implications for the Child*, 19 Burns 501, 1993.

Mason, S., and Hillier, V. F., *Young, Scarred Children and Their Mothers — A Short-Term Investigation into the Practical, Psychological, and Social Implications of Thermal Injury to the Preschool Child. Part III: Influencing Outcome Responses*, 19 Burns 507, 1993.

Mellins, R. B., *Complications of Smoke Inhalation in Victims of Fires*, 87 J. Ped. 1, 1975.

Micak, R. P., et al., *Temperature Changes During Exercise Stress Testing in Children with Burns*, 14. J. Burn Care Rehab. 427 (July-Aug.), 1993.

Monato, W. W., *Initial Management of Burns*, 335 N. Engl. J. Med. 1581 (Nov. 21), 1996.

Munster, A. M., and Gale, B. R., *Accelerated Tumor Growth Following Experimental Burn*, 17 J. Trauma 3737, 1977.

Nduka, C. C., *Cause and Prevention of Electrosurgical Injuries in Laparoscopy*, 179 J. Am. Coll. Surg. 161 (Aug.), 1994.

Neilan, B. A., et al., *T Lymphocyte Rosette Formation After Major Burns*, 228 J.A.M.A. 493, 1977.

Nguyen, T. T., et al., *Current Treatment of Severely Burned Patients*, 223 Ann. Surg. 14 (Jan.), 1996.

Noyes, R., *Stressful Life Events and Burn Injuries*, 19 J. Trauma 141 (Mar.), 1979.

Patterson, D. R., et al., *Factors Predicting Hypnotic Analgesia in Clinical Burn Pain*, 45 Int. J. Clin. Exp. Hypn. 377 (Oct.), 1997.

Pessina, M. A., and Ellis, S. M., *Burn Management: Rehabilitation*, 32 Nurs. Clin. North Am. 365 (June), 1997.

Petro, J. A., et al., *Burn Accidents and the Elderly: What is Happening and How to Prevent It*, 44 Geriatrics 26 (Mar.), 1989.

Ratnayake, B., et al., *Neurological Sequelae Following a High-Voltage Electrical Burn*, 22 Burns 574 (Nov.), 1996.

Rose, J. K., and Herndodn, D. N., *Advances in the Treatment of Burn Patients*, 23 Burns (Suppl.) S19 (Mar.), 1997.

Rubin, L. R., *The Burned Female Breast*, 75 N.Y. St. J. Med. 865, 1975.

Rutan, R. L., et al., *Growth Delay in Postburn Pediatric Patients*, 125 Arch. Surg. 392 (March), 1990.

Shuck, J. M., et al., *Dynamics of Insulin and Glucagon Secretions in Severely Burned Patients*, 17 J. Trauma 706 (Sept.), 1977.

Silverberg, R., et al., *A Survey of the Prevalence and Application of Chest Physical Therapy in U.S. Burn Centers*, 16 J. Burn Care Rehabil. 154 (Mar.-Apr.), 1995.

Staley, M. J., and Richard, R. L., *Use of Pressure to Treat Hypertrophic Burn Scars*, 10 Adv. Wound Care 44 (May-June), 1997.

Staley, M. J., et al., *Functional Outcomes for the Patient with Burn Injuries*, 17 J. Burn Care Rehabil. 362 (July-Aug.), 1996.

Thomas, S. S., *Electrical Burns of the Mouth: Still Searching for an Answer*, 22 Burns 137 (Mar.), 1996.

Thomson, H. G., and Shore, B., *The Bathtub Burn — A Pediatric Disaster*, 14 Canad. J. Surg. 399, 1971.

Tobiasen, J. M., et al., *Burns and Adjustment to Injury: Do Psychological Coping Strategies Help?* 25 J. Trauma 1151, 1985.

Tompkins, R. C., et al., *Significant Reductions in Mortality for Children with Burn Injuries through the Use of Prompt Eschar Excision*, 208 Ann. Surg. 577, 1988.

Turegun, M., et al., *Burn Scar Carcinoma with Longer Lag Period Arising in Previously Grafted Area*, 23 Burns 496 (Sept.), 1997.

Tyack, Z. F., et al. *Postburn Dyspigmentation: Its Assessment, Management, and Relationship to Scarring — A Review of the Literature*, 18 J. Burn Care Rehabil. 435 (Sept.-Oct.), 1997.

Weiler-Mithoff, E. M., et al., *Burns of the Female Genitalia and Perineum*, 22 Burns 390 (Aug.), 1996.

Winfree, J., and Barillo, D. J., *Burn Management: Nonthermal Injuries*, 32 Nurs. Clin. North Am. 275 (June),1997.

Wise, D. L., editor, *Burn Wound Coverings*, CRC Press, Boca Raton, Fla., 1984.

Wolf, S. E., et al., *The Cornerstone and Directions of Pediatric Burn Care*, 12 Pediatr. Surg. Int. 312 (July), 1997.

(B) PLASTIC REPAIR AND HAND SURGERY

Achauer, B. M., *Lasers in Plastic Surgery: Current Practice*, 99 Plast. Reconstr. Surg. 1442 (Apr.), 1997.

Aiach, G., and Monaghan, P., *Treatment of Over-Reduction of the Nose and Subsequent Deformities*, 33 Br. J. Oral Maxillofac. Surg. 250 (Aug.), 1995.

al-Quattan, M. M., et al., *Carpal Tunnel Syndrome in Children and Adolescents with No History of Trauma*, 21 J. Hand. Surg. [Br.] 108 (Feb.), 1996.

Berkel, J., et al., *Breast Augmentation: A Risk Factor for Breast Cancer?*, 326 N. Engl. J. Med. 1649, 1992.

Bowers, D. G., and Radlauer, C. B., *Breast Cancer After Prophylactic Subcutaneous Mastectomies and Reconstruction with Silastic Prosthesis*, 44 Plastic & Recon. Surg. 541, 1969.

Chang, J., et al., *Scarless Wound Healing: Implications for the Aesthetic Surgeon*, 19 Aesthetic Plast. Surg. 237 (May-June), 1995.

Dawson, W. J., *The Spectrum of Sports-Related Interphalangeal Joint Injuries*, 10 Hand Clin. 315 (May), 1994.

Deapen, D. M., et al., *The Relationship Between Breast Cancer and Augmentation Mammaplasty: An Epidemiologic Study*, 77 Plast. Reconstr. Surg. 361, 1986.

Dillerud, E., *Suction Lipoplasty: A Report on Complications, Undesired Results, and Patient Satisfaction Based on 3,511 Procedures*, 88 Plast. Reconstr. Surg. 329 (Aug.), 1991.

Edworthy, S. M., *A Clinical Study of the Relationship Between Silicone Breast Implants and Connective Tissue Disease*, 25 J. Rheumatol. 254 (Feb.), 1998.

Emerson, E. T., et al., *Anatomy, Physiology, and Functional Restoration of the Thumb*, 36 Ann. Plast. Surg. 180 (Feb.), 1996.

Epply, B. L., *Alveolar Cleft Bone Grafting: Primary Bone Grafting*, 54 J. Oral Maxillofac. Surg. 74 (Jan.), 1996.

Estes, E. H., Jr., et al., *Silicone Gel Breast Implants*, 270 J.A.M.A. 2602 (Dec. 1), 1993.

Fisher, J., *The Silicone Controversy: When Will Silicone Prevail?*, 326 N. Engl. J. Med. 1696 (June 18), 1992.

Freeland, A. E., and Benoist, L. A., *Open Reduction and Internal Fixation Method for Fractures at the Proximal Interphalangeal Joint*, 10 Hand Clin. 239 (May), 1994.

Fuleihan, N. S., *Current Concepts in Plastic Surgery of the Nose*, 44 J. Med. Liban. 150 (No. 3), 1996.

Goldwyn, R. M., editor, *The Unfavorable Result in Plastic Surgery: Avoidance and Treatment*, 2d ed., 2 vols., Little, Brown and Company, Boston, 1984.

Goldwyn, R. M., *The Patient and the Plastic Surgeon*, 2d ed., Little, Brown & Co., Boston, 1991.

Hardy, S. P., et al., *Ocular Staphyloma Associated with Facial Clefting*, 8 J. Craniofac. Surg. 326 (July), 1997.

Hennekens, C. H., et al., *Self-Reported Breast Implants and Connective-Tissue Disease in Female Health Professionals: A Retrospective Cohort Study*, 275 J.A.M.A. 616 (Feb. 28), 1996.

Hertz, R. P., et al., *Risk Factors for Occupational Hand Injury*, 28 J. Occup. Med. 36, 1986.

Hoffman, J., et al., *Staple Gun Carpal Tunnel Syndrome*, 27 J. Occup. Med. 848, 1985.

Holmberg, L., et al., *Psychosocial Adjustment after Mastectomy and Breast-Conserving Treatment*, 64 Cancer 969, 1989.

Howard, P. S., et al. *Complications in Endoscopic Plastic Surgery*, 22 Clin. Plast. Surg. 791 (Oct.), 1995.

Hunstad, J. P., *Addressing Difficult Areas in Body Contouring with Emphasis on Combined Tumescent and Syringe Techniques*, 23 Clin. Plast. Surg. 57 (Jan.), 1996.

Hutchison, D. T., et al., *Upper Extremity Tourniquet Tolerance*, 18A Hand. Surg. 206 (Mar.), 1993.

Johnson, C. H., et al., *Oncological Aspects of Immediate Breast Reconstruction Following Mastectomy for Malignancy*, 124 Arch. Surg. 819, 1989.

Lawrence, W. T., and Banes, A. J., *Plastic Surgery Research*, 23 Clin. Plast. Surg. 173 (Jan.), 1996.

Leslie, B. M., et al., *Congenital Carpal Tunnel Syndrome — A Case Report*, 8 Orthopedics 1165, 1985.

Light, T. R., and Bednar, M. S., *Management of Intra-Articular Fractures of the Metacarpophalangeal Joint*, 10 Hand Clin. 303 (May), 1994.

Malerich, M. W., and Eaton, R. G., *The Volar Plate Reconstruction for Fracture-Dislocation of the Proximal Interphalangeal Joint*, 10 Hand Clin. 251 (May), 1994.

Miller, M. J., and Schusterman, M. A., *Secondary Deformities Following Mandibular Reconstruction*, 24 Clin. Plast. Surg. 551 (July), 1997.

Nyren, O., et al., *Breast Implants and Risk of Neurologic Disease: A Population-Based Study in Sweden*, 50 Neurology 956 (Apr.), 1998.

Park, A. J., et al., *Silicone Gel-Filled Breast Implants and Connective Tissue Diseases*, 101 Plast. Reconstr. Surg. 261 (Feb.), 1998.

Phillips, L. G., *What's New in Plastic Surgery*, 184 J. Am. Coll. Surg. 187 (Feb.), 1997.

Rosenberg, G. J., and Gregory, R. D., *Lasers in Aesthetic Surgery*, 23 Clin. Plast. Surg. 29 (Jan.), 1996.

Rudolph, *Problems in Asthetic Surgery: Biological Causes and Clinical Solutions*, C. V. Mosby Company, St. Louis, 1986.

Salter, R. B., *The Physiologic Basis of Continuous Passive Motion for Articular Cartilage Healing and Regeneration*, 10 Hand Clin. 211 (May), 1994.

Schenck, R. R., *Advances in Reconstruction of Digital Joints*, 24 Clin. Plast. Surg. 175 (Jan.), 1997.

Schenck, R. R., *The Dynamic Traction Method: Combining Movement and Traction for Intra-Articular Fractures of the Phalanges*, 10 Hand Clin. 187 (May), 1994.

Sheen, J. H., *Aesthetic Rhinoplasty*, The C. V. Mosby Co., St. Louis, 1978.

Spiera, H., *Scleroderma after Silicone Augmentation Mammaplasty*, 260 J.A.M.A. 236, 1988.

Spurgeon, D., *Breast Implants Do Not Appear to Pose Cancer Risk*, 145 Can. Med. Assoc. J. 1990 (Dec. 15), 1991.

Wang, T. D., *Rhytidectomy for Treatment of the Aging Face*, 64 Mayo Clin. Proc. 780, 1989.

Winer, E. P., et al., *Silicone Controversy: A Survey of Women with Breast Cancer and Silicone Implants*, 85 J. Nat'l Cancer Inst. 1407 (Sept. 1), 1993.

Weiner, S. R., et al., *Chronic Arthropathy Occurring After Augmentation Mammaplasty*, 77 Plast. Reconstr. Surg. 185, 1986.

§ 31.97. Legal references.

Anthony, J., et al., *Silicone Implants: The Coming Legal Tidal Wave?*, 26 Trial Law. Forum 11, 1992. (Publication of Texas Trial Lawyers Association).

Aschinger, E. C., *The Selling of the Perfect Breast: Silicone, Surgeons, and Strict Liability*, 61 UMKC L. Rev. 399 (Winter), 1992.

Belli, M. M., *Transsexual Surgery*, 239 J.A.M.A. 2143, 1978.

Broder, A. J., *Summation in Burn Injury Case*, 1982 Pers. Inj. Deskbook 873.

Burn Injuries, 65 Case & Com. 16, 1960.

Dalgaard, J. B., *Burns and Freezing as a Cause of Peptic Ulceration*, J. For. Med. 16, 1958.

Direct Examination of Plaintiff's Doctor, A Plastic Surgeon — Serious Burn Case, 24 Med. Trial Tech. Q. 345 (Winter), 1978.

Goff, G. W., *Man's Hand: Its Injuries and Values*, 1 Amicus Cur. 5, 1956.

Goldwyn, R. M., *Cutaneous Scars*, 7 Lawyers Med. J. 79, 1971.

Hand Injuries, 27 Current Med. 19, 1960.

Hanover, R., *Use of Prosthetic Implants: Cosmetic Enlargement of the Healthy Female Breast; Legal Implications of Resulting Disfigurement*, 34 Med. Trial Tech. Q. 1, 1987.

Injuries from Electronic Power Sources, 19 Clev. St. L. Rev. 323, 1970.

Johanson, G., and Saldeen, T., *Identification of Burnt Victims with the Aid of Tooth and Bone Fragments*, 16 J. For. Med. 16, 1969.

Kelleher J. C., *What Can Plastic Surgery Do for Traumatized Patients?* 29 Ohio Bar 951, 1956.

King-Cameron, K. A., *Carving Another Exception to the Learned Intermediary Doctrine: Application of the Learned Intermediary Doctrine in Silicone Breast Implant Litigation*, 68 Tul. L. Rev. 937 (Mar.), 1994.

Kosieradzski, M. R., and Thorson, B. R., *Loss of Earnings Claims for Facial Disfigurement*, 29 Trial 18 (Aug.) 1993.

Lawrence, E. A., *Managing the Defense of a Flammable Fabrics Lawsuit*, 17 For the Defense 133 (Oct.), 1976.

Lees-Haley, P., *Disfigurement and Economic Loss*, 23 Trial 64 (May), 1987.

Lehr, H. B. *Fractures of the Bones of the Face*, 5 Lawyer's Med. J. 273, 1969.

Lewis, J. R., Jr., *Burns and Their After Effects*, 2 Amicus Cur. 19, 1957.

Liability for X-ray Burns, 9 Current Med. 28, 1955.

Lichtenstein, S., *A Discussion of the Silicone Gel-Filled Breast Implant Controversy,* 12 Rev. Litig. 205 (Fall), 1992.

Macgregor, F. C., Psychic *Trauma of Facial Disfigurement,* 33 Trial 90, 1984.

Masters, F. W., and Robinson, D. W., *Outpatient Injuries of the Hand,* 13 Clev.-Mar. L. Rev. 473, 1964.

Medical Testimony in a Burn Case with Shock and Skin Grafting, Showing the Direct and Cross-examination of the Orthopedic Surgeon, 7 Med. Trial Tech. Q., 1960 Annual, 69.

Medico-legal Aspects of Burns, 2 Current Med. 19, 1955.

Meyer, K. B., *Silicone Breast Implants and Hospital Liability: A New Forum for Hybrid Transections,* 99 Dick. L. Rev. 439 (Winter), 1995.

Nakles, N. J., *Electrical Injuries in Pennsylvania,* 74 Dick. L. Rev. 389, 1970.

Nelkin, D., *Reporting Risk: The Case of Silicone Breast Implants,* 5 Risk Health Safety & Env't 233 (Summer), 1994.

Nielsen, K. G., et al., *Device and Methods for the Measurement of Energy Transfer in Experiments Involving Thermal and Electrical Injuries of Skin,* 17 For. Sci. Int'l 203 (May-June), 1981.

O'Neil, J. H., *Endoscopic Carpal Tunnel Release Systems: Exposing the Risks,* 13 Prof. Liab. L. Rep. 93 (June), 1994.

Panarites, Z., *Breast Implants: Choices Women Thought They Made,* 11 N.Y.L. Sch. J. Hum. Rts. 163 (Fall), 1993.

Robertson, J. D., and Keavy, W. T., *Plastic Surgery Malpractice and Damages,* John Wiley & Sons, Somerset, N.J., 1990.

Roh, L., and Papero, G., *Detection of Accelerants on a Burn Victim,* 28 J. For. Sci. 292 (Apr.), 1983.

Ryan, D. B., III, and Lawn, T. R., *Strict Liability Claims Against Health Care Providers in Breast Implant Litigation,* 29 Tort & Ins. L.J. 818 (Summer), 1994.

Schumer, W., *Burns: Physiological Bases for Treatment,* 7 Med. Trial Tech. Q., 1960 Annual, 1.

Shafer, N., *The Burned Patient,* 5 Lawyer's Med. J. 377, 1970.

Smialek, J. E., et al., *Automobile Cigarette Lighter Burns,* 25 J. For. Sci. 631 (July), 1980.

Smith, E. P. A., and Buck, G. S., "Defense of Flammable Fabrics Cases," in *Products Liability: Practical Defense Problems II,* D. J. Hirsch, editor, Defense Research Institute, Inc., Milwaukee, 1976.

Stajduhar-Djuric, Z., *Duodenal Ulceration in Cases of Burns,* 5 J. For. Med. 84, 1958.

Stine, K. R., *Silicone, Science, and Settlements; Breast Implants and a Search for Truth,* 63 Def. Couns. J. 491 (Oct.), 1996.

Straith, C. L., "Plastic and Reconstructive Surgery," in *Courtroom Medicine,* M. Houts, editor, Charles C Thomas, Publisher, Springfield, Illinois, 1958.

Straith, C. L., *Reconstructive Surgery,* 34 Mich. St. B.J. 13, 1955.

Sturim, H. S., *Electrical Burns,* 5 Lawyer's Med. J. 183, 1969.

Swartz, E. M., "Handling Cases Involving Extensive Burns" in *American Trial Lawyers Association, 1970 Convention Proceedings,* D. L. Runyan, editor, The W. H. Anderson Co., Cincinnati, 1971.

Swartz, E. M., "Malpractice from the Viewpoint of the Trial Attorney," in *The Unfavorable Result in Plastic Surgery: Avoidance and Treatment,* R. M. Goldwyn, editor, Little, Brown and Company, Boston, 1972.

Trevor, E., *Representing a Burn Survivor,* 32 Trial 40 (Sept.), 1996.

Wall, R. M., *Evaluating Facial Scars on a Minor,* 26 Prac. Law. 39 (July 15), 1980.

Waugh, F. F., *Recent Burn Damage Awards,* 10 Clev.-Mar. L. Rev. 295, 1961.

§31.98. American Law Reports.

16 A.L.R.2d 912. Liability to patron of public amusement for accidental injury from cause other than assault, hazards of game or amusement, or condition of premises. Fire and burns, §12.

42 A.L.R.2d 930. Liability for injury to or death of child from burns caused by hot ashes, cinders, or other hot waste material.

58 A.L.R.2d 216. Malpractice, nose and throat. Burns, §5.

79 A.L.R.2d 401. Liability of manufacturer or seller for injury caused by medical and health supplies, appliances, and equipment. X-ray equipment, §3; vaporizer, §7; hot-water bottles and bags, §8; sun lamp, §10.

79 A.L.R.2d 431. Liability of manufacturer or seller of hair preparations, cosmetics, soaps and other personal cleansers, and the like, for injury caused by the product.

97 A.L.R.2d 473. Malpractice in connection with care and treatment of burns.

11 A.L.R.3d 9. Excessiveness or adequacy of damages awarded to injured person for injuries to arms, legs, feet, and hands. Ankle burns, §6; arm burns, §12; finger burns, §21; foot burns, §25; hand burns, §28; knee burns, §36; leg burns, §43.

11 A.L.R.3d 9. Excessiveness or adequacy of damages awarded to injured person for injuries to arms, legs, feet, and hands. Skin grafting, injury necessitating — ankle injury, §§6, 8, 26; arm injury, §§9, 11, 12, 16; fingers, loss of, §19; foot injury, §§24 to 26; hand injury, §§28, 30; knee abrasion, §36; leg injuries, §§41, 43 to 45; thumb injury, §19; toe injuries, §§26, 46.

11 A.L.R.3d 370. Excessiveness or adequacy of damages awarded to injured person for injuries to head or neck. Plastic surgery, injuries necessitating, §§5, 9, 10, 12, 21.

12 A.L.R.3d 117. Excessiveness or adequacy of damages awarded to injured person for injuries to trunk or torso. Burns — abdomen, §3; back, §5; breast or chest, §7; buttocks, §9; hip, §14; ribs, §17.

12 A.L.R.3d 475. Excessiveness or adequacy of damages awarded to injured person for injuries to organic systems and processes of body. Electrical burns, §76; other burns, §77.

29 A.L.R.3d 1065. Liability of hospital for negligence of nurse assisting operating surgeon. Inflicting burns by use of hot applications or heating devices, §8.

31 A.L.R.3d 1163. Competency of general practitioner to testify as expert witness in action against specialist for medical malpractice. Plastic surgeon, §4[c].

54 A.L.R.3d 1255. Liability of physician or hospital in the performance of cosmetic surgery upon the face.

63 A.L.R.3d 1020. Duty of physician or surgeon to warn or instruct nurse or attendant. Burns, §7.

88 A.L.R.3d 117. Cost of future cosmetic plastic surgery as element of damages.

1 A.L.R.4th 251. Products liability: flammable clothing.

2 A.L.R.4th 775. Transsexual surgery as covered operation under state medical assistance program.

16 A.L.R.4th 1127. Excessiveness or adequacy of damages awarded for injuries to, or conditions induced in, sensory or speech organs and systems. Burns, §11.

34 A.L.R.4th 958. Workers' compensation: liability of successive employers for disease or condition allegedly attributable to successive employments. Hand injury, §§9, 10[b], 11[a].

50 A.L.R.4th 13. Future disease or condition or anxiety relating thereto, as elements of recovery. Burns, §20.

72 A.L.R.4th 905. Workers' compensation: reasonableness of employee's refusal of medical services tendered by employer. Cosmetic surgery, §6.

75 A.L.R.4th 763. What services, equipment, or supplies are "medically necessary" for purposes of coverage under medical insurance. Cosmetic surgery, §§17, 18.

12 A.L.R.5th 195. Excessiveness or inadequacy of punitive damages awarded in personal injury or death cases. Plastic surgery, § 13[b].

19 A.L.R.5th 563. Malpractice in treatment of skin disease, disorder, blemish, or scar.

20 A.L.R.5th 1. Necessity of expert testimony on issue of permanence of injury and future pain and suffering. Scars, § 61.

24 A.L.R. 5th 1. Arbitration of medical malpractice claims. Cosmetic surgery, §§ 9[a], 18, 23[a].

26 A.L.R.5th 401. Sufficiency of evidence to prove future medical expenses as result of injury to back, neck, or spine. Plastic surgery, §§ 8, 12, 24[c].

28 A.L.R.5th 497. Medical malpractice in connection with breast augmentation, reduction, or reconstruction.

42 A.L.R.5th 1. Establishing standard of care and breach of that standard. Plastic surgery, § 10[a].

48 A.L.R.5th 129. Excessiveness or adequacy of damages awarded for injuries to trunk or torso, or internal injuries. Burns, §§ 4, 11, 19.

52 A.L.R.5th 1. Excessiveness or adequacy of damages awarded for injuries causing mental or psychological damages. Plastic surgery, §§ 3([a], 4[a], 7[c, e], 8[a, c, d], 9[c, d].

§ 31.99. Cases.

In the following list of cases, no attempt has been made to include all the decisions on topics covered in Chapter 31. The cases selected are those that the editors believe will best aid the reader in further research on the medicolegal issues involved.

Cases are arranged under the following headings:

(A) MALPRACTICE ACTIONS INVOLVING TREATMENT OF BURNS, PLASTIC SURGERY OR HAND SURGERY

(B) BURNS WHILE UNDER MEDICAL SUPERVISION

(C) OTHER PERSONAL INJURY CASES INVOLVING BURNS

(D) WORKERS' COMPENSATION CASES

(E) DISFIGUREMENT FROM INJURIES OTHER THAN BURNS

(A) MALPRACTICE ACTIONS INVOLVING TREATMENT OF BURNS, PLASTIC SURGERY OR HAND SURGERY

[See also § 31.11.]

United States: Campbell v. Oliva (C.A.-6 Tenn., 1970) 424 F.2d 1244 (action against plastic surgeon for negligence in repair of woman's jaw; evidence suggested that he underestimated seriousness of condition; directed verdict for defendant reversed).

Nunley v. Kloehn (D.C. Wis., 1995) 888 F. Supp. 1483 (in a malpractice action against a plastic surgeon involving several lip augmentation and corrective procedures with the experimental substance Bioplastique, a dermatologist was qualified to testify as to the applicable standard of care; even though the witness had not been trained in the use of Bioplastique, he had performed many lip augmentations using similar silicone-based substances and was familiar with the scar tissue that formed following such procedures).

Alabama: Campbell v. Williams (Ala., 1994) 638 So. 2d 804 (steel company employee who was seen at hospital emergency department for burns on face from molten steel was not intubated; she suffered respiratory distress and lapsed into coma from which she died one month later; appellate court affirmed jury award for $4 million in punitive damages against hospital and physician).

Alaska: Korman v. Malin (Alaska, 1993) 858 P.2d 1145 (question whether plastic surgeon adequately disclosed risk of painful and unsightly scarring before patient consented to breast reduction surgery).

California: Gluckstein v. Lipsett (1949) 93 Cal. App. 2d 391, 209 P.2d 98 (action by fifty-year-old woman against surgeon for negligence in plastic surgery to breasts and abdomen allegedly resulting in disfigurement, pain, and malignant growths in breasts; judgment of $115,000 for plaintiff upheld; extensive medical testimony regarding procedure and results).

Carrasco v. Bankoff (1963) 220 Cal. App. 2d 230, 33 Cal. Rptr. 673, 97 A.L.R.2d 464 (six-year-old severely burned child treated for 53 days in ten-bed ward of small community hospital which did not have facilities for treatment of major burn cases; no substantial skin grafting or definitive treatment administered; isolation techniques not employed; extensive evidence on failure to follow established standards of medical practice in such cases; judgment for plaintiffs affirmed).

Rosburg v. Minnesota Mining & Mfg. Co. (Cal. App., 1986) 226 Cal. Rptr. 299 (manufacturer not liable for deflation of McGhan-sytle 90 saline-filled breast implant six years after implantation; ordinary consumer shold have expected possibility of deflation and package contained warning of such a possibility).

Miller v. Silver (Cal. App., 1986) 226 Cal. Rptr. 479 (psychiatrist competent to testify in negligence action against plastic surgeon regarding defendant's failure to administer prophylactic antibiotics prior to performing breast reconstruction surgery).

Selden v. Dinner (Cal. App., 1993) 21 Cal. Rptr. 2d 153 (unsuccessful action by patient against plastic surgeon for emotional distress allegedly caused by his cancellation of scheduled breast reconstruction surgery).

Colorado: Short v. Downs (1975) 36 Colo. App. 109, 537 P.2d 754 (punitive damages awarded against osteopath who performed breast augmentation by injections of silicone labeled "not for human use").

Spoor v. Martorano (Colo. App., 1992) 852 (doctrine of res ipsa loquitur was applicable in an action against a plastic surgeon for the failure of a muscle flap and skin graft procedure to properly cover an ulcer on the patient's neck, which had been caused by radiation therapy, notwithstanding expert testimony that the procedure failed due to an insufficient blood supply resulting from the patient's long history of cigarette smoking).

District of Columbia: Harris v. Cafritz Mem. Hosp. (App., 1976) 364 A.2d 135 (res ipsa loquitur inapplicable in action involving failure of skin grafts to heal properly).

Florida: Porter v. Rosenberg (Fla. App., 1995) 650 So. 2d 79 (recipient of allegedly defective breast implant did not have strict liability action against physician who implanted it).

Winson v. Norman (Fla. App., 1995) 658 So. 2d 625 (in a complaint involving a failed breast implant, a physician who had not practiced medicine for more than a decade and who had apparently confined his activities to acting as a "litigation expert" did not meet the qualifications necessary to execute the verified written opinion as defined by the provision on screening requirements under the Florida medical malpractice statute).

Georgia: Fulton Cty. Hosp. v. Hyman (1988) 189 Ga. App. 613, 376 S.E.2d 689 (infant's lacerated thumb negligently treated at hospital; upper part of distal joint had to be surgically removed; additional surgery likely; $118,000 award).

Hoffman v. Wells (Ga., 1990) 397 S.E.2d 696 (plaintiff had claim for punitive damages against surgeon who operated on wrong hand, where evidence established that defendant made error in entry in patient's medical records on her first visit to office and failed to correct error during two subsequent visits).

Hawaii: Keomaka v. Zakaib (Haw. App., 1991) 811 P.2d 478 (patient's alleged negligence in permitting incision in leg to become infected, and in injuring leg while swimming, were claimed by defense to be superseding causes in action against surgeon for failing

269

to inform patient of risks of, and alternatives to, transplanting portion of sural nerve from lower leg to finger).

Craft v. Peebles (Haw., 1995) 893 P.2d 138 (in a medical malpractice action against a surgeon by a patient who claimed that she had suffered injury from the release of silicone into her body from a ruptured breast implant, court did not err in admitting evidence that her symptoms might have been related to her drug use and not solely to the effects of silicone).

Ditto v. McCurdy (Haw. App., 1997) 947 P.2d 952 (surgeon did not have an affirmative duty to disclose his qualifications or lack of experience to the patient before performing a breast augmentation).

Ditto v. McCurdy (Haw. App., 1997) 947 P.2d 961 (punitive damages were justified where the evidence established that the surgeon who performed the patient's breast augmentation had not properly informed her of the risks or complications involved in the operation; had failed to properly suture her incisions, which resulted in a bloody discharge; had failed to detect an obvious infection; had failed to document the patient's medications; and had sent her home despite the presence of complications to make room for other patients in his recovery room).

Illinois: Anderson v. Beers (1979) 74 Ill. App. 3d 619, 30 Ill. Dec. 516, 393 N.E.2d 552 (failure to warn patient of possible unsatisfactory outcome of breast reconstruction surgery).

Novey v. Kishwaukee Comm. Health Servs. Ctr. (Ill. App., 1988) 531 N.E.2d 427 (plaintiff, whose severely cut hand had been repaired by plastic surgeon, claimed physical therapist ruptured flexor tendon of left middle finger while administering therapy; issues included whether occupational therapist should have been allowed to testify for plaintiff as to applicable standard of care).

Ramus v. Pyati (1989) 179 Ill. App. 3d 214, 128 Ill. Dec. 290, 534 N.E.2d 472 (hand surgeon accused of failing to obtain informed consent when, in repairing ruptured thumb tendon, he used patient's ring finger tendon for graft instead of wrist tendon as patient had been told; plaintiff claimed stiffness in hand affected work as mechanic).

Gorman v. Shu-Fang Chen, M.D., Ltd. (Ill. App., 1992) 596 N.E.2d 1350 (plastic surgeon who was also board-certified in surgery and thoracic/cardiovascular surgery was qualified to testify as to whether orthopedic surgeon had deviated from standard of care in failing to call in specialist to examine patient with temporomandibular joint (TMJ) problem).

Indiana: Auler v. Van Natta (Ind. App., 1997) 686 N.E.2d 172 (a hospital did not have a duty to obtain a patient's informed consent to have a breast implant inserted, even though it and not the patient's physician provided the patient with the general consent form, where the patient did not allege that the physician was an employee or agent of the hospital, or that the hospital controlled the physician's practice, or that the hospital was aware of the physician's propensity for not obtaining patients' informed consent).

Weinberg v. Geary (Ind. App., 1997) 686 N.E.2d 1298 (in a claim against a plastic surgeon for unsightly scarring following a breast reduction, chin liposuction, and face-lift — allegedly due to the defendant bringing the patient's skin together with too much tension — an orthopedic surgeon was qualified to testify as an expert for the patient where it was established that the witness had special experience in suturing, having spent more than 9,000 hours of service in hospital emergency departments and having sutured more than 100,000 wounds).

Kentucky: Doan v. Griffith (Ky. App., 1966) 402 S.W.2d 855 (facial disfigurement allegedly due to emergency room physician's failure to inform patient that he should have fractured facial bones realigned; directed verdict for defendant reversed).

Harmon v. Rust (App., 1967) 420 S.W.2d 563 (physician charged with malpractice in treating severe leg burn requiring skin grafts from other leg; directed verdict in favor of defendant affirmed; no inference of negligence could be drawn although infection developed in both legs; "We do not believe that laymen have sufficient general knowledge to 'recognize' that infection and slow healing, in treating severe burns and making transplants, are the results of negligence.").

Louisiana: Bush v. St. Paul Fire & Marine Ins. Co. (La. App., 1972) 264 So. 2d 717 (res ipsa loquitur inapplicable in action against plastic surgeon for unsatisfactory face-lift operation).

Bruneau v. Colon (La. App., 1989) 542 So. 2d 560 (plaintiff unsuccessful in recovering damages from plastic surgeon because of scar on tip of her nose following removal of lesion; she failed to offer any evidence as to cause of scar and had signed a consent form recognizing scarring as risk of surgery).

Whiddon v. Elliott (La. App., 1991) 594 So. 2d 449 (obese male patient alleged that surgeon was negligent in performing breast reduction surgery without incorporating skin reduction).

Turner v. Massiah (La. App., 1994), 641 So. 2d 610, *modified*, (La. App., 1995) 656 So. 2d 636 (unsuccessful claim against a plastic surgeon who misdiagnosed breast cancer for scar tissue that occasionally develops following augmentation mammaplasty).

Vedros v. Massiha (La. App., 1994) 646 So. 2d 1120 (insufficient evidence that plastic surgeon who performed subcutaneous mastectomy on plaintiff breached standard of care by failing to inform her of risks involved in treating an infection that developed after breast implantation was performed, where preoperative consultation with plaintiff included information regarding risk of infection; also, evidence was insufficient that surgeon breached standard of care in failing to refer patient to infectious disease expert).

Maine: Hauser v. Bhatnager (Me., 1988) 537 A.2d 599 (plastic surgery patient still suffered from paresthesia of forehead and a "widened, depressed scar" nearly six years after "right eyebrow lift"; paresthesia attributed to injury to supraorbital nerve during surgery; plaintiff awarded $10,000).

Massachusetts: Norton v. Vaughan (1982) 13 Mass. App. 1075, 435 N.E.2d 634 (infection developed under cast applied to burned leg).

Vassallo v. Baxter Healthcare Corp. (Mass., 1998) 696 N.E.2d 909 (despite the absence of evidence of classical epidemiological studies, the plaintiff's medical witnesses, both of whom qualified as experts, had published articles in peer-reviewed journals on silicone-related topics, and had treated hundreds of patients with implants, were permitted to offer testimony based upon animal experiments and controlled and blind clinical studies that silicone gel breast implants caused the plaintiff's atypical connective tissue disease).

Michigan: Palenkas v. Beaumont Hosp. (1989) 432 Mich. 527, 443 N.W.2d 354 (liability was established against plastic surgeon who was absent from hospital for several days after he repaired plaintiff's fractured mandible, during which time plaintiff's jaw began to tip inward, preventing proper alignment of teeth; it was also discovered that defendant had left several pieces of bone and teeth imbedded in plaintiff's jaw).

Minnesota: Roemer v. Martin (Minn., 1989) 440 N.W.2d 122 (while plastic surgeon may have been negligent in repairing severed tendon in plaintiff's thumb, there were several possible causes for plaintiff's injured medial nerve, including original accident, subsequent swelling, scarring, infection, and carpal tunnel syndrome).

Mississippi: Kelly v. Frederic (Miss., 1990) 573 So. 2d 1385 (material issue of fact presented as to whether physician had actually performed tendon repair on patient's finger as claimed).

Barner v. Gorman (Miss., 1992) 605 So. 2d 805 (question whether plastic surgeon had failed to inform patient that results of reconstructive surgery on neck scar could not be guaranteed and that keloid might develop following surgery; boilerplate informed consent form criticized).

Missouri: Barr v. Plastic Surg. Consultants (Mo. App., 1988) 760 S.W.2d 585 (plastic surgeon removed too much tissue during breast reduction, then unsuccessfully attempted to remedy situation with implants; plaintiff claimed breasts shaped "funny," bra continually slipped off, and she could not "camouflage" deformity in "intimate situations").

Cline v. William H. Friedman & Assocs. (Mo. App., 1994) 882 S.W.2d 754 (patient successfully introduced expert testimony in malpractice action against surgeon that established that, during performance of corrective eyelid surgery (bilateral blepharoplasty), defendant removed too much skin and tissue from patient's upper lids).

Nebraska: Turek v. St. Elizabeth Commun. Health Center (Neb., 1992) 488 N.W.2d 567 (fact that nurse had not been licensed to insert catheter into burn patient's subclavian artery, to administer anesthetic, or to use dermatome to perform skin grafting was not sufficient evidence to prove negligence, since licensing statutes create no liability where actor is competent but merely unlicensed).

Burns v. Metz (Neb., 1994) 513 N.W.2d 505 (evidence that a patient's breasts lacked symmetry following a reduction mammaplasty did not mean that the plastic surgeons failed to exercise reasonable care).

Giese v. Stice (Neb., 1997) 567 N.W.2d 156 (even though the hospital supplied the implants used in the patient's augmentation breast surgery, her surgeon, not the hospital, had the duty to warn her of the risk of any side effects involved in the procedure; if hospital personnel had counseled her regarding the possibility of side effects, it could have been interpreted as an unwarranted interference with the physician-patient relationship).

New York: Suria v. Shiffman (N.Y., 1986) 490 N.E.2d 832 (successful malpractice action against plastic surgeon by transsexual patient who claimed his informed consent was not obtained to perform correction of unsuccessful breast augmentation procedure previously undertaken by another surgeon).

Diaz v. Lenox Hill Hosp. (App. Div., 1991) 569 N.Y.S.2d 74 (question of apportionment of damages where diagnosis by supervising physician at hand clinic, who examined patient's hand at request of treating physician, contributed to patient's failure to receive "delayed primary" surgery).

Scariati v. St. John's Queens Hosp. (App. Div., 1991) 569 N.Y.S.2d 189 (conflicting evidence on whether physician's delay in diagnosing severed tendons in patient's hand, in discovering that glass particles were still in wound, and in referring patient to hand surgeon, resulted in patient suffering permanent injury).

Slaybough v. Nathan Littauer Hosp. (App. Div., 1994) 698 N.Y.S.2d 745 (delay of six hours in treating emergency department patient's injured hand was found to be substantial cause of degeneration of tendons, which required surgery, with poor results and eventual permanent impairment).

North Carolina: Easter v. Lexington Mem. Hosp., Inc. (1981) 303 N.C. 303, 278 S.E.2d 253, 17 A.L.R.4th 128 (question of negligence on part of hospital in assigning or permitting obstetrician-gynecologist to treat burn victim who later died from tetanus).

Noell v. Kosanin (N.C. App., 1995) 457 S.E.2d 742 (in facial surgery, the standard of care would probably require that, before the operation, the patient's eyes be taped shut to prevent them from drying out during the procedure).

Pennsylvania: Powell v. Risser (1953) 375 Pa. 60, 99 A.2d 454 (patient at state mental hospital claimed injuries when immersed in hot water and when physician later opened blisters with allegedly unsterile pocketknife; judgment NOV on behalf of defendant).

South Dakota: Van Zee v. Witzke (S.D., 1989) 445 N.W.2d 34 (after patient's finger was fractured by physical therapist, she refused to return for further therapy and sued referring plastic surgeon).

Texas: Wehmeyer v. O'Dell (Tex. App., 1993) 856 S.W.2d 845 (plastic surgeon was not liable to patient for injuries allegedly resulting from his office staff's failure to refer patient to another physician in his absence).

Wisconsin: McManus v. Donlin (1964) 23 Wis. 2d 289, 127 N.W.2d 22 (child burned on leg between ankle and knee from gasoline; in treating patient, physicians accused of: (1) failure to diagnose burn as third degree; (2) failure to use antibiotics to prevent infection; (3) failure to provide round-the-clock care; (4) failure to change dressings as often as necessary; (5) failure to use proper surgical technique in skin grafting; (6) failure to administer proper postoperative care to prevent infections; and (7) discharging patient when he still required care; judgment of nonsuit affirmed for want of expert testimony; doctrine of res ipsa loquitur held inapplicable).

(B) BURNS WHILE UNDER MEDICAL SUPERVISION

United States: Hill v. Gonzalez (C.A.-8 Minn., 1972) 454 F.2d 1201 (patient successful in malpractice case for severe burns to tips of fingers which resulted from use of "Coecal," a "dental stone" substance being used as a "extraoral prosthetic substance" to replace fingertips lost in lawnmower accident; jury verdict of $81,500 reduced to $65,000).

Weeks v. Latter-Day Saints Hosp. (C.A.-10 Utah, 1969) 418 F.2d 1035 (two-year-old child suffered burns from temperature-controlled rubber mattress during heart operation; plastic surgery required; res ipsa loquitur applied and $44,000 verdict for plaintiff upheld).

Hale v. Holy Cross Hosp., Inc. (C.A.-5 Fla., 1975) 513 F.2d 315 (burns and ulcerations on hospital patient's buttocks after application of heating device; doctrine of res ipsa loquitur applicable).

Alabama: Langdon v. Miller (1964) 276 Ala. 195, 160 So. 2d 479 (while undergoing office treatment, patient was burned on back from spilled liquid chemical; jury verdict for $4,000 affirmed).

California: American Bank & Trust Co. v. Community Hosp. of Los Gatos-Saratoga, Inc. (1980) 184 Cal. App. 3d 219, 163 Cal. Rptr. 513 ($198,000 verdict upheld for 49-year-old woman hospital patient who suffered burns to thigh, hip, and groin because of overheated shower water).

District of Columbia: Louison v. Crockett (D.C. App., 1988) 546 A.2d 400 (woman patient burned by diathermy machine; following accident plaintiff claimed she could not sleep, suffered nightmares, heard "voices," and saw "bright lights that were not there"; lost 25 pounds; medical expenses $3,875; jury awarded $725,000, but case remanded for new trial on damages because of conflicting evidence on extent of disability at time of trial).

Florida: West Coast Hosp. Ass'n v. Webb (Fla. App., 1951) 52 So. 2d 803 (hospital patient admitted in diabetic coma subsequently suffered burns from unknown cause; res ipsa loquitur applied and hospital held liable).

Georgia: Porter v. Patterson (1962) 107 Ga. App. 64, 129 S.E.2d 70 (infant allegedly burned at hospital when foot came in contact with electric light bulb used to heat incubator; cause of action found against hospital but not physician).

Hospital Authority of City of St. Mary's v. Eason (1966) 222 Ga. 536, 150 S.E.2d 812 (elderly and partially paralyzed hospital patient burned when bed caught fire apparently from pipe; evidence indicated he had been left alone while smoking despite instructions by family to the contrary; hospital not found liable, however, mainly because of evidence that persons visiting other hospital patients were near his room and may have lighted his pipe).

Clark v. Piedmont Hosp. Inc. (1968) 117 Ga. App. 875, 162 S.E.2d 468 (jury question on negligence raised where 73-year-old hospital patient suffering from pneumonia and vertigo was burned when she tripped over vaporizer that had been placed between bed and bathroom).

Elberton-Elbert County Hosp. Auth. v. Watson (1970) 121 Ga. App. 550, 174 S.E.2d 470 (patient burned in flash fire that erupted around oxygen therapy unit; question whether patient's attempt to light cigarette caused explosion; defendant's motion for summary judgment and motion to dismiss denied).

Davis v. Glaze (Ga. App., 1987) 354 S.E.2d 845 (child suffered severe burns as result of malfunction of electrocautery grounding pad during tonsillectomy).

Illinois: Franck v. Holy Family Hosp., Docket No. 66L-1069, Circuit Ct., Cook County, March 15, 1971 (38-year-old woman alcoholic who was hospitalized for skin disorder developed delirium tremens and hallucinations; all cigarettes and matches were taken from her by hospital personnel at midnight but at 2 a.m. she was found in another patient's room looking for matches; she was returned to her bed and placed in restraints; two hours later she suffered second and third-degree burns attempting to escape by setting fire to her bed; hospital and attending physician were charged with negligence in failing to search her adequately for matches and in leaving the door to her room closed; hospital argued that its personnel did not know she was alcoholic; plaintiff awarded $60,000 against hospital and court directed verdict for physician). Case reported in 23 *The Citation*, July 1, 1971, p. 84.

Burns v. Walker, Docket No. 66L-1390 Circuit Ct., Cook County, March 8, 1971 (pediatrician used glass salad dressing bottle wrapped in towel as makeshift hot water bottle to apply heat to face of ten-month-old child; bottle evidently slipped from under towel during child's convulsion and metal cap touched face, causing third-degree burn that required skin graft; pediatrician found free of liability in damage suit). Case reported in 23 *The Citation*, July 15, 1971, p. 97.

Rolek v. University of Chicago Hosps. and Clinics, Docket No. 69L-6297, Circuit Ct., Cook County, Feb. 20, 1973 (patient undergoing six-hour proctocolectomy and ileostomy suffered three-inch by four-inch wound at end of spine allegedy as result of burn from ground plate of defective electric cautery instrument; defense claimed scar due to pressure necrosis and decubitus ulcer [bed sore]; jury verdict for hospital). Case reported in 27 *The Citation*, September 1, 1973, p. 150.

Indiana: Memorial Hosp. of South Bend, Inc. v. Scott (Ind., 1973) 300 N.E.2d 50 (hospital patient suffering from multiple sclerosis was severely burned while using toilet when he accidently turned knob connected to hot water bed pan flusher; on issue of contributory negligence, court held test to be applied was that of a reasonably prudent man suffering from same disability under like circumstances).

Iowa: Wiles v. Myerly (Iowa, 1973) 210 N.W.2d 619 (patient suffered burns on buttocks while undergoing vascular surgery; award of $25,000 against surgeon, anesthesiologist, and hospital upheld; res ipsa loquitur applied).

Kansas: Smelko v. Brinton (1987) 241 Kan. 763, 740 P.2d 591 (3-month-old infant suffered second- and third-degree burns when placed on heating pad during surgery; burns covered 75-90% of buttocks; hospitalized five weeks; skin-grafting required; permanent scarring; medical expenses $13,476; award of $400,000).

Kentucky: Hamby v. University of Ky. Med. Ctr. (Ky. App., 1992) 844 S.W.2d 431 (malpractice action against radiation oncologist by patient who suffered burned ear during hyperthermia treatment for cancer).

Louisiana: LeBlanc v. Midland Nat'l Ins. Co. (La. App., 1969) 219 So. 2d 251 (elderly patient in nursing home who was allowed to have pipe on request of relatives set himself on fire and was fatally burned; nursing home found not liable).

Clovis v. Hartford Acc. & Indem. Co. (La. App., 1969) 223 So. 2d 178 (if nurses aide's application of hot compresses to patient's leg to relieve cellulitis condition resulted in burns as alleged, such application still did not constitute negligence).

Helms v. St. Paul Fire & Marine Ins. Co. (La. App., 1974) 289 So. 2d 288 (patient who underwent ultraviolet treatment for acne unsuccessful in actions against dermatologist for alleged first degree burns; defense offered testimony that condition was probably caused by a dormant fever blister virus, and that face would have shown more redness and a large amount of superficial blistering if caused by overexposure to ultraviolet rays; theory of res ipsa loquitur held inapplicable).

Louisiana: Reichert v. Barbera (La. App., 1992) 601 So. 2d 802 (child who suffered burns on elbow from acid during removal of wart was entitled to damages of $25,000, where pain had lasted for extended period of time, lesions bled for weeks, and scars, which might require future surgery, were unsightly and disfiguring, causing child to become self-conscious and embarrassed).

Beckham v. St. Paul Fire & Marine Ins. Co. (La. App., 1993) 614 So. 2d 760 (in action by patient who suffered burns and reopening of abdominal incision because of heating pads applied postoperatively by hospital staff, patient was entitled to recover $144,221 award from surgeon because he had supervised application of pads).

Plumber v. State Dep't of Health & Human Resources (La. App., 1994) 636 So. 2d 1347 (patient who suffered chemical burn during chemotherapy claimed she had not been informed of risk).

Mahfouz v. Xanar, Inc. (La. App., 1994) 646 So. 2d 1152 (37-year-old plaintiff suffered severe burn on sole of foot while undergoing removal of plantar wart by laser; attempt to relieve pain by severing nerve endings unsuccessful; past and future medical expenses estimated at $11,334; foot is 50% permanently impaired; plaintiff can no longer work as hair stylist; trial court award of $470,838 reduced by $85,000 on appeal for overestimated loss of future income).

Massachusetts: Regula v. Bettigole (Mass. App., 1981) 425 N.E.2d 768 (patient sustained leg burn during tubal ligation).

McMahan v. Finlayson (1994) 36 Mass. App., 371 632 N.E.2d 410 (plaintiff claimed physician failed to inform her of risk of thermal severance of ureter during laparoscopic cauterization for endometriosis).

Michigan: Hand v. Park Commun. Hosp. (1968) 14 Mich. App. 371, 165 N.W. 2d 673 (while in hospital, stroke patient who was partially paralyzed and confused was found with extensive burns on body; doctrine of res ipsa loquitur applied).

Hilyer v. Hole (1982) 114 Mich. App. 38, 318 N.W.2d 598 (patient suffered bowel perforation from burn during tubal ligation; evidence supported verdicts for osteopaths and hospital).

Minnesota: Swigerd v. City of Ortonville (1956) 246 Minn. 339, 75 N.W.2d 217 (nurse placed heat lamp too close to stroke patient's bed; sheets caught fire and patient died from combination of burns and illness; hospital held liable).

Elm v. St. Joseph's Hosp. of City of St. Paul (1970) 288 Minn. 538, 180 N.W.2d 262 (hospital patient fainted on way to bathroom, burning self on uncovered radiator; directed verdict for hospital reversed and new trial granted).

Olson v. St. Joseph's Hosp. (Minn., 1979) 281 N.W.2d 704 (conditional res ipsa liquitur applicable in action on behalf of spastic quadriplegic who allegedly suffered unexplained burns while hospitalized for throat infection).

Mississippi: Newport v. Hyde (1962) 244 Miss. 870, 147 So. 2d 113 (dental patient suffered burned gums from use of hot dental impression substance; cellulitis developed and tissue sloughed off which exposed jaw bone; judgment for defendant reversed for erroneous instruction requiring patient to show that defendant did not possess skill ordinarily possessed by dentists of good standing in locality and that he did not use ordinary care in applying such skill; action said to be based instead on alleged failure to use reasonable care and diligence in professional dental work).

Missouri: Furlong v. Stokes (Mo. App., 1968) 427 S.W.2d 513 (while undergoing femoral saphenous bypass operation patient allegedly burned by American Sterilizing Company Model ADX Portable Explosion Proof Lamp containing 150 watt bulb; patient claimed burn was caused by placing of lamp too close to his knee; directed verdict for defendant sustained for lack of direct evidence that burn could have been caused in manner claimed; doctrine of res ipsa loquitur held inapplicable).

Racer v. Utterman (Mo. App., 1981) 629 S.W.2d 387 (surgical drapes ignited during operation; jury case for strict liability made against manufacturer).

Hackathorn v. Lester E. Cox Med. Center (Mo. App., 1992) 824 S.W.2d 472 (hospital patient's back burned by heating pad; injuries prevented him from sitting or lying on back and caused two-month delay in surgery to correct herniated disc; $25,000 award affirmed).

Graham v. Thompson (Mo. App., 1993) 854 S.W.2d 797 (doctrine of res ipsa loquitur applicable in action by patient who awoke from ankle surgery to find a third-degree burn under cast on back of her lower leg).

New Jersey: Kent v. County of Hudson (1968) 102 N.J. Super. 208, 245 A.2d 747 (senile hospital patient fatally burned when he set himself on fire with cigarette; defense of contributory negligence rejected and hospital held liable).

New York: Wendover v. State (1970) 63 Misc. 2d 368, 313 N.Y.S.2d 287 (suit on behalf of epileptic patient who was burned on radiator in hospital room while suffering seizure; evidence that patient herself had moved bed to position near radiator and had let side rails down; doctrine of res ipsa loquitur ruled inapplicable; claim dismissed).

Evans v. Newark-Wayne Commun. Hosp., Inc. (1970) 35 App. Div. 2d 1071, 316 N.Y.S.2d 447 (hospital patient fatally burned in oxygen tent fire; evidence introduced that she obtained cigarettes from her purse which had been placed in bureau on other side of room; hospital found free of liability).

Eaton v. Comprehensive Care Am., Inc. (App., Div., 1996) 649 N.Y.S.2d 293 (health care worker left partially paralyzed stroke patient alone with cigarettes and lighter; severe burns plus "shock and fright"; past medical expenses $19,920 and future medical expenses estimated at $250,000; jury award of $1.5 million reduced by $250,000 on appeal).

North Carolina: Schaffner v. Cumberland County Hosp. (N.C. App., 1985) 336 S.E.2d 116 (res ipsa loquitur doctrine was applicable in malpractice action on behalf of child whose hand was burned during performance of an adenoidectomy).

North Dakota: Witthauer v. Burkhart Roentgen, Inc. (N.D., 1991) 467 N.W.2d 439 (distributor of high-intensity surgical lamp failed to warn clinic of danger in using lamp without its heat-protection filter, which resulted in patient being burned).

South Carolina: Burke v. Pearson (1972) 259 S.C. 288, 191 S.E.2d 721 (patient burned by heating pad; insufficient evidence of negligence).

Texas: Rosenblum v. Bloom (Tex. Civ. App., 1973) 492 S.W.2d 321 (physician's nurse assistant applied 100% trichloroacetic acid, instead of 5% solution to woman patient's face for treatment of skin blemishes; $5,000 awarded for pain, anguish, and cost of "face-lift" and corrective chemosurgery; no damages for disfigurement).

Thomas v. St. Joseph Hosp. (Civ. App., 1981) 618 S.W.2d 791 (hospital patient burned to death when gown ignited).

Utah: Dalley v. Utah Valley Reg. Med. Ctr. (Utah, 1990) 791 P.2d 193 (expert testimony not necessary in action by patient who suffered burn on leg while in operating room for Cesarean section).

Virginia: Danville Community Hosp. v. Thompson (1947) 186 Va. 746, 43 S.E. 2d 882 (newborn infant burned while in hospital incubator; doctrine of res ipsa loquitur applied and hospital held liable).

Washington: Clampett v. Sisters of Charity (1943) 17 Wash. 2d 652, 136 P.2d 729 (hospital patient burned when heating pad with defective temperature control overheated; staff was aware of defect but thought it was repaired; hospital held liable).

Wisconsin: Beaudoin v. Watertown Mem. Hosp. (1966) 32 Wis. 2d 132, 145 N.W.2d 166 (hospital patient found to have burns on her buttocks after a dilation and curettage procedure; no evidence as to cause of burns; doctrine of res ipsa loquitur applied).

(C) OTHER PERSONAL INJURY CASES INVOLVING BURNS

United States: MacMullen v. South Carolina Elec. & Gas Co. (E.D. S.C., 1961) 205 F. Supp. 811 (personal injury action involving workman who suffered electrical burns when current was turned on to equipment that he was adjusting; plaintiff, 33 years old, suffered permanent disability of between 65 and 75% of both arms and whole body disability of approximately 65%; future working capacity limited; probability of working life shortened by approximately fifteen years; $75,000 award held adequate).

Collins v. Clayton & Lambert Mfg. Co. (C.A.-6 Ky., 1962) 299 F.2d 362 (39-year-old master plumber severely burned on right arm when "plumber's furnace" exploded; judgment for $65,600 upheld against manufacturer on theory furnace was "imminently dangerous" article).

Darter v. Greenville Community Hotel Corp. (C.A.-4 S.C., 1962) 301 F.2d 70 (hotel owner sued by guest who was burned by extremely hot water while attempting to take bath; plaintiff contended thermostat control valve was defective; defendant claimed contributory negligence; judgment for defendant affirmed).

Southern Natural Gas Co. v. Wilson (C.A.-5 Miss., 1962) 304 F.2d 253 (two oil company roughnecks severely burned from bucket of flaming diesel oil which caught fire on derrick; issues included company's duty to provide working conditions safe from fire; independent contractor involved; awards of $125,000 and $3,000 held not excessive).

Tropea v. Shell Oil Co. (C.A.-2 N.Y., 1962) 307 F.2d 757 (maintenance worker severely burned in service station fire caused by gasoline being washed into drain pipe leading to grease pit; second and third degree burns requiring extensive treatment and 36 days of hospitalization; complications included psychic disturbances, skin sensitivity, and scarring; $35,000 award upheld).

Freeman v. Greenville Towing Co. (N.D. Miss., 1962) 201 F. Supp. 770 (engineer burned extensively from engine explosion and fire, resulting loss of function in hand and fingers and aggravation of preexisting neurological conditions evidenced by headaches, blackouts and personality change; total disability; explosion result of another seaman washing down area with diesel fuel; ship owner held liable under general maritime law and Jones Act; $53,300 awarded for pain and suffering, disability and loss of earnings).

Medlin v. United States (W.D. S.C., 1965) 244 F. Supp. 403 (ten-year-old child burned by pyrotechnic device left on parent's property by military personnel after completion of maneuvers; injuries included first and second degree burns over face and arm and third degree burns over surface of thumb and wrist; hospitalized eighteen days; issues included question of contributory engligence; attractive nuisance doctrine and intervening third party — an eighteen-year-old boy who attempted to ignite explosives; judgment awarded plaintiff under Federal Tort Claims Act).

Caldecott v. Long Island Lighting Co. (S.D. N.Y., 1969) 298 F. Supp. 540 (gas explosion in decedent's home; second and third degree burns with excruciating pain followed by death from suffocation; $50,000 award for conscious pain and suffering held not excessive).

Lightenburger v. United States (C.D. Cal., 1969) 298 F. Supp. 813 (air-plane crash due to negligence of air traffic control personnel; 57-year-old engineering flight test chief mechanic suffered severe second and third degree burns on head and hands with permanent loss of 50% of strength of left hand and 60% of right hand; award of $75,000 special and $40,000 in general damages upheld).

Tucker v. Bethlehem Steel Corp. (C.A.-5 La., 1971) 445 F.2d 390 (welder, employed by independent contractor, suffered burns when engulfed in shower of sparks from other welders' torches; hospitalized forty days; $43,000 awarded in personal injury action).

Armstrong v. Chambers & Kennedy (S.D. Tex., 1972) 340 F. Supp. 1220 ($25,000 damages held appropriate for conscious pain and suffering by ship captain who lived for five to fifteen minutes before jumping overboard in attempt to save himself from fire engulfing ship).

Anderson v. Sears, Roebuck & Co. (E.D. La., 1974) 377 F. Supp. 136 ($1,100,000 awarded for permanent disability and disfigurement suffered by female infant severely burned in fire caused by defective heater; award evaluated in light of specific injuries).

Drayton v. Jiffee Chem. Corp. (N.D. Ohio, 1975) 395 F. Supp. 1081 (one-year-old girl suffered severe burns in spill of drain cleaner; $500,000 awarded for past and future physical and mental suffering).

Ellis v. K-Lan Co. (C.A.-5 Tex., 1983) 695 F.2d 157 (two-year-old boy recovered damages for second- and third-degree chemical burns caused by Master Plumber, an acid-based drain declogger).

Goree v. Winnebago Indus. (C.A.-11, 1992) (quadriplegic who suffered severe burns on his shoeless feet while resting them on floorboard of motor home had cause of action against manufacturer for design defect).

Alabama: Ott v. Faison (1971) 287 Ala. 700, 255 So. 2d 38 (nightclub patron suffered seven-inch burn on hip requiring skin graft when she fell on bottle of liquid drain cleaner containing sulfuric acid; medical expenses $1,600; verdict of $20,000 reduced to $14,000).

Henderson ex rel. Hartsfield v. Alabama Power Co. (Ala., 1993) 627 So. 2d 878 (12-year-old boy came in contact with power line while climbing on transmission tower; suffered deep second-degree burns to face, upper body, and thighs; jury award for $15,304 in compensatory damages and $500,000 in punitive damages upheld on appeal).

Arizona: Wry v. Dial (1972) 18 Ariz. App. 503, 503 P.2d 979 ($401,750 awarded to 41-year-old man in automobile accident who suffered second and third degree burns on neck, shoulder, arm, chest, and thigh, requiring 58 days' hospitalization, and causing some permanent disability in upper right arm; extensive evidence as to economic loss).

Arkansas: Hudson Chevrolet Co. v. Sparrow (1971) 250 Ark. 849, 467 S.W.2d 751 (first and second degree burns on face and 35% of body; $6,683.15 awarded for pain and suffering in suit by tenant against landlord for explosion caused by back-up of sewer gas).

California: Scott v. County of Los Angeles (Cal. App., 1994) 32 Cal. Rptr. 2d 643 (action against social services agency and case worker for negligence in failing to protect three-year-old who was placed in foster care of grandmother who immersed child's legs in scalding water, causing severe burns through skin, fat, and muscle; permanent disability and disfigurement; $2.2 million award affirmed).

Colorado: Uptain v. Huntington Lab, Inc. (Colo., 1986) 723 P.2d 1322 (employee who was burned while using cleaning compound containing 23% solution of hydrochloric acid was unsuccessful in suit against manufacturer because employee failed to use protective rubber gloves as instructed by her supervisor).

McKown-Katy v. Rego Co. (Colo. App., 1989) 776 P.2d 1130 (woman burned in explosion of propane gas and fire in mobile home; evidence that plaintiff was momentarily exposed to temperatures of at least 1,600 degrees Fahrenheit; jury allowed to view 11-minute videotape of plaintiff's painful daily treatment at hospital).

General Elec. Co. v. Niemet (Colo., 1994) 866 P.2d 1361 (utility worker injured when defective and improperly grounded transformer exploded and caught fire; dislocated shoulders and severe burns; jury award of $1.1 million affirmed; fault apportioned 55% to city, 35% to transformer manufacturer, and 10% to worker).

Simon v. Coppola (Colo. App., 1994) 876 P.2d 10 (homeowner suffered second- and third-degree burns when she fell into hot tub that had overheated because of allegedly defective thermostat; $875,000 jury verdict affirmed on appeal).

Connecticut: Oborski v. New Haven Gas Co. (1964) 151 Conn. 274, 197 A.2d 73 (42-year-old workman suffered painful and disfiguring burns to 20% of his body and was left with permanent residual scarring and partial limitation of function in hands; explosion allegedly occurred from accumulated gas leaking from defendant company's gas lines; $60,000 damage award affirmed).

278

Delaware: Dolinger v. Scott & Fetzer Co. (Del Super., 1979) 405 A.2d 690 (defective oil burner exploded in home, covering plaintiff with "molten tar," causing severe burns to shoulder, chest and abdomen; rehospitalized for plastic surgery; $3,200 in special damages; remittitur reducing award to $25,000 reversed and original award of $60,000 reinstated).

Illinois: American Nat. Bank & Trust Co. v. Peoples Gas Light & Coke Co. (1963) 42 Ill. App. 2d 163, 191 N.E.2d 628 ($150,000 awarded to woman injured in explosion when gas company failed to shut off gas service to apartment while work was being done on lines; plaintiff was severely burned over face, both arms, chest and both legs; several operations, including skin grafts, were necessary; permanent disfigurement and disabling keloid formations developed over much of body; also restricted mobility for which therapy would cause much pain).

Traylor v. The Fair (1968) 101 Ill. App. 2d 268, 243 N.E.2d 300 (beauty shop customer burned on application of permanent wave solution; doctrine of res ipsa loquitur held applicable; verdict of $6,000 affirmed).

Rivera v. Rockford Mach. & Tool Co. (1971) 1 Ill. App. 3d 641, 274 N.E.2d 828 (employee's hand severely burned when piston rod broke in plastic injection molding machine; total loss of hand and decreased mobility of forearm; $155,000 award against manufacturer of machine upheld).

Collins v. Sunnyside Corp. (1986) 146 Ill. App. 3d 78, 496 N.W.2d 1155 (action by consumer who was burned on leg while using acetone manufactured by defendant company; pilot light on water heater in utility room ignited vapors; issue concerned adequacy of warnings regarding use only with "adequate ventilation").

Indiana: Northern Ind. Public Serv. Co. v. Otis (1969) 145 Ind. App. 159, 250 N.E.2d 378 (38-year-old woman suffered second and third degree burns over nearly 50% of the body as a result of gas main explosion; 59 days of hospitalization and 64 square inches of skin grafts; permanent scarring on neck and face; personality changes, depression, and threat of nervous breakdown; award of $235,000 upheld).

State v. Tabler (1978) 178 Ind. App. 31, 381 N.E.2d 502 (truck driver suffered burns over 45% of body, over a third of which were third degree, with loss of eyelids, part of nose, ear tips and lips; face, hands, arms and upper torso covered with scar tissue; limited dexterity and freedom of movement in hands and fingers; hospitalized four months; medical bills $31,000; award of $7,500 held inadequate) (nine-year-old boy suffered second and third degree burns over 20% of body; legs amputated; award of $70,000 held inadequate).

Iowa: Ives v. Swift & Co. (Iowa, 1971) 183 N.W.2d 172 (truck driver fell into "hot well" tank at packing company; second and third degree burns over half of body with loss of skin from arms and ankles; issues included contributory negligence, "invitee status"; $50,000 verdict).

Wroblewski v. Linn-Jones FS Services, Inc. (1972) 195 N.W.2d 709 (repairman suffered first and second degree burns from anhydrous ammonia over 25% of body; hospitalized nine days but suffered no permanent disability except three small scars on shoulder and arm; $17,000 damage award upheld).

Kansas: Patterson v. George H. Weyer, Inc. (1962) 189 Kan. 501, 370 P.2d 116 (beauty shop customer burned on application of Rayette Goddess cold wave permanent solution; retailer and manufacturer both held liable; $1,500 awarded).

Slocum v. Kansas Power & Light Co. (1963) 190 Kan. 747, 378 P.2d 51 (fourteen-year-old boy suffered high voltage electrical burns from transmission line while climbing nearby tree; injuries included loss of left hand and forearm and possible future loss of entire arm; severe injuries to right arm; large areas of scarring on stomach and inside and outside of thighs and legs; hospitalized 160 days; award of $95,000 reduced to $60,000).

Cott v. Peppermint Twist Mgmt. Co. (Kan., 1993) 856 P.2d 906 (nightclub customer suffered severe burns to mouth, throat, and esophagus from accidentally being served dishwashing liquid containing sodium hydroxide; development of strictures that must be periodically dilated; replacement of esophagus recommended; increased risk of cancer; $1.1 million awarded for past and future medical expenses, $360,000 awarded for future loss of income, and award of $1.04 million for pain and suffering reduced to $250,000 by statutory cap; in same case, a second customer was awarded $750,000 for similar injuries, which included damage to vocal cords and development of premalignant condition on one cord that will require periodic examinations for lifetime of plaintiff).

Louisiana: Barrois v. Service Drayage Co. (La. App., 1971) 250 So. 2d 135 (yard employee burned when crane came in contact with overhead high voltage line; plaintiff, age forty, underwent numerous operations for repair of arm and ear; pain would continue for life; $175,000 awarded).

Cooksey v. Central La. Elec. Co. (La. App., 1973) 279 So. 2d 242 (43-year-old man suffered severe electrical burns causing loss of left arm and loss of muscle tissue in right leg; some disfigurement; award of $408,000 reduced to $143,000).

Knockum v. Amoco Oil Co. (La. App., 1980) 402 So. 2d 90 (woman injured in propane gas explosion suffered second and third degree burns on face and arms, covering 36% of body; had to undergo three skin graft operations and physical therapy; $180,000 in damages not excessive).

Toups v. Sears, Roebuck & Co. (La. App., 1988) 519 So. 2d 842 (3-year-old boy suffered extensive burns on face, arms, and legs in utility room fire; numerous operations necessary; limitation of motion and some permanent disability; $1,800,000 award).

Thompson v. Petro-United Terminals, Inc. (La. App., 1988) 536 So. 2d 504 (employee of tank cleaning service burned when tank containing toluene exploded; second- and third-degree burns over 45% of body; hospitalized over one month; 25% of body grafted in three major operations; 15-25% disabled and cannot return to work involving exposure to heat or light; also suffered severe posttraumatic distress from witnessing death of brother in same accident; $132,741 award increased on appeal to $157,741).

Casanova v. Ballard (La. App., 1989) 533 So. 2d 1005 (57-year-old male retiree suffered electrical injuries when T.V. antenna he was installing came in contact with power line; third-degree burns of feet, hands, back, and abdomen; posttraumatic stress syndrome; plaintiff was diabetic which delayed healing; decubitus ulcers developed on lower extremities, requiring extensive treatment; medical expenses $29,669; right leg might have to be amputated; award of $229,669 affirmed).

Lajuanie v. Central La. Elec. Co. (La. App., 1989) 552 So. 2d 746 (worker suffered severe electrical burns when he touched bare distribution line; part of foot had to be amputated; several operations and skin grafts required; $214,833 verdict held adequate).

Davis v. Husqvarna Motor (La. App., 1990) 561 So. 2d 847 (44-year-old pulpwood cutter injured when chainsaw caught fire as he was starting it; second- and third-degree burns over 18% of body; total and permanent disability; $279,566 awarded).

Fannin v. Louisiana Power & Light Co. (La. App., 1992) 594 So. 2d 1119 (construction worker injured when cable came in contact with uninsulated high-voltage line running through bridge construction site; second-degree burns to feet, nervous disorder; off work two years; plaintiff continued to suffer from nervousness, headaches, backaches, and leg pain at time of trial; $121,000 award increased by $17,000 on appeal).

Fuselier v. Amoco Prod. Co. (La. App., 1992) 607 La. App. 1044 (vegetation control specialist's bushhog struck pipeline, causing explosion; second- and third-degree burns on leg and arm; hospitalized 24 days; eight debridement procedures and skin grafting; permanent scarring; chronic pain syndrome and depression; special damages $26,588; trial court awarded $210,000, which was increased to $248,588 on appeal).

Villa v. Derouen (La. App., 1993) 614 So. 2d 714 (coworker pointed welding torch toward plaintiff; second-degree burns to penis, scrotum and thighs; symptoms of post-traumatic stress disorder; medical expenses $14,300; plaintiff still unemployed at time of trial; requires psychological rehabilitation; $174,307 jury verdict affirmed).

Weaver v. Valley Elec. Membership Corp. (La. App., 1993) 615 So. 2d 1375 (40-year-old worker suffered electrical injuries while trying to lower transmission line; second- and third-degree burns over 14% of body, mainly left arm and both feet; numerous operations; memory loss; medical expenses $94,553; lost wages $30,206; still unemployable at time of trial; $744,759 award affirmed, including $90,000 for scarring and disfigurement).

Hines v. Remington Arms Co. (La. App., 1993) 630 So. 2d 809 (47-year-old man injured while target shooting when rifle accidentally fired on being loaded, striking canister of gunpowder; burns over 30% of body; hospitalized nine months; bed sores required skin grafts and caused nerve damage rendering plaintiff impotent and incontinent; must use cane or walker; still on medication at time of trial; medical expenses $322,000; $2.3 million award affirmed).

Thomas v. Louisiana Dep't of Transp. & Dev. (La. App., 1995) 662 So. 2d 788 (semi driver in mid-thirties suffered third- and second-degree burns on back, buttocks, and arm from hot asphalt when shoulder of highway collapsed and truck turned over; plaintiff required two painful debridements per day for over two weeks; skin grafts and painful physical therapy; past and future medical expenses estimated at $150,000; permanent scars; can no longer drive big trucks; $1.3 million jury award reduced by $136,552 on appeal following review of claim for lost future income).

Ayres v. Beauregard Elec. Coop. (La. App., 1995) 663 So. 2d 127 (plaintiff injured when electrical explosion ignited oil storage tank; burns over 28% of body, principally thigh, trunk, and under arms; treatment included two skin grafts and physical therapy; residual scarring; medical expenses to time of trial $38,279 and future medical expenses estimated at $1,238).

Oxley v. Sabine River Auth. (La. App., 1995) 663 So. 2d 497 (transformer exploded, causing electricity to strike plaintiff who was standing nearby; severe burns, surgical amputation of lower half of right leg, loss of feeling in left leg, loss of sight of one eye; plaintiff hospitalized 99 days and underwent 30 operations; past and future medical expenses estimated at $500,000; 93% permanent disability; jury verdict for $3.5 million affirmed).

Massachusetts: Nugent v. Sears, Roebuck and Co., No. 89-364 (Super. Ct., Middlesex Cty., Mass., Nov. 27, 1991) (electric blanket caught fire because of defective design; 46-year-old restaurant entertainment director suffered burns over 30% of her body; medical expenses $73,000; manufacturer settled before trial for $1.45 million; jury awarded $4.1 million against Sears, including $100,000 to plaintiff's husband for loss of consortium).

Michigan: Taylor v. Michigan Power Co. (1973) 45 Mich. App. 453, 206 N.W.2d 815 ($50,000 not excessive for death in explosion and fire in view of evidence of "conscious moving and cries for help after the explosion and before death").

Haynes v. Monroe Plumb. & Heat. Co. (1973) 48 Mich. App. 707, 211 N.W.2d 88 (where steam pipe burst, knocking plaintiff's decedent from catwalk, jury was allowed to consider conscious pain and suffering from moment he was scalded by steam until instant of death on striking floor).

Kinzie v. AMF Lawn & Garden (1988) 167 Mich. App. 528, 423 N.W.2d 253 (18-year-old male plaintiff burned when gas-powered lawn mower overturned; severe burns over 50% of body; ten operations by time of trial, and more expected; total disability; severe emotional problems; $5 million award reduced to $1 million because of contributory negligence).

Minnesota: Albert v. Paper Calmenson & Co. (Minn. App., 1994) 515 N.W.2d 59 (worker assisting in removing fuel oil from tank severely burned when blowtorch he was using to loosen manhole cover ignited vapors; second- and third-degree burns over 86% of body; past medical expenses $498,145 and future medical expenses estimated at $18,000; appellate court affirmed jury award of $2.6 million, which included $2 million for past and future pain and suffering).

Mississippi: Illinois Cent. R. Co. v. Nelson (1962) 245 Miss. 395, 146 So. 2d 69 (fifty-year-old tank truck driver severely burned when truck struck by train; survived fourteen days in extreme pain and conscious most of the time; $150,000 award reduced to $115,000).

Mississippi Power & Light Co. v. Walters (1963) 248 Miss. 206, 158 So. 2d 2 (workman suffered electrical shock when "A-Frame" truck touched high-tension wires; first degree burns on right hand and forearm; no blistering; some personality change that "might clear up entirely"; headaches which in time should improve; $25,000 award reduced to $10,000).

Missouri: Vaughn v. Michelin Tire Corp. (Mo. App., 1988) 756 S.W.2d 548 (dump truck driver lost control when tire blew; suffered severe and disabling burns on leg while pinned beneath hot exhaust pipe; $750,000 award).

Washburn v. Grundy Elec. Co-op. (Mo. App., 1991) 804 S.W.2d 424 (adult farmer suffered severe electrical burns to hands and resulting memory loss when grain auger came into contact with power line; father killed in same accident; $25,000 award held adequate).

Montana: Vogel v. Fetter Livestock Co. (1964) 144 Mont. 127, 394 P.2d 766 (neighbor sustained severe burns in explosion while attempting to fight barn fire; question of owner's failure to advise firefighters that barn contained dynamite and other explosives; issues included "invitee versus licensee"; $80,000 award for permanent disability of 30 to 40% held not excessive).

New Hampshire: Marcotte v. Peirce Constr. Co. (1971) 111 N.H. 226, 280 A.2d 105 (roofer suffered electrical burns; issue as to whether injuries resulted from arcing of electricity to plaintiff's hand or from plaintiff negligently contacting "busses" which caused arcing by reason of heavy perspiration from plaintiff's body).

New Jersey: Lewis v. American Cyanimid Co. (N.J. Super., 1996) 682 A.2d 724 (aerosol insecticide room foggers ignited by flames from pilot light on gas range or spark from refrigerator motor; plaintiff suffered burns over 25% of his body; jury awarded plaintiff $275,000 but appellate court reversed for trial court's insufficient instructions on future damages and comparative negligence).

New Mexico: Clay v. Ferrellgas, Inc. (N.M., 1994) 881 P.2d 11 (car being converted to run on propane gas exploded when gas leaked into passenger compartment because of failure to install vapor barrier or outside vent; severely burned female passengers awarded $720,000 and $400,000 respectively; each award included $375,000 in punitive damages).

New York: McSherry v. City of New York (1980) 77 App. Div. 2d 540, 430 N.Y.S.2d 321 ($55,000 held inadequate award for eight-year-old boy seriously burned when bus struck smudge pot near a highway construction site, causing flaming kerosene to splash on his back, arms and legs).

Donohue v. Walter (App. Div., 1989) 548 N.Y.S.2d 435 ($375,000 awarded to 43-year-old commercial pilot who received second-degree burns over 90% of body when apartment house boiler exploded as he was trying to light it).

Wagner v. Kenific (Misc., 1990) 557 N.Y.S.2d 650 (plaintiff suffered first- and second-degree burns to 20% of body when flushed urinal sprayed scalding water; $410,000 awarded to plaintiff and $25,000 to wife for loss of conjugal relations).

Williams v. Niske (N.Y., 1993) 599 N.Y.S.2d 519 (child suffered severe burns when fire started by other children; plaintiff sued five clothing manufacturers, jury award of $2.6 million affirmed).

Cazador v. Greene Ctr. Sch. (App. Div., 1995) 632 N.Y.S.2d 267 (student suffered burns to face and arms from caustic chemical preservative during dissection of frog in science class; after six years, plaintiff's skin was still sensitive to perspiration, heat, and sunlight; $30,000 jury verdict affirmed).

Beck v. Woodward Affiliates (App. Div., 1996) 640 N.Y.S.2d 205 (woman watching parade leaned for five minutes against a building from which a cleaning solution containing hydrofluoride had not been completely removed, resulting in chemical burns to both buttocks; scarred area was small; no evidence of need for skin grafts and no long-term disability; jury award of $450,000 reduced to $75,000 on appeal).

Lyall v. City of New York (App. Div., 1996) 646 N.Y.S.2d 34 (firefighter suffered second- and third-degree burns on knees and one shin from scalding water and embers because he had been furnished with an inadequate uniform; jury award of $ 1 million reduced to $400,000 on appeal).

Ohio: Pasela v. Brown Derby, Inc. (Ohio App., 1991) 594 N.E.2d 1142 (coffeepot placed on table by waitress spilled on child in high chair, causing severe burns to arms, chest, abdomen and leg; permanent scarring; medical expenses $75,000; jury verdict for $102,000 affirmed).

Felden v. Ashland Chem. Co. (Ohio App., 1993) 631 N.E.2d 689 (kettle operator at chemical factory sprayed with acid from ruptured drum when forklift struck steel post; third-degree burns over 23% of body, including face, eyes, arms, leg and side; partial loss of sight; ability to return to job or engage in physical activity of any kind substantially diminished; $3.5 million jury award affirmed).

Oregon: Staples v. Union Pac. R. Co. (Or., 1973) 508 P.2d 426 (welder received two electrical shocks which resulted in prolonged and recurring complications; $66,000 awarded under Federal Employers' Liability Act).

Pennsylvania: Weiner v. White Motor Co. (1972) 223 Pa. Super. 212, 297 A.2d 924 (award of $35,000 for pain and suffering not excessive where truck driver, before dying from third degree burns over 80% of body, endured pain of a duration of probably less than a minute).

Johnson v. Otis Elevator Co. (1973) 225 Pa. Super. 500, 311 A.2d 656 (elevator passenger claimed he was burned and knocked unconscious by bolt of electricity or fire emanating from elevator door's electric eye mechanism; $4,000 award).

O'Malley v. Peerless Petroleum, Inc. (1980) 283 Pa. Super. 272, 423 A.2d 1251 ($400,000 award upheld for apprentice plumber burned when gasoline fumes ignited in sewer; severe burns to head, arms and upper torso; future surgery recommended to reduce deformity to ears; could not return to former occupation).

Takes v. Metropolitan Edison Co. (Pa. Super., 1995) 655 A.2d 138 (industrial painter climbing over housing of energized 4,800-volt capacitor suffered electrical shock and fall of ten feet; electricity created black, leathery entrance and exit wounds; plaintiff also suffered two fractured ribs and fractured shoulder blade; finger had to be amputated; jury verdict of $1.46 million in compensatory damages affirmed; new trial granted on $3 million punitive award).

Texas: Duncan v. Smith (Tex. Civ. App., 1964) 376 S.W.2d 877 (31-year-old truck driver and part-time farmer earning 65 dollars per week awarded $175,000 for severe burns over most of his body; medical testimony that, because of his burns, plaintiff was more susceptible to cancer held proper and not speculative).

Monsanto Co. v. Milam (Tex. Civ. App., 1972) 480 S.W.2d 259 (42-year-old pipefitter suffered first and second degree burns of hands and face and inhalation burns of lungs; even after burns healed, hands and face would "sting" when exposed to heat or cold; $80,000 damage award upheld).

Clark v. McFerrin (Tex. App., 1988) 760 S.W.2d 822 (claim by relatives to recover under homeowner's policy; 13-month-old child suffered severe burns when gas water heater ignited can of paint thinner; medical expenses $2,681; award of $7,650 affirmed).

Loyd Elec. Co., Inc. v. Millett (Tex. App., 1989) 767 S.W.2d 476 (machinery operator injured when electrical switchbox exploded; severe, disfiguring burns on hands and neck, hearing loss, decreased sexual function, weight loss, and psychological problems).

Benefit Trust Life Ins. Co. v. Littles (Tex. App., 1993) 869 S.W.2d 453 (plaintiff burned when he tried to start barbecue grill with gasoline; burns over 21% of body; scarring on neck and lips limited plaintiff in turning head to right, which hindered performance as truck driver; mental anguish; $250,308 award included triple damages and attorney fees for delayed payment of claim by employer's carrier under excess risk coverage).

Transit Mgmt. Co. v. Sanchez (Tex. App., 1994) 886 S.W.2d 823 (wheelchair-bound bus passenger sprayed with oil when hose on hydraulic chair lift ruptured; burns on face and lower lip; plaintiff testified that he was in pain for several months and lip bled periodically; discoloration on cheek; $12,500 jury award affirmed by appellate court).

Washington: Washburn v. Beatt Equip. Co. (Wash., 1992) 840 P.2d 860 (50-year-old maintenance electrician injured when propane pipeline exploded; third-degree burns over 50%-55% of body; ten operations in 18 months; painful therapy; extensive permanent scarring, difficulty in kneeling and walking; posttraumatic emotional distress, anxiety, and embarrassment; $9.5 million award affirmed).

Waite v. Morsette (Wash. App., 1993) 843 P.2d 1121 (liquid propane furnace exploded when tenant tried to light it; burns over 40% of body; county settled for $450,000 and landlord for $10,000, and jury awarded $337,500 against propane supplier; affirmed).

West Virginia: Sargent v. Malcomb (1966) 150 W. Va. 393, 146 S.E.2d 561 (seventeen-year-old girl burned in restaurant fire suffered second and third degree burns on back, buttocks, breast, arm and leg; hospitalized 56 days; numerous skin grafts; extensive scarring; $22,500 award).

Long v. City of Weirton (1975) 158 W. Va. 741, 214 S.E.2d 832 (although there was "optimistic" testimony by plastic surgeon, in view of evidence that child's burn injuries were permanent, and that seven additional operations would be necessary to minimize scarring, $200,000 in damages was not unreasonable).

(D) WORKERS' COMPENSATION CASES

Alabama: Pinto Island Metals Co. v. Edwards (1963) 275 Ala. 351, 155 So. 2d 304 (employee of metals company was using blow torch on metal barrel which contained inflammable material; explosion resulted in burns of leg, face and eyes; eyesight deteriorated after injury and award of 75% total permanent disability was made despite no loss of earning capacity).

Fruehauf Corp. v. Prater (Ala. App., 1978) 360 So. 2d 999 (neurosis developing as result of severe burns suffered during employment held compensable under compensation statute).

Arizona: Alton v. Industrial Comm. (1969) 10 Ariz. App. 472, 459 P.2d 751 (conflicting evidence as to whether woman employee's allergic dermatitis was compensable injury arising out of accident in which flux in brazier furnace caught fire and burned her hands).

Arkansas: Hancock v. Modern Indus. Laundry (Ark., 1994) 878 S.W.2d 416 (Industrial Commission erred in concluding that workers' compensation claim by laundry worker for chemical burns to her arms allegedly suffered during course of employment was a claim for occupational disease, which, under the Arkansas Workers' Compensation Act, required a claimant to prove causal connection by "clear and convincing evidence").

Delaware: A. H. Angerstein, Inc. v. Jankowski (1962) 55 Del. 304, 187 A.2d 81 (workmen's compensation case involving dispute whether welder's paralysis and aphasia were caused by shock from welding machine; no evidence of burns on claimant's skin; award for claimant reversed).

Florida: Martini v. Kapok Tree Inn (1964) 172 So. 2d 829 (claimant successful in disputed workmen's compensation case in which waitress experienced kidney trouble from antibiotics received in treatment for second and third degree burns of the breast suffered when she spilled hot coffee on herself).

Redding v. Cobia Boat Co. (Fla., 1980) 389 So. 2d 1003 (woman who suffered first and second degree burns to face, neck and arms was afraid to return to place of employment where she was injured; temporary total disability benefits awarded on strength of psychiatric testimony).

Baker v. Orange County Bd. of County Commr's (Fla. App., 1981) 399 So. 2d 400 (burns suffered by worker from electrical socks worn outside during cold weather held compensable; socks were not "inherently dangerous instrumentality").

Iowa: Byrnes v. Donaldson's, Inc. (Iowa, 1990) 451 N.W.2d 810 (unsuccessful claim by factory worker that permanent facial scarring from burns incurred during her employment constituted permanent disfigurement, which, under the Iowa Workers' Compensation Act, impaired her future usefulness and earnings).

Louisiana: Jackson v. T. L. James & Co. (La. App., 1962) 141 So. 2d 475 (workmen's compensation claimant failed in argument that chronic nonspecific dermatitis and skin depigmentation were due to earlier burns caused by hot asphalt).

Brown v. Benton Creosoting Co. (La. App., 1962) 147 So. 2d 89 (workman suffered second and third-degree burns of face and arm from blast of burning gas; mild conjunctivitis in eyes; sensitivity to sunlight and heat; order denying compensation for total and permanent disability reversed).

Williams v. Zurich Ins. Co. (La. App., 1963) 159 So. 2d 391 (employee burned when liquid gas escaped from butane tank and splashed over arms and hands; thereafter unable to work around primary irritants and could not work with machinery or tools for long duration; award of total and permanent disability affirmed).

Ryan v. Aetna Cas. & Surety Co. (La. App., 1964) 161 So. 2d 286 (compensation claimant sustained first, second, and third degree burns to head, ears, face, arms and hands; loss of hearing from ear infection; dispute over extent of impairment and disability).

Russell v. Employers Mut. Liab. Ins. Co. of Wis. (1964) 246 La. 1012, 169 So. 2d 82 (workmen's compensation claim; two years after severe electrical burns claimant suffered blackouts, hypotension, electrolyte imbalance, lowered body temperature, infections, and adrenal damage; issue whether there was causal relationship between accident and later difficulties; award for claimant).

Thornton v. American Mut. Liab. Ins. Co. (La. App., 1968) 216 So. 2d 910 (in compensation case, court ruled in error in finding claimant disabled from foot which was burned with molten lead; medical evidence disclosed treatment for three months, skin graft, and residual mild discomfort in the form of skin irritation in periods of extreme hot or cold temperature).

Royer v. E. W. Cantrelle (La. App., 1972) 267 So. 2d 601 (compensation to laundry employee for traumatic neurosis after hand burned in pressing apparatus; no evidence of physical source for pain, but testimony that complaints were "real" to claimant).

Guidry v. Picadilly Cafeterias, Inc. (La. App., 1995) 657 So. 2d 325 (unsuccessful workers' compensation claim by cafeteria worker who suffered first- and second-degree burns when she spilled boiling water on her leg and foot; when burning pain did not subside after burns healed, claimant's physician, based upon clinical examination and results of thermography, opined that claimant had developed reflex sympathetic dystrophy).

Massachusetts: In re Look's case (1962) 345 Mass. 112, 185 N.E.2d 626 (evidence insufficient that plumber was partially disabled by erythema multiforme and allergy to lead which developed after burns from hot leadite).

Michigan: Kaarto v. Calumet & Hecla, Inc. (1962) 367 Mich. 128, 116 N.W.2d 225 (miner who was burned in mine explosion and developed susceptibility to pain in temperature extremes was held not entitled to workmen's compensation benefits where his injuries had not impaired his ability to perform his duties in the mine, even though the mine was shut down and regular mining employment was no longer available in locality).

Missouri: Cox v. GMC (Mo. App., 1985) 691 S.W.2d 294 (insufficient evidence that burn on workers' compensation claimant's forearm was caused by electrical shock from spot welder gun).

New Jersey: Wright v. Purepac Corp. (1963) 82 N.J. Super. 100, 196 A.2d 695 (employee suffered steam burns causing scarring from dorsum of right foot to gluteal area; award of 35% partial permanent disability of right leg held justified despite minor loss of function; 4% partial permanent neurological disability; extensive discussion of disfigurement issue).

Coleman v. Cycle Transformer Corp. (1986) 105 N.J. 285, 520 A.2d 1341 (burns suffered by employee when hair caught on fire while lighting cigarette during lunch break was "risk personal to employee" and was not compensable).

Oklahoma: Burkan Oil Co. v. Notley (Okla., 1971) 488 P.2d 1277 (determination of disability under compensation act from burn injury extending from middle of instep to eight inches below knee).

Pennsylvania: Workmen's Comp. Appeal Bd. v. Allied Chem. Corp. (1975) 20 Pa. Commw. 562, 342 A.2d 766 (third-degree burns of upper torso and limbs in explosion in 1966, together with chemical burn in 1970 which limited range of motion of hand, was held to have "caused or accelerated" worker's death in 1973 from acute myocardial infarction; according to cardiologist worker was "very nervous and apprehensive ... and occasionally depressed secondary to his accident and this ... aggravated his underlying heart disease ... and shortened his life").

(E) DISFIGUREMENT FROM INJURIES OTHER THAN BURNS

United States: Langford v. Chrysler Motors Corp. (C.A.-2 N.Y., 1975) 513 F.2d 1121 (six-year-old child suffered facial injuries causing "slight permanent scar"; damages of $9,000 approved).

Drayton v. Jeffee Chem. Corp. (N.D. Ohio, 1975) 395 F. Supp. 1081 (in case involving disfigurement of girl, jury may consider loss or lessening of prospect for marriage).

Alaska: Martinez v. Bullock (1975) 535 P.2d 1200 (damages of $500 to each of two boys, one of whom was eleven years of age and suffered cut on right side of face, and other was eight years of age and suffered cut on forehead and chin, was held not to be inadequate where at time of trial, approximately 3½ years after accident, both scars "had healed quite well").

Delaware: Ware v. Baker Driveway, Inc. (Del., 1972) 295 A.2d 734 (scar on male claimant's back which was visible for only about five inches above waistline when wearing swimming trunks did not entitle claimant to "disfigurement award" which was available for "disfigurement visible and offensive when body is clothed normally").

Carney v. Preston (Del. Super., 1996) 683 A.2d 47 (13-year-old girl suffered extensive lacerations to face and mouth in automobile accident; between 100 and 150 stitches required to close wounds; permanent scarring; jury returned verdict of $14,000, which trial court held inadequate and increased to $49,000; appellate court affirmed).

Georgia: Crossley v. Collins (1973) 128 Ga. App. 889, 198 S.E.2d 428 ($55,000 award held not excessive where young man's injuries involved a nearly severed ear which required several plastic surgery procedures, and some permanent disfigurement).

Whitley v. Ditta (Ga. App., 1993) 434 S.E.2d 108 (female high school student's face struck windshield in head-on collision; eyelid sliced in half and multiple facial lacerations; painful emergency treatment and five operations to remove scars; dermabrasion required every six months; large permanent scar on cheek; past and future medical expenses $9,869; award of $222,000 held not excessive, but reduced to $209,689 on recalculation of past and future medical expenses).

Illinois: Simon v. Van Steenlandt (Ill. App., 1996) 664 N.E.2d 231 (girl's forehead lacerated in automobile accident; plastic surgeon testified that scar would be permanent but could be made less apparent by reconstructive surgery costing $2,300; jury verdict for $2,600 held adequate by appellate court).

Iowa: Brant v. Bockholt (Iowa, 1995) 532 N.W.2d 801 (male high school student thrown through windshield in auto accident; four operations performed to reduce scarring; some scarring will be permanent; plaintiff graduated and was holding job at time of trial, but still suffers facial numbness; past medical expenses $19,000 and future medical expenses estimated at $31,000; jury awarded total of $85,000, which included $35,000 for past and future pain and suffering, but judgment reversed for erroneous instruction to reduce noneconomic damages to present value).

Foster v. Pyner (Iowa App., 1996) 545 N.W.2d 584 (four-year-old girl bitten by defendant's dog; loose tissue from lacerated lower lip reattached by family physician; medical expenses only $84.00; conflicting testimony by experts as to whether plastic surgery would reduce conspicuous scar or make it worse; defendant's offer of $12,000 refused, and jury returned verdict for $1,084; defendant refused trial court's conditional additur of $10,000, and appellate court granted new trial on damages).

Kentucky: Elmore v. Speicher (Ky. App., 1972) 481 S.W.2d 673 (although rule of law in state prevented recovery of damages for disfigurement as such, plaintiff could recover for past and future pain and suffering).

Louisiana: Ermis v. Governmental Employees Ins. Co. (La. App., 1974) 305 So. 2d 620 (six-year-old child suffered "unsightly" laceration above lip which required two or three cosmetic surgery procedures; $4,500 awarded).

Bobb v. Sears, Roebuck & Co. (La. App., 1975) 308 So. 2d 907 (noticeable and disfiguring scar on leg requiring seventy stitches; $5,000 award).

Adkins v. Fireman's Fund Ins. Co. (La. App., 1975) 313 So. 2d 328 (boy suffered four facial lacerations from dog bite; permanent scarring; injury to teeth would probably necessitate braces; no emotional problems; $5,000 award).

Chmurka v. Southern Farm Bureau Ins. Co. (La. App., 1978) 357 So. 2d 1207 (female suffered seven and one-half inch scar on hip; noticeable when she wore a bathing suit; award of $2,000 held proper).

Garrison v. State (La. App., 1981) 401 So. 2d 528 (jury award of $10,000 reduced to $6,000 where woman plaintiff conceded that facial scar could be concealed by use of cosmetics and plastic surgeon testified that scar could be removed for about $875).

Weaver v. Siegling (La. App., 1990) 569 So. 2d 97 (young girl injured in truck-automobile accident suffered multiple lacerations of face and arms, complicated by adjustment reaction and self-consciousness about scars; jury verdict of $69,000 in general damages reduced to $25,000 on appeal).

Longman v. Allstate Ins. Co. (La. App., 1994) 635 So. 2d 343 (plaintiff who suffered facial injury in automobile accident was left with large scar over eye; also increased risk of cataracts and glaucoma; past and future medical expenses were established at $35,000; jury award of $195,000 included $20,000 for permanent scarring).

Mississippi: D. W. Boutwell Butane Co. v. Smith (Miss., 1971) 244 So. 2d 11 (high school girl awarded $15,000 for injuries to forehead necessitating plastic surgery; some permanent scarring and loss of job as airline hostess).

New Jersey: Balcone v. Branker (1975) 136 N.J. Super. 137, 342 A.2d 875 (guidelines set out for determining "permanent significant disfigurement" under New Jersey's no fault statute).

New York: New v. Cortright (1969) 32 App. Div. 2d 576, 299 N.Y.S.2d 43 ($27,500 awarded to 23-year-old registered nurse for extensive facial lacerations requiring 122 sutures during seven-hour operation, part of which was done without anesthesia; some permanent scarring).

Kelley v. Hitzig (1972) 71 Misc. 2d 329, 336 N.Y.S.2d 122 (attractive woman airline employee bitten on face by passenger's dog resulting in well-healed scar on right side of chin which, with good cosmetic coverage, was only slightly visible; also scar near right earlobe with some disfigurement to ear; $3,000 awarded).

Olsen v. City of Schenectady (App. Div., 1995) 625 N.Y.2d 359 (11-year-old girl struck head on drainage gutter when she dove into city swimming pool; four-centimeter laceration on forehead, which left a permanent, fine-line "Y"-shaped scar; intermittent headaches; $80,000 trial court award affirmed).

Abdulai v. Roy (App. Div., 1996) 647 N.Y.S.2d 778 (male plaintiff suffered facial injuries in an automobile accident that left a deeply colored, line-shaped scar under his right eye and a one-half inch, thickened scar on his nose; according to expert testimony, neither injury could be made less apparent by plastic surgery; appellate court described disfigurement as "significant"; $110,000 jury award affirmed).

Oregon: Nielsen v. Brown (1962) 232 Or. 426, 374 P.2d 896 (admissibility of evidence as to effect on marital relations of scars on plaintiff wife's breasts).

Wisconsin: Zinda v. Pavloski (1966) 29 Wis. 2d 640, 139 N.W.2d 563 (21-year-old salesman suffered disfiguring facial injuries including nine-centimeter scar on forehead, and drooping left eyebrow; plaintiff claimed that despite plastic surgery scar was visible and was impediment in occupation as salesman; medical testimony offered that scar would remain but would "fade a bit as time goes by"; $15,000 awarded).

Sulkowski v. Schaefer (1966) 31 Wis. 2d 600, 143 N.W.2d 512 ($10,000 verdict to twenty-year-old female who sustained facial injuries which required extensive treatment, wearing of bandage for six months, and resulted in permanent scars).

CHAPTER 32

INJURIES TO THE HEAD, SPINAL CORD, AND PERIPHERAL NERVES*

I. INTRODUCTION

---

*Revised by W. Steven Metzer, M.D. Additonal contributors to the current and earlier editions of this chapter include Bruce Wilder, M.D., J.D., A. A. Marinacci, M.D., F. E. Dreifuss, M.B., M.R.C.P., M.R.A.C.P., Albert B. Butler, M.D., M. Louis Offen, M.D., J. de D. Martinez-G., M.D., Richard M. Patterson, J.D., E. S. Sadar, M.D., and C. Thomas Gott, M.D.

IX. ANATOMY AND PHYSIOLOGY OF THE SPINE AND SPINAL CORD

X. INJURY TO THE SPINE AND SPINAL CORD

XI. CLINICAL MANIFESTATIONS OF TRAUMA TO SPINE AND SPINAL CORD

XII. DIAGNOSIS IN SPINAL AND SPINAL CORD INJURIES

I. INTRODUCTION

§ 32.1. Scope of chapter.

This chapter is devoted mainly to injuries and related disorders of the brain, spinal cord, and cranial and peripheral nerves. As for the brain, the chapter deals primarily with physiological aspects as opposed to psychiatric. For psychiatric involvement in brain injuries, see Chapter 20 of this Cyclopedia. For mental conditions generally, see Chapter 17.

With regard to injuries to the spinal cord and peripheral nerves, the approach in this chapter is from the neurosurgical standpoint rather than the orthopedic. The orthopedic approach to disorders such as spinal deterioration, compression fractures, herniated discs, whiplash, etc., can be found elsewhere in the Cyclopedia. See the general index.

§ 32.2. The attorney and cases involving nervous system injury.

The attorney involved in a nervous system injury case should always obtain a careful history of the facts surrounding the injury. In many instances these are just as important as the medical findings. For example, if you ask a person who received a minor head injury whether he had lost consciousness, frequently he will answer no. Yet, after talking to witnesses, you may find that he actually was unconscious for a brief period. Also, it is not surprising to find a person who denies even striking his head in an accident, although an investigation will prove the contrary. One of the characteristics of a brain concussion is amnesia, and the victim not only may fail to remember events after the injury ("anterograde" amnesia), but also before ("retrograde" amnesia).

Determining loss of consciousness is important in a personal injury matter. A period of unconsciousness indicates a concussion and possibly some brain damage — usually, the longer the period of unconsciousness, the more severe the injury.

If the victim was taken to a hospital, the hospital record may reveal that he was disoriented. This is significant; disorientation is suggestive of a preceding stage of unconsciousness. If the hospital stay was lengthy, it is wise to obtain a copy of the complete hospital record (not just a summary) for careful study. Also, the victim's earlier medical history should be explored; his background may show previous injuries or illnesses having a direct bearing on the injury in question.

The X-ray examination made at the hospital may not show the victim's total condition. If the attorney waits until time of trial to study the films, he may be in for a surprise: the hospital may have used only a portable X-ray machine on the patient, or because of his condition complete X-rays may not have been taken; perhaps it was impossible to move him into the necessary positions on the X-ray table. Emergent attention to life-threatening injuries may impede the diagnosis of less severe injuries.

Delayed results in head injuries

The full effect of a head injury may not become apparent immediately. The attorney representing a plaintiff is well advised not to bring about an early disposition of the case. Continued observation of the patient by the doctors with periodic tests such as the electroencephalogram (EEG) or neuropsychological examinations may be indicated.

To illustrate, head injury can result in posttraumatic epilepsy, which may not develop for quite some time after the injury. (See § 32.47 et seq.)[1] Also, minor head injury, so minor that the victim may not recall being struck in the head, can result in a chronic subdural hematoma (blood clot) only evident weeks or even months after the injury. (See § 32.41.)

Personality change

It is well known that after even mild head injuries there can be personality change. This may be the result of physical brain damage, or in some cases, the cause may be purely emotional. When physical, the extent of the damage usually is in direct proportion to the severity of the injury. Where there is change after a relatively minor trauma, the patient often is treated from the psychiatric rather than the physiologic point of view. (See Chapter 20 of this Cyclopedia.) There is now evidence, however, that microscopic or ultrastructural changes probably occur in cases previously believed to be purely emotional or nonorganic. These changes may magnify preexisting psychopathology.

Calling in the specialist

In most cases of moderate head injury, a general practitioner will call in a specialist, usually a neurosurgeon, if one is available. But where the injury appears minor, and skull X-rays show no evidence of fracture, the general practitioner may handle the case on his or her own. Naturally, from a plaintiff's standpoint, it is usually an advantage to have a specialist in on the case. When encountering a general practitioner who believes there is no need for consultation (or the occasional practitioner who is offended whenever the subject of the need for a specialist is raised), some plaintiff's attorneys point out to the practitioner that should the plaintiff's case go to the trial, the practitioner's burden regarding testimony in court will be less if there are specialists who can be called to testify.

---

[1] Where a diagnosis of epilepsy is made, state law may require the doctor to report the patient's name to the bureau of motor vehicles or other agency. Some physicians object to these laws and a few fail to make such reports. (See § 32.59) A physician-witness testifying for a plaintiff may have failed to file this report, and his testimony may suffer seriously if this is brought out on cross-examination.

Medical examination by the defense

The medical examination by the defense of the plaintiff claiming nervous system injury naturally is of great importance. Care must be taken in the selection of a qualified examiner. It is advisable to take the plaintiff's deposition before the examining physician is chosen. This will develop the history and the symptoms of the injury, and will guide the defense in choosing the right specialist. There are a few "defense" doctors who submit negative reports in almost every case in which they examine a plaintiff. This kind of report is not helpful; it does not permit a true evaluation of the injuries for settlement purposes. Even worse, this physician may be made to look ridiculous on the stand under skillful cross-examination.

Difficult causal issues

Head injuries can introduce difficult proximate cause issues. For example, take the visitor who refuses to wear a "hard hat" at a construction site and suffers a fatal head injury. Depending on the circumstances and the parties involved, the case may be defended on assumption of risk, contributory negligence, or a violation of safety rules. The question to be determined may be whether failure to wear the protective headgear was the proximate cause of death. The autopsy report may suggest that the blow could have proven fatal even if the victim had been wearing the protective hat. There could be testimony by a safety expert that hard hats are intended to prevent head injury only from relatively minor blows.

Medical malpractice cases can also raise difficult proximate cause issues. In a Kentucky case, a patient suffered a fall and eventual death from irreversible brain damage. The defendant, a physician working the emergency room of a hospital, apparently was negligent in failing to discover a skull fracture — he merely prescribed aspirin and sent the patient home. But at the trial, the plaintiff was unable to prevail because he could not show that the defendant's misdiagnosis was the proximate cause of the patient's death. The defense successfully argued that the injury was so severe that the patient probably would have died regardless of a correct diagnosis.[2] In another case, a patient who was dazed after an automobile accident appeared at a hospital emergency room suffering from a severe brain concussion, but the hospital personnel thought he was merely intoxicated. He was not admitted and later was found wandering in the street, suffering from numerous additional injuries, apparently from another accident or an assault. A lawsuit against the hospital was unsuccessful for want of proof of proximate cause.[3]

---

[2] Neal v. Welker (Ky. App., 1968) 426 S.W.2d 476.

[3] Sadler v. Sisters of Charity of Providence in Oregon, Inc. (1967) 247 Or. 50, 426 P.2d 747.

Use of depositions

The deposition phase of the case involving a nervous system injury is important. Many cases are won or lost at this stage. Once testimony is under oath and down in writing, it is not easily changed without problems. A deposition is expensive and time consuming, but it is vital. It reduces the number of surprises the attorney will encounter in the courtroom, and it requires both sides to become extremely familiar with the real issues, thus leading to more realistic settlement offers.

Because of the complexities of nervous system injuries, an attorney should never take the deposition of a physician without careful preparation, either through consultation with his or her own medical expert or by way of research in the medical books. In most lawsuits involving central nervous system injuries, the total medical picture is revealed only from thorough depositions based on careful preparation.

Use of the formal medical brief

Attorneys disagree on the value of a formal medical brief in a personal injury case. Some maintain that the medical brief, similar to a legal brief except that it contains supporting medical authorities rather than legal, can be very useful to both the attorney and his medical experts. In a case involving the nervous system, it can be particularly helpful because of the complex nature of most of these injuries.

Attorneys who use the medical brief argue that usually it is of great value to the expert because it contains references to some of the world's best medical literature supporting his or her position. If carefully prepared, it gives the expert confidence and impresses him or her as to the need for thoroughness. For best results, copies of the brief should be forwarded to the experts prior to trial, so they may make additions and suggestions.

Preparation of medical witnesses

Attorneys on both sides of a nervous system injury case are well advised to review carefully the medical authorities to familiarize themselves with the nature of the injury and extent of disability. A pretrial conference with the physicians who are to testify is essential. These witnesses should be informed on matters to be covered on direct examination and those likely to be brought up by opposing counsel.

Physicians frequently misinterpret what is required of them in court. Occasionally they say "My opinion is that the patient suffered a concussion, but I cannot prove it." Obviously, such testimony on behalf of a plaintiff can be detrimental. Physicians should be made to understand that their opinions themselves are a form of proof, and that they have a perfect right to advance any opinion in which they have an honest belief. But they should be cautioned to avoid the use of speculative words such as "It could be." And if the witness is a general practitioner, the attorney may have to offer assurance that he or she has a right to offer an opinion about a complex central nervous system disorder even though he or she does not specialize in the field.

Presenting the medical evidence

In the trial of cases involving central nervous system injuries it is helpful for the medical witnesses to use anatomical charts to explain their testimony to the jury. A plastic skull usually is also very helpful. It is suggested that a real skull not be used because some jurors may be sensitive. Models showing the distribution of nerves also are valuable in most cases. In trials involving minor injuries, however, demonstrative techniques may be overused; the jury may become bored, realize the lack of need for such methods, and conclude that the party is attempting to compensate for a weak case.

Do not overlook the value of lay witnesses in head injury cases; if there have been personality changes, plaintiff's counsel should use members of the family, friends and possibly the employer to testify to this fact.

II. ANATOMY AND PHYSIOLOGY OF THE HEAD

§ 32.3. Introduction.

In order to have a clear understanding of the magnitude of head injuries, their clinical picture and their evolution and sequelae, some knowledge of the anatomy and physiology of the brain and its coverings is essential. It should be emphasized at the beginning that when a neurosurgeon treats head injuries, he is particularly concerned with the damage inflicted to the brain itself. The scalp may be lacerated and the bones of the skull fractured, but as long as the brain itself has not been injured, the results of trauma are not of significance. The scalp and bone can heal without sequelae under proper treatment; however, injury to the brain cannot be repaired, although time and rehabilitation therapy may compensate for some deficit.

§ 32.4. The scalp.

The brain is enclosed in a bony case (skull) covered by the scalp. The scalp is composed of several layers of tissue (**Fig. 1**). The most superficial layer is the skin, or cutis, which is similar to but somewhat thicker than the skin elsewhere on the body. It contains a great number of hair follicles; the presence of the hair on the scalp offers additional protection. Under the skin there is a layer of fatty tissue called subcutaneous tissue; within it are arteries, veins, and nerves. Under the subcutaneous tissue there is a rather firm membrane called the galea. This fibrous membrane in its most anterior and posterior aspects is continued by two

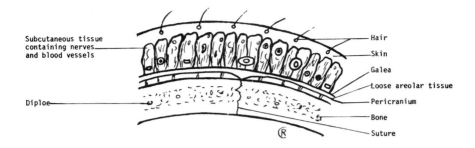

Fig. 1. Cross-section of scalp and skull.

muscles; the frontal muscle over the forehead, and occipital muscle over the back of the head. In the temporal regions (temples), immediately under the galea there are two rather large muscles that give additional protection to the skull. Under the galea, there is space more potential than real, with a small amount of loose tissue. The pericranium forms the inner membrane of this space and serves as connective tissue to the outer table of the skull, carrying to it its blood supply. The scalp as a whole can be moved on the pericranium, thanks to the potential space mentioned above. This fact is very important in injuries where scalp is lost or destroyed, since it allows scalp from other regions to be mobilized and close the wound.

The scalp has a very rich blood supply. The arterial circulation arises from the external carotid arteries, through several vessels which connect freely in the subcutaneous tissue. Since the vessels are lying in loose tissue, they bleed profusely in cases of lacerations of the scalp. The richness of the arterial circulation is a source of protection to the brain, and any cut or localized infection properly treated is likely to heal promptly. Infection occurs only rarely, usually as a result of infected or untreated wounds under the most adverse circumstances where dirt and debris are left in the wound. The veins of the scalp are also numerous and eventually empty into the jugular veins in the neck. Veins of the scalp connect with veins going into the bones and through foramina (openings) in the skull with the veins in the intracranial cavity. The nerves of the scalp originate in the fifth cranial nerve anteriorly, and the first and second cervical nerve roots posteriorly.

§ 32.5. The skull.

Superficial examination of the skull, or cranium, will disclose that the bones of the vault (top) are rather thin in comparison with the massive array of bone at the base. The bones of the vault, however, are not of uniform thickness. Anteriorly, in the midline, there is a thicker area,

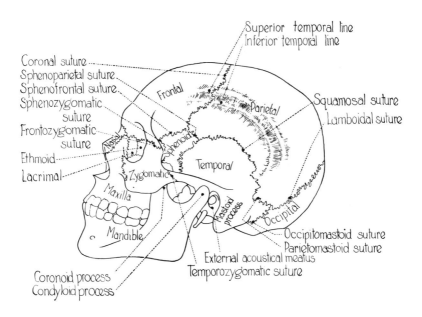

Fig. 2. Anatomy of skull — side view.

and laterally there are three thicker archlike structures continuous with bones of the base. The base of the skull is rather irregular. There are several thin areas, several foramina and also some rather massive structures that are hollow and filled with air. These are the paranasal sinuses in the front and the middle ear and mastoid cavities in the temporal area. **(Fig. 2.)**

The structure of the bones of the vault are rather peculiar to the cranium. The skull here is composed of two layers of hard, compact bone of a few millimeters of thickness. Each is connected by a layer of soft, spongy bone. In the spongy center (diplo/Ue), there are a great number of venous vascular channels that communicate with the scalp veins and the veins of the intracranial cavity. The vault is made of several bones joined together at the suture lines. In a growing child the sutures are open to allow the skull to enlarge as the brain grows, but eventually they fuse and finally close; this is completed between twenty to twenty-five years of age. The names of the different bones of the skull are mentioned only because the names of the areas of the brain underneath correspond to them. The frontal bone, the temporal and parietal bones on each side, and the occipital bone posteriorly, form the vault. The frontal, temporal and occipital bone, together with the ethmoid and sphenoidal bone, form the base of the skull.

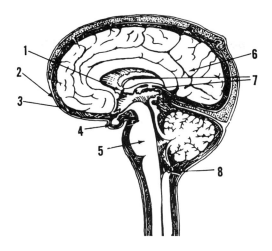

Fig. 3. The brain.

1	Foramen of Monro	5	Pons
2	Dura mater	6	Pia mater
3	Arachnoid	7	Choroid plexus
4	Pituitary gland	8	Foramen of Magendie

§ 32.6. Membranes covering the brain (meninges).

Aside from the protection provided by the skull, the brain is further protected by its covering membranes. These membranes are called meninges and are three in number. The outer meninx is called dura mater or "pachymeninges," from the Greek, meaning thick membrane. The inner two, the "leptomeninges" (Greek for slender membranes) are called arachnoid and pia mater. **(Fig. 3.)** The dura mater is a thick, fibrous membrane composed of two layers that are firmly fused except at the places where they form the venous sinuses. The outer surface is in close contact with the bone to which it serves as connective tissue to the inner table of the skull and as such provides it with blood supply. At the base, the dura is more firmly attached to the bone. It accompanies the nerves and vessels that go out of the skull and blends itself with the coverings of these structures. The potential space between the dura and the bone is called epidural or extradural space. Normally, it is a "virtual space," being real only in pathological conditions in which it may be occupied by blood clots or pus.

From its inner surface, the dura mater forms a strong partition, which serves to divide the intracranial cavity into compartments. One of these partitions starts in the frontal region and goes in the midline as far as the occipital region where it joins the upper part of a transverse partition which extends horizontally to the occipital bones. The first partition

301

mentioned is called the "falx cerebri" — (falx, from the Latin for sickle because of its sickle shape) and separates the cerebral hemispheres. The second is the "tentorium cerebelli" (tent of the cerebellum) and separates the cerebrum from the cerebellum and brain stem. The tentorium also separates the middle fossa from the posterior fossa (the anterior fossa is in the front and is occupied by the frontal lobe) of the skull. There are other partitions formed by the dura that are not as important and will not be mentioned here.

The dural venous sinuses are at the point of attachment of these septa. These are very important structures because they constitute the main avenue of exit of the venous circulation of the brain, meninges and skull. The superior saggital sinus begins in the frontal region, runs under the vertex of the skull at the junction of the dura and falx cerebri as far back as the occipital bone, where it divides into two "transverse sinuses" located at the junction of the tentorium and dura which eventually empty out of the skull into the jugular veins. There are other sinuses at the base of the skull which help to drain the intracranial veins to other veins outside of the skull through the foramina at the base. The cavernous sinus should be particularly mentioned here because it is the only example in the human body of an artery being located inside of a vein. The carotid arteries, the main source of arterial supply to the cerebrum, run for a distance within both cavernous sinuses (right and left). The fourth cranial nerve also runs inside of the cavernous sinuses and other nerves run on its walls. Occasionally a fracture of the base of the skull will tear a carotid artery, giving rise to a free communication of the artery into the cavernous sinus, forming a carotid-cavernous fistula. The walls of the sinuses are rigid, and because of this feature, when lacerated, they may bleed profusely.

Beside the veins, which drain into the sinuses, there are several small constant veins that communicate the intracranial venous circulation with the veins of the scalp, face, and orbit through well-known foramina (holes). These are called emissary veins, and are extremely important in that through them, extracranial infections may spread into the intracranial structures, causing meningitis, brain abscess, etc.

The arterial supply of the dura mater comes from the meningeal vessels, particularly from the middle meningeal arteries. These important vessels enter the skull through foramina at the base (foramina spinosum) and go into the dura. Sometimes these vessels form deep grooves in the temporal bone, which make them vulnerable to injury in fractures of the skull in this region. The venous circulation of the dura goes into the middle meningeal veins or directly into the sinuses.

The leptomeninges are situated under the dura; the pia mater is adherent to the brain and separated from the arachnoid membrane by a space filled with clear fluid (cerebrospinal fluid), called the subarachnoid space. The pia mater is a very thin membrane that follows all of the brain's irregularities (sulci), carrying with it a great number of small blood vessels to supply its surface. The arachnoid membrane is thicker than the pia and does not follow the irregularities in the surface of the brain. It has, however, many attachments to the pia that form a mesh through which the cerebrospinal fluid circulates. In most of the intracranial cavity, the arachnoid membrane and pia mater are fairly close, being separated by some small amount of spinal fluid; however, at the base, and in certain "strategic" places, the subarachnoid space becomes much larger and forms lakes called cisternae. These lakes are situated around the medulla (cisterna magna) and other vital brain stem structures for their protection. The cisternae are part of the pathways through which the spinal fluid passes from its points of origin to the places where its absorption takes place. The large arteries and veins which supply the brain run through for considerable distances in the subarachnoid space. The space between the arachnoid membrane and dura mater is called subdural space and is also normally a potential space that becomes real only in pathological conditions.

§ 32.7. The brain.

Anatomically the brain can be divided into three parts: the forebrain, the midbrain and the hindbrain. The forebrain consists of the cerebral hemispheres, the largest part of the brain, with their connective structures. The midbrain, relatively small, connects the structures of the forebrain with the hindbrain, which is made up of the cerebellum, pons and medulla. The cerebrum occupies most of the intracranial cavity. Its surface is irregular with many grooves, called sulci or fissures, separating the number of elevations known as convolutions, or gyri. (**Fig. 4.**) The most important grooves on the lateral surface of the brain are: the central sulcus (separates the neighboring convolutions and forms the boundaries between the frontal and parietal lobes); the Sylvian or lateral fissure (separates the frontal and parietal lobes from the temporal lobe); and the parieto-occipital fissure (forms the anterior limits of the occipital lobes). On the medial surface outside of the sulci and convolutions, the most prominent feature is the corpus callosum, which is a mass of nervous tissue that connects both cerebral hemispheres.

The corrugated surface of the brain is called the cerebral cortex and is of a different color than the underlying tissue. The cortex has a grayish color and because of that is called the gray matter, while the underlying tissue is white and is called white matter. In the depths of the hemispheres are cavities: the cerebral ventricles, one in each hemisphere. (**Fig. 5.**) They communicate with a central cavity called the third ventricle. Inside the ventricles are the choroid plexus, the organ that produces the cerebrospinal fluid. In close relationship to the ventricles are structures of the same gray color as the cortex, called the basal ganglia.

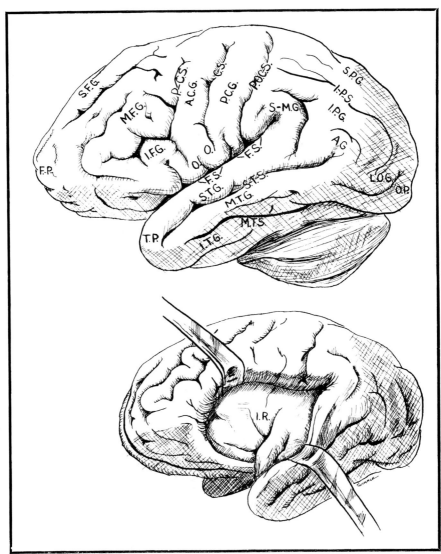

Fig. 4. Lateral surface of the brain, also showing the fissures and major convolutins, among other structures. The abbreviations are as follows: A.C.G. — anterior central gyrus; A.G. — agnular gyrus; C.S. — central sulcus (fissure of Rolando); F.P. — frontal pole; F.S. — fissure of Sylvius; I.F.G. — inferior frontal gyrus; I.P.G. — inferior parietal gyrus; I.P.S. — inter-parietal sulcus; I.R. — island of Reil; I.T.G. — inferior temporal gyrus; L.O.G. — lateral occipital gyrus; M.F.G. — middle frontal gyrus; M.T.G. — middle temporal gyrus; M.T.S. — middle tempral sulcus; O. — operculum; O.P. — occipital pole; P.C.G. — posterior central gyrus; P.C.S. — pre-central sulcus; P.O.C.S. — post central sulcus; S.F.G. — superior frontal gyrus; S.M.G. — supramarginal gyrus; S.P.G. — superior parietal gyrus; S.T.G. — superior temporal gyrus; S.T.S. — superior temporal sulcus; T.P. — temporal pole.

Microscopically, the gray matter is composed mainly of nerve cells (neurons), while the white matter is made up of communicating fibers and has no nerve cells. (There are cells in the white matter (glia) which surround the nerve fibers and help to hold them in place. These glial cells are important in the healing processes after injuries; they also give rise to most brain tumors.)

The midbrain begins in the posterior aspect of the third ventricle and ends at the beginning of the pons. It contains the cerebral peduncles, which connect the cerebrum to the brain stem. Some of the gray matter surrounds the aqueduct of Sylvius, a tube-like structure which connects the third ventricle with the fourth.

The hindbrain consists of the pons, cerebellum, and medulla. Between the pons and cerebellum, the fourth ventricle is located. This cavity communicates by three openings with the subarachnoid cisternae. The pons and medulla are mainly composed of white matter in the form of bundled nerve fibers that connect the cerebrum to the spinal cord, which begin at the lower end of the medulla. Among this white matter, there are many nuclei of gray matter whose nerve cells give rise to the cranial nerves, some of which control such vital functions as breathing, heartbeat, blood pressure, digestion, etc. They also control eye movements, facial sensation and movement, and tongue and vocal cord movement.

The cerebellum, like the cerebrum, has a cortex of gray matter with white matter in the center. This organ controls coordination, but not at the conscious level.

The brain has a very rich blood supply. Four rather large vessels, the two internal carotid and the two vertebral arteries supply all of the intracranial structures. The carotid vessels bring blood to about two-thirds of the cerebrum, while the vertebral vessels supply the hindbrain and the posterior fourth of the cerebral hemispheres. Both carotid and vertebral vessels divide, and each of the branches supplies a certain part of the brain which is more or less constant. Knowledge of the distribution of these vessels and their branches is important to neurologists and more so to the surgeon who may expose them during a surgical procedure.

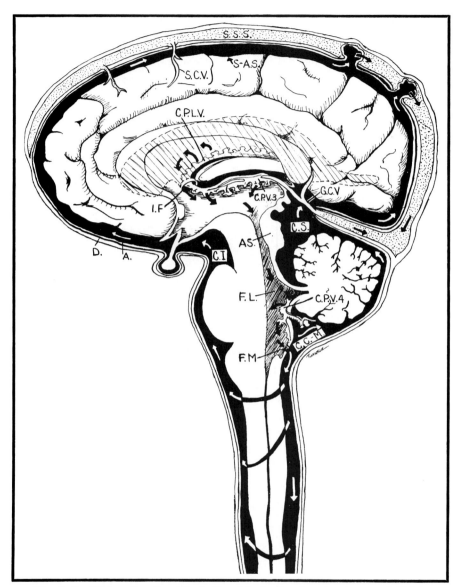

Fig. 5. Sagittal section through skull and brain showing structures and divisions of the brain. Also, in black, the subarachnoid space. Arrows indicate the general flow of the cerebrospinal fluid. The abbreviations are as follows: A. — arachnoid; A.G. — arachnoidal granulation; A.S. — aqueduct of Sylvius; C.C.-M. — cisterna cerebello; C.I. — cisterna interpeduncularis; C.P.L.V. — choroid plexus of lateral ventricle; C.P.V.3 — choroid plexus of third ventricle; C.P.V.4 — choroid plexus of fourth ventricle; C.S. — cisterna superior; D. — dura mater; F.L. — foramen of Luschka; F.M. — foramen of Magendie; G.C.V. — great cerebral vein; I.F. — interventricular foramen (Monro); S.-A.S. — subarachnoid space; S.C.V. — superior cerebral vein; S.S.S. — superior sagittal sinus.

§ 32.8. Physiology of the intracranial structures — Cerebrospinal fluid.

To understand the clinical picture in craniocerebral trauma, that is, the symptomatology and its complications and sequelae, the reader should be aware of the function of the intracranial structures under normal and pathological conditions. As pointed out earlier, the skull is a rigid box containing the brain and its membrane, spinal fluid, and vessels through which blood circulates. All of these elements are in a state of equilibrium as far as volume is concerned. Any increase in volume of any of them results in a reduction in volume of the others, if normal conditions are to prevail; that is, if the intracranial pressure is to remain normal. If no such adaptation takes place, increased intracranial pressure develops. The intracranial volume in adults is fixed and cannot enlarge in size to accommodate large increases in volume of any of the intracranial structures, such as would be caused by a tumor, bleeding, diffuse brain swelling, etc.

In considering the physiology of the intracranial contents, it is well to begin with the spinal fluid, also known as cerebrospinal fluid (CSF). This liquid, which has the appearance of crystal clear water, surrounds the brain and acts as a protective shock-absorber.

The cerebrospinal fluid is produced by filtration from the blood in the choroid plexus, which can be found in all the ventricles, the largest being in the lateral ventricles. About 400-500 cc. of CSF are produced in twenty-four hours. The amount of cerebrospinal fluid in the intracranial cavity is about 50 cc., while the total amount, including that in the spinal subarachnoid space, is about 120 cc. to 140 cc. under normal conditions.

The fluid secreted in the lateral ventricles passes into the third ventricle to the foramina of Monro and then through the aqueduct of Sylvius into the fourth ventricle. This ventricle has three openings into the subarachnoid space, through which the CSF passes to go around the surface of the brain and penetrate the perivascular spaces, then be absorbed back into the venous system by the arachnoidal granulations (pacchionian bodies).

The rate of filtration and production of CSF from the blood depends on the capillary pressure and the osmotic[4] pressure of the blood. A rise in the capillary pressure such as would occur when the venous draining of the brain is blocked will tend to increase the rate of filtration and CSF production. Normally, the blood is isotonic (equal) to the CSF, so under normal conditions the filtration is practically affected only by the capillary pressure. If the osmotic pressure of the blood is low, more fluid will be produced and the converse situation is also true. If the osmotic pres-

---

[4] Editor's Note: "Osmotic" pertains to "osmosis," which is the passage of a solution from a lesser to a greater concentration through a membrane.

sure of the blood is increased, the filtration and CFS production takes place with reabsorption of fluid into the venous circulation. The absorption of the spinal fluid into the venous system mainly depends upon the osmotic pressure of the blood and on the difference of pressure that exists between the subarachnoid space and intracranial venous sinuses. Blockage in the subarachnoid space impedes CSF absorption.

The spinal fluid pressure reflects the intracranial pressure and is normally from 100 to 200 mm. of water. Usually, the intracranial pressure is measured in the lumbar subarachnoid space (lumbar puncture) with the patient in the recumbent position. If the reading is made with the patient sitting up, the pressure is high, and under these conditions one should measure not only the intracranial pressure, but also the hydrostatic pressure over the column of fluid from the head to the needle in the lumbar space. The intracranial pressure can be measured directly from transducers placed in the subarachnoid space, a ventricle, or on the substance of the brain itself.

Normally, the volume of blood entering the intracranial cavity (250 to 400 cc. per minute) through the arteries and leaving through the veins is constant. The blood pressure in the large arteries is as high as it is in the aorta, which is the main artery coming out of the heart. As the artery is divided, the blood pressure falls, so that in the capillaries it is about 50 mm. of mercury. On the venous side the pressure is even lower, reaching as low as 8 mm. of mercury. In an individual in the upright position, the venous pressure in the large venous sinuses may even be negative. The intracranial pressure follows the venous pressure, although it is always somewhat higher. Any change in venous pressure, however, affects the intracranial pressure, as can be readily shown in such commonplace acts as coughing, straining, or holding one's breath (valsalva maneuver). These acts momentarily interfere with the venous drainage of the brain by raising the intrathoracic pressure and interfere with the venous return to the heart.

In pathological conditions, the delicate balance of volume between the cerebrospinal fluid, blood, and brain may become disrupted with the production of increased intracranial pressure. This may occur in several ways. An increase in bulk of the brain may occur in a brain injury in which a bruise has developed (cerebral contusion). At first there is a local extravasation of blood and local swelling, the normal total volume being preserved by diminution in the amount of cerebrospinal fluid and blood. As the swelling increases, the intracranial structures are compressed and the venous flow is impaired, with resulting local and general venous congestion. This venous congestion increases the total volume of the intracranial contents and further increases the intracranial pressure.

Increased intracranial pressure may also be produced by obstruction of the spinal fluid pathways. This situation occurs more often with tumors, particularly fourth ventricle growths produce a back-up of fluid into the ventricles by blocking the circulation of spinal fluid. This condition is known as hydrocephalus. In trauma, when there is a severe subarachnoid hemorrhage, blood may block the spinal fluid pathways and give rise to backing up of fluid and pressure.

§ 32.9. Functions of the brain.

Our present knowledge indicates that various portions of the brain have different microscopic structures, and this suggests that they may have different functions. This knowledge has been acquired gradually through years of study. In 1861, Broca demonstrated that destruction of the left third frontal gyrus resulted in the inability to speak. Today, this area bears his name. (**Fig. 6.**) A few years later it was demonstrated that electrical stimulation of the central gyrus produced movements from muscles in the opposite half of the body. This gyrus is known today as the motor cortex area. Later, similar clinical and pathological studies expanded our knowledge and have shown many functional areas with precision. There are still large areas whose functions are unknown. These are called "silent areas" because their removal fails to show obvious deficit of function. Undoubtedly, as additional studies are carried out, these areas will be found less devoid of function than they now appear.

The hemispheres

The cerebral hemispheres, although they are of similar microscopic structure, are not physiologically equal. There is always a variable degree of dominance of one hemisphere over the other in the control of important functions, such as language and the performance of complex motor acts. This dominance seems to be related to "handedness," so that right-handed individuals are "left-brained" and left-handed ones are "right-brained." The determination of the dominant hemisphere (extremely important in brain surgery) in ambidextrous individuals may be very difficult, and occasionally the surgeon may have to rely on the knowledge of the handedness of the patient's ancestors since heredity seems to play a very important role in this trait, but it is better and more reliable to introduce a brain depressant intra-arterially (Wada test). If the individual is right-handed and left-brained, he should be unable to talk with an injection into the left carotid artery, while if he is right-brained, his speech should not be affected.

At birth, both hemispheres are of equal potential. Dominance begins to develop at about one year of age, but it is not completed for several years. Destruction of the important dominant hemisphere in the first year of life causes a shift of dominance to the opposite side. In an adult, however, destruction of a similar area will lead to serious permanent

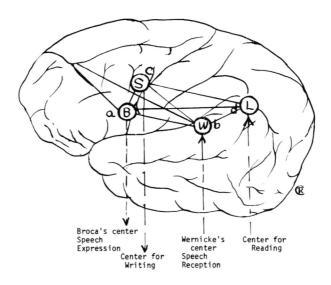

Broca's center
Speech
Expression

Center for
Writing

Wernicke's
center
Speech
Reception

Center for
Reading

a. inferior frontal gyrus

b. superior temporal gyrus

c. precentral gyrus

d. angular gyrus

Fig. 6. Areas of the brain responsible for speech expression and reception, writing, and reading.

disability. This concept is referred to as decreasing plasticity of the brain with increasing age.

In describing the functions of each part of the brain we will first enumerate the functions ascribable to both hemispheres and then the ones that are localized on the dominant side.

Functions of the frontal lobes

The frontal lobes, which are located in the front end of the cerebrum, extend as far back as the rolandic sulcus posteriorly. Injuries or disease to the anterior part of the frontal lobes causes personality changes and disturbance of character, with a loss of executive function of the brain. An individual who before the injury was neat in appearance, circumspect in speech, and fulfilled his duties at work and home, may change into a person who is careless in dress, obscene, and entirely disinterested in his personal affairs. His ability to pay attention and to comprehend may be seriously impaired as may his memory, particularly for recent events. His emotional life may be disturbed, and he may cry or laugh easily and without justification. While before, the patient may have been a composed individual, afterwards his self-control may be affected and he may be subject to outbursts of rage, sexual lapses, or depression.

Injuries or disease to the posterior part of the frontal lobe will cause motor phenomena, such as weakness or paralysis of the muscles of the contralateral side of the body, depending on the part of the motor cortex and adjacent areas injured. Localization in the motor cortex is well known; centers for the foot and leg muscles are in the upper part (which actually is part of the medial aspect of the hemisphere), and centers for the muscles of the thigh, abdomen, shoulder, arm, hand, neck, tongue, and larynx are located in the lower part.

Functions of the parietal, occipital and temporal lobes

Injuries to the parietal lobe cause sensory impairment on the opposite side of the body. Although the sensation is never abolished, such injuries result in inability to localize the sensory stimuli and to appreciate changes of its intensity. The patient may lose the ability to determine the weight of objects and their texture so that if a common object is placed in his hands, such as a coin, although he knows he has something in his hand, he is unable to tell what it is. This inability to recognize objects in one hand is called astereognosis. In addition, right parietel lesions commonly result in impairment of attention and in solving problems involving visuospatial orientation. Left parieto-temporal lesions commonly impair mathematic abilities.

The visual centers are situated in the occipital lobe. Each lobe receives fibers from the same side of each retina of the eye, so that destruction to this area produces blindness in the opposite field of vision. The localization of the visual fields is in the lips of the calcarine fissure, while central vision is diffusely represented all over the occipital lobes, with the result that even in large, destructive lesions in this area, in which there is homonymous hemianopsia (loss of vision on the opposite side of each visual field), central vision is not impaired.

The temporal lobes contain the olfactory (smell) and auditory (hearing) receptive centers. These are bilaterally represented so that a lesion of one temporal lobe alone does not produce serious handicaps along these lines. The optic radiation (fibers that connect the retina of the eye to the centers in the occipital lobe), however, pass in the center of the temporal lobe so that the destructive lesions there also produce blindness in the opposite field, which may vary from complete hemianopsia to small homonymous defects. Central vision is always affected in complete or partial lesions of the optic radiation in the temporal lobe, since both the central and peripheral vision fibers are bundled together in this part of the cerebrum.

Functions of the dominant hemisphere

In addition to the functions outlined in the preceding paragraphs, which are peculiar to both cerebral hemispheres, the dominant hemisphere has functions particularly to itself. These tremendously important functions have to do with the performance of complex motor acts and language. They are peculiar only to the Homo sapiens. Ultimately, herein resides the ability to think. Our thoughts are carried out by using symbols (words). Complete destruction of this area (speech centers) leaves the individual without the ability to recognize or produce the symbols either when heard or seen. This condition is called aphasia.

There are two main types of aphasia: nonfluent (motor; expressive) and fluent (sensory; receptive). Wounds in the frontal lobe produce motor aphasia. The patient is unable to translate ideas or conceptions into words. The muscles of the mouth and larynx are not paralyzed; the patient can make sounds, but the brain is unable to produce speech. This has to be differentiated from a condition in which there is actual paralysis of the muscles used in speech (dysarthia).

Injuries to the upper temporal and lower parietal lobes give rise to sensory aphasia in which the patient can speak, but cannot understand the spoken word. (The language he has spoken all his life sounds to him as a foreign language does to a normal person.) When both areas are destroyed, global aphasia occurs — both the ability to speak and to understand speech are lost. There are many degrees of aphasia, depending upon the site of destruction. For instance, a lesion may produce agraphia, that is, inability to write, while another may produce an inability to read, which may be isolated or mixed with motor or sensory aphasic symptoms.

It is obvious that an individual who is afflicted with aphasia, even in a minimal degree, may be seriously handicapped and sometimes totally disabled, depending on his occupation.

The other important function of the dominant hemisphere is praxis, that is to say the smooth performance of simple and complicated motor acts. This occurs in the absence of paralysis or incoordination by loss of conception of how to carry out the act or inability to make the muscles work in proper sequence to carry out the act. Loss of this important function (apraxia) is also an extremely disabling condition which fortunately is not common, since this lesion usually has to be bilateral and is unusual in head injuries.

§ 32.10.　Basal ganglia.

These structures are situated in the depth of the cerebrum in close proximity to the third and lateral ventricles. There are several basal ganglia. The "corpora striatea" perform as motor centers by many connections with each other (pre-motor cortex, etc.), and thus exert an influence on the motor system. Disease or dysfunction of these structures may produce muscular rigidity, slowing of voluntary movements and the appearance of tremor and other involuntary movements that can be aggravated by emotions or by the patient trying to perform sudden motions.

The other pair of basal ganglia are the "thalami," which are sensory relay stations of impulses coming from the periphery through the peripheral nerves, spinal cord, and brain stem, as well as to these structures through the cerebral cortex. When these impulses reach the thalamus, they are transmitted to the sensory cortex. Destructive lesions of the thalamus can give rise to the so-called "thalamic syndrome" which consists of contralateral diminution of sensation and a spontaneous burning pain of an extremely serious nature. The slightest stimuli, such as touching the skin of the affected site, gives rise to an excessively unpleasant sensation.

The "hypothalamus" (lower continuation of the thalamus) is the main center of the autonomic nervous system in the cerebrum. Its functions are many and among them is the control of temperature regulation, sleep regulation, and metabolic activities.

Another structure, the "cerebellum," co-ordinates most of the activities in such fashion that most voluntary motion can be accomplished. Lesions that destroy part of this structure produce incoordination of movements, hypotonia, (relaxation of muscles), but only minimal weakness on the same side of the lesion. The walk becomes impaired and a staggering gait is a rule with these lesions.

The midbrain and hindbrain are the main avenues through which the cerebrum connects with the spinal cord and peripheral nerves. The nuclei of the cranial nerves are located there so that all lesions in this area produce severe symptoms.

III. PATHOLOGY OF HEAD INJURY

§ 32.11. The meaning of "concussion."

The term "concussion" has acquired a meaning among lay persons and lawyers that does not always correspond to that used by the clinician. A patient sustaining a blow to the head that causes loss of consciousness for a few seconds to minutes has suffered a concussion. This patient must be distinguished from one who has suffered a more severe brain injury, and who remains unconscious for several days or longer. It is obvious that the latter patient has sustained a more severe injury, and is more likely to sustain permanent disability than the patient sustaining a concussion.

The term "concussion" should be reserved for those patients sustaining craniocerebral trauma associated with short-lasting unconsciousness. Although the term concussion, as used by clinicians and others, has assumed no brain damage and no permanent disability, evidence based on neuropsychological testing clearly demonstrates problems in some patients with attention, concentration, memory, and judgment.[5] The pathologic basis for these findings on testing are yet to be determined; however, the majority of patients eventually recover after a mild cerebral concussion.[6]

Some who have considered the subject believe that in a concussion there is a sudden cerebral anemia, caused by the increase of intracranial pressure as a result of the deformation of the skull and brain, and the shaking of the brain substance by the initial blow. Others believe that there is a direct mechanical effect on the brain cells causing a temporary disorder of neuronal metabolism.

Regardless of what theory of concussion one may accept, the above-mentioned changes are sudden, instantaneous, and the associated clinical symptoms may be prolonged in some patients. Concussion is a diagnosis made on the basis of transient loss of consciousness and the associated symptoms that may be evident soon after the accident or for prolonged periods of time. If the state of unconsciousness lasts more than a few minutes, the chances of rapid recovery are less. There is a definite relationship between the length of unconsciousness and the severity of the brain injury. To diagnose a patient who has been unconscious for several hours as having suffered a concussion is misleading. The patient may have suffered contusions (bruises) of the brain that may leave him with permanent disability. The association of prolonged unconsciousness, contusion, cerebral edema, and neurologic deficit establishes a diagnosis of severe brain injury, not a simple concussion.

---

[5] Rimel, R. W., et al., *Disability Caused by Minor Head Injury*, 9 Neurosurgery 221, 1981. The authors studied 538 patients who had sustained minor head trauma (a history of unconsciousness of twenty minutes or less and hospitalization not exceeding 48 hours). Of these patients, 424 were evaluated three months after injury. The follow-up included a history of events since the accident, assessment of subjective complaints and objective measures such as employment status, a neurological examination, a psychosocial assessment designed for estimating life stress, and a neuropsychological test battery to measure higher cortical function. Of these 424 patients, 79% complained of persistent headaches, and 59% described problems with memory. Of the patients who had been employed before the accident, 34% were unemployed three months later. Comparisons were then made between the employed and unemployed groups. Three explanations for the high rate of unemployment were examined. (*a*)

Evidence of organic brain damage: Although the neurological examination was completely normal in nearly all patients, neuropsychological testing demonstrated some problems with attention, concentration, memory, or judgment in most of the 69 patients evaluated. (*b*) *Psychological responses to the injury:* Emotional stress caused by persistent symptoms seems to be a significant factor in long-term disability. (*c*) *Litigation and compensation:* These factors had a minimal role in determining outcome. In conclusion, the most striking observations are the high rates of morbidity and unemployment (up to three months) after a seemingly insignificant head injury and the evidence that many of these patients may have, in fact, suffered organic brain damage.

[6] Rowland, L. P., "Head Injury," in *Merritt's Textbook of Neurology*, 9th ed. (L. P. Rowland, editor), Williams & Wilkins, Baltimore, 1995.

§ 32.12. Significance of a skull fracture.

Another term often given more significance than it should be is "skull fracture." A skull fracture gives an indication of the amount of force of the blow, but it has little value in estimating the severity of the injury to the brain. According to Ver Brugen,[7] 40% of autopsied patients who died of extremely severe brain injuries on his service at Chicago's Cook County Hospital did not show any evidence of fracture of the cranial bone.

In craniocerebral trauma, the injury to the brain is paramount, and the fracture and discontinuity of the bones of the skull *per se* is of little significance at the time, except in the unusual circumstances where complications set in.

According to studies, approximately 30% of patients with craniocerebral injuries have skull fractures, which may be linear, depressed, expressed, or comminuted. These fractures may involve the calvaria, and basilar fractures involve the base of the skull. In closed or simple linear fractures, the skull is intact. In closed brain injury, the dural lining is intact. In open brain injury, there is laceration of the scalp, fracture, and dural tear.

Linear fractures, which constitute about 70% of skull fractures, result from elastic deformation of the skull after impact. The area of impact is inbended, and further out the skull outbends selectively. The outbended portion tears apart from tension with fracture forming that extends toward the area of impact and toward the base of the skull. It extends toward the area of impact because, after the initial inbending, this area becomes outbended and thus constitutes an area of stress concentration. Heavy impacts may cause depression, and depending upon the size of the injuring object, there may be stellate depression or more discrete areas of depression or perforation.

The shape of the injuring object is extremely important. With the same amount of energy, a flat object will cause a linear fracture and a more pointed object impact will cause a depression.

§ 32.13. Classification of head injury.

There is a great deal of confusion in the terminology commonly used in head injuries, and classification is difficult. The following, however, is suggested:

1. **Mild head injuries.** There is a transient loss of consciousness ranging from seconds to a few minutes. There are no or few signs of neurologic deficit, and usually a prompt recovery with few complications. The patient has suffered a cerebral concussion.

---

[7] Ver Brugen, A., *Neurosurgery in General Practice,* Charles C Thomas, Publisher, Springfield, Illinois, 1952.

2. **Moderate head injury.** The period of unconsciousness may last up to one hour. There may be positive neurologic signs, and perhaps a skull fracture. Recovery begins soon after the injury and may be complete in the absence of complications, but less likely than in the patient with a mild head injury.

3. **Severe brain injury.** The patient's unconsciousness may last several hours; neurologic signs may appear; X-rays may or may not show fracture of the skull. In these cases, recovery is slow, and return of consciousness may take from days to weeks. Some of these patients may have to undergo surgical intervention for the removal of clots or decompression for cerebral edema.

4. **Extremely severe brain injury.** If not immediately fatal as a result of trauma to parts of the brain essential to life, the patient shows severe neurologic abnormalities, and sometimes in spite of all possible treatment, he dies in a few hours.

Using this classification, a patient who has received a hammer blow on the right frontal region and has sustained a scalp laceration, a depressed fracture, and a local contusion in the brain, can be said to have had: "a moderate head injury with laceration of the scalp, depressed fracture of the skull, and a contusion of the right frontal lobe of the brain." Such a diagnosis can be visualized by the physicians in talking about the case, and also by the family and lay persons after adequate explanation.

§ 32.14. Mechanisms of injury — Moving head striking object.

The effects of trauma on the brain are varied. The pathological picture could be from severe destruction to no objective evidence of brain damage, depending upon the physical forces at play. The mechanism that will produce a brain injury depends on the circumstances at the time of the accident. In general, when the forward-moving head strikes a stationary flat surface the brain moves forward, first striking the front and base of the skull; the temporal lobes strike the sphenoidal ridge of the skull. The brain stem also moves forward and, although protected by the cisternae around it, may be damaged, especially by torsional forces. Almost immediately after the head is suddenly stopped, the brain itself will go back and, in the process, bruises may occur on the back of the brain (posterior temporal and occipital lobe). This is a "contrecoup" injury, which is extremely common to this type of trauma. Torsional forces can result in diffuse axonal injury.

If the speed of the head moving forward is slow, the actual movement of the brain may be minimal, and the only result could be a cerebral concussion. If the head is moving faster, the forces on the brain are accordingly stronger, and after striking the frontal and temporal bone, may produce bruises in these areas, plus unconsciousness. In these circumstances, there may not be skull fractures, but there may be brain damage that falls under the classification of severe brain injury. (§ 32.13.) If the head is moving at seventy miles an hour in a car and there is a sudden stop, the result would be a severe brain injury. This type of injury is most common in automobile accidents. It is called a closed brain injury if there is no actual opening of the intracranial cavity to the outside.

§ 32.15. Mechanisms of injury — Moving object striking head.

When the head is stationary and is struck by a moving object, the situation is entirely different, depending on the speed of the object. If struck by a slow-moving object such as a bottle or a hammer, the chances are that the scalp would be lacerated, the bone may be fractured in a stellate fashion, and fragments may be driven into the intracranial cavity. If the dura is not torn, a bruise may be produced at the site of the injury. But if the dura is torn, bony fragments may penetrate the brain, which have to be removed at surgery together with the macerated brain. The patient, although sustaining the above-mentioned trauma, may not lose consciousness.

If the bullet of a small caliber gun strikes the head, there may be a laceration of the scalp and brain injury in the form of a tunnel from the portal of entry to the point of exit, yet the victim may not even lose consciousness. Forces generated by the missile result in damage to surrounding brain tissue, and these forces are greater the higher the velocity of the missile; however, soldiers in battle have been so injured and have walked to the nearest aid station. These types of injuries are called open head injuries, since the intracranial cavity has been exposed to the outside and surgical treatment is necessary.

§ 32.15a. Mechanisms of injury — Impact to another part of the body.

The head may suffer injury during an impact to another part of the body. Falling on the buttocks may cause the head to jam against the spine with fracturing about the foramen magnum. A sudden motion of the human trunk may cause the unsupported head to extend or flex, an example of indirect trauma.

§ 32.16. Nature of damage.

During the few moments that the injuring force is acting upon the brain, a certain amount of damage occurs. This may take the form of a contusion (bruise) or laceration (tear of the brain), which are lesions of macroscopic dimensions. With lesser trauma macroscopic lesions in the form of hemorrhages can be seen, but more often the changes are of microscopic dimensions and localized in the nerve cells themselves. Torsional forces can also shear the axons of neurons. These are the primary pathological states in brain injuries. All other phenomena such as edema (swelling) and large hemorrhage are secondary, even if they begin to develop shortly after the trauma.

§ 32.17. Contusions and lacerations — Diffuse lesions.

Contusions are relatively common in craniocerebral injuries. The term contusion is synonymous with bruise and the mechanism of its production is similar to the bruises commonly seen in trauma to soft tissues of the body. In the brain contusions may occur on the surface or deep within its substance. On the surface they appear as reddish-blue discoloration due to extravasation of blood from injured and torn capillaries (small vessels). In the contused area the nerve cells (neurons) are completely destroyed. Depending upon the amount of trauma to the walls of the larger vessels, which may become injured and bleed or become blocked by clotting, the extent of damage to the brain tissue itself may be greatly increased.

Lacerations are actual tears or cuts into the cerebral cortex caused by severe trauma. The laceration is surrounded by a contused area so that one may describe a laceration as a very severe contusion. The pia, the thin membrane covering the brain, is torn as are the superficial cortical vessels. Blood from the torn artery escapes into the subarachnoid space, this mixes with the spinal fluid, causing a subarachnoid hemorrhage. Occasionally a large artery or vein is torn and bleeds into the subdural space where it may give rise to the formation of an acute subdural hematoma. (**Fig. 7.**) With venous bleeding, a subdural hematoma may develop more slowly and manifest in a more chronic fashion. The brain in the depths of the laceration is softened, and without the protection of the dura, may extrude to the outside of the wound. When the dura has been torn, the skull fractured, and the scalp lacerated, the brain tissue from the laceration may be seen extruding into the scalp wound as increased intracranial pressure develops, subsequent to the appearance of edema. Contusions and lacerations are most commonly found on the under-surface of the frontal lobe, and the anterior end of the temporal lobe. Mass movements of the brain may cause it to strike the dural septa and give rise to multiple contusions.

The healing of contusions and lacerations of the brain is the same as in similar lesions elsewhere in the body. In principle, dead tissue is removed and a scar forms. Repair begins by action of special cells (microglia) whose function is to engulf the dead tissue and transport it to the blood vessels for elimination. Other cells (astrocytes) proliferate and occupy some of the space lost, forming what is called a glial scar. The rest of the space, if great, is occupied by spinal fluid through enlargement of the ventricles in that direction, and also by enlargement of the subarachnoid space over the scar, forming an arachnoid cyst.

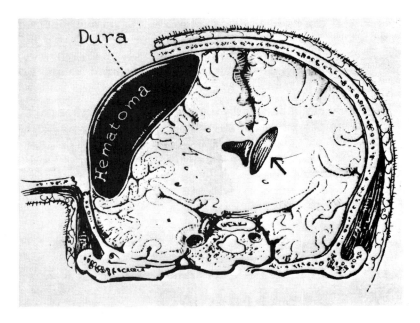

Fig. 7. Arrow indicates displaced ventricles as the result of a large subdural hematoma. Also shown is the nature of brain compression and general displacement of the structures.

In a cerebral laceration in which the dura has been torn by indriven bone in a depressed fracture, a different type scar formation may take place. Connective tissue may grow from the dura and blood vessels into the necrotic area and give rise to a connective tissue scar. Connective tissue does not normally occur in the brain, and such a scar is foreign to nervous tissue. This type of scar, which is the rule elsewhere in the body, contracts and exerts a pull on the cortex and subcortex, causing irritation and in certain cases may give rise to the appearance of late post-traumatic epilepsy.

Contusions and lacerations are macroscopic lesions. In less severe brain injuries, microscopic hemorrhages may occur. These may be barely visible to the naked eye, but are obvious under the microscope. Although a few microscopic hemorrhages (petechial hemorrhage) may be of no clinical significance, a great number of them or repeated episodes of trauma may give rise to the condition popularly called "punch drunk." This condition is rather common in professional boxers, and may occur in any individual who sustains repeated episodes of mild brain injury; it is not uncommon in football players and even horseback riders.

§ 32.18. Unconsciousness.

What is the mechanism of unconsciousness? We cannot answer this with complete certainty in our present state of knowledge, but a great deal of experimental work has been carried out and several theories have been proposed. Some believe the nature of the injury causing unconsciousness is a rather diffuse one, affecting the nerve cells themselves and their axonal connections. This has been explained on the basis of temporary cerebral ischemia (poor circulation causing lack of blood). At the time of trauma, the skull is deformed, and this causes pressure on capillaries and temporary stoppage of circulation. As the circulation is re-established, consciousness gradually returns.

Another theory postulates that in certain types of injury in which the head is accelerated, the sudden deceleration (as when the head strikes a stationary object) causes the intracranial contents to be shaken, and a temporary cessation of the nerve cell function results in unconsciousness. If the shaking has not been severe and no actual damage to the brain has occurred, the patient wakes up in a short time. If the shaking has caused diffused injury, such as multiple contusions or diffuse axonal injury, the length of unconsciousness is prolonged.

These theories, particularly the second, have been widely accepted. In the last few years, however, extremely important neurophysiological work suggests that unconsciousness is the result of injury to the brain stem, particularly the posterior end of the third ventricle and the periaqueductal gray and white matter (gray and white matter around the aqueduct of Sylvius). Depending upon the type of damage, irreversible injury may result. In most cases of severe, profound, and continuous unconsciousness, even coma and death may occur. The brain stem, because of its location, is affected by the acceleration and deceleration (as is the rest of the brain), by shearing torsional forces, and by the sudden increase of intracranial pressure that may come about from the sudden deformation of the skull.

§ 32.19. Pathological changes after injury.[8]

As already pointed out, a certain amount of brain damage is produced at the moment of the trauma. If the force is severe enough to produce a contusion or laceration in a part of the brain indispensable to life (midbrain and hindbrain particularly) death will occur immediately, or at most within a very short time. If the lesion is not located in an area essential to life, partial or full recovery should take place as the healing mechanisms of the body begin to act shortly after injury. This recovery would occur in every case in which the initial injury was compatible with

---

[8]Editor's Note: As to complications of
head injury, see also §§ 32.36 to 32.46.

life, were it not for the fact that complications may change the clinical picture fast. Even in the mildest injury, some swelling takes place or a hemorrhage may occur that not only may aggravate the original damage, but may itself produce injury to vital centers and cause death.

The pathological changes discussed below begin to take place shortly after the original traumatic brain lesion has been produced.

Cerebral edema

Some degree of localized cerebral edema may occur around contusions and lacerations. The actual cause of cerebral edema is a movement of fluid from the damaged capillaries in the injured area and its surroundings into the spaces between the cells within the area of injured brain. This accumulation of protein-rich fluid in the substances of the brain increases its bulk and, when progressive, will increase intracranial pressure. As this process develops, the resultant increased pressure within the brain substance causes venous stasis (stoppage), and a vicious circle develops. In other words, as the process of edema develops in the surrounding brain, the resultant increase in the bulk of the brain and the pressure interferes with the movement of blood out of the brain through the veins, causing increased pressure within the capillaries and the passage of further protein-rich fluid through the damaged walls of these vessels.

This vicious cycle can lead to serious consequences if allowed to go unchecked. If the treatment is unsuccessful and the patient dies, at autopsy the brain will appear swollen entirely out of proportion to the contusion or initial lesion. If there is extensive edema of the white matter, the gyri are noted to be flattened and the ventricles reduced in size. Here, the white matter will be considerably enlarged and wet; on microscopic examination the extracellular spaces are noted to be engorged with protein-rich fluid.

Hemorrhages

In craniocerebral trauma, bleeding may occur from torn vessels in the brain or in its covering membranes. (**Plate 3.**) A fracture in the bone may give rise to bleeding from the diploe and a slight accumulation of blood in the epidural space, which may pass unnoticed. But a similar fracture instead may tear the dura and middle meningeal artery and give rise to an epidural hematoma in a few hours, which unless treated immediately may cause death or considerable morbidity (paralysis of the opposite side of the body, speech disturbances, etc.).

Bleeding from a torn artery in a cerebral laceration may result in an accumulation of blood in the subdural space (acute subdural hematoma). The fact that the patient has an acute subdural hematoma, as a general rule, means that the patient has sustained a severe brain injury that has

produced both lacerations and contusions of the brain. As bleeding occurs, pressure is exerted on the brain, which becomes edematous, and
unless the hematoma is evacuated, death may occur. Often one is unable
to find the bleeding vessel, and multiple surgical procedures may be
necessary to save the patient's life. The difference between acute cerebral edema and a hematoma should be ascertained by computer tomography (CT scan).

Bleeding into the subarachnoid space is the most common type of
bleeding in craniocerebral trauma. Some authors estimate that in patients who have been unconscious for over an hour, about 75% to 85%
will have a subarachnoid hemorrhage. The bleeding usually results from
the tear of a small vessel on the surface of a contused brain and stops
spontaneously. If a vein becomes torn at the time of the accident, especially a vein as large as those going into the superior sagittal sinus,
bleeding in the subdural space may be extensive and life-threatening.

When blood enters the subarachnoid space, it mixes with spinal fluid
which prevents it from clotting. The blood cells are carried by the spinal
fluid towards absorption sites, where they are removed. At times, if the
hemorrhage is severe enough, the absorption pathways may be obstructed by the red cells, causing a backing up of spinal fluid into the
ventricles (hydrocephalus) and increased intracranial pressure. Blood
also acts as an irritant to the leptomeninges, producing meningitis-like
symptoms (headache, stiffness of the neck, photophobia, and mild fever)
that contribute to the restlessness and discomfort of the patient.

Bleeding may occur in the substance of the brain, ranging from microscopic amounts to a large hematoma that may produce serious damage
and even death. At times this requires surgical treatment.

Herniation of the brain

When the brain swells or is encroached upon by an expanding hematoma, increased intracranial pressure develops. Since the skull is a rigid
box, the local increase in volume (edema and hematoma) tends to shift
the brain towards the midline and downwards. As the swelling and
bleeding increases, the undersurface of the temporal lobe may be forced
through the opening of the tentorium cerebelli. (Plate 4.) When this
occurs, the midbrain is pressed upon and displaced to the opposite side
giving rise to symptoms of decerebration (decerebrate rigidity). The third
cranial nerve is usually compressed by herniation, which gives rise to
dilatation (dilation) of the eye pupil on the side of the herniation, a sign
of great importance in the diagnosis of intracranial hematoma. If the
temporal herniation is not relieved by surgical evacuation of the clot,
within a short time death or definite morbidity will occur from brain
stem hemorrhage and compression.

Bleeding in the cerebellar fossa, either in the cerebellum itself or outside, may result in herniation of the cerebellar tonsils (lower part of the cerebellum) into the spinal canal and compression of the medulla. This is an extremely serious complication and almost always fatal. Usually respiration ceases, and although the circulatory centers continue to function, in a matter of minutes the circulation ceases, and the patient dies.

Infections

Intracranial infections have always been a dreaded sequelae to cerebral trauma. In fractures through the base of the skull (sinuses, mastoid, etc.) bacteria may find entrance to the intracranial cavity, causing meningitis, subdural empyema (pus accumulation), or a brain abscess. The presence of foreign matter or bone fragments following a penetrating injury especially promotes infection. Nowadays, this complication is not as serious as it once was because of antibiotics, but it still is a dreaded complication.

IV. CLINICAL MANIFESTATIONS OF HEAD INJURY

§ 32.20. Introduction.

Clinical manifestations of head injuries vary greatly with their severity. All craniocerebral trauma, however, is potentially serious, even in its mildest forms. A patient who has sustained a mild head injury and appears to be doing nicely may suddenly deteriorate and his life may be threatened unless adequate emergency treatment is instituted. In every case a careful history must be obtained. It is important to know how the accident happened, when possible, from an eyewitness. It is particularly important to know the length of unconsciousness and whether it was immediate or delayed.

Soon after the patient is seen, after necessary first aid has been rendered, a complete general and neurological examination should be carried out and recorded. The possibility of associated injuries should always be kept in mind since not uncommonly a patient with a head injury will also have injuries to the chest, abdomen, or spine. An unconscious patient should not be moved more than absolutely necessary without ascertaining whether there has been trauma to the cervical spine. The scalp should be inspected for bruises, and the ears and nose for bleeding. The vital functions should be recorded, i.e., blood pressure, pulse, and respiration. In the early stages, the patient should be re-examined frequently for late-appearing symptoms. Since in a hospital this may be carried out by different individuals, it is important that these findings be carefully recorded. Often such changes are indications of complications requiring early treatment.

The Glasgow Coma Scale (GCS) is widely used to quantify neurological condition after head trauma. This scale rates (1) verbal response from one to five, (2) eye opening to various stimuli from one to four, and (3) motor response to stimuli from one to six. A normal score is fifteen, with any lower score indicating abnormal neurological function. Correlation has been found between the initial score on the GCS and eventual outcome. Serial assessment using the GCS allows for quantitative determination of neurological deterioration in a standardized fashion that is widely utilized.[9]

§ 32.21. Mild head injuries.

As the term implies, these injuries are slight in nature. However, there is loss of consciousness (See § 32.13), which may last from seconds to a few minutes. These patients have suffered a brain concussion. (See § 32.11.)

According to Russell, "Full consciousness is that in which any occurrence in which the patient is actively or passively concerned makes an impression on the memory, and can be subsequently called to mind. Any state of consciousness less than this is to be regarded as a grade of unconsciousness."[10] Under this theory, the appearance of "posttraumatic amnesia," often seen in mild head injuries, indicates that there has been unconsciousness. In these cases, the patient may speak rationally after the injury, but a few hours later may have no recollection of having done so. Russell believes that the fact that the individual is amnesic is in itself evidence of poor cerebration and abnormal cerebral function. Although Russell's definition has a great deal of merit, it is not universally accepted. Some physicians will diagnose a concussion only when the patient has been observed to have been unconscious. Most physicians will concede, however, that a person is conscious only when he is aware of his external environment and is aware of his external environment and is able to respond to external stimuli in a manner intelligible to the observer.

The following case histories contain good examples of clinical manifestations of mild head injury.

Case 1: A male patient seventeen years of age was brought to the emergency room shortly after being hit in the head. According to the history, the patient had been well until two hours before when, while playing football, he was tackled and thrown to the ground. His coach stated the patient received "a knee" in the side of the face. It did not appear to witnesses that he had been rendered unconscious,

---

[9]Teasdale, G., and Jennett, B., *Assessment of Coma and Impaired Consciousness: A Practical Scale*, 2 Lancet 81, 1974; Jennett, B., et al., *Prognosis of Patients with Severe Head Injury*, 4 Neurosurgery 283, 1979.

[10]Cited in Tindall, G. T., et al., editors *Clinical Neurosurgery (Proceedings of the Congress of Neurological Surgeons)*, Vol. 19, The Williams & Wilkins Co. Baltimore, 1972, p. 43.

and he got up slowly and continued to play. But after a couple of plays, it was obvious that he did not know his assignments, and his fellow players noted that he did not appear normal. He was taken out of the game and examined by the team trainer who made him lie down. Apparently he was able to speak rationally, but the trainer believed that he did not look normal and he sent him to the hospital. On arrival at the hospital, the patient was perfectly conscious and complained of generalized headache. He had no recollection of having been hit in the head or of having played for a few moments afterwards. The first thing he remembered was being in the ambulance. The neurological examination in the emergency room was entirely negative, but the patient was admitted for observation. X-rays of the skull failed to show any evidence of bone injury. During the twenty-four hours of his hospitalization, he did nicely, and at the time of discharge, appeared to be asymptomatic. The patient was seen twice after discharge, and appeared to have made a complete recovery. The diagnosis was mild brain injury (concussion).

Case 2: A sixteen-year-old boy was in an automobile accident. He had been riding in the back seat on the right-hand side of a car that was struck broadside by a vehicle traveling about twenty miles an hour. The force of the impact caused the right door to open, the patient was thrown out of the car about ten feet and landed on the grass. Witnesses said the patient was knocked unconscious immediately and remained so until the ambulance arrived five minutes later. On arrival at the hospital, the patient was confused but was able to respond to questions. A few minutes later he was fully conscious. A laceration of the left temple was repaired under local anesthesia. The neurological and general examinations showed no abnormalities. X-rays were negative. The patient was admitted to the hospital for observation and discharged twenty-four hours later, apparently in good condition. Final diagnosis was mild brain injury (concussion), and laceration of the scalp.

The most serious complication of craniocerebral trauma of light nature is bleeding in the epidural space due to a tear or damage to the middle meningeal artery. When this occurs, signs and symptoms (See § 32.22) appear within a few hours, often after a lucid interval.

Patients with mild head injuries may have headache for days to months following the injury. Occasionally, particularly in children, they become nauseated and may vomit several times. Within a few hours, however, this should disappear. At the present time, we allow the patients out of bed as soon as practicable, and they are discharged between twenty-four and forty-eight hours after admission. On discharge the patient is reassured that he has not been seriously injured, and that a complete recovery should be anticipated. He is told, however, that he may have some headache, as well as the possibility that there may be problems with attention, concentration, memory, and judgment. The patient is reassured, but also made aware of the possibility of short-term, and occasionally long-term, problems in these areas. The patient is given a realistic view of his prognosis, yet is encouraged to get in touch with the treating physician should he experience problems in dealing with his normal life after leaving the hospital.

§ 32.22. Moderate to extremely severe head injury.

In the moderate head injury, the period of unconsciousness may last up to an hour. There may be the positive neurologic signs discussed later in this section, and perhaps even a skull fracture, but recovery begins to take place rather quickly, and may be complete without complications.[11]

In severe and extremely severe brain injuries, immediate loss of consciousness is the rule. This may last for hours to months (and in rare cases, even years). Disturbance of consciousness may be profound. "Deep coma" may last from minutes to weeks. If deep coma persists for several days, the outlook is poor.

Painful stimuli, such as pressure on the upper rim of the orbit (eye socket) over the supraorbital nerve give rise to motion activity. Occasionally patients respond to painful stimuli with generalized stiffness of all the extremities. This reaction (decerebrate rigidity) is characteristic of a midbrain injury and is of serious prognostic significance. In stimulating the patient, one may find that there is only motion to one side of the body and the other side may be weak or paralyzed. This is suggestive of contusion in or near the motor cortex or in the brain stem.

Some patients in prolonged coma evolve into what has been referred to as a "persistent vegetative state." These patients may eventually be able to follow moving objects with their eyes and maybe swallow; they may actually appear to be attentive to family members, but there is no evidence of significant cerebral processing. Almost half of patients with an initial GCS score of less than eight will either die or become vegetative. (See § 32.159.)

Stages of consciousness

In an unconscious individual, at first the stimulus has to be rather severe to elicit a motor response, but as the patient improves, less and

---

[11]The tests frequently used to evaluate head injuries are the Glasgow Coma Scale (GCS) and the Swedish Reaction Level Scale (RLS85). In a comparison of these tests, Johnstone et al., in studying a total of 239 patients admitted to a regional head injury unit over a four-month period, found that both the GCS and the RLS85 reliably identified comatose patients and those with minor head injury, but were much less effective in defining the response level in patients considered to have a moderate head injury. Johnstone, et al., *A Comparison of the Glasgow Coma Scale and the Swedish Reaction Level Scale*, 7 Brain Injury 501, 1993.

less stimulus will bring about response. This level of unconsciousness is frequently called stupor. At this stage, the patient may lie quietly in bed as if asleep, but still totally unaware of his surroundings and inaccessible to anyone. Later in this stage he may become restless, thrash about, and at times become violent. At the end of this period of restlessness, some evidence of return of consciousness may be seen. Occasionally, the patient may respond to simple commands and, eventually, to his name. He may remain in this condition from several hours to several days. Later on he may become confused and have spells of delirium in which his behavior may again become violent and difficult to control. Such patients may become abusive in language and in deed, attempt to get out of bed in spite of restraints, and refuse medications. This delirious stage (traumatic delirium) is followed by one of drowsiness, less violence, and some confusion, which gradually progresses to a normal state of consciousness with awareness of surroundings, ability to reason, and ability to remember incidents from day to day.

When the patient regains consciousness, he may have posttraumatic amnesia, with no recollection of even the later stages of his unconscious state (even though during this time he may have appeared to have been in good contact with his environment). This deficit usually includes a period before the injury (retrograde amnesia), and of course he would have no recollection of the injury.

The sequence of events described above, depending upon the severity of the brain injury, may last for hours, days, or even weeks. Usually, once the patient moves from coma to stupor, the stages develop gradually. The last stages may be of longer duration but there is always progressive improvement. When there is a return (either sudden or gradual) from a lighter stage to a deeper stage, the possibility of a surgically treatable complication must be considered. Conversely, the patient who is getting lighter and seems to be regaining consciousness is less likely to be developing a complication of surgical importance. Thus, the state of consciousness is the most important guide in evaluating the progress of a patient who has sustained a brain injury, and any deterioration of this state should alert the physician.

After a severe or extremely severe brain injury, improvement is gradual, occasionally fast at the beginning, but slower later on, over a period of a year or at times longer. It is not unusual for people who have survived such an injury to be left with considerable impairment of memory and judgment, and other personality changes. Residual paralysis and speech impediments are other disabling sequelae due to focal brain injuries which may be of permanent nature.

Although terms such as coma and stupor are often used to describe the condition of these patients, these terms are not precise and should always be accompanied by an objective description of the patient's level of consciousness.

V. TREATMENT OF HEAD INJURY

§ 32.23. Introduction.

The treatment of craniocerebral trauma will vary according to the severity of the trauma and its type. Under certain circumstances, such as in penetrating wounds of the skull, depressed fractures, and hematomata (blood clots), surgery is indicated and may be life-saving. In the majority of cases, however, surgery has little to offer, and conservative treatment, although not as spectacular, may bring about the recovery of what would appear to be a fatally injured patient.

In past years, surgery also has been tried in closed head injuries to relieve edema (swelling). These procedures range from removal of bone to removal of actual contused portions of the brain itself. This aggressive surgery is not widely accepted, and the results vary greatly.

Mild injuries require little treatment other than rest. If the trauma has been severe enough to produce a brain concussion or a fracture of the skull, even without a clearly defined history of concussion, usually the patient should be admitted to the hospital for observation.

§ 32.24. Initial emergency care.

When the physician sees a head injury patient in the emergency room, he or she must size up the situation quickly and decide what needs to be done. In some cases, the physician can immediately examine the patient to determine the extent of brain injury. but often this examination must be postponed to render first aid and treat other potentially life-threatening injuries.

Frequently, a severely injured patient is not only profoundly unconscious but breathing badly. Respiration is slow and noisy, and a quick glance shows that his blood is not being oxygenated. Many of these patients are bleeding from the nose, and sometimes spinal fluid from a fracture at the base of the skull is coming through the nose and pharynx, mixing with the blood, and draining down into the trachea and lungs. Not uncommonly such situations are complicated also by aspiration of vomitus. Under these circumstances the patient is practically drowning in his own secretions. The first and most important thing to do in these cases is to restore the airway. The patient should be suctioned and, if necessary, an endotracheal tube inserted. Further suction can be done through the tube.

The condition of a comatose patient who has trouble breathing often will change dramatically after the airway is cleared. It is not unusual to see such a patient who has failed to respond to any type stimuli react to pain only after a few minutes of normal breathing. Obstruction of the airway increases the intrathoracic pressure, which interferes with the venous return from the head, causing stagnation of the blood and swelling of the already injured brain. Similarly, obstruction interferes with venous drainage of the brain, causing poor circulation of blood that is already poorly oxygenated. This phenomenon causes anoxia (lack of oxygenation) to the brain which aggravates any injury already present.

When the patient's airway has been restored, which should be in a matter of minutes, and breathing is regular, the physician's attention can then be directed to control of hemorrhage and treatment of shock, if present. Most individuals with severe brain injury have cuts and lacerations of the scalp that bleed profusely. The loss of blood alone, when severe enough, may cause the patient to go into shock; a condition characterized by fast, thready pulse, low blood pressure, and a cold, clammy skin.

Bleeding from the scalp can be controlled by pressure on the edges of the wound, or if large vessels are bleeding, by the application of hemostatic clamps, which should be left in place until definite repair is carried out. This is done simultaneously with the airway treatment. The treatment of shock should be started immediately by the administration of intravenous fluid. A solution of 5% glucose in saline is started while the patient's blood is cross-matched so that transfusions can be given in order to restore the blood volume. A patient in shock should be kept warm with blankets and, if possible, the head should be lowered. As shock disappears, the blood pressure comes up gradually to a normal level, the pulse becomes stronger and slower, and the normal color of the skin returns.

As soon as these first-aid measures have been taken care of, a general examination should be carried out. About 70% of the patients with severe brain injuries have associated injuries that may also require emergency treatment. Some chest and abdominal wounds are so extremely serious in themselves that their immediate treatment may take priority over the treatment of the head injury. When bleeding is taking place from internal organs, shock is profound and can only be corrected temporarily until bleeding is stopped by surgical means. Other injuries may not be as important except for injuries to the cervical spine. It is not unusual for a patient, especially one in an automobile accident, to have a cervical spine injury associated with a severe injury to his head. Because of this, a portable X-ray film of the neck should be made to ascertain or rule out this injury. When a cervical injury is present, immobilization of the neck should be carried out to avoid spinal cord damage.

Other injuries, such as broken bones, should be given necessary emergency treatment. Then, a thorough neurological examination should be performed, with quantification of the level of consciousness, using the Glasgow Coma Scale (§ 32.20).

§ 32.25.   Early nonemergency care.

When the patient's condition warrants it, *i.e.*, after he is out of shock and breathing well, an open head wound may be repaired, tetanus antitoxin given, and a CT scan obtained, before transferring the patient to an intensive care unit. It is never justifiable to move a patient in shock or one who is thrashing about to the X-ray unit, since the information to be obtained at this stage is less important than avoiding the risk of further injury. For evaluating head trauma, skull X-rays are of limited value and in most instances been replaced with the CT scan if this procedure is available.

At times, a patient may deteriorate after having first improved after restoring the airway, and signs of brain compression may appear. In that case, another CT scan is advisable, to be sure that the patient does not have an acute epidural or subdural hemorrhage. If these lesions are ruled out, medical treatment with diuretics such as furosemide (Lasix) may be given to reduce the rising intracranial pressure, which is causing the patient's symptoms. This treatment is most effective if administered in conjunction with continuous monitoring of intracranial pressure. Steroids are also administered after head injury, but there is little convincing evidence of their benefit. Osmotic agents such as mannitol are reserved for increasing uncontrolled, life-threatening intracranial pressure.

Treatment of a patient with a severe brain injury requires the closest cooperation of the physician and nursing staff. The physicians in charge must observe the patient closely to detect the possibility of complications as soon as possible. It is only through these combined efforts that the patient with a severe brain injury can be given a chance to recover.

§ 32.26.   Nursing care.

As soon as the patient has been admitted to the intensive care unit, the physician in charge should write the orders to be carried out by the nursing staff. Usually the vital signs such as blood pressure, pulse, and respiration are to be taken every fifteen minutes until stabilized, and then every hour until the patient is obviously on the way to recovery. While carrying out these orders, the nurses should document the patient's level of consciousness and the condition of his pupils. Any change in these signs should be reported to the physician immediately.

An unconscious patient should be turned from his back to either side every two hours to avoid pulmonary complications. The airway should be carefully watched, and the suction machine should be used as often as necessary. When secretions accumulate fast, usually the head of the bed should be lowered to facilitate drainage of the secretions by gravity. In cases of cerebrospinal fluid rhinorrhea or otorrhea (spinal fluid escaping from the nose or ear due to a fracture of the base of the skull), it is advisable to keep the patient's head elevated to encourage the drainage of fluid outwards rather than allow it to pool in the nose or ears. When this pooling occurs, it is easier for bacteria to enter the intracranial cavity. If the patient is breathing without effort, elevation of the head is indicated, as this position tends to lower the intracranial pressure.

Most unconscious patients suffer urinary incontinence; this creates a tremendous nursing problem if allowed to go unchecked. A wet bed tends to macerate the patient's skin and cause bed sores, which almost always become infected. It is better to place an in-dwelling catheter in the patient's bladder to alleviate this difficulty.

All patients with head injuries should receive adequate amounts of fluids. In normal conditions there is about 800 to 1,200 cc. of water lost in the vapor of respiration and in perspiration, about 1,500 cc. or more in the urine, and from 1 to 200 cc. in the feces per day. Total fluid loss under normal conditions is from 2,500 to 3,000 cc. of fluid every twenty-four hours. This loss may be increased with fever, excessive vomiting, or diarrhea.

In the first two or three days in the treatment of an unconscious patient, fluids can be given by vein in the form of normal saline or 5% glucose in saline. If unconsciousness is prolonged, a tube can be placed through the nose into the stomach and fluids given through it, or a gastrostomy tube can be placed directly into the stomach. The patient can also be given a liquid diet through this tube and therefore receive all of the necessary dietary elements (proteins, minerals, vitamins, etc.). No unconscious or semiconscious patient should be given fluids or food by mouth because of the danger of aspiration into the lungs. As soon as the patient is conscious, the stomach tube can be removed and mouth feeding encouraged.

§ 32.27. Medication.

If a patient is unconscious but quiet, medication is not necessary. As consciousness begins to return, he may become restless. This development has to be controlled, because if allowed to go on unchecked, the patient may become violent, interfere with nursing care, and possibly harm himself. There are several drugs available. At one time, one of the most commonly used drugs was sodium phenobarbital, but this has been replaced by tranquilizers that achieve the same results with fewer long-lasting side effects. These are given intramuscularly or intravenously as often as necessary. Opiates should not be routinely used to treat restlessness, although morphine and other narcotics are sometimes used for agitation, especially if the patient's airway and ventilation are being controlled and monitored. Morphine tends to contract the pupils, thus removing one of the most valuable signs in detecting complications.

If convulsions occur, anticonvulsive drugs such as phosphenytoin, phenytoin sodium, or phenobarbital may be given. Occasionally, in spite of these medications, the patient may go into *status epilepticus* (continuous convulsions). In such situations, intravenous administration of anticonvulsants, endotracheal intubation, controlled ventilation, and even general anesthesia may be necessary.

Most patients with head injuries will run a mild fever. Occasionally, the temperature goes higher than 102°; if so, it must be controlled. Alcohol rubs can be used and, if necessary, ice packs or a cooling blanket. While these measures are being carried out, rectal temperature should be taken every fifteen minutes and the cooling measures stopped as soon as the temperature reaches 101°. In mild elevation, aspirin by stomach tube or in suppository form can be used for temperature control.

To date, no effective drug has been developed that will substantially improve the outcome for patients with acute traumatic brain injury. However, basic research in this area is accelerating, and a number of clinical trials are under way or in the late planning stages. Furthest along are studies using *N*-methyl-D-aspartate blockers, including competitive and noncompetitive receptor antagonists, as well as modulators of the polyamine and glycine sites on this receptor.[12]

§ 32.28. Treatment of edema.

The majority of patients with brain injuries will recover with the above-mentioned treatment. Most, after recovering from shock, may show little change for a few hours and then gradually begin to improve. A few patients, however, will remain unconscious and in a state of stupor for longer periods. At times, after a few hours there appears to be a period in which improvement seems to stop, and occasionally there is actual deterioration of the patient's condition. This may be a sign of a complication. If the CT scan reveals no hematoma, and the ventricles of the brain are small, massive edema may have taken place. Edema occurs in all cases of head injury in which there have been contusions or lacerations of the brain. It may be localized around these lesions, but occasionally it is generalized.

Treatment of edema is one of the most difficult aspects in handling head injuries. Over the years, the method of treatment has changed. In the twenties and thirties, subtemporal decompression was used. That was the era of the decompression operation in which a section of the

---

[12]Faden, A. I., *Pharmacologic Treatment of Acute Traumatic Brain Injury*, 276 J.A.M.A. 569 (Aug. 21), 1996. See also Bullock, R., "Experimental Drug Therapies for Head Injury," in *Neurotrauma* (Narayan, R. K., et al., editors), McGraw-Hill Book Co., New York, 1996; Marshall, L. F., and Marshall, S. B., *Pitfalls and Advances from the International Tirilazad Trial in Moder-* ate and Severe Head Injury, 12 Neuroreport 929, 1995; Faden, A. I., *Pharmacological Treatment of Central Nervous System Trauma*, 78 Pharmacol. Toxicol. 12, 1996; Young, B., et al., *Effects of Pegorgotein on Neurologic Outcome of Patients with Severe Head Injury: A Multicenter, Randomized Controlled Trial*, 276 J.A.M.A.. 538 (Aug. 21), 1996.

skull was removed under the temporal muscle, usually on the right side. The dura mater was opened and the brain was allowed to protrude through the opening. The rationale was that the closed intracranial cavity was too small to hold the volume of the brain, and in making the opening, some of the pressure was relieved. After given a thorough trial, it was found that the mortality with this procedure was extremely high, and it lost its popularity.

During the twilight of the decompressive era, dehydration was introduced. Studies have shown that hypertonic (very concentrated) solutions, when introduced intravenously, could absorb water from cerebral tissue and thus reduce swelling. Several substances were tried, among them 25% and 50% concentrations of glucose, sucrose, magnesium sulphate, and sodium chloride. As these solutions were given, water was drawn from the brain and surrounding tissues, which was secreted with the chemicals in the urine, producing a dehydrating effect. But these substances had a serious drawback: although they produced some relief of edema, it was only temporary and, after an hour or two, swelling would return, at times more severe than before. To avoid these so-called "rebound effects," other drugs were tried, with more or less the same result. If the concentrated solutions were given more often to avoid the rebound effects, complications were brought on, mainly general dehydration, which is dangerous in a patient already ill.

As an adjunct to dehydration, at one time lumbar puncture was also used. By removal of cerebrospinal fluid, it was thought that more room was left to be occupied by the swollen brain. Lumbar puncture had many advocates, but many competent neurosurgeons strongly condemned it on the grounds that the volume obtained by the removal of fluid is extremely small, and the removal of fluid can cause a herniation of brain, with possibly fatal results. Thus, lumbar puncture should never be used for this purpose.

None of the above measures are used exclusively. While decompressive procedures are still advocated by many, they are reserved for those rare cases of generalized edema in which all other measures fail. Osmotic diuretics are also used to decrease the size of the brain by reducing its water content. The technique of hypothermia, which is the reduction of the patient's body temperature well below normal, has been used with variable results. Marion et al.[13] compared the effects of moderate hypothermia and normal thermia on eighty-two patients with severe closed head injuries who had a score of five to seven on the Glasgow Coma Scale (§ 32.20) upon admission to the hospital. The patients assigned to the hypothermia group were cooled to 33° C. at a mean of ten hours after injury, kept at 32° to 33° C. for twenty-four hours, and then rewarmed.

---

[13] Marion, D. W., et al., *Treatment of Traumatic Brain Injury with Moderate Hy-* *pothermia*, 336 N. Engl. J. Med. 540 (Feb. 20), 1997.

At twelve months after their injury, 62% of the patients in the five to seven Glasgow Coma Scale group who received hypothermia had good outcomes (moderate, mild, or no disabilities) compared to only 38% of those who received no hypothermia. Hypothermia did not improve the outcomes in the patients with coma scores of three or four on admission.

Steroids are also used in some cases, although there is little evidence that they improve the outcome in this type of cerebral edema.

Lumbar puncture is sometimes used here by neurosurgeons for diagnostic purposes. In such cases, a CT scan should be done first to establish whether there is brain edema and shift. In their absence, lumbar puncture may then be used to establish the diagnosis of meningitis or subarachnoid hemorrhage not visualized on CT.

The treatment of cerebral trauma is now often directed toward the more precise evaluation of increased intracranial pressure (ICP) and the use of a variety of different chemical agents for control.

Operative intervention in the head injured patient is undertaken to relieve intracranial hematoma or to debride contused and lacerated brain. However, in instances where diffuse cerebral edema is a result of traumatic head injury unassociated with a skull fracture or intracranial mass lesion as determined by the CT scan, the aim is to determine as early as possible the level of increased intracranial pressure. Thereafter, it is important to use appropriate techniques to achieve an objective evaluation of the pathophysiologic and metabolic consequences of the diffuse brain injury. Information from this evaluation enables the surgeon to more effectively choose appropriate methods of treatment.

In the specific case of the patient with a severe closed head injury in which a surgically treatable lesion has been ruled out by appropriate radiologic studies, a chronologic evaluation of intracranial pressure is useful to determine the status of the intracranial pressure dynamics and to predict whether the brain has any additional capacity for adapting to further increases in swelling. The accurate measurement of intracranial pressure further allows the surgeon to determine the effectiveness of agents such as barbiturates, steroids, and osmotics in reducing cerebral edema.

An increasing number of neurosurgical facilities are now technically equipped to measure intracranial pressure utilizing pressure-recording devices placed either within the ventricular cavities of the brain, brain tissue, the epidural, or subarachnoid spaces. Because of technical problems associated with the placement of ventricular catheters in compressed ventricles related to severe brain swelling, hollow screws have been designed that can be threaded into the skull through a twist drill hole after the dura and arachnoid have been opened. Devices of this type placed within the subarachnoid space are connected to a transducer after which intracranial pressure recordings can be made. The development of miniaturized pressure transducers that can be implanted in the subdural or epidural spaces has given the neurosurgeon additional reliable means of measuring intracranial pressure. With devices of these types, the surgeon has a visual record of the intracranial pressure and is also able to anticipate complications of clinical significance, often before they produce clinical signs.

When there is an indication from any of these recordings that the intracranial pressure exceeds normal limits, appropriate treatment must be instituted. Elevated intracranial pressure may indicate that a surgically treatable lesion such as subdural or epidural hematoma is developing and suggests that further radiographic studies (repeat CT scans) be performed to determine whether surgical intervention is indicated. If these studies reveal no surgical lesion, attention must then be directed to the possibility of diffuse cerebral edema as the cause of increased intracranial pressure. This determination is now easily made using CT scans or magnetic resonance imaging (MRI).

Cerebral edema that occurs in response to intracranial lesions of a nontraumatic nature has exhibited a much more favorable response to steroids than brain swelling that results from traumatic brain injury. Carefully controlled studies of steroid treatment of patients with closed head injuries indicate a trend toward improved survival rates and quality of life in the treated groups, although the difference has not been shown to be statistically significant. Such studies support the impression of many neurosurgeons that steroids do contribute to improvement of some cases of severe brain edema associated with closed head injuries. Although the indications for the use of steroids in the treatment of traumatic cerebral edema have not been clearly defined, it seems reasonable to use this form of therapy in these patients in combination with careful monitoring of intracranial pressure to determine the effect of their use.

The use of osmotic diuretics such as mannitol in the treatment of cerebral edema is based on the presumed ability of these agents to extract brain water by a process of increasing the osmotic pressure of the circulating blood. These dehydrating agents, although of considerable value in the treatment of brain edema associated with a large number of intracranial disorders, are somewhat less effective in controlling diffuse cerebral edema of traumatic origin. The chronic use of mannitol in combination with careful monitoring of intracranial pressure and measurement of serum osmolality and electrolyte balance have been suggested as a means of more effectively controlling traumatic cerebral edema. Results of this form of treatment have been encouraging, although not as widely used as the administration of mannitol in response to elevations of intracranial pressure. Intravenous barbiturates are sometimes used to control increased intracranial pressure, but there is disagreement as to their effectiveness.

VI. TRAUMA TO THE CRANIAL NERVES

§ 32.29. First cranial nerve.

The first cranial nerve (olfactory) is really part of the brain and ends at the olfactory bulb, which is located at the cribiform plate of the frontal bone. **(Plate 6.)** The two olfactory nerves arise from the bulb and pass through the small foramina to end in the nasal cavity. Basilar fractures through the floor of the frontal fossa may tear these nerves, producing anosmia (lack of the sense of smell) on the side of the lesion. This type of injury is sometimes associated with a spinal fluid leak through the nose (rhinorrhea), predisposing to the development of meningitis.

In unilateral lesions, the patient may not even know that he has partially lost his sense of smell. But in bilateral injury, which fortunately is uncommon, the patient loses his sense of smell completely — and his taste is affected. (Most of the enjoyment of food is derived from the ability to smell its aroma.) These lesions are usually permanent.

§ 32.30. Second cranial nerve.

These two nerves (optic) are also part of the brain itself. The fibers start in the cells of the retina of the eyes, and after partial decussation at the optic chiasm, find their way through the genicular bodies and temporal lobes to the occipital lobes. **(Plate 6.)**

The incidence of optic nerve trauma in head injuries is low, and permanent blindness as a result of trauma is unusual. Loss of sight more commonly results from ocular trauma.

Most optic nerve injuries show a loss of visual acuity and a field defect (blindness in one field of vision). Frequently, these cases begin to improve shortly after the accident, but this improvement ceases after a few weeks, leaving the individual with some permanent impairment of vision.

Injuries to the occipital lobe, as where a patient falls on the back of his head, may cause transient blindness lasting from a few hours to several days. This occurs even if the injury has been only to one occipital lobe. Recovery is usually complete except when the injury is of such magnitude that the lobe is destroyed, as in a gunshot wound, and the patient is left with homonymous hemianopia (blindness on the opposite field of vision), but usually without central vision impairment.

Occasionally the optic chiasm on the ventral surface of the brain is injured. Here, the type of visual deficit will depend on the actual injuries to the visual fibers.

In head injuries, increased intracranial pressure can cause "papilledema," a swelling of the optic nerve. This usually presents no serious problems, as the swelling should recede with control of the intracranial pressure for a complete recovery of visual function. Papilledema produces a temporary enlargement of the "blind spot" and visual blurring. However, when papilledema is prolonged, the result may be optic atrophy and visual loss.

§ 32.31. Third, fourth and sixth cranial nerves.

The third (oculomotor), fourth (trochlear) and sixth (abducens) cranial nerves control the movements of the eyeballs and are essential for proper binocular vision. Dysfunction of these nerves often results in diplopia (double vision) and, if there is involvement of the oculomotor nerve, pupillary changes.

The nuclei of these nerves are in the gray matter around the aqueduct of Sylvius and pons in the brain stem (**Plate 6**), and they are occasionally injured in trauma affecting these areas. However, most injury to these nerves is along their route from the midbrain to the foramina of exit (from the skull) and on the muscles they innervate (the extraocular muscles). In these injuries, it is important to find out whether paralysis occurred immediately after the accident or gradually. Immediate loss of function in any of these nerves may indicate that the nerve has been injured as a direct result of a fracture of the base of the skull. If the loss of function was gradual, even if complete, it is presumptive evidence that the nerve has not actually been cut, but only bruised; therefore recovery should be expected. However, gradual loss of function can also suggest increased intracranial pressure and brain herniation.

Recovery from these injuries may not be 100%, particularly in a third nerve lesion. Complete paralysis of the third nerve would result in a squint, with the eye being pulled toward the outside by the sixth nerve. If the sixth nerve is paralyzed, the eye will be pulled medially. In both cases, double vision will occur. If the fourth nerve is injured, double vision will occur from time to time, when the patient is looking down and inwards. With a third nerve lesion, the pupil is dilated and unresponsive to a light stimulus. Abnormalities of ocular movement also commonly result from orbital trauma.

§ 32.32. Fifth cranial nerve.

The fifth cranial nerve arises from the pons and ends in the gasserian ganglion situated over the petrous pyramid. (**Plate 6.**) From the ganglion it continues with three divisions: the first supplying sensation to the forehead and eye; the second to the cheek, upper gums, and palate; and the third to the skin of the lower jaw, lower gums, and half tongue. Injury to these nerves is unusual as a result of intracranial trauma, but very common in facial fractures in which the nerves are injured or cut at the foramina of exit. The immediate result is lack of sensation over the distribution of the injured nerve. Sometimes pain is a late sequela, resulting from regrowth of the nerve fibers through scar tissue. This is bothersome and may require surgical treatment. This nerve also sup-

337

plies motor fibers to the muscles used in chewing, but fifth nerve injuries rarely result in jaw weakness.

§ 32.33. Seventh cranial nerve.

The facial or seventh cranial nerve arises from the nucleus at the pons and enters the base of the skull through the acoustic foramen; travels through the middle ear to exit the skull at its base; and eventually travels on to innervate the muscles of the face (muscles of expression).

Trauma to this nerve occurs fairly often, particularly at the middle ear. Again, it is very important from the prognostic point of view whether paralysis was instantaneous or occurred progressively. If instantaneous, it is possible that the nerve has been lacerated or avulsed, and return of function will not take place. If the loss of function was late, even if there is complete paralysis, return of function may be expected. But return of function may not be complete, and may be abnormal, in the sense that when the patient wants to move one side of the face, unintended movement may occur. Occasionally, spontaneous motion may result: the patient may grimace uncontrollably on the injured side of the face (hemifacial spasm). This can be extremely annoying, and sometimes surgery must be done in the form of a nerve decompression. However, it is usually treated with botulinum toxin injections. Faulty regeneration of the facial nerve and associated salivary fibers can result (although rarely) in the syndrome of "crocodile tears," which consists of tearing whenever the patient chews.

§ 32.34. Eighth cranial nerve.

The eighth cranial nerve (auditory) consists of two parts, the auditory component (hearing), and the vestibular component, which has to do with equilibrium. These nerves can be injured in basilar fractures of the skull going through the petrous pyramid and middle ear. Complete deafness occurs in about 6% to 8% of the fractures in this area. If the vestibular component is injured, vertigo may result.

§ 32.35. Ninth, tenth, eleventh, and twelfth cranial nerves.

These nerves arise from the hindbrain. The ninth, tenth and eleventh go out of the skull through the jugular foramen. The twelfth goes out through the hypoglossal foramen and into the neck.

Intracranial trauma to these nerves is most unusual, although injury has been reported as a result of a shrapnel wound in the posterior fossa and in skull fracture in the area.

The loss of function of the ninth (glossopharyngeal) nerve would produce numbness in the posterior aspect of the tongue, throat, and pharynx, and would interfere with taste in the posterior aspect of the tongue. The tenth (vagus) nerve innervates the musculature of the pharynx and larynx and supplies nerve control to the heart, lungs, and gastrointestinal tract. Nerve damage here can be extremely disabling to a patient, as he might be unable to swallow and speak normally.

The eleventh (spinal accessory) nerve supplies the sternocleidomastoid muscle and trapezius, both muscles of the neck that may atrophy and produce weakness of certain motions of the neck. Injuries to the twelfth (hypoglossal) nerve would produce atrophy in the same side of the tongue, causing slurred speech.

VII. EVALUATION AND TREATMENT OF COMPLICATIONS OF HEAD INJURY

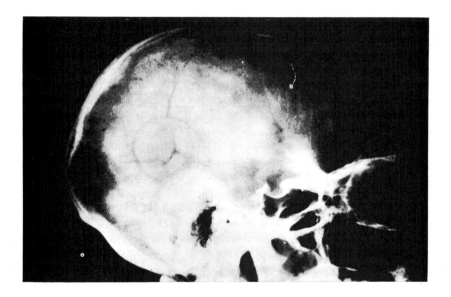

Fig. 8. Depressed fracture in posterior temporal vault from the blow of a policeman's club. There are concentric ring fractures around the point of impact and radiating linear fractures toward and away from the site of impact.

§ 32.36. Skull fractures.

Fractures of the bones of the skull are inconsequential unless they affect the brain, either directly or indirectly. Fractures can be either simple or compound (**Figs. 8 to 10**), depending on whether they are open to the outside due to a laceration of the scalp or communication to the air sinuses (**Plates 8 and 9**).

Simple depressed fractures should be elevated if the depression is deep enough to press on the brain or send bony fragments into it. If the depression is mild, less than one-half of a centimeter, elevation may not be

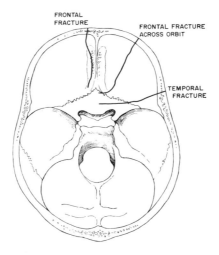

Fig. 9. Characteristic paths of linear fractures radiating from the anterior vault into the base of the skull.

necessary. Elevation is particularly important in younger individuals whose heads may still be growing, since growing of the skull may aggravate the depression. Elevation may help prevent posttraumatic epilepsy.

Depressed fractures, whether compound or simple, that are obviously pressing on the brain with bony fragments (**Plate 8**) should be elevated immediately. Surgical technique may vary, but the aim is debridement (removal of bony fragments), and excision of pulpified brain tissue. The amount of debridement will vary according to the region of the brain involved. The dura (membrane covering brain) should always be closed, if necessary by transplant (fascia lata or temporalis fascia). If the fragments of bone removed are large, they may be replaced in the wound, but if not, a cranioplasty can be done before the scalp is closed. If the wound is contaminated after the dura is closed, the scalp should be closed and the skull defect left to be corrected by cranioplasty at a later date.

If the depression is over the sagittal sinus on top of the head (**Plate 8),** a great deal of judgment has to be used for its repair. If this depression is not severe it may be left untouched, but if it is deep and compound, it should be elevated. The blood pressure on the sagittal sinus is sometimes negative, which may give rise to sucking air into the circulation.

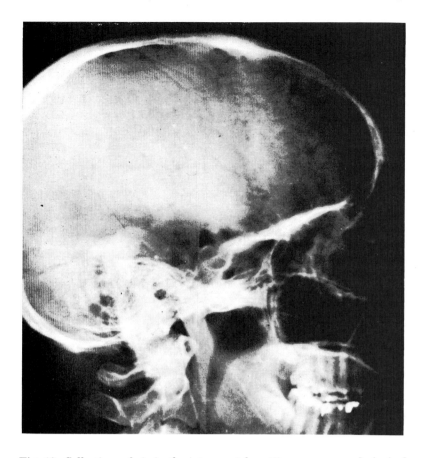

Fig. 10. Collections of air in the intracranial cavities are seen as dark shadows above the pituitary gland and in the frontal poles of the brain. These indicate a compound fracture is present and possible infection.

§ 32.37. Fractures through the air sinuses, cribiform plate, or middle ear.

Fractures at the base of the skull can occur through the air sinuses, cribiform plate, or middle ear. In these cases, the dura (membrane covering the brain) is also torn, so that the spinal fluid in the subarachnoid space will leak into the nose in the first two instances, and into the middle ear in the third. A patient with spinal rhinorrhea, or leaking of spinal fluid through the nose **(Plate 9)**, if conscious, should be kept upright, so that the spinal fluid will leak out rather than pooling in the nose. The patient should also be sedated and instructed not to cough or to do anything that may promote the ingestion of air through the passages.

Some neurosurgeons institute surgical treatment to close the dura and stop the leak as soon as practical. The author is of the opinion, however, that medical treatment should be carried out carefully for at least ten days by giving antibiotics and postural drainage. If the leak does not stop in about two weeks, surgical intervention should be carried out. Usually, spinal fluid leaks stop by themselves within this time. Occasionally a patient's rhinorrhea goes unrecognized, and during the act of coughing or sneezing, he may aspirate air into the brain giving rise to pneumocephalus **(Plate 9).** Trapping of air in the intracranial cavity may cause a dangerous increase in the intracranial pressure.

§ 32.38. Rupture of the internal carotid artery.

Occasionally a fracture at the base of the skull goes through the cavernous sinus and ruptures the internal carotid artery. **(Fig. 11.)** Because of the difference in pressure between the carotid artery and the sinus, the arterial blood goes into the sinus and from there to the veins of drainage, mostly the ophthalmic veins, giving rise to their engorgement in the orbit (eye socket). This produces a carotid cavernous fistula and "pulsating exophthalmus": the eyelids appear swollen, and the eye itself bulges outwards and moves with each pulse wave. The patient usually hears a noise caused by rapid blood flow through the fistula. This condition should be treated as soon as possible if there are signs of visual failure or an increase in intraocular tension, and may require several operations. The carotid artery can be ligated (tied) in the neck, which occasionally takes care of the difficulty. Also, intracranial ligation may be tried, but sometimes this is ineffective, and embolization may have to be done. A newer procedure is occlusion of the arteries or veins through the use of intravascular balloons.

Providing that the collateral circulation is adequate, the loss of the vessel may not be felt by the patient. This condition is extremely serious; if left untreated, it may produce visual loss due to glaucoma, or it may be associated with intracerebral hemorrhage, or in rare instances, severe bleeding from the nose.

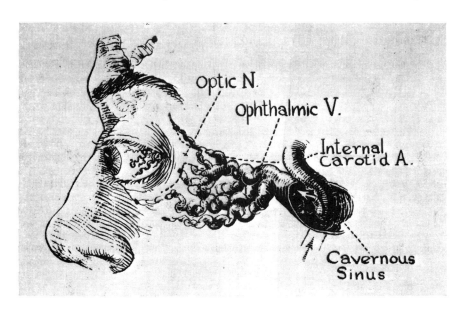

Fig. 11. Artist's illustration shows character of carotid cavernous sinus arterio-venous malformation. White arrow indicates the rupture of the carotid artery into cavernous sinus, with resultant marked backing up of arterial blood pressure into the vessels about the eye, causing marked protrusion of the eye and engorgement of vessels.

§32.39. Intracranial hematomas.

Intracranial hematomas (blood clots) are not unusual complications of head injury. They may occur after mild trauma, so mild in fact, that the occurrence may have passed as a light "bump"; or they may complicate the picture in cases of severe brain injury. In any situation, once the diagnosis is made, surgery and drainage should be considered. These situations may be extreme emergencies. They are best diagnosed by CT scan.

Intracranial hematomas can occur between the bone and dura (membrane covering brain), between the dura and the pia-arachnoid, and in the brain itself. They are classified as extradural (or epidural), subdural, and intracerebral. Their incidence is relatively low, but it is crucial that they are recognized in any patient who is deteriorating, since prompt treatment can produce dramatic improvement, and a delay in treatment may lead to a poor outcome.

§ 32.40.   Extradural (epidural) hematoma.

These hematomas form in the space between the dura mater and the bones of the skull. (**Plate 1.**) Actually, this space does not exist normally, since the dura is practically attached to the bone, but it develops whenever the dura is separated from the bone by a collection of blood.

The most common cause of epidural hematoma is a traumatic tear of the middle meningeal artery or one one of its branches. The bleeding is of arterial origin, and because of the difference in arterial and intracranial pressure, it may continue without stopping until surgery or death. Occasionally, a tear of a venous sinus may give rise to an extradural clot, but its presence may not make itself known for a long period of time. And while arterial bleeding will give rise to the serious symptoms of an epidural hematoma in a matter of hours, in rare occasions, an epidural hematoma of venous origin may produce symptoms only after days or weeks.

The following is a typical case of an epidural hematoma:

> A twelve-year-old boy was accidentally hit with a baseball bat. He fell to the ground and was unconscious for several minutes. On awakening he appeared O.K. except for soreness over his right temple at the site of the blow. He continued playing and, at the end of the game, walked home (about seven blocks). His mother examined him but was not alarmed. About one hour afterwards, the boy complained of headache, and shortly thereafter vomited a few times. After that he lay down and slept for about one hour, when he was awakened for dinner. At that time he was drowsy and complained bitterly of headache. He again became nauseated and vomited, and went back to bed. The family physician was called and a few minutes later the physician found him extremely drowsy, but able to wake up and cooperate. There was little in the way of objective findings on examination, but because of the history, the patient was taken to the hospital, thirty miles away. On arrival the boy was stuporous, but would respond to painful stimuli. There was motion of the right side, but the left side was weak. The reflexes were abnormally active on the left side, and some abnormal reflexes were present, indicating a right cerebral lesion. The right pupil was dilated and failed to contract to stimulation by strong light, indicating paralysis of the third nerve. Blood pressure was normal, the pulse was full and slow, fifty beats per minute. Respiration was noisy and fast. X-rays revealed a linear fracture in the temporal parietal area on the right. A diagnosis of epidural hematoma on the right was made by CT scan. Six and a half hours after the original trauma, surgery was carried out under local anesthesia, and the lesion was verified and evacuated. At the end of the procedure, the patient was perfectly conscious.

The above case represents a typical situation: a history of what appears to be mild head trauma with momentary loss of consciousness, followed by a "lucid interval," after which signs of clouding of the intellect appear that progressively advance to coma and a surgical emergency. Often, however, the "lucid interval" does not appear as clearly as in this case. The physician has to make the diagnosis on signs of gradual deterioration of the patient's neurological status. Computerized tomography (CT) should be done to confirm this diagnosis. In one of the authors' practice (Martinez-G), epidural clots have been evacuated as early as four hours, and as late as fifteen days. In the former, the main branch of the middle meningeal artery had been severed by a temporal bone fracture; in the latter, the clot was found over the left frontal lobe at the vertex, apparently caused by a tear in the sagittal sinus.

Surgical treatment consists of evacuation of the clot as soon as diagnosis is made. There should be no delay since morbidity and mortality are high in patients that have gone long enough to be in very deep coma. In these patients, particularly when both pupils are dilated and fixed, removal of the clot may be too late. There are exceptions, however, and therefore an operation should always be carried out. Martinez-G had two such patients, both teenagers, who not only survived, but after a period of disability returned to normal. (One became an "A" student on returning to school.)

The operation may be done under local anesthesia. The scalp is infiltrated with novacaine, and an incision made about two and one-half inches in length on the temple, about one-half inch in front of and above the ear. The incision is carried down to the galea, and after incising the temporalis fascia, the temporal muscle fibers are separated in the direction of the fibers. A self-retaining retractor is used to separate them, thus exposing the temporal bone. A trephine opening is made in the center of the field, and the clot is visualized. It is usually black and soft, and will begin to extrude through the surgical opening. The original opening is enlarged until enough room is obtained for the removal of the clot, which should be accomplished by suction without difficulty. The bleeding vessel is located and tied with a ligature or cauterized with a coagulating unit. Usually there are several bleeding points, small vessels that go from the dura to the bone, but they should not give much difficulty. However, if the bleeding is severe, the main trunk of the meningeal artery should either be ligated or coagulated at the foramin spinosum, which is the point of entry of this vessel to the intracranial cavity.

Surgical treatment of these hematomas, when carried out early, is very gratifying. It is not unusual to begin a procedure with an unconscious patient, and finish with the patient awake and lucid, and without paralysis or other disability. On the other hand, if surgical treatment is delayed, recovery may not be complete and disability may persist indefinitely.

§ 32.40a.   Classification of subdural hematomas.

The Congress of Neurological Surgeons has classified subdural hematomas according to prognosis and clinical course of the pathologic process. The classifications are (1) acute, (2) subacute, and (3) chronic.

Acute subdural hematomas cause symptoms and signs (deteriorating consciousness and focal manifestations) which require intervention within twenty-four hours. The subacute type causes signs and symptoms that require intervention in two to ten days, and the chronic variety require intervention after eleven days. Acute subdural hematomas have a mortality rate of 63% to 81%, subacute 12% to 25%; and chronic 3% to 12%.

Acute subdural hematomas present clinically much like epidural hematomas. Recently, increased attention has been given to subdural hematomas in children who may have been violently shaken (battered child syndrome).

The age of the patient may be important in the development of the subacute or chronic forms. Since in the older individual there may be a larger potential space available in the subdural region, a large subacute or chronic hematoma may not cause rapidly developing symptoms and signs. In the younger patient, a small hematoma can cause both a large increase in intracranial pressure or intercompartmental herniations.

§ 32.41.   Chronic subdural hematoma.

This lesion results from mild head trauma, in fact the trauma may have been so mild that the patient may have no recollection of it. Only after repeated questioning of the patient and relatives may someone remember a slight bump several weeks before. The bleeding occurs in the subdural space between the dura and the arachnoid. It is usually in very small quantity because, as the intracranial pressure rises, the vein collapses and the bleeding stops. It may take several weeks, at times months, and even years, before its presence gives rise to symptoms severe enough to take the patient to the physician.

These are relatively common lesions. Some authors give their incidence as high as 5% of all craniocerebral trauma. They occur at any age, but are more often seen after the age of fifty. Men are affected more often than women, probably because they are more exposed to trauma.

A chronic subdural hematoma is produced when the head in motion (either forward or backward) is brought to a sudden stop against a stationary surface. The brain moves forward or backward causing the tear of a vein. There may be pain at the site of the impact or at the most, the patient is dazed, but no unconsciousness occurs. This lesion is common in alcoholics who fall and hurt themselves without having any recollection of what has happened. No fracture of the skull is present in most cases.

The bleeding is from one of the veins that pass from the brain surface to the sagittal sinus. In elderly individuals who have some degree of brain atrophy, the portion of these veins in the subdural space is longer, and this makes them more prompt to tear. This is one reason why subdural clots are more common in these individuals.

How much bleeding will take place depends on several factors. In the first place, the venous pressure is very low, and as soon as the intracranial pressure is a little elevated, the bleeding stops with the collapse of the vein walls. As this occurs, clotting within the vessel lumin takes place, which prevents the bleeding from starting up again. How much bleeding can occur before the intracranial pressure stops it will depend on how much potential room is in the subdural space. In patients who have no atrophy and whose brain is flush with the dura, a very small amount of bleeding, perhaps just a film (one-half ounce) on the surface will occur, while in an elderly person with marked brain atrophy, the bleeding may be much greater, perhaps as much as several ounces. **(Plate 2.)** At this time the patient may have some headache, which soon disappears, and there may be nothing in the way of symptoms for a few weeks.

Since the bleeding is in the subdural space, absorption is practically impossible, but apparently some can take place. Author Martinez-G has seen two patients who refused operation and whose hematomas seemed gradually to disappear under follow-up examinations. Small subdural hematomas are now sometimes simply monitored by follow-up CT or MRI.

The dura mater and arachnoid react to the presence of blood by localizing it, and membranes are formed. It takes some time for these membranes to appear, usually a week at least. The blood in the subdural space clots, but soon the red blood cells within the clot begin to disintegrate. The large protein molecules break down into smaller ones, which raises the osmotic pressure in the clot. It is theorized that this causes absorption of water from the subarachnoid space into the cyst, which in turn causes the cyst to grow. This eventually creates intracranial hypertension and produces the symptoms that bring the patient to the physician. This theory of the enlargement of the clot by absorption of water from the subarachnoid space has been accepted by many neurosurgeons. There is some evidence in its favor, for example, the older the clot the more liquid.

Some authors believe that the clot does grow, but as the result of repeated episodes of bleeding from the original vessel, and also from the vessels in the outer membrane. Still other authors believe that the eventual appearance of intracranial hypertension is the result of actual swelling of the brain in reaction to the mass. Be that as it may, the original bleeding gives rise to little trouble, and something happens afterwards that produces increased intracranial pressure. An increase in the size of the clot is certainly the most plausible explanation.

The location of the clot may vary. In the majority of cases the clot is over the convexity of the brain. In about 25% of the cases the clots may be bilateral, although one side is always larger than the other.

The symptoms produced by chronic subdural hematomas are those of gradually increasing intracranial pressure. Most times there is very little in the way of localized findings, and since the history of the trauma sometimes is forgotten, most patients are thought to harbor an intracranial tumor, the true nature of the lesion being discovered only at the time of a CT scan or MRI. The most prominent symptoms, particularly in elderly individuals, are those of mental disorders. The patient may show a definite change in personality, with loss of memory and lack of interest. Drowsiness may be a prominent symptom; the patient may sleep a great deal, but when awakening, may appear perfectly normal. Occasionally, a patient may show weakness in one side of the body and have some difficulty in speaking. Most patients will have headaches, nausea, and vomiting, which are the symptoms of increased intracranial pressure, as is the gradual clouding of the intellect, which results from elevated pressure prior to the onset of coma. Occasionally, a patient also may complain of gradual loss of vision.

The treatment of these lesions can be very simple, and the results are gratifying. In most cases, burr holes are made in the posterior parietal area, the dura is entered, and the outer membrane of the clot is brought into view. On opening this outer membrane, the liquid gushes out under pressure. The opening is then enlarged and the clot washed out with normal saline. A drain is usually left in for twenty-four hours and the wound closed. Very seldom an osteoplastic bone flap is necessary.

Surgery should be instituted soon after the diagnosis is made. In cases in which coma has been present for several hours, drainage of the hematoma may not bring about recovery, and the patient may be left with permanent paralysis of the opposite side of the body and continued mental difficulties.

§ 32.42. Subdural hygroma.

Subdural hygromas (also called hydromas) are unusual lesions that can result from mild head trauma. Their origin stems from a small tear in the pia-arachnoid that allows cerebrospinal fluid to invade the subdural space. This fluid may become encapsulated in more or less the same fashion described in chronic subdural hematomas. Since the fluid is stagnant, it acquires more protein. It is likely that this high protein content makes the hygroma absorb spinal fluid and thus enlarge as in subdural clots, eventually raising the intracranial pressure.

Not all hygromas, which may be bilateral, are encapsulated. Sometimes the mechanism at the site of the tear allows the fluid to leak into the subdural space and produce relatively early symptoms of increased intracranial pressure. In these cases, the fluid from the subarachnoid space may be pushed into the already tense subdural space by the patient's coughing, sneezing, or straining.

The symptoms of these lesions are those described in chronic subdural hematomas. Headaches are more prominent, however, and the patient may have no periods of well-being as is common in chronic clots. Encapsulated hygromas take longer to produce symptoms than the ones in which no capsule is present.

Treatment of these lesions is surgical and will depend on the type encountered. When well-formed membranes are present, the subdural space may be washed out and drained as in chronic subdural hematomas. The results are gratifying, and it is unusual to have a reaccumulation of fluid. Hygromas that are not fully encapsulated, however, sometimes present a very difficult therapeutic problem. In these cases, drainage alone is not sufficient because more fluid will enter the subdural space, and a craniotomy has to be performed to seal the arachnoidal tear. This can be a tremendous problem since the tear may be almost anywhere from the convexity to the base of the brain. At times, both a subdural hematoma and an encapsulated hygroma may be found in the same patient.

§ 32.43. Intracerebral hematomas.

Nontraumatic origin

Cerebral hemorrhage can occur "spontaneously," (i.e., in the absence of previous trauma). Actually, hemorrhagic lesions are among the most common lesions affecting the central nervous system. Most are the result of arterial disease, either acquired (arteriosclerosis) or congenital (arteriovenous malformation — aneurysms, etc.). Also, some are caused by brain tumors and others by blood disorders.

Only a few spontaneous hemorrhages are treated surgically. In congenital lesions and tumors, surgery is directed at the primary cause. In hemorrhage of arteriosclerotic origin, the bleeding may be small in amount (although it can cause serious disability and even death), and surgery is of no help. Occasionally, however, such hemorrhages reach a size to produce not only local symptoms, but also increased intracranial pressure; on occasion, these have been treated surgically with gratifying results.

Arteriosclerotic hemorrhage has a predilection for certain areas of the brain, the most common being the internal capsule where a relatively small amount of bleeding leaves the patient with paralysis of the opposite side of the body. One particular vessel, the lenticulostriate artery, seems to be more susceptible to bleed, and for many years has been called the "artery of cerebral apoplexy." Hematomas not of arteriosclerotic origin, however, do not seem to have a predilection for any particular area or vessel. They occur perhaps more commonly in the temporal lobes, but are seen everywhere in the brain.

Spontaneous intracerebral hematomas have been the object of intensive study for many years. Their evolution is different. Some clots, when in close proximity to spinal fluid, either at the cortex or next to the ventricles, probably grow in size by the same mechanism that causes a subdural clot to grow (§ 32.41), and may become encapsulated and chronic. The pathological mechanism that produces these lesions has been a subject of considerable speculation. Several opinions have been put forth by neuropathologists as to how the bleeding begins. Some believe that a small aneurysm suddenly ruptures. Others believe the lesions occur in a previous area of "softening," an area of the brain that is devoid of blood supply and is dying. (Brain tissue without blood supply first becomes soft and then is gradually absorbed; when a blood vessel has no adequate support from surrounding brain tissue, bleeding may occur.)

Traumatic origin

Intracerebral clots also may follow any type of head trauma. They have been reported in patients with mild brain injuries, usually (but not always) with some unconsciousness. The patient often regains consciousness and has a "lucid period," before going downhill with symptoms of an acutely expanding intracranial lesion. A CT scan will reveal intracerebral bleeding in 4% to 23% of patients with head injury.

Computerized tomography (CT scan) is extremely helpful in diagnosing the cause of delayed worsening following head injury. In addition to showing epidural and subdural hematomas, it can demonstrate intracerebral hemorrhage due to a "shear" injury of the brain or a contusion, which typically is manifested by scattered areas of hemorrhage intermixed with low-density areas of edema.

Traumatic intracerebral hematomas originate from a contused area of the brain in which a vessel has been torn and bleeds. It is usually a small artery: thus, the similarity in clinical picture to the epidural hematoma. The main difference between the two is the length of the lucid interval — usually longer in intracerebral hematomas, and this interval is not entirely free of symptoms, since the patient may have headache, nausea, and bouts of vomiting from the beginning. This can be explained by the fact that some blood reaches the subarachnoid space and irritates the meninges, causing meningism (symptoms of meningitis). Signs of local nature such as weakness develop before the symptoms of pressure appear.

Convulsions are seen in these patients. Eventually, the patient becomes drowsy and stuporous, and eventually coma will set in unless the brain is decompressed by removing the clot. In most cases, signs of brain compression appear in three to five days, but the lucid interval may last ten days to two weeks, in which case the possibility of chronic subdural hematoma is entertained at the time of surgery. The treatment of this condition is drainage of the clot (§ 32.41). Once the lesion is localized by CT scan, a brain needle may be introduced at the site of the clot and the lesion aspirated. This may be sufficient treatment, but at times an incision in the brain is made into the clot, which is then removed by suction. The cavity is washed out, and bleeding points are stopped before closing the wound. The prognosis is good in about 25% of these cases when surgically treated. The sequelae, if any, will depend on the site of damage and the amount of brain destroyed.

Late traumatic apoplexy is a condition in which there is sudden intracerebral hemorrhage, several weeks and sometimes months, after a head injury. In these patients, the trauma may be relatively mild, and after apparent complete recovery, there is the apoplectic onset of symptoms such as headache, nausea and vomiting, weakness of one side of the body, somnolence, and poor cerebration. The suddenness of the onset makes the diagnosis of a vascular accident very likely, and as symptoms continue, an intracerebral hematoma may be diagnosed and verified.

Establishing causation

The legal implications in these cases are obvious. Since hemorrhage may occur "spontaneously," a great deal of thought must be given by the neurosurgeon before accepting a history of trauma as the cause of a hematoma. In young patients with no prior history of arterial disease, a head injury followed in a few weeks by a massive lesion would suggest traumatic origin, particularly if the injury was severe and if some symptoms continued through the so-called "lucid interval." (See § 32.41.) On the other hand, in the elderly individual with hypertension or arteriosclerosis, the causal relationship between trauma and thrombotic or hemorrhagic lesion may be very difficult to establish. But even in the presence of arterial disease, if there was a history of head trauma, followed in a few weeks by a thrombosis or hemorrhage in an area of the brain not usually favored by spontaneous bleeding, the significance of the trauma, although difficult to assess, should be strongly considered.

§ 32.44. Infections.

One of the most significant complications of head injury is intracranial infection. Even the most innocuous appearing scalp lacerations, if improperly treated, may give rise to local infections, bone infections, and brain abscesses.

The scalp has a very rich blood circulation and most lacerations, if properly treated, will heal without any difficulties. However, if the wound has been closed with hair and dirt inside, infection will set in. When detected, the infected wound should be debrided. If this is done immediately, there is a good chance that healing will eventually take place. At times, however, local infection is neglected and it spreads further into the scalp. There may be little pain with this, and the patient may fail to go to the doctor.

Osteomyelitis of the skull is a very serious complication in head injury and should be treated as soon as the diagnosis is made. It takes about a month for X-rays of the skull to show some evidence of this disease. Treatment is removal of the infected bone (leaving the skull defect to be repaired at least a year later). The wound should be drained for several days and allowed to heal from the bottom. At the time of operation, cultures should be taken of the diseased bone in order to administer antibiotics. The antibiotics should be given for at least six weeks.

Compound fractures at the base of the skull into the sinuses or middle ear may become infected in spite of every effort at prevention. The infection may be in the form of meningitis and lead to a brain abscess. Occasionally a patient with rhinorrhea or otorrhea (leakage of spinal fluid through the nose or ear) who appears to be doing nicely may suddenly develop high temperature, convulsions, and clouding of the intellect. Under these circumstances, a lumbar puncture should be done to rule out meningitis, and a CT scan should be done to evaluate any subdural empyema (brain abscess), a very serious condition that carries a high mortality. Before antibiotics, mortality from subdural empyema was close to 100%. Now, with surgical drainage and antibiotics, a few patients are saved.

A posttraumatic brain abscess may result from embedded bony fragments that may not have been removed at the time of elevation of a depressed fracture. The treatment of a brain abscess depends on its location. If in a "silent" area of the brain, the abscess can be removed in toto. However, if the abscess is in a dominant hemisphere and near important brain centers, suction and drainage may be the treatment of choice. Here again, intravenous antibiotics play an important role.

§ 32.45. Additional complications.

Posttraumatic epilepsy

A major complication of head injury is posttraumatic epilepsy. Because of the medicolegal significance of this topic, it is discussed separately and extensively in Part VIII of the chapter. See §§ 32.47 to 32.59.

Another major complication is postconcussion syndrome. This condition, which is usually approached from the psychiatric as well as the neurologic standpoint, is covered in Chapter 20 of this Cyclopedia.

Pulmonary dysfunction may be caused by trauma to the nervous system. Immediately after injury, difficulty in breathing (apnea or tachypnea) may result from brain stem dysfunction. Hypothalamic and brain stem involvement may cause pulmonary vasoconstriction with alveolar edema, collapse of lung tissue and inadequate oxygen exchange. With a lowered respiratory rate, there may be carbon dioxide retention and an increase in the level of arterial pressure. This may result in cerebral edema.[14]

Hydrocephalus

Hydrocephalus refers to any of several neurological conditions marked by abnormal enlargement of the brain's system of internal cavities, the ventricles, and excessive accumulation of cerebrospinal fluid (CSF), a liquid ordinarily water-like in appearance within those spaces. These conditions may be congenital or acquired.

Trauma is one cause of acquired hydrocephalus. The hydrocephalus may follow the original head injury by weeks, months, or even years. Increased use of newer neuroradiological methods (CT scan and MRI) has led to more frequent recognition of posttraumatic hydrocephalus *ex vacuo,* obstructive, or communicating in type.

Hydrocephalus *ex vacuo* reflects shrinkage of the brain and compensatory enlargement of the ventricles. This is a natural process of aging, during which time some loss of brain matter occurs routinely. Atrophy following head trauma carries with it unfavorable implications for functional recovery. Ventricular enlargement of this sort has been reported in more than 25% of severe injuries; it may be evident on a CT scan as early as two weeks postinjury.

Obstructive hydrocephalus and communicating hydrocephalus, on the other hand, arise from actual disturbances in the circulation of cerebrospinal fluid, this causing the expansion of the ventricles. (In hydrocephalus *ex vacuo,* there is no disturbance in cerebrospinal fluid flow; enlargement of the ventricular spaces is simply a "passive" consequence of brain shrinkage.) In obstructive hydrocephalus, cerebrospinal fluid does not circulate normally because outflow from the ventricles, where cerebrospinal fluid is produced, has been blocked at one or more points in its usual course of flow through certain narrow openings. Thus, the fluid cannot pass unimpeded out to the external surfaces of the brain, where absorption takes place. Intracranial pressure may rise as a consequence. In communicating hydrocephalus, sometimes called nonobstructive hydrocephalus, cerebrospinal fluid has not been blocked at any point along its course of flow. Instead, circulation is usually abnormal because of blockage in the subarachnoid space or because of inadequate absorption of cerebrospinal fluid over the cerebral hemispheres. If the spinal fluid

---

[14]Editor's Note: Injuries involving the pulmonary system are covered in Chapter 33 of this Cyclopedia.

pressure is normal, this type of communicating hydrocephalus is also called "normal pressure" or "low pressure" hydrocephalus.

Hydrocephalus *ex vacuo* requires no therapy. Indeed, none is possible. This condition correlates with injury type and severity and suggests that significant mental and physical impairment will persist in the future. Hydrocephalus *ex vacuo* ought not be thought of as an "active" neuropathological process, but rather as something like a scar, that is, a residual of the injury. Accordingly, the recognition of this form of hydrocephalus is helpful, but rarely critical.

For obstructive or communicating hydrocephalus, however, correct and early recognition is very important. These conditions can account for substantial neurological dysfunction beyond that directly incident to the original trauma. The neurological decline associated with these forms of hydrocephalus can be progressive, and prompt treatment can sometimes prevent irreversible changes.

Though said to be rare, posttraumatic obstructive hydrocephalus is well-documented. Subarachnoid hemorrhage is a frequent occurrence in major head trauma and presumably it leads to the formation of clots and debris in the basal cisterns, especially in the cisterna ambiens, thus blocking the outflow of cerebrospinal fluid from the ventricular system. (If cerebrospinal fluid can escape the ventricular system normally, the hydrocephalus must be a communicating type.) Posttraumatic hydrocephalus of this sort can remain clinically "silent," only discoverable by special studies (*e.g.*, CT scan), or it may declare itself by certain symptoms and signs, those characteristic of increased intracranial pressure (*e.g.*, headache, papilledema, paresis, obtundation). Often a shunt must be surgically implanted to divert cerebrospinal fluid from the blocked ventricles, thereby relieving this pressure.

Communicating hydrocephalus has been reported in 1% to 2% of head trauma cases. Again, hemorrhage may be important in the pathogenesis of this condition, resulting in fibrosis and adhesions of the meninges or other impediments to the normal circulation and absorption of cerebrospinal fluid. Central nervous system infection is another possible factor in the etiology of this condition. Communicating hydrocephalus may go undiagnosed until a patient who has recovered to a considerable degree from injury develops new symptoms — dementia, gait disturbance, and incontinence (the "classic," though inconstant, triad). X-ray and nuclear medicine diagnostic studies aid in the diagnosis, but uncertainty may remain despite such studies, especially when not all the findings are "classic." In some large series, good improvement after shunting has been reported in 25% to 50% of those with posttraumatic communicating hydrocephalus. Unfortunately, no satisfactory criteria have been developed that can identify preoperatively those who will respond favorably to this surgery.

When obstructive or communicating hydrocephalus of any etiology antedates head trauma, it is possible for the head trauma, even though mild, to cause significant neurological decompensation. Thus, a previously unrecognized hydrocephalic condition may be brought to light for the first time, or a previously recognized condition may suddenly worsen. Typically, such might occur given preexisting aqueductal stenosis (a common type of obstructive hydrocephalus), whether or not a shunt was in place. Normal pressure hydrocephalus (a type of communicating hydrocephalus) may also be affected adversely by head trauma, as can pseudotumor cerebri, a nonhydrocephalic condition that entails incompletely understood disturbances of cerebrospinal fluid circulation and diffusely increased intracranial pressure.

§ 32.46. Trauma and neurological disease.

Head trauma can contribute to general stress, which could temporarily increase the severity of degenerative neurological conditions such as multiple sclerosis and Parkinson's disease, but head trauma has never been shown to cause either of these diseases. According to Williams et al.,[15] the case for an etiological association between head trauma and dementia is unsupported by the evidence, as is trauma and the development of parkinsonism, Parkinson's disease, or amyotrophic lateral sclerosis. Also, head trauma is unlikely to be a risk factor in the development of Alzheimer's disease in mentally competent survivors, and that reports of such a relationship are likely due to consistent bias resulting from the use of surrogate respondents. Williams and his associates base their conclusions on a review of the medical records of 821 patients who had suffered head trauma with presumed brain injury and who were more than forty years old at the time of their last medical examination.

§ 32.46a. Early and late outcome of contusions and concussions.

Eide and Tysnes[16] evaluated eighty-six head injury patients with focal or multifocal (unilateral or bilateral) brain contusions revealed by CT scanning. The outcome was also evaluated in 117 patients hospitalized for brain concussion. Three months after injury (early outcome), 43% of the eighty-six patients with multifocal contusions as shown by the CT scan had died. As evaluated by the Glasgow Coma Scale (§ 32.20), all of the fifty-seven patients with a focal brain contusion as well as the 117 patients with brain concussion made a good recovery or were only moderately disabled.

[15] Williams, D. B., et al., *Brain Injury and Neurologic Sequelae: A Cohort Study of Dementia, Parkinsonism, and Amyotrophic Lateral Sclerosis*, 41 Neurology 1554 (Oct.), 1991.

[16] Eide, P. K., and Tysnes, O. B., *Early and Late Outcome in Head Injury Patients with Radiological Evidence of Brain Damage*, 86 Acta Neurol. Scand. 194 (Aug.), 1993.

Late outcome (one to five years after injury) was evaluated in seventy-eight of the contusion patients and eighty-five of the concussion patients. Complaints of impaired adaptive functioning were frequent in both groups. Occurrence of headaches, dizziness, and sleep problems did not significantly differ between the groups, but in the patients with focal or multifocal brain contusions on CT scan, there was an increase in the frequency of impaired memory, impaired concentration, speech problems, weakness in arms and legs, and seizures with loss of consciousness. In patients with a focal contusion in the temporal lobe, cognitive deficits and speech problems were especially common. Late adaptive and social functioning were most markedly impaired in patients with multifocal bilateral contusions.

VIII. POSTTRAUMATIC EPILEPSY

§ 32.47. Nature of the syndrome.

Epilepsy is characterized by a persistent tendency to seizures.[17] In most epileptic attacks, there is impairment of thought, awareness, and responsiveness, and there may or may not be convulsive movements or automatisms (nonreflex acts without conscious volition). In attacks in which the disorder remains localized, consciousness may not be impaired. The seizures may be associated with structural disease of the brain or a toxic cause, but more frequently, there is no discoverable, organic brain disease. Some forms of epilepsy appear genetically determined.

Furthermore, epilepsy is not a single clearly defined disease. The individual who has consumed a fifth of whiskey a day for forty years with resultant brain atrophy; the woman whose brain is irritated by a tumor; the child who blinks his eyes, smacks his lips, and then resumes normal activity; and the child who falls to the ground, convulses, bites his tongue, and becomes incontinent do not all suffer from the same disease. They do, however, suffer from one of the manifestations of epilepsy — they have in common a disturbance of the normal pattern of electrical activity in the brain.

The proximate dysfunction in epilepsy is instability of the cell membrane of the nerve cells resulting in changes in electrical polarization. This is related to the passage of charged particles across the membrane which, in turn, is dependent upon energy metabolism. The chemical

---

[17]The term "epilepsy" actually describes a symptom (convulsive state). Most epilepsy is not "posttraumatic"; there are other causes. Also, there is a tendency toward certain types of seizures in the absence of any structural abnormality of the brain. See § 32.47a, *infra.* See also Hansen, W. A., "Incidence and Prevalence," in *Epilepsy: A Comprehensive Textbook* (Engle, J. Jr., and Pedley, T. A., editors), Lippincott-Raven, Philadelphia, 1997.

environment of the cell, the adequacy of the nutrients and circulation all contribute to maintaining the ionic membrane equilibrium. Although epilepsy is determined at the nerve cell level, its clinical expression is that of a system dysfunction in which abnormal electrical discharge is propagated in such a way that its traces can be defined by electroencephalographic (EEG) recording, either from the surface or the depths of the brain.

§ 32.47a. Classification of epilepsy.

Epilepsy might be best defined as the persistent liability to occasional seizures. It is not in itself a disease, but rather a symptom of disordered brain function. The ultimate causes are many. In many persons with seizures, no cause can be ascertained; this epilepsy is called either "idiopathic" or "cryptogenic." When the cause is known, the epilepsy is termed "symptomatic." In symptomatic epilepsy, the causes include birth injuries, biochemical abnormalities, the administration of toxic substances, degenerative diseases of the nervous system, mechanical causes (which would include head injury), vascular disease of the brain, tumors both benign and malignant, abscesses and other inflammatory lesions.

In the following sections, the principal concern is with seizures following head trauma, but it is essential for the sake of perspective and an understanding of the semantics involved to present a general classification of the epilepsies at the outset. There are several classifications. The one used here is the classification of the International League Against Epilepsy, which categorizes seizures according to whether they are generalized or focal (limited or attributed to involvement of one small part of the brain). Generalized seizures involve the whole brain from the beginning. Focal (localized or partial) seizures have a focal onset and may remain such or become generalized.

§ 32.48. Classifications of seizures.

The epilepsies may be classified in the following manner as adapted from the classifications proposed by the International League Against Epilepsy.

INTERNATIONAL CLASSIFICATIONS OF EPILEPTIC SEIZURES
I. Partial Seizures (seizures beginning locally)
  A. Partial seizures with elementary symptomatology (generally without impairment of consciousness)
    1. With motor symptoms (including Jacksonian seizures)
    2. With special sensory or somatosensory symptoms
    3. With autonomic symptoms
    4. Compound forms

   B. Partial seizures with complex symptomatology (generally with im-
      pairment of consciousness)
      1. With impairment of consciousness only
      2. With cognitive symptomatology
      3. With affective symptomatology
      4. With "psychosensory" symptomatology
      5. With "psychomotor" symptomatology (automatisms)
      6. Compound forms
   C. Partial seizures secondarily generalized
II. Generalized Seizures (bilaterally symmetrical and without local
    onset)
      1. Absences (petit mal)
      2. Bilateral massive epileptic myoclonus
      3. Infantile spasms (Hypsarhythmia)
      4. Clonic seizures
      5. Tonic seizures
      6. Tonic-clonic seizures (grand mal)
      7. Atonic seizures
      8. Akinetic seizures
III. Unilateral Seizures (or predominantly)[18]

§ 32.49. Partial (focal) seizures.

Focal or partial seizures have a localized site of origin and are always
symptomatic of underlying focal (local) disease. These seizures may remain focal or become generalized after their focal signature is declared
in the form of an aura, which is that part of the seizure occurring before
consciousness is lost and for which the patient retains awareness afterwards. When a focal seizure becomes generalized, it is presumed that it
does so by activating the central portions of the brain, which then send
their impulses back to both halves of the cerebral cortex. Focal seizures
may thus result in generalized tonic-clonic motor activity and it may
require an electroencephalogram to detect the nature of the responsible
seizure focus.

The nature of the focal seizure depends on the area in which the focus
is located. If in the motor cortex, the focal seizure will result in a movement of the part or parts innervated by nerve cells originating from the
region of the focus. Because the hand and fingers in the primate have the
largest cortical representation, seizures frequently commence in the
upper limb, particularly in the hand and fingers. The seizure may then
spread proximally up the limb to the face and to the lower extremity on
the same side. This is known as a "Jacksonian march," and a focal motor
seizure of this variety is known as a Jacksonian seizure. At any stage,

───────────

   [18] Adapted from *Classification and Terminology of the International League Against
Epilepsy*, 22 Epilepsia 489, 1981.

the seizure may spread into the depths, and a generalized tonic-clonic seizure may result. On the other hand, the seizure may remain limited to the first involved extremity.

When the seizure begins in the parietal region, spreading sensory phenomena occur, particularly numbness or pins and needles. In the case of seizures begining in the occipital region, bright flashing lights on the side opposite the discharging focus are frequently experienced.

Focal seizures beginning in the temporal lobe are known as "complex partial seizures" and are manifested by visual, auditory, and memory hallucinations with alteration of consciousness. Complex visual and auditory hallucinations, emotional experiences, distortions of vision (such as objects appearing very small or very large), dreamlike states, and occasionally automatisms may occur. The patient may continue to engage in various complex (but not goal-directed or motor) activities that may or may not be relevant to the situation in which he finds himself and for which he may have no memory after the seizure. Hallucinations of smell, lip smacking, or chewing movements may be seen, and occasionally a peculiar feeling is experienced in the pit of the stomach during the attack. The electroencephalogram (EEG) may be helpful where seizures have a cortical focus of origin and may show abnormal discharges of electrical activity recorded from the electrode in the region of the abnormal cortex. In many instances, the EEG between seizures is normal, and special techniques may be required to activate the abnormal focus, such as sleep deprivation or monitored withdrawal of medication.

Following a focal seizure there may be local weakness or paralysis that may persist for as long as twenty-four hours (postictal or Todd's paralysis) which is probably due to exhaustion of the nerve cells that have been actively involved in the seizure.

§ 32.50. Generalized seizures.

Generalized seizures comprise (1) absence (petit mal); (2) generalized tonic-clonic (grand mal); (3) myoclonic; and (4) atonic.

1. *Absence (petit mal)*. This is not of great concern in this discussion because absence of seizure is not a sequel to head injury. It is characterized by onset in childhood, frequent occurrence (often as many as 100 times a day), and a short lapse of consciousness, in which the subject suddenly ceases activities for a few seconds and then regains his senses without a period of confusion. Posttraumatic partial complex seizures are often mislabeled as "petit mal" seizures.

2. *Generalized tonic-clonic (grand mal)*. Some patients experience a vague ill-defined warning before a seizure but the majority lose consciousness without any premonitory symptoms. There is a sudden tonic (tense, persistent) contraction of muscles. When this

359

involves the respiratory muscles, there is a cry or moan and the patient falls to the ground in a tonic (stiffened) state occasionally injuring himself in falling. He lies rigid on the ground, and during the tonic stage respiration is inhibited and the patient may become blue. The tongue may be bitten, and urine may be passed involuntarily. The tonic stage then gives way to a clonic (jerking) convulsive stage lasting a variable period of time. Here there are small gasps of respiration between the convulsive movements, but usually the patient remains blue and saliva may froth from the mouth. At the end of this stage, there is a deep inspiration and the muscles relax. Breathing then may be stertorous (noisy) and labored, and the patient will remain unconscious for a variable period of time. On regaining his senses, he usually is confused and stiff and sore all over. The frequency of grand mal seizures varies from one or two a day to one every few weeks or months. True generalized tonic-clonic seizures are usually not seen after trauma, although posttraumatic partial seizures with secondary generalization are commonly misdiagnosed as such.

   3. *Myoclonic.* This form of seizure is characterized by a sudden, shock-like contraction of muscles resulting in a violent jerk; consciousness may be lost at this time but only momentarily. Myoclonic seizures are often seen after diffuse hypoxic brain injury.

   4. *Atonic.* With these seizures, there may be a sudden loss of muscle tone and the patient may fall to the ground or drop what he is holding.

In generalized seizures, the EEG finding is that of a generalized spike and wave pattern affecting all parts of the brain. The origin is probably deep within the central portion of the brain, and the spread is to both halves simultaneously.

§ 32.51. Relationship of epilepsy to head trauma.
Open head wounds

   An open head wound is one in which the intracranial contents communicate with the exterior. This can be brought about either by a penetrating wound or by a fracture through one of the sinuses, the mastoid air cells, or the middle ear. The distinction between open and closed head injuries is important because in open wounds, where there is communication of the intracranial contents with the outside, infection is apt to be introduced with devastating results.

   The missile or penetrating injury presents a special problem with an object forced into the cranial cavity at the point of entry. If the dura, which is the tough outer membrane covering the brain, is torn, the missile and fragments are forced into the brain substance itself, causing a laceration and severe focal brain damage. Despite the severity of such an injury, because it occurs in a localized area of the brain and may not produce generalized effects, in many cases the patient remains conscious and may walk away from the scene of the accident with brain matter leaking from the wound. On the other hand, sufficient generalized damage may lead to loss of consciousness.

Closed head injuries

Here there is no penetration. Closed head injuries are caused by an external blow to the cranium that may or may not be sufficient to fracture the skull. The effect of such an injury will depend entirely on the mechanical factors involved. For example, the patient's head may be crushed between two railroad cars and the skull fractured like an egg shell; yet, despite his injuries, the patient may remain conscious. On the other hand, if the head is in motion and strikes a stationary object or if a fast moving object strikes the stationary head, sudden deceleration or acceleration of the brain within the skull occurs. This may lead to contusion of the brain at the point of impact between brain and skull, which is most commonly seen in the frontal and temporal lobes. An acute "kinking" occurs at the site where the brain is relatively tightly anchored to the skull, that is, where the brain stem is closely invested by the membranous tentorium of the cerebellum and the bony foramen magnum where the spinal cord exits from the skull. Here compression may lead to immediate loss of consciousness. This situation is seen in a blow to the point of the chin or when the forehead strikes the automobile windshield. The sudden loss of consciousness that accompanies this trauma is referred to as a concussion.

Generally, if any impairment of consciousness remains after twenty-four hours, the injury is assumed to be more severe than a concussion. This more severe injury is usually a bruising (contusion) of the brain, a laceration of the brain, or a hemorrhage into (or compressing) the brain.

If concussion occurs frequently, as in boxers, gradually progressive permanent changes can lead to the "punch drunk" syndrome. The long-term effects of contusion or lacerations depend on the site of the brain injury and may include deterioration of judgment, memory, and intellect; paralysis on one or both sides of the body; speech disturbances; tremors; rigidity; or blindness.

A patient rendered unconscious by a head injury usually suffers a period of amnesia that extends beyond the period during which he appears to be unconscious. The patient may apparently regain consciousness, hold conversations, take food, and even perform purposeful acts such as walking to the bathroom, yet, when he finally regains his faculties, he may have no memory for the period during which he has performed these acts. This is known as the period of posttraumatic amnesia.

361

In the case of severe head injuries, the patient may suffer a certain period of amnesia that encompasses time prior to the occurrence of the accident (retrograde amnesia).

An epileptic seizure is the result of increased excitability of individual nerve cells that may be the result of irritation or of the removal of an inhibitory factor. How a head injury alters the balance between excitation and inhibition in favor of excitation is not known. It has been postulated that the contraction of a cerebral scar alters the blood supply to surrounding brain and makes it vulnerable to epilepsy. Also, damage to individual nerve cells has been produced in experimental animals by the application of penicillin, freezing, or alumina cream. This causes alterations in the nerve cells and in the supporting cells that help to nourish the nerve cells. Abnormal concentrations of neurotransmitter chemicals, such as acetylcholine and gamma-aminobutyric acid, as well as excitatory neurotransmitters, have been observed in epileptogenic areas. One or another of these mechanisms may be responsible for the maintenance of the focus of overactive electrical discharge.

§ 32.52.   Early posttraumatic seizures.

Epilepsy may be an early or a late sequel of head trauma. As an early sequel it may occur immediately following the injury or may be delayed for a day or two. It would appear that the acute disruption of the brain tissue during the injury, particularly if severe, may produce an immediate seizure such as is occasionally encountered during the occurrence of a spontaneous brain hemorrhage. In a small group of patients, seizures may occur immediately following trivial head injuries; it may be that these individuals are predisposed to seizures by heredity or other long-standing factors, and that the seizure is only precipitated by the blow. Early posttraumatic seizures occur in 3% to 5% of brain-injured individuals.

In most cases, the prognosis in patients who suffer immediate or early posttraumatic epilepsy is favorable, but as many as 30% will develop later epilepsy. It has been found that a large number of persons who suffer late epilepsy suffered an early seizure. Early posttraumatic seizures are a risk factor for epilepsy in adults, but not in children.

§ 32.53.   Late posttraumatic seizures.

The majority of patients who suffer posttraumatic seizures fall into the delayed-onset group. While seizures may occur any time following head injury, there seems to be a definite pattern: few develop seizures prior to two months following the injury and few develop seizures later than three years following the injury. The peak on the distribution curve falls between six months and two years. In children, the onset may be delayed many years. There is no convincing evidence that mild head injury increases the risk of later epilepsy. Moderate head injury, however, may increase the risk of epilepsy for up to five years, and severe head injury may increase the risk for up to fifteen years.

The epilepsy is of either grand mal or focal variety, with the majority suffering from grand mal. This is because most of these patients actually have partial seizures with secondary generalization.

§ 32.54. Incidence relative to type of injury.

The frequency of seizures after a head injury is quite variable. Some patients suffer only one seizure, but the great majority continue to exhibit epilepsy once the first seizure has occurred. In general, the more frequent the seizures, the less chance of spontaneous remission. Spontaneous remission does, however, occur.

In nearly all of the large series dealing with posttraumatic epilepsy, the most frequent epileptogenic wounds appear to be those involving the parietal lobes of the brain, followed in order by frontal lobes, temporal lobes, and occipital lobes. This is quite different from what occurs in patients with focal seizures without a history of head trauma, where the responsible lesions are most frequently found in the temporal lobes.

The incidence of posttraumatic epilepsy varies according to the severity of the responsible injury. Here, there is a large distinction between what we have called the open and the closed head injury. The incidence of epilepsy following civilian closed head injuries is 0.5% to 5%, and most authors use the average figure of about 2.5% of all closed head injuries.

Most investigations have concerned war injuries, and considerable data have accumulated from the study of head injuries during the first and second world wars and the Korean and Vietnam conflicts. While the treatment of head injuries has improved tremendously over the years, the frequency of epilepsy following head injury has not significantly altered and this is probably due to the survival of many severely head injured patients who formerly would have died. On the other hand, this is offset by the fact that wound infections that add tremendously to the incidence of posttraumatic epilepsy during the world wars were seen less frequently in the head-injured of the Korean and Vietnam conflicts.

One of the most important factors determining whether epilepsy will develop in an open head wound is whether the dura is torn or intact. In cases with penetration of the dura, the incidence of posttraumatic epilepsy is around 50% which is at least four times that in injuries in which the dura is intact. When metal fragments are driven into the brain and infection occurs, the incidence is higher. The overall incidence of posttraumatic epilepsy from war statistics is approximately 35%. A family history of epilepsy does not appear to increase the risk of epilepsy that occurs following a severe head injury.

The highest risk factors for late posttraumatic epilepsy include: (1) loss of consciousness for longer than twenty-four hours; (2) the occurrence of early epilepsy (in adults); (3) torn dura; (4) depressed skull fracture; and (5) intraparenchymal bleeding.

§ 32.55. Cessation of seizures.

Statistics on cessation of posttraumatic epilepsy are difficult to interpret. Some patients eventually stop having seizures, while others exhibit them indefinitely. A carefully studied series of patients by Caveness (who defined cessation as remission of attacks for at least two years prior to the last follow-up) showed fifty-eight cessations out of 109 patients.[19] There appeared to be no difference in these fifty-eight patients compared to the others with regard to (1) penetrating versus nonpenetrating injury; (2) time of onset of seizures; (3) attack patterns; (4) site of injury; or (5) severity of injury. The only difference was in regard to frequency: 85% of those patients who suffered less than four seizures had cessation, but only 21% of those patients who suffered multiple seizures did. Treatment did not appear to significantly affect the ultimate prognosis.

§ 32.56. Arriving at a diagnosis.

In cases of suspected posttraumatic seizures, there are several questions that must be answered.

1. Is the patient actually suffering from seizures? There are a variety of causes of transient loss of consciousness. A skillfully obtained history and frequently careful observation are required to distinguish these. Transient cerebral ischemic attacks (insufficient blood supply) due to disease of the cerebral blood vessels or of the heart, vasovagal syncope (fainting caused by instability of the vascular system or pressure on the tenth cranial nerve), hypoglycemia (low blood sugar), migraine, hysteria, and panic attacks all may mimic the epileptic seizure. Also, a skillful malingerer can imitate a seizure.

2. Did the patient suffer head trauma of a type or severity that might be followed by seizures? A blow on the head from an open cupboard door may daze the patient and raise a large scalp hematoma, but it is unlikely to cause seizures. There is little increase in the risk of epilepsy following a mild head injury in which there is amnesia or loss of consciousness of less than thirty minutes.

3. What is the causal relationship between the injury and the seizures? This is most difficult; invariably it involves speculation. The least controversy arises where there has been a focal brain lesion (§ 32.49), and the subsequent seizures have a pattern consistent with origin in the injured area. The greatest speculation

---

[19] Caveness, W. F., and Liss, H. R., *Incidence of Post-Traumatic Epilepsy*, 2 Epilepsia 123, 1961.

occurs with patients in whom a head injury of relatively mild severity is followed by epilepsy. Some of these have a history of convulsions in childhood. Here, the injury may have triggered seizures in a predisposed individual. Patients with brain tumors, cerebrovascular disease, HIV infection, advanced syphilis, or chronic alcoholism are all liable to suffer seizures that may manifest for the first time following a head injury.

Seizures are diagnosed primarily from careful history taking and, when possible, by observing an attack. There is no objective ancillary test that can establish the diagnosis, although confirmatory evidence may accrue from such investigations. The electroencephalogram (EEG) is frequently confirmatory, but in many cases it will be normal or only nonspecifically abnormal in the interseizure period; this is true whether the seizure disorder is of unknown or traumatic origin. The main value of the EEG is to help distinguish types of seizures and detect the focus in the brain from which the abnormal discharges, when present, arise. Likewise, radiological studies are frequently noncontributory, but in some cases may be helpful. A complete physical examination and spinal fluid examination may indicate other disease processes responsible for the seizures, irrespective of head injury.

Computerized tomography (CT scan) has replaced skull X-rays for evaluating the cranium. CT shows details of the cranial contents, including the presence of blood, distortion, or an increase in the size of the fluid spaces within the brain, thus indicating brain atrophy or focal damage. The procedure is a most valuable test and should be performed on all persons suffering from focal seizures. However, magnetic resonance imaging (MRI) is even more sensitive than CT scanning for this purpose. Also, functional neuroimaging procedures are increasingly being utilized in these cases.

There are usually quite marked EEG changes during the acute phase of head injury. With loss of consciousness, there is usually loss or irregularity of the normal alpha rhythm. Also, there may be suppression of electrical activity, and diffuse random slow waves may be seen. In less severe injuries, the EEG returns to normal in a few days whereas in more severe injuries, the abnormalities tend to persist for longer periods. There is often some correlation between the EEG and clinical improvement but, paradoxically, the EEG may remain grossly abnormal despite clinical improvement and in other cases it returns to normal without evidence of clinical improvement. Often, as generalized abnormality regresses, focal abnormality becomes evident as the expression of focal damage. The incidence of residual EEG abnormality is greater in more severe injuries, and in penetrating rather than in closed injuries. While it is greater in patients who develop posttraumatic epilepsy than in those who do not, the presence or absence of EEG abnormality is not a good prognostic indicator of the development of seizures, although persistence and deterioration or recurrence of slow wave foci are seen with increased risk of epilepsy. The presence of a spike or sharp wave focus in the resting EEG or in response to activating procedures such as sleep or hyperventilation, is evidence of focal cortical instability of potentially epileptic significance.[20]

While in the posttraumatic variety of seizures, focal EEG abnormalities in the form of spikes, sharp waves, or slow activity are most frequently seen, the more generalized subcortical EEG pattern is not infrequently encountered. In such cases, it is difficult to state with certainty that a similar pattern did not antedate the injury.

§ 32.57. Treatment.

Prophylactic treatment

Depressed fractures should probably be elevated, and in case of penetrating head wounds, the wound should be explored, bone fragments removed, and devitalized tissue and blood clot excised. Metallic foreign bodies are usually removed if they are easily accessible. Good closure of the dura is essential. Antibiotics to prevent infection are administered routinely.

The use of steroids to reduce brain swelling is common in acute head injury. However, there are at present no published studies of the effect of steroids on the incidence of posttraumatic epilepsy.

Anticonvulsants have frequently been recommended for use prophylactically. Experimental evidence has suggested that prophylactic anticonvulsant therapy is of some benefit in preventing the development of posttraumatic epilepsy in animals. It has been shown that drugs can modify the development of seizures in "kindled" animals, that is, animals in which repeated electrical stimulation ultimately produces epilepsy. While some authorities believe that anticonvulsants administered after head trauma may slightly reduce the risk of subsequent epilepsy in humans, this must be weighed against the risk of the potential side effects of such treatment. Clinical judgment is required in these cases.

Treatment of seizures

The sheet anchor of seizure treatment is the administration of drugs, principally: (1) phenytoin; (2) phenobarbital; (3) primidone; (4) carbamazepine; (5) ethosuximide; (6) valproic acid; (7) gabapentin; and (8) lamotrigine.

The chief drugs used in the treatment of convulsive attacks of the generalized tonic-clonic and the focal variety consist of phenytoin, phe-

---

[20] Editor's Note: The electroencephalogram (EEG) is discussed in Chapter 22 of this Cyclopedia.

nobarbital, carbamazepine or valproic acid. Usually, one drug of these drugs is given alone to produce a therapeutic blood level, a range that is specific for each drug. If seizures continue despite the attainment of such blood levels, combinations of the drugs are used.

Most anticonvulsant drugs have some deleterious side effects, but these are less frequently seen with the newer medications now available. The most commonly used drugs are phenytoin and carbamazepine.

The majority of patients with traumatic seizures respond to drug therapy, and their seizures are adequately controlled. There remains a small group of patients who, despite medication, continue to have a distressing number of seizures. In this group are some patients who may benefit from surgery. Patients with closed head injuries whose seizures emanate from the frontal or temporal pole may be amenable to frontal or temporal lobectomy (removal of a section of brain). A clean surgical scar in brain tissue is less liable to act as an epileptic factor than the original traumatic scar.

Surgical treatment of seizure disorders is highly specialized, and should not be undertaken without adequate electrophysiological studies and monitoring by an experienced team of physicians and surgeons.

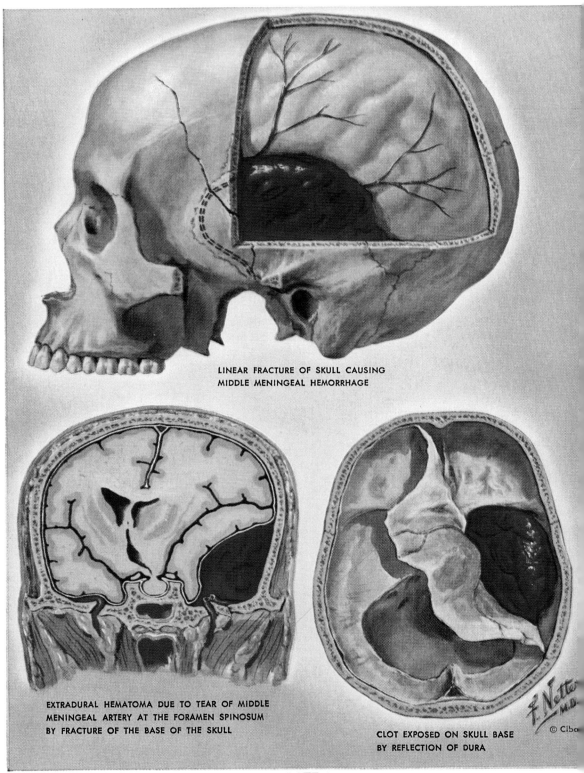

LINEAR FRACTURE OF SKULL CAUSING
MIDDLE MENINGEAL HEMORRHAGE

EXTRADURAL HEMATOMA DUE TO TEAR OF MIDDLE
MENINGEAL ARTERY AT THE FORAMEN SPINOSUM
BY FRACTURE OF THE BASE OF THE SKULL

CLOT EXPOSED ON SKULL BASE
BY REFLECTION OF DURA

PLATE 1

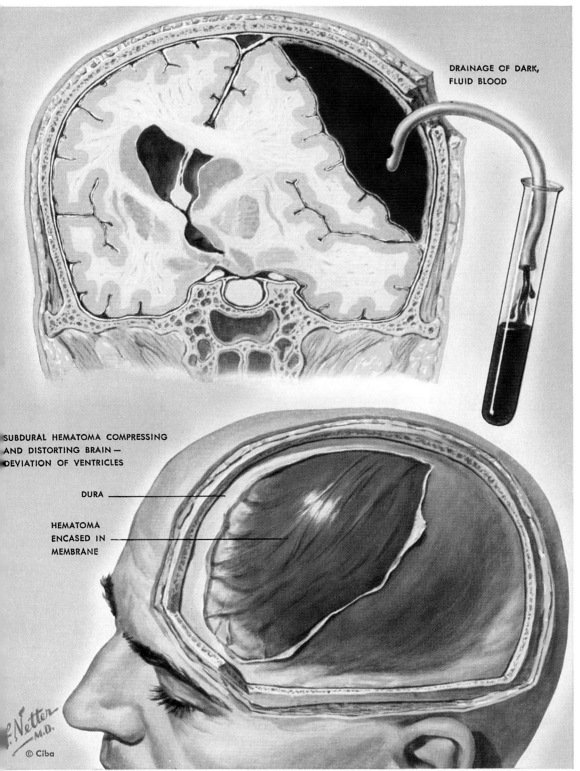

DRAINAGE OF DARK, FLUID BLOOD

SUBDURAL HEMATOMA COMPRESSING AND DISTORTING BRAIN — DEVIATION OF VENTRICLES

DURA

HEMATOMA ENCASED IN MEMBRANE

PLATE 2

Chronic subdural hematoma in an adult. (© Copyright 1953, 1972 CIBA Pharmaceutical Company, Division of CIBA-GEIGY Corporation. Reproduced, with permission, from THE CIBA COLLECTION OF MEDICAL ILLUSTRATIONS by Frank H. Netter, M.D. All rights reserved.)

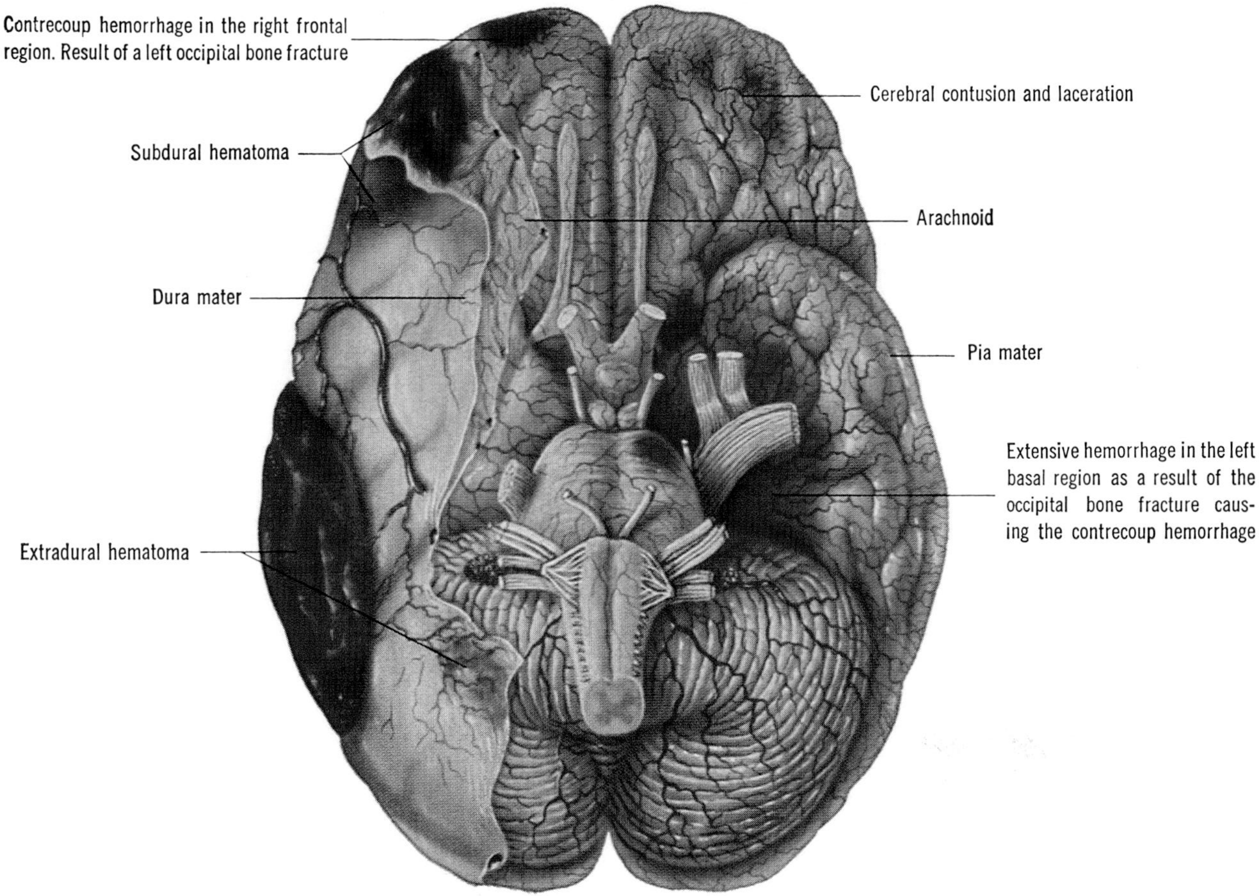

Contrecoup hemorrhage in the right frontal
region. Result of a left occipital bone fracture

Cerebral contusion and laceration

Arachnoid

Pia mater

Extensive hemorrhage in the left
basal region as a result of the
occipital bone fracture causing the contrecoup hemorrhage

Subdural hematoma

Dura mater

Extradural hematoma

PLATE 3

Traumata of the brain, inferior view. (Courtesy, Lederle Laboratories.)

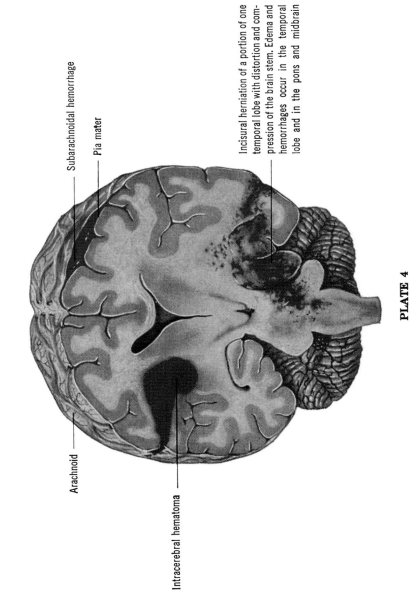

Subarachnoidal hemorrhage

Pia mater

Arachnoid

Intracerebral hematoma

Incisural herniation of a portion of one temporal lobe with distortion and compression of the brain stem. Edema and hemorrhages occur in the temporal lobe and in the pons and midbrain

PLATE 4

Traumata of the brain, frontal view in cross section. (Courtesy, Lederle Laboratories.)

371

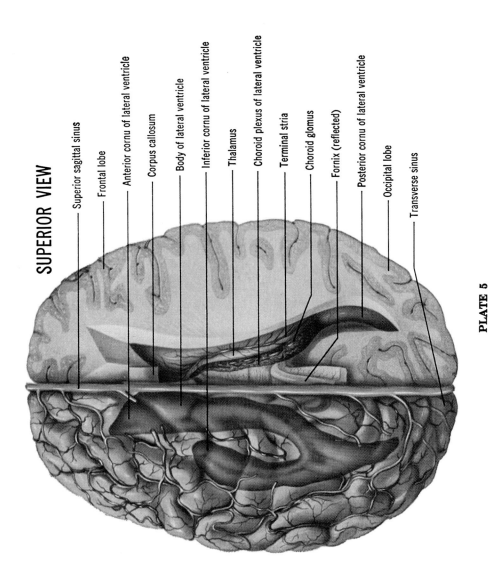

SUPERIOR VIEW

Superior sagittal sinus

Frontal lobe

Anterior cornu of lateral ventricle

Corpus callosum

Body of lateral ventricle

Inferior cornu of lateral ventricle

Thalamus

Choroid plexus of lateral ventricle

Terminal stria

Choroid glomus

Fornix (reflected)

Posterior cornu of lateral ventricle

Occipital lobe

Transverse sinus

PLATE 5

Ventricles of the brain, superior view. (Courtesy, Lederle Laboratories.)

PLATE 6 (opposite)

Anatomy of the brain. (Courtesy, Lederle Laboratories.)

1 Anterior cerebral artery
2 Trunk of corpus callosum
3 Head of caudate nucleus
4 Anterior communicating artery
5 Middle cerebral artery
6 Hypophisis
7 Posterior communicating artery
8 Superior cerebellar artery
9 Basilar artery
10 Internal cerebral vein
11 Choroid artery and vein
12 Choroid plexus of lateral ventricle
13 Inferior cornu of lateral ventricle
14 Vertebral artery
15 Frontal lobe
16 Ophthalmic nerve
17 Maxillary nerve
18 Posterior cerebral artery
19 Mandibular nerve
20 Pons
21 Intermediate nerve
22 Temporal lobe
23 Cerebellum
24 Left transverse sinus

CRANIAL NERVES

I Olfactory nerve
II Optic nerve
III Oculomotor nerve
IV Trochlear nerve
V Trigeminal nerve
VI Abducens nerve
VII Facial nerve
VIII Acoustic nerve
IX Glossopharyngeal nerve
X Vagus nerve
XI Accessory nerve
XII Hypoglossal nerve

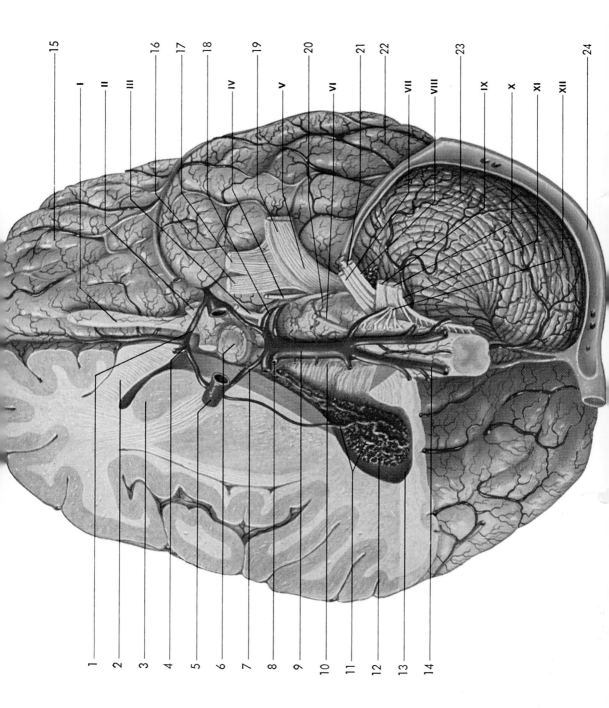

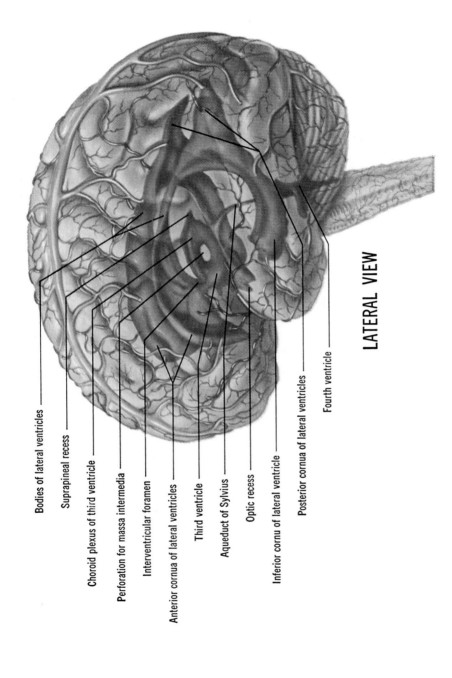

Bodies of lateral ventricles

Suprapineal recess

Choroid plexus of third ventricle

Perforation for massa intermedia

Interventricular foramen

Anterior cornua of lateral ventricles

Third ventricle

Aqueduct of Sylvius

Optic recess

Inferior cornu of lateral ventricle

Posterior cornua of lateral ventricles

Fourth ventricle

LATERAL VIEW

PLATE 7

Ventricles of the brain, lateral view. (Courtesy, Lederle Laboratories.)

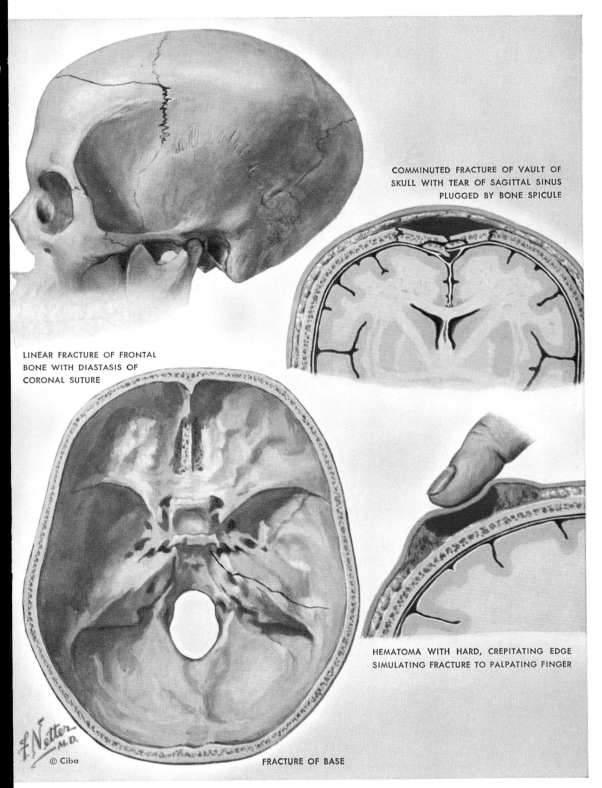

COMMINUTED FRACTURE OF VAULT OF
SKULL WITH TEAR OF SAGITTAL SINUS
PLUGGED BY BONE SPICULE

LINEAR FRACTURE OF FRONTAL
BONE WITH DIASTASIS OF
CORONAL SUTURE

HEMATOMA WITH HARD, CREPITATING EDGE
SIMULATING FRACTURE TO PALPATING FINGER

FRACTURE OF BASE

PLATE 8

Fractures of the skull. (© Copyright 1953, 1972 CIBA Pharmaceutical Company, Division of CIBA-GEIGY Corporation. Reproduced, with permission, from THE CIBA COLLECTION OF MEDICAL ILLUSTRATIONS by Frank H. Netter, M.D. All rights reserved.)

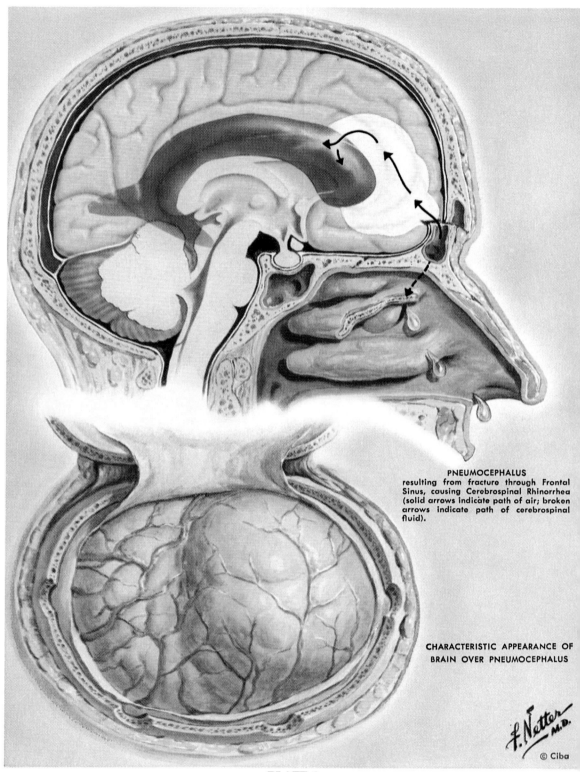

PNEUMOCEPHALUS
resulting from fracture through Frontal
Sinus, causing Cerebrospinal Rhinorrhea
(solid arrows indicate path of air; broken
arrows indicate path of cerebrospinal
fluid).

CHARACTERISTIC APPEARANCE OF
BRAIN OVER PNEUMOCEPHALUS

PLATE 9

Traumatic pneumocephalus. (© Copyright 1953, 1972 CIBA Pharmaceutical Company, Division of CIBA-GEIGY Corporation. Reproduced, with permission, from THE CIBA COLLECTION OF MEDICAL ILLUSTRATIONS by Frank H. Netter, M.D. All rights reserved.)

§ 32.58. Rehabilitation.

A most important feature in the treatment of seizure disorders is reha-bilitation. The patient should not be unduly restricted, although certain safeguards have to be taken, such as prohibition of the operation of motor vehicles, swimming in deep water unaccompanied, and working in high places. If the attacks are reasonably controlled, however, there is no reason why persons should not engage in normal activities, gainful em-ployment, and recreation. Children should attend school in a normal way and take part in all normal childhood activities. Undue restrictions make chronic invalids of persons who are, to all intents and purposes, normal apart from an occasional attack of loss of consciousness.

For patients with severe head injuries, for example, a gunshot wound, the seizures may be only a part of the problem. These patients may be blinded or paralyzed on one or both sides as well as aphasic (unable to speak). Special rehabilitative measures and retraining are essential in these cases.

Because many posttraumatic seizures do not begin for several years following the original injury, a patient at risk, particularly one with a penetrating head wound, is ill-advised to settle his insurance or tort claim too quickly after apparent complete recovery from an accident.

§ 32.59. Physically impaired drivers — Physicians' responsibili-ties.

Driving risks for people with seizures are not well-established because most reports have been based on anecdotal observations or uncontrolled studies. Even the few studies that have addressed this issue more scien-tifically have been hampered by methodological problems, such as iden-tifying an unbiased study population.

Although data are limited, people with epilepsy seem to have a rela-tively increased risk for traffic accidents.[21] In one study,[22] accident rates for reported drivers with epilepsy were nearly twice that of the popula-tion at large. However, these rates for epilepsy are similar to rates for other often less strictly regulated chronic medical conditions.[23] More-over, only 11% of all accidents involving people with epilepsy are re-ported as being due to seizures,[24] with most due to driver error, the same

[21] Naughton, T. J., and Waller, J., *Feasi-bility of Developing a Medical Condition Collection System for Driver Licensing,* Na-tional Highway Safety Administration, Washington, D.C., 1980; Waller, J. A., *Chronic Medical Conditions and Traffic Safety,* 273 N. Engl. J. Med. 1413, 1965; Crancer, A., Jr., and McMurray, L., *Acci-dent and Violation Rates of Washington's*

Medically Restricted Drivers, 205 J.A.M.A. 74, 1968; Hansotia, P., and Broste, S.K., *The Effect of Epilepsy or Diabetes Mellitus on the Risk of Automobile Accidents,* 324 N. Engl. J. Med. 22, 1991.

[22] Waller, supra.

[23] Id., Crancer and McMurray, supra; Hansotia and Broste, supra.

[24] Waller, supra.

major cause of accidents as in the general population.[25] Indeed, personal responsibility and variables, such as age and sex, may be the major determinants of relative driving risks, as supported by the observation that women with epilepsy have lower accident rates than men without epilepsy.[26]

Although the relative traffic accident risks for patients with epilepsy may be above average, the total risk for traffic accidents, particularly fatal accidents, due to seizures appears to be low.[27] A study of driving records in the Netherlands, for example, found that one accident per 10,000 traffic accidents and one fatality per 10,000 traffic deaths is attributed to a seizure while driving.[28] By comparison, in the United States, from 500 to 1,000 accidents per 10,000 traffic accidents and 5,000 deaths per 10,000 traffic deaths are reported to have alcohol as a contributing factor.[29] Moreover, six per 10,000 traffic accidents are caused by natural death at the wheel of a car.[30] Accidents caused by seizures are reported in one study to be less severe than average and less often involve another vehicle or result in serious injury.[31] Seizure disorders may pose some additional driving risks, but these risks are not extreme[32] and are, to a degree, predictable, so they may be limited.

State laws vary as to driving restrictions placed on epileptic patients and the responsibility of physicans to report such patients to the authorities. Some states require a seizure-free interval before an epileptic patient may resume driving.[33] Under such circumstances, it is reasonable to expect a physician to warn an epileptic patient of these restrictions. For the physician's benefit, such a warning should be documented.

A physician's duty to report a physically impaired driver to the motor vehicle authorities outweighs the physician's duty of confidentiality regarding the patient's medical history.[34] Medical ethics prohibit a physician from revealing information about a patient unless required to do so by law or unless it becomes necessary to protect the welfare of the patient or the community.[35] It would appear that a good-faith report to

[25] Naughton, supra; Masland, R.L., *The Physician's Responsibility for Epileptic Drivers*, 4 Ann. Neurol. 485, 1978; Doege, T. C., and Engelberg, A. C., editors, *Medical Considerations Affecting Drivers*, American Medical Association, Chicago, 1986.

[26] Crancer and McMurray, supra; Masland, supra.

[27] van der Lught, P. J. M., *Traffic Accidents Caused by Epilepsy*, 167 Epilepsia 747, 1975; Waller, supra; Masland, supra.

[28] van der Lught, supra.

[29] Perrine, M. W., *Alcohol Involvement in Highway Crashes: A Review of the Epidemiologic Evidence*, 2 Clin. Plast. Surg. 11, 1975.

[30] Baker, S. P., and Spitz, W. U., *An Evaluation of the Hazard Created by Natural Death at the Wheel*, 283 N. Engl. J. Med. 405, 1970.

[31] van der Lught, supra.

[32] Id.; Waller, supra; Masland, supra.

[33] Editor's Note: See Chapter 13A, § 13A.99(D), of this Cyclopedia.

[34] Wiecking, D. K., *Physician Reporting of Physically Impaired Drivers*, 97 Va. Med. Mon. 702, 1970. See also Harden v. Allstate Ins. Co., (D. Del., 1995) 883 F. Supp. 963.

[35] "Principles of Medical Ethics of the American Medical Association," in *Opinions and Reports of the Judicial Council,*

authorities concerning a patient whose epileptic condition definitely would create a driving hazard falls within the class of allowable disclosures for the furtherance of the health and safety of both the patient and society.

The American Medical Association supports the reporting of conditions that obviously contribute to hazardous driving, but it objects to any law requiring physicians to report on a large number of conditions that may or may not lead to unsafe driving, since any such law would deter some patients from seeking necessary examination or treatment.[36]

Actions against physicians

Civil actions have been brought against physicians whose patients have caused automobile accidents where it appeared that had the physician reported the patient's condition to the authorities, the patient's driving privileges probably would have been suspended. As early as 1968, an action for damages was filed against a California physician of an epileptic patient in just such a situation. Rather than let the case go to trial, the defense settled for $95,000.[37] To some observers, it appeared that the defense may been to quick to settle, even in California, where for the past decade physicians had been highly vulnerable in all kinds of civil lawsuits. Under the law that prevailed at the time, it was doubtful that a court would find that third parties had a cause of action against a physician in such a situation. Five years later, however, the Supreme Court of Iowa ruled that they did.

In Freese v. Lemmon,[38] it was held that a pedestrian who was injured when struck by an automobile driven by a patient suffering from seizures had a cause of action against the patient's physician for failing to diagnose the condition and thereby permitting the patient to drive his automobile, which the plaintiff claimed resulted in the accident causing the plaintiff's injury. The plaintiff, who was struck while walking along the edge of the road, alleged that the driver had lost control of the automobile when he became unconscious because of a seizure. She claimed further that it was not the first seizure that the driver had suffered, and that less than three months earlier he had consulted the defendant-physician because of this problem. She alleged that the physician was responsible for her injuries because of the following specific acts of negligence:

1. Failing to ascertain the cause of the first seizure and to learn of its recurrence;

American Medical Association, Chicago, 1979, p. 5.

[36] See American Medical Association Committee on Medical Aspects of Automotive Safety, *The Role of the Physician in Driver Licensing*, 206 J.A.M.A. 2305, 1968.

[37] Wiecking, D. K., *Physician Reporting of Physically Impaired Drivers*, 97 Va. Med. Mon. 702, 1970, citing 17 The Citation 163, 1968.

[38] (Iowa, 1973) 210 N.W.2d 576.

2. Negligently failing to advise the patient not to drive an automobile;
3. Negligently failing to warn the patient of the dangers involved in driving an automobile;
4. Negligently failing to employ recognized and appropriate tests for diagnosing the cause of the patient's first seizure;
5. Negligently failing to take a spinal tap;
6. Negligently advising the patient that he could drive an automobile;
7. Negligently failing to consult a specialist to whom the patient had been referred prior to advising the patient that he could drive an automobile.

The plaintiff further charged that the physician's conduct was willful and wanton and she was entitled to punitive damages.

In the trial court, the physician's attorneys moved to dismiss the complaint for failing to state a claim upon which any relief could be granted, asserting that the plaintiff failed to allege a violation of any duty owed by the physician to the injured pedestrian. The defense claimed that, if there was any duty to diagnose and treat the patient's condition, it was owed only to the patient and not to a third party. The defense argued also that any negligence predicated upon the allegation that the physician advised his patient to operate an automobile or that he failed to advise him not to operate an automobile must be based on knowledge that the physician knew that the physical condition of the patient would be dangerous to the general public or to the plaintiff in particular and that there were no operative facts alleged to this effect. In fact, argued the defense, the plaintiff had alleged that the physician was not aware of any condition suffered by the patient that would preclude his being able to drive an automobile.

The trial court sustained the defense's motions to dismiss. But on appeal, the Supreme Court of Iowa, in a five to four decision, reversed the trial court and held that the plaintiff's claim stated a cause of action. In the majority opinion, the court held that the specifications of negligence asserted by the plaintiff adequately served to charge the physician with negligence in failing to employ recognized procedures to determine the cause of his patient's first seizure, in failing to advise his patient not to drive, in failing to warn him of the dangers of driving, and in advising him that he could drive. These charges were so specific, said the reviewing court, that it could not say that the plaintiff failed to state a claim on which relief may be granted.

In a concurring opinion, it was held that Section 311(1) (b) of the Restatement of Torts (Second) should apply in this case. This Restatement section states: "One who negligently gives false information to another is subject to liability for physical harm caused by action taken by the other in reasonable reliance upon such information, where such harm results ... to such third persons as the actor should expect to be put in peril by the action taken."

The concurring opinion went on to hold that a jury case would be presented if the plaintiff introduced evidence at trial from which the jury could reasonably find that: (1) the physician negligently advised the patient he could drive; (2) in the exercise of due care the physician should have expected that members of the public would thereby be put in peril; (3) that the patient drove in reasonable reliance upon the physician's advice; (4) that the patient suffered a recurrence of his malady; (5) that the patient's automobile struck the plaintiff as a result; and (6) that the plaintiff was thereby damaged.

In a dissenting opinion, in which four of the nine justices participated, it was held that no cause of action should be found because there was no reported authority suggesting that under the circumstances the physician should have anticipated reliance by a third party upon his conduct. The consequences of the majority opinion, said the dissenters, are "both far-reaching and indefensible." The dissenting opinion went on to cite authority from cases that did not involve physicians and patients.[39]

In subsequent cases, the decision usually has turned on foreseeability. In an action against an Arizona physician whose patient lost control of the vehicle while suffering an epileptic seizure, where the evidence established that seventeen years had passed since the physician had advised the driver that he could discontinue using his anticonvulsive medication, it was held that the accident was not foreseeable, that the physician did not owe a duty to protect the plaintiff, and that the physician's advice was not a substantial factor in causing the plaintiff's injuries.[40]

While there is still some inconsistency among jurisdictions, the trend has been to find physicians liable. In a case decided under Delaware law, it was held that a physician's intentional refusal to report a patient's epilepsy to the state motor vehicle department as required by statute (the defendant believed that the statute violated the physician-patient privilege of confidentiality) did not amount to negligence *per se*, but his liability to the plaintiffs, who were injured in an automobile accident that apparently resulted from the patient's seizure, was supportable un-

---

[39] In an action against an Arizona physician whose patient lost control of the vehicle while suffering an epileptic seizure, where the evidence established that seventeen years had passed since the physician had advised the driver that he could discontinue using his anticonvulsive medication, it was held that the accident was not foreseeable, that the physician did not owe a duty to protect the plaintiff, and that the physician's advice was not a substantial factor in causing the plaintiff's injuries. Davis v. Mangelsdorf (Ariz., 1983) 673 P.2d 951.

[40] Davis v. Mangelsdorf (Ariz., 1983) 673 P.2d 951.

der the physician's common-law duty to warn third parties of such a danger.[41]

IX. ANATOMY AND PHYSIOLOGY OF THE SPINE AND SPINAL CORD

§ 32.60. Introduction.

Injuries and disease of the body may affect the bony structures of the spine as well as the ligaments and soft tissues that unite them. The delicate spinal cord and spinal roots, sheltered within the bony spinal column, may be involved as well. Violent injury also can cause damage to the extensions of the nervous system outside the spinal canal — the peripheral nerves. Commonly, injury affects musculoskeletal and nervous structures together.

The discussion in the following sections should acquaint the reader with the anatomical features of these body systems. Several terms are used to convey orientation between and among body structures. These include "anterior," meaning toward the front; "posterior," toward the rear; "medial," toward the midline; and "lateral," away from the midline. "Dorsal" means toward the spine, or back, while "ventral" means the opposite, or toward the belly wall. "Up" and "down" in the erect subject is indicated by "superior" and "inferior," respectively. "Cephalad" means toward the head, while "caudad" means toward the tail.

§ 32.61. Bony structures.

The vertebral column, or spinal column, is formed as a stacked array of thirty-three bones. Of these, twenty-four become the "true" vertebrae, distributed as follows: seven cervical (neck), twelve thoracic (chest), and five lumbar (low back). Five fuse to form the broad spade-like sacrum, while the remaining four form the inconspicuous coccyx just below the sacrum.

Loss of the normal cervical curvature is one indication of mild to moderate neck injury. The lumbar curvature (lordosis) is less often affected by injury that does not disrupt the bony integrity, but lateral tilting or rotation (scoliosis) may be seen. Some degree of rotation always accompanies lateral curvature, since the connections between the bones prevent one movement without the other. The thoracic curvature is well-maintained by the twelve pairs of thoracic ribs and is lost only in patients with major spinal disease or extremely violent injury.

---

[41] Harden v. Allstate Ins. Co. (D. Del., 1995) 883 F. Supp. 963.

§ 32.62. Spinal canal.

Behind the bulky spinal column is the relatively narrow spinal canal, in which lies the spinal cord and its many root fibers. The canal is formed by the posterior part of the body of vertebrae and the processes that arise from the vertebral bodies. It is lined by the several smooth ligaments that span one or more intervertebral spaces. **(Fig. 12.)** Two stalk-like "pedicles" extend backward from each vertebral body, one from each side, forming the side walls of the bony spinal canal.

The pedicles support a complex mass of bone that has extensions in several directions. Toward the head, each vertebra has a bony process bearing the superior articular facet for connection with the vertebra next above. Toward the feet is the corresponding inferior articular process with its facet, for connection with the vertebra next below. To each side of the vertebral body are the paired transverse processes, which serve as levers and points of attachment for strong paraspinous muscles that produce twisting and lateral tilting movements of the trunk. A bony arch arises from the intersection of these three processes on each side of each vertebra. This arch has a "Y" shape, with the two arms of the "Y" formed by the plate-like laminae that bound the posterior canal. Dorsally, the spinous process projects from the arch, like the stem of the "Y." This protuberance may be felt as a firm lump in the midback. The aggregate of spinous processes forms the bumpy ridge along the spine. The overlap of laminae increases with extension of the spine as the interspinous distance shortens. With flexion, the laminae separate to open the interlaminar space and the interspinous distance widens.

The cervical vertebrae **(Fig. 13)** differ in some respects from the thoracic vertebrae. They have in common the vertebral body, pedicles, laminae and dorsal spine, but they differ in the shapes and angles formed by them. A further distinctive difference is the lack of rib articulations that are present in the thoracic spine.

Fractures of the bony prominences may produce pain and instability of the spine. More importantly, the delicate nervous tissue of the spinal cord and spinal roots and nerves may be compressed and injured by displaced bony fragments. Further injury to the nervous tissue may result from interruption of the blood supply.

§ 32.63. Intervertebral articulations and the intervertebral disc.

The connections or "articulations" between vertebrae permit bending and twisting movements of the neck and trunk, while maintaining alignment of the spinal canal to prevent cord or spinal root injury. The paired posterior articular facets of adjacent vertebrae meet at an angle that varies with position along the spine. This angle and the curvature of the articular surfaces determines which motions can take place. Each of these "apophyseal" (projecting) joints has a tough fibrous capsule and is

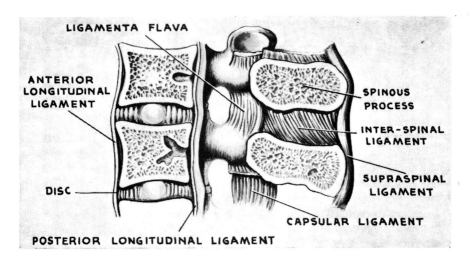

Fig. 12. Cross-section drawing of spine, showing the relationships between the bones and the ligamentous and muscular structures.

lined by a smooth synovial membrane, which is lubricated with synovial fluid.

The largest articulation between vertebrae (and between the fifth lumbar vertebra and the sacrum) occurs through the intervertebral disc. This has three components. A tough fibrous sleeve surrounds each interspace and retains the contents when pressure is applied; this is the "annulus fibrosus." Next, a cartilaginous plate lies above and below each intervertebral space, closely applied to the adjacent vertebral body. Finally, the nucleus pulposus lies within the bounds of these structures.

The normal nucleus pulposus is a soft cartilaginous mass that acts according to the law of fluids and thus cannot be compressed. When force is applied to it, it is transmitted to the annulus fibrosus as well as the cartilaginous plates above and below, allowing minimal deformity in the nucleus pulposus itself. In normal motions of the spine, such as tilting sideways or bending forward, minimal deformity occurs. With age, the nucleus pulposus loses its fluid content and may not behave in the above-mentioned fashion. If the force applied to it is great, it may cause an extrusion through a weakened annulus fibrosus.

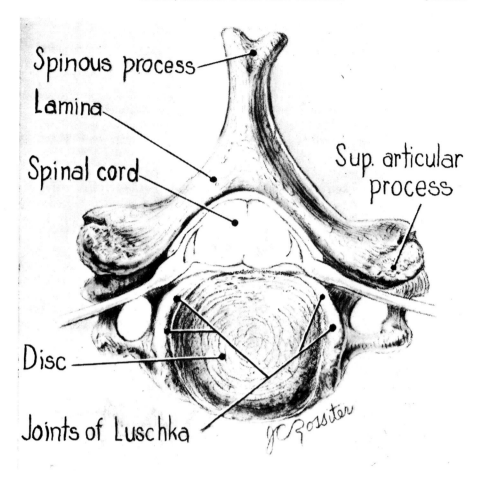

Fig. 13. Cross section through a cervical disc. Note the proximity of the nerve roots to the intervertebral discs, thus subjecting the nerve roots to irritation or compression by displacement of the discs.

§ 32.64. Ligaments.

Major ligaments of the spine include the anterior longitudinal ligament, which is firmly knitted to the anterior surface of the spinal column, and the posterior longitudinal ligament, which runs along the posterior bodies of the vertebrae in the anterior wall of the spinal canal **(Figs. 12 and 14)**. The anterior ligament functions to limit extension of the spine, and is by far the stronger of the two. Flexion is limited in part by the posterior ligament, but to a greater degree by the ligamentum flavum and interspinous ligaments that run along the posterior aspect of

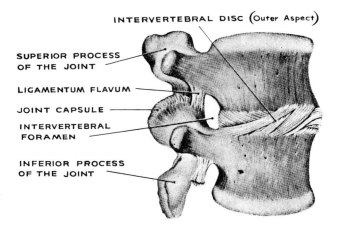

INTERVERTEBRAL DISC (Outer Aspect)

SUPERIOR PROCESS
OF THE JOINT

LIGAMENTUM FLAVUM

JOINT CAPSULE

INTERVERTEBRAL
FORAMEN

INFERIOR PROCESS
OF THE JOINT

Fig. 14. External view of two lumbar vertebrae. The articulations together with the intervertebral discs act as a cushion, allowing the spinal column not only to hold the body erect but also to permit a wide range of movement.

the spinal canal. The ligamentum flavum is a landmark in spinal surgery: it lies just beneath and between the laminae and bounds the posterior wall of the spinal canal.

The tough, band-like annulus fibrosus may be considered also as a ligament. It is firmly attached to the bony margins of the vertebrae above and below the interspace. As noted, it limits and confines the nucleus pulposus to the intervertebral space. It further aids in limiting extreme excursion of the spinal column.

The check function of the ligaments on spinal movements is significantly augmented by reflex contractions of the powerful spinal muscles, which are called into play by conscious as well as by unconscious spinal reflex mechanisms. When the muscles and reflex mechanisms are disabled, as by general anesthesia, the ligaments alone may prove inadequate to protect the spine. Injury may result if improper positioning is permitted.

The annulus fibrosus is thinnest posteriorly, toward the spinal canal. It is reinforced in the central part by the posterior longitudinal ligament. The weakest point of the annular ligament complex is found laterally where the posterior longitudinal ligament is also thin. This helps explain the high frequency of herniated nucleus pulposus in the posterolateral direction, producing the well-known syndrome of "ruptured disc" with nerve root (radicular) symptoms.

§ 32.65. Motions of spine.

The intervertebral articulations provide both for stable weightbearing and complex motions in several planes. Movements may be described analytically into forward and backward bending (flexion and extension), bending to left and right (lateral bending), and twisting (axial rotation). All of these require small motions of the apophyseal joints and adjustments in the intervertebral discs. The maximum permissible degree and direction of movement varies with level of the spinal column.

The cervical region is the most mobile, with a particularly large range of motion (up to 120 degrees) in flexion and extension. The parallel alignment of the curving posterior articular surfaces (facets) permits the necessary anterior-posterior gliding movements. Rotation of the cervical spine up to at least forty degrees is possible. In the thoracic region, the rib attachments and numerous ligaments limit mobility and enhance stability and strength. Lumbar spine movements include a good range of motion in flexion-extension, lateral bending, and rotation.

These various motions are important in determining spinal injuries from trauma. Certain regions of the spine undergo inordinate ligamentous strain at the limits of motion. Examples are the fourth and fifth, fifth and sixth, and sixth and seventh cervical vertebrae in the neck and the fourth and fifth lumbar and fifth lumbar and first sacral vertebrae in the lower spine. When traumatic force is applied to a joint already at the limits of motion, concentrated stress on the supporting ligaments is likely to produce injury at that point. Complex motions of rotation and bending also cause concentration of stress on certain structures which come to lie in the direction of applied force. Under these circumstances, when the forces are not distributed and dissipated in the usual manner, various failures may occur. Examples are compression fractures of the vertebral bodies, crushing of the articular processes, fractures of the laminae, extrusion (herniation) of the intervertebral disc, etc.

Similar accentuation of stresses occurs at the cervicothoracic and thoracolumbar junctions where flexible and relatively rigid spinal segments meet. Whip-like motions in severe flexion-extension injuries may concentrate forces on these junctions to produce increased risk of compression fracture and fracture-dislocation. The seventh cervical and first thoracic vertebrae junction is a hazardous location, because the shoulder frequently blocks the lateral X-ray beam and fracture-dislocation there may go undetected at the time of injury.

The lumbosacral junction is prone to injury when anatomical variants occur and modify the distribution of forces through this heavily-stressed, weight-bearing region. Examples are defects of the posterior bony arches (spondylolysis), slippage of the lumbosacral or low lumbar intervertebral junctions (spondylolisthesis), and abnormal articulations (sacralization of the fifth lumbar vertebra and lumbarization of the sacrum).

§ 32.66. Strength of spine.

The ligamentous and fibroelastic composition of the intervertebral articulations imparts elasticity and resilience to the spine. The shock-absorbing and stress-dissipating effects reduce the incidence of structural damage in trauma. Experimental data show that forces of 330 to 750 pounds are needed to produce fracture of a healthy vertebra. Schmorl and Junghanna[42] quote a figure of 1,300 pounds for compression fracture of a healthy lumbar vertebra. Lesser forces suffice in disease bone (cancer, osteoporosis, or demineralization), and when position caused abnormal stress concentrations. Estimates of forces needed to disrupt physiologically intact ligaments range from 140 to 330 pounds.[43] Lesser forces are needed in the more highly mobile cervical region.

§ 32.67. Craniovertebral junction.

The junction between the skull and upper cervical spine merits special consideration. Here the cranial mass of ten to fifteen pounds is balanced on and supported by the slender and relatively delicate upper cervical spinal column. Two specialized articulations provide a remarkably wide range of motion. At the atlanto-occipital junction, the occipital condyles (articulating surfaces at the base of the skull) meet the corresponding surfaces of the atlas (the first cervical vertebra). The large oblong gliding surface of this junction permits a large movement in flexion-extension of the head on the neck. Excessive movement is checked by a strong fibrous capsule and associated ligaments.

The second articulation of note is that between the atlas and the axis (second cervical vertebra). The atlas is a ring-shaped bone, which lacks the usual vertebral body and dorsal spine. Lying within the sheath of upper cervical ligaments, it is interposed like a thick washer between the skull and the axis. Unlike any other true vertebra, it has no intervertebral disc above or below it. With the skull, it revolves like a hub around the odontoid process, which extends upward from the axis. In embryogenesis, the odontoid arises from primordial tissue that belongs to the vertebral body of the first cervical vertebra. The tissue fuses to the body of the second cervical vertebra. A very strong and important structure, the cruciate ligament, develops across the arch of the atlas. It fits snugly behind the odontoid, and prevents forward slipping of the atlas on the axis (atlanto-axial dislocation). It is so snug that the odontoid is nearly always in contact anteriorly with the arch of the atlas. The odontoid process is further tethered by the cruciate ligament to the skull, by

---

[42]Schmorl, G. and Junghanns, H., *The Human Spine in Health and Disease*, 2d Amer. ed., Grune & Stratton Inc., New York, 1971, p. 35.

[43]Udvarhelyi, G. B., and Walker, A. E.,

"Injuries to the Spinal Column and Spinal Cord (Neurosurgical)" in *Lawyers' Medical Cyclopedia*, Vol. 4, The Allen Smith Company, Indianapolis, 1960, p. 497.

the apical odontoid ligament to the anterior margin of the foramen magnum, and by the alar ligaments and lateral tectorial membrane to its lateral margin. Whereas flexion-extension movements occur mainly at the atlanto-occipital junction, rotation occurs in greatest part at the atlanto-axial junction.

Congenital anomalies of the craniovertebral junction disrupt the coordinated motions of these several structures in ordinary movements. Anomalies may cause pain and deformity, and predispose to increased severity in instances of injury. Particularly hazardous injuries are fractures through the base of the odontoid, and disruption of the cruciate ligaments. Congenital nonunion of the odontoid is of similar import, although this anomaly may be concealed for years by fibrous union, until manifested by a traumatic blow. These lesions permit disastrous excursion of the atlanto-axial junction, producing compression or transection of the upper cervical spinal cord by a pincers mechanism. The anterior and posterior longitudinal ligaments continue on to the base of the skull, lending further support and strength to the craniovertebral junction. These ligaments are secondary in importance to the cruciate ligaments. Fluid-filled, membrane-lined articular capsules surround all articulations, including those between major ligaments (e.g., cruciate) and bone (odontoid) or cartilage.

§ 32.68. Spinal cord.

The spinal cord is a marvelously compact, slender column of nervous tissue that channels communications between the brain and the muscles, skin, organs, and other tissues of the body. Moreover, it possesses complex reflex pathways that maintain normal posture and gait, control the bladder and bowels, and subserve sexual functions. Characteristic aberrations are seen when intrinsic reflex cord mechanisms are "released" by interruption of the modulation influences from above, by bruising or cutting the cord, or by disease. These are discussed later in the sections on trauma.

The cord has both longitudinal and transverse organization. In the cephalo-caudal (head-tail) direction, it serves as a conduit for descending motor fibers that direct contraction of the muscles, producing movements of bones and joints in the performance of locomotion or skilled movements of limbs or trunk. Certain descending fibers establish the resting tension, or "tone," of the muscles. Interruption of these pathways produces abnormalities in tone ranging from flaccidity to the intense sustained contraction of rigidity.

Ascending longitudinal pathways convey "sensory" information to the brain, alerting it to force and stresses acting on the body; signaling the temperature of the environment; relaying the direction and rate of movement of the body's parts; relaying tensions in contracting muscles; and

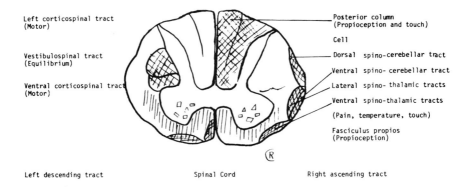

Left corticospinal tract
(Motor)

Vestibulospinal tract
(Equilibrium)

Ventral corticospinal tract
(Motor)

Posterior column
(Propioception and touch)

Cell

Dorsal spino-cerebellar tract

Ventral spino-cerebellar tract

Lateral spino-thalamic tracts

Ventral spino-thalamic tracts

(Pain, temperature, touch)

Fasciculus propios
(Propioception)

Left descending tract   Spinal Cord   Right ascending tract

Fig. 15. Cross-section of spinal cord.

informing about the presence of painful or other noxious influences on
skin, bone, muscle, and gland.

These various pathways hold their relative positions throughout most
of the cord (**Fig. 15**), but their cross-sectional areas change in size as
fibers terminate at destination neurons along the spinal cord.

In the entry zones of the dorsal roots, the afferent (brain-bound) sensory fibers enter the cord, segregated by size. Smaller fibers terminate on
cell bodies in the substantia gelatinosa of the outer dorsal horns of the
central gray matter of the cord. Fibers mediating pain and temperature
sensations are among these. Other larger fibers enter more
dorsomedially and pass without synapsing into the dorsal columns of the
cord. These fibers generally subserve touch and position sensibilities.
They also contact cells near the entry zone via collateral, or branch,
fibers. Anatomical and electrophysiological studies indicate that interaction between incoming fibers and the entry-zone cells may modify (possibly select, attenuate or filter) information that proceeds via nervous
impulses to the higher cord and brain.

A mechanism has been hypothesized for modifying painful sensations
in this entry zone. It has been theorized that two types of peripheral
nerve fibers convey information to the cord about possibly painful stimuli. One of these is the large, myelinated, rapidly conducting fibers such
as those in the dorsal columns. The others are the small, slower-conduct-
ing fibers. Both types synapse (make contact) with and activate a neuron
in the central gray area that relays pain information to the brain where
it may become conscious.

Another neuron (an "interneuron") acts on this same effector neuron
to modify its output. Branches of both large and small fibers act on the
interneuron to modify its output and thereby alter the activity of the
effector neuron. However, these two fiber groups act oppositely on the

interneuron so that the effector output ("pain information") is decreased by the large fiber activity and increased by the small fibers. Since the fast-conducting large fibers stimulate the interneuron first, they may condition or bias the interneuron in such a way the following small fiber activity is discriminated against and not transmitted upward in the cord to the brain. Activity in this entry zone is modified by descending supraspinal input.

A prediction of this theory is borne out in practice, namely, that selective disruption of the large fibers by peripheral nerve injury leads to an increase in pain. This is explained as release of small-fiber activity from inhibition by the gate mechanism.

§ 32.69. Spinal nerves.

The spinal nerves are identified by numbers. In the neck, the first cervical nerve exits above the first cervical vertebra, while successive nerves (second and third cervical) exit below vertebrae one through seven, respectively. There is one more cervical nerve than vertebrae. In the thorax and lumbar spine, each nerve exits below the corresponding numbered vertebra. There are twelve thoracic nerves and five lumbar. The five important sacral roots pass through foramina (openings) in the solid bony sacrum.

Figure 14 best shows the intervertebral foramina. Each is bounded above by the lower margin of one pedicle and below by the upper margin of another. The posterior margin is the posterior articulation (apophyseal joint) between the two vertebrae. The anterior margin is the intervertebral disc or adjacent vertebral body, depending on the level of the spine. Nerve roots passing through these foramina are subject to injury in fractures of the vertebra, of the pedicles, or at the apophyseal joints. In particular, the typical posterolateral herniation of an intervertebral disc can compress the nerve root, producing the classical "radicular" syndrome of muscle spasm and weakness and peculiar sensation (dysesthesia) along the distribution of the spinal nerve.

In general, successive spinal nerves innervate successive areas of skin from the neck above to the sacral area below. There is generous overlap on the trunk, so that interruption of a single spinal root may produce no significant sensory loss on the skin. In the extremities, the dermatomes (skin area) are more discreet, and specific spinal nerve deficits are readily recognized. Spinal nerves five through eight cervical and one thoracic supply the upper limbs, while the first through fifth lumbar and first and second sacral supply the lower extremities. The third through fifth sacral nerves innervate the perianal region between the buttocks.

Interesting topographical consequences of the innervation pattern in the limbs are evident. Since the cervical spinal nerves supply the upper extremities, there is a discontinuity in supply to the trunk; sensory fibers of the fourth cervical, near the clavicles (collarbones), are contiguous with fibers of the second thoracic. In the genital region, the first lumbar supply to the thigh is contiguous with the third sacral. Along the limbs, an "axial line" separates areas innervated by upper plexus fibers from those innervated by lower plexus fibers. Thus the axial line of the upper extremity separates the fifth cervical from the first thoracic innervation, while in the lower extremity the first through fourth lumbar innervation is separated by the axial line from that of the second sacral. Despite these anatomical discontinuities, sensory function and point localization are smoothly continuous.

§ 32.70. Peripheral nerves.

As the spinal roots enter the intervertebral foramina they acquire a covering of dura mater that continues as the perineurium (outer sheath) of the peripheral nerve. The spinal nerve is thickened in the intervertebral canal by the dorsal root ganglion (group of nerve cell bodies), wherein lie the cell bodies of the sensory (dorsal) fibers. These sensory cells have a peculiar T-shaped axon. The stem of the "T" arises from the neuron body; one limb of the "T" proceeds centrally as the dorsal root fiber; and the other runs in the peripheral nerve as a constituent nerve fiber.

Outside the spinal axis, the spinal nerve becomes a peripheral nerve, and bifurcates into dorsal and anterior primary rami (branches). The dorsal ramus supplies the muscle and skin of the midback and deep spinal regions. The anterior ramus passes laterally and forward to supply the remaining tissues of a body segment.

Nerve fibers of many spinal nerves intermingle to form mixed peripheral nerves. Complex interchanges occur in the cervical, brachial, and lumbar plexi (networks). Thus, fibers from a single cord segment (and spinal nerve) may be distributed among several peripheral nerves, and a given peripheral nerve may carry fibers of several spinal cord segments. These fibers resegregate themselves as they approach their terminations, so that they still innervate tissues of their own dermatomes (sensory area of the skin) and myotomes (muscles supplied by the segmental root).

Knowledge of the patterns of combination and resegregation permits clinical localization of many peripheral nerve lesions. When the injury is proximal, that is, near the spinal nerve, all peripheral functions of the segment are affected save possibly those of the posterior primary ramus (which branches soon after exiting from the intervertebral foramen). In these cases, electrodiagnostic techniques provide unique differential diagnostic information.

Most cutaneous nerves subserve all or a portion of one dermatome, or possibly parts of several dermatomes. For example, the ulnar nerve supplies the skin of the ring and little fingers, in the distal distribution of the eighth cervical dermatome. The medial antibrachial cutaneous nerve innervates the adjacent proximal eighth cervical dermatome. In contrast, the supraclavicular nerve carries fibers of the fourth and fifth cervical and first through third thoracic, while the intervening nerves (sixth through eighth cervical) go to the upper limb via the brachial plexus. Patterns of distribution vary considerably from person to person, and sometimes to a lesser degree from side to side in the same person.

The major peripheral nerves are considered individually in §§ 32.138 to 32.151.

§ 32.71. Autonomic nervous system.

The autonomic nervous system is a special division of the nervous system, with two generally antagonistic subdivisions, the parasympathetic and sympathetic. Its functions include the regulation of the organs, glands, and nonskeletal muscle of the body, such as the muscles in the stomach, intestines, etc.

The *parasympathetic division* issues from cell groups in the brain and from the sacral segments of the spinal cord, and has the synonym "craniosacral." Its functions include slowing of the heart rate, tearing, salivation, stimulation of digestive secretions and movements, and penile erection during sexual excitement. The *sympathetic division* stems from cells in the thoracic and lumbar regions of the cord; hence the synonym "thoracolumbar." Its activity is regulated by the hypothalamus, which lies at the base of the brain near the pituitary gland, via diffuse descending pathways in the central regions of the spinal cord. The sympathetic outflow dilates the pupil of the eye, whereas the parasympathetic system constricts it. The sympathetic division also slows the actions to the digestive organs, accelerates the heart rate, increases sweating, releases sugar into the blood by catalyzing conversion of glycogen to sugar in the liver, and brings about ejaculation in sexual intercourse. It is generally regarded as a "fight-or-flight" system, because it prepares the body for strenuous exertion in the face of challenge or danger.

Parasympathetic fibers are confined to cranial nerves and to peripheral nerves of the pelvic plexi. Sympathetic fibers leave the spinal canal with the ventral roots and enter and return from the sympathetic chain of fibers and ganglia, and are distributed with the peripheral nerves to the organs and glands of the body. This sympathetic division plays a key role in certain posttraumatic pain syndromes, in particular, in the disabling syndrome of causalgia. In various nerve injuries, altered sweating helps identify the site of injury.

X. INJURY TO THE SPINE AND SPINAL CORD

§ 32.72. Introduction.

Integrity of the spinal cord and peripheral nerves is essential for the mechanisms of body support, as well as to the variety of willed and unconscious movements of the head and limbs, for which the spine provides a mobile platform.

Severe trauma is needed to produce spinal injury, although the prospect of injury is enhanced by various mechanisms of stress concentration. Intuitively we expect that the healthy spine, as in the young, muscular and athletically conditioned, will best withstand the stress of trauma. Conversely, preexisting congenital or acquired deformities, with inherent instability or stress-concentrating discontinuities of support, increase the severity of injury in trauma. Similarly, the presence of degenerative changes of aging or disease also magnify the risk. Notorious examples are the fragile hips of the aged, softened by loss of calcium, which often fracture when the victim has a minor fall. Pathological fractures, as in bone eroded by cancer or other growth, may fracture simply on arising from a chair. The painful, rigid arthritic neck or back does not fare well in trauma.

When scrutinized in detail, the results of trauma are manifold. However, the significance of injury is measured in terms of pain, deformity and loss of function. In the matter of function, it is the spinal cord and nerves that are the issue, more than the bone or ligaments or muscles. The severity of injury need not be reflected in the appearance on the X-ray film. Indeed, the cord may be destroyed to the point of loss of life, while the bones appear in perfect position on the X-ray. Ligamentous tear may lead to later slippage of bones with nervous system injury and loss.

The following discussion of spinal trauma deals with injury of bone per se, spinous ligaments, blood vessels and meninges (fibrous coverings of the cord). Direct muscle injury, while almost inevitably coexistent with serious spinal injury, is not specifically discussed. The important subject of intervertebral disc protrusion, or "herniated disc," is treated separately.

§ 32.73. Injury to bone.

Injury of bone *per se* may be of surprisingly little consequence, depending on the site and circumstances of the fracture. Linear fracture of the dorsal spine or spinous process usually produces no injury to nervous tissue whatsoever. It is significant only as an indicator of the severity of the causative trauma, and as a prognosticator of painful soft tissue injury in its vicinity. Fractures of the transverse processes, which protrude laterally from the posterior bony arch of the vertebrae in the lumbar and cervical regions likewise may produce no neurological damage. Again, the injury is associated with much pain and muscle spasm; but no visible deformity or loss of function ensues other than temporary protective splinting[44] due to pain. Vascular Injury may occur in the neck, however. (See § 32.75.)

Fractures of the laminae over the spinal canal are of more concern, for bony fragments may impinge on the spinal cord or the spinal roots, producing varying degrees of neurological deficit. Laminar fractures may be inconspicuous on the X-ray film, since the bone is thin and light in density compared to larger structures whose shadows overlap on the X-ray. Fractures of the pedicles or of the articular facets threaten the closely proximate spinal nerves as they exit through the intervertebral foramina. Moreover, fracture through a pedicle removes some of the stabilizing influence of the posterior bony arch on the vertebral column, so that one vertebral body may slide or rotate on another even while the apophyseal joints and dorsal lamina remain intact. Spondylolysis designates a cleavage through the pars interarticularis ("part between the articulations") of the posterior articular mass. Many patients with this disorder develop the slippage of the vertebral body described, which is called spondylolisthesis. Compression of nerve roots is common, and chronic pain of moderate severity is the rule.

These injuries, generally inconsequential in terms of permanent neurological deficit, are often associated with more ominous lesions. The vertebral body itself may undergo compression fracture without displacement, and perhaps without neural injury. More severe blows may fragment the vertebra (bursting fracture) with dispersal of the bone in several directions. Direct backward extrusion of bony fragments is likely, with probable devastating injury to the spinal cord. Even with little evidence of disruption of the vertebral body on X-ray, there often is extrusion of the intervertebral disc into the spinal canal with dire consequences. The disc protrusion often occurs one or more interspaces removed from an obvious vertebral injury, again demonstrating that the X-ray findings must be interpreted with caution. Irreversible spinal cord injuries with permanent paralysis often occur in association with these severe bursting and "tear-drop" injuries of the vertebral bodies and backward disc extrusions.

Simple compression fractures of the vertebrae often produce no instability of the spine. Since the ligamentous structures remain intact, dislocations and shearing injury to cord and roots often do not occur. This explains why neurological damage may be minimal or absent.

In the neck, the odontoid process of the axis (second cervical) prevents dislocation of the atlas on the upper cervical spine. With fracture of the odontoid, the transverse portion of the cruciate ligament of the atlas no

---

[44]Editor's Note: "Splinting," as the term is used here, means the rigidity of muscles that occurs when a patient attempts to avoid pain by not moving an injured body part.

397

longer limits forward displacement of the first cervical on the second cervical vertebra when the head is flexed (inclined forward). When dislocation occurs gradually, there is local pain that tends to cause reflex muscle spasm and cessation of the motion; spinal cord compression may also occur. When dislocation is sudden, the spinal cord ordinarily is transected with prompt death. The mechanism of death is respiratory paralysis, with interruption of all motor fibers to the respiratory muscles and diaphragm. Theoretically, immediate implementation of artificial respiration might prolong life, but quadriplegia (total paralysis of all four limbs) would be expected to persist permanently. Uncommonly, marked dislocation at the first and second cervical vertebrae occurs with only slight neurological deficit.

The neck also has an increased incidence of fractures of the articular masses and facets, because the marked mobility of the neck in flexion-extension and rotation tends to produce stress concentrations on the posterior articular processes in trauma. Injuries of these structures may be elusive on X-ray examination, and functional examination with X-rays taken in various positions of the head and neck may be needed. Sometimes only follow-up examination some weeks or months later will reveal a traumatic bone injury through the development of late degenerative changes.

Again in the neck, fracture of a transverse process assumes a more serious nature. For one thing, such injury is almost sure to involve some of the peripheral nerves in the cervical and/or brachial plexi, since these nerves lie beside or on the transverse processes. In addition, the vertebral arteries pass through the foramina transversaria (foramina of the transverse process) between the second and sixth cervical vertebrae, inclusive. Injury to or compression of these arteries may lead to ischemia (lack of blood supply) of the brain stem and occipital lobes, with serious and even fatal consequences. The patient may be blind or have double vision; he may be unable to swallow and may choke or aspirate (inhale) saliva or food. Vertebral arteriography may be needed to evaluate these vessels for possible remediable injury.

Plain X-rays of the spine are useful in the evaluation of possible spine injury. When acute injury is suspected on clinical or radiographic grounds, CT scan, if available, is the diagnostic study of choice. Bone and blood are very well visualized with CT, even without the use of a contrast medium; however, herniated discs and the spinal cord itself are often not well-visualized with CT and are imaged more effectively with MRI or positive contrast myelography.

Pantopaque was an oil-based contrast medium often used in the past with myelography (see § 32.95); however, the procedure was sometimes complicated by the developement of a painful inflammatory arachnoiditis, especially if performed with blood in the subarachnoid space. Pantopaque has now been replaced by water-soluble contrast media such as metrizamide. Also, electromyography can be very useful in the diagnosis and localization of peripheral nervous system injuries, but it has limited application in the evaluation of acute injuries.

§ 32.74.   Injury to ligaments.

Injuries that disrupt the tough supporting ligaments so crucial in maintaining structural alignment of the spinal column are truly alarming. With such injuries, the spinal column becomes inherently unstable, and even a modest stress in flexion or extension may precipitate a disastrous dislocation and compression of the spinal cord.

When the anterior or posterior longitudinal ligaments are torn, the vertebral bodies are maintained in alignment only by the strength of the intervertebral disc and its annulus fibrosis (if intact, as is unlikely), and by the posterior articular processes and the posterior ligaments. One may never assume the integrity of these other structures when the longitudinal ligaments are disrupted, for the forces and displacements attendant on rupture of those ligaments is certain to damage the other structures to some degree. Fractures may or may not be evident following ligamentous injury; if present, fractures may be secondary in importance to the ligamentous disruption.

Rupture of the ligamentum flavum and the adjacent interspinous ligaments of the posterior bony arch, permits excessive flexion (forward bending) to occur with angulation of the vertebral axis and compromise of the spinal canal. This is most likely to be seen in the neck, especially at the fifth and sixth and sixth and seventh cervical vertebrae where normal mobility is greater in the adult.

Rupture of the transverse portion of the cruciate ligament at the atlanto-axial junction has been mentioned. The resultant instability is akin to that in an odontoid process fracture. Dislocation with spinal cord compression may be immediate or delayed. Occasionally, a patient will show no neurological deficit just after the accident. Pain and muscle spasm may limit displacement of the bones, so that an X-ray examination shows no fracture and no other irregularity of the bony alignment. Later, when pain and spasm subside, the patient may develop a severe sudden deficit as a result of an unguarded movement that produces the latent dislocation. Needless to say, such a situation is a great tragedy for the patient and his family and can be a legal nightmare for the physician.

§ 32.75.   Injury to blood vessels — Hematoma.

Another aspect of spinal trauma is damage to the blood supply. The perispinal venous plexus is rich and invariably is disrupted to a degree in any injury of ligament or bone. A hematoma (blood clot) develops at the site, but bleeding ordinarily stops spontaneously as the site of injury becomes bathed in blood under slight pressure. The blood loss is usually tolerated in closed wounds, although bleeding into paraspinous tissues may sometimes lead to shock and require blood transfusions.

The hematoma serves as a matrix for proliferation of reparative cells (fibroblasts, chondroblasts, osteoblasts) that lead to bony bridging and healing of fracture elements. Neurologically, the hematoma usually is innocuous if outside the spinal canal. At times, pressure on spinal nerves will produce symptoms.

Hematoma formation within the spinal canal often is associated with direct injury to the spinal cord. It is important to distinguish whether observed posttraumatic dysfunction of spinal cord or roots is due to original direct trauma or to pressure subsequently from a hematoma. Unfortunately this distinction often cannot be accurately made. Operative intervention may be crucial to relieve pressure from a compressing hematoma, whereas the results of operation on directly injured spinal cord are less encouraging.

Acute epidural hematoma resulting in spinal cord compression is readily diagnosed by CT scan, MRI, or, if MRI is not available, by myelography. It is crucial to recognize the possibility of a late-occurring hematoma and to perform the proper diagnostic test. Early diagnosis and intervention are of paramount importance.

Damage to the arterial supply of the cord also may produce irreversible and catastrophic damage to nervous tissue. The spinal cord is nourished by segmental arteries derived from the aorta and its major branches. Certain of these branches are preeminent in significance for the cord's blood supply, while others are essentially insignificant. The best-known branch is the artery of Adamkiewicz, which enters the spinal canal at the eleventh and twelfth thoracic level. Interruption of this vessel by trauma or by subsequent surgery for decompression of the spinal canal may lead to infarction of entire lumbosacral region of the cord, with resultant paraplegia (motor paralysis and sensory numbness below the waist). This artery can also be damaged during the surgical repair of an abdominal aortic aneurysm.

In the neck, the possible compromise of the vertebral artery course through the foramina transversaria has been discussed. (§ 32.74.)

§ 32.76.   Injury to meninges — Traumatic cysts.

A lesser mechanism of injury to nervous tissue is that of the traumatic arachnoidal cyst. When the meninges (the thin fibrous coverings of the spinal cord in the spinal canal) are torn, there may be outpouching of the delicate arachnoid layer through the rent in the dura. This herniated segment may fill with fluid from the spinal canal by a ball-valve mechanism that admits fluid into the cyst and retains it there. The resulting expansion of the cyst into a firm, compressive mass may cause pain and injury to nearby nerve roots.

Nerve roots may even herniate into dural tears, producing kinking of the root with production of radicular pain and dysfunction resembling that of a "ruptured disc." Such cysts sometimes result from the surgical trauma of lumbar disc surgery, with the unfortunate consequence that the subsequent nerve root entrapment perpetuates the radicular symptoms for which the surgery was originally performed. The situation ordinarily can be clarified by MRI or by repeat lumbar myelography, when contrast material fills the cyst. When detected, such postoperative extradural arachnoidal cysts should be repaired surgically. In chronic situations, surgical section of the trapped nerve roots may be needed for relief of pain.

A second variant of extradural arachnoidal cyst has a congenital etiology. These cysts may occur anywhere throughout the spine, but more often in the thoracic and sacral regions. Nerve fibers are not contained in the structure of these cysts. Severe symptoms are rare, but may be seen, including weakness or paralysis below the neck.

Another variant of meningeal spinal cyst is the perineurial cyst of Tarlov, named after the man who discovered them in cadavers. These are most common in the spinal canal of the sacrum where they may compress sacral nerve roots and also may enlarge the bony sacral canal from within. Tarlov cysts can mimic the symptoms of herniated nucleus pulposus (ruptured disc) and hence arouse medicolegal interest. Symptoms are thought to include backache, urinary difficulties, sexual impotence, rectal sphincter abnormalities, sciatic pain, and changes in sensory, motor and reflex function in the legs. Controversy about the symptomatology of Tarlov cysts exists because these lesions are often found coexistent with ruptured discs. Thus, it is difficult to be sure which disorder is the source of symptoms. However, Tarlov cysts are uncommon causes of low back pain and sciatica in clinical practice.

§ 32.77. Injury to the spinal cord.

Spinal cord injury in trauma to the spine may range in severity from minimal to profound, in location from the upper neck to the sacral roots, and in time from temporary to permanent. At the lighter end of the scale, a transient decrease in strength or in sensation below the level of a spinal injury identifies the lesion as a spinal cord "concussion." Mechanisms that produce concussion include stretching and blunt injury to cord or roots. There may or may not be identifiable structural injury to the spinal column or its ligaments. Specific injury situations might include blows to the neck (as in a judo chop), whip-like, flexion-extension injuries (as in auto crashes), and high-velocity missiles that pass near, but not make actual physical contact with, the spinal cord.

Concussion

Pathologically, "concussion" is thought to produce only edema and tiny "petechial" (pin point) hemorrhages. These findings are those seen in experimental animals, since human spinal concussions typically survive the injury and therefore are not seen by the pathologist. Later, a slight loss of the myelin sheaths of injured nerve fibers is thought to occur. Clinically, recovery is complete, and the injury may become inapparent within a few hours.

Contusion

"Contusion" designates a more severe injury in which clinical effects persist more than twenty-four hours, but which may be reversible. This injury often presents as paraparesis (bilateral weakness below the waist) that gradually clears over several days. Pathologically, experimental work shows the presence of small hemorrhages, edema, and histological destruction of small focal areas. Like concussion, contusion may arise from shock effects of traumatic forces applied at some distance and without demonstrable displacement of bony structures. More likely, though, this injury will be associated with momentary subluxation (partial dislocation) of the spinal column, whether documented or merely hypothesized.

Lacerations

"Laceration" designates a tearing or physical disruption of the cord, with production of hemorrhage, edema, and necrosis (tissue death) of the cord. Permanent neurological deficit of some degree is the rule. Penetrating injuries such as stab wounds and gunshot wounds and fracture-dislocations of the spine are apt to lacerate the cord with production of permanent deficit. Paraplegia, or paralysis of both legs, is a common finding in lesions of the cord below the shoulders.

Transections

Complete "transections" of the cord almost always involve direct contact of the cord by the destructive object. Foreign bodies, missiles, and fragments of fractured bone are prime instruments of these injuries. Bone fragments are often thrust into the spinal canal in bursting fractures of the vertebrae, crushed pedicles, and fractured laminae. An expanding hematoma (blood clot) within the spinal canal behaves similarly, with production of severe progressive compression injury to the cord.

Hemorrhage

Cord injury may be increased following trauma by hemorrhage into the cord substance, a condition known as "hematomyelia." The blood clot compresses the surrounding cord from within. Bleeding is often confined to the central gray region, largely sparing the longitudinally arrayed white matter tracts, but still may extend over several segments of the cord.

Functional transection

"Functional transection," leading to paraplegia or a worse deficit, results from occlusion (blockage) of the spinal cord blood supply. The pathological process is called "ischemic infarct" (bloodless scar) and is akin to the better known "cerebral infarct" or "stroke." In both, inadequate blood supply leads to nervous tissue death and corresponding functional deficit.

Prognosis

The eventual outcome of spinal cord injury can rarely be predicted with confidence immediately after the traumatic event. Recovery and compensation mechanisms may produce a remarkable restoration of function. It is true that many lesions leave a residua of significant permanent disability, but nearly all lesions improve somewhat with time, even if only at the cord segments adjacent to (above or below) the region of maximal cord damage. This hope of marginal improvement leads to surgical exploration in a great many instances of otherwise hopeless destructive lesions of the cord.

§ 32.78. Combined injury of spinal column and nervous tissue.

Traumatic injury seldom occurs in isolation in a single structural element, i.e., in bone, or ligament, or nervous tissue alone. By the nature of the process, force is spent and damage done in a region of the body, affecting all the elements therein. In spinal injury, then, there is typically a combination of injuries to the vertebrae, the ligaments, the blood vessels, and often the spinal cord and roots.

For example, in "whiplash" injuries of the neck, the severe alternating flexion-extension movements of the neck characteristically produce painful stretching of the muscles and ligaments. There may be mild stretch injury and/or concussion of the cord and roots. The nonneural component of injury may be the most disabling because of the associated pain. In fracture-dislocation, ligaments may be torn or severely distended, pedicles and vertebral body may be fractured, and the bony fragments may impinge on the spinal canal. The cord thus may be lacerated, while the nerve roots are compressed and the blood supply compromised through compression by bone fragments and expanding blood clot. Except for the fracture of bone, this sequence also may occur in severe ligamentous injury with dislocation or subluxation (incomplete dislocation in which the articular processes never lose all contact with one another).

X-rays may not reveal injury

When there is no bony lesion, or when this aspect is of minor degree or otherwise inconspicuous, the X-ray appearance may correlate poorly with the clinical severity of injury. Direct injuries of the cord by penetrating objects also may be invisible on plain X-rays. Transient subluxation may contuse or even transect the cord at the moment of impact, yet the spinal column appears in normal alignment on subsequent radiological study. On the other hand, alarming displacement may be seen in the absence of significant neurological injury.

Acutely herniated intervertebral discs may give rise to radicular (single spinal nerve) symptoms by compression of spinal roots or to multiple spinal nerve and cord symptoms when larger or centrally placed. Compression of the spinal cord or the sensitive terminal "conus medullaris" region (end of cord) (around the first lumbar vertebral body) may occur in higher lesions. Again, the X-ray may be totally unrevealing in such cases, especially when the herniation is acute. However, angulation of the spine and visible bony injury may implicate an injury of the disc. A similar implication holds in chronic instances if there are degenerative changes or loss of height at the intervertebral space.

As noted earlier, the most effective and least invasive method of imaging a herniated disc is with MRI. However, positive contrast myelography and CT scan are sometimes used in place of MRI or to provide supplemental diagnostic information.

Injury and degenerative changes

Injury that is confined initially to the spinal column and its soft tissue supports may result in delayed neurological damage. Such trauma may initiate or accelerate ongoing degenerative changes, causing reduced flexibility, loss of normal spinal curvatures, and narrowing of the spinal canal by bony overgrowth (osteophytes). This occurs most commonly with osteoarthritis. Similar degenerative changes follow medical disorders such as osteomyelitis (bone infection), epiphysitis (inflammation or infection of the epiphyseal plate region of the vertebral body), and as a result of occupational stresses (as in operators of vibrating equipment and workers engaged in heavy labor, etc.). The syndrome of spondylotic caudal radiculopathy results from progressive bony overgrowth in the spinal canal, accompanied by hypertrophy or thickening of the ligamentum flavum along the posterior margin of the spinal canal. Low back pain, radicular pain, numbness, and weakness are seen and may simulate one or more ruptured discs.

For medicolegal purposes, these medical disorders should not be confused with the consequences of acute trauma. After some time (months to years), however, it may prove difficult to differentiate the late results of trauma from these diverse processes. It is important to recognize the increased susceptibility to injury in persons suffering from preexisting degenerative processes of whatever type.

§32.79. Injury to spinal roots.

The delicate spinal roots traverse the spinal canal from their origins in paired dorsal (sensory) and ventral (motor) rows along the spinal cord to the intervertebral foramen where they exit to form the spinal nerves. They may be adversely affected by any mass intruding into the spinal canal, whether it be bony (osteophyte, fracture fragment), cartilagenous (herniated nucleus pulposus), tumor, (meningioma, neurofibroma, lipoma, metastatic tumor, or lymphoma), or vascular (arteriovenous malformation). Spinal roots may be transected in scissor-like manner in fracture-dislocation; if at a level above the first lumbar vertebra, the spinal cord will be involved also. The injury may be chronic or acute. Degenerative bony spurs and tumor, as well as many intervertebral disc protrusions, may produce chronic compression with root irritation and edema. Motor and sensory roots may be affected preferentially, depending on the location of the offending lesion.

Acute, traumatic injury but may be superimposed on a baseline of chronic dysfunction. Herniated discs, fracture fragments, pincer or scissor-like shearing in dislocations, and penetrating objects are some agents of injury to roots. Roots may be injured by stretching over otherwise silent protrusions during forceful flexion or extension in trauma. Common protrusions of note are chronically herniated intervertebral disc, osteophytes of degenerative joint disease, and hypertrophied ligamentum flavum (which buckles and impinges on the posterior cord in severe extension of the neck). Roots of one or several spinal nerves may be affected. Symptomatology will depend on the precise injury, but will include deficits of motor, sensory, and reflex function in the myotome and dermatome[45] of each affected segment.

Autonomic nervous system (specifically, sympathetic)[46] deficits may be produced by involvement of the ventral (motor) roots of the thoracic and lumbar cord, since the preganglionic sympathetic nervous system fibers exit the spinal cord in these regions with the somatic motor roots to skeletal muscle. In the sacral roots (second through fourth sacral) runs the parasympathetic nervous innervation of the bladder. Urinary dysfunction, specifically urinary retention, is a common result of compression of these roots or of the conus medularis from which they arise.

---

[45] A "myotome" is a group of muscles innervated from a single spinal segment; a "dermatome" is a sensory root field on the skin supplied by a single posterior spinal root.

[46] Editor's note: The autonomic nervous system is described in §32.71.

§ 32.80. Factors predisposing to spinal injury.

Any structure with less than optimal strength runs increased risk of injury when sudden severe forces are applied, as in trauma. Factors that increase the chance of damage to the spine and its supporting tissues also threaten the spinal cord and its attached roots within the spinal canal. Local defects or lesions establish a "locus minoris resistentiae," or point of least resistance, where damage may be focused in trauma.

Many processes of congenital or acquired nature present themselves in an unobtrusive "subclinical" manner. Even cancer sometimes demonstrates this tendency; for example, the first sign of breast cancer may be a fracture of bone weakened by metastatic disease from an undetected primary tumor in the breast. When pain or disability appear following trauma, it is natural to link one to the other in a causal manner. However, when there is preexisting subclinical disease, injury may elicit its first signs and symptoms. The severity of injury, the degree of distress, and the rate of recovery all may differ markedly from the expected in such cases. Many congenital and degenerative disorders are prevalent in the population. These important factors, which predispose to injury and modify the effects of trauma, must be dealt with in the numerous instances of posttraumatic litigation.

Malformations of the vertebra

Congenital defects include malformations of the vertebra. In the deformity known as "hemivertebra," only one-half of a vertebral body develops, while the other half remains unformed. "Butterfly vertebra" is a related anomaly in which both halves of the vertebra develop, but a central defect remains through the vertebral body. This defect is attributed to persistence of a prominent notochord. The name is derived from the appearance on plain X-ray. Neither of these conditions is necessarily associated with neurological deficit.

Spina bifida

Another congenital defect is spina bifida, wherein there is failure of fusion of the dorsal bony arch over the posterior spinal canal. The spinal meninges (dura, arachnoid, and pia mater) may bulge into the bony defect, forming a hernial protrusion called a meningocoele. These lesions also lack serious neurological consequences, although the association of lipomas (fatty tumors) may result in spinal nerve or cord compression. A more serious lesion is myelomeningocoele, with bulging of spinal cord and root tissue as well as the spinal meninges outward through the bony defect in the spine. The protruding mass of tissue has the form of a rounded ball, with thin walls of disorganized nervous and scar tissue, and a central core filled with cerebro-spinal fluid. Inclusion of deformed and dysfunctional nervous tissue in the myelomenigocoele sac deprives the lower body of motor and sensory innervation, as well as trophic influences essential to normal development. Paralysis, loss of sensation and deformity of the lower extremities are the result. Bladder and bowel dysfunction typically coexist.

Spondylolysis and spondylolisthesis

A less catastrophic congenital defect of the vertebra is spondylolysis in which the pars interarticularis (the bony bridge between the superior and inferior articular facets) either fails to fuse normally or fractures early in postnatal life. This occurs most often at the low lumbar level, and less often in the cervical spine. The affected vertebral body is released from the normal restraining forces (transmitted through the pedicles), which are important for maintaining alignment of the spine. With the stress and strain of usual activities, the vertebral body begins to shift over the one below, resulting in spondylolisthesis. (**Fig. 16.**) Persons with this spinal defect are prone to spontaneous pain and disability, and are especially vulnerable to traumatic injury. A minor fall or twist of normally inconsequential degree may precipitate prolonged painful disability. Eventually, surgical fusion of the spine may be needed for relief of pain and stabilization of the defective region.

Previous trauma or surgery

Previous trauma or surgical injury contributes directly to spinal weakness through detachment and rupture of supporting ligaments, and secondarily through subsequent arthritic degeneration. The later changes result from the increased mobility permitted by the ligamentous changes and original bony injury. Osteophytes, "spurs," and ridges or bars develop along the margins of the vertebral bodies and at the intervertebral foramina. Narrowing of the spinal canal and foramina results (acquired canal stenosis). This narrowing alone may compromise the nervous tissue space sufficiently to cause symptoms by direct compression of cord or roots. In addition, since the bony excrescences form at the spots where instability is present, there is decreased tolerance to stress and movement. These changes render the cord and roots more susceptible to injury in trauma, as when the cervical spine is forcefully flexed and extended in a "whiplash" injury.

Congenital narrowing of the spinal canal

Narrowing of the spinal canal (stenosis) also results from thickening of the posterior elements. Bony thickening or sclerosis of the lamina, and hypertrophy of the ligamentum flavum, both reduce the anterior-posterior diameter of the spinal canal. Congenital narrowing of the spinal canal affects all dimensions. This disorder may be familial, as in such unfortunates as achondroplastic dwarfs. Many of these persons suffer

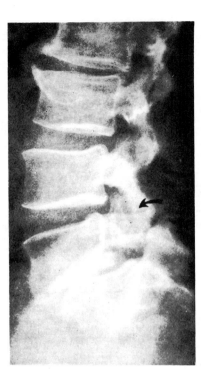

Fig. 16. (58-year-old man.) Lateral X-rays of the lumbar spine, showing a defect in the pars interarticularis of L4, allowing a spondylolisthesis (forward slipping) of L4-L5. Secondary arthritic changes are seen at this level.

severely from compression of the roots in the cauda equina, and even of the spinal cord, as they approach middle age. This narrowing tends to increase with time and age and not uncommonly results in paraplegia.

Arthritic degeneration

In severe arthritic degeneration, the range of motion of the vertebral column becomes reduced nonuniformly by scattered spontaneous intervertebral fusions. Movements of unfused joints, and consequently the stresses and forces of further degeneration, are thereby increased. This accelerated progression of degenerative arthritis may be seen after trauma or surgery or in patients with osteoarthritis, but is most prominent in ankylosing spondylitis of the Marie-Strumpell or Bechterew types. In dramatic instances, degenerative bony spurs may protrude anteriorly sufficiently to press upon the esophagus and cause difficulty in swallowing. Atlanto-axial subluxation of the cervical spine is most uncommon with rheumatoid arthritis.

Inflammatory diseases

Scheuermann's disease (epiphysitis vertebrae) is a disease of the epiphyseal plates of the vertebral bodies. Inflammation sets up degenerative processes that lead to vertebral collapse in the upper thorax, with resultant kyphosis ("humpback") deformity, and marked susceptibility to traumatic injury of nerve roots or cord. Other inflammations, such as osteomyelitis (bacterial infections of the bone), granuloma (sarcoid, tuberculosis, brucellosis), and typhoid infection of the spine also predispose to traumatic injury. Tuberculosis of the spine (Pott's disease) especially may first be detected following injury. Even neurosyphilis has become manifest in Charcot joints of the spine, when the interruption of innervation to the vertebrae permits destructive changes to progress with little discomfort to the victim.

Tumors

Neoplastic disease such as metastatic cancer, primary bone tumors and multiple myeloma (a disease of the blood-forming tissue) may weaken the bone and predispose to injury. Nervous tissue tumors such as meningiomas, neurofibromas, and ependymomas may impinge on nervous tissue spontaneously through growth, or at the time of injury. Tumors within the cord substance (gliomas, ependymomas) may be present for months or years, then first diagnosed after spinal injury. Similarly, the cystic disorder of the cervical cord known as syringomyelia may result in paralysis of both legs after a simple fall.

Defects of the craniovertebral junction

Again, special consideration of the craniovertebral junction is in order. A variety of congenital defects have been noted. Several of these involve abnormal fusions between the first cervical vertebra and the base of the skull, often combined with indentation of the base of the skull (basilar impression and platybasia). These defects prevent the usual range of motion in rotation at this important junction, resulting in additional rotational stresses on the lower cervical spine. Maldevelopment of the odontoid process or cruciate ligament, or failure of the odontoid process to fuse with the axis (second cervical), disrupts the stability of the "hub" mechanism for head turning (rotation), and causes serious potential for severe or fatal injury. Minor trauma in such cases may have disastrous consequences, such as quadriplegia or death from respiratory paralysis.

Other conditions

Laxity of the cruciate ligament appears in children after pharyngitis. Similar ligamentous laxity and progressive instability are associated with the Trisomy 21 chromosomal disorder, also known as Down's syndrome (and formerly, mongolism). Congenital fusions with formation of block vertebrae, as in Klippel-Feil syndrome, mimics the effects of late ankylosing spondylitis.

Occasionally, a benign congenital anomaly will be discovered in the course of evaluation of a traumatic injury. If not recognized, some may be mistaken for injury or fractures. In infants, for example, the cruciate ligament is less taut than in older children and adults. Up to 3 mm. displacement between the posterior aspect of the anterior arch of the first cervical vertebra and the anterior border of the odontoid process of the second cervical vertebra may be seen normally in flexion of the head. Such a finding in larger individuals would probably result in immobilization of the head on suspicion of odontoid fracture. The "butterfly vertebra," mentioned earlier, may be mistaken for a new fracture. Also, a "limbus vertebra," which is due to nonfusion of an epiphyseal line of the vertebral body, is another innocuous developmental anomaly that may be misinterpreted as a fracture.

XI. CLINICAL MANIFESTATIONS OF TRAUMA TO SPINE AND SPINAL CORD

§ 32.81. Musculoskeletal injury.

Pain is a hallmark of trauma to muscle and bone. It may be instantaneous with the injury, or it may be delayed, but it is rarely absent. It tends to increase with time after the injury, reaches a peak in one to three days, then declines slowly with healing. In contrast, peripheral nerve injury may be painless at the time of injury and for days thereafter, only to result in distressing paresthesias (aberrant sensations) or agonizing "burning" pains (dysesthesia) with time and healing. Pain and the fear it engenders are the basis of many legal claims for compensation following trauma.

Deformity of structure accompanies disruptive trauma to bone, with changes in length and angulation of formerly straight contours. Torn and ruptured muscles produce lesser changes in the profiles of limbs or trunk.

Both pain and deformity contribute to loss of function, with the profound consequences to the victim that this may entail. Strength, sensation, skilled movements, even ambulation may be impaired. Old life styles may be shattered, the mode of livelihood lost. Bowel, bladder, and sexual function may be irreversibly altered. Return of function varies widely and depends on many factors, among which are: the age and pretraumatic health of the victim; the type and severity of the injury; the intensity and availability of rehabilitation services; and that indefinable, essential element of success, the will and determination of the subject.

This final crucial element of will and determination in turn depends on many factors, among them support and encouragement by family and friends, professional encouragement by physicians and staff, self-image and self-esteem of the patient. Adverse factors are numerous. The psychological status known as "compensation neurosis" ranks high among them. When a patient stands to benefit materially from his disability, he is much more likely to maintain this condition despite the efforts of others at rehabilitation. The chance for sudden gain, even instant wealth, for sympathy and recognition for his suffering, for release from odious personal and family responsibilities, or from the drudgery of "the job" — all these factors powerfully influence the outcome. When these factors operate at the conscious level, it is called "malingering." When unconscious, and not recognized by the patient, it is called "conversion disorder" (and formerly, "hysteria").

§ 32.82. Spinal cord injury.

Injury to the spinal cord may result in any combination of motor and sensory deficits in the body below the level of the lesion. The severity may range from mild motor weakness or minimal numbness and tingling at one extreme, to paralysis or severe loss of sensation. Disability and dependency threaten the victim, and death is a real possibility in certain cases.

Immediately after injury to the spinal cord, there may be a large measure of reversible dysfunction. We know that complete destruction (necrosis) of areas of the spinal cord produces irreversible deficits. Thus, clinically we attribute reversible deficits to concussion or contusion, and irreversible deficits to spinal cord necrosis or anatomical severance. Whenever a trauma victim succumbs and undergoes autopsy examination, an important opportunity arises to compare precisely the observed clinical deficits and the extent of pathological change.

§ 32.83. Spinal shock.

The term "spinal shock" refers to certain changes that follow immediately on severe cord injury. Motor strength is lost, only to return slowly, if ever. Deep tendon reflexes (ankle jerk, knee jerk) are absent, as are the plantar reflex (Babinski sign) and the superficial skin reflexes (abdominal, cremasteric). Sacral cord reflex mechanisms for emptying the bladder and evacuating the colon become inoperative, and retention of urine and feces occurs. A period of immobility of the bowels (paralytic ileus) also occurs for a short period (several days to two weeks). If neglected, paralytic ileus leads to gastric dilation, with risk of massive emesis and aspiration (inhalation of acid stomach contents); and to abdominal distention, with elevation of the diaphragms and possible respiratory embarrassment. These considerations dictate use of an indwelling Foley bladder catheter, rigorous attention to bowel cleansing, and withholding of oral food and fluids until peristaltic activity returns to the stomach and intestines. Nasogastric tube suction may be required to prevent or relieve abdominal distention and thereby aid enfeebled respiratory efforts.

The period of spinal shock typically persists for two weeks to two months. As it clears, signs of spasticity appear in the muscles below the lesion, and troublesome aberrant reflexes may develop. This is discussed further under "motor deficits" in the next section.

The severity of spinal shock varies with the level of cord injury. While present in low cervical injury, it is more striking in mid- and low-thoracic lesions. The extent of initial spinal shock correlates with the eventual severity of spasticity.

§ 32.84. Motor deficits.

Motor lesions are divided into lower motor and upper motor neuron types. The former refers to injury to the anterior horn cells of the spinal cord or to its axons which comprise the peripheral innervation to skeletal muscle. The latter refers to lesions in the higher spinal cord or brain.

The lower motor neuron is involved either in disease or injury to the spinal cord, spinal roots, or peripheral nerves. Contusions and lacerations of the cord are likely to involve anterior horn cells at the level of injury. This is a segmental type of injury, which will affect those muscles or portions of muscles that are innervated by the injured cord segment. Such muscle fibers show denervation potentials, hyporeflexia, paralysis, or weakness of contraction, and eventual atrophy and fibrous scarring.

Upper motor neuron lesions affect the descending pathways which activate the anterior horn cells in the spinal cord, but do not directly affect the lower motor neuron "final common pathway" to the muscles. The descending pathways are compactly organized and stratified with successive levels (myotomes) represented by adjacent fibers in the tracts. A lesion of the corticospinal tracts tends to involve a region of musculature rather than a specific muscle or group of muscle fibers below the level of the lesion. Initially, there is marked weakness or even paralysis. Later, some strength may return, but much of the observed functional improvement often reflects hypertrophy of unaffected musculature. Hyper-reflexia, spasticity, and pathological reflexes (i.e., Babinski sign)[47] can be seen.

§ 32.85. Motor deficits — Spasticity.

Concomitantly, the signs of spasticity develop with upper motor neuron lesions of the cord. Muscle tone tends to increase, particularly in muscles of extension ("antigravity muscles"). Classically, the heightened tone has a "clasp-knife" quality, in that it gives way suddenly and com-

---

[47] The Babinski sign is the raising of the great toe on stimulation of the sole of the foot, which indicates pathology of the central nervous system.

pletely when flexion is attempted forcefully. Deep tendon reflexes are exaggerated, and the repeated reflexive muscular contractions of "clonus" may be present. Reflex activity may spread abnormally to muscles not ordinarily involved in a physiological reflex arc. An example is the "crossed adductor reflex," in which a tap on the medial knee (or even on the patellar tendon, as in elicitation of the knee jerk) produces adduction of the legs toward one another.

Other abnormal reflex muscular responses develop, many of them triggered by cutaneous (skin) stimuli. Of particular note are spasms of the limbs in flexion or extension. These may be triggered even by light touch, or by the need to urinate or defecate, or by attempts to move some other muscle. The contractions are abrupt and forceful, sometimes throwing the patient off-balance and causing a fall. They may be the source of pain, as well as of great embarrassment. When severe, they seriously impede rehabilitative efforts, and may require surgical intervention to lessen their intensity.

The eventual picture of spasticity varies with the level of the cord lesion. In the high thoracic region, lesions tend to produce "spasticity-in-extension," with spasms that cause forceful extension of the lower limbs. In midthoracic lesions, "spasticity-in-flexion" is the rule. This type of spasm is the more troublesome of the two, and more often necessitates surgical relief. In the low thoracic region, injuries lead to prominent mass reflexes involving the intact, but isolated conus medullaris (urination, defecation, erections, ejaculation). Slightly lower, lumbar lesions involve the cauda equina as well as the conus medullaris, and a mixed picture of combined upper and lower motor neuron lesions results.

Spasticity is often treated medically. Muscle relaxants sometimes used include Robaxin (methocarbamol), Flexeril (cyclobenzaprine), and Soma (carisoprodol). Also, Dantrium (dantrolene sodium) relieves spasticity by inhibiting calcium metabolism in muscle. Prominent side effects can include liver toxicity and fatigue. Lioresal (baclofen) is a commonly used drug that enhances the effect of an inhibitory neurotransmitter in the central nervous system. This is also accomplished with Valium (diazepam), a benzodiazepine. Zanaflex (tizanidine) is a newer drug used to treat spasticity, which acts on the effect of the neurotransmitter epinephrine in the central nervous system. Other recent innovations in treating spasticity include the continuous delivery of baclofen into the subarachnoid space via a subcutaneous pump and periodic injection of botulinum toxin into spastic muscles.

§ 32.86. Motor deficits — Cervical lesions.

The cervical region is a special case. The important phrenic nerve to the respiratory diaphragm arises from the third through fifth cervical levels. High cervical transections seldom reach medical attention, since instant paralysis of the diaphragm occurs, accompanied by interruption of descending motor fibers and paralysis of the intercostal muscles of respiration. This combination of motor deficits is virtually always fatal. Low cervical lesions spare the diaphragm, but paralyze the intercostal musculature (first through twelfth thoracic). The victim then makes do with one-half of his normal respiratory musculature. Adequate ventilation can be maintained at basal conditions, but such patients often clear their airways of secretions poorly, and are prone to develop pneumonia or atalectasis (partial lung collapse). Vigorous attention to the pulmonary status is one key to survival in the early weeks after these injuries. It is interesting that victims of cervical transection tend to develop somewhat less spasticity than do those with thoracic injury. This is thought to be due to the effect of descending inhibitory fibers from the brachial plexus to the lower cord; these are preserved in cervical lesions, but lost in thoracic.

Cord lesions at the sixth cervical vertebra level spare fifth cervical and higher cord segments and with them some functions of the upper limb. In particular, preservation of the fifth cervical segment leaves the ability to elevate the shoulder and externally rotate the arm. Lesions sparing the sixth cervical segment and above permit flexion of the arm at the elbow, and pronation and supination of the hand as well. Preservation of the seventh cervical segment permits flexion and extension of the wrist and extension of the forearm at the elbow. Preservation of the eighth cervical segment permits function of the intrinsic muscles of the hand and preserves the important function of grasp. Knowledge of these expected functions is most important in determining the specific type of rehabilitation needed, and in predicting the ultimate outcome of the injury.

§ 32.87. Sensory deficits.

Sensory deficits may result from spinal cord injury in any or several of the modalities and to any degree. Complete transection of a major pathway may produce virtual anesthesia of a region of the body, although partial reductions in sensation (hypesthesia) are much more common. Occasionally, increased sensitivity to stimulation (hyperesthesia) will result. When dorsal root fibers are affected, as they often are at the level of cord injury, the sensory result may be aberration (paresthesias) or acute unpleasantness of normally innocuous stimuli (hyperpathia) in that dermatome.

The specific anatomical pathways have been discussed above, in the section on the spinal cord anatomy. Consideration of specific lesions follows. In general, a characteristic of sensory loss in cord injury is its regional distribution, i.e., involving a sequence of adjacent dermatomes (sensory root fields on the skin). In many cases this is a terminal region, i.e., a lower body quadrant in a thoracic lesion, or one-half of the body below the neck in a cervical lesion. An interesting exception is the preservation of sensation about the rectum and genitalia in severe but incomplete spinal cord transections. This "sacral sparing" is attributed to a diffuse dispersion of the relevant sensory fibers throughout the cord, outside of the classical tracts. Thus, some of these important fibers remain functional in all but the most severe injury.

In cleanly penetrating wounds such as knife stabbings, there may be little associated cord dysfunction due to edema. This is in marked contrast to the situation of diffuse injury, as in violent blunt trauma or fracture-dislocation. Well-localized cord injuries provide insight into the structure and function of the nervous system. Such a case was reported by Brown-Sequard[48] in 1861, when he described the now classical syndrome of spinal cord hemisection. Brown-Sequard's patient suffered a stab wound that cleanly divided one side (lateral one-half) of his spinal cord. Immediately, there was complete paralysis below the lesion on the same side, accompanied by loss of deep tendon reflexes and superficial skin reflexes (i.e., spinal shock). The patient was unable to perceive the position of the lower limb on the side of the injury, could not detect motion when the limb was moved by the examiner, and had impaired ability to differentiate between a single stimulus and two stimuli applied there simultaneously. A narrow band of sensory loss was present at the level of the lesion on both sides. Sensibility to pain (pin-prick), temperature, and light touch remained otherwise intact on the side of the lesion, but were lost on the opposite side below the lesion. Although difficult to demonstrate clinically in thoracic lesions, in these injuries, there is also a band-like loss of skeletal motor (anterior horn cell) innervation and a vasomotor paralysis of similar distribution on the side of the lesion.

These findings are now known collectively as the Brown-Sequard syndrome. The classical picture is rarely seen, but numerous variants due to partial hemisection injuries are encountered among gunshot and stabbing wounds of the spine. The lesion is inordinately important for its instructive value, however, for it tells much about the organization of the human spinal cord.

The descending motor pathways (corticospinal tracts) and the ascending sensory pathways for position, kinesthesia (movement) and two-point discrimination (all in the dorsal or posterior white columns) run up the cord without crossing. It is known from other contexts that both tracts cross or "decussate" at higher levels. The dorsal column fibers synapse (make contact) with secondary neurons in the upper medulla oblongata of the brain stem; these secondary fibers decussate at once to form the medial lemniscus to the thalamus. The corticospinal tracts have no synapses en route, but they cross at a conspicuous decussation on the

[48] Brown-Sequard, E., *Lectures on the Diagnosis and Treatment of the Principal Forms of Paralysis of the Lower Extremities*, Collins, Philadelphia, 1861.

ventral surface of the neuraxis near the craniovertebral junction. This decussation is taken as the boundary between the upper cervical spinal cord and the lower border of the medulla oblongata of the brain stem.

Sensory fibers subserving pain and temperature sensations (the lateral spinothalamic tract) ascend one or two spinal segments from the level of entry, then cross near the central cord to take up their characteristic positions. These are actually secondary fibers, derived from synaptic contacts of the entering primary sensory fibers (with cell bodies in the dorsal root ganglia). They ascend without further crossing to the thalamus in the base of the brain. Interruption of the already-crossed fibers from one or two segments below accounts for the sensory loss of the opposite lower body. Finally, direct injury to the anterior horn cells and the intermediolateral cell column of sympathetic motor neurons accounts for the segmental loss, on the same side, of skeletal motor and vasomotor function.

§ 32.88. Other syndromes.

Complete cord transection results in segmental anterior horn cell and vasomotor loss on both sides at the level of the lesion. Irritation of dorsal root fibers entering at that level may give rise to a band of paresthesias (abnormal sensations, like "pins-and-needles") or radicular pain. Complete cord lesions are not rare in spinal trauma, whether caused by penetrating injury, crushing injury, or fracture-dislocation. Usually, however, there is some discrepancy between the level of lesion on the two sides. "Classical" lesions that correlate precisely with known neuroanatomy are quite uncommon, and bilateral lesions vary in cross-sectional area, left-right symmetry, and axial extent along the cord. Deficits frequently are incomplete, with patchy loss or diminution in the motor or diverse sensory spheres.

In the "acute anterior cervical spinal cord syndrome," the anterior and central regions of the cord are damaged, while the posterior (dorsal columns) are preserved. Motor strength is lost completely below the level of the lesion. The sensibilities of pain, temperature, and light touch are also diminished or lost. The sensibilities of position, kinesthesia, and two-point discrimination are preserved, so that a "sensory dissociation" results between the several modalities. This syndrome can be caused by direct mechanical trauma to the cord or by vascular impairment involving the anterior spinal artery.

A second syndrome has also been described: an acute central cervical spinal cord injury in which motor loss is greater in the arms than in the legs. The arms may be completely paralyzed, but the legs are merely weak. The bladder is nonfunctional, and urinary retention results. variable sensory loss occurs with no distinct pattern. This syndrome may result from insufficiency of the vertebral arterial blood supply or from cord contusion in cervical subluxation or fracture-dislocation injury. Contusion has been seen in severe hyperextension injuries, particularly where the cervical canal is narrowed anteriorly by osteophytes (bony spurs) or posteriorly by thickened ligamentum flavum.

Where a compressing herniated cervical disc is suspected, emergency myelogram using water soluble radiopaque dyes, plus computerized tomography (CT) or magnetic resonance imaging (MRI) of the spine and spinal cord may clearly define the presence of an acute herniated disc or other cause of compression, such as hematoma or bone fragments. The current diagnostic test of choice in this situation is MRI. The use of these studies sometimes eliminates the need for immediate surgical exploration.

§32.89. Autonomic effects.

Interruption of descending sympathetic nervous system pathways in the spinal cord leads to loss of sweating and temperature control mechanisms (piloerection) below the lesion on the same side. Loss of vasomotor tone in the same distribution causes impairment of circulatory reflexes. Marked postural hypotension (low blood pressure) results, with precipitous fall in the venous return and systemic blood pressure when the patient is placed in head-up position.

Disturbance of the delicately balanced mechanisms for bladder function is another serious consequence. Both sympathetic and parasympathetic innervation is involved. In the early posttraumatic period of spinal shock, the bladder is hypotonic or flaccid. Urine accumulates and leads to marked distention of the bladder musculature, with possibly permanent effects. Early mechanical drainage via intermittent urinary bladder catheterization is needed to prevent this complication. Later, some degree of bladder recovery occurs. Several types of "neurogenic bladder" may develop, each deficient in motor power, sensation or both. With spinal cord (upper motor neuron) lesions, the patient typically develops a spastic bladder with limited capacity. With cauda equina (lower motor neuron) lesions, the patient typically develops a large, hypotonic bladder. Common to them all is inadequate bladder emptying, urinary retention, and potential for infection. Often, ascending urinary infections lead to kidney infections (pyelonephritis) or stone formation (nephrocalcinoses). Kidney complications, specifically renal insufficiency brought on as a result of the above disorders, is probably the leading cause of death in paraplegics several years after the injury.

Loss of rectal sphincter tone and sensation, and impairment of colonic-evacuation reflexes, leads to constipation, fecal impaction, and rectal incontinence. Vigilant bowel care is needed to avoid obstipation (intractable constipation), and observant nursing care is needed to avoid skin breakdown due to the incontinence. The personal embarrassment caused by fecal incontinence is obvious.

Sexual potency also frequently suffers. Priapism, which is a sustained penile erection in the absence of appropriate stimulation, is a troublesome complication of serious cord injury above the sacral outflow. The mechanism of priapism is not fully understood, but is thought to result from vascular engorgement of the corpora cavernosa of the penis due to decreased vasoconstrictor sympathetic tone. The mechanism of ejaculation appears to depend in part on activity of sympathetic centers between the sixth thoracic and third lumbar vertebrae; this function also may be deficient.

§ 32.90. Metabolic factors.

Marked anorexia (loss of appetite) and weight loss often occur in serious spinal injury. This appears due largely to the catabolic condition of increased protein breakdown that follows trauma, which is difficult to reverse by dietary means. Inanition (weakened physical condition resulting from lack of food) is enhanced by the poor oral intake of patients with paralytic ileus (inhibited bowel motility). Anemia and tendency to edema (fluid accumulation) result.

There is a marked tendency of insensitive skin to atrophy and breakdown. Impaired temperature regulation and sweating mechanisms may contribute to this fragility. Lack of sensation and motor paralysis prevent the small frequent postural adjustments that occur normally and tend to relieve local skin pressure and prevent such breakdown.

Infection of the bladder or of open decubitus ulcers of the skin accelerate the catabolic process. Appetite is further depressed by the toxic effects of the infection, even while caloric consumption is increased by fever. This sorry cycle is better prevented than treated, but vigorous nursing care is needed to this end. Pressure on protruding bony prominences must be avoided by careful padding and frequent turning. The skin must be kept dry and free of soiling.

The further metabolic hazard of renal stones has been mentioned. Accelerated mobilization of calcium in the bedridden patient leads to an increase in the urine. Unless a good state of hydration is maintained, precipitation to form calcium stones is likely. Alterations of urinary acidity (pH) by bladder or kidney infections also tends to enhance stone formation.

§ 32.91. Psychological factors.

The psychological aspects in spinal injury are profound. Trauma frequently strikes the young and fit, the athletic, the young parent and breadwinner. The victim suddenly assumes the role of invalid, more or less helpless, unable to perform usual vocational and family duties. Loss of self-esteem may be severe, to the point of contemplated or attempted suicide in some. Pharmacological treatment of depression may be indicated. A positive but realistic approach can help these persons accept their handicaps and regain maximum possible function. Recent years have seen the development of spinal injury centers, staffed with teams of specialists. These coordinated approaches offer much hope for successful rehabilitation. But, as always, the insecurities of funding must be faced. Thus, the actual delivery of care may fall short of the otherwise presently attainable ideal.

XII. DIAGNOSIS IN SPINAL AND SPINAL CORD INJURIES

§ 32.92. Introduction.

As medical sophistication advances, detailed technical examinations become commonplace. Under the stimulus of increasing litigation potential, many examinations are carried out solely for legal reasons, with adverse effects on the economics of medical care. A "me-too" attitude prevails, in which some practitioners adopt whatever new test is proclaimed important by an "expert"—often an academician with strong research bent, but restricted clinical practice. The result is a spiraling pattern of complexity and cost as the profession struggles to "do everything" and avoid exposure to lawsuit. It is unfortunate that medical practice is burdened by the need for this defensive posture. Still it cannot be denied that the patient stands to benefit by studies, carefully chosen, from this ever-increasing catalogue of tests.

§ 32.93. Initial examination.

The clinical method[49] of diagnosis is based upon the patient's medical history and physical examination. This method is as valid today as ever. Clinical judgment remains the best guide to the selection of suitable technical procedures to document critical diagnoses or to differentiate between diagnostic alternatives when the treatment depends upon this distinction (e.g., a fractured cervical vertebra versus a cervical sprain).

The medical history is especially valuable in dictating initial management of injury. A paraplegic patient with a single bullet wound in the midback, with the bullet lodged in a vertebral body, may be in shock from his spinal cord injury. In contrast, a paraplegic who broke his back in a motorcycle accident, and who likewise is in shock, needs urgent study for possible hemorrhage from ruptured internal organs. The patient with painful neck injury suffered in a low-velocity auto collision may be studied for extent of injury on arrival at the hospital, whereas a patient with partial paralysis from a fall on his neck must be protected

[49]Editor's Note: The "clinical method" pertains to the clinic or bedside, founded upon actual observation of patients before and after treatment, as distinguished from the theoretical or experimental approach.

zealously while limited essential information is gathered about a possible cervical fracture. In such a patient, studies involving rotation, flexion or stress on the spine must be eschewed until nonstressed studies such as plain X-rays and computed tomography (CT scan) have defined the likelihood of spinal instability.

Priorities must be assigned in emergency care of the injured. The bleeding patient with respiratory distress must be assured an airway before elaborate attempts to stem the bleeding are undertaken. Decompression of an injured spinal cord must await repair of massively bleeding internal organs, and so on.

In cervical injuries, the history suggests the type if not the degree of injury. Flexion injuries, as produced by severe blows or falls on the back of the head, may produce highly unstable fracture-dislocations of the upper spine. Extension injuries, especially when combined with turning of the head, are much more likely to produce stable fractures of the posterior structures (laminae or articular facets).

The initial examination should include a survey of all major systems for unsuspected injury. With regard to the spine, the examining physician should look for the presence of deformity, pain, and limitation of motion. Grossly visible angulation or palpable steppage in the contour of the spine usually denotes severe injury to bone and supporting ligaments, and is likely to be associated with neurological deficits. Spontaneous pain, or the production of pain by pressure over bony structures, alerts one to the possibility of fracture or ligamentous damage (sprain). Inability of the patient to bend through a normal range of motion may indicate direct muscle injury or reflex muscle spasm due to other structural damage.

The spinal cord and peripheral nerves are examined by inference, through evidence of loss of function. Motor weakness or paralysis may result from either, but the pattern of paralysis will differ. Injury to one side of the cord produces the Brown-Sequard syndrome (§ 32.87). Ordinarily, variants of this pattern (motor and position sense loss on the side of the lesion, and loss of pain and temperature sensation on the other side, all below the lesion) will be seen. The location of an injury to the spinal cord can usually be localized precisely by careful physical examination alone.

Peripheral nerve injuries result in motor or sensory losses, or both. Frequently, the sensory complaint is of "numbness" or "pins-and-needles" sensations in a limb below an injury. The acute injury is not particularly painful, although exposed nervous tissue in a wound does give rise to unpleasant paresthesias and shock-like tingling. A number of well-defined patterns of loss are known in peripheral nerve injury, and these are detailed in Part XVI of this chapter.

§ 32.94. Radiography.

Plain radiographs (X-rays) of the spine have become standard practice in most injuries or painful conditions in which spinal injury is considered. There is no simpler or more useful screening examination for bony fracture or displacement. However, when the findings on examination are limited to muscle pain or spasm, the prospects are slim for findings of significance on plain X-ray.

In suspected "ruptured discs," the plain X-ray films usually show little of diagnostic value. In the lumbar spine, there may be changes of degeneration with altered disc space, but these findings are widespread in the population and poorly correlated with clinical symptoms. In painful back syndromes, X-rays may confirm the clinical observation that the back is held to one side or the other to minimize the pain. The normal cervical or lumbar curves may be reduced or lost due to muscle spasm after trauma. Caution is needed to avoid overinterpretation of such "soft" findings, since up to 70% of uninjured necks lose the lordotic curve when the patient lies supine on an X-ray table (the usual position in the emergency room X-ray unit). In the thorax, the spinal canal bounds the delicate cord more snugly, leaving little space for displaced bone, disc material, or tumor growth before signs of spinal cord or root injury appear. The region of most concern remains the neck, with its greater mobility and risk of injury. Here, as in the thorax, a reduction in the radiolucent intervertebral disc space is more likely to herald a clinically significant disc protrusion.

The lateral cervical spine film is the first to be obtained in most cases of suspected cervical injury, for it is the view most likely to reveal serious injury. It is essential to visualize all vertebrae down to the cervicothoracic junction (seventh cervical and first thoracic); numerous celebrated instances of fracture-dislocation have been missed when they lay unrevealed in the shadow of a bulky shoulder which overlays the region. A second standard view is the anterior-posterior, or "A-P," which shows major spinal angulation, rotation, and displacement. In the "open-mouth A-P," the crucial odontoid process of the second cervical vertebra is seen to best advantage; this is an essential view when neck pain or limitation of motion result from flexion-extension injuries of the neck.

If the injury is slight by physical examination, oblique views may be done to show the intervertebral foramina and pedicles. The latter may be fractured and displaced into the foramen, with compression of the nerve roots therein. Some evaluation of the articular pillars can be made from the oblique views, but some authors suggest a caudally angled view to visualize both sides at once. If stability appears good, one may proceed cautiously to lateral views of the neck in flexion and extension. These maneuvers bring out excessive displacement of one vertebral body over another when ligamentous injury is present. Inability to obtain good films often results from pain-limited neck movements, and in such a case, suspicion must remain high that structural damage exists even if none is demonstrated on the films. If there is a reasonable suspicion of significant bony injury or instability, or if there is evidence of cervical cord injury, a better course is to forego these several views and proceed to CT scans of the neck.

Plain X-rays of the spine, despite their limitations, are definitely indicated to help differentiate between possible herniated disc and other painful conditions. Several disorders have characteristic X-ray appearances. Osteomyelitis is an inflammation of bone and often of surrounding structures, caused by an infectious organism. Osteoarthritis is a degenerative noninfectious process which leads to formation of often painful bony spurs and increased bone density at the edges of joint surfaces. Developmental anomalies include spina bifida (cleft spine resulting from imperfect closure of the embryonic sclerotomes) and spondylolisthesis in which one vertebra slips over another and produces stress concentrations on adjacent ligaments. Metabolic disorders such as hyperparathyroidism and Paget's disease cause sclerosis or increased calcium density in affected bones, and are sometimes productive of pain. Fractures may be traumatic or pathological, *i.e.*, resulting from weakening of bone by demineralization (osteoporosis) or lysis (as by tumor).

Finally, plain spine X-rays are a technical aid to the neuroradiologist or surgeon who contemplates contrast studies (§ 32.95) or surgery.

§ 32.95. Myelography.

Bony injury to the vertebral column is of concern *per se* because of the pain and disability that result, and because its presence dictates a period of rest and limited activity to facilitate healing. Ligamentous sprains have a similar significance. In either case, healing usually occurs in due course. Either injury may be shown on plain films by altered density of bony shadows, irregularities of cortical outline, or by physical displacement.

Even more important is injury to the nervous system elements enclosed within the spinal canal, namely, the spinal cord and roots. Not only pain, but the ability to move and feel, and to carry out the body's functions, are at stake. The spinal cord is exquisitely delicate and has been known to suffer permanent dysfunction merely from gentle retraction to one side during surgery. The nerve roots also are delicate, but their flexibility and mobility reduce the chance of injury. The spinal nerves at the intervertebral foramina have the qualities of peripheral nerves and can withstand traction and pressure forces with less dysfunction and better prospects of recovery than can the spinal cord.

Nervous tissue is not shown by usual X-ray techniques. Muscle, blood clot, body fluids, and nervous tissue all have similar radiodensities. A technique of great utility for demonstrating the spinal cord and roots is positive contrast myelography. A radio-opaque contrast fluid is introduced into the subarachnoid space of the spinal canal via needle puncture of the lumbar or upper cervical meninges. Normally, a sample of spinal fluid is removed at this opportunity, and studied for protein, cell counts, and serology (test for syphilis). These results may suggest an etiology of the condition under consideration in certain atypical cases.

Myelography provides an indirect disclosure of a lesion in the spinal canal. Normally, the contrast material ("dye") surrounds the spinal cord and roots, out to the limits of the surrounding dural sac. In the low lumbar region of common interest, the slender and long nerve roots may be barely seen or not at all, save where they penetrate the dura at the segmental outpouchings. Since the spinal cord itself terminates at the first lumbar level above, the cord is not visualized at the low lumbar level. The symmetrical fullness of the normal lumbar sac is exemplified in the illustration. When a disc or other lesion impinges on the nervous tissue space, it is shown by the absence of dye in its usual place. The dural sac appears "indented," and the nerve roots may be seen to be pushed aside.

A "positive" myelogram is not the *sine qua non* for diagnosis of ruptured disc or spinal axis lesion, which was once the popular belief. In fact, the number of myelograms performed has been considerably reduced in favor of magnetic resonance imaging (MRI). Actually, the above diagnoses can often be made with reasonable certainty from the patient's medical history and physical examination. Sudden onset, an association with physical stress, characteristic radiating pain in dermatomal (skin area) distribution that increases with lifting, bending, and straining at the stool — all tend to favor the clinical diagnosis of intervertebral disc protrusion or "ruptured disc." Reproduction of the radiating pain by elevation of the leg also supports the diagnosis. Sensory loss and reflex change, plus weakness in muscles supplied by the affected spinal nerve, help localize the lesion. (Electromyography (see §§ 32.152 to 32.156) also may be of aid here.)

The myelogram may fail to show the presence of a surgical intraspinal lesion, especially in the vicinity of the fifth lumbar and first sacral vertebrae. This is possible because of the presence of a spacious fat pad that surrounds the lumbar dural sac. A ruptured disc may lie within this space, exerting subtle but significant pressure on the nearby roots, yet not announce its presence by indentation of the contrast column. And too, a bony spur (osteophyte) without clinical import may imitate the indentation of a ruptured disc, and lead the examiner to a "false positive" diagnosis, and the patient to surgery.

Risks involved

Myelography is not without some risks, which, in itself, makes it important in a medicolegal discussion. In the short term, there is the very slight possibility of nerve root or spinal cord damage (depending on the level of puncture) by the myelography needle. Infectious organisms from the skin or atmosphere rarely may be introduced into the subarachnoid space, producing purulent meningitis. Protracted headache is known commonly to follow lumbar puncture and may last for days to weeks in severe instances. It is of interest that the incidence of such headache is correlated with the expectation, and that the fact of informing the patient about the possibility tends to bring it on. Finally, inflammation of the spinal roots and meninges may be incited by the dye, leading to the painful state of "arachnoiditis," with scar formation and fixation of roots to the arachnoid and dura in later months or years. It happens that late recurrent pain from this condition may mimic the original complaint, and lead the patient again to the surgeon's exploring knife in vain. Allergic reactions to the iodinated contrast material are known, and on rare occasions may be severe. Finally, the procedure is variably stressful to the patient; it may range from the inconsequential to the stoic, emotionally stable patient, to an anguishing torment for the anxious and nervous individual.[50]

For these reasons some clinicians have chosen to diagnose on clinical grounds and forego the possible benefits of myelography to avoid the risks and inconveniences. Other surgeons will require the additional information that myelography provides, especially where the clinical picture is not characteristic of a known disorder. The myelogram may help greatly in locating a migrating fragment of extruded nucleus pulposus that has traveled from its point of rupture to an unsuspected position in the epidural space. Myelography is best in those infrequent cases, unknown in advance except possibly by clinical intuition, when the lesion is a mass of abnormal blood vessels (arteriovenous malformation), or a tumor, or the scarring of arachnoiditis. The myelogram may reveal the presence of multiple lesions at more than one level and thereby save the patient from a second operation for a lesion left behind at surgery.

In summary, the myelogram is a likely aid, a possible hazard, sometimes dispensable and sometimes not, but, in unpredictable circumstances, it can be of invaluable utility in avoiding surgical error, and is still favored by many experienced clinicians. However, the procedure is not infallible and may misinform both about the presence of a surgically treatable lesion, and about its absence.

---

[50]Editor's Note: In a New York workers' compensation case, the claimant refused to submit to a myelogram because she felt it was too hazardous. She had suffered a lumbrosacral sprain in a fall in the company cafeteria, and her attending physician recommended myelography when she continued to complain of increased back pain long after her condition, if not serious, should have improved. In reviewing the case, the New York Supreme Court, Appellate Division, concluded that her fears were unjustified, that myelography was not hazardous, and that compensation benefits should be suspended. Zanotti v. New York Tel. Co. (1975) 48 App. Div. 2d 192, 368 N.Y.S.2d 880.

Gas myelography

When blood is present in the subarachnoid space, the use of iodine-containing contrast materials is thought to increase the risk of post-myelographic arachnoiditis. A typical case is one of spinal injury with loss of function, in which there is need to study the spinal canal for impingement of bone or disc on nervous tissue. Gas myelography (negative contrast myelography) has been employed more safely. Room air, oxygen, or carbon dioxide may be used. Special tomographic equipment must be available for an adequate study. Gas myelography is limited by the poorer resolution that results from the decreased contrast between tissue and gas, as compared to that between iodinated contrast "dye" and tissue. The risk of misdiagnosis makes the study unsuitable for many examinations for tumor and ruptured disc, although for foramen magnum tumors it has been a useful adjunctive test. Another drawback is the risk of introducing gas into the head, which can produce a severe headache characteristic of pneumoencephalography. For these reasons, the procedure is rapidly becoming obsolete.

How myelography is performed

Most patients tolerate myelography without event. At best, it is an inconvenience with little pain. For the anxious patient, however, it may be a trial of anguish and torment. The patient's confidence is essential to a happy outcome. His cooperation aids greatly in obtaining maximum information from the test and is essential for doing the test at all. The necessary rapport can be created in many cases if the examiner informs the patient in advance about the test and what can be expected. The examiner should answer questions and allay the often wildly imaginative fears that some patients harbor. The unfounded spectre of paralysis haunts the minds of many. Tale has fed tale, so that the "spinal tap" has come to represent a frightening ordeal to many.

The procedure is carried out in the X-ray suite, with provision for fluoroscopy and regular X-ray films at hand. Rapport is maintained and anxiety should be allayed by an explanation of each step prior to its performance. The patient's back is cleansed with antiseptic solution. The site of puncture should be selected to avoid a needle entry at a level where a lesion is suspected, so that perplexing "needle artifacts" will not obscure the real findings. The selected site should lie below the first and second lumbar interspace if at all possible, for at that level the conus medullaris of the lower spinal cord begins. A small-gauge needle is used to infiltrate the proposed puncture site with local anesthetic. Under favorable circumstances, this may be the most painful part of the procedure. Next, a twenty or twenty-two gauge lumbar puncture needle, with internal stylet to prevent entry of blood and tissues into the tip of the needle as it moves, is passed through the anesthetized skin into the spinal canal.

A patient's distress increases sharply if a misdirected needle fails to enter the spinal canal promptly and multiple puncture attempts are required. This may happen if there is much bony change of the arthritic type, as in the elderly; when the spine is curved or rotated, as in scoliosis; when the fluid-bearing subarachnoid space is distorted and diminished by the scarring or arachnoiditis; when the subarachnoid space is "dry" due to a blockage of the spinal canal by disc, tumor or bony spurs; when the patient is restless and uncooperative; or when the examiner is inexperienced or just "off-stride." Several of these impediments can be overcome through judicious use of fluoroscopy to guide the passage of the needle to its target.

Deep penetration of a lumbar puncture needle through the muscles, interspinous ligaments and dura mater is only slightly painful, and is easily tolerated on a single pass. On multiple attempts, anxiety mounts and distress escalates. Sometimes, the needle tip contacts an intradural nerve root, producing shock-like or burning pain that radiates into the distribution of the affected root. Repetitions of this unpleasantness also sour the patient's recollections of the occasion. Some examiners anticipate the worst and medicate the patient with sedatives and narcotic analgesics before the test.

Entry of the needle tip into the subarachnoid space is usually felt as a characteristic "popping" sensation as the dura is penetrated. When the stylet is withdrawn, a flow of clear cerebrospinal fluid is usually found. The pressure may be measured by attaching a manometer to the hub of the needle. Cerebrospinal fluid dynamics may be evaluated when spinal block is considered as a possibility.

Next, the patient is positioned face-down on a motorized tilting table and carefully secured with padded straps and pillows. Under fluoroscopic control, several cubic centimeters (from 6 to 15 cc.) of iodinated contrast material are introduced through the needle and allowed to pool in the bottom of the lumbar sac. Thereafter, the patient is maneuvered by turning and tilting the table, so that the heavier-than-water (and cerebrospinal fluid) contrast material flows by gravity into all regions of interest. As the head is lowered, contrast material flows up the spinal canal, outlining the nerve roots and spinal cord throughout the length of the spine. If indicated, the spinal needle is removed, and the patient turned on his back to permit better visualization of the posterior cord surface and subarachnoid space. The dye may be carried to the foramen magnum and base of the skull if desired. Throughout the procedure, the progress of the dye is monitored on the fluoroscope screen and representative "spot films" and full-size X-rays are taken to document the presence or absence of pathological lesions. In lumbar myelography for suspected disc disease, attention is focused in turn on the fifth lumbar and first

sacral and fourth and fifth lumbar interspaces, then on the higher interspaces up to the midthorax. The low thorax must always be visualized
since lesions here may mimic disease of the lumbar spine, and might
otherwise be missed.

Headache for one to several days is not uncommon after myelography
or even after lumbar puncture alone. The reasons for this are speculated
to be a leakage of cerebrospinal fluid through the puncture site in the
lumbar meninges into the soft tissue of the back. This is thought to
reduce the buoyant support of the brain by the fluid, and produce traction on pain-sensitive bridging veins between the brain and dura mater
of the skull. Ordinarily, mild analgesics and bed rest for a day or two are
adequate therapy. In exceptional cases, headaches have been relieved
after many weeks by means of a "dural patch," produced by injecting
several cubic centimeters of the patient's own blood into the tissues surrounding the puncture site. Spillage of contrast material into the intracranial cavity generally causes exacerbation of the headache.

For many years, nonwater-soluble contrast material (Pantopaque) was
used, and the practice was to attempt to remove as much as possible at
the completion of the study. Today, almost all myelography is performed
with water-soluble, iodinated contrast, which is completely absorbed
within twenty-four to forty-eight hours and need not be removed. Another advantage of the water-soluble contrast is that the patient may
undergo computerized tomography (CT) while the contrast is present,
which greatly enhances the quality of diagnostic information that can be
gained by the clinician.

Ultimately a decision must be made about treatment. As noted above,
technical procedures are valuable aids, but they are not infallible. Sometimes the radiologist and clinician differ in interpretation of the myelographic study. In such cases, the clinical information must dictate the
course of management. Since it is the surgical specialist who has the
broadest knowledge of the problem, it is usually best to accept his or her
judgment as to what should be done.

§ 32.95a. Computerized tomography (CT scan).

The increasing use of computer tomography (CT scan) in the evaluation of the spine has added a new dimension to the radiographic examination of patients exhibiting a wide variety of spinal disorders. Computerized tomography of the spine is particularly beneficial in examining
the patient who has sustained acute trauma to the vertebrae with or
without injury to the spinal cord or nerve roots. Any area of the spine
can be examined immediately following routine X-rays to define not only
bony injury, but also the presence and extent of disc prolapse, cord swelling, intra- or extradural hemorrhage, displacement of bone fragments
into neural elements, and the extent of vertebral displacement.

Computerized tomography examinations of the spine immediately following myelography using water-soluble dyes provide a means for even more accurately defining the degree of displacement of the dural sac by hematoma, disc prolapse, bony fragments, and vertebral displacement. Similarly, computerized tomography of the spine, either with or without the introduction of water-soluble contrast media, provides even better definition of disc prolapse in both the cervical and lumbar regions where compression of either the nerve root or the spinal cord by herniated disc is suspected. Computer reconstruction of the images in a sagittal plane is useful in defining the degree of narrowing of the spinal canal by arthritic bars in both the lumbar and cervical canal. Congenital or acquired stenosis of the spinal canal can be defined with great accuracy using the CT scan to obtain multiple transverse sections through the spinal canal at the appropriate level as determined by preliminary plain X-rays.

§ 32.95b. Magnetic resonance imaging.

Magnetic resonance imaging (MRI) involves the absorption and emission of electromagnetic energy by nuclei in a static magnetic field after excitation by radiofrequency pulses. Through this combination, information can be obtained regarding the location and interrelation of atomic nuclei within the human body. A computer then generates an image similar to a computerized tomography scan.

This relatively new technique has received wide clinical application, and some authorities believe that eventually it will replace myelography altogether. The technique involves no radiation exposure and provides visualization of the spine and its neural elements, the spinal cord and nerve roots, the brain, and many other structures. If a spinal tumor is suspected, MRI is the test of choice; however, the procedure is not the best method for imaging bone.

§ 32.96. Discography.

Discography is an alternative method of investigating lesions of the intervertebral discs. In this technique, a long needle is passed through the skin of the back, beside but not through the spinal sac, and into each of several disc spaces in the region under study. (**Fig. 17.**) Usually there are two parts to the study. In the first, the disc space is distended with saline to reproduce the patient's pain symptoms, then the pain is relieved with injected local anesthetic. If these maneuvers are consistent, the conclusion is reached that the patient's pain is due to disease at that level. In the second phase, radio-opaque contrast material is injected directly into the disc space, through the same needle, and X-rays taken. Ruptured discs produce a rent or tear in the posterior longitudinal ligament and/or annulus fibrosus, and the tear and the disc fragment tract are often shown by extravasated dye that leaks along the pathway of the

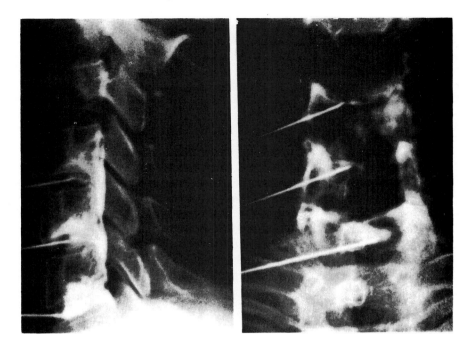

Fig. 17. Cervical discograms. Left: lateral. Right: antero-posterior. Made by the injection of approximately 0.5 cc. of 35% diodrast into the intervertebral spaces between C4-5, C5-6, and C6-7. The discs at all three interspaces are degenerated.

fragment. Possible points of confusion are the fact that the needle itself makes a tract and rent in the annulus, and may produce a spurious "false positive" test. Also, finding of extravasated dye alone does not prove that pain or disability is arising from that level; the first phase of pain reproduction and anaesthetic relief help prevent this misinterpretation. A final limitation of this alternative to myelography is that it tells nothing of the status of the intraspinal canal and the spinal cord and roots, i.e., it does not show directly the impingement on nervous tissue.

Critics of discography once claimed that too many false-positive results show up in discograms of normal cervical spines; that relatively few normal cervical discograms are obtained in individuals who have passed the age of thirty; and that, as a result, plaintiffs' attorneys routinely directed their clients to willing physicians for discograms.[51] Proponents of cervical discography argued that critics condemned the procedure because "they expect it to be a laboratory test that will *make* a positive diagnosis, *localize* the disk lesion, and give indisputable indication for surgical treatment."[52] According to one of the originators of the proce-

[51] Holt, E. P., Jr., *Further Reflections on Cervical Discography*, 231 J.A.M.A. 613, 1975.

[52] *Cervical Discography Defendant* (Letter), 233 J.A.M.A. 862, 1975.

dure, Ralph B. Cloward, M.D., cervical discography was devised "to assist in, or to confirm, the diagnosis of a symptomatic cervical disk lesion in which the pathology and localization are known or suspected from clinical information." If the results of the discogram do not coincide with clinical findings, said Cloward, the procedure should be disregarded in favor of other diagnostic techniques.[53] The early controversy over the procedure has died down, however: with the development of neuroimaging procedures such as MRI, discography now has limited utility.

§ 32.97. Electrodiagnosis.

Certain electrical properties of nerve and muscle are useful in evaluating the locus and degree of injury, and in following the progress of recovery after injury. Electrical stimulation may be applied to the motor nerve of a skeletal muscle, ordinarily via electrodes placed on the skin over the course of the nerve. The nerve becomes excited to the point of "firing" or impulse conduction. The nerve impulse travels along a fiber to the neuromuscular junction, where chemical transmitter (acetylcholine) is released.

The skin resistance is an electrical property of the skin, and is markedly affected by the pseudomotor activity of the skin (under sympathetic nervous system control). When a nerve is interrupted, the denervated region of skin shows a markedly increased skin resistance. The size of the abnormal area may identify the nerve(s) of supply. In recovery, progressive decrease in size of the affected area suggests that nerve regeneration is proceeding, while a stationary region suggests that no regeneration is taking place. While this process was once thought promising in evaluating nerve injury, it has lost favor and is rarely used today.

The above should not be confused with electromyography, which is a valuable technique in the diagnosis of lower motor neuron disorders such as motor neuron disease, nerve root disease, plexus lesions, and peripheral neuropathy. This procedure involves investigation of the intrinsic electrical activity of muscle fibers and is usually performed in conjunction with the determination of nerve conduction velocities.

See Part XVIII of this chapter for a discussion of electromyography.

XIII. TREATMENT OF SPINAL AND SPINAL CORD INJURIES

§ 32.98. First aid.

The primary objective of the care of spinal injuries is to safeguard the function of the nervous system. Secondary objectives are the relief of pain and suffering, and the minimization of deformity. Obviously a pa-

---

[53] Id.

tient who has evidence of neurological involvement should be moved with extreme care to prevent further injury to the spinal cord. With a suspected cervical injury, first aid involves splinting of the neck with sandbags until the patient is taken to the hospital. If the injury is below the neck, the patient should be placed on a rigid stretcher, and any movement of the body should be avoided. Of course, other essential needs must be ministered to. The patient who chokes or aspirates vomitus while immobilized on his back should be turned face down so that the airway may be cleared. Once the patient arrives at the hospital, a thorough neurological examination should be done.

§ 32.99.   Treatment of spinal column injury.[54]

If a patient has suffered a bony injury to the spine without evidence of neurologic involvement, the patient should be treated according to the severity of the injury. The aims are to reduce the misalignment and stabilize disrupted joints. Usually rest in bed and later immobilization with a cast or a brace are all that is necessary. In cervical spine injuries, skeletal traction should be immediately applied in order to realign the deformed vertebrae. This is accomplished by the use of skeletal traction utilizing Gardner-Wells tongs or halo. The aim here is to prevent injury to the spinal cord itself. If the fracture or fracture dislocation is unstable and the vertebral body is badly compressed or even shattered, fusion may be indicated. The amount of traction needed for the reduction of the fracture varies. In upper cervical spine injuries, ten to fifteen pounds may be all that is necessary, but in lower cervical spine injuries more traction has to be applied, up to twenty to thirty pounds for several hours, before the realignment of the vertebrae can be accomplished. Frequent X-ray examination while applying weights will aid in achieving the appropriate degree of traction.

After reduction of spinal deformity is accomplished and spinal cord compression or nerve root compression has been corrected or ruled out, fixation is then instituted by means of bracing, halo-vest application, or body cast or jacket, depending upon the type and location of the instability.

Linear fractures of the laminar and transverse processes should be treated by immobilization and only rarely is surgery indicated. Minor cervical spine injuries can be treated by immobilization with a soft collar. Mild injuries of the thoracic or lumbar spine may have to be treated symptomatically with the use of analgesics and muscle relaxant medication.

The most common types of vertebral injuries are compression fractures. Depending on the magnitude, there may be some transient neuro-

---

[54]Editor's Note: Treatment of spinal column injury is also discussed in Chapter 16 of this Cyclopedia.

logic deficit that disappears on immobilization. This type of mild injury is most commonly produced by a fall onto the buttocks or a sudden loading of the spine by falling weight from above. A medical cause has been electroshock therapy for severe psychiatric disorders in which the resultant tonic-clonic convulsive movements are sufficiently severe to collapse one or more vertebral bodies. (Electroshock therapy is now usually done under general anesthesia, which reduces this risk.) Often the anterior surface of a vertebral body collapses, producing a wedge-shaped vertebra in the lateral X-ray view. Low thoracic and upper lumbar vertebrae are most often involved, with 60% at the twelfth thoracic to the second lumbar. Simple compression fractures are usually stable, and, if minor in degree, are treated like the simple linear fractures described above.

More severe compression fractures do better if immobilized, as in a body brace or cast, usually in hyperextension. A spring device for treatment of thoracolumbar fractures has been developed that attaches to the lamina of healthy vertebrae on either side of the fracture. The pull of the strong springs keeps the spine in extension during the period of healing and beyond.

Indications for surgery

Criteria for surgical intervention in major spinal column injuries such as fracture dislocation vary with the surgeon, but certain guidelines are widely agreed upon. Surgery is indicated in spinal injuries: (1) where there is an appearance of neurological deficit that progresses and a surgically correctable lesion is identified; (2) where there is instability that is likely to persist even after prolonged external immobilization; and (3) when there are compound fractures that are obviously contaminated and involve the spinal canal.

"Halo-vest" apparatus

The halo-vest method of external fixation is widely used in unstable cervical spinal injuries and may obviate the need for internal fixation with or without fusion. Also, the halo vest may be used for immobilization after surgical fusion until the fusion has healed. A metal ring (the "halo") is attached to the skull via four threaded pins around the periphery. Each pin is sunk into the outer portion of the skull (outer table) by tightening with a calibrated torque wrench under local anesthesia. These pins securely attach the ring to the skull. The ring then is supported by four metal posts, which in turn are attached to the patient's torso via a body cast or plastic jacket. The assembly is light in weight, yet strong and stable. It provides the numerous advantages of early mobilization; lessened skin irritation from prolonged bed confinement; decreased calcium mobilization and excretion associated with recumbency with lessened chance of renal or ureteral stone formation; avoidance of muscle atrophy from inactivity; maintenance of cardiovascular tone and postural reflexes; and improvement in morale by reducing boredom and dependency. Some problems associated with the apparatus are skin irritation, where the cast rests on the iliac regions, and malodorous aromas due to restricted bathing under the body cast. Occasionally, the pins may penetrate the skull and cause subdural empyema or brain abscess.

§ 32.100. Treatment of spinal cord injury.

The treatment of spinal cord injury is an area of active interest, although still with often less than gratifying results. Open or contaminated wounds warrant surgical cleaning (debridement) and closure, if possible, to reduce the likelihood of infection in the spine and nervous system. Clean stab wounds may not need to be explored, depending on the clinical condition of the patient. Missile wounds have less predictable consequences.

If the patient has lost every evidence of neurologic function below the lesion at the time of the accident, and on arrival to the hospital shows complete loss of motor power and sensory loss below the lesion, one can assume that the trauma probably has been severe enough to cause either an anatomical section or at least a physiological transection of the spinal cord. Under those circumstances, surgery is only rarely indicated. However, such a patient may be in spinal shock (§ 32.83).

Occasionally, a witness to the accident makes a statement that, immediately after the trauma, the patient sat up or even walked. In these cases, if a CT scan or MRI are not available, the surgeon may decide that exploration is in order to decompress the spinal cord, the rationale being that something happened after the accident to make the patient completely paralyzed. Possibly there is bleeding at the site of the trauma or a herniated disc pressing on the spinal cord. The results from such surgery however, are usually disappointing. If CT or MRI are available, usually exploratory surgery is unnecessary.

Results of surveys during the Vietnam conflict showed that, despite prompt treatment, no victims of a complete cord deficit following injury exhibited any signs of recovery, even when the cord appeared normal at operation. On the other On the other hand, patients who have sustained spinal cord injury that is not complete and shows some evidence of neurologic function below the lesion present an entirely different situation. If the lesion is in the cervical spine and a deformity is present, these patients should be placed on skeletal traction immediately and the bony canal restored to normal if possible. This in itself may decompress the spinal cord and accelerate return of function.

When dislocation is present in the thoracic or lumbar spine, if reduction is indicated, it usually requires an open operation with fixation, using metal rods in conjunction with fusion.

If a patient who has sustained a partial cord injury begins to deteriorate rather than improve, every effort should be made to find out the cause. A CT scan or MRI should be done, and if a block or some obstruction is found, surgery should be carried out to decompress the spinal cord. The decompression may be in the form of a laminectomy (removal of the posterior arch of the vertebra) if the pressure is from the back, or an anterior decompression followed by a fusion if the pressure is in the front. However, with some exceptions, most patients who have a partial cord injury, and whose spinal canal is not very deformed as revealed by X-ray, will do nicely under immobilization and conservative treatment.

§ 32.101. High-dose corticosteroid therapy for cord injury.

There has been a long-standing interest in developing some form of emergency treatment that might preserve function after spinal cord injury. In 1990, Bracken and colleagues reported beneficial effects on subsequent neurological function if high-dose corticosteroids were administered within eight hours of a cord injury. This practice has now become widely accepted in the emergency management of these patients. The recommended regimen is the administration of a 30 mg/kg intravenous bolus of methylprednisolone followed by 5.4 mg/kg per hour for twenty-three hours.[55] Other substances, including naloxone and GM1 ganglioside, have not been found to provide a definite protective effect.

There is also considerable interest in the application of substances to promote the regeneration of neural tissue after cord injury. Currently, the focus is primarily on nerve-growth factors, although at this time, this research remains experimental.

XIV. INTERVERTEBRAL DISC PROTRUSIONS

§ 32.102. Introduction.[56]

Herniations of the intervertebral disc are common. Usually, the patient claims that he hurt his back while doing some lifting or bending

---

[55] Bracken, M. R., et al., *Methylprednisolone or Naloxone Treatment After Acute Spinal Cord Injury*, 322 N. Engl. J. Med. 1405, 1990; Bracken, M. R., et al., *A Randomized Controlled Trial of Methylprednisolone or Naloxone in Treatment of Acute Spinal Cord Injury: One-Year Follow-Up Data*, 76 J. Neurosurg. 23, 1992.

[56] Editor's Note: The lawyer should be aware that two different specialists commonly treat patients with intervertebral disc protrusion — the orthopedist and the neurosurgeon. Either may be equipped by training and experience to treat the condition successfully. Historically, the orthopedist struggled with low back and sciatic pain problems long before neurosurgery emerged as a specialty. At first, brain and spinal tumors and nerve repairs were the principal work of the neurosurgeon. In the course of operating for a suspected spinal tumor, pioneer neurosurgeons occasionally removed a "cartilaginous tumor" that, in retrospect, was a disc protrusion. A neurosurgeon and an orthopedist (W. J. Mixter and J. S. Barr) collaborated in the discovery

over to pick up a heavy object from the floor, often something that he has been doing for years without any trouble.

In the case of the employee performing physical labor, we find co-workers doing the same type of work, day in and day out, who go through life to retirement without developing ruptured discs. On the other hand, a person who does sedentary work may develop such a lesion by barely bending over to tie his own shoes. In order to explain this, we have to refer again to the anatomy of the spinal column. The intervertebral discs are located between each vertebra. The nucleus pulposus is a hyalin cartilage (jelly-like material) that is enclosed by the cartilaginous plate of the vertebra above and the one below. The annulus fibrosus protects and holds the nucleus pulposus in place. Then, there are the anterior and posterior spinal ligaments that reinforce the annulus fibrosus. This ligament is very strong in the midline and fades away in the lateral aspects of the intervertebral disc.

The function of the normal intervertebral disc is to allow mobility to the spine. When compression takes place, the pressure exerted is transmitted in all directions and the consistency of the nucleus pulposus is not affected.

But with age and minor traumas, weakness of the joints may allow the nucleus pulposus to be traumatized. This will cause a loss of fluid, so that the nucleus pulposus, which once behaved as a liquid, begins to behave as a solid. When pressure is applied to the front of the nucleus pulposus, the reaction is for the disc to shift backwards against the annulus fibrosus. Since the weaker part of the annulus fibrosus is its lateral aspect, when enough pressure is exerted, the nucleus pulposus may rupture the annulus and herniate, pressing on the nerve and causing pain in the distribution of the affected nerve roots.

Synonyms for intervertebral disc protrusions include "herniated disc," "ruptured disc," "slipped disc," "disc syndrome," and "herniated nucleus pulposus."

§ 32.103. Clinical picture.

The clinical picture of a ruptured disc may vary from very acute to a chronic situation. The most common history is that of a patient in the middle thirties or forties with recurring attacks of lower back pain, usu-

---

of the disc protrusion as a proven clinical entity in 1934. Some orthopedists consider that removal of bone, ligaments, and fibro-cartilage makes laminectomy (removal of portion of vertebra) exclusively an orthopedic procedure. A large group of neurosurgeons maintains that the operation is primarily directed to relieve compromised nerve tissue, therefore the problem is their domain. However, most physicians recognize that both specialists are capable of successfully treating the patient, and know that the combined talent of both specialties is necessary to provide relief for the many patients who suffer from this painful and disabling problem.

ally brought on by lifting or bending over; these attacks may have been present for years, lasting for a few days at a time, and gradually getting worse. Eventually transient attacks of root pain (nerve pain) may be present. This results from the nucleus pulposus bulging through the annulus fibrosus and pressing on the nerve roots. Eventually, as the annulus becomes thinner from this pressure, it breaks and the nucleus pulposus herniates out, causing severe pressure on the root and severe pain (pain on the distribution of the nerve affected). When this occurs, the pain is so severe that surgical treatment may be indicated.

In acute cases, although there may have been a history of recurring attacks of low back pain as previously mentioned, there is a sudden onset of low back pain and bilateral leg pain that may last for a few hours only, to be followed by paralysis of the lower extremities, usually below the knee, accompanied by paralysis of the bladder and rectum. This constitutes a surgical emergency, and usually means that the whole nucleus pulposus has herniated through the annulus fibrosis and posterior spinal ligament, pressing on the cauda equina. **Figure 18** shows a disc which was removed at surgery. This patient fortunately made a good recovery and had practically complete return of function.

Typically, one or both components of the pain (back and leg) increase with coughing, sneezing, straining, or bending. With lumbar discs, sitting, standing, and walking increases the pain, while rest relieves it. Cervical disc pain similarly increases with activity and subsides with rest, although recumbency may bring exacerbation rather than relief.

Pain and disability are neither fixed nor relentlessly progressive. Symptoms tend to fluctuate with time, and may vary with mood, fatigue, even with the weather. Pain from muscle spasm may be improved by massage or mild activity, while that of nerve root compression is increased. Disability is partial in most cases, rather than complete, with the patient's capacity for work or play depending to a large degree on his motivation and tolerance for discomfort.

Sensitivity to pin-prick, temperature and light touch is commonly decreased in a nerve root distribution. Position sense, kinesthesia,[57] and vibratory sense usually remain intact, since these modalities are conveyed over multiple spinal nerves and roots. Hyperesthesia, with increased sensitivity to noxious stimuli, may occur in the dermatome (sensory root field on the skin) or along its margins. Muscle weakness may appear in the myotome (group of muscles innervated by a single spinal segment) and range in severity from mild paresis to paralysis with atrophy. Tendon reflexes may be diminished in the myotome.

---

[57]Editor's Note: "Kinesthesia" is the perception of movement; the sense by which muscular motion, weight and position are perceived.

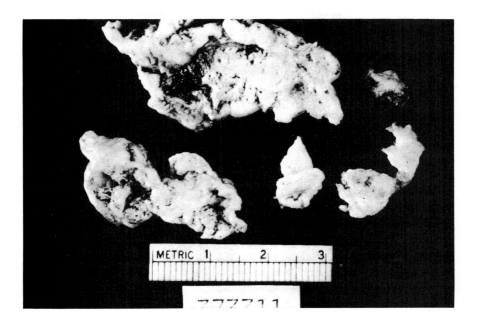

Fig. 18. Ruptured disc removed by surgery.

An affected limb often is splinted[58] involuntarily by the patient because of pain. Consequently, other muscle groups quickly undergo disuse atrophy, and the limb becomes stiff. In neglected cases, a complicated and confusing pattern may develop, falsely suggesting multiple root lesions with secondary weakness, atrophy, and the resultant pain and stiffness of an unused limb. This is most likely to occur in an upper extremity.

While these general symptoms are characteristic of disc protrusion throughout the spine, distinctive features are present in cervical, thoracic, and lumbar disc herniations. Accordingly, each group will be discussed separately herein. (See § 32.105 et seq.)

---

[58]Editor's Note: "Splinted" or "splinting," as the term is used here, means the rigidity of muscle that occurs when a patient attempts to avoid pain by not moving an injured part of the body.

§ 32.104. Psychological complications.

No matter how stoic or strong-willed the patient may be, chronic severe pain from herniated discs can lead to disability and despair. The threat to personal and financial security is great and cannot fail to take a psychological toll. For a few, mild disc symptoms provide the opportunity to mask personal inadequacy in a cloak of respectable invalidism, and the opportunity is tenaciously seized to withdraw from onerous responsibilities. If such a situation is suspected, attention should be given to diagnosis and management of abnormal psychological reactions to real or imagined physical disability.

§ 32.105. Cervical disc syndromes.

Cervical intervertebral disc protrusion may occur at any level, but is most frequent between the fifth and sixth and sixth and seventh cervical vertebrae. The next most frequent sites are between the fourth and fifth cervical vertebrae. From top to bottom, these herniations affect the fifth, sixth, and seventh spinal nerves. Common to them all are neck pain, muscle spasm, and limitation of active and passive movement of the head and neck. The patient may hold his head to one side to relieve pressure on the affected roots. Pains may increase and radiate to the arm on coughing, sneezing, and straining, and on movement of the neck and shoulder. According to some studies, trauma is related to the onset of symptoms in the cervical region in 10% of the cases. The spinal cord is uncommonly involved by simple ruptured discs; however, late degenerative changes of bony bars and intervertebral instability may eventually compromise the cervical cord and produce the long-tract signs of myelopathy (disease of the spinal cord).

Root lesions at the fifth cervical (C5) (fourth and fifth cervical vertebrae disc protrusion) lead to weakness of shoulder elevation by the supraspinatus and deltoid muscles and even of arm flexion by the biceps and brachioradialis muscle. Paresthesias (numbness, tingling, "pins-and-needles" sensation) and sensory changes appear in the upper outer arm. Pain is felt in the neck, shoulder, outer arm, and in the back between the shoulder blades. The biceps and brachioradialis tendon reflexes may be altered. If the fifth cervical root compression is neglected, irreversible atrophy (wasting away, reduction in size) of the shoulder musculature occurs within one to a few weeks. This may result in a weak and possible "frozen," painful shoulder. The potential disability may be devastating to a manual or skilled worker.

Lesions at the sixth cervical (C6) produce paresthesias and sensory loss in the thumb, forefinger, and adjacent outer forearm. Motor weakness in the biceps and brachioradialis muscles occurs, with weakness of flexion of the forearm and loss of the corresponding biceps and brachioradialis deep tendon reflexes.

Lesions at the seventh cervical (C7) affect sensation in the middle and ring fingers and produce motor weakness of the wrists as well as loss of the triceps deep tendon reflex.

Ruptured discs at the seventh cervical (C7) and first thoracic (T1) affecting the eighth cervical spinal nerve root affect sensation in the ring and little fingers of the hand. Motor weakness results in most of the intrinsic muscles of the hand. Significant loss of hand function may become irreversible within days or weeks of the disc rupture. This is an unfortunate and serious outcome for anyone who works with his hands, and an early surgical attempt should be considered to prevent it.

§ 32.106. Thoracic disc syndromes.

Simple herniation of thoracic discs seldom occurs, presumably because mobility of the thoracic spine is restricted by the support of the rib cage. They are usually seen only after major trauma and then most often in the tenth, eleventh, and twelfth thoracic vertebrae. Pain radiates from the back around to the front, at or below the umbilicus. Little local motor weakness or sensory loss can be demonstrated, because of the extensive overlap of segmental innervation on the trunk. However, the superficial abdominal skin reflex may be diminished or lost on the side of the lesion. This reflex involves a brief contraction of abdominal muscles of one side, causing the umbilicus to move briefly in that direction, and is elicited by scratching the skin on that side of the abdomen.

A large or centrally placed disc protrusion may compress the lower spinal cord. This can be a surgical emergency with serious disability if unrelieved by prompt surgical decompression. Otherwise, paralysis of both legs, loss of sensation below the waist, and impairment of bowel, bladder, and sexual function may result.

§ 32.107. Lumbar disc syndrome.

The most frequent site of herniated nucleus pulposus is the lumbar spine, where 85% of lumbar disc lesions occur between the fourth and fifth lumbar vertebrae and the fifth lumbar vertebra and first sacral vertebra. Protrusions at between the third and fourth lumbar vertebrae occur less often, and lesions between the first and second and second and third lumbar vertebrae are unusual. Clinical hallmarks of lumbar disc protrusion include local and radicular pain, postural and gait changes, and resultant disability. The patient may lean toward or away from the side of the lesion, and the back is often curved to one side (scoliosis). He may limp or walk with an "antalgic gait" (marked by avoidance of weight-bearing on affected side). Lumbar paraspinous muscle spasms are common and help account for the altered posture and gait. Pressure over the site of rupture increases the local and radicular pain. There may

439

be tenderness to pressure over the sciatic notch at the lower border of the buttock as well.

Pain often radiates with "shock-like" quality from hip to leg or ankle, while paresthesias (especially "pins-and-needles") are felt in the leg and foot. Back and radicular pain may be reproduced by raising the leg on the affected side (*i.e.*, flexing the straight leg on the trunk — the LaSegue test). This movement stretches the involved spinal roots over the protruding disc. A "positive" test results if the radicular symptoms are reproduced by this maneuver. This is a valuable clinical sign in the diagnosis of ruptured disc, although it does not indicate the level of disc herniation. More reliable is the finding of a positive "crossed straight-leg raising test," in which symptoms are reproduced on the affected side by elevating the opposite leg. When present, this finding indicates a ruptured disc with perhaps 95% reliability.

Each spinal nerve in the lumbar region leaves the spinal canal through the intervertebral foramen, behind the lower aspect of the vertebral body, which bears the same number. Thus, the fifth lumbar roots form the spinal nerve and exit behind the fifth lumbar vertebral body, just above the fifth lumbar and first sacral vertebrae interspace. The first sacral roots cross this interspace at the lateral boundary, en route to the foramen below. The crossing root is the one that is ordinarily compromised by a disc protrusion; this holds true throughout the lumbar spine.

The majority of disc protrusions occur in the posterolateral direction, thereby affecting a single root. In large or central disc protrusions, two or more nerve roots may be compressed, even to the point of paraplegia and bladder dysfunction as in central thoracic discs. Disc fragments that are completely extruded into the spinal canal may migrate to atypical sites, giving rise to unusual single or multiple root symptoms.

Typical ruptured discs between the third and fourth lumbar vertebrae affect the fourth lumbar root, producing weakness of the quadriceps femoris muscle (which extends the knee) and altered knee jerks. Paresthesias and sensory changes appear along the inner calf. Femoral nerve stretch is performed by pulling the leg backwards into hyperextension. This may reproduce the pain, just as straight-leg raising does in fifth lumbar and first sacral root compression.

Fourth and fifth lumbar vertebrae disc protrusions produce weakness of the great toe and foot extensors, possibly leading to foot drop. Paresthesias and sensory changes occur in the great toe, medial foot, and lateral calf. There are no characteristic reflex changes.

Fifth lumbar and first sacral vertebrae lesions affect the first sacral roots, as noted, causing weakness of the gastrocnemius muscle in the calf of the leg and difficulty in rising up on the toes. Sensory loss extends to the lateral foot and little toe, and variably to the sole of the foot. The Achilles reflex (ankle jerk) is usually depressed or absent.

The term "sciatica" is applied to the pain of fifth lumbar and first sacral root compression, since the course of radiating pain is along the sciatic nerve (back of the hip, thigh, knee, and calf to the heel). There may be tenderness to palpation of the nerve as well, as reflected in the painful response on pressure over the sciatic notch.

§ 32.108. Conservative treatment of disc protrusions.

In about 85% of intervertebral disc protrusions, conservative or medical management suffices. The patient is treated symptomatically as local pain and sciatica (or arm pain, in cervical discs) develop. Bedrest, possibly traction, local heat and massage, and muscle relaxants are combined with analgesics as needed. A bed board or firm mattress is often advised. In most instances the pain subsides, and the syndrome abates for months or perhaps years before returning. Treatment is repeated as needed, usually with success.

Back-strengthening exercises may help prevent recurrence by improving posture and muscular strength. Braces or spinal supports are rarely indicated, for they lead to atrophy (wasting away, reduction in size) and increased weakness of the spine. Except in cases of a structural defect of the spine, the use of braces is self-defeating.

For mild cervical symptoms, home cervical traction may be of benefit. However, some clinicians have found that conservative treatment is less successful in ruptured cervical discs than in lumbar and advocate surgical repair early as the course of choice.

§ 32.109. Surgical treatment of disc protrusions.

Surgical treatment of ruptured disc is seldom performed as an emergency procedure. Surgery is urgent in unusual cases that present (1) progressive loss of neurological function or (2) involvement of bladder or bowel function. Indications for elective surgery are (1) intractable pain uncontrolled by conservative measures and (2) repeated recurrence of the disc syndrome on conservative therapy, with intolerable morbidity and disruption of normal living patterns.

§ 32.110. Surgical treatment — Cervical disc protrusions.

Several surgical approaches for treatment of cervical disc disease are employed. Some prefer the anterior interbody decompression and fusion. Incision is made in the anterolateral neck, and blunt dissection is carried to the spinal column. The trachea and esophagus are retracted medially and the carotid artery and associated structures laterally. Cervical muscle attachments are carefully stripped away. The offending interspace is identified, and a hole is drilled through it to the spinal canal. (A guard prevents overpenetration.) Loose disc fragments are extracted through the drill holes, and any lateral osteophytes are removed from the posterior vertebral margins. A fitted plug of bone is taken from another site, such as the iliac crest, and placed in the hole. Strong cervical traction aids in seating the plug snugly. Immediate stabilization is achieved, and the patient may be ambulated in a few days wearing only a soft cervical collar for support.

In the more conventional posterior approach (laminectomy), which is performed by most experienced neurosurgeons, a midline dorsal incision is made and carried to the spine, with separation of the paraspinous muscles in the midline. This approach is relatively bloody because a large muscle mass must be traversed and numerous veins of moderate caliber are encountered, but this should be no problem to an experienced surgeon. The appropriate laminae are removed with rongeurs and currettes[59] and the ligamentum flavum incised, exposing the interspace. The root is carefully retracted and the protruded disc fragment removed. Traction on the spinal cord must be assiduously avoided to prevent potential cord infarct or other disastrous complication. Results are generally good, although moderate but transient exacerbation of root inflammation may result from manipulation of the exposed root. Spinal fusions may also be done via the posterior route, but these are indicated only in unusual circumstances, such as in the case of spinal instability.

§ 32.111. Surgical treatment — Thoracic disc protrusions.

Thoracic disc lesions are rare. In the past they were removed through the posterior approach, which meant that the dura mater (membrane covering spinal cord) and spinal cord had to be retracted to remove the lesion, often with less than gratifying results. Weakness of the legs and even paralysis of the legs have been reported. Now, however, the lateral approach is being used, which does not require spinal cord retraction. Much better results are being obtained as far as morbidity is concerned.

§ 32.112. Surgical treatment — Lumbar disc protrusions.

Lumbar disc protrusions generally are approached from behind. The incision and exposure (laminectomy) are as described above under cervical discs. Steady bleeding from torn epidural veins is a technical hazard that may impair visibility. The root is carefully retracted and the protruded disc fragments removed. Many surgeons then clear the disc space of additional degenerated disc material, while others leave the interspace untouched to avoid possibly deleterious further disruption of the interspace and also to help maintain normal intervertebral structural relationships. Adherents of disc space evacuation believe it significantly lessens the risk of recurrent herniation, one of the known causes of surgical failure.

---

[59]Editor's Note: A *rongeur* is a forceps designed for cutting bone, and a *currette* (or *curet*) is a spoon-shaped instrument for removing material from the walls of cavities.

The spinal canal around the dura mater is carefully explored with instruments to ensure removal of all extruded fragments. The intervertebral foramen (large opening formed by vertebral body and arch) is also explored, and if snug, it is unroofed by removal of additional bone. All attempts are made to free the root from compression or tension.

§ 32.113. Convalescence.

Following surgery, the patient soon begins cautious ambulation. The preferred regimen of convalescence varies widely with different surgeons. Many ambulate patients to the bathroom on the day of surgery, while others advocate bedrest for a number of days. Treatment must be individualized to allow for special circumstances. Generally, the period of postoperative hospitalization is becoming increasingly shorter. At some hospitals, patients go home one week after surgery, having ambulated gradually starting the day after surgery. The return to light duties is usually allowed in about six weeks, but full activity is not permitted for several months.

§ 32.114. Prognosis.

Approximately 15% of patients with diagnosed intervertebral disc protrusion actually undergo surgery. Most of these obtain good relief of symptoms; however, they have a better than average chance of another disc protrusion in the future, either at the same or at a different site. Surgical treatment of the most common ruptured discs (fourth and fifth lumbar and fifth lumbar and first sacral vertebrae) is acceptably safe, and increased neurological deficit after the procedure is most unusual. Known causes of failure of surgical treatment include recurrence of the disc herniation, excessive perineural scarring, and adhesive arachnoiditis. Myelography with iodinated compounds, especially when performed multiple times, appears to have contributed significantly to the last of these.

Because of the chronicity of intervertebral disc protrusion syndromes, settlements of claims are often delayed. It is necessary to allow sufficient time to evaluate the extent of recovery and residual disability. On the other hand, in some cases, the fact of pending litigation appears clearly to work against the patient's recovery and best long-term interest. Hence, from a medical standpoint, settlement is advised promptly after the lapse of a reasonable period of time; one year is suggested as a suitable period in many instances.

§ 32.115. Chemonucleolysis.

An alternative approach to disc surgery is chemonucleolysis, or chemical digestion of degenerated disc material by an enzyme called "chymopapain." This material is extracted from the papaya plant, and is widely used as a meat tenderizer. A needle is placed into a defective intervertebral disc for administration of the enzyme. General anesthesia is employed because of moderately severe pain of the injection, and fluoroscopic control is needed to guide the needle through the skin and deep lumbar muscles into the target interspace. Selection is necessary for this treatment. Completely extruded disc fragments are not likely to be benefited by injection into the interspace. Postprocedure morbidity and pain are less than with laminectomy. A rare but worrisome complication is anaphylactoid shock, a form of allergic response that may occur in response to the chymopapain.

An early proponent of chemonucleolysis, John McCulloch, M.D., of the University of Toronto, reported a 70% success rate using chymopapain in 6,000 patients from 1969 to 1982. He stated that the type of patient who responds best to chymopapain satisfies five clinical criteria that define disc herniation, (1) dominant leg pain, (2) neurological symptoms, (3) significant reduction in straight leg raising, (4) neurological signs, (5) supportive investigations such as myelography, venography, discogram, and CT scan. Conditions unresponsive to chemonucleolysis were degenerative disc disease, facet joint disease, spinal or recess stenosis, and in many cases where the disc fragment has extruded into the canal.[60]

When there is failure in chemonucleolysis, there is usually a disabling sciatica six weeks after injection or disabling back pain three months later. McCulloch cited the sequestered or extruded fragment as the most common cause of his failures, with a lateral recess stenosis being second most common. Discussing chymopapain's safety, he stressed the importance of injecting only in the nucleus, warning that chymopapain in the subarachnoid space can cause bleeding and subsequent arachnoiditis. He cites cauda equina syndrome and anaphylaxis as the worst complications of discolysis with chymopapain. About 20% of his patients had muscle spasm with significant back pain, and 2% had inflammation of the disc. Although none had cauda equina problems, one in 300 exhibited anaphylactic reactions. He treated them with epinephrine and fluid replacement. Since the worldwide anaphylaxis incidence is about .5-1% with chymopapain, McCulloch believed that the best management is to assume that every patient is at risk and to be prepared with an anesthesiologist standing by.

Orthopedist Mark Brown, M.D., of the University of Miami School of Medicine, reported that the use of either chymopapain or collagenase, a similar enzyme, is five times safer than surgery. Brown stated that both drugs are effective in dissolving the offending disc, but he himself felt a lot safer with collagenase, because, at the time, there were no reported

---

[60] *Collagenase and Chymopapain Assessed,* Intradiscal Therapy Rev., August, 1983, p. 2.

allergic reactions with this enzyme. In his opinion, if chymopapain fails, the area can be reinjected at the same level with collagenase without the fear of anaphylaxis. Brown added that the only deaths from anaphylaxis with chymopapain occurred with the patient under general anesthesia, suggesting that the risk of an allergic reaction might be lessened with the use of local anesthesia.[61]

In a review of the use of chymopapain, Nordby found allergic reaction to be the most serious complication, occurring in about 1% of the patients and resulting in four deaths. At the time, these statistics compared with those of laminectomy.[62] However, while described as complications, some of the undesirable occurrences that accompanied chemonucleolysis may have been unrelated to it. A patient who had an injection into a cervical herniated nucleus pulposus without a prior myelogram, and who had initial relief, became paralyzed and subsequently died; however, the cause of death was found to be a malignant tumor. There was also a case of transverse myelitis and paralysis following chemonucleolysis, but, at the time, this was not proven to be related to the use of the enzyme.[63]

With marked narrowing of the intervertebral space following chemonucleolysis, settling of the facet joints may occur and cause back pain, usually of a temporary nature. According to Nordby, the most common adverse experience following injection of chymopapain was back muscle spasm, which may last for a few hours to a few days. It was reported in 30% to 40% of the patients. Septic discitis was also reported, but usually responded to appropriate antibiotics and rest.[64]

On July 19, 1984, Smith Laboratories, Inc., manufacturer of chymopapain (under the trade name Chymodiactin), concerned about additional reports of neurological complications among patients undergoing chemonucleolysis, issued a "Dear Doctor" letter to the medical profession. The following are the essential portions of that letter.

Dear Doctor:

Recent communications have called to your attention the serious neurological adverse experiences, particularly paraplegia/paraparesis, cerebral hemorrhage, and transverse myelitis, that have been reported following chemonucleolysis with chymopapain. Although a cause and effect relationship to chymopapain itself has not been established for these events, review of the available data strongly suggests that modification of the current procedural recommendations for chemonucleolysis be considered.

Table 1 provides data on the 30 cases of serious neurological complications reported in association with Chymodiactin® as of June, 1984. Similar serious neurological problems have also been reported in the Discase® literature,

----

[61] *Orthopedist Prefers Collagenase,* Intradiscal Therapy Rev., August, 1983, p. 1.
[62] Nordby, E. J., *Chymopapain in Intradiscal Therapy,* 56A J. Bone & Joint Surg. 1350, 1983.

[63] Id.
[64] Id.

including subarachnoid hemorrhage, cerebrovascular accidents, and paraplegia.

Avoidance of Discography

As shown in Table 1, 28 of the 30 patients had discography performed as part of their chemonucleolysis procedure. Eleven of the events reported in Table 1 have either been documented, or appear likely to be related, to the entry of contrast agents used in discography (Renografin®, Hypaque®, Conray®, and Amipaque®) and chymopapain into the spinal fluid. The patients in this group have the rapid onset of some or all of the following signs and symptoms: severe headache, hypertension, motor and sensory loss of function in the legs, and loss of sphincter function either immediately or within hours of chemonucleolysis. Diagnostic lumbar puncture invariably produces grossly bloody spinal fluid. These cases all involved discography performed immediately prior to the injection of chymopapain. Discography performed 3-4 days prior to chymopapain injection has not been implicated in the neurological problems.

Further evidence that concurrent entry of contrast agent and chymopapain into the spinal fluid may be responsible for neurotoxicity has been obtained in a recently completed toxicology study in baboons. In this study, seven groups of nine baboons each were administered Chymodiactin® or one of the contrast agents (either alone or in combination) directly into the lumbar spinal fluid. The doses used were close approximations of the human doses administered to treat one disc. When combinations of contrast agent and Chymodiactin® were administered, the contrast agent was injected 15 minutes prior to Chymodiactin®, again following the human procedure.

The results from this study appear in Table 2 and clearly demonstrate that the administration of the contrast agent followed by Chymodiactin® produces significantly more neurotoxicity, including paralysis and death, than the single agents. It is particularly pertinent to note that none of the animals had adverse reactions when injected with Chymodiactin® alone. When the contrast agents were administered alone, Renografin® produced toxicity.

Although discography has been a generally accepted procedure, **IN VIEW OF THE ANIMAL DATA AND THE HUMAN EXPERIENCE IT IS STRONGLY RECOMMENDED THAT DISCOGRAPHY NOT BE PERFORMED AS PART OF THE CHEMONUCLEOLYSIS PROCEDURE.**

Verification of Needle Placement

Surgeons performing chemonucleolysis may wish to consider the injection of saline or water into the nucleus pulposus (saline or water acceptance test) as an alternative to discography. The use of this test plus careful evaluation of high quality AP and lateral X-ray views of the disc are sufficient to confirm proper needle placement in the nucleus pulposus.

If high quality X-ray equipment including an image intensifier is not available to perform chemonucleolysis, the procedure should not be carried out. If there is any question about satisfactory needle placement, or if needle placement is difficult, requiring repeated attempts, the procedure should be terminated.

Potential Role of Multiple Disc Injections

Review of the serious neurological complications listed in Table 1 demonstrates that 15 of the 30 patients (50%) had two or more disc spaces injected. Information from over 47,000 post-marketing surveillance reports submitted to Smith Laboratories demonstrates that only about 25% of all patients undergoing chemonucleolysis have had two or more discs injected.

Based on the increased frequency of two or more disc level injections in the patients with neurological adverse reactions, CHEMONUCLEOLYSIS SHOULD BE LIMITED TO THE ONE DISC PRODUCING THE PATIENT'S SYMPTOMS UNLESS DEFINITIVE SIGNS, SYMPTOMS, AND DIAGNOSTIC PROCEDURES INDICATE THAT MORE THAN ONE DISC IS AT FAULT.

Potential Relation to General Anesthesia

Review of the serious neurological complications reported in Table 1 demonstrates that 27 out of 29 of these events for which data are available have occurred when general anesthesia was used.

The use of supplemented local anesthesia in preference to general anesthesia provides an awake patient, more likely to experience pain and complain if the needle impinges on nerve tissue. In addition, it is likely that a patient under local anesthesia will not tolerate an excessive number of attempts to place the needle. Local anesthesia is also associated with a lower frequency of anaphylaxis than general anesthesia (0.4% vs. 0.6%, respectively).

Based on the above, IT IS RECOMMENDED THAT SUPPLEMENTED LOCAL ANESTHESIA BE USED FOR CHEMONUCLEOLYSIS WHENEVER POSSIBLE.

Need for Adequate Physician Training

Lastly, it is important to call to your attention the following statement in the product labeling:

CHYMOPAPAIN SHOULD ONLY BE USED BY PHYSICIANS WHO ROUTINELY CARE FOR PATIENTS WITH HERNIATED LUMBAR INTERVERTEBRAL DISCS, WHO ARE QUALIFIED BY TRAINING AND EXPERIENCE TO PERFORM LAMINECTOMY, DISCECTOMY, OR OTHER SPINAL PROCEDURES, AND WHO HAVE RECEIVED SPECIALIZED TRAINING IN CHEMONUCLEOLYSIS.

Table 1

30 SERIOUS NEUROLOGICAL COMPLICATIONS AMONG
72,000 (ESTIMATED) CHYMODIACTIN® PATIENTS

	NO. OF DISCS INJECTED	ANES-THETIC USED	DISCOG-RAPHY
8 CEREBRAL HEMORRHAGE			
5 Deaths			
4 Unrelated			
1 Cerebral Aneurysm	2	G	C

	NO. OF DISCS INJECTED	ANES-THETIC USED	DISCOG-RAPHY
3 Cerebral Vascular Malformation	1,1,1	L,L,G	R,NO,R
1 Etiology unknown, probably unrelated	1	G	C
2 Cerebrovascular Accidents	1,1	U,G	YES-U,C
1 Comatose State Documented injection of contrast agent and chymopapain into CSF	3	G	R
1 QUADRIPLEGIA Hemorrhagic myelitis, suspected injection of contrast agent and chymopapain into CSF	2	G	H
1 HEMIPARESIS Transient episode with recovery. No discogram. Suspected injection of chymopapain into CSF	1	G	NO
20 PARAPLEGIA/PARAPARESIS			
4 Acute Transverse Myelitis (ATM) Onset at 2-3 weeks. 1 patient had transdural discography	3,1,2,2	G,G,G,G	C,R,R,R
1 Possible ATM Onset at 5 weeks	1	G	R
1 Possible ATM Onset of encephalomyeloneuritis at 7 weeks	3	G	R
1 Probable Thrombotic Event During cerebral angiography at 2 weeks	1	G	R
9 Documented or Probable Injection of Contrast Agent and Chymopapain into CSF	1,3,2,1, 2,2,1,2, 1	G,G,G,G, G,G,G,G, G	C,C,H,H, R,R,R,R, A
1 Extruded Fragment Complete recovery post-laminectomy	1	G	C
1 Lumbar Subdural Hematoma Probable needle trauma	2	G	YES-U
1 Transdural L5-S1 Needle Approach	2	G	C
1 Etiology Unknown Onset 2 weeks post chemonucleolysis and 2 days post anticoagulant therapy for a pulmonary embolus. Hemorrhagic arachnoiditis at laminectomy.	3	G	R

U = UNKNOWN
G = GENERAL ANESTHESIA
L = LOCAL ANESTHESIA
H = HYPAQUE®
A = AMIPAQUE®

YES-U = DISCOGRAPHY DONE BUT
       AGENT UNKNOWN
R = RENOGRAFIN®
C = CONRAY®
NO = DISCOGRAPHY NOT DONE

Table 2

BABOON STUDIES
ALL TREATMENTS VIA LUMBAR CSF
ALL ANIMALS SACRIFICED AT 48 HOURS

TREATMENT GROUP	N	RESULTS
1. CHYMODIACTIN, 50 units/kg	9	ALL NORMAL
2. CONRAY, .033 ml/kg	9	ALL NORMAL
3. AMIPAQUE, .033 ml/kg	9	ALL NORMAL
4. RENOGRAFIN, .033 ml/kg	9	2 SEIZURES-DEATH 7 NORMAL
5. CONRAY, .033 ml/kg + CHYMODIACTIN, 50 units/kg	9	4 PROSTRATE/1 PARALYZED 5 NORMAL
6. AMIPAQUE, .033 ml/kg + CHYMODIACTIN, 50 units/kg	9	2 PROSTRATE/1 PARALYZED 7 NORMAL
7. RENOGRAFIN, .033 ml/kg + CHYMODIACTIN, 50 units/kg	9	5 PROSTRATE/1 SEIZURES-DEATH 4 NORMAL

Following the issuance of the above letter, the use of chemonucleolysis decline markedly in the United States.

§ 32.116. Spinal fusion.

Spinal fusion is not a primary treatment for intervertebral disc protrusion, but is reserved for unusual cases of chronic backache, spinal instability, and congenital defects. To this group should be added people who have a weak back and who have had two or three discs removed. These individuals have a considerable amount of motion in the spine and are not competent to do heavy work. Under the circumstances a fusion may be beneficial to strengthen their back.

Sumbar spinal fusion is more extensive and stressful than simple laminectomy for ruptured disc extraction. A larger incision and greater bone exposure lead to greater blood loss, often with need for risky blood transfusions. Convalescence is prolonged, because the spine must remain nearly immobile for several weeks as bony healing (fusion) begins. A body cast often is needed for many weeks more. Up to one year may pass before the patient can resume near-normal activities.

The fusion is done in the hope that pain may be reduced by eliminating movements between degenerated or deformed vertebrae, and secondarily to reduce the risk of recurrent herniation of disc fragments. Results vary widely, but a considerable incidence of fair to poor results is encountered.

§ 32.117. Arthritic changes — Osteophytes.

A late consequence of disc protrusion is the formation of arthritic changes known as "osteophytes" or "bony spurs." This process is initiated by slight elevation of the periosteum (fibrous outer lining of the bone) adjacent to a protruding disc. Reactive bone formation fills the space thus formed. This process progresses with time, producing bony deformity, laxity of supporting ligaments, and painful slight movements due to instability at the intervertebral space. Osteophytes grow until they also may compress the spinal cord in the neck or roots in the neck or lumbar spine years after the disc protrusion has regressed and ceased to be a problem. Treatment of this condition at times requires surgery in the form of a foraminotomy in which there is removal of bone around the compressed nerve root to give the nerve root more room. The results are not as dramatic as after removal of a disc, but in the long run may be gratifying.

XV. PERIPHERAL NERVE INJURIES

§ 32.118. Introduction.

The subject of peripheral nerve injury is complicated. (The anatomy and physiology of the peripheral nervous system is covered in § 32.70.) First, the variety of possible injurious processes is wide, and includes laceration, crushing, stretching, tearing, burning, electrical injury, chronic pressure, and the shock effect of impact or of grazing missile wounds. Second, the extent of nerve involvement cannot be predicted reliably from the circumstances of injury, and neither can prognosis for recovery be predicted from physical examination, nor even from operative exploration in most cases. Instances of complete nerve disruption are exceptions to this rule, however, since permanent nonfunction is highly probable. Third, the outlook for development of chronic pain syndromes is unpredictable in any circumstance. Finally, the consequences of a peripheral nerve injury are greatly dependent on several factors: (a) the distance from the point of focal injury to the site of action of the nerve endings; (b) whether the nerve has a single function or is mixed motor and sensory; (c) whether a motor nerve supplies one or many muscles; and (d) the precision of movement required of the muscles to be reinnervated.

§ 32.119. The physiology of disordered function—Severity of injury.

Traumatic dysfunction of peripheral nerves results from anatomical or physiological interruption[65] of the constituent axons (nerve fibers). Several classifications have been offered, but that of Seddon[66] is usefully simple and widely known. According to Seddon, there can be three types of injury to individual axons: (1) neurotmesis; (2) axonotmesis; and (3) neurapraxia.[67]

Neurotmesis

Neurotmesis is the term for complete physical interruption of an axon and of the adjacent supportive connective tissue. Nerve fiber regeneration is not effectual because the essential intraneural pathways (endoneurial tubules) are not available to guide the axon tip effectively toward the target tissues. The healing process results only in a mass of nonfunctional and often painful scarring, known as a "neuroma." With regenerative attempts, the neuroma comes to resemble a tangled skein, consisting of intermingled fibrous Schwann cells and bundles of abortively regenerated axons.

An occasional axon may traverse the neuroma and enter the distal stump, but a few random reconnections of this type have no functional significance. In complete transections, an end-bulb neuroma develops at the proximal end (nearest the spinal cord), whereas a neuroma-in-continuity develops as a fusiform enlargement along the course of a peripheral nerve that is only contused or partially transected. These neuromata are identical in internal structure and significance.

Axonotmesis

Axonotmesis is an intermediate degree of injury, in which the axon and its insulating myelin sheath are functionally disrupted while the connective tissue framework remains intact. Such axons cannot conduct impulses across the site of injury. Degenerative changes occur proximal to the injury, with swelling of the neuron body, changes in the ribonucleic acid structures (Nissl bodies) of its cytoplasm, and displacement of the nucleus to one side of the cell. This is part of the "axonal reaction" of the neuron, and it signals the onset of a hypermetabolic state that appears to prepare the neuron for the regenerative effort which is soon to be directed toward the severed axon.

---

[65] In "anatomical interruption" the nerves have been cut; in "physiological interruption" they are intact but are not functional.

[66] Seddon, H. J., *Three Types of Nerve Injury,* 66 Brain 238, 1943.

[67] This classification is not strictly applicable to the entire peripheral nerve, since all axons are not affected equally.

Proximal to the injury site, the axon and its myelin sheath degenerate for a short distance. Distally, the process called "Wallerian degeneration" becomes evident in a few days. The myelin sheath breaks into small fatty globules, which are engulfed ("phagocytized") by specialized cells known as macrophages. The axon itself becomes beaded and unable to conduct.

The axonal reaction occurs in both neurotmesis and axonotmesis. Regenerative attempts occur in both, but are successful only when the endoneurial tubules remain to direct regenerating axons toward appropriate effector structures. In neurotmesis, destruction of the tubules precludes successful restoration of function. Meticulous surgical approximation of the damaged ends can improve upon the natural chaotic organization of the neuroma, but still cannot achieve the precise alignment of the undamaged or axonotmetic nerve. Thus, the surgeon will accept spontaneous healing so long as function continues to improve with time. In most instances, the result exceeds that obtainable by surgical repair.

Wallerian degeneration begins in several days in both of the above types of injury. Until then, the distal nerve segment responds normally to electrical stimulation. Thus, this persistent electrical responsiveness in the distal nerve segment has no differential diagnostic or prognostic value. Two to three weeks after injury, muscles that lose their innervation because of this degeneration begin to show the membrane hyperirritability and spontaneous electrical potentials of fibrillation. If present sooner than about eighteen days after nerve injury, these potentials signify preexisting disease that cannot be attributed to the recent injury.

Neurapraxia

Neurapraxia is the mildest degree of axonal injury. Like cerebral concussion in the central nervous system, this is a physiological injury without anatomical disruption of axon or surrounding tissues. Some axons receive this degree of injury in serious nerve injury, but more often it results from brief pressure, stretching, or shock of mild impact on a nerve.

Neurapraxic nerves appear normal on inspection. The distal axon also is normal, without Wallerian degeneration. The deficit in neurapraxia is thought to result from local biochemical changes in the myelin at the site of injury. Functional loss is greatest in large myelinated fibers which subserve motor activity and the sensations of touch and position. The smaller fibers which subserve pain and temperature sensations are selectively spared. Physiological nerve impulses do not cross the injured site unless some uninjured axons remain. However, electrical stimulation may break through the blockade and produce muscular twitching on the distal side. Nerve conduction is normal in the distal nerve segment, and the electromyographic record from the muscle may be normal.

§ 32.120. Time factor in regeneration.

Recovery from peripheral nerve injury depends on the severity of axonal and other intraneural injury. In neurapraxia, there is good return of function in four to six weeks. More serious injuries take longer, since the damaged axon must regenerate from the point of injury.

In axonotmesis, about two weeks is required for regeneration to occur just proximal to the injury, in the region of retrograde degeneration that accompanies Wallerian (distal or "downstream") degeneration. In neurotmesis, when the nerve ends are surgically freshened, about four weeks is required for regeneration to proceed across the suture line. Thereafter, in both types of injury, axons grow down the endoneurial tubules of the distal stump at approximately 1.5 mm. per day. Regrowth is faster in children than in adults and also faster when the site of injury is near the spinal cord than when it is more distant. When the regenerating axon reaches the target tissue, an additional delay of weeks to months may occur before "maturation" of the axon results in a functional connection to the muscle.

Clinically, a figure of one inch per month is taken as the average expected rate of functional regeneration for motor fibers. As discussed elsewhere, functional return in sensory fibers is less predictable, but these fibers also regenerate at this approximate rate.

If no return of physiological function can be seen or elicited by electrical stimulation at six to eight weeks, neurotmesis must be presumed to have occurred. This is a signal to abandon conservative waiting, and to consider surgical exploration of the nerve. Spontaneous recovery still is not ruled out, however, and evidence for regeneration should be sought at the operating table by electrical stimulation before resection of the neuroma is performed.

§ 32.121. Limitation on motor regeneration.

Totally denervated muscle fibers soon undergo histological changes in their internal structure. Clinically, atrophy and weakness are noted. Fibrosis (scarring) develops progressively, so that by twelve months the prospects of successful reinnervation are much reduced. By two years the muscle fibers may be completely replaced by inert, functionless scarring. The clinical rule is predicated on these facts, i.e., that the effective limit on the extent of motor reinnervation is the distance that can be satisfactorily regenerated in one year. On the average, this amounts to about twelve inches. Muscles that derive their innervation from a point more distant than twelve inches below a severe lesion are unlikely ever to regain function. Undue delay in resection of a neuroma and suture of the nerve ends further adds to loss, since the regeneration restarts anew at time of nerve repair, while the muscle changes start at time of injury.

§ 32.122.   Mechanisms of injury.

Lacerations

Lacerations may produce complete or partial severance of peripheral nerves. Involved fibers suffer neurotmesis, but other fibers in the nerve may remain intact or suffer only neurapraxia (§ 32.119). Contusions commonly result from bony fractures and direct blows to soft tissue and are common in proximity to high-speed bullet tracts. Nerves may be entrapped within a bony fracture, and suffer further loss, including avulsion of a section of nerve, when the fracture is reduced.

Stretch injuries

Stretch injuries arise in the upper arm from excessive traction on the limb and from direct blows to the top of the shoulder and adjacent clavicular region. A variety of serious lesions may result, including cervical root avulsion. Traction injuries also result from severe hyperextension of joints and from stretching of nerves over displaced bone in dislocations of shoulder or hip. Damage is distributed along the nerve, rather than confined to a single locus; thus surgical treatment is inappropriate for these injuries. Occasionally, significant spontaneous improvement occurs, but no useful prognostic test is available for predicting the eventual outcome.

Compressive lesions

Compressive lesions with neuronal ischemia (insufficient oxygen supply) also produce extended nerve injury. Confined wound hematoma (blood clot) or expanding arteriovenous fistula (communication between artery and vein) or aneurysm ("ballooning" of a weakened vessel wall) may be at fault when initial neurological deficit is found to progress.

Other causes of compression lesions include: pressure on unprotected nerve by a tight cast or by prolonged application of a tourniquet; improper positioning while under general anesthesia; and pressure on unguarded limbs while intoxicated or comatose from other cause, such as "Saturday night palsy," a disabling wrist drop due to radial nerve compression found in intoxicated persons who, in slumping in a chair, create pressure on the back of the upper arm.

"Crutch palsy" results from axillary pressure by crutch pads that cause lower brachial plexus injury (roots seven and eighth cervical and first thoracic) that produces symptoms along the distribution of the derivative ulnar nerve, including weakness of the intrinsic muscles of the hand ("claw-hand" deformity) and sensory loss over the little and ring fingers and adjacent hand and forearm.

"Peroneal palsy" results from pressure on the peroneal nerve where it crosses the head of the fibula at the lower outer margin of the knee. It causes "footdrop" and weakness of eversion (turning the foot outward from the normal position). This injury can result from trauma to the side of the leg, from pressure during anesthesia or coma, and from pressure from the top of a tight boot. It is also occasionally seen in card players who sit long hours with their leg crossed over their knee.)

"Entrapment" syndromes

Other chronic causes of peripheral nerve injury are the several "entrapment" syndromes. In the "carpal tunnel syndrome," the median nerve is compressed by surrounding tissue as it lies in the narrow passageway beneath the tough carpal ligament of the wrist. It results in sensory loss over the thumb and first two digits, and inability to flex the thumb to the remaining digits. These losses are disruptive to performance of skilled manual tasks. Fortunately, early treatment by surgical release of the nerve from the tunnel will minimize permanent deficit, but neglect soon leads to irreversible loss and development of a flattened "ape hand." However, many mild cases can be treated conservatively.

Ulnar nerve entrapment may occur in the groove where it passes behind the medial malleolus of the elbow. Weakness of the intrinsic muscles of the hand and a consequent "claw-hand" deformity is seen, along with sensory loss on the little finger and adjacent hand. Complicated deficits can occur in the upper limb as a result of the "thoracic outlet syndrome," with vascular and brachial plexus compression in the axillary region. However, true neurogenic thoracic outlet syndrome is rare.

Volkmann's contracture

Volkmann's contracture is the disastrous consequence of crushing injury to the forearm. Posttraumatic swelling in the anterior compartment of the forearm produces paralysis by compression of the median nerve. Also, blood supply to the nerve and muscle is compromised by the pressure. Unless relieved promptly by surgical decompression, ischemic injury leads to a painful, useless limb with marked atrophy and fibrosis of muscle and nerve.

Electrical burns

Electrical burns may cause destruction of nerve for considerable distances, and gaps of destroyed nerve tissue may result.[68]

---

[68] Editor's Note: Electrical injuries are discussed in Chapter 26 of this Cyclopedia.

Injection injuries

Medical injections into peripheral nerve is a cause of injury with prominent legal implications. Common sites of such mishap are the sciatic nerve in the buttock, and the radial nerve behind the upper arm. Injection of antibiotics, analgesics, and other drugs can produce a focal irritative neuritis. A local intraneural hematoma also may result and lead to dysfunction by pressure on the nerve fibers. Eventually, a neuroma-in-continuity may develop, with permanent neurological deficit in the lower limb as well as pain. The indications for surgical repair are the same as for any other neuroma.[69]

If promptly detected, further injection of 50 to 100 cc of normal saline into the same region may dilute the irritative drug and thereby reduce the ultimate injury. By similar reasoning, open exploration and irrigation of the nerve might be of benefit, but this is not widely practiced.

XVI. CLINICAL MANIFESTATIONS OF PERIPHERAL NERVE INJURY

§ 32.123. Introduction.

Injury to peripheral nerve, like injury to spinal nerve, manifests in altered function, and to a lesser extent, in pain. Contrary to common thought, peripheral nerve injuries often are not painful in the acute stage. Observed motor and sensory dysfunctions include total absence (paralysis, anesthesia), diminution (weakness, hypesthesia), perversion (paresthesias) and imbalance (excessive sweating). The type and degree of deficit depend on the absolute and relative contents of nerve fibers subserving motor, sensory, and autonomic functions. Because of segregation of spinal nerve fibers in forming the diverse peripheral nerves, deficits may involve single modalities or any combination of functions.

§ 32.124. Motor loss.

Motor weakness (paresis) or paralysis of voluntary movement results from injury to motor fibers. Electrical stimulation beyond the point of injury elicits full muscular contraction until the changes of Wallerian degeneration (§ 32.119) become established. After reinnervation, electrical stimulation of the nerve at this time will elicit muscular contractions.

---

[69] Editor's Note: "Neuromas" are discussed in §§ 32.119 and 32.128.

§ 32.125.   Sensory loss.

Sensory loss may occur alone or in association with motor loss. The larger, myelinated fibers are injured preferentially in peripheral nerve injury. Such fibers subserve the modalities of touch and position sense, as well as motor function. When the larger fibers are damaged, while the smaller myelinated and unmyelinated fibers remain, a condition of sensory imbalance results. Bizarre and unusual sensations (paresthesias) such as tingling, numbness, and "pins-and-needles" are reported. Ordinary stimuli may acquire peculiar, noxious qualities (allodynia). In recovery from peripheral nerve injury, these aberrations may be increased and constitute a source of some distress to many patients.

The cutaneous pattern of altered sensation frequently identifies the injured nerve. Soon after injury, the boundaries of sensory loss decrease rapidly as sensation is conveyed by overlapping innervation from adjacent nerves. The boundary zone between normal and anesthetic skin is often hyperesthetic, with increased sensitivity to stimulation. Paresthesias and other sensory aberrations are prominent at the boundary.

Complete recovery of sensation may occur even in total nerve disruption, in cases where extensive overlap of sensory innervation exists. Thus, loss of a single intercostal nerve may become undetectable by clinical examination. Other nerves, such as the median and ulnar nerves of the hand and forearm, have small autogenous zones that are innervated by no other nerve. Preservation of such nerves (but especially the median) is important if maximal function is to be retained.

§ 32.126.   Reflex activity.

Deep tendon reflexes may be lost when either the afferent fibers (sensory; carrying information to the brain and spinal cord) or efferent fibers (motor; carrying impulses to the periphery) are interrupted. This loss is not important to the patient and may not be recognized. It reflects the altered muscle tonus that results from the nerve injury, and is useful to the physician as one indicator of that injury. Important tendon reflexes are the biceps brachii (musculocutaneous nerve), brachioradialis and triceps brachii (radial nerve), quadriceps femoris or "knee jerk" (femoral nerve), and Achilles tendon reflex or "ankle jerk" (tibial nerve via sciatic).

§ 32.127.   Autonomic dysfunction.[70]

Fibers of the sympathetic nervous system accompany motor and sensory fibers in the peripheral nerves and are thus subject to injury. Normally, these fibers subserve temperature regulation and control of

---

[70] The autonomic nervous system is described in § 32.71.

sweating, piloerection ("goose bump" formation) and constriction of small arterioles (tiny arteries). When the sympathetic fibers are interrupted, these functions are lost. The skin becomes dry for lack of sweating and flushed and warm as the arterioles dilate and increase blood flow through the skin. The absence of sweating increases the electrical resistance of the skin; this fact, as well as the direct demonstration of lack of moisture, is useful in delineating the extent of peripheral nerve interruption. Other autonomic functions are important, such as bladder, bowel, and sexual functions, but these are not germane to this discussion of peripheral somatic nerves. Participation of the sympathetic fibers in late sequelae of nerve injury is dealt with below.

§ 32.128. Pain.[71]

Pain is not a conspicuous early feature of peripheral nerve injury; unpleasant sensory aberrations may arise, as mentioned above. Late in regeneration, pain may arise from pressure on neuromata[72] and may be sufficiently severe to require surgical resection of the neuroma, proximal section of the nerve itself, or even ablative procedures on the pain pathways in the spinal cord or brain stem.

§ 32.129. Causalgia.

A notable and dreaded instance of post-nerve-injury pain is "causalgia." This syndrome arises in perhaps 5% of peripheral nerve injuries. It is most often seen in incomplete injuries to the median nerve, alone or in conjunction with injury of the ulnar or radial nerve, and in the tibial nerve. Grazing injuries, such as those caused by a bullet passing nearby through the tissue, are especially prone to produce causalgia. Considerable evidence supports the concept of a "short circuit" etiology and implicates the sympathetic nervous system fibers in the mechanism. Efferent sympathetic impulses are thought to activate damaged and unmyelinated sensory fibers in the region of the nerve damage. The resultant afferent (sensory) impulses are interpreted by the central nervous system as a most distressing form of pain, usually described as burning in quality.

Causalgia is a specific syndrome with characteristic features, and should be differentiated from the variety of atypical pain syndromes that may follow trauma. Causalgia pain develops early after injury, from a few hours to one or two weeks. The pain is triggered by the slightest stimulus of ordinarily nonnoxious qualities, and the victim appears to

---

[71] For a discussion of pain generally, see Chapter 44A of this Cyclopedia.

[72] Editor's Note: "Neuromata" (plural for "neuroma"), as the term is used here, are nonfunctional and often painful masses of nerve fibers and cells that develop after trauma to the nerve; they are the "scarring" in the healing process. (The term neuroma is used also in describing a tumor of the nerve.) Traumatic neuroma is discussed earlier in § 32.119.

suffer intensely from the burning sensation. Striking alterations in auto-nomic function develop. The affected limb is usually moist, cold, and bluish or pink compared to its mate. With time, atrophic changes develop in the skin, and it becomes glossy and pale. The muscles become wasted and weak, and the bone undergoes decalcification. The joints become fibrotic, and motion is reduced or lost. Early in the disorder, before re-versible dystrophic changes are established, a diagnostic feature of cau-salgia is the complete relief of pain by anesthetic injection of the appro-priate sympathetic ganglion.

The impression is easily drawn that the sufferer has a psychoneurosis as the basis of his complaints. This is not the case; the bizarre behavioral aspects appear to be the result and not the cause of this pain syndrome. This conclusion is supported by the prompt reversal of the psychoneu-rotic features upon appropriate treatment.

Sympathectomy produces permanent relief in perhaps 95% of properly selected cases. Only persons showing full relief by sympathetic ganglion block are likely to derive permanent benefit. Stripping of adhesions around the injured site ("neurolysis") or stripping of sympathetic fibers from adjacent arterial walls are not effective. Resection of a neuroma with end-to-end suture of the stumps has been advocated as effective, but this should not be done if further motor function may be lost. Extirpation of the central sympathetic ganglia or their connections is the treatment of choice.

The role of the sympathetic nervous system in the maintenance of pain in causalgia is questioned by some authorities, although there is no doubt that the above described syndrome can occur after peripheral nerve injury. Causalgia is sometimes now included under the rubric of "complex regional pain syndrome" and treated by certain membrane-sta-bilizing drugs such as the anticonvulsant carbamazepine and the antiarrhythmic mexilitine.

§ 32.130. Sympathetic dystrophy.

Sympathetic dystrophy is a syndrome related to causalgia, with in-volvement of the sympathetic nervous system,[73] which occurs following trauma to a limb in which there is no specific injury to a major nerve. It usually develops after injury, often mild in degree, to a joint such as a wrist or ankle. Pain begins soon thereafter, and the hand or foot becomes pale, swollen, clammy, and cyanotic (bluish). The limb is held immobile and protected. Sudeck's atrophy[74] develops, with atrophic wasting of soft tissues and spotty decalcification of the bone. Functional use of the limb is lost.

---

[73] Editor's Note: The sympathetic nervous system is discussed in § 32.71.

[74] Editor's Note: "Sudeck's atrophy," or "posttraumatic osteoporosis," is loss of bone substance following injury in which there is nerve damage.

Physical therapy and active usage despite the pain has reversed this process in a few patients. Most patients, however, require relief of pain. Sympathetic nerve block and sympathectomy produce dramatic relief early in the course of the disorder. Repeated sympathetic blocks alone have sometimes sufficed to reverse the progressive disability and permit adequate rehabilitative efforts to be carried out.

Some believe that sympathetic dystrophy of the hand arises from injury to the median nerve in the carpal tunnel. Surgical decompression has produced relief in a few cases. This relatively simple operation has been advocated by some clinicians before undertaking the more reliable but more extensive procedure of sympathectomy.

The pain of sympathetic dystrophy is now often referred to as "complex regional pain syndrome," and some question whether the sympathetic nervous system even plays a role in maintaining the pain after a trauma that does not involve peripheral nerve injury. Such patients can be very difficult to manage medically, as do many with chronic pain. The potential role of financial and secondary gain should not be overlooked in these cases.

§ 32.131. Disuse atrophy.

The role of simple disuse cannot be discounted in the cause of the above syndromes. It is well known that disuse of a limb results in painful stiffness and limited motion of the part. Interstitial edema (accumulation of fluid in the interstitial spaces, between the cells) appears when active muscle contractions cease, since their action is needed to drive extravascular fluids into lymphatic channels as part of the body's endolymphatic circulation. A remarkable degree of objective physical change can result following immobilization for even a minor sprain. The changes of osteoporosis, atrophy of skin, fibrosis of joints and tendons, cyanosis, and excessive sweating develop in a limb that is protected and held immobile.

Patients who lack sufficient motivation to endure the unavoidable discomfort of using a recently immobilized extremity are prone to development of this greater, more disastrous misfortune of disuse atrophy. Such patients tend to be dependent types who readily resort to inadvisable surgical attempts to alleviate their pain. Since any surgical intervention produces pain of its own, this only compounds the problem. Some observers emphasize the part played by an unsettled compensation claim or a personal injury suit in the outcome, as well as the secondary gain that disability offers a person who is inadequate or maladjusted in his job, home, or personal life. Satisfactory settlement of pending claims for compensation seems an indispensable first step toward recovery in these patients. Formal psychiatric intervention also offers much assistance in discovering unconscious emotional stresses and in generating the requisite motivation for self-efforts at rehabilitation.

§ 32.132. Causes of pain other than trauma.

In atypical cases, explanations other than trauma for peripheral nerve pain should be considered. The "shoulder-hand syndrome" of painful disability mimics posttraumatic sympathetic dystrophy. It is recognized by its association with angina pectoris and coronary insufficiency. Interestingly, it may even respond well to sympathetic blockade or to sympathectomy. Trauma plays no known role in this syndrome.

The various neuritides (nerve inflammations) of viral origin, (such as herpes zoster or "shingles"), collagen diseases (such as periarteritis nodosa and systemic lupus erythematosis), and metabolic disease (pernicious anemia or Vitamin B12 deficiency, alcoholic or thiamine-deficiency neuropathy, diabetic neuropathy, etc.) may produce peripheral nerve damage with associated pain that is unrelated to trauma. Tabes dorsalis, an advanced stage of syphilis, produces bilateral lancinating pain that might be mistaken for traumatic nerve pain. Arachnoiditis, or inflammation of the spinal meninges, produces troublesome and confusing pain syndromes.

XVII. TREATMENT OF PERIPHERAL NERVE INJURIES

§ 32.133. General principles.

The objectives in treatment of peripheral nerve injuries are those in treatment of all trauma, namely, prevention of infection, optimal healing with least disfigurement, and preservation of maximal function. Open or contaminated penetrating wounds need early surgical exploration and debridement. Control of bleeding is essential to prevent nerve compression by blood clots. Major nerves with retained anatomical continuity should be replaced in the wound after debridement and covered with a protective layer of skin or soft tissue.

§ 32.134. Indications for surgery.

Immediate suture may be performed if a major nerve is cleanly transected, in whole or in part. This is not an urgent matter, however, and should be delayed if complications of healing are expected because of contamination, damaged blood supply, extensive soft tissue loss, etc. Analysis of wartime nerve injuries showed that early repair failed in half of the cases, requiring subsequent resection of the injured segment and resuture of the nerve ends. Suture is never performed unless the cut ends can be joined without tension on the suture line. Thus, immediate suture is not advised when a segment of nerve has been lost. Instead, the cut ends are tagged with metal clips or otherwise and replaced in the wound for later repair (delayed suture).

Nerve injuries due to stretching, ischemia, and electrical burns are not suitable for surgical exploration at any time. In these instances, damage

461

is distributed unevenly and patchily along the length of the nerve. Only discrete (not continuous), focal injury (laceration, contusion) stand to yield a better result from surgery than would be expected from spontaneous recovery.

Focal lesions of the peripheral nerve warrant exploration only when recovery of function or regeneration does not proceed at the expected pace for motor nerves of approximately one inch per month. Sufficient time must pass to allow the nature and severity of the injury to manifest. However, indefinite delay cannot be brooked since the time limit for useful motor innervation is about one year from injury. In practice, exploration and surgical repair are considered when no evidence of functional recovery exists at six to eight weeks after injury.

Recovery of cutaneous sensation is not a reliable guide to regeneration since overlapping innervation from other sensory nerves may play a prominent role in early return of function. Sensory innervation also differs from motor in that there is no definite time limit, so that continued recovery can continue for two or more years. This fact justifies surgical repair of sensory nerve lesions at great distances from the nerve endings, which would be fruitless in motor nerves.

The presence of "Tinel's sign" is favorable, but not conclusive evidence for regeneration in a mixed motor-sensory nerve. This sign reflects irritability of the regenerating nerve endings; the patient reports radiating sensations of "pins-and-needles" in the distribution of the sensory component of the nerve when the site of injury is lightly percussed. With time, the sensitive segment extends down the nerve, paralleling regeneration of the nerve. Because this is a phenomenon of the sensory component only, it tells nothing about regeneration of the motor part of the nerve. Thus, Tinel's sign can mislead the examiner into a conclusion that regeneration is proceeding satisfactorily, when in fact the motor part may be totally dysfunctional.

§ 32.135. Reunion of nerve ends.

If at exploration a discontinuous lesion is found (i.e., a severed nerve with scarred, retracted ends) the treatment is resection of the damaged stumps and reunion of the nerve by careful surgical suture of the stumps. It is essential for good results that the entire extent of scarring be removed, so that the joined ends are fresh and show the fascicular structure of the nerve. There must be good blood supply to the ends, but active bleeding must be gently stemmed before reunion. Alignment of the stumps must be retained, so that rotation does not result in maldistribution of the fibers to the distal stump.

Nerve anastomoses (reunions) must be free of tension at the suture line. Both stumps must be mobilized sufficiently to permit this, even if the skin incision must be carried far from the site of injury. Transposition to a straighter path, and flexion of interposed joints, provides the needed length in most instances. Postoperatively, the suture line may require protection by immobilization of the limb in flexion, using plaster casts or other devices for fixation. As healing proceeds, the casts are changed at intervals and the limb gradually restored to normal position over a period of many weeks.

§ 32.136. Nerve grafts.

Use of nerve grafts may be considered to cover unclosed gaps in certain instances. No more than six to eight centimeters can be bridged satisfactorily in this manner. Grafts also have the disadvantage of two suture lines, a problem common to instances of multiple focal injuries along a single nerve. Considerable attrition and shuffling of fibers occurs at each suture line, and the eventual result may be so unsatisfactory as to hardly justify the surgical procedure. Still, in extreme cases a nerve graft is preferable to no treatment at all. In the special instances of the facial nerve and digital nerves of the fingers, nerve grafts give a useful functional result.

§ 32.137. Treatment of "neuroma-in-continuity."

If the injured nerve is found to be continuous, the damaged site will be apparent as a hardened fusiform enlargement. This is a neuroma-in-continuity and consists of tangled whorls of fibrous scar and regenerated nerve fibers. Various numbers of these fibers lie entrapped within the fibrous maze, while others wander uselessly toward the soft tissue outside. Still others wend their way circuitously into channels (endoneurial tubules) of the distal stump, destined for connections at effector sites in the body. An inevitable attrition of fibers in transit occurs at every juncture, whether of accidental or deliberate (surgical) traumatic origin. Functional attrition occurs as well, as motor and sensory fibers become "shuffled" into inappropriate channels of the distal stump. This shuffling accounts for some remarkable late effects of nerve injury, such as sensory mislocalization on the skin and mass action of small muscles of the hand and fingers when fine skilled movements are attempted.

The functional state of regeneration through a neuroma-in-continuity cannot be accurately assayed by inspection alone. The most improbable-looking mass may convey an adequate number of axons (nerve fibers) through its bulk to the distal nerve. Electrical stimulation is needed for a functional evaluation at the time of surgery. A bipolar electrical stimulus is delivered to the nerve proximal to the injury, and conducted impulses or actual motor contraction sought along the distal nerve. Absence of either finding at six to eight weeks after injury indicates complete and irreversible nerve injury. The treatment is complete excision of the neuroma and end-to-end suture (neurorrhaphy) as described above.

Conversely, if conducted impulses are detected at surgery, the neuroma-in-continuity should be left alone. This finding implies the pres-

463

ence of functioning large myelinated nerve fibers across the injury site and prognosticates eventual recovery at least equal to that to be expected from surgical repair. If sensory return but no motor function exists at eight weeks, the prognosis is inconclusive, and optimal treatment is not established at this time.

Some advocate the procedure of neurolysis, or surgical release of a neuroma from the fibrous bands that connect it to surrounding soft tissue after injury. Others suggest that any favorable results after neurolysis of a neuroma-in-continuity merely reflect the favorable natural course of such lesions rather than a benefit of treatment. On theoretical grounds, neurolysis seems of dubious benefit, for it is thought to be the internal scarring within the neuroma that leads to misdirection of nerve fibers and prevents their establishment of functional connections.

§ 32.138. Specific nerve injuries — Treatment and evaluation of disability.[75]

The general anatomical features of the peripheral nervous system have been described above. Each spinal cord segment innervates the tissues of its dermatome and myotome[76] via paired spinal nerves. Multiple spinal nerves combine in the neck to form the cervical and brachial plexi and in the low back to form the lumbar and lumbosacral plexi. Intermingling of fibers from diverse spinal roots gives rise to trunks of the brachial plexus, and further shuffling occurs to form the divisions, the cords, and the mixed peripheral nerves to the arm. Throughout the body, intermingled spinal root fibers in peripheral nerves resegregate to terminate in tissues derived from their respective dermatome or myotome.

The intricacies of the peripheral innervation provide features that aid in evaluation of the site and probable severity of nerve lesions by clinical examination and by supplementary diagnostic procedures. We will deal here with details of the major named nerves that are commonly of interest in traumatic circumstances.

The proportion of sensory fibers in motor nerves has a large bearing on the likelihood of success in surgical repair, since misdirection of regenerating sensory fibers along previous motor pathways causes significant loss of function. For sensory nerves, the precise region of supply, the extent of overlap by adjacent nerves, and the required degree of tactile

---

[75] Editor's Note: In testifying to the permanent impairment of the peripheral nerves, many physicians rely on the tables established by the American Medical Association's Committee on Rating of Mental and Physical Impairment, which set out in terms of percentages the impairment of the important body parts and their relation to impairment of the body as a whole. These tables are reprinted in Chapter 27 of this Cyclopedia.

[76] Editor's Note: A "dermatome" is a sensory root field on the skin supplied by a single posterior spinal root; a "myotome" is a group of muscles innervated from a single spinal segment.

sensitivity in the area all determine the seriousness of interruption of the nerve. When overlap is extensive, the loss of a sensory nerve will have little practical consequence. Motor nerves are more discretely distributed, with little overlap, so that injury results in characteristic loss of affected muscle fibers. Some major bulky muscles, such as the pectoralis (innervated by the fifth cervical and first thoracic) and quadriceps femoris (second to fourth lumbar via the femoral nerve) receive numerous twigs from the main nerves of supply. Interruption of several of these twigs may produce no permanent functional deficit because of compensatory hypertrophy of remaining intact neuromuscular units. Thus, the consequences of motor denervation depend strongly on the site of injury, the muscles affected, and the possibility of compensation for lost function by other adjacent structures. The limits on effective motor regeneration are approximately one foot of length and one year in time.

§ 32.139. Radial nerve.

The radial nerve is a mixed peripheral nerve of the arm with minor sensory components. It arises as a continuation of the lateral cord, derived from all three trunks of the brachial plexus and carries fibers from the fifth through eighth cervical spinal nerves. Important motor supply is to the triceps muscle of the arm (which extends the forearm), and the extensors of wrist and fingers in the forearm. The clinical deficit of extensor palsy is called "wrist-drop." The brachioradialis muscle (assists in forearm flexion) also is supplied, but this muscle is of secondary importance because its functions may be performed by other nearby muscles. There is no sensory "autonomous zone," so that total interruption of the radial nerve may produce no detectable sensory loss whatsoever. This is true even though the nerve supplies the back of the hand and wrist.

In testing for radial dysfunction, one must beware of trick movements. For example, flexion of the wrist passively produces slight extension of the digits; this should not be confused with active extension, nor taken as a sign of radial nerve integrity. Electrical stimulation over the lower lateral arm (just above the outer side of the elbow) will elicit extension of the wrist and digits if the nerve is intact below that point.

The radial nerve is most commonly injured by pressure or traction near the mid-humerus of the arm, where it lies in the humeral groove. Numerous medical malpractice claims arise because injury is often blamed on intravenous injection or infusion in the antecubital fossa. This charge is seldom substantiated. A frequent cause of these injuries is "Saturday night palsy," a trauma induced by pressure on the back of the arm while lying in a drunken stupor.

Suture at the elbow leads to restoration of wrist extension in two months, of finger extension in four months, and thumb extension (via the long extensor muscle) in six months. The most distal muscle is the short extensor of the thumb; this does not regain function after nerve suture at the elbow or above; and attention should be directed toward substitution for this short extensor by early tendon transfer.

After suture at the mid-humerus level, brachioradialis function returns early. Wrist extension returns in four months, finger extension in six. Thumb extension (the long extensor) takes eight to nine months.

At the level of the axilla, multiple nerve injury is probable, with loss of the triceps (save a few possible higher branches) as well as innervation of the forearm extensors. Suture restores triceps function in three months and wrist extension in six months. No return of thumb extension is expected.

Because the sensory innervation of the radial nerve is unimportant, no attempt should be made to preserve it by nerve suture. Rather, return of motor function only should be sought, with the expectation of 80 to 90% good results. The high success rate is attributable to the relatively few sensory fibers in the nerve, so that shuffling of sensory and motor fibers is kept to a minimum. Moreover, the shuffling of motor fibers among several individual muscles is unimportant because the resultant mass action is acceptable in the muscles of extension. Finally, adequate function of the wrist and digital extensors is possible with less than full return of strength. All in all, the radial nerve is an ideal candidate for surgical repair.

§ 32.140.　Median nerve.

The median nerve is an important mixed motor-sensory peripheral nerve of the arm. It is derived from the lateral and medial cords via the anterior divisions of all three trunks of the brachial plexus and carries fibers from the fifth cervical through first thoracic spinal roots. The autonomous sensory zone includes the tips of the thumb and the first two fingers. For some time after injury, until sensory function is taken over by adjacent nerves, the sensory loss includes the lateral two-thirds of the palm and the contiguous palmar surfaces of the thumb and first two fingers. This autonomous sensory region is essential to skilled movements of manipulation between thumb and fingers; hence, preservation of median nerve sensory function is even more important than retention of its motor function.

Motor supply by the median nerve includes part of the flexors of the wrist (on the side with the thumb), and the flexors of the thumb and first two fingers. Also, it supplies the important muscles for fine movement of the thumb, including the opponens pollicis muscle, which permits pinching movements of thumb against other finger tips. Although essential, this motion can be duplicated by tendon transfer, so that loss of median motor function is less damaging than might at first be supposed.

The median nerve is most often injured at the wrist, where it passes into the palm of the hand through the carpal tunnel, beneath a tough band called the flexor retinaculum of the wrist. Mechanisms of injury include penetrating wounds, pressure in acute post-traumatic swelling in the carpal tunnel, and chronic arthritic swelling.

Injuries to this nerve, like the radial nerve, are sometimes alleged after injection at the antecubital fossa and therefore are the subject of malpractice claims. This seldom happens, however. Again, most cases result from compression at a higher level, such as along the medial aspect of the arm. Unconscious and comatose persons who lie with their arm draped over the hard edge of bed or chair may compress this nerve, as well as the ulnar and even radial nerves.

The median nerve supplies three muscles situated at the base of the thumb in the hand: the short flexor and adductor (toward the palm), and the opponens. Finger flexors (index and middle) are also supplied by this nerve, but in the upper forearm. Any loss of finger flexion in a wrist lesion implies injury to the long flexor tendons that also run through the carpal tunnel, but does not indicate injury of the median nerve at that point.

Certain trick movements may disguise median nerve dysfunction, *e.g.*, the abductor pollicis longus (radial nerve) and flexor pollicis brevis (with a strong ulnar contricution) can act together to mimic opponens action.

Median neurorrhaphy (suture of the transected nerve) at the wrist leads to contraction of the thenar group of muscles on electrical stimulation in three months and to voluntary contraction at four to five months.

Median interruption at the elbow causes loss of flexors to the thumb and first two fingers as well as loss of the thenar group and some intrinsic hand muscles. The resulting deformity is described as "violin hand," because of the resemblance to the fingering hand of a violinist. Suture at the elbow leads to return of function in the wrist flexors (flexor carpi radialis) and palmarus longus (tightens the palm) in two months. Flexor indicis (to the index finger) returns in four months, and flexor pollicis longus (to the thumb) in six months. The thenar group may recover in ten to twelve months, or they may not recover at all. Sensory return will be satisfactory in time, however.

Median suture at the axilla leads to return only of the proximal forearm musculature (*i.e.*, flexor carpi radialis) in six months. No return of finger flexors of thenar muscles is to be expected. Repair is still indicated for return of sensory innervation, however.

Entrapment of the median nerve at the carpal tunnel of the wrist is a common problem. It can result in pain as well as motor and sensory deficit distal to the wrist (carpal tunnel syndrome). The clinical features of the syndrome are quite variable. Diagnosis should always be established by nerve conduction velocity testing, especially before surgery. The role of repetitive hand movements in the development of carpal tunnel syndrome has significant medicolegal importance and is controversial.[77] Pregnancy, diabetes mellitus, and hypothyroidism all predispose to the development of such entrapment neuropathies. Many carpal tunnel syndrome cases can be treated conservatively with a wrist splint and physical therapy. Injection of corticosteroids into the carpal tunnel has been attempted with little success. If conservative treatment fails, most patients respond well to surgical release of the carpal tunnel.

§ 32.141. Ulnar nerve.

The ulnar nerve is a mixed motor-sensory peripheral nerve of the arm, arising from the medial cord via the anterior division of the lower trunk of the brachial plexus. It carries fibers of the seventh cervical through the first thoracic spinal roots. Motor supply is to the flexors of wrist and digits in the forearm (flexor carpi ulnaris, and flexor digitorum superficialis and profundis to the ring and little fingers). At the wrist, it divides into deep and superficial branches. The deep branch supplies many small intrinsic muscles of the hand, as well as two muscles of the thumb (adductor pollicis and flexor pollicis brevis). The superficial branch supplies the hypothenar group of the little finger and one-half of the ring finger. The autonomous sensory zone is the palmar tip of the little finger and one-half of the ring finger. This sensory innervation is not indispensable, and may be sacrificed without serious disability.

The important aspect of ulnar function is the supply to intrinsic hand muscles. When these are denervated, the balance with extensor muscles to the ring and little fingers is upset, and these digits are pulled into a "claw-hand" position. A helpful diagnostic finding is "Froment's sign," in which attempted adduction (toward the palm) of the thumb results in flexion of the distal phalanx (tip) of the thumb. This occurs because the denervated adductor pollicis (ulnar nerve) is substituted for by the long flexor of the thumb (median nerve).

Injury is most common in the ulnar groove behind the medial elbow, either by laceration or by pressure. Persons who sit long hours with elbows on their knees, such as habitual television watchers or persons with chronic lung disease, may develop bilateral ulnar neuropathy. The nerve may also be injured in the wrist, where it passes superficial to the transverse carpal ligament. In the hand, traumatic ulnar neuropathy results from using the hand as a hammer; denervation potentials and clinical dysfunction in such cases appear only in the intrinsic muscles of the first two fingers.

When segments of the ulnar nerve are torn away, up to 10 cm. in length can be gained by transposition of the nerve from back to front of the elbow, combined with flexion of the wrist and elbow. The added length is maintained by holding the arm flexed in a cast until nerve

---

[77] Editor's Note: On repetitive motion injuries, see Chapter 10, § 10.45 of this Cyclopedia. Carpal tunnel syndrome is also discussed in Chapter 31, § 31.42a.

healing begins, then gradually extending the limb through a series of cast changes over several months.

Suture of the ulnar nerve at the wrist produces good sensory return in three months. Motor return to the hypothenar muscles also takes three months, while the return of index finger intrinsic muscles (first dorsal interosseus) requires six months.

At the elbow, sensory return is good in time, but motor return is only fair. At both wrist and elbow, reinnervation leads to poorly co-ordinated action of the intrinsic muscles (lumbricales) of the ring and little fingers. Only one in six patients regain independent finger movements. Tendon transfer may be needed to stabilize the affected fingers and prevent formation of the "claw-hand" deformity.

Results of suture at the axilla are poor. The nerve should be sutured only if totally discontinuous, with the sole expectation of some sensory return. The motor fibers will not regenerate from the axilla, and early tendon transfer is indicated.

Compression of the ulnar nerve

In contrast to the carpal tunnel syndrome, little information was available in the past about compression of the ulnar nerve at the elbow (cubital tunnel syndrome). Ulnar nerve compression is believed to occur as often as median nerve compression; however, the symptoms are less likely to bring the patient to a physician because the ulnar nerve at the elbow is mainly a motor nerve rather than sensory, so the symptoms mostly involve atrophy of muscle.

Ulnar nerve compression at the elbow was recognized only relatively recently. It was first reported that the ulnar nerve lesion at the elbow, called "tardy ulnar neuritis," was usually due to compression of the nerve rather than to traction or friction. However, a band of fibrous tissue ("arcuate ligament") was found bridging the origins of the flexor carpi ulnaris muscle in a manner similar to the transverse carpal ligament's compression of the median nerve.

Cubital tunnel syndrome usually has an insidious onset. The symptoms may follow an episode of trauma, such as a blow to the extremity at any level from the shoulder to the hand. Usually symptoms of ulnar nerve compression do not appear until some weeks after the injury. Some patients note vague symptoms of weakness, heaviness, and easy fatigue without any history of trauma. The symptoms may persist as a minor annoyance until an increase in activity aggravates the problem. In more advanced cases, the patient may have various combinations of symptoms such as sensory impairment and tingling in the ring and little fingers, which may be precipitated by resting the elbow on a hard surface, or pain in the ulnar side of the hand and aching in the ulnar side of the forearm. The pain may involve the inner aspect of the arm and extend to the axilla. Some women complain of pain involving the area of the breast adjacent to the axilla.

Any activity that elevates the extremity aggravates the symptoms, such as using a paint brush, putting the hand on the steering wheel of a car, and combing the hair. The patients are often awakened by episodes of numbness in the fingers at night. The pain at the ulnar side of the forearm is more severe at night.

There are a number of useful tests for diagnosing and localizing compressions of the ulnar nerve. One such test evaluates sensation in the pulp of the fingers by comparison with the opposite hand. The quality of sensation is evaluated by lightly stroking the pulp of the finger in the involved hand simultaneously with the corresponding finger in the normal hand. Another test checks for the presence of atrophy in the hypothenar area (the ridge on the palm along the bases of the fingers and the ulnar margin). A third test checks abduction of the fingers, i.e., ability to spread the fingers apart.

A fourth test determines flexion at the distal joint of the ring and little fingers. This evaluates the component of the deep flexor muscle of these fingers that is supplied by the ulnar nerve. A fifth test checks the muscularity of the upper forearm just beyond the elbow. A decrease in muscular tonicity may be demonstrated by a comparison with the opposite side. In more advanced cases, localized atrophy of the flexor muscles supplied by the ulnar nerve results in a depression in the forearm. A sixth test checks for paresthesia along the course of the ulnar nerve. Lastly, there is a seventh test that checks for tenderness of the ulnar nerve above the elbow by gently compressing the nerve against the medial epicondyle of the humerus.

Treatment of ulnar nerve compression of the elbow consists of excising the ligament. It may be necessary in some cases that the patient wait up to a year to make any conclusions about the result of nerve decompression operation. In older patients, muscular atrophy is less apt to be reversible.

In the past, compressive ulnar neuropathy was frequently misdiagnosed as a cervical radiculopathy or as carpal tunnel syndrome. However, with modern electrodiagnostic equipment, it is now usually a simple matter to establish the diagnosis and localize the lesion, which should always be done prior to attempting cubital tunnel release and ulnar nerve transposition for entrapment neuropathy.

§ 32.142. Combined lesions of median and ulnar nerves.

Combined noncompressive lesions of the median and ulnar nerves have a poor outlook, with only a 5% chance of the patient regaining useful function by nerve suture at wrist or the elbow. Even so, suture is indicated to regain sensation in the tips of the thumb and first two fingers — the important autonomous zone of the median nerve. Some slight thumb innervation may also be possible. Tendon transfers are needed to provide grip and pincer movements between the thumb and index finger.

§ 32.143. Brachial plexus.

Injury to the brachial plexus occurs by direct blows to the clavicular region or neck, by dislocation of the shoulder, by penetrating stab and gunshot wounds, and by severe stretching of the arm. These are serious injuries. Motor function returns only in proximal muscles of the shoulder and arm. No return at all is expected in muscles of the forearm and hand. Sensory return may be useful in time.

The brachial plexus has three trunks: the upper (from the fifth and sixth cervical spinal roots), the middle (seventh cervical) and lower (eighth cervical and first thoracic). Injury of the upper trunk produces the syndrome of Erb-Duchenne, or Erb's palsy. The arm hangs at the side, rotated inward, while the hand assumes the expectant "porter's tip" position.

Suture of the upper trunk, and its derivative posterior and lateral cords, may restore useful function in the deltoid and supraspinatous muscles (elevation of the shoulder) and the biceps and triceps muscle (flex and extend the arm). Two other muscles of note, the brachioradialis (helps flex the forearm) and extensor carpi radialis (extends the wrist) are supplied through these structures via the radial nerve. Suture may restore some function in the former, but none at all in the latter.

In traction injuries, preservation of sensation is encouraging, but is no guarantee of motor return. Function in a "signal" muscle of the shoulder should be seen by six weeks. If no return is seen, the injury should be explored on the chance that a reparable lesion may be found in the upper trunk or posterior or lateral cords. Suture of the upper trunk leads to return of deltoid function in five months. Repair of the lateral cord leads to return of biceps function in three to four months.

The forearm and hand are innervated through the middle and lower trunks of the brachial plexus via the radial, median, and ulnar nerves. Injury to the lower trunk produces the syndrome of Klumpke or Duchenne-Aran, with paralysis of the intrinsic hand muscles, ulnar nerve sensory loss, and Horner's syndrome (see below). Mild injury to the lower trunk may result from pressure of a poorly fitted crutch pad ("crutch palsy"). Because of the large distances involved and the one-year limitation on effective motor regeneration, there is probably no point in surgical repair of the lower trunk or medial cord. No motor function will return below the elbow, and the involved sensation (ulnar nerve distribution) is not essential.

471

Certain clues aid in localization of injury, and in predicting eventual outcome. Innervation to the serratus anterior muscle is via the long thoracic nerve (fifth through seventh cervical), which arises from the spinal roots prior to formation of the brachial plexus. Denervation produces a "winged scapula," with posterior protrusion of the shoulder blade when the arm is lifted and pushed forward against resistance. Loss of serratus anterior function after trauma implies avulsion of the fifth through seventh cervical roots from the spinal cord. This possibility can be documented by cervical myelography or by electromyography. The grim prospects for total uselessness of such a denervated limb are such as to warrant consideration of disarticulation of the limb.

The appearance of Horner's syndrome results from interruption of the sympathetic innervation that accompanies the ventral roots of the eighth cervical and first thoracic spinal nerves. These fibers branch off prior to formation of the brachial plexus. The patient with this syndrome has a constricted pupil, drooping eyelid, sunken appearance to the eye, and lack of sweating over the face, all on the side of the lesion. This sympathetic nervous system lesion has mainly cosmetic significance, except in that it reveals that the lower brachial plexus roots may have been avulsed. The prospect for recovery of denervated intrinsic hand muscles is nil.

Other disorders that may mimic brachial plexus trauma include tumor (primary or metastatic) of the cervical spinal cord, herniated cervical intervertebral disc, osteoarthritis of the cervical spine, progressive spinal muscular atrophy, and brachial plexitis (neuritis of the brachial plexus).

§ 32.144. Peroneal nerve.

The peroneal nerve in the leg is one of the two main branches of the sciatic nerve at the popliteal fossa (behind the knee). Like the radial nerve, it serves extensor motor functions (anterior tibial muscle, for foot-toe dorsiflexion and foot eversion), and has little important sensory function. The sensory autonomous zone is confined to a small patch on the dorsum of the foot, although initially after injury there is widespread loss over the anterior-lateral calf and foot. Electrical stimulation of the nerve is important for early detection of returning function, since voluntary movements return several weeks after the return of evoked electrical activity. In traction injuries with no evidence of return within six weeks, the prognosis for recovery is poor.

The peroneal nerve is most frequently injured of all nerves in the leg. It is particularly vulnerable to laceration or contusion where it crosses the head of the fibula at the lower lateral border of the knee. It is subject to stretch injury in the lateral popliteal space by dislocation of the knee. The most important motor loss is evident as "foot-drop," or inability to clear the ground in the forward swing of the foot in walking. A slapping sound by the sole of the foot follows the heel-strike in walking, since the descent of the foot is uncontrolled by the normal tone of the dorsiflexor muscles. Coexistent denervation in muscles supplied by the tibial nerve, or in muscles of the opposite leg, suggests peripheral neuritis, rather than trauma, as the cause of observed deficit.

The main point in repair of the peroneal nerve is to achieve useful dorsiflexion of the foot for walking. If nerve repair fails, this can be achieved by means of a spring brace or an ankle-foot orthotic (AFO) brace. Only 60% of nerve repairs at the popliteal level are adequate in this regard. A fusion procedure (triple arthrodesis) of the ankle also permits swing-through of the foot in walking, and is another alternative treatment. It is imperative to avoid undue tension on the suture line in peroneal nerve repair. The nerve can be mobilized proximally as far as the hip to achieve length, and fixation of the limb in knee flexion and hip extension lends further length. Avulsion of the suture line is a common occurrence when these precautions are disregarded.

Following suture at the popliteal level, return of peroneal muscle function (foot eversion) should occur in about four months. Tibialis anticus function (foot dorsiflexion) should return in six months. Return of toe extensors (extensor digitorum and extensor hallucis longus) follows later.

The peroneal portion of the sciatic nerve is a distinct division in the posterior thigh, and is selectively involved in dislocation of the hip and in hip surgery complicated by stretch injury of the nerve. The lateral hamstring muscles (biceps femoris) are supplied by this branch. Injuries more than eight inches above the head of the fibula (i.e., at midthigh or above) result in poor return of ankle dorsiflexion. A failure rate of 80% has been reported after hip dislocations with traction injury of the peroneal muscle at the hip.

§ 32.145. Tibial nerve.

The tibial nerve passes medially in the popliteal fossa behind the knee to supply the muscles of the calf, the flexor muscles of the posterior tibial group, and the intrinsic muscles of the foot. The sensory supply to the sole of the foot, via the medial and lateral plantar branches, is very important, for the autonomous zone includes the entire weight-bearing surface of the foot. Preservation of this sensation is needed to prevent trophic ulceration. Following nerve suture, painful paresthesias often develop in this plantar distribution, and have discouraged some from repair of the tibial nerve. However, these pains pass with time, and should be endured, for the gains in plantar sensory innervation are well worth the price in pain. The plantar nerves also may be injured at the ankle, by traumatic blows or by ill-fitting shoe-tops or by entrapment in the tarsal tunnel.

Motor loss in tibial nerve lesions includes the inability to plantarflex the foot (rise on the toes), due to denervation of the gastrocnemius and soleus muscles of the calf. Also involved are the tibialis posterior muscle (inversion of the foot) and long flexors of the toes and intrinsic muscles of the foot. Loss of intrinsic muscles may lead to a "claw-foot," just as loss of ulnar and median nerve do in the hand. Abduction of the great toe may be lost, if this motion is in the repertoire of the patient prior to injury.

Electrical nerve stimulation is needed for evaluation of the progress of motor and sensory recovery. Electrical responsiveness precedes voluntary movement by a month or more, although reflex contraction of muscles may appear simultaneously with return of electrical responsiveness. In suture at the popliteal level, 60% have return of useful plantar flexion. Recovery of plantar sensation takes up to one year.

§ 32.146. Combined lesions of peroneal and tibial nerves.

The peroneal and tibial components of the sciatic nerve are separate and distinct branches in the thigh. Injury or recovery of one does not predict the outcome in the other. It is more important to recognize and repair injury of the tibial component, for the major peroneal nerve deficit (foot-drop) is easily corrected via a foot brace or ankle fusion, while the tibial nerve sensory loss (plantar surface of the foot) is potentially disabling.

At the midthigh level, peroneal exploration is not worthwhile unless the tibial component is also damaged. Tibial nerve repair at midthigh leads to useful plantar flexion in 50% of the cases and to adequate plantar sensation in 50%. Motor branches to the hamstrings come off high, so that knee flexion is seldom involved in midthigh injury. Repair of sciatic nerve branches at the hip or sacral plexus level has little to offer.

§ 32.147. Femoral nerve.

The femoral nerve arises from the lumbar plexus (first through fourth lumbar), and supplies the quadriceps femoris (knee extensors) and sartorius muscles. The main trunk divides two to four centimeters below the inguinal ligament of the groin, into superficial and deep branches. The superficial branch supplies the skin of the medial thigh, and motor innervation to the sartorius muscle (the "tailor's" muscle, which crosses the leg). The deep branch divides repeatedly about five centimeters below the inguinal ligament, sending numerous muscular twigs to the quadriceps group, while a sensory component (the saphenous nerve) continues on to the skin of the anteromedial calf and foot.

The femoral nerve may suffer stretch injury in hyperextension of the hip. Penetrating wounds such as gunshot injury produce a serious injury in this region. Clean lacerations of the femoral trunk are uncommonly treated, since associated involvement of the femoral artery usually leads to loss of life or limb. When multiple motor twig injury has occurred, there is usually severe associated damage to the muscle bundles, so that attempted surgical repair is pointless. Functional recovery then depends on hypertrophy of remaining undamaged neuromuscular units of the quadriceps muscle. If quadriceps function is completely lost, or nearly so, a lock-knee brace will permit walking. Sensory function of the femoral nerve is unimportant, and is not an indication for attempted nerve repair.

§ 32.148. Obturator nerve.

The obturator nerve also arises from the lumbar plexus. It supplies the muscles of adduction of the medial thigh (for closing the knees together). The obturator nerve is seldom injured, since it enjoys a sheltered position. Extreme abduction, as by a forced lateral "split" of the legs, may produce a stretch injury. This sometimes occurs in obstetrical patients when placed in stirrups on the examination or delivery table.

§ 32.149. Lumbosacral plexus.

The lumbosacral plexus is derived from the fourth and fifth lumbar and first through third sacral spinal nerves. It supplies motor innervation to the paraspinous muscles of the low back, and the gluteal musculature of the buttocks. It then continues on as the sciatic nerve, with its two distinct major components, the peroneal and tibial nerves. These branches supply all the muscles and most of the skin below the knee.

Lumbar plexus (first through fourth lumbar) and lumbosacral plexus injury may be claimed after abdominal and pelvic surgery, respectively. Evaluation of such claims requires study of the several branches at varying distances from the spinal canal. Serial electromyographic (EMG) study is important to determine the onset of appropriate denervation potentials in affected areas (and only these) between eighteen and twenty-one days after the alleged injury. Without such findings, the claim of injury at surgery cannot be sustained. Sciatic nerve injury may be claimed after medical injection, and in fact does occur. The same rules regarding appropriately distributed denervation potentials, appearing at eighteen to twenty-one days, must hold to substantiate the alleged injury.

Other causes of neurological dysfunction in the lower extremities include plexus neuritis, spinal cord tumor, amyotrophic lateral sclerosis, poliomyelitis, and peripheral neuropathy of various causes. Bilateral lesions are unlikely in trauma, and findings of changes outside the known distribution of an allegedly injured nerve rule out trauma as the cause of deficit.

§ 32.150. Miscellaneous nerve injuries.

The *cervical plexus* (first through fourth cervical) may be injured by direct blows or prolonged pressure on the side of the neck. The injury is frequently seen in hod carriers. Muscular denervation is confined to the trapezius muscle.

The *dorsal scapular nerve* (fourth and fifth cervical) supplies the rhomboid muscles, between the scapulae. It may be stretched or injured by a direct blow. Evidence of denervation in other muscles from the same spinal levels (supraspinatus, infraspinatus, trapezius) rules out trauma as the cause of dysfunction.

The *long thoracic nerve* (fifth through seventh cervical) supplies the serratus anterior muscle. It can be stretched or contused by direct blow. One confusing but rarely encountered cause of dysfunction is neuritis from horse serum, but this is seldom confined to this nerve alone.

The *suprascapular nerve* (fifth and sixth cervical) supplies the supraspinatus (elevates the shoulder) and infraspinatus (rotates the arm externally) muscles. Traumatic swelling of the shoulder joint may affect only the latter. Lesions of this serve or these muscles must be differentiated from disuse atrophy secondary to other injury, hysteria, or malingering.

The *axillary nerve* (fifth and sixth cervical) supplies the deltoid (shoulder elevation) and teres minor muscles (external rotation of the arm, with infraspinatus). It may be injured in posterior dislocations of the shoulder or associated with stretch injury of the upper trunk or lateral cord of the brachial plexus. It is affected by neuritis of the brachial plexus also.

The *musculocutaneous nerve* (fifth through seventh cervical) innervates the biceps brachii muscle (flexes the arm) and supplies sensory innervation to the lateral forearm as the lateral cutaneous nerve of the forearm. The denervated biceps muscle is flat, flabby, and inert. Rupture of the biceps tendon may produce a similar state of disuse atrophy, but the muscle will not show denervation potentials on electromyography. This nerve may be injured in the arm or may be involved via lesions of the upper trunk or lateral cord of the brachial plexus.

The *plantar nerves* convey sensory and motor fibers of the tibial nerve to the foot. There are two main branches, medial and lateral. They may be injured by blows or fractures of the ankle, by tight, ill-fitting shoes, or by entrapment in the tarsal tunnel. Injury causes diminished sensation of the soles of the feet, and loss of intrinsic muscle function (with denervation potentials) in the feet.

Meralgia paresthetica is also a common problem, which results from entrapment of the *lateral femoral cutaneous nerve* at the inguinal ligament and causes numbness of the anterolateral thigh. Patients sometimes experience mild neuropathic pain, but significant pain is rare.

Since this is a sensory nerve, it does not cause weakness or electromyographic changes. It is sometimes misdiagnosed as lumbar radiculopathy or femoral neuropathy.

Some cranial nerves are of passing interest. In general, injury to cranial nerves is permanent and irreversible. One notable exception is the *trigeminal nerve* (cranial nerve V), which supplies sensory innervation to the face. It is often subjected to alcohol block and even avulsion injury in the treatment of facial pain (tic douloureux), but is notorious for its capacity to regenerate with return of sensation (and pain). The *facial nerve* (cranial nerve VII) and hypoglossal nerve (XII) show excellent regeneration after nerve suture and even after nerve graft. Cross-nerve anastomosis of XII to VII is successful in restoring facial expression after injury to the facial nerve, as in severe Bell's palsy, certain instances of skull fracture, and damage during removal of an acoustic nerve Schwannoma in the posterior fossa of the skull. The resulting movements from cross-grafting are of the mass-action type, with little individuality of contraction of the various facial muscles and consequent limited range of expression.

§ 32.151. Rehabilitation.

In consideration of peripheral nerve injury, it must be stressed that the primary objective of treatment is the recovery of functional use of the injured part. Slavish compulsion to re-establish the integrity of each damaged nerve is not always appropriate. Often, a certain amount of permanent deficit must be accepted as the baseline on which rehabilitative efforts must build.

Physical therapy

Regeneration of nerve injuries is long and slow and the patient must begin to use the injured part before the process is complete.

New motions may be learned to compensate for deficient ones. Physical therapy, with active and passive "range-of-motion" exercises, maintains muscle tone and prevents flexion contractures. Suitable splints to maintain position of parts, such as the fingers of the hand, may be helpful. Padding must be used to protect desensitized areas. Continued usage prevents the painful consequences of the unused limb, and greatly reduces the psychological disability that results from prolonged invalid status.

Electrical stimulation

Electrical stimulation of denervated muscles is a superficially appealing technique touted to maintain muscle integrity and strength while nerve regrowth is going on. Unfortunately, to be effective it is necessary to stimulate each affected muscle about one-half hour daily, always

against resistance. The time demands of this approach render it impractical, and the results are not worthy of the effort expended.

Substitutive mechanics

Substitutive mechanics is an invaluable approach for speeding functional return. Tendon transfers permit old muscles to perform unfamiliar
tasks, replacing muscles denervated by nerve injury. These are particularly useful in the hand. For example, the "opponens" of the thumb
(median nerve supply) may be replaced by an ulnar-innervated flexor
tendon. Similar substitutions may be made for intrinsic hand muscles
(ulnar nerve supply) and wrist extensors (radial nerve). In foot-drop, a
brace may be adequate. Bony fusions of ankle, wrist, or other joint may
improve function of remaining muscle groups to a satisfactory degree.

XVIII. ELECTROMYOGRAPHY

§ 32.152. The electromyogram.

Electromyography (EMG) is a laboratory procedure that measures and
records the electrical activity generated within the skeletal muscles.

The instrument used is the electromyograph, which consists of the
following components: electrode system, electric amplifier, cathode-ray
oscilloscope (TV-like tube), and loud speaker. By the insertion of the
needle electrode into the muscle, the activity is picked up, led into the
electromyograph for amplification, and converted into various kinds of
sounds and visual muscle waves (electromyogram) that can be heard and
seen. Interpretation of the EMG is dependent upon the characteristic
sound heard from the loud speaker and the type of muscle waves seen on
the oscilloscope. This is possible because each genuine muscle wave produces its own characteristic sound. However, there are many different
kinds of waves that can closely resemble each other and can only be
identified by the sound they generate. In a sense, the EMG comprises
more than a laboratory procedure. The examiner must be a physician
who is an expert not only in the interpretation of the sounds generated
by the system, but one who is also familiar with the anatomy and physiology of the neuromuscular pathways, and the muscles supplied by the
individual nerves.

In practice, measurement of motor and sensory nerve conduction velocities is often performed in conjuction with electromyography, and both
are included under the rubric of EMG. Such electrodiagnostic testing is
valuable in the diagnosis and localization of peripheral nervous system
problems; however, the procedure has little value in the evaluation of
spinal cord lesions and no value in the evaluation of brain lesions.

§32.153. The medicolegal problem.

The evaluation of a *true* peripheral nerve injury is a relatively simple one and may present no problem to the attorney. If the plaintiff has indeed experienced an injury, he often can present a scar, sometimes a fracture, and usually some degree of motor disability. Also suggestive of a true injury is a history of the onset of disability immediately after the incident. The problem is that many alleged injuries are indefinite and do not present a clear-cut picture. In addition to the case of an intentionally exaggerated claim, a patient's imagination and emotional response to the situation can be influenced by an unconscious effort to obtain compensation.

Many individuals with alleged nerve injuries present an atypical clinical picture, thus giving rise to variable medical opinion and speculative diagnosis that makes the task of impairment rating more complicated. To add to this confusion, there are several nontraumatic diseases of the peripheral nerves that may have played a causative role in the accident, even though the patient honestly believes his disability was the result of the mishap. The problem becomes even more troublesome when certain diseases of the nerves themselves present a manifestation of nerve injury. The EMG can often be used to resolve these issues.

The usefulness of the EMG is based upon the fact that each local nerve injury or disease produces its own specific EMG changes, often indicating the causative factor of the disability. In nerve injuries, the changes take place in the neuromuscular pathway only beyond the point where the nerve was injured; that is, active denervation activity is present only in the muscle group supplied by the injured nerve and distal to the point of injury. If any other changes occur or the alleged location of the injury differs from the point indicated by the EMG, the disability is not due to the alleged accident.

§32.154. Sources of misinterpretation.

The EMG findings in traumatic nerve lesions do not vary with age. The same findings are found in infancy, childhood, adolescence, adult life, and old age. There are some nontraumatic factors that can produce minor changes (from a few complex motor units to a minimal degree of denervation activity). Among the most common possibilities are: (1) congenital variations of the neuromuscular system (especially in the lumbosacral region) that often produce trains of positive sharp waves on the EMG that might be misinterpreted as a nerve root compression syndrome; (2) congenital bony defects of this region (as in unstable back); (3) alterations from arthritic changes in the vertebral column; (4) residuals of minor nonparalytic infections (such as anterior poliomyelitis, meningitis, and neuronitis); (5) everyday wear and tear on the peripheral nerves, such as excessive stretching of the extremities, minor injuries to the nerve (hitting the "funny bone" or ulnar nerve at the elbow), using the hand as a hammer (ulnar and median nerve changes), sleeping on the arm (mild Saturday night paralysis of the radial nerve), prolonged or repeated leg-crossing (peroneal nerve), dangling a leg over a chair (tibial nerve), or wearing ill-fitted shoes (plantar nerve of the feet, especially in women); (6) the usual deterioration of the vascular system as in atherosclerosis; (7) numerous systemic factors that may produce similar changes (diabetes, mild anemia, avitaminosis, mild nephritis, obesity and often the worst offender, "moderate" use of alcohol); and (8) the common process of aging. These variations can be misinterpreted by an inexperienced electromyographer and therefore can be a source of error.

The sum total of the changes that can be disclosed by the EMG represent not only the influence of the assumed trauma to the nerve, but may represent the combined result of variable alterations by the above-named or coincidental factors. One must differentiate critically between the true traumatic nerve lesion and the nontraumatic variety.

§ 32.155.   "Time and location" principle in nerve injuries.

This principle is based upon two fundamental events: (1) the actual time active denervation appears and (2) the precise location from where this activity is recorded. The time-active denervation appears is based on sound neuromuscular physiology — the law of innervation and denervation of the skeletal muscle system. The genesis of this principle is formulated during embryological development. In intrauterine life, as the muscle develops it becomes an independent organ; it twitches, producing fibrillation waves (twitching), and it is hyperirritable, producing positive sharp waves.

This hyperirritability is due to the excitable envelope of the muscle fiber called sarcolemma. As the skeletal muscle becomes innervated by the nerve, it ceases to be an independent organ, hence, fibrillation and positive sharp wave activity ceases and normal (motor) activity is born. Henceforth, the innervated muscle becomes completely under the control of the nerve. It now contracts and relaxes as directed by the superior control of the nerve. This mechanism constitutes voluntary function that is responsible for all kinetic activity of the body. The functioning of this system starts to a minor degree during the fourth month of pregnancy when the mother begins to feel movements of the fetus. It begins in the muscles of the neck and spreads to the shoulders and back, the upper, and finally the lower extremities when the fetal movements have become even more vigorous. Thus, the maturity of the neuromuscular system proceeds from head to foot.

In certain instances, not all the muscles become innervated during this development. In some infants, the nerves, instead of going down to the legs, curl into a sac in the low back — the result of a congenital defect called meningomyelocele. The muscles ordinarily supplied by these nerves will continue to remain independent, generating fibrillation and positive sharp waves. This defect results in absence of voluntary function and paralysis of both lower extremities; the result of total lack of innervation of the muscles. There is another congenital defect that is partial in nature, in which the excitable sarcolemma has escaped the nerve control, which may result in specific muscle spasm called myotonia congenita (muscular weakness). In this instance no twitching (fibrillation) results, but trains of high-frequency, positive sharp waves are recorded on the EMG. The nerve has only partial control over the muscle; it has control over the contraction of the muscle, but not over its excitability. Thus, voluntary function is dependent upon a sound neuromuscular system, hence the injury to either the nerve or the muscle results in impaired function, muscular weakness, or paralysis.

Time factor

From the above foundation, we can now logically proceed to the factor of *time* of traumatic nerve lesions. The clinical significance of peripheral nerve injury stems from the fact that, if at any time during the life of an individual he sustains an injury, infection, or degeneration of the peripheral nerves, the control of the nerve upon the muscle is lost. In case of complete nerve degeneration, the muscle, freed from its nerve control, reverts back to being an independent organ and hence again generates fibrillation and positive sharp waves that constitute denervation activity.

The nerve does not surrender its control upon the muscle immediately at the time of the injury. The influence is completely lost only after the axis cylinder has completely degenerated. The period of time for this complete degeneration varies according to the size of the animal. In humans, it takes about twenty-one days. Thus, the time element at which the active denervation activity is detected by the EMG is of specific aid in the evaluation of workers' compensation and personal injury cases. In humans, a true nerve injury is not manifested until active denervation activity is recorded in its pathway (muscle group) three weeks after the actual date of the mishap or complaint. If active denervation activity occurs before this period, *the nerve lesion preceded the traumatic episode.* Furthermore, there is no valid nerve injury if there is no active denervation, but normal activity is recorded three weeks after the actual date of the mishap.

Location factor

The second fundamental principle to be considered is that of the precise *location* of the nerve injury. It must be remembered that the peripheral nervous system is formed by repeated branching from every part of the nerves, and each branch supplies its own specific muscle group, thus establishing neuromuscular pathways for the transmission of the nerve impulses for voluntary function. These nerve impulses originate in the brain and travel to their destination via the spinal cord, the nerve roots, and the peripheral nerves, each entering a specific muscle group that they innervate for kinetic activity. A survey by the EMG of these neuromuscular pathways leads to the precise location of the lesion because every nerve root trunk, cord, or peripheral nerve supplies its own specific muscle group. Therefore, the basic principle of valid nerve lesion is based upon finding active denervation activity in the neuromuscular pathway (muscle group) only beyond the point where the nerve is injured or compressed. For example, when one finds active denervation activity only in the muscles supplied by the peroneal nerve, a valid peroneal nerve lesion exists at the level of the back of the fibula. In the following section examples of the clinical application of this principle will be presented.

§ 32.156. Application of "time and location" principle.

A single EMG examination will be of value in establishing the location of a nerve injury and the degree of involvement (minimal, slight, moderate, or severe). This information is significant in determining whether such a lesion is consistent with an alleged traumatic or compressive origin, or whether the findings are suggestive of some other disorder. For example, if motor weakness is present in the form of a foot-drop, a single EMG examination will tell the location of the lesion: whether it has occurred somewhere along a peripheral nerve or at the nerve root (as a herniated disc), or whether the paralysis is but the focal manifestation of a more generalized infectious or degenerative disease. In such a case, it would have been helpful if the time element could have been established by repeated EMG checks, beginning with the onset of muscular weakness followed by residuals in the course of the disorder. However, this rarely occurs.

Alleged surgical complications

Take for example the case of the patient who developed weakness in the right lower extremity following hernia repair and alleged that his condition was the direct result of the operation. An EMG done on the fifth postoperative day showed widespread active denervation (neuronitis). Because such findings were not consistent with trauma-induced denervation in time of appearance or location (the time not yet twenty-one days and the location of the lesion too widespread — see § 32.155), this evidence immediately ruled out any nerve injury associated with the surgery, thus preventing a possibly successful malpractice claim.

Another case involved a woman who complained of a minor weakness in her left lower leg following a hysterectomy under spinal anesthesia. Electromyograms performed in the first, second, and third postoperative weeks were all normal and showed no evidence of nerve injury in the spinal cord, spinal nerve roots, plexuses, or the peripheral nerves. The patient was discharged from the hospital. However, five weeks later she returned, complaining that the weakness had worsened. This time, an EMG revealed severe partial involvement of the left tibial nerve from the back of the knee downward. However, the lumbosacral nerve roots and the rest of the peripheral nerves were normal. On further questioning, the patient admitted that, three weeks after her discharge from the hospital, she was standing on her left toes while reaching upward for an object in her cupboard when she noted a severe pain in the left leg and foot. Despite this admission, she argued that her problem was the result of the spinal anesthetic given at the time of surgery. Her claim was successfully defended, but it would have been difficult without the aid of the EMG, because she found other physicians who were of the opinion that the anesthetic agent could have been responsible for the disability.

Industrial cases

A night watchman alleged a fall resulted in a herniation of the left fifth lumbar disc, which caused an immediate foot drop. An EMG done in the first two weeks revealed no denervation activity, but in the third week, another EMG showed active denervation in all the muscles supplied by the left peroneal nerve. These findings (left peroneal nerve) suggested that the lesion was not in the spine (the lumbosacral nerve roots were still normal), but in the neck of the fibula, the smaller of the two bones in the lower leg. In this instance, the situation was consistent with the time but not with the location. It was suspected that the patient sustained the nerve injury as a result of prolonged leg-crossing while asleep.

In another industrial case, a patient alleged a nerve injury resulting in weakness of the left shoulder with inability to abduct the arm. His physician reported a fifth cervical nerve root compression. An EMG done four days after the injury revealed active denervation activity in the distribution of the fifth and sixth cervical nerve roots. Thus the findings were consistent with the location of alleged injury, but not with the time element; the condition must have preexisted the alleged mishap by at least two weeks.

The "time and location" principle also has been helpful in evaluating conversion disorders (formerly hysterical paralysis) and malingering. For instance, a woman employee fell while working and immediately became paralyzed in the right lower extremity. She was taken by ambulance to a hospital where the examining physician stated her paralysis was possibly due to a right sciatic nerve injury; however, EMG examinations on admission and during the following five weeks were entirely normal. These findings ruled out any valid nerve injury. A diagnosis of functional paralysis was made; with the help of psychotherapy, the patient made a gradual recovery and returned to work seven weeks after the fall.

IXX. RELATED TOPICS

§ 32.157. Role of litigation in prolonged postconcussion conditions.[78]

Is the prospect of monetary gain through litigation a significant factor in the protraction of symptoms following head injury? Some authors used to answer in the affirmative. Moreover, the medical literature continues to imply that the postconcussion syndrome is probably a product of the litigious patient's attempt to fake disability to recover damages. This notion, however, became a simplistic and arbitrary interpretation of a complex condition for which no ready medical explanation could be found. Greed will always be a part of our society. The diagnostician will remain responsible for sorting out, through medical and psychological considerations, what is a genuine complaint and what is a fraudulent claim. Methodologically sound studies of the last two decades, however, have lent no support to the notion that feigning or the deceitful exaggeration of symptoms plays a major role in the syndrome.

In a study by Rimel et al.,[79] only six out of 424 concussed patients were involved in litigation three months after their injury, and only one of these had not returned to work. The authors concluded that "litigation and compensation ... have a minimal role in determining outcome after minor head injury." There is ample evidence that seemingly trivial head trauma can lead to protracted symptomatology in the absence of any prospect of monetary gain.[80] In cases that involve litigation, research shows that patients often resume work prior to settlement.[81] In addition, the myth that patients who have been unemployed due to a prolonged postconcussion condition typically return to work symptom-free after financial settlement is reached has also been refuted.[82]

---

[78] Nemeth, A. J., *Litigating Head Trauma: The "Hidden" Evidence of Disability*, 12 Am. J. Tr. Advoc. 239, 1988.

[79] Rimel, et al., *Disability Caused by Minor Head Injury*, 9 Neurosurg. 221, 1981.

[80] See generally Russell, *Cerebral Involvement in Head Injury*, 55 Brain 549, 1932. But see Rutherford, et al., *Symptoms at One Year Following Concussion from Minor Head Injury*, 10 Injury 225, 1979.

[81] See Kelly, *The Post-Traumatic Syndrome: An Iatrogenic Disease*, 6 Forensic Sci. 17, 1975; Oddy, et al., *Subjective Impairment and Social Recovery after Closed Head Injury*, 41 J. Neurol. Neurosurg. & Psychiat. 611, 1978; Wrightson and Gronwall, *Time Off Work and Symptoms after Minor Head Injury*, 12 Injury 445, 1981.

[82] See Kelly and Smith, *Post-Traumatic*

§ 32.158. Executive deficits following mild head injury.[83]

Because the sequelae of moderate, severe and catastrophic injuries are so visible, persons suffering from these injuries are likely to receive rehabilitation services. Those with mild injuries may not be so fortunate. Their disabilities are often subtle and can go unrecognized. One area worthy of particular attention, and an area that is exceedingly difficult to measure and appreciate, is that of *executive deficits*. The essence of executive deficits is contained in the word "execute." Clients with executive deficits are unable to execute their plans or to formulate plans at all. They are unable to be self-directed and self-initiating. In much the same manner that an administrative executive plans, organizes, directs and controls an enterprise, so too does one's inner executive accomplish these tasks. These mildly injured clients may appear intact, perform well on structured tasks, and be enthusiastically involved in structured work experiences. They may give assurances that they can perform adequately and give the impression of competence when, in reality, they are unable to follow through and execute their plans. They are notorious for talking a good game, but their self-description may bear scant resemblance to the reality of their life.

These executive deficits are virtually invisible, extremely difficult to document and may account for up to 90% of the failure in vocational rehabilitation efforts. Thus, it may be readily appreciated how difficult it is to concretely and realistically estimate the amount of earnings loss for the head-injured individual, let alone present a convincing case to a jury.

§ 32.159. Vegetative state after closed-head injury.[84]

The essential feature of the persistent vegetative state (PVS) has been characterized by Jennett and Plum[85] as "the absence of any adaptive response to the external environment." Posttraumatic PVS patients are distinguished from other survivors of severe head injury who are capable of making a "consistently understandable response to those around them" either by word or by gesture.[86] Despite the inability to obey commands and no comprehensible speech, patients who survive head injury in a vegetative state may exhibit eye opening and pursuit eye movements. Few recent studies have focused on the PVS, particularly in relation to head injury. Of 110 PVS patients studied by Higashi and co-

---

Syndrome: Another Myth Discredited, 74 J. Royal Soc'y Med. 275, 1981; Merskey and Woodforde, *Psychiatric Sequelae of Minor Head Injury,* 95 Brain 521, 1972; Steadmon and Graham, *Head Injuries: An Analysis and Follow-up Study,* 63 Proc. Royal Soc'y Med. 23, 1970.

[83]Vogenthaler, D., et al., *Vocational Experts Help Assess the "Silent Epidemic,"* Mass. Lawyers' Weekly, Dec. 9, 1991.

[84]Primary source: Levin, H. S., et al., *Vegetative State after Closed-Head Injury: A Traumatic Coma Data Bank Report,* 48 Arch. Neurol. 580 (June), 1991.

[85]Jennett, B., and Plum, F., *Persistent Vegetative State after Brain Damage,* 1 Lancet 552, 1981.

[86]Id.

workers,[87] only thirty-eight had sustained a head injury. These investigators reported a one-year mortality of 41% overall (26% among the head-injured), which increased to 73% over five years. Although 10% of these PVS patients partially recovered, only three became communicative.

Jennett and Plum[88] did not specify the minimum duration for post-traumatic vegetative state to be considered persistent; however, serial observations have shown that severely head-injured patients rarely are capable of comprehending simple commands within one year if they have not done so by six months.[89] Of the patients who eventually obeyed commands by one year, Bricolo and coworkers[90] found that only 1.5% of the patients began to follow commands after six months. Limitations of the Bricolo study include the retrospective selection of patients and lack of computed tomographic scan information. In a retrospective study of 134 closed-head-injured patients who were in a coma persisting over thirty days, Sazbon and Groswasser[91] found that seventy-two patients (54%) subsequently recovered consciousness, most of them during the second and third month. Of the patients who did not recover consciousness during the study period, approximately two-thirds died within the first year. Analysis of acute findings revealed that signs of hypothalamic damage (e.g., generalized sweating) and a flaccid motor response most clearly differentiated the recovered from the nonrecovered patients, while epilepsy and hydrocephalus were the late complications that most clearly discriminated the two groups.

Braakman's[92] analysis of the International Coma Data Bank of 1,373 patients with severe head injury revealed that 140 (10%) were vegetative one month after trauma. Fifty-nine (42%) of the vegetative patients regained consciousness within one year after the onset of coma, including fourteen patients (all younger than forty years) who became independent. The authors reported that age, pupillary reactivity to light, and the best motor response were the most useful prognostic factors for death or continued vegetative state at various time points.

To elucidate the clinical course of the vegetative state after severe closed-head injury, the Traumatic Coma Data Bank was analyzed for outcome at the time of discharge from the hospital and after follow-up

[87] Higashi, K., et al., *Five-Year Follow-up Studies of Patients with Persistent Vegetative State*, 44 J. Neurol. Neurosurg. Psychiat. 552, 1981; Higashi, K., et al., *Epidemiological Studies on Patients with a Persistent Vegetative State*, 40 J. Neurol. Neurosurg. Psychiat. 876, 1977.

[88] Jennett and Plum, supra.

[89] Bricolo, A., et al., *Prolonged Posttraumatic Unconsciousness*, 52 J. Neurosurg. 625, 1980.

[90] Id.

[91] Sazbon, L., and Groswasser, Z., *Outcome in 134 Patients with Prolonged Posttraumatic Unawareness, I: Parameters Determining Late Recovery of Consciousness*, 72 J. Neurosurg. 75, 1990.

[92] Braakman, R., et al., *Prognosis of the Posttraumatic Vegetative State*, 95 Acta Neurochir. 49, 1988.

intervals ranging up to three years after injury.[93] Of 650 patients with closed-head injury available for analysis, ninety-three (14%) were discharged in a vegetative state. In comparison with conscious survivors, patients in a vegetative state sustained more severe closed-head injury as reflected by the Glasgow Coma Scale scores and pupillary findings and more frequently had diffuse injury complicated by swelling or shift in midline structures. Of eighty-four patients in a vegetative state who provided follow-up data, 41% became conscious by six months, 52% regained consciousness by one year, and 58% recovered consciousness within the three-year follow-up interval. A logistic regression failed to identify predictors of recovery from the vegetative state.[94]

§ 32.160. Posttraumatic tremor.[95]

Tremor[96] is well known as a late consequence of severe head trauma[97] and usually appears a few months after the event. The frequency ranges from 4 to 6 Hz.[98] The tremor, which is typically proximal and may worsen with kinetic movement, resembles severe cerebellar postural tremor.[99] Lesions have been found in the superior cerebellar peduncle and in the cortical white matter. The tremor may respond to propranolol or stereotaxic thalamotomy.[1] Tremor resembling essential tremor[2] can

---

[93] Levin, H. S., et al., *Vegetative State after Closed-head Injury: A Traumatic Coma Data Bank Report,* 48 Arch. Neurol. 580 (June), 1991.

[94] Id.

[95] Primary source: Hallett, M., *Classification and Treatment of Tremor,* 266 J.A.M.A. 1115 (Aug. 28), 1991.

[96] Tremor is an involuntary movement characterized by rhythmic oscillations of a part of the body. There are many types of tremor, and appropriate therapy depends on the correct diagnosis. A useful classification scheme categorizes tremor by the situation in which it appears. The first division is based on whether the tremor appears at rest or with movement. Tremors with movement are subdivided into those occurring (1) with maintained posture (postural or static tremor); (2) with movement from point to point (kinetic or intentional tremor); and (3) only with a specific type of movement (task-specific tremor). Postural movement can be examined by having the patients hold their arms out in front of them, and kinetic movement by the finger-to-nose test.

[97] Andrew, J., et al., *Tremor after Head Injury and Its Treatment by Stereotactic Surgery,* 45 J. Neurol. Neurosurg. Psychiat. 815, 1982.

[98] Sabra, A. F., and Hallett, M., *Action Tremor with Alternating Activity in Antagonist Muscles,* 34 Neurology 151, 1984.

[99] Cerebellar postural tremor has a frequency of 2.5 to 4 Hz and may wax and wane in amplitude, increasing progressively with prolonged posture. The tremor affects proximal muscles more than distal ones and may involve the head and trunk. It persists or worsens with goal-directed movement and is associated with dysmetria, which is an inability to fix the range of a movement in muscular activity (rapid and brisk movements are made with more force than necessary).

[1] Andrew et al., supra note 20. Stereotaxic thalamotomy refers to a selected destruction of a portion of the thalamus.

[2] Essential tremor often occurs in families. It may appear in childhood or late in life and typically runs a slowly progressive course. It is usually a postural tremor, but in some patients it increases with kinetic movement and in others it is primarily associated with kinetic movement and is

result from mild head trauma and may respond to clonazepam, primidone, or propranolol.[3]

Tremor also can be a conversion symptom.[4] Hysterical tremor can take many forms, but the most common are tremors with movement. These tremors may be of irregular frequency or variable intensity and may have a tendency to diminish or disappear when the patient's attention is distracted. Because these cases can be difficult, a positive psychiatric diagnosis should be sought.

§ 32.160a.   Spasmodic torticollis.[5]

Spasmodic torticollis, which is also called cervical dystonia, is a neurological disorder in which the nerves controlling the neck muscles cause them to contract at the wrong time. Until the mid-1960s, most physicians considered the condition a psychological disorder; however, it is now believed that head injury, and perhaps heredity, may play a role in some cases.

Dystonia in general is an involuntary movement disorder characterized by sustained involuntary contraction of muscles, which can result from head trauma, the most common scenario being the development of hemidystonia after moderate or severe head injury. There is evidence that segmental dystonia — such as torticollis — can result from both head or neck trauma.[6]

Spasmodic torticolis, which may affect more than 80,000 persons in the United States, can begin with a nagging ache in the base of the neck, involuntary turning of the head, or slight tremors associated with neck and muscle pain. The pain usually grows more intense and, as the muscles contract, the chin may be pulled down to the chest or shoulder. The contractions may last for hours or may occur intermittently, in which case they may cause "shaking" movements of the head.

---

called essential intentional tremor. It rarely persists at rest. Although all parts of the body can be affected, it most commonly occurs in the distal upper extremities. Individual fingers can be affected and a side-to-side finger tremor is characteristic. The head can be affected, with flexion and extension or rotational movements (titubation). The vocal tract can also be affected, giving a tremulous quality to the voice.

[3] Biary, N., et al., *Posttraumatic Tremor,* 39 Neurology 103, 1989.

[4] Editor's Note: Conversion disorders are discussed in Volume 3A of this Cyclopedia. See the General Index under this entry.

[5] *Spasmodic Torticollis: Progress in Treatment and Awareness Help Outlook,* 14 Mayo Clin. Health Ltr. 6 (July), 1996. See

also Van Zandijcke, M., *Cervical Dystonia (Spasmodic Tortcollis): Some Aspects of the Natural History,* 95 Acta Neurol. Belg. 210 (Dec.), 1995; Clapool, D. W., et al., *Epidemiology and Outcome of Cervical Dystonia (Spasmodic Torticollis) in Rochester, Minnesota,* 10 Mov. Disord. 608 (Sept.), 1995; Braun, V., et al., *Selective Peripheral Denervation for Spasmodic Torticollis: Is the Outcome Predictable?,* 242 J. Neurol. 504 (Aug.), 1995.

[6] Weiner, W. J., and Lang, A. E., *Movement Disorders: A Comprehensive Survey,* Futura Publishing Co., Mt. Kisco, N.Y., 1989; Jankovic, J., and Tolosa, E., *Parkinson's Disease and Movement Disorders,* 2d ed., Williams & Wilkins, Baltimore, 1993.

In the past, physicians usually prescribed muscle relaxants or pain-killers for torticollis, which were not always effective. At a few medical centers, a surgical procedure has been performed in which nerves to the affected muscles are severed. About 80% of patients who have undergone this treatment reported improvement. However, at present the most common treatment for torticollis is botulinum toxin, which is injected into the involuntarily contracting muscles.

§ 32.161. Abnormalities after mild head injury revealed by CT scan.[7]

A study reported in 1993 suggests that there may be a subgroup of victims of mild, closed-head injury that is deserving of a higher level of suspicion by examining physicians, especially if the patient is over sixty or the mechanism of injury suggests the potential for more diffuse injury.

The study involved a prospective trial of 712 consecutive patients with blunt head trauma who had Glasgow Coma Scale (GCS) scores of 15 (minimal injury), but who reported amnesia or loss of consciousness. All of the patients underwent computed tomographic (CT) scanning. In approximately 10% of the patients, the CT detected abnormalities. In these patients, one-half had multiple abnormalities, including cerebral contusion, intracerebral and extracerebral hematoma or hemorrhage, and basilar and other skull fractures.

The abnormalities were found to be three times more common in patients more than sixty years of age than in those between eighteen and sixty. Also, patients with clinical evidence of a basilar skull fracture, as well as those whose injury occurred by assault or who were pedestrians injured by a vehicle, were more likely to have abnormalities.

§ 32.162. Discharging patients with mild head injury.[8]

Closed head injuries account for approximately 20% to 30% of all hospital trauma admissions. The majority of these patients — just under 90% — sustain mild head injuries (*i.e.*, a temporary alteration in consciousness without persistent deficit). However, a small number of these patients who are awake upon examination will deteriorate and require neurosurgical intervention. Evaluation of the head injury patient who is awake presents a difficult problem for the emergency department physician.

A review of 407 consecutive patients with head injuries treated at an adult regional trauma center identified 310 individuals with Glasgow Coma Scores of 15, all of whom were admitted as inpatients. Five of

---

[7] Jeret, J. S., et al., *Clinical Predictors of Abnormality Disclosed by Computed Tomography after Mild Head Trauma*, 32 Neurosurgery 9, 1993.

[8] Taheri, P. A., et al., *Can Patients with Minor Head Injuries Be Safely Discharged Home?*, 128 Arch. Surg. 289 (Mar.), 1993.

these patients required intervention for intracranial abnormality, and all five had skull fractures and or neurological deficits. Based on this and other studies, the authors suggest that criteria for discharge should be (1) a Glasgow Coma Score of 15, (2) no deficit except amnesia, (3) no signs of intoxication, and (4) no evidence of basilar fracture upon clinical examination or linear fracture on screening skull X-rays. The authors suggest that, using such criteria, safe discharge without universal CT scan evaluation or hospital admission is possible.

§ 32.163. Transferring multiply injured patients for neurosurgical opinions.[9]

In many cases, patients with intracranial injuries who require a neurosurgical opinion during the early course of their management are transferred from the primary place of treatment to a neurosurgical unit, especially if CT scanning facilities or image-transmission facilities are not available at the referring facility. For the multiply injured patient, this can be dangerous. Missed injuries, initial mismanagement, and deterioration during transfer compound the problem of a transfer to a unit that may not have on-site access to other surgical specialties.

The problem is not new and has been reported before. In one of the latest reports, the authors studied the records of twenty-one consecutive patients with multiple injuries admitted to a London neurosurgical unit over a one-year period, and found that injury assessment was deficient in nine cases, four patients developed hypovolemic shock during transfer, and in five patients resuscitation was inadequate. Four of the patients died. There were seven missed injuries. The authors concluded that interhospital transfer of such patients carries significant risks, may occasionally be unnecessary, and may delay other surgical priorities.

§ 32.164. Quantitative electroencephalography (brain-activity mapping).[10]

Quantitative electroencephalography (QEEG), commonly called "brain-activity mapping," involves the use of multiple electroencephalograph (EEG)[11] recordings to create a computer-generated topographical map of the brain that allows local cortical activity to be visualized. Advantages of the procedure are that it involves no radioactive isotopes, can be performed in any EEG laboratory, and is inexpensive.

Some neruologists have claimed that, while originally used as a research tool, brain-activity mapping promises to have some important

---

[9] Lambert, S. M., and Willett, K., *Transfer of Multiply Injured Patients for Neurosurgical Opinion: A Study of the Adequacy of Assessment and Resuscitation*, 24 Injury 333, 1993.

[10] Bernad, P. G., *Closed-Head Injury: A Clinical Source Book*, The Michie Company, Charlottesville, Va., 1994, pp. 94-6.

[11] Editor's Note: The EEG is discussed extensively in Chapter 22 of this Cyclopedia.

clinical applications. As an instrument for evaluating head injuries, however, the emphasis is still on research, and clinical applications are limited. Large parts of the brain are always active, and the cortical activation pattern changes throughout life, which raises questions of reliability and accuracy of brain activity calculated by computer methods.[12] Also, the American Academy of Neurology does not recommend routine use of brain activity mapping for mild head injury because "the sensitivity and specificity fail to substantiate a role for these tests in the clinical diagnostic evaluation of individual patients."[13]

§ 32.165. Sensory-evoked potentials.[14]

Sensory-evoked (event-related) potentials are responses of the sensory pathways to appropriate sensory or electrical stimuli that involve the auditory, visual, or somatosensory (tactile sense) system. (Examples of such stimuli include a flash of light, an audible click, or an electrical shock.) Evoked potentials can be of value in the diagnostic workup of trauma, since they can provide accurate information on the functional integrity of the brain stem, the hemispheres of the brain, and the peripheral sensory systems. Also, significant changes in arterial oxygenation, carbon dioxide content, intracranial pressure, cerebral blood flow, cerebral perfusion pressure, and hypothermia may alter or obliterate these evoked potentials.

Tests for evoked potentials are noninvasive and pose no serious risk to the patient. They can be performed at the patient's bedside, and they are not seriously influenced by the level of coma or by central nervous system depressants used to manage brain-injured patients.

Thus far, most of the studies evaluating the efficacy of evoked potentials have involved severely injured patients. There is a need to further evaluate these tests for routine use in cases of mild head injury and postconcussion syndrome before widespread application to these patients.

§ 32.166. Variations in assessment of Glasgow Coma Scale scores.[15]

Rapid treatment of patients with head injury frequently includes prehospital endotracheal intubation and sedation, which can compro-

---

[12] Pfurtscheller, G., et al., "Brain Electrical Activity Mapping in Normal and Ischemic Brain", in *Brain Ischemia: Quantitative EEG and Imaging Techniques. Progress in Brain Research* (G. Pfurtscheller, et al., editors), Elsevier Science Publishers, New York, pp. 287-301.

[13] American Academy of Neurology, *EEG Brain Mapping*, 39 Neurology 1100, 1989.

[14] Bernad, P. G., *Closed-Head Injury: A Clinical Source Book*, The Michie Company, Charlottesville, Va., 1994, pp. 97-8.

[15] Marion, D. W., and Carlier, P. M., *Problems with Initial Glasgow Coma Scale Assessment Caused by Prehospital Treatment of Patients with Head Injuries: Results of a National Survey*, 36 J. Trauma 89 (Jan.), 1994.

mise the ability to obtain an accurate Glasgow Coma Scale (see § 32.20) for these patients' score in the emergency department. To determine how initial GCS scores are obtained when these or other complicating circumstances exist, researchers from the Department of Surgery, University of Pittsburgh School of Medicine, surveyed trauma teams at seventeen major head injury centers in the United States. Responding centers were questioned as to who determines the initial GCS scores, when and where the patients are assessed, how the scores are assigned for patients who receive medication or were intubated before arrival, and how patients who are hypotensive, hypoxic, or have severe periorbital swelling are scored.

It was found that most neurosurgeons assess the initial GCS scores in the emergency department within one hour after the discovery of the patient by prehospital personnel, that at most centers patients with hypotension and hypoxia are stabilized before the initial GCS scores are assessed, and that intubated patients receive a nonnumerical designation. However, the majority of nonneurosurgical emergency department personnel determine the initial GCS scores immediately after the patient arrives in the emergency department, regardless of hypotension or hypoxia. Also, there were significant discrepancies between attending neurosurgeons and residents with regard to who actually assesses the GCS scores and how the scores are determined for patients who have received neuromuscular paralysis or sedation as well as those who have severe periorbital swelling.

ANNOTATIONS

§ 32.196. Medical references.

The following additional references may aid in further research on the material covered in Chapter 32. For a guide to the abbreviations used in referring to medical periodicals, see Chapter 3, § 3.36.

References are arranged under the following headings:

- (A) NEUROLOGY AND NEUROSURGERY IN GENERAL
- (B) HEAD INJURIES
- (C) SPINAL CORD INJURIES
- (D) OTHER SPINAL DISORDERS
- (E) COMPLICATIONS OF TREATMENT
- (F) EPILEPSY
- (G) PERIPHERAL NERVE INJURIES

(A) NEUROLOGY AND NEUROSURGERY IN GENERAL

Adams, R. D., et al., *Principles of Neurology*, 6th ed., McGraw-Hill, New York, 1997.

Agur, A. M. R., *Grant's Atlas of Anatomy*, 9th ed., Williams & Wilkins, Baltimore, 1991.

Allen, M. B., Jr., and Miller, R. H., *Essentials of Neurosurgery*, McGraw-Hill, New York, 1995.

Carpenter, M. B., *Core Text of Neuroanatomy*, 4th ed., Williams & Wilkins, Baltimore, 1991.

Greenberg, J. O., *Neuroimaging*, McGraw-Hill, New York, 1995.

Haerer, A. F., et al., *Functional Disability Associated with Major Neurologic Disorders*, 43 Arch. Neurol. 1000, 1986.

Ropper, A. H., *Neurological and Neurosurgical Intensive Care*, 3d ed., Raven Prewss, New York, 1993.

Rowland, L. P., *Merritt's Textbook of Neurology*, 9th ed., Williams & Wilkins, Baltimore, 1995.

Salzman, S. K., and Faden, A. I., *The Neurobiology of Central Nervous System Trauma*, Oxford University Press, New York, 1994.

Schott, G. D., *Mechanisms of Causalgia and Related Clinical Conditions: The Role of the Central and the Sympathetic Nervous Systems*, 109 Brain 717, 1986.

Youmans, J. R., *Neurological Surgery*, 4th ed., W. B. Saunders Co., Philadelphia, 1996.

(B) HEAD INJURIES

Adams, J. H., et al., *Diffuse Axonal Injury in Non-Missle Head Injury*, 54 N. Neurol. Nurosurg. Psychiatry 481, 1991.

Arcia, E., and Gualtier, C. T., *Association Between Patient Report of Symptoms after Mild Head Injury and Neurobehavioral Performance*, 7 Brain Injury 481, 1993.

Bell, D. S., *Medico-Legal Assessment of Head Injury*, Charles C Thomas, Springfield, Ill., 1992.

Bernad, P. G., *Closed-Head Injury: A Clinical Source Book*, The Michie Company, Charlottesville, Va., 1994.

Biary, N., et al., *Post-Traumatic Tremor*, 39 Neurology 103, 1989.

Boyle, M. J., et al., *Role of Drugs and Alcohol in Patients with Head Injury*, 84 J. Roy. Society Med. 608 (Oct.), 1991.

Cavallo, M. M., et al., *Problems and Changes after Traumatic Brain Injury: Differing Perceptions Within and Between Families*, 6 Brain Inj. 327 (July-Aug.), 1992.

Childs, N. L., and Mercer, W. N., *Brief Report: Late Improvement in Consciousness After Posttraumatic Vegetative State*, 334 N. Engl. J. Med. 24 (Jan. 4), 1996.

Clark, W. C., et al., *Analysis of 76 Civilian Craniocerebral Gunshot Wounds*, 65 J. Neurosurg. 9, 1986.

Cooper, P. R., *Head Injury*, 3d ed., Williams & Wilkins, Baltimore, 1993.

Crow, W., *Neuroradiology of Head Injury*, 2 Neurosurg. Clin. North Am. 321, 1991.

Davis, J. R., et al., *Natural and Structured Baselines in the Treatment of Aggression Following Brain Injury*, 8 Brain Inj. 589 (Oct.), 1994.

Dearden, N. M., et al., *Effect of High-Dose Dexamethasone on Outcome in Severe Head Injury*, 64 J. Neurosurg. 81, 1986.

Dikman, S., et al., *Psychosocial Outcome in Patients with Moderate to Severe Head injury: 2-Year Follow-Up*, 7 Brain Inj. 113, 1993.

Eslinger, P. J., et al., *Developmental Consequences of Childhood Frontal Lobe Damage*, 49 Arch. Neurol. 764 (July), 1992.

Ewert, J., et al., *Procedural Memory During Post-traumatic Amnesia in Survivors of Severe Closed Head Injury: Implications for Rehabilitation*, 46 Arch. Neurol. 911, 1989.

Feiring, E. H., editor, *Brock's Injuries of the Brain and Their Complications*, 5th ed., Springer, New York, 1974

Fleischer, A. S., et al., *Cerebral Aneurysms of Traumatic Origin*, 4 Surg. Neurol. 233, 1975.

Gaffan, E. A., *Amnesia Following Damage to the Left Fornix and to Other Sites*, 114 Brain 1297, 1991.

Gentry, L. R., et al., *MR Imaging of Head Trauma: Review of the Distribution and Radiopathologic Features of Traumatic Lesions*, 150 Am. J. Radiol. 663, 1988.

Grafman, J., et al., *Intellectual Function Following Penetrating Head Injury in Vietnam Veterans*, 31 Brain 169, 1988.

Graves, A. B., et al., *Association Between Head Trauma and Alzheimer's Disease*, 131 Am. J. Epidemiol. 491, 1990.

Grigsby, J., and Kaye, K., *Incidence and Correlates of Depersonalization Following Head Trauma*, 7 Brain Injury 507, 1993.

Gutman, M. B., et al., *Risk Factors Predicting Operable Intracranial Hematomas in Head Injury*, 77 J. Neurosurg. 483, 1992.

Hackney, D. B., *Skull Radiography in the Evaluation of Acute Head Trauma: A Survey of Current Practice*, 181 Radiology 711 (Dec.), 1991.

Horn, L. J., and Zasler, N. D., *Medical Rehabilitation of Traumatic Brain Injury*, C. V. Mosby Co., St. Louis, 1996.

James, H. E., *Emergency Management of Acute Coma in Children*, 48 Am. Fam. Physician 473 (Sept. 1), 1993.

Jennett, B., "Head Trauma," in *Diseases of the Nervous System*, 2d. ed. (A. K. Asbury, et al., editors), W. B. Saunders Co., Philadelphia, 1992.

Johnstone, A. J., et al., *A Comparison of the Glasgow Coma Scale and the Swedish Reaction Level Scale*, 7 Brain Injury 501, 1993.

Kanter, R. K., et al., *Association of Arterial Hypertension with Poor Outcome in Children with Acute Brain Injury*, 24 Clin. Pediatr. 320, 1985.

Kelly, J. P., et al., *Concussion in Sports: Guidelines for the Prevention of Catastrophic Outcome*, 266 J.A.M.A. 2867 (Nov. 27), 1991.

Koenig, S., and Schultze, C., *Long-Term Follow-Up of Children with Head Injuries-Classified as "Good Recovery" Using the Glasgow Outcome Scale: Neurological, Neuropsychological and Magnetic Resonance Imaging Results*, 156 Eur. J. Pediatr. 230 (Mar.), 1997.

Krefting, L., et al., *Measuring Long-Term Outcome after Traumatic Brain Injury*, 83 Can. J. Pub. Health S64 (July-Aug., Supp. 2), 1992.

Lahz, S., and Bryant, R. A., *Incidence of Chronic Pain Following Traumatic Brain Injury*, 77 Arch Phys. Med. Rehabil. 889 (Sept.), 1996.

Lee, L., et al., *Early Seizures after Mild Closed-Head Injury*, 76 J. Neurosurg. 435, 1992.

Levin, H. S., and Grossman, R. G., *Behavioral Sequelae of Closed Head Injury*, 35 Arch. Neurol. 720 (Nov.), 1978.

Levin, H. S., et al., *Impairment of Olfactory Recognition After Closed Head Injury*, 108 Brain 579, 1985.

Lewis, R. J., et al., *Clinical Predictors of Post-Traumatic Seizures in Children with Head Trauma*, 22 Ann. Emerg. Med. 7 (July), 1993.

Mackay, L. E., et al., *Maximizing Brain Injury Recovery*, Aspen Publishers, Inc., Gaithersburg, Md., 1997.

Marion, D. W., and Carlier, P. M., *Problems with Initial Glasgow Coma Scale Assessment Caused by Prehospital Treatment of Patients with Head Injuries: Results of a National Survey*, 36 J. Trauma 89 (Jan.), 1994.

Masters, S. J., et al., *Skull X-ray Examinations After Head Injury: Recommendations by a Multidisciplinary Panel and Validation Study*, 316 N. Engl. J. Med. 84, 1987.

Mazmanian, P. E., et al., *A Survey of Accredited and Other Rehabilitation Facilities: Education, Training, and Cognitive Rehabilitation in Brain Injury Programmes*, 7 Brain Injury 319 (July-Aug.), 1993.

McLean, A., et al., *Psychosocial Recovery after Head Injury*, 74 Arch. Phys. Med. Rehab. 1041, 1993.

McPherson, K. M., and Pentland, B., *Disability in Patients Following Traumatic Brain Injury*, 20 Int. J. Rehabil. Res. 1 (Mar.), 1997.

Michaud, L. J., et al., *Predictors of Survival and Severity of Disability after Severe Brain Injury in Children*, 31 Neurosurgery 254 (Aug.), 1992.

Miller, J. D., et al., *Early Insults to the Injured Brain*, 240 J.A.M.A. 434, 1978.

Morgan, M. K., et al., *Intracranial Carotid Artery Injury in Closed Head Trauma*, 66 J. Neurosurg. 192, 1987.

Nelson, W. E., et al., *Minor Head Injury in Sport: A New System of Classification and Management*, 12 Physician Sports Med. 103, 1984.

Peters, J. D., *Litigating the Brain-Damaged Baby Case: From the Initial Interview to the Trial*, 70 Mich. B.J. 1063 (Oct.), 1991.

Peters, S., *Using a Neuropsychologist in a Closed Head Injury Case*, 11 Prod. Liab. L. Rep. 185 (Nov.), 1992.

Pollack, D. A., *Temporal and Geographic Trends in the Autopsy Frequency of Blunt and Penetrating Trauma Deaths in the United States*, 269 J.A.M.A. 1525 (Mar. 24), 1993.

Ponsford, J. L., et al., *A Profile of Outcome: Two Years After Traumatic Brain Injury*, 9 Brain Inj. 1 (Jan.), 1995.

Rakier, A., et al., *Head Injuries in the Elderly*, 9 Brain Inj. 187 (Feb.-Mar.), 1995.

Reitan, R. M., and Wolfson, D., *The Influence of Age and Education on Neuropsychological Performances of Persons with Mild Head Injuries*, 4 Appl. Neuropsychol. 16, 1997.

Rimel, R. W., et al., *Disability Caused by Minor Head Injury*, 9 Neurosurgery 221, 1981.

Rivari, J. B., et al., *Family Functioning and Children's Academic Performance and Behavior Problems in the Year Following Traumatic Brain Injury*, 75 Arch. Phys. Med. Rehabil. 369, 1994.

Ropper, A. H., et al., *Acute Traumatic Midbrain Hemorrhage*, 18 Ann. Neurol. 80, 1985.

Rose, J., et al., *Avoidable Factors Contributing to Death After Head Injury*, 2 Brit. Med. J. 615 (Sept.), 1977.

Ruff, R. M., et al., *Predictors of Outcome Following Severe Head Trauma: Follow-Up Data from the Traumatic Coma Data Bank*, 7 Brain Injury 101, 1993.

Rutherford, W. H., et al., *Sequelae of Concussion Caused by Minor Head Injuries*, 1 Lancet 1 (Jan.), 1977.

Saul, T. G., et al., *Steroids in Severe Head Injury: A Prospective Randomized Clinical Trial*, 54 J. Neurosurg. 596, 1981.

Schwartz, M. F., et al., *Cognitive Theory and the Study of Everyday Action Disorders after Brain Damage*, 8 J. Head Trauma Rehab. 59 (Mar.), 1993.

Schynoll, W., et al., *A Prospective Study to Identify High-Yield Criteria Associated with Acute Intracranial Computed Tomography Findings in Head-Injured Patients*, 11 Am. J. Emerg. Med. 321 (July), 1993.

Seelig, J. M., et al., *Traumatic Acute Subdural Hematoma*, 304 N. Eng. J. Med. 1511, 1981.

Sharples, P.M., et al., *Avoidable Factors Contributing to Death of Children with Head Injury*, 300 Br. Med. J. 87, 1990.

Smith, R. J., et al., "Evaluation of Head Trauma," in *Neuropsychology. Human Brain Function: Assessment and Rehabilitation* (G. Goldstein, et al., editors), Plenum Press, New York, 1998.

Smith-Seemiller, L., et al., *Neuropsychological Function in Restrained Versus Unrestrained Motor Vehicle Occupants Who Suffer Closed Head Injury*, 11 Brain Inj. 735, 1997.

Sosin, D. M., et al., *Head Injury-Associated Deaths in the U.S. from 1979 to 1986*, 262 J.A.M.A. 2251, 1989.

Stambrook, M., et al., *Effects of Mild, Moderate, and Severe Closed Head Injury on Long-Term Vocational Status*, 4 Brain Inj. 183, 1990.

Stein, S. C., et al., *Minor Head Injury: A Proposed Strategy for Emergency Management*, 22 Ann. Emerg. Med. 103 (July), 1993.

Taheri, P. A., et al., *Can Patients with Minor Head Injuries Be Safely Discharged Home?*, 126 Arch. Surg. 289 (Mar.), 1993.

Thomas, S. et al., *Effectiveness of Bicycle Helmets in Preventing Head Injury in Children: Case-Control Study*, 308 Brit. Med. J. 173, 1994.

Thompson, R. S., et al., *A Case-Control Study of the Effectiveness of Bicycle Safety Helmets*, 320 N. Engl. J. Med. 1361 (May 25), 1989.

Tuel, S. M., et al., *Functional Improvement in Severe Head Injury after Readmission for Rehabilitation*, 6 Brain Inj. (July-Aug.), 363, 1992.

Uomoto, J. M., et al., *Traumatic Brain Injury and Chronic Pain: Differential Types and Rates by Head Injury Severity*, 74 Arch. Phys. Med. Rehab. 61 (Jan.), 1993.

Uzzell, B. P., et al., *Visual Field Defects in Relation to Head Injury Severity: A Neuropsychological Study*, 45 Arch. Neurol. 420, 1988.

Wasserman, R. C., et al., *Bicyclists, Helmets and Head Injuries: A Rider-Based Study of Helmet Use and Effectiveness*, 78 Am. J. Public Health 1220, 1988.

Weisz, G. M., et al., *Transient Blindness Following Minor Head Injuries*, 6 Injury 348, 1975.

White, R. J., et al., *The Diagnosis and Initial Management of Head Injury*, 327 N. Engl. J. Med. 1507 (Nov. 19), 1992.

Williams, D. B., et al., *Brain Injury and Neurologic Sequelae: A Cohort Study of Dementia, Parkinsonism, and Amyotrophic Lateral Sclerosis*, 41 Neurology 1554 (Oct.), 1991.

Zuger, R. R., et al., *Vocational Rehabilitation Counseling of Traumatic Brain Injury: Factors Contributing to Stress*, J. Rehab. 28 (Apr.-June), 1993.

(C) SPINAL CORD INJURIES

Alfred, W. G., et al., *Vocational Development Following Severe Spinal Cord Injury: A Longitudinal Study*, 68 Arch. Phys. Med. Rehab. 854, 1987.

Aisen, P. S., and Aisen, M. L., *Shoulder-Hand Syndrome in Cervical Spinal Cord Injury*, 32 Paraplegia 588 (Sep.), 1994.

Berczeller, P. H., and Bezkor, M. F., *Medical Complications of Quadriplegia*, Year Book Medical Publishers, Chicago, 1986.

Bracken, M. B., et al., *A Randomized, Controlled Trial of Methylprednisolone or Naloxone in the Treatment of Acute Spinal Cord Injury*, 322 N. Engl. J. Med. 1405 (May 17), 1990.

Byrne, T. N., *Spinal Cord Compression from Epidural Metastases*, 327 N. Engl. J. Med. 614 (Aug. 27), 1992.

Chen, L. S., et al., *Acute Central Cervical Cord Syndrome Caused by Minor Trauma*, 108 J. Pediatr. 96, 1986.

Crawford, P. M., et al., *Hyperextension Injuries to the Cervical Cord in the Elderly*, 299 Br. Med. J. 669, 1989.

DeVivo, M. J., et al., *Causes of Death During the First 12 Years after Spinal Cord Injury*, 74 Arch. Phys. Med. Rehab. 248 (Mar.), 1993.

DeVivo, M. J., et al., *Cause of Death for Patients with Spinal Cord Injuries*, 149 Arch. Intern. Med. 1761, 1989.

DeVivo, M. J., et al., *The Influence of Age at Time of Spinal Cord Injury and Rehabilitation Outcome*, 47 Arch. Neurol. 687 (June), 1990.

DeVivo, M. J., et al., *Spinal Cord Injury: Its Short-Term Impact on Marital Status*, 66 Arch. Phys. Med. Rehabil. 501, 1985.

Ducker, T. B., *Treatment of Spinal Cord Injury*, 332 N. Engl. J. Med. 1459 (May 17), 1990.

Fehlings, M. G., and Louw, D., *Initial Stabilization and Medical Management of Acute Spinal Cord Injury*, 54 Am. Fam. Physician 155 (July), 1996.

Formal, C. S., et al., *Spinal Cord Injury Rehabilitation. Functional Outcomes*, 78 Arch. Phys. Med. Rehabil. S59 Mar., Suppl. 3), 1997.

Fuhrer, M. J., et al., *Pressure Ulcers in Community-Resident Persons with Spinal Cord Injury: Prevalence and Risk Factors*, 74 Arch. Phys. Med. Rehab. 1172 (Nov.), 1993.

Garfin, S. R., and Northrup, B. E., *Surgery for Spinal Cord Injuries*, Raven Press, New Yorks, 1993.

Green, B. G., et al., *Penile Prostheses in Spinal Cord Injured Patients: Combined Psychosexual Counseling and Surgical Regimen*, 24 Paraplegia 167, 1986.

Jeffrey, D. L., *The Hazards of Reduced Mobility for the Person with a Spinal Cord Injury*, 52 J. Rehab. 59, 1986.

Johnston, R. A., *Management of Old People with Neck Trauma: Injury to the Cervical Cord is Common but May Be Overlooked*, 299 Br. Med. J. 633, 1989.

Kosieradzski, M. R., editor, *Legal Guide to Spinal Cord Injuries and Expert Testimony*, John Wiley & Sons, Somerset, N.J., 1995.

Krause, J. S., *Employment after Spinal Cord Injury*, 73 Arch. Phys. Med. Rehab. 163 (Feb.), 1992.

Krause, J. S., and Crewe, N. M., *Prediction of Long-Term Survival Among Persons with Spinal Cord Injury: An 11-Year Prospective Study*, 32 Rehab. Psychol 205, 1987.

Krause, J. S., *The Relationship of Productivity to Adjustment Following Spinal Cord Injury*, 33 Rehab. Coun. Bull. 188, 1990.

Krengel, W. F., III., et al., *Early Stabilization and Decompression for Incomplete Paraplegia Due to a Thoracic-Level Spinal Cord Injury*, 18 Spine 2080, 1993.

Kuhlemeier, K. V., et al., *Long-Term Followup of Renal Function After Spinal Cord Injury*, 134 J. Urol. 510, 1985.

Maeder, K., et al., *Methicillin-Resistant Staphylococcus Aureus (MRSA) Colonization in Patients with Spinal Cord Injury*, 31 Paraplegia 639 (Oct.), 1993.

Maroon, J. C., *"Burning Hands" in Football Spinal Cord Injuries*, 238 J.A.M.A. 2049, 1977.

Marshall, L. F., et al., *Deterioration Following Spinal Cord Injury*, 66 J. Neurosurg. 400, 1987.

Piepmeier, J. M., *The Outcome Following Traumatic Spinal Cord Injury*, Futura Publishing Co., Inc., Mt. Kisco, N.Y., 1992.

Relethford, J. H., et al., *Trends in Traumatic Spinal Cord Injury: New York*, 40 M.M.W.R. 535, 1991.

Rossier, A. B., et al., *Posttraumatic Cervical Syringomyelia*, 108 Brain 439, 1985.

Rubayi, S., et al., *Diagnosis and Treatment of Iliopsoas Abscess in Spinal Cord Injury Patients*, 74 Arch. Phys. Med. Rehab. 1186 (Nov.), 1993.

Schurch, B., et al., *Posttraumatic Syringomyelia (Cystic Myelopathy): A Prospective Study of 449 Patients with Spinal Cord Injury*, 60 J. Neurol. Neurosurg. Psychiatry 61, 1996.

Sipski, M. L., et al., *Long-Term Use of Computerized Bicycle Ergometry for Spinal Cord Injured Subjects*, 74 Arch. Phys. Med. Rehab. 238 (Mar.), 1993.

Sobus, K. M., et al., *Undetected Ausculoskeletal Trauma in Children with Traumatic Brain Injury or Spinal Cord Injury*, 74 Arch. Phys. Med. Rehabil. 902 (Sep.), 1993.

Stover, S. L., and Fine, P. R., *Spinal Cord Injury: The Facts and Figures*, University of Alabama at Birmingham, Birmingham, 1986.

Tate, D. G., et al., *The Effects of Insurance Benefit Coverage of Functional and Psychosocial Outcomes after Spinal Cord Injury*, 75 Arch. Phys. Med. Rehabil. 407, 1994.

Torg, J. S., et al., *The Relationship of Developmental Narrowing of the Cervical Spinal Canal to Reversible and Irreversible Injury of the Cervical Spinal Cord in Football Players*, 78 J. Bone Joint Surg. Am. 1308 (Sept.), 1996.

Varghese, G., et al., *Spinal Cord Injuries Following Electrical Accidents*, 24 Paraplegia 159, 1986.

Waites, K. B., et al., *Epidemiology and Risk Factors for Urinary Tract Infection Following Spinal Cord Injury*, 74 Arch. Phys. Med. Rehab. 691, 1993.

Walker, J., et al., *Cardiac Risk Factors Immediately Following Spinal Injury*, 74 Arch. Phys. Med. Rehab. 129 (Nov.), 1993.

Welch, R. D., et al., *Functional Independence in Quadriplegia: Critical Levels*, 67 Arch. Phys. Med. Rehabil. 235, 1986.

Whiteneck, C. G., *Evaluating Outcome After Spinal Cord Injury: What Determines Success?*, 20 J. Spinal Cord Med. 179 (Apr.), 1997.

Yamashita, Y., et al., *Chronic Injuries of the Spinal Cord: Assessment with MR Imaging*, 175 Radiology 849 (June), 1990.

Yarkony, G. M., et al., *Benefits of Rehabilitation for Traumatic Spinal Cord Injury*, 44 Arch. Neurol. 93, 1987.

Yarkony, G. M., et al., *Spinal Cord Injury Rehabilitation. Assessment and Management During Acute Care*, 78 Arch. Phys. Med. Rehabil. S48 (Mar., Suppl. 3), 1997.

(D) OTHER SPINAL DISORDERS

Braackman, R., *Management of Cervical Spondylitic Myelopathy and Radiculopathy*, 57 J. Neurol. Neurosurg. Psychiatry 257, 1994.

Chen, L. S., et al., *Multiple Thoracic Disc Herniations — Case Report*, 66 J. Neurosurg. 290, 1987.

DiMarco, A., et al., *Postoperative Management of Primary Spinal Cord Ependymomas*, 27 Acta Oncologica 371, 1988.

Editorial, *Chymopapain and the Intervertebral Disc*, 2 Lancet 843, 1986.

Isu, T., et al., *A Reappraisal of the Diagnosis in Cervical Disc Disease: The Posterior Longitudinal Ligament Perforated or Not*, 28 Neuroradiology 215, 1986.

Javid, M. J., *Efficacy of Chymopapain Chemonucleolysis*, 62 J. Neurosurg. 662, 1985.

Maciunas, R. J., et al., *The Long-Term Results of Chymopapain Chemonucleolysis for Lumbar Disc Disease*, 65 J. Neurosurg. 1, 1986.

Rowland, L. P., *Surgical Treatment of Cervical Spondylitic Myelopathy: Time for a Controlled Study*, 42 Neurology 5, 1992.

Woolsey, R. M., and Young, R. R., *Neurologic Clinics: Disorders of the Spinal Cord*, W. B. Saunders Co., Philadelphia, 1991.

(E) COMPLICATIONS OF TREATMENT

Allen, M. B., Jr., and Miller, R. H., *Essentials of Neurosurgery*, McGraw-Hill, New York, 1995.

Arego, D. E., et al., *Bacteriuria in Patients with Spinal Cord Injury*, 21 Hosp. Pract. 87, 1986.

Beck, R. W., et al., *Post-Decompression Optic Neuropathy*, 63 J. Neurosurg. 196, 1985.

Diringer, M. N., *Management of Sodium Disturbances in Patients with CNS Lesions*, 6 Clin. Neuropharmacol. 427, 1992.

Glaser, J. A., et al., *Complications Associated with the Halo-Vest*, 65 J. Neurosurg. 762, 1986.

Landolt, A. M., editor, *Complications in Neurosurgery*, S. Karger, New York, 1984.

Lanza, D. C., et al., *Predictive Value of the Glasgow Coma Scale for Tracheotomy in Head-Injured Patients*, 99 Ann. Otol. Rhinol. Laryngol. 38, 1990.

McDonald, J. V., et al., *Intraspinal Epidermoid Tumors Caused by Lumbar Puncture*, 43 Arch. Neurol. 936, 1986.

Mollman, H. D., et al., *Risk Factors for Postoperative Neurosurgical Wound Infection*, 64 J. Neurosurg. 902, 1986.

Narayan, R., et al., *Intracranial Pressure: To Monitor or Not To Monitor. A Review of Our Experience with Head Injury*, 56 J. Neurosurg. 650, 1982.

Ropper, A. H., *Neurological and Neurosurgical Intensive Care*, 3d ed., Raven Prewss, New York, 1993.

(F) EPILEPSY

Abarbannell, N. R., *Prehospital Seizure Management*, 11 Am. J. Emerg. 210 (May), 1993.

Beckhung, E., et al., *Motor and Sensory Dysfunctions in Children with Mental Retardation and Epilepsy*, 6 Seizure 43 (Feb.), 1997.

Camfield, C., et al., *Outcome of Childhood Epilepsy: A Population-Based Study with a Simple Predictive Scoring System for Those Treated with Medication*, 122 J. Pediatr. 861 (June), 1993.

Chadwick, D., et al., *Outcomes After Seizure Recurrence in People with Well-Controlled Epilepsy and the Factors that Influence It: The MRC Antiepileptic Drug Withdrawal Group*, 37 Epilepsia 1043, 1996.

Chaplin, J. E., et al., *National General Practice Study of Epilepsy: The Social and Psychological Effects of A Recent Diagnosis of Epilepsy*, 304 Br. Med. J. 1416 (May 30), 1992.

Dan, N. G., et al., *The Incidence of Epilepsy After Ventricular Shunting Procedures*, 65 J. Neurosurg. 19, 1986.

Diamantopoulos, N., et al., *The Effect of Puberty on the Course of Epilepsy*, 43 Arch. Neurol. 873, 1986.

Devinsky, O., et al., *Clinical and Electroencephalographic Features of Simple Partial Seizures*, 38 Neurology 1347, 1988.

Editorial, *Surgery for Temporal Lobe Epilepsy*, 8620 Lancet 1115, 1988.

Fiordelli, E., et al., *Epilepsy and Psychiatric Disturbance: A Cross-Sectional Study*, 163 Brit. J. Psychiat. 446, 1993.

Gold, J. M., et al., *Schizophrenia and Temporal Lobe Epilepsy*, 51 Arch. Gen. Psych. 265, 1994.

Jones, S. C., et al., *Multiple Forms of Epileptic Attack Secondary to a Small Chronic Subdural Hematoma*, 299 Br. Med. J. 439, 1989.

Koch-Weser, M., et al., *Prevalence of Psychologic Disorders after Surgical Treatment of Seizures*, 45 Arch. Neurol. 1308, 1988.

Lee, L., et al., *Early Seizures after Mild Closed-Head Injury*, 76 J. Neurosurg. 435, 1992.

Lewis, R. J., et al., *Clinical Predictors of Post-Traumatic Seizures in Children with Head Trauma*, 22 Ann. Emerg. Med. 7 (July), 1993.

Pellock, J. M., et al., *A Routine Guide for Blood Monitoring in Patients Receiving Antiepileptic Drugs*, 41 Neurology 961, 1991.

Phillips, S. A., et., *Etiology and Mortality of Status Epilepticus in Children*, 46 Arch Neurol. 74, 1989.

Rosenstein, D. L., et al., *Seizures Associated with Antidepressants: A Review*, 54 J. Clin. Psychiat. 289 (Aug.), 1993.

Saunders, M., *Epilepsy in Women of Childbearing Age*, 299 Br. Med. J. 581, 1989.

Simon, R. P., *Alcohol and Seizures,* 319 N. Engl. J. Med. 715, 1988.

Spudis, E. V., et al., *Driving Impairment Caused by Episodic Brain Dysfunction — Restrictions for Epilepsy and Syncope,* 43 Arch. Neurol. 558, 1986.

Temkin, N. R., et al., *Posttramautic Seizures,* 2 Neurosurg. Clin. North Am. 425, 1991.

Toone, B. K., *The Psychoses of Epilepsy,* 84 J. Royal Society Med. 457, 1991.

Trimble, M. R., and Bolwig, T. G., editors, *Aspects of Epilepsy and Psychiatry,* John Wiley & Sons, Inc., New York, 1986.

Walker, A. E., et al., *The Fate of World War II Veterans With Post-Traumatic Seizures,* 46 Arch. Neurol. 23, 1989.

Weiss, G. H. et al., *Predicting Posttraumatic Epilepsy in Penetrating Head Injury,* 43 Arch. Neurol. 771, 1986.

Wyllie, E., et al., *Outcome of Psychogenic Seizures in Children and Adolescents Compared with Adults,* 41 Neurology 742, 1991.

Wyllie, E., *The Treatment of Epilepsy,* 2d ed., Lea & Febiger, Philadelphia, 1997.

(G) PERIPHERAL NERVE INJURIES

Dawson, D. M., et al., *Entrapment Neuropathies,* 2d ed., Little, Brown & Co., Boston, 1990.

Dyck, P. J., and Thomas, P. K., *Peripheral Neuropathy,* 3d ed., W. B. Saunders Co., Philadelphia, 1993.

Omer, G.. E., Jr., et al., *Management of Peripheral Nerve Problems,* 2d W. B. Saunders Co., Philadelphia, 1998.

Rayan, G. M., *Surgical Management of Peripheral Nerve Injuries,* 79 J. Okla. State Med. Assoc. 398, 1986.

Rettig, A. C., et al., *Anterior Subcutaneous Transfer of the Ulnar Nerve in the Athlete,* 21 Am. J. Sports Med. 836, 1993.

Schott, G. D., *Induction of Involuntary Movements by Peripheral Trauma: An Analogy with Causalgia,* 2 Lancet 712, 1986.

§ 32.197. Legal references.

The following additional references may aid in further research on the material covered in Chapter 32.

References are arranged under the following headings:

    (A) HEAD INJURIES GENERALLY
    (B) COMPLICATIONS OF HEAD INJURIES
    (C) SPINAL CORD AND NERVE INJURIES
    (D) NEUROLOGICAL TESTS
    (E) PREPARATION AND TRIAL
    (F) NEGLIGENCE ACTIONS AGAINST PHYSICIANS

(A) HEAD INJURIES GENERALLY

Alverson, J. B., and Smagac, S. S., *Brain Mapping: Should This Controversial Evidence Be Excluded?,* 48 Fed'n Ins. & Corp. Couns. Q. 131 (Winter), 1998.

Barry, H. J., et al., *Brain and Spinal Cord Injuries Related to Trauma,* 24 Ins. Couns. J. 272, 1957.

Bell, D. S., *Misleading Expert Testimony About Head Injury,* 3 J.L. & Med. 346 (May), 1996.

Bernad, P. G., "Forensic Issues," in *Closed-Head Injury: A Clinical Source Book* (P. G. Bernad), The Michie Company, Charlottesville, Va., 1994.

Braithwaite, B., *Head Injury Litigation,* 142 New L.J. 942 (July 3), 1992.

Cahn, G., and Miller, S., *Closed Head Injuries,* 24 Trial 33 (April), 1988.

Camps, F. E., *Investigation and Interpretation of Head Injuries,* 27 Ins. Couns. J. 178, 1960.

Cantor, P., *Injuries, Diseases and Congenital Abnormalities of Central Nervous System,* 1959 Trial & Tort Trends 50.

Crandall, P. H., *Frontal Injuries of the Skull,* 7 Clev.-Mar. L. Rev. 429, 1958.

Evans, J. P., *Acute Head Injury,* 4 Lawyer's Med. J. 23, 1968.

Freeman, M. J., *Differential Diagnosis — Head Trauma,* 14 Trial 28 (Mar.), 1978.

Grossman, R. G., *Diagnosis and Management of Acute Head Injuries,* 6 Lawyer's Med. J. 97, 1970.

Harvey, F. H. and Jones, A. M., *Typical Basal Skull Fracture of Both Petrous Bones: An Unreliable Indicator of Head Impact Site,* 25 J. For. Sci. 280 (Apr.), 1980.

Harvey, F. H., *The Significance of the Amount of Fluid Surrounding the Brain to the Recognition of Brain Swelling (or Atrophy) at Autopsy: A New and Routinely Applicable Method of Diagnosing Abnormal Brain Size,* 25 J. For. Sci. 287 (Apr.), 1980.

Hunter, A. R., *Basic Consideration in the Conservative Care of Head Injuries,* 30 Ins. Couns. J. 163, 1963.

Montgomery, R. B., Jr., et al., *Injuries to the Brain,* 23 Ins. Couns. J. 411, 1956.

Segerson, J. A., *Brain Injury,* 24 J. B.A. Kan. 336, 1956.

Seletz, E., *Brain Injuries (Cerebral Concussion, Contusion, Laceration and Hemorrhage),* 5 Med. Trial Tech. Q. 1, 1958.

Shafer, N., *Parkinson's Disease and Trauma,* 2 Lawyer's Med. J. (Second Series) 223, 1974.

Symposium on Brain Injuries, 11 Clev.-Mar. L. Rev. 521, 1962.

(B) COMPLICATIONS OF HEAD INJURIES

Arieff, A. J., *Amnesia,* Med. Trial Tech. Q., 1955 Annual, 17.

Averbach, A., *Problems of Traumatic Epilepsy as Viewed by the Trial Lawyer,* 1957 Trial & Tort Trends 52.

Bell, D. S., *The Medico-Legal Hazard of Denial After Brain Damage,* 69 Austl. L.J. 455 (June), 1995.

Bernad, P. G., "Complications and Unusual Clinical Presentations," in *Closed-Head Injury: A Clinical Source Book* (P. G. Bernad), The Michie Company, Charlottesville, Va., 1994.

Bernad, P. G., "Psychiatric Complications," in *Closed-Head Injury: A Clinical Source Book* (P. G. Bernad), The Michie Company, Charlottesville, Va., 1994.

Christovich, A. R., Jr., et al., *Multiple Sclerosis and Related Conditions Including the Role of Trauma,* 24 Ins. Couns. J. 107, 1957.

Coburn, F. E. and Fahr, S. M., *Amnesia and the Law,* 41 Ia. L. Rev. 369, 1956.

Dalgaard J. B., *Brain Injury as a Cause of Oesophago-Gastroduodenal Ulceration,* 4 J. For. Med. 110, 1957.

Donnelly, J., *Traumatic Neuroses Associated with Brain Injury,* 1 Amicus Cur. 38, 1955.

Duttman, M. R., *Anosmia in Head Injury,* Med. Trial Tech. Q., 1957 Annual, 33.

Epileptic Seizures and Criminal Mens Rea, The Army Lawyer 65 (Feb.), 1990.

Feldman, W. S., *Episodic Cerebral Dysfunction: A Defense in Legal Limbo,* 9 L. Psych. & L. 193 (Summer), 1981.

Flaxman, N., *Delayed Traumatic Apoplexy,* 5 Med. Trial Tech. Q. 29, 1958.

Frank, L. M., *Effects of Trauma to the Nervous System,* 1 Amicus Cur. 14, 1956.

Galski, T., and Carnevale, G., *Proving Cognitive and Behavior Brain Injuries,* 32 Trial 47 (Sept.), 1996.

Graber, B., et al., *Brain Damage Among Mentally Disordered Sex Offenders,* 27 J. For. Sci. 125 (Jan.), 1982.

Honor, S., *Head Injury, Neuropsychological Sequelae, and Personal Injury Litigation,* 40 Med. Trial Tech. Q. 42, 1993.

Keys, J. G., et al., *Epileptic Automobile Driver in Ohio,* 35 Ohio Bar 63, 1962.

Legal Problems of Epilepsy, 29 Temp. L.Q. 364, 1956.

Lowis, S., *Subdural Hematomas: From Diagnosis to Prognosis,* Med. Trial Tech. Q., 1975 Annual 349.

Nielson, J. M., *Traumatic (Jacksonian) Epilepsy,* 1 Med. Trial Tech. Q. 27, 1955.

Note, *Amnesia: A Case Study in the Limits of Particular Justice,* 71 Yale L.J. 109, 1961.

O'Doherty, D. S., *Personal Injury and Multiple Sclerosis,* 8 Prac. Law. 31, 1962.

Perr, I. N., *Epilepsy and the Law,* 7 Clev.-Mar. L. Rev. 280, 1958.

Perr, I. N., *Post-traumatic Epilepsy and the Law,* 8 Clev.-Mar. L. Rev. 129, 1959.

Peters, J. D., *Cerebral Palsy,* 20 Trial 34 (Dec.), 1984.

Policastro, N. C., *Neurological and Psychiatric Disabilities from Head and Brain Injuries,* 22 Trauma 47 (Dec.), 1980.

Sexual Disturbances Following Head Injuries, 27 Current Med. 26 (Nov.), 1980.

Schutte, J. W., and Howell, M. F., *Refuting Common Defenses in Traumatic Brain Injury Cases,* 33 Trial 32 (Jan.), 1997.

Smith, B. H., *Subdural Hematoma,* 5 Lawyer's Med. J. 317, 1970.

Stolker, C. J., *The Unconscious Plaintiff: Consciousness As a Prerequisite for Compensation for Non-Pecuniary Loss,* 39 Int'l & Comp. L.Q. 82 (Jan.), 1990.

Tuchler, M. L., *Review of the Amnesic States: The Significance of Retrospective Falsification,* 2 J. For. Sci. 263, 1957.

Walker, A. E., *Posttraumatic Epilepsy,* 4 Lawyer's Med. J. 1, 1968.

Wecht, C. H. and Perper, J. A., *Medicolegal Implications of Epilepsy,* 27 Med. Trial Tech. Q. 9 (Summer), 1980.

Weller, M. P. I., *The Statute of Time Limitation in Post-Traumatic Epilepsy,* 136 New L.J. 409 (May 2), 1986.

(C) SPINAL CORD AND NERVE INJURIES

Barry, H. J., et al., *Brain and Spinal Cord Injuries Related to Trauma,* 24 Ins. Couns. J. 272, 1957.

Begam, R. G., *Day in the Life of a Quadriplegic,* 14 Trial 25 (Mar.), 1978.

Belli, M. M., *Representing the Quadriplegic Client,* 18 Trial 48 (June), 1982.

Cantor, P., *Injuries, Diseases and Congenital Abnormalities of Central Nervous System,* 1959 Trial & Tort Trends 50.

Frank, L. M., *Effects of Trauma to the Nervous System,* 1 Amicus Cur. 14, 1956.

Gabrielsen, M. A., and Olenn, J. R., *Swimming Pool Litigation: Educating for Safety,* 18 Trial 38 (Feb.), 1982.

Gordon, E. J., *Disorders of the Upper Extremity,* 10 Law. Med. J. 759 (May), 1982.

Gosnold, J. K., and Sivaloganathan, S., *Spinal Cord Damage in a Case of Non-Accidental Injury in Children,* 20 Med., Sci. & Law 54 (Jan.), 1980.

Kosieradzki, M. R., *Litigating Spinal Cord Injuries: Law, Medicine, and Economics,* Wiley Law Publishers, Colorado Springs, Col., 1995.

Nerve Injuries, 4 Current Med. 11, 1957.

Pegalis, S. E., et al., *Thoracic Spinal Cord Paraplegia: Its Cause and Avoidability,* 1981 Pers. Inj. Ann. 179.

Policastro, N. C., *Injuries to Nerves Arising from Lumbar, Sacral and Coccygeal Plexuses,* 22 Trauma 5 (Aug.), 1980.

Policastro, N. C., *Injuries to Spinal Cord, Nerve Roots, Plexuses and Peripheral Nerves,* 21 Trauma 37 (April), 1980.

Schlomann, B., *Medico-legal Aspects of Spinal Cord Injuries,* 6 S. T. L.J. 247, 1962.

Smialek, J. L., et al., *Secondary Intracranial Subarachnoid Hemorrhage Due to Spinal Missile Injury,* 26 J. For. Sci. 431 (April), 1981.

(D) NEUROLOGICAL TESTS

Anchor, K. N., et al., *Fundamentals of Disability Determination and Rehabilitation: A Higher Ground for the Applied Neurobehavioral Sciences,* 36 Defense L.J. 363 (July), 1987.

Arieff, A. J., *Electrodiagnosis in Peripheral Nerve Injuries*, Med. Trial Tech. Q., 1956 Annual, 33.

Bauder, R. I., *Proving up the Electromyogram*, 3 Med. Trial Tech. Q. 41, 1956.

Bernad, P. G., "Neurodiagnostic Procedures and Examinations," in *Closed-Head Injury: A Clinical Source Book* (P. G. Bernad), The Michie Company, Charlottesville, Va., 1994.

Bernstein, L., *Myelography in Low Back Pain Diagnosis*, 1 Amicus Cur. 29, 1955.

Blanton, F., et al., *E.E.G. — A Trial Aid*, 30 Ala. Law. 460, 1969.

Byrne, A., and Nilges, R. G., *The Brain Stem in Brain Death: A Critical Review*, 9 Issues L. & Med. 3 (Summer), 1993.

DeCaro, J., *Handling the Aquatic Diving Injury Case*, 22 Barrister 25 (Winter), 1991-92. (Publication of Pennsylvania Trial Lawyers Association).

Duttman, M. R., *Brain Injuries: Proving and Disproving By Vestibular Tests; Some Medical-Legal Misconceptions*, Med. Trial Tech. Q., 1954 Annual, 1.

Fuller, P. L., *Brain Injuries and the E.E.G.*, 15 Fed'n Ins. Couns. Q. 14, 1965.

Goodgold, J., *Electromyography as a Diagnostic Aid*, 4 Lawyer's Med. J. 369, 1969.

Guilmette, T. J., and Matazow, G. S., *Proving Brain Damage from Mild Head Injury*, 28 Trial 56 (Aug.), 1992.

Hall, R. E., *Using Improvements in Medical Technology to Prove Timing of Newborn Brain Injury*, 41 Fed'n Ins. & Corp. Couns. Q. 495 (Summer), 1991.

Horan, D. J., *Cross-Examination Concerning Electroencephalographic Studies*, 15 Trial Law. Guide 15, 1971.

Incagnoli, T., *Clinical Neuropsychologists*, 21 Trial 60 (June), 1985.

Kadushin, F. S., *How to Assess Brain Damage*, 26 Trial 64 (Oct.), 1990.

Katz, H. A., and Schur, J., *Electromyography (EMG): Objective Proof of Disability in Nerve and Muscle Cases*, 1957 Trial & Tort Trends 737.

Kiloh, L. G., *Electroencephalogram in Psychiatry*, 30 Ins. Couns. J. 632, 1968.

Kosieradzski, M. R., editor, *Legal Guide to Spinal Cord Injuries and Expert Testimony*, John Wiley & Sons, Somerset, N.J., 1995.

Lawrence, R. M., *Electroencephalogram (EEG) and the Law*, 10 Med. Trial Tech. Q. 57, 1963.

Leestma, J. E., *The Neuropathologist as an Expert Witness*, 36 Med. Trial Tech. Q. 170, 1989.

Levy, L. L., *Electromyography and Electroencephalography*, 2 Amicus Cur. 4, 1956.

Nemeth, R. S., *Litigating Head Trauma: The "Hidden" Evidence of Disability*, 39 Defense L.J. 377, 1990.

Nolan, J. R., *Myelography and the Myelogram*, 6 Med. Trial Tech. Q. 9, 1959.

Paschke, R. E., and Moch, J. W., *Neuropsychological Evaluation in Traumatic Head Injury — A New Tool for Attorneys*, 30 Trial Law. Guide 442, 1987.

Peters, J. D., *Litigating the Brain-Damaged Baby Case: From the Initial Interview to the Trial*, 70 Mich. B.J. 1063 (Oct.), 1991.

Riley, P. W., *Handling Swimming Pool Injury Cases*, 11 Prod. Liab. L. Rep. 145 (Aug.), 1992.

Roberts, A. C., et al., *Litigating Head Trauma Cases*, Wiley Law Publications, Colorado Springs, 1989.

Smith, B. H., *Methods of Neurological Diagnosis and Their Critical Assessment*, 27 Ins. Couns. J. 169, 1960.

Smith, L. J., *Significant Tests for Back and Neck Injuries*, 19 Prac. Law. 17, 1973.

Stern, B. H., *The Neuropsychologist in a Mild Traumatic Brain Injury Case: How to Conduct the Direct Examination*, 31 Trial 66 (June), 1995.

Sykes, R. B., and Vilos, J. D., *The Brain Injury Case: Preparation and Discovery*, 3 Utah B.J. 14 (March), 1990.

Udvarhelyi, G. B., *The Diagnosis of Craniocerebral Injuries*, 2 Lawyer's Med. J. (Second Series) 1, 1974.

Wasyliw, O. E., and Golden, C. J., *Neuropsychological Evaluation in the Assessment of Personal Injury*, 3 Behavioral Sci. & L. 149, 1985.

(E) PREPARATION AND TRIAL

Braithwaite, B., *Head Injury Litigation*, 142 New L.J. 942 (July 3), 1992.

Check List for Objective Signs of Brain Injury Which Can Be Demonstrated at Trial, 3 Current Med. 25, 1956.

Hirson, H. L., *Preparation and Trial of Head Injury Cases*, 3 Prac. Law. 56, 1957.

Horan, D. J., *Cross-Examination Concerning Electroencephalographic Studies*, 15 Trial Law. Guide 15, 1971.

Lay, D. P., *Medical-Legal Proof of Cervical Nerve Root Irritation*, 1957 Trial & Tort Trends 448.

Lees-Haley, P., *Mild Brain Injury: Proving Lost Earnings*, 23 Trial 83 (Nov.), 1987.

Magee, D. J., and Leestma, J. E., *Use of Neuropathologic Evidence in Will Contests*, 33 Med. Trial Tech. Q. 121 (Fall), 1986.

McCarthy, J. P., *Football-Helmet Brain Injury — Cross Examination of a Defense Medical Expert*, 1981 Pers. Inj. Ann. 255.

McNeal, H. J., *Defensing the Plaintiff's Headaches*, 10 Defense L.J. 49, 1961.

Medical Testimony in a Fracture of the Cribiform Plate, Skull and Brain Injury Case Resulting in Loss of Sense of Smell (Anosmia) and Knee Joint Injury — Showing the Direct and Cross-Examination of the General Practitioner and the Otolaryngologist, 3 Med. Trial Tech. Q. 75, 1957.

Medical Testimony in a Head Injury Case with Headache, Showing the Direct and Cross-Examinations of the Internist and the Neurosurgeon, 8 Med. Trial Tech. Q. 67, 77, 1962.

Medical Testimony in a Herniated Intervertebral Disc Case, Showing the Direct and Cross Examination of the Neurosurgeon, 6 Med. Trial Tech. Q. 65, 1959.

Medical Testimony in a Traumatic (Jacksonian) Epilepsy Case Showing the Direct and Cross-Examination of the Medical Witnesses — Includes the Roentgenologist, Neurosurgeons and Otolaryngologist, 1 Med. Trial Tech. Q. 63, 1955.

Medical Trial Technique in an Aggravation of Preexisting Multiple Sclerosis Case, 1 Med. Trial Tech. Q. 108, 1954.

Nonpecuniary Damages for Comatose Tort Victims, 61 Georgetown L. J. 1547, 1973.

Pollock, L. J., *Examination of Motor and Sensory Function as Related to Opinion Evidence*, 6 Med. Trial Tech. Q. 41, 1959.

Sorensen, H. C., *Defending "Traumatic Epilepsy" Cases*, 21 Defense L.J. 589, 1972.

Spevack, S., *Cross Examination in a Traumatic Epilepsy Case*, 7 Trial Law. Q. 15, 1970-71.

Stevens, M. D., *Case for Extended Recovery in Posttraumatic Epilepsy*, 27 Med. Trial Tech. Q. 201 (Fall), 1980.

Trial Technique: Medical Testimony in a Subdural Hematoma Case, Showing the Direct and Cross Examination of the Pathologist, the Ambulance Surgeon, Motion for a Directed Verdict, and Affidavits of Neurosurgeons, a Neurologist, and the Pathologist, 9 Med. Trial Tech. Q. 71, 1962.

(F) NEGLIGENCE ACTIONS AGAINST PHYSICIANS

Napoli, J. P., *Neurosurgical Malpractice — Or, the Improper Diagnosis and Treatment of Lawsuits*, 10 Trial Law. Q. 7, 1974.

§ 32.198. American Law Reports.

29 A.L.R.2d 501. Malpractice: diagnosis and treatment of brain injuries, diseases, or conditions.

54 A.L.R.2d 273. Malpractice: diagnosis of fractures or dislocations. Skull fractures, §§ 3, 4, 9.

66 A.L.R.2d 1082. Admissibility of opinion evidence as to cause of death, disease, or injury. Brain injury, §§ 4, 5[a], [e], [g], 7[b]; spinal injury, §§ 4, 5[a], [f], [g], 6, 7[b].

2 A.L.R.3d 487. Proof that mental or neurological condition resulted from accident or incident in suit. Cerebral conditions, §§ 4-7, 9; ataxia, § 3; epilepsy, § 8; multiple sclerosis, § 15; neurasthenia, § 16; neuritis, § 17; miscellaneous neurological conditions, § 18.

11 A.L.R.3d 370. Excessiveness or adequacy of damages awarded to injured person for injuries to head or neck. Brain injuries, §§ 3, 4; epilepsy, injuries resulting in, §§ 3, 4, 15, 20, 23; nervous system, §§ 3, 4, 23; skull fracture, § 23; spine injuries, §§ 3, 15, 19, 20.

12 A.L.R.3d 475. Excessiveness or adequacy of damages awarded to injured person for injuries to organic systems and processes of body. Nerves and nervous system, generally, §§ 28-34.

30 A.L.R.3d 988. Malpractice in connection with diagnosis and treatment of epilepsy.

31 A.L.R.3d 1163. Competency of general practitioner to testify as expert witness in action against specialist for medical malpractice. Neurosurgeon, § 4[e].

37 A.L.R.3d 464. Malpractice: surgeon's liability for inadvertently injuring organ other than that intended to be operated on. Nerves, §§ 4-15; brain, § 23.

45 A.L.R.3d 731. Medical malpractice: liability for injury allegedly resulting from negligence in making hypodermic injection. Improper injection into spinal cord or nerves, §§ 12-14.

89 A.L.R.3d 87. Sufficiency of evidence to prove future medical expenses as result of injury to head or brain.

14 A.L.R.4th 328. Excessiveness or adequacy of damages awarded for injuries to head or brain, or for mental or nervous disorders.

15 A.L.R.4th 294. Excessiveness or adequacy of damages awarded for injuries to back, neck, or spine.

20 A.L.R.5th 1. Necessity of expert testimony on issue of permanence of injury and future pain and suffering. Brain injuries, §§ 16, 17; nerve injuries or paralysis, § 48.

50 A.L.R.5th 1. Excessiveness or adequacy of damages awarded for injuries to head or brain.

51 A.L.R.5th 467. Excessiveness or adequacy of damages awarded for injuries to nerves or nervous system.

52 A.L.R.5th 1. Excessiveness or adequacy of damages awarded for injuries causing mental or psychological damages.

§ 32.199. Cases.

In the following list of cases, no attempt has been made to include all the decisions on topics covered in Chapter 32. The cases selected are those that the editors believe will best aid the reader in further research on the medicolegal issues involved.

Cases are arranged under the following headings:

    (A) HEAD INJURY AND ITS CONSEQUENCES
    (B) EPILEPSY
    (C) BRAIN TUMOR AND TRAUMA
    (D) SPINAL INJURY
    (E) PERIPHERAL NERVE INJURY
    (F) ALLEGED MALPRACTICE OR INJURY WHILE UNDER MEDICAL SUPERVISION

(A) HEAD INJURY AND ITS CONSEQUENCES

[See also Chapter 20, § 20.99.]

[For traumatic epilepsy see (B) below.]

United States: Gaskins v. Ryder Truck Lines, Inc. (C.A.-4 S.C., 1962) 299 F.2d 236 (traumatic amnesia, facial scars, and severe spine injuries).

Higgs v. Grissom (C.A.-6 Tenn., 1972) 455 F.2d 951 (award of $300,000 upheld on behalf of eighteen-year-old male who suffered severe head injuries requiring tracheotomy, emergency brain surgery and plastic surgery; partial paralysis and inability to speak for several months after accident; probability that convulsions requiring medication will be permanent; psychological impairment).

Anderson v. Pittsburgh & Lake Erie R. Co. (W.D. Pa., 1962) 217 F. Supp. 956 (severe blow to jaw causing cerebral concussion with amnesia for day before and day after injury).

McCall v. United States (E.D. Va., 1962) 206 F. Supp. 421 (laceration on forehead of eight-year-old boy with brain tissue extruding and depressed fragments of bone driven into brain tissue, requiring graft of dura mater, removal of considerable brain tissue, and insertion of plastic plate to replace portion of skull, with probable personality changes, possible future epilepsy, but no impairment of cerebral function).

Rafferty v. Rainey (E.D. Tenn., 1968) 292 F. Supp. 152 (proposed $1,500 settlement for injuries to eight-year-old boy was not approved where he continued to suffer malfunctioning of brain two years following injury and sustained a residual injury to back of forebrain reflected by minimal abnormal result on an electroencephalogram, notwithstanding that settlement was urged by father and counsel).

Powell v. Hellenic Lines, Ltd. (E.D. La., 1972) 347 F. Supp. 855 (54-year-old longshoreman who was struck in face by ship's jackstaff awarded $15,000 for post-concussion syndrome).

French v. Farmers Ins. Co. (E.D. Mo., 1972) 354 F. Supp. 105 (high school girl who was good student suffered permanent brain damage from head injuries which affected her grades; $75,000 awarded).

Robertson v. Emory Univ. Hosp. (C.A.-5 Ga., 1980) 611 F.2d 604 (examining neurosurgeon overlooked fact that head injury patient was experiencing weakness of right side, and neurosurgical resident who did notice weakness failed to report fact to superiors).

Arizona: Esmeier v. Industrial Comm'n (1969) 10 Ariz. App. 435, 459 P.2d 523 (subdural hematoma and brain damage; medical testimony that claimant would have "considerable amount of difficulty going about his ordinary way of life" because of "80 per cent mortality with this particular type of injury").

California: Solorio v. Lampros (1969) 2 Cal. App. 3d 522, 82 Cal. Rptr. 753 (although neurosurgeon admitted he missed seeing head injury patient's subdural hematoma when he inspected skull through burr holes, and both he and neurologist admitted that they probably would have discovered it if they had ordered an arteriogram, there was insufficient evidence that defendants were guilty of below-standard practice).

Niles v. City of San Rafael (1974) 42 Cal. App. 3d 230, 116 Cal. Rptr. 733 (eleven-year-old boy rendered quadriplegic and mute from head injuries; damages exceeding $4,000,000 upheld).

Fortman v. Hemco, Inc. (1989) 211 Cal. App. 3d 241, 259 Cal. Rptr. 311 (5-year-old girl fell out of Jeep because of defective door; brain damage and multiple injuries; plaintiff is paraplegic and will function at level of 5-year-old for remainder of her life; no bladder or bowel control; will need total care at estimated average cost of $180,000 per year for life expectancy of 70.9 years; $23,000,000 award).

Colorado: Maryland Cas. Co. v. Kravig (1963) 153 Colo. 282, 385 P.2d 669 (evidence insufficient that rupture of congenital aneurysm and subarachnoid hemorrhage were caused by blow to head coupled with emotional excitement).

Lee's Mobile Wash v. Campbell (Colo., 1993) 853 P.2d 1140 (unsuccessful personal injury action by truck driver in rear-end collision whose head struck both rear window and steering wheel; although medical expenses over $6,000, jury award of no damages was upheld in view of conflicting evidence of injury to brain and evidence suggesting that plaintiff's problems were caused by other than accident).

Connecticut: Wood v. City of Bridgeport (Conn., 1990) 583 A.2d 124 (53-year-old male slipped and fell on icy sidewalk; skull fracture and epidural hematoma; memory loss and depression; 9% reduction in I.Q.; will require medication for epileptic seizures for life; medical expenses approximately $7,000; award of $400,000 approved).

Lutynski v. B. B. & J. Trucking Co. (Conn. App., 1993) 628 A.2d 1 (plaintiff injured in automobile-truck collision; cerebral contusion and facial injuries, including spasmodic muscular contraction on left cheek; some permanent brain damage; greater susceptibility to further head injury with accompanying fear and anxiety; award of $150,026 affirmed).

Delaware: Episcopo v. Minch (Del., 1964) 203 A.2d 273 (slight collision with no apparent injuries causing plaintiff's blood pressure to rise, resulting in rupture of aneurysm).

District of Columbia: Hooks v. Washington Sheraton Corp. (1977) 188 App. D.C. 71, 578 F.2d 313 (teenage boy awarded $6,000,000 and parents $1,000,000 as result of quariplegia from striking head on bottom of hotel swimming pool; remittiturs of $1,500,000 and $820,000 ordered in lieu of new trial on damages).

Florida: Vanguard Pest Control v. Turner (Fla. App., 1987) 501 So. 2d 66 (worker's compensation benefits for total disability awarded employee whose dormant multiple sclerosis was exacerbated by surgery necessitated by industrial accident).

Georgia: Central of Georgia Ry. Co. v. Brower (1962) 106 Ga. App. 340, 127 S.E.2d 33 (retrograde amnesia as explanation of plaintiff's inability to recall details of collision).

State v. Birditt (1986) 181 Ga. App. 356, 352 S.E.2d 203 (permanent partial disability benefits could not be paid under workmen's compensation for nurse's stuttering, loss of memory, loss of concentration and sluggishness, all of which resulted from head injury, because injuries had not reached "maximum improvement" so as to qualify as "permanent").

J. B. Hunt Transp., Inc. v. Bentley (Ga. App., 1993) 427 S.E.2d 499 (state DOT employee injured when tractor-trailer rig swerved off highway at construction site and struck pickup truck; concussion followed by development of three blood clots; organic brain damage; three craniotomies performed; plaintiff suffered cardiac arrest during one surgery; plaintiff now unemployable; jury awarded $6.55 million to plaintiff and wife, which included $3 million in punitive damages against trucking company and driver; punitive awards reduced on appeal to statutory caps of total of $1 million).

Illinois: Redmond v. Huppertz (1966) 71 Ill. App. 2d 254, 217 N.E.2d 85 (brain injury resulting in loss of smell, partial loss of taste and emotional control, and a degree of epileptic activity).

Robin v. Miller (1978) 67 Ill. App. 3d 656, 24 Ill. Dec. 22, 384 N.E.2d 889 ($800 held adequate damages for salesman who suffered "mild concussion" in auto accident and was unable to work for one week due to headache).

Lynch v. Board of Educ. (1980) 82 Ill. 2d 415, 45 Ill. Dec. 96, 412 N.E.2d 447 (head injury during high school "powder puff" football game; brain wave permanently altered, personality change, behavior problems; $60,000 award not excessive).

Burke v. 12 Rothschild's Liquor Mart, Inc. (Ill., 1992) 593 N.E.2d 522 (25-year-old shipping department worker struck head on being ejected from liquor store and struck head again on way to jail; permanent quadriplegia; $7.4 million jury award affirmed).

Yates v. Chicago Nat'l League Ball Club, Inc. (Ill. App., 1992) 595 N.E.2d 570 (10-year-old boy struck in head by foul ball at baseball game; hospitalized five days;

surgery required; severe headaches for almost 90 days; still suffered from occasional headaches and double vision at time of trial; has stopped participating in sports; $67,500 award affirmed).

Wagner v. City of Chicago (Ill. App., 1993) 626 N.E.2d 1227 (19-year-old's motorcycle struck by pickup truck; plaintiff sustained severe and permanent brain damage and requires 24-hour companion care; jury award of $4.3 million, reduced to $4.25 million by trial court for overestimation of future medical care, affirmed by appellate court).

Indiana: Kmart Corp. v. Beall (Ind. App., 1993) 620 N.E.2d 700 (customer struck on head and neck by box containing electrical receptacles; reflex sympathetic dystrophy and extreme sensitivity to pain; underwent numerous orthopedic, neurological, and osteopathic treatment programs with only temporary relief; physicians recommend pain center program costing $28,000; although formerly employed as sales consultant, due to difficulty concentrating, plaintiff can perform only clerical and computer data entry work; poor prognosis for recovery; $883,500 award affirmed).

Iowa: Kallel v. Petersen (Iowa App., 1993) 498 N.W.2d 413 (60-year-old homeowner who was trimming tree injured when visitor pulled rope tied to limb, causing limb to strike him in head; hematoma; surgery to remove clot and 40 days of hospitalization; medical expenses $37,388; off work over five months; parties found equally at fault; $59,846 jury verdict held adequate).

Kansas: Morgan v. Auto Transports, Inc. (1963) 192 Kan. 139, 386 P.2d 230 (skull fracture and cerebral concussion with continuing headaches but no organic brain damage and conflicting testimony as to functional brain injury and extent of permanent impairment).

Louisiana: Normand v. Bankers Fidelity Life Ins. Co. (La. App., 1962) 148 So. 2d 154 (medical evidence that fatal cerebral hemorrhage had its onset at most several hours before death and could not have been caused by head injury six days before).

Freeman v. Royal Indem. Co. (La. App., 1963) 157 So. 2d 315 (headaches and dizziness attributed to hypertension rather than concussion).

Smolinski v. Tauli (La. App., 1973) 285 So. 2d 577 (child awarded $75,000 for permanent brain damage which caused hyperkinesia and resulted in retarded psychomotor development affecting ability to learn, speak, think, and perform).

Glazer v. Louisiana Trailer Sales, Inc. (La. App., 1975) 313 So. 2d 266 (where injuries consisted of cut on crown of head which caused headaches for "one to two years" plus other bruises, award of $2,000 was proper).

Prats v. Moffett (La. App., 1980) 391 So. 2d 1299 (65-year-old woman suffered brain concussion in rear-end collision; nausea, dizziness, headaches, and hallucinations; continued to take medication at time of trial; $180,000 award not excessive).

Favorite v. Texas Road Gin (La. App., 1986) 499 So. 2d 531 (issue was whether worker who sustained head injuries was entitled to partial permanent or total permanent disability benefits for recurring dizziness).

Keyes v. Rockwood Ins. Co. (La. App., 1987) 502 So. 2d 223 (conflicting evidence as to whether worker was temporarily totally disabled from post-traumatic syndrome following head injury).

Bradford v. Pias (La. App., 1988) 525 So. 2d 134 (plaintiff injured in fight at nightclub; two linear temporal fractures of skull and basilar skull fracture; concussion; broken nose and facial lacerations; medical expense $4,300; $29,300 award reduced 30% for plaintiff's comparative fault).

Riche v. City of Baton Rouge (La. App., 1988) 541 So. 2d 905 ($60,000 awarded to 9-year-old boy whose bicycle struck displaced street barricade; skull fracture and cerebral concussion; severe headaches, dizziness and vomiting persisted nearly three years after accident; special damages $10,000; jury awarded $60,000).

Molbert v. Toepfer (La. App., 1989) 540 So. 2d 577 (28-year-old male plaintiff suffered brain damage in automobile accident; in coma for one month; now has mentality of 7- or 8-year-old; past and future medical expenses $300,000; loss of earnings $600,000; jury award of $1,050,000 affirmed).

Rosell v. ESCO (La. App., 1990) 558 So. 2d 1360 (elevator door struck plaintiff's face, causing her to fall and strike head; epileptic seizure disorder; 30% comparative negligence; award of $500,000 held adequate).

Whatley v. Regional Transit Auth. (La. App., 1990) 563 So. 2d 1194 (27-year-old practical nurse suffered head injury in bus crash; vertigo with episodes of nystagmus (jerky eye movement) and ringing in ears; 40% comparative negligence; verdict for $220,500).

Bush v. Winn-Dixie, Inc. (La. App., 1990) 573 So. 2d 508 (two-year-old boy suffered head injuries when van rear-ended by truck; two episodes of seizures; conflicting medical evidence on alleged diminished intellectual capacity and hyperactivity; $75,000 award held adequate).

Coley v. State (La. App., 1993) 621 So. 2d 41 (17-year-old student suffered head injury when she lost control of automobile in water that had flowed onto highway; brain concussion resulting in continuing headaches and blurred vision; $24,550 trial court award affirmed on appeal).

Laing v. American Honda Motors, Inc. (La. App., 1993) 628 So. 2d 196 (25-year-old farmer injured when three-wheeled ATV turned over; severe brain injury; plaintiff in coma for two weeks; hospitalized seven months; suffers spastic hemiparesis and speech impairment; requires daily living assistance; $5.75 million award affirmed).

Arneneaux v. Howard (La. App., 1993) 633 So. 2d 207 (18-year-old plaintiff suffered head injury in automobile accident; had first seizure ten days after injury and a second one 14 months later; may have to take antiseizure medication for life; trial court concluded that injury did not cause seizures and awarded only $2,781; appellate court held that trial court should have applied presumption in favor of plaintiff and increased award to $47,742).

Sinor v. National Cas. Co. (La. App., 1993) 633 So. 2d 720 (yard worker resting on swing in defendant's yard was struck in head by falling crossbeam; headaches, neck pain, blurred vision, postconcussion syndrome, and depression; still out of work 60 weeks and still taking prescription drugs at time of trial; will need future psychiatric treatment costing an estimated $5,000, although such treatment not totally due to accident; $49,042 trial court award affirmed on appeal).

Orillion v. Carter (La. App., 1994) 639 So. 2d 461 (plaintiff sustained fracture through wall of frontal sinus in head-on automobile accident; injury to frontal lobes and right temporal lobe; no surgery; plaintiff returned to work, but terminated two years later for personality problems; conflicting evidence as to whether problems were injury-related; trial court awarded $415,000, which included $250,000 for impairment of earning capacity).

Kramer v. Continental Cas. Co. (La. App., 1994) 641 So. 2d 557 (17-year-old female high school student suffered severe closed head injury in automobile accident; IQ reduced 20 points and cognitive difficulties; past medical expenses $197,255 and estimated future medical expenses $750,000; jury award, as adjusted by trial court, of $2.6 million, which included $1 million in general damages, affirmed on appeal).

Maryland: Abraham v. Moler (1969) 253 Md. 215, 252 A.2d 68 ($100,000 for plaintiff in slip-and-fall case; chronic brain syndrome, loss of memory, further surgery likely).

Massachusetts: Fogerty's Case (1975) 3 Mass. App. 737, 326 N.E.2d 347 (circulatory ailments implicated as cause of dizziness and blackouts in compensation claim by worker who fell from truck).

Stuart v. Town of Brookline (Mass., 1992) 587 N.E.2d 1384 (jewelry clerk earning $8.00 per hour suffered head injury in automobile accident; right hemisphere damage resulting in memory loss, poor concentration, decreased organizational abilities, erratic behavior, and depression; also exacerbation of preexisting epilepsy; medical expenses $12,824; lost wages $4,800; trial court awarded $125,000 under statute limiting recovery from public employers and municipalities).

Michigan: Williams v. State Highway Dep't (1972) 44 Mich. App. 51, 205 N.W.2d 200 (sixteen-year-old girl suffered brain stem injury causing permanent aphasia, vocabulary of eight-year-old, mental maturity of seven-year-old, and possible reduced life span; medical expenses $35,000; award of $1,100,000 upheld).

Frohman v. City of Detroit (Mich. App., 1989) 450 N.W.2d 59 (college student suffered closed head injury in auto crash; comatose for six weeks; memory loss and continuing manic episodes; permanent disability; $2.25 million verdict held not excessive).

Minnesota: Capriotti v. Beck (1962) 264 Minn. 39, 117 N.W.2d 563 (severe skull fracture in 3½-year-old boy, requiring removal of part of bone, removal of brain tissue, and insertion of metal plate, and resulting in future inability to pursue hazardous occupations and possible impairment of cerebral function).

Mester v. Fritze (1963) 265 Minn. 242, 121 N.W.2d 335 (concussion and possible subdural hematoma from automobile accident, causing headaches for 21 months, partial loss of memory, confusion, facial paralysis, slurring of speech, and personality changes, all temporary in nature).

State v. Peterson (1963) 266 Minn. 77, 123 N.W.2d 177 (evidence that brain damage from previous accident caused lapse of memory and staggering gait that would give appearance of intoxication).

Patterson v. Donahue (Minn., 1971) 190 N.W.2d 864 (driver's head "scraped" top of car, resulting in stiff neck, severe headaches, two unsuccessful operations, apparently to relieve nerve damage, and $8,000 in medical expenses and lost wages; award of $57,000 upheld).

Fifer v. Nelson (Minn., 1973) 204 N.W.2d 422 (farmer struck in forehead by silo blower lever lost only 1½ days of work and incurred only $144 in specials; symptoms included post-concussion syndrome, slight loss of cervical spine curvature and slight motion limitation; recurrent headaches; $27,500 award reduced to $22,500).

Erickson v. American Honda Motor Co. (Minn. App., 1990) 455 N.W.2d 74 (12-year-old boy suffered severe brain damage when all-terrain vehicle he was driving tipped over; plaintiff in periodic unconscious state and experiences pain; $2.9 million award held adequate).

Mississippi: Faulkner Concrete Pipe Co. v. Fox (1963) 248 Miss. 50, 157 So. 2d 804 (skull fracture and concussion followed by permanent blindness in one eye).

General Motors Corp. v. Jackson (Miss., 1994) 636 So. 2d 310 (six-week-old infant injured when vehicle overturned, allegedly because of defective rear axle; profound brain damage; I.Q. below 35 at age five; requires permanent cranial shunt because of hydrocephalic condition; medication required to control seizures; visual, speech, and motor control impairment; $5 million jury verdict not excessive).

Missouri: Schaeffer v. Craden (Mo. App., 1990) 800 S.W.2d 165 ($2,500 pain and suffering verdict for auto accident victim's closed head injury, which resulted in headaches and ringing in ears, held adequate despite medical bills of over $3,000).

Patrick v. Alphin (Mo. App., 1992) 825 S.W.2d 11 (driver struck head on windshield when he ran into ditch to avoid two trucks stopped on highway; temporal lobe disorder, causing organic brain syndrome and extreme mood swings; plaintiff unemployable; $1.15 million jury award upheld).

Magnuson ex rel. Mabe v. Kelsey-Hayes Co. (Mo. App., 1992) 844 S.W.2d 448 (wheel broke loose from passing pickup truck and struck four-year-old child in head; contrecoup brain injury; permanent right-side hemiparesis, retarded growth of right arm and leg, visual and auditory impairment, aphasia, fine motor-skill defects, poor balance, diminished cognitive thinking, decreased IQ, defective abstract thinking, memory loss, poor concentration, and emotional behavior problems; probably will be unemployable; $4.75 million award affirmed).

Montana: Knudson v. Edgewater Automotive Div. (1971) 157 Mont. 400, 486 P.2d 596 ($99,907 awarded for multiple skull fractures affecting taste, hearing, and vision, which still caused pain and discomfort after six years).

Pachek v. Norton Concrete Co. (1972) 160 Mont. 16, 499 P.2d 766 (79-year-old man awarded $20,000 for subdural hematoma requiring surgery, considerable hospitalization and extensive postoperative therapy).

Simchuk v. Angel Island Commun. Ass'n (Mont., 1992) 833 P.2d 158 (light pole on tennis/basketball court fell on guest; permanent brain damage affecting ability to remember new information; $177,000 verdict affirmed).

Nevada: General Elec. Co. v. Bush (Nev., 1972) 498 P.2d 366 ($3,000,000 awarded in defective product case to 39-year-old worker whose skull was crushed when load slipped on truck-type vehicle; plaintiff could neither communicate with others nor care for himself, being totally paralyzed below neck).

New Jersey: Sobin v. M. Frisch & Sons (1969) 108 N.J. Super. 99, 260 A.2d 228 (tree trimmer who suffered brain concussion in fall sued manufacturer and distributor of rope which gave way; plaintiff unconscious or semiconscious for 100 days; condition considered "insanity" and cause of action ruled not to have commenced until plaintiff was of "sane mind").

Lesniak v. County of Bergen (1989) 117 N.J. 12, 563 A.2d 795 (branch fell from tree in park, striking 7-year-old boy in head; severely depressed skull fracture; $170,000 jury verdict reversed and new trial on damages ordered for trial court's error in not allowing jury to properly consider plaintiff's future earning capacity).

Ryan v. KDI Sylvan Pools, Inc. (N.J., 1990) 579 A.2d 1241 (social guest struck head on bottom of swimming pool; in halo device for three months; permanent numbness and spasticity of hands; body spasms; urinary frequency and urgency; sexual dysfunction; 50% chance of future surgery; life expectancy of 32 years; $550,000 verdict held adequate).

New Mexico: Sanchez v. Molycorp, Inc. (N.M., 1985) 703 P.2d 925 (in claim for total disability benefits by miner who struck head in fall, fact that two medical experts who testified that disability was caused by accident did not have access to results of another physician's brain stem test on claimant went to weight and not to admissibility of their testimony).

New York: Kozminsky v. Sobel (1969) 31 App. Div. 2d 759, 297 N.Y.S.2d 635 (award reduced to $1,500 for infant who suffered skull fracture; bone fragment driven into brain; permanent tissue damage; operation left hole in the head).

Nelson v. State (1980) 105 Misc. 2d 107, 431 N.Y.S.2d 955 (evidence sufficient to support finding that woman who suffered severe brain injury which resulted in permanent "vegetative state" experienced pain while hospitalized and therefore was entitled to damages for pain and suffering in amount of $350,000).

Pavia v. Rosato (App. Div., 1989) 546 N.Y.S.2d 140 (adult male automobile accident victim suffered head injuries resulting in permanent paralysis, spasticity of left side and severe speech impediment; jury awarded $3.6 million for past and future medical expenses, $562,000 for loss of earnings, and $2.1 million for pain and suffering; pain and suffering award reduced to $1 million on appeal).

Cayuto v. Lilledah (Misc., 1990) 555 N.Y.S.2d 901 ($6,000 award adequate for 14-year-old girl who suffered skull fracture in automobile accident; rapid recovery and return to active social life despite continuing headaches, which, according to defense medical testimony, could have been caused by use of alcohol and birth-control pills).

Mirand v. City of New York (App. Div., 1993) 598 N.Y.S.2d 464 (17-year-old high school student struck in head by hammer while attempting to stop fight; headaches lasted six months; "black spots before eyes"; lacerated scalp; jury returned verdict of $50,000, but trial court found no liability and set award aside; appellate court reversed and reinstated verdict).

511

Marx v. Pross (App. Div., 1993) 603 N.Y.S.2d 84 (30-year-old plaintiff with 29.2 years' work expectancy suffered head injury in automobile collision; severe concussion exacerbating minimal brain dysfunction sustained in earlier accident; decreased functioning of brain and weakening of right side of body will prevent full-time employment; jury awarded $318,500, but plaintiff found 87.5% at fault for following too closely).

Raucci v. City School Dist. (App. Div., 1994) 610 N.Y.S.2d 653 (17-year-old high school junior claimed coach at summer football camp struck him 13 or more times in head with foam rubber tackling dummy during agility drill; medical evidence revealed permanent neurological injuries, emotional disorders, impaired learning abilities, depression, and social withdrawal; jury awarded $25,000 for past pain and suffering, but nothing for future pain and suffering or economic loss; appellate court affirmed, noting conflicting and inconsistent testimony, evidence of preexisting hydrocephalic condition that would account for many of plaintiff's symptoms, and evidence that plaintiff's social activities had not been materially affected).

Bartlett v. Snappy Car Rental, Inc. (App. Div., 1995) 626 N.Y.S.2d 499 (head injury suffered in automobile accident resulted in worsening of woman's preexisting tremors; plaintiff also experienced severe headaches, which she claimed prevented her from leading normal, active life; jury awarded $700,000, which included $535,000 in past and future pain and suffering; reduced by $150,000 on appeal).

North Dakota: Froemke v. Hauff (N.D., 1966) 147 N.W.2d 390 (malfunction of olfactory nerve one of several injuries growing out of auto accident and resulting in verdict of $28,810 in damages).

Strandness v. Montgomery Ward (N.D., 1972) 199 N.W.2d 690 ($5,000 awarded in slip-and-fall case to woman for four-inch cut on head which caused concussion, dizziness, headaches, nausea, and partial disability for sixteen months).

Nitschke v. Barnick (N.D., 1975) 226 N.W.2d 785 (child suffered slight concussion causing headaches and dizziness with nightmares and emotional problems; $500 award held proper).

Oregon: Newman v. Murphy Pac. Corp. (1975) 20 Or. App. 17, 530 P.2d 535 (iron worker who had suffered two head injuries claimed post-concussion headaches were aggravated by heat and noise encountered in his work).

Miller v. Coast Packing Co. (1987) 84 Or. App. 83, 733 P.2d 97 (insufficient evidence linking employee's paranoid psychosis to previous head injury; also testimony that employee had predisposition to mental condition prior to accident).

Pennsylvania: City of Philadelphia v. Shapiro (1965) 416 Pa. 308, 206 A.2d 308 (trauma to head resulting in histamine cephalalgia, evidenced by pain in face and head, flushing of face, and other discomforts).

Masters v. Alexander (1967) 424 Pa. 65, 225 A.2d 905 ($100,000 not excessive recovery for compound comminuted fractures of right frontal portion of skull; laceration of dura and arachnoid brain coverings, requiring removal of a portion of the brain itself; fracture of right orbital area and levator muscle controlling right eyelid; injury to optic nerve of right eye and multiple scarring of face and head, with deformity and depression of right frontal area; the totality of these injuries resulting in permanent memory defects, impairment of earning capacity, and educational disability in ten-year-old child).

DiChiacchio v. Rockcraft Stone Prods. Co. (1967) 424 Pa. 77, 225 A.2d 913 (blow on head from falling plank resulting in post-concussion syndrome consisting of dizziness, headaches, and personality changes; $25,000 awarded).

Commonwealth v. Stoltzfus (1975) 462 Pa. 43, 337 A.2d 873 (even though physician's testimony that victim "died as a result of a blow to the left side of head producing a depressed skull fracture" was not stated in terms of "beyond a reasonable doubt," testimony was sufficient to meet prosecution's burden of proof as to causal connection between death and criminal act).

Workmen's Comp. Appeal Bd. v. Adley Express Co. (1975) 20 Pa. Commw. 251, 340 A.2d 924 (pathologist's testimony that there were changes in brain of worker who fell from forklift truck compatible with "clinical trauma" to head, and that blow produced spasms of blood vessels which dislodged plaque from walls of vessels causing vessel blockage resulting in paralysis and death; conflicting testimony by autopsy pathologist).

Berman v. Radnor Rolls, Inc. (Pa. Super., 1988) 542 A.2d 525 (plaintiff, an adult male, struck head when he fell while roller skating on allegedly defectively designed skating rink; mild organic brain dysfunction, weakness in one side of body, memory loss, and difficulty in learning and retaining information; condition probably permanent; $463,000 award less 40% for plaintiff's negligence).

Haines v. Raven Arms (Pa., 1994) 640 A.2d 367 (handgun accidentally discharged, striking 14-year-old girl in head, causing permanent brain damage; plaintiff underwent seven operations over five-year period, also rehabilitation therapy and special schooling; medical expenses $125,000; at time of trial, she had weakness on right side of body, visual impairment on right side, and loss of cognitive skills; round-the-clock care will be required for life; jury awarded $11.3 million, which was reduced to $8.3 million on appeal).

DeVita v. Durst (Pa. Commw., 1994) 647 A.2d 636 (female plaintiff involved in automobile accident claimed closed head injury resulted in organic brain disorder, posttraumatic stress disorder, severe anxiety, and depression; defense challenged medical opinions and introduced evidence of preexisting emotional problems; $120,000 award affirmed).

South Carolina: Kennedy v. Williamsburg County (1963) 242 S.C. 477, 131 S.E. 2d 512 (assault and blows to head found to have precipitated paranoid schizophrenia).

Scott ex rel. McClure v. Fruehauf Corp. (S.C., 1990) 396 S.E.2d 354 (worker injured by wheel rim that came loose during tire inflation; most of frontal lobes of brain destroyed; plaintiff requires 24-hour care; $2.25 million award).

Tennessee: Ferrill v. Southern Ry. Co. (Tenn. App., 1972) 493 S.W.2d 90 (woman suffered deep laceration from center of nose to end of cheek which severed two facial nerves, one of which controlled facial movement; permanent numbness of lip and partial paralysis of face with twitch at corner of mouth; award of $91,250 reduced to $50,000).

Texas: Fort Worth & Denver Ry. Co. v. Coffman (Tex. Civ. App., 1965) 397 S.W.2d 544 (award of $160,000 to conductor who sustained brain concussion which resulted in headaches, loss of equilibrium, mental disturbances and other disabilities permanent in nature).

Gerland's Food Fair, Inc. v. Hare (Tex. Civ. App., 1980) 611 S.W.2d 113 (woman who suffered seizures and depression following head injuries entitled to recover $250,000).

Kennedy v. Missouri Pac. R. Co. (Tex. App., 1989) 778 S.W.2d 552 ($1,135,086 awarded to minor male for frontal lobe brain damage incurred in car-train collision; conflicting evidence on extent of brain damage and its manifestations).

Reagan v. Vaughn (Tex., 1990) 804 S.W.2d 463 (bar manager hit patron in head with baseball bat during altercation; severe brain injury; plaintiff functions on level of six- or seven-year-old; 40% comparative negligence; jury award of $2.4 million).

Enochs v. Brown (Tex. App., 1994) 872 S.W.2d 312 (child struck by automobile while riding bicycle; permanent brain damage; medical expenses $311,578; court-approved settlement for $2.3 million, which was total of policy limits).

St. Elizabeth Hosp. v. Graham (Tex. App., 1994) 883 S.W.2d 433 (36-year-old patient who was recuperating in hospital from craniotomy fell from recliner chair in which nurse has placed him without restraints; plaintiff received left-sided brain injury resulting in aphemia, aphasia, and right hemiplegia; will need lifetime care; $1.25 million jury award affirmed).

Vermont: Scrizzi v. Baraw (1968) 127 Vt. 315, 248 A.2d 725 (post-concussion syndrome with blackouts, dizzy spells, fits of depression and vision problems; $19,000 awarded to 56-year-old man).

Melford v. S. V. Rossi Constr. Co. (Vt., 1973) 303 A.2d 146 (studio musician entitled to damages for loss of sense of rhythm as result of head injury).

Washington: Harvey v. Wight (1966) 68 Wash. 2d 205, 412 P.2d 335 ($24,000 verdict for disability resulting from depressed skull fracture which required surgery and elevation; other injuries).

Pybus Steel Co. v. Department of Labor & Indus. (1975) 12 Wash. App. 436, 530 P.2d 350 (seemingly conflicting testimony by neurologist regarding permanent disability of worker who suffered brain concussion but whose headache would, "by its very nature," improve without medical treatment).

Wyoming: Coulthard v. Cossairt (Wyo., 1990) 803 P.2d 86 (adult male plaintiff suffered skull fracture in truck accident; part of brain removed; difficulty in speaking and forming sentences; placed in bottom percentile for language and mathematic skills; $1.7 million verdict held adequate).

(B) EPILEPSY

United States: United States v. Gilligan (C.A.-2 N.Y., 1966) 363 F.2d 961 (experts in disagreement as to whether thirteen-year-old charged with murder was experiencing psychomotor epileptic attack at time of homicide; question of sanity brought into issue).

King v. Gardner (C.A.-6 Tenn., 1967) 370 F.2d 652 (claimant subject to epileptic seizures every six to eight weeks not disabled).

Figueroa v. Secretary of Health, Educ. & Welfare (C.A.-1 P.R., 1978) 585 F.2d 551 (where evidence indicated that recurrence of social security disability claimant's epileptic seizures were in large part preventable through medication, and that his condition did not impair his functional residual capacities except for an inability to tolerate heights and moving machinery, it appeared that the claimant, an electrician, could perform a variety of other jobs and was not disabled).

Smith v. Kenosha Auto Transp. (D. Mont., 1964) 226 F. Supp. 771 ($180,000 award to truck driver disabled as result of petit mal seizures and psychological disorder resulting from trauma).

Bagwell v. Celebrezze (W.D. S.C., 1964) 232 F. Supp. 989 (epileptic seizures with increase in frequency rendered claimant disabled for Social Security purposes).

Wright v. Charles Pfizer & Co. (D. S.C., 1966) 253 F. Supp. 811 ($150,000 verdict in favor of 37-year-old male who sustained blow to head which resulted in traumatic epilepsy).

Duran v. City of Tampa (M.D. Fla., 1977) 430 F. Supp. 75 (according to medical experts, childhood epilepsy did not disqualify applicant for police force).

Arizona: H. P. Foley Elec. Co. v. Industrial Comm'n (1972) 18 Ariz. App. 332, 501 P.2d 960 (successful claim for traumatic epilepsy after head injury in fall on concrete).

Terrell v. Industrial Comm'n (1975) 24 Ariz. App. 389, 539 P.2d 193 (issue whether worker's seizures were due to earlier work injury or were result of toxic or metabolic disturbance).

Davis v. Mangelsdorf (Ariz., 1983) 673 P.2d 951 (in action against physician of driver who lost control of vehicle while suffering epileptic seizure, where accident occurred approximately seventeen years after physician advised driver to discontinue use of his anticonvulsive drug, accident was not foreseeable as matter of law and physician did not owe duty to protect plaintiff, nor was physician's advice substantial factor in causing plaintiff's injuries).

Thomas v. Arizona Dep't of Transp. (1985) 144 Ariz. 579, 698 P.2d 1298 (seizure disorder standard recommended by medical advisory board could not be applied to deny epileptic a driver's license when standard had not been officially promulgated as a department rule).

Arkansas: Eddington v. City Elec. Co. (1964) 237 Ark. 804, 376 S.W.2d 550 (convulsive seizures after blackout and fall due to heavy work in extreme temperature).

Jackson v. Southland Life Ins. Co. (1965) 239 Ark. 576, 393 S.W.2d 233 (death not accidental where insured fell into ditch and drowned during epileptic seizure).

Connecticut: Wood v. City of Bridgeport (Conn., 1990) 583 A.2d 124 (53-year-old male slipped and fell on icy sidewalk; skull fracture and epidural hematoma; memory loss and depression; 9% reduction in I.Q; medical expenses approximately $7,000; will require medication for epileptic seizures for life; award of $400,000 approved).

Illinois: Redmond v. Huppertz (1966) 71 Ill. App. 2d 254, 217 N.E.2d 85 (award of $90,000 to sixteen-year-old girl who sustained brain injury which resulted in degree of epileptic activity, loss of smell, and partial loss of taste and emotional control).

Morris v. Stewart (Ill. App., 1972) 280 N.E.2d 746 (issue as to whether epileptic seizures caused by head injury in automobile accident or fall at work; plaintiff's physician testified seizures began two months following accident but no mention was made in hospital report; $75,000 verdict for 25-year-old truck driver).

Louisiana: Bush v. Winn-Dixie, Inc. (La. App., 1990) 573 So. 2d 508 (two-year-old boy suffered head injuries when van rear-ended by truck; two episodes of seizures; conflicting medical evidence on alleged diminished intellectual capacity and hyperactivity; $75,000 award held adequate).

Rosell v. ESCO (La. App., 1990) 558 So. 2d 1360 (elevator door struck female plaintiff's face, causing her to fall and strike head; epileptic seizure disorder; 30% comparative negligence; award of $500,000 held adequate).

Esteve v. Iberia Parish Hosp. (La. App., 1989) 539 So. 2d 727 (survivors of epileptic patient claimed patient died because hospital staff did not suction fluid and vomit from her airway).

Maryland: Katz v. Holsinger (1972) 264 Md. 307, 286 A.2d 115 (child fell through second floor porch railing to concrete pavement, suffering fractured skull; convulsions began six months after injury and epilepsy discovered; $71,500 judgment against landlords).

Michigan: Hall v. Strom Constr. Co. (1962) 368 Mich. 253, 118 N.W.2d 281 (settlement for concussion from falling concrete block set aside when grand mal epilepsy later developed).

Minnesota: Lieberman v. Korsh (1962) 264 Minn. 234, 119 N.W.2d 180 (evidence tending to indicate that epileptic symptoms in fourteen-year-old girl were related to natural causes, including hormonal imbalance incident to puberty, rather than to head injury in automobile accident).

Missouri: Love v. Land (Mo. App., 1962) 356 S.W.2d 105 (grand mal epileptic seizure as possible cause of cardiac asystole causing death).

Wallace v. Bounds (Mo., 1963) 369 S.W.2d 138 (evidence did not require finding that accidental injuries aggravated preexisting epilepsy and caused suicide).

Hawkins v. Nixdorff-Krein Mfg. Co. (Mo., 1965) 395 S.W.2d 247 (petit mal epilepsy found causally related to carbon monoxide poisoning).

New Jersey: Lanier v. Kieckhefer-Eddy Div. of Weyerhaeuser Timber Co. (1964) 84 N.J. Super. 282, 201 A.2d 750 (employee suffering seizure resembling epileptic seizure fell while left unattended by first-aid attendant and sustained fatal head injuries).

Brennan v. Biber (1966) 93 N.J. Super. 351, 225 A.2d 742 (virus infection as possible cause of petit mal and grand mal seizures).

Oklahoma: Atchison, Topeka & Santa Fe Ry. Co. v. Coulson (1962) 371 P.2d 914 (epilepsy appearing eight years after head injury which caused twelve hours' unconsciousness and possible encephalitis).

Oregon: Pendergrass v. State (1985) 74 Or. App. 209, 702 P.2d 444 (government agencies liable for failure to suspend or prevent renewal of license of epileptic driver who suffered seizure and stuck bicyclist).

South Carolina: Gamble v. Travelers Ins. Co. (1968) 251 S.C. 98, 160 S.E.2d 523 (positive medical testimony that, absent a history of epilepsy, the only way to determine the presence of the disease is by an electroencephalogram).

(C) BRAIN TUMOR AND TRAUMA

United States: Minyen v. American Home Assur. Co. (C.A.-10 Okla., 1971) 443 F.2d 788 (preexisting brain tumor prevented recovery under accident policies for death after head injury).

Arizona: Reynolds Metals Co. v. Industrial Comm'n (1965) 98 Ariz. 97, 402 P.2d 414 (trauma to head aggravating preexisting tumor, resulting in death).

Louisiana: Phillips v. Liberty Mut. Ins. Co. (La. App., 1968) 209 So. 2d 795 (rear-end automobile collision not shown to have activated or accelerated development of preexisting brain tumor which first manifested symptoms approximately one month after accident).

Griffin v. Phoenix Ins. Co. (La. App., 1968) 213 So. 2d 73 (fall not shown to have aggravated preexisting unknown brain tumor).

Maryland: Subsequent Injury Fund v. Rinehart (1971) 12 Md. App. 649, 280 A.2d 298 (fatal astrocytoma, a malignant brain tumor, was aggravated by employee's fall).

New York: Speregon v. Downtown Delicatessen, Inc. (1965) 23 App. Div. 2d 901, 258 N.Y.S.2d 883 (conflicting evidence as to whether trauma to head aggravated and accelerated brain tumor, with finding in the affirmative).

Flanagan v. Stella D'Oro Biscuit Co. (1965) 23 App. Div. 2d 912, 258 N.Y.S. 2d 907 (meningeoma, a slow growing tumor, allegedly aggravated and accelerated by automobile accident; finding no causal connection).

Oklahoma: City of Duncan v. Sager (Okla., 1968) 446 P.2d 287 (action for compensation for death of workman struck on head; hospital doctors diagnosed cause of death as malignant brain tumor and medical witness, in response to hypothetical question, attributed death to cerebral hemorrhage).

Tennessee: Gipson v. Memphis Street Ry. Co. (1962) 51 Tenn. App. 31, 364 S.W.2d 110 (fatal glioblastoma multiform not aggravated nor death accelerated by electric shock).

Morristown Chest Co. v. Morgan (1963) 212 Tenn. 441, 370 S.W.2d 513 (moderate exertion as contributing cause of rupture of cerebral hemangioma and death ten days later).

Texas: Insurance Co. of N. Am. v. Myers (Civ. App. 1966) 399 S.W.2d 932 (severe head and neck injury with medical testimony that the injury aggravated a preexisting brain tumor which resulted in death).

(D) SPINAL INJURY

United States: Ammar v. American Export Lines, Inc. (C.A.-2 N.Y., 1964) 326 F.2d 955 (quadriplegia resulting from severed spinal cord).

Wright v. Standard Oil Co. (N.D. Miss., 1970) 319 F. Supp. 1364 (five-year-old child became "high-level paraplegic" as result of transected spinal cord).

Caporossi v. Atlantic City, New Jersey (D. N.J., 1963) 220 F. Supp. 508 (severe damage to spinal cord from striking submerged pipe while swimming, with quadriplegia alleviated only by limited shoulder and wrist motions; $600,000 verdict approved for 24-year-old teacher and bridegroom).

McLaughlin v. Eastern Eng'g Co. (E.D. Pa., 1963) 218 F. Supp. 380 (evidence that exertion in handling heavy oil drum caused vascular lesion and atrophy of cervical cord with paralysis and numbness of arms).

Alabama: Precise Eng'g, Inc. v. Lacombe (Ala., 1993) 624 So. 2d 1339 (construction worker suffered spinal injury in collapse of scaffold pole; despite numerous operations and medical procedures, plaintiff continues to suffer pain in back and legs; permanent loss of bladder and bowel control; medical expenses $41,375; loss of income $77,902 and future loss of income estimated at $478,406; award of $2.9 million plus settlements of $214,000 affirmed).

Arizona: Castillo v. Industrial Comm'n (1975) 24 Ariz. App. 315, 538 P.2d 402 (medical evidence of no permanent disability held sufficient in compensation case involving low back injury despite fact that physicians did not use electromyogram in their examination of claimant).

Arkansas: Lewis v. Crowe (1988) 269 Ark. 175, 752 S.W.2d 280 (male plaintiff injured in automobile accident suffered compression fracture of vertebra and nerve damage causing numbness of leg; 5% permanent impairment; medical expenses $12,000; lost wages $20,000; award of $269,799).

California: Mann v. Workmen's Comp. Appeals Bd. (1968) 265 Cal. App. 2d 333, 71 Cal. Rptr. 237 (award to claimant who sustained spinal and pelvic fractures with resultant lack of sensation in rectum and buttocks area was inadequate to extent that factors relating to bowel dysfunction were not included in request for rating of permanent disability).

Colorado: Miler v. Solaglas (Colo. App., 1993) 870 P.2d 559 (unbelted plaintiff rendered quadriplegic after being ejected through windshield that popped out when truck struck light pole; windshield replacers found liable and jury awarded $2.6 in economic damages, $2.5 for mental pain and suffering, and $1 in punitive damages; affirmed).

Florida: Jeep Corp. v. Walker (Fla. App., 1988) 528 So. 2d 1203 (29-year-old female plaintiff suffered spinal cord injury when Jeep overturned following collision; quadriplegia, complicated by diabetes; $9.5 million award).

Hawaii: Masaki v. General Motors Corp. (Haw., 1990) 780 P.2d 566 (28-year-old auto mechanic run over by van when it apparently "self-shifted" into reverse gear; spinal cord injury resulting in quadriplegia; $6.77 million award).

Illinois: Varilek v. Mitchell Eng'g Co. (Ill. App., 1990) 558 N.E.2d 365 (32-year-old ironworker rendered quadriplegic after falling off roof; $3.9 million jury verdict, but case remanded for new trial on damages because court limited testimony of plaintiff's economist on cost of future care and treatment).

Indiana: William H. Stern & Son, Inc. v. Rebeck (Ind. App., 1971) 277 N.E.2d 15 (award of $80,000 "liberal but not excessive" for nerve root injury to cervical spine, paralysis of arms, and loss of control of right leg).

Kansas: Hampton v. State Highway Comm'n (1972) 209 Kan. 565, 498 P.2d 236 (twenty-year-old man sustained complete paraplegia due to spinal cord severance; medical expenses $15,641.47; award of $450,000 not excessive).

Cooper v. Eberly (1973) 211 Kan. 657, 508 P.2d 943 (male with 51.9 years life expectancy suffered broken neck causing permanent loss of 20% of use of body and constant threat of quadriplegia and death; award of $54,797.85 affirmed).

Louisiana: Williams v. United States Cas. Co. (La. App., 1962) 145 So. 2d 592 (paralysis of lower part of body as result of severance of spinal cord by bullet).

Pacaccio v. Avondale Shipyards, Inc. (La. App., 1963) 158 So. 2d 841 (myelographic evidence of traumatic arachnoiditis of lumbar cord discounted because of faulty technique).

Falgoust v. Richardson Indus., Inc. (La. App., 1989) 552 So. 2d 1348 (male high school student injured in above-ground swimming pool diving accident; quadriplegia with sterility, impotency, and loss of bowel and bladder functions; limited dexterity and strength in arms and hands; sight, hearing and speech unaffected; $975,000 verdict held adequate).

McGowan v. Sewerage & Water Bd. (La. App., 1990) 555 So. 2d 472 (mildly retarded adult suffered compression injury to cervical spine, resulting in quadriparesis, when bicycle fell into uncovered catch basin at curb; plaintiff unable to walk without assistance; $2 million verdict affirmed).

Martino v. Sunrall (La. App., 1993) 619 So. 2d 87 (college student injured spinal cord when he dived into shallow creek at campground; requires 24-hour care; past medical expenses $318,733 and future medical expenses estimated at $3.9 million; total award of $7.1 million, which included $2.5 million for pain and suffering, affirmed on appeal).

Jenkins v. State, Dep't of Transp. & Dev. (La. App., 1993) 619 So. 2d 1188 (25-year-old waitress thrown from pickup truck when it failed to negotiate curve on elevated highway; cervical fracture at C5-C6, resulting in quadriplegia; plaintiff totally dependant on others for 24-hour care; trial court awarded $8.1 million, which included $5 million for future medical and life care, subject to statutory cap on general damages).

Mathieu v. Imperial Toy Corp. (La. App., 1994) 632 So. 2d 375 (38-year-old mental patient suffering from schizophrenia shot by police officers after he pointed toy gun at them; injury rendered him paraplegic; treatment complicated by preexisting mental condition, depression, and pressure sores and infections; medical expenses $203,600 and future medical expense and care estimated at $3.7 million; award of $5 million affirmed by appellate court).

Poche v. Louisiana Dep't of Transp. & Dev. (La. App., 1994) 633 So. 2d 913 (plaintiff injured in crash allegedly caused by poorly constructed shoulder of roadway, suffered crushed thoracic vertebra causing paralysis below rib cage; past medical expenses and attendant care totalled $296,161; future medical expenses and attendant care estimated at $3 million; trial court award of $3.4 million, which included only $500,000 in general damages, increased to $5.9 million by appellate court).

White v. Louisiana Dep't of Pub. Safety & Cors. (La. App., 1994) 644 So. 2d 648 (56-year-old female plaintiff who was married and led active life despite being confined to wheelchair since childhood was rendered quadriplegic in automobile accident; as result of injury, she was dependant upon tracheostomy, incontinent, totally unable to care for herself, and confined to residential treatment center; past medical expenses $58,399 and future medical expenses and care estimated at $3.9 million; award of $4.5 million affirmed by appellate court).

Pitre v. Louisiana Tech Univ. (La. App., 1995) 655 So. 2d 658 (20-year-old university student struck light post in campus parking lot while sliding down hill following ice/snow storm; fractures of cervical and thoracic spine; permanently paralyzed below midchest; despite injuries, plaintiff eventually graduated and enrolled in law school; past medical expenses $128,771; estimated present value of life care plan $1.16 million; award of $3.8 million affirmed).

Minnesota: Roman v. Minneapolis Street Ry. Co. (1964) 268 Minn. 367, 129 N.W.2d 550 (degenerative spinal cord changes traced to injury which had occurred twenty years previously).

Nierengarten v. State, Dep't of Highways (1969) 282 Minn. 231, 163 N.W. 2d 862 (arteriovenous malformation and burst blood vessels caused block in spinal cord).

Busch v. Busch Constr., Inc. (Minn., 1977) 262 N.W.2d 377 (woman with life expectancy of 29.4 years suffered quadriplegia following spinal injury; prolonged hospitalization; permanently confined to a wheelchair; annual medical expenses estimated at $36,000; $1,800,000 award following remittitur of $275,000).

Lind v. Slowinski (Minn. App., 1990) 450 N.W.2d 353 (female in her early thirties suffered severe cervical spine injury in automobile accident; 25% permanent partial disability; Brown-Sequard syndrome, manifested by muscular deficit on one side of body with corresponding loss of feeling on other side; $323,074 jury verdict reduced to $277,448 on appeal for insufficient evidence of future medical expenses).

Missouri: Coffman v. St. Louis-San Francisco Ry. Co. (Mo., 1964) 378 S.W.2d 583 (award of $220,000 to youth who sustained multiple injuries to spinal cord which resulted in complete paralysis of lower extremity and partial paralysis of upper extremity).

Dean v. Young (Mo., 1965) 396 S.W.2d 549 (compression fracture, dislocation of cervical vertebra and damage to spinal cord, resulting in partial paralysis; $390,000 verdict reduced on appeal to $250,000).

Nebraska: Smith v. Stevens (1962) 173 Neb. 723, 114 N.W.2d 724 (disability found by preponderance of evidence to have been caused by trauma to neck and spinal cord rather than by Guillain-Barre syndrome of nontraumatic origin).

New Jersey: Lombardo v. Hoag (N.J. Super., 1993) 634 A.2d 550 (college student injured in truck-automobile accident; fracture-subluxation of spine resulting in compression of cord; incomplete paraplegia at 6th cervical vertebra and loss of bladder and bowel control secondary to C4-C5 subluxation; spine realigned with tongs and patient had to wear halo device during five months of inpatient treatment; ten months of treatment as outpatient; left arm lacks normal range of motion; loss of sensation below waist; plaintiff returned to college but had to change major from law enforcement to accounting; jury award of $200,000 held adequate on appeal).

New York: Flanagan v. Stella D'Oro Biscuit Co. (1965) 23 App. Div. 2d 912, 258 N.Y.S.2d 907 (finding that meningeoma which was removed from dorsal spine, resulting in paraplegia, was aggravated and accelerated by the first of three automobile accidents).

Garcia v. Gallo Original Iron Works, Inc. (1970) 34 App. Div. 2d 1077, 312 N.Y.S.2d 467 (employee suffered strain in lifting sofa; eventually hospitalized with paralysis in both legs; diagnosis of schistosomiasis, a parasitic infection, of the spinal cord).

Bartlett v. State (1973) 40 App. Div. 2d 267, 340 N.Y.S.2d 63 (21-year-old man who was totally paralyzed in lower extremities and who suffered extensive paralysis of upper extremities with no feeling or mobility below shoulder blade was expected to be confined to bed or wheelchair for remainder of life; award of $666,444.06 upheld).

Zanotti v. New York Tel. Co. (1975) 48 App. Div. 2d 192, 368 N.Y.S.2d 880 (compensation claimant refused to submit to myelogram to evaluate back injury). (See § 32.95.)

Nowlin v. City of New York (App. Div., 1992) 582 N.Y.S.2d 669 (24-year-old law student suffered spinal injury in one-car accident due to faulty road sign; paraplegia; plaintiff finished law school and, at time of trial, was city attorney in Dallas, Texas; jury returned verdict of $7.75 million for past and future pain and suffering, $1.5 million for future equipment costs; $4.7 million for future health care assistance, and $225,000 for appropriate residence; appellate court reduced economic damages to $5 million for a total award of $7.5 million).

Pennsylvania: Smith v. Brooks (Pa. Super., 1990) 575 A.2d 926 (elderly male suffered crippling spinal compression in truck-automobile accident; also evidence of neurologic brain disorder; at time of trial, plaintiff still experienced crying spells, loss of memory, swelling of limbs, muscle twitches, gait disorder, and chronic pain; jury award of $1.25 million affirmed).

Smith v. Brooks (Pa. Super., 1990) 575 A.2d 926 (elderly male suffered crippling spinal compression in truck-automobile accident; also evidence of neurologic brain disorder; at time of trial, plaintiff still experienced crying spells, loss of memory, swelling of limbs, muscle twitches, gait disorder, and chronic pain; jury award of $1.25 million affirmed).

Rhode Island: Thibault v. Berkshire Hathaway, Inc. (R.I. 1973) 302 A.2d 755 (workman who suffers permanent loss of use of legs from spinal cord injury entitled to specific award under statute providing compensation for loss of use of bodily member even though no direct trauma to legs).

South Carolina: Mickle v. Blackmon (1969) 252 S.C. 202, 166 S.E.2d 173 (seventeen-year-old girl impaled on gear shift lever which penetrated upper thoracic spine, fracturing and pushing vertebra against spinal cord causing immediate and permanent paralysis of body below upper chest level; award of $780,000 approved).

Texas: Port Terminal R. Ass'n v. Inge (Civ. App., 1975) 524 S.W.2d 801 (43-year-old engineer suffered compression of nerve roots at fifth, sixth, and seventh cervical levels; unable to work at profession; $265,000 award under F.E.L.A. upheld).

National Cty. Mut. Fire Ins. Co. v. Howard (Tex. App., 1988) 749 S.W.2d 618 ($3.3 million verdict (less 10% for contributory negligence) for male plaintiff with 23.2 years' life expectancy who became quadriplegic following spinal cord injury in automobile accident).

Clayton W. Williams, Jr., Inc., v. Olivo (Tex. App., 1995) 912 S.W.2d 319 (action against representative of oil and gas lease operator by oil drilling company worker who suffered spinal injury in fall from pipe rack; plaintiff partially paralyzed and able to walk only with great difficulty; jury award of $2.02 million affirmed).

Miles v. Ford Motor Co. (Tex. App., 1996) 922 S.W..2d 572 (14-year-old boy suffered severe spinal injury in pickup truck accident in which "tension eliminator" prevented shoulder harness webbing from respooling after he leaned forward prior to collision; plaintiff, a quadriplegic, requires round-the-clock care and can breathe only with a ventilator; jury awarded $30 million compensatory damages and $10 million punitive damages against manufacturer; punitive award remanded for new trial on questions of gross negligence and malice).

Washington: Carabba v. Anacortes Sch. Dist. No. 103 (1967) 72 Wash. 2d 939, 435 P.2d 936 (high school wrestler suffered severance of spinal cord during match).

Curtiss v. Young Men's Christian Ass'n (1972) 7 Wash. App. 98, 498 P.2d 330 (seventeen-year-old girl received directed verdict against manufacturer of parallel bars and awarded $100,000, including $59,859.80 in general damages, for spinal injuries when bar came apart during gymnastic exercise; strict liability applied; case against Y.M.C.A. dismissed).

West Virginia: Johnson v. General Motors Corp. (W. Va., 1993) 438 S.E.2d 28 (passenger in rear seat in head-on collision suffered fractured spine resulting in paralysis; plaintiff has colostomy and is mostly confined to wheelchair; injuries, which included severed stomach muscles and lacerated intestines, were allegedly more severe because of lap-only seat belt; $223,227 incurred in medical expenses; $3.1 million jury verdict).

(E) PERIPHERAL NERVE INJURY

[see also (F) below.]

Alabama: Coca-Cola Bottling Co. v. Hammac (Ala., 1972) 261 So. 2d 893 (waitress awarded $8,000 for nerve injury in arm from exploding bottle; neurofibroma developed which caused sensation similar to electric shock whenever arm was touched, and which caused whatever plaintiff was holding in hand to be dropped).

Pacifico v. Jackson (Ala., 1990) 562 So. 2d 174 (patient suffered injury to median nerve during securing of monitoring device to his arm prior to heart bypass surgery; patient, who was surgeon himself, awarded $1.65 million for loss of future earnings).

Cates v. Colbert Cty. — N.W. Ala. Healthcare Auth. (Ala., 1994) 641 So. 2d 239 (where, following abdominal surgery during which straps were placed on patient's arms while she was sedated, it was discovered that she had suffered injury to interior interosseous nerve of her right arm, court held that "even a layman" could infer that something happened during the operation).

Georgia: Copeland v. Houston Cty. Hosp. Auth. (Ga. App., 1994) 450 S.E.2d 235 (evidence insufficient that nurse violated standard of care that requires that intramuscular injections in buttocks be administered in upper outer quadrants of buttock to avoid injuring sciatic nerve).

Iowa: Harrison v. Keller (1962) 254 Iowa 267, 117 N.W.2d 477 (amyotrophic lateral sclerosis progressive but not attributable to nerve injury sustained in fall).

Kentucky: McVey v. Berman (Ky. App., 1992) 836 S.W.2d 445 (spouse not entitled to loss of consortium in action by husband for nerve damage to leg during abdominal surgery).

Louisiana: Rodriguez v. Underwood Glass Co. (La. App., 1962) 140 So. 2d 176 (disability of nervous origin from blow on shoulder at base of neck).

Nixon v. Pittsburgh Plate Glass Co. (La. App., 1964) 161 So. 2d 361 (evidence that tetanus shot administered after minor injury was injected into or close to radial nerve, resulting in complications which led to amputation).

LeBlanc v. R. F. Ball Constr. Co. (La. App., 1964) 162 So. 2d 716 (injury to low back and groin, with dispute as to presence of meralgia paraesthetica, a form of nerve irritation).

Bailey v. Employers Liab. Assurance Corp. (La. 1971) 244 So. 2d 356 (plantar neuroma which developed between second and third toes attributed to earlier injury involving fracture of first metatarsal caused by piece of iron being dropped on foot).

Brown v. Manchester Ins. & Indem. Co. (La. App., 1975) 313 So. 2d 275 ($5,000 award upheld for Horner's syndrome [restriction of pupil of eye, drooping of eyelid, sinking of eyeball into socket, and dilation of ocular blood vessels] caused by paralysis of cervical sympathetic nerve).

Thompson v. Colony Ins. Co. (La. App., 1987) 520 So. 2d 1158 (male computer programmer and electronics technician involved in auto accident suffered contusion and nerve injury to upper left arm; plaintiff missed between two and three weeks' work; evidence at trial suggesting 10% to 15% permanent disability was thrown out by court of appeal as inconclusive; $51,468 jury verdict reduced to $31,468).

Goodwin v. Hartford Acc. & Indem. Co. (La. App., 1988) 530 So. 2d 1218 (35-year-old female manager of travel agency involved in rear-end auto accident suffered stretch injury of ulnar nerve in right arm; pain still present at time of trial, causing 1% to 5% impairment of plaintiff's work on computer terminal; plaintiff also suffered cervical sprain; medical expenses $261; jury awarded $9,011 which court of appeal increased to $12,261).

Foster v. Town of Manou (La. App., 1993) 616 So. 2d 837 (pedestrian walking in alley at night fell into unmarked ditch; nondisplaced cortical fracture of os calcis (heel bone) complicated by reflex sympathetic dystrophy; fracture healed in six weeks without surgery, but RSD required three spinal nerve blocks by time of trial and was expected to require two or three more; $150,000 trial court award held excessive and reduced to $53,000 on appeal).

Falkowski v. Maurus (La. App., 1993) 637 So. 2d 522 (claim that emergency medical technicians' negligence in establishing IV to treat nonresponsive diabetic patient caused damage to patient's ulnar nerve).

Robertson v. Hospital Corp. of Am. (La. App., 1995) 653 So. 2d 1265 (anesthesiologist, surgeon, and hospital all liable for ulnar nerve injury suffered by patient during abdominal surgery).

Massachusetts: Solimene v. B. Grauel & Co. (1987) 399 Mass. 790, 507 N.E.2d 662 (product liability action: female machine operator's hand caught in machine for 20-40 minutes, resulting in carpal tunnel syndrome followed by reflex sympathetic dystrophy; plaintiff off work nine months; $275,000 award less 5% for comparative fault).

Michigan: A'Eno v. Lowry (1962) 367 Mich. 657, 116 N.W.2d 730 (electromyography used to investigate cause of injury to seventh cervical nerve root or ulnar nerve).

Mississippi: Luther McGill, Inc. v. Clark (1962) 244 Miss. 707, 146 So. 2d 338 (fall causing unconsciousness, followed by pain in arms and back and urological complications).

Missouri: Davis v. Brezner (Mo. App., 1964) 380 S.W.2d 523 (trauma to shoulder with conflict of medical evidence as to whether injury to suprascapular nerve had caused limitation of shoulder motion).

New Mexico: Mireles v. Broderick (N.M. App., 1992) 827 P.2d 847 (in res ipsa loquitur case, although patient who suffered ulnar nerve injury during bilateral mastectomy was under care of more than one physician during surgery, expert testimony as to anesthesiologist's ultimate responsibility for positioning patient's arms was sufficient to create jury question on exclusive control issue).

New York: Burns v. Gooshaw (App. Div., 1996) 639 N.Y.S.2d 528 (plaintiff suffered permanent injury to sciatic nerve in fall on steps; medical expenses $19,362 and lost earnings $26,361; jury verdict for $69,362 held inadequate, and new trial granted).

South Carolina: Wilkes v. Moses (S.C. App., 1987) 354 S.E.2d 403 (male plaintiff injured in assault; ulnar nerve damage resulted in permanent impairment to arm and hand; two fingers numb; small muscles in hand will eventually atrophy; $2,478 compensatory damages and $45,000 punitive).

Texas: Twin City Fire Ins. Co. v. Grimes (Tex. App., 1987) 724 S.W.2d 956 (worker exposed to lead fumes developed peripheral neuropathy which left him unable to perform any manual labor).

Washington: Horner v. Northern Pac. Beneficial Ass'n Hosps., Inc. (1963) 62 Wash. 2d 351, 382 P.2d 518 (brachial plexus injury while under general anesthesia resulting in paralysis of arm which gradually diminished over four-year period).

Benedict v. Department of Labor & Indus. (1963) 63 Wash. 2d 12, 385 P.2d 380 (conflicting evidence supported finding that decedent was disabled by occupational vibration disease rather than by Addison's disease).

Wisconsin: Erickson v. Department of Indus., Labor & Hum. Relations (1970) 40 Wis. 2d 114, 181 N.W.2d 495 (compensation claimant stated that while carrying large timbers he stepped in a hole, felt something snap in his back and felt a "pain running down the side of his leg"; condition diagnosed as herniated nucleus pulposus causing sciatica; laminectomy necessary; history of prior episodes of sciatic pain).

(F) ALLEGED MALPRACTICE OR INJURY WHILE UNDER MEDICAL SUPERVISION

United States: Evans v. United States (C.A.-1 Mass., 1963) 319 F.2d 751, aff'g 212 F. Supp. 648 (evidence supported finding that paralysis in year-old child was not caused by scarring of sciatic nerve from intragluteal injection of penicillin in Army hospital).

Christopher v. United States (E.D. Pa., 1965) 237 F. Supp. 787 (spinal cord contused by gauze during surgery, resulting in paraplegia).

Corson v. United States (E.D. Pa., 1969) 304 F. Supp. 155 (catheter broke in patient's arm who was under light anesthesia in preparation for surgery; damage to median nerve).

Frost v. Mayo Clinic (D. Minn., 1969) 304 F. Supp. 285 (surgery patient suffered permanent partial paralysis following disc operation; $50,000 awarded).

Toal v. United States (D. Conn., 1969) 306 F. Supp. 1063 (negligence to leave pantopaque dye in patient's spinal cord after myelogram).

Downs v. American Employers Ins. Co. (C.A.-5 La., 1970) 423 F.2d 1160 (patient alleged needle struck nerve during penicillin injection and caused atrophy of arm).

Luna v. Nering (C.A.-5 Tex., 1970) 426 F.2d 95 (question of whether lateral cord of median nerve severed by injury or during operation).

Tyminski v. United States (C.A.-3 N.J., 1973) 481 F.2d 257 (FTCA case against VA physicians for failing to diagnose and remove an epidural hematoma which formed in operative site and which put pressure on the patient's spinal cord and resulted in paraplegia; complication arose out of operation for lesion of thoracic area of spine; patient lived twelve years after the initial operation during which time he was operated upon nineteen times in attempts to remedy his paralysis; $175,000 awarded).

Robertson v. Emory Univ. Hosp. (C.A.-5 Ga., 1980) 611 F.2d 604 (examining neurosurgeon overlooked fact that head injury patient was experiencing weakness of right side, and neurosurgical resident who did notice weakness failed to report fact to superiors).

Baber v. Hospital Corp. of Am. (C.A.-4, W. Va., 1992) 977 F.2d 872 (hospital emergency personnel did not violate Emergency Medical Treatment and Active Labor Act in performing medical screening of patient who died from head injury).

Porter v. Lima Mem. Hosp. (C.A.-6 Ohio, 1993) 995 F.2d 629 (unsuccessful action against hospital for nurses' negligence in failing to properly monitor vital signs of infant who became paralyzed following automobile accident).

McGeshick v. Choucair (C.A.-7 Wis., 1993) 9 F.3d 1229 (question whether clinic's failure to perform second MRI in timely fashion caused patient to become paralyzed from progressive spinal cord disease).

Lareau v. Page (D. Mass., 1993) 840 F. Supp. 920 (where radioactive contrast dye Thorotrast had been used to facilitate postoperative observation of abscess cavity in patient's brain, advice from neurosurgeon, 14 years later, that it was theoretically possible that dye could have induced tumor "activated a duty to investigate" on the part of the patient, and her reluctance to do so did not toll statute of limitations, even if she was "incompetently advised" or even if medical community was divided on the issue).

Simmons v. United States (E.D. La., 1993) 841 F. Supp. 748 (action for negligence of Veterans' Administration hospital personnel in permitting infection to develop in patient's left hand at site of intravenous injection that allegedly resulted in deterioration of motor skills and weakness and numbness of entire left side of body).

Marchand v. Mercy Med. Center (C.A.-9 Idaho, 1994) 22 F.3d 933 (attorney fees and costs of malpractice action were properly assessed against defendant physician where there was no reasonable basis for him to refuse to submit to patient's request for admission that patient's paralysis had been caused by movement of his spine that could have been avoided had spine been properly immobilized).

Rios v. Bigler (D. Kan., 1994) 847 F. Supp. 1538 (action against physician for failing to refer patient suffering from reflex sympathetic dystrophy (RSD) to appropriate specialist).

Alabama: Peden v. Ashmore (Ala., 1989) 554 So. 2d 1010 (family physician mistook patient's intracranial bleeding for migraine headache, but plaintiff failed to prove that if patient's true condition was diagnosed sooner, outcome would have been any different).

University of Alabama Health Servs. Found. v. Bush (Ala., 1994) 638 So. 2d 794 (claim that either neurosurgeon or neurological resident had been negligent in diagnosing and treating infant's meningitis).

Cates v. Colbert Cty. — N.W. Ala. Healthcare Auth. (Ala., 1994) 641 So. 2d 239 (where, following abdominal surgery during which straps were placed on patient's arms while she was sedated, it was discovered that she had suffered injury to interior interosseous nerve of her right arm, court held that "even a layman" could infer that something happened during the operation).

Williams v. Spring Hill Mem. Hosp. (Ala., 1994) 646 So. 2d 1373 (insufficient evidence that earlier steroid intervention would have arrested or improved patient's paraplegia).

Arizona: Gaston v. Hunter (1978) 121 Ariz. 33, 588 P.2d 326 (question of informed consent to use of experimental procedure chemonucleolysis as treatment for disc disorder).

Borja v. Phoenix Gen. Hosp. (Ariz. App., 1986) 727 P.2d 355 (emergency room physicians allegedly failed to make timely diagnosis of injured plaintiff's subdural hematoma).

California: LeMere v. Goren (1965) 233 Cal. App. 2d 799, 43 Cal. Rptr. 898 (injection of novocaine at base of neck allegedly causing nerve injury and permanent disability to hand and arm).

Solorio v. Lampros (1969) 2 Cal. App. 3d 522, 82 Cal. Rptr. 753 (although neurosurgeon admitted he missed seeing head injury patient's subdural hematoma when he inspected skull through burr holes, and both he and neurologist admitted that they probably would have discovered it if they had ordered an arteriogram, there was insufficient evidence that defendants were guilty of below-standard practice).

Schnear v. Boldrey (1971) 22 Cal. App. 3d 478, 99 Cal. Rptr. 404 (patient lost sight in one eye after exploratory operation on spine for suspected syringomyelia; judgment for defendant neurologist).

Connecticut: Camp v. Booth (1970) 160 Conn. 10, 273 A.2d 714 (where one-year-old child fell from crib in hospital, suffered fractured skull, and as a result, became irritable and for three months refused to be lifted by anyone except his mother, and even then exhibited fear at being picked up, $5,000 award was not held excessive).

Kiniry v. Danbury Hosp. (1981) 183 Conn. 448, 439 A.2d 408 (skull fracture patient's death attributed to failure to obtain prompt consultation by neurosurgeon).

Sheinitz v. Greenberg (Conn., 1986) 509 A.2d 1023 (woman complained that she had suffered chronic headache for over eight years because neurosurgeon had permitted her to ambulate only ten minutes after undergoing myelogram).

Mather v. Griffin (1988) 207 Conn. 125, 540 A.2d 666 (negligent treatment of infant during delivery and post-delivery period; brain damage and cerebral palsy secondary to neonatal asphyxia; $9,000,000 award).

Florida: Reeves v. North Broward Hosp. Dist. (Fla. App., 1966) 191 So. 2d 307 (evidence of symptoms of subdural hematoma sufficient to present jury question as to negligence of hospital in failing to render proper treatment).

North Broward Hosp. Dist. v. Johnson (Fla. App., 1988) 538 So. 2d 871 (negligence resulted in newborn infant suffering permanent brain damage; borderline or mild retardation will require special education and rehabilitation for several years; $750,000 award).

Myron v. South Broward Hosp. Dist. (Fla. App., 1997) 703 So. 2d 527 (pediatrician was qualified to offer an opinion as to a neurosurgeon's negligence in failing to perform a spinal tap, and the witness' unchallenged testimony that the defendant deviated from the acceptable standard of care caused or substantially contributed to the patient's further brain damage provided the necessary elements of malpractice).

Georgia: Richmond County Hosp. Auth. v. Haynes (1970) 121 Ga. App. 537, 174 S.E.2d 364 (diabetic hospital patient recovered for injuries to wrists and hands, including median nerve damage, as a result of being restrained with leather wrist straps on admission for diabetic coma).

Parrott v. Chatham County Hosp. Auth. (1978) 145 Ga. App. 113, 243 S.E.2d 269 (in suit against hospital and several physicians by emergency room patient who claimed he was released despite fact he had suffered skull fracture which was not diagnosed until five days later when attending physician received X-rays, directed verdict for defendants was upheld because plaintiff failed to produce medical evidence showing that he would have had less pain or discomfort if he had been correctly diagnosed and treated earlier).

Hewett v. Kalish (Ga. App., 1993) 436 S.E.2d 710 (in action against podiatrist for negligence in performing posterior tibial nerve resection and epineuroplasty, board-certified orthopedic surgeon was held not to be competent to provide affidavit supporting plaintiff's claim, where he failed to show that he had performed procedures similar to those employed in podiatry).

Copeland v. Houston County Hosp. Auth. (Ga. App., 1994) 450 S.E.2d 235 (evidence insufficient that nurse violated standard of care that requires that intramuscular injections in buttocks be administered in upper outer quadrants of buttock to avoid injuring sciatic nerve).

Idaho: Hale v. Heninger (1964) 87 Idaho 414, 393 P. 2d 718 (transverse myelitis following myelogram and laminectomy was not result of negligence on part of physicians and hospital).

Smallwood v. Dick (1988) 114 Idaho 860, 761 P.2d 1212 (failure to diagnose compression fracture resulted in severance of patient's spinal cord; $775,500 in special damages; $356,714 verdict increased to $1,033,530 on appeal; also separate settlement for $375,000).

Illinois: Estell v. Barringer (Ill. App., 1972) 278 N.E.2d 424 (where "posterior fossa" method used in performing operation to sever trigeminal nerve for purpose of reducing pain was one of the most common methods of treatment of this condition, surgeon was not liable for patient's resulting paralysis of face, loss of eyelid control, loss of hearing in left ear, and some loss of sense of balance, where medical experts could not explain cause of these injuries).

Richter v. Northwestern Mem. Hosp. (1988) 177 Ill. App. 3d 247, 126 Ill. Dec. 584, 532 N.E.2d 269 (physician treated 35-year-old attorney for headache for six years without diagnosing acoustic neuroma; then hospital staff negligent in postoperative treatment; severe brain damage, paralysis and loss of sight and hearing; $15,787,555 award).

Fisher v. Slager (Ill. App., 1990) 559 N.E.2d 118 (patient who sued neurosurgeon for negligence in treating him for massive brain hemorrhage and abscess ignored advice to undergo inpatient therapy and instead followed only outpatient home therapy plan).

Kemnitz v. Semrad (Ill. App., 1990) 565 N.E.2d 1 (discussion of standard of care in retracting and avoiding injury to radial nerve during surgery to repair fractured humerus).

Bombagetti v. Amine (Ill. App., 1993) 627 N.E.2d 230 (trial court's determination that spinal surgery patient's pain and suffering was caused by surgeon's negligence in performing laminectomy was supported by evidence, which included testimony that patient experienced "snapping" in his back following surgery).

Rockwood v. Singh (Ill. App., 1994) 630 N.E.2d 873 (question whether trial court erred in barring medical malpractice plaintiff from making any references to defendant neurosurgeon's failure to become board-certified).

Indiana: Yaney v. McCray Mem. Hosp. (Ind. App., 1986) 496 N.E.2d 135 (failure of hospital emergency room nurse to take child's vital signs not proximate cause of child's ultimate injury resulting from subdural hematoma where child had been under direct care of duly licensed physician who did not request such information during his examination and treatment).

Vogler v. Dominguez (Ind. App., 1993) 624 N.E.2d 56 (in action against neurosurgeon by patient who developed nerve palsy following right frontal craniotomy, defendant was not entitled to summary judgment in view of expert testimony by orthopedic surgeon that nerve palsy was not an accepted risk of the procedure and that it might have been prevented with reasonable prudence).

Kansas: Funke v. Fieldman (1973) 212 Kan. 524, 512 P.2d 539 (res ipsa loquitur not applicable against anesthesiologist for nerve damage allegedly the result of negligence in administering spinal anesthetic; issues included charge of lack of informed consent).

Kentucky: McVey v. Berman (Ky. App., 1992) 836 S.W.2d 445 (spouse not entitled to loss of consortium in action by husband for nerve damage to leg during abdominal surgery).

Louisiana: Herbert v. Travelers Indem. Co. (La. App., 1970) 239 So. 2d 367 ($50,000 awarded 34-year-old self-employed businessman who sustained injury to nerve roots during administration of spinal anesthetic).

Isom v. Page (La. App., 1972) 257 So. 2d 720 (unsuccessful suit by patient who underwent rhizotomy [severing of nerve root] based mainly on allegations that surgeon became confused during eight-hour operation and spent needless time tracing "recognizable bones" in attempt to find nerve root; defendant blamed delay on grossly abnormal spinal bone structure).

Thomas v. West Calcasieu-Cameron Hosp. (La. App., 1986) 497 So. 2d 375 (award upheld in action against hospital by plaintiff who suffered injury to median or ulnar nerve because of medical technician's negligence in attempting to draw blood).

Esteve v. Iberia Parish Hosp. (La. App., 1989) 539 So. 2d 727 (survivors of epileptic patient claimed patient died because hospital staff did not suction fluid and vomit from her airway).

Norfleet v. Southern Baptist Hosp. (La. App., 1993) 623 So. 2d 891 (obstetrical patient suffered sciatic nerve injury and "foot-drop" as result of intramuscular injection negligently administered by hospital employee).

McGraw v. Louisiana State Univ. Med. Ctr. (La. App., 1993) 627 So. 2d 767 (question whether failure to surgically implant shunt to relieve intracranial pressure in infant suffering from meningitis was cause of neurological impairment).

Falkowski v. Maurus (La. App., 1993) 637 So. 2d 522 (claim that emergency medical technicians' negligence in establishing IV to treat nonresponsive diabetic patient caused damage to patient's ulnar nerve).

Pfiffner v. Correa (La. App., 1994) 640 So. 2d 281 (even though plaintiff failed to present expert testimony as to applicable standard of care, directed verdicts for defense were properly denied in action against general practitioner and neurosurgeon for negligent treatment of patient who suffered seizure, lost consciousness, and never awoke after treatment for head injury, since standard of care was established on plaintiff's cross-examination of physicians).

Melancon v. LaRocca (La. App., 1995) 650 So. 2d 371 (doctrine of res ipsa loquitur was not applicable in action against surgeon by patient who suffered injury to right recurrent laryngeal nerve and resulting paralysis of vocal cord following anterior cervical spinal fusion, where expert testimony established that such injury could occur in absence of negligence).

Robertson v. Hospital Corp. of Am. (La. App., 1995) 653 So. 2d 1265 (anesthesiologist, surgeon, and hospital all liable for ulnar nerve injury suffered by patient during abdominal surgery).

Massachusetts: Lynch v. Egbert (Mass., 1971) 271 N.E.2d 640 (verdict for defendant where plaintiff alleged injury to median nerve from intravenous injection of anesthetic Brevitol; medical testimony that nerve could have been irritated by other means and that plaintiff was alcoholic significant).

Harlow v. Chin (1989) 405 Mass. 697, 545 N.E.2d 602 (emergency department physician failed to order neurological examination of patient who had fallen and struck head and neck, which would have revealed herniated disc at C-4, C-5 level; defendant spent no more than five minutes with plaintiff, during which time he only "felt the back of the plaintiff's neck and tapped his elbows and kneecaps"; plaintiff is now quadriplegic).

Michigan: Podvin v. Eickhorst (1964) 373 Mich. 175, 128 N.W.2d 523 (progressive paralysis allegedly resulting from failure of physicians properly to examine and diagnose extent of spinal injuries).

Rostron v. Klein (1970) 23 Mich. App. 283, 178 N.W.2d 675 (summary judgment for physician reversed in suit against him and hospital for death of patient from epidural hematoma; physician testified that when he saw patient in hospital emergency room he thought that he had only suffered seizure as he had on previous occasion and that patient did not tell him nor did he ask patient if he had suffered a head injury).

Minnesota: Schneider v. Buckman (Minn., 1988) 433 N.W.2d 98 (patient claimed spinal injury aggravated while being transferred from hospital bed to ambulance cart; plaintiff felt "snapping" in back, followed by paralysis below knees and painful burning sensation; able to walk after surgery, but pain in ankle, diminished stamina, and bowel and bladder problems still present at time of trial; $125,000 award).

Schendel v. Hennepin Cty. Med. Center (Minn. App., 1992) 484 N.W.2d 803 (physicians accused of failing to diagnose patient's cervical spinal fracture and immobilize neck, and later initiating rehabilitation therapy too soon after spinal fusion; plaintiff suffered decreased ability to use hands and arms, severe neck pain, and permanent causalgia from nerve root damage).

Mississippi: Ross v. Hodges (Miss., 1970) 234 So. 2d 905 (physician gave sufficient information to woman patient for her informed consent when he told her that her surgery would involve the shaving of her head, the sawing of a hole in her skull to remove a bony lesion, and that there was a remote possibility of damage to dura and paralysis).

Turner v. Temple (Miss., 1992) 602 So. 2d 817 (fact that orthopedic surgeon and neurosurgeon, in performing spinal fusion, had acted in dual role and performed to some extent in each other's specialty did not imply negligence, where expert witnesses testified that much of the work of two specialties overlapped and they would have done nothing different than what defendants had done).

Missouri: Burns v. Owens (Mo., 1970) 459 S.W.2d 303 (nerve injury due to nurse's injection of Demerol into lower third of upper arm; admitting physician and physician who prescribed injection not vicariously liable).

Nebraska: Swierczek v. Lynch (Neb., 1991) 466 N.W.2d 512 (doctrine of res ipsa loquitur applicable in action by patient who entered hospital for extraction of teeth and left with injuries to nerves in arms and hand).

New Jersey: Gould v. Winokur (1969) 104 N.J. Super. 329, 250 A.2d 38 (no causal connection shown in malpractice suit between surgeon's activity and any involvement of seventh and eighth cranial nerves).

Adamski v. Moss (N.J. App., 1994) 638 A.2d 1360 (under learned treatise rule, plaintiff could not introduce medical-legal treatises as proof concerning standard of care in negligence action against surgeon by patient who claimed defendant injured nerve in her arm during removal of nonmalignant lump in her neck; treatises must be established as authority either by judicial notice or by testimony of qualified expert witness).

New Mexico: Mireles v. Broderick (N.M. App., 1992) 827 P.2d 847 (negligence action against anesthesiologist by patient who claimed she developed ulnar neuropathy from being improperly positioned during surgery).

New York: Zeleznik v. Jewish Chronic Disease Hosp. (1975) 47 App. Div. 2d 199, 366 N.Y.S.2d 163 (occlusion of brachial artery during angiogram).

Taype v. City of New York (1981) 82 App. Div. 2d 648, 442 N.Y.S.2d 799 (jury found cesarean section patient's paraplegia caused by physicians' compression of artery to stop hemorrhaging, resulting in stoppage of flow of blood to spinal cord).

Hunter v. Szabo (App. Div., 1986) 499 N.Y.S.2d 426 (insufficient evidence that patient suffered nerve root injuries as a result of a fluoroscopic machine striking plaintiff's lower back during performance of a myelogram; machine allegedly struck a needle which had been inserted in his spine for the injection of contrast material).

Olivieri v. Schwartz (App. Div., 1986) 502 N.Y.S.2d 252 (unsuccessful action by patient who claimed he received negligent care by hospital personnel following performance of myelogram).

Trocchia v. Long Island College Hosp. (App. Div., 1986) 503 N.Y.S.2d 651 ($400,000 award adequate for 78-year-old patient who developed quadriparesis after undergoing laminectomy in view of evidence that patient suffered from preexisting neurological disease which could have contributed to quadriparesis).

Tarantola v. Bennett (1988) 141 App. Div. 2d 716, 529 N.Y.S.2d 827 (hypertensive patient who had temporarily lost consciousness after striking head was released from emergency department after negative neurological exam; several hours later she suffered stroke, leaving her partially paralyzed; $800,000 jury verdict).

Marmo v. Southside Hosp. (1988) 143 App. Div. 2d 891, 533 N.Y.S.2d 402 (patient's "excruciatingly painful headache," vomiting, and fainting spells diagnosed as intestinal virus, and no neurological examination was performed; patient had aneurysm and week later suffered subarachnoid hemorrhage, resulting in severe brain damage; jury awarded $1.28 million).

North Carolina: Lentz v. Thompson (1967) 269 N.C. 188, 152 S.E.2d 107 (severance of spinal accessory nerve held to be inherent risk in operation to remove malignant lymph glands from posterior cervical triangle and, where removal was accomplished according to accepted medical standards, severance did not constitute malpractice on part of surgeon).

Hussey v. Montgomery Mem. Hosp. (N.C. App., 1994) 441 S.E.2d 577 (where patient suffered head injury in fall from hospital gurney, medical evidence supported defendant's claim that cause of action accrued at time of fall, notwithstanding plaintiffs' allegations that patient's injury was not readily apparent at such time and that plaintiffs had no knowledge of specific nature of injury until more than two years later).

Ohio: Cooper v. Sisters of Charity of Cincinnati, Inc. (1971) 27 Ohio St. 2d 242, 272 N.E.2d 97 (unsuccessful suit against physician who failed to diagnose fatal basal skull fracture in sixteen-year-old patient examined at hospital emergency room).

Oregon: Mayor v. Dowsett (1965) 240 Or. 196, 400 P.2d 234 (paralysis following injection of anesthetic into spine prior to delivery of child).

Brannon v. Wood (1968) 251 Or. 349, 444 P.2d 558 (res ipsa loquitur doctrine inapplicable in suit against thoracic surgeon by patient whose lower body was paralyzed following use of cellulose substance to stop hemorrhaging after operation for removal of posterior mediastinal tumor).

Simpson v. Sisters of Charity of Providence (1978) 284 Or. 547, 588 P.2d 4 (hospital X-ray technicians negligent in failing to obtain a clear film showing patient's cervicothoracic junction as ordered by physicians; patient paralyzed when fracture compressed during ambulation).

Pennsylvania: Hurchick v. Falls Township Bd. of Supervisors (1964) 203 Pa. Super. 1, 198 A.2d 356 (myelogram performed after back injury; dye material entered preexisting meningocele, irritating cyst and causing disability).

Tobash v. Jones (1965) 419 Pa. 205, 213 A.2d 588 (spinal cord excision for biopsy purposes, resulting in cord damage and permanent disability).

Mitzelfelt v. Kanrin (Pa., 1990) 584 A.2d 888 (in negligence action against neurosurgeon, evidence established that patient's stystolic blood pressure was allowed to drop 30 points during operation which, according to expert, could have compromised blood flow to spinal cord, causing paralysis).

Texas: Chasco v. Providence Mem. Hosp. (Tex. Civ. App., 1972) 476 S.W.2d 385 (unsuccessful action against physician and hospital for diagnosing as alcoholic a patient who was suffering from subdural hematoma).

Miller v. Hardy (Tex. Civ. App., 1978) 564 S.W.2d 102 (where patient allegedly suffered spinal cord injury when rolled from stretcher to operating table, doctrine of res ipsa loquitur was not applicable against surgeons since they were in control only of actual operation itself).

Duff v. Yelin (App., 1986) 721 S.W.2d 365 (unsuccessful malpractice action against neurosurgeon for improper positioning of patient during neck surgery which resulted in injury to right ulnar nerve).

Tilotta v. Goodall (Tex. App., 1988) 762 S.W.2d 160 (claim against neurosurgeon for damage to thyroid gland during frontal cervical spinal surgery dismissed on evidence that patient's symptoms probably were caused by immunological disorder).

Brown v. Bettinger (Tex. App., 1994) 882 S.W.2d 953 (family practitioner, although not trained in neurology, was qualified to testify as to standard of care required in administering spinal taps and that plaintiff, as result of having to undergo "traumatic" series of three taps in attempt to determine cause of severe headaches and double vision, sustained herniated disk).

Crawford v. Hope (Tex. App., 1995) 898 S.W.2d 937 (unsuccessful action against a physician who took a patient off barbiturates that she had been taking for seizures for years and put her on the anticonvulsant Zarontin (ethosuximide), which she claimed caused her to have a seizure that resulted in her falling and suffering a head injury).

Virginia: Lawhorne v. Harlan (1973) 214 Va. 405, 200 S.E.2d 569 (intern working in University of Virginia Hospital emergency room failed to diagnose skull fracture, but together with other hospital employees was found free of liability under Virginia's sovereign immunity rule which protects state employees who are guilty of simple negligence in performing duties involving judgment or discretion).

Washington: ZeBarth v. Swedish Hosp. Med. Ctr. (1972) 81 Wash. 2d 12, 499 P.2d 1 (hospital liable for paralysis due to spinal cord injury allegedly resulting from negligent application of radiation therapy during treatment for Hodgkin's disease; res ipsa loquitur held applicable; informed consent an issue).

Younger v. Webster (1973) 9 Wash. App. 87, 510 P.2d 1182 (doctrine of res ipsa loquitur applicable in malpractice action in which patient lost sensory perception in lower half of body after administration of spinal anesthetic).

Wisconsin: Black v. Gundersen Clinic, Ltd. (1989) 152 Wis. 2d 247, 448 N.W.2d 247 (no liability on part of neurosurgeon even though he misrepresented to patient risk of developing personality or intellectual deficiencies from brain surgery; chances of such impairment were so remote that misrepresentation did not subject patient to "unreasonable risk of harm").

CHAPTER 32A

AUTOPSIES*

I. THE MEDICOLEGAL AUTOPSY (CORONER OR MEDICAL EXAMINER)

II. THE HOSPITAL AUTOPSY

III. AUTOPSY PROCEDURE — THE INTERNAL EXAMINATION

---

*Revised by John C. Hunsaker III, M.D., J.D. Additional contributors to the current and earlier editions of this chapter include Diane M. Hunsaker, M.D., Gregory J. Davis, M.D., Cyril H. Wecht, M.D., J.D., Geoffry Mann, M.D., and Richard M. Patterson, J.D.

I. THE MEDICOLEGAL AUTOPSY (CORONER OR MEDICAL EXAMINER)

§ 32A.1. Introduction.

The medicolegal autopsy is a specialized type of autopsy performed in the public interest, ideally by board-certified forensic pathologists. The forensic pathologist is a licensed physician who, following an internship and standard training in anatomic pathology, including the postmortem examination of individuals who have died in hospitals following medical therapy, spends further time training in one of several accredited medicolegal investigative offices (coroner or medical examiner) to learn the skills required in the investigation of persons dying without medical attendance or under violent, unusual, or suspicious circumstances. A successful completion of an examination by the American Board of Pathology confers board certification.

The number of medicolegal autopsies performed each year in the United States varies considerably from jurisdiction to jurisdiction, which may be an entire state, a county, or a city. Many factors, including the population of the jurisdiction, the formulation of the enabling law, the breath and structure of the investigative office, and the funding agency's commitment to financial support, substantially affect the quality of official investigations; however, improvement has been steadily evident following the establishment of recommended guidelines and credentialing mechanisms by the National Association of Medical Examiners (NAME), the opportunity for board certification in forensic pathology by the American Board of Pathology, and the development of practice guidelines for forensic pathology by the College of American Pathologists.[1]

§ 32A.2. Purpose and objectives.

Medicolegal autopsies are performed for three reasons: First, to aid in the discovery and prosecution of (or to rule out the commission of) a crime; second, to disclose hazards to public health, such as dangerous drugs or chemicals, communicable, contagious or infectious diseases such as AIDS or Hanta virus pulmonary syndrome, or occupational diseases such as "black lung"; and third, in the administration of civil justice, such as in disputed life or health and accident insurance claims, workers' compensation cases, or similar problems involving questions of civil liability.

The medicolegal autopsy seeks to discover, in the context of a comprehensive death investigation: the identification of the decedent; the time (as nearly as possible) and place of death; the exact cause of death, and in cases of violent death, the circumstances and manner in which the fatal injuries were sustained. Naturally, the evidence uncovered in these au-

---

[1] Randall, B. B., et al., *Practice Guidelines for Forensic Pathology*, 122 Arch. Path. Lab. Med. 1056 (Dec.), 1998.

topsies is also frequently involved in identifying the person and instrument responsible for the death.

Medicolegal autopsy is not an automatic procedure. On the contrary, it should be painstakingly thorough and systematic, the yield of which often directly relates to the skill and training of the pathologist. Not all medicolegal autopsies are conducted in the same way, each having to be directly related to the circumstances of the death so far as they are known at the time of the examination.

Ideally, all medicolegal autopsies should be performed by board-certified forensic pathologists. However, due to the lack of trained personnel in this field, a substantial number of these autopsies in the United States are performed by hospital-based pathologists, many of whom have had no further training in the subspecialty of forensic pathology. But these examinations can be satisfactory, particularly when the hospital pathologist has ready access to a certified forensic pathologist for pre- and post-autopsy consultation.

In sum, the medicolegal autopsy may be viewed as an indispensable laboratory procedure whose initial goal is to identify the decedent. In the context of a general death investigation, the medicolegal autopsy is also helpful in answering questions about the time and place of death. In cases of unnatural death, the evidence obtained is often determinative of the circumstances in which the fatal injuries were sustained so as to settle issues about the manner of death. Also, from these autopsies one can frequently identify the lethal instrumentality, which in some cases may lead to the person responsible for the death.

§ 32A.3.　Identifying the victim.

Accurate identification of the victim is the *sine qua non* of a competent death investigation; however, this is not always easy, especially when there has been an effort to mislead the authorities. Fingerprints are most useful, and even in decomposing bodies may be restored by the subcutaneous injection of various materials. Bodily markings such as scars, deformities, amputations, occupational markings, moles, and tattoos should be photographed and carefully described.

In any case where identification is expected to be difficult, such as occurs in severely decomposed bodies, or in any case of suspected child abuse, total body X-rays should be made. These may reveal evidence of old fractures or unique bone anatomy that can be compared to medical records. The teeth should always be examined for the same reason and an accurate dental record made at the time of examination. This is best accomplished by a specialist skilled in forensic practices, such as a forensic odontologist or forensic anthropologist, but in most cases may be adequately performed by a pathologist. To a well-trained examiner, the condition of the teeth also can give a relatively accurate indication of the age of the decedent.

Determination of the sex of badly decomposed bodies can be attempted from the contours of the pelvis and skull, size and contour of the long bones, and physical or chemical analysis of teeth. Cytologic examination of well-preserved tissue may aid in the finding of sex chromatin or the Barr body in the epithelial cells that are present in about 50% of females.

A corpse has been identified by comparing antemortem and postmortem computed tomographic (CT scan) images of the subject's spine. On each set of images, the authors found, in identical locations, a posterolateral disc herniation at L5-S1 on the right side, Schmorl's nodes, and a lucency in the ilium. Also, the authors found characteristic similarities in the vertebral bodies, spinous processes, transverse processes, and neural arches of the spine.[2]

Other recently employed techniques include the use of computer software coupled with photographic superimpositions on the skull. Also, forensic anthropologists have enjoyed some degree of success by sculpting skulls out of clay to reconstruct facial features.

The most outstanding recent advance in forensic identification involves the application of recombinant deoxyribonucleic acid (DNA) by molecular biologists. Except for monozygotic siblings (twins derived from a single fertilized ovum), DNA is unique to each individual. All cells with chromosomes or mitochondria may be analyzed if the tissues are appropriately collected. Extremely small amounts of DNA that may be too small or poorly preserved for study by conventional methods may be used to construct DNA profiles, even with fixed, embalmed, or mummified specimens.[3]

§ 32A.4. Violent or unusual death — Examination of the scene.

Long before the medicolegal autopsy in any case is begun, there should be a painstaking collection of all available information pertaining to the case. The initial investigation in most jurisdictions will be conducted by the police, and this information will be immediately reported to the medical examiner or coroner. This should include the identity of the victim if known, the exact location where he was found, and the identification and statements of the individual or individuals who discovered the body. One must know the time the decedent was last seen alive, and by whom. If persons were present at the time of the death, a detailed chronology of all the circumstances, including any special complaints by the decedent, must be noted and recorded. Any past medical attention, medication, or history of injury must be elicited and recorded. A thorough description of the scene of death that relates the individual to his surroundings, should be made. With this information the initial medical investigator can make a reliable decision as to whether he or she should personally visit the scene.

---

[2] Riepert, T., et al., *Identification of an Unknown Corpse by Means of Computed Tomography (CT) of the Lumbar Spine,* 40 J. Forensic Sci. 126 (Jan.), 1995.

[3] Editor's Note: The use of DNA for identification purposes is discussed in Chapter 24 of this Cyclopedia.

In some violent deaths, examination by the forensic pathologist at the scene is mandatory for an accurate correlation of the autopsy findings and the physical facts uncovered during the investigation. In violent or suspected violent death, extensive photographs of the scene should be made. These investigations are most satisfactorily carried out through the team approach by the police department, forensic specialists, and criminologists.

In many cases, a knowledge of the scene of death may well yield more direct information than the most painstaking autopsy. A case in point involved a middle-aged plumber found floating face down in approximately a foot and a half of water in a cellar in which he had been working. Careful investigation of the scene disclosed a malfunctioning water pump that had bare wires extending into the water, but a careful examination of the body revealed no evidence of direct electrical contact. Autopsy further revealed no evidence of drowning. Arteriosclerotic heart disease of a moderate degree was present, but was not believed by the pathologist to be severe enough to explain the death of this individual. The actual cause of death was established with the help of the local electric company which, through special instrumentation, showed that the water pump that had been plugged in at the time the decedent was found could have delivered a high level of current into the water in the cellar. Thus, it was only through a correlation of the physical evidence at the scene and the information delivered through a painstaking autopsy, that the exact cause of death of this individual was ascertained.

By gathering facts at the scene, sometimes an autopsy may be avoided. For example, if an elderly man is seen to collapse and die while transacting business, and in his pocket is found a bottle of nitroglycerine tablets, and external examination of the body reveals no injury, but does reveal the signs of sudden coronary insufficiency, the public interest in the case probably is fulfilled without a complete autopsy.

Bodies are frequently found in rural or secluded areas. During the growing season, green plants under a body will lose their chlorophyll and become pale in about eight days. This information may help in determining the time of death; however, usually time of death may only be roughly estimated even by a careful external and internal examination of the body.

§ 32A.5. Violent or unusual death — External examination of the body.

The external examination of the body is most useful in determining the difficult question of the postmortem intervalas well as the cause of death. Beginning at the time of death, the body undergoes a series of physical and chemical changes that continue until the body is ultimately destroyed. At best, however, using all available data, a pathologist is only able to make an estimate of the time of death. Some of the traditional criteria used are subject to wide variation, depending upon the physical and environmental circumstances and the range of time involved.

Body temperature (algor mortis)

In the first twenty-four hours, the steady fall of body temperature is the most reliable guide in determining how long the person has been dead. Under average conditions, about 2° Fahrenheit are lost hourly for the first six hours and from 1 to 2° Fahrenheit for the next six hours. However, calculations based on these figures may be upset by extremes in temperature, the amount of clothing worn, ventilation, and the environment.

Lividity (livor mortis)

Postmortem lividity (discoloration from settling of blood by gravity) begins to appear in about thirty minutes to two hours in plethoric (ruddy, red-faced) individuals and in about four hours in anemic individuals. Changes are usually complete in about twelve hours. Lividity represents the settling of blood in dependent portions of the body, and use can be made of its appearance in determining the position of the body at the time of death. Lividity usually becomes permanently fixed in about six to ten hours. If a body is moved after death within this time interval, the lividity may shift, and this determination is of extreme importance to the forensic pathologist.

Skin color

As well as lividity, the color of the skin may be a useful sign. The cherry-pink color imparted by carbon monoxide poisoning is well known. A pinkish discoloration of the skin also occurs in cases of freezing. A dark red color of the skin is found in cyanide poisoning, but it is important to note that small amounts of cyanide (0.03 mgs.%) may be formed by putrefaction. A gray color may result from methemoglobinemia (presence of an abnormal form of hemoglobin in the blood) due to poisoning by such chemicals as potassium chlorate, or due to the ingestion of well water rich in nitrogenous compounds. Jaundice or a yellow discoloration of the skin should alert the pathologist that he or she is dealing with a possible case of infectious hepatitis. A bronze color to the skin may indicate that death was due to a form of septicemia.

Rigor mortis

The stiffening of skeletal muscles after death is called rigor mortis, which is caused by a form of coagulation of the muscle protein and plasma, comparable in a way to the coagulation of blood. The chemical reaction of living muscle protoplasm is alkaline; after death, this reaction changes to form acid, which causes loss of flexibility. The process generally begins in two to four hours, first in the muscles of the face, jaw, and upper extremities, and then eventually in the trunk and lower extremities. Once begun, rigor mortis usually takes about two hours for stiffening of the whole body, but it may not be complete for up to six or eight hours. Rigor usually lasts from twelve to forty-eight hours. It disappears in the same order in which it appears, beginning with the muscles of the face.

Rigor mortis is hastened or delayed by many factors; for example, poisoning with strychnine, atropine, pilocarpine, or such factors as heat, cold, age, general health, and size of the individual.

Hair

The hair must always be carefully examined. Any disarray or evidence of bleeding should alert the pathologist to a possible underlying fatal injury. Contrary to popular belief, hair does not grow after death. Measurement of hair growth, however, may be used to certain advantages. Whiskers grow about one millimeter in twenty-four hours. In males, if the time of the last shave of the decedent is known, this may be of some value in determining the time of death.

Opacification of cornea

The extent of the opacification (clouding) of the cornea of the eye should be noted; however, the rate of corneal opacification varies with environmental conditions and increases over time.

Contusions

The skin must always be carefully examined for the presence of any lacerations, abrasions, or contusions. Within certain variable limitations, contusions or bruises may be dated as they evidence certain color changes with the passage of time if inflicted upon a live individual. But it must be remembered that persons on anticoagulant or blood-thinning therapy, obese females, fair-skinned individuals, and people with chronic dietary insufficiencies are frequently apt to develop large contusions following minor injuries.

Decomposition

Bacterial decomposition of a human body usually starts about thirty-six to forty-eight hours postmortem, beginning with a green discoloration of the abdomen. Later it invades the vascular system, with hemolysis or the breakdown of blood and gas production resulting in distention of the vascular system in the body generally. In unembalmed bodies that have been buried in the ground, unless subjected to destruction by animals or other external means, the soft parts are completely destroyed in three to four years; the fibrous tissue in five years or more; and the skeleton itself in ten years.

One week in air is equivalent to about two weeks in water or eight weeks in soil insofar as the rate of bacterial decomposition is concerned. The rate of decomposition is influenced by the general health of the individual, environmental temperature, and the way the body is dressed.

Insect infestation

Blowflies will lay eggs in warm bodies, especially in the corners of the eyes, mouth, and the vulva of females. These eggs develop into larvae in two to three days, and change to pupae in seven to ten days. Thus, presence of pupae indicate death at least two weeks earlier. Body lice will survive three to six days after the death of the host. It is often useful to collect insect species in varying stages of maturation and submit them to a forensic entomologist for examination.

Special clues as to cause of death

Examination of the eyes should be made, and the color and size of the pupils should be noted. The presence of punctate (resembling points or dots) hemorrhages in the conjunctival portion of the eye should alert the pathologist to the possibility of strangulation and thus would direct special attention to the structures of the neck. The body should be carefully examined for the presence of any underlying fractures, or dislocation of the hyoid bone and cartilaginous structures within the neck regions.

The skin of the extremities should be inspected for needle puncture marks, recent or old, as they are often present in drug abusers. A careful search for needle puncture marks also should be made on the lips, the inner linings of the mouth, the richly vascular undersurface of the tongue, the vagina, and the penis. The tongue should also be examined for the presence of any lacerations or bitemarks which could alert the medical investigator to the possibility of a seizure or convulsion preceding death.

Photographs

Before the performance of any autopsy, a routine identification photograph of the decedent should be made. This should include the identification number of the case and an indication of the date upon which the autopsy is to be performed. In any case of violent death, in addition to extensive photographs of the decedent at the scene before disturbance of the body, complete photographs of the decedent, clothed (if found that way) and unclothed, showing any external wounds should be taken.

Semen stains

The staining of semen must be identified and preserved for further definitive testing. It may be possible to recover DNA from the semen and thereby more accurately determine the identification of the perpetrator of a sex crime. The external genitalia and mouth should be always thoroughly examined, particularly when there is any question of sexual assault. Swabs of the vagina, anus, and mouth should be made. One swab should be smeared on a glass microscopic slide and preserved for staining and microscopic search for the presence of spermatoza. The other swab should be delivered to the forensic serologist for the determination of acid phosphatase, a chemical found in male prostatic fluid, a large component of the ejaculate.

Hands and fingernails

Scrupulous examination of the hands and fingernails should be made for any evidence of defense marks; that is, indications that the decedent may have been attempting to ward off an attacker. It is important in the case of a homicidal assault that the condition of the hands be diligently preserved for future examination. This may necessitate tying a paper bag around each hand at the scene of the crime before the body is removed. If this is not done, it is possible for blood spillage from the victim to soil the hands and make comparison tests forensically useless.

On autopsy, the fingernails should be cut and any dirt, human debris, or other materials preserved, sealed and labeled. Human skin from an assailant may be subsequently identified. Dried blood from beneath the fingernails may contain DNA of the assailant. Hair recovered from beneath the fingernails likewise may be identified. A close examination of the fingernails may reveal white streaks or "Mee's lines" and alert the pathologist that he or she is dealing with a case of arsenic poisoning.

In gunshot cases, painstaking examination of the victim's hands sometimes reveals areas of staining from firearms residues. This material can be collected by various means, appropriately identified and packaged, and then submitted to the crime laboratory for more definitive chemical and microscopic tests for the identification of these residues.

Teeth

If loose teeth are found at the scene, they should be collected and properly preserved for examination by a forensic odontologist to determine if they are from the victim's mouth or possibly from an assailant. If any tissue is attached to the tooth, it may be possible to express sufficient blood for DNA analysis. Also, DNA may be recoverable from the dental pulp, which would be of obvious importance if the tooth does not belong to the victim.

Clothing

Clothing should be examined for any evidence of perforating wounds, for the "pattern" of blood that may indicate the direction of flow, and for any exogenous staining. In hit-and-run cases, if paint stains or paint flakes are found, they should be noted and preserved, since they may be later compared with material retrieved from suspected vehicles. Imprints found on clothing also may be helpful in determining the instrument that caused the death.

Only after the clothing has been examined for any evidence it may yield should it be removed from the body. Clothing should not be cut from the body, but should be very carefully removed, labeled, and stored for possible future examination. In the case of gunshot wounds, each clothing perforation may be thoroughly examined chemically for powder residues. It should be noted that the paraffin test is obsolete, and other methodologies are now used for the identification of powder residues.

§ 32A.6. Gunshot and stab wound cases.

The entire skin of the victim must be examined for evidence of any kind of wounding. Any wound should be photographed, measured, and diagramed for possible future comparison with an instrument. All gunshot and stab wounds should be fully documented both by photography and diagrams. Notation must be made of any adjacent residues, as well as the size, shape, and direction of these wounds. It has been found to be most satisfactory to measure the distance of all wounds from a fixed anatomic landmark, such as the top of the head or from the heel, and the distance of each wound from the left or right of midline. This is most useful information, especially if it can be correlated with physical evidence found at the scene of a homicide.

Gunshot — Entry wounds

DiMaio[4] has provided a workable classification of gunshot wounds that has been adopted by most forensic pathologists in the United States. All gunshot wounds are either penetrating (no exit from the body) or perforating (through-and-through). Entry wounds are characterized by distance between the muzzle of the weapon and the target. The following broad categories apply, but overlap may exist between each.

  1. *Contact wounds.* These wounds indicate complete or partial apposition of the muzzle of the weapon against the target on discharge. Variation in the surface appearance of such wounds depends upon whether they are hard, loose, angled, or incomplete.

---

[4]DiMaio, V. J. M., *Gunshot Wounds: Practical Aspects of Firearms, Ballistics,* and Forensic Techniques, 2d ed., CRC Press, Boca Raton, Fla., 1999, pp. 65-122.

With variation, these wounds are characterized by the presence of searing and deposits of soot at the margins. Many of components that exit the barrel, among which are soot, powder, and the bullet, are present within the internal wound track.

2. *Near-contact or close-entry wounds.* These are created when the muzzle is not against the target, yet close enough so that powder that exits the muzzle does not impact the circumferential skin. Typically, in these cases the muzzle was no greater than several inches from the surface on discharge.

3. *Intermediate range.* The hallmark of intermediate-range gunshot entry wounds are deposits of "powder tattooing and stippling" on the target around the bullet hole. These deposits represent abrasions of skin by burning, burned, or unburned powder grains. Embedded powder grains cause the tattooing. As the muzzle-target distance increases, the diameter of stippling and tattooing expands. Typically, these changes do not occur when the muzzle is greater than thirty-six inches from the target. However, the most accurate means of measuring the muzzle-target distance in intermediate-range entry wounds is to test-fire the suspected weapon with the same type of commercial ammunition in the laboratory setting.

4. *Distant or indeterminate entry wounds.* These wounds are characterized by a perforation of the skin with marginal abrasion. In the absence of an interposed target between the muzzle and the victim, such wounds occur at distances greater than twenty-four inches. As before, laboratory testing is necessary to accurately determine muzzle-target distances.

The foregoing categorization of entry wounds does not apply in cases of graze wounds, projectile recochet, malfunctioning firearms, or in the presence of interposed targets between the muzzle of the weapon and the victim.

Gunshot — Exit wounds

Exit wounds have several general features. Although typically larger than entry wounds, they can in some instances be smaller. Their appearance is variable in that they may be star-shaped, slit-like, crescentic, circular, or without specific geometric feature. The vast majority of cutaneous exit wounds exhibit no marginal abrasion. Shored or supported exit wounds are an exception to this rule. Such wounds, which may resemble entry wounds, have abraded and contused margins if the victim's skin at the exit site had a firm object pressing against it.

Estimating direction and distance of gunshot

Bullet wounds must be extensively examined and described. A hand lens is very useful for this. Through this means entrance and exit wounds can be initially differentiated. When a gun is fired, hot gases and particulate debris issue from the barrel. They are followed abruptly by the missile and more hot gases and products of combustion. Depending upon the weapon and ammunition, a shot fired at a distance of about eighteen inches to two feet will show a rounded hole and no burning or gunpowder tattooing of the skin. There will be a circular "abrasion collar" around the hole. This is because the skin is a relatively elastic structure, and stretches to an extent as the bullet perforates. A "hard contact" (also called "tight contact") shot, where the muzzle of the gun is held in firm contact with the skin, may have the same appearance, but examination of the underlying tissues will show burning and the presence of gunpowder and combustion products.

In a shot fired at close range (six to twelve inches) there is usually a circular wound, but the edges may show some splitting. The abrasion collar is present, and grease and grime (fouling) are often found on the edges of the wound. A flame burn, smudging, and tattooing of powder may be visible on the skin. In a "soft contact" (also called "loose contact") wound, where the muzzle is held loosely against the skin, the edges of the wound may be widely split and often everted. No burning or tattooing may be visible, but as in the hard contact shot, carbon monoxide, powder residues, and products of combustion may be found in the subcutaneous tissues. The size of entry and exit gunshot wounds is dependent upon myriad factors. Typical exit wounds lack the abrasion collar characteristic of entrance wounds, show no evidence of powder residues, and characteristically show everted skin margins or tags.

Suicides versus accidental deaths

In gunshot cases, the victim's arm length should be measured from the armpit to the end of the index finger to determine if it would have been physically possible for him to have shot himself without an auxillary device. This is especially important in shooting cases involving rifles or shotguns.

In cases of self-inflicted wounds, unexploded shells in the gun or near the gun or the body may suggest that the decedent was loading or unloading the gun rather than having deliberately loaded it for the purpose of suicide. Accounts that the decedent had a habit of twirling the gun or playing pranks may be useful to show that the purpose was not suicide. Showing that the gun was purchased, borrowed, or assembled for no apparent purpose would serve in determining that suicide was the motive.

Accidental shooting would be favored by evidence showing that the gun was old, rusty, "tricky," "easy on the trigger," had no safety device or a defective one, or could be discharged in a variety of ways without pulling the trigger. Absence of powder residue on the hands may be significant where it can be shown that the discharge of the gun by ordinary means customarily produced such deposits. Evidence showing whether the decedent had an adequate knowledge of firearms and their use should always be searched for.

Examination prior to organ removal

All gunshot and stab wound tracts should be examined in situ before any organs are removed. This is particularly important in the presence of multiple wounds, since this is the only opportunity that the pathologist will have to determine their exact course, nature, and extent.

In cases where the victim underwent surgery prior to death from a gunshot or stab wound, it is highly desirable for the pathologist to speak directly with the surgeon before starting the autopsy to determine if a surgical incision was made through a preexisting skin wound, what the surgeon found internally, and what the operation consisted of. Otherwise, wounds may be misinterpreted or missed completely.

§ 32A.7. Bodies recovered from fires.

In the examination of a body recovered from fire the pathologist should be able to determine early in the investigation whether the subject was alive or dead when the fire began. This is most easily accomplished by searching for the cherry-pink discoloration of the skin, blood, and internal organs due to the inhalation of carbon monoxide, the consistent product of incomplete combustion. This may be extremely difficult if not impossible in bodies that have undergone extensive charring of the skin, but can be readily determined by examining the blood of the decedent. Rapid screening tests easily performed in the autopsy room for a rough quantitation of the amount of carbon monoxide are available, and these should be immediately followed up and verified by exact quantitation by skilled toxicologists.[5]

If the pathologist initially discovers a negative or low carbon monoxide level in the blood of the victim, he or she must immediately consider that either this victim died of natural causes before the fire began or he was the victim of homicide with the fire used to conceal the crime. In case of flash fires, however, victims who die as a result of the fire quite commonly have normal or even low levels of carbon monoxide.

The victim's tracheobronchial tree should be examined for deposits of soot. If none is present, it is quite unlikely that the victim was alive and breathing after the fire started. It is also necessary to keep other toxic substances (*e.g.*, plastic) in mind when ordering toxicologic and physicochemical analyses on fire victims, their clothing, and other materials

---

[5] Editor's Note: For an extensive discussion of carbon monoxide determinations in the human body, see Chapter 24 of this Cyclopedia.

from the scene. Often, victims are incapacitated by the thermal degradation products of various substances, for example cyanide, that are found ubiquitously in wood and plastic furniture, plastic wire insulation, office, and home equipment, etc. Such scientific findings could have great medicolegal significance in civil litigation related to conflagrations.

§ 32A.8. Bodies recovered from water.

A body found in water, which may range from subfreezing fresh water through salty seawater to tap water in a bathtub, requires that the pathologist exhaustively consider many questions. When did the victim die? How long was the victim in the water? Was he dead or alive before submersion? What was the cause of death? Did injuries found on the body occur before or after death?

Drowning is a diagnosis of exclusion and rests upon data gathered from circumstantial evidence — from investigation of the scene, from laboratory studies, and from the postmortem examination. Despite reports suggesting the use of certain laboratory criteria for the diagnosis of drowning, no such criteria have gained acceptance by medicolegal death investigators in the United States. Many investigators initially heralded certain tests, including a comparison of chloride levels in the right and left heart chambers and the observing of diatoms (microscopic algae) in the lungs, but these procedures lack sufficient specificity and sensitivity to serve as definitive drowning tests. Moreover, there are no specific autopsy findings indicative of drowning. Deaths due to drowning result from asphyxiation and cerebral anoxia. Although pulmonary edema is a common finding at autopsy, the mere presence of water and aquatic debris is not definitive. For example, especially in children, the lungs may be over-inflated with pulmonary edema as a result of laryngeal spasm (so-called dry drowning).

The victim's gastric contents should be examined, the sinuses of the skull should be evaluated for watery fluid, and middle-ear hemorrhage in the basilar skull should be looked for. Natural disease processes and traumatic injuries should be noted, and differentiation must be made between actual ante-mortem injuries and post-mortem artifacts (e.g., injuries to the body from a boat propeller, floating log, or fish or other aquatic animals, etc.).

§ 32A.9. Automobile accident cases.

The external examination of the fatal automobile accident victim includes a general description of the body with special attention to injuries of the head, trunk, and extremities, such as abrasions, contusions, lacerations, perforation wounds of the skin, and external evidences of fractures.

When external injuries of the head appear, they may suggest internal head and neck injuries. In chest trauma, particularly when fractured ribs can be felt, it may indicate a "stove-in" type of chest injury. Chest injuries are the most common causes of death in automobile accident cases. Head injuries are next in frequency, especially in pedestrian fatalities. In most crash-deaths, combined chest and head injuries are found.

The pathologist should note also the presence of foreign material, car fragments, dirt or gravel. Occasionally, characteristic marks occur on the skin, such as tire burns, gravel burns, and similar contact wounds. These should be described accurately, measured, and recorded in the autopsy report. Usually it is desirable to photograph these wounds.

A careful study of abrasions and lacerations that show beveled edges may be helpful in determining the direction and type of a "scraping force." Neck lacerations may suggest broken windshield injuries. Multiple fractures of the bones of the legs may suggest bumper injuries, common of course in pedestrian accidents. Black eyes and bleeding from the ears are suggestive of basilar skull fractures.

The external examination in automobile fatality cases is particularly useful in reconstructing the events at the scene. And the experienced pathologist, through a visit to the scene, can usually determine which injuries are primary impact injuries and which are secondary.

The advent of restraints and airbags has introduced a new set of considerations for the pathologist in evaluating occupant-related vehicular deaths. Not infrequently, patterned abrasions and contusions on the anterior torso indicate whether the occupant was wearing a lap or a three-point restraint. Malfunctioning restraints may form a partially encircling noose around the victim's neck and cause death by mechanisms akin to hanging. Short-statured persons may experience a fatal blunt injury of the head and torso upon impact by rapidly deployed airbags. Correlation with the vehicle's design is imperative in these cases.

The internal examination of a victim of an automobile accident generally is conducted in the manner of the usual autopsy (See Part III of this chapter), with special attention to the usual findings in vehicle cases; for example, steering wheel injuries of the chest and heart. Also, where the cause of the accident is unknown, the pathologist should look for evidence of disease involvement or the possibility of other physiological influences, such as alcohol, drugs, carbon monoxide poisoning, etc.

II. THE HOSPITAL AUTOPSY

§ 32A.10. Introduction.

The hospital autopsy (also called the "permission," or "consent" autopsy) in almost all cases is performed in the hospital or medical center. Generally these autopsies involve patients who have been under treatment and are performed only with the consent of the decedent's relatives. Some, of course, have legal implications, especially where the death could have been the result of complications of surgery, anesthesia, or the administration of drugs or other therapy.

While suggesting that each hospital establish its own specific recommendations for autopsies through consultation between the hospital pathologist and the rest of the medical staff, the College of American Pathologists (CAP), recommends the following indications for hospital autopsies:

1. Deaths in which an autopsy might help explain unknown an unanticipated medical complications to the attending physician;
2. All deaths in which the cause of death is not known with certainty on clinical grounds;
3. Deaths in which an autopsy might help to allay concerns of the family or the public regarding the death, and to provide reassurance to them regarding same;
4. Unexpected or unexplained deaths occurring during or following any dental, medical, or surgical diagnostic procedures or therapies;
5. Deaths of patients who have participated in clinical trials (protocols) approved by institutional review boards;
6. Unexpected or unexplained deaths that are apparently natural and not subject to a forensic medical jurisdiction;
7. Natural deaths that are subject to, but waived by, a forensic medical jurisdiction such as (a) persons dead on arrival at hospitals, (b) deaths occurring in hospitals within twenty-four hours of admission, and (c) deaths in which the patient sustained or apparently sustained an injury while hospitalized;
8. Deaths resulting from high-risk infectious and contagious diseases;
9. All obstetric deaths;
10. All neonatal and pediatric deaths;
11. Deaths at any age in which it is believed that an autopsy will disclose a known or suspected illness that also may have a bearing on survivors or recipients of transplant organs;
12. Deaths known or suspected to have resulted from environmental or occupational hazards.[6]

Hospitals fully accredited by the Joint Commission on Accreditation of Healthcare Organizations (JCAHO)[7] require that a pathologist or physi-

---

[6] *Autopsies Serve as Valuable Quality Improvement Tool*, 11 JCAHO Perspect. 4 (Jan./Feb.), 1991.

[7] The Joint Commission on Accreditation of Healthcare Organizations (JCAHO) is the recognized national accrediting body for hospitals in the United States and Canada. It is sponsored and supported by the American Medical Association, American Hospital Association, Canadian Medical Associa-

cian qualified in anatomic pathology perform or supervise each hospital autopsy. Other JCAHO requirements include: (1) a pathologist must prepare a descriptive diagnostic report of each autopsy performed; (2) provisional anatomic diagnoses must be recorded in the patient's clinical record within three days after the autopsy, and a complete protocol must be made part of the patient's clinical record within sixty days, unless the hospital's clinical staff establishes exceptions for special studies; (3) gross and microscopic reports must be included in the patient's clinical record; (4) all microscopic interpretations must be made by a pathologist qualified in anatomic pathology; (5) appropriate refrigeration must be available for the body in case a delay occurs in performing the autopsy.[8]

The hospital autopsy differs in several respects from the medicolegal or coroner's autopsy. In the hospital autopsy, the decedent's medical history almost always is available. The attending physician usually can speculate as to the cause of death, at least generally, but wants to confirm the diagnosis. The major duty of the hospital pathologist, therefore, is to observe and describe the conditions of the body as it is found on dissection.

The hospital autopsy is performed substantially in the same professional manner as any operation. If possible, it is performed with a minimum of disturbance of the body. Ordinarily, only medical personnel are present: in most cases, only the pathologist and his or her assistants, interns, resident physicians, and the patient's attending physician.

Most hospitals maintain a staff pathologist. Traditionally, the cost of the autopsy has been absorbed by the hospital. If a patient dies outside the hospital, however, a reasonable fee generally is charged by the hospital pathologist.

A thorough hospital autopsy takes a variable amount of time, depending upon the complexity of the case. Afterwards, preferably under the direct guidance of the pathologist, a laboratory technologist will prepare tissues for later microscopic examination by the pathologist. A final report is prepared by the pathologist, which becomes a permanent record for the hospital and the decedent's attending physician.

Hospital autopsies are encouraged by the medical profession. Until 1970, the performance of autopsies in 25% of patient deaths was necessary for maintaining adequate levels of postgraduate medical education in teaching hospitals under internship and residency programs approved by the Council on Medical Education of the American Medical Association. Also, the performance of autopsies was necessary for the maintenance of high standards of patient care under the standards of the Joint

---

tion, American College of Physicians, American College of Surgeons, and similar organizations. The Joint Commission determines minimum standards of administration, operation, and practice which all hospitals must meet to enjoy accreditation.

[8] *1996 Accreditation Manual for Pathology and Clinical Laboratory Services: Standards*, Joint Commission on Accreditation of Healthcare Organizations, Oakbrook Terrace, Illinois, 1996, pp. 128-29.

Commission on Accreditation of Healthcare Organizations (then called the Joint Commission on Accreditation of Hospitals). At present, however, no specific number of autopsies is required by the JCAHO.

Notwithstanding the recommendations of the College of American Pathologists, the phenomenon of continually diminishing autopsy rates for hospital deaths continues unabated. The national average is now below 9%, and, despite a substantial number of hospital deaths, some hospitals have autopsy rates at nearly zero. Yet, as confirmed by many reports over the last thirty years, the discordance rate between clinical diagnoses and autopsy findings approaches 45%.[9] There is, in other words, yet a huge chasm between what high-technology diagnostic medicine performs prior to death and what is discovered upon autopsy.

Although the causes for the severe decline in autopsy rates may be unclear, it is indisputable that the autopsy provides answers to many relevant questions that are often not answered by current high-tech clinical medicine. An active debate is ongoing over the resolution of these issues, which have a definite impact upon the reasons for autopsies in the first place: namely, accurate death certificates and vital statistics; assessment of the quality of medical practice; elucidation of emerging diseases; determination of the effectiveness of therapies, including medications, operations, and implantation of medical devices; correlation of premortem and postmortem diagnoses; and monitoring the public health.[10]

§ 32A.11. Establishing a final diagnosis.

When a patient dies without the attending physician knowing the exact cause, if consent can be obtained from the next of kin, an autopsy should be performed to determine the diagnosis. If the patient has been under treatment, the autopsy findings are correlated carefully with the patient's medical record. The method of treatment is reviewed, and the various diagnostic tests the patient received are evaluated. As a result, the course of the patient's illness usually is established, and the value of the therapy and diagnostic measures often can be determined. In some cases this information may be used to save the lives of future patients in similar situations.[11]

---

[9] Lundberg, G. D., *Low-Tech Autopsies in the Era of High-Tech Medicine*, 280 J.A.M.A. 1273 (Oct. 14), 1998.

[10] Id.

[11] "To secure the consent of the family for autopsy, one of two motives usually must be actuated: self-interest or altruism. Self-interest may be evoked if the family is concerned about the possibility of a hereditary factor in the patient's disorder, or if they are intensely interested in why the patient complained of some unrelated difficulty over a period of years. Altruism, however, is the motive most frequently and successfully actuated. The physician explains to the family the importance of the findings on autopsy to medical education and to society. Most persons when carefully and considerately approached will consent to the scientific investigation desired." McCormack, L.

An autopsy can also be valuable to the patient's surviving family members: a major benefit may be knowledge gained concerning the true nature of the disease as it affects the lives of survivors. For example, siblings and descendants may benefit greatly from information regarding inherited or familial diseases. Also, in the case of the death of a newborn infant, where the advisability of future pregnancy is in doubt, the final answer may be obtained only by postmortem examination.

The confirmation of a diagnosis by autopsy also has a significance that frequently is overlooked: compilation of accurate vital statistics on the death rates of various diseases. This information is important not only for purposes of public health and scientific research but also because it is carefully considered by life and health insurance companies in computing potential risks in offering insurance coverage. Were it not for such statistics, insurance companies, cautious by nature, would seldom offer coverage to individuals suspected of being poor health risks. Vital statistics compiled from death records verified by autopsy reports enable insurance companies to evaluate potential risks more effectively.

The medical profession has been criticized for carelessness in the completion of ordinary death certificates. The fact that a patient had cirrhosis of the liver, pulmonary tuberculosis, and arteriosclerosis does not necessarily mean that he died of coronary thrombosis, although this conclusion would be common in certifying his death. Actually, an autopsy might show that the patient died of a massive spontaneous hemorrhage into the gastrointestinal tract secondary to cirrhosis, or from liver failure, or from some completely different cause.

Often the physician completing the death certificate lists symptoms or symptom complexes instead of a definite and recognized pathologic condition. Studies have shown that the accuracy in death certificates can be improved. The autopsy is the most reliable, and in many cases the only, method of determining the true cause of death.

§ 32A.12. Standards for postoperative autopsies.

Pathologists consider postoperative autopsies to be among the most difficult. For this reason, and because of the legal implications that may be involved, conscientious pathologists observe certain basic procedural standards when time and circumstances permit: (1) If several pathologists are available, the most experienced should perform the autopsy; (2) the help of an assistant pathologist is desirable; (3) the pathologist should consult with the surgeons who performed the operation, the anesthesiologist in attendance, and other medical personnel at the operation; (4) before starting the autopsy, the pathologist should become thoroughly familiar with the operative report, the patient's case history, and

J., *The Pathologist and the Autopsy*, 6
Clev.-Mar. L. Rev. 205, 207, 1957.

the results of all X-ray and laboratory examinations; (5) if such information is not available, the autopsy should be delayed until it is obtained; (6) the autopsy technique should fit the situation — for example, incisions should not be carried through operative wounds that should be viewed from both outer and inner aspects before they are opened and inspected, no tension should be applied to sutures, and the sutured region should be widely excised and then prepared for microscopic study; (7) drains should not be removed before their precise location has been established; (8) instructive views of all decisive phases of the autopsy should be documented by photographs; and (9) an autopsy report should be dictated by the pathologist during the actual inspection and dissection of organs.

§ 32A.13. Official autopsies in deaths of hospital patients.

Occasionally, a patient under treatment at a hospital dies suddenly without explanation. The hospital authorities and the physicians want an autopsy, but the patient's next-of-kin will not consent. Perhaps because of the fear of a possible contagious disease or maybe because of an anticipated malpractice suit, the hospital calls the local coroner's office requesting an official autopsy, the kind authorized by law in the case of death under unusual circumstances. Coroner's offices are wary of such requests, especially where a matter of public health obviously is not involved, and the only apparent reason is the possible threat of a civil suit. Coroner's offices cannot arbitrarily perform autopsies. They must take each case on its merits. Coroners themselves can be subjected to a lawsuit for performing an unnecessary autopsy. (See § 32A.43.) Therefore, if the attending physician believes the death should be reported to the coroner or medical examiner, the report should be made *before* the patient's next-of-kin are asked about autopsy permission.

III. AUTOPSY PROCEDURE —
THE INTERNAL EXAMINATION

§ 32A.14. Introduction.

Only after a thorough external examination, photographic records, the preparation of diagrams, and the careful preservation and labeling of available evidence is the pathologist ready to begin the internal examination of the decedent.

During the examination the pathologist should be assisted by an autopsy technologist. It is the responsibility of this individual to provide assistance as directed by the pathologist. These duties are normally limited in scope, consisting principally of opening the body cavities prior to the internal examination, removing and weighing the individual organs after the pathologist has examined them *in-situ*, and closing the body upon completion of the internal examination.

§ 32A.15. Opening incision — Abdominal cavity — Chest.

The internal examination of the body generally is begun by a Y-shaped incision beginning at the tip of each shoulder, joining in the midline over the lower part of the breastbone, then extending downward across the abdomen adjacent to (but not through) the umbilicus to the level of the pubic bone. The skin flaps are then dissected and reflected, with careful note being made of any disease or injury to the tissues underlying the skin. At this point, the abdominal cavity is examined for the presence of any fibrous scars, fluid, or foreign body. In the female, breasts can be examined by making multiple serial cuts extending toward but not through the skin surface.

Rib fracture or lung perforation

If indicated, before the chest is opened the examiner should check for the presence of any entrapped air that might occur from a rib fracture with a perforation of the lung. This can readily be done by creating a pocket, one margin of which is the chest wall and the other the reflected skin flap. This pocket can be filled with water, the chest subsequently punctured with a scalpel beneath the level of the water, and the amount of escaping air if present can be evaluated.

The breastbone or sternum is then removed by cutting the ribs along each side with a curved scissor or oscillating saw made for this purpose. Ribs or cartilages should not be cut with a knife or similar sharp instrument because a cut or laceration of underlying tissues may be accidentally inflicted during the process and subsequently cause confusion in the evaluation of any wounds.

The breastbone once freed is removed, and before any large vessels are cut the pleural cavity or space between each lung and the rib cage is examined for the presence of fluid or blood resulting from an injury. An accurate measurement of the amount and its location is made, since this may be of importance later in estimating the approximate time interval the individual survived following his injuries.

Withdrawal of blood

After the above procedure, the pericardium or sac around the heart should be opened and its contents inspected and noted. At this point, blood should be withdrawn from the heart by the use of a chemically clean syringe and should be placed in properly labeled tubes for further tests. A blood-alcohol determination should be routinely made on a high percentage of cases that come to the attention of the medical examiner and should be properly preserved at the time of autopsy for chemical tests later. However, for an alcohol determination, care should be taken not to utilize blood exclusively from the right heart, particularly the inferior vena cava, since this blood courses directly from the liver and may give a falsely high result. For this reason, and because of the post-mortem redistribution of various drugs, the examiner should collect blood from multiple arterial and venous sites. In cases of questioned identity and all cases of suspected homicide, a bloodstain on clean filter paper should be obtained for DNA analysis.

Embolisms

The pulmonary artery, the main artery leading from the heart to the lungs, should be opened in situ before the heart is removed and examined for the presence of any embolism.[11] The emboli are usually blood clots that have formed in another part of the body, have become detached, and have traveled in the circulation to a distant part. They are a frequent cause of sudden unexpected death and may be related to an earlier injury to an extremity, having formed there as a result of thrombophlebitis or circulatory stagnation due to immobilization.

§ 32A.16. Removal and examination of organs.

There have been numerous methods developed over the years for the systematic removal and examination of organs on autopsy, but each pathologist usually adopts the method that he or she has found the most useful. Rather than remove all organs of the chest, abdominal, and pelvic cavities in one block, a careful examination of these organs *in situ*, and then a systematic removal and examination of each, generally yields the best results.

At the time of autopsy, all organs removed should be weighed and their weights compared with recognized normal weights for the organs of an individual of a given size and age. Also, representative sections of normal and diseased tissue from every organ should be placed in a chemical called a "fixative." In most cases this chemical is a formalin preparation, and serves to harden the tissue and stop any further autolysis (enzymatic digestion of cells) or decomposition. These tissues may then be prepared for microscopic study at a later time.

§ 32A.17. Heart.

The heart is removed with long segments of all its great vessels. It is imperative that the coronary arteries, which supply blood and deliver oxygen to the muscles of the heart, be examined with the utmost care,

---

[11] Editor's Note: An "embolus" is any matter foreign to the blood vessel, *i.e.*, blood clot, tissue, air bubble, fat, clump of bacteria, splinter, etc. An "embolism" is the blockage, or occlusion, of a vessel by an embolus (plural —"emboli").

since they yield useful evidence as to the extent of arteriosclerotic heart disease.

Evidence of heart attack

The normal function of the heart is dependent upon a supply and demand principle. As more work is demanded by the heart, blood rich in oxygen must be delivered to the myocardium (heart muscle) through these coronary arteries. If they are narrowed through the process of the formation of a blood clot, or as is much more frequently the case through their progressive and relentless destruction in atherosclerosis,[12] then an adequate amount of oxygen may not be delivered to the heart muscle in a given demand situation, and a fatal episode of coronary insufficiency with cardiac standstill or a fatal arrhythmia (irregular heart rhythm) may develop.

The examination of the coronary arteries is, with rare exception, performed by making minute transverse serial sections through their entire course. In this way any thrombosis[13] will be revealed. The coronary arteries may also be dissected out longitudinally with a scissor, but the pathologist must use constant caution not to displace a thrombus with the tip of the scissor. Since a heart attack (myocardial infarction) results in damage to the heart muscle, the wall of this muscle must be thoroughly examined for any evidence of old scarring or recent damage.

If an individual survives an occlusion of a coronary artery for approximately eight to ten hours, then the muscles supplied by that involved artery may well show some softening and paleness at the time of the autopsy. If he survives longer, well-documented changes, including hemorrhage and eventual scarring of the muscle, occur and can be dated. If, however, the victim dies before that eight- to ten-hour interval, at gross autopsy no changes may be apparent. It should be noted also that, in this time interval, even extensive microscopic examination of the tissues may reveal only minimal evidence of myocardial ischemia.

The size of the chambers of the heart should be recorded, as well as the condition of the heart valves and great vessels. The valves themselves may show evidence of disease that may be responsible for the victim's death.

Special stains and histochemical studies can be done to demonstrate acute myocardial changes from ischemia in those cases in which a heart attack is suspected as the cause of sudden death. Coronary artery spasm

---

[12]Editor's Note: "Arteriosclerosis" is a general term referring to the hardening and narrowing (sclerosis) of arteries. "Atherosclerosis" refers to the disorder in which lipid (fatty) material, including cholesterol, is deposited in and beneath the lining of the arteries. These deposits are called atheromata and may become so extensive that the artery is markedly reduced or even blocked (occlusion). This disease process is discussed in Chapter 34 of this Cyclopedia.

[13]Editor's Note: A "thrombosis" is the formation of a blood clot, or "thrombus" (plural—"thrombi"), in a blood vessel.

and cardiac arrhythmia, neither of which is demonstrable at autopsy, must also be considered as the possible mechanism in cases of sudden death where there is insufficient anatomic evidence of pathology to explain the cause.

§ 32A.18. Organs of the throat and neck.

The neck organs should be removed, including the tongue, and examined in conjunction with the respiratory apparatus. The tongue may show evidence of injury (for example, bite marks if the deceased was an epileptic), or burns and tissue destruction as the result of ingestion of poisonous compounds.

A trap-door-like structure, the epiglottis, is present slightly below the tongue and serves to prevent foreign material from entering the airways during swallowing or vomiting. In cases of coma from alcohol, barbiturates, or other causes, the reflexes that control the epiglottis may be depressed, and a fatal aspiration of stomach contents may be allowed to enter the airways, thereby obstructing them and causing sudden death. The epiglottis itself is subject to assault by infections, particularly in children, and may become rapidly swollen and cause airway obstruction. This phenomenon may also occur in allergic reactions to insect bites or drugs.

Occasionally, large aggregates of food, particularly meat, may be found lodged in the upper airway. Pathologists frequently encounter this in people who collapse in restaurants and are brought to the morgue or to the hospital with an apparent heart attack. Usually a moderate level of alcohol in the decedent's blood is found; it would appear that the ingestion of alcohol before the meal, while heightening the appetite, depresses the reflexes. Under these circumstances a person is apt to ingest a larger amount of food than he can comfortably handle, which becomes lodged in the upper airways, causing sudden unconsciousness and death. The frequent misdiagnosis of this condition in the past has led to the eponym "cafe coronary."

The hyoid bone in the neck should be carefully examined because fracture in this structure often suggests manual strangulation. For the same reason, the laryngeal cartilages (thyroid and cricoid) should be examined. The cartilaginous rings of the trachea, the cervical vertebrae, and all the overlying and surrounding soft tissues of the neck, including the fascia and strap muscles, should be carefully dissected to look for evidence of injury in suspected cases of manual or ligature strangulation.

§ 32A.19.   Lungs.

The arteries in the lungs must be dissected to discover any clots that might be present. Emboli in the lungs are frequently the result of an injury in another part of the body that may have occurred days to weeks before the fatal event. The substance of the lung is examined by numerous serial sections. Infectious diseases of public health importance such as tuberculosis are not uncommonly found. Examination of the lungs also may reveal the effects of an industrial or occupational hazard.[14] In appropriate cases, numerous representative sections of lung tissue should be preserved for routine and special stains, together with fresh frozen pieces, to determine if the deceased suffered from a pneumoconiosis ("dust disease"). Special perfusion tests can be performed in selected cases to analyze pulmonary function capacity in retrospective fashion.

In cases of questionable stillbirth, the lungs should be removed and placed in water. In general, if the infant has been born alive and has taken several breaths, the lungs will float. However, this float test is neither a truly sensitive nor specific procedure. Gases of putrefaction can also accumulate in the lung and cause it to float when placed in water. Fortunately, it has been found that if the putrefied lungs of stillborns are subjected to manual compression, the gases of putrefaction can be expressed, and the lungs will sink precipitously when placed in water. On the other hand, if the infant was born alive and breathed, despite external compression the air breathed into the tiny alveoli or air sacs will not be extruded, and these lungs will continue to float when placed in water.

§ 32A.20.   Esophagus.

The esophagus, which courses from the throat to the stomach, should be left attached to the stomach and removed with it. The examination of the contents of the esophagus can be of considerable importance from a legal standpoint. Not infrequently, staining of its lining or any adherent material may indicate an indication of the ingestion of a drug. In this case, the pathologist must be careful to retain all stomach contents at the time of the examination of this organ in order that definitive toxicological tests can be performed. Any corrosives that have been ingested will be apparent in the lining of the esophagus as areas of injury, and if no evidence of burning in the mouth or about the lips had occurred, such findings may be the first indication to the pathologist of a possible suicide case. Beneath the delicate lining of the esophagus are large numbers of blood vessels. In a case in which cirrhosis of the liver is present, these blood vessels frequently become partially obstructed and markedly dilated. This condition is known as esophageal varices, and rupture of a

---

[14] Editor's Note: Occupational lung disorders are discussed in Chapter 33 of this Cyclopedia.

varix from increased pressure is not infrequently the cause of a rapid loss of blood (exsanguination). Because of the large amount of blood spilled, these cases are often misinterpreted at the scene of the investigation as being the result of a homicidal assault.

§ 32A.21.   Stomach and intestines.

The stomach should be opened lengthwise along its greater curvature and in many cases its contents preserved and measured. Ingested food usually leaves the stomach as a grumous (clotted, lumpy) material called "chyme" approximately two to four hours after it is eaten. Thus the amount of food present in the stomach or in the upper intestine may give an indication as to the time of death of the decedent if the time of his last meal is known. The rate of travel of food through the remainder of the gastrointestinal tract also can be determined.

The color of the stomach contents should be noted and often is very helpful in identifying some of the more frequently ingested drugs. Seconal, for example, will impart a red color to the gastric contents and will stain the lining of the stomach red. In the ingestion of phosphorus, the stomach contents may be luminous. Many lethal substances that are ingested, for example cyanide and chloroform, have distinctive odors.

The lining of the stomach should be routinely examined for injury or for the presence of any peptic ulcer that may have eroded through the relatively thin wall of the stomach and been responsible for a fatal hemorrhage into the abdominal cavity.

The structure and content of the remainder of the gastrointestinal tract should be carefully examined. The intestinal contents may be preserved for further toxicologic study.

§ 32A.22.   Anus and rectum.

The anus should be scrupulously checked for any untoward bruising or tearing and for the presence of foreign bodies. Anal swabs for microscopic and other studies, including acid phosphatase determination, must be procured in cases of suspected sexual assault involving anal intercourse. A rigid foreign object introduced into the rectum during the course of an assault or errant sexual activity may have been responsible for perforation, leakage of feces into the abdominal cavity, and eventually a fatal infection. Considerable labor on the part of the pathologist may be necessary in a case of this type to localize the area of perforation and thereby deduce the offending object. Not infrequently, a previously undiagnosed carcinoma or inflammatory disease of the bowel may be found to be responsible for a perforated intestine and unexpected death.

In both apparent and suspected cases of child abuse, rape, or sexual assault, the perianal and rectal areas should be thoroughly examined for any evidence of old, as well as recent, injury.

§ 32A.23. Spleen.

The spleen appears to be particularly vulnerable to injury. It is a somewhat disc-shaped organ, slightly larger than a coffee mug, and comprises many blood channels. At the time of an assault or traumatic injury, it may become ruptured and lead to fatal blood loss in a matter of hours or even minutes. It is not unusual for the spleen to be bruised, bleed within itself, and unexpectedly rupture several days after an injury that initially was judged of no consequence. The capsule of the spleen is readily torn, and the organ should be examined for small tears, in the presence of blood in the abdomen, before it is removed.

§ 32A.24. Liver.

The liver is a large organ situated in the right upper part of the abdominal cavity that also is frequently ruptured during traumatic injuries. It therefore must also be thoroughly examined before being removed from the abdominal cavity. Alcoholic cirrhosis of the liver is a well known disease in our society and is responsible in itself for many deaths that come under the purview of the medical examiner's office. In chronic alcoholism, an acute alcoholic debauch, or situations of marked anemia, the liver cells may rather rapidly become infiltrated by large globules of fat. The development of an acute fatty liver is well recognized by forensic pathologists as a cause of sudden and unexpected death. The exact underlying physiological mechanism remains obscure.

Any evidence of infectious hepatitis discovered at the time of autopsy is of utmost public health importance, since any contacts of the decedent must be found, evaluated, and possibly treated. Massive necrosis of the liver may be a useful clue as it is found in many cases of intentional or accidental poisoning with numerous agents including commercial products such as cleaning fluids, carbon tetrachloride, and industrial and therapeutic chemicals and drugs.

§ 32A.25. Gallbladder.

The gallbladder is a sac located on the under surface of the middle portion of the liver that is used to store bile for the process of digestion of fats. Its presence should be noted as well as its surgical absence, and any gallstones or other abnormality of the bladder or its duct system should be described by the pathologist. This may prove of considerable benefit later on in the case of an unidentified victim. These facts also may be used as an important component of the medical history of the decedent.

§ 32A.26. Pancreas.

The pancreas is an organ that serves two distinct physiological functions. One is the production of insulin necessary for the body's utilization of glucose, and the other is the release of digestive enzymes into the intestinal tract.

Particularly in alcoholics, the pancreas may be the seat of a rather rapid and devastating disease in which the organ becomes inflamed, releases enzymes that digest itself, and subsequently produce extensive local hemorrhage, autolysis (cell breakdown) and necrosis. In the medical examiner's office, this acute hemorrhagic pancreatitis is a not unusual finding as a cause of unexpected death in the medical examiner's office, particularly among the nomadic and often solitary members of the alcoholic communities.

§ 32A.27. Adrenal glands.

The adrenal glands are paired organs that sit atop each kidney. They are comprised of an outer portion of cortex that produces cortisone-like compounds and enables the body to withstand long periods of stress. The cortex also releases chemicals that help control water and electrolyte metabolism. The inner portion of each adrenal gland is called the medulla and serves principally to produce adrenalin to be used in times of stress or emergency.

Diseases such as tuberculosis may affect the adrenal gland, leading to a condition known as Addison's disease. In rare cases, adrenal failure and sudden circulatory collapse and death may be caused by hemorrhage in the adrenal glands. This should alert the pathologist that he or she may be dealing with a generalized, previously undiagnosed infection, particularly one involving meningococcus bacteria. This phenomenon is called Waterhouse-Friderichsen syndrome.

§ 32A.28. Kidneys and urinary bladder.

The kidneys, which are found in the posterior portion of the abdominal cavity, are not usually implicated in cases of sudden death. However, they can be ruptured in traumatic injuries and lead to a slow, relentless blood loss that may go unrecognized clinically. Microscopically, the kidneys may show degenerative changes in some poisoning cases.

The kidneys are connected to the urinary bladder by two small muscular tubes called ureters. The urinary bladder itself should be carefully examined for any evidence of perforation or instrumentation, as must the urethra, which is the tube for passage of urine from the urinary bladder to the surface of the body. On autopsy, it is important to note the amount, color, and chemical nature of urine, and in many cases it should be preserved, since it constitutes a ready medium for toxicologic analyses and drug screening. On occasion, foreign bodies are encountered within the urinary bladder.

§ 32A.29. Sex organs in the female.

The sex organs of the female may be of critical importance in a forensic case. The ovaries are paired organs located on either side of the uterus in the pelvis. Their examination may give evidence of a recent pregnancy. The Fallopian tubes, which are also paired structures, carry the eggs released by the ovary to the uterus. They may be severely abscessed or scarred by gonorrhea, a fact of public health and epidemiologic importance. Not infrequently, a pregnancy may become ectopically established in a Fallopian tube rather than in the uterus. In this case, the pregnancy may well develop for several weeks before it becomes too large to be contained within the tube. At this point rupture occurs with rapid blood loss into the abdominal cavity. Cases of this sort are seen infrequently in a coroner's or medical examiner's office as a cause of sudden, unexpected death.

The wall of the uterus and its outer coat must be diligently searched for any evidence of perforation such as might occur during an abortion, and the condition of the endometrium or lining of the uterine cavity must be thoroughly examined. There are cases on record of perforation of the uterus by means of an intrauterine contraceptive device. This may lead to hemorrhage or a generalized infection. The neck of the uterus terminates in the cervix. This should always be examined for the presence of any injury.

An examination of the vaginal wall and the lining of the vagina is most important, and sections of tears or bruises must be excised and prepared for microscopic examination. As has been noted, careful vaginal smears and swabs should be made and preserved for further study in all cases of suspected or alleged rape. A "hanging drop" slide may be examined at the beginning of the autopsy to determine if motile spermatazoa are present.

§ 32A.30. Major blood vessels.

In examining the organs of the abdomen and pelvis, the pathologist must not neglect to make careful note of the major arteries and veins. Certain drugs and oral contraceptive pills in particular have been implicated in causing thrombosis of major veins and may be responsible for deaths in young people. A frequent cause of unexpected death in middle aged and older individuals is the spontaneous rupture of an aneurysm or bulging weak part of the wall of the distal abdominal aorta, usually due to severe arteriosclerosis. In situations in which the decedent has suffered trauma to the abdomen at some time prior to the rupture of an aneurysm, evaluation of all history and factual evidence about the case is imperative before a final decision is reached as to the possible role of the trauma.

§ 32A.31. Rib and vertebral bone marrow.

Samples of rib and vertebral bone marrow may need to be examined because they may give early evidence of such diseases as leukemia, anemia, and other dyscrasias. On occasion, bone marrow may be analyzed for carbon monoxide content when, due to the marked destruction of a body, the blood cannot be examined.

In appropriate cases, X-ray examination is especially valuable in studying the skeleton for evidence of old, healed fractures, which is extremely important in suspected child-abuse cases. Bone studies are also important in cases requiring identification of bodies.

§ 32A.32. Spinal cord.

The spinal cord itself can be examined with ease. This is done most simply by making an incision in the back of the body and removing the posterior portion of the bony vertebral column or by an anterior approach after evisceration. The cord can then be examined in situ and removed for further study. This should be done in cases of trauma involving the vertebral column, as well as in cases of possible central nervous system infection and various neurological disorders.

§ 32A.33. Brain and skull.

Access to the brain is gained by an incision behind both ears extending across the crown of the head. The skin flaps thus created are deflected anteriorly and posteriorly and note should be made in the subgaleal tissues of any evidence of hemorrhage. In many cases, at this point, an injury to the head is disclosed that previously went unrecognized because of difficulty in viewing the scalp through the hair. In the case of a thick-haired individual, a sizable blow to the head may be concealed by the hair.

The calvarium, the bone comprising the top of the head (skull cap), is examined and then removed through the use of an oscillating saw. This process exposes the thick outer membrane covering the brain (dura mater). In cases of head injury, bleeding may rapidly occur either between the dura and the skull (epidural) or beneath the dura, between it and the brain (subdural). Individuals with these injuries are generally rendered unconscious and death may ensue rapidly. The presence of a subdural hematoma is probably one of the most frequently encountered unexpected causes of death in any medical examiner's office.

On concluding that the dura is unremarkable and shows no evidence of trauma or infectious disease such as meningitis, the pathologist should

561

carefully incise it in the midline. Representative sections of any blood clot or abnormality in the dura are taken for microscopic study, as epidural and subdural hematomas can be extensively studied and may be quite accurately dated.

Once the dura is removed, two other very thin membranous coverings intimately applied to the brain — the arachnoid and pia maters — will be exposed. While an epidural or subdural hemorrhage is generally the result of a traumatic injury, isolated subarachnoid hemorrhage is often a manifestation of natural death. In most cases this is caused by the rupture of a congenital or arteriosclerotic aneurysm of the arteries comprising the Circle of Willis at the base of the brain. An individual may die within minutes or hours of the development of a subarachnoid hemorrhage, and may manifest erratic or belligerent behavior in the few minutes between the time the vessel ruptures and the time he loses consciousness. A diligent search by the pathologist will generally enable the exact point of bleeding to be defined. Cases of traumatic subarachnoid hemorrhage do occur, but are generally in the company of more characteristic subdural hemorrhage.

The brain is removed from the skull by cutting across the twelve cranial nerves at its base and across the upper cervical spinal cord with which it is continuous. In the hospital autopsy, the brain is generally hardened in a formaldehyde solution for two weeks before being sectioned and examined further. However, it is useful in the majority of medicolegal autopsies to make multiple coronal sections of the brain at the time of autopsy. This may aid greatly in the clarification of suspected head injuries, or may disclose a hemorrhage deep within the substance of the brain due to high blood pressure or other natural causes.

Traumatic hemorrhages are often found opposite the area that was directly exposed to trauma. These are called "contrecoup" injuries and in general terms result from the fact that the brain freely moves within its membranes and neurovascular attachments within the rigid cranial cavity. Identification and differentiation between coup and contrecoup injuries may be significant in determining whether an individual died from a fall or blows to the head.

At the base of the brain there extends downward a small stalk that is continuous with the pituitary gland. The gland itself sits within a bony case called the "sella turcica." The bones that comprise the base of the skull, after the dura has been stripped away, can be examined for any evidence of fracture or perforation. At this time the "foramen magnum," the hole at the base of the skull through which the spinal cord exits, is palpated and offers the pathologist an opportunity to evaluate the position and degree of integrity of the upper cervical vertebrae. These frequently become dislocated in traumatic injuries, and although not necessarily cutting into the spinal cord, may produce bleeding that can compress or bruise it. Both of these phenomena, when occurring in the upper portions of the spinal cord, may cause sudden death.

§ 32A.34. Eyes.

Should it be necessary to examine the eyes, the bony plate in the front of the skull may be removed and the globe of the eye examined and removed for further study. This procedure is especially indicated in cases of head injury in infants and children for the purpose of microscopic evaluation of retinal bleeding.

§ 32A.35. Examining the fetus and infant.

The postmortem examination of a fetus or newborn infant is a complicated procedure and frequently requires more time and study than a routine adult autopsy. In cases of a fetus or newborn infant, exact measurements of both length and weight must be ascertained. This is necessary to evaluate the gestational age. X-rays may be useful in displaying centers of ossification or centers of bone formation, which occur at well known intervals.

In an abandoned fetus or newborn infant, evidence of birth trauma must be searched for and evaluated. This may include subcutaneous edema (fluid accumulation) and hemorrhage of the scalp and tears in the meninges.

§ 32A.36. Exhumations.[15]

Often it becomes imperative to perform an autopsy on a body after it has been buried or to re-examine after burial a body that has previously been autopsied. In most areas of the country, a judicial order is required to do this. In some jurisdictions this is a simple procedure, in others rather complicated.

Generally, the procedural steps in exhuming a human body are as follows: (1) application containing the reason for the exumation is made to a court; (2) if the application is granted, a copy of the court order is sent to the cemetery, pathologist, undertaker, and any other persons whose presence may be required (*e.g.*, dentist, fingerprint expert, photographer, etc.); (3) notice is given to all other interested parties of the time and place of exhumation; (4) the autopsy is performed and the body is reburied; and (5) the results of the exhumation and autopsy are reported to the court.

Embalmed bodies that have been exhumed are generally satisfactory for an autopsy. Preservation is usually quite good, although it is dependent on a number of factors, namely: the thoroughness of the embalming

---

[15]Editor's Note: The terms "exhumation" and "disinterment" are used interchangeably and mean merely the removal of a body from the earth or burial vault.

procedures, the type of casket, the characteristics of the burial ground and whether a vault was used. It is not uncommon for bodies buried many years to reveal as much information on autopsy by an experienced forensic pathologist as would be elicited from a recently deceased individual. This is especially true in suspected poisonings because of sophisticated techniques now employed by the toxicologist; recovery and identification of lethal materials has been greatly enhanced despite the presence of embalming fluids. It is impossible to predict the value of an individual exhumation and examination, but the majority will provide satisfactory results.

Decomposed bodies in every case should be subjected to the most searching examination accompanied by a high index of suspicion. Although in many instances the examination of a decomposing, maggot-infested cadaver may be unpleasant, often the thorough forensic examiner will be rewarded by solving a case that to the uninitiated appeared impossible.

In civil and criminal cases, exhumations (disinterments) have proven valuable in determining:

1. Cause of death;
2. Manner of death (especially in a suspicious death, as in a murder disguised by a fire);
3. Identity or verification of identity of the body;
4. Cause of an accident in a civil case;
5. Presence of a natural disease;
6. Possibility of medical liability in a malpractice case;
7. Time of death (*e.g.*, in a civil proceeding to determine which spouse was the first to die); and
8. Possibility of child abuse.

Also, exhumations are used to collect forensic evidence such as bullet fragments and hair, and in some cases to make up for an inadequate postmortem examination by an inexperienced pathologist.

Once authority for an exhumation is obtained and the casket opened, the contents are photographed and the remains are removed and placed on the autopsy table. If the exhumation is for identification purposes, the body is measured, weight is estimated, and color and description of hair is documented. Fingerprints may remain. There may be a heavy growth of mold on the exposed parts of the body, and this may have to be scraped or rubbed off to reveal scars, tattoos, or birthmarks. All of this is documented. If the casket has not been tightly sealed, water may have caused some damage to a body that has not been properly embalmed, and there also may be damage from worms, insects, or small animals. The body should be cleaned.

Dental structures should be compared to the subject's dental charts, if available, and a forensic dentist should be called in if necessary. The dental region and other important parts of the body should be documented by X-ray. Any injuries, including skeletal damage, entry and exit wounds, and stabs and cuts should be documented and, if possible, identified as offensive or defensive in nature. X-rays should be taken to demonstrate such injuries and to detect the presence of any foreign objects, such as bullets, powder flakes, orthopedic prostheses, or traces of metal or grease (which would be important, for example, in a suspected hit-and-run case). If necessary, samples can be taken and toxicological tests run to uncover evidence of poison, carbon monoxide, or drugs.

§ 32A.37. Illustrative autopsy reports.

The following are two reports of autopsies (redacted for anonymity) performed at the Office of the Associate Chief Medical Examiner, Centralized Laboratory Facility, Frankfort, Kentucky.

Autopsy reports, whether based upon a hospital autopsy or an autopsy of an official medicolegal nature, appear in a variety of forms. However, they all should contain the same essential information: (1) a summary of background information, including the medical history of the deceased; (2) objective descriptions of the external body surfaces and major body cavities including the organs and structures therein; (3) results of relevant laboratory tests; (4) microscopic descriptions of selected tissues; (5) an outline of findings or diagnoses based upon the pathologist's investigation and review; and (6) a summarizing statement of the examiner's principal conclusions, which may be very brief or quite long, especially where there are hospital reports containing extensive clinicopathological correlation.

The medicolegal death investigation system in Kentucky is mixed: the major participants being (1) elected lay county coroners who authorize the official autopsy examination and (2) forensic pathologists who serve as appointed state medical examiners and perform the autopsies. Other jurisdictions may be either strictly coroner-based or have appointed medical examiners in which the relevant enabling law prescribes the lines and extent of investigative authority.

The first of the following autopsy reports involves the fatal shooting of a twenty-five-year-old man who was believed to have been involved in a street drug deal that "went bad." Here, the cause of death was not a central issue. Because of conflicting statements by eyewitnesses to the shooting, the critical questions concerned the range of fire of the firearm that caused the lethal injury and the direction of the multiple projectile paths. The second autopsy report concerns a sixty-year-old truck driver who was involved in a relatively minor collision and then died after a brief hospitalization. The key question in the death investigation was whether the man died from natural or accidental causes.

The findings in each report include anatomic diagnoses, a summary of investigative information, and results of laboratory analyses. The actual laboratory reports containing the signatures of the analysts and the chain of custody forms for evidentiary items are retained in the case file folder, where they are later made available for use in any subsequent legal proceedings.

COMMONWEALTH OF KENTUCKY
Justice Cabinet
OFFICE OF THE ASSOCIATE CHIEF MEDICAL EXAMINER
Centralized Laboratory Facility
100 Sower Boulevard - Suite 202
Frankfort, Kentucky 40601
(502) 564-4545

AUTOPSY REPORT   Case No.   ME-C 98-00-000

Name   Doe, Johnathan   Age   25   Race   Black   Sex   Male

Address   516 Average Street, Elsewhere, Kentucky

Pronounced

Date and Time of: Death   4:17 p.m.   3-XX-98   Autopsy   3-XX1-98   10:45 a.m. - 2:50 p.m.

Autopsy Authorized by: Mr. Earnest Quincy, Deputy Coroner, Elsewhere County

Identified by: Hospital Identification Labels

Prosector   Dr. ME Pathologist   Site of Examination: CLF, Frankfort, Ky.

Witnesses:

Detectives David Seeker and Tim Sleuth, Local P.D.

Autopsy Technician: Ms. Busy Assistant

CAUSE OF DEATH:	INTERNAL CERVICOTRUNCAL HEMORRHAGE AND CEREBRAL EDEMA
DUE TO:	PERFORATING PROJECTILE INJURIES OF THE MEDIASTINUM, UPPER LOBE OF LEFT LUNG, AND BRAIN
DUE TO:	MULTIPLE GUNSHOT WOUNDS OF THE HEAD AND NECK
ICD-9 CODE:	E 965.0

MANNER OF DEATH: _____ Natural Causes   _____ Accident   _____ Suicide

                       XXX Homicide   _____ Undetermined - Pending Investigation *

_____4/x/98_____   _UE Pathlgist_____ M.D.

Date Signed   Medical Examiner

See Conclusion, Page 4

MEDICAL EXAMINER PROGRAM - 1 (5/90)

DOE, JOHNATHAN
ME-C 98-00-000

COMMONWEALTH OF KENTUCKY
Justice Cabinet
OFFICE OF THE ASSOCIATE CHIEF MEDICAL EXAMINER
Centralized Laboratory Facility
100 Sower Boulevard - Suite 202
Frankfort, Kentucky 40601
(502) 564-4545

FINDINGS

I. **Investigative History:** Reported Altercation With Another Individual; Decedent Sustained "Gunshot Wounds to the Head and Neck. . . Reportedly Over a Drug Deal."

II. Multiple Gunshot Wounds.

    A. Gunshot wound perforating upper right ear and penetrating head, right postauricular temple (GSW "A") [indeterminate range through cloth garment].

        1. Perforations of upper right external ear, skull and brain.

        2. Acute subscalpular hemorrhage.

        3. Acute intracranial hemorrhage (subdural and subarachnoid).

        4. Basilar skull fracture, right parasagittal sphenoid bone.

        5. Brain swelling (1,560 gms.).

        6. Projectile recovery: left globus pallidus, cerebrum, brain.

    B. Penetrating gunshot wound of mid right lateral neck (GSW "B") [indeterminate range through cloth garments].

        1. Perforations of right anterolateral subcutaneous cervical muscle and blood vessels, upper trachea, mediastinum, upper lobe of left lung, and left anterolateral third intercostal muscle/vessels.

        2. Penetration with fracture, left anterolateral fourth rib.

        3. Cervical hematoma, large.

        4. Hemomediastinum.

        5. Left hemothorax (460 ml.).

-2-

DOE, JOHNATHAN
ME-C 98-00-000

FINDINGS - CONT.

    6.   Aspiration of bloody fluid, lower airways.

    7.   Visceral pallor, mild.

    8.   Projectile recovery: left anterolateral fourth rib.

  C.   Cutaneous graze wound, left facial temple, with perforation of upper left external ear (GSW "C") [intermediate range].

    1.   Cutaneous/subcutaneous laceration, left facial temple.

    2.   Perforating projectile wound, posterior left pinna.

    3.   Acute cutaneous contusions, lateral left upper/lower eyelids.

  D.   Penetrating gunshot wound of the face, posterior left preauricular cheek(GSW "D") [close range].

    1.   Perforations of left parotid gland, masseter muscle, maxillary and nasal sinuses.

    2.   Projectile recovery: subcutis, anterior right cheek.

III. Blunt Force Injuries of the Face: Multifocal Cutaneous Abrasions, Right Forehead and Right Periorbital Region.

IV. Status Post Brief CPR.

 V. Atherosclerosis, Aorta, Mild.

VI. Pulmonary Edema and Hyperemia, Mild (870 gms.).

-3-

DOE, JOHNATHAN
ME-C 98-00-000

COMMONWEALTH OF KENTUCKY
Justice Cabinet
OFFICE OF THE ASSOCIATE CHIEF MEDICAL EXAMINER
100 Sower Boulevard Suite 202
Frankfort, Kentucky 40601
(502) 564-4545

Recommended formulation for Parts I and II on Certification of Death:

25. TIME OF DEATH PRONOUNCED 4:17 p.m.	26. DATE PRONOUNCED DEAD *(Month, Day, Year)* 3-XX1-98	27. WAS CASE REFERRED TO MEDICAL EXAMINER/CORONER? *(Yes or No)* Yes

28. PART I. Enter the diseases, injuries, or complications that caused the death. Do not enter the mode of dying, such as cardiac or respiratory arrest, shock or heart failure. List only one cause on each line.		Approximate interval between onset and death
IMMEDIATE CAUSE (Final disease or condition resulting in death)	a. INTERNAL CERVICOTRUNCAL HEMORRHAGE AND CEREBRAL EDEMA DUE TO (OR AS A CONSEQUENCE OF)	_____
	b. PERFORATING PROJECTILE INJURIES OF THE MEDIASTINUM, UPPER LOBE OF LEFT LUNG, AND BRAIN DUE TO (OR AS A CONSEQUENCE OF)	_____
Sequentially list conditions, if any, leading to immediate cause. Enter UNDERLYING CAUSE (Disease or injury that initiated events resulting in death) LAST	c. MULTIPLE GUNSHOT WOUNDS OF THE HEAD AND NECK DUE TO (OR AS A CONSEQUENCE OF)	Minutes
	d. _____ DUE TO (OR AS A CONSEQUENCE OF)	_____

PART II. Other significant conditions contributing to death but not resulting in the underlying cause given in Part I	28a. WAS AUTOPSY PERFORMED? (Yes or No) YES	28b. WERE AUTOPSY FINDINGS AVAILABLE PRIOR TO COMPLETION OF CAUSE OF DEATH (Yes or No) YES

29. MANNER OF DEATH		30a. DATE OF INJURY 3-XX1-98	30b. TIME OF INJURY Abt. 3:30 p.m.	30c. INJURY AT WORK (Yes or No) No	30d. DESCRIBE HOW INJURY OCCURRED Shot by Another Person
❑ Natural	❑ Pending Investigation				
❑ Accident	❑ Could not be determined	30e. PLACE OF INJURY At home, farm, street, factory, office building, etc. (Specify) Home		30f. LOCATION (street and number or Rural Route number, City or Town) 516 Average Street, Elsewhere, Kentucky	
❑ Suicide					
XⓍX Homicide					

[Portion of FORM V.S. NO. 1-A (Rev. 9/88)]

CONCLUSION

In my opinion, Mr. Doe died as a result of internal cervicotruncal hemorrhage and cerebral edema due to perforating projectile injuries of the mediastinum, upper lobe of left lung, and brain due to multiple gunshot wounds of the head and neck.

Brief investigative history supplied by Deputy Coroner E. Quincy is summarized on the "Findings" sheet.

The principal findings at necropsy, to which the decedent's death is attributed, consisted of multiple gunshot wounds of the head and neck. All changes referable thereto are catalogued on the "Findings" sheet and detailed in the appended autopsy protocol.

In addition to those traumatic changes, there were patchy cutaneous abrasions on the right upper half of the side of the face.

No significant underlying natural disease was present.

Postmortem toxicology: see separately attached report.

-4-

DOE, JOHNATHAN
ME-C 98-00-000

CLOTHING EXAMINATION: When first viewed, the decedent's nude body is received in a white body bag to which a hospital identification tag with the decedent's name and identifying data is tied. The body is covered by a white blanket and overlies a white cloth sheet. Several blue/white paper chucks, focally blood-soaked, are present in the large bag as well.

Delivered at the early stages of the necropsy by Detective Tim Sleuth, Local P.D., are various items of clothing including the following upper garments: 1] green/black/brown camouflage-type jacket; and 2] black, hooded sweatshirt ("BIKE®"); both exhibit extensive resuscitation-related scissors cuts. On the posterolateral aspect of the right collar of the camouflage-type jacket there is a single, 3/16 inch in diameter perforation of cloth. On the right lower aspect of the hood of the black sweatshirt there are four, separate perforations of cloth, all measuring slightly less than 1/4 inch in diameter. [see attached clothing diagrams.]

After inspection and photography, these items are remanded to the custody of Detective Sleuth.

EVIDENCE OF THERAPY: A hospital identification bracelet with the decedent's name and identifying data is around the right wrist, and a similar-appearing hospital identification tag is tied to the right great toe. A patent endotracheal tube is in situ, inserted through the right side of the mouth. An intravenous line is inserted percutaneously in the left antecubital fossa. Needle punctures are present at the following sites: one in the right lateral subclavian chest, one in the mid anterior right upper arm, and one in the right antecubital fossa.

AUTOPSY PROTOCOL:

The body is that of a well developed, well nourished moderately muscular adult black male, measuring 5 feet 6 1/4 inches and weighing 144 pounds (in body bag as received). His appearance is consistent with the reported age of 25 years.

INJURIES, INTERNAL AND EXTERNAL:

Multiple gunshot wounds of entry with associated internal tracks are noted to be present on the decedent's head and neck. Their features and paths are described in detail below. The listing below is for purposes of convenience only, not implying sequence of fire.

GUNSHOT WOUND PERFORATING UPPER RIGHT EAR AND PENETRATING HEAD, RIGHT POSTAURICULAR TEMPLE (GSW "A") [INDETERMINATE RANGE THROUGH CLOTH GARMENT]:

ENTRY: The inshoot wound of the right upper external ear is centered at a point 4 3/4 inches below the top of the head, 4 inches to the right of midline. The entrance wound on the outer aspect of the right external ear consists of a 3/16 inch in diameter circular perforation of skin with a hairline marginal abrasion collar and superficial laceration superiorly. No fouling is present. The projectile pierces the underlying cartilage, and exits on the superior aspect of the right external ear, creating a similar-appearing circular cutaneous defect with minimal marginal abrasion. The projectile enters the head by perforating the right upper postauricular hair-bearing temple, creating a 1/8 inch in diameter circular perforation of skin with a fine circumferential marginal abrasion and a superficial marginal laceration directed posteriorly and superiorly.

DIRECTION OF TRACK: From entry, the gunshot wound track is directed from right to left, slightly upward, and minimally from back to front.

-5-

DOE, JOHNATHAN
ME-C 98-00-000

BODY STRUCTURES INVOLVED: After perforating the skin/subcutis, the projectile enters the cranial cavity by perforating the upper aspect of the right squamous temporal bone, creating a 1/4 inch in diameter perforation of skull with internal beveling. After perforating the subjacent dura mater, it traverses the brain by perforating the right middle and inferior temporal gyri, creating a gaping hemorrhagic track of laceration with pulpifaction on the undersurface of the right temporal lobe, crossing the midline above the optic chiasm and coming to rest within the left globus pallidus, cerebrum.

EXIT: None present.

PROJECTILE RECOVERY: A mangled, mushroomed small gray metal slug with copper-colored wash is recovered from the point of final lodgment noted above. The base is concave. It is placed in an appropriately labeled envelope and delivered to the custody of Detective T. Sleuth at 2:40 p.m. on 3-XX1-98.

SECONDARY EFFECTS: In addition to the changes noted above, there is acute subscalpular hemorrhage on the right side. Small amounts of thinly layered and fluid acute subdural hemorrhage accumulate over the cerebral convexities. There is mild acute generalized subarachnoid hemorrhage. A hairline basilar skull fracture with osseous hemorrhage is present on the right parasagittal sphenoid bone. A focal light blue/green cutaneous contusion occupies the medial aspect of the right lower eyelid. The brain is moderately swollen and edematous, weighing 1,560 gms. and characterized by generalized flattening of the cerebral gyri and narrowing of the structures in the region of the basilar cisterns.

PENETRATING GUNSHOT WOUND OF MID RIGHT LATERAL NECK (GSW "B") [INDETERMINATE RANGE THROUGH CLOTH GARMENTS]:

ENTRY: The inshoot wound of the mid right lateral neck is centered at a point 7 3/4 inches below the top of the head, 3 3/4 inches to the right of midline. It consists of a 1/8 inch in diameter circular perforation of skin with a slightly eccentric marginal abrasion directed posteriorly and superiorly. No fouling is present.

DIRECTION OF TRACK: From entry, the internal wound track is directed from right to left, back to front, and moderately downward, in that the projectile comes to rest at a point 7 inches below the wound of entry.

BODY STRUCTURES INVOLVED: After perforating the skin/subcutis, the projectile creates a hemorrhagic track of laceration through the subcutaneous musculature including the sternocleidomastoid muscle and right lateral cervical musculature. It courses posterior to the right jugular vein and common carotid artery. It next perforates the proximal trachea, on the right side at a point 1 3/4 inches and on the left side 2 inches distal to the glottis. It perforates the structures of the anterior mediastinum and enters the left pleural cavity, perforating the apex and mid segment of the anterior surface of the left upper lobe of the lung at three locations. Exiting the lung, the projectile next perforates twice the left third anterolateral intercostal muscle/vessels, and comes to rest by penetrating with fracture the left anterolateral fourth rib.

EXIT: None present.

PROJECTILE RECOVERY: Recovered from the point of final lodgment is a similar-appearing metal projectile, dented on one side. It is similarly packaged and delivered.

DOE, JOHNATHAN
ME-C 98-00-000

SECONDARY EFFECTS: In addition to the changes noted above, large amounts of clotted and fluid blood invest the anterolateral cervical musculature. A prominent hemomediastinum is present. A measured 460 ml. of clotted bloody fluid are recovered from the left pleural cavity. Small amounts of bloody fluid accumulate within the distal trachea and the branching bronchial tree bilaterally. All major viscera are slightly pale.

CUTANEOUS GRAZE WOUND, LEFT FACIAL TEMPLE, WITH PERFORATION OF UPPER LEFT EXTERNAL EAR (GSW "C") [INTERMEDIATE RANGE]:

ENTRY: The inshoot wound is centered at a point 5 inches below the top of the head, 2 1/2 inches to the left of midline. It consists of a deep cutaneous "gutter wound" of skin in the left facial temple. The defect is oblong, and oriented obliquely inferiorly to the left; it measures 1 3/8 inches long by up to 1/2 inch wide posteriorly. On the mid and lateral aspect of the left upper eyelid and lateral orbital area there is a confluent light blue/green cutaneous contusion; peppered within the contusion and in the left posterior orbital area are patchy punctate and slightly larger dark brown cutaneous abraded contusions, compatible with powder stippling. The overall array of stippling defects measures 1 1/4 inches transversely by 1 3/8 inches longitudinally. Light green contusions are also present on the medial aspect of the left upper eyelid and on the inferior left eyelid

At the posterior aspect of the gutter wound, region of upper left pinna, there is a 5/16 inch in diameter perforation of subcutaneous tissue.

Separated from the anterior/inferior margin of the graze wound anteriorly by a small bridge of intact epidermis, there is a 1/4 inch in diameter oval laceration of skin. Inferior to that defect, on the left posterior cheek there is a 7/16 inch long transverse linear abrasion.

DIRECTION OF TRACK: The graze wound is directed from front to back, minimally from right to left, and slightly downward.

BODY STRUCTURES INVOLVED: The projectile after grazing the left temple perforates the upper posterior aspect of the left external ear.

PROJECTILE RECOVERY: None.

EXIT: The outshoot wound is centered at a point 5 1/4 inches below the top of the head, 2 9/16 inches to the left of midline. It consists of an irregular laceration of skin measuring 1/4 inch in diameter with circumferential dark blue cutaneous contusion.

PENETRATING GUNSHOT WOUND OF THE FACE, POSTERIOR LEFT PREAURICULAR CHEEK (GSW "D") [CLOSE RANGE]:

ENTRY: The inshoot wound of the posterior left preauricular cheek is centered at a point 6 1/2 inches below the top of the head, 2 1/2 inches to the left of midline. It consists of a 1/16 inch in diameter circular perforation of skin. Deposited at the margin of the defect is a corona of black foreign material, having an overall diameter of 1/2 inch. Also present at the margin of the wounds are patchy punctate dark maroon cutaneous contusions, compatible with powder stippling.

-7-

DOE, JOHNATHAN
ME-C 98-00-000

DIRECTION OF TRACK: From entry, the internal wound track is directed from left to right, back to front, and slightly upward.

BODY STRUCTURES INVOLVED: After perforating the skin/subcutis, the projectile perforates the underlying parotid gland and left masseter muscle, without striking the mandible. It creates a hemorrhagic track of fracture through the left maxillary sinus, the posterior nasal bones, and the right maxillary sinus, coming to rest below the skin in the right mid lateral cheek.

EXIT: None present.

PROJECTILE RECOVERY: A subcutaneous palpable bullet is present on the right mid lateral cheek, centered at a point 6 inches below the top of the head and 2 inches to the right of midline. It underlies a 1/4 inch in diameter brown rectangular cutaneous abrasion. A distorted, mushroomed projectile, similar in appearance to those previously described, is placed in an appropriately labeled enveloped and delivered, as above.

SECONDARY EFFECTS: There is intrasinusoidal hemorrhage of the mid face, associated with bloody fluid distributed through the upper and lower respiratory tract to the branching bronchial tree bilaterally; sections of both lungs exhibit a patchy aspiration pattern characterized by hemorrhagic macules.

No other gunshot-related traumata or sequelae thereof are noted. The above changes, having been mentioned once, will not be repeated below.

BLUNT FORCE INJURIES OF THE HEAD:

A composite cluster of linear parallel, obliquely oriented (inferior/posterior) cutaneous abrasions is present on the right lateral forehead, and right periorbital region. The individual brown/red cutaneous abrasions range in diameter from punctate up to 1 inch long. Underlying facial bones in these regions are intact.

No other blunt force injuries are noted. The above changes, having been mentioned once, will not be repeated below.

EXTERNAL EXAMINATION:

HEAD: The scalp is fully covered by black hair, arranged in a corn row pattern, and has tails posteriorly measuring up to 1 1/2 inches long. Two needle punctures are present in the left ear lobule, and one in the right. The irides are brown; pupils are equal, measuring 5 mm. in diameter bilaterally. The conjunctivae are pale white. Small amounts of bloody fluid accumulate within the nares and oral cavity. The dentition is natural, intact and in good repair; two gold-colored metal rims are present on the left central and lateral maxillary incisors, respectively. There are no lacerations/contusions of the tan smooth glistening mucosa of the lips and oral cavity. A sparse mustache is present together with a sparse goatee and focal clusters of facial hair on the posterior cheeks bilaterally.

NECK: No scars or false mobility.

CHEST: Symmetrical, moderately muscular, and normally developed. No notable scars/recent trauma.

ABDOMEN: Flat and minimally taut. No scars/recent trauma.

-8-

DOE, JOHNATHAN
ME-C 98-00-000

EXTERNAL GENITALIA: The penis is circumcised; two testes are palpated in the scrotum.

UPPER EXTREMITIES: Symmetrical, moderately muscular, and normally developed. No notable scars or hesitation marks. No fouling is noted on the forearms or hands. Fingernail beds are gray, and all nails are intact, moderately long, with patchy accumulations of dark brown and red subungual foreign material.

LOWER EXTREMITIES: Symmetrical, moderately muscular, and normally developed. Focal patches of hypopigmented skin are present in the mid anteromedial left thigh. A small cutaneous scar is present on the medial aspect of the right knee. A slightly raised and hyperpigmented 1/2 inch in diameter circular cutaneous scar is present on the upper anteromedial right thigh. No ankle edema present.

BACK: No scars/recent trauma.

Rigidity is complete, overcome with marked difficulty; minimal light violet lividity is present posteriorly with blanching at pressure points.

INTERNAL EXAMINATION:

The abdominal panniculus measures 1/4 inch thick. No aromatic odor is noted in the tissues.

MESOTHELIAL SURFACES: Smooth and glistening. There are no abnormal fluid accumulations in the peritoneal or right pleural cavities. Pericardial sac with smooth glistening lining contains a measured 8 ml. of clear serous fluid.

HEART: Weight: 315 gms. Intact. Epicardial surfaces are smooth and glistening with mild focal fat. Extramural coronary arteries: normal distribution and wide patency. Foramen ovale is closed. Endocardial surfaces are smooth and glistening; there is mild light red acute subendocardial hemorrhage within the left ventricle. The cardiac valves are intact and freely flexible, free of vegetations with normal coaptation. Rare atheromas within the aortic valvular sinuses of Valsalva. Myocardium, light red/brown and firm, is free of fibrosis/hemorrhage, measuring 1.1 cm. in thickness concentrically in the left ventricle and 0.4 cm. in the right. The intact aorta exhibits mild atherosclerosis characterized by patchy atheromatous streaks and atheromas extending from the arch to the abdominal segment. All major branches are widely patent.

LUNGS: Combined weight: 870 gms. Except for trauma noted previously, pleural surfaces are smooth and glistening, light pink anterolaterally and livid posteriorly with mild anthracotic pigmentation. Pulmonary arteries and veins arise and branch normally with wide patency. Cut surfaces of the mainstem bronchi are patent, oozing small amounts of bloody fluid; mucosal lining is smooth and glistening. On section, the lungs are subcrepitant, light red on the left side and maroon on the right side in areas free of trauma, oozing moderate amounts of edema fluid with compression; hyperemia is generalized and moderate. There is no evidence of masses or consolidation. Hilar and mediastinal lymph nodes exhibit mild anthracosis without masses.

NECK ORGANS: Gunshot-related trauma is noted above. The lumen of the airway is subtotally occluded by bloody fluid and clot, which extends from the posterior oral cavity via larynx and trachea to the carina; mucosal lining is otherwise smooth and glistening. Bony and other cartilaginous structures of the neck are intact. The thyroid gland, of normal size and shape, exhibits uniformly light tan/red colloid. There are no fractures of the cervical vertebrae. The tongue is free of lacerations/contusions.

GASTRO-INTESTINAL TRACT: Intact. The esophagus contains small amounts of gastric contents. The stomach, prominently distended by gas, contains a measured 50 ml. of dark green mucoid chyme with light tan/white bits of food material, not otherwise identified. No pills, capsules or tablets are identified. Mucosa is intact with normal rugae. Duodenum contains dark green mucoid chyme. Vermiform appendix is present. Remainder of the gastro-intestinal tract is unremarkable.

-9-

DOE, JOHNATHAN
ME-C 98-00-000

LIVER: Weight: 1,500 gms. The light brown/red capsular surfaces are smooth and glistening. The margins are sharp and, on section, the parenchyma is of the same color and firm, free of fibrosis, hemorrhage or tumor. The gallbladder contains a measured 4 ml. of brown/yellow fluid bile without calculi. The hepatobiliary tree courses normally and is widely patent. Lymph nodes, porta hepatis are not enlarged.

SPLEEN: Weight: 70 gms. The slate gray capsular surfaces are smooth and glistening. On section, the firm parenchyma is uniformly maroon with easily identifiable white pulp.

ADRENAL GLANDS: Weight: 14 gms. The organs are of normal size and shape and, on section, exhibit a golden yellow cortex and brown/gray medulla.

PANCREAS: The coarsely lobulated structure is light tan/brown.

KIDNEYS: Combined weight: 260 gms. The capsules strip with ease exhibiting smooth glistening cortical surfaces. On section, the organs are light brown/red and firm, with cortices measuring 0.8 cm. thick, well-defined corticomedullary junctions, and unremarkable pelvocalyceal systems. Renal arteries and veins: UNK.

URETERS AND URINARY BLADDER: The patent ureters course normally with smooth glistening urothelium. The urinary bladder contains a measured 50 ml. of clear light yellow urine. Mucosal lining is smooth and glistening.

INTERNAL GENITALIA: The prostate gland is round, smooth, firm and not enlarged. Multiple coronal sections exhibit no focal abnormality.

SKELETAL SYSTEM: Except for gunshot-related fractures noted previously, the appendicular and axial skeleton is intact and unremarkable.

HEAD: Brain weight: 1,560 gms. Gunshot-related craniocerebral trauma is noted above. There is no evidence of epidural hemorrhage. Leptomeninges are thin and glistening. Cerebral convexities have normally formed convolutions. The vessels at the base of the brain, in the circle of Willis, arise and branch normally and are widely patent. Multiple coronal sections of the brain disclose no other focal abnormalities. The organ is firm. The pituitary gland is of normal size, shape, and appearance.

TOXICOLOGY: Samples of heart blood, urine, bile, vitreous humour, bilateral nasal swabs, all of the gastric contents, and bloody fluid from the left chest cavity are submitted to the Toxicology Laboratory, Cabinet for Health Services, Frankfort, Kentucky, for blood alcohol and drug screen.

SPECIAL STUDIES: A sample of vitreous humour is submitted for ASTRA-6. Heart blood is retained on a DNA card.

ADDITIONAL EVIDENCE COLLECTION: A sample of heart blood is placed on a DNA blot card. Bilateral fingernail clippings/scrapings are collected at the start of the necropsy. The firearms residue test of both hands is completed at the same time. All these items are appropriately labeled, packaged, and delivered to the custody of Detective Sleuth at 2:40 p.m. on 3-XX1-98.

-10-

DOE, JOHNATHAN
ME-C 98-00-000

COMMONWEALTH OF KENTUCKY
Justice Cabinet
OFFICE OF THE ASSOCIATE CHIEF MEDICAL EXAMINER
Centralized Laboratory Facility
100 Sower Boulevard - Suite 202
Frankfort, Kentucky 40601
(502) 564-4545

MICROSCOPIC DESCRIPTION

CARDIOVASCULAR

HEART (1 H & E), LEFT VENTRICLE:	Focal acute subendocardial hemorrhage
CORONARY ARTERIES (2 H & E):	No pathologic change (NPC)
AORTA, ABDOMINAL (1 H & E):	Mild atherosclerosis
LUNGS (3 H & E):	Acute intra-alveolar, subpleural, and intrabronchiolar hemorrhage
LIVER (1 H & E):	NPC
SPLEEN (1 H & E):	NPC
PANCREAS (1 H & E):	NPC
KIDNEY (2 H & E):	NPC
PROSTATE GLAND (1 H & E):	NPC
TESTIS (1 H & E):	NPC
ADRENAL GLANDS (1 H & E):	NPC
THYROID GLAND (1 H & E):	Acute periglandular hemorrhage
CENTRAL NERVOUS SYSTEM	
PITUITARY GLAND (1 H & E):	Acute subarachnoid hemorrhage
LEFT SUPERIOR FRONTAL GYRUS, CEREBRUM (1 H & E):	Perineuronal clearing consistent with interstitial edema
RIGHT MIDDLE TEMPORAL GYRUS, CEREBRUM (MARGIN OF GUNSHOT WOUND ENTRY (1 H & E):	Hemorrhagic laceration
PONS & MEDULLA (1 H & E):	NPC

GUNSHOT ENTRY WOUNDS:

"C," AT LEFT LATERAL EYEBROW (1 H & E):	Cutaneous abrasions with focally imbedded foreign material consistent with powder grains; acute cutaneous hemorrhage
"D," LEFT CHEEK AT MARGIN (1 H & E):	Hemorrhagic laceration of skin and subcutis with patchy carbon deposition on epidermis and within subcutaneous track

DOE, JOHNATHAN
ME-C 98-00-000

COMMONWEALTH OF KENTUCKY
Justice Cabinet
OFFICE OF THE ASSOCIATE CHIEF MEDICAL EXAMINER
Centralized Laboratory Facility
100 Sower Boulevard - Suite 202
Frankfort. Kentucky 40601
(502) 564-4545

LABORATORY RESULTS

CRIMINALISTICS:

    Serology: Not requested
    DNA: Not requested
    Firearms Residue Test, Hands: Negative for Antimony, Barium, Lead, and Copper
    Fingernail Clippings/Scrapings: All nails were intact. Traces of dirt and blood were identified in the
        outer and inner surfaces of most nails

CHEMISTRIES – VITREOUS HUMOUR:

    Sodium: 139 mmol/L
    Potassium: 8.7 mmol/L
    Chloride: 121 mmol/L
    Glucose: < 20 mg/dL
    Urea Nitrogen: 8 mg/dL
    Creatinine: 1.1 mg/dL

TOXICOLOGY

    Blood – Heart   Vitreous Humour

        Ethyl alcohol: 0.073 gm/100 ml.   Ethyl alcohol: 0.070 gm/100 ml.
        Cocaine: < 0.03 mg/L
        Dextromethorphan: < 0.05 mg/L

    Bloody Fluid – Chest   Nasal Swabs

        Ethyl alcohol: 0.80 gm/100 ml.   Negative for Cocaine

    Urine:

        Benzoylecgonine
        Cannabinoids

    Bile:

        Ethyl alcohol: 0.176 gm/100 ml.

COMMONWEALTH OF KENTUCKY
DEPARTMENT OF JUSTICE
OFFICE OF THE ASSOCIATE CHIEF MEDICAL EXAMINER

Name: DOE, JONATHAN   Case No: ME-C 98-00-000

Race: B   Age: 25   Date: 3-XXI-98

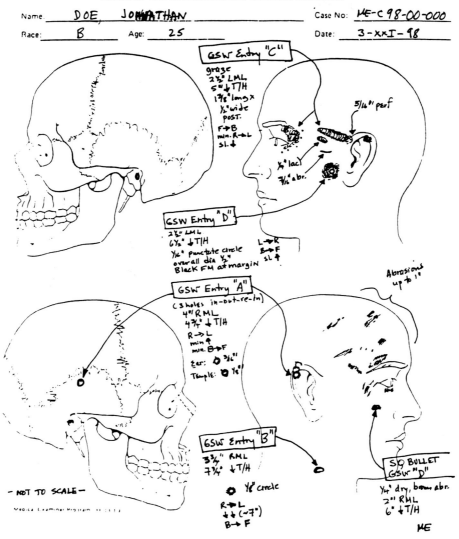

GSW Entry "C"
graze
2½" LML
5" ↓ T/H
1⅞" long x
½" wide
post.
F→B
min. R→L
sl. ↓

5/16" perf

¼" lac)
7/16" abr.

GSW Entry "D"
2⅝" LML
6½" ↓ T/H
7/16" punctate circle
overall dia ½"
Black FM at margin

L→R
B→F
sl. ↓

GSW Entry "A"
(3 holes in-out-re-in)
4" RML
4¾" ↓ T/H
R→L
min ↑
min. B→F
ear: ⊘ 3/16"
Temple: ⊘ ⅛"

Abrasions
up to 1"

GSW Entry "B"
3¾" RML
7¾" ↓T/H

⊘ ⅛" circle

R→L
↓↓ (~7°)
B→F

S/O BULLET
GSW "D"
¼" dry, brown abr.
2" RML
6" ↓T/H

ME

- NOT TO SCALE -

Medical Examiner Program

COMMONWEALTH OF KENTUCKY
DEPARTMENT OF JUSTICE
OFFICE OF THE ASSOCIATE CHIEF MEDICAL EXAMINER

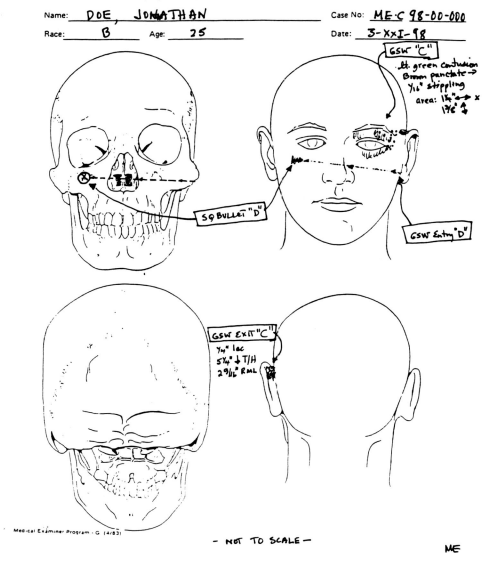

Name: DOE, JONATHAN   Case No: ME·C 98-00-000

Race: B   Age: 25   Date: 3-XxI-98

GSW "C"
lt. green contusion
Brown punctate →
Y₁₆" stippling
area: 1¼" → x
1⅜" ↑

S9 Bullet "D"

GSW Entry "D"

GSW Exit "C"
Y₄" lac
5¼" ↓ T/H
29¾" RML

Medical Examiner Program - G (4/83)

– NOT TO SCALE –

ME

580

COMMONWEALTH OF KENTUCKY
DEPARTMENT OF JUSTICE
OFFICE OF THE ASSOCIATE CHIEF MEDICAL EXAMINER

Name: _DOE, JOHNATHAN_   Case No: _MEC 98-00-000_

Race: _B_   Age: _25_   Date: _3-XXI-98_

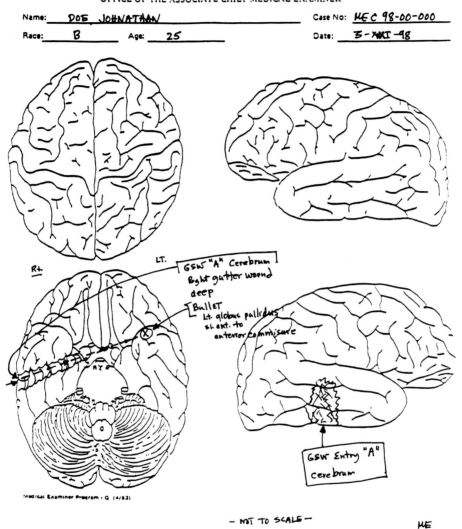

GSW "A" Cerebrum
Right gutter wound
deep

Bullet
Lt. globus pallidus
sl. ant. to
anterior commisure

GSW Entry "A"
cerebrum

Medical Examiner Program - Q (4/83)

— NOT TO SCALE —   ME

COMMONWEALTH OF KENTUCKY
DEPARTMENT OF JUSTICE
OFFICE OF THE ASSOCIATE CHIEF MEDICAL EXAMINER

Name: DOE, JOHNATHAN Case No: MEC 98-00-000

Race: B Age: 25 Date: 3-XXI-98

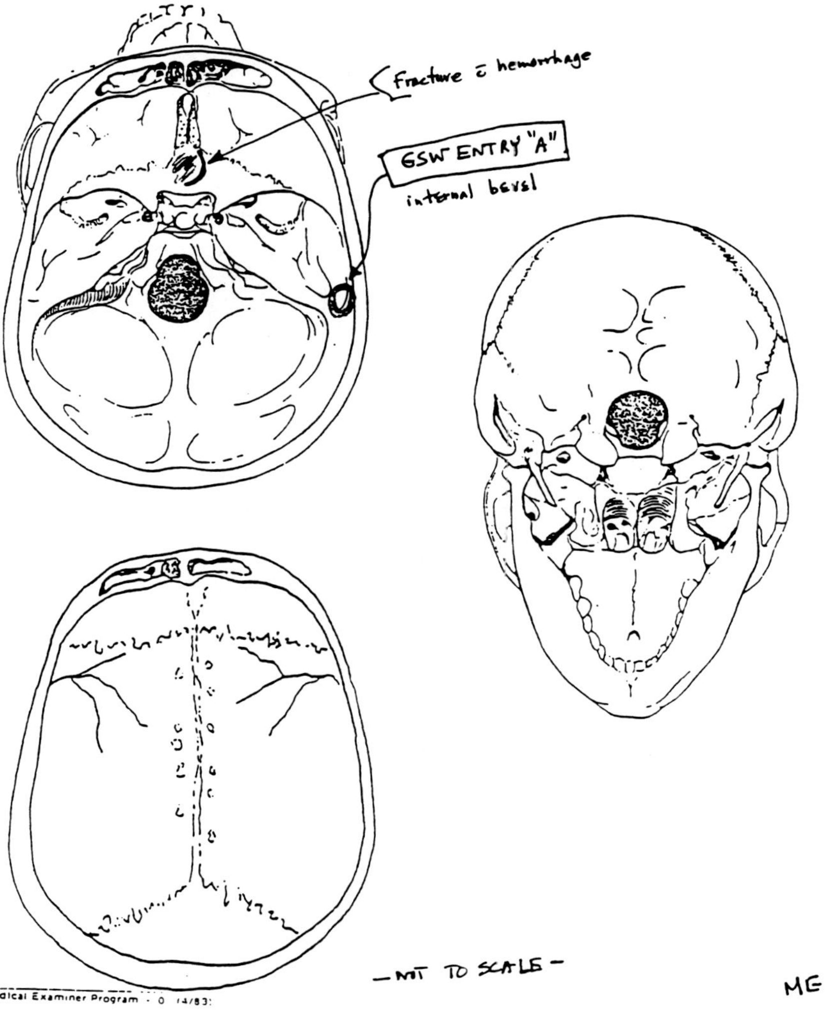

Fracture c̄ hemorrhage
GSW ENTRY "A"
internal bevel

— NOT TO SCALE —

Medical Examiner Program ... (4/83)

ME

COMMONWEALTH OF KENTUCKY
DEPARTMENT OF JUSTICE
OFFICE OF THE ASSOCIATE CHIEF MEDICAL EXAMINER

Name: DOE, JOHNATHAN   Case No: MEC 98-00-000

Race: B   Age: 25   Date: 3-XXI-98

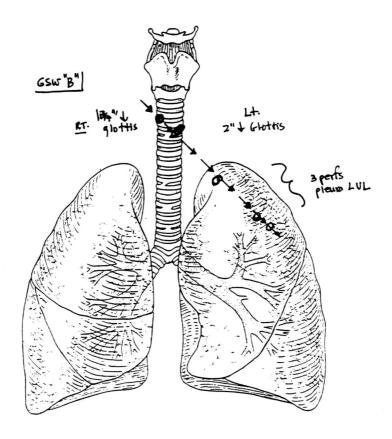

GSW "B"

RT. 1¾" ↓ glottis

Lt. 2" ↓ Glottis

3 perfs pleura LUL

Medical Examiner Program - NN (4/83)

— NOT TO SCALE —

ME

COMMONWEALTH OF KENTUCKY
DEPARTMENT OF JUSTICE
OFFICE OF THE ASSOCIATE CHIEF MEDICAL EXAMINER

Name: DOE, JOHNATHAN   Case No: MEC 98-00-000

Race: B   Age: 25   Date: 3-XXI-98

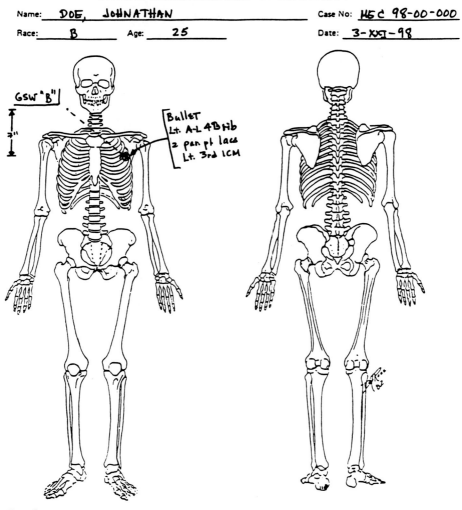

GSW "B"

7"

Bullet
Lt. A-L 4B rib
2 pen pt lacs
Lt. 3rd ICM

Medical Examiner Program - AA (4/83)

— NOT TO SCALE —

ME

584

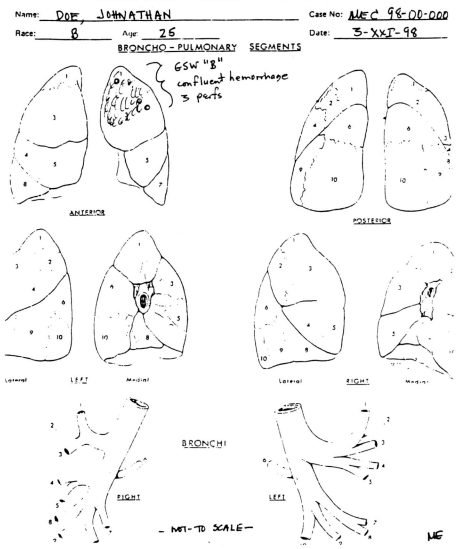

COMMONWEALTH OF KENTUCKY
DEPARTMENT OF JUSTICE
OFFICE OF THE ASSOCIATE CHIEF MEDICAL EXAMINER

Name: DOE, JOHNATHAN   Case No: MEC 98-00-000

Race: B   Age: 25   Date: 3-XXI-98

BRONCHO - PULMONARY SEGMENTS

GSW "B"
confluent hemorrhage
3 perfs

ANTERIOR

POSTERIOR

Lateral   LEFT   Medial

Lateral   RIGHT   Medial

BRONCHI

RIGHT

LEFT

— NOT-TO SCALE —

ME

COMMONWEALTH OF KENTUCKY
JUSTICE CABINET

OFFICE OF THE ASOCIATE CHIEF MEDICAL EXAMINER

NAME: DOE, JOHNATHAN   CASE No.: MEC 98-00-000

RACE: B   AGE: 25   DATE: 3-XXI-98

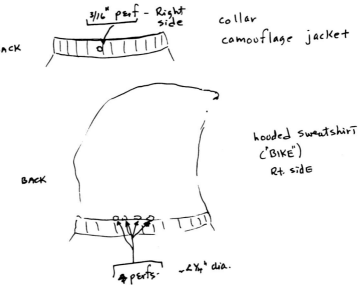

BACK   3/16" perf - Right side   collar
                                                camouflage jacket

BACK   hooded sweatshirt ("BIKE")
              Rt. side

              4 perfs. ~ <¼" dia.

CLOTHING c̄ BULLET HOLES

Medical Examiner Program – CE (4/83)
                    — NOT TO SCALE —

                                                ME

COMMONWEALTH OF KENTUCKY
Justice Cabinet
OFFICE OF THE ASSOCIATE CHIEF MEDICAL EXAMINER
100 Sower Boulevard Suite 202
Frankfort, Kentucky 40601
(502) 564-4545

AUTOPSY REPORT   Case No. ME 00-00-000

Name   Doe, John   Age 60   Race White   Sex Male

Address   123 Elsewhere Avenue, Anywhere, Kentucky

Pronounced
Date and Time of: Death   5:00 p.m. 10-XX-00   Autopsy   10-XXI-00   2:15 p.m. – 5:15 p.m.

Autopsy Authorized by   Mr. Vigorous Investigator, Deputy Coroner, Elsewhere County

Identified by: Hospital Identification Bracelet and Tag; Coroner's Identification Tag

Prosector: Dr. M.E. Pathologist   Site of Examination: CLF, ME Suite, Frankfort
Witnesses:

Deputy Coroner Investigator

Autopsy Technician: Ms. Busy Assistant

CAUSE OF DEATH: CEREBRAL INFARCTION (STROKE)

DUE TO: INTRAMURAL DISSECTION, AORTA (DEBAKEY TYPE I)

DUE TO: HYPERTENSIVE AND ATHEROSCLEROTIC CARDIOVASCULAR
DISEASE (SUDDEN COLLAPSE WHILE DRIVING MOTOR
VEHICLE)

ICD-9 CODES: 402.90; 414.0; 441.2; 442.82; 433.8

MANNER OF DEATH: XXX Natural Causes   ____ Accident   ____ Suicide
____ Homicide   ___ Undetermined - Pending Investigation *

___11/XXV/00___   ___M.E. Pathologist___ M.D.
Date Signed   Medical Examiner

See Conclusion, Page 5

DOE, JOHN
ME 00-00-000

COMMONWEALTH OF KENTUCKY
Justice Cabinet
OFFICE OF THE ASSOCIATE CHIEF MEDICAL EXAMINER
Centralized Laboratory Facility
100 Sower Boulevard - Suite 202
Frankfort, Kentucky 40601
(502) 564-4545

FINDINGS

I.   Summarized INVESTIGATIVE HISTORY: Tractor-Trailer Driver – Left Interstate Highway With Minor Roadside Impact (11:15 p.m.,10-XV-00); Reported History of Antecedent Chest Pain.

II.   Calcific Atherosclerotic and Hypertensive Cardiovascular Disease.

    A.   Aortic dissection with intramural hematoma, ascending aorta to arch (DeBakey Type I), with 40% stenosis of proximal right innominate artery.

    B.   Segmental atherosclerosis of all major extramural coronary arteries with multiple foci of critical (greater than 75%) stenosis.

    C.   Cardiomegaly, mild-moderate (465 gms.) with moderate concentric left ventricular myocardial hypertrophy.

    D.   Aorta, moderately severe; abdominal aortic aneurysm, distal, with small thrombus.

    E.   Arterial and arteriolonephrosclerosis.

    F.   Cerebrovascular atherosclerosis, multifocal, moderately severe

    G.   Hemorrhagic infarct, right frontal and parietal lobes, brain , recent (distribution of right middle cerebral artery).

III.   Floppy (Prolapsed) Mitral Valve, Both Leaflets, Mild (Grade I); Focal Endocardial Fibrosis; Subvalvular Posterior Mitral Valve Leaflet (Salizar Lesion).

IV.   Blunt Force Injuries.

    A.   Head.

        1.   Superficial cutaneous lacerations and contusions, right lateral eyebrow/orbit, healing.

        2.   Focal cutaneous contusion, right upper forehead.

        3.   Subdural hematoma, right cerebrum, brain, small, resolving.

        4.   Acute subarachnoid hemorrhage, right cerebrum, brain, mild.

2

FINDINGS – CONT.

    B.   Chest.

        1.   Focal cutaneous contusion, right lower lateral chest, resolving

        2.   Transverse fracture, right posterolateral 9th rib.

    C.   Extremities – Patchy cutaneous scabbed abrasions, left anterior upper arm and back of right hand.

V.   Status Post Brief Hospitalization (CH, 10-XV to 10-XX-00) With Development of Coma and Delayed Death:

    A.   Mini celiotomy (diagnostic peritoneal lavage), lower periumbilical region.

    B.   Mucosal edema, laryngeal aperture, associated with multifocal purulent mucosal ulcers, larynx and upper trachea (status post endotracheal intubation).

    C.   Patchy mucosal hyperemia, urinary bladder (status post foley catheterization).

    D.   Mucosal petechiae, fundus of stomach (? Nasogastric intubation).

    E.   Hypoxic encephalomalacia, brain (1,565 gms., fixed).

        1.   Cerebral edema, marked.

        2.   Herniation of right uncus.

        3.   Secondary (Duret) hemorrhages, midbrain and rostral pons.

    F.   Cutaneous decubitus ulcer, upper medial right buttock (Stage I).

VI.   Pulmonary Edema and Hyperemia, Marked (1,785 gms.).

VII.   Chronic Obstructive Pulmonary Disease.

    A.   Pulmonary centrilobular emphysema, bilateral, moderate-marked.

    B.   Anthracosis, pleurae and parenchyma of lungs, hilar and mediastinal lymph nodes, marked.

    C.   Subpleural apical bleb, right apex.

    D.   Increased A-P diameter, chest.

    E.   Atherosclerosis, proximal pulmonary arterial trunk, mild.

    F.   Concentric right ventricular myocardial hypertrophy, heart, mild.

VIII.   Congestive Hepatosplenomegaly, Moderate-Marked (Liver: 2,465 gms.; Spleen: 435 gms.).

3

DOE, JOHN
ME 00-00-000

FINDINGS—CONT.

IX.   Hemorrhagic Necrosis, Left Psoas Muscle, Marked, Diffuse.

X.   Diverticulosis Coli, Descending and Sigmoid Colon, Mild.

XI.   Nodular Hyperplasia, Prostate Gland, Mild.

4

DOE, JOHN
ME 00-00-000

COMMONWEALTH OF KENTUCKY
Justice Cabinet
OFFICE OF THE ASSOCIATE CHIEF MEDICAL EXAMINER
100 Sower Boulevard Suite 202
Frankfort, Kentucky 40601
(502) 564-4545

Recommended formulation for Parts I and II on Certification of Death:

25. TIME OF DEATH PRONOUNCED	26. DATE PRONOUNCED DEAD (Month, Day, Year)	27. WAS CASE REFERRED TO MEDICAL EXAMINER/CORONER? (Yes or No)
5:00 p.m.	10-XX-00	Yes

28 PART I Enter the diseases, injuries, or complications that caused death. Do not enter the mode of dying, such as cardiac or respiratory arrest, shock or heart failure. List only one cause on each line		Approximate interval between onset and death
IMMEDIATE CAUSE (Final disease or condition resulting in death)	a. CEREBRAL INFARCTION (STROKE)	DAYS
	DUE TO (OR AS A CONSEQUENCE OF)	
	b. INTRAMURAL DISSECTION, ASCENDING AORTA	DAYS
Sequentially list conditions if any leading to immediate cause Enter UNDERLYING CAUSE (Disease or injury that initiated events resulting in death) LAST	DUE TO (OR AS A CONSEQUENCE OF)	
	c. HYPERTENSIVE AND ATHERSCLEROTIC CARDIOVASCULAR DISEASE	YEARS
	DUE TO (OR AS A CONSEQUENCE OF)	
	d.	
	DUE TO (OR AS A CONSEQUENCE OF)	

PART II Other significant conditions contributed to death but not resulting in the underlying cause given in Part I	28a. WAS AUTOPSY PERFORMED?	28b. WERE AUTOPSY FINDINGS AVAILABLE PRIOR TO COMPLETION OF DEATH (Yes or No)
	Yes	Yes

29. MANNER OF DEATH		30a. DATE OF INJURY	30b. TIME OF INJURY	30c. INJURY AT WORK (Yes or No)	30d. DESCRIBE HOW INJURY OCCURRED
XX Natural	☐ Pending Investigation				
☐ Accident		30e. PLACE OF INJURY - At home, farm, street, factory, office building, etc. (Specify)		30f. LOCATION (street and number or Rural Route number. City or Town)	
☐ Suicide	☐ Could not be determined				
☐ Homicide					

[Portion of FORM V.S. NO. 1-A (Rev. 9-88)]

CONCLUSION

In my opinion, Mr. Doe died as a result of cerebral infarction (stroke) due to intramural dissection, aorta (DeBakey Type I) due to be hypertensive and cardiovascular disease (sudden collapse while driving motor vehicle).

According to Deputy Coroner Investigator and review of the decedent's medical records from Charity Hospital, Elsewhere, Kentucky and various records supplied by Mr. Ima Barrister, Attorney at Law, Elsewhere, Kentucky, the decedent was driving a tractor-trailer on Interstate US in Elsewhere County, during the late evening hours of 10-XV-00. At around 11:15 p.m. on that date he was noted to be driving erratically following which he left the roadway with apparent minor impact of the truck against roadside objects. Paramedics were called to the scene, instituting CPR and delivering the decedent to the ER of CH, with formal admission shortly after midnight on that date.

5

CONCLUSION – CONT.

On initial assessment he was noted to be hypotensive and diagnostic peritoneal lavage yielded bloody fluid. Neurologically, he was awake but confused, demonstrating a left hemiplegia. Both eyes were noted to deviate to the right. Drug screen taken during initial assessment yielded no drugs present. Emergency CT scan of the head showed questionable evidence of fluid collection in the right frontal area without shift of midline structures, findings possibly representing an infarct in the distribution of the right middle cerebral artery. A computed tomographic (CT) scan of the head within 24 hours of admission then demonstrated findings consistent with hemorrhagic infarct in that distribution. including the anterior cerebral arterial territory as well, associated with shift of midline structures from right to left. Abdominal CT scan showed evidence of aneurysmal dilatation of the abdominal aorta, free of evidence of retroperitoneal hemorrhage. On the day of admission bilateral carotid arteriography was carried out via the right transfemoral approach and showed essentially no abnormalities. A dynamic CT scan of the chest on that date was unremarkable with a specific note that there was no evidence to suggest aortic dissection. Serial chest X-rays on that day of admission showed essentially unremarkable findings, with a minimally displaced fracture of the right posterolateral ninth rib. A subsequent peritoneal tap on 10-XVI was reported "negative" in contrast to an earlier one reported as "positive." By 8:30 p.m. on 10-XVI he experienced an abrupt change in mental status with less responsiveness. That evening he experienced an episode of cyanosis and apnea, requiring resuscitation. Thereafter he became progressively obtunded. He remained in coma, experiencing progressive cardiopulmonary deterioration and dying with formal pronouncement of death at 5:00 p.m. on 10-XX-00. slightly less than 5 days after the vehicular mishap.

Past medical history was remarkable for systemic hypertension, which was treated pharmacologically with Lopressor®, hyperlipidemia, glaucoma, diverticulosis, and Chronic Obstructive Pulmonary Disease. In 3-00 he underwent evacuation of a hematoma of the abdominal wall. Evaluation of recurrent headaches ten years prior to death culminated in excision of a right sphenoid mucocele (sphenoidectomy) together with excision of a right frontal sinus mucocele. Also reported was a history of fairly regular, "heavy" ethyl alcohol consumption.

The principal findings at necropsy, to which decedent's death is attributed, involved the cardiovascular and central nervous system. Specifically, there was a dissecting mural hematoma of the ascending aorta (DeBakey Type I), a process which extended to involve the proximal right innominate artery, leading to approximately 40% stenosis in that region. Associated with that change was a complication of such stenosis, mainly hemorrhagic infarction of portions of the right cerebral hemisphere. [**COMMENT**: systemic hypertension is the most common underlying and predisposing factor for such an event. His clinical presentation is consistent with the notion that the full extent of the dissection had not occurred immediately after the motor vehicular mishap or during the early stages of evaluation. but within less than 24 hours after hospital admission, associated with the acute change in mental status. Clinical findings suggest that there was some degree of compromise, less severe, prior to that time. The clinical history of chest pain shortly prior to his leaving the roadway suggests that the acute process probably started at that time, however]. All such changes regarding this condition are catalogued on the "Findings" sheet and detailed in the appended autopsy protocol.

Various forms of blunt force injuries were noted, externally and internally, most prominently involving the head region, but none of these injuries, which consisted of a small right cerebral subdural hematoma and subarachnoid hemorrhage, was sufficient to account for his death directly. Of course, the stress associated with such trauma may have induced elevated blood pressure so as to contribute to the aortic dissection.

Also catalogued and detailed are various forms of changes due to therapy and various types of minor natural disease involving various organ systems.

Postmortem toxicology was negative.

6

DOE, JOHN
ME 00-00-000

REFERENCES:

1. DeSanctis, RW, Doroghazi, RM, Austen, WG, and Buckley, MJ. Aortic dissection [medical progress]. N Engl J Med 1987: 317(17); 1060-1067.

2. Prahlow, JA, Barnard, JJ, Milewicz. Familial thoracic aortic aneurysms and dissections. J Forensic Sci 1998: 43(6); 1244-1249.

7

DOE, JOHN
ME 00-00-000

CLOTHING EXAMINATION: None present with body. When first viewed, the decedent's nude body is received in a white body bag to which a Coroner's identification tag with the decedent's name and identifying data is tied.

EVIDENCE OF THERAPY: Two hospital identification bracelets with the decedent's name and imprint are on the left wrist, and a hospital identification tag with similar imprint is tied to the left great toe.

Needle punctures are present at the following sites: right subclavian region, one each in the right and left antecubital fossae, scabbed punctate defects on the back of the left hand and one in the right inguinal region with light green/blue ecchymoses. A ½ inch long longitudinal cutaneous surgical incision is present in the lower abdomen, in the midline below the umbilicus.

Internally, there is mild submucosal edema within the laryngeal aperture, associated with multifocal punctate and slightly larger mucosal ulceration with gray/green exudate in the ulcer beds, involving the mid epiglottis, associated with patchy mucosal hyperemia (status post endotracheal intubation). There is patchy mucosal hyperemia of the urinary bladder (status post foley catheterization). Patchy punctate and slightly larger mucosal "suction" hemorrhages are present within the fundus and proximal body of the stomach (? status post nasogastric intubation). At necropsy, no tubing is in situ.

Within the upper right parasagittal buttock there is a focal region of irregular maroon cutaneous discoloration with superficial epidermal erosion, measuring up to 1 ½ inches in greatest diameter, free of suppuration or subcutaneous necrosis.

AUTOPSY PROTOCOL:

The body is that of a well-developed, well-nourished adult white male, measuring 5 feet 10 inches and weighing an estimated 185-190 pounds. His appearance is consistent with the reported age of 60 years.

INJURIES, INTERNAL AND EXTERNAL:

HEAD: A ¾ inch in diameter violaceous contusion with small centrally placed scabbed laceration is present in the mid right forehead. Three superficial cutaneous scabbed lacerations are present at the lateral border of the right eyebrow, each measuring ½ inch long and all being oriented parallel to each other transversely, associated with focal circumferential violaceous contusion. Underlying craniofacial bones are intact.

Small amounts of thinly layered light brown/yellow subdural hemorrhage as a thin membrane accumulate over the right frontoparietal convexity. In addition, patchy amounts of moderate acute dark blue subarachnoid hemorrhage are present over the right cerebral convexity, primarily involving the posterior frontal and parietal regions. No contusions are noted.

CHEST: A 3-inch in diameter light green/blue irregular cutaneous contusion is present on the right lateral chest. Internally, there is minimal blunt force trauma of the thoracic cage, with a minimally displaced fracture noted to occupy the right posterolateral ninth rib.

EXTREMITIES: Patchy punctate cutaneous scabbed abrasions are present on the mid anterior left upper arm, and two discrete linear cutaneous scabbed abrasions are present on the back of the right hand, one measuring approximately ¾ inches long and the other at the distal right second knuckle, measuring ½ inch long. Appendicular skeleton is intact.

The above changes, having been mentioned once, will not be repeated below.

8

DOE, JOHN
ME 00-00-000

EXTERNAL EXAMINATION:

HEAD: The scalp is partially covered by curly black hair with gray streaks, arranged in a pattern of moderate frontal balding and measuring up to 5 inches long. Recent trauma is noted above. Prominent linear creases are present in each ear lobule. Tan/brown liquid accumulates within the oral cavity. Otherwise, the skin of the forehead, face and ears is unremarkable. The irides are light brown with dark brown specks; pupils are symmetric, measuring 5 mm. in diameter bilaterally. The conjunctivae are pale white, free of hemorrhage or icterus, demonstrating patchy horizontal slightly raised pale yellow pingueculae. Arcus senilis is present and circumferential. The decedent is edentulous. There are no lacerations/contusions of the lips and buccal mucosa. The face is clean-shaven.

NECK: No evidence of scarring or recent trauma. No false mobility.

CHEST: Symmetrical, slightly muscular and normally developed with slightly increased A-P diameter. No evidence of significant remote scarring/trauma.

ABDOMEN: Slightly scaphoid and soft. An old, well-healed 3 inch long transverse cutaneous linear surgical scar is present in the mid left lower quadrant. Cutaneous hair in the region of the right inguinal ligament is recently shaved.

EXTERNAL GENITALIA: The penis is circumcised; two testes are palpated in the scrotum.

UPPER EXTREMITIES: Symmetrical, slightly muscular, and normally developed. No significant remote trauma noted. No hesitation marks present. Fingernail beds are gray/violet, with slight accumulations of subungual dirt.

LOWER EXTREMITIES: Symmetrical, slightly muscular, and normally developed. No evidence of significant scarring or trauma. A mild degree (1+/4+) of pitting edema is present in the region of the right ankle, so that it is slightly enlarged compared to the left side. Prominent blue/red serpiginous and tortuous subcutaneous varicosities are noted on the calves and shins.

BACK: No evidence of remote scarring/trauma.

Rigidity is complete, overcome with moderate difficulty; pink/violaceous lividity is present posteriorly with blanching at pressure points.

INTERNAL EXAMINATION:

The abdominal panniculus measures up to 7/8 inches thick. No aromatic odor is noted in the tissues.

MESOTHELIAL SURFACES: Smooth and glistening with the following exception: a focal patch of peritoneal adhesion is present within the lateral aspect of the inferior left upper quadrant, measuring up to 2 inches in greatest surface dimension, subjacent to the previously-described cutaneous scar. There are no abnormal fluid accumulations in the peritoneal cavity. Pleural surfaces are smooth and glistening, each containing an estimated 30 ml. of yellow/brown serous fluid (60 ml. in toto). Pericardial sac is intact with a smooth glistening lining, and its cavity contains an estimated 10 ml. of bloody fluid.

HEART: Weight: 465 gms. Please refer to separately attached report entitled "Cardiovascular Findings."

9

DOE, JOHN
ME 00-00-000

LUNGS: Combined weight: 1,785 gms. The lungs fully occupy their respective pleural cavities. Pleural surfaces are smooth and glistening, pale gray anteriorly and violaceous (livid) posteriorly with moderate-marked anthracotic pigmentation. A 1-inch in diameter subpleural apical bleb is present on the right side. Pulmonary arteries and veins arise and branch normally and are widely patent; patchy punctate and slightly larger pale yellow atheromas are present within the proximal pulmonary arterial tree. Cut surfaces of the mainstem bronchi ooze moderate accumulations of tan/gray liquid; bronchial mucosa is smooth and glistening, slightly hyperemic. On section, the lungs are markedly subcrepitant, uniformly light maroon/violet, oozing marked amounts of edema fluid without compression; hyperemia is generalized and marked. Multiple sections of both lungs display a mild-moderate pattern of centrilobular emphysema, upper lobes more greatly affected than lower lobes, with individual expansion of air spaces measuring up to 3/16 inches in greatest diameter. Hilar mediastinal lymph nodes are uniformly anthracotic and, on section, several such lymph nodes are subtotally effaced by punctate and slightly larger pale yellow calcific granulomas.

NECK ORGANS: Except as noted previously, essentially unremarkable. There are no fractures of the cervical vertebrae. The bony and cartilaginous structures of the neck are intact. The tongue is free of lacerations or contusions. The airways are patent. The thyroid gland, of normal size and shape, exhibits uniformly light red/brown colloid, free of hemorrhage, calcification or masses.

GASTRO-INTESTINAL TRACT: The esophagus courses normally, has a smooth glistening lining, and is patent. The stomach is slightly distended, containing a measured 128 ml. of light green liquid. No pills, capsules, or tablets are present. Mucosa is intact with normal rugation, free of varices or masses. Vermiform appendix is present. Patchy outpouchings of the wall of the descending and sigmoid colon, consistent with diverticulosis coli, are noted, individually measuring up to 3/8 inches in greatest diameter, free of perforation, inflammation or suppuration. Remainder of the gastro-intestinal tract is normally configured and patent; there is moderate generalized flatus.

LIVER: Weight: 2,465 gms. Intact. The light red/brown capsular surfaces are smooth and glistening. The margins are round, the organ is moderately increased in size and, on section, is uniformly light red/brown and moderately soft with a "nutmeg" pattern of chronic passive congestion, associated with prominent centrilobular hyperemia. The gallbladder is markedly distended, containing a measured 40 ml. of dark green slightly viscous fluid bile without calculi. The hepatobiliary tree arises and courses normally and is widely patent to the ampulla of Vater. Lymph nodes of the porta hepatis are unremarkable.

SPLEEN: Weight: 435 gms. Maroon/gray capsular surfaces are intact, smooth and glistening. Rare punctate well-circumscribed hyalinized granulomas are noted on the capsular surfaces. On section, the organ is soft and uniformly maroon with identifiable white pulp.

ADRENAL GLANDS: Combined weight: 12 gms. There is moderately prominent periadrenal fat. The organs are of normal size and shape with a pale yellow thin cortex and brown/gray medulla. No masses or hemorrhages are noted.

PANCREAS: Intact. The organ is a moderately soft, coarsely lobulated structure, free of fibrosis, hemorrhage or tumor. There is moderate postmortem autolytic change appearing as multifocal areas of maroon discoloration.

KIDNEYS: Combined weight: 335 gms. There is prominent perinephric adiposity. The capsules strip with ease demonstrating coarsely granular surfaces admixed with patchy indented and pitted cortical scars, measuring up to ¼ inch in greatest surface dimension. In addition, patchy, well-circumscribed 1/8 inch in diameter cortical retention cysts are noted on both sides, having smooth glistening linings and filled with clear light yellow fluid. On section, the organs are slightly soft, light violet, otherwise with normal cortical thicknesses, well-defined corticomedullary junctions, and unremarkable pelvocalyceal systems. Renal arteries and veins arise and course normally and are widely patent.

10

DOE, JOHN
ME 00-00-000

URETERS AND URINARY BLADDER: The configuration of the ureters is unremarkable. The urinary bladder is contracted, containing an estimated 2 ml. of tan/yellow creamy fluid. Mucosal lining is smooth and glistening.

INTERNAL GENITALIA: The prostate gland is round, firm, smooth and minimally enlarged; multiple coronal sections display mild nodular hyperplasia, characterized by patchy well-circumcised whorled and bosselated white nodules, measuring up to ¼ inch in greatest diameter, free of calcification or necrosis. Prostatic urethra is patent.

SKELETAL SYSTEM: The skeleton is intact, except for rib fracture noted previously. There is diffuse maroon hemorrhagic necrosis of the left psoas muscle, free of suppuration or calcification.

HEAD: Brain weight: 1,565 gms. Please refer to separate appended consultation report entitled "Brain Description." The pituitary gland is of normal size and shape; it is moderately soft without hemorrhage.

TOXICOLOGY: Samples of heart blood, urine, vitreous humor, and bile are submitted to the Toxicology Laboratory, Cabinet for Health Services, CLF, for blood alcohol and drug screen.

SPECIAL STUDIES: A sample of vitreous humour is submitted for ASTRA-5. Heart blood is retained on a DNA card. Samples of heart blood, lung (RLL) are submitted for routine bacteriology.

11

CARDIOPATHOLOGY CONSULTATION

GROSS HEART AND AORTA DESCRIPTION

The specimen is examined in detail in the presence of Dr. William Valentine, Cardiac Pathologist on 11-XX-00 in the autopsy suite. The specimen is formalin fixed and, as a block, consists of the heart, with portion of ascending aorta attached and the remainder of the aorta as a separate segment. In addition, the aorta has been previously sectioned longitudinally, anteriorly throughout the complete length of the specimen, including the proximal ascending portion.

The heart portion weighs 465 gms.

Epicardial surfaces are smooth and glistening, the epicardial adiposity is moderate.

Extramural coronary arteries arise and branch normally with right-sided dominance. Multifocal critical (greater than 75% stenosis) atherosclerosis is present associated with a moderate degree of mural calcification. 70% - 80% stenosis proximally of the left anterior descending artery is noted with clear distal course. The left circumflex artery reveals 60% stenosis proximally with critical stenosis immediately distal to the origin of the obtuse marginal branch. The right coronary artery shows focal calcific and atheromatous stenosis of approximately 70% at 2 cm. from its origin over a span of 3 to 4 mm. As the artery descends down the interventricular sulcus posteriorly a 50% stenosis is noted, primarily atheromatous plaque, with a mild degree of calcification.

The foramen ovale is closed. Endocardial surfaces are smooth and glistening. The aortic valve, tricuspid vale, and pulmonary vale cusps are normal in configuration, intact, and free of vegetations, and flexible. Both leaflets of the mitral valve shows mild ballooning (grade I, floppy mitral valve) with interchordal hooding. A small fibrotic plaque is noted 4-5 mm. beneath the posterior leaflet of the mitral valve (="jet [Salizar] lesion"). The myocardium is uniformly firm and dark brown in a fixed state, free of gross scarring or recent infarction. Thicknesses are as follows: left ventricular freewall and septum – 1.7 cm.; right ventricular freewall – 0.6 cm.

The aorta arises and branches normally, demonstrating severe ulcerative atherosclerosis, characterized by multifocal fibrous pale yellow to brown ulcerated calcific plaques, extending from the supravalvular aorta to the distal terminus of the specimen; the process is more prominent in the distal portion of the specimen.

A dissecting hematoma (dissecting "aneurysm") of the ascending and arcual aorta is present. A jagged transverse intimal tear, 2.5 cm. in length is located 1 cm. above the left cusp of the aortic valve. The tear of the intima is in a region uninvolved by significant atherosclerotic plaque. From this entry point a false channel is demonstrable in the aortic media, revealing a non laminated dark brown blood clot. The dissection distally ascends circumferentially to the base of the right innominate artery, and continues dorsally to involve the left common carotid, extending to but not including the left subclavian artery. The dissection exists as adventitial hematoma only at the level of the left subclavian artery, and demonstrates 40% compromise of

12

DOE, JOHN
ME 00-00-000

patency in only the proximal innominate artery off the aorta. There is no organization of the hematoma noted grossly.

The ostia of both right and left main coronary arteries are not grossly involved with the dissection, however adventitial hematoma of the left and right main coronary arteries is present. The patency of these arteries does not appear to be compromised by the adventitial hematoma. The dissection descends proximally to involve myocardium and ¾ of the circumference of the aortic valve ring, sparing the anterior ½ of the left coronary cusp. The circumference of the supravalvular aorta is 8 cm. (COMMENT: No rupture of the dissection into the pericardial space was detected in the fresh state at autopsy.)

An intimal tear is noted dorsally in the arcual aorta at the proximal border of the origin of the innominate artery. This tear is oriented longitudinally to the course of the aorta, and measures approximately 2 cm. in length. This tear is felt to be the re-entry tear, however communication with the dissection channel is difficult to demonstrate.

The remainder of the aorta, as noted previously, demonstrates advanced atherosclerotic plaque formation with ulceration. Immediately distal to the origin of the renal arteries an aneurysmal dilatation with indwelling mural thrombus is noted. External transverse diameter of aorta at this point is 5 cm. Proximal stenosis of both common iliac arteries is noted, with aneurysmal dilatation of the right common iliac artery. There is no occlusion of the common iliac arteries.

DIAGNOSES

I.   Hypertensive and Calcific Atherosclerotic Cardiovascular Disease.

     A.   Multifocal critical stenosis, all major extramural coronary arteries.

     B.   Atherosclerosis of aorta, marked.

II.   Intramural Dissection, Aorta (DeBakey Type I, Daily Type A).

     A.   Intimal tear, proximal ascending aorta, above superior aortic valve ring.

     B.   Antegrade and retrograde mural dissection, propagated to aortic valve ring and base of left subclavian artery.

     C.   Marked dissection, wall of innominate artery, with 40% stenosis of lumen, by coagulated hematoma within false channel.

William Valentine, M.D.
Cardiopathologist

13

NEUROPATHOLOGY - CONSULTATION

BRAIN DESCRIPTION

The weight of the fresh brain is 1,565 gms. Beneath the dura over the right cerebral hemisphere there is a smooth, shiny brown membrane, representing a subacute subdural hematoma. Cutting across this thin mass allows leakage of brick red-colored thick fluid. The cerebral hemispheres are roughly symmetrical. The gyri are flattened and the sulci narrowed throughout both hemispheres. The surfaces of the cerebral hemispheres are soft. Over the right frontal and parietal lobes there are areas of dark red focal hemorrhage. On the inferior surfaces of the brain there are marked extraction artifacts and severe softening. In the region of the right medial temporal lobe there is marked softening and shallow groove approximately 1.7 cm from its most medial surface. The surfaces of the brainstem are soft. The surfaces of the cerebellum are softened and irregular. The major arteries at the base of the brain arise and distribute in the usual fashion and contain multifocal atherosclerotic plaques. In the proximal portion of the right middle cerebral artery, just after it arises from the internal carotid artery there is marked stenosis, although the lumen is not completely compromised. Coronal sections of the cerebral hemispheres reveal the aforementioned cerebral edema shown by marked flattening of the gyri and narrowing of the sulci. In the distribution of the right middle cerebral artery in the mid frontal and anterior parietal lobe there are large areas of hemorrhagic encephalomalacia. These involve the superior, middle and inferior frontal gyri and the mid inferior parietal lobule. The hemorrhages are brick red and primarily involve the cerebral cortex and subcortical white matter. A small area of hemorrhage is also present in middle frontal gyrus in the frontal pole. There is a skip area of approximately 2 cm. behind the right frontal pole in which no obvious areas of hemorrhagic infarction is present. There is generalized softening of the brain but the medial right temporal lobe shows poor differentiation between cortex and white matter and the tissue there fractures readily. The basal ganglia, thalami and hypothalami are roughly intact though soft to the touch. The septum pellucidum is absent and there is a major fracture in the middle portion of the corpus callosum. Serial sections through the remnants of brainstem reveal midline dark hemorrhages in the midbrain-pons junctions and pons. There is softening in the cerebellum along the roof of the fourth ventricle. Coronal sections of the cerebellum reveal diffuse areas of hemorrhage in the right superior cerebellar hemisphere. There is an overall redness to much of the cerebellum. [**COMMENT:** this probably reflects hypoxia and poor fixation.]

DIAGNOSES:

I.   Hemorrhagic infarction, right frontal and parietal lobes (distribution of right middle cerebral artery).

II.   Diffuse hypoxic encephalopathy.

III.   Cerebral edema, severe.

IV.   Herniation of right uncus into tentorium.   [CONTINUED ON NEXT PAGE]

14

600

V.   Duret hemorrhages of midbrain and pons

VI.   Subdural hematoma, convexity of right cerebral hemisphere, small.

_____
Robert Nervous, M.D.
Neuropathologist

15

DOE, JOHN
ME-C 00-00-000

COMMONWEALTH OF KENTUCKY
Justice Cabinet
OFFICE OF THE ASSOCIATE CHIEF MEDICAL EXAMINER
Centralized Laboratory Facility
100 Sower Boulevard - Suite 202
Frankfort. Kentucky 40601
(502) 564-4545

LABORATORY RESULTS

CHEMISTRIES – VITREOUS HUMOUR:

    Sodium: 121 mmol/L
    Potassium: 8.0 mmol/L
    Chloride: 112 mmol/L
    Glucose: 14 mg/dL
    Urea Nitrogen: 67 mg/dL
    Creatinine: 2.6 mg/dL

TOXICOLOGY

    Blood – Heart: Negative

    Urine: Negative

    Bile: Negative

    Vitreous Humour: Negative

MICROBIOLOGY – ROUTINE BACTERIOLOGY:

    Heart blood: No growth

    Lung (RLL): No growth

COMMONWEALTH OF KENTUCKY
Justice Cabinet
OFFICE OF THE ASSOCIATE CHIEF MEDICAL EXAMINER
Centralized Laboratory Facility
100 Sower Boulevard - Suite 202
Frankfort, Kentucky 40601
(502) 564-4545

MICROSCOPIC DESCRIPTION

CARDIOVASCULAR:

HEART
LEFT VENTRICLE (1 H & E) — Mild myocyte hypertrophy with focal interstitial and perivascular fibrosis; patchy wavy fiber change without inflammation; extensive autolysis

RIGHT VENTRICLE (1 H & E): — Mild autolysis; no pathologic change (NPC)

CORONARY ARTERIES (5 H & E with decalcification):
LEFT MAIN: — Adventitial hemorrhage without compromise of vascular lumen

PROXIMAL LAD: — Calcific atherosclerotic plaque with dystrophic calcification and intimal hyperplasia; 85% stenosis

PROXIMAL LEFT CIRCUMFLEX: — Atherosclerotic plaque with dystrophic calcification and intimal hyperplasia; 60% stenosis

PROXIMAL RCA: — Atherosclerotic plaque with dystrophic calcification and intimal hyperplasia; 75% stenosis; also exhibits focal dissecting hemorrhage of the media without compromise of the vascular lumen

PDA: — Atherosclerotic plaque with dystrophic calcification and intimal hyperplasia; 70% stenosis

AORTA:

DISTAL ABDOMINAL, REGION OF ANEURYSM (1 H & E): — Calcific atherosclerosis with ulceration and organized intraluminal thrombus

ASCENDING (2 H & E): — Dissecting medial hemorrhage with fibrin; diffuse medial necrosis in uninvolved segments; calcific atherosclerosis

603

DOE, JOHN
ME-C 00-00-000

MICROSCOPIC DESCRIPTION - CONTINUED

INNOMINATE ARTERY (1 H & E):	Circumferential medial dissection by hemorrhage with 40% luminal compromise; mild intimal hyperplasia
LUNGS (5 H & E):	confluent pleural, interstitial, perivascular and peribronchiolar anthracosis with focal fibrosis; centrilobular emphysema, moderate; intra-alveolar and interstitial edema with abundant macrophages, rare polymorphonuclear leukocytes; mild hypertrophy of alveolar lining cells
LIVER (2 H & E):	Sinusoidal hyperemia, marked, with perivenous hemorrhage and hepatocytic necrosis without inflammation
SPLEEN (1 H & E):	Subcapsular hyalinized granuloma; sinusoidal hyperemia, marked
PANCREAS (1 H & E):	NPC; autolysis
KIDNEY (2 H & E):	Focal subcortical/interstitial fibrosis with parenchymal dropout and multifocal peritubular lymphocytic aggregates; mild intimal hyperplasia of interstitial arteries
PROSTATE GLAND (1 H & E):	Glandular and stromal hyperplasia, mild, with focal chronic prostatitis; periprostatic venous thrombosis, postmortem
TESTIS (1 H & E):	NPC
ADRENAL GLANDS (2 H & E):	Lipid depletion of cortices
THYROID GLAND (1 H & E):	NPC
LEFT PSOAS MUSCLE (1 H & E):	Diffuse hemorrhage with necrosis of myocytes; no inflammation

DOE, JOHN
ME-C 00-00-000

MICROSCOPIC DESCRIPTION - CONTINUED

CENTRAL NERVOUS SYSTEM (8 H & E):

DURA MATER:	Convexity of left cerebrum: NPC Convexity of right cerebrum: Intact and fragmented erythrocytes with fibrin; fibroblastic layer of 2-4 cells thick on dural side; rare pigment-laden histiocytes
RIGHT PARIETAL AND RIGHT FRONTAL LOBE:	Patchy acute subarachnoid hemorrhage. Extravasated blood effacing parenchyma with compression of adjacent parenchyma; anoxic (eosinophilic) neuronal and glial changes, cytotoxic and vasogenic edema; hyperplastic microglia; prominence of histiocytes/macrophages at periphery of liquefactive necrosis
LEFT FRONTAL LOBE:	Ischemic change and edema: autolysis
RIGHT HIPPOCAMPUS:	Ischemic neuronal change (eosinophilia of neurons with pyknosis and karyorrhexis) in Sommer sector; edema; autolysis
CEREBELLUM, RIGHT:	Ischemic changes with interstitial edema and patchy hemorrhage: ischemia (eosinophilia) of Purkinje cells
MIDBRAIN/ROSTRAL PONS:	Neuronal ischemia: multifocal punctate and larger areas of parenchymal hemorrhage (Duret)

605

COMMONWEALTH OF KENTUCKY
DEPARTMENT OF JUSTICE
OFFICE OF THE ASSOCIATE CHIEF MEDICAL EXAMINER

Name: DOE, JOHN   Case No: ME 00-00-000

Race: W   Age: 60   Date: 10-XXI-00

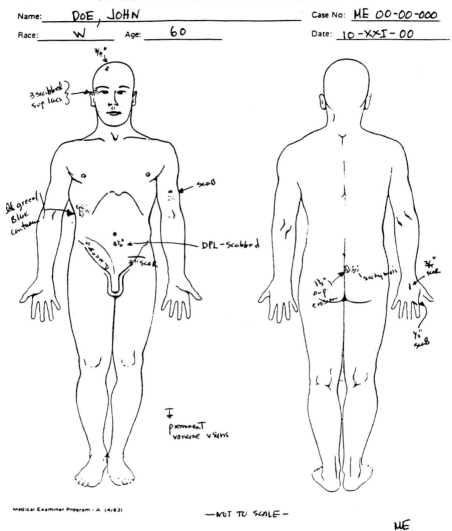

Medical Examiner Program · A (4/83)

—NOT TO SCALE—

ME

606

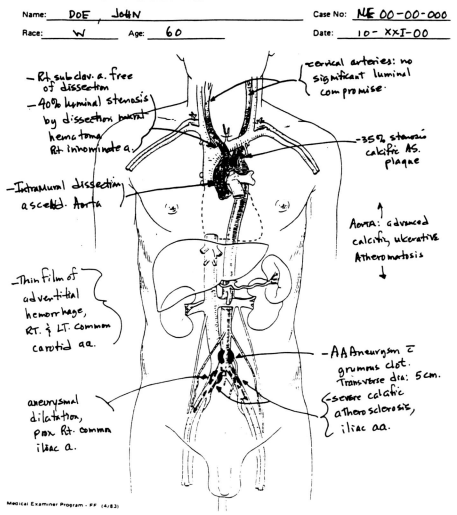

COMMONWEALTH OF KENTUCKY
DEPARTMENT OF JUSTICE
OFFICE OF THE ASSOCIATE CHIEF MEDICAL EXAMINER

Name: DOE, JOHN   Case No: NE 00-00-000

Race: W   Age: 60   Date: 10- XXI-00

- Rt. subclav. a. free of dissection
- 40% luminal stenosis by dissection mural hematoma Rt innominate a.

cervical arteries: no significant luminal compromise.

-35% stenosis calcific AS. plaque

-Intramural dissection ascedd. Aorta

Aorta: advanced calcific, ulcerative Atheromatosis

-Thin film of adventitial hemorrhage, RT. & LT. common carotid aa.

-AA Aneurysm c̄ grumous clot. Transverse dia: 5cm.
-severe calcific atherosclerosis, iliac aa.

aneurysmal dilatation, prox Rt. common iliac a.

Medical Examiner Program - FF (4/83)

- NOT TO SCALE -   WE

607

COMMONWEALTH OF KENTUCKY
DEPARTMENT OF JUSTICE
OFFICE OF THE ASSOCIATE CHIEF MEDICAL EXAMINER

Name: DOE, JOHN   Case No: ME 00-00-000

Race: W   Age: 60   Date: 10-XXI-00

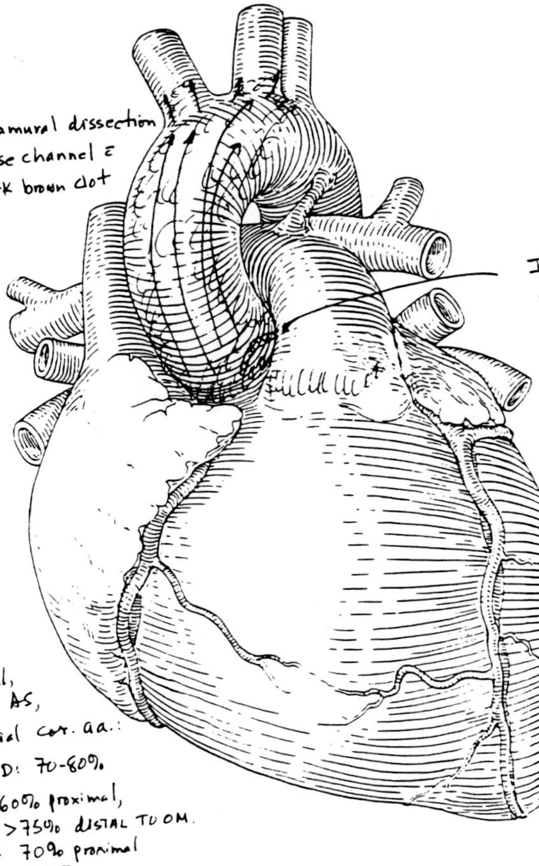

Intramural dissection,
False channel c̄
dark brown clot

Intimal Tear—Entry
transverse 2.5cm long,
1 cm. above Lt.
cusp. of AV

Segmental,
Calcific AS,
Epicardial cor. aa.:
- prox LAD: 70-80%
- circ: 60% proximal,
    >75% distal to OM.
- RCA: 70% proximal
- PDA: 50%

Medical Examiner Program - HH (4/83)

— NOT TO scale—

ME

COMMONWEALTH OF KENTUCKY
DEPARTMENT OF JUSTICE
OFFICE OF THE ASSOCIATE CHIEF MEDICAL EXAMINER

Name: DOE, JOHN   Case No: ME 00-00-000

Race: W   Age: 60   Date: 10-XXI-00

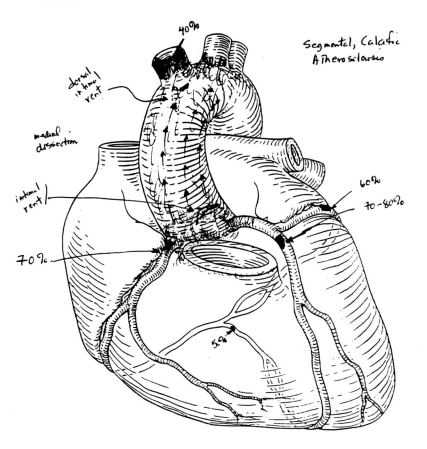

Medical Examiner Program · KK (4/83)   — NOT TO Scale —   ME

COMMONWEALTH OF KENTUCKY
DEPARTMENT OF JUSTICE
OFFICE OF THE ASSOCIATE CHIEF MEDICAL EXAMINER

Name: DOE, JOHN   Case No: ME 00-00-000

Race: W   Age: 60   Date: 10-XXI-00

RESPIRATORY SYSTEM

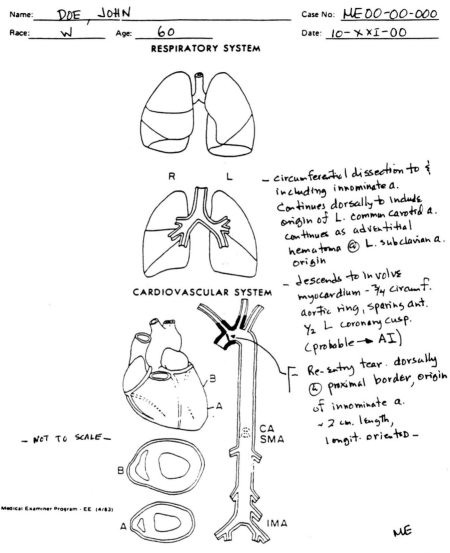

R   L

CARDIOVASCULAR SYSTEM

— circumferential dissection to &
including innominate a.
continues dorsally to include
origin of L. common carotid a.
continues as adventitial
hematoma @ L. subclavian a.
origin

— descends to involve
myocardium – ¾ circumf.
aortic ring, sparing ant.
½ L coronary cusp.
(probable → AI)

— Re-entry tear. dorsally
@ proximal border, origin
of innominate a.
~2 cm. length,
longit. orientsed —

— NOT TO SCALE —

B

A

3
A

CA
SMA

IMA

Medical Examiner Program · EE (4/83)

ME

610

COMMONWEALTH OF KENTUCKY
DEPARTMENT OF JUSTICE
OFFICE OF THE ASSOCIATE CHIEF MEDICAL EXAMINER

Name: DOE, JOHN   Case No: ME 00-00-000

Race: W   Age: 60   Date: 10-XX-I-00

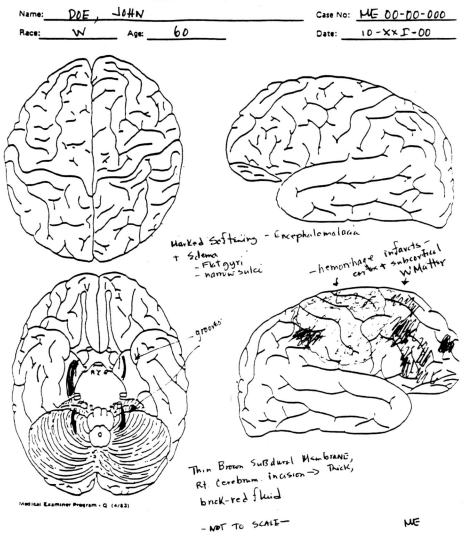

Marked Softening - Encephalomalacia
+ Edema
- Flat gyri
- narrow sulci

- hemorrhage infarcts - cortex + subcortical W. Matter

- grooves

Thin Brown Subdural Membrane,
Rt. Cerebrum incision → Thick,
brick-red fluid

- NOT TO SCALE -   ME

Medical Examiner Program - Q (4/83)

COMMONWEALTH OF KENTUCKY
DEPARTMENT OF JUSTICE
OFFICE OF THE ASSOCIATE CHIEF MEDICAL EXAMINER

Name: _DOE , JOHN_   Case No: _ME 00-00-000_

Race: _W_   Age: _60_   Date: _10-XXI-00_

RT

Segmental AS,
cerebral aa.
>50% stenosis

Medical Examiner Program - LL (4/83)   —NOT TO SCALE—   ME

Brain, optic chiasm and mammillary bodies

Name _DOE, John_   Autopsy No. _ME 00-00-000_

Age _60_   Race _W_   Sex _M_   Date _10/xxII 00_

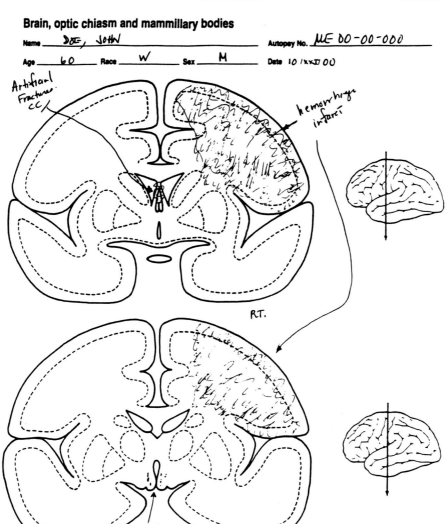

Artificial Fractures CC

hemorrhage infarct

RT.

Duret hemorrhages

Medical Examiner Program S-2   — NOT TO SCALE —   ME

Brain, thalamus and pineal gland

Name _DOE, JOHN_____   Autopsy No. _ME 00-00-000_____

Age ___60___   Race ___W___   Sex ___M___   Date _10 /XXI/00___

hemorrhage
infarct

RT

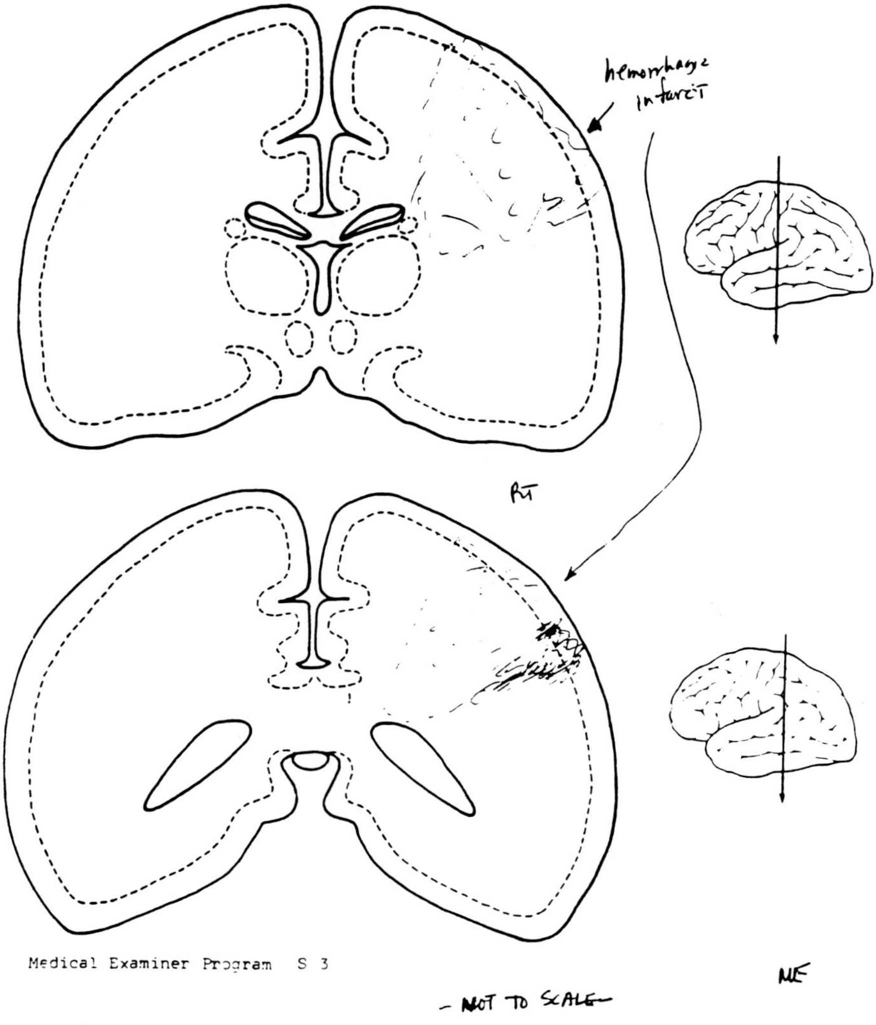

Medical Examiner Program   S 3

— NOT TO SCALE—

ME

Brain stem, pons, medulla and cerebellum

Name _DOE, JOHN_   Autopsy No. _ME 00-00-000_

Age _60_   Race _W_   Sex _M_   Date _10 1xx1100_

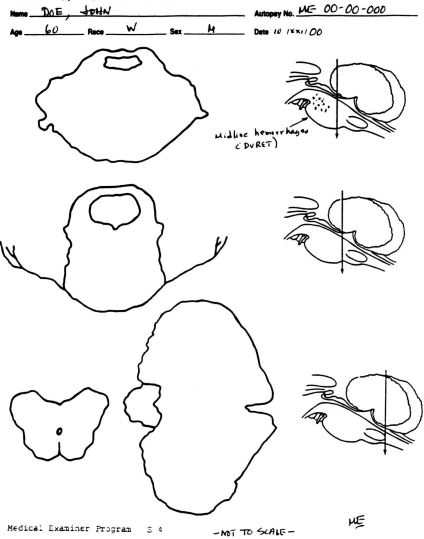

Midline hemorrhages
(DURET)

Medical Examiner Program   S 4   —NOT TO SCALE—   ME

615

IV. LEGAL PROBLEMS ASSOCIATED WITH AUTOPSIES*

§ 32A.38. Introduction.

No medical procedure is more frequently involved in litigation than the autopsy. Except those autopsies performed purely for the advancement of medical knowledge or to satisfy hospital accreditation requirements, nearly every postmortem examination stems from pending or anticipated civil or criminal litigation. Frequently, the autopsy itself initiates or aborts a personal injury lawsuit or the filing of a criminal charge.

Possible malpractice claim

It is true that many hospital autopsies are performed merely to verify the attending physicians' opinions as to the true cause of death. Also, many are requested to evaluate therapy methods, and a number must be performed in teaching hospitals for the benefit of medical students and postgraduate trainees. But also, many hospital autopsies are requested because hospital officials or physicians foresee a possible negligence action arising out of the patient's death. (See § 32A.48.)

Official autopsies

Official autopsies, or those authorized or required by law because of violent, suspicious or unusual circumstances surrounding the death, usually are performed because a possible crime has been committed. (See § 32A.43.)

Autopsies as the cause of litigation

Both hospital and official autopsies have given rise to numerous civil lawsuits by surviving relatives who claim damages for mental and emotional suffering due to the mutilation of the deceased's body. Most of these actions are based on the charge that the autopsy was unauthorized. (See § 32A.42.) Occasionally, the lawsuit is filed because of the method used in the autopsy, or because of negligence in the procedure. (See § 32A.41.) And in a few instances, autopsies have been performed solely by mistake. (See § 32A.45.)

Insurance autopsies

As would be expected, disputed insurance claims often cause demands for autopsies. Under most state workmen compensation laws, upon proper application and a showing of just cause, an employer or its insurer may order an autopsy on the body of a deceased employee. A post-

---

*By the editors.

mortem examination becomes important in these cases because it may be the method of distinguishing an accident from a disease, a job-related injury from a non-job-related injury, or an occupational disease from a nonoccupational disease.

Nearly every insurance policy offering death benefits contains a provision giving the company the right to request an autopsy if not prohibited by law. (See § 32A.47.) Usually the clause is utilized to distinguish an accidental death from death by disease. Occasionally, an autopsy is ordered to establish the onset of a disease, for example where it is uncertain whether an insured's condition existed prior to the effective date of the policy.

The autopsy can be important also in determining the exact disease from which the insured suffered. Many health policies exclude benefits for expenses resulting from certain conditions; namely, drug-overdose, alcoholism, and venereal disease. Also, many health policies are issued with endorsements excluding or at least limiting benefits for conditions suffered by the insured prior to applying for the policy. Similarly, the autopsy provision comes into play also in the specialty policy; for example, the policy offering coverage only for expenses or death associated with an automobile accident, or the policy paying benefits only for a catastrophic disease such as polio or cancer.

From a practical standpoint, however, since the insurance company assumes the expense of the autopsy, the provision is not utilized unless the policy benefits in question substantially exceed the cost of the autopsy.

§ 32A.39. Possession and control over disposition of body.

In most states, disposition of a dead body and authorization for an autopsy are governed by statute. In situations where these statutes do not apply, and there are many, the case law on the subject, which is extensive, must be consulted.

Surviving spouse has superior right

Unless prescribed otherwise by statute, the surviving spouse generally has the right of possession of the body.[16] This is not a "property right,"

---

[16]Larson v. Chase (1891) 47 Minn. 307, 50 N.W. 238, 14 L.R.A. 85, 28 Am. St. Rep. 370; Steagall v. Doctors Hosp. (1948) 84 App. D.C. 214 171 F.2d 352; Aetna Life Ins. Co. v. Lindsay (C.A.-7 Ill., 1934) 69 F.2d 627; Parker v. Quinn-McGowen Co. (1964) 262 N.C. 560, 138 S.E.2d 214; Edwards v. Franke (Alaska, 1961) 364 P.2d 60; Terrill v. Harbin (Tex. Civ. App., 1964) 376 S.W.2d 945; Travelers Ins. Co. v. Welch (C.A.-5 La., 1936) 82 F.2d 799; Simpkins v. Lumbermens Mut. Cas. Co. (1942) 200 S.C. 228, 20 S.E.2d 733; In re Autopsy of Kyle (Okla., 1957) 309 P.2d 1070; Mutual Life Ins. Co. of New York v. Griesa (D. Kan. 1907) 156 Fed. 398.

however, at least in the usual or commercial sense,[17] but a kind of quasi-property interest that gives the spouse the power to determine who shall have custody of the body until burial.[18] A dead body is not property as such, but something special for which specific rules regarding possession and disposition have developed over a period of years.[19]

It has been said that even the executor or administrator of the deceased's estate does not have a right superior to the surviving spouse (or next of kin) regarding control over the disposition of the body,[20] although the deceased's own wishes in the form of testamentary disposition should be considered,[21] at least where there is no surviving spouse.[22] Also, a person may authorize his own autopsy by entering into an insurance contract containing a provision giving this right to the company.[23] (See § 32A.47.) Furthermore, an individual can make legally binding arrangements for the performance of an autopsy following his death under the provisions of the Uniform Anatomical Gift Act.[24]

---

[17] Parker v. Quinn-McGowen Co. (1964) 262 N.C. 560, 138 S.E.2d 214; Cohen v. Groman Mortuary, Inc. (1964) 231 Cal. App. 2d 1, 41 Cal. Rptr. 481; Huntly v. Zurich Gen. Acc. & Liab. Ins. Co. (1929) 100 Cal. App. 201, 280 Pac. 163; Gray v. Southern Pac. Co. (1937) 21 Cal. App. 2d 240, 68 P.2d 1011; Deeg v. City of Detroit (1956) 345 Mich. 371, 76 N.W.2d 16.

[18] Cohen v. Groman Mortuary, Inc. (1964) 231 Cal. App. 2d 1, 41 Cal. Rptr. 481; Barela v. Frank A. Hubbell Co. (1960) 67 N.M. 319, 355 P.2d 133; Parker v. Quinn-McGowen Co. (1964) 262 N.C. 560, 138 S.E.2d 214; Simpkins v. Lumbermens Mut. Cas. Co. (1942) 200 S.C. 228, 20 S.E.2d 733; Stephenson v. Duke Univ. (1932) 202 N.C. 624, 163 S.E. 698; Patrick v. Employers Mut. Liab. Ins. Co. (1938) 233 Mo. App. 251, 118 S.W.2d 116; Medical College v. Rushing (1907) 1 Ga. App. 468, 57 S.E. 1083.

[19] See Larson v. Chase (1891) 47 Minn. 307, 50 N.W. 238, 14 L.R.A. 85, 28 Am. St. Rep. 370; Whaley v. County of Tuscola (C.A.-6 Mich., 1995) 58 F.3d 1111 (next-of-kin had claim for infringement of property rights under due process clause for assistant medical examiner's removal of decedent's corneas without consent.

[20] O'Donnell v. Slack (1899) 123 Cal. 285, 55 Pac. 906; Mutual Life Ins. Co. of New York v. Griesa (D. Kan., 1907) 156 Fed. 398; Burney v. Children's Hosp. in Boston (1897) 169 Mass. 57, 47 N.E. 401, 38 L.R.A. 413, 61 Am. St. Rep. 273; In re Estate of Mgurdichian (1968) 30 App. Div. 2d 732, 291 N.Y.S.2d 453.

[21] Travelers Ins. Co. v. Welch (C.A.-5 La., 1936) 82 F.2d 799. See "Validity and Effect of Testamentary Direction as to Disposition of Testator's Body," 7 A.L.R.3d 747.

[22] Snouffer v. Peoples Trust & Sav. Co. (1965) 140 Ind. App. 491, 212 N.E. 2d 165. See also "Enforcement of preference expressed by decedent as to disposition of his body after death," 54 A.L.R.3d 1037.

[23] Aetna Life Ins. Co. v. Lindsay (C.A.-7 Ill., 1934) 69 F.2d 627. See also § 32A.47, infra.

[24] Uniform Anatomical Gift Act (U.L.A.). Editor's Note: Section 7 of the Act, which discusses the rights and duties of the parties at the death of the donor of an anatomical gift, states, under subsection (d), that "The provisions of this Act are subject to the laws of this state prescribing powers and duties with respect to autopsies." Under the Official Comments to this section, the Commissioners on Uniform State Laws state that "Subsection (d) is necessary to preclude the frustration of the important medical examiners duties in cases of death by suspected crime or violence. However, since such cases often can provide transplants of value to living persons, it may prove desirable in many if not most states to reexamine and amend the medical examiner statutes to authorize and direct medical examiners to expedite their autopsy pro-

In at least one case it has been held that, generally speaking, the person whose duty it is to care for the body of a deceased is entitled to the possession of that body.[25] If the surviving spouse is separated from the deceased at the time of death, the length and nature of the separation may be considered in determining the spouse's right to control over the body.[26] A New York court has said: "Absolutes are rare in the physical sciences. They are even rarer in the law. Therefore, this court believes no inflexible rule concerning rights of the surviving spouse can be formulated that will be attuned to all the nuances of situations arising when the couple have been living apart at the date of one partner's death. This court believes that a surviving spouse who had been living apart does have some rights concerning the funeral and burial of her husband."[27]

That a surviving spouse does not take immediate steps to assume responsibility for the deceased's funeral arrangements will be considered, and may result in his or her waiver of any later rights, including the right to an action for an unauthorized autopsy.[28] A separation prior to the deceased's death, but not during his last days, probably will not affect the spouse's rights regarding possession of the body.[29]

Where an Oklahoma statute establishing who had the right to authorize the dissection of a dead body gave such right to "any husband or next of kin," the Oklahoma court refused to construe the statute to mean a deceased husband's sisters had a right superior to his widow; the court assumed the legislators, when they drafted the law, wanted to include a surviving wife as well as a surviving husband under its provisions.[30]

Where there is no spouse

In the absence of statute, if there is no surviving spouse, the right to possession of a dead body usually belongs to the next-of-kin[31] in the order of relation to the deceased.[32] In California it was held that on the death of the surviving spouse the right passes to the children apparently to be exercised by majority decision.[33]

Most states have statutes that provide that nonofficial autopsies may be performed upon the authorization of only one surviving relative or

cedures in cases in which the public interest will not suffer."

[25] Deeg v. City of Detroit (1956) 345 Mich. 371, 76 N.W.2d 16.

[26] See Feller v. Universal Funeral Chapel (1953) 124 N.Y.S.2d 546; In re Estate of Barner (1966) 50 Misc. 2d 517, 270 N.Y.S.2d 678.

[27] In re Estate of Barner (1966) 50 Misc. 2d 517, 270 N.Y.S.2d 678.

[28] Dutton v. Brashears Funeral Home (1962) 235 Ark. 120, 357 S.W.2d 265.

[29] Thompson v. Pierce (1914) 95 Neb. 692, 146 N.W. 948.

[30] In re Autopsy of Kyle (Okla., 1957) 309 P.2d 1070.

[31] Travelers Ins. Co. v. Welch (C.A.-5 La., 1936) 82 F.2d 799; In re Autopsy of Kyle (Okla., 1957) 309 P.2d 1070; Edwards v. Franke (Alaska, 1961) 364 P.2d 60; Thompson v. Pierce (1914) 95 Neb. 692, 146 N.W. 948.

[32] Edwards v. Franke (Alaska, 1961) 364 P.2d 60.

[33] Smith v. Vidovich (1966) 242 Cal. App. 2d 206, 51 Cal. Rptr. 196.

next of kin. The Illinois statute was tested and held valid.[34] (See § 32A.40 infra.)

Death of child

In the death of a child, it has been held that the rights of the mother and father to possession of the body are equal.[35] There is some early authority, certainly questionable under today's standards, that in the case of an unauthorized autopsy of a child, the father has the right of bringing legal action in preference to the mother.[36] Of course, much will depend upon whether the parents are living together and who is present at the time of the child's death.[37]

Additional exceptions to rule

Exceptions to the rule that the surviving spouse and next of kin are entitled to possession and control of a deceased's remains have been compared to those instances that would deprive a natural guardian of the custody of a living child.[38] There is a form of sacred trust established for the benefit of all persons allied to the deceased by the ties of family or friendship, and if this trust is violated by neglect or misuse, the courts may intercede.[39]

The right to control over a dead body can be affected also by the manner in which the death occurs. If the death occurs by violence or under unusual circumstances, suggesting that a crime has been committed, the survivors' right to possession and control will be subordinated by statute to an overriding public interest. The body may be placed temporarily under the custody of the authorities for a postmortem examination and autopsy without regard to the wishes of the survivors. (See § 32A.43 infra.)

A dead body also may be examined and an autopsy performed without the consent of the survivors for the promotion of truth in private litigation.[40] Usually this involves a deceased who has given an insurance company the right to an autopsy under the terms of the policy. (See § 32A.47 infra.)

The right to possess and control the disposition of a dead body apparently ends with burial. It has been held that a surviving spouse who once

---

[34] Leno v. St. Joseph Hosp. (1973) 55 Ill. 2d 114, 302 N.E.2d 58.

[35] Coty v. Baughman (1926) 50 S.D. 372, 210 N.W. 348.

[36] Stephenson v. Duke Univ. (1932) 202 N.C. 624, 163 S.E. 698; Burney v. Children's Hosp. in Boston (1897) 169 Mass. 57, 47 N.E. 401, 38 L.R.A. 413, 61 Am. St. Rep. 273.

[37] See Coty v. Baughman (1926) 50 S.D. 372, 210 N.W. 348.

[38] Thompson v. Pierce (1914) 95 Neb. 692, 146 N.W. 948.

[39] Larson v. Chase (1891) 47 Minn. 307, 50 N.W. 238, 14 L.R.A. 85, 28 Am. St. Rep. 370.

[40] Travelers Ins. Co. v. Welch (C.A.-5 La., 1936) 82 F.2d 799. See also Aetna Life Ins. Co. v. Lindsay (C.A.-7 Ill., 1934) 69 F.2d 627.

buries her husband does not have an absolute right to disinter the body for reburial elsewhere over the objections of other close relatives of the deceased, the granting of such a right being within the sound discretion of a court.[41]

§ 32A.40. Consent requirements for hospital autopsies.

For maximum protection against liability, an autopsy requiring the consent of surviving relatives or next of kin probably should be performed only with the permission of all members of the nearest class of relatives of the deceased. Most states, however, have statutes providing that a nonofficial autopsy may be performed upon the authorization of only one surviving relative or next of kin.

The validity of such a statute was challenged in Illinois in 1972. The case arose when a hospital obtained the consent of only one of two surviving brothers of a deceased patient. The brother whose consent had not been sought filed suit for damages, alleging that the autopsy on his dead brother had caused him emotional suffering. He charged that his constitutional rights were violated in that he had a form of "property right" in his brother's body which was interfered with when the autopsy was performed without notice.

The plaintiff was successful in the trial court; the statute was held unconstitutional and damages in the amount of $1,000 were awarded. On appeal, however, the lower court's decision was overturned and the statute held valid, at least as to the specific question of whether it was fundamentally unfair to deprive a person of the right claimed by the plaintiff without some reasonable provision of notice. A contention not decided by the reviewing court was whether the statute, which includes in the definition of surviving relative only adult survivors, discriminates against minors. Since the plaintiff in the instant case was an adult, the court ruled he had no standing to challenge the statute on this ground.[42]

The following form has been suggested for use by hospitals in obtaining authorization for autopsies.[43]

---

[41] Hickey v. Hickey (Ind. App., 1973) 298 N.E.2d 29. See also Mutual of Omaha Ins. Co. v. Garrigan (1971) 31 Ohio Misc. 1, 285 N.E.2d 395 (under statute only "next of kin," from which spouse has been excluded, may disinter).

[42] Leno v. St. Joseph Hosp. (1973) 55 Ill. 2d 114, 302 N.E.2d 58.

[43] Form supplied through the courtesy of the Law Division of the American Medical Association, 535 North Dearborn Street, Chicago, Illinois 60610.

AUTHORIZATION FOR AUTOPSY AND
DISPOSITION OF REMAINS

I (We) hereby represent that I am (we are) the (state relationship) _____ of the deceased (name of patient) _____ and that I (we) have the right to control the disposition of the remains of said deceased.

IF THE AUTHORIZATION IS SIGNED BY ONE OTHER THAN THE SURVIVING SPOUSE THE FOLLOWING IS TO BE SUPPLIED.

Other surviving relatives are named below:

Adult children: _____

_____

Minor children (Under 18 years): _____

_____

Father: _____
Mother: _____
Adult brothers and sisters: _____

_____

Minor brothers and sisters (Under 18 years): _____

_____

On behalf of myself and the surviving relatives of the deceased (name of patient) _____ including all of those relatives named above, I request and authorize the physicians and surgeons in attendance at the _____ Hospital to perform a complete autopsy on the remains of the deceased (name of patient) _____ and I authorize the removal and retention or use for diagnostic, scientific or therapeutic purposes of such organs, tissues and parts as such physicians and surgeons deem proper.

This authority is granted subject to the following restrictions:

_____

_____

(If no restrictions, write "None.")

The following special examinations shall be made:

_____

_____

I (We) wish the remains to be released to:

_____   _____   _____ _____

(name of undertaking establishment)   (city)   (state)

Signed _____

Signed _____

Witnesses:

_____

_____

Name of person obtaining Authorization:

_____

Date _____ Time _____

§ 32A.40a. Religious or sentimental objections to autopsies.[44]

In some cases families of the deceased voice strong religious and senti-

---

[44]Jones, J. T. R., *Evidentiary Autopsies,*
61 U. Colo. L. Rev. 567, 1990.

mental objections to any autopsy of their loved one. Many of these cases involve the religious objections of decedents and their survivors who are adherents of Orthodox Judaism, which strongly condemns any autopsies of the bodies of the faithful. Some states have statutes that address the conflict that arises between religious or sentimental feelings on the one hand and the legitimate needs of the party demanding an autopsy on the other. In most jurisdictions, however, resolution of the conflict is left to the discretion of the court hearing the autopsy request.

While some courts refuse to order autopsies when faced with the religious objections of the decedent or the decedent's surviving relatives, courts normally refuse only when an autopsy is not really "necessary" or the need for it is outweighed by the objections.[45] When an autopsy is needed to determine cause of death or some other material and disputed point, courts generally reject objections.[46] Some courts endeavor to balance the respective interests of the parties,[47] while others hold that religious and sentimental objections can never defeat an autopsy request when the autopsy is clearly needed.[48] At least one state, California, provides by statute that an autopsy may not be performed against the will of a decedent or the decedent's family, but that as a consequence the family will probably be unable to recover whatever benefits to which it might otherwise have been entitled.[49]

§ 32A.41. Actions arising out of authorized autopsies.

Nature and scope of authorization

In the absence of statute, an authorization by the surviving spouse or next of kin for an autopsy need not be in writing to be valid, but for the protection of the pathologist, it is essential that witnesses be present at the time of agreement.[50] If written consent is required by statute, it behooves hospital and its pathologist to comply with it.[51] A verbal agree-

---

[45] See, e.g., Atkins v. Medical Examiner (1979) 100 Misc. 2d 296, 418 N.Y.S.2d 839; Weberman v. Zugibe (1977) 90 Misc. 2d 254, 394 N.Y.S.2d 371; Wilensky v. Greco (1973) 74 Misc. 2d 512, 344 N.Y.S.2d 77.

[46] See, e.g., Sykes v. Commercial Travelers' Mut. Acc. Ass'n (M.D. Pa., 1963) 32 F.R.D. 335; Labiche v. Certain Ins. Cos. (E.D. La., 1961) 196 F. Supp. 102; Snyder v. Holy Cross Hosp. (1976) 30 Md. 317, 352 A.2d 334; Robinson v. Nashville Mach. Co. (Tenn., 1973) 503 S.W.2d 90.

[47] See, e.g., In re Asbestos Litigation (D. Del., 1988) 123 F.R.D. 84; In re Certain Asbestos Cases (N.D. Tex., 1986) 112 F.R.D. 427; Snyder v. Holy Cross Hosp. (1976) 30 Md. App. 317, 352 A.2d 334; cf. Life Investors' Ins. Co v. Heline (Iowa, 1979) 285

N.W.2d 31; In re Disinterment of Body of Jarvis (1953) 244 Iowa 1025, 58 N.W.2d 24.

[48] See, e.g., Sykes v. Commercial Travelers' Mut. Acc. Ass'n (M.D. Pa., 1963) 32 F.R.D. 335; Robinson v. Nashville Mach. Co. (Tenn., 1973) 503 S.W.2d 90.

[49] Cal. Lab. Code § 5707. See also Holm v. Superior Ct. (1986) 187 Cal. App. 3d 1241, 232 Cal. Rptr. 432; Greenwell v. Industrial Acc. Comm'n (1933) 132 Cal. App. 653, 23 P.2d 422; Morrison v. Industrial Acc. Comm'n (1941) 42 Cal. App. 2d 685, 109 P.2d 770.

[50] See Tackett v. Terrill (Tex. Civ. App., 1966) 404 S.W.2d 158.

[51] See Bambrick v. Booth Mem. Med. Ctr. (App. Div., 1993) 593 N.Y.S.2d 252.

ment to the performance of a limited autopsy, for example the opening of a previous operative incision, creates a great risk of litigation because of the possibility of misunderstanding.[52]

It has been held that consent to an autopsy necessarily implies consent to disinterment or exhumation (removal of body from burying place),[53] and that an autopsy may be performed by a physician other than the one to whom consent is given.[54] But conditional authorizations will be upheld; for example, a person may designate the place at which the autopsy is to be performed,[55] or agree to the autopsy only on the condition that the body organs not be removed permanently.[56]

Where a surviving spouse signed a consent form for an autopsy that a physician mistakenly told her was required by law, she had no cause of action against the physician.[57]

Removal of organs

An authorization for the performance of an autopsy to determine the cause of death implies permission to conduct the examination in the approved and usual manner practiced by competent pathologists.[58] Where the person authorizing the autopsy understands the purpose of the postmortem examination is to ascertain cause of death and clearly consents to the autopsy for that purpose, if the removal of some of the deceased's organs for microscopic examination is necessary, the pathologist, by such removal, is not guilty of any actionable wrong.[59]

There even is some authority that removed organs do not necessarily have to be returned to the body,[60] unless this is a part of the agreement authorizing the autopsy,[61] or unless a timely demand for their return is made and there is no apparent valid reason for their further retention.[62] And it has been said that organs do not have to be returned to their original location if it is not the customary practice of the pathologist to

---

[52] See Terrill v. Harbin (Tex. Civ. App., 1964) 376 S.W.2d 945.

[53] Aetna Life Ins. Co. v. Lindsay (C.A.-7 Ill., 1934) 69 F.2d 627.

[54] Division of Labor Enforcement, Dept. Industrial Relations v. Gifford (1955) 137 Cal. App. 2d 259, 290 P.2d 281.

[55] Hill v. Travelers Ins. Co. (1927) 154 Tenn. 295, 294 S.W. 1097. But see Dean v. Chapman (Okla., 1976) 556 P.2d 257 (unsuccessful action by daughter of deceased against medical examiner for conducting autopsy in public to draw attention to state legislators' failure to appropriate additional funds requested by medical examiner's office).

[56] See, e.g., Winkler v. Hawkes & Ackley (1905) 126 Iowa 474, 102 N.W. 418.

[57] McDonald v. Goodman (Ky., 1951) 239 S.W.2d 97.

[58] Winkler v. Hawkes & Ackley (1905) 126 Iowa 474, 102 N.W. 418.

[59] Id. See also Allinger v. Kell (1981) 102 Mich. App. 798, 309 N.W.2d 547.

[60] Palmer v. Broder (1891) 78 Wis. 483, 47 N.W. 744; Gray v. Southern Pac. Co. (1937) 21 Cal. App. 2d 240, 68 P.2d 1011; Lashbrook v. Barnes (Ky. App., 1969) 437 S.W.2d 502.

[61] Winkler v. Hawkes & Ackley (1905) 126 Iowa 474, 102 N.W. 418.

[62] Palmquist v. Standard Acc. Ins. Co. (S.D. Cal., 1933) 3 F. Supp. 358.

do so.[63] Such practice has been held not to be "mutilation" of a dead body.[64]

On the other hand, an early Texas court held that if the autopsy authorization contains the express limitation that the body should not be mutilated, it clearly negates permission to sever and remove any portion of the body.[65] And a federal court deciding New York law has made it very clear that the authorization for an autopsy does not always include the giving of the right to retain body organs, even if the pathologist is well motivated.[66] And this court believed that one should not be primarily concerned with the extent of physical mishandling or injury to the body per se, but rather with whether such action causes mental suffering to the survivors.[67]

When an autopsy is performed under the right granted an insurance company in a policy, the right contemplates the removal of internal organs, but not their retention after a demand for their return.[68]

§ 32A.42. Actions for unauthorized autopsies.

It has been said that mankind can imagine no clearer or dearer right than the right to bury the dead in peace,[69] and that a survivor has the right to bury the body in the condition in which death leaves it.[70] Any interference with these rights by another, including mutilating or disturbing the body, is an actionable wrong.[71] This includes an unauthorized autopsy,[72] since it is a matter of common knowledge that an autopsy disfigures the human body in such a way as to "shock the sensibilities" of the family of the deceased.[73]

Right to bring action

The right to bring a legal action for an unauthorized autopsy belongs to the person having the right of custody of the body for purposes of

---

[63] Lashbrook v. Barnes (Ky. App., 1969) 437 S.W.2d 502.

[64] Id. See also Burgess v. Perdue (Kan., 1986) 721 P.2d 239 (plaintiff had no claim for outrageous conduct when, after giving instructions that her deceased son's brain was not to be examined during autopsy, she received call from hospital that they had her son's brain "in a jar" and wanted to know what she wanted done with it).

[65] Hill v. Travelers Ins. Co. (1927) 154 Tenn. 295, 294 S.W. 1097.

[66] Hendrikson v. Roosevelt Hosp. (S.D. N.Y. 1969) 297 F. Supp. 1142.

[67] Id.

[68] Palmquist v. Standard Acc. Ins. Co. (S.D. Cal., 1933) 3 F. Supp. 358.

[69] Koerber v. Patek (1905) 123 Wis. 453, 102 N.W. 40.

[70] Parker v. Quinn-McGowen Co. (1964) 262 N.C. 560, 138 S.E.2d 214; Terrill v. Harbin (Tex. Civ. App., 1964) 376 S.W.2d 945; McPosey v. Sisters of the Sorrowful Mother (1936) 177 Okla. 52, 57 P.2d 617.

[71] Larson v. Chase (1891) 47 Minn. 307, 50 N.W. 238, 14 L.R.A. 85, 28 Am. St. Rep. 370.

[72] Id. French v. Ochsner Clinic (La. App., 1967) 200 So. 2d 371.

[73] Young v. College of Physicians & Surgeons of Baltimore City (1895) 81 Md. 358, 32 Atl. 177. See also French v. Ochsner Clinic (La. App., 1967) 200 So. 2d 371.

burial.[74] Perhaps the theory behind allowing such an action is based partly on the wrongdoer's interference with the survivor's responsibility, especially a surviving spouse, to protect and care for the departed until last laid to rest.[75] It is permissible, therefore, to consider whether the survivor's responsibility in this regard was met: a court may review the survivor's conduct immediately after the death to determine if there was in effect an abandonment of the body. If so, it may defeat an action for an unauthorized autopsy.[76]

Nature of action and damages

An unauthorized autopsy is regarded as an intentional tort,[77] and has been likened to wrongs such as false imprisonment, seduction, and breach of promise of marriage,[78] a class of torts for which recovery can be had in damages on mental suffering alone without proof of physical injury to the plaintiff.[79]

Awards in cases involving only mental anguish on the part of the survivor have been fairly moderate, and this has not gone unnoticed by reviewing courts.[80] There may be some consideration of the manner in which the unauthorized procedure was conducted; for example, whether the examination was performed in a "decent and scientific manner," or whether there was mutilation of the body visible at the time of the funeral.[81] Where the defendant's conduct has been highly unreasonable or grossly negligent punitive damages have been deemed proper.[82]

In a case in which negligence against a hospital was alleged, it was held that governmental immunity, if applicable, does not cease on the death of the patient.[83]

---

[74]Simpkins v. Lumbermens Mut. Cas. Co. (1942) 200 S.C. 228, 20 S.E.2d 733; Burney v. Children's Hosp. in Boston (1897) 169 Mass. 57, 47 N.E. 401, 38 L.R.A. 413, 61 Am. St. Rep. 273.

[75]Koerber v. Patek (1905) 123 Wis. 453, 102 N.W. 40.

[76]See Meyers v. Clarke (1906) 122 Ky. 866, 90 S.W. 1049.

[77]McPosey v. Sisters of the Sorrowful Mother (1936) 177 Okla. 52, 57 P. 2d 616; Hill v. Travelers Ins. Co. (1927) 154 Tenn. 295, 294 S.W. 1097.

[78]Larson v. Chase (1891) 47 Minn. 307, 50 N.W. 238, 14 L.R.A. 85, 28 Am. St. Rep. 370; Alderman v. Ford (1937) 146 Kan. 698, 72 P.2d 981; Aetna Life Ins. Co. v. Burton (1938) 104 Ind. App. 576, 12 N.E.2d 360.

[79]Crenshaw v. O'Connell (1941) 235 Mo. App. 1085, 150 S.W.2d 489; Koerber v. Patek (1905) 123 Wis. 453, 102 N.W. 40.

[80]See Crenshaw v. O'Connell (1941) 235 Mo. App. 1085, 150 S.W.2d 489. But see also French v. Ochsner Clinic (La. App., 1967) 200 So. 2d 371.

[81]See Cook v. Walley (1891) 1 Colo. App. 163, 27 Pac. 950; Crenshaw v. O'Connell (1941) 235 Mo. App. 1085, 150 S.W.2d 489; Jackson v. Rupp (Fla. App., 1969) 228 So. 2d 916; (Fla., 1970) 238 So. 2d 86; Young v. College of Physicians & Surgeons of Baltimore City (1895) 81 Md. 358, 32 Atl. 177.

[82]Patrick v. Employers Mut. Liab. Ins. Co. (1938) 233 Mo. App. 251, 118 S.W.2d 116; Parker v. Quinn-McGowen Co. (1964) 262 N.C. 560, 138 S.E.2d 214; Medical College v. Rushing (1907) 1 Ga. App. 468, 57 S.E. 1083.

[83]Lane v. City of Knoxville (1936) 170 Tenn. 482, 96 S.W.2d 769.

Who is liable

In a case of unauthorized autopsy, potentially liable parties include all persons who "assisted, advised, abetted, incited, commanded, countenanced, or co-operated" in conducting the examination and those who "approved of it after it was done, if it was done for their benefit."[84] Mere observers having only an academic interest in the procedure are not to be held liable,[85] and probably an attending physician who objectively reports the circumstances of the death to the coroner will not be in danger of liability, even though he actually attends the autopsy, if he did not otherwise participate in reaching the decision to order the examination.[86]

A mortuary seldom will be held liable, having no duty to interfere with an autopsy ordered by a coroner.[87] A Pennsylvania court has said that a mortuary does not even have a duty to notify the deceased's family that the coroner has taken possession of the body.[88]

The physicians who performed an autopsy at the request of a coroner who wrongfully ordered it were held as guilty as the coroner himself,[89] but physicians who performed an autopsy on the wrong patient because of a nurse's mistake in attaching identification tags to the bodies were found free of liability, as were a deputy coroner and the hospital involved.[90] A physician associated with a school district escaped liability on charges that he induced the coroner to order an unauthorized autopsy on the body of a custodian who died the morning after he suffered an apparently minor head injury while at work; the court felt that the investigation commenced by the physician was as much for the protection of the custodian's family's claim as it was for the interests of the school district.[91]

An insurance company will be held liable for ordering an autopsy without obtaining authorization,[92] but a physician who observed an autopsy at the request of an insurance company, and who was unaware that authorization had not been obtained, was found free of liability.[93]

---

[84] Streipe v. Liberty Mut. Ins. Co. (1932) 243 Ky. 15, 47 S.W.2d 1004. See also Deeg v. City of Detroit (1956) 345 Mich. 371, 76 N.W.2d 16.

[85] Streipe v. Liberty Mut. Ins. Co. (1932) 243 Ky. 15, 47 S.W.2d 1004.

[86] Frick v. McClelland (1956) 384 Pa. 597, 122 A.2d 43.

[87] Gurganious v. Simpson (1938) 213 N.C. 613, 197 S.E. 163; Frick v. McClelland (1956) 384 Pa. 597, 122 A.2d 43.

[88] Frick v. McClelland (1956) 384 Pa. 597, 122 A.2d 43.

[89] Gurganious v. Simpson (1938) 213 N.C. 613 197 S.E. 163. See also Streipe v. Liberty Mut. Ins. Co. (1932) 243 Ky. 15, 47 S.W.2d 1004.

[90] Schwalb v. Connely (1947) 116 Colo. 195, 179 P.2d 667.

[91] Frick v. McClelland (1956) 384 Pa. 597, 122 A.2d 43.

[92] Streipe v. Liberty Mut. Ins. Co. (1932) 243 Ky. 15, 47 S.W.2d 1004.

[93] Id.

§ 32A.43. Autopsies authorized by law — Official autopsies.

When death occurs under suspicious or unusual circumstances, suggesting the possibility of foul play, medical examiners or coroners have a statutory right to order an autopsy without seeking the consent of the survivors of the deceased. These generally are called "official" autopsies. Here, the survivor's right to control over the body becomes subordinate in the interest of public welfare.[94]

The statutes giving public officials the right to postmortem examinations vary somewhat from state to state and should be consulted. Courts generally do not favor autopsies, however,[95] and an extensive body of case law has developed in this area that discloses the limits placed upon the public right by the courts in their attempt to balance the public's interest against the interests of the survivors.

The function of the coroner is to aid in the administration of the criminal laws of the state,[96] and it has been said that a coroner acting under the law in ascertaining the circumstances surrounding a suspicious death takes on the character of a judicial inquiry.[97] A coroner does not, however, have unlimited discretionary powers in deciding when an autopsy may be performed.[98]

Under the majority rule, unless authorized by statute,[99] a coroner may not order an autopsy merely to arrive at a cause of death where there is no indication of a possible crime.[1] He or she may act only for the public good and not for private interests.[2] He or she may not order an autopsy at the request of an insurance company,[3] to obtain a fee for a pathologist,[4] or even to advance science.[5]

---

[94] Kingsley v. Forsyth (1934) 192 Minn. 468, 257 N.W. 95; Gahn v. Leary (1945) 318 Mass. 425, 61 N.E.2d 844; Allinger v. Kell (1981) 102 Mich. App. 798, 309 N.W.2d 547.

[95] See, e.g., In re Assbestos Litig. (D. Del., 1988) 123 F.R.D. 84.

[96] Streipe v. Liberty Mut. Ins. Co. (1932) 243 Ky. 15, 47 S.W.2d 1004.

[97] See Kingsley v. Forsyth (1934) 192 Minn. 468, 257 N.W. 95.

[98] Patrick v. Employers Mut. Liab. Ins. Co. (1938) 233 Mo. App. 251, 118 S.W.2d 116; Crenshaw v. O'Connell (1941) 235 Mo. App. 1085, 150 S.W.2d 489; Kingsley v. Forsyth (1934) 192 Minn. 468, 257 N.W. 95.

[99] See Young v. College of Physicians & Surgeons of Baltimore City (1895) 81 Md. 358, 32 Atl. 177; Rushing v. Medical College of Georgia (1908) 4 Ga. App. 823, 62 S.E. 563; Gray v. Southern Pac. Co. (1937) 21 Cal. App. 2d 240, 68 P.2d 1011.

[1] Rupp v. Jackson (Fla., 1970) 238 So. 2d 86; Wilensky v. Greco (1973) 344 N.Y.S.2d 77; Weberman v. Zugibe (1977) 90 Misc. 2d 254, 394 N.Y.S.2d 371; Patrick v. Employers Mut. Liab. Ins. Co. (1938) 233 Mo. App. 251, 118 S.W.2d 116; Coty v. Baughman (1926) 50 S.D. 372, 210 N.W. 348; Woods v. Graham (1918) 140 Minn. 16, 167 N.W. 113. Statutes requiring death certificates generally apply to attending physicians and not coroners. See Rupp v. Jackson (Fla., 1970) 238 So. 2d 86.

[2] Patrick v. Employers Mut. Liab. Ins. Co. (1938) 233 Mo. App. 251, 118 S.W.2d 116.

[3] Streipe v. Liberty Mut. Ins. Co. (1932) 243 Ky. 15, 47 S.W.2d 1004; Patrick v. Employers Mut. Liab. Ins. Co. (1938) 233 Mo. App. 251, 118 S.W. 2d 116; Kingsley v. Forsyth (1934) 192 Minn. 468, 257 N.W. 95. See § 32A.47 regarding contractual rights of insurance companies to request autopsies on policyholders.

[4] Kingsley v. Forsyth (1934) 192 Minn. 468, 257 N.W. 95.

[5] Patrick v. Employers Mut. Liab. Ins. Co.

But if a coroner's decision to order an autopsy is challenged, every reasonable supposition should be indulged in favor of honesty of purpose;[6] it should be presumed the coroner acted properly and lawfully according to his or her best judgment,[7] and in the absence of evidence of bad faith, if the determination was made within the coroner's jurisdiction, it should not be questioned.[8] Since the coroner is a public official, in many states he or she cannot be held liable for ordering an autopsy unless there is proof of wanton and willful misconduct.[9] And authorization by the deceased's survivors has been held to relieve a coroner from liability for an autopsy not authorized by statute.[10]

If a coroner fails to order an autopsy, a court may do so, even though there are no civil or criminal proceedings pending.[11]

§ 32A.44. What constitutes violent, suspicious or unusual deaths.

Death "by violence," as the term is used in statutes giving coroners and medical examiners the authority to order autopsies without the consent of the deceased's survivors, does not mean that the death must have occurred by an apparently unlawful exercise of physical force. Under these statutes death by violence implies any death from other than natural means,[12] and would include nonviolent deaths such as those caused by poisoning[13] and even under certain circumstances, an overindulgence in alcohol.[14]

Under statutes providing for autopsies where the circumstances of the death are "suspicious," this term connotes "foul play,"[15] and in most instances it would include an examination to establish or rule out the possibility of suicide.[16]

Where a statute states that an autopsy may be performed on bodies of "persons as are supposed to have died by violence," the language should

---

(1938) 233 Mo. App. 251, 118 S.W.2d 116. But the coroner may order an autopsy to investigate the possibility of a contagious disease that could reach epidemic proportions. Young v. College of Physicians & Surgeons of Baltimore City (1895) 81 Md. 358, 32 Atl. 177.

[6] Gahn v. Leary (1945) 318 Mass. 425, 61 N.E.2d 844.

[7] Huntly v. Zurich Gen. Acc. & Liab. Ins. Co. (1929) 100 Cal. App. 201, 280 Pac. 163; Kingsley v. Forsyth (1934) 192 Minn. 468, 257 N.W. 95.

[8] Gahn v. Leary (1945) 318 Mass. 425, 61 N.E.2d 844.

[9] See, e.g., Donnelly v. Guion (C.A.-2 Conn., 1972) 467 F.2d 290; Stearns v. County of Los Angeles (1969) 275 Cal. App.

2d 134, 79 Cal. Rptr. 757 (plaintiff claimed allegedly negligent autopsy resulted in his being charged with murder).

[10] Crenshaw v. O'Connell (1941) 235 Mo. App. 1085, 150 S.W.2d 489.

[11] In re Bernardi (1971) 132 Ill. App. 2d 186, 267 N.E.2d 717.

[12] Gahn v. Leary (1945) 318 Mass. 425, 61 N.E.2d 844.

[13] Id.

[14] Id.

[15] Rupp v. Jackson (Fla., 1970) 238 So. 2d 86.

[16] See Brown v. Broome County (1960) 8 N.Y.2d 330, 207 N.Y.S.2d 657, 170 N.E.2d 666, 83 A.L.R.2d 952; Kingsley v. Forsyth (1934) 192 Minn. 468, 257 N.W. 95.

be interpreted to mean "supposed" by anyone within the knowledge of the coroner or medical examiner, and not to mean that there must be a supposition of violence by the coroner or medical examiner himself, except where he might happen to know of his own personal knowledge of such a death.[17]

Death occurring on the job

The New York Court of Appeals has said that in the case of a death occurring on the job, when the nature of the victim's work, the site of the work, and the scene of the death all disclose conditions which often accompany accidents, there must be substantial reasons present to justify the need for an official autopsy.[18] For example, the finding of the dead body of a railroad worker, whose duties included assisting in the assembling and coupling of freight cars, between the tracks in the railroad yard with his left hand partially severed did not warrant an official autopsy.[19] However, in a later Second Circuit case involving New York law the death of a farm worker, occurring two years after a fall from a truck which apparently involved no "foul play," evidently justified an official autopsy by the county coroner, since the court held the operating physicians, charged with unauthorized autopsy and mutilation of a human body, were free from liability under the coroner's authorization.[20]

And where there was no charge of bad faith on the part of the coroner, a Pennsylvania court held that he could not be liable for performing an alleged unauthorized autopsy on the body of a miner who collapsed and died while working in a mine.[21]

Also in Pennsylvania, where a high school custodian struck his head while working, was treated for a laceration by a fellow employee, continued to work the remainder of the day, spent a normal evening at home, but was then found dead the following morning, the county coroner was held free of liability for performing an official autopsy under a statute giving this right "in all cases where death is sudden or violent or is of a suspicious nature and character."[22] And where a California man died at work, and a coroner's autopsy report showed the cause of death as "angina pectoris," there was no abuse of discretion in the performance of a second autopsy to determine the effect of a bruise found on the victim's forehead.[23]

---

[17] Gahn v. Leary (1945) 318 Mass. 425, 61 N.E.2d 844.

[18] Brown v. Broome County (1960) 8 N.Y.2d 330, 207 N.Y.S.2d 657, 170 N.E.2d 666, 83 A.L.R.2d 952.

[19] Id.

[20] Chaparro v. Jackson & Perkins Co. (C.A.-2 N.Y., 1965) 346 F.2d 677.

[21] Hirko v. Reese (1945) 351 Pa. 238, 40 A.2d 408.

[22] Frick v. McClelland (1956) 384 Pa. 597, 122 A.2d 43.

[23] Huntly v. Zurich Gen. Accident & Liab. Ins. Co. (1929) 100 Cal. App. 201, 280 Pac. 163.

In an early Maryland case, a coroner's autopsy was ruled justified where an exceptionally healthy railroad worker's leg was severely injured in an accident and he died the following day. The defense successfully raised was that the injury itself should not have caused the death, and that perhaps a disease, possibly contagious, was the real cause.[24]

Sudden death without evidence of external injury

The finding of a man dead on the sidewalk without any evidence of injury was held not to have justified by law a Missouri coroner's autopsy.[25] And in a North Carolina case, it was held that the plaintiffs had a cause of action for unauthorized autopsy against a coroner where a boy was found drowned in a Y.M.C.A. swimming pool with no outward appearances of injury.[26]

But in Connecticut, a coroner was found free of misconduct when he ordered an autopsy on a sixteen-year-old boy found dead in his bed at boarding school. The boy had a medical history of Marfan's syndrome, a congenital heart defect. Death often occurs from a ruptured aneurysm in these patients, but the school physician who first examined the boy testified that his records indicated recent X-rays had not shown an aneurysm in the boy's case, and that the common indications of death from Marfan's syndrome were not present. There were no external indications as to the cause of death. Most helpful to the defendant's case was the wording of the Connecticut statute in force at the time which, as interpreted, permitted an official autopsy where the cause of a death was obscure.[27]

Death while under medical treatment

A directed verdict for a Florida physician was reversed where an unauthorized autopsy was performed on an elderly woman who died after surgery for a broken hip incurred in a fall from her hospital bed.[28] The defendant, a pathologist at the hospital and also an associate county medical examiner, requested permission for the autopsy from the patient's son. The request was denied, but the autopsy was performed anyway, because, according to the defendant, of the possibility that the death was due to the fall, because of "reasons of insurance or possible litigation," and also for purely "medical" reasons. (The autopsy showed death was caused by an intestinal obstruction and cancer of the colon.) A District Court of Appeals ruled the death was not within the Florida

---

[24] Young v. College of Physicians & Surgeons of Baltimore City (1895) 81 Md. 358, 32 Atl. 177.

[25] Crenshaw v. O'Connell (1941) 235 Mo. App. 1085, 150 S.W.2d 489.

[26] Gurganious v. Simpson (1938) 213 N.C. 613, 197 S.E. 163.

[27] Donnelly v. Guion (C.A.-2 Conn., 1972) 467 F.2d 290.

[28] Jackson v. Rupp (Fla. App., 1970) 228 So. 2d 916.

statute providing for an autopsy in cases of deaths "of criminal violence, by casualty, by suicide, suddenly when in apparent good health and when unattended by any physician ... or in any suspicious or unusual manner." A writ of certiorari to the Florida Supreme Court was discharged.[29]

A forty-year-old woman was admitted to a New York hospital for acute abdominal distress. Her past medical history was negative. Examination disclosed distention of the abdomen, considerable gas in the bowels and free air under the diaphragm, which indicated a perforation of some organ. A pelvic abscess was drained, but the patient refused an exploratory operation. A convulsion developed suddenly on the third day suggesting a pulmonary embolism. The patient died six days later. The husband refused to authorize an autopsy.

The matter was referred to the county medical examiner's office. An assistant medical examiner reviewed the hospital record and chart. The fact that no final diagnosis was entered in the record was noted, but the examiner testified later that he did not know the husband had refused to permit an autopsy. An autopsy was performed on the basis of a "suspicious" or "unusual" death,[30] and it was found that the patient had suffered from a devastating parasitic infection which had caused a perforated sigmoid colon and other deterioration.

A suit was filed by the husband for an unauthorized autopsy. A jury returned a verdict of $12,500. On appeal the reviewing court said the defendant's motion to dismiss the action should have been granted because there could be no recovery unless the circumstances were such that there was "no possible scope for the reasonable exercise of discretion" on the part of the assistant medical examiner in interpreting the application of the statute pertaining to unusual deaths.[31]

A South Dakota coroner could not escape liability for an unauthorized autopsy on a child which he claimed was performed because it appeared the child had died from neglect. At the trial, the only proof he could offer that would suggest neglect was that the parents had allowed the child, who suffered from tuberculosis, to be treated by a chiropractor.[32]

---

[29] Jackson v. Rupp (Fla., 1970) 238 So. 2d 86.

[30] At the trial the defendant testified that there was a valid question whether the patient had been poisoned. In a Massachusetts case, a court held that conflicting diagnoses in a hospital patient's records, some of which suggested the possibility of lead poisoning, was sufficient evidence of death "by violence" to authorize an official autopsy. Gahn v. Leary (1945) 318 Mass. 425, 61 N.E.2d 844.

[31] Cremonese v. City of New York (1965) 23 App. Div. 2d 861, 259 N.Y.S. 2d 235. (Through a procedural error, however, the judgment was reversed only on the ground of excessive amount, and the plaintiff was allowed to accept a reduced judgment of $9,000.)

[32] Coty v. Baughman (1926) 50 S.D. 372, 210 N.W. 348.

Religious objections to official autopsies[33]

Under a county ordinance requiring a medical examiner to perform autopsies which in his opinion are necessary to establish the cause of death, or to determine the means or manner of death, a New York court held that an autopsy could not be performed over the religious objections of the deceased's spouse where the deceased had been struck by an automobile, where there were no criminal charges brought against the driver, and where the only reason for the autopsy was to determine the precise cause of death.[34] In another New York case, the deceased's next-of-kin, Orthodox Jews who did not believe in the desecration of a body after death, had a cause of action for damages against a hospital that failed to notify the medical examiner's office of the plaintiffs' objections, and the court held that there was no support to the defense that the traffic accident in which the deceased was killed had given rise to the possibility of a criminal prosecution, where the police report merely showed that the deceased, while crossing the street, was struck by the rear of a truck making a turn.[35]

In contrast, a Maryland court held that state's power to determine the cause of death under a medical examiner's statute was superior to religious objections of the nearest of kin. The fact situation, however, was considerably different than in the New York case. An eighteen-year-old boy died suddenly and unexpectedly at home. He had not been under the care of a physician, and a Maryland statute grants the state medical examiner the authority to perform an autopsy under such circumstances to determine the cause of death. A lower court refused to grant an injunction to prevent the autopsy, and the state appellate court upheld the ruling.[36]

§ 32A.45. Autopsies performed by mistake.

In a Louisiana case,[37] the patient died following extensive surgery for lung cancer. Immediately after his death the widow was asked to authorize an autopsy. She refused, but later an autopsy was performed, limited to the thoracic and abdominal cavities. The autopsy did not result in disfigurement or mutilation noticeable at the funeral, and the widow did not discover that it had been performed until she read the death certificate several days after the funeral. When she called the hospital, the

---

[33] See also § 32A.40a.

[34] Weberman v Zugibe (1970) 90 Misc. 2d 254, 394 N.Y.S.2d 371 See also Begay v. State (N.M. App., 1985) 723 P.2d 252 (relatives of deceased Navajo had a cause of action against a state medical investigator under thee Civil Rights Act for authorizing an autopsy that violated traditional Navajo religious beliefs).

[35] Rotholz v. City of N.Y. (Sup. Ct., N.Y. County, 1992) 582 N.Y.S.2d 366.

[36] Snyder v. Holy Cross Hosp. (1976) 30 Md. App. 317, 352 A.2d 334.

[37] French v. Ochsner Clinic (La. App., 1967) 200 So. 2d 371.

chief of the surgical service apologized for what he described as an error
by hospital employees.

The widow sued the hospital for damages, claiming mental anguish,
pain and suffering. At the trial the chief of the hospital surgical service
testified that the unsigned authorization form had gotten into the patient's record when it was sent to the hospital morgue, and apparently
because the form contained the signatures of two witnesses (a doctor and
a nurse had signed it before it was presented to the widow), the autopsy
was performed under the mistaken impression that permission had been
granted. This doctor's testimony, however, was ruled hearsay because he
admitted that he was out of town at the time of decedent's death and did
not return until more than a week later. (There was no explanation as to
why the hospital employees involved did not testify on this point.)

The doctor did testify that the autopsy was of medical importance
because it revealed that the type of cancer in the decedent was not the
kind usually caused by smoking.[38]

The widow testified that during his lifetime her husband had expressed objections to having an autopsy performed in the event of his
death, and that she felt that he had "gone through enough" and "there
was no reason for any more." She also testified that after learning of the
autopsy she was unable to sleep, waking up "... many a night, wondering
if Mr. French was really dead when they did it." This testimony was
confirmed in substance by a close friend of the widow.

The case was defended on the basis that (1) there could be no recovery
for mental anguish because the unauthorized autopsy in no way mutilated the dead body or interfered with the burial, and (2) since the widow
did not learn of the autopsy until approximately ten days after her husband's death, and since she was already suffering from the grief and
sadness normally attendant upon the death of a loved one, any additional mental anguish associated with learning that an autopsy had
been performed could result only in such damages as are "de minimus"
and therefore not compensable.

As to the defendant's first argument, which was not successful in trial
court, the reviewing court held that it was true there was no interference
with the burial of the deceased, but it also was true that the widow did
not receive the body in the same condition that it was in at the time of
death.[39] There was a dissection, said the court, and this constituted mutilation. However, the dissection should not be the primary consideration,

---

[38] At the time of this trial, a controversy
was raging over the possible liability of cigarette manufacturers for lung cancer in
smokers. Feeling was especially strong in
Louisiana where several lawsuits were
pending.

[39] Testimony was given on behalf of the

hospital by the pathologist who supervised
the autopsy which established that two
body cavities, thoracic and abdominal, were
entered through the standard anterior "Y"
shaped incision. The various organs were
then removed and examined, and tissue
samples were taken.

held the court, but its effect on the feelings of the family. Thus, the second argument of the defendant also was rejected. In regard to damages, the reviewing court not only disagreed with the contention that the damages were "de minimus," but increased the trial court's award.

In an earlier Colorado case, an autopsy was performed on the wrong hospital patient as a result of a nurse's mistake in attaching identification tags to the bodies. The Supreme Court of Colorado, calling the incident "unfortunate and regrettable," but clearly an occurrence resulting from "untoward happenings," refused to find the physicians involved liable for the nurse's error. The nurse was not made a party to the action.[40]

§ 32A.46. Autopsy reports as evidence.

Autopsy reports, like other hospital records kept in the ordinary course of business, are admissible under the Uniform Business Records Act in most states, at least with regard to the facts contained therein.[41] Mere opinions or conclusions of the pathologist, on the other hand, as opposed to the reported findings, may be inadmissible as an invasion of the province of the jury.[42]

In at least one case it has been held that in actions for malpractice, an autopsy report, for evidentiary purposes, should not be placed in the same category as other hospital records.[43] Most hospital records are prepared primarily for the benefit of the patient, and only secondarily for the benefit of the doctors and the hospital staff; thus, there is a natural desire to see that they are accurate and dependable. But an autopsy, it is argued, is often performed to obtain information useful in defending a lawsuit, and the autopsy report may reflect a less than objective point of view, especially when prepared by a member of the staff of a hospital that could be named a defendant.[44] Both the autopsy report and photo-

---

[40] Schwalb v. Connely (1947) 116 Colo. 195, 179 P.2d 667.

[41] See Brennan v. St. Luke's Hosp. (1971) 446 Pa. 339, 285 A.2d 471; Carroll v. Houtz (1966) 93 N.J. Super. 215, 225 A.2d 584; Abbe v. Woman's Hosp. Ass'n (1971) 35 Mich. App. 429, 192 N.W.2d 691.

[42] St. Luke's Hosp. Ass'n v. Long (1952) 125 Colo. 25, 240 P.2d 917, 31 A.L.R.2d 1120; People v. Hampton (1972) 38 App. Div. 2d 772, 327 N.Y.S. 2d 961. See also People v. Fiddler (1970) 45 Ill. 2d 181, 258 N.E.2d 359; Neas v. Snapp (1968) 221 Tenn. 325, 426 S.W.2d 498; Schelberger v. Eastern Sav. Bank (1983) 93 App. Div. 2d 188, 461 N.Y.S.2d 785, aff'd 60 N.Y.2d 506, 470 N.Y.S.2d. 548, 458 N.E.2d 1225. But see

People v. Carbona (1975) 27 Ill. App. 3d 988, 327 N.E.2d 546 (pathologist's testimony in murder cases that it was "physical impossibility for the subject to have shot himself" was not invasion of province of jury); Malekar v. State (1975) 26 Md. App. 498, 338 A.2d 328 (admission of conclusion contained in autopsy report to effect that death was homicide was not erroneous nor prejudicial where conclusion stemmed from obvious fact that victim was strangled, and was consistent with defense's theory of case).

[43] Horn v. Sturm (Okla., 1965) 408 P.2d 541.

[44] Id.

graphs taken in connection with the report often contain evidence prejudicial to a party in a personal injury action and may be inadmissible on these grounds.[45] In the case of a post-autopsy photograph, the party introducing the document may be prevented from showing a relevant injury or physical condition of the deceased because the photographs show the entire body and thus the "distressing" effects of the pathologist's dissection.[46]

The rule is similar in criminal cases, especially as to photos that are gruesome or show the incision made during the autopsy procedure,[47] unless the photos are necessary to explain the testimony of the witness who performed the autopsy[48] or to identify the victim or the fact or manner of death.[49]

§ 32A.47. Autopsy provision in insurance policies.

Provision valid and enforceable

A person may authorize his own autopsy by entering into an insurance contract containing a provision giving this right to the company.[50] Most life, health, and accident policies contain such a provision that usually states simply that the insurer at its own expense shall have the right and opportunity to order an autopsy in case of death where it is not forbidden by law.[51] In most cases, however, if the deceased's family resists the request, the insurer will be required to show that it is reasonably certain that the autopsy will reveal something otherwise undiscoverable that affects the rights of the parties involved.[52] In the case of worker's compensation, it has been held that, if under the statute an employer has the right to order an autopsy, the employer's insurance company has the same right.[53]

The standard provision in a life, health, or accident policy providing for an autopsy is valid and enforceable,[54] but a clause merely giving an

---

[45]St. Luke's Hosp. Ass'n v. Long (1952) 125 Colo. 25, 240 P.2d 917, 31 A.L.R.2d 1120.

[46]Id.

[47]State v. Watson (Ohio, 1991) 572 N.E.2d 97; State v. Lundgren (Ohio, 1995) 653 N.E.2d 304.

[48]United States v. Davidson (C.A.-8 Ark., 1997) 122 F.3d 531.

[49]Frybach v. State (Ind., 1980) 400 N.E.2d 1128; State v. Buie (Kan., 1978) 575 P.2d 555.

[50]Aetna Life Ins. Co. v. Lindsay (C.A.-7 Ill., 1934) 69 F.2d 627.

[51]Some policies contain an additional provision that no surgical examination of the body of an insured shall be made at the instance of his representatives without due notice having been first given to the company so that its medical officers can be present. See, e.g., Labiche v. Certain Insurance Companies or Underwriters at Lloyd's, London, England (E.D. La., 1961) 196 F. Supp. 102.

[52]Deneen v. New England Mut. Life Ins. Co. (C.A.-Mich., 1980) 615 F.2d 396.

[53]Simpkins v. Lumbermens Mut. Cas. Co. (1942) 200 S.C. 228, 20 S.E.2d 733.

[54]Standard Acc. Ins. Co. v. Rossi (C.A.-8 Ark., 1929) 35 F.2d 667; Clay v. Aetna Life Ins. Co. (D. Minn., 1931) 53 F 2d 689; Cohen v. Guardian Life Ins. Co. (1955) 207 Misc. 266, 138 N.y.S.2d 794.

insurance company the right to "examine the person" of the insured has been held not include the right to an autopsy.[55]

The purpose of the autopsy provision in a policy is to enable the insurance company to determine whether the cause of death asserted by the claimant is within the terms of the policy.[56] It is understandable that companies retain this right; a postmortem examination can be very important in claims in which murder or suicide is suspected, and autopsies frequently are performed to differentiate death by injury from death by disease — an important determination when benefits are payable only for accidental death.[57]

Scope of autopsy

The autopsy provision includes the right to remove, if necessary, the internal organs of the deceased insured, but not the right to retain such organs after they are no longer needed and a demand for their return has been made.[58] Nor does the provision give the right to mutilate a body by unnecessary dissection.[59]

Provision strictly construed

The policy provision authorizing an autopsy has been strictly construed by some courts.[60] This is justified, it is said, not only because the provision has been drafted by the insurance industry for its own benefit,[61] but because an unreasonable exercise of the right of autopsy entails a course of action that is abhorrent to the sensibilities of the relatives of the deceased and involves in some instances desecration of the grave.[62] This view has been criticized.[63]

---

[55] Ewing v. Commercial Travelers' Mut. Acc. Ass'n of Am. (1900) 55 App. Div. 241, 66 N.Y.S. 1056; Sudduth v. Travelers' Ins. Co. (D. Ky., 1901) 106 Fed. 822.

[56] Maryland Cas. Co. v. Harris (C. A.-3 Pa., 1932) 60 F.2d 810.

[57] The fact that a jury concludes that an insured's death was the result of an accident rather than disease does not prevent a court from later holding that a beneficiary is precluded from recovering under an accident insurance policy for refusing to allow the company to order an autopsy, since an autopsy might have revealed a condition that would have influenced the jury to reach a different conclusion. Dvorkin v. Commercial Travelers Mut. Acc. Ass'n of Am. (1940) 258 App. Div. 501, 17 N.Y.S.2d 109.

[58] Palmquist v. Standard Accident Ins. Co. (S.D. Cal., 1933) 3 F. Supp. 358.

[59] Travelers Ins. Co. v. Welch (C.A.5 La., 1936) 82 F.2d 799.

[60] Gath v. Travelers Ins. Co. of Hartford, Conn. (1925) 113 Ohio St. 369, 149 N.E. 389; Bernstein v. Metropolitan Life Ins. Co. (1931) 142 Misc. 516, 255 N.Y.S. 591; McCulloch v. Mutual Life Ins. Co. of New York (C.A.4 W. Va., 1940) 109 F.2d 866; Mutual of Omaha Ins. Co. v. Garrigan (1971) 31 Ohio Misc. 1, 285 N.E.2d 395.

[61] Bernstein v. Metropolitan Life Ins. Co. (1931) 142 Misc. 516, 255 N.Y.S. 591; McCulloch v. Mutual Life Ins. Co. of New York (C.A.-4 W. Va., 1940) 109 F.2d 866.

[62] McCulloch v. Mutual Life Ins. Co. of New York (C.A.-4 W. Va., 1940) 109 F.2d 866.

[63] Howes v. United States Fidelity & Guar. Co. (C.A.-9 Wash., 1934) 73 F.2d 611.

Insurer must initiate proceedings

The right under the autopsy provision is to be exercised by the company. The beneficiary is under no obligation to initiate proceedings for an autopsy,[64] and has no duty to tender the body of the deceased for this purpose until a demand is made.[65] If the beneficiary denies the insurer's request, the insurer should seek court action to determine its right.[66]

Noncompliance by beneficiary — Effect

Refusal by the beneficiary to permit an autopsy that (1) is authorized by the terms of the policy, (2) apparently necessary, and (3) requested within a reasonable period of time after the company receives notice of the insured's death constitutes a breach of the contract and can preclude recovery of benefits.[67] When the autopsy would have established positively the cause of death, the effect of the refusal presents a question of law for a court to decide rather than a question of fact for the jury.[68] But if the insured's body cannot be produced for autopsy through no fault of the beneficiary, e.g., if the body was destroyed by fire or lost at sea, recovery under the policy cannot be denied under the autopsy clause.[69]

The autopsy provision has been construed to be a "present demand, calling for present compliance or refusal."[70] Where an insurance company forwarded proof of loss forms to a beneficiary after she had refused to authorize an autopsy in a written statement in which she said she decided to "defer decision as to permitting autopsy after burial, pending further investigation and consideration," a court held the company did not waive its defense under the policy on grounds of noncompliance with the autopsy provision.[71]

Demand on the right party

There is some uncertainty in situations in which the beneficiary under the policy is not the person having the legal right to authorize the autopsy. One court has said that in such cases the beneficiary's consent or refusal means nothing,[72] but in a case involving a policy on the life of the

[64]Travelers Ins. Co. v. Welch (C.A.5 La., 1936) 82 F.2d 799; Employers' Liab. Assurance Corp., Ltd., of London, England v. Dean (C.A.-5 Ga., 1930) 44 F.2d 524.

[65]Ocean Accident & Guarantee Corp. v. Schachner (C.A.-7 Ill., 1934) 70 F.2d 28.

[66]Travelers Ins. Co. v. Welch (C.A.-5 La., 1936) 82 F.2d 799.

[67]Powell v. Commericial Travelers Mut. Acc. Ass'n, (Ga. App., 194) 137 S.E.2d 759; Employers' Liab. Assur. Corp., Ltd., of London, England v. Dean (C.A.-5 Ga., 1930) 44 F.2d 524; Standard Acc. Ins. Co. v. Rossi (C.A.-8 Ark., 1929) 35 F.2d 667; Howes v.

United States Fidelity & Guar. Co. (C.A.-9 Wash., 1934) 73 F.2d 611; Clay v. Aetna Life Ins. Co. (D. Minn., 1931) 53 F.2d 689.

[68]Howes v. United States Fidelity & Guar. Co. (C.A.-9 Wash., 1934) 73 F.2d 611.

[69]Ocean Acc. & Guarantee Corp. v. Schachner (C.A.-7 Ill. 1934) 70 F.2d 28.

[70]Johnson v. Bankers' Mut. Cas. Co. (1915) 129 Minn. 18 151 N.W. 413.

[71]Hurley v. Metropolitan Life Ins. Co. (1936) 296 Mass. 130, 5 N.E.2d 16.

[72]Travelers Ins. Co. v. Welch (C.A.-5 La., 1936) 82 F.2d 799.

president of a corporation which named the corporation as beneficiary another court has suggested the insurer's demand should have been made on the corporation rather than on the deceased's widow.[73] A demand on a beneficiary's son has been deemed insufficient, where it should have been apparent to the insurer that the demand was not forwarded to the beneficiary.[74]

Affirmative action may be necessary

When a beneficiary remains silent on an insurer's demand for an autopsy, the insurer is left to pursue any lawful course of action necessary to secure its rights.[75] In some jurisdictions, it appears the insurer must take affirmative action through the courts, rather than just sit back and let the beneficiary file suit under the policy.[76]

Reasonable and unreasonable demands

An insurance company's defense to a contested claim based on a beneficiary's refusal to permit an autopsy on the insured may be defeated if the company's demand for the autopsy was unreasonable. Occasionally, a demand will be found unreasonable because of the manner in which it was made, but usually the problem stems from an unreasonable delay in making it.

Manner in which demand made

If a beneficiary refuses to permit an autopsy because she does not fully understand the implications of the autopsy clause, the company can lose its right to enforce the clause if its representatives do not make a special effort to explain it to her.[77] The company has an obligation to "leave nothing to intendment" in making the demand.[78] If the demand is made immediately before the funeral, which has been considered an unreasonable request,[79] the company and not the beneficiary has the duty to suggest a more reasonable alternative — a beneficiary is not expected to make counter propositions regarding arrangements.[80]

A company representative's erroneous advice to an insured's widow that an autopsy on her husband would take several days, when in fact it

[73] Waldo Fertilizer Co. v. Mutual Life Ins. Co. of New York (C.A.-8 Ark., 1934) 72 F.2d 203.

[74] Gath v. Travelers' Ins. Co. of Hartford, Conn. (1925) 113 Ohio St. 369, 149 N.E. 389.

[75] Employers' Liab. Assur. Corp., Ltd., of London, England v. Dean (C.A.-5 Ga., 1930) 44 F.2d 524.

[76] Travelers Ins. Co. v. Welch (C.A.-5 La., 1936) 82 F.2d 799; Employers' Liab. Assur. Corp., Ltd., of London, England v. Dean (C.A.-5 Ga., 1930) 44 F.2d 524.

[77] Johnson v. Bankers' Mut. Cas. Co. (1915) 129 Minn. 18, 151 N.W. 413.

[78] Id.
[79] Id.
[80] Id.

could have been performed in two or three hours, was held to justify the widow's refusal to consent to the autopsy.[81]

An insurer has lost a decision involving a dispute over the exact form of its request. The beneficiary's attorney agreed verbally to an autopsy and asked for forms to give to his client. The company's representative referred him to the pathologist at a local hospital. The pathologist, who had not been told of the specific reason for the autopsy, furnished the attorney with usual hospital forms designed for autopsies performed for purely medical reasons, providing for unlimited dissection of the body. When the beneficiary saw these forms, she refused to sign. Although evidence at the trial showed that a later attempt was made by the company to persuade the beneficiary to change her mind, there was insufficient proof as to whether there was an attempt to explain the difference between limited and unlimited autopsies. The jury, under an instruction by the court that it was the duty of the defendant to make a demand "in a manner and method in keeping with the proprieties of the occasion," found for the beneficiary and the verdict was upheld on appeal.[82]

Timeliness of demand

An insurance company may not delay in its demand for an autopsy merely because the policy provision is silent as to when the autopsy should be performed.[83] An unreasonable delay in demanding the autopsy will defeat the company's right to enforce the provision.[84] However, an insurance company's failure to demand an autopsy before the insured is buried should not necessarily forfeit its right to the autopsy, but should be considered among other evidence in determining whether the demand was reasonable and reasonably made under all circumstances of the case.[85]

Whether there has been an unreasonable delay depends on when the company received notice of (1) the insured's death and (2) the need for an autopsy.[86] Notice of the death of an insured apparently from natural causes does not constitute notice for purposes of the autopsy provision

[81] Employers' Liab. Assurance Corp., Ltd., of London, England v. Dean (C.A.-5 Ga., 1930) 44 F.2d 524.

[82] Hemrich v. Aetna Life Ins. Co. (1936) 188 Wash. 652, 63 P.2d 432.

[83] Bernstein v. Metropolitan Life Ins. Co. (1931) 142 Misc. 516, 255 N.Y.S. 591.

[84] Brunson v. Beneficial Fire & Cas. Ins. Co. (C.A.-5 Tex., 1969) 407 F.2d 841; Reardon v. Mutual Life Ins. Co. of New York (1952) 138 Conn. 510, 86 A.2d 570; Order of United Commercial Travelers of Am. v. Moore (C.A.-5 Ga., 1943) 134 F.2d 558; Cavallero v. Travelers Ins. Co. of Hart-ford, Conn. (1936) 197 Minn. 417, 267 N.W. 370; Provident Life & Acc. Ins. Co. v. Green (1935) 172 Okla. 591, 46 P.2d 372; General Acc., Fire & Life Assur. Corp. v. Savage (C.A.-8 Colo., 1929) 35 F.2d 587; Trueblood v. Maryland Assur. Co. of Baltimore 1933) 129 Cal. App. 102, 18 P.2d 90.

[85] Insurance Co. of N. Am. v. Achor (Fla. App., 1970) 230 So. 2d 166.

[86] Gould v. Travelers' Ins. Co. (1935) 244 App. Div. 274, 279 N.Y.S. 892; Deneen v. New England Mut. Life Ins. Co. (C.A.-6 Mich., 1980) 615 F.2d 396.

should the beneficiary later claim accidental death benefits and the autopsy is needed to determine the true cause of death.[87]

Notice to an authorized agent of the company is sufficient.[88] It has been held that the policy clause stating that no person other than an officer of the company has the power to bind the company regarding information not contained in the application does not apply to a notice to an agent of an impending claim for accidental death benefits.[89]

In deciding whether a company was unreasonable in delaying a demand for an autopsy, a court should consider whether the beneficiary was caused any greater distress by the delay.[90] Generally, the timeliness of the demand is for the jury to decide unless the demand was made so promptly or so tardily after notice of death that reasonable minds could not fairly differ on the question.[91] Delays of only two days[92] and ten days[93] have been held reasonable as a matter of law; delays of five weeks,[94] four months[95] and one year[96] have been held unreasonable as a matter of law; and juries have been given the question in cases involving delays of one week,[97] ten days,[98] three weeks,[99] sixty-five days,[1] and five weeks.[2]

In an early Minnesota case, a company received notice of the insured's death at 11 a.m. A claims adjuster was dispatched the same day for the home of the insured, a farm in another county of the same state. The adjuster arrived at the nearest town, which was two miles from the insured's home, at approximately 7:30 that evening. He spent the remainder of the evening inquiring around town about the death. The next morning he called at the insured's home and found that the funeral was scheduled for 1 p.m. that afternoon. At 10:18 a.m. he informed the widow's mother that his company wanted an autopsy. This was conveyed to the widow who refused, claiming that "it was too close to the time of

---

[87] Id.

[88] See 45 C.J.S. Insurance § 982(3).

[89] Reardon v. Mutual Life Ins. Co. of New York (1952) 138 Conn. 510, 86 A.2d 570.

[90] Clay v. Aetna Life Ins. Co. (D. Minn. 1931) 53 F.2d 689.

[91] Order of United Commercial Travelers of Am. v. Moore (C.A.-5 Ga., 1943) 134 F.2d 558; Cavallero v. Travelers Ins. Co. of hartford, Conn. (1936) 197 Minn. 417, 267 N.W. 370.

[92] Howes v. United States Fidelity & Guar. Co. (C.A.-9 Wash., 1934) 73 F.2d 611.

[93] Employers' Liab. Assur. Corp., Ltd., of London, England v. Dean (C.A.-5 Ga., 1930) 44 F.2d 524.

[94] Cavallero v. Travelers Ins. Co. of Hartford, Conn. (1936) 197 Minn. 417, 267 N.W. 370.

[95] Brunson v. Beneficial Fire & Cas. Ins. Co. (C.A.-5 Tex., 1969) 407 F.2d 841.

[96] Bernstein v. Metropolitan Life Ins. Co. (1931) 142 Misc. 516, 255 N.Y.S. 591.

[97] Maryland Cas. Co. v. Harris (C.A.-3 Pa., 1932) 60 F.2d 810.

[98] General Accident, Fire & Life Assur. Corp. v. Savage (C.A.-8 Colo. 1929) 35 F.2d 587 (held unreasonable).

[99] Reardon v. Mutual Life Ins. Co. of New York (1952) 138 Conn. 510, 86 A.2d 570 (held unreasonable).

[1] Order of United Commercial Travelers of Am. v. Moore (C.A.-5 Ga., 1943) 134 F.2d 558 (held unreasonable).

[2] Waldo Fertilizer Co. v. Mutual Life Ins. Co. of New York (C.A.-8 Ark., 1934) 72 F.2d 203.

the funeral." The adjuster said nothing and left. The claim was denied and suit was filed. The widow was allowed to recover under the policy on the theory that the company's demand was not made within a reasonable time "nor on a proper occasion." The court felt the adjuster could have arranged to hold the autopsy earlier, or possibly after the funeral.[3]

Exhumation (disinterment)

At the turn of the century, when the autopsy provision was first considered by insurance companies, it was predicted that a company insisting on the right to dig up and examine the body of an insured would sell few policies.[4]

Courts generally have construed the autopsy provision to include the right to exhume the body,[5] although there has been some resistance.[6] The right has been deemed waived where the company had ample time and reason to demand the autopsy prior to the burial.[7] Where a representative of the company knew of the death of the insured the day after it occurred, a delay until the day after the funeral in demanding the autopsy was held unreasonable as a matter of law.[8] And where a claims adjuster for a workers' compensation insurer learned within three weeks after the death of an employee that no autopsy had been performed, the court properly refused a request by the insurer for exhumation eight months later.[9] But where a company learned of the death the morning of the funeral, it was suggested that it would have been unreasonable for the company to have ordered an autopsy that afternoon.[10]

A company must have a very good reason to demand an autopsy after burial. It must be reasonably certain that an exhumation will reveal something bearing on the rights of the parties which could not otherwise be discovered.[11] An insurer cannot obtain an autopsy after burial merely

---

[3] Johnson v. Bankers' Mut. Cas. Co. (1915) 129 Minn. 18, 151 N.W. 413.

[4] Ewing v. Commercial Travelers' Mut. Accident Assn. (1900) 55 App. Div. 241, 66 N.Y.S. 1056.

[5] Cohen v. Guardian Life Ins. Co. of Amer. (1955) 207 Misc. 266, 138 N.Y.S. 2d 794; Howes v. United States Fidelity & Guar. Co. (C.A.-9 Wash., 1934) 73 F.2d 611. This rule is important, since in many cases an insurance company does not learn of an insured's death until after burial.

[6] Brunson v. Beneficial Fire & Cas. Ins. Co. (C.A.-5 Tex., 1969) 407 F.2d 841; Mutual of Omaha Ins. Co. v. Garrigan (1971) 31 Ohio Misc. 1, 285 N.E. 2d 395.

[7] Trueblood v. Maryland Assur. Co. of Baltimore (1933) 129 Cal. App. 102, 18 P.2d 90. See also Gath v. Travelers' Ins. Co. of Hartford, Conn. (1925) 113 Ohio St. 369, 149 N.E. 389; Clay v. Aetna Life Ins. Co. (D. Minn., 1931) 53 F.2d 689; Insurance Co. of N. Am. v. Achor (Fla. App., 1970) 230 So. 2d 166.

[8] Root v. London Guar. & Accident Co. (1904) 92 App. Div. 578, 86 N.Y.S. 1055.

[9] Huey Bros. Lumber Co. v. Anderson (Tenn., 1975) 519 S.W.2d 588.

[10] General Acc., Fire & Life Assur. Corp v. Savage (C.A.-8 Colo., 1929) 35 F.2d 587.

[11] McCulloch v. Mutual Life Ins. Co. of New York (C.A.-4 W. Va. 1940) 109 F.2d 866.

on a hope that in the course of the examination something may turn up that will relieve it from liability.[12]

In a federal court case decided in West Virginia, an insured under accidental death coverage suffered a fatal skull fracture in a fall at his club. After two months of investigation, the company's best evidence for justifying exhumation and autopsy was that the insured had been a frequent user of alcohol, and that the death had erroneously been reported in a newspaper as due to a heart attack. The company's request was denied and the denial upheld.[13]

But in a Louisiana case, also tried in federal court, a man insured for accidental death benefits was found dead in his bathtub. The local coroner, who lived just next door, immediately ordered an autopsy and the initial pathologist's findings showed nothing to indicate an accidental death. The insured was buried. Three weeks later the coroner issued an official report listing the death as accidental due to "bone marrow and fat embolism to lungs." These findings were said to be the result of a later examination of microscopic slides of tissue samples taken during the autopsy. The coroner concluded that the deceased must have fractured one or more bones, causing the release of bone marrow and fat which found their way to the lungs. The autopsy report, however, had revealed no fracture. The insurance company requested exhumation which was refused, but the court ruled it was justified.[14]

Respect for the dead militates against granting motions in a court of law for exhumations. Nevertheless, where the interest of justice appears to require it, exhumation will be ordered. Where an insurance company has been denied through no fault of its own the right to produce proof that a claim is invalid, and exhumation is the only means of obtaining this proof, exhumation will be ordered despite the mental anguish caused the survivors.[15]

Attempts to prevent insurance exhumations by claiming that the standard policy language "unless it is forbidden by law" applies to statutes making it unlawful to disinter, mutilate or remove a dead body ("grave robbing statutes") generally have been unsuccessful.[16] A Minnesota court has held that should the beneficiary refuse to consent to exhumation, such a law would prevent the company from exhuming, but the beneficiary's refusal would preclude recovery under the policy.[17] Recov-

---

[12] Ibid. See also Mutual of Omaha Ins. Co. v. Garrigan (1971) 31 Ohio Misc. 1, 285 N.E.2d 395.

[13] Id.

[14] Labiche v. Certain Insurance Companies or Underwriters at Lloyd's, London, England (E.D. La., 1961) 196 F. Supp. 102.

[15] Id.

[16] Howes v. United States Fidelity & Guar. Co. (C.A.-9 Wash., 1934) 73 F.2d 611; Aetna Life Ins. Co. v. Lindsay (C.A.-7 Ill. 1934) 69 F.2d 627; General Accident, Fire & Life Assur. Corp. v. Savage (C.A.-8 Colo., 1929) 35 F.2d 587; Standard Acc. Ins. Co. v. Rossi (C.A.-8 Ark., 1929) 35 F.2d 667.

[17] Clay v. Aetna Life Ins. Co. (D. Minn., 1931) 53 F.2d 689.

ery was also denied in a Georgia case in which a beneficiary failed to notify the insurer of the insured's death until after burial, then rejected the insurer's request for disinterment seventeen days later.[18]

§ 32A.47a. Organ transplants.[19]

In 1975, the Supreme Court of Bronx County, New York was asked to define by declaratory judgment the term "death" as used in that state's version of the Uniform Anatomical Gifts Act, and to clarify the duties of the New York City Medical Examiner with regard to requests by physicians for organ transplants.[20] The controversy arose on March 4, 1975, when Richard Smith, aged twenty-seven, was transferred from Lincoln Hospital to the Neurological Service at Bronx Municipal Hospital Center in a comatose condition from a gunshot wound to the left temporal area of the brain. The patient was found to be totally unresponsive with no spontaneous respiration or movement, and was placed on mechanical respiratory support systems. Tests were conducted in accordance with generally accepted medical standards and it was determined that the patient was neurologically dead on March 5, 1975. The parents of the patient authorized physicians to remove both kidneys and eyes for transplant purposes.

Even though the patient was a suitable donor and appropriate consents had been obtained, the physicians did not remove the organs because of potential legal problems associated with the legal definition of death, and further by policy of the Chief Medical Examiner, city of New York, prohibiting removal of organs from homicide victims. On March 6th the patient, in addition to neurological failure, suffered cardiovascular failure and was pronounced dead. The organs were still not removed, because of the prohibition, and as a result two transplant patients were deprived of kidneys.

The two patients awaiting kidney transplants were prepared to undergo transplant surgery at Montefore Hospital and Medical Center. There were twenty-three such patients whose genetic and immunological tests were found to be compatible for receipt of Mr. Smith's kidneys.

On March 5, 1975 at 9:47 p.m., another patient, Daniel Sulsona, aged twenty-one years, was admitted to the Neurological Service at Bronx Municipal Hospital Center in a comatose condition suffering from a gunshot wound to the right parietal region of the brain. The patient, unresponsive, with no spontaneous respiration or movements, was placed on mechanical respiratory support systems. Tests were conducted in accordance with generally accepted medical standards, and it was determined

---

[18] Powell v. Commerical Travelrs Mut. Acc. Ass'n (Ga. App., 1959) 137 S.E.2d 759.

[19] Editor's Note: Transplantation of organs and tissue in discussed in Chapter 30B of this Cyclopedia.

[20] New York City Health & Hosps. Corp. v. Sulsona (1975) 81 Misc. 2d 1002, 367 N.Y.S.2d 686, 76 A.L.R.3d 905.

that he was neurologically dead on March 6, 1975. Mrs. Maria Sulsona, mother of the patient, authorized the removal of the patient's kidneys for transplant purposes.

Given the almost identical fact pattern in the Susona case with that of patient Smith, the hospital commenced court action to permit physicians to declare Sulsona dead and to authorize the removal of his kidneys for transplantation. On March 7, patient Sulsona, in addition to neurological failure, suffered cardiovascular failure and was pronounced dead. The physicians, on the advice of counsel, removed his kidneys and successfuly transplanted them in two recipients who were matched for genetic and immunological compatibility.

In its petition, the hospital stressed that the Smith and Sulsona cases typify circumstances that occur virtually on a daily basis in the municipal hospitals and which, therefore, lend even greater urgency for judicial resolution of the issue. In support of the petition the court heard District Attorney Mario Merola of Bronx County; Dr. Jack Fein, Assistant Professor, Neurological Surgery at the Albert Einstein College of Medicine; Dr. Julius Korein, Professor of Neurology at New York University Medical Center and Chief of Electroencephalography at Bellevue Medical Center; Dr. Samuel L. Kountz, Professor and Chairman of the Department of Surgery, State University of New York, Downstate Medical Center in Brooklyn; Dr. Frank J. Veith, Professor of Surgery at Albert Einstein College of Medicine, Co-Director of the Transplant Unit at Montefoire Hospital and Chairman of the Transplant Advisory Committee for the New York-New Jersey Regional Transplant Program; and Dr. Louis N. Baker, Director of the New York-New Jersey Regional Transplant Program.

Each of the above witnesses was accepted by all parties as recognized experts in their fields, and there was unanimous agreement among the doctors that kidneys obtained from donors whose deaths are diagnosed on the commonlaw criteria of cardiac and respiratory failure have an 88% incidence of postoperative renal failure, while kidneys resulting from "brain death" criteria[21] are indistinguishable from kidneys obtained from living donors and therefore have the optimal chance of successful transplantation (only 10% to 20% chance of postoperative renal failure).

Samuel L. Kountz, M.D., testified that in the New York-New Jersey region there are about 800 to 1,000 patients each year who suffer renal failure and that the number of patients in this region in "end-stage renal

---

[21] On this issue the court said: "... there presently exists a discrepancy between the common law criteria for determining death which are the easily observable absence of heartbeat and respiration ... and the medically recognized concept of 'brain death' as defined by criteria formulated by the Harvard Medical School's Ad Hoc Committee to Examine the Definition of Brain Death...." Id., 367 N.Y.S. 2d at 687. For a discussion of the criteria used for determination of death, see Chapter 30B of this Cyclopedia.

disease" approximate a public health crisis. He further testified that the absence of a clear, legal definition of death has a "chilling effect" upon transplant surgery in that it causes undue emotional distress on the part of the next of kin who wish to donate organs of the deceased. Hospital administrators do not know how to proceed in implementing the Uniform Anatomical Gifts Act and physicians are reluctant to expose themselves to possible liability.

A representative of the State Attorney General argued that it was the duty of the court to construe the statute as constitutional if there was any reasonable interpretation of the term "death." An attorney for the New York City Medical Examiner's office testified that that office took no position on a definition of death, but was concerned with the postmortem duties imposed upon his office in such cases.

At the conclusion of the evidence, which included a tentative memorandum of policy offered by the New York City Chief Medical Examiner regarding organ transplants in cases falling under his jurisdiction, the court held that in enacting the Uniform Anatomical Gifts Act, it was "with clear legislative understanding" that the legislature intended that the act "would be effectuated by duly licensed medical doctors acting in accordance with generally accepted medical standards," and that the context in which the term "death" was used "implies a definition consistent with the generally accepted medical practice of doctors primarily concerned with effectuating the purposes of this statute."

As an appendix to the decision, the court set out the memorandum of policy of the Chief Medical Examiner, incorporated it into the decision, and approved it for cases in which physicians desire to perform organ transplants.

POLICY REGARDING ORGAN TRANSPLANTS IN ALL CASES WHICH FALL UNDER THE JURISIDICTION OF THE OFFICE OF CHIEF MEDICAL EXAMINER

This statement sets forth the policy of the Medical Examiner with respect to requests for organ transplants in cases falling under his jurisdiction. This statement of policy is adopted in view of the existing law and is subject to change in the event of any pertinent change in law affecting this subject.

In all cases in which physicians desire to perform organ transplants, the following procedure should be followed:

1. The attached Medical Examiner's notification form for transplant donor shall be filled out in its entirety by one of two physicians certifying to the death of the donor and having no connection with the proposed transplant, both of whom shall certify every entry on the form.

2. One of the physicians certifying to the death who is fully familiar with the facts and circumstances of the case, shall notify, by telephone, the Medical Examiner's Office of the certification of death and the request for permission to perform organ(s) transplants. Such Doctor shall advise the Medical Examiner of all the information set forth on the form which the Medical Examiner shall require.

3. After organ(s) are removed for transplantation purposes, the member hospital and its physicians shall furnish the following data and materials to the Chief Medical Examiner:

(a) A copy of the donor's medical record;

(b) A copy of the consent form or testamentary document authorizing removal of organ(s) for transplantation purposes;

(c) The microscopic preparation (slides from organ biopsy); and

(d) The Medical Examiner's Notification Form for Transplant donors, which is to be filled out in its entirety.

The above data and materials shall accompany the body of the donor.

It shall be the policy of the Medical Examiner in all such cases to permit the removal of the organ(s) for transplant purposes, unless under the circumstances, the Medical Examiner shall determine for good cause that the removal of the organ(s) shall impair the ability of the Medical Examiner to perform his duties under Law and to establish the cause of death in any Court proceeding.

I am confident that these policy guidelines will facilitate transplantation of organs while at the same time ensuring the Office of the Chief Medical Examiner can continue to fulfill its statutory duties and responsibilities.

> (s) Dominick J. DiMaio, M.D.
> Dominick J. DiMaio, M.D.
> Chief Medical Examiner
> City of New York

MEDICAL EXAMINER'S NOTIFICATION FORM FOR TRANSPLANT DONOR

1. Hospital _____

2. Patient's Age _____ Sex _____

3. Patient's Name _____

4. Circumstances Surrounding Patient's Admission, Whether Illness, Injury, Foul Play, Homicide, etc. (Note: Circumstances of the Injury, such as Type, Time, Location, Witnesses, etc., should be set forth if available).

_____

_____

_____

_____

5. Hospital Course Including Evidence of Cessation of Cardiac Function or Brain Death (Tests Performed, Neurological Evaluation, Neurosurgical Evaluation, EEG Findings, Cerebral Angiography, etc.)

_____

_____

_____

_____

_____

6. Permission Granted By _____

   Relationship to Donor _____

   (NOTE: A COPY OF THE CONSENT FORM IS TO BE SIMULTANEOUSLY SUBMITTED WITH THIS FORM)

7. Complete Chart with Operative Findings of Organ(s) Transplant Donor and Organ(s) Biopsy.

   Organ biopsy must be taken from the organ(s) removed. Reports and slides must be given to the Medical Examiner in order that he may incorporate the same in his autopsy protocol and thereby establish a permanent to be maintained in the Office of the Chief Medical Examiner.

   Once organ biopsies have been taken, the Medical Examiner's presence will not be required in the operating room. However, the Surgeon must forward a surgical report of his operative technique with the complete description of the organ(s) removed, since they will be made a part of protocol.

8. Name of Medical Examiner Contacted by Telephone _____

_____

9. Time of Death of Donor _____ Date _____
The undersigned Attending Physicians do hereby certify the fact of the decedent's death; and do further certify to the truth of all the entries set forth in this Medical Examiner's Notification Form.

_____ M.D.
Attending Physician
_____ M.D.

(NOTE: THE TIME OF DEATH SHALL BE CERTIFIED BY THE ATTENDING PHYSICIAN AND ONE OTHER PHYSICIAN. NEITHER PHYSICIAN SHALL PARTICIPATE IN THE PROCEDURE FOR REMOVING OR TRANSPLANTING THE ORGAN. PENDING CLARIFICATION OF THE LAW CONCERNING DEFINITION OF DEATH, AUTHORIZATION TO RE-MOVE ORGANS FROM VICTIMS OF HOMICIDES WILL ONLY BE GRANTED FOLLOWING CERTIFICATION BY PHYSICIANS OF CESSA-TION OF SPONTANEOUS HEART FUNCTION.)

V. AUTOPSY FINDINGS IN THE MEDICAL MALPRACTICE CASE*

§ 32A.48. Value of the autopsy.

A request for an autopsy would be a very good idea in every malprac-tice claim involving a death. The days of embarking upon malpractice litigation in scientific darkness because of the absence of a conclusive diagnosis obtainable from postmortem findings should be gone by now. There should be sufficient sophistication on the part of the bar to realize that attorneys do themselves and their clients great injustice if they do not take advantage of the autopsy.

Many facts can be ascertained quickly and easily from a postmortem examination, some that will always defy discovery, and some that re-main in the controversial area of pure medical opinion. While pathology is far more concrete and tangible, and thus probably more of a true science than other branches of medicine, attorneys should not assume, as some laymen do, that everything in pathology is unequivocal. If an attor-ney were to go to a meeting of any pathology society — national, state, or local — where slides are reviewed by the group, he or she would be surprised to see that ten board-certified pathologists may arrive at ten different diagnoses on the same case. Of course, this does not occur fre-quently in practice, but then again it is not at all rare.

Unexplainable deaths do occur. As a matter of fact, the better the examiner, the higher percentage of "undetermined" deaths you might find among his or her reports. Good pathologists can afford to be honest

---

*Except where otherwise noted, the opin-ions expressed in these sections are those of Cyril E. Wecht, M.D., J.D.

because they are secure in the knowledge of their own competency. One can find many coroners' jurisdictions where inept offices may have no cases listing an undetermined cause or manner of death.

Consultation is always available in pathology. Pathologists can send slides around for other opinions. For example, they can send them to the Armed Forces Institute of Pathology in Washington, D.C., where there are numerous specialists, and to various other national experts in subspecialty fields of pathology.

§32A.49. Value of an informed pathologist.

The attorney can help his client by helping the pathologist. A hospital pathologist might not be aware of all of the possible medicolegal ramifications of a particular case. The attorney should see to it that the pathologist is apprised of what the attorney may suspect went wrong.

§32A.50. A problem in hospital autopsies.

Hospital autopsies are not always conducted under ideal circumstances. Many times the hospital pathologist will not even have the patient's record at hand when he or she is scheduled to perform the examination. This is wrong — the pathologist should always consult the record before beginning the autopsy. However, too often the hospital's record procedure leaves much to be desired. The patient's chart may have been sent down from the nursing station directly to the hospital medical record librarian because the nursing staff did not know that an autopsy was to be performed. Occasionally, the pathologist will find that the record has been misplaced or lost somewhere in the hospital. Or, the pathologist may discover that the attending physician has kept the chart to make "progress notes" on the patient's last few days. And not infrequently, the physician will hold the chart and come down to the autopsy room to complete his notes only after he has learned what the pathologist has turned up on examination.

§32A.51. Some malpractice case histories.

Death following injection of contrast medium

A patient presented with a possible renal cyst that had been suggested on routine X-rays. The radiologist wanted to inject a contrast medium into the area for better visualization. He inserted a needle laterally in the patient's back directed in a medial fashion toward the region of the vertebral column, in the area where the kidney should be found. He withdrew fluid to see where the needle was, and, indeed, he got back clear fluid. He then proceeded to inject the dye. A short time later, however, the patient suddenly died.

In many situations, depending upon the location and circumstances, an autopsy might not have been done. It was in this case, however, and the pathologist found that the dye had been injected into the spinal canal. The fluid that the radiologist had withdrawn was not the contents of the renal cyst, but spinal fluid. The needle had gone too far and the radiologist had done, unknowingly, a lateral spinal puncture. The patient had died from spinal shock.

Cervical spinal tap

In a similar case, an individual had a cervical spinal tap done and death ensued soon thereafter. Here, the autopsy revealed that the needle had gone into the upper cervical spinal column, the part just below the foramen magnum, and the patient had died as a result of intraspinal hemorrhage and spinal shock.

Sternal bone-marrow tap

From time-to-time death occurs during or immediately following a sternal bone-marrow tap. In this procedure, the physician uses a syringe with a fairly thick needle that usually has some kind of adjustable guard on it to keep it from going too far. The physician punctures the sternum (breastbone) and then uses the aspirated material for a bone marrow study. Autopsies in several of these cases have revealed hemopericardium (blood in the pericardial sac) as a result of the needle having gone past the sternum into the patient's heart. Contrary to what many laymen believe, the heart is not located way over on the left side of the chest. Part of the heart is to the right of the midline, and the bulk of the heart is immediately to the left of the midline. Thus, this sort of thing can happen if the guard on the needle is not properly placed or if the pressure is too great.

Cardiac catheterization and air embolism

Sudden death has occurred following cardiac catheterization. In some of these cases, the autopsy has revealed that death was due to an air embolism. In an examination for air embolism, caution must be taken during the autopsy. Once the pathologist has opened the body and compromised the circulatory system's integrity, he or she will not be able to demonstrate the presence of air. Unlike blood clots, bone marrow, fat, and other emboli following traumatic episodes, air will be quickly lost because it will simply pass off into the atmosphere. The body, therefore, must be opened using special techniques.

Surgical errors

In cases involving deaths from suspected surgical errors, several things are commonly looked for on autopsy — such things as failure to have properly ligated or cauterized the stump of an appendix with resultant postoperative leakage and peritonitis leading to septicemia, or in the case of a hysterectomy, an improper ligation of uterine vessels or other pelvic vessels that results in intra-abdominal postoperative bleeding.

Unfortunately, some surgical procedures are performed badly. This is particularly true in the case of gallbladder resections, which can be a very difficult procedure. One of the reasons why the incidence of post-gallbladder complications is so high is because there are some surgeons doing these operations who are not fully qualified. If you ask a hospital pathologist what is the worst kind of hospital autopsy, the answer probably will be "where somebody's gallbladder was removed and then there were two or three more surgical procedures to correct postoperative complications." This is a difficult autopsy for the pathologist, and thus a complex legal situation for the attorney to evaluate.

Lethal drug dosage

A thirty-three-year-old woman entered the hospital for an elective hysterectomy. The operation was completed with no apparent complications, but twelve hours later the patient suddenly died. An autopsy was performed, but nothing conclusive was found. In this case, however, the hospital pathologist was alert; he suspected something of an atypical nature and sent blood and tissue specimens to a private laboratory. The results showed a 3.3 mg level of meperidine (Demerol) in the body at death; however, according to the laboratory report, this amount was "within therapeutic range."

The attorney handling the case was not satisfied with the report; suspecting that this was not a correct opinion, he sent the results to several forensic toxicologists, and they all agreed that, in the absence of other findings, in this case only about a one mg% level of meperidine would be sufficient to cause them to consider death from acute meperidine toxicity.

The attorney went back to the hospital record and studied the physician's order sheets. Here it said "Demerol; 100 mg given preoperatively along with scopolamine." This was correct preoperative medication, but there was also a note: "Demerol ordered 100 mg every 2 hours times 12 postoperatively." This Demerol was not ordered "PRN" (as necessary), but every two hours — for a 115-pound woman — twelve times postoperatively. That is why the patient had a 3.3 mg level of meperidine at death. And that is also why the defendant in this case, a board-certified obstetrician-gynecologist, enjoyed a reputation for surgical procedures that usually caused no postoperative pain. Further investigation revealed that there had been two similar deaths involving this physician's patients in the previous twelve months. He was guilty of using a good drug in a way that the manufacturer never had intended.

Blood transfusion reactions

Where a patient dies after a blood transfusion, the autopsy often reveals things that routine antemortem studies do not reveal. At autopsy, the pathologist may find evidence of "hemoglobinuric nephropathy," which means hemoglobin crystals were found deposited in the renal tubules. This tells the pathologist that probably there was a reaction to the blood transfusion.

Respiratory ailments

What about the patient who dies after being treated in an emergency room for pneumonitis and sent home, or dies after being treated over the phone by the physician with an antibiotic order. Many times these cases are "signed out" on the death certificate as lobar or bronchial pneumonia. If an autopsy is ordered, the pathologist may instead find a myocardial infarction.

With regard to lobar pneumonia, certainly the days are gone when one could walk into a hospital ward and immediately pick out twenty people with classic lobar pneumonia. However, we still see the disease in the coroners' and medical examiners' offices. Many times the diagnosis of lobar pneumonia is missed or has been treated improperly. Frequently, the physician has ordered some kind of throat lozenge or given the patient one shot of an antibiotic, instead of medication over a seven-day period or longer after first obtaining appropriate specimens for a bacteriology culture and sensitivity tests.

Brain injuries

Cases in which people die following treatment in a hospital emergency room should always merit an autopsy. Instances of undiagnosed cranial-cerebral injury often occur. In a medium-sized metropolitan area, probably thirty such cases are seen each year on autopsy. In a larger city like New York or Los Angeles, there might be well over 100 cases annually where people have had skull fractures or subdural or epidural hemorrhages that have not been diagnosed. Pathologists have even found patients with foreign objects inside their brains in cases where X-rays were not taken or follow-up studies done, and the patient was not kept in the hospital overnight for observation.

Trauma to the chest and abdomen

Similarly, patients with undiagnosed ruptured thoracic or abdominal viscera following automobile accidents or other kinds of blunt force chest or abdominal trauma often turn up in the coroner's office. A classical situation involves the case of a blunt force trauma to the chest with only some slight degree of chest pain. This patient usually feels reasonably well, and a chest X-ray frequently reveals either a normal chest shadow or only a slight suggestion of mediastinal widening. These chest pains continue, however, and sometimes a chest X-ray is done again (but sometimes it is not) with still no findings. Should this patient die, the autopsy may reveal a ruptured, slowly leaking thoracic aortic aneurysm that was caused by the trauma. This is usually a "dissecting" aneurysm, one that has sealed itself off spontaneously and then later ruptures.

There was the case of a nineteen-year-old boy involved in an automobile accident who continued to complain of pain in his epigastric region. He returned to his general practitioner periodically for several months after the accident, but despite complaints of pain and generalized malaise, no thorough examination was ever done, and no flat plate of the abdomen or chest X-ray was ever made. One night, while lying on the couch in his living room, this boy suddenly died. The autopsy revealed a "black mass" in his left chest region. *It was the patient's stomach.* The stomach had evidently made its way up through a ruptured diaphragmatic hernia and had become incarcerated in the left thorax. It subsequently became gangrenous and caused a collapse of the entire left lung. The boy had died from pulmonary atelectasis (lung collapse), congestion, and shock secondary to the gangrenous stomach.

Blood disorders

There are some disorders with which the pathologists cannot help the attorney: matters that remain very much in the realm of speculation. A good example are the blood (hematological) disorders; specifically the dyscrasias, such as aplastic anemia, agranulocytosis, the leukemias, etc. Usually a diagnosis can be established with ease, but when the case involves a malpractice claim that the disorder is associated with a particular drug the patient was taking, the pathologist seldom can come up with a firm, unequivocal answer for the attorney. However, where the clinical history and temporal relationships are strongly suggestive, then a direct causal relationship may be established with a reasonable degree of medical probability or certainty.

Tumors

In tumor cases, the malpractice issue often involves the age of the tumor. This question no pathologist can answer with scientific certainty. Valid opinions have been given on both sides of these cases by competent medical experts, but scientifically, a pathologist cannot look at a tumor, either a primary lesion or one of metastases, and say that "this is a five-month old cancer." The use of these so-called doubling-time calculations can be helpful in certain cases, depending on the histological nature of the tumor and the clinical history, but this concept should not be applied as if it were a universally consistent and scientifically absolute law.[22]

Deaths under anesthesia

Possibly the most difficult cause-of-death case for the pathologist is the request to pinpoint the etiology and mechanism of an anesthesia death. Most of these deaths are due to inadequate ventilation that leads to hypoxia (oxygen deficiency), arrhythmia (irregular heart rhythm), and cardiac arrest. However, the pathologists cannot see or demonstrate arrhythmia or cardiac arrest at autopsy; in fact, approximately 35% of so-called "heart attack" deaths do not reveal specific, significant morbid anatomy on the autopsy table. Careful, thorough analysis of the anesthesiology and operative records is required to evaluate these cases properly.

Allergic reactions

Fatal allergic reactions also are difficult to determine at autopsy. In many cases, it is a negatively arrived-at diagnosis. The pathologist usually will find something on the order of pulmonary edema (fluid accumulation) and congestion, and perhaps some laryngeal (throat area) edema. Eosinophylia (an abnormal increase in the number of eosinophils, *i.e.*, leukocytes, or other granulocytes in the blood that are characteristic of allergic states) is an important laboratory finding, but a complete autopsy must be performed to rule out other causes. Obviously, the clinical history in such a case is extremely important.

Drug interactions

Drug interactions also are difficult to diagnose postmortem. These cases do not necessarily involve toxicity of a particular drug as such, but the formidable problem of demonstrating in tangible fashion the physiological complications produced by the adverse interaction of two or more drugs. The question is often should the physician have ordered drug A in the presence of drug B? Or should only one-half dose of drug C have been given in conjunction with drug D?[23] The pathologist may not always be of definitive assistance in these cases. However, a thorough autopsy to rule out other cases, correlated with a detailed medical history, may

---

[22] Editor's Note: The "doubling-time" concept in tumor growth is discussed in Chapter 38, § 38.42, of this Cyclopedia.

[23] Editor's Note: For summaries of drug allergy and drug interaction cases that have reached the courts, including jury verdicts and settlements, see the latest edition of *Drugs in Litigation: Damages Awards Involving Prescription and Nonprescription Drugs*, LEXIS Law Publishing, Charlottesville, Va.

enable the pathologist to arrive at a diagnosis of drug reaction with a reasonable degree of medical certainty.

§ 32A.52. Exhumations.

If a malpractice case concerns a possible fracture, epidural or subdural hematoma, certain toxic substances, or in some instances surgical error, and no autopsy was ordered at the time of death, the plaintiff's attorney might be able to accomplish something by requesting an exhumation of the body. In Pittsburgh, in a wrongful death case involving a suspected perforation of a patient's uterus during surgery, an exumation was ordered a year and a half after the patient's death. On autopsy it was found that the woman's pubic organs were the best preserved of any organs in the body, and it was easily determined that there had been perforation. The noted forensic pathologist Dr. Alan Moritz once had a case in which he exhumed and autopsied a woman that had been dead seven years and found a subdural hematoma.

If a case concerns barbiturates, heavy metals, or carbon monoxide, one may go back months and maybe even years later to detect such evidence in the embalmed body. With many drugs, however, there can be no value in exhumation. This would be true with volatile compounds and those that are destroyed by embalming fluid.

§ 32A.53. Conclusions.

While autopsies are not necessarily always the beginning and the end of a medical malpractice case, and while the pathologist's testimony frequently is just one more medical expert's opinion, the autopsy findings are usually important and in some instances can supply the total medical answer for that particular case. Any attorney experienced in bringing medical malpractice actions knows that it is best not to get too far involved in the matter unless there really is provable theory. Trying to deceive oneself and others in a case by not having an autopsy performed when there is an opportunity to do so can be extremely foolish, costly, and embarrassing.

VI. RELATED TOPICS

§ 32A.54. College of American Pathologists' guidelines for autopsy technique.

According to guidelines for autopsy technique established by the Autopsy Committee of the College of American Pathologists,[24] autopsy inci-

---

[24]Hutchins, G. M., and The Autopsy Committee of the College of American Pathologists, *Practice Guidelines for Autopsy Pathology: Autopsy Performance*, 118 Arch. Path. Lab. Med. 19 (Jan.), 1994.

sions should be sharply and cleanly cut. A "Y" incision is recommended for the basic examination of both sexes and is modified to conform with any autopsy limitations. Care should be exercised to protect the entire face, forehead, and exposed parts of the body from damage.

In the performance of the cranial examination, it is preferable that the scalp not be reflected anterior to a normal hairline, since reflection beyond this point may create a crease in the skin that may be difficult for the embalmer to efface. The recommended technique for cranial examination is a transverse incision of the scalp, made from mastoid to mastoid, posterior to the vertex of the skull. In the removal of the calvarium, the temporal muscles should not be excised; a single, horizontal cut with slight reflection of the muscle to allow for appropriate saw cuts should be made. To avoid overriding of the replaced calvarium, it is suggested that the occipital bone be sawed as far posteriorly as possible. In the temporal area, the anterior and posterior cuts through the calvarium should form an obtuse angle. On completion of the intracranial examination, a small amount of absorbent material may be placed within the cranial cavity, the calvarium replaced, and a few sutures placed in the scalp to temporarily hold the calvarium in position. Care should be exercised to avoid distortion of facial features of the body during the performance of the cranial examination.[25]

Incisions in the posterior or lateral abdominal or thoracic walls should be avoided, if at all possible, to prevent embalming fluid leakage. Incisions close to the anterior midline should be utilized whenever possible. The breast plate should be completely removed and replaced in the body on completion of the autopsy. The testes should be removed through the inguinal canals. Unless the investigation of specific pathologic changes requires alternative approaches in removing the pelvic organs, it is preferable that the pelvic floor and labia not be cut, a generous cuff of rectum be left, and the uterus be removed with a short piece of vagina, leaving a generous cuff. In removing the neck organs, the carotid and subclavian arteries should be dissected free and left intact with an adequate length of vessel.[26]

§ 32A.55.　Psychological autopsies.[27]

Effective mental health assessments typically require the participation and cooperation of the examinee. At the very least, it is considered essential that the examinee be available for the evaluation. However, some legal questions arise that necessitate an examination of a decedent's mental state prior to his or her death. Mental health evaluations

[25] Id.
[26] Id.
[27] Primary source: Ogloff, J. R. P., and Otto, R. K., *Psychological Autopsy: Clinical and Legal Perspectives*, 37 St. Louis L.J. 607 (Spring), 1993, reprinted in 43 Defense L.J. 597 (Winter), 1994.

that address such concerns — "psychological autopsies," "psychiatric autopsies" or "reconstructive psychological evaluations" — are receiving an increasing amount of attention in both legal and mental health arenas.

Psychological autopsy[28] is a relatively unstructured clinical technique in which a mental health professional attempts to discern the mental state of a deceased person at some previous point in time. Because the subject of inquiry is not available for interview and examination, this type of evaluation is substantially different from most evaluations conducted by mental health professionals for either therapeutic or forensic purposes.

Compared to more traditional evaluations, psychological autopsy is a relatively new and unrefined technique. Nonetheless, expert testimony based on psychological autopsies has been admitted by courts in both civil and criminal cases with increasing frequency.[29]

There are some differences of opinion regarding the definition of psychological autopsy and what it entails. Although psychological autopsies historically focused on determining the manner of death, suicide versus accidental death, natural death, or homicide, the technique can be defined more broadly to include techniques or a group of techniques whereby a mental health professional attempts to describe or discern the mental state of a deceased or missing person at some prior point in time. Bruce W. Ebert defined the psychological autopsy as "a process designed to assess a variety of factors including behavior, thoughts, feelings, and relationships of an individual who is deceased."[30] Given this more expansive definition, psychological autopsy describes not only investigations/assessments designed to determine mode of death, but also any assessments of the prior mental state of a deceased person.

Psychological autopsies differ from other types of mental state evaluations with which judges and attorneys are familiar. Competency or capacity evaluations that are frequently performed for the courts, such as

---

[28]For purposes of this discussion, no distinction is made between psychological autopsy and psychiatric autopsy. Most writers make little distinction between the two techniques, and the and goals of both techniques are virtually identical.

[29]See Campbell v. Young Motor Co. (Mont., 1984) 684 P.2d 1101 (workers' compensation); Harvey v. Raleigh Police Dep't (N.C. App., 1987) 355 S.E.2d 147 (worker's compensation); Rodriguez v. Henkle Drilling & Supply Co. (Kan. App., 1992) 828 P.2d 1335 (workers' compensation); Kackman v. North Dakota Workers' Comp. Bur. (N.D., 1992) 488 N.W.2d 623 (workers' compensation); Evans v. Provident Life & Acc.

Ins. Co. (Kan., 1990) 815 P.2d 550 (life insurance claim); Estate of Skulina (Mich. App., 1988) 425 N.W.2d 135 (intent as to intestate succession); Mache v. Mache (Ill. App., 1991) 578 N.E.2d 1253 (alleged undue influence on testator); Thompson v. Mayes (Tex. App., 1986) 707 S.W.2d 951 (murder or suicide); Gaido v. Weiser (N.J. Super., 1988) 545 A.2d 1350 (medical malpractice); Beaver v. Hamby (M.D. Tenn., 1983) 587 F. Supp. 88 (murder or suicide); Jackson v. State (Fla. App., 1989) 553 So. 2d 719 (suicide allegedly result of child abuse).

[30]Ebert, B. W., *Guide to Conducting a Psychological Autopsy,* 18 Prof. Psychology: Res. & Prac. 52, 1987.

guardianship, competency to stand trial, and competency to testify, differ from psychological autopsies in two important ways. In these competency or capacity evaluations, the focus is on current mental state and adjustment, and the individual of interest is available for interview and evaluation. Although criminal responsibility/sanity evaluations, like psychological autopsies, require the examiner to offer some opinion about the examinee's mental state at some prior point in time, these evaluations, like capacity/competency evaluations, differ from psychological autopsies in that the subject of interest is available for examination.

The technique of the psychological autopsy

There is no agreed upon format for conducting psychological autopsies. It largely consists of the analysis of third-party information, which typically is derived from two sources — interviews with significant others, and records of various types. Persons close to the deceased, such as spouse, parents, children, co-workers, friends, physicians, and supervisors, can provide both historical information, such as whether there was a history of depression or suicide attempts and how the individual typically responded to stress, and information about more recent developments and behaviors such as whether the deceased was under any financial pressure, what the deceased's mood was like at the point in time of interest, and whether the deceased made any plans for the future. Both kinds of information may be relevant to assessing and determining one's mental state at a particular point in time.

Those conducting psychological autopsies also rely heavily on various types of archival information, both recent and remote. Hospital, mental health, medical, and school records, letters and diaries written by the deceased and videotapes on which the deceased appears all may provide information relevant to assessing the person's mental state at a particular point in time.

Ebert[31] and Shneidman[32] offer guidelines for conducting psychological autopsies. Both writers, however, note that their guidelines are not fixed and inflexible. They encourage practitioners to work from the guidelines, and to adapt the technique to their particular situation. Thus, despite publication of these guidelines, there remains no standard technique or approach for conducting a psychological autopsy. Therefore, the term "psychological autopsy" still describes a goal of an inquiry as much as a particular technique.

Limitations of Psychological Autopsies

There are a number of shortcomings inherent in psychological autopsies, many of which are generally shared by therapeutic or forensic eval-

---

[31] Id.
[32] Shneidman, E. S., *The Psychological*   *Autopsy,* 11 Suicide to Life-Threatening Behav. 325, 1981.

uations. These limitations are presented to demonstrate how they may affect the nature of the investigation. Clearly, the greatest limitation of the psychological autopsy is that the individual of interest is not available for examination. This feature, of course, distinguishes psychological autopsies from virtually every other kind of mental health evaluation. It could be argued that availability of the subject is not relevant because it is past mental state, not present mental state, that is at issue. This argument is a weak one, since it is acknowledged that there is typically some relationship between present mental state and past mental state, though it may be a tenuous one in some cases. Moreover, availability of the subject also provides the examiner with the opportunity to question the individual of interest about his or her thoughts, emotions, and reactions at the time of interest — factors that are clearly relevant to determining mental state.

In defending the autopsy technique and the fact that the individual of interest cannot be assessed or interviewed, Bendheim asserted that the psychiatric autopsy "appears to be more objective and less controversial than the analysis of the living examinee."[33] Such a claim is interesting and, if true, would suggest that mental health professionals should consider, as a matter of standard practice, not interviewing examinees directly, even when they are available for such examination. Of course, whether a more objective evaluation can be obtained with or without interviewing the patient is an empirical question that is subject to study.

A major part of many mental health evaluations, for psychologists at least, is psychological testing. Standardized tests have been developed to measure psychopathology and many psychological constructs. Furthermore, some tests, such as protective measures, lack face validity and, as such, are less vulnerable to dissimulation (i.e., conscious distortion) on the part of the examinee in order to appear a particular way to the examiner. Thus, one clear limitation of psychological autopsies is the impossibility of psychological test administration.[34] The second major weakness of the psychological autopsy is its retrospective nature. The examiner is required to offer observations or opinions about past mental state, which is rarely, if ever, an objective of therapeutic evaluations. Memories and recollections of third parties are likely to suffer over time. Of course, this concern also applies to some forensic evaluations such as sanity/diminished capacity evaluations.

---

[33] Bendheim, O. L., *The Psychiatric Autopsy; Its Legal Application*, 7 Bull. Am. Acad. Psychiatr. & L. 400, 1979.

[34] Of course, any psychological tests that the deceased completed prior to death might provide helpful information. While a psychologist might be able to complete some psychological tests once he or she has accumulated a significant amount of information about a subject during a psychological autopsy, such reconstructive testing would be of questionable reliability and validity.

Another limitation of the psychological autopsy is that third-party informants may distort representations of the decedent for a variety of reasons. In cases in which a psychological autopsy is conducted for the purpose of determining mode of death, significant others may find it difficult to conclude that the decedent committed suicide, and they may unconsciously distort their impressions of the decedent as a result. Additionally, the accuracy of the survivors' observations or recollections may be affected by their grief.

When the psychological autopsy is being performed for some kind of forensic purpose, those close to the decedent may have a personal stake in particular conclusions, and they may purposefully distort their reports. Prospective heirs may be motivated to distort their description of the decedent's testamentary capacity or succession wishes prior to death for personal gain. Of course, the potential for purposeful distortion on the part of the examinee or third parties is an issue with many types of forensic mental health evaluations.

Shaffer and his colleagues[35] noted the potential for mental health professionals conducting psychological autopsies to feel obligated to offer explanations regarding mode of death or mental state, even when reasonable conclusions cannot be offered. Of course, this potential also exists when mental health professionals are conducting a variety of therapeutic and forensic evaluations. Similarly, there appears to be considerable pressure on professionals conducting psychological autopsies to offer conclusory and "ultimate issue" opinions, even when a conclusory opinion cannot be supported and should not be offered.

Shaffer and his colleagues[36] also noted that the lack of a standard technique for psychological autopsies increased the possibility of unreliable assessments. In response to this, they recommended use of a structured and normed instrument, assessing a variety of behaviors of the deceased, which could be completed by persons close to the deceased.

The above limitations, in combination with the fact that there have been few studies examining the reliability and validity of psychological autopsies, suggest that producers and consumers of psychological autopsies should limit their confidence in the procedure and opinions.

§ 32A.56. Accuracy of death certificates.[37]

In the United States, every death must be reported to state authorities on a prescribed form designed for reporting the "underlying cause of

---

[35] Shaffer, J. W., et al., *Assessment in Absentia: New Directions in the Psychological Autopsy,* 130 Johns Hopkins Med. J. 308, 1972.

[36] Id.

[37] Messite, J., and Stellman, S. D., *Accuracy of Death Certificate Completion: The Need for Formalized Physician Training,* 275 J.A.M.A. 794 (Mar. 13), 1996. See also Kingsford, D. P., *A Review of Diagnostic Inaccuracy,* 35 Med. Sci. Law 347 (Oct.), 1995.

death," which has been defined as "the disease or injury that initiated the train of morbid events that led directly to death, or the circumstances of an accident or violence that produced the fatal injury."[38] This section of the death certificate is usually completed by a licensed physician.

The death certificate is a public health surveillance tool with essential legal and public health functions. On the legal side, it is relied upon in settling estates and payment of life insurance benefits. In some cases, the underlying cause of death section is extremely important, especially in claims under health insurance and accidental death policies, as well as under double-indemnity clauses of life policies. Cause of death can also be significant is personal injury and wrongful death cases, and in some criminal cases.

From the standpoint of public health, data included in the death certificate are a major means of identifying community health problems and evaluating the effectiveness of programs designed to deal with them. For example, the allocation of public funds for disease prevention and research programs depends largely on the interpretation of trends in mortality rates obtained from death certificates.

Notwithstanding the importance of death certificates, a study has raised questions as to the accuracy of the certifying physicians' statements regarding the underlying cause of death. Using written cases of hospital deaths adapted from materials from the National Center for Health Statistics, researchers from the New York Academy of Medicine and the American Health Foundation, New York City, tested twelve practicing internists, twenty-one internal medicine residents, and thirty-five senior medical students on accuracy in completing the cause-of-death section of the death certificate used in New York City. The underlying cause of death recorded by each participant was compared with the correct cause as determined by a nosologist (expert in the classification of diseases). The overall level of agreement for the practicing internists was only 56.9%, which was only slightly higher than the internal medicine residents (56%) and the medical students (55.7%).[39]

According to the researchers, who found a substantial underreporting of death from circulatory diseases and diabetes, the variation in the

---

[38] World Health Organization, *Manual of the International Statistical Classification of Diseases, Injuries, and Causes of Death, Based on the Recommendations of the Ninth Revision Conference, 1975*, World Health Organization, Geneva, Switzerland, 1977.

[39] A review in 1995 of autopsy reports also revealed startling evidence of clinical diagnostic inaccuracy. The major clinical diagnosis was not confirmed by autopsy evidence in up to 45% of the cases, with typical error rates of up to 30% In as many as 24% of the cases, the patient received the wrong treatment. The author of the report found that, despite the current widespread use of advanced diagnostic modalities, these clinical error rates have changed little from those reported in a similar study conducted in 1912. Kingsford, D. P., *A Review of Diagnostic Inaccuracy*, 35 Med. Sci. Law 347 (Oct.), 1995.

extent of agreement on cause of death appears to reflect a lack of training in death certificate completion at all levels of medical experience, which strongly suggests the need to include such training as part of physician education.

ANNOTATIONS

§ 32A.96. Medical references.

The following additional references may aid in further research on the material covered in Chapter 32A. For a guide to the abbreviations used in references to periodicals, see Chapter 3, § 3.36.

Adelson, L., *The Forensic Pathologist*, 237 J.A.M.A. 1585 (April 11), 1977.

Adelson, L., *The Pathology of Homicide*, Charles C. Thomas, Publisher, Springfield, Ill., 1974.

Anderson, G. S., *The Use of Insects to Determine Time of Decapitation: A Case-Study from British Columbia*, 42 J. Forensic Sci. 947 (Sept.), 1997.

Avis, S. P., *Death Investigation in Canada*, 43 J. Forensic Sci. 377 (Mar.), 1998.

Baselt, R. C., and Cravey, R. H., *Disposition of Toxic Drugs and Chemicals in Man*, 4th ed., Charles C. Thomas, Publisher, Springfield, Ill., 1986.

Bass, M., et al., *Death-Scene Investigation in Sudden Infant Death*, 215 N. Engl. J. Med. 100, 1986.

Bernstein, M. L., "Forensic Odontology," in *Introduction to Forensic Sciences*, 2d ed. (W. G. Eckert, editor), CRC Press, Boca Raton, Fla., 1997.

Bierig, J. R., *Actions for Damages Against Medical Examiners and the Defense of Sovereign Immunity*, 18 Clin. Lab. Med. 139 (Mar.), 1998.

Bierig, J. R., *A Potpourri of Legal Issues Relating to the Autopsy*, 120 Arch. Pathol. Lab. Med. 759 (Aug.), 1996.

Breitenecker, R., *Shotgun Wound Patterns*, 52 Am. J. Clin. Path. 258, 1969.

Briglia, E. J., et al., *The Distribution of Ethanol in Postmortem Blood Specimens*, 37 J. Forensic Sci. 991 (July), 1992.

Brody, G. I., et al., *The Identification and Delineation of Myocardial Infarcts*, 84 Arch. Path. 312, 1970.

Burke, T. W., and Rowe, W. F., *Bullet Ricochet: A Comprehensive Review*, 37 J. Forensic Sci. 1254 (Sept.), 1992.

Burrows, S., *The Postmortem Examination: Scientific Necessity or Folly?*, 233 J.A.M.A. 441, 1975.

Byrne, A., and Nilges, R. G., *The Brain Stem in Brain Death: A Critical Review*, 9 Issues L. & Med. 3 (Summer), 1993.

Campbell, K., *Post-Mortems: How and Why They Are Carried Out*, 93 Nurs. Times 52 (Apr. 16), 1997.

Caplan, Y., editor, *Medicolegal Death Investigation: Treatises in the Forensic Sciences*, The Forensic Sciences Foundation Press, Colorado Springs, Colo., 1997.

Chandramohan, D., et al., *Verbal Autopsies for Adult Deaths: Issues in Their Development and Validation*, 23 Int. J. Epidemiol. 213 (Apr.), 1994.

Charlton, R., et al., *Autopsy and Medical Education: A Review*, 87 J. Royal Soc. Med. 232 (Apr.), 1994.

Coe, J. I., and Austin, N., *The Effects of Various Intermediate Targets on Dispersion of Shotgun Patterns*, 13 Am. J. Forensic Med. 281 (Dec.), 1992.

Cotran, S.. R., et al., editors, *Robbins Pathologic Basis of Disease*, 6th ed., W. B. Saunders Company, Philadelphia, 1999.

Damjanov, I., and Linder, M. D., editors, *Anderson's Pathology*, 10th ed., 2 vols., Mosby-Year Book, Inc., St. Louis, 1996.

Davis, J. H., *Bodies Found in Water*, 7 Am. J. Forensic Med. Pathol. 291 (Dec.), 1986.

Degaetano, D. H., et al., *Fungal Tunneling of Hair from a Buried Body*, 37 J. Forensic Sci. 1048 (July), 1992.

Dijkhuis, H., et al., *Medical Examiner Data in Injury Surveillance: A Comparison with Death Certificates*, 139 Am. J. Epidemiol. 637 (No. 6), 1994.

DiMaio, D. J., and DiMaio, V. J. M., *Forensic Pathology*. 2d. ed., CRC Press, Boca Raton, Fla., 1999.

DiMaio, V. J. M., and Dana, S. E., *Handbook of Forensic Pathology*, Landes Bioscience, Georgetown, Tex., 1998.

Donoghue, E. R., et al., *Criteria for the Diagnosis of Heat-Related Deaths*, 18 Am. J. Forensic Med. Pathol. 11 (Mar.), 1997.

Eckert, W. G., et al., *Disinterments: Their Value and Associated Problems*, 11 Am. J. Forensic Med. 9, 1990.

Eckert, W. G., editors, *Introduction to Forensic Sciences*, 2d ed., CRC Press, Boca Raton, Fla., 1997.

Enticknap, J. B., *Biochemical Changes in Cadaver Sera in Fatal Acute Heart Attacks*, 7 J. For. Med. 135, 1960.

Fitzpatrick, J. J., and Macaluso, J., *Shadow Positioning Technique: A Method for Postmortem Identification*, 30 J. Forensic Sci. 1226, 1985.

Flynn, L. L., *Collection of Fiber Evidence Using a Roller Device and Adhesive Lifts*, 37 J. Forensic Sci. 106 (Jan.), 1992.

Froede, R. C., editor, *Handbook of Forensic Pathology*, College of American Pathologists, Northfield, Il., 1990.

Fuller, R. H., *The Clinical Pathology of Human Near-Drowning*, 56 Proc. Royal Soc. Med. 33, 1963.

Gillett, R., and Warburton, F. G., *Barbiturate Blood Levels Found at Necropsy in Proven Cases of Acute Barbiturate Poisoning*, 23 J. Clin. Path. 435, 1970.

Glassman, D. M., and Dana, S. E., *Handedness and the Bilateral Asymmetry of the Jugular Foramen*, 37 J. Forensic Sci. 140 (Jan.), 1992.

Gowitt, G. T., and Hanzlick, R., *Atypical Autoerotic Deaths*, 13 Am. J. Forensic Med. Pathol. 115, 1992.

Guileyardo, J. M., et al., *Renal Artery Bullet Embolism*, 13 Am. J. Forensic Med. 288 (Dec.), 1992.

Hagland, W. D., and Ernst, M. F., *The Lay Death Investigator: In Search of a Common Ground*, 18 Am. J. Forensic Med. Pathol. 21 (Mar.), 1997.

Hagland, W. D., and Reay, D. T., *Problems of Recovering Partial Human Remains at Different Times and Locations: Concerns for Death Investigators*, 38 J. Forensic Sci. 69 (Jan.), 1993.

Hagland, W. D., and Sorg, M. H., editors, *Forensic Taphonomy*, CRC Press, Boca Raton, Fla., 1997.

Hagland, W. D., and Sperry, K., *The Use of Hydrogen Peroxide to Visualize Tattoos Obscured by Decomposition and Mummification*, 38 J. Forensic Sci. 147 (Jan.), 1993.

Hanzlick, R., and Combs, D., *Medical Examiner and Coroner Systems: History and Trends*, 279 J.A.M.A. 870 (Mar 18), 1998.

Hanzlick, R., and Mills, D. H., "Cause-of-Death Statements and the Death Certificate" in *Medicolegal Death Investigation: Treatises in the Forensic Sciences* (Y. Caplan, editor), The Forensic Sciences Foundation Press, Colorado Springs, Colo., 1997.

Hanzlick, R., and Parrish, R. G., *Death Investigation Report Forms (DIRFs): Generic Forms for Investigators (IDIRFs) and Certifiers (CDIRFs)*, 39 J. Forensic Sci. 629 (No. 3), 1994.

Hanzlick, R., and Parrish, R. G., *Epidemiologic Aspects of Forensic Pathology*, 18 Clin. Lab. Med. 23 (Mar.), 1998.

Hanzlick, R., and Parrish, R. G., *The Role of Medical Examiners and Coroners in Public Health Surveillance and Epidemiologic Research*, 17 Ann. Rev. Public Health 383, 1996.

Hanzlick, R., *BLURB: A Coding Scheme for Toxicologic Data*, 14 Am. J. Forensic Med. Pathol. 34 (No. 1), 1993.

Hanzlick, R., *Data Quality Assurance Measures (DQAMs) for Electronic Investigation Data*, 15 Am. J. Forensic Med. Pathol. 58, 1994.

Hanzlick, R., *Death Certificates: The Need for Further Guidance*, 14 Am. J. Forensic Med. Pathol. 249, 1993.

Hanzlick, R., *Embalming, Body Preparation, Burial, and Disinterment: An Overview for Forensic Pathologists*, 15 Am. J. Forensic Med. Pathol. 122 (June), 1994.

Hanzlick, R., et al., *Cause of Death Statements and Certification of Natural and Unnatural Deaths: Protocols and Opinions*, College of American Pathologists, Northfield, Ill., 1997.

Hanzlick, R., *Lawsuits Against Medical Examiners and Coroners Arising from Death Certificates*, 18 Am. J. Forensic Med. Pathol. 119 (No. 2), 1997.

Hanzlick, R., *Obtaining Permission of Postmortem Examination*, 121 Arch Pathol. Lab. Med. 9, 1997.

Hanzlick, R., *On the Need for More Expertise in Death Investigation (and a National Office of Death Investigation Affairs)*, 120 Arch. Pathol. Lab. Med. 329, 1996.

Hanzlick, R., *Practice Protocol for Writing Cause-of-Death Statements for Natural Causes*, 156 Arch Intern. Med. 25, 1996.

Hanzlick, R. *Principles for Including or Excluding "Mechanisms" of Death When Writing Cause-of-Death Statements*, 121 Arch. Pathol. Lab. Med. 377, 1997.

Hanzlick, R., *Protocol for Writing Cause-of-Death Statements or Deaths Due to Natural Causes*, 156 Arch. Intern. Med. 25, 1996.

Hanzlick, R., *Quality Assurance of Medical Expert Testimony*, Atlanta Med. 25 (July), 1992.

Hanzlick, R., *The Impact of Homicide Trials on the Forensic Pathologist's Time: The Fulton County Experience*, 42 J. Forensic Sci. 533 (No. 3), 1997.

Hanzlick, R., *The Relevance of Queries and Coding Procedures to the Writing of Cause-of-Death Statements*, 17 Am. J. Forensic Med. Pathol. 319, 1996.

Hanzlick, R., *Sharpening of Autopsy Tools*, 14 Am. J. Forensic Med. Pathol. 82, 1993.

Hanzlick, R., *Survey of Medical Examiner Office Computerization*, 15 Am. J. Forensic Med. Pathol. 110 (No. 2), 1994.

Hartshorne, N. J., et al., *Fatal Head Injuries in Ground-Level Falls*, 18 Am. J. Forensic Med. Pathol. 258 (Sept.), 1997.

Hellman, F. N., *Forensic Pathology's Dilemma: State Death Certificate*, 94 Pa. Med. 22, 1991.

Hewan-Lowe, K. O., et al., *The Role of Postmortem Electron Microscopy in the Diagnosis of Infectious Diseases*, 6 Emory U. J. Med. 232, 1992.

Hill, R. B., *The Current Status of Autopsies in Medical Care in the USA*, 5 Qual. Assur. Health Care 309 (Dec.), 1993.

Houts, M., et al., *Courtroom Toxicology*, 7 vols., Matthew Bender & Co., Inc., New York, 1998.

Hyma, B. A., and Rao, V. J., *Evaluation and Identification of Dismembered Human Remains*, 12 Am. J. Forensic Med. 291 (Dec.), 1991.

Isaacs, T. W., et al., *Postmortem Identification by Means of a Recovered Intraocular Lens*, 18 Am. J. Forensic Med. Pathol. 404 (Dec.), 1997.

Iyasu, S., et al., *Guidelines for Death Scene Investigation of Sudden Unexplained Infant Deaths: Recommendations of the Interagency Panel on Sudden Infant Death Syndrome*, 1 J. SIDS & Inf. Mort. 183 (No. 3), 1996.

James, D. S., and Leadbetter, S., *The Use of Personal Health Information in the Coroner's Inquiry*, 31 J. R. Coll. Physicians Lond. 509 (Sept.-Oct.), 1997.

Jason, D., et al., *A National Survey of Autopsy Cost and Workload*, 42 J. Forensic Sci. 270 (Mar.), 1997.

Jason, D., *The Role of the Medical Examiner/Coroner in Organ and Tissue Procurement for Transplantation*, 15 Am. J. Forensic Med. Pathol. 192 (Sept.), 1994.

Jeffreys, A. J., et al., *Individual Specific "Fingerprints" of Human DNA*, 316 Nature 76, 1980.

Jentzen, J. M., and Ernst, M. F., *Developing Medicolegal Death Investigator Systems in Forensic Pathology,* 18 Clin. Lab. Med. 279 (June), 1998.

Jones, A. W., *Disappearance Rate of Ethanol from the Blood of Human Subjects: Implications in Forensic Toxicology,* 38 J. Forensic Sci. 104 (Jan.), 1993.

Johnson, G., and Saldeen, T., *Identification of Burnt Victims with the Aid of Tooth and Bone Fragments,* 16 J. For. Med. 16, 1969.

Jordan, J. M., and Bass, M. J., *Errors in Death Certificate Completion in a Teaching Hospital,* 16 Clin. Invest. Med. 249, 1993.

Karch, S. B., *Introduction to the Forensic Pathology of Cocaine,* 12 Am. J. Forensic Med. 126 (June), 1991.

Karch, S. B., *The Pathology of Drug Abuse,* CRC Press, Boca Raton, Fla., 1996.

Karkola, K., and Heikki, N., *Diagnosis of Drowning by Investigation of Left Heart Blood,* 18 For. Sci. Intl. 149 (Sept.-Oct.), 1981.

Kaufman, S. R., *Autopsy: A Crucial Component of Human Clinical Investigation,* 120 Arch. Pathol. Lab. Med. 767 (Aug.), 1996.

Kidwell, D. A., *Analysis of Phencyclidine and Cocaine in Human Hair by Tandem Mass Spectrometry,* 38 J. Forensic Sci. 272 (Mar.), 1993.

Killam, E. W., *The Detection of Human Remains,* Charles C. Thomas, Springfield, Ill., 1990.

Kintz, P., et al., *Evaluation of Nicotine and Cotinine in Human Hair,* 37 J. Forensic Sci. 72 (Jan.), 1992, 38 J. Forensic Sci. 72 (Jan.), 1993.

Kintz, P., et al., *Nicotine Analysis in Neonates' Hair for Measuring Gestational Exposure to Tobacco,* 38 J. Forensic Sci. 119 (Jan.), 1993.

Knight, B., *Forensic Pathology,* 2d ed., Oxford University Press, New York, 1996.

Knight, B., *The Obscure Autopsy,* 16 For. Sci. Intl. 237 (Nov.-Dec.), 1980.

Knight, B., *The Post-Mortem Demonstration of Early Myocardial Infarction,* 5 Med. Sci. & L. 31, 1965.

Kohn, W. G., and Jeger, A. N., *Identification of Drugs by Their Near-Infrared Spectra,* 37 J. Forensic Sci. 35 (Jan.), 1992.

Krogman, W. M., and Iscan, M. Y., *The Human Skeleton in Forensic Medicine,* 2d ed., Charles C. Thomas, Publisher, Springfield, Ill., 1986.

Lamendin, H., et al., *A Simple Technique for Age Estimation in Adult Corpses: The Two Criteria Dental Method,* 37 J. Forensic Sci. 1373 (Sept.), 1992.

Laposata, E. A., *The Need for Scientific Approaches in Forensic Pathology,* 12 Am. J. Forensic Med. 278 (Dec.), 1991.

Lifschultz, B. D., and Donoghue, E. R., *Forensic Pathology of Heat- and-Cold-Related Injuries,* 18 Clin. Lab. Med. 77 (Mar.), 1998.

Lipsky, M. S., *Autopsy: The Role of the Family Physician,* 15 Am. Fam. Physician 1605 (May), 1993.

Maeda, H., et al., *Evaluation of Postmortem Oximetry with Reference to the Causes of Death,* 87 Forensic Sci Int. 201 (June 23), 1997.

Mangin, P. D., and Ludes, B. P., *A Forensic Application of DNA Typing: Paternity Determination in a Putrefied Fetus,* 12 Am. J. Forensic Med. 161 (June), 1991.

Mann, R. W., *A Method for Siding and Sequencing Human Ribs,* 38 J. Forensic Sci. 151 (Jan.), 1993.

Mant, A. K., *The Postmortem Diagnosis of Hypothermia,* 2 Brit. J. Hosp. Med. 1095, 1969.

Marshall, T. K., *Temperature Methods of Estimating the Time of Death,* 5 Med. Sci. & L. 224, 1965.

Mason, J. K., editor, *Pediatric Forensic Medicine and Pathology,* Chapman and Hall, London/New York, 1989.

Meadows, L., and Jantz, R. L., *Estimation of Stature from Metacarpal Lengths,* 37 J. Forensic Sci. 147 (Jan.), 1992.

McGinnis, J. M., and Foege, W. H., *Actual Causes of Death in the United States,* 270 J.A.M.A. 2207 (Nov. 10), 1993.

Mellen, P. F., et al., *Electrocution: A Review of 155 Cases with Emphasis on Human Factors*, 37 J. Forensic Sci. 1016 (July), 1992.

Messite, J., and Stellman, S. D., *Accuracy of Death Certificate Completion: The Need for Formalized Physician Training*, 275 J.A.M.A. 794 (Mar. 13), 1996.

Micozzi, M. S., *Postmortem Change in Human and Animal Remains: A Systematic Approach*, Charles C Thomas, Springfield, Ill., 1991.

Miller, J. J., *A Technique for Developing and Photographing Ridge Impressions on Decomposed Water-Soaked Fingers*, 38 J. Forensic Sci. 197 (Jan.), 1993.

Mittler, D. M., and Sheridan, S. G., *Sex Determination in Subadults Using Auricular Surface Morphology: A Forensic Science Perspective*, 37 J. Forensic Sci. 1068 (July), 1992.

Moore, W. G., *The Prototype Internet Autopsy Database*, 120 Arch. Pathol. Lab. Med. 125, 1996.

Murphy, G. K., *Cancer and the Coroner*, 237 J.A.M.A. 786, 1977.

Murray, K. A., and Rose, J. C., *The Analysis of Cremains: A Case Study Involving the Inappropriate Disposal of Mortuary Remains*, 38 J. Forensic Sci. 98 (Jan.), 1993.

Needleman, S. B., et al., *Creatinine Analysis in Single Collection Urine Specimens*, 37 J. Forensic Sci. 1125 (July), 1992.

Nelson, D. E., et al., *Sensitivity of Multiple-Cause Mortality Data for Surveillance of Deaths Associated with Head or Neck Injuries*, 42 MMWR 29 (SS-5), 1993.

Nelson, R., *A Microscopic Comparison of Fresh and Burned Bone*, 37 J. Forensic Sci. 1055 (July), 1992.

Nickerson, B., et al., *Methodology for Near-Optimal Computational Superimposition of Two-Dimensional Digital Facial Photographs and Three-Dimensional Cranial Surface Meshes*, 36 J. Forensic Sci. 480, 1991.

1996 Accreditation Manual for Pathology and Clinical Laboratory Services: Standards, Joint Commission on Accreditation of Healthcare Organizations, Oakbrook Terrace, Illinois, 1996, pp. 128-29.

Norton, L. E., et al., *Drug Detection at Autopsy: A Prospective Study of 247 Cases*, 27 J. For. Sci. 66 (Jan.), 1982.

Ohtani, S., and Yamamoto, K., *Estimation of Age from a Tooth by Means of Racemization of an Amino Acid*, 37 J. Forensic Sci. 1061 (July), 1992.

Oliver, W. R. *Image Processing in Forensic Pathology*, 18 Clin. Lab. Med. 151 (Mar.), 1998.

Pellegrino, E. D., *The Autopsy: Some Ethical Reflections on the Obligations of Pathologists*, 120 Arch. Pathol. Lab. Med. 739 (Aug.), 1996.

Pisanelli, D. M., and Russi-Mori, A., *Converting the Representation of Medical Data: Criteria to Code the Underlying Cause of Death*, 29 Methods Inf. Med. 220, 1990.

Prahlow, J.A., and Lentz, P. E., *Medical Examiner/Death Investigator Training Requirements in State Medical Examiner Systems*, 40 J. Forensic Sci. 55 (Jan.), 1995.

Ranson, D., and Dodd, M., *Cardiac Surgery and Pathology*, 5 J.L. & Med. 18 (Aug.), 1997.

Reay, D. T., *Death in Custody*, 18 Clin. Lab. Med. 1 (Mar.), 1998.

Redsicker, D. R., and O'Connor, J. J., editors, *Practical Fire and Arson Investigations*, 2d ed., CRC Press, Boca Raton, Fla., 1997.

Renz, B., and Hanzlick, R., *Penetrating Wounds of the Female Breast*, 6 Emory U. J. Med. 29, 1992.

Resnick, J. M., et al., *Postmortem Angiography of Catheter-Induced Pulmonary Artery Perforation*, 37 J. Forensic Sci. 1346 (Sept.), 1992.

Rieders, F., "Toxic Considerations in Deaths Associated with Anesthesia," in *Legal Medicine Annual*, C. H. Wecht, editor, Appleton-Century-Crofts, New York, 1969.

Riepert, T., et al., *Identification of an Unknown Corpse by Means of Computed Tomography (CT) of the Lumbar Spine*, 40 J. Forensic Sci. 126 (Jan.), 1995.

Saferstein, R., *Criminalistics: An Introduction to Forensic Science*, Prentice-Hall, Inc., Edgewood Cliffs, N.J., 1990.

Sanbar, S. S., et al., editors, *Legal Medicine*, 4th ed., Mosby, Inc., St. Louis, 1998.

Saracci, R., *Is Necropsy a Valid Monitor of Clinical Diagnosis Performance?*, 303 Br. Med. J. 898 (Oct. 12), 1991.

Saracci, R., *Problems with the Use of Autopsy Results as a Yardstick in Medical Audit and Epidemiology*, 5 Qaul. Assur. Health Care 339 (Dec.), 1993.

Schmidt, G., and Kallieris, D., *Use of Radiographs in Forensic Autopsy*, 19 For. Sci. Intl. 263 (May-June), 1982.

Schoning, P., *Frozen Cadaver: Antemortem Versus Postmortem*, 13 Am. J. Forensic Med. 7 (Mar.), 1992.

Seow, E., and Lau, G., *Who Dies at A & E? The Role of Forensic Pathology in the Audit of Mortality in an Emergency Medicine Department*, 82 Forensic Sci. Int. 201 (Oct. 25), 1996.

Setlow, V. P., *The Need for a National Autopsy Policy*, 120 Arch. Pathol. Lab. Med. 773 (Aug.), 1996.

Shapiro, H. A., *The Diagnosis of Death from Delayed Air Embolism*, 12 J. For. Med. 3, 1965.

Smith, O. C., et al., *Characteristic Features of Entrance Wounds from Hollow-Point Bullets*, 38 J. Forensic Sci. 323 (Mar.), 1993.

Song, Y., et al., *A Modified Method for Examining the Cardiac Conduction System*, 86 Forensic Sci. Int. 135 (Apr. 18), 1997.

Spitz, W. U. and Fisher, R. S., editors, *Medicolegal Investigation of Death: Guidelines for the Application of Pathology to Crime Investigation*, 2d ed., Charles C Thomas, Publisher, Springfield, Illinois, 1980.

Spitz, W. U., *Essential Postmortem Findings in the Traffic Accident Victim*, 90 Arch. Path. 451, 1970.

Stevens, P. J., *Fatal Civil Aircraft Accidents: Their Medical and Pathological Investigation*, John Wright & Sons, Ltd., Bristol, England, 1970.

Swalwell, C. I., et al., *Sudden Death Due to Unsuspected Coronary Vasculitis*, 12 Am. J. Forensic Med. 306 (Dec.), 1991.

Stone, I. C., *Characteristics of Firearms and Gunshot Wounds as Markers of Suicide*, 13 Am. J. Forensic Med. 275 (Dec.), 1992.

Stuart, R. D., and Cotton, D. W., *The Meta-Autopsy: Changing Techniques and Attitudes Towards the Autopsy*, 5 Qual. Assur. Health Care 325 (Dec.), 1993.

Stimson, P. H., and Curtis, A. M., editors, *Forensic Dentistry*, CRC Press, Inc., Boca Raton, Fla., 1997.

Thompson, D. D., *Microscopic Determination of Age at Death in an Autopsy Series*, 26 J. For. Sci. 470 (July), 1981.

Troxel, D. B., et al., *Problem Areas in Pathology Practice Uncovered by a Review of Malpractice Claims*, 18 Am. J. Surg. Pathol. 821 (Aug.), 1994.

Ubelaker, D. H., *Hyoid Fracture and Strangulation*, 37 J. Forensic Sci. 1216 (Sept.), 1992.

Vass, A. A., et al., *Time Since Death Determinations of Human Cadavers Using Soil Solution*, 37 J. Forensic Sci. 1236 (Sept.), 1992.

Wecht, C. H., *Cause of Death*, Dutton Signet, New York, 1993.

Wecht, C. H., editor, *Forensic Sciences*, 5 vols., Matthew Bender & Co., New York, 1998.

Wecht, C. H., "Pathology" in *Preparing and Winning Medical Negligence Cases*, Vol. 3, 2d ed., (C. H. Wecht, et al., editors, The Michie Company, Charlottesville, Va., 1994.

Wecht, C. H., and Ravano, P. Q., "The Pathology of Soft Tissue Injuries," in *Handling Soft Tissue Injury Cases: Medical Aspects*, Vol. 2, 2d ed. (C. H. Wecht, et al., editors), The Michie Company, Charlottesville, Va., 1993.

Weedn, V. W., *Postmortem Identifications of Remains*, 18 Clin. Lab. Med. 115 (Mar.), 1998.

Weedn, V. W., and Roby, R. K., *Forensic DNA Testing*, 117 Arch. Pathol. Lab. Med. 486, 1993.

Wetli, C. V., et al., *Practical Forensic Pathology*, Igaku-Shojn Medical Publishers, Inc., New York/Tokyo, 1988.

Wirthwein, D. P., and Pless, J. E., *Carboxyhemoglobin Levels in a Series of Automobile Fires. Death Due to Crash or Fire?*, 17 Am. J. Forensic Med. Pathol. 117 (June), 1996.

Zumwalt, R. E., *Applications of Molecular Biology to Forensic Pathology*, 20 Human Pathol. 303, 1989.

§ 32A.97. Legal references.

The following additional references may aid in further research on the material covered in Chapter 32A.

Affeck, W. B., *Coroners' Inquests*, 7 Crim. L. Q. 459, 1965.

Anderson, R. E., et al., *The Autopsy: Past, Present, and Future*, 22 Trauma 2 (Dec.), 1980.

Asnaes, S., and Paaske, F., *Uncertainty of Determining Mode of Death in Medico-Legal Material Without Autopsy: A Systematic Autopsy Study*, 15 For. Sci. Intl. (Jan.-Feb.), 1980.

Bechard, B., *The Issue of Granting Standing at Inquests*, 34 Crim. L.Q. 55 (Nov.), 1991.

Biff, E., *Psychological Autopsies: Do They Belong in the Courtroom?*, 24 Am. J. Crim. L. 123 (Fall), 1996.

Brotherton v. Cleveland: Property Rights in the Human Body — Are the Goods Oft Interred with Their Bones?, 37 S.D. L. Rev. 429, 1992.

Bucklin, R., *Forensic Pathology for Attorneys*, 12 Calif. Western L. Rev. 197 (Winter), 1976.

Byrne, A., and Nilges, R. G., *The Brain Stem in Brain Death: A Critical Review*, 9 Issues L. & Med. 3 (Summer), 1993.

Coleman, H., and Swendson, E., *DNA in the Courtroom: A Trial Watcher's Guide*, Genelex Corporation, Seattle, 1994.

Compulsory Removal of Cadaver Organs, 69 Colum. L. Rev. 693, 1969.

Cragie, A. W., *Burial of a Tort: The California Supreme Court's Treatment of Tortious Mishandling of Remains in* Christianson v. Superior Court, 26 Loy. L.A. L. Rev. 909 (Apr.), 1993.

Curphey, T. J., *Role of the Forensic Pathologist in the Medicolegal Certification of Modes of Death*, 13 J. For. Sci. 163, 1968.

De Saram, G. S. W., et al., *Post-Mortem Temperature and the Time of Death*, 46 J. Crim. L. 562, 1955.

Diagnosing the Dead: The Admissibility of the Psychiatric Autopsy, 18 Am. Crim. L. Rev. 617 (Spring), 1981.

Enticknap, J. B., *Biochemical Changes in Cadaver Sera in Fatal Acute Heart Attacks*, 7 J. For. Med. 135, 1960.

Feegel, J. R., *Legal Aspects of Laboratory Medicine*, Little, Brown and Company, Boston, 1974.

Fitzpatrick, J. J., and Macaluso, J., *Shadow Positioning Technique: A Method for Postmortem Identification*, 30 J. Forensic Sci. 1226, 1985.

Frederiksen, V., et al., *The Value of the Hospital Autopsy: A Study of Causes and Modes of Death Estimated Before and After Autopsy*, 21 For. Sci. Intl. 23 (Jan.-Feb.), 1983.

Gatter, K., and Bowen, D. A. L., *A Study of Suicide Autopsies*, 20 Med., Sci. & Law 37 (Jan.), 1980.

Gerber, S. R., *Postmortem Examinations*, 6 Clev.-Mar. L. Rev. 194, 1957.

Gianelli, P., *The Admissibility of Laboratory Reports in Criminal Trials: The Reliability of Scientific Proof*, 49 Ohio St. L.J. 671, 1988.

Gilmour, J. M., *"Our" Bodies: Property Rights in Human Tissue*, 8 Can. J. L. & Soc'y 113 (Fall), 1993.

Goodman, R. S., *The Clinical-Legal-Pathological Conference*, 13 Leg. Aspects Med. Pract. 1 (Sept.), 1985.

Graham, M. A., and Hanzlick, R., *Forensic Pathology in Criminal Cases*, Lexis Law Publishing, Carlsbad, Cal., 1997.

Halkier, E., *Forensic Autopsy Material*, 2 J. For. Med. 217, 1955.

Hannemann, B. G., *Body Parts and Property Rights: A New Commodity for the 1990s*, 22 Sw. U. L. Rev. 399, 1993.

Hanzlick, R., and Mills, D. H., "Cause-of-Death Statements and the Death Certificate" in *Medicolegal Death Investigation: Treatises in the Forensic Sciences* (Y. Caplan, editor), The Forensic Sciences Foundation Press, Colorado Springs, Colo., 1997.

Hanzlick, R., and Parrish, R. G., *Death Investigation Report Forms (DIRFs): Generic Forms for Investigators (IDIRFs) and Certifiers (CDIRFs)*, 39 J. Forensic Sci. 629 (No. 3), 1994.

Hanzlick, R., *Data Quality Assurance Measures (DQAMs) for Electronic Investigation Data*, 15 Am. J. Forensic Med. Pathol. 58, 1994.

Hanzlick, R., *Death Certificates: The Need for Further Guidance*, 14 Am. J. Forensic Med. Pathol. 249, 1993.

Hanzlick, R., *Death Registration: History, Methods, Legal Issues*, 42 J. Forensic Sci. 265, 1997.

Hanzlick, R., et al., *Cause of Death Statements and Certification of Natural and Unnatural Deaths: Protocols and Opinions*, College of American Pathologists, Northfield, Ill., 1997.

Hanzlick, R., et al., *Standard Language in Death Investigation Laws*, 39 J. Forensic Sci. 637 (No. 3), 1994.

Hanzlick, R., *Lawsuits Against Medical Examiners and Coroners Arising from Death Certificates*, 18 Am. J. Forensic Med. Pathol. 119 (No. 2), 1997.

Hanzlick, R., *Obtaining Permission of Postmortem Examination*, 121 Arch Pathol. Lab. Med. 9, 1997.

Hanzlick, R., *On the Need for More Expertise in Death Investigation (and a National Office of Death Investigation Affairs)*, 120 Arch. Pathol. Lab. Med. 329, 1996.

Hanzlick, R., *Practice Protocol for Writing Cause-of-Death Statements for Natural Causes*, 156 Arch Intern. Med. 25, 1996.

Hanzlick, R. *Principles for Including or Excluding "Mechanisms" of Death When Writing Cause-of-Death Statements*, 121 Arch. Pathol. Lab. Med. 377, 1997.

Hanzlick, R., *Quality Assurance of Medical Expert Testimony*, Atlanta Med. 25 (July), 1992.

Hanzlick, R., *The Impact of Homicide Trials on the Forensic Pathologist's Time: The Fulton County Experience*, 42 J. Forensic Sci. 533 (No. 3), 1997.

Hanzlick, R., *The Relevance of Queries and Coding Procedures to the Writing of Cause-of-Death Statements*, 17 Am. J. Forensic Med. Pathol. 319, 1996.

Houts, M., et al., *Courtroom Toxicology*, 7 vols., Matthew Bender & Co., Inc., New York, 1998.

Iyasu, S., et al., *Guidelines for Death Scene Investigation of Sudden Unexplained Infant Deaths: Recommendations of the Interagency Panel on Sudden Infant Death Syndrome*, 1 J. SIDS & Inf. Mort. 183 (No. 3), 1996.

Jaffe, F. A., *Some Limitations of the Medico-Legal Postmortem Examination*, 17 Crim. L. Q. 178 (Mar.), 1975.

Johnson, G., and Saldeen, T., *Identification of Burnt Victims with the Aid of Tooth and Bone Fragments*, 16 J. For. Med. 16, 1969.

Jones, J. T. R., *Evidentiary Autopsies*, 61 U. Colo. L. Rev. 567, 1990.

Jordan, J. M., and Bass, M. J., *Errors in Death Certificate Completion in a Teaching Hospital*, 16 Clin. Invest. Med. 249, 1993.

Karkola, K., and Heikki, N., *Diagnosis of Drowning by Investigation of Left Heart Blood*, 18 For. Sci. Intl. 149 (Sept.-Oct.), 1981.

Kiel, F. W., *Psychiatric Character of the Assailant as Determined by Autopsy Observations of the Victim*, 10 J. For. Sci. 263, 1965.

Kesan, J. P., *An Autopsy of Scientific Evidence in a Post-Daubert World*, 84 Geo. L.J. 1985 (May), 1996.

Knight, B., *The Obscure Autopsy*, 16 For. Sci. Intl. 237 (Nov.-Dec.), 1980.

Knight, B., *The Post-Mortem Demonstration of Early Myocardial Infarction*, 5 Med. Sci. & L. 31, 1965.

Lapi, A., *Role of the Pathologist in the Investigation of Unexplained Death and in Examination of Trace Evidence*, 28 U. Kan. City L. Rev. 113, 1960.

Leestma, J. E., *The Neuropathologist as an Expert Witness*, 36 Med. Trial Tech. Q. 170, 1989.

Marshall, T. K., *Temperature Methods of Estimating the Time of Death*, 5 Med. Sci. & L. 224, 1965.

McClure, M., *Odontology: Bite Marks as Evidence in Criminal Trials*, 11 Computer & High Tech. L.J. 269 (July), 1995.

Moenssens, A. A., *Novel Scientific Evidence in Criminal Cases: Some Words of Caution*, 84 J. Crim. L. 1 (Spring), 1993.

Moorhead, R., *Exhumation and Autopsy in Civil Cases for Evidential Purposes*, S.C. Trial Law. B. (Fall), 1991, p. 12. (Publication of South Carolina Trial Lawyers Association).

Nickerson, B., et al., *Methodology for Near-Optimal Computational Superimposition of Two-Dimensional Digital Facial Photographs and Three-Dimensional Cranial Surface Meshes*, 36 J. Forensic Sci. 480, 1991.

Norton, L. E., et al., *Drug Detection at Autopsy: A Prospective Study of 247 Cases*, 27 J. For. Sci. 66 (Jan.), 1982.

Norwood, D., *Dead Reckoning: Evidence and Proof of Death*, 15 Est. & Tr. J. 65 (Sept.), 1995.

O'Carroll, T. L., *Over My Dead Body: Recognizing Property Rights in Corpses*, 29 J. Health & Hosp. L. 238 (July/Aug.), 1996.

Ogloff, J. R. P., *Psychological Autopsy: Clinical and Legal Perspectives*, 37 St. Louis L.J. 607 (Spring), 1993.

Oppenheim, E. B., *The Medical Records As Evidence*, LEXIS Law Publishing, Charlottesville, Va., 1998, § 2-19, The Autopsy.

Owen, T., *Deaths in Custody*, 141 New L.J. 1421 (Oct. 18), 1991; 1444 (Oct. 25), 1991.

Petty, C. S., *The Devil's Dozen: Popular Medicolegal Misconceptions*, 1 Lawyer's Med. J. (Second Series) 331, 1973.

Prutting, J. M., *Autopsy and the Law*, 7 Lawyer's Med. J. 229, 1972.

Psychological Autopsy: A New Tool for Criminal Defense Attorneys?, 24 Ariz. L. Rev. 421, 1982.

Ranson, D., and Dodd, M., *Cardiac Surgery and Pathology*, 5 J.L. & Med. 18 (Aug.), 1997.

Ranson, D., *The Coroner and the Rights of the Terminally Ill Act of 1995*, 3 J.L. & Med. 169 (Nov.), 1995.

Reals, W. J., and Reals, J. F., *Aviation Pathology: Finding the Answers*, 14 Trial 32 (Aug.), 1978.

Reals, W. J., and Reals, J. F., *Use of Aviation Pathology and Aviation Medicine as Proof of Liability and Damage*, 44 J. Air. L. 297, 1978.

Redsicker, D. R., and O'Connor, J. J., editors, *Practical Fire and Arson Investigations*, 2d ed., CRC Press, Inc., Boca Raton, Fla., 1997.

Rieders, F., "Toxic Considerations in Deaths Associated with Anesthesia," in *Legal Medicine Annual*, C. H. Wecht, editor, Appleton-Century-Crofts, New York, 1969.

Saferstein, R., *Criminalistics: An Introduction to Forensic Science*, Prentice-Hall, Inc., Edgewood Cliffs, N.J., 1990.

Sanbar, S. S., et al., editors, *Legal Medicine*, 4th ed., Mosby, Inc., St. Louis, 1998.

Schmidt, G., and Kallieris, D., *Use of Radiographs in Forensic Autopsy*, 19 For. Sci. Intl. 263 (May-June), 1982.

Schmidt, S., *Consent for Autopsies*, 250 J.A.M.A. 1161 (Sept. 2), 1983.

Schwar, T. G., *Guide for Filing Medico-legal Necropsy Data*, 9 J. For. Med. 61, 1963.

Scottolini, A. G., and Weistein, S. R., *The Autopsy in Clinical Quality Control,* 13 Leg. Aspects Med. Pract. 6 (Sept.), 1985.

Shapiro, H. A., *The Diagnosis of Death from Delayed Air Embolism,* 12 J. For. Med. 3, 1965.

Skegg, P. D. G., *Human Corpses, Medical Specimens and the Law of Property,* 4 Anglo-Am. L. Rev. 412 (Oct.-Dec.), 1975.

Stahl, C. J., III, *The Pathologist in Quality Assurance Programs,* 13 Leg. Aspects Med. Pract. 3 (Sept.), 1985.

Sullivan, J. T., *When Death Is the Issue: Uses of Pathological Testimony and Autopsy Reports at Trial,* 19 Willamette L. Rev. 579 (Summer), 1983.

Thompson, D. D., *Microscopic Determination of Age at Death in an Autopsy Series,* 26 J. For. Sci. 470 (July), 1981.

Wecht, C. H., *Cause of Death,* Dutton Signet, New York, 1993.

Wecht, C. H., *Role of the Forensic Pathologist in Criminal Cases,* 37 Tenn. L. Rev. 669, 1970.

Wecht, C. H., "Significance of Autopsy Findings in Evaluating Malpractice Claims," in *Exploring the Medical Malpractice Dilemma* (C. H. Wecht, editor), Futura Publishing Company, Inc., Mount Kisco, New York, 1972.

Wecht, C. H., and Collom, W. D., "Medical Evidence in Alleged Rape," in *Legal Medicine Annual* (C. H. Wecht, editor), Appleton-Century-Crofts, New York, 1969.

Wecht, C. H., and Perper, J. A., *The Forensic Medical Expert,* 2 Lawyer's Med. J. (Second Series) 355, 1974.

§ 32A.98. American Law Reports.

12 A.L.R.2d 1264. Proof of death or injury from external and violent means as supporting presumption or inference of death by accident means within policy of insurance.

17 A.L.R.2d 1078. Absence of accused during making of tests or experiments as affecting admissibility of testimony concerning them. Postmortem examinations; autopsies, § 4.

21 A.L.R.2d 538. Power of court to order disinterment and autopsy or examination for evidential purposes in civil case.

30 A.L.R.2d 837. Time for making autopsy or demand therefor under insurance policy.

31 A.L.R.2d 693. Necessity, in homicide prosecution, of expert medical testimony to show cause of death.

56 A.L.R.2d 1447. Admissibility in homicide prosecution of opinion evidence that death was or was not self-inflicted.

66 A.L.R.2d 1082. Admissibility of opinion evidence as to cause of death, disease, or injury.

73 A.L.R.2d 769. Admissibility of photograph of corpse in prosecution for homicide or civil action for causing death.

85 A.L.R.2d 722. Presumption against suicide as overcome as a matter of law by physical facts related to death in action on accident or life insurance policy.

86 A.L.R.2d 722. Homicide: identification of victim as person named in indictment or information.

7 A.L.R.3d 8. Right of accused in state courts to inspection or disclosure of evidence in possession of prosecution. Report of autopsy or postmortem examination, § 21[b]

7 A.L.R.3d 747. Validity and effect of testatmentary direction as to disposition of testator's body.

28 A.L.R.3d 413. Construction and effect of "visible sign of injury" and similar clauses in accident provision of insurance policy.

54 A.L.R.3d 1037. Enforcement of preference expressed by decedent as to disposition of his body after death.

63 A.L.R.3d 1294. Disinterment in criminal cases.

65 A.L.R.3d 283. Necessity and effect in homicide prosecution of expert medical testimony as to cause of death.

71 A.L.R.3d 1265. Admissibility of testimony of coroner or mortician as to cause of death in homicide prosecution.

81 A.L.R.3d 1071. Validity, construction, and application of statutes making it a criminal offense to mistreat or wrongfully dispose of dead body.

18 A.L.R.4th 858. Liability for wrongful autopsy.

27 A.L.R.4th 680. What are "records" of agency which must be mae available under state Freedom of Information Act. Autopsy reports, § 15.

27 A.L.R.4th 1188. Right of accused in state courts to have expert inspect, examine, or test physical evidence in possession of prosecution — modern cases. Autopsy report, §§ 6, 11[a].

53 A.L.R.4th 349. Dead bodies: liability for improper manner of reinterment.

53 A.L.R.4th 360. Civil liability of undertaken in connection with transportation, burial or safeguarding of body.

54 A.L.R.4th 1214. Statutes authorizing removal of body parts for transplant: validity and construction.

70 A.L.R.4th 1091. Homicide: cremation of victim's body as violation of accused's rights.

§ 32A.99. Cases.

In the following list of cases, no attempt has been made to include all the decisions on topics covered in Chapter 32A. The cases selected are those that the editors believe will best aid the reader in further research on the medicolegal issues involved.

Cases are arranged under the following headings:

(A) ACTIONS QUESTIONING AUTHORITY FOR AUTOPSY
(B) AUTOPSY REPORTS, PHOTOS, AND TESTIMONY AS EVIDENCE
(C) INSURANCE AND WORKERS' COMPENSATION CASES
(D) ACTIONS FOR NEGLIGENCE IN PERFORMING AUTOPSIES
(E) MISCELLANEOUS CASES

For a general discussion of the legal problems associated with autopsies, see §§ 32A.38 to 32A.47.

(A) ACTIONS QUESTIONING AUTHORITY FOR AUTOPSY

[See also §§ 32A.39, 32A.40, 32A.42 to 32A.45]

United States: Donnelly v. Guion (C.A.-2 Conn., 1972) 467 F.2d 290 (coroner sued for performing autopsy without consent on sixteen-year-old boy found dead in bed at boarding school; boy had history of Marfan's syndrome, a congenital heart defect, but death not typical of such disease and boy had recent X-ray which showed no aneurysm, the usual cause of death in such cases; defendant found free of liability under Connecticut law which permitted official autopsy where death "obscure").

Watson v. Manhattan & Bronx Surface Transit Operating Auth. (D. N.J., 1980) 487 F. Supp. 1273 (in an action involving the payment of a decedent's retirement benefits, in which the decedent's sister alleged foul play on the part of the decedent's wife in the decedent's death, it was held that the court, under New Jersey law, could not order disinterment of the body, because the statutes on disinterment were intended for public purposes only, being the protection of public health, welfare, and safety, and they provided no basis to secure evidence in a private matter).

In re Asbestos Litigation (D. Del., 1988) 123 F.R.D. 84 ("It is not difficult to imagine that in many instances, upon the death of a spouse or close relative the obligation to have an autopsy performed will not be a pressing matter to the survivor. In some cases the obligation may be completely overlooked. In some instances the next of kin may be emotionally unable to authorize an autopsy. If the order is not complied with under these conditions, is the Court going to penalize the survivors? And if so, how? The Court is unwilling to risk involvement in such a predicament by routinely ordering all plaintiffs and their next of kin to be prepared to have an autopsy performed immediately upon the death of the plaintiff.").

Stephens v. National Gypsum Co. (M.D. Ga., 1988) 685 F. Supp. 847 ("Disinterment for the purpose of examination or autopsy [in asbestos case] will be ordered upon showing of good cause and urgent necessity and upon a strong showing that the examination or autopsy will establish the facts sought.").

Yang v. Sturner (D. R.I., 1990) 728 F. Supp. 845 (action against state's chief medical examiner for unauthorized autopsy of 23-year-old son of family from Laos who were members of Hmong community, which prohibits any mutilation of the body, including autopsies or the removal of organs during an autopsy).

Whaley v. County of Tuscola (C.A.-6 Mich., 1995) 58 F.3d 1111 (next of kin had claim for infringement of property rights under due process clause of Constitution for removal of decedent's corneas by medical examiner's assistant without plaintiffs' consent).

California: Huntly v. Zurich Gen. Acc. & Liab. Ins. Co. (1929) 100 Cal. App. 201, 280 Pac. 163 (where man died at work, and coroner's autopsy report showed cause of death to be "angina pectoris," there was no abuse of discretion in the performance of second coroner's autopsy to determine effect of bruise found on victim's forehead).

Division of Labor Enforcement, Dept. of Industrial Relations v. Gifford (1955) 137 Cal. App. 2d 259, 290 P.2d 281 (not improper for autopsy to be performed by associate of doctor to whom authorization was given).

Colorado: Schwalb v. Connely (1947) 116 Colo. 195, 179 P.2d 667 (physicians and deputy coroner not liable where autopsy performed on wrong patient due to nurse's mistake in attaching identification tags to bodies).

In re Estate of Tong (Colo. App., 1980) 619 91 (a probate court, upon sufficient showing of necessity, has the authority to order an exhumation and autopsy of a body located within its jurisdiction).

Florida: Rupp v. Jackson (Fla., 1970) 238 So. 2d 86 (fact that death certificate was required by law did not serve as authorization for hospital pathologist, who was also associate county medical examiner, to perform autopsy on patient to determine cause of death; statute requiring death certificate related to attending physician and made no mention of recourse to medical examiner if cause of death could not be determined).

Georgia: Clark v. Arras (Ga. App., 1994) 443 S.E.2d 277 (plaintiff failed to establish intentional infliction of emotional stress in action against county medical examiner for performing unauthorized autopsy on stillborn fetus where defendant claimed that he considered stillbirth to be unexplained, and it was immaterial whether fetus was determined to be a "person" under statute authorizing autopsies in unexplained deaths of persons after birth but before seven years of age).

Illinois: Cybart v. Michael Reese Hosp. & Med. Ctr. (1977) 50 Ill. App. 3d 411, 8 Ill. Dec. 616, 365 N.E.2d 1002 (directed verdict for defendants upheld in action by deceased hospital patient's relatives for an unauthorized autopsy; patient had been undergoing treatment for Hodgkin's disease, but cause of death was not known, and no physician would sign death certificate; court held defendants were only following law and that plaintiffs could offer no evidence for compensatory damages to support their claim of mental anguish.

Indiana: Stath v. Williams (1977) 174 Ind. App. 369, 367 N.E.2d 1120 (where decedent who otherwise appeared to be in "good health" was found dead in wrecked automobile, where there appeared to have been no application of brakes prior to accident, and where body was intact and was not bloody despite impact of vehicle with bridge, county coroner had duty to assume jurisdiction and require autopsy).

Kansas: Alderman v. Ford (1937) 146 Kan. 698, 72 P.2d 981 (actions for unauthorized autopsies compared to those involving intentional assault without physical violence, false imprisonment or seduction).

Kentucky: McDonald v. Goodman (Ky. App., 1951) 239 S.W.2d 97 (surviving spouse who authorized autopsy had no cause of action against physician who mistakenly advised her that autopsy was required by law).

Lashbrook v. Barnes (App., 1969) 437 S.W.2d 502 (failure to return heart to body after authorized autopsy not "mutilation" of body where it was necessary for pathologist to take heart to laboratory for dissection and microscopic examination, nor was there mutilation in placing brain in stomach instead of returning it to skull where pathologist explained that this was his customary practice because replacing brain sometimes caused seepage to outside area of skull).

Maryland: Young v. College of Physicians & Surgeons of Baltimore City (1895) 81 Md. 358, 32 Atl. 177 (it is common knowledge that autopsy disfigures human body and gives it appearance that would "shock the sensibilities" of family of deceased).

Massachusetts: Gahn v. Leary (1945) 318 Mass. 425, 61 N.E.2d 844 (conflicting information in hospital patient's records, some of which suggested possibility of lead poisoning, was sufficient evidence of death "by violence" to authorize official autopsy).

Michigan: Deeg v. City of Detroit (1956) 345 Mich. 371, 76 N.W.2d 16 (widow of traffic victim involved in accident with streetcar had cause of action against city for unauthorized autopsy apparently performed to determine if victim had been drinking; evidence revealed that city's medical representative requested county medical examiner to remove certain organs from body for tests).

Allinger v. Kell (1981) 102 Mich. App. 798, 309 N.W.2d 547 (deputy medical examiner was acting in such capacity and immune from suit under statute in severing hands from plaintiff's daughter's corpse where it was necessary to retain such portions of body for further criminal investigation).

Minnesota: Larson v. Chase (1891) 47 Minn. 307, 50 N.W. 238 (decision establishing right to cause of action for unauthorized autopsy).

Missouri: Patrick v. Employers Mut. Liab. Ins. Co. (1938) 233 Mo. App. 251, 118 S.W.2d 116 (coroner does not have unlimited discretion in deciding when autopsies should be performed; punitive damages allowed in action for unauthorized autopsy).

Crenshaw v. O'Connell (1941) 235 Mo. App. 1085, 150 S.W.2d 489 (authorization by deceased's next of kin would relieve coroner of liability for autopsy not authorized by statute).

New Hampshire: Kusky v. Laderbush (N.H., 1950) 21 A.2d 536 (defendant in a personal injury action arising out of an automobile accident was entitled to request an autopsy to determine if the plaintiff's decedent's death eleven months after the accident were due to cancer rather than the effects of the accident, even though the defendant may have had other sources of proof on this issue).

New Mexico: Begay v. State (N.M. App., 1985) 723 P.2d 252 (relatives of deceased Navajo had cause of action against state medical investigator under civil rights act for authorizing autopsy that violated their traditional Navajo religious beliefs.

New York: Brown v. Broome County (1960) 8 N.Y.2d 330, 207 N.Y.S.2d 657, 170 N.E.2d 666, 83 A.L.R.2d 952 (under New York statute providing for official autopsies in cases of suspicious or unusual deaths, coroners' powers limited to deaths that indicate possibility of either crime or suicide; where death occurs on job at site disclosing conditions which often accompany accidents, there must be substantial reasons present to justify official autopsy).

People v. Miller (1975) 82 Misc. 2d 72, 368 N.Y.S.2d 788 (district attorney refused permission by court to exhume body of automobile accident victim to establish cause of death and "buttress the evidence" in vehicular homicide charge against other driver where it was not adequately explained why hospital records and testimony of physicians who attended victim were not adequate to supply such proof.)

Weberman v. Zugibe (1977) 90 Misc. 2d 254, 394 N.Y.S.2d 371 (autopsy could not be performed over religious objections of deceased's spouse where deceased had been struck by automobile, where driver was not facing criminal charges, and where only reason for autopsy was to determine precise cause of death).

Rotholz v. City of New York (Sup. Ct., New York Cty., N.Y., 1992) 582 N.Y.S.2d 366 (plaintiffs had a cause of action for civil damages against hospital that failed to notify medical examiner's office that deceased's family, who were Orthodox Jews and thus did not believe in the desecration of a body after death, had raised an objection to the performance of an autopsy; there was no support for defense that traffic accident in which deceased was killed had given rise to possibility of criminal prosecution where police report merely showed that he was killed while attempting to cross street and was struck by rear end of truck making right turn).

Bambrick v. Booth Mem. Med. Center (App. Div., 1993) 593 N.Y.S.2d 252 (widow and son of deceased had cause of action for civil liability against hospital for performing autopsy in violation of statute that required written consent of person or persons legally entitled to give consent).

North Carolina: Gurganious v. Simpson (1938) 213 N.C. 613, 197 S.E. 163 (undertaker not liable in unauthorized autopsy case because he failed to object to coroner's improper order).

Parker v. Quinn-McGowen Co. (1964) 262 N.C. 560, 138 S.E.2d 214 (punitive damages allowable in action for unlawful autopsy where conduct malicious or grossly negligent).

Oklahoma: Dean v. Chapman (1976) 556 P.2d 257 (unsuccessful action by daughter of deceased against medical examiner for conducting autopsy in public place; autopsy was performed in an open and public site adjacent to National Guard Armory apparently to create publicity and draw attention to state legislature's failure to appropriate additional funds requested by medical examiner's office).

Pennsylvania: Hirko v. Reese (1945) 351 Pa. 238, 40 A.2d 408 (in absence of charge of bad faith on part of county coroner, he could not be held liable for alleged unauthorized autopsy on body of miner who collapsed suddenly and died while at work; fact that autopsy was performed without state inspector of mines being present not material since state law pertaining to deaths of miners applied to inquests and not to autopsies).

Frick v. McClelland (1956) 384 Pa. 597, 122 A.2d 43 (physician attached to school district found free of liability on charges that he induced county coroner to order alleged unauthorized autopsy on body of custodian who died after minor head injury on job; court felt investigation commenced by physician was as much for benefit of deceased's family as for school district).

South Dakota: Coty v. Baughman (1926) 50 S.D. 372, 210 N.W. 348 (fact that child had been under treatment of chiropractor not sufficient evidence of neglect to warrant official autopsy).

Wisconsin: Scarpaci v. Milwaukee County (1980) 96 Wis. 2d 663, 292, N.W.2d 816, 18 A.L.R.4th 829 (parents of deceased child had cause of action against county for wrongful performance of autopsy).

(B) AUTOPSY REPORTS, PHOTOS, AND TESTIMONY AS EVIDENCE

[See also § 32A.46]

United States: Hamilton v. Chaffin (C.A.-5 Miss., 1975) 506 F.2d 904 (testimony of state chemist in action for wrongful death of juvenile while in police custody admissible even though autopsy was performed without compliance under authorization statutes, where defendants were not involved in procuring autopsy, and autopsy was not performed with malice or "intentional wrongful actions").

United States v. Davidson (C.A.-8 Ark., 1997) 122 F.3d 531 (no error to admit photos taken during the autopsy of a murder victim, where the photos, although graphic, were less gruesome than photos that had been taken at the scene of the murder, and where the autopsy photos helped explain the testimony of the witness who performed the autopsy).

Alabama: Mobile Infirmary v. Eberlein (Ala., 1960) 119 So. 2d 8 (mortician with 20 years' experience who saw body shortly after death and was present during autopsy was qualified to testify that death was caused by strangling from exterior pressure).

Atkins v. Lee (Ala., 1992) 603 So. 2d 937 (report by pathologist established that heart catheterization performed on child 90 minutes before seizure was cause of death; pathologist reported that puncture wound pointed "upward toward tip of intravenous catheter" and concluded that heart had been pierced from inside out during catheterization, which resulted in escape of blood and fatal cardiac tamponade).

Colorado: St. Lukes Hosp. Ass'n v. Long (Colo., 1952) 240 P.2d 917 (in an action by the parents of a child who had strangled to death in a hospital bed, the admission of a photograph of the entire body of the child, which showed incisions and sutures made during the autopsy, was irrelevant to the issues and prejudicial, where the only possible purpose of the photo was to show a mark on the child's lower cheek, which could have been shown by a photo of the head only).

Illinois: People v. Fiddler (1970) 45 Ill. 2d 181, 258 N.E.2d 359 (copy of coroner's death certificate prepared after autopsy held inadmissible in murder case as prima facie evidence of cause of victim's death on ground that determination of cause of death could have been result of "complex value judgment" made by examining pathologist from autopsy; "the doctor's opinion as to the cause of death is not converted into a fact by the process of including it in a certified copy of the coroner's death certificate").

People v. Carbona (1975) 27 Ill. App. 3d 988, 327 N.E.2d 546 (in murder case, pathologist's testimony after autopsy that it was "physical impossibility for the subject to have shot himself" was not invasion of province of jury).

Indiana: Fryback v. State (Ind., 1980) 400 N.E.2d 1128 (color photo of a murder victim's body on the autopsy table was admissible, even though it showed an unsightly and roughly sewn zigzag incision made during the autopsy, because it was relevant to the identity of the victim and the fact of death, and the tendency to inflame the passions of the jury or to engender excessive sympathy was minimal).

Kansas: State v. Buie (Kan., 1978) 575 P.2d 555 (photos of a murder victim's body taken during the autopsy were admissible, where they did not show how the body was cut open for the autopsy, but merely showed the location and direction of the bullet wounds, thus indicating the manner in which the victim was shot).

Louisiana: Giroir v. Pann's of Houma, Inc. (La. App., 1976) 341 So. 2d 1346 (orthopedic surgeon's testimony as to slip-and-fall victim's cause of death based upon his reading of autopsy report was not inadmissible on grounds that he had not performed autopsy himself, that he was not present at time of death nor that he did not examine deceased postmortem).

Maryland: Malekar v. State (1975) 26 Md. App. 498, 338 A.2d 328 (admission of conclusion contained in autopsy report to effect that death was homicide was not erroneous or prejudicial where conclusion stemmed from obvious fact that victim was strangled and was consistent with defense's theory of case).

Michigan: Abbe v. Woman's Hosp. Ass'n (1971) 35 Mich. App. 429, 192 N.W. 2d 691 (in malpractice case involving death of 26-year-old woman hospital patient after mastectomy, trial court's refusal to admit pathologist's autopsy report under Business Records Act prejudicial error where pathologist present and available for cross-examination).

New Jersey: Petrosino v. Public Serv. Coordinated Transp. (N.J. Super., 1948) 61 A.2d 746 (in a wrongful death action, a physician could offer an opinion as to the cause of death, even though another physician performed the autopsy, where the witness was present during the autopsy as an observer, examined tissue, and formed his own diagnosis, and his testimony was corroborated by the physician who performed the autopsy).

Carroll v. Houtz (1966) 93 N.J. Super. 215, 225 A.2d 584 (autopsy report prepared by assistant county physician admitted under Uniform Business Records Act).

New York: Weinstein v. Prostkoff (Misc., 1959) 191 N.Y.S.2d 310 (it was error to admit microscopic slides in the absence of proof of their possession during the six or eight weeks between the gross autopsy and the microscopic examination).

People v. Hampton (1972) 38 App. Div. 2d 772, 327 N.Y.S.2d 961 (opinion in autopsy report that secondary cause of death was "battered child syndrome," was ruled inadmissible).

Schelberger v. Eastern Savings Bank (1983) 93 App. Div. 2d 188, 461 N.Y.S.2d 785, aff'd. 60 N.Y.2d 506, 470 N.Y.S.2d 548, 458 N.E.2d 1225 (report of medical examiner offering opinion that death of insured resulted from suicide was hearsay).

Ohio: State v. Watson (Ohio, 1991) 572 N.E.2d 97 (in a murder case, it was not error to admit photographs of the body at the crime scene, taken at different angles and distances, where the photos had probative value in showing how the murder took place and were not especially gruesome, but it was an error to admit photos taken during the autopsy that were cumulative and potentially prejudicial, when the manner and cause of death were not in dispute and no issue was raised as to the killer's intent; however, the error did not call for a reversal because it could not be said that, had the autopsy photos not been admitted, the result of the trial would have been different).

State v. Lundgren (Ohio, 1995) 653 N.E.2d 304 (error to admit autopsy photos that were repetitive and whose probative value did not outweigh their prejudicial effect, but the error was harmless in view of overwhelming evidence of guilt).

Pennsylvania: Brennan v. St. Luke's Hosp. (1971) 446 Pa. 339, 285 A.2d 471 (autopsy report of consulting pathologist in private practice admitted under Uniform Business Records Act where pathologist, who supervised preparation of autopsy, testified at trial as to specific findings and conclusions).

Workmen's Comp. Appeal Bd. v. Adley Express Co. (1975) 20 Pa. Commw. 251, 340 A.2d 924 (positive testimony of qualified expert pathologist that employment injury is related to employee's death is sufficient to support finding of such causation despite contradictory testimony by other equally competent witnesses).

Capan v. Divine Providence Hosp. (Pa. Super, 1979) 410 A.2d 1282 (in medical malpractice action, trial court did not err in excluding medical testimony relative to autopsy report because witness was an anesthesiologist and not a pathologist).

Tennessee: Perkins v. Park View Hosp., Inc. (1970) 61 Tenn. App. 458, 456 S.W.2d 276 (in considering in a malpractice case the question of whether the plaintiff should be allowed to testify as to what a pathologist personally told him about the cause of his wife's death, a trial court was upheld in ruling that the fact that the hospital selected the pathologist to perform the autopsy did not make him an agent of the hospital, even though he had an office in the hospital basement).

Texas: Pan American Life Ins. Co. v. Youngblood (Tex. Civ. App., 1978) 569 S.W.2d 951 (uncontradicted testimony by pathologist that sole cause of an insured's death was arteriosclerotic cardiovascular disease, which resulted in heart attack and caused him to fall and sustain head injury, was not binding on jury).

Wisconsin: Milbauer v. Transport Employees Mut. Benefit Soc'y (Wis., 1973) 205 N.W.2d 135 (medical expert's opinion testimony based upon contents of autopsy reports that he read or heard about at trial was admissible since reports were in record and were assumed to be true).

(C) INSURANCE AND WORKERS' COMPENSATION CASES

[See also § 32A.47]

United States: General Acc., Fire & Life Assur. Corp. v. Savage (C.A.-8 Colo., 1929) 35 F.2d 587 (insurance company's delay of ten days in demanding autopsy found unreasonable by jury; upheld on appeal).

Employers' Liab. Assur. Corp., Ltd., of London, England v. Dean (C.A.-5 Ga., 1930) 44 F.2d 524 (if party claiming under policy remains silent after company's request for autopsy on insured, company should take affirmative action to enforce right, and not merely wait until claimant files suit and then defend on theory of noncompliance with policy provision; where company representative erroneously advised beneficiary that autopsy on her husband would take several days when in fact it could have been performed in several hours, beneficiary was justified in refusing to permit autopsy).

Clay v. Aetna Life Ins. Co. (D. Minn., 1931) 53 F.2d 689 (in deciding whether insurance company was unreasonable in delaying demand for autopsy, court should look to see if beneficiary was caused any greater distress by delay).

Palmquist v. Standard Acc. Ins. Co. (S.D. Cal., 1933) 3 F. Supp. 358 (autopsy provision in insurance policy contemplates right to removal of internal organs but not their retention after demand for their return).

Ocean Acc. & Guar. Corp. v. Schachner (C.A.-7 Ill., 1934) 70 F.2d 28 (insurance claim should not be defeated if autopsy cannot be granted through no fault of the beneficiary).

Waldo Fertilizer Co. v. Mutual Life Ins. Co. of New York (C.A.-8 Ark., 1934) 72 F.2d 203 (where corporation was beneficiary of life insurance policy on its president, demand for autopsy should have been made on corporation rather than on deceased's widow).

Howes v. United States Fidelity & Guar. Co. (C.A.-9 Wash., 1934) 73 F.2d 611 (refusal to permit autopsy granted by insurance policy provision, if demand is made reasonably and seasonably, constitutes breach of contract and precludes recovery of benefits).

Travelers Ins. Co. v. Welch (C.A.-5 La., 1936) 82 F.2d 799 (if beneficiary denies request for autopsy, insurance company should seek court action to determine its right).

Aetna Life Ins. Co. v. Lindsay (C.A.-7 Ill., 1934) 69 F.2d 627 (clause in standard autopsy provision granting insurance company right to demand autopsy "where it is not forbidden by law" does not apply to the criminal statute prohibiting grave robbing).

McCulloch v. Mutual Life Ins. Co. of New York (C.A.-4 W. Va., 1940) 109 F.2d 866 (autopsy provision in insurance policy should be strictly construed by the courts not only because it has been drafted by the insurance industry for its own benefit, but also because it entails a course of action abhorrent to the sensibilities of the relatives of the deceased, and may involve desecration of the grave).

Order of United Commercial Travelers of Am. v. Moore (C.A.-5 Ga., 1943) 134 F.2d 558 (jury found delay of 65 days by insurance company in demanding autopsy unreasonable).

Labiche v. Certain Ins. Cos. or Underwriters at Lloyd's, London, England (E.D. La., 1961) 196 F. Supp. 102 (insurance company was granted right to exhume body where coroner who ruled death accidental was found to be neighbor of insured and initial autopsy findings revealed nothing to indicate accident caused death).

Brunson v. Beneficial Fire & Cas. Ins. Co. (C.A.-5 Tex., 1969) 407 F.2d 841 (four months between notice of insured's death and demand for autopsy held unreasonable as matter of law, even in presence of some evidence that autopsy would have been "fruitful"; standard autopsy provision in insurance policy permits autopsy only before interment).

Deneen v. New England Mut. Life Ins. Co. (C.A.-6 Mich., 1980) 615 F.2d 396 (under the rule that an insurance company has a right to order disinterment and autopsy of a deceased insured if (1) through no fault of the insurer it was impractical to order an autopsy before interment and (2) it is reasonably certain that an autopsy would reveal something otherwise undiscoverable bearing on the parties' rights, an insurer failed to meet the second condition in a claim for accidental death benefits on behalf of an insured who died in a one-car accident, where the strongest evidence supporting the insurer's motion to disinter was the testimony of a physician that the accident could have been caused by the insured suffering a stroke).

Stephens v. National Gypsum Co. (M.D. Ga., 1988) 685 F. Supp. 847 (court would allow the disinterment of a worker's body for a limited autopsy to determine whether the deceased suffered from asbestosis, where the defendant showed good cause and urgent necessity and made a strong showing that the examination would establish the facts being sought).

Connecticut: Reardon v. Mutual Life Ins. Co. of New York (1952) 138 Conn. 510, 86 A.2d 570 (for purposes of determining whether insurance company acted within reasonable time in demanding autopsy, clause in policy stating that no person other than officer of company has power to bind company by "accepting any representations or information not contained in the written application for this policy" was not applicable to notice to agent of impending claim for accidental death benefits).

Florida: Insurance Co. of N. Am. v. Achor (Fla. App., 1970) 230 So. 2d 166 (failure of insurance company to demand autopsy before burial should not necessarily forfeit company's right to autopsy under policy, but should be considered in determining whether demand was seasonably and reasonably made under all circumstances of case).

Georgia: Mutual Benefit Health & Acc. Ass'n v. Hickman (Ga. App., 1959) 365 N.Y.S.2d 154 (insurance company, which unequivocally denied liability under an health and accident policy, waived its right to an autopsy when it did not demand it until five months after receiving notice of the insured's death).

Powell v. Commercial Travelers Mut. Acc. Ass'n (Ga. App., 1964) 137 S.E.2d 759 (where a beneficiary did not notify the insurer of the insured's death until after burial, and where the insurer requested disinterment and an autopsy within 17 days of the death, which request was refused by the beneficiary, the beneficiary could not recover on the policy).

Iowa: Life Investors Ins. Co. v. Heline (Iowa, 1979) 285 N.W.2d 31 (where (1) there was very little evidence to determine the exact cause of the insured's death; (2) there was a reasonable likelihood that an autopsy would provide this evidence, and (3) no claim had been made that disinterment would endanger the public health or offend the dead, the fact that the feelings of the insured's relatives would be offended by disinterment and autopsy was insufficient to prevent the court from issuing such an order).

Massachusetts: Hurley v. Metropolitan Life Ins. Co. (1936) 296 Mass. 130, 5 N.E.2d 16 (where insurance company forwarded proof of loss forms after beneficiary wrote that she was deferring decision to allow autopsy, company did not waive its defense under the policy of noncompliance with the autopsy provision).

Minnesota: Cavallero v. Travelers Ins. Co. of Hartford, Conn. (1936) 197 Minn. 417, 267 N.W. 370 (where insurance company's demand for autopsy was made approximately five weeks after notice of death, demand was too late as matter of law, and issue should not have been submitted to jury).

Roepke v. Rice County (Minn., 1977) 260 N.W.2d 464 (order for an autopsy in a workers' compensation action was properly denied where the party seeking the order could not show a reasonable probability that the autopsy would reveal whether the deceased was dead or alive at the time of the accident).

New York: Bernstein v. Metropolitan Life Ins. Co. (1931) 142 Misc. 516, 255 N.Y.S. 591 (insurance company may not delay demand for autopsy on insured merely because policy provision is silent as to when it should be performed; autopsy clause should be construed against insurance company because it is the party that benefits from it).

Dvorkin v. Commercial Travelers Mut. Acc. Ass'n of Am. (1940) 258 App. Div. 501, 17 N.Y.S.2d 109 (fact that jury finds insured's death was result of accident and not disease does not prevent court from holding beneficiary precluded from recovering under accident policy for refusing to allow autopsy, since autopsy might have revealed condition that would have influenced jury to arrive at different conclusion).

Cohen v. Guardian Life Ins. Co. of Am. (1955) 207 Misc. 266, 138 N.Y.S.2d 794 (the standard autopsy provision in an insurance policy includes the right to exhume an insured's body, and an insurer was entitled to an exhumation where the claimant's demand for double indemnity benefits was not made until after the insured was buried).

Saperstein v. Commercial Travelers Mut. Acc. Ass'n (N.Y., 1975) 365 N.Y.S.2d 154, 324 N.E.2d 539 (absence of readily available documentary evidence that would assure the reasonableness of an insurer's request for disinterment and autopsy raises and issue of fact to be resolved in court).

Buntin v. Guardian Life Ins. Co. (App. Div., 1987) 521 N.Y.S.2d 258 (an insurer, who had the consent of the insured's heirs, was entitled to delay litigation and obtain an order for disinterment on presenting evidence that the cremated remains might not be those of the insured).

Tennessee: Hill v. Travelers' Ins. Co. (Tenn., 1927) 294 S.W. 1097 (widow had a cause of action against an insurance company which, after requesting an autopsy on her husband, removed and retained certain vital organs against her instructions).

Robinson v. Nashville Mach. Co. (Tenn., 1973) 503 S.W.2d 90 (under the workers' compensation act, the employer has a right to request an autopsy when the cause of death is obscure or disputed, but the trial court did not err in denying a request by an employer and it's insurer for disinterment and autopsy where the request was not made until nine months after they first had knowledge that an autopsy was needed and where, in addition, two physicians were available to testify as to the cause of death).

Huey Bros. Lumber Co. v. Anderson (Tenn., 1975) 519 S.W.2d 588 (court properly refused request by workmen's compensation insurance company exhumation of body of worker eight months after death where claim adjuster for company learned within three weeks after death that no autopsy had been performed).

Texas: Pan American Life Ins. Co. v. Youngblood (Tex. Civ. App., 1978) 569 S.W.2d 951 (uncontradicted testimony by pathologist that sole cause of an insured's death was arteriosclerotic cardiovascular disease, which resulted in heart attack and caused him to fall and sustain head injury, was not binding on jury).

(D) ACTIONS FOR NEGLIGENCE IN PERFORMING AUTOPSIES

United States: Lawyer v. Kernodle (C.A.-8 Mo., 1983) 721 F.2d 632 (pathologist engaged by coroner to perform autopsy on woman found dead in her home was immune from civil liability in negligence action by woman's husband who was charged, but never tried, for her murder).

Illinois: Courtner v. St. Joseph Hosp. (Ill. App., 1986) 500 N.E.2d 703 (widow failed to state cause of action against hospital for negligent infliction of emotional distress caused by hospital's failure to preserve her husband's body in a condition suitable for an open casket funeral; body had decomposed because of malfunctioning of refrigeration unit in hospital morgue).

Kansas: Burgess v. Perdue (Kan., 1986) 721 P.2d 239 (woman had no claim for outrageous conduct when, after giving instructions that her deceased son's brain was not to be examined during autopsy, she received phone call from physician at hospital informing her that he "had her son's brain in a jar" and wanted to know what she wanted him to do with it).

New Mexico: Flores v. Baca (N.M., 1994) 871 P.2d 962 (when body exhumed for autopsy, family discovered that only upper half had been embalmed; widow suffered long-term and severe emotional distress evidenced by depression, crying spells, and "feelings that husband's body had been disgraced"; appellate court affirmed jury award of $100,000 in compensatory damages and remanded case for trial on issue of punitive damages).

New York: Groeger v. Col-Les Orthop. Assoc. (1989) 149 App. Div. 2d 973, 540 N.Y.S.2d 109 (pathologist could not be held liable for failing to determine whether tumor was benign or malignant, in absence of evidence that, in examining tissue, he did not deviate from accepted practice).

Young-Myun Rho v. Ambach (N.Y., 1989) 546 N.E.2d 188 (deputy chief medical examiner could not be disciplined on charges that he had committed negligence "on more than one occasion" for multiple acts of negligence during performance of single autopsy).

North Carolina: Epps v. Duke Univ., Inc. (N.C. App., 1994) 447 S.E.2d 444 (plaintiffs had cause of action against medical examiner in his individual capacity in which they alleged that defendant had "excessively mutilated" decedent's body in authorizing or supervising autopsy that involved unnecessary procedures unrelated to cause of death).

Wisconsin: Scarpaci v. Milwaukee County (Wis., 1980) 292 N.W.2d 816 (cause of action against the county for allegedly mutilating the body of a child during the performance of an autopsy).

(E) MISCELLANEOUS CASES

United States: Brotherton v. Cleveland (C.A.-6 Mich., 1991) 923 F.2d 477 (action by wife for wrongful removal of deceased husband's corneas for donation under Anatomical Gift Act).

Perry v. St. Francis Hosp. & Med. Ctr. (D.C. Kan., 1994) 863 F. Supp. 724 (widow of the deceased was the only person who could pursue a claim against the Red Cross for converting bones and tissues that were removed from the deceased's body during a donation procedure that allegedly exceeded the family's authorization).

Alabama: Wint v. Alabama Eye & Tissue Bank (Ala., 1996) 675 So. 2d 383 (deceased's family, which had refused to donate his eyes to eye bank, filed suit against eye bank when pathologist, in performing autopsy on deceased, discovered that both eyes were missing).

Colorado: Denver Pub'g Co. v. Dreyfus (Colo., 1974) 520 P.2d 104 (certain autopsy reports in the possession of manager of the department of health and hospitals constituted "public records" within the meaning of the Open Records Act).

Connecticut: Galvin v. Freedom of Information Comm'n (1986) 518 A.2d 64 (autopsy report prepared by Chief Medical Examiner's Office not accessible to general public under Freedom of Information Act; report excepted from Act by state statute setting forth more restrictive guidelines limiting disclosure of such records).

Georgia: Washington v. City of Columbus (1975) 136 Ga. App. 682, 222 S.E.2d 583 (two-year-old child brought to emergency room not breathing and without a pulse; after attempts at resuscitation, child was pronounced dead and "four-quadrant taps" were performed by emergency room physician to determine cause of distended abdomen; autopsy report later suggested child not dead when taps performed; plaintiff alleged performance of taps was "mutilation of the body, but court did not agree).

Mallory v. State (Ga., 1991) 409 S.E.2d 839 (murder defendant's due process rights not violated by prosecution's exhumation of victim's body on eve of trial for further identification purposes, even though court orders did not give defendant right to be present at autopsy that followed exhumation, where, under court orders, defendant could have exhumed body and conducted independent examination of remains).

Louisiana: Succession of Moody (La., 1955) 80 So. 2d 93 (in an action challenging a deceased's testamentary capacity, the court's refusal to order an exhumation and autopsy was held proper, since even if the autopsy showed that the deceased was mentally ill at the time of death, this fact alone would not prove the absence of testamentary capacity).

Alexander v. State Dep't of Health & Hosps. (La. App., 1994) 648 So. 2d 11 (evidence supported trial court's finding that patient had died as result of physician's failure to treat her for bacterial infection rather than from adrenal infarction as stated in coroner's report).

Michigan: Sillery v. Michigan Dep't of Licensing & Reg. Bd. of Med. (Mich., 1985) 378 N.W.2d 570 (medical examiner charged with overstating the scope of an autopsy performed on behalf of a pharmaceutical manufacturer in a product liablity action).

Swickard v. Wayne Cty. Med. Examiner (Mich., 1991) 475 N.W.2d 304 (in view of state Freedom of Information Act, county medical examiner was not justified in withholding report of postmortem examination of chief judge of district court who was found shot to death in mother's home).

Nebraska: Schleich v. Archbishop Bergan Mercy Hosp. (Neb., 1992) 491 N.W.2d 307 (fact that hospital nurse notified county coroner of unusual circumstances surrounding comatose patient's death did not render hospital liable to patient's mother for negligent infliction of emotional distress allegedly caused by police investigating death and questioning her).

New Jersey: Strachan v. John F. Kennedy Mem. Hosp. (1988) 109 N.J. 523, 538 A.2d 346 (hospital held negligent for withholding release of "brain dead" son to his parents, allegedly in order to attempt to persuade parents to allow patient's organs to be removed for donation to transplant program).

Camilli v. Immaculate Conception Cemetery (N.J. Super., 1990) 583 A.2d 417 (claimant in will contest failed to show that five years after the decedent's death from Alzheimer's disease, an exhumation and autopsy of the decedent's brain would, in all reasonable probability, establish evidence of dementia and lack of testamentary capacity three years before her death).

New York: In re Band (App. Div., 1986) 498 N.Y.S.2d 67 (before exercising benevolent discretion in sanctioning disinterment and autopsy, a court must consider the facts and circumstances peculiar to each case).

Gross v. Ambach (1988) 71 N.Y.S.2d 859, 522 N.E.2d 1043 (when performing autopsy, pathologist is engaging in "practice of medicine").

Liebowitz v. Hirsch (App. Div., 1990) 562 N.Y.S.2d 41 (although state law permitted delegation of some physicians' duties to properly supervise physician's assistants, New York City regulations governing medical examiners required licensed physicians to investigate death scenes).

People v. Radtke (App. Div., 1991) 578 N.Y.S.2d 827 (trial court did not abuse discretion in denying murder defendant's motion to exhume body of six-day-old victim to determine whether body had been cut by sharp instrument or bitten by dog where autopsy findings showed that victim had been cut by sharp instrument and where autopsy was videotaped and extensively photographed).

Diaz v. Lukash (N.Y., 1993) 624 N.E.2d 156 (registered nurse convicted of killing twelve patients with excessive doses of lidocaine had right to inspect autopsy records in medical examiner's office upon learning of doctoral dissertation by toxicologist that would allegedly show that high concentrations of lidocaine in victims' bodies were not necessarily lethal).

Janis v. Ladas (App. Div., 1994) 620 N.Y.S.2d 342 (since paternity statute did not contemplate posthumous testing, motion to exhume a decedent's body to perform blood and genetic marker tests to determine paternity was properly denied).

North Carolina: Batcheldor v. Boyd (N.C. App., 1992) 423 S.E.2d 810 (court properly ordered exhumation of body to perform DNA sampling to determine whether claimant against estate was the decedent's son born out of wedlock).

Ohio: Alexander v. Alexander (Ohio Misc., 1988) 537 N.E.2d 1310 (court properly ordered exhumation of body on motion of alleged illegitimate child of deceased who sought to prove paternity through genetic testing).

Pennsylvania: Wawrykow v. Simonich (Pa. Super., 1994) 652 A.2d 843 (in deciding a paternity claim, the court erred in denying a motion for exhumation and DNA testing of the decedent without first determining the sufficiency of the claimant's allegations of parentage and whether a lapse of three years since the decedent's death and embalming would render retrieval of blood and tissue samples improbable or highly unlikely to produce results from which the testing could be performed).

INDEX

A

ABDOMEN.
Autopsy examination, §32A.15.
Reduction of size of abdomen through surgery, §31.27.

ABORTION.
Autopsy evidence, §32A.29.

ACID.
Burns caused by acid, treatment, §31.7b.

ACIDOSIS.
Burns as cause of disturbance of acid base, §31.5.
Ketoacidosis, in diabetics, §30A.15(B).
Lactic acidosis in diabetics, §30A.15(B).

ACROMEGALY.
Diabetes mellitus associated with, §30A.7.

ADACTYLY.
Definition, §31.31.

ADRENAL GLANDS.
Autopsy examination, §32A.27.
Diabetes, tumor of adrenal medulla associated with, §30A.7.

ALCOHOL.
Atrophy of brain, excessive use of alcohol as cause, §32.47.
Black coffee, value in "sobering up," §32.47.
Brain syndrome, alcohol as cause, §32.47.
Cirrhosis of liver.
    Autopsy examination for, §§32A.20, 32A.24.
Epileptic seizures, alcoholics prone to, §32.56.
Peripheral nerve pain, alcoholism as cause, §32.132.

ALKALI.
Burns caused by alkali, §31.7b.

ALLERGIES.
Autopsy evidence of allergic reactions, §§32A.18, 32A.51.

AMNESIA.
Epilepsy, relationship to, §32.54.
Head injury, amnesia following, §32.2.
    Mild head injury, §32.21.
    Moderate to severe head injury, §32.22.

AMPUTATION.
Replantation surgery, §§31.27a, 31.27c.
Severed parts.
    Replantation, §§31.27a, 31.27c.

685

AMYOTROPHIC LATERAL SCLEROSIS.
Lower extremity dysfunction, as cause of, §32.149.
Trauma and, §32.46.

ANAPHYLAXIS.
Autopsy findings in death from, §32A.51.

ANEMIA.
Spinal cord injury as cause, §32.90.

ANESTHESIA.
Autopsy evidence of anesthesia deaths, §32A.51.
Brain injured patients, use of anesthesia, §31.15.
Cardiac arrest during anesthesia.
    Autopsy, difficult to determine on, §32A.51.
Chemonycleolysis, use of general anesthesia, complications, §32.115.

ANEURYSM.
Autopsy examination for, §32A.30.

ANGINA PECTORIS.
"Shoulder-hand syndrome," §32.132.

ANKLE.
Burn injuries, contractures restricting motion, §31.8.

ANOREXIA.
Spinal cord injury as cause, §32.90.

ANTIGENS.
Transplantation of organs and tissue, role in, §30B.4.

ANUS AND ANAL CANAL.
Autopsy examination, §32A.22.

APHASIA.
Brain injury as causing, §32.9.
Description, §32.9.

APOPLEXY.
Traumatic apoplexy, §32.43.

ARACHNOIDITIS.
Peripheral nerve pain, may cause, §32.132.

ARTERIES.
Autopsy examination of major arteries, §32A.30.

ARTERIOSCLEROSIS AND ATHEROSCLEROSIS.
Brain hemorrhage, as cause of, §32.43.

ARTHRITIS.
Spinal arthritis.
    Osteophytes as late consequence of disc rupture, §32.117.
    Predisposing factor to injury, §32.80.

AUTOMOBILES.
Autopsy examination of automobile accident victims, §32A.9.

AUTOPSIES—Cont'd
Hospital autopsies—Cont'd
    Malpractice suspected. (*See within this heading*, "Medical malpractice cases").
    Mistake, autopsies performed by, §32A.45.
    Official autopsies on hospital patients, §32A.13.
    Procedure generally, §32A.10 to 32A.13.
    Purpose, §32A.38.
    Reports, §§32A.37, 32A.47.
    Standards, §§32A.10, 32A.12.
    Value of routine autopsies questioned, §32A.11.
Identification of victim, §§32A.3, 32A.5.
Insurance policies, autopsy provision, §§32A.38, 32A.47, 32A.99(C).
Kidneys, examination, §32A.28.
Leukemia, examination for, §32A.31.
Liver, examination, §32A.24.
Lungs.
    General examination, §32A.19.
    Misdiagnosis of respiratory ailments, autopsy evidence, §32A.51.
    Perforation, examination for, §32A.15.
    Pulmonary function tests, postmortem, §32A.19.
Medical examiners and coroner systems, described, §32A.1.
Medical malpractice cases, §32A.48 to 32A.53.
    Case histories, §32A.51.
    Pathologist's role, §32A.49.
    Problems encountered by attorney, §32A.50.
    Value of autopsy, §§32A.48, 32A.53.
Medicolegal autopsies described, §32A.1.
Mistake, autopsies performed by, §32A.45.
Mutilation of body, actions for, §§32A.41, 32A.42.
Negligent performance of autopsy, actions for, §§32A.41, 32A.42.
Official autopsies.
    Definition, §32A.1.
    Legal authority for, §§32A.43, 32A.44.
Opening incision, procedure, §32A.15.
Organ transplant requests.
    Failure to release organs, §30B.11(A).
    Guidelines for coroners and medical examiners, §32A.47a.
    Uniform Anatomical Gift Act, autopsies under, §32A.39.
Ovaries, examination, §32A.29.
Pancreas, examination, §32A.26.
Pathologists.
    Forensic pathologist defined, §32A.1.
    Hospital pathologist, role in autopsies, §32A.10 to 32A.12.
    Medical malpractice cases, pathologist's role, §32A.49.
"Permission" autopsy. (*See within this heading*, "Hospital autopsies").
Poisonings, autopsy evidence, §§32A.21, 32A.24, 32A.31.
Psychological autopsies, §32A.55.
Purpose of autopsies, §§32A.2, 32A.11, 32A.38.
Rectum, examination, §32A.22.
Religious objections to autopsies, §§32A.40a, 32A.44.

AUTOPSIES—Cont'd
Removal of organs, procedure, §32A.16.
Reports, autopsy.
    Illustrative reports, §32A.37.
    Use as evidence, §§32A.46, 32A.99(B).
Rigor mortis defined, §32A.5.
Scene of death, examination, §32A.4.
Sentimental objections to autopsies, §32A.40.
Sex cases, examination and autopsy evidence, §§32A.5, 32A.22, 32A.29.
Skull, examination, §32A.33.
Spinal cord, examination, §32A.32.
Spleen, examination, §32A.23.
Stab wound cases, §32A.6.
Stomach contents, examination, §32A.21.
Strangulation, autopsy evidence, §32A.18.
Surgical errors, examination for, §32A.51.
Time of death, determining, §§32A.5, 32A.21.
Unauthorized autopsies, actions for, §§32A.42, 32A.99(A).
Urinary bladder, examination, §32A.28.
Uterus, examination, §32A.29.
Vagina, examination, §32A.29.
"Violent, suspicious or unusual death" defined, §32A.44.
Vital statistics, role of autopsies, §32A.11.

AXONOTMESIS.
Description, §32.119.

B

BALANITIS.
Diabetes as cause, §30A.17(D).

BIRTHMARKS.
Surgical correction, §31.33.

BLADDER (URINARY).
Autopsy examination of bladder, §32A.28.
Spinal cord injuries as cause of bladder dysfunction, §§32.83, 32.85, 32.88, 32.89.

BLEPHAROPLASTY.
Description, §31.22.

BLOOD.
Autopsies.
    Blood disorders, autopsy evidence, §32A.51.
    Withdrawal of blood, §32A.15.
Dyscrasia, blood.
    Autopsy evidence, §32A.51.

BLOOD TRANSFUSIONS.
Autopsy evidence in transfusion reactions, §32A.51.

BLOOD VESSELS.
Autopsy examination, §32A.30.

BONE.
Marrow, bone.
    Autopsy examination of, procedure, §32A.31.
        Sternal bone marrow tap, death following, §32A.51.
Pain, musculoskeletal.
    Description, §32.81.
    Factors contributing to, §32.128.

BRACHYDACTYLIA.
Description, §31.31.

BRAIN.
Abscess of brain.
    Trauma, as complication of, §32.44.
Activity-mapping, brain, §32.164.
Air in cranial cavity, §32.37.
Anatomy and physiology, §§32.7, 32.9.
Areas of brain connected with bodily functions, §32.9.
Atrophy of brain.
    Alcohol use as cause, §32.47.
    Elderly more susceptible to hematoma due to, §32.41.
Autopsy examination, §§32A.33, 32A.51.
Blood clot on. (*See within this heading*, "Hematoma").
Blood supply, §32.7.
Bodily functions, areas of brain connected with, §32.9.
Brain death, determination, §30B.14.
Cancer, brain. (*See within this heading*, "Tumors").
Cerebellum, description and function, §§32.7, 32.10.
    Lesions of, §32.10.
Cerebrum, description and function, §32.7.
Compression of brain.
    Contusion as cause, §32.17.
    Laceration as cause, §32.17.
Concussion of brain. (*See within this heading*, "Trauma to brain").
Corpora striatae, §32.10.
Corpus callosum, §32.7.
Cortex, cerebral.
    Description and function, §32.7.
    Motor cortex area, §32.9.
Death, brain, §30B.14.
Dura, injury to, and epilepsy, §32.54.
Edema, cerebral, trauma as cause. (*See within this heading*, "Trauma to brain").
Fissures of brain, §32.7.
Forebrain, description, §32.7.
Function of brain generally, §§32.8, 32.9.
Ganglia, basal, description and function, §32.10.
Gray matter, §32.7.
Hearing, area of brain controlling, §32.9.

BRAIN—Cont'd

Pressure, intracranial—Cont'd
    Optic nerve affected by increase in, §32.30.
    Subarachnoid hemorrhage may increase, §§32.8, 32.19.
    Trauma causing increase in, treatment, §32.28.
Reading ability, area of brain controlling, §32.9.
"Silent areas" of brain, §32.9.
Speech expression and reception, area of brain controlling, §32.9.
Stem, brain.
    Injury to, §§32.14, 32.18.
    Role in causing unconsciousness, §32.18.
Sulci of brain, §32.7.
Surgery involving brain, §32.23 to 32.28.
    Malpractice actions, §32.199(F).
Syndrome, brain.
    Alcohol as cause, §32.47.
Thalamus, description and function, §32.10.
    Lesions of, §32.10.
Trauma to brain.
    Abducens nerve injury, §32.31.
    Abscess as complication, §32.44.
    Aggravation of preexisting disease, §32.46.
    Amyotrophic lateral sclerosis, trauma and, §32.46.
    Anesthesia, use on brain injured patients, §31.15.
    Aphasia resulting from, §32.9.
    Apoplexy, late traumatic, §32.43.
    Athletic injuries, §32.17.
    Auditory nerve injury, §32.34.
    Blindness as result of, §32.30.
    Blood clot, formation of. (*See* within this subheading, "Hematoma").
    Brain-mapping, use in diagnosis, §32.164.
    Bullet penetrating brain, nature of injury, §32.15.
    Cerebellum, traumatic lesions usually fatal, §32.10.
    Cerebrospinal fluid, production increased by trauma, §32.8.
    Closed brain injury, §32.14.
    Coma following injury.
        Unconsciousness. (*See* within this subheading, "Unconsciousness").
    Concussion.
        Brain cells, possible effect on, §32.11.
        Cerebral anemia, as cause of, §32.11.
        Definition of term, §32.11.
        Early and late outcome, §32.46a.
        Hematoma following. (*See* within this subheading, "Hematoma").
        Litigation and prolonged postconcussion conditions, §32.157.
        Mechanism of concussion, §32.11.
        Mild head injury, concussion and, §32.13.
        Symptoms, §32.21.
        Treatment.
            Generally, §32.23 to 32.28.
            Mild concussion, §32.23.

BRAIN DEATH.
In determination of death, §30B.14.

BRAIN-MAPPING.
Description, §32.164.

BREAST.
Augmentation through surgical implants, §31.25.
Cancer of breast.
    Reconstruction following surgery, §31.26a.
Implants, problems with, §§31.25, 31.49, 31.99(A).
Plastic surgery, §§31.25, 31.26, 31.26a.
Reconstruction, §31.26a.
Reduction through surgery, §31.25.
Silicone implants, §§31.25, 31.49, 31.99(A).

BROWN-SEQUARD SYNDROME.
Spinal cord injury as cause, §§32.87, 32.93.

BURNS.
Acid burns, §31.7b.
Alkali burns, §31.7b.
Antibiotics, use in treatment, §31.4.
Autopsies on burned bodies, §32A.7.
Chemical burns, §31.7b.
Classification of burn wounds, §31.3.
Complications of burns, §31.5.
Degrees of burns, §31.3.
Depth of burn, determination, §31.3.
Early treatment, §31.4.
Electrical burns, §§31.2, 31.7a.
Emotional damage, §§31.8, 31.47.
Fatalities in burn cases, cause of death, §§31.5, 32A.7.
Fluid loss, replacement, §§31.4, 31.5.
Free flaps, use in treatment, §31.8.
Gasoline, contact with, mistaken for flame burn, §31.7b.
Growth delay in children, §31.5.
Historical development of treatment, §31.1.
Impairment rating, §31.9a.
Incidence and common causes of burns, §§31.1, 31.2, 31.9.
Infection, §§31.4, 31.5, 31.11.
Keloids, §31.48.
Kidney failure, §31.5.
Litigation involving burns, §§31.9 to 31.11, 31.99.
    Flammable fabrics, §§31.9, 31.10.
    Medical malpractice, §§31.11, 31.99(A), 31.99(B).
    Product liability actions, §§31.9, 31.10, 31.99(C).
Lung damage, treatment, §31.4.
Lye burns, §§31.2, 31.7b.
Magnesium burns, §31.7b.
Medical treatment, burns suffered while under, §31.99(B).
Muscle flaps, use in treatment, §31.8.

CANCER—Cont'd
Growth rate of cancer.
 Cannot be determined on autopsy, §32A.51.
Transplantation of cancer from organ donors, §30B.18(B).

CARDIAC DEATH.
In determination of death, §30B.14.

CAROTID ARTERY.
Injury to, in skull fractures, §32.38.

CARPAL TUNNEL SYNDROME.
Description, §§31.42a, 32.140.
Endoscopic release, risks involved, §31.42a.
Sympathetic dystrophy as result of median nerve injury, §32.130.

CAT SCANS. (*See* TOMOGRAPHY).

CAUSALGIA.
Description, §32.129.

CEREBROSPINAL FLUID.
Amount of fluid in normal system, §32.8.
Brain hemorrhage into subarachnoid space, clotting prevented by fluid, §32.19.
Circulation of fluid, §32.8.
Diagnostic use of spinal tap, §32.8.
Function, §32.8.
Leakage of fluid.
 Nose, fluid leaking from, §32.57.
 Pneumocephalus as complication, §32.37.
Production of fluid, §32.8.
Spinal rhinorrhea, skull fracture as cause, §32.37.
Trauma to brain as increasing production, §32.8.

CEREBRUM.
Description and function, §32.7.

CHEEKBONE.
Cheek implants, cosmetic, §31.20.
Injuries to, §31.14 to 31.17.
 Fractures, §31.17.

CHEMONUCLEOLYSIS.
Description, §32.115.

CHEST.
Autopsy examination of chest, §32A.15.
 Misdiagnosis of injuries, §32A.51.
Fatal injuries.
 Value of autopsy, §32A.51.
Trauma to chest.
 Autopsy examination, §32A.15.
  Misdiagnosis of injuries, §32A.51.

CUBITAL TUNNEL SYNDROME.
Description, §§31.42c, 32.141.

CUSHING'S SYNDROME.
Diabetes associated with, §30A.7.

D

DEAD BODIES.
Autopsies. (*See* AUTOPSIES).
Exhumation, §§32A.36, 32A.47, 32A.52.
Possession and control over disposition of body, §32A.39.

DEATH.
Determination of death, methods, §30B.14.
Time of death, determining, §§32A.5, 32A.21.

DEATH CERTIFICATES.
Accuracy of cause of death information, §32A.56.

DERMABRASION.
Description and complications, §31.23.

DERMATOME.
Definition, §32.138.

DIABETES MELLITUS.
Accidents, diabetes as cause, §30A.18.
    Diabetics as drivers of motor vehicles, §30A.99(E).
Acromegaly, diabetes associated with, §30A.7.
Adrenal gland tumor, diabetes associated with, §30A.7.
Adult onset, §30A.5.
Autonomic neuropathy as complication, §30A.17(C).
Blindness, diabetes as cause, §§30A.17(A), 30A.23, 30A.28.
Blood glucose (sugar) tests, §§30A.8, 30A.9.
Causes of diabetes generally, §30A.4 to 30A.7.
Circulatory disorders and diabetes, §§30A.17(A), 30A.17(B).
Coma, diabetic, §30A.15(B).
Complications of diabetes, §§30A.14, 30A.14 to 30A.17, 30A.17, 30A.28.
Coronary disease and diabetes, §30A.17(B).
Cushing's syndrome, diabetes associated with, §30A.7.
Description of disease, §§30A.1, 30A.2.
Diabetes Control and Complications Trial (DCCT), §§30A.9, 30A.17.
Diagnosis of diabetes, criteria, methods, §§30A.8, 30A.23, 30A.28.
Diet and diabetes, §§30A.2, 30A.9.
Drugs as cause of diabetes, §§30A.7, 30A.19.
Drugs used to treat diabetes, §30A.9 to 30A.13.
Exercise and diabetes, §30A.9.
Finger-stick test, §30A.8.
Gangrene as result of trauma to diabetic, §30A.17(B).
General practitioners, quality of care, §30A.23.
Genetic testing for potential diabetics, §30A.4.
Gestational diabetes, §30A.8.

DIABETES MELLITUS—Cont'd

Trauma.

    As aggravating diabetes, §§30A.16(D), 30A.20, 30A.99(D).

    As cause of diabetes, §§30A.7, 30A.19, 30A.99(D).

Treatment of diabetes, §§30A.9 to 30A.13, 30A.23.

    Antidiabetic drugs, §30A.9 to 30A.13.

    Malpractice, §§30A.23, 30A.99(A).

    Primary care physicians, §30A.28.

    Transplantation of pancreas, §§30A.13, 30B.19.

Types of diabetes, §§30A.1, 30A.4 to 30A.6.

University Group Diabetes Program (UGDP), §30A.11.

Workers' compensation and diabetes, §§30A.20(B), 30A.99(B).

DIENCEPHALON.

Role in epilepsy, §32.49.

DISCOGRAPHY.

Complications, §32.115.

Controversy over value, §32.96.

Description and use in diagnosis of disc disorders, §32.96.

DISFIGUREMENT.

Litigation involving, §31.99(C).

Psychological effect, §31.47.

Treatment. (*See* PLASTIC SURGERY).

DISUSE ATROPHY.

Following peripheral nerve injury, §32.131.

DOWN'S SYNDROME.

Predisposing factor to spinal injury, §32.80.

DROWNING VICTIMS.

Autopsy examination of bodies recovered from water, §32A.8.

DRUGS.

Acarbose, §§30A.11, 30A.12.

ACE-inhibitors, §30A.17(A).

Acetohexamide, §30A.11.

Antibiotics (antimicrobials).

    Burns, use in treatment, §31.4.

Antidiabetic drugs, §30A.11.

Antilymphocyte antibody preparations, §30B.6.

ATG, §30B.6.

Autopsy examination for drug reactions or complications, §§32A.18, 32A.30, 32A.51.

Azathioprine, §30B.6.

Baclofen, §32.85.

Botulinum, §§32.33, 32.160a.

Carbamazepine, §32.57.

Carisoprodol, §32.85.

Chlorpropamide, §30A.11.

Chymopapain, §32.115.

Cyclobenaprine, §32.85.

Cyclosporine, §30B.6.

DURA MATER.
Description, §32.6.

DYNAMOMETER.
Use in measuring grasping power, §31.35.

E

EAR.
Congenital anomalies, §31.30.
Deformed ear, methods of correction, §31.30.
External ear.
    Deformities of, methods of correction, §31.30.
Middle ear.
    Basal skull fractures through, §32.37.

EDEMA.
Cerebral edema in head injuries, §32.28.
Spinal cord injury as cause, §32.90.

ELBOW.
Burn injuries, contractures restricting motion, §31.8.

ELECTRICAL INJURIES.
Burn injuries, §§31.2, 31.7a, 31.7b.
Children.
    Lip burns from electrical cords and outlets, §31.2.
Neurological injuries, §32.122.

ELECTROENCEPHALOGRAPHY (EEG).
Brain death, determination of, §30B.14.
Brain injury.
    Epilepsy, §§32.49, 32.50, 32.56.
Brain-mapping, §32.164.
Brain waves.
    Epilepsy, §§32.49, 32.50, 32.56.
Epilepsy.
    Brain-wave activity, §§32.49, 32.50, 32.56.
Quantitative encephalography, §32.165.

ELECTROLYTES.
Burn injuries, replacement of fluid loss, §31.4.

ELECTROMYOGRAPHY (EMG).
Description and use, §§32.97, 32.152 to 32.156.

EMBOLISM.
Autopsy examination for embolism, §§32A.15, 32A.19, 32A.51.

EMPYEMA.
Subdural empyema as complication of head injury, §32.44.

EPENDYMOMA.
Predisposing factor to spinal cord injury, §32.80.

704

EPILEPSY.
Accidents, epilepsy as factor in, §32.59.
    Physicians' duty to report epileptic drivers, §32.59.
Alcoholics susceptible to, §32.56.
Amnesia in, §32.54.
Brain hemorrhage as cause, §32.52.
Brain tumor, seizures in persons suffering from, §32.56.
Classifications, §32.47a.
    Seizures, §32.48.
Definition of epilepsy, §§32.47, 32.47a.
Diagnosis, §32.56.
Head injury.
    Amnesia, relationship of posttraumatic epilepsy, §32.54.
    Brain hemorrhage as cause of epilepsy, §32.52.
    Description of epilepsy following, §32.47.
    Diagnosis of epilepsy following, §32.56.
    Prevention of epilepsy following, §32.57.
    Relationship between head injury and epilepsy, §32.51 to 32.54.
    Seizures following head injury, classification, description. (*See within this heading,* "Seizures").
Litigation involving, §32.199(B).
Posttraumatic epilepsy. (*See within this heading,* "Head injury").
Rehabilitation of epileptics, §32.58.
Restrictions on activities, §§32.58, 32.59.
Seizures.
    Atonic, §32.50.
    Brain hemorrhage as cause, §32.52.
    Brain tumors and, §32.56.
    Cessation of, §32.55.
    Classification, §32.48.
    Conditions which mimic, §32.56.
    Delayed onset, §32.53.
    Drugs used in control, §32.57.
    Early posttraumatic, §32.52.
    Focal type, §32.49.
    Generalized, §32.50.
    Grand mal, §32.50.
    Hallucinations during seizure, §32.49.
    Head injury as cause, §32.51 to 32.54.
    Imitated seizures, §32.56.
    Incidence relative to type of injury, §32.54.
    Injury to third party, physician's liability, §32.59.
    Jacksonian type, §32.49.
    Myoclonic, §32.50.
    Partial type, §32.49.
    Petit mal, §32.50.
    Psychomotor, §32.49.
    Surgery for, §32.57.
    Syphilis patients, seizures in, §32.56.
    Time of onset, §§32.52, 32.53.

EPILEPSY—Cont'd
Todd's paralysis, §32.49.
Traumatic epilepsy. (*See within this heading*, "Head injury").
Treatment, §§32.57, 32.58.

ERB-DUCHENNE'S SYNDROME.
Description, §32.143.

ESOPHAGUS.
Autopsy examination of esophagus, §32A.20.

EXECUTIVE DEFICIT.
Sequela of mild head injury, §32.158.

EXHUMATIONS.
For autopsy examinations, §§32A.36, 32A.47, 32A.52.

EXOPHTHALMOS.
Skull fracture as cause, §32.38.

EXTREMITIES.
Replantation of extremities, §31.27a.

EYE.
Autopsy examination of eyes, §32A.34.
"Bags" under eyes, cosmetic surgery to remove, §31.22.
Brain damage indicated by abnormalities in eyes, §32.19.
Hypertelorism, §31.32.
Impaired vision. (*See* VISION).
Injuries to eye.
    Oculomotor nerve injury resulting in "squint," §32.31.
Lower-lid fat resection, §31.22.
Orbit.
    Injuries to.
        Engorgement in skull fractures, §32.38.
        Pulsating exophthalmus, §32.38.
Pupil.
    Dilation as symptom of hematoma (blood clot), §32.19.
"Squint" resulting from injury to oculomotor nerve, §32.31.
Tears (lacrimation).
    "Crocodile tears" description and cause, §32.33.
"Wide eye" deformity, description and treatment, §31.32.

F

FACE.
Face-lift, §31.21. (*See also* PLASTIC SURGERY).
Injuries to face.
    Emergency care, §31.15.
    Facial tic, injury as cause, §32.33.
    Fracture of facial bones.
        Treatment, §31.17.
    Lacerations, treatment for, §31.16.

706

707

HAND—Cont'd
Dupuytren's contracture, §§31.42d, 31.44, 31.44a.
"Shoulder-hand syndrome," §32.132.
Trauma to hand, §31.39 to 31.45.
    Diseases complicating injuries generally, §31.44.
    Nerve injuries, §31.42.
    Rehabilitation, §31.45.
    Replantation surgery, §31.27a.
    Tendon injuries, §31.41.
    Treatment, §31.40.
        Complications, §31.43.
        Medical record, importance of, §31.40.
"Violin hand" as result of nerve injury, §32.140.

HARELIP.
Cleft plate, §31.29.

HEADACHE.
Head injury, headache following, §32.21.

HEAD INJURIES.
Classifications of injuries, §32.13.
Cranial nerve injury, §§32.29 to 32.35, 32.150.
Disability awards, §32.199(A).
Examination and treatment generally, §32.23 to 32.28.
    Facial injuries, §31.14 to 31.17.
    Skull fractures, §§32.12, 32.36 to 32.38.
Personal injury actions.
    Generally, §32.199(A).
    Points to consider, §32.2.
Personality change following head injury, §32.2.

HEARING.
Brain area controlling hearing, §32.9.

HEART.
Autopsy examination of heart, §32A.17.
Cardiac death, §30B.14.
Catheterization, cardiac.
    Autopsy examination for death following, §32A.51.
Coronary arteries.
    Autopsy examination for disease, §32A.17.
Pain associated with heart disorders.
    "Shoulder-hand syndrome," §32.132.
Transplants, heart, §§30B.11, 30B.19. (*See* TRANSPLANTATION).

HEMANGIOMA.
Surgical correction, §31.33.

HEMIANOPIA (HEMIANOPSIA).
Description, §32.30.
Homonymous hemianopia resulting from head injury, §32.30.

IDENTIFICATION.
Dead bodies, §§32A.3, 32A.5.

IMMUNE SYSTEM.
Beneficial effects of system, §30B.3.
Immunity and rejection of tissue. (*See* TRANSPLANTATION).

IMPAIRMENT RATING.
Burns, §31.9a.

IMPOTENCE.
Diabetes mellitus as cause, §30A.17(C).
Spinal cord injury as cause, §§32.85, 32.89.
Spinal nerve root cysts as cause, §32.76.

INFECTIOUS DISEASES.
Stethoscopes as source of disease, §31.11.

INSULIN.
Diabetes mellitus, use in treatment, §30A.10.

INTERVERTEBRAL DISC.
Discography, use in detecting disc disorders, §32.96.
Herniated disc.
    Cervical disc, §32.105.
    Common occurrence, §32.102.
    Discography, use of, §32.96.
    Electromyography, use in evaluating nerve damage, §32.156.
    Lumbar disc, §§32.107, 32.112.
        Orthopedic *versus* neurosurgical approach, §32.102.
        Surgical removal of disc, §32.109 to 32.113.
            Anterior *versus* lateral approach, §32.110.
            Complications, §32.114.
            Laminectomy, §§32.110, 32.112.
            Period of convalescence, §32.113.
            Prognosis, §32.114.
    Nerve-root compression, §§32.103, 32.105, 32.107.
    Orthopedic *versus* neurosurgical approach to, §32.102.
    Pain associated with herniation.
        Description, §32.103.
        Leg pain, §32.107.
        Lumbar disc, §32.107.
        Onset, §32.103.
        Psychological effects, §32.104.
        Tranquilizers to relieve, §32.104.
    Preexisting weakness, §32.102.
    Symptoms, §§32.103, 32.105, 32.107.
    Tarlov cyst may mimic, §32.76.
    Thoracic disc, §§32.106, 32.111.
    Treatment, §32.108 to 32.116.
        Cervical discs, §32.110.

L

LAMINECTOMY.
Use in removing herniated discs, §§32.110, 32.112.

LASEGUE TEST.
Spinal examination, use in, §32.107.

LASER RESURFACING.
Cosmetic procedure, §31.24a.

LEUKEMIA.
Autopsy examination for, §32A.31.

LIPOSUCTION.
Description, §31.27.

LIVER.
Autopsy examination, §§32A.20, 32A.24.
Transplants, §§30B.11, 30B.19. (*See* TRANSPLANTATION).

LOBECTOMY.
Frontal or temporal lobectomy as treatment for posttraumatic epilepsy, §32.57.

LUNGS.
Brain injury, pulmonary complications, §32.45.
Transplants. (*See* TRANSPLANTATION).

M

MAGNETIC RESONANCE IMAGING (MRI).
Description, §32.95b.
Use in evaluating spinal disorders, §§32.73, 32.88, 32.95b.

MALINGERING.
Back injury cases, §32.81.
Brain concussion cases, §32.157.
Electromyography, use in detecting malingering, §32.156.
Peripheral nerve injury, refusal to use limb following, §32.131.

MAMMAPLASTY.
Augmentation mammaplasty, §31.25.
Reduction mammaplasty, §31.26.

MANDIBLE.
Fractures of mandible, §31.17.

MARIE-STRUMPELL DISEASE.
Predisposing factor to spinal injury, §32.80.

MASTOPEXY.
Description, §31.26.

MAXILLA.
Fractures of maxillary bone, §31.17.

N

NERVES—Cont'd

Auditory nerve.
    Function, §32.34.
    Injuries to, §32.34.
Autonomic nervous system.
    Anatomy and physiology generally, §32.71.
    Causalgia, effect on autonomic function, §32.129.
    Parasympathetic division.
        Function, §32.71.
        Nerve root lesions as affecting, §32.79.
    Spinal cord injury, effect of, §32.89.
    Sympathetic division.
        Dysfunction, §§32.127, 32.130.
        Function, §32.71.
        Nerve root lesions as affecting, §32.79.
        Peripheral nerve injury, effect on sympathetic nerves, §32.130.
Axillary nerve, injury to, §32.150.
Axon, definition, §32.119.
Brachial plexus.
    Anatomy and function, §32.143.
    "Crutch palsy," §§32.122, 32.143.
    Duchenne-Aran's syndrome, §32.143.
    Erb-Duchenne's syndrome, §32.143.
    Erb's palsy, §32.143.
    Horner's syndrome, §32.143.
    Injury to, §32.143.
    Klumpke's syndrome, §32.143.
Central nervous system.
    Peripheral nerves. (*See within this heading*, "Peripheral nerves").
Cervical plexus, injury to, §32.150.
Cranial nerves.
    Anatomy of, §32.29 to 32.35.
    Eighth. (*See within this heading*, "Auditory nerve").
    Eleventh. (*See within this heading*, "Spinal accessory nerve").
    Fifth. (*See within this heading*, "Trigeminal nerve").
    First. (*See within this heading*, "Olfactory nerve").
    Fourth. (*See within this heading*, "Trochlear nerve").
    Function of, §32.29 to 32.35.
    Impairment of, evaluation, §32.29 to 32.35.
    Injury to, §§32.29 to 32.35, 32.150.
    Ninth. (*See within this heading*, "Glossopharyngeal nerve").
    Second. (*See within this heading*, "Optic nerve").
    Seventh. (*See within this heading*, "Facial nerve").
    Sixth. (*See within this heading*, "Abducens nerve").
    Tenth. (*See within this heading*, "Vagus nerve").
    Third. (*See within this heading*, "Oculomotor nerve").
    Twelfth. (*See within this heading*, "Hypoglossal nerve").
Diabetic neuropathy, §§30A.17(D), 32.132.
Disuse atrophy, §32.131.
Electromyogram (EMG), use in detection of nerve disorders, §32.152 to 32.156.

716

NERVES—Cont'd
Peripheral nerves—Cont'd
    Trauma to nerve—Cont'd
        Personal injury actions, §32.199(E).
        Regeneration following, §§32.120, 32.121.
        Rehabilitation following, §32.151.
        Seddon classification of severity of injury, §32.119.
        Stretch injuries, §32.122.
        Sudeck's atrophy following, §32.130.
        Surgical repair.
            Anastomosis, §32.135.
            Indications for, §32.134.
            Nerve grafts, §32.136.
            "Neuroma-in-continuity," §32.137.
            Reunion of nerve ends, §32.135.
            Types of injuries unsuited for, §32.134.
        Sympathetic dystrophy following, §32.130.
        Sympathetic nervous system dysfunction, §32.127.
            Sympathetic dystrophy, §32.130.
        Symptoms of, §32.123.
        "Time and location" principle in evaluating nerve injuries, §§32.155, 32.156.
        "Tinel's sign," §32.134.
        Treatment.
            Electrical stimulation, §32.151.
            Physical therapy, §32.151.
            Substitutive mechanics, §32.151.
            Surgery. (*See* within this subheading, "Surgical repair").
        Types of injury, §§32.119, 32.122.
    Vitamin B-12 deficiency as cause of pain, §32.132.
Peroneal nerve.
    Anatomy and function, §32.144.
    "Foot-drop," §32.144.
    Injury to, §32.144.
Plantar nerve, injury to, §32.150.
Plexus neuritis as cause of lower extremity dysfunction, §32.149.
Radial nerve.
    Injury to, §32.139.
Regeneration of nerves, §§32.120, 32.121.
Roots of nerves. (*See within this heading*, "Spinal nerves").
Scapular nerve (dorsal), injury to, §32.150.
Spinal accessory nerve.
    Anatomy, §32.35.
    Function, §32.35.
    Injury to, §32.35.
Spinal nerves.
    Description and function, §32.69.
    Injury to.
        Root injury. (*See* within this subheading, "Nerve roots").
        Treatment, §32.99.

NERVES—Cont'd
Spinal nerve—Cont'd
  Nerve roots.
    Conditions mistaken for root compression, §32.154.
    Description, §32.79.
    Electromyographic evaluation in suspected nerve root compression, §32.156.
    Injury to, §32.79.
    Lesions as affecting autonomic nervous system, §32.79.
    Perineurial cysts, §32.76.
    Tarlov cysts, §32.76.
    Traumatic cysts, §32.76.
  Suprascapular nerve, injury to, §32.150.
  Sympathetic nervous system. (*See within this heading*, "Autonomic nervous system").
  Thoracic nerve, injury to, §32.150.
  Thoracic outlet syndrome.
    Anatomy and function, §32.145.
    Injury to, §§32.145, 32.146.
  Trauma to nerves. (*See within this heading*, "Injury to nerve").
  Trigeminal nerve.
    Anatomy, §32.32.
    Injury to, §§32.32, 32.150.
  Trochlear nerve.
    Anatomy, §32.31.
    Function, §32.31.
    Injury to, §32.31.
  Ulnar nerve.
    Anatomy and function, §32.141.
    "Froment's sign," §32.141.
    Injury to, §§32.141, 32.142.
  Vagus nerve.
    Anatomy, §32.35.
    Function, §32.35.
    Injury to, §32.35.

NEURAPRAXIA.
Description, §32.119.

NEURITIS.
Lower extremity dysfunction, plexus neuritis as cause, §32.149.

NEUROFIBROMA.
Neck pain, as cause of.
  Cord compression, associated with, §32.80.

NEUROSIS.
Compensation neurosis, §32.81.
  Musculoskeletal injury and, §32.81.

NEUROTMESIS.
Description, §32.119.

NOSE.
Cosmetic surgery to reshape nose, §31.19.

NOSE—Cont'd
Fractures and other injuries.
    Treatment, §31.17.
Rhinoplasty, §31.19.
Spinal fluid leaking from nose, §32.27.

O

OSTEOMYELITIS.
Head injury, as complication of, §32.44.

OSTEOPHYTES.
Description, §32.117.
Trauma as aggravating body overgrowth, narrowing of spinal canal, §§32.78, 32.80.

OVARIES.
Autopsy examination of ovaries, §32A.29.

P

PAIN.
Causalgia, §32.129.
"Gate control" theory.
    Spinal cord and, §32.68.
Head pain.
    Brain concussion, as symptom of, §32.21.
Musculoskeletal pain, §32.80.
    Contributing factors, §32.81.
Post-nerve-injury pain, §§32.128, 32.129.
"Shoulder-hand syndrome," §32.132.

PALSY.
"Crutch palsy," §§32.122, 32.143.
Peroneal palsy, §32.122.
"Saturday night palsy," §§32.122, 32.139, 32.154.

PANCREAS.
Autopsy examination, §32A.26.
Transplantation of pancreas, §§30A.13, 30B.11, 30B.19.
Trauma to pancreas.
    Diabetes caused by, §§30A.7, 30A.19.

PAPILLEDEMA.
Head injury as cause, §32.30.

PARALYSIS.
Todd's paralysis following epileptic seizure, §32.49.

PARESTHESIA.
Spinal cord injury as cause, §§32.81, 32.87.

PATHOLOGISTS.
Autopsies, role of pathologist, §§32A.10 to 32A.12, 32A.49.

719

PATHOLOGISTS—Cont'd
Medical malpractice cases, pathologist's role, §32A.49.

PENIS.
Diabetics susceptible to inflammation of glans penis (balanitis), §30A.17(D).

PHALANGES.
Description, §31.35.

PHARYNX.
Laxity of cruciate ligament following pharyngitis, §32.80.
Numbness of pharynx, glossopharyngeal nerve damage as cause, §32.35.

PHEOCHROMOCYTOMA.
Diabetes associated with, §30A.7.

PHYSICAL THERAPY (PHYSIOTHERAPY).
Nerve injuries, treatment for, §32.151.

PHYSICIANS AND SURGEONS.
Epileptic drivers, physicians' duty to report, §32.59.
Malpractice.
 Autopsy findings, use in malpractice cases, §32A.48 to 32A.53.
 Burn cases, §§31.11, 31.99(A).
 Diabetes mellitus, treatment of, §§30A.23, 30A.28, 30A.99(A).

PLASTIC SURGERY.
Abdomen, reduction, §31.27.
Anxiety in cosmetic surgery patients, §31.46.
"Bags" under eyes, removal, §31.22.
Birthmarks, removal, §31.33.
Blepharoplasty, §31.22.
Breasts.
 Augmentation, §31.25.
 Fat transplantation, §31.25.
 Implants, §31.25.
 Reconstruction following mastectomy, §31.26a.
 Reduction, §31.26.
Buttocks, reduction, §31.27.
Cheek implants, cosmetic, §31.20.
Chin implants, cosmetic, §31.20.
Cleft lip and palate, correction, §31.29.
Collagen injections, §31.16.
Congenital deformities, correction, §31.28 to 31.33. (*See also* CONGENITAL ANOMALIES
 AND DEFORMITIES).
Cosmetic surgery, §31.18 to 31.27.
Dermabrasion, §31.23.
Ear deformities, correction, §31.30.
Face-lift, §§31.21, 31.21a.
Face-peel.
 Chemical, §31.24.
 Laser, §31.24a.
Facial implants, §31.20.

PSYCHOLOGICAL AUTOPSIES.
Description, §32A.55.

Q

QUECKENSTEDT TEST.
Description, §32.8.

R

RADIATION.
Hazards of radiation.
    Burns, §31.7c.

RADIATION THERAPY.
Benign conditions, use of radiation therapy for, §31.48.
Keloids, treatment with radiation, §31.48.

RAPE AND SEXUAL ASSAULT.
Examination of victim.
    Autopsy examinations, §§32A.5, 32A.22, 32A.29.

RECTUM.
Autopsy examination, §32A.22.

REFLEX SYMPATHETIC DYSTROPHY.
Description, §32.130.

REHABILITATION.
Burn patients, §31.8.
Head injury patients.
    Executive deficits, §32.158.
    Vegetative state, §32.159.

RESPIRATION.
Kussmaul respiration in lactic acidosis, §30A.15(B).

RETINA.
Diabetes, retinal damage due to, §30A.17(A).

RHINOPLASTY.
Description, §31.19.
    Complications, §31.19.

RHINORRHEA.
Spinal rhinorrhea as result of skull fracture, §32.37.

RHYTIDECTOMY.
Description, §31.21.

RIGOR MORTIS.
Description, §32A.5.

S

SCALP.
Anatomy of scalp, §32.4.

SCAPULA.
Scapular and suprascapular nerve injuries, §32.150.
"Winged scapula," §32.143.

SCARS.
Acceptable scars, §31.48.
Description of scar tissue, §31.48.
Disfigurement generally.
    Litigation involving, §31.99(C).
    Wound healing and scars, §31.48.
Myths regarding scars, §31.48.

SCHEUERMANN'S DISEASE.
Predisposing factor to spinal injury, §32.80.

SCIATIC PAIN.
Perineurial cysts as cause, §32.76.
Spinal nerve root cysts as cause, §32.76.
Tarlov cysts as cause, §32.76.

SEX CHANGE.
Psychiatric consultation, §31.33a.
Surgical sex change, §§31.33a, 31.33a to 31.33c, 31.33b.

SHOCK.
Burn cases, §31.5.
Spinal shock, severe cord injury as cause, §32.83.

SHOULDER.
Pain in shoulder.
    Eleventh cranial nerve injury as cause, §32.35.
"Shoulder-hand syndrome," §32.131.

SILICONE BREAST IMPLANTS.
Litigation involving, §§31.49, 31.99(A).

SINUSES (FACIAL).
Skull fractures, injuries to sinuses, §32.38.

SKIN.
Dermabrasion, §31.23.
Diabetic dermopathy, §30A.17(D).
Nerves supplying skin (dermatomal distribution), §32.70.
Shin spots, diabetes as cause, §30A.17(D).

SKULL.
Anatomy of skull, §§32.4, 32.5.
Autopsy examination, §32A.33.
Bones of skull, §32.5.
Fractures of skull.
    Abducens nerve injury, §32.31.

SPINAL CORD—Cont'd

Blood vessels supplying, §32.75.

Compression of cord.

    Trauma as cause. (*See within this heading*, "Trauma to spinal cord").

"Gate control" theory of pain and spinal cord, §32.68.

Medical malpractice actions involving, §32.199(F).

Motor fibers within, §32.68.

Trauma to spinal cord.

    Appetite loss as result, §32.90.

    Autonomic nervous system, effect on, §32.89.

    Bedsores as complication, §32.90.

    Bladder dysfunction, §§32.83, 32.85, 32.88, 32.89.

    Blood clot causing pressure on cord, §§32.75, 32.77.

    Blood vessel injury associated with, §§32.75, 32.77.

    Bowel dysfunction, §§32.83, 32.85, 32.89.

    Brown-Sequard syndrome, §§32.87, 32.88, 32.93.

    Cervical cord injuries.

        Acute anterior cervical spinal cord syndrome, §32.88.

        As "special cases," §§32.86, 32.88.

    Compression of cord.

        Causes blood clot, §§32.75, 32.77.

    Concussion of cord, §32.77.

    Contusion of cord, §32.77.

    Cysts, traumatic (Tarlov), §32.76.

    Diagnosis, §§32.78, 32.92 to 32.97.

        Myelography, use of, §32.95.

        X-ray examination, §§32.72, 32.78, 32.94.

    Disability awards, §32.199(D).

    Effect of trauma generally, §§32.72, 32.82.

    Emotional aspects, §32.91.

    Examination, initial, §32.93.

    Fever accompanying, §32.90.

    Hematoma associated with, §§32.75, 32.77.

    Hemorrhage within or around cord, §§32.75, 32.77.

    Hyperpathia, §32.87.

    Hypesthesia, §32.87.

    Impairment.

        Paralysis, §§32.77, 32.84 to 32.86, 32.100.

        Sensory, §§32.87, 32.88.

        Sexual, §32.89.

    Infection as result, §32.90.

    Laceration of cord, §32.77.

        Transection, §§32.77, 32.86, 32.88.

    Lower extremity dysfunction, as cause of, §32.149.

    Metabolic complications, §32.90.

    Motor deficits, §32.82 to 32.84.

    Myelography, use of, §32.95.

    Nerve roots, spinal. (*See* NERVES, SPINAL).

    Paralysis--*See* within this subheading, "Impairment.".

        Syringomyelia as predisposing factor to paralysis, §32.80.

STOMACH.
Autopsy examination, §32A.21.

STRESS.
Posttraumatic stress disorder (PTSD).
   Burn injuries, §31.8.

STROKE.
Autopsy report of stroke victim, §32A.37.
Brain hemorrhage as cause, §32.43. (*See also* BRAIN).

SUICIDE.
Autopsy examination to determine, §32A.6.

SURGERY.
Autopsy examinations for surgical errors, §32A.51.
Hand surgery. (*See* HAND).
Microvascular surgery, §31.27b.
Replantation of limbs and digits, §§31.27a, 31.27c.
Sex change operations, §§31.33a, 31.33b.
Transplantation of organs. (*See* TRANSPLANTATION).

SURGICAL IMPLANTS.
Breast implants. (*See* BREAST).

SYNDACTYLY.
Definition, §31.31.

SYPHILIS.
Seizures in patients with advanced syphilis, §32.56.

SYRINGOMYELIA.
Posttraumatic, description, §32.86a.
Predisposing factor to paralysis following spinal cord trauma, §32.80.

T

TARLOV CYSTS.
Description, §32.76.

TEETH.
Autopsy examination of teeth, §§32A.3, 32A.5.

TENDONS.
Hand, tendon injuries of, §31.41.
Reflex loss in peripheral nerve injury, §32.126.

TESTS.
Brain-activity mapping, §32.164.
Clycosolated hemoglobin test, §30A.9.
Diabetes, tests for, §§30A.8, 30A.9.
Froment's sign, §32.141.
Glasgow Coma Scale, §§32.20, 32.22, 32.25, 32.28, 32.159, 32.161, 32.162, 32.166.
Glucose tolerance tests, §30A.8.
Glycated hemoglobin test, §30A.9.

UTERUS.
Autopsy examination of uterus, §32A.29.

V

VAGINA.
Autopsy examination of vagina, §32A.29.
Vaginitis.
    Diabetics susceptible to, §30A.17(D).

VEINS.
Autopsy examination of major veins, §32A.30.

VERTEBRAE.
"Articulations" between vertebrae, §32.63.
"Block vertebrae" as predisposing factor to spinal injury, §32.80.
"Butterfly vertebra" mistaken for fracture, §32.80.
Craniovertebral junction, disorders of, §§32.67, 32.80, 32.99.
    Predisposing factor to injury, §32.80.
Description of vertebrae, §32.61.
Fractures of vertebrae.
    "Butterfly vertebra" mistaken for fracture, §32.80.
    Compression fractures, §32.99.
        Without instability or neurological damages, §32.73.
    Description and treatment generally, §§32.73, 32.99.
    Healthy vertebrae, amount of weight necessary to fracture, §32.66.
    "Limbus vertebra" mistaken for fracture, §32.80.
    Spinal cord injury, types of fractures resulting in, §32.73.
"Half vertebra," §32.80.
Hemivertebra, §32.80.
    Predisposing factor to injury, §32.80.
"Limbus vertebra" mistaken for fracture, §32.90.
Malformations of vertebrae and spinal injury, §32.80.
Odontoid process.
    Maldevelopment, as predisposition to injury, §32.80.
Spinal canal, relationship of vertebrae to, §32.62.
"True" vertebrae, §32.61.

VERTIGO.
Head injury as cause, §32.34.

VISION.
Blind spot.
    Optic nerve injury as enlarging, §32.30.
Brain area controlling vision, §32.9.
Double vision.
    Injury as cause, §§31.17, 32.31.
Hemianopia (hemianopsia), §32.30.
Impairment of vision.
    Central visual acuity.
        Head injury as cause, §32.30.
        Optic nerve injury as cause, §32.30.

INDEX

VISION—Cont'd
Impairment of vision—Cont'd
 Diabetes as cause, §30A.17(A).
 Trauma as cause, §§31.17, 32.30, 32.31.

VITAMINS.
Peripheral nerve pain caused by Vitamin B-12 deficiency, §32.132.

VOLKMANN'S CONTRACTURE.
Causes, description, treatment, §32.122.

W

WALLERIAN DEGENERATION.
Description, §32.119.

WATERHOUSE-FRIDERICHSEN SYNDROME.
Description, §32A.27.

WRIST.
"Wrist-drop" following nerve injury, §§32.141, 32.142.

X

X-RAY.
Spinal conditions, X-ray diagnosis of, §§32.78, 32.94.

Z

ZYGOMA.
Fracture of, §31.17.